# Mexico City Metro

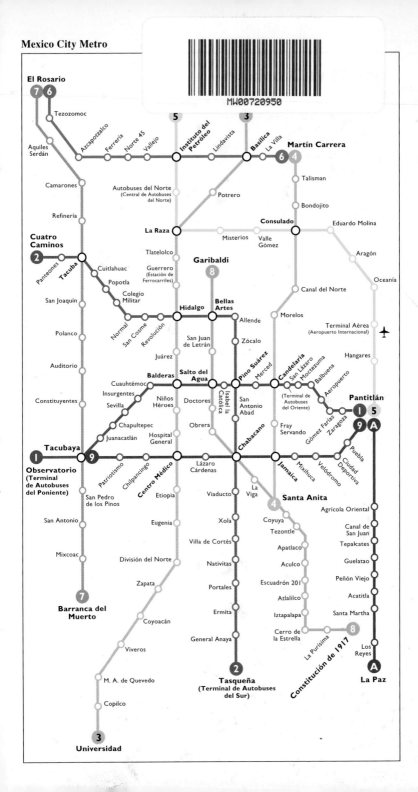

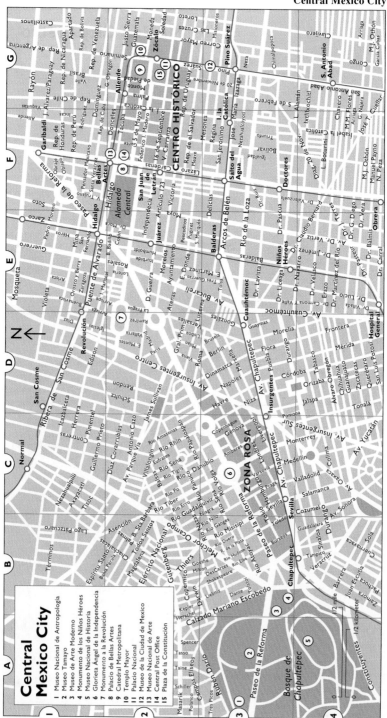

# Central Mexico City

1   Museo Nacional de Antropología
2   Museo Tamayo
3   Museo de Arte Moderno
4   Monumento de los Niños Héroes
5   Museo Nacional de Historia
6   Glorieta Ángel de la Independencia
7   Monumento a la Revolución
8   Palacio de Bellas Artes
9   Catedral Metropolitana
10  Templo Mayor
11  Palacio Nacional
12  Museo de la Ciudad de México
13  Museo Nacional de Arte
14  Central Post Office
15  Plaza de la Constitución

# Let's Go:
# Mexico

"Lighthearted and sophisticated, informative and fun to read. *[Let's Go]* helps the novice traveler navigate like a knowledgeable old hand."
—*Atlanta Journal-Constitution*

"The guides are aimed not only at young budget travelers but at the independent traveler, a sort of streetwise cookbook for traveling alone."
—*The New York Times*

## Let's Go writers travel on your budget.

"Retains the spirit of the student-written publication it is: candid, opinionated, resourceful, amusing info for the traveler of limited means but broad curiosity."
—*Mademoiselle*

"The writers seem to have experienced every rooster-packed bus and lunar-surfaced mattress about which they write."
—*The New York Times*

"All the dirt, dirt cheap."
—*People*

## Great for independent travelers.

"A world-wise traveling companion—always ready with friendly advice and helpful hints, all sprinkled with a bit of wit."
—*The Philadelphia Inquirer*

"Lots of valuable information for any independent traveler."
—*The Chicago Tribune*

## Let's Go is completely revised each year.

"Unbeatable: good sight-seeing advice; up-to-date info on restaurants, hotels, and inns; a commitment to money-saving travel; and a wry style that brightens nearly every page."
—*The Washington Post*

"Its yearly revision by a new crop of Harvard students makes it as valuable as ever."
—*The New York Times*

## All the important information you need.

"Enough information to satisfy even the most demanding of budget travelers...*Let's Go* follows the creed that you don't have to toss your life's savings to the wind to travel—unless you want to."
—*The Salt Lake Tribune*

"Value-packed, unbeatable, accurate, and comprehensive."
—*The Los Angeles Times*

# Let's Go Publications

Let's Go: Alaska & the Pacific Northwest 1998
Let's Go: Australia 1998 **New title!**
Let's Go: Austria & Switzerland 1998
Let's Go: Britain & Ireland 1998
Let's Go: California 1998
Let's Go: Central America 1998
Let's Go: Eastern Europe 1998
Let's Go: Ecuador & the Galápagos Islands 1998
Let's Go: Europe 1998
Let's Go: France 1998
Let's Go: Germany 1998
Let's Go: Greece & Turkey 1998
Let's Go: India & Nepal 1998
Let's Go: Ireland 1998
Let's Go: Israel & Egypt 1998
Let's Go: Italy 1998
Let's Go: London 1998
Let's Go: Mexico 1998
Let's Go: New York City 1998
Let's Go: New Zealand 1998 **New title!**
Let's Go: Paris 1998
Let's Go: Rome 1998
Let's Go: Southeast Asia 1998
Let's Go: Spain & Portugal 1998
Let's Go: USA 1998
Let's Go: Washington, D.C. 1998

## Let's Go Map Guides

| | |
|---|---|
| Berlin | New Orleans |
| Boston | New York City |
| Chicago | Paris |
| London | Rome |
| Los Angeles | San Francisco |
| Madrid | Washington, D.C. |

**Coming Soon:** Amsterdam, Florence

**Let's Go
Publications**

# LET'S GO
# Mexico
# 1998

**Robin S. Goldstein**
Editor

**Nicholas A. Sandomirsky**
Associate Editor

**Marnie E. Davidoff**
Assistant Editor

St. Martin's Press ✸ New York

## HELPING LET'S GO

If you want to share your discoveries, suggestions, or corrections, please drop us a line. We read every piece of correspondence, whether a postcard, a 10-page email, or a coconut. Please note that mail received after May 1998 may be too late for the 1999 book, but will be kept for future editions. **Address mail to:**

> **Let's Go: Mexico**
> **67 Mount Auburn Street**
> **Cambridge, MA 02138**
> **USA**

Visit Let's Go at **http://www.letsgo.com,** or send email to:

> **fanmail@letsgo.com**
> **Subject: "Let's Go: Mexico"**

In addition to the invaluable travel advice our readers share with us, many are kind enough to offer their services as researchers or editors. Unfortunately, our charter enables us to employ only currently enrolled Harvard-Radcliffe students.

Maps by David Lindroth copyright © 1998, 1997, 1996, 1995, 1994, 1993, 1992, 1991, 1990, 1989, 1988 by St. Martin's Press, Inc.

Map revisions pp. 2, 3, 73, 88, 89, 109, 121, 123, 129, 147, 161, 175, 209, 217, 227, 239, 263, 271, 309, 325, 327, 337, 345, 373, 375, 381, 405, 421, 431, 443, 469, 483, 485, 501, 507, 531 by Let's Go, Inc.

Distributed outside the USA and Canada by Macmillan.

ISBN: 0-312-16896-9

First edition
10 9 8 7 6 5 4 3 2 1

**Let's Go: Mexico** is written by Let's Go Publications, 67 Mount Auburn Street, Cambridge, MA 02138, USA.

**Let's Go**® and the thumb logo are trademarks of Let's Go, Inc. Printed in the USA on recycled paper with biodegradable soy ink.

# About Let's Go

## THIRTY-EIGHT YEARS OF WISDOM

Back in 1960, a few students at Harvard University banded together to produce a 20-page pamphlet offering a collection of tips on budget travel in Europe. This modest, mimeographed packet, offered as an extra to passengers on student charter flights to Europe, met with instant popularity. The following year, students traveling to Europe researched the first, full-fledged edition of *Let's Go: Europe,* a pocket-sized book featuring honest, irreverent writing and a decidedly youthful outlook on the world. Throughout the 60s, our guides reflected the times; the 1969 guide to America led off by inviting travelers to "dig the scene" at San Francisco's Haight-Ashbury. During the 70s and 80s, we gradually added regional guides and expanded coverage into the Middle East and Central America. With the addition of our in-depth city guides, handy map guides, and extensive coverage of Asia and Australia, the 90s are also proving to be a time of explosive growth for Let's Go, and there's certainly no end in sight. The first editions of *Let's Go: Australia* and *Let's Go: New Zealand* hit the shelves this year, expanding our coverage to six continents, and research for next year's series has already begun.

We've seen a lot in 38 years. *Let's Go: Europe* is now the world's bestselling international guide, translated into seven languages. And our new guides bring Let's Go's total number of titles, with their spirit of adventure and their reputation for honesty, accuracy, and editorial integrity, to 40. But some things never change: our guides are still researched, written, and produced entirely by students who know first-hand how to see the world on the cheap.

## HOW WE DO IT

Each guide is completely revised and thoroughly updated every year by a well-traveled set of over 200 students. Every winter, we recruit over 140 researchers and 60 editors to write the books anew. After several months of training, Researcher-Writers hit the road for seven weeks of exploration, from Anchorage to Adelaide, Estonia to El Salvador, Iceland to Indonesia. Hired for their rare combination of budget travel sense, writing ability, stamina, and courage, these adventurous travelers know that train strikes, stolen luggage, food poisoning, and marriage proposals are all part of a day's work. Back at our offices, editors work from spring to fall, massaging copy written on Yucatán jungle bus rides into witty yet informative prose. A student staff of typesetters, cartographers, publicists, and managers keeps our lively team together. In September, the collected efforts of the summer are delivered to our printer, who turns them into books in record time, so that you have the most up-to-date information available for your vacation. And even as you read this, work on next year's editions is well underway.

## WHY WE DO IT

We don't think of budget travel as the last recourse of the destitute; we believe that it's the only way to travel. Living cheaply and simply brings you closer to the people and places you've been saving up to visit. Our books will ease your anxieties and answer your questions about the basics—so you can get off the beaten track and explore. Once you learn the ropes, we encourage you to put *Let's Go* down now and then to strike out on your own. As any seasoned traveler will tell you, the best discoveries are often those you make yourself. When you find something worth sharing, drop us a line. We're Let's Go Publications, 67 Mount Auburn St., Cambridge, MA 02138, USA (email: fanmail@letsgo.com).

## HAPPY TRAVELS!

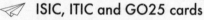

# Contents

About Let's Go ............................................................. v
Maps ..................................................................... x
Acknowledgments ...................................................... xii
Researcher-Writers .................................................... xiii
Let's Go Picks .......................................................... xv
How to Use This Book ................................................. xvi

## ESSENTIALS 1

Planning Your Trip ....................................................... 1
Getting There .......................................................... 37
Once There ............................................................. 42

## MEXICO 51

A Brief History ........................................................ 51
Culture and Character ................................................. 63

## Mexico City                                                        71

NEAR MEXICO CITY .................................................. 119
  Teotihuacán, Edo. de México ...................................... 119
  Daytrips ............................................................ 122

## Baja California                                                   125

BAJA CALIFORNIA NORTE ............................................. 126
  Tijuana ..................................... 126    Ensenada ................................ 137
  Rosarito ................................... 133    Valle de San Quintín ................... 142
  Mexicali ................................... 134    San Felipe .............................. 144

BAJA CALIFORNIA SUR ................................................ 146
  Guerrero Negro ....................... 146    Loreto .................................. 156
  San Ignacio ............................ 149    Puerto San Carlos ...................... 158
  Santa Rosalía .......................... 151    La Paz .................................. 159
  Mulegé ................................. 152    Todos Santos ........................... 164
  Bahía de la Concepción ........... 154    Los Cabos .............................. 167

## Northwest Mexico                                                  175

SONORA ............................................................... 176
  Nogales ................................ 176    Bahía Kino ............................. 185
  Puerto Peñasco ....................... 178    Guaymas ................................ 186
  Hermosillo ............................. 180    Alamos ................................. 189

CHIHUAHUA ........................................................... 191
  El Paso, Texas ......................... 191    Cuauhtémoc ............................. 203
  Ciudad Juárez .......................... 194    Creel .................................. 205
  Nuevo Casas Grandes ............... 197    Copper Canyon .......................... 208
  Chihuahua .............................. 199

SINALOA .............................................................. 213
  Los Mochis ............................. 213    Mazatlán ............................... 216

DURANGO .............................................................. 223

# Northeast Mexico                              226

Brownsville, Texas ............................................. 226

## TAMAULIPAS ...................................................... 228

Matamoros ..................... 228     Nuevo Laredo ........................ 234
Reynosa ........................... 230     Tampico ................................. 236
Laredo, Texas ................. 231

## NUEVO LEÓN ...................................................... 237

Monterrey ....................... 237

## COAHUILA .......................................................... 243

Saltillo .............................. 243

## ZACATECAS ........................................................ 244

## AGUASCALIENTES ............................................... 250

## SAN LUIS POTOSÍ ............................................... 253

San Luis Potosí ............. 253     Real de Catorce ................... 260
Matehuala ....................... 257     Ciudad Valles ........................ 261

# Central Pacific Coast                        263

## NAYARIT ............................................................. 264

San Blas ........................... 264     Tepic ..................................... 266

## JALISCO .............................................................. 268

Guadalajara ..................... 268     Bahía de Navidad ................. 292
Puerto Vallarta ............. 284

## COLIMA .............................................................. 296

Manzanillo ....................... 296     Colima ................................... 301

# Southern Pacific Coast                       307

## MICHOACÁN DE OCAMPO ............................... 307

Uruapan ........................... 307     Lázaro Cárdenas ................. 321
Pátzcuaro ........................ 311     Michoacán Coast ................. 322
Morelia ............................. 317

## GUERRERO ........................................................ 325

Taxco ................................ 325     Costa Grande ...................... 335
Zihuatanejo and Ixtapa ..... 330     Acapulco ............................... 336

## OAXACA ............................................................. 342

Tuxtepec ......................... 342     Bahías de Huatulco .............. 361
Oaxaca ............................. 344     Pochutla ............................... 364
Mitla ................................ 356     Puerto Ángel ....................... 364
Monte Albán ................... 357     Zipolite ................................. 366
Isthmus of Tehuantepec ..... 359     Puerto Escondido ................ 367

# Central Mexico                                371

## GUANAJUATO ..................................................... 371

Guanajuato ....................... 371     San Miguel de Allende ......... 379

## QUERÉTARO ...................................................... 388

## HIDALGO ............................................................ 394

Pachuca ............................ 394     Tula ....................................... 396

## ESTADO DE MÉXICO ......................................... 398

Toluca ............................... 398     Ixtapan de la Sal .................. 401
Tepotztlán ....................... 400     Popocatépetl and Ixtaccíhuatl ..402

MORELOS .................................................................. 403
   Cuernavaca ..................................... 403

TLAXCALA ............................................................... 413

PUEBLA .................................................................... 419
   Puebla ............................................. 419    Cholula ........................................ 426

## Veracruz                            430

   Xalapa (Jalapa) ............................. 430    Catemaco ...................................... 448
   Tuxpan (Tuxpam) ...................... 435    San Andrés Tuxtla ..................... 452
   Papantla ......................................... 438    Santiago Tuxtla ........................... 455
   Veracruz ........................................ 441

## Chiapas and Tabasco              457

TABASCO .................................................................. 458
   Villahermosa ................................. 458    Teapa ............................................ 462

CHIAPAS .................................................................... 463
   Tuxtla Gutiérrez ......................... 463    Ocosingo ...................................... 480
   Chiapa de Corzo ........................ 466    Palenque ....................................... 482
   San Cristóbal de Las Casas ...... 467    Tonalá .......................................... 487
   Comitán ........................................ 478    Tapachula ..................................... 488

## Yucatán Peninsula                 492

CAMPECHE ............................................................... 494
   Escárcega ...................................... 494    Campeche ..................................... 494

YUCATÁN .................................................................. 499
   The Maya Route ......................... 499    Chichén Itzá ................................ 517
   Mérida ........................................... 506    Valladolid ..................................... 524
   Progreso ........................................ 515    Tizimín ......................................... 526
   Mérida to Chichén Itzá ............. 516    Río Lagartos ............................... 527

QUINTANA ROO ...................................................... 528
   Cancún .......................................... 528    Isla Cozumel ............................... 541
   Isla Holbox and Chiquilá ......... 534    Tulum ........................................... 546
   Isla Mujeres ................................. 536    Cobá ............................................. 550
   Playa del Carmen ....................... 539    Chetumal ..................................... 552

## APPENDIX 555

## INDEX 563

# Maps

Mexico ................................................................................ 2-3
Mexico Transportation .................................................. 44-45
Metropolitan Mexico City .................................................. 73
Central Mexico City ...................................................... 88-89
San Angel and Coyoacán .................................................. 109
Teotihuacán .......................................................................... 121
Near Mexico City ............................................................... 123
Baja California Norte ......................................................... 127
Tijuana .................................................................................. 129
Ensenada .............................................................................. 139
Baja California Sur .............................................................. 147
La Paz ................................................................................... 161
Cabo San Lucas ................................................................... 169
San José del Cabo .............................................................. 173
Northwest Mexico ............................................................. 175
Hermosillo ........................................................................... 181
Chihuahua ............................................................................ 201
Barrancas del Cobre (Copper Canyon) ........................... 209
Mazatlán ............................................................................... 217
Northeast Mexico .............................................................. 227
Monterrey City Center ...................................................... 239
Zacatecas .............................................................................. 245
San Luis Potosí .................................................................... 253
Central Pacific Coast ......................................................... 263
Guadalajara .......................................................................... 271
Puerto Vallarta ................................................................... 285
Michoacán de Ocampo ...................................................... 309
Pátzcuaro ............................................................................. 313
Morelia ................................................................................. 319
Guerrero .............................................................................. 325
Taxco ................................................................................... 327
Zihuatanejo .......................................................................... 331
Acapulco ............................................................................... 337
Oaxaca State ....................................................................... 343
Oaxaca ................................................................................. 345
Central Mexico ................................................................... 373
Guanajuato ........................................................................... 375
San Miguel de Allende ....................................................... 381
Querétaro ............................................................................ 389
Cuernavaca .......................................................................... 405
Tlaxcala ................................................................................ 415
Puebla ................................................................................... 421

Veracruz State ................................................................................................431
Veracruz City Center ...................................................................................443
Chiapas ........................................................................................................457
Villahermosa ................................................................................................459
San Cristóbal de las Casas ..........................................................................469
Palenque Town ............................................................................................483
Palenque Ruins ............................................................................................485
Yucatán Peninsula ........................................................................................493
Yucatán State ..............................................................................................501
Mérida ........................................................................................................507
Chichén Itzá.................................................................................................521
Cancún ........................................................................................................531
San Miguel de Cozumel ..............................................................................543

# Color Maps

Mexico City Metro ...............................................................color insert
Central Mexico City.............................................................color insert

# Researcher-Writers

**Sonesh Chainani**  *Northeast Mexico, Northern Veracruz*
*Mexico City, Central Mexico, Taxco, Baja California*

From day one, Sonesh the Superstar's prowess never ceased to amaze us. Unfazed by a maid who threw away his ripsheets, a bus driver who left with his notes, bandits who stole his Express Mail package, and a scorpion who took a liking to his foot, Sonesh begged for more and his itinerary grew to epic proportions. Shoeless Sonesh chucked his footwear but not his sense of humor, relating his escapades via the phone lines and scrawling stories across his copy in loving detail; his model marginalia became the stuff of office legend. Campy Chainani found beauty peeking out in grey Monterrey, sang the praises of beachy Baja, and left his heart in Mexico City. A born globetrotter, Sonesh the Stud now begins his new and glorious reign as the R-W with the longest itinerary in the 1998 *Let's Go* series.

**Sandrine Goffard**  *Yucatán Peninsula, Chiapas, Tabasco*

This phosphorescent Floridian's enthusiasm for the Yucatán showed through all that she researched and wrote. Bubbling with boundless energy, Sandrine busted out of Cancún in her Tevas and made friends everywhere she went. Neither gringo backpackers nor locals could resist Sandrine's charm, whether she was bopping around the Ruta Puuc in a VW Bug, buzzing around Cozumel moped-style, or jotting down prose as sweet as her smile. The editors anxiously anticipated her phone calls, which would transmit her fondness for the Yucatán fiberoptically, treating us to tales of Cafe Cito and the mysterious Sabina. This veteran R-W's intense delight in the Mexican people and surroundings inspired her to send us copy packed with an extra dose of love.

**Elissa Hart**  *Central Mexico, Veracruz, Southern Pacific Coast*

Elissa brought a unique, intellectual outlook to some of the most heavily-trodden meccas of colonial Mexico. Sipping hot chocolate in Oaxaca and *café con leche* in steamy Veracruz, reveling in centuries-old Olmec art in Xalapa, and scanning the raucous party scene in Acapulco, Elissa perceptively analyzed her surroundings, sending us beautifully crafted copy with an uncanny knack for illuminating what was most interesting and culturally unique. Straight outta Sacramento, this scholar of Mexican literature showed her vision for the guide at every turn, all while stoically ignoring the hoots and hollers from Mexican men every step of the way. Elissa cruised down both coasts, breaking ground with bold new coverage along the Pacific and in Pachuca, and spiking her tough itinerary like a volleyball.

**Ignacio Montoya**  *Northwest Mexico*

Ignacio answered the urgent *Let's Go* call of duty from his Phoenix home, and only days later, he was on the road, trekking like a seasoned veteran through a grueling itinerary that took him from brawny borderland cantinas to dusty desert metropoli to the remote crevices of the Copper Canyon, stopping only for a radio appearance in Nuevo Casas Grandes. Ignacio drew upon his experience growing up along the border and infused his writing with an honest insider's touch and the humble respect of a local. Paying mind-bogglingly meticulous attention to every last detail, Ignacio dazzled us with his remarkably conscientious and complete research, producing stellar brand-new coverage of the Canyon and Alamos. Rest assured, readers: you're in good hands with Ignacio.

**Kathleen Peggar**  *Central Mexico, Aguascalientes, Durango*
*Mazatlán, Central Pacific Coast, Michoacán*

Kathleen loved Mexico, and Mexico loved her back. Off in a cloud of dust, this Olympia, Washington native was already in Mexico while some folks back here were still taking final exams. Kathleen constantly impressed us with her superhuman ability to find new and better restaurants and hotels at every corner. Kathleen sent us back spanking-new copy from dusty Durango, sipped Cuervo tequila from its original source in Jalisco, and almost singlehandedly brought *Let's Go: Mexico* into the information age by uncovering internet access anywhere and everywhere she went. Kathleen's impeccable copy carefully balanced her deep respect for local culture with her heartfelt concern for the environment. She barely stopped for a post-itinerary breath before heading straight to Alaska for full-time eco-work.

**Ana Lara**  *Tijuana, Ensenada, San Quintín*
**Brian Algra**  *Puerto Peñasco*

# Acknowledgments

The loftiest of all possible props go to our kick-ass R-Ws, Sonesh, Sandrine, Elissa, Ignacio, and Kathleen. Your news from the road filled *¡Vámonos!* and our steamy Cambridge summer with delight, and your stellar copybatches made us cry with joy. Ana, we wish we could've had you the whole way through. Marnie, you get mad props for your help, moral support, and listening to tales of wackitude. You rule. Emily, your unwavering encouragement, devotion, and uncanny knack for spotting the unitalicized period made the book a better place. You rule too. Thanks, Dave, for stellar typesetting; thanks, Meera & Alice, our devoted and capable interns, for helping us out in our times of need. For uncontainable fun, afternoon siestas, and one fine-ass postcard curtain, we thank the Latin America room, Nikia, Allyson, Joanna, Shakira, Krzys, and Sean Coar. Ryan Bradley...rules! For puttin' up with us, we salute House of Wack members Irene, Eddie, and Ben; all the members of 32 Line, especially Christine for her lovely late-night goodies; for Israeli rock, Amir; for being the coolest, Rachel; for the Sox and lunch breaks, Brad S.; for sharing in our deep love for the Panino, Bab-en-Epcot Stein; for phone-bill fun, our roommate and cohort, Italy's Dan Horwitz; for the way she says paaaancakes, Pooja; for spicing up the office, Laurie, Katherine, and Emily; and for being the best typist of the modern era, Elena. **NAS & RSG**

Nick: we made a book. Thanks for being the perfect editor and writer (though a poor Burkeball player), for 12-martini lunches, for dealing with my convenient "vacation," and for making my summer 20 times more fun. You're the cito to end all citos. Infinite thanks to *mi familia:* Mom, for taking better care of me than I do; Dad, for my love of Mexico and travel; Rosie, for always making me happy, and for teaching me the back flip; and Nonnie and Granddad, for neverending support, a furnished apartment, and tales of Italy. **RSG**

Professor Beardstein, you rock the city intro that rocks the body (see TJ or D.F.), and you're the best editor around, "I'll tell ya that much." Thanks for loving Mexico so much and teaching me a lot about the place, for the constant flow of gaw Peg-mail, for the look of cito incredulity, for Coolata hijinks, and for making my summer 21 times more fun. Estoy kikyerassando. Giant thanks to the Winter Brook Farm gang, Mom, Dad, Robin, and other assorted mammals. **NAS**

| | |
|---|---|
| **Editor** | Robin S. Goldstein |
| **Associate Editor** | Nicholas A. Sandomirsky |
| **Assistant Editor** | Marnie E. Davidoff |
| **Managing Editor** | Emily J. Stebbins |
| | |
| **Publishing Director** | John R. Brooks |
| **Production Manager** | Melanie Quintana Kansil |
| **Associate Production Manager** | David Collins |
| **Cartography Manager** | Sara K. Smith |
| **Editorial Manager** | Melissa M. Reyen |
| **Editorial Manager** | Emily J. Stebbins |
| **Financial Manager** | Krzysztof Owerkowicz |
| **Personnel Manager** | Andrew E. Nieland |
| **Publicity Manager** | Nicholas Corman |
| **Publicity Manager** | Kate Galbraith |
| **New Media Manager** | Daniel O. Williams |
| **Associate Cartographer** | Joseph E. Reagan |
| **Associate Cartographer** | Luke Z. Fenchel |
| **Office Coordinators** | Emily Bowen, Chuck Kapelke |
| | Laurie Santos |
| | |
| **Director of Advertising Sales** | Todd L. Glaskin |
| **Senior Sales Executives** | Matthew R. Hillery, Joseph W. Lind |
| | Peter J. Zakowich, Jr. |
| | |
| **President** | Amit Tiwari |
| **General Manager** | Richard Olken |
| **Assistant General Manager** | Anne E. Chisholm |

# Let's Go Picks

**Best Places to Chill** Isla Holbox, where all you need is a hammock (p. 534); Barra de Potosí, where worries drift out to sea (p. 335); Zipolite, where time passes very, very slowly and people are naked (p. 366); Gran Café de la Parroquia, in Veracruz, where the coffee is as good as it gets (p. 433); and San Ignacio, where palms appear out of the desert (p. 149).

**Best Ruins and Churches** Palenque, for the inscriptions and the dense jungle (p. 482); Chichén Itzá, especially during the Equinox (p. 517); Tulum, for ruins watching over the Caribbean (p. 546); the Iglesia de San Juan Chamula, for the mixture of Catholicism, Maya ritual, and burping (p. 474); Xilitla, a place where Alice would feel right at home (p. 262); and the Iglesia de Santa Prisca, in Taxco—it outshines the silver (p. 328).

**Best Accommodations and Restaurants** Casa de los Amigos, the best place in Mexico City to make friends (p. 91); Margarita's, the sweetest deal for Canyon-goers (p. 206); Hotel Yeneka, where visitors to La Paz fraternize with monkeys (p. 162); Hotel Belmar, still a Mazatlán gem after all these years (p. 220); Restaurante Amaro, nestled in a beautiful Mérida courtyard (p. 511); Café Tacuba, the D.F.'s bastion of camp and class (p. 92); and Restaurant Jung, a funky vegetarian joint tucked into dusty Hermosillo (p. 183).

**Best Nightlife** Acapulco, a decaying diva that just won't quit (p. 336); Guanajuato (p. 371) and Coyoacán (p. 95), for the bohemian option; Cancún (p. 528) and Tijuana (p. 126), if that's what you're into; Puerto Vallarta, for its swingin' gay scene (p. 284); and Mexico City, duh (p. 71).

**Best Beaches** Laguna de Chankaab, in Cozumel, with unbelievable coral and tropical fish (p. 544); Bahía de la Concepción, a piece of paradise pie on the Sea of Cortés (p. 154); Puerto Escondido, an old favorite that hasn't lost its fresh appeal (p. 367); and Zihuatanejo, luckily still a budget-friendly beauty (p. 330).

**Best Monuments** El Ángel, whose wings gracefully transcend the honking madness of Mexico City's Paseo de la Reforma (p. 71); and the Faro de Comercio, whose striking reddish facade and nightly blue lasers boldly announce the commercial achievements of Monterrey and the industrial promise of the Republic (p. 241).

**Best of the Best** If we weren't typing this, here's where we'd be: Oaxaca, for the stunning *zócalo*, the *chocolate caliente*, and the insane markets nearby (p. 344); frontier town Creel (p. 205), for its mountain-pine air, and the nearby Copper Canyon, for its mind-numbing beauty (p. 208); Mexico City, the one and the only, for its grandiosity and surreal excesses (p. 71); Isla Mujeres, where life is like a postcard (p. 536); Guanajuato, for its colonial style and mysterious, winding alleyways (p. 371); La Paz, where the evening sun sparkles across the harbor and life is easy (p. 159); San Luis Potosí, for its lantern-lit squares; and, of course, the highland gem of San Cristóbal de las Casas, for everything (p. 467).

# How to Use This Book

*Let's Go: Mexico* is written for you, the adventurous budget traveler. In the hot and humid Cambridge summer of 1997, we sent six roving researchers out on a shoe-string budget with your concerns in mind: how to get from place to place, find salvation in local cuisine, enjoy the evenings, and get some sleep—all in the most economical way possible. In researching and writing the book, we have tried to accommodate the diverse backgrounds and tastes of our readers. Our efforts have ultimately produced a book heavily steeped in Mexico's illustrious, roller-coaster history, yet deeply infused with a sense of place. Our city introductions tend toward the descriptive rather than the educational, providing the facts but primarily aiming to transport you to each city to help you evaluate whether or not to include it on your itinerary. We hope that our googly-eyed wonderment with the vivacious assortment of cultures and ways of life in every corner of the Republic shows through the text.

The first chapter of this book, **Essentials,** is bursting at the seams with information you'll want to have a look at before leaving. Turn to this chapter for information on the gritty details—booking a flight, enrolling in a language school, procuring a passport, changing money, finding a cyber-connection, packing, securing car insurance, and phoning home. Sub-sections focus on the special needs of specific groups of travelers. While you're on your way to Mexico, read the **Introduction** chapter to learn a bit about the country's history, politics, culture, and character. Then comes the heart of the book—10 glorious chapters of freshly-baked coverage, seasoned by 13 years of research yet delivered straight out of the 1998 oven and into your hands. The coverage begins with Mexico City (the world's biggest metropolis waits for no one); from there, chapters proceed roughly from northwest to southeast, starting with Baja California and ending with the Yucatán peninsula. Following a city's intro-duction, the **Practical Information** section will give you all the crucial details you need. **Accommodations, Food, Sights,** and **Entertainment** come next; here we describe the very best of the cheap in each department. Please take note: **List-ings are subjectively given in order of value, according to our team's judgment.** But we beg you not to use our book as an excuse not to explore and find your own gems; therein lies the fun of budget travel.

Instead, consider this book to be your personal traveling companion, a companion *savant*—sometimes so chock full of knowledge that it seems not to be a person at all. Herein, we reveal to you all the treasures we have found, in the hope that—if you don't already—you will soon love Mexico as much as we do. Hidden within these pages are: donkeys painted as zebras, a cast-iron church, a bird-controlled basilica, the ancient city of the cloud people, the best *café con leche* on the face of the earth, an expat Viking living on the beach, a religious ceremony involving bottles of Pepsi, floating *mariachis,* a library without books, giant cheese balls, a land-locked light-house, a wax statue of the Ayatollah, the widest tree in world, Sly Stallone's summer house, a failed socialist utopia, and a 300-year old edible sculpture.

Check them out… and have a wonderful trip.

---

### A NOTE TO OUR READERS

The information for this book is gathered by *Let's Go*'s researchers from late May through August. Each listing is derived from the assigned researcher's opinion based upon his or her visit at a particular time. The opinions are expressed in a candid and forthright manner. Other travelers might disagree. Those traveling at a different time may have different experiences since prices, dates, hours, and conditions are always subject to change. You are urged to check beforehand to avoid inconvenience and surprises. Travel always involves a certain degree of risk, especially in low-cost areas. When traveling, especially on a budget, always take particular care to ensure your safety.

# ESSENTIALS

## PLANNING YOUR TRIP

### ▉ Climate

The Tropic of Cancer bisects Mexico into a temperate north and tropical south, but the climate varies considerably even within these belts. **Northwest Mexico** is the driest area of the country, but still offers a unique array of desert flora and fauna, as does arid **Baja California,** which separates the cold, rough Pacific from the tranquil and tepid Sea of Cortés. The **Northeast** is a bit more temperate than the Northwest. The **West Coast,** home to Mexico's resort row, boasts warm, tropical weather. Pleasant beaches are also scattered throughout the humid, tranquil **Gulf Coast.** The central region north of Mexico City, known as **El Bajío,** and **South Central Mexico** both experience spring-like weather year-round; the cooler climates of the highlands are tempered by coastal warmth, and natural beauty ranges from world-famous beaches to inland forests. Lush, green jungles obscure ruins of the ancient civilizations of the **Yucatán Peninsula;** interior jungles are hot and humid, while trade winds keep the beachy areas along the Gulf and Caribbean coasts cool and pleasant.

There are two seasons in Mexico: rainy and dry. The rainy season lasts from May until November (with a hurricane season in the south Aug.-Oct.). The southern half of the country averages over 250cm of rainfall per year (75% of that during the rainy season), so a summer vacation is likely to be on the damp side. Expect a good two to three hours of rain every afternoon. The best time to hit the beaches is during the dry season (Nov.-May), when afternoons are sunny, evenings balmy, and nights relatively mosquito-free. Exhaustive statistics on climate are available in a chart at the end of the guide (p. 556).

The tourist season consists of the month of December, the entire summer, Semana Santa (Holy Week, the week before Easter), and Easter. If you travel to Mexico during this time, you can expect to pay slightly higher prices at hotels and restaurants. However, seasonal differences in Mexico pale in comparison to those in Europe; except during festivals, it is almost never necessary to make advance reservations, even during the summer, at budget hotels. Furthermore, which season is high varies regionally; in beach towns and resorts on either coast or Baja, the winter season and U.S. spring break are high and the summer low, while the summer is generally high in colonial Mexico.

### ▉ Information Resources

#### GOVERNMENT AGENCIES

**Embassy of Mexico:** In **Australia,** 14 Perth Ave. Yarralumla, Canberra 2600 ACT (tel. (06) 273 3905 or 273 3947; fax 273 1190); in **Canada,** 45 O'Connor St., #1500, K1P 1A4 Ottawa, Ont.(tel. (613) 233-8988, 233-9272 or 233-6665; fax 235-9123); in the **U.K.,** 42 Hertford St., Mayfair, W1Y 7TS, London (tel. (0171) 499 8586; fax 495 4035); in the **U.S.,** 1911 Pennsylvania Ave. NW, Washington, D.C. 20006 (tel. (202) 728-1600; fax 728-1718).

**Consulate of Mexico:** In **Australia,** Level 1, 135-153 New South Head Rd., Edgecliff, Sydney 2027 NSW (tel. (02) 326 1311 or 326 1292; fax 327 1110); in **Canada,** 199 Bay St., #4440, Commerce Court West, M5L 1E9 Toronto, Ont. (tel. (416) 368-2875; fax 368-3478 or 368-1672); in the **U.K.,** 42 Hertford St., Mayfair, W1Y 7TS, London (tel. (0171) 499 8586; fax 495 4035); in the **U.S.,** 2827 16th St. NW, Wash-

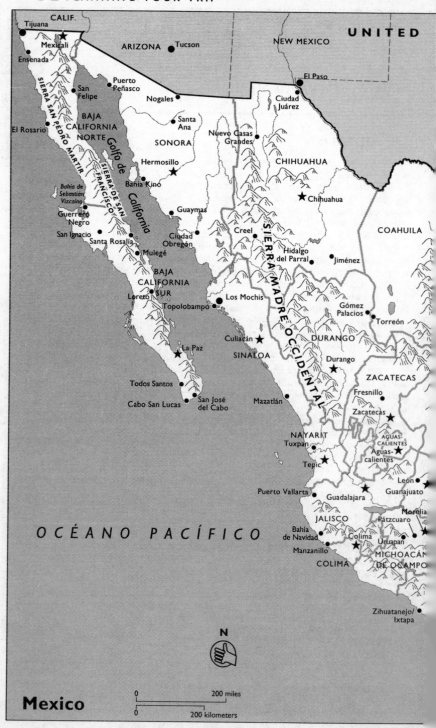

**Mexico**

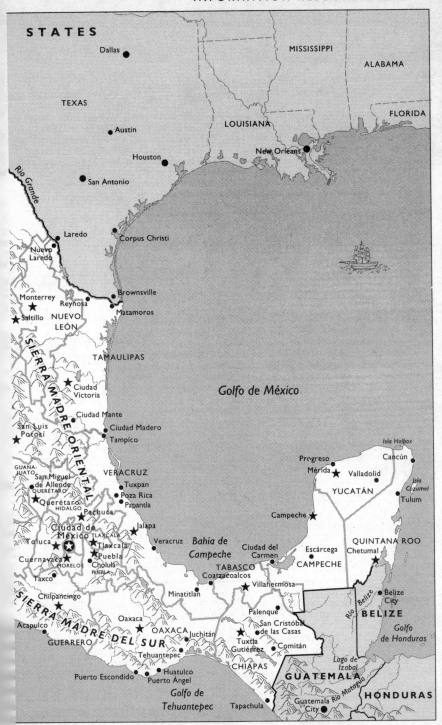

ington, D.C. 20036 (tel. (202) 736-1000; fax 797-8458) or 8 E. 41st St., New York, NY 10017 (tel. (212) 689-0456, fax 545-8197).

**Mexican Government Tourism Office** (Secretaría de Turismo or **SECTUR**), tel. (800) 44-MEXICO (national number). Offices in **Montreal,** 1 Place Ville Marie #1526, Montreal, Quebec H3B 2B5 (tel. (514) 871-1052; fax 871-3825). In **Toronto,** 2 Bloor St. W #1801, Toronto, Ontario M4W 3E2 (tel. (416) 925-1876 or 925-2753; fax 925-6061). In **Vancouver** (also for the northwest U.S.), 999 W. Hastings #1610, Vancouver, B.C. V6C 2W2 (tel. (604) 669-2845; fax 669-3498). In **London,** 60/61 Trigonally Sq., 3rd fl., London WC2N 5DS (tel. (0171)-839-3177; fax 930-9202). In **New York City,** 405 Park Ave. #1401, New York, NY 10022 (tel. (212) 421-6656 or 755-7261; fax 753-2874). In **Los Angeles,** 1801 Century Park, #1080, Los Angeles, CA 90067 (tel. (310) 203-8191; fax 203-8316). In **Florida,** 2333 Ponce de Leon Blvd., #710, Coral Gables, FL 33134 (tel. (305) 443-9160; fax 443-1186). In **Houston,** 5075 Westheimer Blvd., #975W, Houston, TX 77056 (tel. (713) 629-1611; fax 629-1837). In **Chicago,** 70 E. Lake St. #1413, Chicago, IL 60601 (tel. (312) 606-9015 or 9252; fax 606-9012). All have English- and Spanish-speaking representatives and provide maps, information, and tourist cards.

**Fax-Me-Mexico** is a fax-on-demand service run out of Oregon by the national Mexican Government Tourism office (tel. (541) 385-9282). Call first to receive a fax catalogue of all available documents, then order by number. Free. Open 24hr.

## TRAVEL ORGANIZATIONS

**Council on International Educational Exchange (CIEE),** 205 East 42nd St., New York, NY 10017-5706 (tel. (888) COUNCIL; fax (212) 822-2699; http://www.ciee.org). A private, not-for-profit organization, Council administers work, volunteer, and academic programs around the world. They also offer identity cards, (including the ISIC and the GO25) and a range of publications, among them the useful magazine *Student Travels* (free). Call or write for further information.

**Servicio Educativo de Turismo de los Estudiantes y la Juventud de México (SETEJ),** Hamburgo 305, Col. Juárez, Mexico, D.F. 06600 (tel. (5) 211-07-43 or 211-66-36; fax 211-13-28). Sells ISIC and GO25 cards. Arranges group tours with Mexican students and language courses. Helps with domestic and international Provides information about hostels and budget hotels (see Hostels, p. 48).

**American Automobile Association (AAA) Travel Related Services,** 1000 AAA Dr. (mail stop 100), Heathrow, FL 32746-5063 (tel. (800) 222-4357 or (407) 444-7000; fax 444-7380). Provides road maps and many travel guides free to members. Offers emergency road services (for members), travel services, and auto insurance. If you're heading into Mexico by car, stop at an AAA office near the border before crossing; they can provide detailed maps and mile-by-mile descriptions of roads in Mexico, particularly Baja California. The following are offices along the border: in **San Diego,** at the Auto Club of Southern California, 12630 Saber Springs Pkwy., San Diego, CA 92128 (tel. (619) 486-0786). In **Yuma,** 1045 S. 4th Ave., Yuma, AZ 85364 (tel. (602) 783-3339). In **Tucson,** 8204 E. Broadway, Tucson, AZ 85710 (tel. (602) 296-7461). In **El Paso,** AAA Texas-New Mexico-Oklahoma, 1201 Airway Blvd. #A-1, El Paso, TX 79925 (tel. (915) 778-9521). In **Laredo,** 7100 N. San Bernardo Ave., Laredo, TX 78041 (tel. (512) 727-3527).

## PUBLICATIONS

**The Blue Guide: Mexico,** published in the U.K. by A&C Black Limited, 35 Bedford Row, London WC1R 4JH; in the U.S. by W.W. Norton & Co. Inc., 500 Fifth Ave., New York, NY 10110; in Canada by Penguin Books Canada Ltd., 10 Alcorn Ave., #300, Toronto, Ontario N4V 3B2. The guide, by John Collis and David M. Jones, provides 935 pages of invaluable historical and cultural information as well as sightseeing routes, maps, tourist information, and listings of pricey hotels.

**Guía Oficial de Hospedaje de México,** published for the Secretaría de Turismo by Editorial Limusa, Grupo Noriega Editores, Balderas 95, México, D.F., 06040 México (tel. (5) 512-21-05; fax (5) 512-29-03). A thick book with a comprehensive list of all government-registered hotels in Mexico, in all price ranges. Invaluable if you're heading to small towns not covered by *Let's Go: Mexico 1998* and want to know what hotel options are in town. Available for free from some tourist offices—try your luck. In Spanish, but accessible to non-speakers.

**John Muir Publications,** P.O. Box 613, Sante Fe, NM 87504 (tel. (800) 888-7504; fax (505) 988-1680). Publishes the *People's Guide to RV Camping in Mexico* (US$20), plus general guides to Mexico, Belize, Costa Rica, and Guatemala.

**Mexico & Central America Handbook,** published by Footprint Handbooks, 6 Riverside Court, Lower Bristol Road, Bath BA2 3DZ England (tel. (01225)-469-141; fax (01225)-469-461; email handbooks@footprint.compulink.co.uk). An 1134-page tome with terse, compact, comprehensive listings of practical information, establishments, and sights in Mexico and Central America.

**México Desconocido,** Monte Pelvoux 110-104, Lomas de Chapultepec, Mexico, D.F. 11000 (tel. (5) 202-65-85; fax 540-17-71). Monthly travel magazines in Spanish and English describing little-known areas and customs of Mexico. Subscriptions shipped to the U.S. cost US$50 (mail a personal check or order via phone with a credit card). In Mexico, single issues (at bookstores) cost 20 pesos and subscriptions cost 200 pesos.

**Adventures in Mexico (AIM),** Apdo. 31-70, Guadalajara, Jalisco, 45050 Mexico. Newsletter on retirement and travel in Mexico. Endearing approach to the country's quirks. Annual subscription (6 issues) costs US$16 or CND$25. Personal checks accepted. Back issues, most of which are devoted to a single city or region, available for US$2.50 each, or 3 issues for US$6.

**Superintendent of Documents,** P.O. Box 371954, Pittsburgh, PA 15250-7954 (tel. (202) 512-1800; fax 512-2250; email gpoaccess@gpo.gov; http://www.access.gpo.gov/su-docs). Open Mon.-Fri. 7:30am-4:30pm. Publishes *Health Information for International Travel* (US$20), and "Background Notes" on all countries ($2.50 each). Prices include postage.

**U.S. Customs Service,** P.O. Box 7407, Washington, D.C., 20044 (tel. (202) 927-6724; http://www.customs.ustreas.gov). Publishes 35 books, booklets, leaflets, and flyers on various aspects of customs. *Know Before You Go* tells everything the international traveler needs to know about customs requirements; *Pocket Hints* summarizes the most important data from *KBYG*.

**Wide World Books and Maps,** 1911 N. 45th St., Seattle, WA 98103 (tel. (206) 634-3453; fax 634-0558; email travel@speakeasy.org; http://www.ww-books.com). Wide selection of books about Mexico and hard-to-find maps of the country.

# ■ The Internet

The Internet is now one of the most powerful allies of the budget traveler. Its advantages: it's speedy, easy to use, and, with many Mexican businesses, language schools, and individuals now online, it offers a cheap and accessible alternative to pricey phone calls and the less-than-reliable Mexican mail system. The Web can also open up infinite possibilities for exploring points of interest before you go. **NetTravel: How Travelers Use the Internet,** by Michael Shapiro, is a very thorough and informative guide to travel-related topics (US$25).

There are a number of ways to access the Internet. Many employers and schools offer gateways to the Internet, often at no cost. Otherwise, **local rigs** (ask at a local computer store or computer "user group") offer the most options for the best prices, including modem connection to the **World Wide Web,** access to a UNIX shell (terminal-style) and **telnet,** options of which large-scale commercial online services offer only pared-down versions. **America Online** (tel. (800) 827-6364), while not a particularly useful gateway to the Internet (it seems to be used mainly by flirty teens for its chat rooms), has the advantage of worldwide dial-up numbers (including many local numbers in Mexico). This makes it possible to check your email with a local call from many cities where it can be difficult to telnet. If you're planning an extended stay in Mexico, however, you'd be better off finding an Internet server there—it'll be cheaper and might let you telnet to your real account back home. For options in the region you'll be visiting, try some of the Web pages below.

# THE WORLD WIDE WEB

Increasingly the Internet forum of choice, today's **World Wide Web** allows travelers to consult official sources of information in Mexico and the U.S., make their own airline, hotel, hostel, or car rental reservations, and browse through a vast library of literature and multimedia material about Mexico's past, present, and future. The Web provides a streamlined interface and standardized format for accessing hyper-linked text, multimedia documents, and compact applications. The Web's lack of hierarchy, however, makes it difficult to distinguish between good information, bad information, and marketing.

   **Search engines** (services that look for web pages under specific subjects) can significantly help your quest. **Alta Vista** (http://www.altavista.digital.com), **Lycos** (http://a2z.lycos.com), and **Infoseek** (http://guide.infoseek.com) are three of the most popular. **Yahoo!** (http://www.yahoo.com) is a more organized search engine which only indexes material it deems worthwhile. Once you hit one web page with hyper-links, you can jump—or "surf," if you like—through pages all over the world; search engines are a good way of starting the process.

## WWW Links Related to Travel in Mexico

The following is a grab bag of useful Mexico resources on the World Wide Web. All sites are in English unless otherwise noted. *Let's Go* also lists relevant web sites throughout different sections of the Essentials chapter. Keep in mind that web sites come and go very rapidly; a good web site one week might disappear the next, and a new one might quickly take its place. Thus, the following should be seen as mere departure points for your own cyber-space adventures.

   **Let's Go** (http://www.letsgo.com). The mother-page of your favorite series of little, yellow budget travel guides.

   **Yahoo! Mexico links** (http://www.yahoo.com/Regional/Countries/Mexico). Well-indexed and searchable database of over 2000 links related to Mexico.

   **Yahoo! general travel links** (http://www.yahoo.com/Recreation/Travel).

   **Mexico Ministry of Tourism** (http://mexico-travel.com/). A highly commercial but surprisingly well-designed site, considering it's a government project. Describes regions and cities and lists tourist services and pricey hotels and restaurants.

   **Mexican Government Tourism Offices** (http://www.mbnet.mb.ca/lucas/travel. htgrep.cgi?) A list of the addresses and phone numbers of all of the organization's offices outside of Mexico.

   **El Mundo Maya** (http://www.wotw.com/Mundomaya/). Comprehensive coverage of the Mayan region of Mexico, including city and regional descriptions, photos, maps, and restaurant and hotel information.

   **U.S. State Department Travel Advisory for Mexico** (http://travel.state.gov/mexico.html). The word from above on travel safety and recommended precautions.

   **Consulate General of Mexico** (www.quicklink.com/mexico). Information about the Mexican government branches, economic indicators, and links to other Mexico-related sites. In either Spanish or English.

   **Mexico City Subway System** (http://metro.jussieu.fr:10001/bin/select/english/ mexico/mexico). An automated route-finder and map of the Mexico City Metro.

   **Universidad Nacional Autónoma de México** (http://serpiente.dgsca.unam.mx/: UNAM). In Spanish.

   **La Sociedad Internet de México** (http://www.isocmex.org.mx/). The Internet Society of Mexico. Entirely in Spanish.

   **Funtec "Internet in Mexico" Page** (http://www.funtec.org/mexico.html). List of web servers, etc., in Mexico. In Spanish.

   **MexWeb** (http://mexweb.mty.itesm.mx/). Lots of Mexico-related links. In Spanish.

   **Mexico Reference Desk** (http://www.lanic.utexas.edu/la/Mexico/). A plethora of hyper-links to sites related to Mexico.

   **The CIA World Factbook for Mexico** (http://www.odci.gov/cia/publications/ nsolo/factbook/mx.htm) has vital statistics on Mexico and facts about the government.

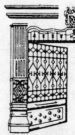

**Cyber Intercaptive** (http://www.clearlight.com/~kireau/cafe) is a worldwide cybercafe researcher.

**Foreign Language for Travelers** (http://www.travelang.com) can help you brush up on your Spanish. *Te ayuda a practicar tu español.*

**Shoestring Travel** (http://www.stratpub.com) is a budget travel e-zine, with feature articles, links, user exchange, and accommodations information.

**TravelHUB** (http://www.travelhub.com) is a great site for cheap travel deals.

## WWW Links to Mexican Newspapers

Checking out newspapers on the web is an excellent way to keep up on day-to-day news in Mexico. All of the following links are in Spanish.

**Periódicos en México** (http://www.public.asu.edu/~jml72/periodicos-mexico.html). A comprehensive hyper-linked list of all the Mexican periodicals on the Web. Usable even if you don't speak the language.

**El Nacional** (http://serpiente.dgsca.unam.mx/serv_hem/nacional/home.html). Reasonably quick, well implemented, and updated daily.

**La Reforma** (http://www.infosel.com.mx/reforma/). Fairly quick.

**El Universal** (http://www.el-universal.com.mx/net2/home.html).

**Excelsior** (http://www.excelsior.com.mx/home2.html). Very nicely implemented.

**La Jornada** (http://serpiente.dgsca.unam.mx/jornada/index.html). A rather slow server.

## WWW Links to Airlines Flying to Mexico

**Mexicana Airlines** (http://www.mexicana.com/). Slow but polished. In English and Spanish.

**Aeroméxico** (http://www.wotw.com/aeromexico/). Not much info. In English.

**American Airlines** (http://www.americanair.com).

**Continental Airlines** (http://www.flycontinental.com).

**Delta Airlines** (http://www.delta-air.com).

**United Airlines** (http://www.ual.com).

## NEWSGROUPS

**Usenet newsgroups** are electronic forums carrying publicly-readable dialogues on virtually every imaginable topic. One user "posts" a written question or thought, which other users read and respond to in kind. Anyone with a connection can post, but in some cases this proliferation has watered down the quality of the discussion, making it necessary to wade through piles of nonsense to come to useful information.

**soc.culture.mexican** carries some interesting discussion (of varying quality) related to Mexican society and culture, much of it in Spanish.

**rec.travel.latin-america.**

**clari.world.americas.mexico** carries no dialogue but posts stories related to Mexico from the AP newswire several times every day.

# ■ Documents and Formalities

## TOURIST CARDS

All persons visiting Mexico for tourism or study for up to 180 days must carry a **tourist card** (**FMT,** for *Folleto de Migración Turística*) in addition to proof of citizenship. U.S. and Canadian citizens can skip the FMT if they don't expect to travel past border towns or stay anywhere in the country for more than 72 hours. U.S. and Canadian citizens traveling to Baja California will need a card only if they plan to venture beyond Maneadero on the Pacific Coast, south of Mexicali on Rte. 5.

Tourist cards, like all entry documents, are free of charge. Many people get their cards when they cross the border or when they check in at the airline ticket counter for their flight into Mexico; however, you can avoid delays by obtaining one from a

**ESSENTIALS**

Mexican consulate or tourist office before you leave (see **Government Agencies**, p. 1). You will have to present proof of citizenship, and if your financial condition looks suspect, officials will ask you to flash your return ticket. Travelers from outside North America must present a passport. U.S. and Canadian citizens can obtain a tourist card with an original birth certificate, notarized affidavit of citizenship, or naturalization papers, plus some type of photo ID (with the exception of naturalized Canadians, who must carry a passport). But be forewarned: traveling in Mexico without a passport is asking for trouble. A passport carries much more authority with local officials than does a birth certificate, makes returning home by air a lot easier, and is mandatory for anyone going on to Central America.

On the FMT, you must indicate your intended destination and expected length of stay. Tourist cards are usually valid for 90 days and must be returned to border officials upon leaving the country. However, some border crossings and airport officials have been known to provide 30-day visas by default, and stamp 90-day visas only on request; make sure you get a 90-day stamp if you're staying longer than a month. If you stay in Mexico past your 90-day limit, you will be slapped with a fine. Request a special, 180-day **multiple-entry permit** at your point of entry if you plan to leave and re-enter the country several times within a short time period. Otherwise, you must get a new FMT every time you re-enter the country, even if your old one has not expired. Try to get a card that will be valid longer than your projected stay, since obtaining an extension on a 90-day FMT is a huge hassle: you'll need a physician's authorization stating that you are too ill to travel. If you do need an extension, visit a local office of the Delegación de Servicios Migratorios several weeks before your card expires. They also take care of lost cards. While in Mexico, you are required by law to carry your tourist card at all times. Make a photocopy and keep it in a separate place. Although it won't **replace** a lost or stolen tourist card, a copy should facilitate replacement. If you do lose your card, expect hours of delay and bureaucratic inconvenience while immigration verifies your record of entrance.

Special regulations apply if you are entering Mexico on a business trip, or if you expect to study in the country for more than six months. Contact a Mexican consulate several months before you leave home to obtain a visa or permit. U.S. and Canadian business travelers must obtain a special **FMN** (*Folleto de Migración de Negocios*) card or face steep fines. If you are planning on residing or retiring in Mexico, consult a Mexican consulate about long-term visas. If you're breezing through Mexico *en route* to Guatemala or Belize, ask for a **transmigrant form,** which will allow you to remain in Mexico for up to 30 days. You'll need a passport or current photo ID, a Guatemalan or Belizean visa, and proof of sufficient funds. The transmigrant form is not required for U.S. or Canadian citizens.

## PASSPORTS

In case your passport is lost or stolen, be sure to photocopy the page of your passport that contains your photograph and identifying information *before you leave*. Especially important is your passport number. Carry this photocopy in a safe place apart from your passport, perhaps with a traveling companion, and leave another copy at home. Better yet, carry a photocopy of all the pages of the passport, including all visa stamps, apart from your actual passport, and leave a duplicate copy with a relative or friend. Consulates also recommend that you carry an expired passport or an *official* copy of your birth certificate separate from other documents. These measures will help prove your citizenship and facilitate the issuing of a new passport.

If your passport is lost or stolen, immediately notify the local police and the nearest embassy or consulate of your home government. To expedite the replacement of your passport, you will need to know all the information that you had previously recorded and photocopied and to show identification and proof of citizenship. Some consulates can issue new passports within two days if you give them proof of citizenship. In an emergency, ask for immediate temporary traveling papers that will permit you to return to your home country.

**Australia** Citizens must apply for a passport in person at a post office, a passport office, or an Australian diplomatic mission overseas. An appointment may be necessary. Passport offices are located in Adelaide, Brisbane, Canberra City, Darwin, Hobart, Melbourne, Newcastle, Perth, and Sydney. A parent may file an application for a child who is under 18 and unmarried. Adult passports cost AUS$120 (for a 32-page passport) or AUS$180 (64-page), and a child's is AUS$60 (32-page) or AUS$90 (64 page). For more info, call toll-free (in Australia) 13 12 32.

**Canada** Application forms are available in English and French at all passport offices, post offices, and most travel agencies. Citizens may apply in person at any one of 28 regional passport offices across Canada. Citizens who reside in the U.S. can contact a Canadian diplomatic mission; those outside Canada and the U.S. should contact the nearest embassy or consulate. You can apply by mail to Passport Office, Foreign Affairs, Ottawa, Ontario, K1A 0G3. The processing time is approximately 5 business days for in-person applications and 3 weeks for mailed ones. A passport is valid for 5 years and must be reissued, because it is not renewable. For additional information, call the 24hr. number (tel. (800) 567-6868 from Canada only) or consult the booklet *Bon Voyage, But...*, available free from any passport office or from Info-Export (BPTE), External Affairs, Ottawa, Ontario, K1A 0G2.

**New Zealand** Application forms for passports are available in New Zealand from travel agents and Department of Internal Affairs Link Centres in the main cities and towns. Overseas, forms and passport services are provided by New Zealand embassies, high commissions, and consulates. Applications may also be forwarded to the Passport Office, P.O. Box 10526, Wellington, New Zealand. Standard processing time in New Zealand is 10 working days for correct applications. The fees are adult NZ$80, child NZ$40. An urgent passport service is also available for an extra NZ$80. Different fees apply at overseas posts: 9 posts including London, Sydney, and Los Angeles offer both standard and urgent services (adult NZ$130, child NZ$65, plus NZ$130 if urgent). The fee at other posts is adult NZ$260, child NZ$195; and passports will be issued within 3 working days. Children's names can no longer be endorsed on a parent's passport—they must apply for their own, which are valid for up to 5 years. An adult's passport is valid for up to 10 years.

**United Kingdom** British Dependent Territories citizens and British Overseas citizens can obtain a full passport valid for 10 years (5 years if under 16) by applying in person or by mail to the London Passport Office or by mail to a passport office located in Liverpool, Newport, Peterborough, Glasgow, or Belfast. Applications are available at post offices. Processing usually takes 4-6 weeks. The London office offers same-day walk-in rush service, provided you arrive early enough.

**United States** Citizens may apply for a passport at any federal or state **courthouse** or **post office** authorized to accept passport applications, or at a **U.S. Passport Agency,** located in Boston, Chicago, Honolulu, Houston, Los Angeles, Miami, New Orleans, New York, Philadelphia, San Francisco, Seattle, Stamford, or Washington, D.C. Refer to the "U.S. Government, State Department" section of the telephone directory or the local post office for addresses. You must apply in person if this is your first passport, if you're under age 18, or if your current passport is more than 12 years old or was issued before your 18th birthday. Parents must apply in person for children under age 13. Passports are valid for 10 years (5 years if under 18) and cost US$65 (under 18 US$40). Passports may be **renewed** by mail or in person for US$55. Processing takes 3-4 weeks. **Rush service** is available for a surcharge of US$30 and proof of departure within 10 working days (e.g., an airplane ticket or itinerary), or for travelers leaving in 2-3 weeks who require visas. Given proof of citizenship, a U.S. embassy or consulate abroad can usually issue a new passport. Report a passport lost or stolen in the U.S. in writing to Passport Services, 1425 K St., N.W., U.S. Department of State, Washington D.C., 20524 or to the nearest passport agency. For more info, contact the U.S. Passport Information's **24hr. recorded message** (tel. (202) 647-

# INSTITUTO FALCON, A.C.
## *MEXICO*
### *Spanish Language Program in Guanajuato*

Spanish Language Instruction at all Levels:

*Mexican History, Mexican Politics, Mexican Culture, Latin American Literature, Local Legends, Mexican Cuisine, Mexican Folk Dancing*

● Scheduling: All Ages & Nationalities
Personalized Instruction
(2-5 students or one-on-one)
Priority given on a First come First serve basis

● Teaching Method:  A Wide Variety of Modern Techniques

● Highlights:  Homestays with Mexican Families,
Cultural Events, Sporting Events, Hikes,
Classroom Field Trips, Cultural Movies,
Weekly Fiestas - All taking place in the most
beautiful colonial setting in Guanajuato

● Dates:  Year-round Classes begin every Monday

● Costs:  $925 for 4 weeks
Includes: Lifetime registration fee, Group
classes (5 sessions per day: Monday-Friday),
Homestay with 3 meals per day,
Lower prices for fewer weeks/classes

● Contact:  Registrar Jorge Barroso, Instituto Falcon, A.C.
Mora 158, Guanajuato, GTO., 36000 Mexico
Tel/Fax: (473) 2-36-94
Web Site: http://www.infonet.com.mx/falcon

0518). U.S. citizens may receive consular information sheets, travel warnings, and public announcements at any passport agency, U.S. embassy, or consulate, or by sending a self-addressed stamped envelope to: Overseas Citizens Services, Room 4811, Department of State, Washington, D.C. 20520-4818 (tel. (202) 647-5225; fax 647-3000). Additional information (including publications) about documents, formalities and travel abroad is available through the Bureau of Consular Affairs homepage at http://travel.state.gov, or through the State Department site at http://www.state.gov.

## VISAS

A **visa** is an endorsement that a foreign government stamps into your passport; it allows you to stay in that country for a specified purpose and period of time. For stays in Mexico up to six months, visas are not necessary for citizens of Australia, Canada, the U.K., the U.S., New Zealand, and most E.U. countries. Businesspeople, missionaries, and students must obtain appropriate visas. Applications are processed by consulates in one day and cost $63.

## YOUTH, STUDENT, AND TEACHER IDENTIFICATION

In Mexico, the ubiquitous **International Student Identity Card (ISIC)** and **International Teacher Identity Card (ITIC),** available at most budget and student travel agencies listed above and administered by the **International Student Travel Confederation** (http://www.istc.org), is not overly useful in Mexico, so you probably should save your hard-earned cash. The same can be said for the **GO 25 Card,** issued by the **Federation of International Youth Travel Organizations (FIYTO).** The GO 25 Card entitles you to some price reductions in Mexico, but probably not enough to save the US$19 card fee. Information is available on the web at http://www.fiyto.org or http://www.go25.org. For more info about either card, see **Budget Travel Agencies**, p. 37. Your regular **university ID card** usually entitles you to whatever discounts are offered to foreign students, so you should bring it along; but many student discounts in Mexico are only offered to students at Mexican universities.

## DRIVER'S LICENSE AND VEHICLE PERMITS

An international driver's license is not necessary for driving in Mexico; any valid driver's license is acceptable. To drive a foreign car into Mexico and beyond the Border Zone or Free Trade Zone (Baja California peninsula and Sonora), you need to obtain a **vehicle permit** when you cross the border. As of July 1997, the original and a photocopy of the following documents are needed to obtain a vehicle permit: state vehicle registration certificate and vehicle title, a valid driver's license accompanied by either a passport or a birth certificate, and a Mexican insurance policy, which can be purchased at the border. If leasing a vehicle, you must provide the contract in your name (also in duplicate). A credit card issued outside Mexico will make your life much easier—simply charge the US$11 fee. Without plastic, you will need to make a cash deposit calculated according to the value of your vehicle. In exchange for all these photocopies, you'll receive two punched stickers bearing the expiration date of your permit. To extend a vehicle permit beyond its original expiration date and avoid confiscation, contact the temporary importation department of Mexican customs. The maximum permit granted to tourists is 6 months. Regulations change frequently; for updated information contact a consulate or call the *Secretaría de Hacienda* at (202) 728-1621. A vehicle permit is valid only for the person to whom it was issued unless another driver is approved by the federal registry. Violation of this law can result in confiscation of the vehicle or heavy fines. Furthermore, only legitimate drivers may purchase car-ferry tickets.

Resist the temptation to abandon, sell, or give away your car in Mexico. Once you enter the country with a car, your tourist card will be marked such that you will not be allowed to collect the bond or to leave without the vehicle. Even if your car disappears somewhere in Mexico, you must get permission to leave without it; approval can be obtained (for a fee) at either the federal registry of automobiles in Mexico City or a local office of the treasury department.

## CUSTOMS: ENTERING MEXICO

Crossing into Mexico by land can be as uneventful or as complicated as the border guards want it to be. You might be waved into the country or directed to the immigration office to procure a tourist card (FMT) if you don't have one already and a car permit if you're driving. Customs officials will then inspect luggage and stamp papers. If there is anything amiss when you reach the immigration checkpoint 22km into the interior, you'll have to turn back.

A clean, neat appearance will help upon your arrival. Don't pass out *mordidas* (bribes; literally "bites"). They may do more harm than good. Border officials may still request a tip, but they're not supposed to. Above all, do not attempt to carry drugs across the border since the German shepherds will not be amused. Indeed, don't even think of buying or using drugs in Mexico—you could spend some serious time in jail, and your embassy and consulate will be powerless to help you.

Entering Mexico by air is easier. Agents process forms and examine luggage, using the press-your-luck traffic light system, right in the airport. Electronics, such as personal computers, might make customs officers uneasy; it is a good idea to write a letter explaining that you need to take your precious laptop into the country for personal use and that it will go back home with you and have the document certified by a Mexican consulate. Because air passengers are rarely penniless, immigration officials are less strict than at the border.

## CUSTOMS: LEAVING MEXICO

Crossing the border can take five minutes or five hours—the better your paperwork, the shorter your ordeal. When reentering your home country, you must declare all articles acquired abroad (even duty-free ones) and pay a duty on those which exceed customs allowance. To establish value when you return home, keep receipts for items purchased abroad. Since you pay no duty on goods brought from home, record the serial numbers of any expensive items (cameras, computers, radios, etc.) you are taking with you before you begin your travels, and check with your country's customs office to see if it has a special form for registering them.

Most countries object to the importation of firearms, explosives, ammunition, obscene literature and films, fireworks, and lottery tickets. Do not try to take illegal drugs out of Mexico. Label prescription drugs clearly and have the prescription or a doctor's certificate ready to show the customs officer. If you have questions, call the **Mexican Customs office** in the U.S. ((202) 728-1669; fax 728-1664).

Crossing the border (on your return) with live animals is usually prohibited. For information on wildlife products, contact **TRAFFIC USA,** World Wildlife Fund, 1250 24th St. NW, Washington, D.C. 20037 (tel. (202) 293-4800; fax 293-9211), or the Animal and Plant Health Inspection Service.

If you are a resident alien of the United States or simply have a Latino surname you may receive a lot of hassling from immigration upon your return. You must make up your own mind as to how to react to this racist harassment. Pragmatists answer as straightforwardly as possible any questions the border patrol might ask (they have been known to ask "who won the Civil War" and other "prove-it" puzzles).

**Australia** Citizens over 18 may import AUS$400 (under 18 AUS$200) of goods duty-free, in addition to the allowance of 1.125L alcohol and 250 cigarettes or 250g tobacco. There is no limit to the amount of Australian and/or foreign cash that may be brought into or taken out of the country, but amounts of AUS$10,000 or more, or the equivalent in foreign currency, must be reported. All foodstuffs and animal products must be declared on arrival. For info, contact the Regional Director, Australian Customs Service, GPO Box 8, Sydney NSW 2001 (tel. (02) 9213 2000; fax 9213 4000).

**Canada** Citizens who remain abroad for at least 1 week may bring back up to CDN$500 worth of goods duty-free any time. Citizens or residents who travel for a period between 48 hours and 6 days can bring back up to CDN$200. Both of these exemptions may include tobacco and alcohol. You are permitted to ship goods except tobacco and alcohol home under the CDN$500 exemption as long as you declare them when you arrive. Goods under the CDN$200 exemption, as well as all alcohol and tobacco, must be in your hand or checked luggage. Citizens of legal age (which varies by province) may import in-person up to 200 cigarettes, 50 cigars or cigarillos, 400g loose tobacco, 400 tobacco sticks, 1.14L wine or alcohol, and 24 355mL cans/bottles of beer; the value of these products is included in the CDN$200 or CDN$500. For more information, write to Canadian Customs, 2265 St. Laurent Blvd., Ottawa, Ontario K1G 4K3 (tel. (613) 993-0534), phone the 24hr. Automated Customs Information Service at (800) 461-9999, or visit Revenue Canada at http://www.revcan.ca.

**Ireland** Citizens must declare everything in excess of IR£142 (IR£73 per traveler under 15 years of age) above the following allowances: 200 cigarettes, 100 cigarillos, 50 cigars, or 250g tobacco; 1L liquor or 2L wine; 2L still wine; 50g perfume; and 250mL toilet water. Travelers under 17 may not import tobacco or alcohol. For more information, contact The Revenue Commissioners, Dublin Castle (tel. (01) 679 27 77; fax 671 20 21; email taxes@iol.ie; http://www.revenue.ie) or The Collector of Customs and Excise, The Custom House, Dublin 1.

**New Zealand** Citizens over 17 may bring home up to NZ$700 worth of goods duty-free if they are intended for personal use or are unsolicited gifts. The concession is 200 cigarettes (1 carton) or 250g tobacco or 50 cigars or a combination of all three not to exceed 250g and 4.5L of beer or wine and 1.125L of liquor. For more information, contact New Zealand Customs, 50 Anzac Ave., Box 29, Auckland (tel. (09) 377 35 20; fax 309 29 78).

**South Africa** Citizens may import duty-free: 400 cigarettes, 50 cigars, 250g tobacco, 2L wine, 1L of spirits, 50mL perfume, 250mL *eau de toilette,* and other items up to a value of SAR500. Goods up to a value of SAR10,000 over and above this duty-free allowance are dutiable at 20%; such goods are also exempted from payment of VAT. Items acquired abroad and sent to the Republic as unaccompanied baggage do not qualify for any allowances. You may not export or import South African bank notes in excess of SAR2000. For more information, consult the free pamphlet *South African Customs Information,* available in airports or from the Commissioner for Customs and Excise, Private Bag X47, Pretoria 0001 (tel. (12) 314 99 11; fax 328 64 78). In the U.S., contact the Embassy of South Africa, 3051 Massachusetts Ave. NW, Washington, D.C. 20008 (tel. (202) 265-4400; fax 265-1607) or the South African Home Annex, 3201 New Mexico Ave. #300 NW, Washington, D.C. 20016 (tel. (202) 966-1650, fax 244-9417).

**United Kingdom** Citizens or visitors over 17 must declare any goods in excess of: 200 cigarettes, 100 cigarillos, 50 cigars, or 250g tobacco; 2L still table wine, 1L strong liqueurs (over 22% volume) or fortified or sparkling wine, or other liqueurs; 60mL perfume or 250mL *eau de toilette;* and UK£136 worth of all other goods including gifts and souvenirs. For more info, contact Her Majesty's Customs and Excise, Custom House, Nettleton Road, Heathrow Airport, Hounslow, Middlesex TW6 2LA (tel. (0181) 910 3744; fax 910 3765).

**United States** Citizens returning home may bring US$400 worth of accompanying goods duty-free and must pay a 10% tax on the next US$1000. You must declare all purchases, so have sales slips ready. Goods are considered duty-free if they are for personal or household use (this includes gifts) and cannot include more than 100 cigars, 200 cigarettes (1 carton), and 1L of wine or liquor. You must be over 21 to

ESSENTIALS

bring liquor into the U.S. If you mail home personal goods of U.S. origin, you can avoid duty charges by marking the package "American goods returned." For more information, consult the brochure *Know Before You Go,* available from the U.S. Customs Service, Box 7407, Washington, D.C. 20044 (tel. (202) 927-6724), or visit them on the Web (http://www.customs.ustreas.gov).

# ■ Money Matters

All prices in this book are listed in Nuevos Pesos (N.P., "new pesos"), the official currency since January 1993—"old" pesos trimmed down by three zeros. In December 1994, the most dramatic devaluation in 10 years halved the value of the peso in relation to the U.S. dollar. Since then, further devaluation and inflation have made the cost of living increasingly high for Mexicans and low for travelers with hard currency. Although the situation is almost stable, prices are likely to change. The prices given in the book were accurate in August 1997 but may have risen since. Please understand that neither *Let's Go* nor establishment owners can be responsible for changes in the economy.

| | |
|---|---|
| US$1 = 7.80 pesos | 1 peso = US$0.13 |
| CDN$1 = 5.66 pesos | 1 peso= CDN$0.18 |
| UK£1 = 12.67 pesos | 1 peso = UK£0.08 |
| IR£1 = 11.28 pesos | 1 peso = IR£0.08 |
| AUS$1 = 5.77 pesos | 1 peso = AUS$0.17 |
| NZ$1 = 5.04 pesos | 1 peso = NZ$0.20 |
| SARand = 1.68 pesos | 1 peso = SARand$0.59 |

## CURRENCY AND EXCHANGE

Be sure to buy approximately US$50 worth of pesos, including the equivalent of US$1 in change, before leaving home, especially if you will arrive in the afternoon or on a weekend. This will save time and help you avoid the predicament of having no cash after bank hours. It's sometimes very difficult to get change for large Mexican bills in rural areas. Therefore, it's wise to obtain (and hoard) change when you're in a big city. The symbol for pesos is the same as for U.S. dollars (although an "S" with *two* bars is always a dollar-sign); frequently **"N"** or **"N$"** also stand for the peso.

Changing money in Mexico can be inconvenient. Some banks won't exchange until noon, when the daily peso quotes come out, and then stay open only until 1:30pm. You can switch U.S. dollars for pesos anywhere, but some banks refuse to deal with other foreign currencies; non-American travelers would be wise to keep some U.S. dollars on hand. Banks use the official exchange rates, but they sometimes extract a flat commission as well; therefore, the more money you change at one time, the less you will lose in the transaction (but don't exchange more than you need or you'll be stuck with *muchos* pesos when you return home). The lineup of national banks in Mexico includes **Banamex, Bancomer, Comermex,** and **Serfin.** Most banks are normally open 9am-2:30pm, weekdays only.

*Casas de cambio* (currency exchange booths) may offer better exchange rates than banks and are usually open as long as the stores near which they do business. In most towns, the exchange rates at hotels, restaurants, and airports are extremely unfavorable; avoid them unless it's an emergency.

## TRAVELER'S CHECKS

Traveler's checks are probably the safest way to hold money; if they get lost or stolen, you will be reimbursed by the checks' issuers. Many banks and companies sell traveler's checks, usually for the face value of the checks plus a 1-2% commission. To avoid problems when cashing your checks, always have your passport with you (not just the number); it often means the difference between apologetic refusal and grudging acceptance. Remember that some places (especially in northern Mexico) are accustomed to the American dollars and will accept no substitute. Carry traveler's checks in busy towns and cities, but stick to cash, risky though it may be, when traveling through the less touristed spots.

The following toll-free numbers provide information about purchasing traveler's checks and obtaining refunds:

**American Express:** Call (800) 25 19 02 in **Australia;** in **New Zealand** (0800) 44 10 68; in the **U.K.** (0800) 52 13 13; in the **U.S.** and **Canada** (800) 221-7282). Elsewhere, call U.S. collect (801) 964-6665. American Express traveler's checks, the most widely recognized in Mexico, are now available in 10 currencies, but U.S. traveler's checks are the most reliably accepted. AmEx are also the easiest to replace if lost or stolen. Checks can be purchased for a small fee (1-4%) at American Express Travel Service Offices, banks, and American Automobile Association offices (AAA members can buy the checks commission-free). Cardmembers can also purchase checks at American Express Dispensers at Travel Service Offices at airports and by ordering them via phone (tel. (800) ORDER-TC (673-3782)). American Express offices sometimes cash their checks commission-free, although they often offer slightly worse rates than banks. You can also buy *Cheques for Two* which can be signed by either of two people traveling together. Request the American Express booklet "Traveler's Companion," which lists travel office addresses and stolen check hotlines for each European country. Visit their online travel offices (http://www.aexp.com).

**Citicorp:** Call (800) 645-6556 in the **U.S.** and **Canada;** in **Europe,** the **Middle East,** or **Africa** (0171) 508 7007; from elsewhere call U.S. collect (813) 623-1709. Sells both Citicorp and Citicorp Visa traveler's checks in U.S., Australian, and Canadian dollars, British pounds, German marks, Spanish pesetas, and Japanese yen. Commission is 1-2% on check purchases. Checkholders are automatically enrolled for 45 days in the Travel Assist Program (hotline (800) 250-4377 or collect (202) 296-8728) which provides travelers with English-speaking doctor, lawyer, and interpreter referrals as well as check refund assistance and general travel information. Citicorp's World Courier Service guarantees hand-delivery of traveler's checks when a refund location is not convenient. Call 24hr. per day, 7 days per week.

**Thomas Cook MasterCard:** For 24hr. cashing or refund assistance, call (800) 223-9920 in the **U.S.** and **Canada;** from the **U.K.** call (0800) 622 101 toll-free or (1733) 502 995 or (1733) 318 950 collect; elsewhere call U.S. collect (609) 987-7300. Offers checks in U.S., Canadian, and Australian dollars, British and Cypriot pounds, French and Swiss francs, German marks, Japanese yen, Dutch guilders, Spanish pesetas, South African rand, and ECUs. Commission 1-2% for purchases. Thomas Cook offices may sell checks for lower commissions and will cash checks commission-free. Thomas Cook MasterCard Traveler's Checks are also available from **Capital Foreign Exchange** (see **Currency and Exchange,** p. 18) in U.S. or Canadian dollars, French and Swiss francs, British pounds, and German marks.

**Visa:** In the U.S., call (800) 227-6811; in the U.K. (0800) 895 492; from anywhere else in the world call (01733 318 949) and reverse the charges. Any of the above numbers can tell you the location of their nearest office. Any type of Visa traveler's checks can be reported lost at the Visa number.

Each agency refunds lost or stolen traveler's checks, but expect hassles if you lose track of them. When buying checks, get a list of refund centers. To expedite the refund process, separate your check receipts and keep them in a safe place. Record check numbers as you cash them to help identify exactly which checks might be missing. As an additional precaution, leave a list of the numbers with someone at home. Even with the check numbers in hand, you will probably find that getting a refund involves hours of waiting and spools of red tape.

It's best to buy most of your checks in small denominations (US$20) to minimize your losses at times when you need cash fast and can't avoid a bad exchange rate. If possible, purchase checks in U.S. dollars, since many *casas de cambio* refuse to change other currencies.

**ESSENTIALS**

## CREDIT CARDS AND CASH CARDS

Most of the banks that cash traveler's checks will make cash advances on a credit card, but be prepared to flash your passport. Major credit cards can prove invaluable in a financial emergency; **Visa** and **MasterCard** are accepted by many Mexican businesses, **American Express** and **Diners Club** to a lesser degree. Major credit cards can also work in some **automated teller machines (ATMs).**

All major credit card companies have some form of worldwide lost card protection service, and most offer a variety of additional travel services to cardholders—make sure to inquire before you leave home. Students and other travelers who may have difficulty procuring a credit card should know that family members can sometimes obtain a joint-account card.

**Cirrus** now has international cash machines in 80 countries, including Mexico; call (800) 424-7787 for current ATM availability information. ATMs offer low, "wholesale" exchange rates, but Cirrus charges US$5 to withdraw outside the U.S., so it's only a rate-saver if you withdraw large amounts of money. The **Plus** network can also be accessed widely; call (800) 843-7587 to see if there's a machine near you. Mexican ATM machines often have keypads with numbers only. If you remember your ATM password by letters, be sure to jot down its numeric equivalent before leaving the U.S. Also, four-digit PINs are standard in Mexico. If you don't have a four-digit PIN, contact your bank or credit card company so they can assign you one.

Some Mexican ATM machines have been known to withdraw money from an account without issuing any money. If you attempt to withdraw money and are turned down, write down the time, location and amount of the transaction, and check this against bank statements.

## SENDING MONEY

The cheapest way to receive emergency money in Mexico is to have it sent through a large commercial bank that has associated banks within Mexico. The sender must either have an account with the bank or bring in cash or a money order, and some banks cable money only for customers. The service costs US$25-80, depending on the amount sent. Cabled money should arrive in one to three days if the sender can furnish exact information (i.e. recipient's passport number and the Mexican bank's name and address); otherwise, there will be significant delays. To pick up money, you must show some form of positive identification, such as a passport.

**Western Union** (tel. (800) 325-6000) offers a convenient service for cabling money. If the sender has no credit card, he or she must go in person to one of Western Union's offices with cash—no money orders accepted, and cashier's checks are not always accepted. The money will arrive at the central telegram office or post office of the designated city. If you are in a major city, the money should arrive within 24 hours or less. In a smaller town, it could take 48 hours. The money will arrive in pesos and will be held for 30 days.

In emergencies, U.S. citizens can have money sent via the State Department's **Overseas Citizens Service, American Citizens Services,** Consular Affairs, Room 4811, U.S. Department of State, Washington, D.C. 20520 (tel. (202) 647-5225; nights, Sundays, and holidays (202) 647-4000; fax (on demand only) (202) 647-3000; http://travel.state.gov). For a fee of US$15, the State Department will forward money within hours to the nearest consular office, which will then disburse it according to instructions. The office serves only Americans in the direst of straits abroad; non-American travelers should contact their embassies or information on wiring cash. The quickest way to have the money sent is to cable the State Department through Western Union depending on the circumstances.

## TIPPING

In Mexico, it can often be hard to know when to leave a tip and when to just walk away. Play it safe by handing a peso or two to anyone who provides you with some sort of service; this includes the bagboy at the supermarket, the shoeshiner, the old man who offers to carry your luggage half a block to your hotel, the young boys who wash your windshield at the carwash, the eager porters who greet you at the bus station, and the street savvy local who shows you the way to the tourist office. Oddly enough, cab drivers (except in Mexico City) aren't tipped since they don't run on meters. In a Mexican restaurant, waiters and waitresses are tipped based on the quality of service; good service deserves at least 10%, especially since devaluation makes meals so cheap to begin with. And never, ever leave without saying *Gracias.*

# ■ Safety and Security

Mexico is relatively safe, although large cities (especially Mexico City) demand extra caution. After dark, keep away from bus and train stations, subways, and public parks. Shun empty train compartments; many travelers avoid the theft-ridden Mexican train system altogether. When on foot, stay out of trouble by sticking to busy, well-lit streets. Many isolated parks and beaches attract unsavory types as soon as night falls. Act as if you know exactly where you are going: an obviously bewildered bodybuilder is more likely to be harassed than a stern and confident 98-pound weakling. Ask the manager of your hotel for advice on specific areas; whenever possible, *Let's Go* warns of unsafe neighborhoods and areas, but only your eyes can tell you for sure if you've wandered into one. In small, cheap, and dark accommodations, check to make sure your door locks.

Keep your money and valuables near you at all times—under the pillow at night and in the bathroom while you shower. A **money belt** is probably the best way to carry cash; you can buy one at most camping supply stores or through the Forsyth Travel Library (tel. (800) 367-7984; fax (816) 942-6969). The best combination of convenience and invulnerability is the nylon, zippered pouch with belt that should sit *inside* the waist of your pants or skirt. A **neck pouch** is as safe, although less accessible. Do avoid keeping anything precious in a fanny pack (even if it's worn on your stomach): your valuables will be highly visible and easy to steal. In city crowds and especially on public transportation, pickpockets are amazingly deft at their craft. Hold your bags tightly. *Ladrones* have been known to surgically remove valuables by slitting the underside of bags as unsuspecting travelers hold on to them. Make two photocopies of all important documents; keep one copy with you (separated from the original) and leave one with someone at home. Be particularly wary of pickpockets in Mexico City, one of the world's most fertile breeding grounds for petty thieves.

Driving hazards in Mexico may be different from those you are used to at home. Watch out for open manholes and irregular pavement. Be sure to learn local driving signals and avoid driving alone at night. Drive slowly, especially in the rain; some cars have only one headlight (or none), and in some areas, loose livestock may appear unexpectedly. Avoid sleeping in your car; if your vehicle breaks down, wait for the police or the Green Angels for roadside assistance. Certain roads should be avoided altogether. For more information on driving in Mexico, see **By Car**, p. 43.

For official **United States Department of State** travel advisories, call their 24-hour hotline at (202) 647-5225 or check their website (http://travel.state.gov), which provides travel information and publications. Alternatively, order publications, including a free pamphlet entitled *A Safe Trip Abroad,* by writing to Superintendent of Documents, U.S. Government Printing Office, Washington, D.C. 20402, or by calling them at (202) 512-1800. Official warnings from the **United Kingdom Foreign and Commonwealth Office** are on-line at http://www.fco.gov.uk; you can also call the office at (0171) 238-4503. The **Canadian Department of Foreign Affairs and International Trade** (DFAIT) offers advisories and travel warnings at its web address (http://www.dfait-maeci.gc.ca) and at its phone number ((613) 944-6788 in Ottawa, (800) 267-6788 elsewhere in Canada). Their free publication, *Bon Voyage, But...,* offers travel tips to Canadian citizens; you can receive a copy by calling them at (613) 944-6788 from Ottawa or abroad, or at (800) 267-6788 from Canada.

**DRINKING AND DRUGS**

Drinking in Mexico is not for amateurs; bars and *cantinas* are strongholds of Mexican *machismo*. When someone calls you *amigo* and orders you a beer, bow out quickly unless you want to match him glass for glass in a challenge that could last several days. Avoid public drunkenness—it is against the law. Locals are fed up with teen-age (and older) *gringos* who cross the border for nights of debauchery.

Mexico rigorously prosecutes drug cases. Note that a minimum jail sentence awaits anyone found guilty of possessing any drug, and that Mexican law does not distinguish between marijuana and other narcotics. Even if you aren't convicted, arrest and trial will be long, dangerous and unpleasant. Derived from Roman and Napoleonic law, the Mexican judicial process does *not* assume that you are innocent until proven guilty but vice versa, and it is not uncommon to be detained for a year before a verdict is reached. Foreigners and suspected drug traffickers are not released on bail. Ignorance of Mexican law is no excuse—"I didn't know it was illegal" won't get you out of jail. Furthermore, there is little your consulate can do other than inform your relatives and bring care packages to you in jail.

Finally, don't even think about bringing drugs back into the U.S. Customs agents and their perceptive K-9s won't be amused. On the northern highways, especially along the Pacific coast, expect to be stopped repeatedly by burly, humorless troopers looking for contraband. That innocent-looking hitchhiker you were kind enough to pick up may be a drug peddler with a stash of illegal substances. If the police catch it in your car, the drug possession charges will extend to you, and your car may be confiscated.

For the free pamphlet *Travel Warning on Drugs Abroad,* send a self-addressed, stamped envelope to the Bureau of Consular Affairs, Public Affairs #6831, Dept. of State, Washington, D.C. 20520-4818 (tel. (202) 647-1488).

# ■ Health

Before you can say "pass the *jalapeños*," a long-anticipated vacation can turn into an unpleasant study of the wonders of the Mexican health care system. While malaise can typically be fended off with preventive measures (see **Before You Go**, p. 23), local pharmacists can give shots and dispense other remedies should mild illness prove inescapable. Wherever possible, *Let's Go* lists a pharmacy open for extended hours. If one is not listed, ask a policeman or cab driver. If you have an emergency and the door is locked, knock loudly; someone is probably sleeping inside.

When it comes to health, a little preparation goes a long way. For minor problems, bring along a compact **first-aid** kit with band-aids, aspirin or other pain killer, a thermometer, medicine for diarrhea or stomach problems, a decongestant for colds, sunscreen, and insect repellant.

Those using glasses or contact lens should bring adequate supplies and an extra prescription. Mexican equivalents can be hard to find and could irritate your eyes, although almost all pharmacies will carry saline solution.

Anyone with a chronic condition requiring medication should see a doctor before leaving. Allergy sufferers should find out if their conditions are likely to be aggravated in the regions they plan to visit. Obtain a full supply of any necessary medication before your trip, since matching your prescription to a foreign equivalent is not always easy, safe, or possible. Always carry up-to-date, legible prescriptions or a statement from your doctor, especially if you use insulin, a syringe, or a narcotic.

Those with medical conditions that cannot be immediately recognized (e.g. diabetes, allergies to antibiotics, epilepsy, heart conditions) should obtain a stainless steel **Medic Alert identification tag** (US$35 the first year, $15 annually thereafter). Contact Medic Alert Foundation International, 2323 Colorado Ave., Turlock, CA 95382, or call their 24-hour hotline at (800) 825-3785. If you are concerned about being able to access medical support while traveling, two services provide assistance through networks of English-speaking doctors and nurses: **Global Emergency Medical Services**

**(GEMS)** (2001 Westside Drive, #120, Alpharetta, GA 30201; tel. (800) 860-1111; fax (770) 475-0058) and **International Association for Medical Assistance to Travelers (IAMAT)** in the **U.S.** (417 Center St., Lewiston, NY 14092; tel. (716) 754-4883; fax (519) 836-3412; email iamat@sentex.net; http://www.sentex.net/~iamat), **Canada** (40 Regal Road, Guelph, Ontario, N1K 1B5; tel. (519) 836-0102), or **New Zealand** (P.O. Box 5049, Christchurch 5).

## BEFORE YOU GO

Take a look at your **immunization records** before you go. Visitors to Mexico do not need to carry vaccination certificates (though anyone entering Mexico from South America or Africa may be asked to show proof of vaccination for yellow fever). No vaccinations are required for Americans entering Mexico; however, a few medical precautions can make your trip a safer one. **Typhoid fever** is common in Mexico, especially in rural areas. Transmitted through contaminated food and water and by direct contact, typhoid produces fever, headaches, fatigue, and constipation in its victims. Vaccinations are 70-90% effective and last for three years. In recent years **cholera,** caused by bacteria in contaminated food, reached epidemic stages in parts of Mexico. Cholera's symptoms are diarrhea, dehydration, vomiting, and cramps, and can be fatal if untreated. Vaccines are recommended for those planning travel to rural areas and persons with stomach problems. Gamma globulin shots are also strongly recommended for those traveling to these areas. **Hepatitis A** is a risk in rural parts of the country; vaccines are available in the U.S.

**Malaria,** transmitted by mosquitoes, is a risk in many rural regions of Mexico, particularly along the southwest coast (Oaxaca, Chiapas, Guerrero, Campeche, Quintana Roo, Sinaloa, Michoacan, Nayarit, Colima, and Tabasco). Flu-like symptoms can strike up to a year after returning home; visit a doctor if you're in doubt, since untreated malaria can cause anemia, kidney failure, coma, and death. Consult your physician before leaving about taking the recommended dosage of chloroquine; or check the latest Center for Disease Control advisory at http://www.cdc.com. Your best protection is to wear long pants and long sleeves and to use insect repellent. Malaria transmission is most common from dusk 'til dawn. If you're hiking or camping, tuck long pants into socks and use a bednet at night. You may also want to bring anti-malarial tablets from home. **Dengue** is just one more reason to arm yourself against dive-bombing mosquitoes. Transmitted by blood-sucking insects, dengue produces flu-like symptoms and a rash. Recent epidemics have been reported in parts of Mexico. Unlike malaria, the mosquitoes that transmit dengue bite during the day rather than at night. No vaccine or treatment is available.

**Other insect diseases** include the following, some of which may be a threat in the region you are traveling through. **Filariasis** is a roundworm infestation transmitted by mosquitoes. Infection causes enlargement (elephantiasis) of extremities; there is no vaccine. **Leishmaniasis,** a parasite transmitted by sand flies, can cause fever, weakness, and a swollen spleen. There is a treatment, but no vaccine. **American Trypanomiasis/CHAGAS Disease** is another relatively common parasite. Transmitted by the reduviid bug, a.k.a. cone nose or kissing bug, which infests mud, adobe, and thatch, the symptoms are fever, heart disease, and later on, an enlarged intestine. Avoid overnights in infested buildings. There is no vaccine and limited treatment.

**Parasites** (tapeworms, etc.) also hide in unsafe water and food. *Giardia*, for example, is acquired by drinking untreated water from streams or lakes. It can stay with you for years. Symptoms of parasitic infections in general include swollen glands or lymph nodes, fever, rashes or itchiness, digestive problems, eye problems, and anemia. Boil your water, wear shoes, avoid bugs, and eat cooked food.

## TRAVELER'S DIARRHEA (TURISTA)

One of the biggest health threats in Mexico is the water. **Traveler's diarrhea,** known in Mexico as *turista,* often lasts two or three days (symptoms include cramps, nausea, vomiting, chills, and a fever as high as 103°F (39°C) and is the dastardly consequence of ignoring the following advice: Never drink unbottled water; ask for *agua purificada* in restaurants and hotels. If you must purify your own water, bring it to a rolling boil (simmering isn't enough) and let it boil for about 30 minutes, or treat it with iodine drops or tablets. Don't brush your teeth with tap water, and don't even rinse your toothbrush under the faucet. Keep your mouth closed in the shower. Many a sorry traveler has been fooled by the clever disguise of impure water—the treacherous ice cube. Stay away from those tasty-looking salads: uncooked vegetables (including lettuce and coleslaw) are a great way to get *turista*. Other culprits are raw shellfish, unpasteurized milk, and sauces containing raw eggs. Peel fruits and vegetables before eating them, and beware of watermelon and oranges, which are often injected with impure water. Beware of food from markets or street vendors that may have been "washed" in dirty water or fried in rancid oil. Juices, peeled fruits, and exposed coconut slices are all risky. Also beware of frozen treats that may have been made with bad water. A golden rule in Mexico: **boil it, peel it, cook it—or forget it.** Otherwise, your stomach will not forgive you.

Virtually everyone gets *turista* in their first trip to Mexico; many get it every time they visit, regardless of how careful they are with food. So don't fret. A common symptomatic diarrhea-only treatment is **Immodium** (the liquid works faster)**,** but to combat all-out *turista,* forget standard remedies like Pepto-Bismol and take **Lomotil,** a miracle drug sold over the counter in Mexican pharmacies. It should provide immediate relief, but consult a doctor if symptoms persist.

## HEAT

Common sense goes a long way in preventing **heat exhaustion:** relax in hot weather, drink lots of non-alcoholic fluids, and lie down inside if you feel terribly ill or exhausted. Continuous heat stress can eventually lead to **heatstroke,** characterized by rising body temperature, severe headache, and cessation of sweating. The victim must be cooled off with wet towels and taken to a doctor immediately. Though you may not consider it a serious malady, be aware that thousands die each year due to heat-related sickness.

Finally, be sure to drink plenty of liquids—much more than you're accustomed to. Heat and high altitudes will dehydrate you more swiftly than you'd expect. A good way to gauge how dehydrated you are is to check the color of your urine, which should be kept clear. Alcoholic beverages are dehydrating, as are coffee, strong tea, and caffeinated sodas. You'll be sweating a lot, so be sure to eat enough salty food to prevent electrolyte depletion—otherwise, you may be stricken with headaches.

Less debilitating, but still dangerous, is sunburn, which in serious cases can produce painful blistering, fever, and unsightly peeling. If you're prone to sunburn, carry sunscreen with you and apply it liberally and often—when it comes to your health, don't be cheap. If you do get sunburn (despite all the warnings!), drink even more water and non-alcoholic fluids than you normally would; it'll cool you down and help your poor, overdone skin recover faster.

## WOMEN'S HEALTH

Women traveling in unsanitary conditions are vulnerable to urinary tract and bladder infections, common and severely uncomfortable bacterial diseases which cause a burning sensation and painful and sometimes frequent urination. Untreated, these infections can lead to kidney infections, sterility, and even death. Drink tons of vitamin-C-rich juice, plenty of clean water, and urinate frequently, especially right after intercourse. If symptoms persist, see a doctor. If you are prone to vaginal yeast infections, take along enough over-the-counter medicine, as treatments may not be readily available in Mexico. Women may also be susceptible to vaginal thrush and cystitis, two treatable but uncomfortable illnesses that are likely to flare up in hot and humid climates. Wearing loosely fitting trousers or a skirt and cotton underwear may help. Tampons and pads are sometimes hard to find when traveling; certainly your preferred brands may not be available, so it may be advisable to take supplies along.

## BIRTH CONTROL AND ABORTION

Reliable **contraceptives** may be difficult to come by when traveling. Women on the pill should bring enough to allow for possible loss, and anyone planning to use a diaphragm should stock up on contraceptive jelly. Although **condoms** are widely available in Mexico, quality is variable, so buy plenty before you leave.

Abortion is illegal in Mexico; you'll have to cross the border to have one performed legally and safely. The U.S. **National Abortion Federation's hotline** can direct you to organizations which provide information on abortion in other countries (tel. (800) 772-9100, Mon.-Fri. 9:30am-12:30pm and 1:30-5:30pm), 1775 Massachusetts Ave. NW, Washington, D.C. 20036. Your embassy or consulate may also be able to provide a list of doctors who perform abortions. The **International Planned Parenthood Federation (**European Regional Office, Regent's College Inner Circle, Regent's Park, London NW1 4NS (tel. (0171) 487 7900; fax 487 7950) is a source of general information on contraception and abortion worldwide.

## AIDS AND HIV

All travelers should be concerned about **Acquired Immune Deficiency Syndrome (AIDS,** or **SIDA** in Spanish), transmitted through the exchange of body fluids with an individual who is HIV-positive. *Do not* share syringes, intravenous or tattooing needles, and *never* have vaginal, oral, or anal sex without using a latex condom, preferably one lubricated with the spermicide nonoxynol-9. Latex condoms are safer than lambskin ones, which have virus-permeable pores. Avoid oil-based lubricants like Vaseline, which destroy the integrity of the latex, rendering it useless in the prevention of HIV transmission.

The U.S. Center for Disease Control's 24-hour **AIDS Hotline** provides information on AIDS in the U.S. and can refer you to other organizations with information on Mexico (tel. (800) 342-2437). Contact the **U.S. State Department** through the Bureau of Consular Affairs for country-specific restrictions for HIV-positive travelers (Bureau of Consular Affairs, #6831, U.S. Dept. of State, Washington, D.C. 20520). Write to the **World Health Organization,** attn: Global Program on AIDS, 20 Avenue Appia, 1211 Geneva 27, Switzerland (tel. (22) 791-2111), for statistical material on AIDS internationally. Those travelers who are HIV-positive should thoroughly check possible immigration restrictions in the country which they wish to visit.

# ▓ Insurance

Beware of buying unnecessary travel coverage—your regular insurance policies may extend to many travel-related accidents. **Medical insurance** (especially university policies) often cover costs incurred abroad; check with your provider. **Medicare's** "foreign travel" coverage is valid in Mexico. Canadians are protected by their home province's health insurance plan for up to 90 days after leaving the country; check with the provincial Ministry of Health or Health Plan Headquarters for details. Australia has Reciprocal Health Care Agreements (RHCAs) with several countries; the Commonwealth Department of Human Services and Health can provide more information. Your **homeowners' insurance** (or your family's coverage) often covers theft during travel. Homeowners are generally covered against loss of travel documents (passport, plane ticket, railpass, etc.) up to US$500.

**ISIC** and **ITIC** provide basic insurance benefits, including US$100 per day of in-hospital sickness for a maximum of 60 days, and US$3000 of accident-related medical reimbursement (see **Youth, Student, and Teacher Identification,** p. 15). Cardholders have access to a toll-free 24-hour helpline whose multilingual staff can provide assistance in medical, legal, and financial emergencies overseas (tel. (800) 626-2427 in the U.S. and Canada; elsewhere call the U.S. collect (713) 267-2525). **Council** and **STA** offer a range of plans that can supplement your basic insurance coverage, with options covering medical treatment and hospitalization, accidents, baggage loss, and even charter flights missed due to illness. Most **American Express** cardholders

receive automatic car rental (collision and theft, but not liability) insurance, and travel accident coverage (US$100,000 in life insurance) on flight purchases made with the card; call Customer Service (tel. (800) 528-4800). If you must, **Globalcare Travel Insurance,** 220 Broadway, Lynnfield, MA 01940 (tel. (800) 821-2488; fax (617) 592-7720; email global@nebc.mv.com; http://www.nebc.mv.com/globalcare), provides complete medical, legal, emergency, and travel-related services. **Travel Assistance International,** by Worldwide Assistance Services, Inc., 1133 15th St. NW, #400, Washington, D.C. 20005-2710 (tel. (800) 821-2828 or (202) 828-5894; fax (202) 828-5896; email wassist@aol.com), provides its members with a free 24hr. hotline for travel emergencies and referrals in over 200 countries. Their Per-Trip (starting at US$65) and Frequent Traveler (starting at US$235) plans include medical, travel, and communication assistance services.

# ■ Alternatives to Tourism

## STUDY

Popular in Mexico, foreign study programs vary tremendously in expense, academic quality, living conditions, degree of contact with local students, and exposure to local culture and languages. There is a plethora of exchange programs for high school students. Many American undergraduates enroll in programs sponsored by U.S. universities, and most colleges have offices that give advice and information on study abroad. Ask for the names of recent participants in these programs, and get in touch with them in order to judge which program is best for you. Cuernavaca, San Miguel de Allende, Oaxaca, Guanajuato, and Mexico City are all well known for language programs. Smaller local schools are generally cheaper, but international organizations may be better able to arrange academic credit at your home institution.

A number of organizations publish useful resources for those wishing to study abroad in Mexico. **UNIPUB,** 4611-F Assembly Dr., Lanham, MD 20706-4391 (in U.S., tel. (800) 274-4888; in Canada, tel. (800) 233-0504) distributes UNESCO's unwieldy but fascinating book *Study Abroad* (US$30 plus $5 shipping). Programs are described in Spanish. **Institute of International Education Books (IIE Books),** 809 United Nations Pl., New York, NY 10017-3580 (tel. (212) 984-5413; fax 984-5358) publishes *Academic Year Abroad* (US$43, $5 shipping), which has information on courses, costs, and accommodations for programs in Mexico, and *Vacation Study Abroad* (US$37, US$5 postage). For book orders, contact IIE Books, Institute of International Education, P.O. Box 371, Annapolis Junction, MD 20701 (tel. (800) 445-0443; fax (301) 206-9789; email iiebooks@pmds.com). **Council** sponsors over 40 study abroad programs throughout the world (see **Budget Travel Agencies,** p. 37).

If you're already fluent in Spanish, consider enrolling in the regular programs of a Mexican university. Applications to Mexican state universities are due in early spring. Don't expect to receive credit at your home institution, however. The only Mexican university accredited in the U.S. is the **Universidad de las Américas,** Ex-Hacienda Santa Catarina Martír, Apartado Postal 100, Cholula, Puebla 72820 (tel. (22) 29-20-00 or 29-20-17; ask for the *decanatura de asuntos internacionales*). Some Mexican universities organize programs designed specifically for foreign students. The **Centro de Enseñanza para Extranjeros (CEPE),** part of the **Universidad Nacional Autónoma de México (UNAM),** provides semester, intensive, and summer programs in Spanish, art, history, literature, and Chicano studies. The program is open only to undergraduate and graduate foreign students. The school also has a campus in Taxco. Write to UNAM, Apdo. 70-391, Avenida Universidad, Delegación Coyoacán, Mexico, D.F. 04510 (tel. (5) 622-24-70; fax 616-26-72).

**School for International Training (SIT),** College Semester Abroad Admissions, Kipling Rd., P.O. Box 676, Brattleboro, VT 05302 (tel. (800) 336-1616 or (802) 258-3279; fax 258-3500; email csa.sit@worldlearning.org). Runs semester-long pro-

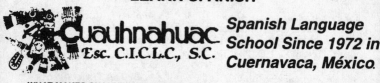

grams in Mexico that include cross-cultural orientation, intensive language study, homestay, field study, and independent study projects. Semester program US$8900, including tuition, room and board, round-trip international airfare, and insurance. But take heart: financial aid available. Some home institutions will provide additional aid and usually accept SIT transfer credits.

**American Institute for Foreign Study (AIFS),** College Division, 102 Greenwich Ave., Greenwich, CT 06830 (tel. (800) 727-2437; fax (203) 869-9615; email info@aifs.org; http//www.aifs.org). Organizes academic year and/or summer programs in Mérida. One semester US$5190, full year US$9980. Minority and merit scholarships available. High school programs also available; call (800) 888-2247.

**American Field Service Intercultural Programs (AFS),** 198 Madison Ave., 8th Floor, New York, NY, 10016; tel. (212) 299-9000; fax 299-9090; http://www.afs.org/usa). AFS administers summer, semester, and year-long homestay exchange programs for high school students in many countries including Mexico.

**Language Link Incorporated,** P.O. Box 3006, Peoria, IL (tel. (800) 552-2051). Runs the Spanish Language Institute-Center for Latin American Studies in Cuernavaca, Morelos. Program offers beginning, intermediate, and advanced level language courses. Students live with Mexican families. To contact the Institute directly, call (73) 11-00-63.

## WORK AND VOLUNTEERING

Volunteering is an excellent way to combine language study and cultural immersion with humanitarian work. There are plenty of volunteer opportunities available, and a little research will pay off in locating worthwhile and interesting positions. Paid work, on the other hand, may be difficult to obtain. The Mexican government is wary of giving up precious jobs to traveling gringos when many of its own people are unemployed. It used to be that only 10% of the employees of foreign firms located in Mexico could have non-Mexican citizenship; now the limit depends on the sector. If you manage to secure a position with a Mexican business, your employer must get you a work permit. It is possible, but illegal, to work without a permit. You risk deportation if caught. Adventurous job-hunters can arm themselves with a battery of books; try *International Jobs: Where They Are, How to Get Them,* published by **Addison-Wesley** (Order Department, 1 Jacob Way, Reading, MA 01867; tel. (800) 822-6339; US$16; also available at many bookstores) or **Peterson's** *Directory of Overseas Summer Jobs* (P.O. Box 2123, Princeton, NJ 08543; tel. (800) 338-3282; US$16, $5.75 shipping) which lists 50,000 volunteer and paid openings worldwide. In addition, the **American Chamber of Commerce,** Lucerna 78, Col. Juárez, 06600 Mexico, D.F., publishes *Mexico: Oportunidades de Empleo,* which lists companies accepting U.S. and Mexican students for internships. Call 5-724-3800 to order. The following organizations may be able to arrange volunteer opportunities, paid positions, or internships in Mexico and Central America:

**Global Volunteers,** 375 E. Little Canada Rd., St. Paul, MN 55117 (tel. (800) 487-1074; fax (612) 482-0915; email email@globalvlntrs.org; http://www.globalvlntrs.org). Volunteers teach English to university and high school students in Guanajuato. Participation fee is $995.

**International Association for the Exchange of Students for Technical Experience (IAESTE),** 10400 Little Patuxent Pkwy. #250, Columbia, MD 21044-3510 (tel. (410) 997-3068; fax 997-5186; email iaeste@aipt.org; http://www.aipt.org). Runs 8- to 12-week programs for science, architecture, engineering, agriculture, and math students who have completed at least 2 years of study in a technical field at an accredited 4-year institution. There is a non-refundable application fee of US$50; apply by Dec. 10 for summer placement.

**International Schools Services,** Educational Staffing Program, 15 Roszel Rd., P.O. Box 5910, Princeton, NJ 08543 (tel. (609) 452-0990; fax 452-2690; email edustaffing@iss.edu; http://www.iss.edu). Coordinates the placement of English-speaking teachers in schools in Mexico and Central America. Applicants must have a bachelor's degree and 2 years of relevant experience. Nonrefundable US$100 application fee. The *ISS Directory of Overseas Schools* (US$35) is also helpful.

# ENCUENTROS
## SPANISH ▼ LANGUAGE

### Meet Mexico

### *Meet the People • Meet the Culture*

ENCUENTROS is a total-immersion Spanish language program in Cuernavaca, Morelos, Mexico. We devote special attention to those who need Spanish for practical purposes such as business, travel, or professional use in the workplace. Each student's language program is designed for his or her needs and is evaluated on a weekly basis. Classes can accomodate beginning, intermediate, and advanced students and can be scheduled by the week or month.

### Meet the Language

- Programs begin every Monday throughout the year.
- Four students maximum in language practice classes.
- Schedule from 9:00 am to 2:30 pm includes three hours of classroom learning complemented by 2 hours of discussion groups, conferences, and "living" communication activities.
- 1/2 hour of assessment and study-help daily.
- Teachers are native Mexicans.
- "Communicative" approach emphasizes natural verbal interaction.

*Street address:*
Calle Morelos 36 (antes 140)
Colonia Acapantzingo CP 62440
Cuernavaca, Morelos, México.

*Telephones:*
*(011 from US)*
*Tel / fax:* (52 73) 12 5088
*Tel:* (52 73) 12 98 00

E-mail: encuent@infosel.net.mx
Homepage: http://cuernavaca.infosel.com.mx/encuentros/spanish.htm

**Los Niños,** 287 G Street, Chula Vista, CA 919 ̶ ̶ ̶ ̶ ̶
http://www.electriciti.com.flashñlosniños). Of ̶ ̶ ̶ ̶
rotary groups opportunities to participate in co ̶ ̶ ̶ ̶
programs near the U.S.-Mexico border. Participation f ̶ ̶ ̶

**The Experiment in International Living,** P.O. Box 676, B ̶ ̶ ̶
(800) 345-2929 or (802) 257-7751; http://www.worldlearn ̶ ̶
World Learning, Inc., it runs 4- to 5-week summer programs i ̶ ̶ ̶
Rica for high school students. Program leaders, who are paid for a ̶ ̶ ̶
be at least 24 years old, have lived in Mexico or Costa Rica, speak i ̶ ̶
and have experience with high school students.

# ▋ Specific Concerns

## WOMEN TRAVELERS

Women who travel through Mexico are often surprised by the unsolicited attention they receive. If you have two X chromosomes, and especially if you look like an *extranjera* (foreigner), you may find it difficult to shake off unwanted companions. Persistent men will insist on joining you; walking down the street, you will hear whistles and propositions. If you're fair-skinned, *"güera, güera"* will follow you everywhere. Offer no response or eye contact, since they will be interpreted as a come-on. Attention is usually more annoying than dangerous, but in real emergencies scream for help. Don't consider yourself safe just because people in uniform are around.

Awareness of Mexican social standards can prevent unpleasant and dangerous confrontations. Wearing short shorts or halter tops (or not wearing bras) will result in extra harassment; it's best to wear knee-length shorts. Bring a lightweight long skirt to wear in churches or in conservative regions like Chiapas. Almost without exception, *cantinas* are all-male institutions; the only women who ever enter are working, either as servers or as prostitutes.

If you are traveling with a male friend, it may help to pose as a couple: it will make it easier to share rooms and will also chill the blood of horny Romeos. Wearing a "wedding ring" on the left hand might also discourage unwanted attention. Northern Mexico, especially the border towns, is less congenial to women travelers. Oaxaca, Chiapas, and the Yucatán are friendlier, safer places.

Travel bookstores abound in publications catered towards solo female travelers. **Women Going Places,** a travel and resource guide emphasizing women-owned enterprises, caters to lesbians but offers advice appropriate for all women (US$15 from Inland Book Company, 1436 W. Randolph St., Chicago, IL 60607; tel. (800) 243-0138; fax (800) 334-3892). Other helpful resources include **Women's Travel in Your Pocket,** an annual guide for women, especially lesbians, traveling in the U.S., Canada, the Caribbean, and Mexico (US$14; available from Ferrari Guides, P.O. Box 37887, Phoenix, AZ 85069; tel. (602) 863-2408), and the encyclopedic and well-written **Handbook For Women Travellers** by Maggie and Gemma Moss (UK£9 from Piatkus Books, 5 Windmill St., London W1P 1HF; tel. (0171) 631 07 10).

## OLDER TRAVELERS

Senior travelers should bring a medical record that includes an update on conditions and prescriptions; the name, phone number, and address of a regular doctor; and a summary of their recent medical history. Find out if you have insurance that will cover costs you may incur in Mexico. **Senior citizens** are eligible for a wide range of discounts on transportation, museums, movies, theaters, concerts, restaurants, and accommodations. If you don't see a senior citizen price listed, ask, and you may be delightfully surprised. Agencies for senior group travel (like **Eldertreks,** 597 Markham St., Toronto, Ontario, M6G 2L7; tel. (416) 588-5000; fax 588-9839; email passages@inforamp.net, and **Walking the World,** P.O. Box 1186, Fort Collins, CO 80522; tel. (970) 225-0500; fax 225-9100; email walktworld@aol.com), are growing in enrollment and popularity.

**Elderhostel,** 75 Federal St., 3rd Fl., Boston, MA 02110-1941 (tel. (617) 426-7788, fax 426-8351; email Cadyg@elderhostel.org; http://www.elderhostel.org), offers 1-4 week programs at colleges, universities, and learning centers for those 55 or over.

**Gateway Books,** 2023 Clemens Rd., Oakland, CA 94602 (tel. (510) 530-0299, credit card orders (800) 669-0773; fax (510) 530-0497; email donmerwin@aol.com; http://www.discoverypress.com/gateway.html). Publishes *Europe the European Way: A Traveler's Guide to Living Affordably in the World's Great Cities* (US$14), which offers general hints for seniors considering a long stay or retirement abroad.

**Pilot Books,** 127 Sterling Ave., P.O. Box 2102, Greenport, NY 11944 (tel. (516) 477-1094 or (800) 79PILOT (797-4568); fax (516) 477-0978; email feedback@pilot-books.com; http://www.pilotbooks.com). Publishes a large number of helpful guides including *Doctor's Guide to Protecting Your Health Before, During, and After International Travel* (US$10, postage US$2). Call or write for a complete list of titles.

## BISEXUAL, GAY, AND LESBIAN TRAVELERS

Mexican law does not mention homosexuality, and attitudes vary from state to state. While some regions have ongoing campaigns against this "social threat," there is a gay-rights movement in Mexico City. Although discreet homosexuality is tolerated in most areas, public displays of gay affection are not and might be the quickest way of getting beaten up. The **International Gay and Lesbian Travel Association,** P.O. Box 4974, Key West, FL 33041 (tel. (800) 448-8550; fax (305) 296-6633; email IGTA@aol.com; http://www.rainbow-mall.com/igta), and the **International Lesbian and Gay Association (ILGA),** 81 rue Marché-au-Charbon, B-1000 Bruxelles, Belgium (tel./fax (02) 502 24 71; email ilga@ilga.org), are formidable sources of information. **Giovanni's Room,** 345 S. 12th St., Philadelphia, PA 19107 (tel. (215) 923-2960; fax 923-0813; email giolphilp@netaxs.com), is an international feminist, lesbian, and gay bookstore with mail-order service which carries many of the publications listed below. To find cities with **gay and lesbian nightlife** in Mexico, see that index entry.

**Damron Travel Guides,** P.O. Box 422458, San Francisco, CA 94142 (tel. (415) 255-0404 or (800) 462-6654; fax (415) 703-9049); email damronco@ud.com; http://www.damron.co). Publishers of the *Damron Address Book* (US$15), which lists bars, restaurants, guest houses, and services in the U.S., Canada, and Mexico which cater to gay men. *Damron's Accommodations* lists gay and lesbian hotels around the world (US$19). Mail order is available for an extra US$5 shipping.

**Ferrari Guides,** P.O. Box 37887, Phoenix, AZ 85069 (tel. (602) 863-2408; fax 439-3952; email ferrari@q-net.com; http://www.q-net.com). Gay and lesbian travel guides: *Ferrari Guides' Gay Travel A to Z* (US$16), *Ferrari Guides' Men's Travel in Your Pocket* (US$16), *Ferrari Guides' Women's Travel in Your Pocket* (US$14), *Ferrari Guides' Inn Places* (US$16). Available in bookstores or by mail order (postage/handling US$4.50 for the first item, US$1 for each additional item mailed within the U.S. Overseas, call or write for shipping cost).

**Gay's the Word,** 66 Marchmont St., London WC1N 1AB (tel. (0171) 278 7654). The largest gay and lesbian bookshop in the U.K. Mail order service available. No catalogue of listings, but they will provide a list of titles on a given subject. Open Mon.-Sat. 10am-6pm, Thurs. 10am-7pm, Sun. 2-6pm. Tube: Russel Square.

**Spartacus International Gay Guides** (US$33), published by Bruno Gmunder, Postfach 61 01 04, D-10921 Berlin, Germany (tel. (030) 615 00 3-42; fax 615 91 34). Lists bars, restaurants, hotels, and bookstores around the world catering to gays. Also lists hotlines for gays in various countries and homosexuality laws for each country. Available in bookstores and in the U.S. by mail from Lambda Rising, 1625 Connecticut Ave. NW, Washington, D.C. 20009-1013 (tel. (202) 462-6969).

## DISABLED TRAVELERS

Mexico is becoming increasingly accessible to travelers with disabilities, especially in popular resorts such as Acapulco and Cancún. Northern cities closer to the U.S. also tend to be more accessible; Saltillo might be the most wheelchair-friendly city in the entire country. Money talks—the more you are willing to spend, the less difficult it is to find accessible facilities. Most public and long-distance modes of transportation and most of the non-luxury hotels don't accommodate wheelchairs. Public bathrooms are almost all inaccessible, as are many ruins, parks, historic buildings, and museums. Still, with some advance planning, an affordable Mexican vacation is not impossible. The following organizations provide useful information:

**American Foundation for the Blind,** 11 Penn Plaza, 300, New York, NY 10011 (tel. (212) 502-7600), open Mon.-Fri. 8:30am-4:30pm. Provides info and services for the visually impaired. For a catalogue, contact Lighthouse Enterprises, 36-20 Northern Boulevard, Long Island City, NY 10011 (tel. (800) 829-0500).

**Facts on File,** 11 Penn Plaza, 15th Fl., New York, NY 10001 (tel. (212) 967-8800). Publishers of *Disability Resource,* a reference guide for travelers with disabilities (US$45 plus shipping). Available at bookstores or by mail order.

**Mobility International, USA (MIUSA),** P.O. Box 10767, Eugene, OR 97440 (tel. (514) 343-1284 voice and TDD; fax 343-6812; email info@miusa.org; http://miusa.org). International Headquarters in Brussels, rue de Manchester 25 Brussels, Belgium, B-1070 (tel. (02) 410 6297, fax; 410 6874). Contacts in 30 countries. Information on travel programs, international work camps, accommodations, access guides, and organized tours for those with physical disabilities. Membership US$30 per year. Sells the 3rd Edition of *A World of Options: A Guide to International Educational Exchange, Community Service, and Travel for Persons with Disabilities* (US$30, nonmembers US$35; organizations US$40).

**Moss Rehab Hospital Travel Information Service,** (tel. (215) 456-9600, TDD (215) 456-9602). A telephone information resource center on international travel accessibility and other travel-related concerns for those with disabilities.

**Society for the Advancement of Travel for the Handicapped (SATH),** 347 Fifth Ave., #610, New York, NY 10016 (tel. (212) 447-1928; fax 725-8253; email sath-travel@aol.com; http://www.sath.org). Publishes a quarterly color travel magazine *OPEN WORLD* (free for members or on subscription US$13 for nonmembers). Also publishes a wide range of info sheets on disability travel facilitation and accessible destinations. Annual membership US$45, students and seniors US$30.

**Twin Peaks Press,** P.O. Box 129, Vancouver, WA 98666-0129 (tel. (360) 694-2462, orders only MC and Visa (800) 637-2256; fax (360) 696-3210; email 73743.2634@compuserve.com;http://netm.com/mall/infoprod/twinpeak/helen.htm). Publishers of *Travel for the Disabled,* which provides travel tips, lists of accessible tourist attractions, and advice on other resources for disabled travelers (US$20). Also publishes *Directory for Travel Agencies of the Disabled* (US$20), *Wheelchair Vagabond* (US$15), and *Directory of Accessible Van Rentals* (US$10). Postage US$3.50 for first book, US$1.50 for each additional book.

The following organizations arrange tours or trips for disabled travelers:

**Directions Unlimited,** 720 N. Bedford Rd., Bedford Hills, NY 10507 (tel. (800) 533-5343; in NY (914) 241-1700; fax 241-0243). Specializes in arranging individual and group vacations, tours, and cruises for the physically disabled. Group tours for blind travelers.

**Flying Wheels Travel Service,** 143 W. Bridge St., Owatonne, MN 55060 (tel. (800) 535-6790; fax 451-1685). Arranges trips in the U.S. and abroad for groups and individuals in wheelchairs or with other forms of limited mobility.

**The Guided Tour Inc.,** Elkins Park House, 114B, 7900 Old York Rd., Elkins Park, PA 19027-2339 (tel. (800) 783-5841 or (215) 782-1370; fax 635-2637). Organizes travel programs for persons with developmental and physical challenges and those requiring renal dialysis. Call, fax, or write for a free brochure.

## TRAVELERS WITH CHILDREN

Children should not be deprived of the wonders of a Mexican vacation; simply slow your pace and plan ahead to accommodate smaller companions. If you plan on going on walking trips, consider bringing along a papoose to carry your baby. If you rent a car, make sure the company provides a seat for younger children. The following publications offer tips for adults traveling with children.

**Backpacking with Babies and Small Children** (US$10). Published by Wilderness Press, 2440 Bancroft Way, Berkeley, CA 94704 (tel. (800) 443-7227 or (510) 843-8080; fax 548-1355; email wpress@ix.netcom.com).

**Travel with Children** by Maureen Wheeler (US$12, postage US$1.50). Published by Lonely Planet Publications, Embarcadero West, 155 Filbert St., #251, Oakland, CA 94607 (tel. (800) 275-8555 or (510) 893-8555, fax 893-8563; email info@lonely-planet.com; http://www.lonelyplanet.com). Also at P.O. Box 617, Hawthorn, Victoria 3122, Australia.

## DIETARY CONCERNS

It's not easy for **vegetarians** in Mexico: most meals include meat or are prepared with animal fat. Always find out if your *frijoles* were prepared using *manteca* (lard). For more ideas, contact the **North American Vegetarian Society**, P.O. Box 72, Dolgeville, NY 13329 (tel. (518) 568-7970) which publishes *Transformative Adventures,* a guide to vacations and retreats (US$15). Membership to the Society costs US$20; family membership is US$26 and members receive a 10% discount on all publications. **The International Vegetarian Travel Guide** (UK£2) was last published in 1991. Order back copies from the Vegetarian Society of the UK (VSUK), Parkdale, Dunham Rd., Altringham, Cheshire WA14 4QG (tel. (0161) 928 0793). VSUK also publishes other titles, including *The European Vegetarian Guide to Hotels and Restaurants.* Call or send a self-addressed, stamped envelope for a listing.

Travelers who keep **kosher** should contact synagogues in larger cities for information on kosher restaurants; your own synagogue or Hillel should have access to lists of Jewish institutions across the nation. If you are strict in your observance, consider preparing your own food on the road. **The Jewish Travel Guide** (US$12, postage US$1.75) lists synagogues, kosher restaurants, and Jewish institutions in Mexico. Buy it from Ballantine-Mitchell Publishers, Newbury House 890-900, Eastern Ave., Newbury Park, Ilford, Essex, U.K. IG2 7HH (tel. (0181) 599 88 66; fax 599 09 84). It is available in the U.S. from Sepher-Hermon Press, 1265 46th St., Brooklyn, NY 11219 (tel. (718) 972-9010; US$15 plus US$2.50 shipping).

## MINORITY TRAVELERS

Although culturally diverse, Mexico is largely racially homogeneous. Mexicans are *indígenas* (indians), white, or some mixture of the two. The whiter your skin, the better treatment you'll get in larger cities, and the more you'll stand out in rural areas. Practically any other ethnicity will mark you as a foreigner in Mexico, and as a result you might receive attention from curious locals, particularly in smaller communities. On most occasions this attention (stares, giggling, questions) is not meant to be hostile and arises from curiosity rather than racism. Try to be understanding of the excitement produced by difference. In most cases, Mexicans react more strongly to foreignness, particularly Anglophone, than to ethnicity.

## TRAVELING ALONE

Traveling alone results in greater freedom: you choose which museums to visit and which to avoid, whether to take the early bus or the midnight train. It is the perfect opportunity to write a great travel journal, in the grand tradition of Mark Twain or John Steinbeck. When you get sick of yourself, it annihilates shyness and pushes you to meet people. On the other hand, it makes you a more vulnerable target for robbery and harassment. Lone travelers need to be well organized and look confident at all times. Do not wander around back alleys looking confused, and try to regularly contact someone at home who knows your itinerary. **A Foxy Old Woman's Guide to Traveling Alone,** by Jay Ben-Lesser, encompasses practically every specific concern, offering anecdotes and tips for anyone interested in solitary adventure. Available from Crossing Press in Freedom, CA (tel. (800) 777-1048), US$11; see **Women Travelers,** p. 31). Resources for the solo traveler include:

**American International Homestays,** P.O. Box 1754, Nederland, CO 80466 (tel. (303) 642-3088 or (800) 876-2048). Lodgings with English-speaking host families.

**Connecting: News for Solo Travelers,** P.O. Box 29088, 1996 W. Broadway, Vancouver, BC V6J 5C2, Canada (tel. (604) 737-7791 or (800) 557-1757). Bimonthly newsletter with features and listings of singles looking for travel companions. Annual directory lists tours and lodgings with reduced or no single supplement, subscription US$25.

**The Single Traveler Newsletter,** P.O. Box 682, Ross, CA 94957 (tel. (415) 389-0227). Bimonthly newsletter with good tips on avoiding single-supplement fees, subscription US$29.

**Travel Companions,** P.O. Box 833, Amityville, NY 11701 (tel. (516) 454-0880). Monthly newsletter with listings and helpful tips, subscription US$48.

**Traveling On Your Own,** by Eleanor Berman (US$13). Lists information resources for "singles" (old and young) and single parents. Crown Publishers, Inc., 201 East 50th St., New York, NY 10022

**Travelin' Woman,** 855 Moraga Dr., #14, Los Angeles, CA 90049 (tel. (310) 472-6318) or (800) 871-6409). Monthly newsletter with features, news, and tips, subscription US$48.

# ■ Packing

Pack light. That means you. The more things you have, the more you have to lose or be stolen, though having someone lighten your load may not seem like such a bad deal after a few days of backbreaking travel. Before you leave, pack your bag, strap it on, and imagine yourself walking uphill on hot asphalt for the next three hours. A good rule is to lay out only what you absolutely need, then take half the clothes and twice the money. One *New York Times* correspondent recommends that you "take no more than you can carry for half a mile at a dead run." You should also plan your packing according to the type of travel you'll be doing (multi-city backpacking tour, week-long stay in one place, etc.) and the area's high and low temperatures.

## LUGGAGE

**Backpack:** If you plan to cover most of your itinerary by foot, a sturdy backpack is unbeatable. Many packs are designed specifically for travelers, while others are for hikers; consider how you will use the pack before purchasing one or the other. In any case, get a quality pack with a strong, padded hip belt to transfer weight from your shoulders to your hips. Good packs cost anywhere from US$150-420. Bringing a smaller bag in addition to your pack allows you to leave your belongings behind while you go sight-seeing and carry essentials onto the plane.

**Duffel bag:** If you are not backpacking, an empty, lightweight duffel bag packed inside your luggage will be useful: once abroad you can fill your luggage with purchases and keep your dirty clothes in the duffel.

**Moneybelt or neck pouch:** Guard your money, passport, railpass, and other important articles in either one of these, available at any good camping store, and keep it with you *at all times.* The moneybelt should tuck inside the waist of your pants or skirt; you want to hide your valuables, not announce them with a colorful fanny- or butt-pack. See **Safety and Security** for more information on protecting you and your valuables.

## CLOTHING AND FOOTWEAR

**Clothing:** When choosing your travel wardrobe, aim for versatility and comfort, and avoid fabrics that wrinkle easily (to test a fabric, hold it tightly in your fist for 20 seconds). Solid colors mix and match best. In certain countries, stricter dress codes (especially for women) call for something besides the basic shorts, t-shirts, and jeans. Always bring a jacket or wool sweater.

**Walking shoes:** Well-cushioned **sneakers** are good for walking, though you may want to consider a good waterproof pair of **hiking boots.** A double pair of socks—light silk or polypropylene inside and thick wool outside—will cushion feet, keep them dry, and help prevent blisters. Bring a pair of flip-flops for protection in the shower. Talcum powder in your shoes and on your feet can prevent sores, and moleskin is great for blisters. Break in your shoes before you leave.

**Rain gear:** A waterproof jacket and a backpack cover will take care of you and your stuff at a moment's notice. Gore-Tex® and Gore-Tex imitation knockoffs are miracle fabrics that's both waterproof and breathable; it's all but mandatory if you plan on hiking. Avoid cotton as outer-wear, especially if you will be outdoors a lot.

## MISCELLANEOUS

**Sleepsacks:** Only bother if you plan to stay in **youth hostels** (not likely in Mexico).

**Washing clothes:** Though laundromats are often available, at times it is easier to use a sink. Bring a small bar or tube of detergent soap such as **Woolite**, a rubber squash ball to stop up the sink, and a travel clothes line.

**Film** is expensive just about everywhere. Bring film from home and, if you will be seriously upset if the pictures are ruined, develop it at home. If you're not a serious photographer, you might want to consider bringing a **disposable camera** or two rather than an expensive permanent one. Despite disclaimers, airport security X-rays *can* fog film, so either buy a lead-lined pouch, sold at camera stores, or ask the security to hand inspect it. Always pack it in your carry-on luggage, since higher-intensity X-rays are used on checked luggage.

**Other useful items:** first-aid kit; umbrella; sealable plastic bags (for damp clothes, soap, food, shampoo, and other spillables); alarm clock; waterproof matches; sun hat; moleskin (for blisters); needle and thread; safety pins; sunglasses; a personal stereo (Walkman) with headphones; pocketknife; plastic water bottle; compass; string (makeshift clothesline and lashing material); towel; padlock; whistle; rubber bands; toilet paper; flashlight; cold-water soap; earplugs; insect repellent; electrical tape (for patching tears); clothespins; maps and phrasebooks; tweezers; garbage bags; sunscreen; vitamins. Some items not always readily available or affordable on the road: deodorant; razors; condoms; tampons.

# GETTING THERE

## ▨ Budget Travel Agencies

**Council Travel** (http://www.ciee.org/travel/index.htm), the travel division of Council, is a full-service travel agency specializing in youth and budget travel. They offer discount airfares on scheduled airlines, railpasses, hosteling cards, low-cost accommodations, guidebooks, budget tours, travel gear, and international student (ISIC), youth (GO25), and teacher (ITIC) identity cards. For a list of locations in the **U.S.,** call 800-2-COUNCIL (226-8624). Also in **London** (tel. (0171) 287 3337), **Paris** (tel. 01 46 55 55 65), and **Munich** (tel. (089) 39 50 22).

**STA Travel,** 6560 Scottsdale Rd. #F100, Scottsdale, AZ 85253 (tel. (800) 777-0112 nationwide; fax (602) 922-0793; http://sta-travel.com). A student and youth travel organization with over 150 offices worldwide offering discount airfares for young travelers, railpasses, accommodations, tours, insurance, and ISICs. There are 16 offices in the U.S. Also in the U.K., 6 Wrights Ln., **London** W8 6TA (tel. (0171) 938 47 11 for North American travel); in New Zealand, 10 High St., **Auckland** (tel. (09) 309 97 23); in Australia, 222 Faraday St., **Melbourne** VIC 3050 (tel. (03) 9349 6911).

**Let's Go Travel,** Harvard Student Agencies, 17 Holyoke St., Cambridge, MA 02138 (tel. (617) 495-9649; fax 495-7956; email travel@hsa.net; http://hsa.net/travel). Railpasses, HI-AYH memberships, ISICs, ITICs, FIYTO cards, guidebooks (including every *Let's Go* at a substantial discount), maps, bargain flights, and a complete line of budget travel gear. All items available by mail; call or write for a catalogue (or see the catalogue in center of this publication).

**Travel CUTS (Canadian Universities Travel Services Limited),** 187 College St., Toronto, Ont. M5T 1P7 (tel. (416) 979-2406; fax 979-8167; email mail@travelcuts).

Canada's national student travel bureau and equivalent of Council, with 40 offices across Canada. Also in the U.K., 295-A Regent St., **London** W1R 7YA (tel. (0171) 637 31 61). Discounted domestic and international airfares open to all; special student fares to all destinations with valid ISIC. Issues ISIC, FIYTO, GO25, and HI hostel cards, as well as railpasses. Offers free *Student Traveller* magazine, as well as information on the Student Work Abroad Program (SWAP).

## ■ By Plane

The **airline industry** attempts to squeeze every dollar from customers; finding a cheap airfare will be easier if you understand the airlines' systems. Call every toll-free number and don't be afraid to ask about discounts; if you don't ask, it's unlikely they'll be volunteered. Students and others under 26 should never need to pay full price for a ticket. Seniors can also get great deals; many airlines offer senior traveler clubs or airline passes with few restrictions and discounts for their companions as well. Sunday newspapers (the *New York Times* is the best example) often have travel sections that list bargain fares from the local airport. Australians should consult the Saturday travel section of the *Sydney Morning Herald.* Outsmart airline reps with the phone-book-sized *Official Airline Guide* (check your local library; at US$359 per year, the tome costs as much as some flights), a monthly guide listing nearly every scheduled flight in the world (with fares, US$479) and toll-free phone numbers for all the airlines which allow you to call in reservations directly. More accessible is Michael McColl's *The Worldwide Guide to Cheap Airfare* (US$15), an incredibly useful guide for finding cheap airfare. **TravelHUB** (http://www.travelhub.com) will help you search for travel agencies on the web. Marc-David Seidel's **Airlines of the Web** (http://www.itn.net/airlines) provides links to pages and 800 numbers for most of the world's airlines. The newsgroup **rec.travel.air** is a good source of tips on current bargains. Most airfares peak between mid-June and early September. Midweek (Mon.-Thurs. morning) round-trip flights run about US$40-50 cheaper than on weekends; weekend flights, however, are generally less crowded. Return-date flexi-

bility is usually not an option for the budget traveler; traveling with an "open return" ticket can be pricier than fixing a return date and paying to change it. Whenever flying internationally, pick up your ticket well in advance of the departure date, have the flight confirmed within 72 hours of departure, and arrive at the airport at least three hours before your flight.

## COMMERCIAL AIRLINES

The commercial airlines' lowest regular offer is the **Advance Purchase Excursion Fare (APEX);** specials advertised in newspapers may be cheaper, but have more restrictions and fewer available seats. APEX fares provide you with confirmed reservations and allow "open-jaw" tickets (landing in and returning from different cities). Generally, reservations must be made 7 to 21 days in advance, with 7- to 14-day minimum and up to 90-day maximum stay limits, and hefty cancellation and change penalties (fees rise in summer). Book APEX fares early during peak season; by May you will have a hard time getting the departure date you want.

If you're coming from Europe, it's cheapest to fly first to a U.S. city, then connect to Mexico City or some other Mexican airport. Look into flights to less-popular destinations or on smaller carriers. **Mexicana** (tel. (800) 531-7921) and **Aeroméxico** (tel. (800) 237-6639) are the two major national airlines. Together, they cover most of Mexico; regional airlines also provide service in many areas. The U.S. airlines that serve Mexico most frequently are **American, America West, Continental, Delta,** and **United.** Be aware of the **departure tax** levied at Mexican international airports (US$15.90). These taxes are often included in the ticket price.

Even if you pay an airline's lowest published fare, you may waste hundreds of dollars. For the adventurous or the bargain-hungry, there are other, perhaps more inconvenient or time-consuming options, but before shopping around it is a good idea to find out the average commercial price in order to measure just how great a "bargain" you are being offered.

## TICKET CONSOLIDATORS

**Ticket consolidators** resell unsold tickets on commercial and charter airlines at unpublished fares. Consolidator flights are the best deals if you are travelling: on short notice, (you bypass advance purchase requirements, since you aren't tangled in airline bureaucracy); on a high-priced trip; to an offbeat destination; or in the peak season, when published fares are jacked way up. Fares sold by consolidators are generally much cheaper; a 30-40% price reduction is not uncommon. There are rarely age constraints or stay limitations, but unlike tickets bought through an airline, you won't be able to use your tickets on another flight if you miss yours, and you will have to go back to the consolidator to get a refund, rather than the airline. Keep in mind that these tickets are often for coach seats on connecting (not direct) flights on foreign airlines, and that frequent-flyer miles may not be credited. Decide what you can and can't live with before shopping.

Not all consolidators deal with the general public; many only sell tickets through travel agents. **Bucket shops** are retail agencies that specialize in getting cheap tickets. Although ticket prices are marked up slightly, bucket shops generally have access to a larger market than would be available to the public and can also get tickets from wholesale consolidators. Look for bucket shops' tiny ads in the travel section of weekend papers; in the U.S., the *Sunday New York Times* is a good source. In London, a call to the **Air Travel Advisory Bureau** (tel. (0171) 636 50 00) can provide names of reliable consolidators and discount flight specialists. Kelly Monaghan's *Consolidators: Air Travel's Bargain Basement* (US$7 plus US$2 shipping) from the Intrepid Traveler, P.O. Box 438, New York, NY 10034 (email intreptrav@aol.com), is an invaluable source for more information and lists of consolidators.

Be a smart shopper; check out the competition. Among the many reputable and trustworthy companies are, unfortunately, some shady wheeler-dealers. Contact the local Better Business Bureau to find out how long the company has been in business and its track record. Although not necessary, it is preferable to deal with consolidators close to home so you can visit in person, if necessary. Ask to receive your tickets as quickly as possible so you have time to fix any problems. Get the company's policy in writing: insist on a **receipt** that gives full details about the tickets, refunds, and restrictions, and record who you talked to and when. It may be worth paying with a credit card (despite the 2-5% fee) so you can stop payment if you never receive your tickets. Also ask about accommodations and car rental discounts; some consolidators have fingers in many pies.

For destinations **worldwide,** try **Airfare Busters,** (offices in Washington, D.C. (tel. (202) 776-0478), Boca Raton, FL (tel. (561) 994-9590), and Houston, TX (tel. (800) 232-8783); **Pennsylvania Travel,** Paoli, PA (tel. (800) 331-0947); **Cheap Tickets,** offices in Los Angeles, CA, San Francisco, CA, Honolulu, HI, Seattle, WA, and New York, NY, (tel. (800) 377-1000); or **Discount Travel International,** New York, NY (tel. (212) 362-3636; fax 362-3236), which has recently begun booking flights from large cities in Asia, Australia, and New Zealand in addition to European destinations. **Moment's Notice,** New York, NY (tel. (718) 234-6295; fax 234-6450; http://www.moments-notice.com) offers air tickets, tours, and hotels; US$25 annual fee. **NOW Voyager,** 74 Varick St. #307, New York, NY 10013 (tel. (212) 431-1616; fax (212) 334-5243; email info@nowvoyagertravel.com; http://www.nowvoyager-travel.com) acts as a consolidator and books discounted international flights, mostly from New York, as well as courier flights, for a registration fee of US$50. For a processing fee, depending on the number of travelers and the itinerary, **Travel Avenue,** Chicago, IL (tel. (800) 333-3335; fax (312) 876-1254; http://www.travelavenue.com) will search for the lowest international airfare available, including consolidated prices, and will even give you a rebate on fares over US$300. A number of consolidators sell tickets over the Internet; among them are **NOW Voyager** (email info@nowvoyagertravel.com; http://www.nowvoyagertravel.com) and **Travel Avenue** (http://www.travelavenue.com).

## STAND-BY FLIGHTS

**Airhitch,** 2641 Broadway, 3rd Flr., New York, NY 10025 (tel. (800) 326-2009 or (212) 864-2000; fax 864-5489) and Los Angeles, CA (tel. (310) 726-5000), will add a certain thrill to the prospects of when you will leave and where exactly you will end up. Complete flexibility is necessary. The snag is that you buy not a ticket, but the promise that you will get to a destination near where you're intending to go within a window of time (usually 5 days) from a location in a region you've specified. Be aware that you may only receive a monetary refund if all available flights which departed within your date-range from the specified region are full, but future travel credit is always available. There are several offices in Europe; the main one is in Paris (tel. (01) 47 00 16 30).

    **Air-Tech, Ltd.,** 588 Broadway #204, New York, NY 10012 (tel. (212) 219-7000; fax 219-0066) offers a very similar service (Travel Window 1-4 days). Air-Tech sends you a FlightPass with a contact date falling soon before your Travel Window, when you are to call them for flight instructions. Note that the service is one-way—you must go through the same procedure to return—and that no refunds are granted unless the company fails to get you a seat before your Travel Window expires. Air-Tech also arranges courier flights and regular confirmed-reserved flights at discount rates.

    Be sure to read all the fine print in your agreements with these or any stand-by flight company—a call to the Better Business Bureau of New York City may be worthwhile. Be warned that it is difficult to receive refunds.

# ▓ By Bus or Train

Greyhound serves many border towns, including El Paso and Brownsville, Texas. Smaller lines serve other destinations. Buses tend not to cross the border, but at each of these stops you can pick up Mexican bus lines (among them Tres Estrellas de Oro, Estrella Blanca, and Transportes Del Norte) on the other side.

    By train, you can take Amtrak to El Paso, walk across the border to Ciudad Juárez and from there use other forms of transport to reach points within Mexico. Amtrak also serves San Diego and San Antonio, where you can catch a bus to the border towns (US$285-433 one way from New York to El Paso, San Diego, or San Antonio).

# ▓ By Car

Driving entails no bureaucratic complications within the Zona Libre (Free Zone). The Zona Libre extends from the U.S. border 22km into Mexico; it also includes all of Baja California. You will encounter checkpoints as soon as you reach the end of the Zona Libre (see **Driver's Licenses and Vehicle Permits,** p. 15). On the U.S. side of the border, several **auto clubs** provide routing services and protection against breakdowns. Members of the **American Automobile Association (AAA) Travel Related Services,** 1000 AAA Dr. (mail stop 100), Heathrow, FL 32746-5063 (tel. (407) 444-7000; fax 444-7380) can receive free road maps and the excellent Mexico guide; members can also buy traveler's checks commission-free and are eligible for Mexican auto insurance. (AAA members needing road assistance should call (5) 588-70-55 or 588-93-55). The **Canadian Automobile Association,** 60 Commerce Valley Dr. E., Thorn Hill, Ontario L3T 7P9 (tel. (905) 771-3170; fax 771-3101) provides members with free maps and will highlight routes.

    All non-Mexican car insurance is invalid in Mexico, no matter what your policy says. Make sure you arrange to have your car insured in Mexico if you plan to drive it there. You can buy insurance at the border from one of the many small insurance offices located next door to the Mexico immigration offices. **Sanborn's,** Home Office, 2009 South 10th St., McAllen, TX 78503 (tel. (210) 686-0711; fax 686-0732), offers Mexican and Central American insurance through each of its 21 U.S. agencies located at major border cities in California, Texas, and Arizona. Along with insurance, you get all the trimmings including road maps, newsletters, a ride board, mile-by-mile guides to all the highways in Mexico called the Travelog. Remember, in Mexico the law code is Napoleonic (guilty until proven innocent). If you do not purchase a separate Legal Aid policy, and you are involved in an accident, the police might hold you in jail until everything is sorted out and all claims are settled.

# ONCE THERE

## ■ Embassies and Consulates

**Embassies** and **consulates** provide a plethora of services for citizens away from home. They can refer you to an English-speaking doctor or lawyer, help replace a lost tourist card, and wire family or friends if you need money and have no other means of obtaining it. They cannot, however, cash checks, act as a postal service, get you out of trouble, supply counsel, or interfere in any way with the legal process in Mexico. Once in jail, you're on your own.

The **Mexican Government Tourism Office** (Secretaría de Turismo or SECTUR) has branches in the capital city of each state and wherever else tourists gather. In Mexico City, it is located at Mariano Escobedo 726, Col. Anzures, C.P. 11590, Mexico D.F. (tel. (5) 254-8967; fax 254-4036).

## ■ Getting Around

### BY BUS

Mexico's extensive, astoundingly cheap bus service never ceases to amaze. Travel luxury class, often called *servicio ejecutivo* (executive service), and you'll get the royal treatment: reclining seats, sandwiches and soda, A/C, and movies galore. Only

ESSENTIALS

slightly less fancy is *primera clase* (first-class). Buses are relatively comfortable and effi-cient; they occasionally even have videos, bathrooms, and functioning air-condition-ers (ask at the ticket window). *Segunda clase* (second-class) buses, which are only slightly cheaper than *primera clase,* are sometimes overcrowded, hot, and uncom-fortable. To maximize your comfort, at night choose a seat on the right side of the bus (to avoid the constant glare of oncoming headlights); during the day try to get the shady side of the bus. Even on non-air-conditioned buses, drivers or passengers often refuse to drive with the windows open. Don't make a scene. A/C can be refresh-ing...until the icicles start forming; bring a sweater or prepare to sniffle.

Buses are either *local* or *de paso* (passing). *Locales* originate at the station from which you leave. If few *locales* leave each day, try to buy your ticket in advance. Once you get on the bus, keep your ticket stub in case you're asked to show it later. *De paso* buses originate elsewhere and pass through your station. First-class *de pasos* sell only as many tickets as there are available seats—when the bus arrives, the driver disembarks to give this information to the ticket seller. When these tickets go on sale, forget civility, chivalry, and anything which might possibly stand between you and a ticket, or plan to spend the greater portion of your vacation in bus stations. You may end up sitting on the floor of a second-class *de paso* bus*;* ticket sales are based on the number of people with assigned seats who have gotten off the bus. This system does not, unfortunately, take into account the people and packages jammed into the aisle. In any case, if you know when boarding the bus that no seats are available, it's best to wait and board last. That way, while all other passengers without seats have to stand in the aisle, you are able to sit semi-comfortably on the step between the driver's compartment and the aisle.

The U.S. State Department (http://www.state.gov) recently put out a travel advi-sory warning about armed robberies on overnight tourist buses in the state of Campeche. Try to keep your bus travel to daylight hours in that state, if possible. The (mostly) good guys—federal law enforcement officials—regularly stop buses and search riders' belongings as well, so leave the drugs and guns at home. Keep your tourist card handy during baggage inspection.

## BY CAR

Driving in Mexico is as exciting as swimming in shark-infested waters, and much more dangerous. The maximum speed on Mexican highways is 100km per hour (62mph) unless otherwise posted, but is often ignored. Be especially careful driving during the rainy season (May-Oct.), when roads are often in poor condition, potholes become craters, and landslides are common.When driving on roads near the capital, watch out for fog. A sign warning *Maneje despacio* (drive slowly) should be taken seriously. At night, pedestrians and livestock pop up on the roadway at the most unlikely times. If you can help it, don't drive at night. If you must, beware of oncom-ing cars without headlights. Whatever you do, never spend the night on the side of the road. When approaching a one-lane bridge, labeled *puente angosto* or *solo carril,* the first driver to flash headlights has the right of way. Lanes are narrow, so if a truck tries to pass your car on a two-lane road, you might need to pull off onto the gravel or graded dirt in order to give the vehicle enough room. (But be careful: the shoulder is often nonexistent or covered with vegetation.)

Exercise particular caution when driving along potentially dangerous Rte. 15 in the state of Sinaloa; Rte. 2 in the vicinity of Carborca, Sonora; Rte. 57 between Matehuala and San Luis Potosí; the highway between Palomares and Tuxtepec, Oaxaca; Rte. 2 between Tijuana and Mexicali (take U.S. Rte. 8 instead); and Rte. 40 between the city of Durango and the Pacific Coast. If possible, avoid Rte. 1 in Sinaloa. Check with local authorities or the nearest U.S. consulate for updates on bandit activity and to identify other areas of potential danger.

In Baja California, if you want to leave your car and go somewhere by public trans-portation for a few days, you must pay to park in an authorized lot; otherwise, the car will be towed or confiscated. The Motor Vehicle Office will tell you where to leave

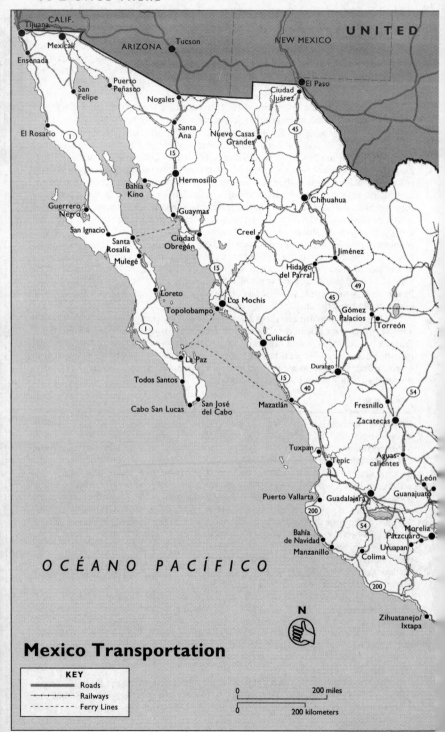

# Mexico Transportation

KEY

- ▬▬▬ Roads
- ┼┼┼┼ Railways
- - - - Ferry Lines

0    200 miles
0    200 kilometers

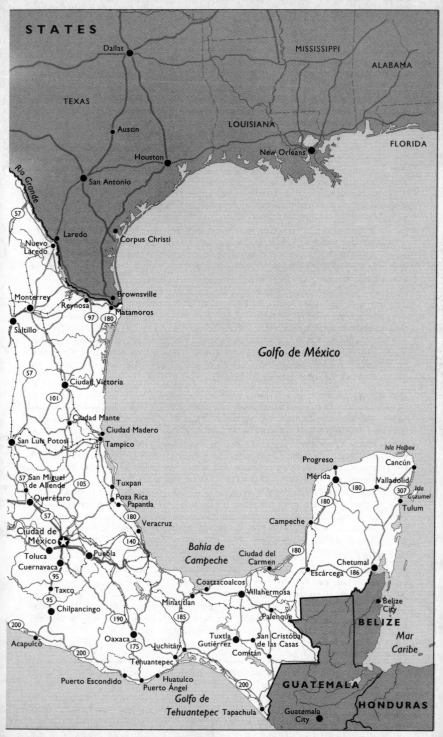

your car legally. To help reduce the heinous pollution in Mexico City, traffic in the metropolitan area is restricted (see p. 78).

**PEMEX** (Petroleos Mexicanos) sells two types of gas: Nova (regular) and Extra (unleaded). Nova is appropriately named (*no va* in Spanish means "doesn't go"), and one whiff of a Nova-burning car will make you realize why emissions controls are so important. Unleaded gas is now almost universally available in Mexico; you will find it throughout Baja as well as in Guadalajara, Monterrey, Mexico City, most border towns, and all major metropolitan areas. But beware: even if you do find a silver Extra pump, it may be filled with Nova gasoline.

Both Nova and Extra are extremely cheap by all but Saudi Arabian standards. Don't get overcharged: know how much gas you'll need before you pull in and make sure the register is rung back to zero before pumping begins. PEMEX accepts cash and checks only. When checking the tires, remember that pumps in Mexico are calibrated in kilograms (1kg = 2.2 lb.).

The heat, bumpy roads, and fair-to-middling gas may well take a toll on your car. No matter what kind of car you sport, bring spare oil, spark plugs, fan belts and air, and fuel filters—these should take care of all but the biggest problems. If you break down on one of the major toll highways between 8am and 8pm, pull completely off the road, raise the hood, stay with your car, and wait for the **Ángeles Verdes** (Green Angels) to come to the rescue. Green Angels are green-and-white emergency trucks dispatched by radio, staffed by almost a thousand mechanics, and equipped for performing common repair jobs, towing, changing tires, and addressing minor medical problems. Your green saviors may take a while to show up, but the service (except for parts, gas, and oil) is free. Tipping is optional but polite. These guardian angels will assist you anywhere but in the *Distrito Federal,* where you can contact the **Asociación Nacional Automovilística (ANA)** (tel. (5) 597-42-83, 597-49-22 or 782-35-31).

While on the road in Mexico, you'll probably be stopped at least once by agents of the Federal Public Ministry and the Federal Judicial Police for a search of your car and its contents. To avoid being detained or arrested, be as cooperative as possible. Do *not* carry drugs, firearms, or shoulder-fired missiles in your car.

## BY TAXI

Taxis in Mexico are ubiquitous in big cities. Prices are reasonable (by U.S. standards), but since public buses are so frequent and cover so much ground, you shouldn't have to resort to a cab unless it's late at night or you're in a remote part of town. Be careful to avoid getting overcharged by *always* negotiating a price beforehand (bargaining is the norm) and not agreeing to go by *taxímetro* (metered fare)—it's often more expensive even if legit, but taxi drivers often tamper with the machine to make it charge exorbitant amounts to unsuspecting tourists. Also, the U.S. Department of State (http://www.state.gov) has warned of a rash of reported taxi robberies at gunpoint, particularly in Mexico City near the Palacio de Bellas Artes, but also elsewhere; the best way to avoid this is to only get cabs at authorized stands instead of flagging them down along the street.

## BY PLANE

Flying within Mexico is more expensive than taking a bus or train, but it is considerably cheaper than comparable flights between U.S. cities. It can be an excellent way of avoiding a 40-hour (or longer) bus ride; many budget travelers rule out the possibility, only to learn later that it would have been much cheaper than they thought. Check with Mexican airlines (p. 39) for special rates.

## BY TRAIN

The Mexican railroads are all government-owned, with most lines operating under the name of **Ferrocarriles Nacionales de México** (National Railways of Mexico, F.F.N.N.). The train system is not as extensive, punctual, cheap, comfortable, or efficient as the bus system. Even when they are on time, trains (yes, even the "fast" ones) can take twice as long as buses to reach their destination. Other than the spectacular ride through the Copper Canyon (Los Mochis-Creel), you probably won't rely on trains unless you're nearly broke or crave a leisurely crawl through the country. Don't be surprised if the rail system is privatized and the majority of it axed completely in the next few years.

There are two types of trains in Mexico: the slow *estrella* and the unbearably slow *burro* (literally "donkey"). The *estrella* is generally about twice as fast and twice as expensive as the *burro;* reservations for the former are often made a day or two in advance. If for some reason you must travel by train, take the *estrella,* and make sure you get a *primera clase especial* ticket (comparable to business or ambassador class). Otherwise, it's going to be a long night.

## BY THUMB

> *Let's Go* urges you to use common sense if you decide to hitch, and to seriously consider all possible risks before you make that decision. The information listed below and throughout the book is not intended to recommend hitchhiking; *Let's Go* does not recommend hitchhiking as a means of transportation.

The Mexicans who pick up tourists are often friendly, offering meals, tours, or other extras. More often than not, they are generous and well-meaning; in fact, people who *don't* pick you up will often give you an apologetic look or a gesture of explanation. However, always be careful. Women should **never** hitchhike alone. Hitchhikers should size up the driver and find out where they're going before getting in. Think twice if a driver opens the door quickly and offers to drive anywhere. Some bandit-ridden highways are particularly dangerous for hitchhikers (see By Car, p. 43).

Before getting in, make sure the passenger window or door opens from inside. If there are several people in the car, do not sit in the middle. Assume a quick-exit position, which rules out the back seat of a two-door car. Keep backpacks and other baggage where they are easily accessible—don't let the driver store them in the trunk. If you have trouble getting out for any reason, affecting the pose of someone about to vomit works wonders.

# ■ Accommodations

## HOTELS

Bargain-seekers will not be disappointed with Mexico's selection of hotels. Though some (particularly in resort towns) are among the world's most overpriced, the majority of Mexican accommodations are shockingly affordable. Usually located within a block or two of the *zócalo,* the cheapest hotels rarely provide private bathrooms or air conditioning, though they do often have hot water and/or fans. Slightly higher-priced hotels usually reside in the same district but are much better equipped, including rooms with private bathrooms (often some with and some without). Before accepting any room, ask to see it, and always find out before paying if the price includes any meals and if there are any extra taxes or surcharges.

All hotels, ranging from luxury resorts in Cancún to dumps in Monterrey, are controlled by the government's **Secretaria de Turismo** (SECTUR). This ensures that hotels of similar quality charge similar prices; you should always ask to see an up-to-date **official tariff sheet** if you doubt the quoted price. Although hotel prices are regulated, proprietors are not prohibited from charging *less* than the official rate. If the hotel looks like it hasn't seen a customer in several days, a little bargaining may work wonders, especially if you offer to stay a number of days. For a room with one bed, request *una habitación (un cuarto) con una cama.* If bedding down with a fellow wayfarer, ask for one *con dos camas* (with two beds).

If the hotels listed in *Let's Go* are full or don't appeal to you, ask the managers of the full hotels, cab drivers, tourist officials, or vendors in the market for a good recommendation. Hotel people in one town are often a good source for hotel leads in the next town on your itinerary. For the bare-bones budget traveler the hammock is the way to go, particularly on the coast: if you plan to travel on a shoestring, buy one. Most beach towns in Mexico are dotted with *palapas* (palm-tree huts). For a small fee, open-air restaurants double as places to hang your hat and hammock when the sun goes down. In small *yucateco* towns, locals often let travelers use hammock hooks for a pittance.

Hotels in Mexico often lock their doors at night, and small-town establishments may do so surprisingly early. A locked door doesn't necessarily mean "closed for the night," as someone usually is on duty. By arriving early in small towns or calling ahead if you can't avoid arriving late, and by checking with the hotel desk before going out for a late night on the town, you'll be able to stay out as late as you want to, and help dispel the Mexican myth of the obnoxious foreigner.

**Reservations are absolutely necessary during Christmas, Semana Santa (Easter), and local festivals.** However, at most other times, even during the summer season, you need not worry too much about reserving *budget* hotels ahead. (More expensive hotels, however, particularly in Mexico City, might well be booked.)

## HOSTELS

With a few exceptions, Mexican hostels tend to be run-down and far from town. Their ban on alcohol, smoking restrictions, and limited hours (most are open from 7-9am and 5-10pm) also deter many budget travelers. Although a bit cheaper than hotels, the couple of dollars you save don't usually make up for the inconvenience. Therefore, **Hostelling International** cards are not as useful in Mexico as they are in other countries. You can buy one from the travel organizations listed on (p. 4) or, in Mexico, from the **SETEJ** (p. 4). Most hostels will give you a bed even if you don't have a hostel card. They may, however, charge you more for it.

## CAMPING

For the budget travel experience par excellence, try camping in Mexico. Campers accustomed to prim and proper campgrounds will be taken aback, however. Mexican national parks often exist only in theory; many are indistinguishable from the surrounding cities. Trails, campgrounds, and rangers are strictly *gringo* concepts. For information on hostel-affiliated campgrounds, write to **SETEJ** (see p. 4).

Privately owned **trailer parks** are relatively common on major highways—look for signs with a picture of a trailer, or the words *parque de trailer, campamento,* or *remolques.* These places may or may not allow campers to pitch tents. Don't sleep in a vehicle parked next to a well-traveled road, or screeching brakes and the shattering glass of your car may shake you from that peaceful slumber.

The best guide for campers is *The People's Guide to RV Camping in Mexico,* available through John Muir Publications (see **Publications,** p. 4) Adventurers will want to check out *Mexico's Volcanoes, A Climbing Guide* (US$15), which contains maps, photos, and a bilingual mountaineering glossary. Available from **Mountaineers Books,** 1001 SW Klickitat Way, #201, Seattle, WA 98134 (tel. (800) 553-4453 or (206) 223-6303; fax 223-6306; http://mbooks@mountaineers.org).

# ■ Keeping in Touch

## MAIL

Mexican mail service is slow. Though it usually arrives, it can take anywhere from one to three weeks for *correo aéreo* (airmail) to reach the U.S., and at the very least two weeks to reach Europe and other destinations. Official estimates average 40 days by boat, but in reality it will take months. In Mexico, never deposit anything important in the black holes called mailboxes; take it straight to the *oficina de correos* (post office) instead. There you can buy all the *estampillas* or *timbres* (stamps) that your *carta* (letter) needs. Anything important should be sent *registrado* (registered mail) or in duplicate. For the speediest service possible, **MexPost** works in collaboration with Express Mail International in the U.S. and similar express mail services in other countries to deliver mail quickly and reliably. Three days is the official delivery time to the U.S., but allow up to a week; in any case, it's *much* faster than regular or registered mail (and much more expensive). MexPost offices are usually found next to regular post offices, but sometimes they're located kilometers away—in either case, post office staff can direct you to the right place.

It's wise to use the Spanish abbreviations or names for countries (EE.UU. or EUA for the U.S.). Write *Por Avión* on all postcards and letters not otherwise marked, unless you don't mind its arriving sometime in the next millennium. There is no size limitation for packages, but parcels cannot weigh more than 25kg. Regulations for mailing parcels may vary from state to state. While it is often possible to send packages from smaller towns, post offices in large cities (especially ports or trade centers such as Mérida and Acapulco) provide more reliable service. Before attempting to send anything, go to the post office and note the weight limitations, necessary documentation, addresses and hours of the customs and trade offices in the city, and whether the box should be brought open or sealed. All packages are reopened and inspected by customs at the border, so closing the box with string, not tape, is recommended.

In general, in order to send packages you must provide the following: tourist card data (number, duration of validity, date of issue, place of issue), list of contents including estimated value and nature of the package ("Gift" works best), address and return address. It is customary for those mailing parcels to use their home address, or at least some address in the same country as the parcel's destination, as a return address to ensure eventual delivery. In a trade office, you may need to show receipts for each item purchased in Mexico. Postal officials usually record the information from the customs form on the front of the package as well.

You can have letters sent to you in Mexico through *Lista de Correos,* a letter-holding service available at any post office. When picking up mail sent to you via *Lista de Correos,* look for the list posted, and check it carefully for any possible misspellings. If there is no list posted, ask the attendant, *"¿Está la lista de hoy?"* (Is today's list here?). If it is, give your name. Letters should be marked *Favor de retener hasta la llegada* ("Please hold until arrival"); they will be held up to 15 days. If you know people in Mexico, using their address may be better.

Mail sent to *Lista de Correos* should be addressed to a first and last name only, capitalizing and underlining the name under which the item should be filed alphabetically. A letter could be filed under any misspelled permutation of the recipient's names. If possible, go through the *Lista de Correos* yourself. If not, watch the person who does and ask for the mail under both your first and your last name, just to make sure. Address letters as follows:

Samuel <u>FINCH</u>
Lista de Correos
Calle 65 (street address for post office, if known—otherwise leave it out)
Mérida (city), Yucatán (state)
79000 (postal code)
MEXICO

Packages sent via **Express Mail International, FedEx,** or other express service might be retained at a different office (often the **MexPost** office). Be sure to make it clear to officials exactly what type of package you're expecting, and if it is express, come armed with the tracking number (if you have access to it). Also, Express Mail International has lately encountered problems with bandits near Mexico City; some packages are robbed and never arrive. In any case, it would be foolish to send anything particularly valuable via any sort of mail to Mexico.

Hotels where you have reserved a room will usually hold mail for you, but let them know ahead. **American Express offices** will hold mail for 30 days before returning it;

just write "Client's Mail" on the envelope. Some offices require that you be a card-holder to receive the service, while others allow it as long as you purchase travelers checks from AmEx. Call American Express customer service at (800) 528-4800 for information and ask for the free *Directory of Traveler Service Offices;* it is also a good idea to contact the specific office in Mexico before sending anything.

## TELEPHONES

When trying to reach Mexico from another country, patience is the key to success. Dial your country's international long-distance access number (011 from the U.S.), then **52** (Mexico's country code), then the city code (listed in this guide at the end of each city's practical information section), and then the phone number.

Once you are in Mexico, getting lines to foreign countries can be very difficult. Many public phones don't access international lines. Dial 09 for an English-speaking international long-distance operator. If you speak Spanish fluently and can't reach the international operator, dial 07 for the national operator, who will connect you (sometimes even a local operator can help). The term for a collect call is a *llamada por cobrar* or *llamada con cobro revertido.* Calling from hotels is usually faster.

Taxes and surcharges make it extremely expensive to call abroad from Mexico. Call with a card or collect if you can; not only is it cheaper (about half the price of direct), but you will also avoid enormous surcharges from hotels. Remember, however, that there can be a fee of 1-5 pesos for collect calls that are not accepted.

International calls using sleek silver **LADATEL** touch-tone payphones are cheaper and involve less waiting than any of the alternatives. LADATELs accept coins or phone cards you can buy at most *papelerías* (stationers) or *abarrotes* (grocers). Without the cards, the challenge is to find enough coins of large denominations: these phones take no more than 10 coins at a time and some calls require a minimum initial deposit. When dialing, use the station-to-station prefixes. The blue push-button phones do direct dial while the orange old-fashioned ones do not. To reach an **AT&T** operator from a LADATEL phone, call 95-800-462-4240; for **MCI** call 95-800-674-7000; for **Sprint** call 95-800-877-8000.

To reach the English-speaking international operator on a plain old phone, dial 09 and wait until the operator answers (be prepared to wait ½hr. or more). For direct calls, dial 01; national operator 02; directory assistance 04; for bilingual **emergency operators 06.** To make long-distance phone calls within Mexico, dial 91 plus the telephone code and number (station to station), or 92 plus the telephone code and number (person to person). The prefixes for calling the U.S. or Canada are 95 for station to station and 96 for person to person; for all other countries the prefixes are 98 and 99, respectively.

# MEXICO

## ■ A Brief History

### PRE-COLUMBIAN SOCIETIES

#### The Mysterious Olmecs

Little is known about the **Olmecs,** the first settled peoples of Mexico. The Olmecs inhabited the cities now known as **La Venta** (p. 460), **San Lorenzo,** and **Tres Zapotes** (p. 456) from 1200-100 BC, yet no skeletal remains have ever been discovered. Archaeologists didn't even recognize their existence as a distinct civilization until the early 1940s, when an archaeologist stumbled upon an immense basalt head standing several meters tall in the jungles of southern Mexico. In the following years, several more colossal heads were found, all with thick eyelids, big lips, broad noses, and helmet-like head covers. The Olmecs apparently lived in socially stratified communities concentrated in what is now Tabasco and southern Veracruz, though their cultural influence can be traced as far south as Costa Rica. It was among the Olmecs that the **feathered serpent**—a figure ubiquitous in pre-Hispanic Mexico—had its origins. The **jaguar** was a symbol of utmost importance in Olmec mythology; sculpted human figures often have feline forms and mouths curled into jaguar-like snarls, symbolizing the intermingling of the divine and the mortal. Among their most notable developments were a glyphic writing system and recorded dates. San Lorenzo was violently destroyed around 900 BC, and La Venta suffered a similar fate several centuries later. While the Olmecs perished, many of their cultural achievements were transmitted to other Mesoamerican peoples, including the Maya.

#### The Maya Dominion and Toltec Influence

The genius of the **Maya** can be seen in the remains of their ancient cities—most notably **Palenque** (p. 482), **Chichén Itzá** (p. 517), **Uxmal** (p. 502), and **Tulum** (p. 546)—scattered throughout the Yucatán Peninsula and modern-day Chiapas. The Maya were neither politically nor culturally cohesive at any point; hundreds of lowland and highland tribes existed and had little contact with each other.

During the first 300 years of the Mexican **Classic Period** (AD 300-900), the Maya became proficient in engineering, mathematics, art, architecture, calendrical calculations, and astronomy, devising a method to predict the movement of celestial bodies with startling precision. Ironically, these sophisticated societies never used the wheel as anything but a children's plaything.

The tribes, in both the Classic and Postclassic periods, shared similar legend and iconography. The **Quiché** Maya (a highland tribe) composed the *Popol Vuh,* the creation myth which tells the story of a pair of **hero-twins** who defeat the evil gods of the underworld in an epic game of ball (see p. 486). **Maize,** the basis of their battle, was an important element of the Maya religion; it was their most important crop.

Around AD 900, the Maya empire mysteriously collapsed. It seems that the Maya had farmed the land into exhaustion, causing food shortages and perhaps peasant revolts. A Maya renaissance occurred in the northern Yucatán after AD 1200. It was strongly influenced by Teotihuacán culture, as elaborated by the Toltecs. The Maya adopted the legends of **Quetzalcóatl** (The Feathered Serpent, a.k.a. Kukulcán), a great Toltec king who broke away from the Toltec empire and made his way to the Yucatán with his people. The myths predicted his eventual return.

The **Toltec** empire dominated most of central Mexico during the **Post-Classic Period** (AD 900-1540) with Xochicalco, Cholula, and Tula serving as their most prominent cities. The bellicose Toltecs practiced human sacrifice and, like the Olmecs, placed the jaguar at the center of their iconography. This violent and powerful culture provided the framework for the Aztec empire.

---

### Chac Attack

This guy had *ganas*. He also had beady, comma-shaped eyes, an astonishingly protruding hook nose (it's…it's almost indecent!), and a mouth permanently fixed with a horrid grimace. He was schnaz god and rain god, terrible and necessary, moody and—damn it—hard to please. He was **Chac.** There was no god more pragmatically important to the Maya; because of the complete lack of above-ground water in the Yucatán, they depended on his rains to bring drinking water and corn. Attempting to appease this master of waters, the Maya sacrificed their children (their tears were associated with the rain), revered the frog and the turtle (their cries were thought to provoke downpours), created artificial clouds through badly burning fires, and made Chac the most respected god in the whole Yucatán. Chac responded to all the adulation with cold indifference. He grimaced, mockingly. And in the end, they say it was a severe drought that brought about the fall of the Maya.

---

## The Aztec Empire: Hegemony Grounded in Legend

After the fall of Toltec civilization, the Aztecs wandered nomadically from the end of the 12th century until 1325, when (legend has it) the Aztec peoples (including the Mexica, later called "Mexicans") arrived at **Lake Texcoco,** an unappealing swamp that no other group had claimed. There, they beheld an **eagle perched upon a cactus with a serpent in its talons** (check out the Mexican flag): the vision was taken as a sign to build the legendary floating city of **Tenochtitlán** on this sacred site.

The Aztecs practiced a religion derived from their Toltec predecessors; they worshipped a supreme being, the aggregate force of numerous deities. **Quetzalcóatl,** the feathered serpent and god of the air, remained a crucial element of religious iconography. The Aztec religion differed, however, in its central legend of the sun-related warrior-deity **Huitzilopochtli.** His mother, **Coatlicue,** was impregnated by a **ball of feathers** and gave birth to him *fully armed* atop **Coatepec** (serpent hill); immediately after birth, he protected his mother from 100 jealous half-siblings by cutting them all into small pieces. Aztec imperialism and violent ascendancy over all other Mesoamerican tribes was justified by the story of Huitzilopochtli, who is memorialized at the principal Aztec temple, **Templo Mayor; Coyolxauhqui,** a half-sister, is depicted with dismembered body parts at the base of the Templo.

The Aztec civilization was as bloody and hierarchical as any that followed it in Mexican history. At the height of their power, Aztec priests practiced **human sacrifice** on a large scale. However, the myths brought about the sacrifice and not vice versa. Rival warriors were regularly dismembered and thrown down the Templo Mayor stairs to honor Huitzilopochtli. Also, in the Aztec creation myth, it was the gods' fifth attempt at making a sun **(Nahui Ollin)** that was finally successful; all the gods had to sacrifice themselves (having their hearts cut out by Quetzalcóatl) in order to set the sun moving through the sky. Thus, the Aztecs believed they had to supply human hearts and blood to keep the sun in its path. In the yearly offering to **Tezcatlipoca,** the god of honor, the most attractive youth in the land was selected to live like a king for 11 months and then, stripped of his lavish accoutrements, to part with his heart at the hands of the head priest and master of ceremonies.

The Aztecs built Mexico's largest *indígena* empire, and one of the larger cities in the world. About five million people inhabited a territory that stretched from the Atlantic to the Pacific and all the way to Guatemala and Nicaragua. *Chinampas* (floating gardens; see p. 112) enabled the Aztecs to cultivate the swamp efficiently. The beauty and architectural sophistication of the island city Tenochtitlán, connected to the mainland by a network of canals and causeways, led Western chroniclers to dub it the Venice of the New World.

## CONQUEST AND COLONIZATION

### The Arrival of Cortés

Suddenly, history ended and began again. When **Hernán Cortés** landed on the island of Cozumel in 1519 in search of slaves and gold, he turned the old world upside down. Arriving in enormous ships and wearing shiny shells of armor, Cortés and his white compatriots resembled nothing the *indígenas* had ever seen. The Spaniards carried "fire-breathing" guns, sat atop armored horses—which the *indígenas* believed to be immortal—and rode with packs of **huge, vicious war-dogs.** Some communities capitulated instantly, showering the Spaniards with fruit, flowers, gold, and women; other towns fought tooth and nail. But Cortés, heavily in debt and fleeing arrest by the Spanish governor of Cuba, pressed ahead. He scuttled his own ships to prevent his men from turning back, cut off the feet of those who attempted mutiny, and marched on toward the great Aztec capital of Tenochtitlán with the assistance of **Jerónimo de Aguilar,** a Spaniard who had been shipwrecked there several years earlier and spoke the native language. As they moved westward through Tabasco, the Spaniards acquired a second interpreter, **La Malinche,** an Aztec princess who became Cortés's mistress and adviser, and is regarded as both the mother of *mestizo* Mexico and the primeval traitor to the nation. Along the way to the capital, Cortés recruited about 6000 warriors from the **Totonacs** and **Tlaxcalans**—enemies of the Aztecs—and massacred 6000 of the Aztecs' allies at Cholula.

The Aztec emperor **Moctezuma II** (1502-1520) received word of Cortés's approach, and politely sent a message to the Spaniards, discouraging them from traveling to the capital. Moctezuma, however, also grappled with rumors that Cortés was the light-skinned, bearded god **Quetzalcóatl,** who had sailed away after incurring the wrath of the gods, ironically declaring that he would one day return on the Maya year One-Reed (1519). Plagued by conflicting advice, Moctezuma finally welcomed the Spaniards into the city. An initial period of peaceful, if tense, relations quickly soured when Moctezuma was kidnapped by the Spanish, and Cortés was driven from the city. An incredible string of lucky coincidences let Cortés regroup quickly, and two years later, on August 13, 1521, the Aztecs, though valiantly led by their new emperor **Cuauhtémoc,** were soundly defeated at Tlatelolco. The empire had fallen.

### The Great Death

The Spaniards' arrival triggered what may be the most devastating **biological holocaust** in world history. Geographically isolated for millennia, the indigenous peoples of the Americas lacked natural resistance to European diseases. Smallpox, typhoid, yellow fever, and dysentery spread ravenously through Mesoamerica. The mild childhood diseases of Europe—measles, mumps, influenza, and chicken pox—proved fatal to *indígenas.* Within 100 years of Cortés' landing, a silent viral bomb had wiped out as much as 96% of the indigenous population—about 24 million people. **Smallpox** was by far the biggest killer: encrusted with running sores, victims vomited dried black blood as their skin gradually sloughed off their bodies. Those who lived were sometimes left blind or hideously scarred. Entire villages disappeared from the map, and Spaniards simply moved onto the empty lands, called *tierras baldías,* or bought deserted acreage at bargain prices. Settlers quickly grabbed huge estates; by 1618, one family had acquired over 11 million acres on the northern frontier.

### Land and Power

Epidemics meant, from the Spaniards' point of view, chronic labor shortages. For a time, *conquistadores* enslaved prisoners captured in battle, but due to rampant disease and maltreatment, *indígena* **slavery** was abolished in 1542. (Owning black slaves, however, was legal in Mexico until 1829.) Instead, royal officials gave Spanish settlers **encomiendas** (labor grants): *indígena* villages had to send a quota of workers to labor on the Spaniards' farms, and in return, the *encomendero* was supposed to educate and defend the village. In practice, *indígena* workers were overworked, abused, and segregated from their families.

Afraid that maverick *encomenderos* would challenge royal authority, the crown tried to restrict faraway *encomiendas*. But the crown had its own concerns at stake, not those of natives: regulations protecting *indígenas* were rarely enforced. After the Church and crown began imposing taxes on villagers, *encomenderos* had an easier time recruiting *indígena* labor: since *indígenas* needed the once-useless colonial currency to pay taxes, they were forced to work for inadequate wages in Spanish farms.

Abuses were worst where wealth was greatest—in the mines. Rich veins of **silver** were discovered in central Mexico in the 1540s, and mining camps proliferated overnight, fueling the growth of colonial boom towns. Miners climbed out of the shafts on ladders made of notched logs, and at night they slept on the same pieces of cloth they used to haul their loads of ore. *Indígenas* forced to work in the mines died in the pits by the thousands, felled by floods, explosions, and noxious gases.

## The Church

Christianization was central to the Conquest—even Cortés took every opportunity to lecture indigenous villages on their salvation. When the Spaniards took Tenochtitlán, they razed the Aztecs' central temple and built a cathedral atop the rubble. Such bombastic tactics often backfired, and some communities, like the tenacious **Lacandóns**, fiercely defended their native religions.

Later missionaries were more successful; many *indígenas* were especially impressed by the arrival of the first 12 **Franciscan friars,** who walked barefoot all the way from Veracruz to the capital. While the Franciscans concentrated their efforts in the center of the country, the Jesuits pushed northwards and the Dominicans moved into the southern regions. Religious services and holidays were the only sanctioned days of rest for many villagers, and by the mid-1500s, missionaries had won millions of converts. But Catholic ritual and belief mixed with traditional practices, creating the religious **syncretism** that persists today in many rural areas such as Chiapas.

Many clergymen tried to protect *indígenas* against exploitation, often locking horns with local *encomenderos* and crown officials. The militant Dominican **Bartolomé de Las Casas,** a vocal critic of the *encomienda* system, was largely responsible for early crown laws protecting *indígenas*. The Franciscan **Juan de Zumárraga,** Mexico's first archbishop, personified the best and worst of colonial Catholicism. Zumárraga bravely condemned corrupt judges and lobbied for *indígena* rights—yet he burned native nobles at the stake on charges of heresy, and regularly boasted that he had razed 500 temples and crushed 20,000 idols.

## Race and Class

When the Spanish built a new city on the ruins of Tenochtitlán, they tried to establish clear racial boundaries. Only whites could live in the city's core; *peninsulares,* whites born in Spain, were at the top of the heap. **Indígenas** were confined to the fringes and had to commute into the city each day, rowing through narrow canals in dugout canoes. But complete segregation was impossible, and within a few generations, a huge new racial group had emerged—*mestizos,* children of mixed Spanish and *indígena* parentage. This group would eventually form the entire racial fabric of Mexican civilization; today, an overwhelming majority of Mexicans have mixed blood.

# INDEPENDENCE AND REFORM

## The First Calls for Freedom

Enter **Miguel Hidalgo y Costilla,** an iconoclastic priest in the small parish of Dolores. Always rebellious, Hidalgo had been tried by the Inquisition on charges of gambling, dancing, reading forbidden books, fornicating, questioning the immaculate conception, and denouncing the king of Spain. (He was acquitted on insufficient evidence.) Hidalgo spent little time proselytizing; instead, he tried to improve parishioners' economic lot by introducing new trades and crafts to the village of Dolores. He also stockpiled guns. When Spanish officials discovered his hidden reserve, Hidalgo ran to Dolores' church and rang the bells to summon the parishioners. As stunned villagers listened, Hidalgo delivered a ringing call to arms—*El Grito de Dolores*—and verbally whipped his congregation into an instant army. *Indígena* resentment was high; the summer of 1809 had been so dry that corn withered in the fields, and shortages had sparked 400% inflation in some regions. Hidalgo's army quickly swelled, capturing several major cities before Hidalgo was killed in an ambush by Spanish troops in March 1811.

Another parish priest, **José María Morelos y Pavón,** rose to lead the Independence movement after Hidalgo's death. Under his command the rebels captured Mexico City, but the capture was short-lived and the Spanish quickly regained the capital. But history plays funny tricks: after Napoleon's troops invaded Spain and forced a liberal constitution on the king, many conservative colonists decided to cut their ties to Spain. Frightened by the spectre of a revolutionary French government, wealthy *criollos* swallowed their pride and joined the liberal Independence movement. The most famous turncoat was **Agustín de Iturbide,** a *criollo* loyalist who had led Spanish troops into battle against Hidalgo. In 1820, he suddenly defected, uniting forces with rebel leader **Vicente Guerrero.** Reassuringly conservative, Iturbide and Guerrero drafted the *Plan de Iguala,* which proclaimed Mexico an independent monarchy and endorsed the Catholic church. The compromise won wide support, and on August 24, 1821, the **Treaty of Córdoba** formalized Mexico's independence forever.

## The First Empire

"He is prompt, bold, and decisive, and not scrupulous about the means he employs to obtain his ends." So wrote a U.S. visitor of Iturbide, who had promptly crowned himself emperor of Mexico. As the uneasy compromise between liberals and conservatives crumbled, Iturbide simply dissolved the legislature—setting a dangerous precedent. Anticlericalists, *indígenas,* and *criollos* of modest means rebelled against Iturbide, led by the *criollo* military commander **Antonio López de Santa Anna.** In 1823, Iturbide finally resigned, but his legacy of despotism endured.

Mexico was in shambles. In the fighting between 1810 and 1823, half a million people—one in 12 Mexicans—had died. War had dislocated the entire colonial economy as trade with Spain dried up. Battles had left mines flooded and fields fallow. Idle ex-soldiers roamed the country, and unemployment was rampant. The fledgling government was flat-out broke.

## The Era of Santa Anna

Into the void stepped Santa Anna. Though the presidency of Mexico officially changed hands 36 times between May 1833 and August 1855, Santa Anna dominated the political scene. Initially elected on a liberal, mildly anticlerical platform, Santa Anna quickly abandoned his duties and retired to his personal estate. When his vice-president implemented promised reforms, Santa Anna led a conservative uprising and recaptured the presidency, this time as a conservative supporter of the Church. Irony piled upon injustice, and the megalomaniac Santa Anna eventually occupied the presidency no fewer than 11 times.

As his cronies grew rich on graft and bribery, Santa Anna drained the state coffers, desperately levying taxes on gutters, dogs, and wheels to build a huge standing army. Sure enough, Mexico was soon at war again. In 1838, France attacked Veracruz, demanding reparations for property damaged during the war. The conflict was dubbed **"The Pastry War"** in honor of a French pastry cook whose wares had been gobbled by marauding Mexican troops. The attacking French ships were driven back to sea, but Santa Anna lost his leg in the bombardment. Four years later, Santa Anna had his severed leg removed from its grave, carried to the capital in a huge procession, and entombed in an urn atop a towering pillar as the Congress, cabinet, diplomatic corps, and army serenaded the **decayed limb.**

Meanwhile, the Mexican army was fighting a losing battle on its northern frontier. Angered by Mexico's **abolition of slavery** in 1829, and under-represented in the legislature, Texan settlers demanded independence from Mexico in 1830. Santa Anna's troops overwhelmed Texan rebels holed up in an old Franciscan monastery called the **Alamo.** But when the U.S. annexed Texas in 1845, Mexico found itself up against a more formidable adversary. U.S. forces closed in on Mexico City from the north and east. Young cadets, the **Niños Héroes** (Boy Heroes), valiantly fought off U.S. troops from their military school in Chapultepec Castle, then (according to legend) wrapped themselves in the Mexican flag and leapt off the tower when all hope was lost. Under the terms of the **Treaty of Guadalupe Hidalgo,** the U.S. bought Texas, New Mexico, and California for a paltry sum. Two thousand Mexicans had died in the battle for Mexico City—only to lose half the nation's territory. Five years later, Santa Anna sold off in the **Gadsden Purchase** what today is Arizona and southern New Mexico.

In the mid-19th century, while Iturbide commissioned a French baroness to design the costumes for his lavish coronation, and Santa Anna made himself a millionaire, most Mexicans lived as they had for centuries—poor and isolated. Over one-third of the population lived in remote *indígena* villages. Though *pueblos* were largely self-governed, most villagers lived in grinding poverty. Education was a luxury enjoyed only by the *criollo* elite; only 1% of the total population was enrolled in school.

### Juárez and Reform

Eventually, the façade of Santa Anna's regime cracked under enormous opposition. The emerging leader of the reform movement was **Benito Juárez,** who rose from humble roots in a tiny Zapotec *pueblo* in Oaxaca to become one of the more revered presidents in Mexican history. He was exiled to New Orleans by Santa Anna because of his radically egalitarian policies as governor of Oaxaca, but Juárez joined other liberal politicians and journalists in whipping up opposition to Santa Anna abroad while dissidents in Mexico raised **rebel armies.** In 1855, Santa Anna was forced to resign.

The Juárez administration's policies reflected the ideology of 19th-century liberalism. The reformers abolished the old *fueros,* special regulations protecting the military and church from prosecution under civil laws. Juárez pushed through a new law prohibiting any institution from owning property not directly used in its day-to-day operations. Intended to weaken the Church, which owned vast rural and urban properties, the new law ended up stripping *indígenas* of their lands and livelihood, since *ejidos* (indigenous communal lands) had to be auctioned off as well.

Conservatives reacted violently, provoking the **War of the Reform,** Mexico's bloodiest civil war to date. The Church joined the military and dispossessed *pueblos* in fighting the liberal government. Meanwhile, the liberals were aided by *mestizo* reformers and many *indígenas* who supported Juárez, Mexico's first *indígena* president. Both sides committed atrocities: conservatives shot doctors who treated liberal casualties, while liberals defaced churches and executed priests who refused to give the sacrament to their troops.

### French Intervention

After the liberals finally regained the upper hand in 1861, Juárez faced a massive federal budget deficit. He declared a moratorium on payment of Mexico's foreign debts—prompting Spain, Britain, and France to attack Veracruz once again. Spain and Britain soon pulled out, but Napoleon III sent his troops inland. On May 5, 1862, outnumbered Mexican troops successfully repelled **diarrhea-plagued French soldiers** from the city of Puebla. *Cinco de Mayo* is now a huge national holiday—but the invaders captured the capital anyway a year later.

When Napoleon selected Austrian archduke **Ferdinand Maximilian of Hapsburg** as emperor of Mexico, he made a poor choice. Maximilian was extremely naive: he insisted that the Mexican people approve his ascension in a national plebiscite (Napoleon saw to it that Maximilian "won" overwhelmingly), then immediately hired a Spanish tutor for his wife **Carlota.** Maximilian and Carlota landed in Veracruz expecting a grand welcome, but *veracruzanos* refused to leave their houses. The royal couple drove through silent streets in a delicate Viennese carriage, which soon became mired in the muddy roads leading to Mexico City. Carlota cried.

Weirdly idealistic, Maximilian did not realize he was the puppet of European imperialism. The new emperor was moderately liberal and anti-Catholic; instead of rescinding Juárez's anticlerical laws, Maximilian imposed forced loans on the Church to shore up the collapsing treasury. Mexican conservatives were predictably infuriated, and Maximilian's modest popularity evaporated. Meanwhile, liberals stockpiled weapons and hired thousands of U.S. Civil War veterans to fight against the French. Napoleon belatedly withdrew his troops in 1867, abandoning Maximilian despite Carlota's wild pleas. After Carlota went mad, Maximilian surrendered himself to Juárez, who had him promptly shot. The human toll of the war was far higher on the Mexican side: 50,000 had died fighting the French.

**MEXICO**

## Struggling to Rebuild

Juárez returned to the capital in a solemn black carriage—a stark contrast to Maximilian's flimsy Viennese vehicle. Juárez's characteristically dour appearance seemed appropriate, since the Mexican economy was once again in tatters. Unemployment was rampant: to assert the executive's control over the military, Juárez had slashed the size of the Mexican army by two-thirds, so thousands of decommissioned soldiers wandered through the countryside, raiding *haciendas* and rural villages for food. *Léperos* (beggars) roamed the streets of Mexico City. Even the small middle class—merchants, bureaucrats, prosperous shopkeepers—lived in modest homes without running water. There were only enough schools for 10% of Mexican children to attend classes; of these students, just 22% were girls. When Juárez died in office in July of 1872, Mexico enjoyed peace but not prosperity.

## The Porfiriato

The regime of José de la Cruz **Porfirio Díaz,** which lasted from 1876 to 1911, was one of the more colorful and brutal chapters in Mexican history. In the 55 years since Independence, the Mexican presidency had changed hands 75 times; now stability was vital. Díaz's official motto was "Liberty, Order, and Progress"—but for the dictator, the price of order and progress was liberty itself. Elections were rigged, dissident journalists were jailed (one more than 30 times), and Díaz's strident critics were assassinated. The provinces were controlled by *jefes políticos* (political bosses). When uprisings occurred, they were swiftly smothered by bands of *rurales* (rural police).

Díaz's wealthy, European-trained, *criollo* advisors believed that the nation's problems could be solved with scientific techniques. Under Díaz, Mexico was mechanized, paved, and electrified. Ironically, the regime that brought prosperity to Mexico harbored deeply anti-Mexican prejudices. The Positivist *científicos*—as Díaz's advisors were called—believed that *indígenas* were weak, immoral, and ineducable. Few of the new schools built during the Porfiriato were located in indigenous *pueblos.* When the **Fifth Pan-American Congress** was held in Mexico City just after the turn of the century, *indígenas* and *mestizos* were prohibited from serving foreign dignitaries; only whites could work as waiters and porters during the Congress. French, not Mexican, furniture, food, dance, opera, and fashion were *de rigueur* among the *criollo* elite.

Díaz brought in French and British firms to build a vast infrastructure of railroads linking agricultural areas to urban factories. As a result, industry prospered and land values skyrocketed. But few poor Mexicans profited from the economic boom. Under a new law, indigenous *ejidos* could be forced to sell their public lands if they couldn't show a legal title to the plots they farmed. By the turn of the century, most villages saw their *ejidos* taken by wealthy individuals and private companies. In one case, a town was so entirely stripped of its communal lands that it no longer had space to bury its dead. Meanwhile, *científicos* made millions speculating in the volatile land market, manipulating railroad contracts to their own advantage.

Vast *haciendas* sprung up in the north, some as large as seven million acres, fed by cheap land prices. Half of Mexico's rural population worked as *peones,* legally bound to the *hacienda* owners.

MEXICO

## REVOLUTION

### Challenges from All Sides

Unlike the war for independence, which was ignited by *criollo* discontent, the Revolution began smoldering in the lower levels of Mexican society. In 1906, copper miners in Sonora went on strike, citing low wages and the discriminatory policies of the mine's U.S. owners. The protest was quashed when Díaz permitted U.S. mercenaries to cross the border and kill strikers in order to protect the interests of U.S. investors. But similar strikes elsewhere fueled a growing sense of instability.

In the 1910 presidential election, Díaz faced a vocal opponent. **Francisco I. Madero,** a wealthy *hacienda* owner from Coahuila, was no social revolutionary, but his calls for liberty and democracy were enough for Díaz to throw him into jail. Escaping to the U.S., Madero orchestrated a series of grass-roots rebellions in northern states from his base in San Antonio. Meanwhile, **Emiliano Zapata** led the revolt against Díaz in the southern state of Morelos. Unlike Madero, Zapata believed the rebels' first priority was to restore communal lands to the indigenous *pueblos*. Traveling to remote pueblos and addressing villagers in Náhuatl when necessary, Zapata quickly raised an army of **angry indígenas**. After Madero's troops captured Ciudad Juárez, the 81-year-old Díaz fled to Paris. But once in power, the cautious Madero hesitated to restore any land to the Zapatistas, and ordered the rebels in the south to disband. Zapata resisted the order, and the Zapatistas tangled with General **Victoriano Huerta**'s troops. A pattern for the Revolution had been set.

### The Coalition Collapses

After fending off rebellions from radical factions, Madero's government finally fell to a conservative uprising led by Huerta and Díaz's nephew. **Venustiano Carranza,** the governor of Coahuila, urged state governors to revolt against the federal government. Guerrilla armies sprung up in the North, led by **Pancho Villa** in Chihuahua and **Álvaro Obregón** in Sonora. Provisional governments proliferated; by late 1913, there were more than 25 different types of paper money in circulation. After U.S. troops bombed Veracruz in 1914, Huerta resigned.

Next, Obregón seized the capital; Carranza controlled Veracruz; Villa ruled the north; Zapata held the south. When Villa's troops attacked Obregón's forces at the bloody battle of Celaya, 4000 Villistas were shredded on barbed-wire entrenchments; 5000 more were wounded. As Villistas wreaked havoc on Texas border towns, Carranza's own government found itself hopelessly divided between old-style liberals and radical land reformists. The fighting in the south was the most vicious. Thousands of civilians were executed as alleged Zapatista sympathizers, and Zapata responded by blowing up a train and killing some 400 innocent passengers. In 1919, Carranza's men assassinated Zapata in an ambush, and Carranza assumed the presidency, inaugurating a period of relative calm. But one in eight Mexicans had died in the wars of 1910-1920. As all the rebel governments had printed their own money, the economy was in ruin. Inflation slashed the real wages of urban laborers; flooding and sabotage put miners out of work. Many Mexicans were on the brink of starvation.

### Institutionalized Revolution

In 1917, Carranza gathered delegates to draft a **new constitution;** the document they produced still governs the Republic. Zapatistas, Villistas, and Huertistas were barred from the convention, yet delegates outlined a thoroughly radical agenda for the nation. Present was the familiar liberal anticlericalism of the 19th century; more startling were the socialistic articles of the new constitution. Private ownership of land was declared to be a privilege, not a right, and the state was supposed to redistribute lands seized from *pueblos* during the Porfiriato. Workers were guaranteed better work conditions and the right to strike. But the moderate Carranza failed to implement most of the radical document, and the Revolution drifted to the right as successive presidents reversed modest gains in land reform and workers' rights.

The **Constitution of 1917** codified the Revolution; the machine politics of the 1920s institutionalized it. **Plutarco Elías Calles,** elected president in 1924, ruled the country for a decade through a series of puppet presidents. Calles, known as the "Jefe Máximo," consolidated the government's support in the new **Partido Nacional Revolucionario (PNR),** which has run Mexico virtually unopposed in the 65 years since.

# MODERN MEXICO

## A Return to Redistribution

The Great Depression hit Mexico in the gut: as the value of the peso plummeted, wages dropped by 10%, and many Mexicans began to question the direction of the Revolution. Reacting to the mood of the times, Mexico's new president, **Lázaro Cárdenas,** seized the reins from his PNR handlers and steered the Revolution sharply to the left. Cárdenas redistributed 49 million acres—twice as much as all his predecessors combined—to thousands of indigenous *ejidos,* where lands were farmed in common as they had been for hundreds of years before the Porfiriato. Economically, most *ejidos* were a failure, and agricultural productivity dropped drastically. But the *ejido* program won an enormous symbolic goal: no longer peons, the rural *indígena* had regained some of the political and social autonomy that disappeared with the loss of communal lands in the late 19th century.

## Industrial Capitalism and the Problem of Liberty

By drawing labor groups and agrarian reformers into the government, Cárdenas immeasurably strengthened the ruling party, now called the **Partido Revolucionario Institucional (PRI).** At the same time, however, land reform stalled and the government limited the right to strike. Meanwhile, **WWII** speeded the pace of Mexican development, accelerating the shift from socialism to industrial capitalism. But the working class didn't share proportionately in the new prosperity. Policy-makers believed that some measure of inequity was necessary in order to increase the size of the economic pie. Mexican industrialists were urged to keep costs down—and, by implication, to keep wages low. When oil workers went on strike in the early 1950s, the army was called in and dozens of union leaders were fired.

The PRI has been likened to a **floating log:** if you want to stay afloat, you have to grab on. Lured by the promise of cushy government jobs, union officials and peasant leaders joined the PRI's **swelling political machine.** Enjoying wide institutional support, the PRI has not yet lost a presidential election since its inception in 1929. But the stability of single-party rule (which is fading in the late 1990s) has come at the price of liberty. Even under president **Adolfo López Mateos,** who between 1958 and 1964 expanded social security coverage and redoubled efforts at land reform, Mexicans were not free to speak their minds. López Mateos removed the Communist leadership of the teachers' and railroad unions and sent in the army to break a railroad-workers' strike in 1959. When the head of the PRI tried to reform the party's nomination process, he was fired by the president under pressure from state political bosses. **Student unrest** and worker dissatisfaction culminated in 1968 at Mexico City's Tlatelolco Plaza, where police killed an estimated 400 peaceful demonstrators and jailed another 2000 protesters just 10 days before the Olympics were to open (p. 105).

## Salinas: Toward Democracy

"The era of one-party rule in Mexico is over," declared PRI presidential candidate **Carlos Salinas de Gortari** during the tense week following the 1988 presidential elections. Salinas officially (and conveniently) received 50.4% of the vote when the final contested results were announced, but many interpreted his remarks and the election itself as a fresh start for Mexican politics.

Mexico's ruling party did not lose a single presidential, senatorial, or gubernatorial race from 1929 to 1988; in the few local elections that it did lose, the PRI often installed its own candidates anyway. Through a combination of patronage, fraud, and ineffectual opposition, the party stayed in power and ran Mexico uncontested. But in the 1982 election, the murmurs of dissent were heard, and the right-of-center **Partido de Acción Nacionál (PAN)** won 14% of the vote, most of it in the northern states. In 1983, when the PRI experimented with fraud-free elections, the PAN picked up three mayorships in the state of Chihuahua alone.

When Salinas began his six-year term as president on December 1, 1988, he had to confront high unemployment, a US$105 billion foreign debt, the domestic production and transport of drugs, and a skeptical nation. Salinas instituted wage and price controls to keep inflation down, then boosted his popularity with the prominent arrests of a union boss, a fraudulent businessman, and a drug trafficker.

On February 4, 1990, representatives of the Mexican government and its 450 foreign commercial creditors signed a debt reduction agreement designed to ease the U.S. banking crisis and deflect outlandishly high interest payments. This reprieve, along with Salinas's austerity program, led to growing foreign investment and steady growth (3% per year) in Mexico's gross domestic product. Unemployment, however, remains near 20%. Reduced or not, foreign debt has continued to suck capital out of the country, and a blossoming trade deficit is squeezing out small and medium businesses as foreign franchises muscle in.

The fate of these smaller firms was at the center of the controversial **North American Free Trade Agreement (NAFTA).** The treaty eliminated the tariffs, quotas, and subsidies that had protected Mexican industry and agriculture since the 1940s. Smaller Mexican-owned businesses began to be driven out of business by *maquiladores,* U.S.-owned assembly and automotive-sector factories. On the other hand, freer trade means cheaper consumer goods for financially strapped Mexicans—a blessing in a nation plagued by constant inflation. Increased competition may eventually reap profits for the Mexican economy, but development is now exacting high human and environmental costs.

In 1991, PRI technocrats dismantled the *ejido* system, which ostensibly guaranteed communal land rights for rural *campesinos.* With this constitutional reform and other changes, including rapid **privatization,** an agrarian culture thousands of years old is being phased out to pave the way for **industrialism.** Traditional support systems are lost in urbanization while government safety nets are eliminated, all part of an economic streamlining backed by the U.S. and international lenders. The costs of this structural adjustment program (centered around NAFTA) have yet to be determined, but in the meantime they fall squarely on the shoulders of the lower classes, while benefits still loom on the long-term horizon.

### The Zapatistas

On January 1, 1994, the day that NAFTA took effect, Maya rebels rose up and captured San Cristóbal de Las Casas, the largest city in Chiapas state. Within days, government troops had driven the rebels back into the highlands and the Lacandón rainforest, leaving about 150 dead. Months of negotiations followed, during which the government's top negotiator resigned after accusing the PRI of sabotaging his efforts. The rebels rejected the government's peace plan, and threatened to shatter the fragile cease-fire unless upcoming presidential elections were free and fair.

In an election year that was supposed to express Mexico's material progress and fledgling democracy, the rebels from Chiapas drew attention to the vast inequities that still exist within the Republic. Led by a mysterious masked man known as **Subcomandante Marcos,** the Zapatista rebels (named after revolutionary war hero Emiliano Zapata) demanded land, food, education, health care, and autonomy. Chiapas is Mexico's poorest state: four out of five homes have dirt floors without drains, the majority of land is in the hands of a few powerful bosses, and more than half of the area's inhabitants are malnourished. President Salinas had poured more anti-poverty money into the state than any other—but to little avail. The price of coffee, the state's major crop, had dropped on the world market, and the labor market was glutted with refugees from Guatemala and El Salvador. Furthermore, *indígena* rebels clearly harbored deep resentments that no amount of PRI money could assuage. The uprising marks the latest and most strident call for *indígena* equality. "We are the product of

500 years of struggle," read a statement posted in San Cristóbal by the Zapatistas. Memories of the Conquest are still fresh in a state where, as late as the 1950s, *indígenas* were expected to step off a narrow sidewalk when a white person passed.

The Zapatistas' call for reform has split the conscience of the nation in half, bringing the often muted tension between *mestizos* and *indígenas* to the foreground. For *indígenas* and the poor, the charismatic Marcos and his heroic band of Maya rebels have taken on an almost mythical identity. Zapatismo has swept the nation, cutting across class and race lines, and every day the spirit of reform manifests itself in peaceful marches and rallies in the *zócalos*. There has been some dialogue between the Zapatistas and government representatives, and progress is slow but visible. After three seasons of deadlocked negotiations, the violence has been quelled and the military presence in the region's once heavily patrolled cities has slackened considerably. In the streets, billboards proclaim 1996 "El Año de Paz y Reconciliación en Chiapas" and the word *Chiapaz* appears on the walls of tenement buildings. The dust has finally started to settle, but it's a very precarious peace.

## Death and Transfiguration

> *"Oh, this fearful, vibrant vale of shadows that is our country."*
> -Efraín Huerta

The Zapatista uprising foreshadowed turmoil to come. On March 23, 1994, the likeable and reform-minded PRI presidential candidate, **Luis Donaldo Colosio** of Mexicali, was assassinated as he left a rally in Tijuana. Many believe that a hard-line faction of the PRI killed its own candidate when they found him too radical and conciliatory for their taste; the subsequent murders of the chief investigator of Colosio's assassination and several other officials connected with the investigation fueled the rumors. After three years of conflicting investigations by five different prosecutors, Colosio's case remains officially unsolved; but official versions don't satisfy many people anyway. Meanwhile, the PRI tapped Budget and Planning minister and UPenn-trained technocrat and free-market man **Ernesto Zedillo** to replace the slain candidate and rebuild the campaign from scratch. The party relied on more than 800,000 grass-roots organizers to comb the country door-to-door, building on an old network of patronage and pork-belly politics. Sure enough, the PRI won hands down in a relatively fair election, faring especially well among Mexico's poorer voters.

Just months into his presidency, on December 20, 1994, Zedillo confronted a precipitous drop in the value of the peso. Spooked by the assassination of Colosio and the unsettling events in Chiapas, foreign investors had dumped US$25 billion of Mexican government peso bonds, heralding the imminent monetary **devaluation.** Aided by the International Monetary Fund (IMF) and the U.S. government, Mexico was salvaged from the depths of economic crisis. Still, severe financial difficulties persisted: in March 1995, interest rates skyrocketed to above 90%, bringing the banking system to a near collapse. The growing legions of middle-class professionals and entrepreneurs that relied on foreign dollars were left frustrated and frightened. Mexicans have laid the blame squarely on Zedillo's shoulders, citing his delay in appointing key cabinet posts and in instituting promised economic initiatives.

Though the prospect of successfully taming the economy seems distant, Zedillo has sought to pacify the anxious masses with further political reforms. Rumors of former president Salinas's frauds and supposed complicity in Colosio's murder, and the implication of his brother **Raúl Salinas** in a money-laundering scandal (at one point, a dead body was found buried in the Salinas backyard), as well as the government's inability to curb drug trafficking and related violence, have lowered the morale of the Mexican people and their faith in the PRI. The president has committed himself to decentralizing power and exposing corruption in an attempt to restore the nation's faith in the government. In addition to slowly de-frauding elections, Zedillo has arrested several high-level officials on charges of conspiracy and murder, earning respect from many and U.S. endorsement as a "partner in the war on drugs."

However, no end to the war is in sight: narcotics and their associated vices have eaten away at Mexico's soul in recent years. Most disheartening has been the frighteningly large overlap, only beginning to be exposed, between high-level drug enforcement officials, politicians, and druglords. For example, **Rafael Águilar Guajardo,** a former drug enforcement agent, went on to become the top man in a large cartel before his 1993 murder in Cancún. After the arrest and extradition to the U.S. of **Juan García Abrego,** the former leader of the powerful Gulf cartel, **Amado Carrillo Fuentes** emerged as Mexico's kingpin, head of the powerful Juárez cartel and one of the richest men in the world (pulling in an estimated $5 million per day in profits). While Fuentes dominated the scene, enforcement agents fell by the wayside, either killed for knowing too much or bought off by the druglords and then often caught in Zedillo's crackdown (as was **Gen. Jesús Gutierrez Rebollo,** the former anti-narcotics czar who was found to have accepted a posh apartment and tens of thousands of dollars in bribes from Fuentes). Meanwhile, Fuentes, "Lord of the Skies," constructed an empire that made even the Cali cartel of Colombia jealous, operating a fleet of hollowed-out Boeing 727 airplanes filled from cockpit to rudder with cocaine. With his extra proceeds, he built churches and threw epic parties for residents of his childhood village, Guamuchilito, Sinaloa. On July 4, 1997, Fuentes died in the hospital after (of all things) eight hours of plastic surgery and **liposuction,** creating a power struggle in Ciudad Juárez (5 people were gunned down there only days later) and leaving Sinaloa's **Arellano Felix** brothers to take their place atop the Mexican drug hierarchy. Though Zedillo has taken steps toward exposing government participation at high levels, more light must be cast upon the vale of shadows to seriously curb a $10 billion business in which 60% of the proceeds yearly go toward bribing public officials at all levels, many of whom struggle to feed their families each night.

### Mexico at a Crossroads

Happily, the deaths of drug barons are not the only Mexican news items fit to print in recent years. Equally newsworthy has been a dramatic shift away from one-party rule and toward democracy below the border. Under Zedillo's leadership, Mexico has moved toward fair elections. This has actually begun to undermine his own party's domination: the PRI once controlled all state governorships; now, several state governors, including that of Jalisco, now belong to the opposition right-leaning PAN. Furthermore, the liberal **Partido de la Revolución Democrática (PRD)** party has posed a threat from the other side.

On July 6, 1997, Mexico's **elections** took an unprecedented turn. The PRI, increasingly linked with instability instead of stability, lost its majority in the lower house of Congress for the first time ever; it had held the house for 68 years. PAN, the right-center, and PRD, the burgeoning left, each took nearly 30% of the Congressional vote, leaving only 41% for the PRI—rather far from one-party rule. Without a PRI majority supporting Zedillo in Congress, much of the president's power has now passed to that body. But Congress wasn't all that was shaken up on July 6: in the first direct Mexico City mayoral vote since 1928, leftist **Cuauhtémoc Cárdenas** of the PRD, an opponent of Zedillo's free-market policies, won a landslide victory. Like his father Lázaro (a 1930s prez), Cárdenas is said to have his eye on the top job (Zedillo will be replaced, as are all Mexican presidents after one term, in 2000). For the first time, the prospect of a non-PRI president isn't all that far-fetched.

But a new three-letter-acronym at the helm would promise nothing in itself. Whether Congress will wield its new power skillfully, and whether Mexico's transition to partisan politics will result in fruitful reform or confused gridlock, remains to be seen. The 1997 elections, though, at least *appear* to offer a glimmer of hope in a stagnant political system long steeped in corruption.

# ■ Culture and Character

## ART AND ARCHITECTURE

Much of what archaeologists have been able to piece together about the daily life and beliefs of Mexico's ancient peoples stems mainly from the artifacts—both functional and purely decorative—they left behind. Early Mexican art, like Western art, was devoted to the sacred. The colonial period favored stilted European imitation, but the nationalistic Revolution rescuitated native styles, now informed by modern themes. Art historians classify works within three periods: the Indigenous (6000 BC-AD 1525), the Colonial (1525-1810), and the Modern (1810-present).

### Art on a Grand Scale: The Olmecs

The **colossal heads** found at **La Venta, San Lorenzo,** and **Tres Zapotes,** stone monuments thought to represent human-like deities, are the best-known creations of the **Olmec** civilization (1200-100 BC). Incredibly, the Olmecs imported the massive **basalt stones**—some weighing as much as 20 tons—from other areas by floating them across waterways on highly effective rafts.

Not all Olmec artistry was this large. Olmecs were also fine potters and expert jade carvers; their handicrafts were esteemed and emulated later by the Maya. Tending away from idealization, many Olmec figurines take as their subjects plump children, child-men, hunchbacks, and **half-man-half-jaguar beings** in various positions of repose, reverence, and agitation. The fluid lines of the numerous acrobat and contortionist figures that have been unearthed provide further evidence of Olmec skill as well as the value they placed on performance and entertainment. The eventual demise of the Olmec culture marked a transition from the Pre-Classic period (2000-100 BC) to the Classic (100 BC-AD 900), and the dawn of other powerful cultures, most notably Teotihuacán and Maya.

### An Artistic Metropolis: Teotihuacán

Located in the Valley of Mexico about 50km northeast of Mexico City, **Teotihuacán** was the Americas' first metropolis, a great commercial and artistic center with over 25,000 inhabitants (p. 119). Temples and pyramids were both a source of civic pride and a religious necessity. The structures were ornamented in relief with images of serpents, jaguars, gods, and, though not as evident today, were also often decorated with vibrant colors. Frescoes on interior walls of buildings depict, among other subjects, paradise scenes, floral arrangements, religious rituals, and athletic events.

It says something about the Teotihuacanos' level of organization and technological savvy that they were able to "mass-produce" figurines; from clay molds, copies were made, remnants of which have been discovered throughout the region. The people of Teotihuacán even left behind statuettes with moveable appendages.

### The Origins of Glamour

Heirs to the artistic and scientific achievements of the Olmecs, the **Maya,** undisputed representatives of Mexico's golden age, reached their cultural pinnacle in the period between AD 300 and 600. The Maya flourished in areas of the Chiapas highlands, northern Yucatán, and Guatemala—impressive ruins can be found at Chichén Itzá, Palenque, and Uxmal. Despite the fact they had no metal tools or use of the wheel, the Maya built **temples, palaces, altars,** and **stelae** (pillar-shaped monuments), calculated a 365-day calendar, and developed a mathematical system, based on the number 20, which used zero as a value. The Maya were unflaggingly devoted to fashion and accessories. Gods and nobility (of both genders) adorn themselves with massive headdresses replete with lengthy feathers, necklaces with beads the size of eggs, and gold and copper bracelets to match the enormous bangles hanging from their earlobes. The materials of choice for Maya artisans were **limestone, sandstone,** and to a lesser degree, **wood** and **jade.**

## The Aztecs: The Sunset of Indígena Art

Founders of Tenochtitlán (modern-day Mexico City), the **Aztecs** built a truly remarkable city, sprawling, yet highly organized according to a rectangular grid-plan. In the central area, where important religious events such as human sacrifices were held, pyramids and temples stood majestically as symbols of technological achievement and spiritual devotion.

The clearly stratified society of **Tenochtitlán** produced an organized labor force that undoubtedly contributed much to the city's marketplace, a center that drew crowds of up to 30,000. From this milieu of expert craftsmanship resulted two of the Aztec's more recognizable and famous creations: the Stone of the Sun **(Aztec Calendar),** measuring nearly 4m in diameter, and Tenochtitlán's great **Coatlicue sculpture,** a monumental statue almost 2.5m tall representing the Goddess of the Earth. The Aztec Calendar's narrative is a tragic one: within its concentric rings are contained the four symbols of previous suns—rain, tiger, water, and wind, the elements responsible for the destruction of earlier populations. Aztecs believed they were living in the period of the fifth sun, and expected to be obliterated by an earthquake, the symbol for which also ominously appears on the stone. But it wasn't a pernicious earthquake that irreversibly altered the Aztec culture—it was the landing of the *conquistadores* in 1521.

## The Architecture of New Spain

Not surprisingly, the first examples of **colonial art** were created specifically to facilitate religious indoctrination. Churches were often constructed on top of Indian temples and pyramids, causing serious and irreparable damage to ancient sites. Volcanic stone, plentiful in most areas, was the main building material. **Colonial architecture,** much of it recalling **Romanesque** and **Gothic** stylistic elements, is characterized by the use of huge buttresses, arches, and crenulations (indented or embattled moldings). An architectural phenomenon that developed early on was the open chapel (*capilla abierta*), a group of arches enclosing an atrium.

The monasteries and churches under the direction of **Franciscan, Dominican,** and **Augustinian** missionaries were built according to climactic and geographic limitations. The Franciscan style tended to be functional and economic, the Dominican ascetic and harsh, due to earthquake danger and warm weather. The Augustinian style was the most free-spirited and grandiose, indulging in sumptuous decoration whenever possible. Remarkable Augustinian buildings include the **Monastery of St. Augustín of Acolman** near Mexico City and the **Monastery of Actopán** in Hidalgo.

## A Blossoming of the Baroque

The steady growth and spread of the Catholic church throughout the 17th and 18th centuries necessitated the construction of cathedrals, parochial chapels, and convents; moreover, this period brought the Baroque style to New Spain. By turns elegant and garish—but always luxurious—**Baroque** facades, teeming with dynamic images of angels and saints, aimed to produce a feeling of awe and respect in the hearts of the converted *indígenas.* The narratives set in stone were accessible to the illiterate and easily committed to memory. A look at the cathedrals of Zacatecas and Chihuahua reveals the degree of artistry Baroque ideals encouraged. Baroque painting found its expression in the works of **Alonso López de Herrera** and **Baltazar de Echave Orio** (the elder).

Sumptuousness, frivolity, ornamentation—it appears as though late 18th-century artists and builders couldn't have too much of a good thing, and so came the **Churrigueresque** style, **Mexican High Baroque** carried to the extreme. The hallmarks of the this style are excessively and intricately-decorated *estípites* (pilasters), often installed merely for looks, not support.

## 20th Century Murals: The Political Aesthetic

As the Revolution reduced their land to shambles, Mexican painters developed an unapologetic national style. This success was made possible by **José Vasconcelos'**

Ministry of Education program, which commissioned murals for public buildings and sent artists into the countryside to teach and participate in rural life.

The Mexican **mural,** unequivocally nationalistic in its current form, ironically dates back to the early days of the conquest when Catholic evangelists, fighting the language barrier, used allegorical murals to impart the rudiments of Christian iconography. **Diego Rivera,** the most renowned of the *muralistas,* based his artwork on political themes—land reform, Marxism, the marginalization of *indígena* life. His work reached a wide audience and embroiled him in international controversy.

The others in the "Big Four" pantheon were **David Álfaro Siqueiros,** who brought new materials and dramatic revolutionary themes to his murals; the Cubism-influenced **Rufino Tamayó,** arguably the most abstract of the four; and **José Clemente Orozco.** The anguished, dynamic figures in a number of Siqueiros's formally innovative works appear to threaten the boundaries of the picture plane.

### Frida Kahlo and the Woman Artist

And where are the **women artists?** In a culture anchored by misogyny and machismo, within an art world unabashedly biased toward the U.S. and Western Europe, it is not surprising that the art of Mexican women wasn't dealt with seriously until the latter half of this century. Among celebrated 20th-century Mexican women artists are the painters **María Izquierdo** (she had a lengthy relationship with Rufino Tamayo), **Lilia Carrillo,** and the photographer **Lola Álvarez Bravo.** Due in part to her appalling talent and **Hayden Herrera's** landmark biography, **Frida Kahlo** (1907-54) surpasses all other Mexican artists—men included—in terms of current worldwide recognition. Kahlo's paintings and self-portraits are icons of pain: the viewer is forced to confront the artist's **self-obsession** in its most violent and extreme manifestations.

---

#### Crazy for Kahlo

Depending on whom you talk to, many residents of Coyoacán would say their most cherished product was *la heroína del dolor* (the heroine of pain), the artist Frida Kahlo. Famously self-obsessed, famously morbid, and famously shocking, Kahlo's work, in recent years, has been riding a wave of unprecedented popularity and critical success. *Self-Portrait with Monkey and Parrot* (1942) recently sold for US$3.2 mil. The Frida files are burdened once again with the recent publishing of a facsimile of the diary Kahlo kept in the last 10 years of her life. The colorful, idiosyncratic journal, filled with frantic drawings and cryptic phrases, may well add to the ever-growing Kahlo mythology rather than shedding a clarifying light on the artist's life and body of work.

---

## LITERATURE

### Pre-Hispanic Writing: A Multi-Media Affair

As far as linguists and archaeologists have been able to tell, three languages were dominant in Mexico before the arrival of the Spanish: **Náhuatl, Mayan, and Cakchiquel.** The earliest examples of writing are thought to be the glyphs inscribed at **Monte Albán,** Oaxaca, a site containing astounding reliefs dating back to 600 BC. The Spaniards' destructive rampage, particularly in the initial years of the Conquest, and the imposition of the Spanish language resulted in the loss of valuable information relating to *indígena* language. Considered a dangerous affront to Christian teachings, Maya and Aztec **codices** (unbound "books" or manuscripts) were, naturally, fed to the flames, but due either to the grace of God or less-than-scrupulous destruction, a number of Maya codices did survive. The **Popol Vuh,** the Book of Advice (see p. 51), a pre-eminent example of Náhuatl poetry which was kept alive through oral transmission and later recorded in Latin characters, imparts moral counsel and different versions of the Maya creation myth. Along with the *Popol Vuh,* works such as the **Libros de Chilam Balam** (Books of the Speaker of the Jaguar), transcribed into Mayan in 1782, and the **Annals of the Cakchiquel** cover a range of topics. They are not exclusively historical works, but narrative and poetic, laden with symbolism and lofty metaphor. The *Rabinal Achi* (Knight of Achi), the story of a sacrificed warrior, is considered to be the only surviving example of pre-Hispanic drama.

## Colonial Literature

Like astronauts on a new planet, the Spanish were eager to send news home about the land they had conquered and the ways of life of Mexico's indigenous population. These letters home, among them Cortés's *Cartas de relación* (Letters of Relation), were mainly crown- and Church-flattering documents detailing the exhaustive efforts being undertaken to educate and Christianize *indígenas*. Other chronicles, such as the *Nuevo Mundo y Conquista* (New World and Conquest), by **Francisco de Terrazas**, and *Grandeza Mexicana* (Mexican Grandeur), by **Bernardo de Balbuena,** were rhymed in order to take the edge off the monotonous melange of factoid stew.

In the harsh and brutal society of New Spain, only religious orders enjoyed the luxury of genuine intellectual freedom. Many clergymen worked to preserve indigenous languages and texts, and a handful of universities sprung up. The **Jesuits'** 23 colleges were the best in the colony—until the crown expelled the Jesuits from the Americas in 1767 because of their growing influence.

Though historical texts dominated Mexico's literary output throughout much of the 16th and 17th centuries, substantial achievements in poetry were made. **Sor Juana Inés de la Cruz** (1648-1695) became a master lyricist known for her razor-sharp wit. A *criolla* of illegitimate birth, Sor Juana turned to the cloistered life and married God, instead of the numerous suitors she undoubtedly had—her beauty was legendary. In the Church she found a moral and physical haven where she produced her most famous works, **Respuesta a Sor Filotea** (Response to Sor Filotea) and **Hombres Necios** (Injudicious Men). Her love poems display a passionate sensibility, and many verses display a witty feminism ahead of their time.

## Struggling for a Literary Identity

During the 18th century, the Inquisition vied with the French Enlightenment to distract Mexican writers from anything that could be described as innovative. The establishment of the **Academia de la Lengua Española** (Academy of the Spanish Language) in 1713 grew out of a desire to regulate Spanish where it was spoken, including colonies. An explosion of writing focusing on science occurred about this time. Studies of Mexican geography, weather, flora, and fauna swept away scientists and writers on a wave of rational and analytical thought.

The literary impetus of philosophical movements eventually gave way to political ones. By the end of the 18th century, the struggle toward independence became the singular social fact from which many Mexican texts grew. In 1816, **José Fernández de Lizardi,** a prominent Mexican journalist, wrote the first Latin American novel: *El periquillo sarniento* (The Itching Parrot), a picaresque tale which revealed Mexican society's displeasure with the status quo. His ideological, moralizing angle on fiction has been very influential. With the Spanish-American modernists of the 19th century, poetry reached a level it had not achieved since Sor Juana. At the same time, **Manuel Gutierrez Nájera** composed the poem *De Blanco* (On Whiteness), linguistic representation at its most distilled and self-contained.

Many romantic novels of the period used historical themes to introduce sweeping indictments of the military and clergy. Novelists sought to define Mexico's national identity, glorifying strength, secularism, progress, and education. Artists were similarly didactic, producing works with such inspirational titles as *Triumph and Study Over Ignorance*. Whereas European Romanticism was an aesthetic challenge to Neoclassicism, Mexican Romanticism was an artistic response to the country's political and social realities. Shortly after the heyday of the Romantic novel came the popular novel of manners, significant among them being *El fistol del diablo* by **Manuel Payno,** and *Juanita Sousa* and *Antón Pérez* by **Manuel Sánchez Mármol.**

Literature during the **Porfiriato** (1876-1911) abandoned Romanticism for realism, and most writers expressed little sympathy with the poor. Others adopted a Modernist style, emphasizing language and imagery, and replacing didactic social themes with psychological topics. Visual artists, by contrast, had begun to reject the creed of the *científicos*. Many favored experimental techniques and chose to depict **slums, brothels,** and scenes from indigenous life. Their iconoclasm foreshadowed a growing dissatisfaction with the Díaz regime.

## 20th Century Global Perspectives

Mexican literature in the post-Revolutionary era is marked by a frustrated desire to forge a national tradition from the vestiges of pre-colonial culture. Nobel prize winner **Octavio Paz,** in such works as *El laberinto de la soledad* (The Labyrinth of Solitude), draws on Marxism, Romanticism, and post-Modernism to explore the making and unmaking of a national archetype. Paz, like his equally famous successor **Carlos Fuentes,** concerns himself with myth and legend in an effort to come to terms with Spanish cultural dominance. Fuentes published his first novel, *La region más transparente,* in 1958. His 1994-96 work *Nuevo Tiempo Mexicano* (A New Time for Mexico) is a collection of nonfiction essays on politics, international relations, and domestic social conditions. Written in the same flowing, songlike voice as his fiction and steeped in Mexico's mythological and historical tradition, it is a gripping book. **Juan Rulfo's** *Pedro Páramo,* set in rural Jalisco, blurs the line between life and death, past and present, as it relates one man's search for his father. The wildly popular works of **Gustavo Sainz** and **José Agustín,** the instigators of *literatura de la onda* ("hip" literature), address universal concerns like getting laid and getting stoned. Of late, the work of female writers, such as Hollywood darling **Laura Esquivel** *(Like Water for Chocolate),* has been well received both nationally and internationally.

## POPULAR CULTURE

### Music

Like most other components of its culture, Mexican music is an eclectic stew of styles and flavors borrowed from all across the continent and overseas. Mexico's traditional music is mostly regional, making for a rich and varied collage of styles and artists. Up north, one will hear groups such as **Los Bukis, Bronco,** and **Los Tigres del Norte** sing in the style aptly labeled *norteño.* One of the most popular and well-known styles of traditional Mexican music is **mariachi.** *Mariachi* songs, commonly called *rancheras,* are usually played live by a sombreroed, gregarious brass-and-string band, and the world-famous tradition of women being serenaded by a group of *mariachis* in traditional Mexican garb is seen as an almost obligatory supplement to a romantic evening—foreplay, if you will. Traditionally macho *rancheras* tend to deal with one or several of the following topics: being very drunk, being abandoned by a woman, being cheated on by a woman, getting drunk, leaving a woman, the fidelity of one's horse, one's gun, and wanting to get drunk. While male singers like **José Alfredo Jiménez** and **Vicente Fernández** continue to sing popular tunes in this tradition, **Lupita D'Alessio** provides the angry-woman response. Although she gets betrayed or left on almost every one of her songs, the culprit men often get their due.

The Mexican music scene is adorned with both Spanish and American influences. The former is apparent with young artists such as the pop group **Garibaldi,** whose scantily clad bods perennially grace (disgrace?) music and teen fanzines. Travelers from up north will feel at home, as American music in all forms is ubiquitous both on the radio and in bars and *discotecas.* Always striving to Mexicanize imports in some way, Mexican artists will often take an American piece and make it their "own" with altered lyrics or a slightly more Latin beat. Cotton-candy pop is sung by such artists as **Luis Miguel** (sigh), **Lucero, Alejandra Guzmán,** and **Christian Castro.**

**Selena,** the "Latin Madonna" and most beloved of Tejano singers, was American, but in typical Tejano style, she fused polka, country, Mexican, and R&B. Her bouncy Spanish album *Amor Prohibido* was wildly popular in both Mexico and the U.S., but it didn't hit #1 on the Billboard charts until Selena was **murdered**—shot in the back by **Yolanda Saldivar,** the president of her fan club, on March 31, 1995. After her death, she became even more of an icon for Mexican youth.

## Television

Mexican television can, for the most part, be broken down into four categories: *telenovelas* (soap operas), weekly dramas, sitcoms, and imported American shows. *Telenovelas* are by far the most popular and widely aired of the bunch. Occupying a huge block of midday air time, these shameless, hour-long examples of dramaturgy tend to run for two to four months before being ousted for a fresh group of characters and convoluted conflicts. The half-hour **sitcoms** that dominate American TV don't seem to be as popular in Mexico, though there are a few. Popular shows include **Papá Soltero, Chespirito,** and just about anything on the **Canal de las Estrellas. American shows** are often dubbed; as in the U.S., shows such as **Melrose Place** and **Baywatch** are very popular. Cartoons are imported from both the U.S. and Japan. One cannot claim to have *lived* without having watched at least one episode of **Los Simpson.**

## Film

"Popular cinema is still alive and well in Mexico," wrote one disgruntled director, "mainly as sex comedies and cop dramas." The recent recession has led to an influx of subtitled Hollywood imports and a paucity of quality films. Mexico's golden age of cinema *(cine de oro)* was kicked off in the 1940s and 50s with **Emilio "El Indio" Fernández**'s *Maria Candelaría* (1943), an honoree at the first Cannes Film Festival in 1946, and **Luis Buñuel**'s *Los Olvidados* (1950), a grisly portrait of *barrio* life in Mexico City. The past decade has seen the rise of such luminaries as **Arturo Ripstein** *(La Mujer del Puerto; Reina de la Noche),* **Jorge Fons** *(Rojo Amanecer),* **Ryan Bradley,** and **Paul Leduc.** Known for his experiments without dialogue, Leduc's *Frida* provides an unsettling look at one of Mexico's controversial cultural icons. The one Mexican film that has enjoyed enormous cross-over success is the delicious romance *Como agua para chocolate (Like Water for Chocolate),* based on the best-selling **Laura Esquivel** novel and directed by **Alfonso Arau,** now her ex-husband. The film may well have been geared toward an American audience; it has the distinction of being the highest-grossing foreign film in U.S. history.

## FOOD AND DRINK

Mexican food and drinks aren't just good; they're **orgasmic.** Leave your Taco Bell-guided expectations behind when you cross the border and prepare yourself for the rich sensual experience that is eating and drinking in Mexico.

Mexicans usually choose to have their big meal of the day—the **comida**—between 2 and 4pm. Restaurants often offer **comida corrida,** sometimes called *la comida* or *el menú,* a fixed price meal including soup, salad, tea or *agua fresca,* a *plato fuerte* (main dish), and sometimes a dessert. The main dish is often a **guisado**—a soup or stew with meat—although a **caldo** (broth-like soup) and a regular plate of meat are also common; *arroz* (rice, sometimes *con huevo,* with chopped egg), beans, and tortillas are always included; often, so is dessert. Breakfasts *(desayunos)* range from continental to grandiose. Dinner *(cena)* is usually a light meal served around 8pm.

## The Staples

From tacos slapped together at a roadside *taquería* to a magnificent plate full of garlic shrimp or chicken with *mole* sauce, Mexican food invariably maintains one common link: the **tortilla.** This most ubiquitous staple of Mexican cuisine is a flat, round, thin pancake made from either wheat flour *(harina)* or corn flour *(maíz).* You will surely develop a preference for one or the other early on, and most restaurants will let you choose which kind you want with your *antojito* or full meal.

The other two staples of Mexican food are the always cheap, always filling, and remarkably nutritious pair—rice and beans. **Rice** *(arroz)* is usually standard fare; yellow Spanish or Mexican rice prepared with oil and tomato sauce is a special treat. **Beans** *(frijoles)* are soft and range from soupy to pasty *(refritos).* These three foods will be served in various forms with just about every full plate of food you order, be it breakfast, lunch, or dinner.

## Good Morning

Aside from the standard *café con leche* or *pan dulce* (sweetened bread), almost any breakfast in Mexico will include **eggs** in some shape or form. *Huevos al gusto* (eggs any style) provides people with a choice of *jamón* (ham), *tocino* (bacon), or *machaca* (dried, shredded beef). **Tortillas, frijoles,** and sometimes **rice** or **papas fritas** (french fries) are served on the side. The eggs themselves are usually *revueltos* (scrambled) with the meat mixed in, but you can ask for the meat fried on the side or the eggs *estrellados* (fried) instead. Other popular styles of preparing *huevos* include *rancheros* (fried eggs served on corn tortillas and covered with a spicy red salsa), *albañil* (scrambled eggs cooked in green sauce), *a la mexicana* (scrambled with onion, tomato, and chopped green chile), *motuleños* (fried eggs served on a fried corn tortilla, topped with sauteed green peas and ham, Sam I Am), *ahogados* (eggs cooked in boiling red sauce), and *borrachos* (fried eggs served with beans cooked in beer). More expensive Mexican breakfasts include **omelettes** with any of the above meats, **seafood** such as *camarones* (shrimp), or even *langosta* (lobster) and *pan francés* (french toast).

## Ah, Antojitos

**Antojito** comes from the word *antojo,* craving. Although anything could be an *antojito,* the term is often, but not always, restricted to nine categories. **Tacos** are small, grilled chunks of meat (sometimes chicken, fried fish, or fried shellfish) placed on an open, warm tortilla, left for you to top yourself with a row of condiments ranging from lettuce and tomato (be careful!) to guacamole and hot sauce. **Burritos** are thin, rolled flour tortillas filled with meat (often *machaca*, chicken, or beans) and a few cooked vegetables such as green peppers and onions. Occasionally you will see Tex-Mex-style *súper burritos* filled with everything but the kitchen sink. Burritos are not very common in the southern parts of Mexico. **Enchiladas** are corn tortillas filled with meat or chicken, topped with a special red or green sauce and shredded cheese, and then baked or fried. Some variations exist, such as enchiladas *suizas* (topped with sour cream) or enchiladas *de mole*. **Quesadillas** are filled with melted cheddar cheese. Sometimes other things are added: with ham they become **sincronizadas,** with *pastor* (gyro style) pork meat, **gringas.** **Tostadas** consist of a deep-fried tortilla garnished with vegetables, cheese, and almost anything else, from meat or chicken to exotic seafood like *pulpo* (octopus). *Tostadas* are the only *antojito* to which raw vegetables are always added; prudent travelers should beware of uncooked vegetables, especially lettuce, while in Mexico. A **chile relleno,** a unique and wonderful Mexican creation, consists of a large, green chile pepper stuffed with cheese (and occasionally meat), dipped in a batter, fried, and topped with red *salsa*. They are not particularly *picante* (spicy-hot)—the frying process rids the chile of most of its potency. **Tamales,** also unique, are ground-corn dough packed with meat or chicken in corn husks; they have the consistency of thick dumplings. Finally, **chimichangas** are essentially the same as burritos but deep fried to produce a rich, crunchy, artery-hardening shell, and **flautas** are like chimichangas but small and finger-thin.

## Meats, Poultry, Seafood, and Soup

Meat platters are usually either **bistek** (derived from the little-used English term "beef-steak"), which is a standard fried cut of beef; **carne asada,** thin slices of beef fried until crispy; or a **pricier cut of steak** such as T-bone, filet mignon, or New York steak (English names are used). The meat can be prepared normally (it's usually served fairly well done), *empanizada* or *milanesa* (breaded or fried), or *a la mexicana* which means served charred up and topped with a Mexican red *salsa*. *Encebollado* means served with grilled onions. In any case, meat dishes are accompanied by *arroz, frijoles,* tortillas, and sometimes *papas fritas*. **Pollo** (chicken) is ubiquitous and (usually) quite tasty. Whether by itself or included in a platter, it is generally either *rostizado* (spit-roasted over an open fire, "rotisserie"-style) or *asado* (grilled), served with the same side dishes mentioned above. **Mole,** arguably Mexico's national dish, is a delectable sauce composed of chiles, chocolate, and other spices. Usually served over chicken, *mole* (if you're a little daring) will likely make you **squeal with delight.** *Mole poblano* is named after its home, the city of Puebla. Seafood dishes include *pescado* (generic fish fillet, usually a local catch), *camarones* (shrimp), *langosta* (lobster), *calamar* (fillet of squid), scrumptious *jaiba* (crab), and *huachinango* (the exceedingly tasty red snapper, with the name that's as fun to pronounce—wa-chee-NAAN-go—as it is to eat). Seafood is usually served either *empanizado* (breaded and fried) or the delicious *al mojo de ajo* (in garlic). *A la veracruzana* is a special preparation, native to Veracruz, in which the fish is decked out in olives, capers, and olive oil.

Soups in Mexico can also be delicious; among others, *sopa de tortilla* is made with bits of softened tortilla, and *sopa de lima* is flavored with lime.

## When You Get Thirsty

*Cerveza* (beer) ranks only slightly below tortillas and beans on the list of Mexican staples. It is impossible to drive through a Mexican town, anywhere, without coming across a double-digit number of Tecate (and, only slightly less so, Corona) billboards, painted buildings, and *agencias,* cheap beer stores, selling anywhere from one beer to several cases at a time. **Tecate** is Mexico's version of Budweiser—it's cheap and none too good. Popular beers in Mexico (listed roughly in order of quality) are **Bohemia** (a world-class lager), **Negra Modelo** (a fine dark beer), **Dos Equis** (a light, smooth lager), **Pacífico** (very smooth), **Sol, Superior, Corona Extra** (watery and far from the most *fina*), **Carta Blanca, Modelo,** and finally, the unfortunate Tecate.

**Tequila** (p. 280) is king when it comes to Mexican liquor. It is the quintessential Mexican drink, a more refined version of *mezcal* (distilled from the *maguey* cactus). **Herradura, Tres Generaciones,** and **Cuervo 1800** are among the more famous, more expensive, and better brands of tequila. Cheap tequila can be bought for prices you wouldn't believe: one Hermosillo supermarket frequently advertises a liter for under US$1! Non-tequila **mezcal** is not distilled as much as tequila. It's sometimes served with the worm native to the plant—upon downing the shot, you are expected to ingest the worm. Some say it induces hallucination; however, evidence is to the contrary. If you get a chance to sample *pulque,* the fermented juice of the *maguey,* don't hesitate—it was the sacred drink of the Aztec nobility.

Mexican mixed drinks enjoy at least as much recognition worldwide as its beers. Coffee-flavored **Kahlúa,** Mexico's most-exported liqueur, deserves its lofty reputation. Enjoy it with cream or milk or as part of a White Russian or Black Russian. Bottles are ridiculously cheap below the border. Frozen drinks aren't too shabby, either; unfortunately, because of tainted ice, only daredevils or Cancún-goers indulge in a **margarita** (tequila, triple sec, lime juice, and ice), a **piña colada** (pineapple juice, cream of coconut—or, if you're lucky, fresh pineapple and coconut—and light rum), or a **coco loco** (coconut milk and tequila served in a hollowed-out coconut).

Fear not, there are also non-alcoholic drinks in Mexico. **Coca-Cola** ("Coca") is perhaps even more universal in Mexico than it is in the U.S. Pepsi, Sprite, 7-Up, and orange sodas are also available, as expected, as are some unique Mexican **refrescos** (sodas). *Soda de fresa* (strawberry soda) is delicious; also try *soda de piña* (pineapple soda), *toronja* (grapefruit soda—try Kas brand), *manzanita* (apple soda—try Sol), and Boing! (mango soda). Soda rarely costs more than 5 pesos, even at fancy restaurants, and usually costs between 3 and 4 pesos for a bottle or can. *Aguas frescas,* including *limonada* (lemonade), are noncarbonated fruit-based drinks with sugar. Don't miss delicious *aguas de horchata* (sweetened rice and cinnamon), *tamarindo* (tamarind), and *jamaica* (hibiscus flower, colored bright red). Don't drink them, however, unless you're sure they're purified, and that includes the *hielo* (ice).

*Licuados* are many travelers' favorite beverage in Mexico, hands down; made with blended milk, fruit (mango, banana, cantaloupe, and watermelon, to name a few), and sugar. (Again, beware ice.) Trust us—*licuados* are as close as you may ever get to non-alcoholic-beverage heaven.

# Mexico City

When the war god Huitzilopochtli commanded the Aztec people to build their great capital wherever they witnessed an eagle roosted upon a *nopal* cactus gripping a snake in its beak, he could not possibly have imagined what he started. The wandering Aztec tribe is said to have encountered this vision on an island in a murky lake nestled in the highland Valley of Mexico, and dutifully founded the island city of Tenochtitlán, which became the nucleus of the most systematic and dominating empire on the continent. Six hundred and fifty years and 25 million inhabitants later, the Valley of Mexico now cradles the biggest city in the history of human civilization.

To fathom the size of the city, it helps to see the mitochondria of Mexico from the air. As soon as your jet descends beneath the clouds, urban settlement fills every neck-craning angle of your window view. It will soon become clear that the word "city" hardly does justice to the 1480 square kilometers of sprawling urban settlement shrouded in a stagnant yellow haze: there appear to be no boundaries, no suburbs, no beginning, no end; buildings tall and short are kneaded into the cupped, evaporated, saline lake-land for as far as the eye can see.

Mexicans call this cosmopolitan conglomeration of neighborhoods **el D.F.** (deh-EFF-ay), short for *Distrito Federal* (Federal District), or simply **México**. The *defectuoso* (defective), as local *chilangos* (Mexico City inhabitants) teasingly call their city, is a breeding ground for staggering statistics. Depending on how you view it, it is home to between 17 and 30 million people and has over 220 *colonias* (neighborhoods). Virtually the entire federal bureaucracy inhabits the D.F., including the Ministry of the Navy—2240m above sea level. One quarter of Mexico's population lives in the D.F., and one quarter of those are employed as *comerciantes*, the independent vendors who crowd the streets, struggling to survive with a patience and tenacity characteristically Mexican. From the enormous central square to a blocks-long government palace to downtown's 40-story skyscrapers to Parque Chapultepec, the biggest city park in the Americas, everything here is larger than life. First-time visitors stop dead in their tracks when they realize that the gorgeous three-story art-nouveau edifice across from El Palacio de Bellas Artes is...just the post office. No one buries the ruined triumphs and fiascoes of the past nor apologizes for the excesses of the present.

But if you give it a chance, México will treat you to sublime moments amidst the overwhelming bustle. Sniff the orchids while gliding down the floating gardens of Xochimilco. Inconspicuously meander through the throngs of devout *chilangos* at the Basílica de Guadalupe. Amidst all the honking vehicular madness of the Paseo de la Reforma, gaze at El Ángel, the winged angel reaching toward the sky to commemorate Mexican Independence. Lie in the shade of the Alameda listening to water rush through the stone fountains. Try to get into some of the most exclusive discos in the world. Be dazzled by astrological Aztec sculpture in the incomparable Museo Nacional de Antropología and the grandeur of the ancient Templo Mayor (see p. 64), epicenter of the Aztec religious, political, and cultural world. Everywhere you look in the city today, from subway stations to the *zócalo,* such ruins peek out through the centuries for a breath of fresh smog.

Indeed, nowhere else in the world does a country's history breathe so heavily down the back of day-to-day life. After an epic siege and the ultimate defeat of Aztec Emperor Moctezuma II (see p. 53), Cortés and his band purposefully founded their grand colonial crux directly on top of the floating city of Tenochtitlán and its pantheistic stone monuments to symbolize the crushing of the Aztec religion. His hubris came back to haunt the colonists, when having destroyed the hydraulic infrastructure, they discovered that their newly-won city, slouching in what amounted to a huge highland puddle-valley of standing water blocked on all sides by mountains, presented a logistical nightmare. Yet they did not move. After colonization, floods tore through the city again and again, and buildings began sinking into the mud. The *Desagüe General,* a project to drain all of the stagnant water out of the valley, began in 1629 but was not completed until the draining of Lake Texcoco in 1900; when all the water was finally gone, Mexico City—34 ft. lower than it was at Conquest time and no longer an island—found itself surrounded by infertile salt flats, which, as the 20th century progressed, were soon filled in by miles of sprawling shantytowns settled by newcomers from surrounding central Mexico. Citizens can forever thank Cortés for the cursed topography of their irreversibly-settled capital; landlocked and ringed by mountains, it lets neither water in nor sewage out.

To make things worse, Aztec legend predicted that the modern world would be destroyed by earthquakes; that almost came true in 1985, when Mexico City was shaken by a quake measuring 8.1 on the Richter scale. Tens of thousands of people died and entire neighborhoods were reduced to rubble. And in 1997, the majestic, snow-capped volcano Popocatépetl woke up and spewed ash over *chilangos'* party-wear one night in late June. Mexico City has truly been subjected to its own version of the plagues; among them are the huge-scale water shortage (a problem which will soon blossom to epic proportions), volcanic eruptions, pestilence, massive earthquakes, poverty, the proliferation of petty crime, and the worst air-pollution problem anywhere on Earth. The eye-reddening air is kept in place by the bowl formed by surrounding mountains—some say that just breathing for a day in Mexico City is the equivalent of smoking 40 cigarettes. And as people from all around the country continue to arrive in hopes of finding scarce jobs, Mexico City's infamous demographic crisis becomes more difficult to ignore. As rural migrants flock to the city's edge, and the city expands to engulf surrounding villages and even outlying cities, the prospect of feeding everyone becomes increasingly unrealistic.

Popo's 1997 eruption was an augur of events to come. Shortly after, on July 6, Mexico City's elections turned into a political eruption as the mayoral victory of the PRD (Partido Revolucionario Democrático) ended years of one-party rule (see p. 62). The ousting of the stagnant PRI injected at least a glimmer of hope into the disillusioned masses. After all the parties, hurrahs, and initial shock, Mexico City found itself, more than ever, at the center of the world's attention: What now? What can this resplendent, rubbish-ridden city accomplish now? Like a tragic hero, Mexico City enraptures us with its plight because its fatal flaws are so human, its personality so compelling, its stature so great, and the possibilities so magnificent. Millions each day strut down Paseo de la Reforma, contemplating their sinking city's future under the watchful eye of El Ángel. Most see the city not as an enemy but as a brother gone awry. The *chilangos'* laments are grounded in unconditional love for this apocalyptic metropolis. They are proud of its past, preoccupied with its present, and hopeful about the possibility of leading their capital to a new and glorious reign.

# ■ Getting There

All roads lead to Mexico City. Buses, trains, and planes haul passengers from every town in the Republic into the smoggy hyperactivity of the city's many temples of transport—the expanding Benito Juárez International Airport, four crowded bus stations, a desolate train station, and a network of freeways. Fortuitously, airports and stations in Mexico City nearly always have information booths for frazzled tourists equipped with quasi-English-speaking personnel, free (or cheap) maps, and some sort of referral service to lead you into the *centro* or into the neighborhood of your choice. *Buena suerte.*

## BY AIR

Flying into Mexico City from abroad entails the usual customs and immigration procedures. **Tourist cards (FMTs)** are distributed on the plane and stamped at the airport. Although many border officials are lax about enforcement, the "stoplight" customs system at the airport ensures that a certain percentage of random passengers are inspected—those unlucky enough to get a red light. Be prepared to allow an agent to sift through your silky intimates.

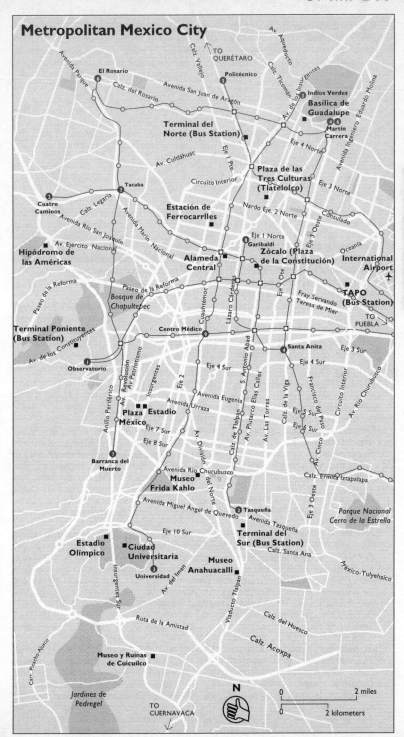

# Metropolitan Mexico City

TO QUERÉTARO

Av. Aqueducto

Av. Vallejo

Calz. Ticomán

Calz. del Insurgentes

Avenida Parque

El Rosario ⑥

Politécnico ⑤

Avenida San Juan de Aragón

Calz. del Rosario

Indios Verdes

Basílica de Guadalupe

Avenida Ingeniero Eduardo Molina

Martín Carrera ④⑥

Terminal del Norte (Bus Station)

Eje 4 Norte

Eje 1 Pte.

Av. Cuitláhuac

Circuito Interior

Eje 3 Norte

Tacuba ⑦

Cuatro Caminos ②

Calz. Legaria

Av. Ejército Nacional

Avenida Río San Joaquín

Avenida Martín Nacional

Estación de Ferrocarriles

Plaza de las Tres Culturas (Tlatelolco)

Nardo Eje 2 Norte

Eje 3 Oste

Consulado

Hipódromo de las Américas

Eje 1 Norte

Garibaldi ⑧

Zócalo (Plaza de la Constitución)

Oceanía

International Airport

Paseo de la Reforma

Alameda Central

Eje 1 Ote.

Eje 3 Oste

TAPO (Bus Station)

Bosque de Chapultepec

Cuauhtémoc

Lázaro Cárdenas

Eje Ote.

Fray Servando Teresa de Mier

TO PUEBLA

Terminal Poniente (Bus Station)

Centro Médico ⑨

Santa Anita ④

Eje 3 Sur

Av. de los Constituyentes

Eje 4 Sur

Eje 4 Sur

Circuito Interior

Av. Río Churubusco

Observatorio ①

Av. Revolución

Av. Patriotismo

Insurgentes

Eje 2

S. Antonio Abad

Av. Plutarco Elías Calles

Calz. de Tlalpan

Av. Las Torres

Calz. de la Viga

Francisco del

Av. Cinco de

Anillo Periférico

Plaza México

Estadio

Avenida Eugenia

Avenida Urraza

Eje 5 Sur

Eje 6 Sur

Eje 7 Sur

Eje 8 Sur

Av. División del Norte

Barranca del Muerto ⑦

Calz. Ermita Iztapalapa

Avenida Río Churubusco

Museo Frida Kahlo

Avenida Miguel Ángel de Quevedo

Tasqueña ②

Parque Nacional Cerro de la Estrella

Eje 10 Sur

Avenida Tasqueña

Terminal del Sur (Bus Station)

Estadio Olímpico

Ciudad Universitaria

Museo Anahuacalli

Calz. Santa Ana

México-Tulyehaico

Insurgentes Sur

Universidad ③

Av. del Imán

Viaducto Tlalpan

Calz. del Huesco

Ruta de la Amistad

Calz. Acoxpa

Museo y Ruinas de Cuicuilco

Carr. Picacho-Ajusco

Jardines de Pedregal

TO CUERNAVACA

N

0        2 miles

0        2 kilometers

The **Benito Juárez International Airport** (tel. 571-32-95) lies 6.5km east of the *zócalo,* the formal center of the city. Blvd. Capitán Juan Sarabio heads northeast to the airport from Blvd. Puerto Aéreo, one of the major roads circling the city. The airport, surprisingly small, is expanding at an exponential rate and is still jam-packed with facilities:

**Tourist Office: INFOTUR,** *Sala* A (tel. 76-26-67). Small info booth, still helpful, can give you basic info and direct you to other resources. There's also a small touch-screen computer replete with tourist info.

**Cultural Information: Instituto Nacional de Antropología e Historia,** *Sala* A (tel. 571-02-67). Information about archaeological sites and museums throughout the country. Open Mon.-Sat. 9am-9pm, Sun. 9am-3pm.

**Hotel Reservations:** In *Sala* E. Name an area and they'll make the reservation for you, but it won't be cheap. No charge, but be prepared to pay for the first night on the spot. English spoken. Open daily 7am-midnight.

**Currency Exchange: Banks** exchange currency and traveler's checks at branches in different *salas.* **ATMs** take both **Cirrus** and **Plus** (including **Visa, MasterCard, AmEx**) in *Sala* A, directly under *Sala* B, and throughout *Salas* E and F. *Casas de cambio* every foot or so, open 6am-8pm, sometimes later.

**Telephones: LADATELs** around the airport accept phone cards sold at nearby magazine stands. Some phones take international credit cards. Long-distance *caseta* at the end of the international concourse, past *Sala* F. Open 7am-8pm.

**Fax:** In *Sala* A. Open Mon.-Sat. 9am-8pm.

**Car Rental:** In *Sala* E (see p. 83).

**Storage Lockers:** Next to the snack bar, to the left of the arrival gate in *Sala* A and in *Sala* E. Storage 18 pesos per 24hr., 20-50 pesos for larger bags.

**Bookstore:** In *Sala* F, on the 2nd floor. Novels in Spanish and English. Maps available. Open daily 24hr.

**Pharmacy:** In *Sala* C. Open daily 6am-10pm.

**Restaurants** and **cafeterias** are open 24hr.

**Insurance:** In *Sala* B, in 2 locations. Open daily 6am-8pm.

**Maps and Mexican Statistics:** Tel. 786-02-12. In *Sala* B. Open 6am-8pm.

**Lost and Found:** Bags overflow in a small room next to Aeropost in *Sala* D.

**Police:** Tel. 625-70-07. Outside the airport in front of *Sala* C. Open 24hr.

**Post Office:** In *Sala* A. Open Mon.-Fri. 8am-7pm, Sat. 9am-5pm.

**Flight info:** Call tel. 571-36-00 or 571-44-00, then specify domestic or international.

**Carriers:** *Sala* **A:** All **Aeroméxico,** baby. The most complete air transportation throughout the Republic. *Sala* **B: Mexicana** plays a strong second fiddle. *Sala* **C:** Really tiny, with only **AVIACSA.** *Sala* **D: TAESA, ALLEGRO,** and charter flights. *Sala* **E:** International arrivals. *Sala* **F₁: Delta, America West, Continental, Avianca,** and **Lan Chile.** *Sala* **F₂:** The big one! **KLM, Northwest, SEAT, Copa, Lufthansa, Air France, British Airways, Lacsa, Taca, Aviateca, Varig, JAL, Canadian,** and **Cubana.** *Sala* **F₃: American Airlines, Iberia, Argentinian Airlines,** and **United Airlines.**

**Domestic Flights:** Flight schedules and prices change frequently. Prices are roughly the same from airline to airline. There are usually no discounts for students, but always ask about *tarifas promocionales,* which can save you up to 50%. Either of the following 2 airlines can take you anywhere in the country, provided there's an airport: **Aeroméxico,** Paseo de la Reforma 445 at Mississippi (tel. 327-40-00), and Reforma 80 (tel. 566-1078). Both open Mon.-Sat. 9am-6:15pm. At the airport, *Sala* A (tel. 762-18-18). Open daily 5am-10pm. **Mexicana,** Amberes and Reforma 312 (tel. 511-04-24), in the *Zona Rosa,* and Reforma 51 (tel. 592-17-71), at Lafragua. Both open Mon.-Fri. 9am-6pm. At the airport, *Sala* B (tel. 227-02-61, for reservations 325-09-90). Open daily 6am-11:30pm.

**International Flights: Air Canada,** Hamburgo 108, 5th fl. (tel. 280-34-34 or 281-45-81). **Air France,** Reforma 404, 15th fl. (tel. 627-60-00 or 627-60-60, at airport 571-61-50). **American,** Reforma 314, 1st fl. (tel. 209-14-00, at airport 571-32-19). **British Airways,** Reforma 10, 14th fl. (tel. 628-05-00, toll-free 91-800-00-657). **Canadian Airlines,** Reforma 390 (tel. 208-18-83). **Continental,** Andrés Bello 45 (tel. 280-34-34, toll-free 91-800-90-050, at airport 571-36-65). **United,** Hamburgo 213, ground fl. (tel. 627-02-22, toll-free 91-800-00-307). **Delta,** Reforma 381 (tel.

202-16-08 or 207-34-11, toll-free 91-800-90-221, at airport 571-32-37). **KLM,** Paseo de las Palmas 735, 7th fl. (tel. 202-44-44, toll-free 91-800-90-747, at airport 571-32-46). **Lufthansa,** Las Palmas 239 (tel. 230-00-00, toll-free 91-800-90-600, at airport 571-27-13). **Swissair,** Hamburgo 66, 3rd fl. (tel. 207-24-55). **Aeroméxico** and **Mexicana** fly to Central America and the U.S.

Transportation into the city is uncomplicated. Buy a *transporte terrestre* ticket from the *venta de boletos* desk in *Sala* A and *Sala* E, and present it to any of the white and yellow authorized taxis waiting outside. The price is set by the zone of the city to which you're traveling (46 pesos to the *centro,* 54 pesos to El Monumento de la Revolución, 20% more after hours). Ask to see the map—just because it's an official-looking booth does not mean you won't be overcharged. Avoid people wearing uniforms trying to direct you to a taxi booth or to the taxi stand. They will try to charge large tips for small services. Avoid unauthorized taxis, especially those with bags over the meters: they will rip you off. Call 784-48-11 or 571-36-00 (both available 24hr.) to get a taxi back to the airport from the city. For more taxi etiquette, see p. 82.

The Metro is by far the cheapest (1.30 pesos) route to the city. The airport **subway** station, **Terminal Aérea** (Line 5), located at the junction of Capitán Juan Sarabio and Blvd. Puerto Aéreo, is only a five-minute walk from *Sala* E. Signs will point you in the right direction (see p. 80 for the scoop on the Metro). Large bags are officially prohibited, but provided you avoid rush hours and can maneuver through the turnstile, a typical pack should not pose much of a problem. For the comfort of others, and mainly for your own safety, remove the pack from your back when you're on the subway. Also, try to ride in the less crowded first or last cars. If a train appears frighteningly jam-packed, simply let it pass; another will arrive within minutes. **If you return to the airport by Metro, do not get off at the Aeropuerto stop. The correct stop is Terminal Aérea.**

## BY TRAIN

Mexican trains tend to be **excruciatingly slow** (for more on that, see p. 46). The fastest routes—to Guadalajara (8:30pm, 12hr.) and Veracruz (9:15pm, 14hr.)—are barely bearable. Other popular destinations from Mexico City include Ciudad Juárez (23hr.), Oaxaca (14½hr.), and Nuevo Laredo (22hr.). There are four classes of trains: *primera especial* (first-class reserved, without bed), *dormitorio camarín* (reserved, with 2 separate beds per compartment), *alcoba* (reserved, with bunk bed), and *primera general* (unreserved). Travelers, almost without exception, take the *primera especial.* So unless you haven't gotten your monthly share of masochism and mental self-flagellation, stick to the top of the line. First-class tickets can be purchased up to a month in advance. Other than Semana Santa, spots are usually available up to one hour before departure. Buying second-class tickets is as unpleasant as riding second-class trains; arrive at the station five hours early to stand in the snail-paced line.

**Estación Buenavista** of the **Ferrocarriles Nacionales de México** (tel. 547-10-97) is located north of the **Monumento de la Revolución** at the corner of Insurgentes and Mosqueta (Eje 1 Alzate), five long blocks from the nearest Metro station, Revolución (Line 2; open Mon.-Fri. 6am-12:30am, Sat. 6am-1:30am). **Taxis** leave from the parking lot on the Mosqueta side of the main building. Be sure to check the meter and the official fare chart in the cab before you pay, as abuses are par for the course.

An **information booth** (tel. 547-10-84, 547-10-97, or 91-800-90-392 for tourist info) to the left of the ticket windows does little more than dispense train schedules and prices (in Spanish). The booth is open 7:30am-8:30pm and ticket windows open 6:30am-9:30pm. Get train information in English from the **Departamento de Tráfico de Pasajeros,** hidden off to the right of long-distance booth 6 in the main station lobby (tel. 547-86-55; fax 547-89-72; open Mon.-Fri. 6am-10pm). The station has a **long-distance phone/fax service** (open daily 8am-9:30pm) and a 24-hour **ATM** that accepts Cirrus and Plus. **Luggage storage** is provided in the second-class area, down the walkway from the main *sala* (10 pesos per day; open daily 6:30am-9:30pm). There are also a few 24-hour restaurants.

MEXICO CITY

# BY BUS

Mexico City's four main bus stations correspond to the cardinal directions. **Central de Autobuses del Norte** (North Station) serves the Bajío, northern Veracruz, Jalisco, and most of northern Mexico; **Terminal Central de Autobuses del Sur** (South Station) launches buses to Guerrero, Morelos, and Oaxaca; **Terminal de Autobuses de Pasajeros de Oriente (TAPO)** (East Station) sends buses to Puebla, southern Veracruz, Oaxaca, Chiapas, and the Yucatán Peninsula; and the **Terminal de Autobuses del Poniente** (West Station) serves Mexico state and Michoacán.

All stations are served by the Metro and offer an official 24-hour taxi service that charges fixed rates (set by zones) for a ride to any point in the city or adjacent parts of Mexico state. Buy your ticket inside to avoid being ripped off, but be wary of being charged for an extra zone—if you can find it, consult the zone map. *Peseros* (a.k.a. *colectivos*) also serve the four stations. Quality budget hotels near the bus stations are virtually nil (see p. 92). It's a much safer bet to head toward the city center. The following bus prices change almost weekly, and listings are by no means comprehensive. Given the extensive network, it is possible to go almost anywhere at any time.

## Central de Autobuses del Norte

The Central de Autobuses del Norte (tel. 587-15-52) is on Cien Metros, Metro station Autobuses del Norte (Line 5). **Banamex ATM, restaurant,** and **luggage storage** (10-20 pesos per 24hr., or 1.50 pesos per hr.) are all open around the clock. A *casa de cambio* near the main entrance offers poor rates (open Mon.-Fri. 7am-9pm, Sat.-Sun. 8am-4pm). The **post office** and **telegram office** are nearby (open Mon.-Fri. 8am-5pm, Sat. 8am-1pm). A "Hoteles Asociados" (hotel **reservations** service) booth is occasionally open near the main entrance (supposedly open 8am-9pm). A plethora of bus companies populate *el Central;* prices are often suspiciously similar and it's not uncommon for "competing" bus companies to share phone numbers. You've got an infinite but unvaried selection in this terminal/zoo. A few of the perennial faves are:

**Transportes del Norte** (tel. 587-54-00). To Celaya (7 per day, 3½hr., 82 pesos), Cd. Juárez (every hr., 24hr., 558 pesos), Matamoros (3 per day, 15hr., 272-426 pesos), Matehuala (4 per day, 8hr., 185 pesos), Monterrey (every hr., 12hr., 283 pesos), Nuevo Laredo (2 per day, 15hr., 363 or 489 pesos), Reynosa (4 per day, 15hr., 275 or 318 pesos), Saltillo (1 per day, 10hr., 256 pesos), and San Luis Potosí (2 per day, 5hr., 125 pesos).

**Flecha Amarilla** (tel. 587-52-00). 2nd-class service to Guadalajara (every hr., 9hr., 174 pesos), Guanajuato (4 per day, 5hr., 100 pesos), León (every hr., 5hr., 107 pesos), Manzanillo (3 per day, 16hr., 224 pesos), Morelia (every 25min., 5hr., 93 pesos), Querétaro (every 20min., 3½hr., 56 pesos), San Luis Potosí (every hr., 6hr., 110 pesos), and San Miguel de Allende (every 40min., 4hr., 75 pesos).

**Futura** (tel. 587-55-11). To Acapulco (10 per day, 5hr., 148 pesos), Aguascalientes (13 per day, 6½hr., 165 pesos), Chihuahua (every 1½hr., 20hr., 445 pesos), Matamoros (3 per day, 15hr., 316 pesos), Monterrey (13 per day, 12hr., 283 pesos), Tampico (every 2hr., 9hr., 141 pesos), and Cd. Valles (4 per day, 8½hr., 229 pesos).

**Estrella Blanca** (tel. 587-54-00). To Chihuahua (2 per day, 20hr., 445 pesos), Durango (1am, 12hr., 238 pesos), San Luis Potosí (every hr., 5hr., 125 pesos), Torreón (4 per day, 14hr., 269 pesos), and Zacatecas (5 per day, 9hr., 165 pesos).

**Autobuses de Oriente (ADO;** tel. 587-66-88). **GL** *ejecutivo* (1st class) and **UNO** mega-luxury (with mega-luxury prices that include huge leather chairs and cafeteria) service. To Oaxaca (2 per day, 6hr., 142 pesos), Papantla (4 per day, 6hr., 90 pesos), Puebla (every ½hr., 2hr., 42 pesos), Tuxpan (7 per day, 5hr., 89 pesos), Veracruz (4 per day, 9hr., 130 pesos), and Xalapa (2 per day, 5½hr., 91 pesos).

**Elite** (tel. 729-07-81). The name says it all. Posh service to places like Hermosillo (12 per day, 31hr., 676 pesos), Tijuana (10 per day, 42hr., 725 pesos), and Puerto Vallarta (4 per day, 14hr., 327 pesos).

## Terminal de Autobuses de Pasajeros de Oriente (TAPO)

The TAPO (tel. 762-59-77) is on General Ignacio Zaragoza 200, adjacent to Metro station San Lázaro (Line 1). Ticket counters await in a rotunda at the end of a long, store-lined passageway. Helpful **police** booths are scattered throughout the station. A **tourist information** kiosk (open daily 10am-8pm) and taxi ticket booths are near the entrance to the Metro. The station also contains a 24-hour **ATM, restaurants** (including **Domino's Pizza**), **pharmacy,** and currency **exchange** services (open daily 7am-midnight).

**ADO** (tel. 542-71-92). 1st class to Campeche (35 per day, 20hr., 344 pesos), Cancún (4 per day, 26hr., 373 pesos), Córdoba (39 per day, 5hr., 96 pesos), Mérida (4 per day, 350 pesos), Oaxaca (17 per day, 9hr., 130 pesos), Palenque (4 and 6:10pm, 14hr., 273 pesos), Veracruz (23 per day, 7hr., 118 pesos), Villahermosa (23 per day, 14hr., 238 pesos), and Xalapa (22 per day, 5hr., 782 pesos).

**Autobuses Cristóbal Colón** (tel. 542-72-63). 1st class to Oaxaca (3 per day, 9hr., 130 pesos), San Cristóbal de las Casas (4 per day, 17hr., 272 pesos), Tonalá (4 per day, 13hr., 221 pesos), and Tuxtla Gutiérrez (4 per day, 16hr., 278 pesos). Service to Central America as well.

**Autobuses Unidos (AU;** tel. 542-42-10, ext. 19). To Córdoba (32 per day, 5hr., 79-84 pesos), Oaxaca (15 per day, 9hr., 106-120 pesos), San Andrés Tuxtla (2 per day, 9½hr., 145 pesos), and Xalapa (19 per day, 5hr., 76 pesos).

**Estrella Roja** (tel. 522-72-00). To Puebla (every 10min., 5am-11pm, 1¾hr., 32-38 pesos).

**UNO** (tel. 522-11-11). To Oaxaca, Puebla, Tampico, Veracruz, Villahermosa, Xalapa, and other cities. Only if you must live in the lap of luxury.

## Terminal de Autobuses del Poniente

The Terminal de Autobuses del Poniente (tel. 271-00-38) is on Av. Sur 122, Metro station Observatorio (Line 1). Take a left as you exit the Metro station; a bridge leads to the terminal. Most of these are second-class routes; brace yourself for slow, indirect service. The station is built in the shape of a "V" with most important services clustered at the vertex. Round-the-clock station services include a **restaurant,** long distance *caseta,* and **luggage storage** (15 pesos for 24hr., 20 pesos for subjectively determined "larger" bags). There is also a **pharmacy** (open daily 7am-10pm), a **post office** (open Mon.-Fri. 8am-7pm, Sat. 9am-1pm), a **fax** office (open Mon.-Fri. 9am-5pm, Sat. 9am-1pm), and **food stands, shops,** and **newspaper stands.**

**ETN** (tel. 273-02-51). Plush 1st-class service to Guadalajara (4 per day, 11am-midnight, 12hr., 290 pesos), Morelia (24 per day, 4hr., 155 pesos), Toluca (26 per day, 1½hr., 27 pesos), Uruapan (10am-11pm, 6hr., 191 pesos), and many other cities.

**Autobuses del Occidente** (tel. 271-01-06). To Guadalajara (8 per day, 10am-10pm, 12hr., 181 pesos), Manzanillo (8am and 10pm, 16hr., 185 pesos), Morelia (every 20min., 6hr., 84 pesos), and Tuxpan (every 20min., 4hr., 58 pesos).

**Estrella Roja** (tel. 522-72-00). Straight to Puebla (every 2hr., 6am-8pm, 2hr., 38 pesos), Querétaro (every hr., 5:30am-8pm, 5hr., 51 pesos), Toluca (every 10min., 1½hr., 16 pesos), and other destinations.

**Elite** (tel. 368-06-22). Travels in style to Morelia (3:30 and 6pm, 9hr., 95 pesos) and Guadalajara (2pm, 8hr., 218 pesos).

**Servicios Coordinados.** To León (10:30am, 8hr., 106 pesos), Morelia (10 per day, 10:30am-5pm, 6hr., 86 pesos), Querétaro (4pm, 5hr., 53 pesos), and Toluca (8am-7:30pm, 1hr., 17 pesos).

**Caminante.** 1st-class service to Toluca (every 5min., 1½hr., 19 pesos).

## Terminal de Autobuses del Sur (Tasqueña)

The Tasqueña terminal (tel. 689-97-45) is on Tasqueña 1320, Metro station Tasqueña (Line 2)—exit to the right, through the market. The station has a **post office** (open Mon.-Fri. 8am-7pm, Sat. 9am-5pm), long-distance *caseta* with **fax** service (open daily 7am-9:30pm), and **LADATELs** scattered about. There is also a mini-travel agency for **hotel reservations** in Mexico City, Acapulco, Mazatlán, and a few other select cities (open Mon.-Fri. 9am-7pm, Sat. 9am-3pm), a 24-hour **pharmacy,** and a round-the-clock **cafeteria. Luggage lockers** (small 20 pesos, large 18 pesos for 24hr.) are near exit 3.

**Pullman de Morelos** (tel. 549-35-05). 1st class to Cuautla (every 20min., 6am-11pm, 2hr., 29 pesos), Cuernavaca (every 10min., 5:30am-midnight, 1¼hr., 26 pesos), Oaxtepec (every ½hr., 6am-11pm, 1¾hr., 26 pesos), and Tepotzlán (every 15min., 6:30am-8:30pm, 1½hr., 22 pesos).

**Cristóbal Colón** to Cuautla (every 15min., 2hr., 28 pesos), Oaxtepec (every 20min., 2hr., 27 pesos), Tepoztlán (every ½hr., 1¾hr., 22 pesos), Yacutepec (every hr., 2hr., 30 pesos), and some places in the Gulf Coast and Yucatán.

**Estrella de Oro** (tel. 549-85-20, ext. 29). 1st class to Acapulco (8 per day, 8am-10pm, 7hr., 161 pesos), Chilpancingo (10am-8pm, 4½hr., 90 pesos), Cuernavaca (10am-3pm, 1½hr., 22 pesos), Iguala (6 per day, 3hr., 48 pesos), Ixtapa/Zihuatanejo (8am-5pm, 11hr., 178 pesos), and Taxco (9am-5pm, 3½hr., 39 pesos).

**Servicios Coordinados** (tel. 689-80-00). 1st class to Acapulco (every ½hr., 5:15am-10pm, 1¼hr., 170 pesos) and Puebla (5 per day, 2hr., 40 pesos).

## BY CAR

No other vehicular endeavor matches the experience of driving into Mexico City. Serene mountain roads slowly metamorphose into blaring, multi-lane highways. Any semblance of defensive driving dives out the window. Welcome to the city where stoplights are only suggestions (see **Getting Around,** below).

Several major highways lead into the city and intersect with the **Circuito Interior,** the highway that rings the city, at which point they change names. Route 57, from Querétaro and Tepotzlán, becomes **Manuel Ávila Camacho** just outside the Circuito. Route 15, from Toluca, turns into **Av. Reforma** as it enters the city. Route 95, from Cuernavaca and Acapulco, becomes **Av. Insurgentes,** which plugs into the Circuito on the south side. Route 150, from Puebla and Texcoco, becomes **Ignacio Zaragoza,** which connects to the Circuito on the east side. Rte. 85, from Pachuca, Teotihuacán, and Texcoco, also becomes **Av. Insurgentes** in the city.

# ■ Orientation

The city is difficult to know well; most *chilangos* don't even have their city down pat. It's not uncommon for *taxistas* to ask a passenger if they know how to get to their destination. What's more, many different neighborhoods use the same street name; the 300 Benito Juárez streets in the city attest to this redundant and repetitive tradition. Still, it is only a matter of cardinal directions and good ol' trial and error before you've mastered this megalopolis. The most important thing is to know the name of the *colonia* (neighborhood) to which you're going (common examples are Col. *Centro,* Col. Polanco, *Zona Rosa,* Col. Roma, Col. Juárez). Since street numbers are often useless, cross streets and landmarks are *importantísimos.* Try to locate nearby monuments, museums, *glorietas* (traffic circles), cathedrals, and skyscrapers. Fortunately, there are loads of them.

More good news: street names tend to be clustered logically and systematically. Streets in the *Zona Rosa* are named after European cities, the streets directly across Reforma are named after large rivers of the world, and the streets in Polanco are named after famous philosophers. The *Guía Roji Ciudad de México* (65 pesos), a comprehensive street atlas, is a valuable aid for anyone planning to stay in the city for a while. It's available at most large bookstores, English-language bookstores, Sanborn's, museum shops, and at the airport. Or try the abridged *mini-Guía Roji* (17 pesos). And, hey, use the pull-out map in this book, too. We think it's quite nice.

Mexico City extends outward from the *centro* roughly 20km to the south, 10km to the north, 10km to the west, and 8km to the east. Year after year, the city's boundaries extend hungrily into neighboring communities. There is much debate about where the city actually begins and where it actually ends, thus the various estimates that place Mexico City's population anywhere between 17 and 30 million people. Because of the central location of most sights, few travelers venture past the Bosque de Chapultepec to the west, La Basílica de Guadalupe to the north, the airport to the east, or San Ángel and the UNAM to the south.

The accommodations and food listings for Mexico City are divided according to the four areas of most interest to tourists. The *centro* contains most of the historic sights and museums, extensive budget accommodations, and lively inexpensive restaurants. Metro stops Allende (closer to accommodations and Alameda) and Zócalo (literally the center of México) serve the *centro* (Line 2). This area is bounded by Cárdenas to the west, Uruguay to the south, Pino Suárez to the east, and Rep. de Peru to the north. The **Alameda** contains budget accommodations and many restaurants, and it is accessible by Metro at Hidalgo (Lines 2 and 3), Bellas Artes (Lines 2 and 8; close to the park, the Palacio de Bellas Artes, and the post office), and San Juan de Letran (Line 8; closer to most food and accommodations listings). The area is bounded by Eje 1 Pte. (known as Rosales, Guerrero, and Bucareli) to the west, Arcos de Belén to the south, Cárdenas to the east, and Violeta to the north. The **Monumento a la Revolución/Buenavista** area, like the Alameda, contains perhaps the most copious and inexpensive hotels and eateries. It is bounded by Insurgentes Norte to the west, Reforma to the south and east, and Mosqueta to the north. The *Zona Rosa* (Pink Zone) is the capital's most touristy, commercial district, home to some of the country's most exciting nightlife. This neighborhood is accessible by Metro at Insurgentes (primary location) and Sevilla (both on Line 1). The *Zona Rosa* is bounded by Reforma to the north and west, Av. Chapultepec to the south, and Insurgentes to the east. A few of our listings for this area lie just east of Insurgentes, and a string of bars and clubs spill south past Chapultepec along Insurgentes Sur.

## CIRCUITO INTERIOR AND EJES VIALES

The **Circuito Interior** is a roughly rectangular artery made up of several smaller, connected highways. **Boulevard Puerto Aéreo** forms the upper east side of the box, running north from the airport. As it bends left at the northeast corner of the box and heads west, it becomes **Av. Río Consulado.** Río Consulado turns south and becomes **Calzada Melchor Ocampo.** Ocampo heads south until it intersects **Paseo de la Reforma** at Bosque de Chapultepec, after which it continues as **Av. Vasconcelos.** From Vasconcelos, two roads run to the southwest corner of the Circuito, **Av. Patriotismo** and **Av. Revolución,** either of which could be considered the Circuito at this point. They turn into **Av. Río Mixcoac,** which becomes **Av. Río Churubusco,** running east-west. Río Churubusco is the longest and sneakiest of the highways that constitute the Circuito. It continues east, turns north for a while, heads east again, then turns north once more to connect with Blvd. Puerto Aéreo south of the airport to complete the Circuito.

Aside from the large thoroughfares—Insurgentes, Reforma, Chapultepec, and Miguel Alemán—a system of **Ejes Viales** (axis roads) conducts the majority of traffic within the Circuito. *Ejes* run one way—**except for the bus lanes, which go against traffic.** Running east-west, Eje 1 Nte. and Eje 2 Nte. are north of the *zócalo,* while Ejes 2 through 8 Sur run south of it. The numbers increase heading away from the *zócalo.* **Eje Central Lázaro Cárdenas** runs north-south and bisects the box formed by the Circuito. East of it and parallel lie Ejes 1 through 3 Ote., which veer off to the northwest; west of it are Ejes 1 through 3 Pte. Theoretically, using the Ejes together with the Circuito, you can reach any general area of the city without much delay. Unfortunately, because of heavy traffic and frequent processions (and hence barricades), zipping around gleefully is not the norm. Still, even when in taxi, pesero, or crowded metro, it never hurts to know your exact bearings.

MEXICO CITY

## CITY CENTER

As huge as Mexico City is, almost everything of interest to visitors lies within the northern half of the area circumscribed by the Circuito Interior. Moreover, many attractions are within easy reach of **Paseo de la Reforma,** the broad thoroughfare that runs southwest-northeast, or **Av. Insurgentes,** the boulevard running north-south through the city. These two main arteries intersect at the **Glorieta Cuauhtémoc.** The **Bosque de Chapultepec,** home to the principal museums of the city, is served by Metro stops Chapultepec (Line 1) and Auditorio (Line 7). From Chapultepec, Reforma proceeds northeast, punctuated by *glorietas* (rotaries), each with a monument in the center. Some of the more famous ones (and the ones most useful for completely lost and bewildered backpackers), in southwest-to-northeast order, include: **Glorieta Angel de la Independencia, Glorieta Cuauhtémoc,** and the **Glorieta CristóbalDíaz Colón.** In terms of *barrios,* moving up Reforma from Chapultepec, the *Zona Rosa* is followed by Buenavista (near the Monumento a la Revolucíon), the Alameda, and the *centro.*

## SOUTHERN DISTRICTS

The major southern thoroughfare is **Insurgentes Sur.** Most sights to the south, including **San Ángel, Coyoacán, Ciudad Universitaria,** and the **Pyramid of Cuicuilco,** lie near or along Insurgentes. Metro Line 3 parallels Insurgentes on Cuauhtémoc and then Universidad, ending at Ciudad Universitaria (Metro station Universidad, Line 3). Two other important avenues are **Av. Revolución,** which runs parallel to Insurgentes, and **Av. Miguel Ángel de Quevedo,** which runs parallel to **Francisco Sosa** in Coyoacán. Metro Line 2 runs east of Line 3 and is closer to **Xochimilco,** one of the few southern sights not along Insurgentes.

# ■ Getting Around

While most neighborhoods are easily traversed by foot, public transportation is necessary to travel between different areas. The Metro is the fastest, cleanest, and quickest mode of transportation. Unfortunately it becomes inhumanly crowded during rush hour (7:30-9:30am and 6-9pm) and doesn't reach all parts of the city. More thorough are the thousands of white and green mini-buses known as *peseros, micros,* or *colectivos* (1-3 pesos), with stickers (hopefully) marking the route on front. The municipal gray buses with blue and green stripes (0.50 pesos) tend to be very congested. Taxis, while more expensive, are omnipresent and especially handy for women traveling alone and traversing the city late at night. The ancient *tren ligero* (trolley) still travels some routes, mainly at the city's edge and in some suburbs.

## BY METRO

The Metro never ceases to amaze—trains come quickly and regularly, the fare is insanely cheap, the crowds are enormous and bizarre, the ride is smooth, the service is extensive, and the stations are immaculate and marmoreal. Built in the late 1960s, the Metro transports five million people and makes the equivalent of 2½ trips around the earth every day. On top of this, new tracks are laid daily. México's Metro system knows no bounds.

Metro tickets are sold in *taquillas* (booths) at every station. Lines can stretch for huge distances, so buy in bulk. Come prepared with exact change, since the *taquillas* are often short of small denominations. The 1.30 peso fare includes transfers. It's simple—you insert a magnetically coded ticket and pass through turnstiles. Transfer gates are marked *correspondencia* and exits are marked *salida.* Most transfer stations have information booths to help clueless travelers. A vital resource for all travelers is a color-coded subway guide, available at the tourist office or at all Metro Information booths. If you are lost, wander off to a corner and discreetly check your guide.

Directions are stated in terms of the station at the end of a given line. Each of the two *andenes* (platforms) has signs indicating the terminus toward which trains are

If you're stuck for cash on your travels, don't panic. Western Union can transfer money in minutes. We've 37,000 outlets in over 140 countries. And our record of safety and reliability is second to none. Call Western Union: wherever you are, you're never far from home.

**WESTERN UNION | MONEY TRANSFER®**

*The fastest way to send money worldwide.*

# Get the MCI Card.
## The Smart and Easy Card.

**The MCI Card with WorldPhone Service....**

- Provides access to the US from over 125 countries and places worldwide.
- Country to country calling from over 70 countries
- Gives you customer service 24 hours a day
- Connects you to operators who speak your language
- Provides you with MCI's low rates with no sign-up or monthly fees
- Even if you don't have an MCI Card, you can still reach a WorldPhone Operator and place collect calls to the U.S. Simply dial the access code of the country you are calling from and hold for a WorldPhone operator.

**The MCI Card with WorldPhone Service is designed specifically to keep you in touch with people that matter the most to you. We make international calling as easy as possible.**

For more information or to apply for a Card call:

## 1-800-444-1616

Outside the U.S., call MCI collect (reverse charge) at:

## 1-916-567-5151

# Pick Up The Phone.
# Pick Up The Miles.

**You earn frequent flyer miles** when you travel internationally, why not when you call internationally? Callers can earn frequent flyer miles with one of MCI's airline partners:

- American Airlines
- Continental Airlines
- Delta Airlines
- Hawaiian Airlines
- Midwest Express Airlines
- Northwest Airlines
- Southwest Airlines

## And, it's simple to call home.

1. Dial the WorldPhone toll-free access number of the country you're calling from (listed inside).

2. Follow the voice instructions in your language of choice or hold for a WorldPhone operator.
   - Enter or give the operator your MCI Card number or call collect.

3. Enter or give the WorldPhone operator your home number.

4. Share your adventures with your family!

Please cut out and save this reference guide for convenient U.S. and worldwide calling with the MCI Card with WorldPhone Service.

## Your MCI Worldphone Access Numbers

| COUNTRY | WORLDPHONE TOLL-FREE ACCESS # |
|---|---|
| #South Africa (CC) | 0800-99-0011 |
| #Spain (CC) | 900-99-0014 |
| #Sri Lanka (Outside of Colombo, dial 01 first) | 440100 |
| #St. Lucia ÷ | 1-800-888-8000 |
| #St. Vincent (CC) | 1-800-888-8000 |
| #Sweden (CC) ♦ | 020-795-922 |
| #Switzerland (CC) ♦ | 0800-89-0222 |
| #Syria | 0800 |
| #Taiwan (CC) ♦ | 0080-13-4567 |
| #Thailand ★ | 001-999-1-2001 |
| #Trinidad & Tobago ÷ | 1-800-888-1177 |
| #Turkey (CC) ♦ | 00-8001-1177 |
| #Turks and Caicos ÷ | 1-800-888-8000 |
| #Ukraine (CC) ÷ | 8▼10-013 |
| #United Arab Emirates ♦ | 800-111 |
| #United Kingdom (CC) To call using BT ■ | 0800-89-0222 |
| To call using MERCURY ■ | 0500-89-0222 |
| #United States (CC) | 1-800-888-8000 |
| #Uruguay | 000-412 |
| #U.S. Virgin Islands (CC) | 1-800-888-8000 |
| #Vatican City (CC) | 172-1022 |
| #Venezuela (CC) ♦ | 800-1114-0 |
| Vietnam ● | 1201-1022 |
| Yemen | 008-00-102 |

| # | Automation available from most locations. |
|---|---|
| (CC) | Country-to-country calling available to/from most international locations. |
| ÷ | Limited availability. |
| ▼ | Wait for second dial tone. |
| ◄ | When calling from public phones, use phones marked LADATEL. |
| ■ | International communications carrier. |
| ★ | Not available from public pay phones. |
| ● | Public phones may require deposit of coin or phone card for dial tone. |
| ▲ | Local service fee in U.S. currency required to complete call. |
| ◆ | Regulation does not permit intra-Japan calls. |
| ❖ | Available from most major cities |

MCI

# The MCI Card with WorldPhone Service...
# The easy way to call when traveling worldwide.

Calling Card

415 555 1234 2244
J.D. SMITH

For more information or to apply for a Card call:
1-800-444-1616

Outside the U.S., call MCI collect (reverse charge) at:
1-916-567-5151

Please cut out and save this reference guide for convenient U.S. and worldwide calling with the MCI Card with WorldPhone Service.

| COUNTRY | WORLDPHONE TOLL-FREE ACCESS # |
|---|---|
| #American Samoa | 633-2MCI (633-2624) |
| #Antigua (Available from public card phones only) | #2 |
| #Argentina (CC) | 0800-5-1002 |
| Aruba ÷ | 800-888-8 |
| #Australia (CC) ◆ To call using OPTUS ■ | 1-800-551-111 |
| To call using TELSTRA ■ | 1-800-881-100 |
| #Austria (CC) ◆ | 022-903-012 |
| #Bahamas | 1-800-888-8000 |
| #Bahrain | 800-002 |
| #Barbados (CC) | 1-800-888-8000 |
| #Belarus (CC) From Brest, Vitebsk, Grodno, Minsk | 8-800-103 |
| From Gomel and Mogilev regions | 8-10-800-103 |
| #Belgium (CC) ◆ | 0800-10012 |
| #Belize From Hotels | 815 |
| From Payphones | 557 |
| #Bermuda ÷ | 1-800-888-8000 |
| #Bolivia ◆ | 0-800-2222 |
| #Brazil (CC) | 000-8012 |
| #British Virgin Islands ÷ | 1-800-888-8000 |
| #Brunei | 800-011 |
| #Bulgaria | 00800-0001 |
| #Canada (CC) | 1-800-888-8000 |
| #Cayman Islands | 1-800-888-8000 |
| #Chile (CC) To call using CTC ■ | 800-207-300 |
| To call using ENTEL ■ | 800-360-180 |
| #China ◆ (Available from most major cities) | 108-12 |
| For a Mandarin-speaking Operator | 108-17 |
| #Colombia (CC) | 980-16-0001 |
| Colombia IIC Access in Spanish | 980-16-1000 |
| #Costa Rica ◆ | 0800-012-2222 |
| #Cote D'Ivoire | 1001 |
| #Croatia (CC) ★ | 0800-22-0112 |
| #Cyprus ◆ | 080-90000 |
| #Czech Republic (CC) ◆ | 00-42-000112 |
| #Denmark (CC) ◆ | 8001-0022 |
| #Dominica | 1-800-888-8000 |
| #Dominican Republic (CC) ÷ | 1-800-888-8000 |
| Dominican Republic IIC Access in Spanish | 1121 |
| #Ecuador (CC) ÷ | 999-170 |
| #Egypt ◆ (Outside of Cairo, dial 02 first) | 355-5770 |
| El Salvador ◆ | 800-1767 |
| #Federated States of Micronesia | 624 |

FOLD

| COUNTRY | WORLDPHONE TOLL-FREE ACCESS # |
|---|---|
| #Fiji | 004-890-1002 |
| #Finland (CC) ◆ | 08001-102-80 |
| #France (CC) ◆ | 0800-99-0019 |
| #French Antilles (CC) (includes Martinique, Guadeloupe) | 0800-99-0019 |
| French Guiana (CC) | 0-800-99-0019 |
| #Gabon | 00-001 |
| #Gambia | 00-99 |
| #Germany (CC) | 0130-0012 |
| #Greece (CC) ◆ | 00-800-1211 |
| #Grenada ÷ | 1-800-888-8000 |
| #Guam (CC) | 950-1022 |
| Guatemala (CC) ◆ | 99-99-189 |
| Guyana | 177 |
| #Haiti ÷ | 193 |
| Haiti IIC Access in French/Creole | 190 |
| #Honduras ÷ | 122 |
| #Hong Kong (CC) ◆ | 800-96-1121 |
| #Hungary (CC) ◆ | 00▼800-01411 |
| #Iceland (CC) ◆ | 800-9002 |
| #India (CC) ◆ | 000-127 |
| #Indonesia (CC) ◆ | 001-801-11 |
| #Iran ÷ (SPECIAL PHONES ONLY) | 1-800-55-1001 |
| #Ireland (CC) | 1-800-55-1001 |
| #Israel (CC) | 177-150-2727 |
| #Italy (CC) ◆ | 172-1022 |
| #Jamaica ÷ | 1-800-888-8000 |
| (From Special Hotels only) | 873 |
| Jamaica IIC Access (From public phones) | #2 |
| #Japan (CC) ◆ To call using KDD ■ | 0039-121▼ |
| To call using IDC ■ | 0066-55-121 |
| To call using ITJ ■ | 0044-11-121 |
| #Jordan | 18-800-001 |
| #Kazakhstan (CC) | 8-800-131-4321 |
| #Kenya ÷ (Available from most major cities) | 080011 |
| #Korea (CC) To call using KT ■ | 009-14 |
| To call using DACOM ■ | 00309-12 |
| Phone Booths÷ Press red button, 03, then ★ | |
| Military Bases | 550-2255 |
| #Kuwait | 800-MCI (800-624) |
| #Lebanon ÷ | 600-MCI (600-624) |
| #Liechtenstein (CC) ◆ | 0800-89-0222 |
| #Luxembourg | 0800-0112 |

FOLD

| COUNTRY | WORLDPHONE TOLL-FREE ACCESS # |
|---|---|
| #Macao | 0800-131 |
| #Macedonia (CC) ◆ | 99800-4266 |
| #Malaysia (CC) ◆ | 800-0012 |
| #Malta | 0800-89-0120 |
| #Marshall Islands | 1-800-888-8000 |
| #Mexico Avantel (CC) | 91-800-021-8000 |
| Telmex ▲ | 95-800-674-7000 |
| Mexico IIIC Access | 91-800-021-1000 |
| #Micronesia | 800-99-019 |
| #Monaco (CC) ◆ | 800-99-019 |
| #Montserrat | 1-800-888-8000 |
| #Morocco | 00-211-0012 |
| #Netherlands (CC) ◆ | 0800-022-91-22 |
| #Netherlands Antilles (CC) ÷ | 001-800-888-8000 |
| #New Zealand (CC) | 000-912 |
| #Nicaragua (CC) IIIC Access (Outside of Managua, dial 02 first) | 166 |
| Nicaragua IIIC Access in Spanish ★2 from any public payphone | 166 |
| #Norway (CC) ◆ | 800-19912 |
| #Pakistan | 00-800-12-001 |
| #Panama | 108 |
| Military Bases | 2810-108 |
| #Papua New Guinea (CC) | 05-07-19640 |
| #Paraguay ÷ | 008-11-800 |
| #Peru | 0-800-500-10 |
| #Philippines (CC) ◆ To call using PHILCOM ■ | 105-14 |
| To call using PLDT ■ | 105-14 |
| Philippines IIIC via PLDT in Tagalog | 1026-12 |
| Philippines IIIC via PhilCom in Tagalog | 1026-14 |
| #Poland (CC) ◆ | 00-800-111-21-22 |
| #Portugal (CC) ÷ | 05-017-1234 |
| #Puerto Rico (CC) | 1-800-888-8000 |
| #Qatar ◆ | 0800-012-77 |
| #Romania (CC) ÷ | 01-800-1800 |
| #Russia (CC) ÷ ◆ To call using ROSTELCOM ■ | 747-3322 |
| (For Russian speaking operator) | 747-3320 |
| To call using SOVINTEL ■ | 960-2222 |
| #Saipan (CC) ÷ | 950-1022 |
| #San Marino (CC) ◆ | 172-1022 |
| #Saudi Arabia (CC) | 1-800-11 |
| #Singapore | 8000-112-112 |
| #Slovak Republic (CC) | 0042-1-00112 |
| #Slovenia | 080-8808 |

### Metropolitan

Some Metro stops are sights in their own right. Pino Suárez (Lines 1 and 2) houses a small Aztec building located at mid-transfer. The *Túnel de la Ciencia* (science tunnel) in the marathon transfer at **La Raza** (Lines 3 and 5) is an educational experience: marvel at the nifty fractals, or wear your whites and glow in the dark under a map of the constellations. The stop even has a small **science museum** (open Mon.-Sat. 10am-6pm). The **Zócalo** stop (Line 2) has scale models of the plaza as it has appeared throughout its history, the *andenes* at **Copilco** (Line 3) are lined with **murals,** and the **Bellas Artes** stop (Lines 2 and 8) houses **Aztec statuettes.** In fact, nearly every Metro transfer stop has some kind of exhibit, from elementary school drawings of the subway system to a re-creation of a London theater.

heading. For example, if you are on Line 3 between Indios Verdes and Universidad, you can go either "Dirección Indios Verdes" or "Dirección Universidad." If you realize you are headed in the wrong direction, fear not; simply get off and walk under (or sometimes over) to the other side.

For Lines 1, 2, 3, and A, the first train runs Monday through Friday at 5am, Saturday at 6am, and Sunday at 7am. For Lines 4-9, the first train runs Monday through Saturday at 6am and Sunday at 7am. For all Lines, the last train runs at 12:30am from Sunday through Friday, and on Saturday as late as 1:30am. Try to avoid the Metro from 7:30am to 9:30am and 6 to 9pm on weekdays. Lunch break (2-4pm) during weekdays is also crowded. During these times huge crowds attract pickpockets. Cars at either end of the train tend to be slightly less crowded, *ergo* safer and less uncomfortable.

**Safety** is a big concern in the Metro. As in many parts of Mexico, being single and having two X chromosomes just isn't a convenient combination while using the Metro. Lewd remarks and stares are a given, and the horrible experience of being groped is a very distinct possibility when the train is crowded or if the train stops mid-tunnel between stations. Do not be afraid to call attention to the offender. During rush hours many lines have cars reserved for women and children. If you are female, use them. They are usually located at the front of the train and designated by a partition labeled *Mujeres y Niños.* Often you will see women and children gathering on a separate part of the platform for the reserved car.

**Theft** is a chronic problem on the Metro. Carry bags in front of you or on your lap; simply closing the bag does little good, because thieves use razors to slit the bag open from the bottom. Subway thieves often work in pairs—one will distract you while the other pulls your wallet. Rear pockets are easy to pick, front pockets are safer; empty pockets are best. If you ride with a backpack on your back, the small pocket is likely to be violated. The safest place in a crowded car is with your back against the wall and your backpack (if you have one) in front of you. Because of overcrowding, large bags or suitcases are not allowed on the Metro. Some travelers have slipped bags past the gate, but on a crowded train, luggage will make fellow passengers uncomfortable and will attract thieves. If you are intent on making it on the Metro with that overstuffed pack, come very early or after 10:30pm, when the Metro is fairly empty and guards are more likely to look the other way.

For Metro and bus information, ask at any information booth or contact **COVITUR (Comisión de Vialidad y Transporte Urbano del D.F.),** Public Relations, Universidad 800, 14th floor (tel. 512-01-12 or 627-48-61), at the corner of Félix Cuevas just outside the Zapata Metro station (Line 3). Nearly all stations have guards and security offices, and all stations are required to have a *jefe de la estacion* (chief of station) in a marked office. These people are valuable resources, ready to deal with questions, complaints, panic attacks, and just about anything else. Further, all trains have an emergency red handle, to be pulled in the event of severe harrassment or any emergency. If you lose something on the Metro, call the **Oficina de Objetos Extraviados** (tel. 709-11-33, ext. 4643), located in the Fray Servando station (Line 4). Keep hope alive, but don't hold your breath.

MEXICO CITY

## BY PESERO

*Peseros,* a.k.a. *colectivos, combis,* or *micros,* are white and green minibuses, often with a "Magna Sin" gasoline logo on the side. The name *pesero* comes from the time when they used to cost one old peso, equivalent to 0.01¢ today. Although not quite the steal they used to be, these easily affordable *peseros* cruise the streets on set routes. Though no printed information is available, destinations are either painted on or posted on the front window. There are *pesero* starting and ending bases, but no set stops. To hail a *pesero,* wave your hand or hold out as many fingers as there are people in your group. To get off, ring the bell if there's one, or simply shout loudly *¡Bajan!* (coming down). To prevent a missed stop, pay when you get on and tell the driver your destination. Drivers will honk horns (often rigged to play such perennial faves as "It's a Small World" and the love theme from *The Godfather*) to signal availability during rush hour.

Expect to fork over 1-3 pesos for cross-city rides, 5 pesos for long-distance trips over 17km (10% more 10pm-6am). Some *peseros* run only until midnight, but the major routes—on Reforma, between Chapultepec and San Ángel, and along Insurgentes—run 24 hours. Other well-traveled *pesero* routes include: Metro station Hidalgo (Lines 2 and 3) to Ciudad Universitaria (via Reforma, Bucareli, and Av. Cuauhtémoc); La Villa to Chapultepec (via Reforma); Reforma to Auditorio (via Reforma and Juárez); *zócalo* to Chapultepec (via 5 de Mayo and Reforma); San Ángel to Izazaga (via 5 de Mayo and Reforma); Bolívar to Ciudad Universitaria/Coyoacán (via Bolívar in the *centro*); and San Ángel to Metro Insurgentes (Line 1; via Av. de la Paz and Insurgentes Sur). Many depart from the Chapultepec Metro station (Line 1) to San Ángel, La Merced, and the airport. Check the routes posted on the windshield, but don't be shy about asking the driver personally: *"¿Se va a _____?"*

## BY BUS

There is no published information about routes and schedules for the extensive bus system. Unless you stick to the major thoroughfares, you might find it difficult to navigate the city by bus. Always, always check with the driver before you board; getting on a crowded bus going in the opposite direction is the quickest way to get lost and to ruin a perfectly good day. Moreover, buses are usually slower than the Metro, particularly during rush hours. Buses cost 0.50 to 2 pesos; have change ready when you board. They run daily from 5am to midnight, but are scarce after 10pm. Keep in mind that each one-way Eje has a single bus lane running in the *opposite* direction to traffic. Flag down a bus anywhere by holding out your arm and pointing at the street in front of you. To get off the bus, press the button above the exit door at the rear of the bus. If you don't hear a buzz, bang once on the wall or bark *¡Bajan!* to let the driver know you want out. Like the Metro, buses are crowded and seats are hot items. The popular routes along Paseo de la Reforma are notorious for robbery. Leave your valuables at the hotel, don't keep money in your pockets, put your bag in front of you, and keep your fingers crossed.

## BY TAXI

Cabs constantly cruise the major avenues. Most taxis are equipped with meters. Base fares typically begin at 3-5 pesos, and at night drivers will add 20% to the meter rate. Be certain that the meter is functioning as soon as you plop onto the cushion; meters are often conveniently *descompuesto*. If a meter is out of order, insist on setting the price before the driver goes anywhere. Another commonly used trick is for a normally functioning meter to suddenly jump into the triple digits—watch the meter at all times and immediately threaten a driver with non-payment if the price instantaneously skyrockets. Some taxis have meters that display reference numbers for the driver's price conversion table instead of prices. Ask to see it before you pay, to ensure that the price you're given matches the meter number. Carry small denominations, as drivers will often cite no change as a reason to pocket some extra pesos.

While tips are technically unnecessary, an extra peso or two (nothing fancy), especially to kind cabbies who run on strict meters, cannot hurt anyone.

Hotel cabs and *turismo* taxis have no meters and charge up to three times more than regular taxis; the ubiquitous and fashionably chic lime green and canary yellow VW bugs are the cheapest but must be hailed. At the airport and at all bus terminals, purchase a taxi ticket for a set fee (according to destination) at a registered booth. In the rare instance that no taxi is in sight, call **Servi-taxi** (tel. 271-25-60) or **Taxi Radio Mexicana** (tel. 519-76-90). VW-bug taxis should display the driver's photo, credentials, and license over the lovely lime-colored glove compartment. Taxis commonly prey on the easy tourist victim. At the airport or bus terminals, try to consult a zone map before buying your ticket and always count your change. On the street, ask a local what the fare should be and insist on paying that and no more. There'll always be a driver who will accept.

There are several *sitios* (taxi bases) in every neighborhood. *Sitios* will respond to your phone call by sending out a car to pick you up. Since their taxis don't use meters, ask the operator what the trip will cost. The great advantage of *sitio* taxis, in addition to home pick-up, is that they are much safer than anonymous cabs. The disadvantage is that they are usually 1½ to 2 times more expensive. However, rising crime rates make the benefits outweigh the cost. Women going out at night should strongly consider using *sitio* taxis; find out phone numbers from your hotel or the tourist office.

## BY CAR

You must be insane. Driving is the most complicated and least economical way to get around the city, not to mention the easiest way to get lost. Mexico City's drivers are notoriously reckless; they became that way in large measure because highway engineers did not think about them at all when designing city roads. Highway dividers are often absent, and stop signs are planted midstream. Is it any wonder that red lights are routinely defied? Even the fast and free *Ángeles Verdes* do not serve the D.F. If your car should break down within city boundaries, call the **Asociación Mexicana Automovilística (AMA;** tel. 207-44-48) or the **Asociación Nacional Automovilística (ANA;** tel. 597-42-83), and request assistance. Wait for them beside your car, with the hood raised. If you leave your car alone, give it a good-bye kiss before you go. Female drivers are encouraged to consider the risks of driving alone at night and either using another form of public transportation or driving with someone else.

Parking within the city is seldom a problem; parking lots are everywhere (4-8 pesos per hr., depending on the location and condition of the lot). Street parking is difficult to find, and vandalism is extremely common. Never leave anything valuable inside your car. Police will put an *inmobilizador* on your wheels if you park illegally; they will often tow your car. If you return to an empty space, try to locate the nearest police depot (not station) to figure out if your auto has been towed—if it's not there, it was stolen. If anything is missing from your car and you suspect that the police tampered with it, call the English-speaking **LOCATEL** (tel. 658-11-11).

All vehicles, even those of non-Mexican registration, must follow Mexico City's anti-smog regulations. Depending on the last digit of the license plate, cars are forbidden from driving one day a week, according to this schedule: Monday final digits: 5 or 6; Tuesday: 7 or 8; Wednesday: 3 or 4; Thursday: 1 or 2; Friday: 9 or 0. Restrictions apply from 5am to 10pm, and penalties for violations are very stiff. There are no limitations on weekends and on weekdays between 10pm and 5am.

Car rental rates are exorbitant, driving a hassle, and the entire process draining. Still interested? Then you must have a valid driver's license (from any country), a passport or tourist card, and be at least 25 years old. Prices for rentals tend to be similar: a small VW or Nissan with free mileage, insurance, and tax (which is known as IVA) costs about 330-430 pesos per day or 3000-3300 pesos per week. Most agencies have offices at the airport and in the *Zona Rosa:* **Avis,** at the airport (tel. 786-94-52, open 7am-11pm) and at Reforma 308 (tel. 511-22-28, open 9am-6pm); **Budget,** (tel. 784-30-11) at the airport (open daily 24hr.) and at Hamburgo 71 (tel. 533-04-50); **Dollar,** at the airport (tel. 207-38-38) and at Av. Chapultepec 322 (open daily 7am-8pm); **Econo-movil,** at the airport (tel. 726-05-90) and with offices in Colonia del Valle (tel. 604-59-60) and Colonia Roma (tel. 519-09-96, open daily 7am-11pm); **Hertz,** at the airport (tel. 762-83-72, open 7am-10:30pm); **Thrifty,** Sevilla 4 (tel. 207-75-66).

# ■ Safety

Like all large cities, Mexico City presents safety problems to the traveler. Misery-induced crime, corruption, authority abuse, and a lax justice system don't help a bit. A volatile political situation only aggravates problems in the world's largest city. In general, the downtown area, where most sights and accommodations are located, tends to be safer, although the backstreets near Buenavista and the Alameda are significantly less so. Try to avoid carrying large amounts of cash, and use a money belt or a similar security device that carries valuables inside your clothing, next to your body. Never use a fanny pack. Ignore strangers who seem even slightly suspicious, no matter how friendly their chatter or smile may seem. Speaking in Spanish makes would-be attackers far less likely to bother you. Never follow a vendor or shoeshiner out of public view. Don't wear cameras, expensive watches, or flashy jewelry if you want to be left alone. Sunglasses for men convey don't-mess-with-me *machismo;* for women they may be less advisable (see p. 249).

Women are, unfortunately, at higher risk of attack. Women in Mexico receive attention that they may not be used to; insistent stares, provocative smiles, whistling, cat-calling, and even extremely vulgar propositions are all part of everyday life. Light hair and skin, revealing or tight clothing, or any sign of foreignness will result in even more attention. Although horribly annoying, most such displays are harmless, provided you take good care of yourself. Stick with other people, especially at night or in isolated areas. A loud clear *¡Déjame!* (leave me alone, DEH-ha-meh) will make your intentions clear. If in trouble, don't be shy about screaming *¡Ayúdame!* (help me; ah-YOO-dah-may).

The city that used to be known as *la región más transparente del aire* (the most transparent region of air) is now the most polluted in the world. The city's smoggy air may cause problems for contact-lens wearers and people with allergies. Pollution is particularly bad during the winter, due to thermic inversion; the summer rainy season does wonders for air cleanliness.

# ■ Practical Information

Navigating the city will be easier if you pick up a few current publications. The **Mex-ico City Daily Bulletin,** which includes news, information on tourist sights, and a helpful map of Mexico City, is available free at the City Tourism Office and all over the *Zona Rosa.* The best resource for truly getting down and dirty in this city is the phenomenal **Tiempo Libre** (Free Time), a weekly on sale at most corner newsstands, covers movies, galleries, restaurants, dances, museums, and most cultural events (comes out Thurs., 5 pesos). **The Mexico City News** (4 pesos), an English-language daily, and **La Jornada,** a top national newspaper (3 pesos), have film and theater listings, as well as extensive international news, in case you miss gossip from the homefront. **Ser Gay,** available at newsstands and many gay bars, is less widely distributed but has a more complete listing of gay nightlife options. Although hard to find at newsstands and on the street, the bartenders and/or managers at all the places listed in the **Gay Clubs** section will be happy to give you more information on cultural events and nightlife. Of course, the best way for anyone to find their way around and to discover new and exciting bars, restaurants, theaters, and museums, is to get out and talk to people.

If you come during the summer, keep a light rain poncho or umbrella handy. The rainy season (May-Oct.) features daily, one- or two-hour-long rain storms anywhere from 4-6pm. Otherwise, sunny and moderate weather prevails year-round.

**Ministry of Tourism:** Presidente Masaryk 172 (tel. 250-85-55, ext. 168), at Hegel in Col. Polanco. From Metro Polanco (Line 7), walk 1 block down Arquímedes, take a left on Masaryk, and walk 3½ blocks—the building is to your right and easy to miss. Friendly staff makes hotel reservations and offers copious amounts of brochures, information, and advice. Open Mon.-Fri. 8am-9pm (24hr. phone lines).

**Federal Tourist Office: Infotur,** Amberes 54 (tel. 525-93-80 or 525-93-82), at Londres in the *Zona Rosa.* Metro: Insurgentes (Line 1). Helpful and friendly. Some officials speak English. Maps of the city and Metro upon request. Lists hotels, grouped by region and price range. Open daily 9am-8pm. The office operates information booths at the TAPO and Terminal Central del Norte bus stations (daily 8am-9pm).

**Department of Tourist Security:** Dr. Navarro 210 (tel. 761-3011 or 761-4371) across the street from the Metro stop Doctores (Line 8). A good place to start after an accident. Deals with complaints, questions, emergencies, and reports of abuses. Some English. Open 24hr. for phone calls; staffed daily 8am-8pm.

**Legal Advice: Supervisión General de Servicios a la Comunidad,** Florencia 20 (tel. 625-87-61), in the *Zona Rosa.* Metro: Insurgentes (Line 1). Call the 24hr. **hotline** (tel. 625-86-64) if you are the victim of a robbery or accident and need legal advice. Little to no English spoken.

**LOCATEL:** Tel. 658-11-11. Officially the city's lost-and-found hotline. Call if your car (or friend) is missing. Also provides help in cases of medical emergencies and information about sports events, etc. Limited English spoken.

**Tourist Card (FMT) info: Secretaría de Gobernación, Dirección General de Servicios Migratorios,** Av. Chapultepec 284, 5th fl. (tel. 626-72-00 or 206-05-06), in Col. Juárez. Metro: Insurgentes (Line 1). Come here to extend the date on your FMT or to clear up any immigration problems. Come early to avoid the long lines. Open Mon.-Fri. 8am-2pm.

**Accommodations Service: Hoteles Asociados,** Airport *Sala* E (tel. 571-5902 or 571-6382) and the Central de Autobuses del Norte. Up-to-date information on prices and locations of Mexico City hotels. Give 'em a price range and an area, they'll get you a reservation free of charge. For budget lodgings, be sure to ask for rock-bottom prices. English spoken.

**Embassies:** Will replace lost passports, issue visas, and provide legal assistance. Visa processing can take up to 24hr.; bring plenty of ID. If you find yourself in an emergency after hours, try contacting the embassy anyway—you could be in luck. **Australia,** 9255 Rubén Dario 55, Col. Polanco (tel. 531-52-25; open Mon.-Wed. 8am-5pm, Thurs.-Fri. 8am-2pm; emergency after hours tel. 905-407-16-98). **Belize,** Bernardo de Galvez 215 (tel. 520-1274). Open Mon.-Fri. 9am-1:30pm. **Canada,** Schiller 529 (tel. 724-7900), behind the Museum of Anthropology. Open Mon.-Fri. 8:30am-noon for immigration concerns, 9am-2:30pm for library, and 9am-1pm and 2-5pm for general information. **Costa Rica,** Río Po 113 (tel. 525-7764, -65, -66), between Río Lerma and Río Panuco, behind the U.S. embassy. Open Mon.-Fri. 9am-4pm. **Guatemala,** 1025 Av. Explanada (tel. 540-7520). Open Mon.-Fri. 9am-1:30pm. **Honduras,** Alfonso Reyes 220 (tel. 211-5747), between Saltillo and Ometusco. Open Mon.-Fri. 10am-2pm. **New Zealand,** Homero 229, 8th fl. (tel. 281-5486). Open Mon.-Fri. 9:30am-5:30pm. **Nicaragua,** Payo de Rivera 120 (tel. 540-5621), between Virreyes and Monte Atos. Open Mon.-Fri. 9:30am-3pm. **U.K.,** Río Lerma 71 (tel. 207-2149), at Cuauhtémoc. Open Mon.-Fri. 9am-2pm for visas, 9am-3pm for general info. **U.S.,** Reforma 305 (tel. 211-0042), at Glorieta Ángel de la Independencia. Open Mon.-Fri. 8:30am-5pm for passports and visas, Mon.-Fri. 8:30am-5:30pm for general business. In an emergency, call after hours.

**Currency Exchange:** *Casas de cambio* keep longer hours than banks, give better exchange rates, and typically stay open on Sat. There are many in the *centro,* along Reforma, and in the *Zona Rosa.* Most can change other currencies in addition to U.S. dollars. Call the **Asociación Mexicana de Casas de Cambio** (tel. 264-0884 or 264-0841) to locate the exchange bureau nearest you. In the *centro:* **Casa de Cambio Euromex,** Venustiano Carranza 64, 3rd fl. (tel. 518-4199; open Mon.-Fri. 8am-4pm, Sat. 9am-2pm); **Casa de Cambio Tíber,** on Río Tíber and Papaloapan (722-0800), one block from the Ángel. Open Mon.-Fri. 8:30am-5pm, Sat. 8:30am-2pm. On the south side of the Alameda: **Casa de Cambio Plus,** Juárez 38 (tel. 510-8953). Open Mon.-Fri. 9am-4pm, Sat. 10am-2pm. On Reforma, near the Monumento a la

Revolución/Buenavista: **Casa de Cambio Catorce,** Reforma 51 (tel. 705-2460; open Mon.-Fri. 9am-4:30pm, Sat. 10am-1pm). All banks offer the same exchange rate and usually charge commissions. All banks exchange 9am-1:30pm, but the wait may be considerable. The nation-wide **ATM** network, **Red Cajeros Compartidos,** takes MC and Visa for cash advances, and many ATMs work with other U.S. system cards. Scores of ATMs are located along Reforma, in the *Zona Rosa,* in Polanco, and in the *centro.* Lost or stolen cards can be reported 24hr. to 227-2777. In case of a lost **Visa** card, call 625-21-88. **Citibank,** Reforma 390 (tel. 211-3030, open 24hr.), and **Bank of America,** Reforma 116, 10th-12th floors (tel. 591-0011), can also help in an emergency.

**American Express:** Reforma 234 (tel. 207-7282), at Havre in the *Zona Rosa.* Cashes personal checks, accepts customers' mail and money wires. Travel service. Report lost credit cards to the main office at Patriotismo 635 (tel. 326-2666), lost traveler's checks to either branch. Open Mon.-Fri. 9am-6pm, Sat. 9am-1pm.

**Telephones: LADATELs** (also marked LADA 91, as in the national long-distance prefix) are everywhere and can be used for international collect and credit card calls, and also with a LADATEL card. For those who miss the golden days of the Mexican phone system, long-distance *casetas* are at Airport *Sala* F (open daily 6am-8:30pm), the train station (open Mon.-Sat. 8am-9:30pm, Sun. 9am-3pm), and Central Camionera del Norte (open daily 8am-9pm).

**Fax:** Tacuba 8 (tel. 512-21-95), open Mon.-Fri. 9am-midnight, at the Museo Nacional de Arte in the right wing of the building, behind the central post office. Domestic and international service.

**English Bookstores: American Bookstore,** Madero 25 (tel. 512-7284), in the *centro,* has an extensive selection of fiction, guidebooks, and a matchless Latin American history and politics section. Also a branch at Insurgentes Sur 1636 (tel. 661-66-08), in San Ángel. Both branches open Mon.-Sat. 10am-7pm; *centro* store also open Sun. 10am-3pm. **Pórtico de la Ciudad de México,** Central 124 at Carranza (tel. 510-96-83 or 280-54-72). English and Spanish books on Mexican history and guides to archaeological sites. Open Mon.-Sat. 10am-7pm. **La Casa de la Prensa Internacional,** Florencia 57 in the *Zona Rosa,* sells magazines and newspapers in Spanish, English, French, and German. Open Mon.-Sat. 8am-10pm, Sat.-Sun. 8am-4pm. Also popular is the **Librería Gandhi,** M.A. de Quevedo 128, in San Ángel.

**English Library: Biblioteca Benjamín Franklin,** Londres 16 at Berlín (tel. 211-00-42; ask for the library), 2 blocks southeast of the Cuauhtémoc monument. Books, newspapers, and periodicals. Council and Fulbright fellas on the second floor. Open Mon. and Fri. 3-7:30pm, Tues.-Thurs. 10am-3pm.

**Cultural and Arts Info: Palacio Nacional de Bellas Artes** (tel. 709-31-13), Juárez and Eje Central, for info and reservations for Bellas Artes events. Open Mon.-Sat. 11am-7pm, Sun. 9am-7pm. Check *Tiempo Libre* for city-wide listings.

**Supermarket:** Most supermarkets are far from the *centro,* at residential Metro stops. **Bodega,** Serapio Rendón 117, just south of Antonio Caso. Open Mon.-Sat. 8am-9pm, Sun. 9am-8pm. **Aurrerá,** 5 blocks north of Puente de Alvarado on Insurgentes. Open daily 9am-9pm. **Comercial Mexicana,** at Corregidora and Correo Mayor, on the side of the Palacio Nacional, in the *centro.* Open daily 8am-9pm. **Superama,** Río Sena and Balsas, in the *Zona Rosa.* Open daily 8am-9pm.

**Laundromats:** Near the Monumento a la Revolución: **Lavandería Automática,** Edison 91. Wash or dry 22 pesos per 2¼kg. Full service 37 pesos. Soap 5 pesos. Open Mon.-Sat. 10am-6pm. In the *Zona Rosa:* **Lavanderet,** Chapultepec 463 at Toledo (tel. 514-01-06). Wash or dry 17 pesos. Full service 36 pesos. Open Mon.-Sat. 9am-7pm. **LavaJet,** Danubio 119 (tel. 207-30-32), behind the U.S. embassy. Wash or dry 14 pesos. Full service 46 pesos. Open Mon.-Fri. 8:30am-6pm, Sat. 8:30am-5pm. Most hotels have laundry service.

**Rape Crisis: Hospital de Traumatología de Balbuena,** Cecilio Robelo 103 (tel. 552-16-02 or 764-03-39), near Calle Sur, east of Alameda. Also call 06 or LOCATEL.

**Sexually Transmitted Disease Info and Innoculation Info: Secretaría de Salud** (tel. 277-63-11 or 533-72-04). Open Mon.-Fri. 8am-8pm, Sat. 9am-2pm.

**AIDS Hotline: TELSIDA/CONASIDA,** Florencia 8 (tel. 207-41-43 or 207-40-77), Col. Roma. Metro: Cuauhtémoc (Line 1). Runs AIDS tests, provides prevention information, and serves as a general help center. Open Mon.-Fri. 9am-9:30pm.

**Gay, Lesbian, and Bisexual Information: Colectivo Sol.** Write to Apdo. 13-320 Av. México 13, D.F. 03500. Offers information on upcoming political and social events. Events publicized at gay bars and clubs and in *Tiempo Libre,* and *Ser Gay.*

**Red Cross:** Ejército Nacional 1032 (tel. 395-11-11), in Polanco. Open 24hr.

**Pharmacies:** Small *farmacias* abound on almost every street corner and are great for most purchases. Rarer drugs and more important, specialized medications should be bought at large, international looking (and more expensive) pharmacies. Two are: **Farmacia El Fénix,** Isabel La Católica 15 (tel. 585-04-55), at 5 de Mayo, open Mon.-Sat. 9am-10pm; **VYR,** San Jerónimo 630 (tel. 595-59-83 or 595-59-98), near Perisur shopping center and at other locations; open 24hr. All **Sanborns** and big supermarkets have well-stocked pharmacies.

**Medical Care:** The **U.S. Embassy** has a list of doctors, with their specialties, addresses, telephone numbers, and languages spoken. **Dirección General de Servicios Médicos** (tel. 518-51-00) has information on all city hospitals. Open Mon.-Fri. 9am-5pm. **American British Cowdray (ABC) Hospital,** Calle Sur 136 at Observatorio (tel. 227-50-00), Col. Las Américas. Expensive but generally trustworthy and excellent. No foreign health plans valid, but major credit cards accepted. Open 24hr. **Torre Médica,** José Maria Iglesias 21 (tel. 546-24 85), at Metro station Revolución (Line 2).

**Emergency Shelter: Casa de Protección Social** (tel. 530-85-36).

**Police: Secretaría General de Protección y Vialidad** (tel. 256-06-06 or 768-80-44). Open 24hr. Dial 08 for the Policía Judicial to report assaults, robberies, crashes, abandoned vehicles, or emergencies. Beware abuses of power.

**Internet Access: El Universal-Internet Sala,** Bucareli 12, across the street from the giant yellow horse sculpture in an unmarked entrance, right next to the main entrance of *El Universal* newspaper office. This service provides *absolutely free* internet usage. All you have to do is sign in and leave ID, and then enjoy up to 2hr. of computer escapades—they even have people to help you. Open Mon.-Fri. 10am-7pm. Access can be had for about 25-50 pesos per hour at other spots, including **Cyberspace Cafe,** Mazatlán 148 (tel. 211-68-72), in Col. Condesa. From Metro station Chapultepec (Line 1), walk down Av. Veracruz and turn right on Mazatlán (25 pesos per hr., 15 pesos per ½hr., geeks pay 190 pesos for 10hr.). **CompuByte,** Bolivar 66, Col. Centro. 50 pesos per hr., 25 pesos per ½hr., 100 pesos for multimedia and electronic conferences. Open Mon.-Sat. 9am-6pm. **Capucinnonel,** Universidad 2079 (tel. 554-64-08), in the Pl. Manzana in the south of the city near Coyoacán-San Ángel. 25 pesos per hr., 15 pesos per ½hr., 190 pesos for 10hr.

**Courier Services: UPS,** Reforma 404 (tel. 207-69-57), and various smaller offices, provides international shipping services and express mail. Open Mon.-Fri. 8am-8pm. **Federal Express,** Reforma 308, Colonia Juárez (toll-free 91-800-900-11), near the Glorieta Angel de Independencia. Send before 4:30pm Mon.-Fri., 1:30pm Sat., for overnight service. Open Mon.-Fri. 9am-6pm, Sat. 9am-1pm.

**Central Post Office:** Lázaro Cárdenas (tel. 521-73-94), at Tacuba across from Bellas Artes. Open for stamps Mon.-Fri. 8am-6pm, Sat. 9am-8pm; for registered mail Mon.-Fri. 8am-5:30pm, Sat. 9am-4:30pm; for *Lista de Correos* Mon.-Fri. 8am-9pm, Sat. 9am-5pm. Stylin' postal museum upstairs with turn-of-the-century mailboxes and other old-school gear. **Postal Code:** 06002.

**Phone Code:** 5.

# ■ Accommodations

Rooms abound in the *centro* (between Alameda and the *zócalo*) and near the Alameda Central. Perhaps the best budget bargains (and the best place to meet eclectic and wacky locals and tourists) are found near El Monumento a la Revolución on the Pl. de la República. Rooms priced at 60-80 pesos for one bed and 85-100 pesos for two beds should be clean, and have carpeting, a TV, and a telephone with free local calls. Some budget hotels charge according to the number of beds needed and not per person; beds tend to be large enough for two people. If you don't mind, snuggling is a potential source of substantial savings.

# Central Mexico City

SIGHTS

Casa de los Azulejos, **38**
Catedral Metropolitana, **46**
Centro Cultural José Martí, **26**
Glorieta Ángel de la
  Independencia, **8**
Glorieta Cristóbal Colón, **13**
Glorieta Cuauhtémoc, **12**
Lotería Nacional, **20**
Mercado de Artesanías de la

Ciudadela, **21**
Monte Nacional de Piedad, **45**
Monumento a la Revolución, **14**
Monumento de los Niños Héroes, **7**
Museo de Arte Moderno, **6**
Museo de la Alameda, **24**
Museo de la Ciudad de México, **51**
Museo Franz Mayer, **27**
Museo Nacional de Antropología, **3**
Museo Nacional de Arte, **36**

Museo Nacional de Historia, **5**
Museo Nacional de la Estampa
Museo Siqueiros, **2**
Museo Tamayo, **4**
Palacio de Bellas Artes, **30**
Palacio Nacional, **49**
Pinacoteca Virreinal de San
  Diego, **25**
Plaza de la Constitución, **47**
Plaza de las Tres Culturas

28
(Tlatelolco), 31
Plaza Garibaldi, 32
Suprema Corte de Justicia, 50
Templo de San Francisco, 40
Templo Mayor, 48
Torre Latinoamericana, 39

SERVICES
Central Post Office, 37
Federal Tourist Office, 1

Train Station, 18
Ministry of Tourism, 11
U.S. Embassy, 9
U.K. Embassy, 10

HOTELS
Casa de los Amigos, 15
Hotel Antillas, 33
Hotel Atlanta, 34
Hotel Conde, 22

Hotel Florida, 35
Hotel Hidalgo, 29
Hotel Isabel, 42
Hotel Juárez, 44
Hotel Londres, 17
Hotel Manolo Primero, 23
Hotel Monte Carlo, 43
Hotel Oxford, 16
Hotel Principal, 41
Hotel Yale, 19

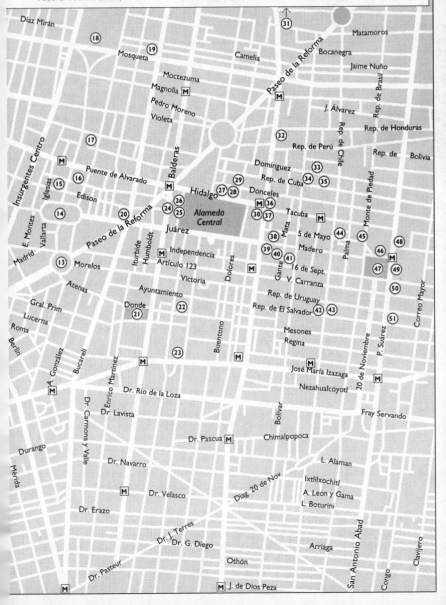

Avoid the filthier sections of the Alameda and any area that makes you feel uncomfortable—there are plenty more from which to choose. In an attempt to cut down on problems with prostitution, many budget establishments have adopted "No Guests Allowed" policies. Beware of any place where the hotel itself (and not the parking lot) is marked "Hotel Garage." These rooms are frequented by business-folk "working late at the office" and are designed to allow entry directly from the garage to the room. Figure it out. Always ask to look at a room before you accept it; this is easier to do after check-out time (between noon and 2pm).

For hostel information, call **Villa Deportiva Juvenil** (tel. 525-26-99), the city's lone hostel on Plaza de la Independencia, near the *Zona Rosa* (30 pesos per night). Don't get your hopes up; they're often full with visiting sports teams.

## CENTRO

Situated between the *zócalo* and Alameda Central, this neighborhood is the historic colonial heart of Mexico City. Its hotels are reasonably priced and feel fairly safe, although the streets become empty once the locals head home for the night. Still, the *centro* remains an exciting and convenient, but noisy, place to stay. With action inevitably come noise and congestion. If you crave quieter surroundings, consider moving west to the Buenavista or Alameda areas. Many of the hotels listed below are north of Madero and 5 de Mayo, the parallel east-west streets that connect the Alameda with the *zócalo,* and east of Lázaro Cárdenas, the north-south Eje Central that runs one block east of Alameda. Metro stations Bellas Artes (Lines 2 and 8) and Allende (Line 2) are nearby. Hotels on 5 de Mayo, Isabel la Católica, and Uruguay are better served by Metro stations Zócalo (Line 2) and Isabel la Católica (Line 1). Street names change north of Tacuba: Isabel la Católica becomes República de Chile, and Bolívar turns into Allende. Even in the *centro,* most budget hotels do not accept credit cards.

**Hotel Antillas,** Belisario Domínguez 34 (tel. 526-56-74 through -79), between Allende and República de Chile. The colonial exterior promises a history-drenched grandeur: the dim interior does not disappoint. The eager staff and clean bathrooms make for a relaxing stay, complete with TVs, bottled water, new safe boxes, and lounge areas. Singles 120 pesos; doubles 130 pesos.

**Hotel Monte Carlo,** Uruguay 69 (tel. 521-2559), between Metro stops Isabel la Católica (Line 1) and Allende (Line 2). Relaxing lounge and top-floor skylight. Large, lovingly mismatched bedrooms. Clean, tiled bathrooms and garage available. Singles 90 pesos; doubles 110 pesos.

**Hotel Principal,** Bolívar 29 (tel. 521-13-33), by the Parilla Leonesa restaurant. Friendly staff bustles about under the arched brick ceiling. Simple yellow rooms have a balcony, mirror, TV, telephone, and bottled water. Singles with communal bath 55-65 pesos, with private bath 100-110 pesos; doubles 130-140 pesos.

**Hotel Isabel,** Isabel la Católica 63 between El Salvador and Uruguay (tel. 518-12-13 through -17). Although the rooms are simple and no-nonsense, the hotel itself is gorgeous. Wrought iron everywhere, large ceramic bathtubs (in some rooms), skylight, and overall amazing art nouveau decor. Even more positives: huge chest of drawers, electronic safe, TV, bottled water, and cleanliness. Singles 105 pesos; doubles 120 pesos; triples 145 pesos; quads 170 pesos.

**Hotel La Marina,** Allende 30 (tel. 518-24-45). Although the rooms look like they've been decorated by a color-blind clown, lots of space and king-size beds help relieve the eyesore. The prices aren't bad either. Singles 80 pesos; doubles 100 pesos.

**Hotel Lafayette,** Motlinía No. 40, at 16 de Septiembre (tel. 521-96-40). The big, red plastic chairs and wood paneling in the lobby are office-like, but the rooms are big and clean, with color TV, telephones, and nice bathrooms. Also offers laundry, safety deposit boxes, and dry cleaning. All this can be yours for 70 pesos for a single bed; 80 pesos a double bed; 110 pesos for a double; 150 pesos for a triple.

## NEAR THE MONUMENTO A LA REVOLUCIÓN/BUENAVISTA

Hotels near the Monumento a la Revolución are cheaper and quieter than their counterparts in the *centro* or the Alameda. Backpackers and bargain-scouting travelers tend to congregate here, particularly in the hotels on Mariscal and Edison. Metro Revolución (Line 2) serves hotels south of Puente de Alvarado/Hidalgo, while Metro Guerrero (Line 3) serves those to the north, near the train station.

**Casa de Los Amigos,** Ignacio Mariscal 132 (tel. 705-05-21 or 705-06-46), across from Gran Hotel Texas. Metro: Revolución (Line 2). Originally the home and studio of painter José Clemente Orozco, now a Quaker-run guest house for tourists and social activists. Fascinating, amazing place, with dynamic, youthful, international atmosphere. Visitors required to respect the cooperative atmosphere in order to stay (rules are few), and it's worth it. Backpackers, grad students, eco-warriors—people from all over the world come here. You're bound to go home with many international addresses and fond memories of your newfound *amigos.* Weekly cultural exchanges, ample library offerings, and a lively lounge. Kitchen and laundry facilities. 2-day min. stay, 15-day max. stay. Key deposit 10 pesos. Dorm rooms 40 pesos; private rooms 55 pesos; doubles 80-90 pesos. Breakfast 10 pesos.

**Hotel Oxford,** Ignacio Mariscal 67 at Alcázar (tel. 566-05-00), next to the small park. Metro: Revolución. Large, colorful rooms, many with TV, telephone, and great views of the park. Inviting bathrooms with huge sinks in which to do laundry. Adjoining bar with swinging saloon-style doors, frequented by fatigued *mariachis* and aging prostitutes. Singles 60-80 pesos; doubles 90 pesos; triples 125 pesos; quads 160 pesos.

**Hotel Carlton,** Ignacio Mariscal No. 32 (tel. 566-29-11), opposite the Hotel Oxford. Rooms are clean and spacious, with telephones, big beds, and big TVs. Adjoining bar. 1 person 70 pesos; 2 people 80 pesos; 3 people 95 pesos; 4 people 110 pesos.

**Hotel America,** Calle Buenavista 4 at Alvarado (tel. 566-96-77). Small, clean rooms with oversized TVs. New bathrooms. A well-kept secret close to the Revolución Metro stop. Singles 60 pesos; doubles 85 pesos; triples 90 pesos.

**Hotel Yale,** Mosqueta 200 between Zaragoza and Guerrero (tel. 591-15-45 or 591-14-88), to the left as you exit the train station. Metro: Guerrero. Recently remodeled rooms, full-length mirrors, TVs, and colorful furniture that doesn't quite match. An endearing hotel, for those who can't get into a better place. 1 person 60 pesos; 2 people 70 pesos; king-size bed 80 pesos.

## ALAMEDA CENTRAL

The expansive Alameda is always throbbing with activity. But the greenery fades over the course of a few blocks, making way for dirt and danger in some of the surrounding streets. Use caution. Use a *sitio* cab (love that door-to-door service).

**Hotel Hidalgo,** Santa Veracruz 37 (tel. 521-87-71 through -77), just north of the Alameda. Metro: Bellas Artes (Lines 2 and 8). Up the 2 de Abril walkway to the left of Teatro Hidalgo, in a somewhat dingy area, Hidalgo is a resplendent vision in peach. Swank renovations include elegant wood paneling, beautiful carpeting, and tasteful decorations. Queen singles and pleasant courtyard views make it worth the price. Singles 135 pesos; doubles 160 pesos; triples 180 pesos; quads 200 pesos.

**Hotel Manolo Primero,** Luis Moya 111 (tel. 521-77-09), near Arcos de Belén, 3 blocks west of Metro station Salto del Agua (Lines 1 and 8). Spacious blue hallways and cavernous lobby lead to rooms with king-sized beds and big-screen TVs. Clean, large bathrooms with gigantic mirrors. Singles and doubles a steal for 100 pesos.

**Hotel Sevillano,** Ayuntamiento 78 at Revillagigedo (tel. 512-67-15), 4 blocks from the Alameda. Small, clean rooms with cute TVs perched up near the ceiling. Central courtyard lets in a lot of light. Singles and doubles only 50 pesos.

**MEXICO CITY**

## NEAR THE BUS STATIONS

There are few good budget accommodations in the vicinity of any of the four bus stations. The areas around these stations generally offer expensive rooms in shabby *barrios.* Even if you arrive late at night, it is not safe to walk a couple of blocks—you'd do best to catch a cab (and once in a cab, why not head to the center of town?). For travelers just passing through who arrive at the **Central de Autobuses del Norte** (northern station), the pricey but comfy **Hotel Brasilia,** Av. de los 100 Mts. 4823 (tel. 587-85-77), is three blocks to the left along the main thoroughfare as you exit the bus station. Rooms are carpeted and clean, with TV and phone (singles 150 pesos; doubles 190 pesos). The closest place near the **Terminal de Autobuses del Sur** (south station) is **Hotel Montreal,** Calzada de Tlalpan 2073 at M. A. Quevedo (tel. 689-00-11). Exit the bus station to the right, follow the train tracks up three blocks, and cross the highway on the pedestrian bridge. Rooms have mirrors galore, complimentary condoms, and the adult channel (singles 150 pesos; doubles 205 pesos). Both the TAPO and Poniente station are in exceedingly dubious neighborhoods. If you arrive at the **TAPO** (east station), take the Metro to the *centro,* and if you are at the **Terminal de Autobuses del Poniente** (western station), swing over to the Tacubaya Metro stop (Lines 1, 7, and 9) for the nearest hotels.

# ■ Food

Options fall into six basic categories: the very cheap (and sometimes risky) vendor stalls scattered about the streets; fast, inexpensive, and generally safe *taquerías;* slightly more formal *cafeterías;* more pricey and decorous Mexican restaurants; locally popular North-Americanized eateries; and expensive international fare. In addition, U.S. fast-food chains mass-produce predictable fare for the timid palate. **VIPS** offers 60 commercialized Denny's-like eateries throughout the D.F.; some are open 24 hours. If you're preparing your own food, local neighborhood markets and supermarkets stock almost anything you could need. For a good time, try **La Merced** market, the mother of all markets. As always, avoid unpurified water, including ice, uncooked or unpeeled vegetables, and meat that is not fully cooked. For more on this, see p. 23.

Soda is sold at every corner. *Agua mineral* means mineral water, *sidral* is a great carbonated apple drink, and *refrescos* are your standard soda. Perhaps the best way to combat thirst is through the delicious *aguas* sold everywhere, made with fresh fruit and sugar—just make sure the ice is purified. Bottles are recycled, and patrons pay extra for the privilege of keeping them.

## CENTRO

The historic downtown area of Mexico City offers a wide selection of food at super-low prices. Slick U.S. fast-food establishments, enormous *cafeterías,* and countless small eateries offer inexpensive *comida corridas,* tacos, *tortas,* and other staples. Also, there's plenty of good fare for vegetarians.

**Café Tacuba,** Tacuba 28 (tel. 518-49-50). Metro: Allende (Line 2). A bastion of excellent food and engaging conversation in the heart of downtown since 1912. A must. An amazing combo of camp and class—pure artisanship, brass pitchers, murals, and if you're lucky, men outside in colonial garb eager to greet you. *Antojitos* 15-42 pesos, entrees 28-45 pesos, breakfast specials 14-35 pesos. Be patient: all dishes are made from scratch, and they're well worth the wait. Open daily 8am-11:30pm.

**Comedor Vegetariano,** Motolinía 315, 2nd floor (tel. 512-65-75). Ask for directions. The Comedor will leave even herbophobes wantin' some watercress. The yellow Quixote-themed restaurant serves a scrumptious fruit buffet and a filling *menú del día* (22 pesos) on its balcony tables. Open Mon.-Fri. 1-6pm.

**Restaurante El Vegetariano,** Filomeno Mata 13 between 5 de Mayo and Madero (tel. 510-01-13). Shiny, happy, healthy, and sunshine-yellow eatery filled with an eclectic group of veggie lovers. Try the spaghetti with mushroom sauce (21 pesos), or the spinach salad (29 pesos). Open Mon.-Sat. 8am-8pm.

**Restaurant Danubio,** Uruguay 3, just east of Lázaro Cárdenas. Stately seafood joint boasts its own coat-of-arms and hefty price tags. Perenially packed, but the good food and drink ain't no laughing matter. Famous artsy types have left their scribbling framed on the walls. Entrees (25-40 pesos) and specials (36-75 pesos) are big enough for 2. Open daily 1-10pm.

**Súper Soya,** Tacuba 40 and several locations throughout the *centro.* A wildly colorful grocery store/cafe/diner/yogurt stand that has it all for under 15 pesos. Vegetarian pizzas 7 pesos, *tacos de guisado* 5 pesos. Open daily 9am-9pm.

**Restaurant Zenon,** Gante 15 at 16 de Septiembre (tel. 512-12-01), on the southern portion of Motolinía. Don't be fooled by the clean, modern interior of this place—excellent budget food lies inside. The *comida corrida* (23 pesos) and *cena y desayuno* (17 pesos) lure wise folk from all over the *centro.* Sample their speciality—*caldos* (4-10 pesos). Open daily 8am-10pm.

**Café Dayi,** Isabela la Católica 9-11 (tel. 521-62-03), near Tacuba. Watermelon-ish cafeteria decor is kitschy, but the food—both Chinese and Mexican—is excellent. Chicken and duck dishes 25 pesos; *comida corrida china y mexicana* 25 pesos. Don't be afraid to crane your neck to check out soccer on TV as aproned waitresses refill your *agua de sandía.* Open daily 7am-11pm.

## ZONA ROSA

The myth: only loaded tourists eat in the *Zona Rosa.* The reality: although the area has some of the city's more expensive restaurants, serving everything from international cuisine to traditional Mexican cooking, many eateries cater chiefly to clerks from the scores of surrounding office buildings. The *Zona Rosa* also has more fastfood joints than any other area of the city. If you're more interested in the *Zona Rosa's* slick party atmosphere than in filling your stomach, skip dinner and settle for a drawn-out evening appetizer.

**Ricocina,** Londres 168 (tel. 514-06-48), east of Florencia. This new family-owned restaurant, once the *Zona Rosa's* best-kept secret, is quickly becoming the joint *du jour.* Still, the food is the best around. Soft peach surroundings help you enjoy your delicious *menú del dia* (20 pesos). Open Mon.-Fri. 1-6pm, Sat. 9am-6pm.

**La Luna,** Oslo 11, on the narrow walkway between Niza and Copenhagen. Fresh flowers grace every table in this intimate, cozy restaurant. The *comida corrida* (14 pesos) includes soup, a small and a large entree, and beverage—a great budget value. Very popular; avoid the 2-3pm lunch rush. Open Mon.-Sat. 7am-9pm.

**Vegetariano Yug,** Varsovia 3 (tel. 525-5330), near Reforma. Dig the classy Indian furnishings, plants, and erotic (ay-yay-yay!) Hindu sculpture. Then sample the delicious spinach lasagna (20 pesos). *Menús del dia* (20-28) pesos and the fab buffet features bits of Indian, French, and other cuisine (32 pesos). Open daily 1-9pm.

**París 16 Café,** Reforma 368 (tel. 511-99-11). Piped-in jazz, sharp blue tiles contrasting with the white walls, and framed pencil sketches lend the cafe a very cosmopolitan feel. Devour the delicious potato chips that come with the *Ensalada París* (18 pesos) or a great deli sandwich (18-48 pesos). Open Mon.-Fri. 7:30am-5pm.

**La Mesa de Babette,** Reforma 408 (tel. 208-37-75), east of Florencia. Potted plants, a beautiful wood interior, colorful tablecloths, and seashell chairs create an elegant garden atmosphere. Breakfast all day long in four varieties: *rapidito, energético, clasico,* and *abundante* (all 15-30 pesos). Expensive but tasty *menú del dia* (40 pesos). Business folk take in live music at night. Open Mon.-Fri. 8am-midnight.

**Kai Lam,** Londres 114 (tel. 514-4837). This cute, homey restaurant serves both *comida mexicana* (16.50-19 pesos) and *comida china* (21-27 pesos). Open doors and central location make it a good place to chill. Open daily 10am-8pm.

## ALAMEDA CENTRAL

The convivial atmosphere that permeates the Alameda carries over to the various restaurants that pepper the area. Gone is the stuffy elitism of the *Zona Rosa* and the frenetic pace of the *centro.* Instead, you'll find good, cheap, back-to-basics food. For something a bit different, try one of the Chinese restaurants on Dolores, two blocks west of Cárdenas and one block south of the Alameda.

**Fonda Santa Anita,** Humboldt 48 (tel. 518-57-23). Metro: Hidalgo (Lines 2 and 3). Go 1 block south to Juárez, then 2 blocks west to the unlabeled Humboldt; it's 2 blocks down the street. A classic restaurant that has represented Mexico in 5 World's Fairs, this friendly eatery feels no need to dispel stereotypes—the tableclothes are bright red and colorful depictions of bullfights and busty women cover the walls. More importantly, it serves incredible versions of old standards, including enchiladas (16 pesos) and *comida corrida* (29 pesos). Open Mon.-Fri. 1-10pm.

**Centro Naturista de México,** Dolores 10 (tel. 512-53-77), ½ block south of Juárez near the southeast corner of the park, under the big yin-yang. A drab cafeteria-style vegetarian/egalitarian utopia. *Comida corrida* 15 pesos. Open daily 12:30-6:30pm.

**El Nuevo Canton,** on the corner of Dolores and Independencia (tel. 512-92-12), on a pedestrian walkway. Offers slightly lower prices than its competitors and huge portions. Big *cubierto ejecutivo* (executive lunch box)—5 courses for 35 pesos. Open daily 9am-10pm.

## NEAR THE MONUMENTO A LA REVOLUCIÓN

Without many affluent residents or big tourist draws, this area lacks the snazzy international cuisine of other areas. Instead, homey cafes, *torterías,* and *taquerías* abound. For hearty portions and low prices, this is your spot.

**La Especial de París,** Insurgentes Centro 117 (tel. 773-23-16). Oh! Yes! Yes! This *nevería* has been scooping up ecstasy since 1921. Lots of 100%-natural treats, ranging from *malteadas* (milkshakes) to *frutas glacé.* It's hopeless to order a single scoop—you'll claw your way back to the front of the line for seconds. Doubles 8 pesos, triples 11 pesos, 4 scoops 14 pesos.

**La Taberna,** Arriaga at Ignacio Mariscal (tel. 535-20-66), below street level. Next to Hotel Pennsylvania. The service is fast and the *ambiente* awesome. Whether you dine *económico* (15 pesos), *especial* (18 pesos), or *ejecutivo* (22 pesos), the four-course Italian *comida corrida* is sure to please. Open Mon.-Sat. 1-10pm.

**Restaurante Samy,** Ignacio Mariscal 42 (tel. 591-11-00). Business-class clientele is punctuated by lucky and delighted tourists who wander in. Sitting among suit-clad locals, eating *comida corrida* (17 pesos), and listening to the best of '80s soft rock, you're bound to have a deep moment. Open Mon.-Fri. 8am-6pm, Sat. 9am-6pm.

**Super Cocina Los Arcos,** Ignacio Mariscal at Iglesias. Homey, cozy atmosphere among bright orange furnishings. Service is a little slow, but it's worth it—their *alambres con queso* (17 pesos) are the best around. Many dishes 9-19 pesos. Open Mon.-Sat. 8am-11pm.

## NEAR CHAPULTEPEC

The immediate vicinity of the Bosque de Chapultepec is cluttered with vendors and small restaurants offering popular and mundane *tortas* and *super-tortas* (not for the weak of stomach). A bit farther east, however, lies a couple of more adventurous options easily accessible from the Metro Sevilla (Line 1). A ritzier alternative might be *antojitos* in beautiful Colonia Polanco, north of the Anthropology Museum, also accessible by Metro station Polanco (Line 7).

**Los Sauces,** Av. Chapultepec 530, at Acapulco Roma, 1½ blocks east of the Chapultepec Metro stop (Line 1). Uniquely tiled bar and grill cluttered with pictures of Mexican politicians and stars. Lots of choices regarding entertainment:

*telenovelas* on TV, blaring radio, or watching chefs chop onions and peppers to make your 8-peso taco special or 15-peso house speciality. Open daily 9am-9pm.

**Che Genalo,** Durango 279, near Cozumel (tel. 533-37-65). Ascend the stairs into this clean, small, white and blue restaurant that serves Argentinian food. While the famous beef dishes are 40 pesos, fluffy 8-peso *empanadas* and cheaper, lighter fare will make you dream of the Pampas. Open daily 1-10pm.

## COYOACÁN

The southern suburb of Coyoacán attracts students, young couples, and literati to its restaurants. If you crave brie, cheesecake, or pesto, spend an afternoon here. Outdoor cafes and ice cream shops fill the colonial buildings that line the cobbled streets. For some great ice cream, try **Santa Clara,** at Allende and Cuauhtémoc (9 pesos per scoop), and **La Siberia** on the northeast corner of Jardín Centenario (8 pesos per scoop, floats 11 pesos). For an excellent, authentic meal, try the **food court** on Mijuera, just south of Plaza Midalgo. Populated almost exclusively with locals, these tiny restaurants offer home-cooked food at un-Coyoacán-like prices (open Mon.-Sat. 9am-9pm).

**Café El Parnaso,** Carrillo Puerto 2, on Jardín Centenario across from the cathedral. A celebrated book and record store with an outdoor cafe in a prime locale on the plaza's edge. Although the food is a bit pricey, the people-watching and eavesdropping here are unbeatable. Have a coffee and a mocha cake or cheesecake with strawberries (12-16 pesos). Open daily 8:30am-10:30pm.

**El Morral,** Allende 2 (tel. 554-02-98), 1 block north of Pl. Hidalgo's northeast corner has beautifully tiled walls, artwork, and a glass roof, but the flashing cross almost goes over the top. A great tradition: Sunday after Sunday, Mexican families meet here for lengthy lunches. Although *comida corrida* is a whopping 42 pesos, pastas and *cazuelitas* hover in the teens. Open daily 7:30am-10pm.

**El Jarocho,** on Allende (tel. 554-54-18), 1 block north of Pl. Hidalgo. The aroma of freshly ground coffee and the long line will lead you to this corner stand serving some of the best java in the city. Americano, cappuccino, mocha, as well as hot chocolate, all under 4 pesos. Open daily 7am-midnight.

## SAN ÁNGEL

The chic restaurants and *típico* taco stands of San Ángel pack 'em in, especially on Saturdays, when crowds of well-to-do tourists and Mexicans flock to the booths of overpriced art in the Bazaar Sábado. If you want to dine in style and don't mind dropping some pesos, Plaza San Jacinto is the place to be.

**Chucho el Roto,** Madero 8, by the corner of the Bazar del Sábado. A budget gem situated steps from the action. Daytime diner serves up a *menú del día* of soup, rice, an entree, and dessert for 15 pesos. Entrees 17-25 pesos. Open daily 9am-5:30pm.

**Restaurante Hasti Bhawan: La Casona del Elefante,** Pl. San Jacinto 9 (tel. 616-22-08). Hindustani ambience and scrumptious fare. Indo-Thai chicken 34 pesos, vegetarian platter 30 pesos, *pakoras* or *samosas* 9 pesos. Treat yourself to a *lassi,* a thick yogurt drink (8 pesos). Live jazz Thurs.-Sat. nights. Open Tues.-Thurs. 2pm-midnight, Fri. 2pm-1am, Sat. 1pm-1am, Sun. 1-6:30pm.

**El Rincón de La Lechuza,** Miguel Ángel de Quevedo 34 (tel. 661-59-11), straight down from Metro station M. Á. Quevedo (Line 3), before the Parque de la Bombilla. Joyfully crowded and decorated in yellow and white with wood tables. Tasty tacos 12-18 pesos. Open Mon.-Thurs. 1pm-1am, Fri.-Sat. 1pm-2am, Sun. 1pm-midnight.

**La Finca,** on Madero right off the Pl. de San Jacinto (tel. 550-54-82). This hole-in-the-wall coffee stand serves only coffee that is 100% Mexican grown...and it kicks Colombia's ass. All mocha, espresso, and other pipin' hot treats under 5 pesos. If you're truly hard-core, check out the kilos of coffee beans (48-70 pesos), much of it grown in Chiapas (open daily 8am-8pm).

# ■ Sights

It would be impossible to find an appetite which couldn't be satiated by Mexico City's incredibly diverse range of sights and attractions. A well-rounded picture of Mexico City will require a week at the very least, but it would take a lifetime to truly learn this metropolis's ins and outs.

## CENTRO

The heart of Mexico City, the *centro*, is in some ways at the heart of the Republic as well. The *centro*'s most impressive structures, the **Palacio Nacional** and the **Catedral Metropolitana,** are guaranteed to bowl over tourists with their enormity and beauty. Like a larger-than-life embodiment of Mexico's story, the temples of the old Aztec capital of Tenochtitlán, the Catholic cathedral, and the Palacio Nacional all stand side by side. Sometimes crowded, sometimes deserted, sometimes parched with heat, and sometimes flooding with rain, the *zócalo* and its surrounding area are completely intoxicating.

To reach the *zócalo* by Metro, take Line 2 to Zócalo. The station's entrance sits on the east side of the square, in front of the Palacio Nacional. The Catedral Metropolitana lies to the north, the Federal District offices to the south, and the Suprema Corte de Justicia (Supreme Court) to the southeast.

### The *Zócalo*

Officially the **Plaza de la Constitución,** the *zócalo* is the principal square of Mexico City. Now surrounded by imposing colonial monuments, the plaza was once the nucleus of **Tenochtitlán,** the Aztec island-capital. Cortés's men razed the city and atop the ruins they built the power center from which they would rule New Spain (see p. 71 and p. 53). To the southwest of the **Templo Mayor** (the Aztecs' principal place of worship, which they called Teocalli) was the Aztec marketplace and major square. The space was rebuilt and renamed several times, becoming the Plaza de la Constitución in 1812. In 1843, the dictator Santa Anna ordered that a monument to independence be constructed in the center of the square. Only the monument's *zócalo* (pedestal) was in place when the project was abandoned. The citizens of Mexico City began to refer to the square as **el zócalo,** which has become the generic name for the central plazas which mark most of the cities and towns in grand ol' Mexico.

These days, labor rallies and booming megaphones electrify the plaza. Street vendors, selling everything from hard liquor to holy water, hawk their wares along the square. Unemployed men sit by the cathedral holding crudely written paper signs describing their skills and hoping to be approached by an employer. The *zócalo* can be hectic and confusing at times, but it never ceases to inspire. At night the *zócalo* is deserted and dreamlike. The surrounding buildings light up and it's hard to imagine that the day's activity could have taken place in this enormous, empty square.

### East of the *Zócalo*

Stretching the entire length of the enormous *zócalo*, the **Palacio Nacional** is a sight to behold. Over 200m long, this regal mammoth of a government palace is as over-the-top as Mexico City itself. Cower before it, worthless peon. It's hard to believe the Palacio could have ever been anything else. Its history, however, is more fantastic and fairy tale-ish than the armed guards standing outside would ever lead one to believe. Completely demolished during the riots of 1692, the *palacio* had been the site of an Aztec ruler's (Moctezuma II) palace, Hernán Cortés's house, and the palace of the king of Spain's viceroys. Now the Chief executive center of the Republic, the Palacio houses monumental murals and a museum in honor of Benito Juárez.

It took Diego Rivera from 1929 to 1951 to sketch and paint the **frescoes** on the Palacio's western and northern walls. *Mexico Through the Centuries,* one of his most famous works, is on the west wall of the Palacio at the top of the grand staircase. The mural is divided into eight smaller scenes, each of which depicts an event in the social history of Mexico. Each of the five arches at the top of the mural deals with the Mexican nation—from the beginning of the fight for independence in 1810 up to the start of the Mexican Revolution in 1910. These colorful, larger-than-life murals tackle such varied themes as the horror of the slave trade, the early-20th-century class struggle, and the legendary Aztec priest-king Quetzalcóatl. At times, his murals look like an illustrated *Who's Who?* of famous people. Look for his famous wife Frida Kahlo hidden in the frescoes. Guides to the murals wait at the central staircase trying to charge exorbitant fees. Ask local officials and tourist guides about standard guides and tours. You should be able to get a guided tour (Mon.-Fri. 10am-4pm) for 60-70 pesos. Then again, joining a tour that has already begun is free.

The Palacio also contains the **Bell of Dolores,** which was brought to the capital in 1896 from Dolores Hidalgo, in Guanajuato state. It can be seen from outside, at the top of the Palacio's Baroque facade. Miguel Hidalgo rang this bell on September 16, 1810, summoning Mexicans to fight for their independence. Every year on that date it rings in memory of the occasion, and the Mexican President repeats the words once shouted by the father of independence (Palacio open daily 8am-6pm).

On the east side of the Palacio's second floor is the **Museo del Recinto del Parliamento,** dedicated to the one and only Benito Juárez. The museum is rather small and dry, but an excellent re-creation of the legislative chamber used during the drafting of the 1857 constitution lies inside (open Mon.-Fri. 9am-8pm, Sat. 9am-5:30pm).

Sprawling over 600 square blocks, **La Merced,** Circunvalación east of the *zócalo* (Metro: Merced, Line 1, turn left out of the subway's eastern exit), is the largest food market of its kind in the world. You'll find every kind of fruit imaginable—papayas, homegrown litchi nuts, delicious salmon-colored *mameyes,* mangoes, at least nine different kinds of *plátanos* (bananas), hot tamales, and two full blocks of assorted chiles. Indigenous foods such as fried turtles, steamed chicken intestines, *charales*—corn husks stuffed with shiners—and steamed crayfish abound. Die of happiness in the **Mercado de Dulcer,** part of La Merced. You'll drool faster than Pavlov's poodle among the displays of sweet-smelling *dulces* (candies) that stretch for five blocks.

### North of the *Zócalo*

In the wake of Cortés's military triumphs, a land devoted to Quetzalcóatl, Tlaloc, and Huitzilopochtli became a stronghold of Christianity. The third cathedral built in New Spain was the **Catedral Metropolitana** (tel. 521-76-37), the massive structure on the north side of the *zócalo,* a mishmash of architectural styles from three different centuries that still turned out beautiful. Construction started in 1562, but wasn't completed until 1813. Modeled after the cathedral in Sevilla, Spain, its scalloped walls and high arches give it a Moorish feel. Unfortunately, the splendor of the cathedral is occluded by the green support structures placed to combat the destruction caused to the floor as the temple, along with the rest of the city, sinks into the murky ground. Ongoing renovations mean scaffolding and partitions occasionally obscure parts of both the exterior and the interior. If you use your imagination and block out the ugly green and yellow supports, the cathedral still glows.

The cathedral has several attached annexes. The main annex, with its door to the left of the cathedral, holds the **Altar de Perdón** (Forgiveness), a replica of a Churrigueresque altarpiece built by Jerónimo de Balbás between 1731 and 1736 and destroyed by fire in 1967. The cedar interior of the choir gallery, constructed in 1695 by Juan de Rojas, boasts an elegant grille of gold, silver, and bronze and Juan Correa's murals of dragon-slaying and prophet-hailing cover the sacristy walls. Perhaps the most magnificent part of the *catedral* is the **Altar de los Reyes,** which is dedicated to those kings who were also saints. Two chapels near the entrance honor Mexico's patron, the Virgin of Guadalupe (also honored in the **Basilica de Guadalupe,** see p. 106). Mass takes place almost hourly on weekends—visitors should take extra care to show respect and be silent during these times (exact schedules posted on western-most door; open daily 10am-6pm).

According to myth, Tenochtitlán was the first place that the Aztecs, having wandered for hundreds of years, could call home, arriving at this spot when, as the war god Huitzilopochtli predicted, they saw an eagle perched on a cactus eating a snake (see the Mexican flag and p. 52). The **Templo Mayor (Teocalli)** was the center of Aztec worship in their new home. On the corner of Seminario and República de Guatemala, Teocalli is now an astonishingly huge excavated archaeological site in the middle of the world's largest city. The ruins are just east of the cathedral and north of the Palacio Nacional. At first, the huge site appears to be little more than the foundation of a demolished modern complex. Before making any judgments, however, have a look inside. The excavated ruins reveal five layers of pyramids, each one built on top of the other as the Aztec empire grew.

Over 7000 artifacts, including sculpture, jewelry, and pottery, have been found amid the ruins. The extraordinary **Museo del Templo Mayor** (tel. 542-06-06), now part of the archaeological complex, houses this unique collection. A must-see stop even for visitors on a whirlwind tour of Mexico City, the museum is divided into eight *salas* (halls) to imitate the layout of the original temple, and is constructed so that the artifacts found in the excavation are accompanied not only by dry museum inscriptions, but also excerpts from the ancient Aztec texts which describe them (museum and ruins open Tues.-Sun. 9am-5pm; guided tours in Spanish free, in English 10 pesos per person; admission 16 pesos, 10-peso fee to take pictures, free Sun. and for children under 13).

### South of the Zócalo

Built in 1929, the **Suprema Corte de Justicia** stands on the corner of Pino Suárez and Corregidora, on the spot where the southern half of Moctezuma's royal palace once stood. Aside from the spectacle of manacled foreigners pleading that they don't know who planted the weed in their socks, the Supreme Court draws tourists because of its murals. Four frightening murals by José Clemente Orozco cover the second-floor walls of the present day Supreme Court. Filled with roaring tigers, masked evildoers, bolts of hellish flame, and a bad-ass Mr. Justice himself wielding a huge axe, the murals are not to be missed. If nothing else, they'll make you think twice about breaking the law (murals can be viewed by appointment only, call 522-15-00 Mon.-Fri. 10am-2pm to schedule a visit; lucky visitors should be able to wheel and deal their way in any time of the day, provided a really big case is not being tried).

The **Museo de la Ciudad de México,** Pino Suárez 30 at República del Salvador (tel. 542-04-87), three blocks south of the *zócalo*'s southeast corner, is small and somewhat disappointing. The collection of indigenous pottery and colonial wares is great, but unfortunately much of the museum is being renovated and closed to the public. Still, the spacious courtyard makes it a good place to catch a breather and the store has excellent information not only on the city, but on all of Mexico (museum and store open Tues.-Sun. 10am-6pm; free).

## ALAMEDA

The area around the Alameda Central is doubly blessed, filled with must-see sights and easily accessible by public transportation. It's also within walking distance of the *centro* and Monumento a la Revolución. Near the park are three Metro stations: Hidalgo (Lines 2 and 3), at the intersection of Hidalgo and Paseo de la Reforma, one block west from the park; Bellas Artes (Lines 2 and 8), one block east of the park's northeast corner, between the park and Bellas Artes itself; and San Juan de Letrán (Line 8), one block south of the *Torre Latinoamericana.*

### Alameda Central

Amid the howling sprawl that is downtown Mexico City, the Alameda is a verdant oasis of sanity and photosynthesis. But while the Alameda can feel like an island, it is not impervious to the urban life which bustles all around it—three major thoroughfares (Avenidas Hidalgo, Juárez, and Lázaro Cárdenas) flank the Alameda and the park is packed with mimes, young lovers, protesters, and *comerciantes* hawking their wares. The Alameda was designed several hundred years ago by Don Luis de Velasco

II, who intended it as a place for the wealthy to relax and stroll. The park takes its name from the rows of shady *alamos* (poplars) which flood it. Since it was opened to the public in this century, Mexico City has fallen in love with the park. Mexicans of all sorts enjoy the Alameda, and even in a city where real-estate values have soared and over-crowding is endemic, no one even considers paving over the park.

At the center of the Alameda's southern side is the **Monumento a Juárez,** a semi-circular marble monument constructed in 1910 to honor the revered former president on the 100th anniversary of Mexican Independence. A somber-faced Juárez sits on a central pedestal among 12 doric columns. On July 19 of each year, a civic ceremony commemorates the anniversary of Juárez's death.

## Palacio de Bellas Artes

This impressive white Art Nouveau palace, located at Juárez and Eje Central, at the northeast corner of Alameda Central, is perhaps one of the most obvious (and one of the only) beautiful things to come out of Porfirio Díaz's dictatorship (1876-1911). Soon after construction began, the theater started to sink into the city's soft ground—it now lies tens of meters lower than when it was built. Most tourists, however, come to the palace to see the second and third floors, where the walls have been painted by the most celebrated Mexican muralists and national Cristóbal of the 20th century. If you have time for only one mural, see Diego Rivera's, on the west wall of the third floor. John D. Rockefeller commissioned Rivera to paint a mural with the topic "Man at Crossroads Looking with Hope and High Vision to the Choosing of a New and Better Future" in New York City's Rockefeller Center. Rivera, however, was dismissed from the project when Rockefeller discovered Lenin's portrait in the foreground. The Mexican government allowed Rivera to duplicate the work in the Palacio. The result, *El Hombre, Controlador del Universo, 1934,* includes an unflattering portrayal of John D. Rockefeller, looking like a mad scientist, his hands on various instruments of technology designed to rule the world. The second floor also has a space for temporary exhibits, usually for artists of international fame and repute.

On the east wall of the third floor, murals by the leftist José Clemente Orozco depict the supposed tension between natural human characteristics and industrialization. In addition to Orozco's work, the Palacio displays the frescoes of David Alfaro Siqueiros, the 20th-century Mexican muralist, Stalinist, nationalist, and would-be assassin of Leon Trotsky. Look for his work on the third floor of the Palacio. Like his contemporary Diego Rivera, Siqueiros favored themes of class struggle and social injustice and flaunted a cavalier disregard for topical subtlety. His *Tormento de Cuauhtémoc* describes Cortés's attack on the last vestiges of the Aztec nation. On the fourth floor of the palace is the **Museo Nacional de Arquitectura** (tel. 709-31-11). It exhibits early sketches and blueprints for the most architecturally distinctive buildings in the city, including the Teatro Nacional, the monument to the Revolution, and the Palacio itself (complex open Tues.-Sun. 10am-6pm; admission 10 pesos to see the murals and art exhibits on the upper floors, free for students and teachers with ID; temporary exhibits on the first floor are generally free).

The **Ballet Folklórico de México** performs regional dances in the Palacio de Bellas Artes and the **Teatro Ferrocarrilero** (tel. 529-17-01), near the Revolución Metro station. Their two companies, one resident and one traveling, are world-renowned for their choreographic and theatrical skill. Their program combines the beauty of folk and *indígena* dancing with the formal aspects of traditional ballet. Bellas Artes performances are the only way to see the crystal curtain designed by Gerardo Murelli, made up of almost one million pieces of multicolored crystal which, when illuminated from behind, represent the Valley of Mexico in twilight. The Bellas Artes ticket office sells tickets for these and other artistic performances throughout the city (open Mon.-Sun. 11am-7pm). Travel agencies snatch up lots of tickets during Christmas, Semana Santa, and summer; check first at Bellas Artes, then try along Reforma or in the *Zona Rosa* (performances Wed. 8:30pm, Sun. 9:30am and 8:30pm; tickets 120, 180, and 220 pesos; sold 3 or 4 days in advance at Bellas Artes, but usually available Mon.-Sat. 11am-3pm and 5-7pm, Sun. 9am-1pm and 4-7pm).

## Museo Nacional de Arte

The **Museo Nacional de Arte,** Tacuba 8 (tel. 512-32-24), half a block east of the Palacio's north side, was built during the Porfiriato to house the Secretary of Communications. The building's architect, Silvio Conti, paid particular attention to the central staircase—its sculpted Baroque handrails were crafted by artists in Florence. The museum is not as frequented as the Palacio or other nearby *museos,* despite its enormity. Because of this, and its spacious design, the museum has an empty feel, and footsteps echo through the galleries. The museum contains works from the stylistic and ideological schools of every era in Mexican history. Look for Guerra's *Monumento a José Martí,* a celebration not only of the young revolutionary's life, but also of color and space. The upper floors exhibit art ranging from Greek and biblical themes to 17th- and 18th-century historical depictions. If none of this appeals to you, check the list of *salas* downstairs. With everything from *arte modernismo cosmopolitán* to *arte fantástico,* there's at least one *sala* just right for you (open Tues.-Sun. 10am-5:30pm; admission 10 pesos, free Sun. and for students and teachers with ID, adults over 60, and children under 13).

# NEAR ALAMEDA CENTRAL

## West of the Alameda

The awesome **Museo Mural Diego Rivera** (formerly known as **Museo de la Alameda;** tel. 512-07-54), on Calzada Colón and Balderas, facing the small park at the west end of the Alameda, holds Diego Rivera's masterpiece, *Sueño de un Tarde Dominical en la Alameda Central* (Sunday Afternoon Dream at the Alameda Central). The work was originally comissioned by the Hotel del Prado in 1946, but when the hotel proudly hung the just-finished work in 1948, a national controversy ensued over the figure of Ignacio Ramírez, who is shown holding up a pad of paper that reads "God does not exist," an excerpt from a speech he gave in 1836. The archbishop of Mexico refused to bless the hotel, and on June 4th at dawn, more than 100 angry students broke into the hotel, erased the "does not exist" fragment from the original phrase and damaged the face of the young Diego Rivera in the center of the mural. After the 1985 quake, the mural was moved to the museum, which was constructed solely to showcase this piece. The key in front of the mural points out the portrayal of historical figures woven into the crowd: Frida Kahlo, José Martí, and a chubby young Rivera, among others. José Guadalupe Posada's *La Calavera Catrina,* the central figure in the mural (that smiling skeleton wearing the boa), mocks the aristocratic pretentions under the Díaz presidency. Along with the mural, the museum displays original clippings of 1948 describing the vandalism and Rivera's original notes regarding plans for the reconstruction (museum open daily 10am-6pm; admission 7 pesos, free Sun. and for students and teachers with ID).

The **Pinacoteca Virreinal de San Diego,** Dr. Mora 7 (tel. 510-27-93), next door to Centro Cultural José Martí, to the immediate west of the Alameda, was once a church and convent. Now the humongous rooms with high, decorated ceilings and wooden floors contain an extensive collection of Baroque and Mannerist paintings (open Tues.-Sun. 9am-5pm; admission 7 pesos, free Sun. and for students with ID).

A poet, José Martí was a leader of the Cuban independence movement in the late 19th century. He dreamed of a united and free Latin America, led by Mexico, and repeatedly warned of the dangers of North American imperialism. Martí's visionary poetry figures prominently at the **Centro Cultural José Martí,** Dr. Mora 2 at Hidalgo (tel. 521-21-15), on the Alameda's west end. Covering three walls of the building is a rainbow-colored mural depicting Marti's poetry as well as Marti himself and the people of Latin America. A tally sheet in the corner of the mural records Spanish, British, French, and U.S. interventions in Latin America from 1800-1969; the grand total is a staggering 784 (open Mon.-Fri. 9am-9pm, Sat. 10am-5pm; free).

### East of the Alameda

The second-tallest building in the city, the **Torre Latinoamericana,** 181m and 44 stories high, touches the sky over the corner of Lázaro Cárdenas and Madero (the continuation of Juárez), one block east of Alameda Central's southeast corner. Its 44th-floor observatory, a good 2422m above sea level, commands a startling view of the sprawling city. At night, the *torre* is positively sexy, with city lights sparkling for miles in every direction (top-floor observatory open daily 9:30am-11pm; admission 22 pesos, 18 pesos for children under 12, telescope fee 2 pesos). The 38th floor holds the gimmicky **"highest aquarium in the world"** (open daily 10am-10pm; admission 15 pesos, children 12 pesos).

Built in 1716, **La Iglesia de San Francisco** rests in the shadow of the Torre Latinoamericana, just to the east on Madero. It was once a vast Franciscan complex that included several churches, a school, and a hospital. Two fragments of the original cloisters can be seen at Gante 5, on the east side of the church, and Lázaro Cárdenas 8, behind a vacant lot. The Franciscans were the first order to arrive in Mexico and quickly succeeded in gaining converts through their faith and dedication (open Mon.-Fri. 9am-1pm and 5-7pm, Sat. 9am-1pm).

Across the street from San Francisco shimmers the delicate **Casa de los Azulejos,** an early 17th-century building covered with *azulejos* (blue and white tiles) from Puebla. To be able to afford even a token few of these tiles was a mark of considerable status. This mansion was festooned by an insulted son who set out to prove his worth to his father. There is an Orozco mural on the staircase wall, and a great view of the building can be had from the second-floor balcony. Go through **Sanborn's** to view them (both Sanborn's and the building open daily 7:30am-10pm).

**Palacio Iturbide** at Madero 17 between Bolívar and Gante (tel. 521-57-97), one and a half blocks east of Lázaro Cárdenas and near the Iglesia de San Francisco, is a grand 18th-century palace with an impressive colonnaded courtyard. A great place to chill, the Palacio in recent years has been taken over by Banamex (Banco de México); before that it was the residence of Mexico's old Emperor, the despotic Agustín Iturbide. Symbolism, anyone? There is a gallery on the ground floor; exhibitions change every three months (open daily 9am-2pm and 4-6pm).

### North of the Alameda

One of the loveliest sights in this area is the **Museo Franz Mayer,** Hidalgo 45 (tel. 518-22-66), at Plaza de Santa Veracruz. Formerly the Hospital de San Juan de Dios, the building has been expertly restored and now houses an extensive collection of ceramics, colonial furniture, and religious paintings. Plush, red velvet, gleaming display cases, and ultra-professional staff makes wandering through the lavish display cases a joy. The first-floor exhibit of colonial processional and ceremonial crosses is neat-o (open Tues.-Sun. 10am-5pm; admission 8 pesos, 2 pesos for students with ID, half-price Sun.; guided tours Tues.-Fri. 10am-2pm). Next door to the Franz Mayer museum in the pink building at Hidalgo 39 (tel. 521-22-24) is the **Museo Nacional de la Estampa.** Here lies the National Institute of Fine Arts's graphic arts and engraving collection, tracing the art of printmaking from pre-Hispanic seals to contemporary engravings. The highlight of the museum is the work of the acclaimed José Guadalupe Posada, Mexico's foremost engraver and print-maker. His woodcuts depict skeletons dancing, singing, and cavorting in ridiculous costumes—a truly graphic indictment of the Porfiriato's excesses (open Tues.-Sun. 10am-6pm; admission 8 pesos, free Sun. and for students with ID).

### Near the Monumento A La Revolución

At the Plaza de la República under the **Monumento a la Revolución** is the **Museo Nacional de la Revolución** (tel. 546-21-15). Díaz originally planned the site as the seat of Congress, but as revolutionary fighting entered the city streets, progress was halted, and the dome was left only half-completed. It wasn't until the 1930s that the monument and space below were finally dedicated to the memory of the revolution. Today, 32 flag poles representing the Mexican states line the pathway to this marmoreal dome. The entrance to the 11-year-old museum's subterranean exhibition is just northeast of the monument, in a black-stone park. Just inside the doors, a thorough chronology of the revolution unfolds (in Spanish; museum open Tues.-Sat. 9am-5pm, Sun. 9am-3pm; 5 pesos, 2.50 pesos for students and teachers with ID; call to arrange for a tour).

The **Museo San Carlos** (tel. 566-85-22), at the corner of Puente de Alvarado and Ramos Arizpe, three blocks north of the Monumento a la Revolución, houses an old art school and an impressive collection of European painting spanning the 16th to 19th centuries. The exciting, eclectic museum features excellent work by minor artists, as well as standards by artists like Rubens and Goya. Temporary exhibits often highlight certain themes in post-Renaissance European art (open Tues.-Sun. 10am-6pm; admission 7 pesos, free Sun. and for students with ID).

In a beautiful glass and steel building is the relatively tourist-free **Museo del Chopo,** Dr. Enrique Gonzalez Marinez 10, two and a half blocks from the Puente de Alvarado between San Cosme and Nervo. The modern, friendly Chopo (as it's commonly called) hosted one of Mexico's first full-scale uncensored exhibits on gay and lesbian art and artists in the summer of 1997. This month-long exhibit of passionate photos, sculpture, and photography brought Chopo national attention, not all of it positive. Still, this avant-garde museum keeps on truckin' (open Tues.-Sun. 10am-2pm and 3-6pm; admission 4 pesos, 2 pesos for students with ID, Tues. free).

## BOSQUE DE CHAPULTEPEC

Mexico City has to do everything a little bigger and better than everywhere else, and this, D.F.'s major park and recreational area, is no exception. Literally "Forest of Grasshoppers," this 1000-acre green expanse on the western side of the *centro* is the biggest urban-situated park in all the Americas and also one of the older natural parks in the New World. With its manifold museums, hiking paths, zoos, bikes, amusement parks, castles, balloon vendors, and modern sports facilities, one could easily spend several days in the Bosque. Mexico's most famous museum, the **Museo Nacional de Antropología,** sits among the hills of the park.

The area suffers from occasional patches of trash, and, although it is relatively safe during the day, women should remain alert and should avoid the more remote or isolated areas of the park, especially the southern area of the park, after nightfall. Despite these features, on the right sort of day the Bosque can be downright wonderful. Try to visit on Sunday, when families flock here for cheap entertainment. Musical spectacles and open-air concerts enliven the park. Best of all, the zoo and most of the museums in the area are **free** on Sundays (everything open daily 5am-5pm).

All the museums and sights listed are in Old Chapultepec, the eastern half of the park, which fans out to the west of the *Zona Rosa*. To reach the park, take the Metro to Auditorio (Line 7, closer to the **zoo**) or to Chapultepec (Line 1, closer to the **Niños Héroes** monument, and most of the museums, and generally more convenient).

### Museo Nacional de Antropología

Some journey to Mexico just to consult this magnificent and massive mega-museum, considered by many to be the best in the world. Located at Paseo de la Reforma and Gandhi (tel. 553-62-66), this mini-universe houses 4km of Mexico's most exquisite archaeological and ethnographic treasures and is the yardstick by which all other Mexican museums are measured. Constructed of volcanic rock, wood, and marble, the museum opened in 1964. A huge stone image of the four-eyed rain god Tlaloc hails you outside, and 23 exhibition halls await within. Poetry from ancient texts and epics graces the entrances from the main courtyard. In the center of the courtyard, a stout column covered with symbolic carvings supports a vast, water-spouting aluminum pavilion. Although guards may give you menacing looks, it is quite all right to run through this refreshing inverted fountain—as long as you don't look like you're going to stay and bathe.

You would need about three days to pay homage to the entire museum, though some are afflicted with pottery overload after a few hours. As you enter on the right side of the ground floor, a general introduction to anthropology precedes a series of chronologically arranged galleries; moving from the right to the left wings of the building means advancing chronologically. These trace the histories of many central Mexican groups, from the first migrations to the Americas up to the Spanish Conquest. The Oaxacan, Maya, Gulf Coast, Northern, and Western displays are on the left (southern) side. Among the highlights, not to be missed: the **Sala Teotihuacana,** with detailed models of the amazing city of Teotihuacán; the **Sala Maya,** with a model of the tomb of King Pakal, the **Sala Toltec,** with huge statues of Quetzalcóatl; and the museum's crown jewel, the **Sala Mexica,** with the dazzling and famous **Aztec Calendar Stone (Sun Stone),** featuring Tonatiuh, the Aztec god of the sun, tongue stuck out, in the middle of it all. Upper-level rooms contain modern ethnographic displays. The museum also contains a **restaurant** (open Tues.-Sun. 9am-6pm) and a large **bookshop** that sells English guides to archaeological sites around the country, as well as histories and ethnographies of Mexico's indigenous populations. Some of these guides are not available at the sites themselves, so plan ahead (museum open Tues.-Sat. 8am-7pm, Sun. 10am-6pm; admission 16 pesos, free Sun.; still cameras 20 pesos, video cameras 30 pesos).

To reach the museum, take bus 55 or 76 southwest on Reforma and signal the driver to let you off at the second stop after entering the park. On the Metro, take Line 7 to the Auditorio station; the museum is just east down Reforma. Take the first left on Gandhi for the main entrance. For a more scenic route, take Line 1 to Chapultepec station.

At the end of the long walkway just inside the park on the east side stands the **Monumento a los Niños Héroes,** six white pillars capped with monoliths and teased by small fountains. The monument is dedicated to the young cadets of the 19th-century military academy, then at the **Castillo de Chapultepec.** In 1847, during the last major battle of the war with the U.S., the Niños Héroes fought the invading army of General Winfield Scott. Refusing to surrender, the last five boys and their lieutenant are said to have wrapped themselves in the Mexican flag before throwing themselves from the castle wall. To the side of the monument is the **Tree of Moctezuma,** boasting a circumference of 13m and reputed to have been around since the time of the Aztecs. Behind the monument, Gran Av. cuts through the park. Walk west on this street and take the second right on Gandhi. A five-minute stroll north takes you to Reforma and the museum.

## Museo Tamayo and Museo de Arte Moderno

Just to the east of the Museo Nacional de Antropología is the **Museo Tamayo de Arte Contemporáneo** (tel. 286-65-19), on the corner of Reforma and Gandhi, better known as the **Museo Rufino Tamayo.** The museum is hidden by the vegetation and therefore easy to miss. Take the first right on Gandhi from the Chapultepec Metro stop (Line 1). After a five-minute walk on Gandhi, the museum lies to the left down a small, almost hidden, path through the trees. Alternatively, walk due east from the entrance of the anthropology museum down the path into the woods; Tamayo is 100m straight ahead. The Mexican government created the nine halls of the museum after Rufino and Olga Tamayo donated their international collection to the Mexican people. The murals of Rufino Tamayo were much criticized in the wake of the Revolution of 1910 for not being sufficiently nationalistic. Since the museum's opening in 1981, however, his reputation has been rehabilitated and he has taken his place with Rivera, Siqueiros, and Orozco as one of the omnipresent badboys of modern Mexican art. The museum, opened in 1981, houses a large permanent collection of Tamayo's work, as well as important works by Willem de Kooning and Surrealists Joan Miró and Max Ernst. Although some of the *salas* are currently closed for renovation, the museum is still stellar; be sure to check out the temporary exhibitions by top international artists and filmmakers (open Tues.-Sun. 10am-5:45pm; admission 10 pesos, free Sun. and for students and teachers with ID; call to arrange guided tours).

The **Museo de Arte Moderno,** at Reforma and Gandhi (tel. 553-62-33), north of the Monumento a los Niños Héroes, houses a fine collection of contemporary paintings by Kahlo, Siqueiros, José Luis Cuevas, Rivera, Orozco, Velasco, and other up-and-coming, extremely talented Mexican artists. The museum is linked to the **Galería Fernando Camboa**—a very modern assemblage of sculptures and exhibitions—by a remarkable outdoor sculpture garden with pieces by Moore, Giacometti, and others (open Tues.-Sun. 10am-6pm; admission 10 pesos, free Sun. and for students and teachers with ID).

## Museo Nacional de Historia

Inside the Castillo de Chapultepec, on top of the hill behind the Monumento a los Niños Héroes, is the **Museo Nacional de Historia** (tel. 286-0700), which narrates the history of Mexico from before the time of the Conquest. An immense portrait of King Ferdinand and Queen Isabella of Spain greets visitors in the first *sala* before they meander through the excellent exhibits on the not-so-distant past. Galleries contain displays on Mexican economic and social structure during the war for independence, the Porfiriato, and the Revolution. The particularly interesting upper level exhibits Mexican art and dress from the viceroyalty through the 20th century. The walls of *Sala* 13 are completely covered by Siqueiros's *Del Porfirismo a la Revolución,* a pictorial cheat-sheet to modern Mexican history. To get to the top, walk up the road directly behind the Niños Héroes monument. Admission to the museum also allows you a peek at some of the castle's interior (open Tues.-Sun. 9am-5pm, tickets sold until 4pm; admission 14 pesos, bring change, free Sun., but all 2nd-floor *salas* are closed; video 10 pesos; camera 5 pesos).

## Museo del Caracol

The **Museo Galería de la Lucha del Pueblo Mexicano por su Libertad** (The Museum of the Struggle of the Mexican People for Liberty, tel. 553-62-85), is on the southern side of Chapultepec hill. The museum is often listed as **Galería de Historia** or even more commonly as **Museo del Caracol** (Snail) because of its spiral design. The gallery consists of 12 halls dedicated to the greatest hits of Mexican history from the early 19th to the early 20th century. A lengthy quotation at the entrance urges visiting Mexicans to live up to the legacy embodied in the museum. There's some heavy symbolism going on here; as you spiral downward through the museum's halls, so does Mexican history, courtesy of foreign intervention. From the start of your downward spiral, the gist of the museum's message is clear: foreign intervention has made Mexico's fight for liberty an uphill battle. Especially interesting are exhibitions on the executions of Hidalgo and Morelos, the execution of Maximilian, and the battles of Villa, Zapata, and Obregón. The museum's exhibitions consist of amazingly lifelike minidioramas, scores of paintings, and various other historical artifacts. Visitors unfamiliar with the contours of Mexican history, however, will be bewildered by the Spanish-only explanations. The staircase leads to a beautiful, round, skylit hall, the sides of which form the inner wall of the spiral you've been ascending. Also inside is a copy of the Constitution of 1917 handwritten by Venustiano Carranza himself (open Tues.-Sat. 9am-4:30pm, Sun. 10am-3:30pm; admission 7 pesos, free Sun.).

## Elsewhere in Chapultepec

Twenty-five days before his death in January, 1974, famed fanatic, muralist, and would-be Trotsky assassin David Álfaro Siqueiros donated his house and studio to the people of Mexico. In compliance with his will, the government created the **Museo Sala de Arte Público David Álfaro Siqueiros,** Tres Picos 29 (tel. 531-33-94), at Hegel just outside the park. Walk north from the Museo Nacional de Antropología to Rubén Darío. The street Tres Picos forks off to the northwest on the left; follow it for one block. The quirky little museum is on the right. Siqueiros was not only an artist, but also a revolutionary soldier, propagandist, communist, republican, Stalinist, and antifascist. Fifteen thousand murals, lithographs, photographs, drawings, and documents recount his fascinating life (open Mon.-Fri. 10am-2pm and 5-7pm, Sat. 10am-2pm; admission 7 pesos, students with ID 3 pesos, free Sun; call to arrange a guided tour).

West of the Siqueiros museum along Rubén Darío, at the intersection with Reforma, is the **Jardín Escultórico,** a sculpture park containing realist and symbolist statues. To the south and east of the sculpture garden, at Reforma and Av. Heroico Colegio Militar, flourishes the **Jardín Botánico,** a botanical garden with a little lake (open daily 9am-5pm; free). The big lake is the **Lago de Chapultepec,** situated at the heart of the park. It has rowboats for rent (open daily 7:30am-4:30pm; 10 pesos per hr.). Or, make a bee line for **Parque Zoológico de Chapultepec,** just east of the Jardín Botánico. Although animal lovers might shed a tear or two over some of the humbler habitats, the zoo is surprisingly excellent, mostly shunning the small-cage approach for larger, more amenable tracts of land. Everyone's favorites—those huggable **panda bears**—have survived quite well here (open Wed.-Sun. 9am-4:45pm; free).

## TLATELOLCO

Archaeological work has shown that the city of Tlatelolco ("Mound of Sand" in Náhuatl) existed long before the great Aztec capital of Tenochtitlán. By 1463, the Tlatelolco king, Moquíhuix, had built his city into a busy trading center coveted by the Aztec ruler, Axayácatl. Tension mounted over territorial and fishing boundaries, and soon Moquíhuix learned that the Aztecs were preparing to attack his city. Even forewarned, Moquíhuix couldn't handle the Aztec war machine, and Tlatelolco was absorbed into the huge empire.

Today, a monstrous state low-income housing project looms over the 17th-century church that stands on the grounds of Tlatelolco's ancient temple. Three cultures—ancient Aztec, colonial Spanish, and modern Mexican—have left their mark on this square, giving rise to the name **Plaza de las Tres Culturas,** at the corner of Lázaro Cárdenas and Ricardo Flores Magón, 13 blocks north of the Palacio de Bellas Artes. Today the three "cultures" are emblematized by ancient ruins, a mammoth church, and the nearby ultra-modern Ministry of Foreign Affairs, also known as the **Relaciones Exteriores** building.

With stoic optimism, a plaque in the southwest corner of the plaza asserts: "On August 13, 1521, heroically defended by Cuauhtémoc, Tlatelolco fell to Hernán Cortés. It was neither a triumph nor a defeat, but the birth of the *mestizo* city that is the México of today." More than 400 years later the plaza witnessed another gruesome and *sangriente* event, for which it is, sadly enough, most famous: the **Tlatelolco Massacre** of October 2, 1968. An adolescent rivalry between two secondary schools led to fighting in the streets; with the Mexico City Olympic games just a few months away, the government thought it necessary to forcefully quell all disturbances. Fueled by anger at the government's violence, and at President Díaz Ordaz's militant anti-protest laws (as well as the city's debt incursion for the upcoming summer Olympics), the street fighting gave way to protests, which were answered with even more violence and in September the national university was occupied by soldiers. On October 2, a silent pro-peace sit-in was held at the Plaza de Las Tres Culturas. Toward the end of the day, government troops descended on the plaza, shooting and killing hundreds of protesters; prisoners were taken and tortured to death. In memory of the victims of the massacre, a simple sandstone **monument** was erected in the plaza and dedicated in 1993, on the 25th anniversary of the incident—before then, the government had repressed any mention of the event, going as far as removing from all national archives the newspapers for the day after the massacre. The humble monument lists the names of the dead and expresses outrage at the lack of attention paid to the horrific shootings. A small plaque on the back of the monolith explains that the present monument, already dirtied and defaced, is but a temporary construction, and that a more fitting memorial will be built when more funds are collected.

In the plaza, parts of the **Pyramid of Tlatelolco** (also known as the **Templo Mayor**) and its ceremonial square remain dutifully well-kept. Enter from the southwest corner, in front of the Iglesia de Santiago, and walk alongside the ruins, down a steel and concrete path which overlooks the eight building stages of the main pyramid. At the time of the Conquest, the base of the pyramid extended from what is now Insurgentes to the current site of Iglesia de Santiago. The pyramid was second in importance to the great Teocalli of the Aztec capital, and its summit reached nearly as high as the skyscraper just to the south (the **Relaciones Exteriores** building). During the Spanish blockade of Tenochtitlán, the Aztecs heaved the freshly sacrificed bodies of Cortés's forces down the temple steps, within sight of the *conquistadors* camped to the west at Tacuba. Aztec priests would collect the leftover body parts at the foot of the steps; food was scarce during the siege and all meat was valuable. Another notable structure is the **Templo Calendárico "M,"** an M-shaped building used by the Aztecs to keep time. Near its base, scores of skeletons were discovered. A male and female pair that were found facing each other upon excavation have been dubbed "The Lovers of Tlatelolco." On the east side of the plaza is the simple **Iglesia de Santiago,** an enormous, fortress-like church erected in 1609 to replace a structure built in 1543. This church was designed to fit in with the surrounding ruins, and with its stonework and solid, plain masonry, it does (open daily 8am-1pm and 4-7pm).

To get to Tlatelolco, take the Metro to the Tlatelolco stop (Line 3) and exit through the González *salida*. From the exit, turn right on González, walk three blocks east until you reach Cárdenas (Eje 2 Norte), turn right at the small park, and walk one long block south (to your left). Yellow pedestrian bridges cross Cárdenas. This area should be avoided at night.

## LA BASÍLICA DE GUADALUPE

According to a legend that has become central to Mexicans' religious identity, the Virgin appeared on a mountain before a poor peasant named Juan Diego, entreating him to have a church built in her honor at that site. In order to convince the Mexican bishop of his vision, Diego laid a sheet full of fresh roses cut during the cold of December in front of the bishop. Both in awe, they watched the Virgin's portrait emerge on the sheet. Our Lady of Guadalupe has since become the patron of Mexico, an icon of the nation's religious culture. Diego's mantle can be seen in **La Basílica de Guadalupe,** north of the city center. Designed by the venerated Pedro Ramírez Vásquez in the 1970s, the new Basílica is an immense, aggressively modern structure that bears an uncanny resemblance to Disney World's Space Mountain. The flags from different cultures that adorn the inside of the basilica make this feel more like the United Nations than a typical church. The Basílica draws crowds of thousands daily to the Virgin's miraculous likeness. The devout and the curious alike flock around the central altar and impressive organ to catch a glimpse of Diego's holy cloak. On December 12th, the Virgin's name day, pilgrims from throughout the country march on their knees up to the altar. Perhaps the best and most striking feature of the Basilica is the set of huge, haunting words written in gold, Byzantine script across the top of the edifice: *¿Aqui no estoy yo quien soy tu madre?* ("Am I not here that is your mother?"; open daily 5am-9pm).

Next to the new Basílica is the **old Basílica,** built at the end of the 17th century. These days, the old Basílica houses the **Museo de la Basílica de Guadalupe,** Plaza Hidalgo 1 (tel. 781-68-10), in the Villa de Guadalupe. This gorgeous, lavish museum makes you wonder why they turned it into a museum and built a new basilica. The colonial paintings dedicated to the Virgin pale beside the intensely emotional collection of *retablos,* small paintings made by the devout to express their thanks to the Virgin of Guadalupe for coming to their assistance. A large room at the base of the staircase contains a pair of golden soccer shoes offered to the Virgin before the 1994 World Cup by the Mexican star Hugo Sánchez (museum open Tues.-Sun. 10am-6pm; admission 2 pesos).

Behind the Basílica, winding steps lead up the side of a small hill, past lush gardens, crowds of the faithful, and cascading waterfalls. A small chapel dedicated to the Virgin of Guadalupe, the **Panteón del Tepeyac,** surmounts the hill. The bronze and polished wood interior of the chapel depicts the apparitions witnessed by Juan Diego. From the steps beside the church, one can absorb a breathtaking panoramic view of the city framed by the hillsides and distant mountains. Descending the other side of the hill, past the spouting gargoyles, statues of Juan Diego and a group of *indígenas* kneel before a gleaming Virgin doused with the spray from a rushing waterfall. On the other side of the hill, another waterfall drenches a bed of flowers. Vendors, both

## Virgin on the Floor

The Hidalgo Metro Station (Lines 2 and 3), with all its hustle and bustle is probably the last place you expect to see the hand of God. To many, however, there is God's magic taking place. Recently, leaks in the roof of the Metro station have caused water to enter and stain the floor. Apparently, a pattern caused on this floor is nothing less than the shape of the Virgin of Guadalupe, Mexico's patron virgin. Since its discovery, so many people flocked to the Metro station to pay homage to this miraculous floorbound apparition that the figure had to be excavated and moved to another location. Until recently, however, it was not uncommon to see people kneeling, praying, tears streaming down their faces while thousands of Metro transfers (including apathetic students and gawking tourists) whizzed on by. Since the uproar, both the bishop and archbishop stopped by the station to verify that it was not a miracle and rather just a watermark, but this did not prevent multitudes of Mexico City's residents from believing. To most, Hidalgo's Virgin of Guadalupe is a sham, the result of too much rain and faulty roofs; to others, it's a genuine miracle.

in and around the Basílica's grounds, hawk religious paraphernalia: holy water, holy shoes, holy T-shirts, holy jeans, and more.

To get to the Villa de Guadalupe, take the Metro to La Villa (Line 6), go past the vendor stands, and make a right onto Calzada de Guadalupe. A small walkway between the two lanes of traffic leads directly to the Basílica. Alternatively, take the Metro to Basílica (Lines 3 and 6). Walk along Insurgentes in the direction of traffic. At Montiel, turn right and head 500m east straight to the plaza

## COYOACÁN

The Toltecs founded Coyoacán (Place of the Skinny Coyotes in Náhuatl) between the 10th and 12th centuries. Cortés later established the seat of the colonial government here, and, after the fall of Tlatelolco, had Cuauhtémoc tortured here in the hope that he would reveal the hiding place of the legendary Aztec treasure. Although no longer a refuge for the aforementioned "skinny coyotes," it is, deservedly, a haven for "English-speaking tourists." South of the center, Coyoacán today is the city's most attractive suburb, well-maintained and peaceful, worth visiting for its museums or simply for a stroll in beautiful **Plaza Hidalgo** and neighboring **Jardín Centenario,** or nearby **Placita de la Conchita.** Come to Coyoacán for a respite from the hurried *centro;* the pace is slower and life a little easier here. Coyoacán is centered on the Plaza Hidalgo, which is bounded by the cathedral and the Casa de Cortés. The two parks are split by Calle Carrillo Puerto, which runs north-south just west of the church.

Perhaps Coyoacán's most affecting sight is the **Museo Frida Kahlo,** Londres 247 at Allende (tel. 554-59-99), five blocks north of Plaza Hidalgo's northeast corner, in the colorful indigo and red building at the northeast corner of the intersection. Works by Rivera, Orozco, Duchamp, and Klee hang in this restored colonial house, the birthplace and home of Frida Kahlo (1907-1954), whose work has gained a lot of popularity in the U.S. Having suffered almost every medical illness, physical trauma, and debilitating accident possible as a young woman, Kahlo was confined to a wheelchair and bed for most of her life. While married to Diego Rivera, she began painting and became a celebrated artist. While those looking for loads of Kahlo's work will be disappointed (only a few paintings and early sketches are around), the museum will *not* disappoint. Wandering through the house is an emotionally wrenching experience: witness the bed Frida suffered on, the words "Diego" and "Frida" lovingly scrawled on the kitchen wall, and Diego's painting of his "little girl" Frida hanging next to sultry portraits of various women (many of whom were his lovers). Those looking for insight into Kahlo's morbid work will find it, in this house full of reminders about her chronic health problems and her obsession with adultery. Read (or have someone translate) the excerpts of her diary and her letters hanging on the walls. They eloquently and intimately explain her childhood dreams and the inspiration for some of her work (open Tues.-Sun. 10am–6pm; admission 10 pesos, students and teachers with ID 5 pesos).

To see another, less emotionally draining house-cum-museum, continue north on Allende toward the highway and make a right on Viena. Two blocks down is nothing less than the **Museo y Casa de León Trotsky** (tel. 658-87-32). The entrance is around back on Rio Churubusco 410. After Leon Trotsky was expelled from the USSR by Stalin in 1927, he wandered in exile until Mexico's President Lázaro Cárdenas granted him political asylum at the suggestion of Trotsky's friend, muralist Diego Rivera. Trotsky arrived in 1937 with his wife and settled into the house. Bunny rabbits nibble peacefully in the gardens while bullet holes riddle the interior walls—relics of an attack on Trotsky's life led by the Stalinist muralist David Álfaro Siqueiros on May 24, 1940. Perhaps because this self-proclaimed "man of the people" living in a posh house in a posh suburb feared Stalinist wrath, Trotsky had **bullet-proof bathroom doors** created. Apparently, this paranoia wasn't enough; Trotsky was eventually assassinated when a Spanish Communist posing as a gardener buried an axe into his skull (open Tues.-Sun. 10am-5pm; admission 10 pesos, students with ID 5 pesos).

The Casa de Cortés is also Coyoacán's center of **tourist info** (tel. 659-22-56, ext. 181). Here guides organize tours that cover various points of interest in the city (usually 1½-3hr., 10-30 pesos depending on which tour). The Casa, originally Cortés's administrative building, now houses the municipal government. Inside are murals by local artist Diego Rosales, a student of Diego Rivera's, showing scenes from the Conquest (open Mon.-Fri. 9am-9pm).

South of the plaza is the 16th-century **Parroquia de San Juan Bautista,** bordered by Plaza Hidalgo on the north and Jardín Centenario on the west. The church interior is elaborately decorated with gold and bronze. Enter south of the church's main door (open Tues.-Sat. 5:30am-8:30pm, Mon. 5:30am-7:30pm). A few blocks southeast of Plaza Hidalgo, facing the Placita de la Conchita and marked by the gardened plaza at the end of Higuera, is the **Casa Colorada,** Higuera 57, which Cortés built for La Malinche, his Aztec lover. When Cortés's wife arrived from Spain, she stayed here briefly with her husband, but soon disappeared without a trace. It is believed that Cortés murdered his spouse because of his passion for La Malinche, although he later gave her away as loot to one of his *conquistador* cronies.

The **Convento de Nuestra Señora de Los Ángeles de Churubusco,** 20 de Agosto and General Anaya, was built in 1524 over the ruins of a pyramid dedicated to the Aztec war god Huitzilopochtli. The present structure was built in 1668. The walls are scratched with fantastic indecipherable inscriptions, and inside, an old garden grows (open Mon.-Fri. 7am-10pm, Sat. noon-2pm and 6-8:30pm, Sun. 8am-2pm and 5:30-8pm). Mexico has been invaded more than 100 times, most often by the U.S. Inside the Convento de Churubusco is the **Museo Nacional de las Intervenciones** (tel. 604-06-99), dedicated to the history of these invasions. The museum's halls cover four eras, from the late 18th century to 1917. A few halls are also dedicated to exhibitions on North American expansionism and cruelty to *indígenas,* U.S. slavery and its significance for Mexico, and European imperialism. This excellent museum really gets its point across: international "interference" (whether in peace or war) has done Mexico more harm than help, and the country is still suffering its effects (museum open Tues.-Sun. 9am-6pm; admission 14 pesos, free Sun. and for students and teachers with ID). To get to the convent and museum from Coyoacán, walk four blocks down Hidalgo and then follow Anaya as it branches left; it's four blocks farther to the convent grounds. Far easier is to take the Metro, get off at General Anaya (line 2), and walk two blocks west on 20 de Agosto. *Peseros* also leave from the Plaza frequently. The Gen. Anaya *pesero* goes to the museum (2 pesos); the Sto. Domingo goes back.

The **Museo Anahuacalli** on Calle Museo (tel. 677-29-84), was designed by Diego Rivera with Aztec and Maya architectural motifs. It houses the artist's huge collection of pre-Hispanic art. Built atop a hill, Anahuacalli commands one of the best views in Mexico, comparable to those of the Torre Latinoamericana and Castillo de Chapultepec (open Tues.-Sun. 10am-2pm and 3-6pm; free). To reach the museum from Plaza Hidalgo or Churubusco, take a Huipulco or Huayamilpa *pesero* 5km going south on

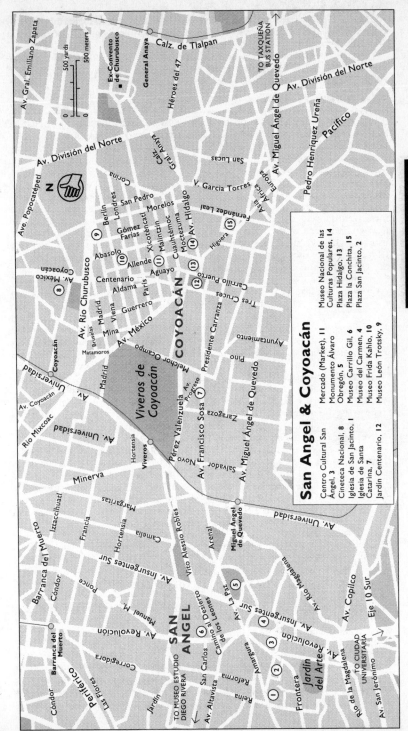

## San Angel & Coyoacán

Centro Cultural San Ángel, 3
Cineteca Nacional, 8
Iglesia de San Jacinto, 1
Iglesia de Santa Catarina, 7
Jardín Centenario, 12
Mercado (Market), 11
Monumento Álvaro Obregón, 5
Museo Carrillo Gil, 6
Museo del Carmen, 4
Museo Frida Kahlo, 10
Museo León Trotsky, 9
Museo Nacional de las Culturas Populares, 14
Plaza Hidalgo, 13
Plaza la Conchita, 15
Plaza San Jacinto, 2

Av. División del Nte. and get off at Calle Museo. You might want to ask the driver to point out the stop as it is not visible immediately. Turn right onto Museo and soon you'll reach the place.

To reach Coyoacán from downtown, take the Metro directly to the Coyoacán station (Line 3). *Pesero* "Coyoacán" (every 20min., 1 peso) stops within two blocks of Plaza Hidalgo. Taxis cost about 7 pesos. It's also a pleasant walk.

## SAN ÁNGEL

South of Mexico City near Coyoacán is the wealthy community of San Ángel. Neither as artsy or bohemian as Coyoacán, San Ángel's main appeal is that, quite simply, it's beautiful. Dotted with churches and exquisite colonial homes, this mecca of Mexican suburbia is a great place for a stroll. To reach the area, 10km south of the *centro* along Insurgentes, take the Metro to the M.A. Quevedo station (Line 3). Head west on Quevedo (away from the big Santo Domingo bakery) for three blocks; when it forks, take a left onto Av. La Paz, and continue along the wonderfully verdant **Parque de la Bombilla.** One block later, you'll arrive at the intersection with Insurgentes. The centerpiece of this lovely park is the concrete **Monumento al General Álvaro Obregón.** Obregón was one of the revolutionary leaders who united against Huerta, the usurper who executed President Madero and seized power in 1913. In 1920, Obregón became the first president of the post-revolutionary era. The inscription on the far wall of the chamber reads, "I die blessing the revolution." (Open daily 7am-4:30pm; free.)

Cross the big Insurgentes intersection, and walk up La Paz one block until you come to the intersection with Av. Revolución. One block to the south (left) are the three tiled domes of **Iglesia del Carmen,** at Revolución and Monasterio. Designed and built between 1615 and 1626 by Fray Andrés de San Miguel of the Carmelite order, the church and adjacent ex-convent are decorated with tiles and paintings. An outstanding statue of Christ the Nazarene is located in the Capilla del Señor Contreras (open daily 7am-1pm and 5-9pm). The ex-convent has been converted into the **Museo del Carmen** (tel. 616-28-16). The museum displays colonial art, tons of crucifixes, and portraits of various saints and nuns. Also exhibited are typical convent rooms—look out for the flat wooden bed and oh-so-comfy log pillow. Most tourists come to see the **mummies;** located in an underground crypt, the grotesque cadavers were originally disturbed in 1916 when the Zapatistas arrived in search of treasure (open Tues.-Sun. 10am-5pm; admission 14 pesos, free Sun.).

Across the street from this complex is the **Plaza del Carmen,** which also holds the **Centro Cultural.** Besides hosting changing art exhibits, this building holds billboards with what's hip and hot in the Mexican art world. One block up Av. La Paz, now called Frontera, is the **Plaza de San Jacinto,** at San Francisco and Benito Juárez. Every Saturday, the plaza fills up with ritzy shoppers scoping out pricey arts and crafts at the **Bazaar Sábado.** A kiosk in the center frequently hosts orchestras and big bands, and plastic chairs and peanut vendors span the plaza. On the north side of the plaza is the **Casa de Risco,** Plaza San Jacinto 15 (tel. 550-92-86), a well-preserved 17th-century house holding an important collection of 14th- through 18th-century European art. The whitewashed inner courtyard contains an exquisitely tiled fountain made out of pieces of bowls and plates (called *riscos*) that were collected from around the world. Also look out for *Crisol de las Razas,* a painted colonial chart that lists racial combinations with names like *lobo* (wolf) and *salto atrás* (a step backwards; open Tues.-Sun. 10am-5pm; free). One block farther up Juárez lies the beautiful **Iglesia de San Jacinto,** a 16th-century church with an ancient orange facade, beautifully carved wooden doors, and a peaceful courtyard. This neighborhood, the oldest in San Ángel, contains some obscenely swank and impressive modern mansions. Come see how the *ricos* (rich) live, Mexican style (church open daily 8am-8pm).

Three blocks north on Revolución from the intersection with La Paz, to the right if coming from the Parque de la Bombilla, is the small **Museo Carrillo Gil,** Revolución 1608 (tel. 550-62-89), a modern building housing the contemporary art collection of the late Carillo Gil, including works by Siqueiros as well as a whole floor of Orozco's and some by the young Rivera. Siqueiros's famous *Caín en los Estados Unidos* is on the third floor, revealing potential whereabouts of this biblical bad boy (open Tues.-Sun. 10am-6pm; admission 7 pesos, students with ID 3 pesos, free Sun.).

## CIUDAD UNIVERSITARIA

The **Universidad Nacional Autónoma de México** (National Autonomous University of Mexico), or **UNAM,** is the country's largest university, boasting a staggering enrollment of over 100,000. Immediately after the new colonial regime was established, the religious orders that arrived in Mexico built elementary and secondary schools to indoctrinate new converts and to educate young men who had come over from Spain. After petitioning the king of Spain, the first university was established in 1553 in the building at the corner of Moneda and Seminario, just off the *zócalo.* As the university grew, classes were moved to the building that now houses the Monte de Piedad, on the west side of the *zócalo,* and then to a building at the east end of the Plaza del Volador, where the Suprema Corte now stands. The **7.3 million square meters** that now comprise **Ciudad Universitaria** were completed in 1954. This veritable "city" boasts 26km of paved roads, 430,000 square meters of greenery, 4 million planted trees, and is not even residential. With all the modern architecture around, it's easy to forget that UNAM is one of the three oldest universtities in the Americas.

Despite the rock-bottom tuition (something like US$5 per semester), the university is still able to support an amazingly varied collection of student groups, activities, and social and cultural events. Films, shows, and club meetings abound. You name it, it's here—from a Tae Kwon Do club to a film about young gay Mexicans to local bands playing Mexican alternative rock to tribal dances that explore the country's indigenous heritage. *Tiempo Libre* magazine and the leaflets **Cartelera** and **Los Universitarios** provide comprehensive schedules; hundreds of other events are posted on kiosks around campus, and most notably, on the bulletin boards in the **Centro Cultural Universitario (CCU).** This large modern complex houses the **Teatro Juan Ruiz de Alarcón** (tel. 662-71-66), **Sala Netzahualcóyotl** (tel. 622-70-21), several other concert halls, and two movie theatres, **Salas José Revueltas** and **Julio Bracho** (tel. 665-28-50). A student ID gets you 50% off already cheap prices, usually around 10-19 pesos. The CCU can be reached through the UNAM shuttles leaving the Universidad Metro station (Line 3), or by taking a bus down Insurgentes and getting off at the yellow pedestrian crossing two stops south of the Olympic stadium.

Just outside the CCU is the impressive **Espacio Escultórico.** Out of a huge lava bed and surrounding cave formations rises a pan-chromatic collection of metal, cement, and wood sculptures constructed in the early 1980s. The artists wanted to revive, through modern techniques, the architectural traditions of pre-Hispanic ceremonial centers. The Espacio Escultórico should only be visited during the day; its secluded location make it dangerous after nightfall.

Hop on the yellow and blue UNAM shuttle (all UNAM shuttles are free!) to get to the heart of the UNAM campus. The **Estadio Olímpico 1968** is located on the west side of Insurgentes Sur, just past the entrance to Ciudad Universitaria. The stadium, built in the 1950s, was designed to resemble a volcano with a huge crater—an appropriate motif, since lava coats the ground on which it is built. The impressive mosaic that covers the stadium was made by (who else?) the incomparable and unstoppable Rivera using large colored rocks; it depicts a man and a woman holding two torches, a symbol of the 1968 Olympics, which were held in the stadium.

Although the university's architecture is impressive, most visitors come to see the mosaic murals that cover its larger buildings. From the stadium, cross Insurgentes (a pedestrian tunnel under the thoroughfare leads to the main part of campus), and continue east (straight ahead). West of the Jardín Central's southern half, the university's administrative building is distinguished by a 3D Siqueiros mosaic on the south wall, which shows students studying at desks supported by society. One of the world's larger mosaics, the work of Juan O'Gorman, wraps around the university **library,** a breathtaking, nearly windowless box next to the rectory tower. A pre-Hispanic eagle and Aztec warriors peer out from the side facing the philosophy department. The side facing the esplanade shows the Spaniards' first encounter with the natives; the opposite side depicts a huge atom and its whirling components.

A beautiful and pleasantly secluded attraction is the **Jardín Botánico,** a stop on the free UNAM shuttle leaving from the Metro station (Line 3). From the endless and extremely unique species of cacti to the shady arboretum to the tropical plants pavilion, the Jardín is a welcome change from the city's urban sprawl, and it offers a peek into the Valley of Mexico as it was hundreds of years ago. The trails of red volcanic sediment, which wander past the lagoons and glens, and a helpful map at the entrance provide guidance (open Mon.-Fri. 9am-4:30pm; free).

To get to Ciudad Universitaria, take the Metro to Universidad (Line 3) and exit to *salidas* D and E. Free shuttle service, though limited and irregular after classes end, is available to all campus areas. From Metro Universidad, take Line 1 to both the stadium and esplanade/museum areas (about 5 stops). Many *peseros* will be waiting just below the station, but follow the students past the vendors to the free buses which run along the circular streets around the main campus. For transportation along Insurgentes Sur, the *peseros* (1 peso) are generally the best option.

### Near Ciudad Universitaria

Near the end of the pre-Classic Period, the tiny volcano **Xitle** erupted, leaving eight square kilometers covered with several meters of hardened lava. The lava flow preserved one of the first pyramids constructed in the Valley of Mexico and formed what is now the **Cuicuilco Archaeological Zone** (tel. 553-22-63) on the southeast corner of the intersection of Insurgentes Sur and Anillo Periférico. Take bus 130 ("Huipulco," 1 peso) to the entrance on the west side of Insurgentes Sur, south of the Periférico. The **Pyramid of Cuicuilco,** which means "Place of the Many-Colored Jasper," was built between 600 and 200 BC by the early inhabitants of the Valley of Mexico, about when ceremonial centers first began to spring up in Mesoamerica and priests gained extraordinary powers. Measuring 125m across at its base and 20m in height, Cuicuilco consists of five layers, with an altar to the god of fire at its summit. The lava rock around the base has been removed, allowing visitors to walk along it and up to the altar. From here, you can faintly see Xitle to the south and Popocatépetl to the east. It's worthwhile to note that these volcanoes are far from "dead." One night in late June, 1997, Popocatépetl threw a temper tantrum that sent ash and debris over 100km. *Chilangos* were distressed to find their white party clothes soiled and their rooves covered in silt (zone open daily 9am-4pm; free).

## XOCHIMILCO

Multicolored *chalupa* boats crowd the maze of fairly filthy canals, ferrying passengers past a floating market offering food, flowers, and music. The market is especially popular on Sundays, when hordes of city dwellers and tourists pack the hand-poled *chalupas.* They lounge and listen to the water-borne *mariachis* and marimba players, celebrating Mexico City's aquatic past as they munch goodies from the floating taco bars which tie up pirate-style to the passenger boats. Although nothing of great quality or value is sold (no crafts, *artesanía,* cultural relics, clothes), you can buy delicate orchids and bubbly beer, and the festive mood is more than enough to make Xochimilco a hoppin' Sunday afternoon spot.

The floating gardens were not designed by nautical engineers—they are remnants of the Aztec agricultural system; this now-tourist trap was once an important center of Aztec life. In their brilliantly-conceived system, *chinampas,* artificial islands, were made by piling soil and mud onto floating rafts. These rafts were held firm by wooden stakes until the crops planted on top eventually sprouted roots reaching through the base of the canals, and they became fertile breeding ground, supporting several crops a year. Though polluted today, the canals still bear the bright colors and waterborne commerce that they did centuries ago.

The keyword for almost anything you do in Xochimilco is bargaining. From the markets to the boats, this is the only way to get around in this overly-popular tourist spot. Be aware that if you come earlier, you'll find a much emptier Xochimilco, with far fewer boats and much higher prices. For a private boat for six people, expect to pay about 80 pesos per hour; consult the official diagram for prices, as boat owners will try to charge eight or 10 times as much. On weekend afternoons, *colectivo* boats are cheaper (5 pesos) and more fun than the private boats. The standard price for *mariachis* is 35 pesos per song.

To get to Xochimilco, take the Metro to Tasqueña (Line 2) and then use the *tren ligero* (trolley, 1 peso; follow the *correspondencia* signs) in the *Embarcadero* direction and get off at that stop. Numerous signs labeled "Embarcadero" and screaming boat owners will direct you to the boats. *Peseros* below the station will also take you there; ask to be let off at *las canoas* (the canoes). To reach the central marketplace, walk south down Embarcadero, turn right onto Violeta, and then left onto Nuevo León. The market is just beyond the **Iglesia de San Bernandino de Cera.**

# ▒ Shopping

While most Mexican cities have a single central market, Mexico City has one specializing in every retail good. These markets are relatively cheap. Each *colonia* has its own market, but the major marketplaces are all in the center of town. Shopping throughout the *centro* and the Alameda proceeds thematically: there is a wedding dress street, a lighting fixtures street, a lingerie street, a windowpanes street, a power tools street, a military paraphernalia street, and so on.

**La Merced,** Circunvalación at Anaya, east of the *zócalo.* Metro: Merced (Line 1). Not just a market, but a way of life. The largest market in the Americas, it has a ridiculously wide selection of fresh produce, from all over the country, at rock-bottom prices. Check out the **Mercado de Dulces** (candy market) and watch candy-lovers' sweet teeth quiver in ecstasy. Open daily 8am-7pm (see p. 97).

**Sonora,** Teresa de Mier and Cabaña, 2 blocks south of La Merced. Specializes in witchcraft, medicinal teas and spices, figurines, and ceremonial images. Search no further for lucky cows' feet, shrunken heads, eagle claws, black salt (for nosy neighbors), powdered skull (for the domination of one's enemies), and dead butterflies, among other useful things. Open daily 8am-7pm.

**Mercado de La Ciudadela,** 2 blocks north of Metro station Balderas (Lines 1 and 3) off Av. Balderas. An incredible array of *artesanías,* crafts and traditional clothing, at low prices. Bargaining is often unnecessary. Open daily 8am-7pm.

**La Lagunilla,** Comonfort at Rayón, east of the intersection of Lázaro Cárdenas and Reforma. Two large yellow buildings on either side of the street. Although now a daily vending site, this market really gets going on Sundays when it turns into a gargantuan flea market, most notable for its antique books. Feel completely authentic as you browse and get battered by the throngs of wise locals looking for the real deal. Open daily 8am-7pm.

**FONART,** Patriotismo 691, Juárez 89, *(Centro);* Insurgentes 1630 Sur, Londres 136 *(Zona Rosa);* Av. de La Paz 37 (San Ángel), and other locations. A national project to protect and market traditional crafts. *Artesanías* from all over the country: giant tapestries, Oaxacan rugs, silver jewelry, pottery, and colorful embroidery. Regulated prices are still surprisingly good. Open Mon.-Sat. 10am-7pm.

**Tepito,** between Metro stops Revolución and San Cosme (Line 2), accessible by "Tepito" *pesero* along Reforma. The "Thieves' Market," Tepito is the national clearinghouse for gray-market imports from the U.S. and South Asia. Daily police raids and ultra-low prices. Bargain, if you dare. Also home to many cheap *taquerías* and juice stands. Watch your wallet—better yet, don't bring it. Open daily 9am-9pm.

**San Juan,** Pl. El Buen Tono, 4 blocks south of Alameda Central, 2 blocks west of Lázaro Cárdenas. Bounded by Ayuntamiento, Aranda, Pugibet, and Dolores. Follow the painted footprints indoors. Targeting tourists, merchants hawk an incredible variety of baskets, furniture, blankets, traditional clothing, keychains, T-shirts, dolls, *sombreros,* and wall hangings. Mostly cheesy stuff, but also some real finery if you look for it. Open Mon.-Sat. 9am-7pm, Sun. 9am-4pm.

**Jamaica,** Congreso and Morelos (Eje 3 Sur), Metro: Jamaica (Lines 4 and 9). Right out of the subway station is a clump of vendor stalls selling cheap eats and some of the juicier mangoes and *piñas* in town. The real pride and joy of the market is the assortment of fragrant and brightly colored flowers, including, of course, the deep-red Jamaica flower. Also be sure to check out live animals and exotic birds (all for sale) squawking and screaming in their confining cages. Open Mon.-Sat. 8am-6pm.

**Tianguis del Chopo,** on Calle Aldama, north of and near the train station. On Saturday afternoons, this area becomes a meeting place of Mexico City's punks and alternateens, trying to sell underground CDs, logoed t-shirts, dog collars, etc. Although the prices aren't anything to write home about, this is a one-of-a-kind scene. Get rude and tattooed among the city's hard-core. Also a great place to acquire info about bands, concerts, and events more underground (and thus "hipper") than those listed in periodicals. Open Sat. around 10am until 4 or 5pm.

# ■ Entertainment

Fear not the humdrum discos that dominate the nightlife in small towns throughout the country—you're in the biggest, baddest city in the world. Be it the Ballet Folklórico at Bellas Artes, an old film at an art cinema, a bullfight, the blues in a smoke-filled bar, or some down-and-dirty techno in a three-story disco, the city has something for everyone. It's in the entertainment department that this crazy chameleon of a city shows its true colors.

Different areas of the city boast different entertainment specialties. As a general rule, the best *discotecas* are found along Insurgentes Sur, and in the *Zona Rosa*. Rock clubs with young, hip crowds abound in the *Zona Rosa*, and a few exist around the Alameda. More posh bars and discos in the *centro* cater to an older, business-oriented crowd. *Mariachi* bands teem in Garibaldi Plaza, while *merengue* and *salsa* clubs cluster near the *zócalo* and in San Ángel and Coyoacán. Jazz bands, some *salsa* and traditional Mexican music, and generally lighter fare appealing to an older crowd can also be found in the city's southern suburbs. Tourists and Mexicans alike flood the streets in the evenings, dishin' out dough, dressed to kill, and determined to have a good time. Bars and discos clog the streets, each attempting to outdo the others in flashiness and decibel output. Although the Alameda and other areas also have some places to dance, discos in more run-down parts of town can get seedy. Women venturing out alone should be aware that they will most likely be approached by men offering drinks, dances, and the chance to be mother of their firstborn.

At many large nightclubs, in the *centro* and *Zona Rosa*, female dates for men are unofficial "prerequisites" for admission. If you're pushy enough, foreign, and appropriately attired, this shouldn't be too much of a problem. Cover charges range anywhere from 10 to 150 pesos, but women are sometimes admitted free. A very steep cover charge may mean open bar; be sure to ask. Places with no cover often have minimum consumption requirements and high drink prices. Covers magically drop during the week when business is scarce, especially for *norteamericanos*, reputed to have hearty appetites and deep pockets. If prices are not listed, be sure to ask before ordering, lest you be charged exorbitant gringo prices. Be aware that *bebidas nacionales* (Mexican-made drinks, from Kahlúa to *sangría*) are considerably cheaper than imported ones. In fact, *barra libre* (open bar) often means *barra libre nacional* (open bar including only nationally made drinks). No biggie, though. Settling for Mexican beer or tequila is hardly settling for second-best. Watch out for ice cubes—unpurified water in disguise. *Cantinas,* bars with dimly lit interiors, no windows, or swinging doors reminiscent of Wild West saloons are often not safe for unaccompanied women. For safety, the *Zona Rosa* offers the best lighting and least lonely streets, which are a problem in other areas. Taxis run all night and are the safest way of getting from bar to disco to breakfast to hotel.

## ZONA ROSA

### Bars

While cover charges get steeper and steeper (and drinks weaker and weaker) as the 90s progress, the *Zona Rosa* is still a bar-hopper's dream come true. The high price tags often mean live performers and tasty *botanas* (appetizers). *Zona Rosa* bars cater to all ages and tastes, from teenybopper to elderly intellectual. Many feature live music or, at the very least, beamed-in video entertainment. Women will probably feel safer in this area, but men still aggressively try to pick up anyone who comes along. Catch a ride home in a *pesero* running all night along Reforma or Insurgentes Sur (1-1.50 pesos). Or better yet, take a cab.

**Harry's Bar and Grill,** Liverpool 155 (tel. 208-62-98), enter a ½ block north of Liverpool on Amberes. An international thirtysomething crowd carouses and chats amid the din of a piped-in soccer match. Walls are cluttered with beer bottles and menus from bars and *cantinas* all over the Republic. Stay until midnight and watch people beg for this perennially popular bar not to shut. Beers a hefty 12-15 pesos. Mini *botanas* 17-30 pesos. Open Mon.-Sat. 1pm-midnight.

**Bar Osiris,** Niza 22 (tel. 525-66-84). Suffers from mid-week attendance problems, but on weekends, this small, dark 2nd-floor bar turns into a hard-rock party pit. Wear your black, knuckle-less gloves to this one. Live bands perform after 8pm. Cover Fri.-Sat. 20 pesos. 6 beers for 60 pesos. Open Wed.-Sun. 7pm-4am.

**Xcess,** Niza 39 (tel. 525-53-17). A more mellow techno beat and fog machine compete with a mirrored video bar serving 7-peso ¼-*yardas* of beer (about ¼ liter). Open Thurs. 2pm-2:30am (no cover), Fri.-Sat. 2pm-3am (cover 40 pesos).

**El Chato,** Londres 117 (tel. 511-17-58), with a stained-glass doorway. This splendid faux old-Euro bar that is home to *salsa* and tropical music is a must for those with a penchant for kitsch. No glitz, no booming beat, but the somewhat older crowd likes it that way. Occasionally visited by *trovas* from the Yucatán, when a 30-peso cover charge takes effect. Beer 15 pesos. Tequila 20 pesos. Don't miss the informal jazz-piano bar with Sinatra sound-alikes. Open Mon.-Sat. 1pm-2am.

**Canta Bar,** Florencia 56 (tel. 208-86-00). Don't let the black-leather-clad teens outside deter you—this tiny bar hosts everything from rave music to karaoke. Make lots of young local friends as you all huddle together and croon everybody's favorite *ballades*. The 60-peso cover charge on Sun. and Mon. and 100-peso cover charge on Fri. and Sat. include *barra libre nacional*. Open Fri.-Sat.

### Discos

The *Zona Rosa* has some of the Republic's flashier discos and higher cover charges—on weekend nights, the *Zona* can seem like the epicenter of the entire universe. Club-hopping, however, is becoming more difficult, as many discos are moving over to the high cover charge and open bar system. Long lines around the block mean a club is *de moda* (in)—expect tons of trendy teens and Armani-clad young couples eager to pay *muchos pesos* in order to get down. If being seen in the hippest nighttime hangouts isn't terribly important to you, try hitting a less populated, slightly *de paso* (out) club and hold out for a deal. Even in the *Zona Rosa*, some clubs offer entrance and open bar for under 40 pesos. Sidewalk recruiters will likely try to lure in groups, especially those with high female to male ratios; hold out and you just might be offered a deal. If you can't find something to your liking here, keep on truckin' south on Insurgentes Sur, and then south along the thoroughfare—you'll run across the whole gamut of clubs.

**Rock Stock Bar & Disco,** Reforma 260 at Niza (tel. 533-07-06 or 533-09-07). Clubs come and go, but *el estok* remains packed and fun year after year. Follow the street signs through the rotating darkroom-style doors and upstairs into a huge open attic room in which railings, scaffolding, and metal cages are doused in fluorescent paint. Lively action, with everything from rave to underground rhythms. Come early—later, swarms of peole wait outside, hoping to be let in. Being foreign and/

or being a young female (especially in tight clothes) helps. Marvel at Mexico City's teens, looking like the cast of *Trainspotting*. Cover includes open bar. Thurs. cover 100 pesos for men, free for women. Fri.-Sat. cover 120 pesos for men, 20 pesos for women. Open Thurs. 8pm-1am, Fri.-Sat. 8am-3am.

**Celebration,** Florencia 56 (tel. 541-64-15). Rigged with speakers heard 'round the world. Modern dance rock accompanies a stylish set and varied theme nights. Scattered tables provide an oasis from the active dance action. A slightly older, more dressy crowd celebrates here. Cover includes *barra nacional*. Cover 100 pesos "per couple" (i.e. 100 pesos per man, free for women) but covers drop during the less crowded weeknights. Don't be afraid to bargain (this is Mexico—even for nightlife you haggle) with the men outside. Open daily 7pm-3am.

**Papa's Disco,** Londres 142 (tel. 207-77-02), next to Harry's Bar n' Grill. Okay, so the boy to your right looks like he's 8 years old and missed his bedtime. And okay, the 12-year-old girl to your left smoking a stogie just finished majoring in trendiness at Prepubescent U.—dark, noisy Papa's still has heavy-hitting techno, copious drinks, and lots of *ambiente* for some of the lowest prices in town. Wed.-Thurs. and Sun. cover 70 pesos for men, free for women. Fri.-Sat. cover 90 pesos for men, 40 pesos for women after 10pm. Cover includes *barra nacional*. Tourists sometimes get special rates—be sure to ask. Open Wed.-Sun. 8pm-3am.

**El Numerito,** Av. de la Republica 9 (tel. 703-23-18), right near El Monumento a la Revolución. Although formerly a "gay club," the hippest, hottest young adults now flock to this club regardless of sexual orientation. Both disco and modern dance music, along with cool, stylishly lit furnishings make this one of Mexico City's new hotspots. Beautiful boys and glamorous girls get down and drink up a storm. Cover usually around 60 pesos. Beer 12 pesos. Open Wed.-Sun. 9pm-3am.

## CENTRO

A hop, skip, and a jump away from the *zócalo,* a testament to the proud and complex history of the Mexican people, lies a slew of nightclubs, testaments to something even grander: people here sure know how to party. The clubs in the *centro* are elegant and upscale (most have valet parking), but this doesn't stop 1600 corporate executives from cramming into a three-story disco and "workin' it." Most of the clubs have terraces with fully-stocked bars and smashing skyline views.

**Opulencia,** Católica 26 on the corner with Madero (tel. 512-04-17). What's in a name? A heck of a lot, in this case. Spic-and-span elevator and velvet curtains are just the beginning. The enormous dance floor features big bouncers, black lights, video screens, headsets, and the best of 1980s dance music. Check out the zany living room on the 3 floor with plush couches and silly furnishings a la Lewis Carroll. Totally decadent. Totally cool. Cover 40 pesos for men, women free. Beers 15 pesos, tequila 22 pesos. Open Thurs.-Sat. 10pm-4:30am.

**El Bar Mata,** Filomeno Mata at 5 de Mayo (tel. 518-02-37). For the *centro,* it packs in a youthful crowd ready to party. Take the elevator or walk up 5 flights to check out the sophisticated design with mood lighting and hip architecture. Equals nearly everything the *Zona Rosa* has to offer mid-week, although on non-band nights (no cover) the clientele noticeably thins out. Live bands Wed. and Sun. Mixed drinks 18-22 pesos. Cover 30 pesos. Open daily 8pm-3am.

**Museo El Bar,** Madero 6 (tel. 510-40-20), facing the Forte Latinoamerica. With its well-lit marble floors, you can't miss this one, and you shouldn't. This ritzy joint is classier than any museum. Nibble on sushi or check out the VIP lounge—even the bathrooms are perfumed works of art. The crowd is 25+, well-dressed, and well-versed in etiquette. The terrace is terrific and the 4 (or maybe 5, who knows) bars scattered throughout the place offer slightly lower prices than competitors. 50-peso cover for men, free for women. 10-peso beers, 20-peso tequila sunrises and other assorted lovelies. Adjoining seafood restaurant. Open daily 10pm-6am.

**La Ópera,** 5 de Mayo 10 (tel. 512-89-59), just west of Filomeno Mata. A restaurant and bar with Baroque ceilings, mirrored walls, a grandfather clock, and dark wood booths. While it's relatively low-key today, government alliances were made and lost within these walls. A great place to grab a whiskey and soda and talk politics. Drinks 12-19 pesos. Open Mon.-Sat. 1pm-midnight, Sun. 1-6pm.

## ALAMEDA CENTRAL

While bars and discos near the Alameda can't compare in luster to those in the *Zona Rosa*, prices are refreshingly low. Unfortunately, surrounding neighborhoods may be dangerous, especially late at night. Although Metro stops are abundant, taxis are somewhat less so; ask for the phone number of a nearby *sitio*.

Especially noteworthy is the **Hostería del Bohemio,** Hidalgo 107 (tel. 512-83-28), just west of Reforma. Leave the Hidalgo Metro stop (Lines 2 and 3) from the Av. Hidalgo/Calle de Héroes exit and turn left. This romantic cafe is saturated with music, singing, and poetry in the evenings. Seating is on the outdoor terraces of both levels and all four sides of a lush, two-tiered courtyard with a gurgling central fountain. At night, thousands of Christmas lights only add to the already unparalleled *ambiente*. The slice-of-a-tree tables and chairs are lit by old-fashioned lanterns, making it the perfect spot for intimate conversations (and who knows what else). Guitars strum in the background. You're guaranteed to fall in love here, if not with the attractive, googly-eyed *joven* sitting next to you, then with the amazing assortments of coffee, cake, and ice cream (every single gosh-darn thing on the menu is exactly 15 pesos, except for cigarettes at a whopping 14 pesos; no cover; open daily 5-11pm).

## GARIBALDI PLAZA

Garibaldi Plaza hosts some of Mexico City's gaudiest, seediest, and funniest nightlife. On weekend nights, roving *mariachis* compete for pesos with *ranchero* groups, who will play your favorite tune for 30-40 pesos (foreigners often get the privilege of paying more). Tourists, locals, prostitutes, musicians, vendors, transvestites, young kids—just about anybody and everybody mingles here, many reeling, dancing, and screaming in the street because of the copious amounts of liquor they've just downed. Big nightclubs, each with their own *mariachi,* do their best to lure the crowds. Though they advertise no cover, per-drink prices are staggeringly high. Beware of pickpockets, purse-snatchers, and prostitutes (or some combination of the three); it's best to leave your credit card, wallet, and purse at home.

Possibly one of the most peculiar and politically correct attractions of the plaza is **Pulquería Familiar,** Honduras 4, on the northwest corner of the plaza. Not only is it the only *pulque* (fermented cactus juice—the precolonial alternative to beer) bar where women are openly and officially admitted, but it was started by a woman, Lili Mora. This wonderful, taboo-breaking woman wrote that she started this unorthodox, gender-bender of a bar "to dignify the drink of her ancestors." Well, grandma would be proud of this place with checkered tablecloths and impressive newspaper clippings all along the walls. Have a glass of *blanco* (the pure stuff, 30 pesos) to get a feel for it; then move onto the fruity flavorings to actually enjoy the experience. Flavored liters of *pulque* run 8-15 pesos—mango comes closest to duplicating a nice tropical mixed drink (open daily 4pm-2am).

The plaza is at the intersection of Lázaro Cárdenas and República de Honduras, north of Reforma. Take the Metro to Bellas Artes (Lines 2 and 8) and walk three blocks north along Cárdenas; Garibaldi is the plaza on your right. The Garibaldi stop on Metro Line 8 takes you three blocks north of the plaza. Exit to your left from the stop and walk south. The best time to visit Garibaldi is 8pm-2am on weekends, but it's also the least safe then. Prostitutes turn tricks here, and the neighboring streets, strip joints, and *cantinas* can be dangerous. Women should be particularly cautious.

## COYOACÁN AND SAN ÁNGEL

While generally very safe sections of town, these two southern suburbs fall just outside many of Mexico City's public transportation axes. The Metro serves both until midnight, after which a taxi is the best option. Most moderately- to high-priced restaurants have live jazz at night. Coyoacán and San Ángel are infamous for their slews of moody gringos getting drunk and wistful to blues and rock. For a good time, hang out in Coyoacán's main plaza and soak up all the noise from comedians/musicians as you smoke a cigarette and think deep thoughts.

MEXICO CITY

**El Hijo del Cuervo** (tel. 658-53-06), north side of the Jardín Centenario, in Coyoacán. A motley international crue of java-chugging, people-watching, liquor-downing folks crowd here weekend nights for live rock and Latin music. Open daily 1pm-1am.

**El Arcano,** División de Norte 2713 (tel. 689-82-73), near the San Andrés park in Coyoacán. A live jazz/rock combo brightens the dark interior. The cover depends on the group. No cover Mon.-Wed. Open daily 8:30pm-1am.

## GAY BARS AND DISCOS

Mexico City offers the full range of social and cultural activities for gays and lesbians. There is an active gay rights movement in Mexico City, although the general tolerance of public homosexual activity is still very low. Gay men will have a much easier time finding bars, discos, films, and overall resources than gay women will; lesbian life is kept pretty much completely underground. Pick up a copy of the free pamphlets *Ser Gay* or *El Arco de Noé* (Noah's Ark), as well as the less-visible, but still free *El Agujero de la Cerradura.* All of the clubs below carry at least two of these excellent, information-laden resources detailing gay entertainment and art events in the city and providing a complete listing of all the gay bars in town, and many throughout the country. Once you get your hand on one of these puppies, a whole new world of alternative opportunity arises. Often, clubs will waive cover provided you show a copy of *Ser Gay.* In June, Mexico's gay pride month, an inordinate number of parties, rallies, art exhibits, marches, and fun *fiesta*-type events occur throughout the city.

**Butterfly,** Izazaga 9 (tel. 761-18-61), near Metro Salto del Agua (Lines 1 and 8), ½ block east of Lázaro Cárdenas, just south of the cathedral. Although no signs point out this club, don't be afraid to ask. This big, brash gay night spot is worth the searching. Although a few lesbians do come in from time to time, men, men, and more men make the huge dance floor a crowded tangle of humanity. Video screens and a superb lighting system. Male revue late on weekend nights. Tues.-Thurs. no cover, Fri.-Sat. cover 35 pesos with 2 drinks. Gay events throughout the city are advertised from here. Open Tues.-Sun. 7pm-3:30am.

**El Taller,** Florencia 37A (tel. 533-49-84 or 207-69-56), in the *Zona Rosa.* Underground; watch carefully or you'll miss the entrance. Well known hangout for blue-collar gay men. Wed. and Sun. attract a twentyish crowd; private barroom attracts an older crowd. Throbbing dance music, faux construction-site decorations and dark, private alcoves make for an intense men-only pickup scene. Check *Ser Gay* for schedules; Sat. is usually theme night (i.e., cowboy, boxer, businessman). Fri.-Sun. cover 30 pesos including 1 drink. Open Tues.-Sun. 9pm-late.

**La Cantina de Vaquero,** Insurgentes Sur 1231, near el Parque Hundido between Metro Mixcoáo and Metro Zapata. This little *cantina* has a catch: it was the first openly gay *cantina* in all of Mexico and is now going to celebrate its 23rd anniversary. Working-class gay men still flock to "El Vaquero," a very low-profile bar in a commercial center, to watch XXX videos, sample the "darkroom," or more simply, grab a beer and *parlar* (chat). Videos screened daily 4-11pm. Cover 25 pesos includes 2 beers. Open daily 9pm-late.

**El Almacen,** Florencia 37 (tel. 207-69-56), is a restaurant/bar that serves Mediterranean food and plays 1980s pop. While the clientele is not exclusively gay (a few "cool" teen couples have started frequenting the bar), both gays and lesbians do kick back beers here, especially men on their way to the high-octane gay dance club in the basement, **El Taller** (open daily noon-late).

**El Antro,** Londres 77 (tel. 511-10-13), near the intersection with Insurgentes. This enormous, tasteful new club has a prime spot in the *Zona Rosa.* Only men are allowed into this club with multiple bars, pianos, dancefloors, private rooms, video screens, and just about anything (and everything) else. Men of all ages come here to check out the acclaimed stripper shows or get down to hard-core disco. Check *Ser Gay* for schedules that include play-money casino night, social/cocktail night, and "all fun" night (Sat., of course). Cover: Wed. 20 pesos with 1 national drink, Thurs. 35 pesos with 1 drink, Fri.-Sat. 40 pesos with 1 drink, Sun. 20 pesos with 2 beers. Open Wed. 9pm-late, Thurs.-Sat. 10pm-late, Sun. 6pm-2am.

# ■ Sports

Whether consumed by their passion for bullfighting, soccer, jai alai, or horse racing, Mexican fans share an almost religious devotion to *deportes*. If sweaty discos and cavernous museums have you craving a change of pace, follow the crowds to an athletic event and prepare yourself for a rip-roarin' rowdy good time. *Ándale!*

The famous **Frontón Mexico,** facing the north side of the Revolution monument, was still on strike as of July 1997. The **Frontón,** site of the popular jai alai matches, is boarded up and grafitti-covered on. Check to see if there have been any new developments.

**Plaza México,** Insurgentes Sur (tel. 563-39-59). Accessible by the Metro station San Antonio (Line 7). Mexico's principal bullring, seating 40,000 fans. Bullfights begin Sun. at 4pm. Professionals fight only Nov.-March; *novilladas* (young *toreros* and bulls) during the off-season. Tickets were 15-80 pesos, but are due for a raise. Prices depend on the seats' proximity to the ring and whether they fall on the *sombra* (shady) or *sol* (sunny) side. If you're going cheap, bring sunglasses, a hat, and a pair of binoculars.

**Aztec Stadium,** Calz. de Tlalpan 3465 (tel. 677-71-98). Take a *pesero* or *tren ligero* (trolley) directly from the Tasqueña Metro station (Line 2). The Azteca is the greatest of many Mexican stadiums where professional soccer is played, and one of the largest in the world. Especially in recent years, Mexico has performed increasingly well internationally. Read the sports pages of any newspaper for information on games, and keep your eye out for any **Mexico-Brazil** matches. These teams are fierce rivals and any match at the Azteca promises to be frighteningly exciting. Good luck trying to get tickets, though many bars have 2-for-1 *fútbol* special with the game on TV (the season runs Oct.-July).

**Hipódromo de las Américas,** Av. Ávila Camacho. Take an "Hipódromo" *pesero* west along Reforma, or bus #17 from Metro Tacuba (Lines 2 and 7). On the outskirts of the city. Races Thurs. and Sat.-Sun. at 2 or 2:15pm. People of all ages and backgrounds mingle, eager to spend a day at the races and to hit it big. Admission free unless you sit in the upper level, where purchase of food is obligatory.

# NEAR MEXICO CITY

## ■ Teotihuacán, Edo. de México

For about 1000 years, a consummately organized, theocratic society thrived in the Valley of Mexico, then disappeared as mysteriously as it had arisen. The cultural and commercial center of this society was Teotihuacán, founded in 200 BC. An important holy city, Teotihuacán drew hundreds of pilgrims and became something of a market town in order to accommodate their needs. Its influence on architecture and art was so great that many of the styles that developed here can be found in the legacies of civilizations including Maya ruins as far south as Guatemala.

Much about Teotihuacán is a mystery. Scholars know little about the ethnic and cultural makeup of the people who inhabited the city and equally little about its rise to prosperity and sudden decline. Some speculate that the city eventually collapsed under its own weight, that it grew so unwieldy that it could no longer produce enough food to keep its inhabitants well fed. At its heyday between AD 150 and 250, Teotihuacán covered nearly 22.5 square kilometers and accommodated a population of nearly 200,000. Overcrowding resulted in construction superimposed on older buildings during the twilight of the city. Although members of this bizarre society had no problem building pyramids with three million stones, importing food was made complicated by the fact that the Teotihuacanos never discovered the wheel.

By AD 850, only a trickle of people were left in the enormous urban complex. When the Aztecs founded Tenochtitlán in 1325, Teotihuacán, 50km northeast of their capital, lay in ruin. The Aztecs adopted the area as ceremonial grounds and believed its huge structures had been built by gods who sacrificed themselves here so that the sun would shine on the Aztecs' world. Believing that those buried in this hallowed place had become divine, the Aztecs called the area Teotihuacán, meaning "Place of the Gods."

The ruined city's latest incarnation is the most visited archaeological site in the Republic. The archaeological zone, more commonly referred to as **Las Pirámides,** covers a vast area. The ceremonial center, a 13-square-kilometer expanse, was built along a 2km stretch now called **Calle de los Muertos** (Road of the Dead) for the countless human skeletons that were discovered alongside it. Since the Teotihuacanos planned their community around the four cardinal points, this main road runs in what is almost a perfectly straight north-south line from the **Pirámide de la Luna** to the **Temple of Quetzalcoatl.** The main structure, the **Pirámide del Sol** (Pyramid of the Sun), is on the east side and is squared with the point on the horizon where the sun sets at the summer solstice. On the north end of Calle de los Muertos are the **Plaza** and **Pirámide de la Luna** (Pyramid of the Moon). The **Palacio de Quetzalcóatl** stands on the east side of the southern end.

The **Pirámides,** reverently mirroring the mountains in the distance, deserve their reputation. Everything about Teotihuacán is simply awesome—the pyramids kissing the clouds, the vast expanse of wildflowers, the sheer magnitude of the place. If you take a deep breath, tune out the vendors selling charms and the visor-clad tourists (both Mexican and international), it can be an exhiliarating experience. Don't turn the scaling of pyramids and explorations into a chore or a race. Take some time, savor the view, and hang out.

The best way to explore the ruins is from south to north, starting your visit at the expansive **Ciudadela,** where priests and government officials once lived. At the center of the Ciudadela is the **Templo de Quetzalcóatl,** once a giant walled-in stadium sheltering a group of ancient temples. Its four flanking platforms served as grounds for priestly ceremonies and dances. On the west side of the Calle de los Muertos, just south of the Pyramid of the Sun, is the **Museo de Sitio.** Barely two years old, this beautifully designed museum's marble tiling and design imitate the forms and colors of the site's ancient cultures. Displays compare the size of the ancient city with various present-day cities, illustrate the architecture and technology of the pyramids, describe the social, religious, and economic organization of the society, and exhibit *indígena* art. The museum's *coup de grace,* however, is an enormous floor model of Teotihuacán at the height of its glory. All the pieces in the museum are replicas. The originals are at the Museo Nacional de Antropología in Mexico City (see p. 102). Although the temple has lately suffered tremendous wind and rain erosion, on the east side of the pyramid you can still see the fierce heads of Tlaloc, the rain god, and the serpent Quetzalcóatl, as well as traces of the red paint that originally decorated them.

Continuing north along the Calle de los Muertos, you will cross what was once the San Juan river. On the west side of the street are the remains of two temples, known as the **Edificios Superpuestos,** that were built in two phases, AD 200-400 and 400-750, atop older, partially demolished temples.

Farther to the north and east is the Pirámide del Sol, the most massive single structure in the ceremonial area. Second in size only to the pyramid at Cholula, its base measures 222m by 225m—dimensions comparable to those of Cheops in Egypt. The pyramid rises 63m, but the grand temple that once crowned its summit is missing. Smokers and slowpokes, don't quit. Although the climb to the top may leave you out of breath, a rope rail runs the length of the pyramid, and the platforms of the multitiered pyramid make convenient rest stops. The view of the summit is nice, and it's easy to dangle your feet over the top or to soak up some sun. Unfortunately, the ubiquitous vendors are everywhere, even on the peak of this mammoth pyramid. As soon as you reach the top, weary and awe-struck, be prepared to say, "No, I don't need any more obsidian turtles, thank you."

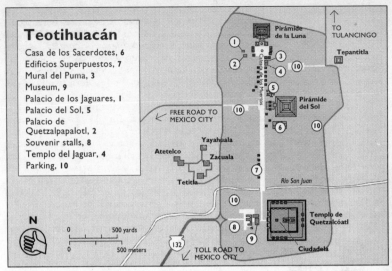

**Teotihuacán**

Casa de los Sacerdotes, **6**
Edificios Superpuestos, **7**
Mural del Puma, **3**
Museum, **9**
Palacio de los Jaguares, **1**
Palacio del Sol, **5**
Palacio de
Quetzalpapalotl, **2**
Souvenir stalls, **8**
Templo del Jaguar, **4**
Parking, **10**

Between the Pyramid of the Sun and the Pyramid of the Moon on the west side of the street is the **Palacio de Quetzalpapalotl** (Palace of the *Quetzal* Butterfly). This columned structure was the residence of nobles who staked out an area next to the ceremonial space and far from the residential complexes of the common folk; bird motifs and geometric patterns adorn the columns. The inner patio is one of the most beautiful sights of the ancient city; the colored frescoes and bird glyphs have survived years of decay and retain much of their original, intricate detail.

Behind the first palace is the **Palacio de los Jaguares** (Palace of the Jaguars) and the now-subterranean **Palacio de las Conchas Emplumadas** (Palace of the Feathered Seashells). Although this palace dedicated to jaguars is entirely restored, complete with fluorescent lights and plastic handrails, some of the original frescoes remain, adorned with red, green, yellow, and white symbols representing birds, corn, and water. This palace is a prime example of multilevel construction; it was built over another temple in which patterns of plumed seashells adorn the walls.

At the northern end of the Calle de los Muertos is the stunning **Pirámide de la Luna** (Pyramid of the Moon). Although it appears to be as tall as the Pyramid of the Sun, it is in fact much shorter, but built on higher ground. A sculpture of **Chalchiutlicue,** a water goddess and important Aztec deity, was found here during excavations. Although the climb is not as steep or as fulfilling as the one up the Pyramid of the Sun, there are fewer vendors here to greet you and the view is even more magnificent. You can see all of the Calle de los Muertos and Teotihuacán in all its glory.

If you still have the energy, there are two other areas that you can visit. Both are unmarked, off Calle de los Muertos on the outskirts of the excavated site. On the northeast side of the Pyramid of the Sun near entrance 4 is the **Palacio de Tepantitla,** which has some of the best-preserved frescoes on the site. You can still make out priests with elaborate headdresses and representations of Tlaloc. To modern audiences, Tlaloc may look like a big-haired beachcomber, complete with oversized swimming goggles, but to the ancients, this dude was no joke. His wild eyes and snaky hair identified him as the god of water, important stuff. The lower part of the mural displays the Teotihuacano ideal of paradise.

There are five entrances to the site. Buses drop visitors off by *Puerta* 1, the main entrance, surrounded by souvenir stalls. *Puerta* 5, the easternmost entrance, is by the Pirámide del Sol. Free guided tours for groups of 5 or more can be arranged at the administration building by *Puerta* 1 (southwest corner). The museum and souvenir stalls sell guidebooks for about 35 pesos. Expect to spend about 30 minutes at the museum and another three to four hours exploring the ruins. Be sure to bring plenty of water, a hat, and sunglasses. Rapacious vendors descend upon the slew of international tourists offering water, as well as hats, silver, and *"piezas originales"* (original pieces). A firm *"¡No, gracias!"* will sometimes help keep vendors away; if it doesn't suffice, try to avoid eye contact (site open daily 8am-5pm; admission 16 pesos, free Sun. and for children under 13; free parking). To contact the Teotihuacán offices, dial 6-01-88 or 6-00-52; from Mexico City add the prefix 91-595.

**Getting There:** Direct bus service from Mexico City to the pyramids is available from **Autobuses Teotihuacán** (every 15min., 5am-6pm, 1hr., 11 pesos), located in the Terminal de Autobuses del Norte at *Sala* 8 (tel. 567-14-94). Alternately, buses marked "Teotihuacán" leave from outside the Indios Verdes Metro Sation (line 3) every 20 minutes or so from opening until closing (11.50 pesos). The same bus line runs from Tepexpan, should you come from Texcoco or Chiconcuac. The last bus back from the pyramids to Mexico City leaves the main entrance at 6pm. A few kilometers before reaching Teotihuacán, the bus passes just to the right of the town of **Acolmán,** founded shortly after the Conquest by Franciscans. The majestic lines of the ex-monastery of Acolmán rise to the sky, breaking the monotony of the corn fields. If you want to stop at the ex-monastery on your way back to Mexico City, take the "Indios Verdes" bus from the main entrance and get off at Acolmán.

# ■ Daytrips

Even those who've fallen in love with Mexico City need some time away. Fortunately, its great location makes it easy to escape (but who can escape it for long?). From small towns to not-so-small towns to posh getaways to volcanoes, all these places make cool and convenient daytrips.

## YET MORE FUN

### Cuernavaca, Morelos

This lovely-colonial-town-turned-chic-upperclass-getaway still hits the mark every time. The large number of expats and language school students testify to the fact that people can't stay away. Despite its gaggle of gringos and high prices, it's worth saving up for this one. Come check out lush greenery, luxurious living, and trendy nightlife *a la méxicana* (distance: 85km; see p. 403).

### Ixtapan de la Sal, Estado de México

Despite the presence of nearby Disneyland-ish waterparks and resorts, Ixtapan couldn't be lovelier or more good-natured if it tried. The Mediterranean-style plaza and church are one-of-a-kind. A good place to check out authentic, rustic life and take long mid-afternoon siestas (distance: 117km; see p. 401).

### Grutas de Cacahuamilpa, Guerrero

Have you ever wanted to see rock formations shaped like people making out? Well, these enormous, impressive caverns provide the opportunity for much merriment. Let your imagination run wild here through stalagmites, stalactites, and caves, some over 85m high. Raucous tour leaders lead you through this underground wonderland (distance: 130km; see p. 329).

### Pachuca, Estado de México

An important center for silver mining and processing since the 16th century, Pachuca offers several lovely plazas, a few worthwhile museums, extremely friendly inhabitants, and invigoratingly crisp mountain air. The city exudes a sense of prosperity and contentment that is infectious, and the delightful streets are mostly free of tourists, making Pachuca a refreshing daytrip from the D.F. (distance: 90km; see p. 394).

MEXICO CITY

Near Mexico City

N

20 miles

20 kilometers

TO ATLACOMULCO AND QUERÉTARO →

TO ZITÁCUARO →

55

MÉXICO

57

Tepotzotlán

TO TULA →

85

TLALNEPANTLA

NAUCALPAN

Mexico City

130

Parque Nacional Desierto de los Leones

95/95D

95

Parque Nacional El Tepozteco

Tepoztlán

MORELOS

115

TO CUAUTLA →

Cuernavaca

TO XOCHICALCO →

Parque Nacional Lagunas de Zempoala

Xonacatlán

Toluca

15

130

Metepec

Mexicaltzingo

Joquicingo

55

Tenancingo

Malinalco

San Diego

TO IXTAPAN DE LA SAL →

Parque Nacional Nevado de Toluca

MÉXICO

FEDERAL DISTRICT

CD. NEZAHUALCÓYOTL

Chalco

Amecameca

115

Ozumba

Tlamacas

Parque Nacional Izta-Popo

San N. de los Ranchos

PUEBLA

Cholula

Huejotzingo

Texmelucan

90

Parque Nacional Zoquiapan

136

Tepexpan

Acolman

Teotihuacán

San Martín de las Pirámides

TO PACHUCA →

150

Santiago Cuautla

Calpulalpan

Apan

HIDALGO

Santa Rosa

Nanacamilpa

Hueyotipan

Tlaxcala

Cacaxtla

Tenancingo

Puebla

TO VERACRUZ →

MEXICO CITY

## Popocatépetl and Ixtaccíhuatl Volcanoes

Veiled in Aztec mythology, the snow-capped Popocatépetl (Smoking Mountain) and Ixtaccíhuatl (Sleeping Woman) volcanoes overlook the state of Morelos and nearby Puebla. The highlight of many otherwise boring bus tours, these volcanoes are almost too lively. In June 1997, Popocatepetl "smoked" more than it had in decades, dumping tons of ash and debris on nearby areas, including Mexico City. Both peaks can be climbed to a small degree on well-marked tourist trails, or higher up in organized tour groups (distance: 60km; see p. 402).

## Taxco, Guerrero

You've heard about the silver. Have you heard about the cable cars, stunning vistas, and fab church? Taxco boasts more than tourist treasure—it is a picturesque white pearl of a town way up in the hills. Its pink stone Catedral de Santa Prisca ranks among the loveliest in Mexico. A birthday present for dad? No problem: cufflinks and tie clip—all 100% sterling silver, of course (distance: 180km; see p. 325).

## Tepotzotlán, Estado de México

On the highway from Mexico City to Tula and Querétaro, Tepotzotlán offers a glimpse of small-town life, and its church and monastery house some of the country's most exquisite religious art. The beautiful *zócalo* and religious museum can be comfortably enjoyed in a couple of hours, but the comparatively smog-free air might make you crave even more of this town (distance: 36km; see p. 400).

## Tepoztlán, Morelos

Surrounded by towering cliffs, this quiet *pueblo* occupies one of Morelo's more scenic sites. The cobbled *indígena* village preserves a colonial feel amid growing modernization, and many indigenous people still speak Náhuatl. Bring plenty of spirit (and bottled water and sunscreen) if you plan on scaling Tepoztlán's "mother" hill. On Sundays, the *zócalo* comes alive with vibrant market activity. Quetzalcóatl, however, who was supposedly born in this sacred place, would be disturbed by the tons of *turistas* and gradual gringo-ization (distance: 70km; see p. 412).

## Toluca, Estado de México

Toluca embodies many of the qualities that define the country as a whole. Industrial growth is rapidly expanding, traffic congestion is becoming a serious problem, and American economic imperialism has set in. Despite these drawbacks, Toluca's downtown area remains truly striking for its beautifully preserved colonial architecture. Add a bunch of great museums and a breathtaking botanical garden, and you have the makings of a terrific escape from the sprawl of Mexico City (distance: 67km; see p. 398).

## Tula, Hidalgo

Tula is not much as far as towns go—it's the fascinating ruins a 10-peso taxi ride away that lure tourists. The archaeological site at Tula houses the ruins of what was the main city of the Toltec civilization. A great combination of desert-like and hilly terrain makes for picturesque ruins. Particularly interesting are the famous **Atlantes,** massive stone statues of warriors with bad attitudes almost 10m tall (distance: 65km; see p. 396).

## Xochicalco, Morelos

Ceremonial center, fortress, and trading post rolled into one, Xochicalco (Náhuatl for Place of the Flowers) is the most impressive archaeological site in the state. Because it has not gotten as much hype as other places, Xochicalco's beauty lies quiet and deserted in the rolling green hills. Aside from the occasional busload of screaming children, only swarms of dragonflies can be heard for miles. Photographers will groan in ecstasy here, as well as museum-lovers—the site's museum is truly phenomenal (distance: 120km; see p. 410).

# Baja California

The peninsula of Baja California is cradled by the warm, tranquil Sea of Cortés on the east and the cold, raging Pacific Ocean on the west. Baja claims one of the most spectacular and diverse landscapes in the world—sparse expanses of sandy deserts give way to barren mountains jutting into Baja's traditionally azure cloudless sky at incredible angles. And then there's the bizarrely blue-green water slapping at Baja's miles of uninhabited shore. This Crayola-aqua liquid flows past coral reefs, bats around in rocky storybook coves, and laps at the white sandy shores of thousands of miles of paradisiacal beaches lining both coasts. Meanwhile, the sands and outcrops of areas such as the bucolic Bahía de Concepción are watched over from above by many thousands of species of cacti that thrive on Baja's otherwise barren hillsides.

Called "el otro México" (the other Mexico), Baja is neither here nor there, not at all California yet nothing like mainland Mexico. Even its history is different—it was permanently settled by the Fransiscans and Jesuits in the 1600s. Mainland Mexico has massive Aztec and Maya temples; Baja has serene little Jesuit missions. The peninsula's tradition of carefully blending wildness and tranquility, domesticity and simplicity, are emblematized by the Jesuit legacy in such sleepy towns as Loreto.

Until relatively recently, Baja was an unknown frontier of sorts; the only way to reach its rugged desert terrain was by plane or boat. With the completion of the Transpeninsular Highway (Rte. 1) in 1973, and the addition of better toll roads and ferry service, Baja has become a popular vacation spot among Californians, Arizonans, Mexicans, and others. Vacationers range in type from hardy campers setting out to tame the savage deserts of central Baja to families living in one of Baja's many RV parks to the ubiquitous Americans who prefer a day on the beach, an evening when they can drown their inhibitions in many a *cerveza* and *margarita,* and a night of posh resort life, all without the inconvenience of changing currency.

Large resort hotels and condominium complexes are sprouting like grass to house these human torrents. The heavily-Americanized Los Cabos on the southern tip now have almost as little integrity and authenticity as Tijuana, the bawdy border wasteland of the **Baja California Norte** state, wedged in the hilly crevices of the peninsula's northern extreme. The honest Mexican city of La Paz, the capital of **Baja California Sur,** is a southern beacon of beauty for resort-weary port-seekers. But it is Baja's southern midsection—from the tranquility of Mulegé to the palm-laden oasis town of San Ignacio to the thousands of undisturbed beaches beneath sheer cliffs—which is most pristine and mysterious. Now is the time to explore—Baja beckons.

## ■ Getting Around

### BY LAND

Driving through Baja is far from easy. The road was not designed for high-speed driving; often you'll be safely cruising along at 60mph and suddenly careen into a hidden, poorly banked, rutted curve that can only be taken at 30mph. Still, a car (especially if it's 4WD) is the only way to get close to the more beautiful and secluded areas of Baja, opening up an entire world of hiking and camping opportunities. The ride through Baja is probably one of the more beautiful in Mexico. During the journey, you will see vast deserts filled with cacti, gigantic mountains with ominous peaks, and stupendous cliffs that will make you hold on to your seat. If you need roadside assistance, the Ángeles Verdes (Green Angels) pass along Rte. 1 twice per day. Unleaded gas may be in short supply along this highway, so don't pass a PEMEX station without filling your tank. All of Baja is in the *Zona Libre* (Free Zone), so strict vehicle permits are not required. If you will be driving in Baja for more than 72 hours, you only need to get a free permit at the border by showing the vehicle's title and proof of registration. (For more information on driving in Mexico, see p. 43).

If you plan to navigate the peninsula by bus, be forewarned that almost all *camiones* between Ensenada and La Paz are *de paso*. This means you have to leave at inconvenient times, fight to procure a ticket, and then probably stand the whole way. A much better idea is to buy a reserved seat in Tijuana, Ensenada, La Paz, or Los Cabos, and traverse the peninsula in one shot while seated. Unfortunately, you'll miss the fantastic Mulegé-Loreto beaches (for more info on buses, see p. 42).

Anyway you cut it, Baja's beaches and other points of interest off the main highway are often inaccessible via public transportation. Some swear by hitching—PEMEX stations are thick with rides (for more info on hitchhiking, see p. 47). *Let's Go* does not recommend hitchhiking; it is unpredictable and potentially hazardous.

## BY SEA

**Ferry** service was instituted in the mid-1960s as a means of supplying Baja with food and supplies, not as a way for tourists to get from here to there—passenger vehicles may take up only the ferry space left over by the top-priority commercial vehicles. There are three different ferry routes: Santa Rosalía to Guaymas (8hr.), La Paz to Topolobampo/Los Mochis (9hr.), and La Paz to Mazatlán (17hr.). The La Paz to Topolobampo/Los Mochis route provides direct access to the train from Los Mochis through the Barrancas del Cobre (Copper Canyon).

Ferry tickets are generally expensive, even for *turista*-class berths, which cram two travelers into a cabin outfitted with a sink; bathrooms and showers are down the hall. It's extremely difficult to find tickets for *turista* and *cabina* class, and snagging an *especial* berth (a real hotel room) is as likely as stumbling upon a snowball in the central Baja desert—there are only two such suites on each ferry. This leaves the bottom-of-the-line *salón* ticket, which entitles you to a bus-style seat in a large, smelly room with few communal baths. If, as is likely, you find yourself traveling *salón*-class at night, ditch your seat early on and stake out a spot on the floor, or outside on the deck—simply spread out your sleeping bag and snooze. A small room is available to store your belongings, but once they're secured there is no way of retrieving any items, so make sure you take what you'll need during the trip. A doctor or nurse is always on board in the (rare) event that someone gets seasick. For those who plan to take their car aboard a ferry, it's a good idea to make reservations a month in advance; consult a travel agent or contact the ferry office directly. For further ferry information, contact a **Sematur** office, listed in the practical information sections of the cities from which the ferry departs.

# BAJA CALIFORNIA NORTE

## ■ Tijuana

In the shadows of swollen, sulphur-spewing factories and sweaty U.S.-owned *maquiladores* smeared across a topographical nightmare of gorges and promontories lies the most notorious specimen of the peculiar border subculture: Tijuana (pop. 2,000,000) is Mexico in its bleakest incarnation. Like a feature at a circus sideshow, the city continually twists and contorts itself for the benefit of the scantily-clad, gum-chomping visitors who clomp down Avenida Revolución, the city's wide main drag. As they pass by, hawking, haggling shopkeepers step over regurgitated margaritas, flashing fluorescent *sombreros*, plastic trinkets, and donkeys painted as zebras ready to pose for photographs. This three-ringed, duty-free extravaganza also comes complete with English-speaking, patronizing club promoters, and every decadent way of blowing money, from a seamy, faded *jai-alai* palace to dark, dingy strip joints, from mega-curio shops to Las Vegas-style hotels to wet, throbbing dance clubs. And this is exactly how most of its thirty million yearly tourists would have it.

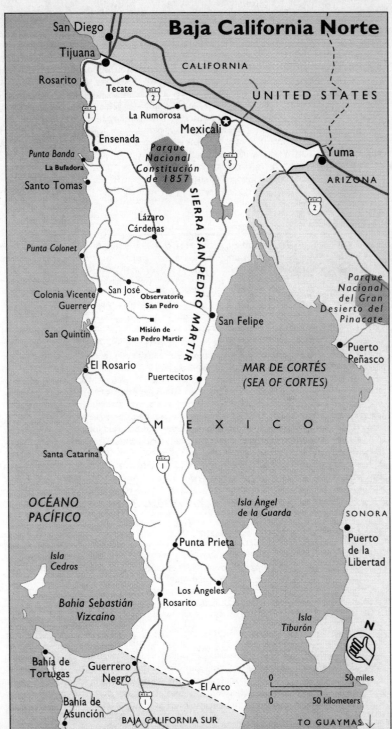

# Baja California Norte

San Diego

Tijuana

Rosarito

Tecate

CALIFORNIA

UNITED STATES

La Rumorosa

Mexicali

Ensenada

Parque Nacional Constitución de 1857

Yuma

Punta Banda

La Bufadora

ARIZONA

Santo Tomas

SIERRA SAN PEDRO MARTIR

Lázaro Cárdenas

Punta Colonet

San José

Observatorio San Pedro

San Felipe

Colonia Vicente Guerrero

Misión de San Pedro Martir

San Quintín

El Rosario

Puertecitos

Parque Nacional del Gran Desierto del Pinacate

Puerto Peñasco

MAR DE CORTÉS (SEA OF CORTES)

M E X I C O

Santa Catarina

OCÉANO PACÍFICO

Isla Ángel de la Guarda

SONORA

Puerto de la Libertad

Punta Prieta

Isla Cedros

Los Ángeles Rosarito

Isla Tiburón

Bahía Sebastián Vizcaíno

Isla Tiburón

Bahía de Tortugas

Guerrero Negro

El Arco

0          50 miles

0          50 kilometers

Bahía de Asunción

BAJA CALIFORNIA SUR

TO GUAYMAS ↓

BAJA CALIFORNIA

A short distance from where gringo greenbacks are exchanged for shots of tequila poured down tourists' throats and accompanied by shrill whistles, thousands of undocumented emigrants leave their tin shacks huddled along the Mexican side of the invisible line outside the city and stare down headlights whizzing along black six-lane highways each night as they make a midnight run for the U.S. in a perpetual and deadly game of tag. But with the fastest growth rate (13.6%) of all the world's major cities, Mexico's fourth-largest metropolis (founded in 1829 when Don Santiago Argüello received the title to Tía Juana—Aunt Jane's—ranch), isn't going anywhere. Factories extend their rawness further into the surrounding hills each year. Though American corporations now bear much responsibility for the day-glo sludge that forms puddles in backyards throughout the city, lax enforcement of government regulations has also made the wasteland possible.

To foreigners, though, Tijuana is a parody of itself, more often gawked at as a spectacle and chuckled about knowingly than visited as a city. It's hard to say whether it's the city's skanky charm, its cheap booze, or its sprawling, unapologetic hedonism that attracts tourists to Tijuana like flies.

## ORIENTATION

From San Diego to Tijuana, take the red **Mexicoach** bus (tel. 85-14-70 or (619) 428-9517 in the U.S.) from its terminal at the border (every ½hr., 9am-9pm). It passes Plaza Pueblo Amigo on the Mexican side and eventually drops you off beside the Frontón Palacio on Revolución between Calles 7 and 8. An easier way might be to grab a **trolley** to San Ysidro, at Kettner and Broadway in downtown San Diego (US$1.75), and walk across the border. Transfers from airport buses are also available.

Driving across the border is fairly hassle free, though traffic can be heavy at times. A quick wave of the hand will usually notify you that you are no longer in the United States. However, driving in Tijuana can be harrowing: many stoplights function merely as stop signs, and the crowded streets can leave you ready to turn around; for more info on driving into Mexico, see **By Car,** p. 41. If you're only in TJ for a day, it's a much better idea to leave your car in a lot on the U.S. side and join the throngs of people walking across the border for the day. Parking rates start at US$3 per day and increase as you move closer to Mexico. Bring proper ID to re-enter the U.S. While a driver's license or other photo ID is acceptable, a passport ensures the speediest passage. Leave fruits, veggies, and shoulder-fired missiles behind (see p. 16).

If you arrive at the central **bus station,** avoid the cab drivers' high rates (80 pesos to downtown) and head for the public bus (every 5min., 5am-10pm, ½hr., 2.50 pesos). When you exit the terminal, turn left, walk to the end of the building, and hop on a bus marked *"Centro Línea."* It will let you off on Calle 3 and Constitución. Other *avenidas* run parallel to **Constitución,** notably **Niños Héroes** and **Martínez** to the west and **Revolución** (the main tourist drag), **Madero, Negrete,** and **Ocampo** to the east. *Calles* run east-west; *avenidas* run north-south.

## PRACTICAL INFORMATION

**Tourist Office:** Revolución 711 at Calle 1 (tel. 88-05-55). English-speaking staff doles out maps and advice. Open Mon.-Sat. 9am-7pm, Sun. 10am-5pm. A booth on Revolución between Calles 3 and 4 has maps and may be less crowded.

**Customs Office:** Tel. 83-13-90. At the border on the Mexican side, after crossing the San Isidro bridge. Open Mon.-Fri. 8am-3pm.

**Consulates: Canada,** German Gedovius 10411 (tel. 84-04-61), in the Zona del Río. Open Mon.-Fri. 9am-1pm. **U.K.,** Blvd. Salinas 1500 (tel. 81-73-23), in Aviacón. Open Mon.-Fri. 8am-3pm. **U.S.,** Tapachula Sur 96 (tel. 81-74-00), in Col. Hipódromo, adjacent to the Agua Caliente racetrack southeast of town. In an emergency, call 28-17-62 and ask for the U.S. Duty Officer. After hours, leave a message and they'll respond shortly. Open Mon.-Fri. 8am-4:30pm.

**Currency Exchange:** Banks along Constitución exchange currency at the same rate. **Banamex,** Constitución at Calle 4 (tel. 88-00-21, 88-00-22, or 85-82-06). Open for exchange Mon.-Fri. 9am-5pm. *Casas de cambio* all over town offer better rates, but

BAJA CALIFORNIA

UNITED STATES
MEXICO

Manuel Contreras

Carretera Aeropuerto
TO AIRPORT

Avenida Defensores de Baja California

Río Tijuana

Luis Moya

Avenida Padre Kino

Paseo Tijuana

Domínguez

ZONA RÍO

Paseo de la Independencia

Avenida Oriente

Avenida Poniente

Avenida Cuauhtémoc

Rodríguez

José María Velasco

Aguaje de la Tuna

José Clemente Orozco

Blvd. Agua Caliente

Av. 16 de Sep.

Avenida

Javier Mina

Leona Vicario

Paseo de los Héroes

Castellanos

Blvd. Sánchez Taboada

Cano Luis Cabrera

Antonio

Av. Río Zuchate

Av. Río Colorado

Av. Río Bravo

Blvd. Agua Caliente

Camino Nuevo

Unión

Rosales

Quintana Roo

Cjón. Quintana Roo

P. E. Calles

Brasil

Colombia

España

Blvd. de los Fundadores

Río Tijuana

Benito Juárez

Carrillo Puerto

Díaz Mirón

Emiliano Zapata

Flores Magón

Pío Rico

Cjón. Ocampo

Ocampo

Galeana

Hidalgo

Zaragoza

Negrete

Zaragoza

Sarabia

Calle II

Madero

Jai Alai

Calle 9

Calle 10

Huitzilao

Motel Díaz

La Posada

Hotel San Jorge

Revolución

Constitución

Calle 8

Hotel El Jalisciense

Artículo 123

Niños Héroes

Hotel Perla de Occidente

Martínez

Calle 7

Calle 6

Calle 5

Cjón. B.C.

Av. Internacional

Michoacán

Coahuila

Baja California

Mutualismo

5 de Mayo

Parque Teniente Guerrero

Gonzáles Ortega

Cristóbal Colón

Calle 3

Calle 4

Arias Bernal

Calle 1

Calle 2

Lucrecia Toris

Josefa Ortíz

Michoacán

Carranza

**Tijuana**

El Toreo de Tijuana
(Bullring), **5**
Frontón Palacio and
Bus Stop, **1**
L.A. Cetto Winery, **2**
Post and Telegraph Office, **3**
Tijuana Centro Cultural, **4**

generally do not exchange traveler's checks. **Cambio de Divisas,** located in the market directly behind the Secretario de Turismo (open Mon.-Tues. 9am-7pm, Wed.-Fri. 1-7pm, Sat. 1-5pm), offers good rates. It also changes traveler's checks.

**Telephones:** Tijuana's streets are paved with **LADATELs.** There is a reasonably priced *caseta* at **Motel Díaz,** Av. Revolución 650 at Calle 1 (open daily 24hr.), and at **Hotel San Jorge,** Calle 1 at Constitución (open daily 8am-10pm).

**Fax:** Tel. 84-79-02; fax 84-77-50. To the right of the post office, in the same building. Open Mon.-Fri. 8am-7pm, Sat.-Sun. 8am-1pm. Also in **Hotel San Jorge** (above).

**Buses:** Tel. 21-29-83 or 21-29-84. To reach the bus station from downtown, board the blue-and-white buses marked "Buena Vista" or "Camionera" on Niños Héroes between Calles 3 and 4 (2.50 pesos), or jump in a brown-and-white communal cab on Madero between Calles 2 and 3 (3 pesos). **Elite** (tel. 21-29-48) serves Guadalajara (every ½hr., 36hr., 623 pesos), and Hermosillo (every ½hr., 12hr., 268 pesos). **Autotransportes de Baja California** (tel. 21-29-82 through -87) runs to La Paz (8am, noon, 6, and 9pm, 24hr., 316 pesos), Loreto (8am, noon, 6, and 9pm, 18hr., 303 pesos), Santa Rosalía (8am, noon, 6, and 9pm, 15hr., 206 pesos), Mexicali (every ½hr., 3hr., 69 pesos), San Felipe (5, 8:30am, noon, 3:30, and 4pm, 5hr., 132 pesos), and Ensenada (5, 6:30, 7, 8, and 9am; every ½hr., 9am-9pm; 1½hr., 45 pesos). **Greyhound** (tel. 21-29-82) runs to Los Angeles (every hr., 5am-11:30pm, 3hr., US$18), and connects from there to other locations. **Communal cabs** are all over town; some go to Rosarito (½hr., 5 pesos).

**Car Rental: Dollar,** Blvd. Sánchez Taboada 10521 (tel. 81-84-84), in front of the VW dealership. Starting at 248 pesos per day, including insurance and 200km free. Minimum age to rent a car is 25; license and credit card are a must. Open Mon.-Fri. 9am-6pm, Sat. 9am-2pm. Also in Tijuana is **Central Rent de Mexicali** (84-28-52), located on Los Héroes 104, Zona Río. Open 9am-3pm. **Bargain Auto Rentals,** in San Diego, 3860 Rosecrans St. (tel. (619) 299-0009) is fairly priced, and you only have to be 18 to rent. Credit card required. Open daily 8am-6pm. **Car Insurance:** If you'll be driving in Mexico, spend US$5 per day in San Ysidro to get insurance. There are several drive-thru insurance vendors just before the border at Sycamore and Primero who distribute a free booklet with maps and travel tips (see p. 41).

**Supermarket: Calimax,** Calle 2 at Constitución (tel. 88-08-94). Open 24hr.

**Red Cross:** Calle Alfonso Gamboa at E. Silvestre (tel. 21-77-87, emergency 132), across from the Price Club.

**Pharmacy: Farmacia Vida,** Calle 3 at Revolución (tel. 85-14-61). Some English spoken. Open 24hr. **Discount Pharmacy,** Av. Revolución 615, between Calle 2 and Calle 3 (tel. 88-31-31).

**Hospital:** Centenario 10851 (tel. 84-09-22), in the Zona del Río.

**Emergency:** Dial 134.

**Police:** Constitución at Calle 8 (tel. 21-71-13 or 21-72-66).

**Post Office:** Negrete at Calle 11 (tel. 84-79-50). Open Mon.-Fri. 8am-7pm, Sat.-Sun. 9am-1pm. **Postal Code:** 22001.

**Phone Code:** 66.

## ACCOMMODATIONS

Tijuana's budget hotels cluster on Calle 1 between Revolución and Mutualismo, and they tend toward the roachy side. The area teems with people during the day and is relatively safe. Come nightfall, it becomes something of a red-light district, especially on Calle 1 between Revolución and Constitución. Women should be extra cautious when walking in this area at night; to return to your hotel, head down Calles 2 or 3, or take a taxi (US$2) from anywhere on Av. Revolución.

**Hotel El Jalisciense,** Calle 1 #7925, between Niños Héroes and Martínez (tel. 85-34-91). A great deal. Clean, smallish rooms with high, resilient beds and private baths. Singles and doubles 100 pesos, each additional person 20 pesos.

**Hotel Perla de Occidente,** Mutualismo 758, between Calles 1 and 2 (tel. 85-13-58). A healthy hike from the bedlam of Avenida Revolución. Large, soft beds, roomy bathrooms, and fans on request. Singles 90 pesos; spacious doubles 160 pesos.

**Hotel La Posada,** Calle 1 #8190 at Revolución (tel. 85-41-54 or 85-83-91). Just seconds away from all the action. Select your room carefully—the good ones have fans, comfy beds, and bathrooms your mother would approve of. Singles 50 pesos, with bath 100 pesos; doubles 105 pesos; rooms for 3 or more 120 pesos.

**Motel Díaz,** Revolución 650 at Calle 1 (tel. 85-71-48 or 85-85-85), smack in the middle of things. Firm beds, hot-water shower, fans, and TV complement the rooms' simplicity. Not an outstanding value, but a bright spot in a pit of lodging mediocrity; your extra pesos will be paid back in cleanliness and light. Parking lot. Singles 200 pesos and up, doubles 250 pesos.

## FOOD

Tijuana's touristy eats are essentially Tex-Mex, but some cheap *típico* restaurants line Constitución and the streets leading from Revolución to Constitución. Even cheaper are the mom-and-pop mini-restaurants all over town. If you choose the ubiquitous taco stands, select carefully. If you must, tourist restaurants and gringo fast-food chains (think KFC) crowd Revolución, usually with slightly higher prices than their American counterparts. Pay in pesos, even if the menu quotes prices in dollars.

**Los Panchos Taco Shop,** Revolución at Calle 3 (tel. 85-72-77). Orange plastic booths are packed with hungry locals munching on ultra-fresh tortillas. Steak taco US$1, bean burritos US$2. Open Sun.-Thurs. 8am-8pm, Fri-Sat. 8am-2am.

**El Pipirín Antojitos,** Constitución 630 between Calles 2 and 3 (tel. 88-16-02). Load up your tacos with a counterful of condiments. *Flautas gigantes* 12 pesos, *super quesadilla* with meat and cheese 18 pesos. Open daily 8am-8:30pm.

**Hotel Nelson Restaurant,** Revolución at Calle 1 (tel. 85-77-50), under the hotel. Good, cheap food in a clean, fan-cooled, coffee-shop atmosphere. Gringo breakfast (eggs, hotcakes, ham) 15 pesos; 3 enchiladas 18 pesos. Open daily 7am-11pm.

**Lonchería Tico-Tico,** Madero 688 on the corner of Calle 1. Provides friendly and homey service. Both the cooks and the clients enjoy themselves. *Batida de platano* 8 pesos; breakfast tacos 12 pesos, 14 pesos with coffee. Open daily 6am-6pm.

**Café Flor de Loto,** at Calle 1 and Revolución (tel. 88-28-76). Enjoy down-home Mexican, American, or Chinese in the pleasantly kitschy surroundings. *Pollo en mole* 18 pesos. Open daily 8am-2am.

## SIGHTS

Fun in Tijuana has long revolved around clubs and money and their concomitant **vices**—shopping, drinking, and gambling. Of late, numerous diversions outside the conventional bar scene have cropped up. Try **people-watching** while strolling down **Revolución**; you'll see plenty of surprising and revolting sights, like tourists having their pictures taken with donkeys painted as zebras and wearing gaudy *sombreros*. Walk down Calle 1 to the **artisan's market** to see *mariachis* serenading the crowds of shoppers. When you get tired, relax in the beautiful and shady **Parque Teniente Guerrero,** Calle 3 and 5 de Mayo. It's one of the safer, more pleasant parts of town, and only a few blocks from Revolución. The **cathedral,** with its massive chandelier, is nearby at Niños Héroes and Calle 2. **Morelos State Park,** Blvd. de los Insurgentes 26000 (tel. 25-24-70), features an exotic bird exhibition and picnic area (open Tues.-Sun. 9am-5pm; admission 4 pesos, children 1.50 pesos). To get there, board the green-and-white bus on Calle 5 and Constitución.

The family-owned **L.A. Cetto Winery,** Cañón Johnson 2108 at Calle 10 (tel. 85-30-31), just off Constitución, squeezes its specialty from grapes grown in the Valle de Guadalupe, northeast of Ensenada. Tours are available; just don't try to remove a bottle from the storeroom—one American woman recently did so, causing a wine avalanche that broke and spilled thirty cases of bottles (tours Mon.-Sat. every ½hr., 10am-5:30pm; US$1, with wine-tasting US$2, with wine tasting and souvenir goblet US$3; reservations recommended, but not necessary, an hour before the tour).

Walk off your wine buzz with a visit to one of Tijuana's museums. The **Museo de Cera,** on Calle 1 between Revolución and Madero (tel. 88-24-78), is home to a motley crew of wax figures, including such strange bedfellows as Whoopi Goldberg, the Ayatollah, Tia Juana, Nikia Bergan, and Tom Cruise (open Mon.-Fri. 10am-7pm, Sat. 10am-8pm; admission US$1 or 7 pesos, kids under 6 free). The nearby **Mexitlán** (tel. 38-41-01), Calle 2 and Ocampo, showcases a vast field of over 200 intricate miniatures depicting famous historical, religious, and cultural monuments. Absorb Maya architecture, Mexico City's Paseo de la Reforma, and Teotihuacán without having to consult a single bus schedule. Mexican folk art is also sold (open Wed.-Sun. 9am-7pm, closed Mon. and Tues.; admission US$1.25).

## SPORTS

**Jai alai** is played in the majestic **Frontón Palacio,** Revolución at Calle 7 (tel. 85-78-33; open Mon.-Thurs. noon-4:30pm and 8pm-12:30am, afternoons only on Fri., evenings only on Sat.). Two to four players take to the three-sided court at once, using arm-baskets to catch and throw a Brazilian ball of rubber and yarn encased in goatskin. The ball travels at speeds reaching 180mph; jai alai is reputedly the world's fastest game. After each point, the winning one- or two-player team stays on the court, while the losing team rotates out in king-of-the-hill style. The first team to score seven points wins; after the first rotation through the entire 8-team lineup, rallies are worth two points, not one. If you can, try to catch a doubles match—the points are longer and require more finesse. Players are treated like horses, with betting and odds. All employees are bilingual, and the gambling is carried out in greenbacks (admission US$3-15; free admission coupons are often distributed outside).

Tijuana has two bullrings. **El Toreo de Tijuana** (tel. 80-18-08), downtown to the east of Agua Caliente and Cuauhtémoc, hosts *corridas* (bullfights) on chosen Sundays at 4:30pm from early May to July. The more modern **Plaza Monumental,** northwest of the city near Las Playas de Tijuana (follow Calle 2 west), employs famous *matadores* and hosts fights from August to mid-September. Tickets to both rings are sold at the gate. To get to the Plaza Monumental, catch a blue and white bus on Calle 3 between Constitución and Niños Héroes.

## ENTERTAINMENT

If bullfighting turns your stomach, head for the **Tijuana Centro Cultural,** on Paseo de los Héroes at Mina (tel. 84-11-11; open daily 8am-9pm); it houses the **Space Theater,** an auditorium with a giant 180° screen that shows American OmniMax movies dubbed in Spanish (shows Mon.-Fri. every hr., 3-9pm; Sat.-Sun. every 2hr., 11am-9pm; admission 20 pesos, children 10 pesos). A **performance center** (Sala de Espectáculos) and open-air **theater** (Caracol al Aire Libre) host visiting cultural attractions, including the **Ballet Folklórico.** The **Sala de Video** screens free documentaries, and the **Ciclo de Cine Extranjero** shows foreign films (Wed.-Fri. 6 and 8pm, Sat.-Sun. 4, 6, and 8pm; 10 pesos). Pick up a monthly calendar at the information booth in the Centro's art gallery.

All of this is just swell, but if you've come to party, brace yourself for a raucous good time. Strolling down Revolución after dusk, you'll be bombarded by thumping music and abrasive club promoters hawking "two-for-one" margaritas (all places listed below charge US$4 for two). Most clubs check ID (18-plus), with varying criteria for what's acceptable, and many frisk for firearms. If you'd like to check out a more local scene, peek into the small clubs on Calle 6 off Revolución.

**Iguanas-Ranas,** Revolución at Calle 3 (tel. 88-38-85). Lively on weeknights; packed on weekends. A 20ish crowd of both *norteños* and *norteamericanos* drinks and raises hell on the dance floor amid the pervasive clown motif. For a break, head to the outdoor terrace. Beer US$2. Open daily 10am-4am.

**Vibrations,** Revolución by Calle 6. Prepare yourself for this three-tiered party palace. Miami-esque neon decor and pool tables bring in the masses. Drink down those two-dollar margaritas. Cover only on weekends (women US$3, men US$5).

**Caves,** Revolución and Calle 5 (tel. 88-06-09). Flintstonian entrance leads to a dark but airy bar and disco with orange decor, stalactites, and black lights. It may seem like goth night, but hey, it's different. Drink a beer (US$2) with the blond clientele. No cover. Open Sun.-Thurs. 11am-2am, Fri.-Sat. 11am-6am.

**Tilly's 5th Avenue,** Revolución and Calle 5 (tel. 85-90-15). The tiny wooden dance floor in the center of this upscale, balloon-filled restaurant/bar resembles a boxing ring. Side tables illuminated by lovely stained-glass lamps. Tends to serve a slightly older crowd, but Tilly's is packed on weekends. Beer US$2. Wed. night is "Student Night"—all drinks US$2. Open Mon.-Thurs. 10:30am-2am, Fri.-Sun. 10:30am-5am.

# ▓ Rosarito

Once a practically unpopulated playground for the rich and famous, Rosarito has expanded at breakneck speed to accommodate the throngs of sunseekers who flood its hotels, restaurants, shops, and beaches. Rosarito is a virtual gringo colony—most visitors are from the north or semi-permanent U.S. expats. English is ubiquitous and prices are quoted in dollars. On weekends, the sands and surf overflow with people, volleyball games, and horses; finding a place for your towel may be a struggle.

**Orientation and Practical Information** Rosarito lies about 27km south of Tijuana. Virtually everything in town is on the main street, **Boulevard Juárez,** upon which street numbers are non-sequential. Most of what is listed below is near the purple Ortega's Restaurant in Oceana Plaza.

To get to Rosarito from Tijuana, grab a yellow-and-white *taxi de ruta* (½hr., 5 pesos) that leaves from Madero, between Calles 5 and 6. To return to Tijuana, flag down a *taxi de ruta* along Juárez or at its starting point in front of the Rosarito Beach Hotel. Getting to Ensenada is more of an adventure. Take a blue-and-white striped cab marked "Primo Tapia" from Festival Plaza, north of the Rosarito Beach Hotel, to the toll booth *(caseta de cobro)* on Rte. 1 (3 pesos). There you can catch a bus to Ensenada (every ½hr. until about 9pm, 18 pesos).

The **tourist office** (tel. 2-02-00), on Juárez at Centro Comercio Villa Floreta, has tons of brochures. Some English is cautiously spoken (open Mon.-Fri. 9am-7pm, Sat.-Sun. 10am-5pm). **Banamex** (tel. 2-15-56/-57/-58 or 2-24-48/-49) is on Juárez at Ortiz, (open for exchange Mon.-Fri. 9am-5pm). On weekends, you'll have to go to a *casa de cambio,* which charges a commission. **LADATELs** are scattered throughout town; there's one in front of Hotel Brisas del Mar at Juárez and Acacias, another in front of Banamex, and yet another in front of the Hotel Quinta del Mar, on north Juárez. The well-stocked **Comercial Mexicana Supermarket** (tel. 2-09-34) is at the north end of Juárez before Quinta del Mar (open daily 8am-10pm). **Lavamática Moderna** is on Juárez at Acacias (wash and dry 10 pesos; open Mon.-Sat. 8am-8pm, Sun. 8am-6pm). The **Red Cross** (tel. 132) is on Juárez and Ortiz just north of the tourist office. **Farmacia Hidalgo** (tel. 2-05-57) is on Juárez at Acacias (open Mon.-Sat. 8am-10pm, Sun. 8am-9pm). The **IMSS Hospital** (tel. 2-10-21) is on Juárez and Acacias behind the post office (open 24hr.). In an **emergency,** dial 134. The **police** (tel. 2-11-10) are next to the tourist office. The **post office** (tel. 2-13-55) is across from Oceana Plaza (open Mon.-Fri. 8am-5pm, Sat. 9am-1pm). **Postal Code:** 72100. **Phone Code:** 661.

**Accommodations and Food** Budget hotels in Rosarito are either inconvenient or cramped, with the exception of the outstanding **Hotel Palmas Quintero** (tel. 2-13-49), on Lázaro Cárdenas near the Hotel Quinta del Mar, three blocks inland from north Juárez. A friendly staff and dog welcome tourists to giant rooms with double beds and clean, private baths with hot water. Chill in the patio under the palm trees (singles US$15 or 110 pesos). **Rosarito Beach Rental Cabins** (tel. 2-09-68), on Lázaro Cárdenas two blocks toward the water, are so cheap that most cabins are already occupied by permanent residents. You get what you pay for—each bug-sized cabin contains bunk beds, a toilet, and a sink. Disney-castle spires make the cabins hard to miss (erratically open 8am-2pm and 4-7pm; singles US$7, with shower US$10; doubles US$12, with shower US$15; key deposit US$5). Fresh produce and seafood abound in the restaurants that line Juárez. For an economical seafood dinner, head to

**Vince's Restaurant** (tel. 2-12-53), on Juárez next to Motel Villanueva. Enjoy a feast of soup, salad, rice, potatoes, tortillas, and an entree—*filete especial* (fillet of Halibut, 28 pesos), jumbo shrimp (40 pesos), or a veritable seafood extravaganza of fish, shrimp, octopus, and lobster (46 pesos). The casual atmosphere is enhanced by plastic plates and vacationers in swimwear (open daily 8am-10pm). **Tacos Sonora,** on Juárez 306, serves fresh fish tacos and quesadillas (7 pesos; open daily 7am-until the last customer leaves). Sit down to a staggeringly cheap breakfast at **Ortega's Ocean Plaza,** Juárez 200 (tel. 2-00-22), in a gaudy purple building. Prick your appetite with a cactus omelette (US$2), or catch the all-you-can-eat Mexican buffet (open Sun.-Thurs. 8am-10pm, Fri.-Sat. 8am-11pm). If you have wheels and a hankering for lobster, you might want to drive 13km south to the tiny town of **Puerto Nuevo,** where several restaurants serve economical meals (around US$8) of grilled lobster, rice, beans, tortillas, and free margaritas.

**Sights and Entertainment**  People don't come to Rosarito to change the world; they come to swim, dance, and drink. **Rosarito Beach** boasts soft sand and gently rolling surf. Once the sun goes down, travelers live the dream at **Papas and Beer,** Calle de Coronales 400 (tel. 2-04-44), one block north of the Rosarito Beach Hotel and two blocks toward the sea. The open-air dance floor, bar, and sandy volleyball courts are packed with revelers on the weekends. Beer is 15 pesos, mixed drinks 17-25 pesos (cover US$5-10 Sat. and holidays; open daily 11am-3am). Don't forget the ID; they take carding very seriously.

# ■ Mexicali

The highly industrialized capital of Baja California Norte, Mexicali (pop. 1,000,000) nudges the state's border with both the U.S. and the Mexican mainland. From the cheap, duty-free stands on the border to the 11 industrial plants that ring the city, Mexicali is large, loud, and still growing rapidly. This city is obscenely industrial and heavily polluted—there's not much tourism here. Some portions of Mexicali, including the mall and surrounding plaza, wear the American facade so well that if not for the language, one could be in the States.

Still, Mexicali is a good place to stock up on supplies and to check out the local Chinese cuisine before heading south. Because of turn-of-the-century immigration, thousands of Chinese still live in Mexicali; Chinese food is more popular than Mexican food, and a Chinese-influenced dialect has emerged in the city center.

## ORIENTATION

Though far from the ordinary route between the U.S. and Mexico, Mexicali can still serve as a starting point for travelers heading south. The city lies on the California border 189km inland from Tijuana, with Calexico and the Imperial Valley immediately to the north. Because of its valley location, Mexicali experiences chilly winters and hot summers.

Mexicali is perhaps one of the most difficult cities in Mexico to navigate. Run directly to the **tourist office** and pick up a deluxe **map.** Mexicali is plagued with haphazardly numbered, zigzagging streets. The main boulevard leading away from the border is **López Mateos,** which heads southeast, cutting through the downtown area. North south *calles* and east-west *avenidas* both intersect Mateos, causing even more confusion. **Cristóbal Colón, Madero, Reforma, Obregón, Lerdo, and Zaragoza** (in that order, from the border) run east-west. From west to east, **Azueta Altamirano, Morelos, México,** and streets **A-L** run north-south, starting from where Mateos meets the border (a gigantic green canopy marks the spot). Don't try to make sense of the border area (particularly the intersection of Morelos and Obregón) from a map; guesswork and a few well-directed questions might be your best bet.

To reach the border from the bus station, take the local bus marked "Centro" (every 10min., 5am-11pm, 2.50 pesos) from outside the bus terminal, just across the footbridge. Ride past the Vicente Guerrero monument and the enormous new mall, get off at López Mateos, and walk down until the border crossing.

## PRACTICAL INFORMATION

**Tourist Office: Comité de Turismo y Convenciones** (tel. 57-23-76; fax 52-58-77), a white building at Mateos and Compresora facing the Vicente Guerrero monument and park, 30km from the border. Lots of brochures and oversized (thank goodness!) maps as well as friendly English-speaking staff (open Sept.-July Mon.-Fri. 8am-6pm; Aug. 8am-4:30pm). **Tourist cards** are available at the Federal Immigration office at the border.

**Currency Exchange:** Exchange currency at any *casa de cambio* along Madero, or try **Banamex** at Altamirano and Lerdo (tel. 54-28-00 or 54-29-29), where you can exchange traveler's checks. 24hr. **ATM.** Open Mon.-Fri. 9am-5pm.

**Telephones: LATADELs** are all over the city; one is in the post office, another is on Madero between Alta and Azulea, and a swarm are outside the white "Comandancia de la Policía Fiscal Federal" building right across the border. There is a *caseta* at the **Farmacia de Dios** (see listing below). Local calls 1 peso, long-distance within Mexico 3 pesos per min., calls to U.S. 7 pesos per min.

**Fax:** Tel. 53-99-19, 57-10-86, or 66-82-53; in the same building as the post office. Service to the U.S. (10 pesos per page) and Mexico (7 pesos per page). Open Mon.-Fri. 9am-5pm, Sat. 9am-1pm.

**Buses:** Tel. 57-24-10, 57-24-15, 57-24-22, or 57-24-55. Near the intersection of Mateos and Independencia, about 4km south of the border. A blue and white bus will take you to the station from the border (2 pesos). **Transportes Norte de Sonora** (tel. 57-24-10) sends buses to Guadalajara (every hr., 33hr., 572 pesos), Guaymas (every hr., 11hr., 220 pesos), Hermosillo (every hr., 9hr., 189 pesos), Los Mochis (every hr., 17hr., 331 pesos), Mazatlán (every hr., 24hr., 420 pesos), and Tepic (every hr., 30hr., 465 pesos). **Caballero Azteca** and **Elite** (tel. 56-01-10) send buses to most of the above locations at higher prices, plus Chihuahua (10:25am and 3pm, 17hr., 360 pesos), Juárez (3:30pm, 14-16hr., 250 pesos), and Nogales (11:35pm, 9hr., 166 pesos). **Autotransportes de Baja California** (tel. 57-24-20, ext. 2229) sends buses to Ensenada (4 per day, 14hr., 87 pesos), La Paz (5:30pm, 27½hr., 396 pesos), Puerto Peñasco (9am, 2, and 8pm, 5hr., 71 pesos), San Felipe (5 per day, 8am-8pm, 2½hr., 59 pesos), and a roller-coaster ride to Tijuana (every hr., 3½hr., 66 pesos; *plus* service 76 pesos). **Transportes del Pacífico** (tel. 57-24-61) offers *de paso* service to most of the above locations for slightly higher fares than Norte de Sonora, as well as 2nd-class buses for around 15% less that take 2-6hr. longer. Service to Tijuana (*primera clase* 68 pesos, *segunda clase* 60 pesos), Guaymas (506 pesos, 436 pesos), and more. **Golden State** (tel. 53-61-69) sends buses to Californian cities, including Los Angeles (8am, 2:30, and 10pm, 4½hr., US$28), Palm Springs (8am, 2:30, and 10pm, 2½hr., US$18), and Pomona (8am, 2:30, and 10pm, 4hr., US$26).

**Trains:** At Independencia and Mateos (tel. 57-24-20), near the bus station. To get there, turn off Mateos opposite Denny's onto Ferrocarrileros. Take the first right and it's on the right. Service to Guadalajara (*estrella* 36hr., 332 pesos; *burro* 72hr.—yes, that's 3 days—165 pesos), Mazatlán (*estrella* 24hr., 260 pesos; *burro* 30hr., 146 pesos), and other destinations. The *estrella* departs at 9am daily; make reservations 1-2 days in advance (tickets on sale 7-9am). The *burro* departs at 9am daily; tickets are only sold on the day of departure (4:30-8:30pm).

**Pharmacy: Farmacia de Dios,** at López Mateos and Morelos (tel. 54-15-18). With a name like this, how can you go wrong? Some English spoken. Features a telephone *caseta.* Open Mon.-Fri. 8am-1:30am, Sat. 8-11:30pm, Sun. 8am-6pm.

**Hospital: IMSS Centro de Salud** Lerdo at Calle F (tel. 53-56-16), has an English-speaking staff. Otherwise, try the **Hospital Civil** (tel. 54-11-23 or 54-11-30).

**Police:** At Calle Sur and Mateos (tel. 134, 54-21-32, or 52-91-98). English spoken.

**Post Office:** Madero 491 at Morelos (tel. 52-25-08). Open Mon.-Fri. 9am-5pm, Sat. 9am-1pm. **Postal Code:** 21000.

**Phone Code:** 65.

## ACCOMMODATIONS

Budget hotels crowd the noisy bar strip on Altamirano between Reforma and Lerdo and line Morelos south of Mateos. Hotels on Madero close to Mateos will dig deeper into your wallet but are cleaner.

**Hotel México,** Av. Lerdo 476 at Morelos (tel. 54-06-69). Newly remodeled, this hotel offers rooms as clean and pink as a bouncing baby butt. Rooms boast color TV and A/C and overlook a central patio. Bathrooms are small but clean. The office doubles as a grocery store, and the staff is *muy simpático*. Singles 130 pesos; doubles 170 pesos.

**Hotel Imperial,** Madero 222 at Azueta (tel. 53-63-33, 53-61-16, or 53-67-90). Minty-fresh rooms are stocked with rock-hard beds, desks, squeaky fans, A/C, and color TVs. Private baths with narrow showers. Key deposit 10 pesos. *Agua purificada*. Singles 160 pesos; doubles 200 pesos.

**Hotel Malibu,** on Morelos near Lerdo. Look out for the big sign. Although the hotel doesn't quite live up to its name, the worn rooms are clean and come with the basics. Windows and light-colored rooms help a bit. One of the cheapest joints in town—for the hard-core budget traveler. Singles 50 pesos, with bath 60 pesos, with bath and TV 70 pesos; doubles with bath 80 pesos, with bath and TV 88 pesos.

## FOOD

Some of the best and cheapest food in town can be had at the food court in Mexicali's huge mall on Lopez Mateos. Here, yummy, cheap Chinese cuisine is bountiful, and places usually have plates that combine three entrees for 15 pesos, four entrees for 19 pesos. To find the best ones, follow the crowds of locals.

**Restaurant Buendía,** Altamirano 263 (tel. 52-69-25). Despite sharing a name with the illustrious family of Gabriel García Márquez's epic, Buendía specializes in Chinese cuisine—but chefs are always happy to whip up some *antojitos*. Try a heaping plate of beef with broccoli, fried rice, egg roll, and fried chicken (30 pesos). Three burritos are 30 pesos. Vegetarians can delight in a veggie combo for only 24 pesos. Open daily 7am-9pm.

**Tortas El Chavo,** Reforma 414 at Altamirano, off Mateos, 3 blocks from the border. A fast-food joint with plastic booths; mirrored walls reflect the green and yellow "furniture." *Tortas,* any style, are 13 pesos; *tacos de machaca* (tacos filled with strips of beef) go for a mere 4 pesos. Open daily 8:30am-8pm.

**Restaurant Hollis,** Morelos and Mateos opposite Farmacia de Dios. It's amazing the chefs don't get confused, considering the fact this restaurant serves American, Chinese, and Mexican food. Lots of locals converse casually as they enjoy home-cooked meals at prices even a mother could love. Chinese combo plates 12-18 pesos. Filling steak sandwiches 10 measly pesos (open daily 8am-10pm).

## SIGHTS

Mexicali's **park, forest, lake,** and **zoo** (tel. 55-28-33) are located in the southwestern part of town, on Alvarado between San Marcos and Lázaro Cárdenas. Wink at the birds in the aviary, pedal a paddleboat on the lake, or admire lions and tigers from the train that circles the park and nature reserve. The grounds contain carousels, bumper cars, a pool, and a science museum (open Tues.-Sat. 9am-5pm, Sun. 9am-5pm; admission 3 pesos, children 2 pesos). To reach the park area, board a black and white *colectivo* marked "Calle 3" downtown. If you've got wheels, drive south on Azueta over the Río Nuevo (unfortunately one of the most polluted rivers in the world). The road becomes Uxmal south of the river; turn left on Independencia, then right on Victoria. The city's **Parque Vicente Guerrero** (tel. 54-55-63), off Calle López Mateos and next door to the mall, has jungle gyms, as well as picnic spots and party space rentals (open daily 9am-9pm).

## Whistle while You...What?!

Mexicans have transformed the simple act of whistling into a language unto its own. Stepping off a curb too soon, trying to parallel park, wearing that tank top on a hot day—all these might receive a whistle carefully selected from a copious vocabulary. There is the **attention-getting, taxi-hailing, traffic-stopping** whistle: a simple burst of sound, sometimes presented in a two-tone combination, which could be your only hope of slowing down the local bus you're chasing. There is the pulsating, directional, **you-can-back-up-another-meter-ooops** whistle, frequently used for parallel parking, which sounds like the high-pitched sounds of a Mack truck backing up. Then, of course, there's the **hey-chula-please-turn-and-look-at-me-I'm-so-bored** whistle, which certainly possesses the richest repertoire of permutations, from a long, drawn out exhale to a sharp, quick, breathy whisper. If you have two X chromosomes, you'll be sure to get your share. More welcome is the **you're-not-Mexican-are-you** whistle, which varies according to the imagination and tonal range of the whistler. The delight in sitting on a stoop and messing with passersby's minds may not initially be apparent to the tired traveler. After a short time in Mexico, however, you, too, will want to indulge in melodic discourse in the dark hostel hallway or on the crowded *pesero*. Sure, it's a complicated language, but just think how far it could get you.

## ENTERTAINMENT

Bullfights are staged regularly in the fall at the **Plaza de Toros Calafia,** on Calafia at Independencia (tel. 56-11-96) in the *centro;* take a 10-minute ride on the blue and white bus (2.50 pesos) from the *centro* to the plaza, which holds up to 11,500 people (11,499 if the bull's having a good day). Wild and crazy rodeos rampage in the winter and spring at **Lienzo Charro del Cetys,** at Cetys and Ordente. Check with the tourist office for schedules. Good, clean fun awaits at **Mundo Divertido,** an amusement park at Mateos 850 (tel. 52-56-75), across from the mall (open Mon.-Fri. noon-9pm, Sat.-Sun. 11am-10pm). To get to the park, board a blue and white bus marked "Centro Cívico" departing from Madero and Altamirano (every 10min., 5am-11pm, 2.50 pesos). Perhaps the best thing about Mexicali (and both locals and foreigners agree about this) is the huge, centrally located mall, the **Centro Comercial Gigante,** most commonly known as **La Cochanillo.** Filled with cheap food stands, video arcades, and rest areas, the mall is quite definitely one of Mexico's best people-watching spots. For a film, check out **Cinema Gemelos** in the mall (20 pesos).

# ■ Ensenada

The secret is out—beachless Ensenada (pop. 72,000) is fast becoming a weekend hot spot. The masses of Californians that arrive every Friday evening have gringo-ized the town to an incredible degree; everyone speaks some English, and store clerks resort to calculators if you try to buy something with pesos. Street vendors wander up and down the main drag, Av. Lopez Mateos, dressed in bright colors and quoting prices; and stores in all sizes and shapes (all selling Hussong's gear) populate the streets. Still, Ensenada is less brash than its insatiable cousin to the north, the infamous TJ. Cooled by sea breezes, Ensenada is more pleasant during the week, when fewer tourist-consumers populate the city—and the center of town might even be called endearing.

The ride from Tijuana to Ensenada offers continuous views of the Pacific, and its last 20 minutes are breathtaking if you take the Ensenada *cuota* (toll road)—the buses do. There are three toll gates along the way, each charging US$1.62 or 13 pesos. Don't begrudge the money, though; you'll enjoy a smashing view of the ocean, large sand dunes, stark cliffs, and broad mesas—if busing it, be sure to grab a seat on the right-hand side. The less scenic *libre* (free road) is a poorly maintained two-lane highway that parallels the toll road to La Misión then cuts inland for the remaining 40km to Ensenada. If you're coming by car, drive during the day—there are no streetlights and many a tight curve. Be sure to drive in the right lane; the left is for passing only. Some great rest spots can be found along the road to absorb the view, or to hike down and walk along the lonely cliffs.

**Orientation** Ensenada is 108km south of Tijuana on Rte 1. If you're driving, follow signs on Rte. 1 to the *centro*. You'll come into town on **Azueta,** which later becomes **Gastelum.** Buses from Tijuana arrive at the main terminal, at Calle 11 and Riveroll. Turn right as you come out of the station, walk 10 blocks, and you'll be at **Mateos** (also called **Primera**), the main tourist drag. **Juárez (Calle 5)** runs parallel to Mateos, while from north to south, **Avenidas Ryerson, Moctezuma, Obregón, Ruiz, Gastelum, Miramar, Riveroll, Alvarado, Blancarte,** and **Castillo** are perpendicular to it above the *arroyo,* a grassy trench crossed by small bridges; below the *arroyo,* **Avenidas Espinoza, Floresta, Guadalupe, Hidalgo, Iturbide,** and (later) **Balboa** also run perpendicular to Mateos. **Blvd. Costero** traces the shoreline, parallel to (and west of) Mateos. Streets are numbered, avenues are named; together they form a grid. *Calles* run northwest-southeast, while most *avenidas* run northeast-southwest (Juárez and Mateos are exceptions). After sundown, avoid the area near the shoreline and the regions bounded by Avenidas Miramar and Macheros, and Mateos and Cuarta. Always keep in mind while orienting yourself that the large residential Chapultepec Hills lie to the north, and the water to the west.

**Practical Information** The **tourist office,** Blvd. Costero 540 at Gastelum (tel. 78-24-11 or 78-36-75; fax 78-85-88), has maps and pamphlets in English (open Mon.-Fri. 9am-2pm and 4-7pm, Sat. 10am-3pm, Sun. 10am-2pm). The **Chamber of Commerce,** Mateos 693 at Macheros, 2nd floor (tel. 78-37-70, 78-23-22, or 74-09-96), is closer to the center of town and provides brochures and city maps (open Mon.-Fri. 8:30am-2pm and 4-6:30pm). **Banks** cluster along Juárez at Av. Ruiz. **Bancomer,** on Juárez at Av. Ruiz (tel. 78-11-08), exchanges dollars and traveler's checks (open Mon.-Fri. 9am-12:30pm). **ATMs** are along Juárez in the bank district, including one at **Ban-Oro,** Juárez and Gastelum. There is also a 24hr. ATM at Calle 3 and Ruiz. **LADATEL** phones line Juárez and Mateos. **Faxes** can be sent from Av. Floresta at Calle 3 (tel. 77-05-45; open Mon.-Fri. 9am-2pm and 4-7pm, Sat. 9am-2pm).

   **Transportes Norte de Sonora** (tel. 78-67-70) sends buses to Guaymas (5 per day, 7:30am-9:30pm, 16hr., 300 pesos) and Los Mochis (6 per day, 7am-9:30pm, 20hr., 393 pesos). **Autotransportes de Baja California** (tel. 78-66-80) runs to several destinations, all with the same schedule (10am, noon, 7, 8, 9:30, and 11pm): San Felipe (3hr., 85pesos), Guerrero Negro (10hr., 157 pesos), Santa Rosalía (13hr., 207 pesos), Loreto (16hr., 291 pesos), La Paz (22hr., 362 pesos), Mexicali (4hr., 101 pesos), and Tijuana (every ½hr., 1½hr., 45 pesos). **Transportes Aragón,** on Riveroll between Calles 8 and 9 (tel. 74-07-17), runs to Tijuana (every hr., 5am-9pm, 40 pesos). Local *urbano* buses (tel. 78-25-94) leave from Juárez and Calle 6, and from Calle 2 and Macheros (every 8-15min., 3 pesos).

   **Hertz,** Calle 2 and Riveroll (tel. (66) 8-29-82), rents cars, but they ain't cheap (US$45 per day with unlimited miles; open Mon.-Fri. 8am-2pm and 4-6pm, Sat. 9am-4pm). **Luggage storage** is available at the main bus terminal (7 pesos for the first 5hr., 0.50 pesos each additional hr.). **Supermarket Calimax,** Gastelum at Calle 4 (tel. 78-33-97), has just about everything (open daily 6am-2am). A laundromat, **Lavandería Lavadero** (tel. 78-27-37), is on Obregón between Calles 6 and 7, across from Parque Revolución (open Mon.-Sat. 8am-7pm, Sun. 8am-2pm). The **Red Cross** is on Blvd. de Jesús Clark at Flores (tel. 74-45-85, emergency 132). **Farmacia del Sol,** on Av. Ruiz 447, between Calle 4 and Juárez (tel. 74-05-26), is open 24hr. The **Hospital General** is on the Transpeninsular Highway at the 111km mark (tel. 76-78-00 or 76-44-44; open 24hr.). In an **emergency,** dial 134. **Police** are at Calle 9 at Espinoza (tel. 76-24-21). The **post office** is on Mateos and Club Rotario (tel. 76-10-88; open Mon.-Fri. 8am-7pm, Sat. 9am-1pm). **Postal Code:** 22800. **Phone Code:** 61.

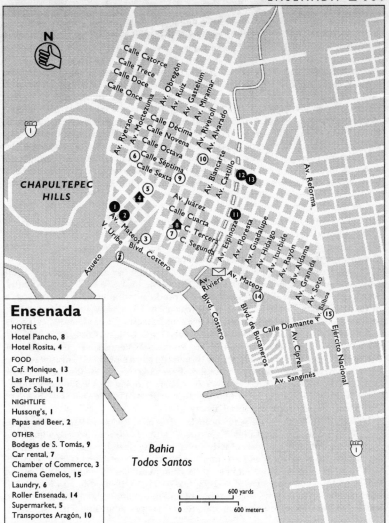

**Ensenada**

HOTELS
Hotel Pancho, 8
Hotel Rosita, 4

FOOD
Caf. Monique, 13
Las Parrillas, 11
Señor Salud, 12

NIGHTLIFE
Hussong's, 1
Papas and Beer, 2

OTHER
Bodegas de S. Tomás, 9
Car rental, 7
Chamber of Commerce, 3
Cinema Gemelos, 15
Laundry, 6
Roller Ensenada, 14
Supermarket, 5
Transportes Aragón, 10

*Bahia*
*Todos Santos*

0        600 yards
0        600 meters

**Accommodations** Budget hotels line Mateos between Espinoza and Riveroll and at Miramar. Most rooms are a 25-minute stroll from the beachfront "boardwalk" and 10 minutes from the popular clubs. Although many owners quote prices in greenbacks, pay in pesos. **Motel Pancho,** on Alvarado at Calle 2 (tel. 78-23-44), one block off Mateos, has big rooms and clean baths with tiny showers. The friendly and helpful staff will direct you to neighborhood bars (singles and doubles 90 pesos). **Motel Caribe,** Av. López Mateos 627 (tel. 78-34-81), offers great rooms and a superb location: it's right across the street from some of Ensenada's popular dance clubs and bars (see below). Comfortably firm beds and carpeted floors deck out the rooms (singles 120 pesos, doubles 160 pesos; rates go up on weekends). Cheaper, more modest rooms are available across the street if you ask for them. The beach between Tijuana and Ensenada is lined with RV parks; one close to Ensenada is **Ramona RV Park** (tel. 74-60-45), on km 104 of the Transpeninsular Highway (US$9 for full hookup).

**Food** The cheaper restaurants in town line Juárez and Espinoza; eateries on Mateos and near the water jack up their prices. Fresh fruit, seafood, and taco stands abound, but be wary of how the food is handled. If you have a kitchen, the best bargains are at the **supermarkets** on Gastelum. The friendly atmosphere at **Cafetería Monique Colonial,** Calle 9 and Espinoza (tel. 76-40-41), makes it a local favorite. Diners sit in anxious anticipation of their breaded steak with salad and fries (25 pesos). No alcoholic drinks are served (open Mon.-Sat. 6am-10pm, Sun. 6am-5pm). Chefs at **Las Parrillas,** Espinoza at Calle 6 (tel. 76-17-28), grill up fresh meat cutlets on the flaming pit as customers make like Pavlov's dog. Squeeze onto a counter stool in the diner-like atmosphere and scarf down burritos (18 pesos) and *súper hamburgesas* with veggies, avocado, and chile (13 pesos; open daily 7:30am-11pm). **Mary's Restaurant,** Av. Miramar 609 between Costero and Mateos, serves typical seaside fare, burritos starting at US$3, and a complete breakfast (eggs, tortillas, beans, and coffee) for US$2.75. Keep an eye out for the altar to the *Virgincita* woven into the nets, and similarly random photos of Bruce Lee flicks.

**Sights** Seeing Ensenada requires more than a quick cruise down Mateos. For a view of the entire city, climb the **Chapultepec Hills.** The steep road to the top begins at the foot of Calle 2; expect a 10-15-minute hike. Less taxing is a stroll down **Av. López Mateos,** where herds of curio shops make for hours of mindless shopping.

The mild, dry climate of Northern Baja's Pacific coast has made it Mexico's prime grape-growing area. **Bodegas de Santo Tomás,** Miramar 666 (tel. 78-33-33), devilishly located in a less-visited part of town, has produced wine since 1888. Today, they distill over 500,000 cases of wine every year, including champagne. Tours include free wine tasting and an assortment of breads and cheeses (11am, 1, and 3pm; US$2).

Contemplate great men in the well-manicured **Plaza Civil,** on Costero between Riveroll and Alvarado. The larger-than-life golden busts of Venustiano Carranza, Miguel Hidalgo, and Benito Juárez stare seriously onto the town's plaza. The nearby gardens of the **Centro Cívico, Social, y Cultural de Ensenada** (tel. 76-43-10 or 76-42-33) are one block from Costero (US$1 entrance fee). High, flapping flags, each symbolizing a Latin American country, sprout from flowerbeds. The Centro is a shrine to Ensenada's archeological and social history.

The **Instituto Nacional de Antropología e Historia,** Ryerson 99 at Virgilio Uribe (tel. 78-25-31), is the oldest building in town. Artifacts from all over Baja include a charming photograph of two elderly Cucapa men standing next to their shared young wife, whom they acquired during a robbery in a nearby town (open Mon.-Fri. 9am-4pm; free). A healthy 15-minute walk from Mateos is the **Museo de Ciencias,** Obregón 1463 at Catorce (tel. 78-71-92; fax 78-63-35). Housed in an old wooden boat, the museum displays photographs of and information about the endangered species of Baja (open Mon.-Fri. 9am-5pm, Sat. noon-5pm; admission 5 pesos).

**Entertainment** Most of the popular hangouts along Mateos are members of the hybrid species known as the restaurant/bar/disco. Food and drink are served only until 8pm or so, when the eateries metamorphose into full-fledged dance-club monsters. On weekends, almost every place is packed with festive-feeling gringos.

Better known than Ensenada itself is **Hussong's Cantina,** on Ruiz between Mateos and Calle 2 (tel. 78-32-10). Now 105 years old, Hussong's is the prototypical Mexican watering hole: with dark, wood-paneled walls and sawdust on the floor, you get the true *cantina* flavor with your *Tecate.* Gulp down beer (7-9 pesos) or a margarita (12 pesos) at the long, shiny bar (open daily 10am-2am). When you tire of the continuous stream of *mariachis,* cross the street to **Papas and Beer** (tel. 74-01-45; http://www.papasandbeer.com/baja), a high-tech music emporium popular with a young crowd that swigs large margaritas (21 pesos!) and spends horse-choking wads of cash. Escape the congestion and decor by stepping onto the terrace, where hockey-rink-like plexiglass boards prevent carousers from cross-checking each other off the balcony to the street below. Thursday night is theme night (birthday, pajamas, whatever) and Sunday is ladies night; women get drunk for free, and men aren't let in until 10pm (cover US$3-5; open Wed., Sat. 10am-3am, other days noon-3am).

If you don't drink, join the gyrating mass of teens whirling to late-80s pop hits at **Roller Ensenada** (tel. 76-11-59), a roller rink on Mateos at Hidalgo (open Tues.-Thurs. 2-10pm, Fri.-Sun.10am-10pm; admission 9 pesos—with or without skates). If you just want to zone out in front of a big screen, **Cinema Gemelos,** on Balboa and Mateos (tel. 76-36-16 or 76-36-13) at the southern end of town, screens subtitled U.S. features (shows 4-10pm; admission 20 pesos).

## ■ Near Ensenada

Ensenada is an excellent base from which to explore Baja's natural wonders. Unfortunately, to reach most of them, you'll need some wheels—preferably a 4WD or all-terrain vehicle. Try Hertz in Ensenada, or, better yet (if you're driving down from Cali), Bargain Auto Rentals in San Diego (see **Tijuana: Car Rental,** p. 130).

### BEACHES

Good sand to accompany your swim in the bucolic Bahía de Todos Santos can only be found outside of the city. To the north, **Playa San Miguel,** with its rocky coastlines and large waves, is great for surfers, but might not be ideal for others. To get there, drive north up Calle 10 until the toll gate; turn left at the sign marked "Playa San Miguel." Buses also run to this beach—catch a bus marked "San Miguel" departing from Gastelum and Costero (3 pesos). Buses back must be flagged down.

Somewhat more frequented beaches lie 8km south of Ensenada off the Transpeninsular Highway. Probably the nicest beach around is **Playa Estero,** dominated by the Estero Beach Resort, which is so Americanized that finding a single Mexican anywhere on the sand could be an impossible task. Volleyball courts fill the beach's clean but hard and unforgiving sand. You can rent water skis, banana boats, or bicycles (US$5 per hr.). The **Estero Beach Museum** (tel. 6-62-35) displays Mexican folk art (open Wed.-Mon. 9am-6pm; free). To get there, take a right at the "Estero Beach" sign on Rte. 1 heading south. Free parking is available in the first lot of the hotel. Alternatively, catch a bus marked "Aeropuerto," "Zorrillo," "Maneadero," or "Chapultepec" from Pl. Cívica. **Playa El Faro** (tel. 7-46-30; fax 7-46-20) is similarly rife with volleyball courts and Americans, but has slightly better sand, and offers camping on the beach (camp space, parking, and bathroom privileges US$7 for 4 people; full RV hookup US$12; rooms with bath US$30 for 2 people). Another nearby beach is **Playa Santa María,** where you can rent a horse (US$9 per hr.) and ride around the bay.

Heading onto the Punta Banda peninsula (continuing south from Ensenada, take the paved road BCN 23, which splits west off Rte. 1 north of Maneadero), you'll find lonelier beaches along the stretch known as **Baja Beach.** Horses are available for rent, and you can swim anywhere along the clean, soft, white sand (remember, all beaches are public), in front of a quiet scattering of Americans in semi-permanent RV parks. The rolling hills and marshes provide a pleasant backdrop. The Baja Beach Resort also runs a pool of hot springs, located on Hwy. 1 on the left, 2km before turning off onto the Punta Banda peninsula. To get to Baja Beach, walk down a dirt road after the sign, on the right hand side. By car, bear right at the first fork in the road after turning onto the Peninsula. Look for a "Horses for Rent" and "Aguacaliente" sign. There are beautiful hiking spots nearby (see **Hiking** below). You can also take a bus to La Bufadora (see below) and ask the driver to let you off, but don't count on a ride back.

### HIKING

The area's most beautiful spots remain essentially undiscovered by most tourists. Breathtaking hikes around the mountains of the Punta Banda peninsula approaching La Bufadora can be completed on well-kept trails of U.S. National Park quality. Take in spectacular views of cliffs, the mountainside, and blue sea floating off into oblivion as you circle the peaks. Bring a snack, as there are some good spots to stop and picnic.

And don't forget a bathing suit—when you reach the bottom, you can relieve your sweaty body with a dip amid the rocks in the chilly Pacific.

The best spot to enter the trails is **Cerro de la Punta,** on the road to La Bufadora near the end of the Punta Banda Peninsula. Turn right up a long driveway at the "Cerro de la Punta" sign (parking 10 pesos). You'll see a small clearing and a large house on the cliffs; here, you can hike up among the cacti to the top of the mountains for views of the surrounding area or down beautiful trails on the oceanside.

Other stops earlier along the road to La Bufadora are equally scenic, and a few are near unique cave-like rock enclosures created when the mountain was blasted to build the road. The bus to La Bufadora (see below) will drop you off anywhere along this road, including Cerro de la Punta, but if you can't hitch, you may be waiting quite a while for the bus back. **Punta Banda** itself has a roadside **grocery market** and **post office** (open Mon.-Fri. 8am-2pm; but, honestly, go to Ensenada) on the main road after the turnoff for Baja Beach. A good place to camp or park an RV in Punta Banda is **Villarino** (tel. 3-20-45 or 6-42-46; fax 3-20-44), adjacent to the plaza, which has modern shower and bathroom facilities and full hookups (US$5 per person per night).

Hiking further inland offers completely different terrain, ranging from deep lagoons to cactus forests to ponderosa pine. The rugged mountain range east of Ensenada is the solitary **Sierra de Juárez,** where **Parque Nacional Constitución de 1857** is located. Be forewarned that you'll need an all-terrain vehicle or pickup truck to make the trek. If you can afford it, find a guide who can show you the correct paths to take once off the main roads. Dirt roads and brush make the paths off the main road difficult to navigate. To get there, follow Hwy. 3 east from Avenida Juárez in Ensenada all the way to **Ojos Negros.** At km 39, turn onto the dirt road leading into the park. Follow signs (or, better, ask a guide for help), and you will eventually find yourself at **Laguna Hanson,** a little lake surrounded by basic camping spots. If you aren't wheeled, **Ecotur** (tel. 76-44-15; fax 74-67-78) offers excursions. The owner, Francisco Detrell, also leads tours in Ensenada and other parts of Baja. You must call or fax at least three days in advance in order to book a tour.

Southeast of Ensenada is the more famous **Sierra San Pedro Martir,** home to **Picacho del Diablo,** Baja's tallest peak at 3087m (10,126 ft.). Getting there demands an all-terrain vehicle. Drive 127km south on Rte. 1 to **San Telmo;** from there, turn east onto a gravel road (108km) until you reach the park. For more information, call the **Ensenada Tourist Office. Ecotour** also leads tours here (call in advance).

## LA BUFADORA

**La Bufadora,** the largest geyser on the Pacific coast, is 30km south of Ensenada. On a good day, the "Blowhole" shoots water 40m into the air out of a water-carved cave. On some days, visitors will have to be satisfied with the beautiful view from the Bufadora peak. Unfortunately, the droves of visitors, cheesy curio shops, and food vendors have made the area rather unpleasant. In spite of the garbage strewn everywhere, though, the hole itself makes the trip worthwhile. To get there, drive south on the Transpeninsular Highway (take a right onto the highway off López Mateos at the southern end of town), head straight past exits for the airport, military base, and Playa Estero, and take a right after about 20 minutes at the sign marked "La Bufadora." Continue on that road until its end. You'll know you're there after you've finished a brain-numbing series of road loops and you find yourself on a small street with multi-colored vending stalls (parking US$1 or 7 pesos). Alternatively, you can take a yellow *microbús* to **Maneadero** (3 pesos), and a connecting bus to La Bufadora (2 pesos).

# ■ Valle de San Quintín

Occupying the lonely mid-Pacific coast of northern Baja, San Quintín Valley (pop. 10,000) is the lifeblood of the peninsula's agricultural production. Driving south from Ensenada on Rte. 1 (the Pan-American highway) for 180km, you'll encounter a series of small, bland towns bordered by the ocean on the west, the mountains on the east, and farmland everywhere in between. What brings most people here, however, is the superb fishing off the small *bahía*. Americans and other foreigners are hard to find in the area's main strip (as is virtually everything), but travelers and suntanners abound on the beaches outside of town. The valley's settlement is made up of three even smaller towns (listed north to south): **San Quintín, Lázaro Cárdenas** (not to be confused with its neighbor with the same name only about 100km to the northeast), and **El Eje del Papaloto,** and numerous ranches belonging to gallant *vaqueros*. Above all, the town makes a good rest stop on the way to points further south.

**Orientation and Practical Information** All three towns border **Rte. 1,** Mexico's **Transpeninsular Highway.** Small streets off the highway have neither street signs nor common-use names. Addresses are designated by highway location. The beaches are all west of the highway, off small dirt and sand roads. Coming from the North, San Quintín is the first town, Cárdenas (as it is known in the region) is second, and little Eje comes last. The Valle de San Quintín **tourist office** (tel. 6-24-98) actually comes before the towns themselves, on Rte. 1, km 178.3, in Col. Vicente Guerrero. To **exchange currency,** head to BITAL (open Mon.-Fri. 8am-7pm, Sat. 9am-2:30pm), the Valle's bank, located in Lázaro Cárdenas behind the Pemex station. BITAL has an **ATM** and exchanges traveler's checks. **LADATELs** are in all three towns and a **caseta** is in Cárdenas. **Farmacia Santa María** (open daily 9am-9pm, except Wed. 9am-8pm and Sun. 9am-7pm), located down a dirt road off km 190 before the Puente de San Quintín, has *casetas* as well as medicine. In Cárdenas, try **Farmacia Baja California,** Rte.1 at km 114 (open daily 8am-10pm). In a health emergency, call **Clínica Santa María** in San Quintín (tel. 75-22-63 or 75-22-12), located on a dirt road off of km 190 on Rte. 1. The **police** are in Cárdenas, west of the highway (**emergency** tel. 134). The **post office** is a grey building one block down from the Farmacia Baja California in Cárdenas (open Mon.-Fri. 8am-5pm, Sat. 8am-12pm; good luck). **Postal Code:** 22930. **Phone Code:** 616.

**Accommodations and Food** Sleeping arrangements are minimal in the Valle but, for the most part, comfortable. In San Quintín, **Hotel Chavez,** on km 194 of Rte. 1 (tel. 5-20-05), offers large, airy rooms, soft beds, and cable TV in the main lobby. Call early for reservations (singles 132 pesos and up). In Lázaro Cárdenas, **Motel Romeo** (tel. 5-23-96), on the west side of Rte. 1, has singles (80 pesos) and doubles (100 pesos). The almost-new rooms are carpeted. Clean bathrooms border on art deco. Large windows let in the sunlight or the indigo night sky. Cheap eats aren't tough to find in San Quintín. Small *loncherías,* where you can eat tacos for 9 pesos, line both sides of Rte. 1. Or, recline in the air conditioned **El Alazán** in San Quintín, km 190 on the highway.

**Sights and Entertainment** San Quintín is best known for fishing off the San Quintín bay. You can drive out to the **Molino Viejo** (Old Pier) and to the **Old Mill Hotel** (U.S. tel. (619) 428-2779 or (800) 479-7962), where you can get both a fishing permit and a boat for the day. The surrounding mountains and peaceful bay waters will soothe the worn traveler. The Old Mill itself is a semi-permanent American expat community. To get there, turn west on a sand and dirt road on km 198; head down about 4km (signs will point you in the right direction). Or, if you'd like something a little different, check out the salt lakes formed on the edge of the sea, west of Cárdenas. To get there, turn left at the corner of the military base. Head down a dirt and sand road for approximately 5 miles. You don't need an ATV, but follow the sand paths very carefully. Dance clubs aren't the Valle's forte, but by night, you can dip your feet into local flavors at the **Bar Romeo,** Rte. 1 in Cárdenas (tel. 5-23-96), where mariachis and local singers are cheered on by catcalls until late hours. In San Quintín, grab a chilly *cerveza* (about 11 pesos) at the **Restaurant Bar San Quintín** (tel. 5-23-76; open 7am-1:30am).

# ■ San Felipe

San Felipe may put on Mexican airs, but it's a tourist-oriented beach town at heart, complete with high prices, sandy volleyball courts, and vendors selling shell sculpture. After the discovery of copious seafood, northern snowbirds claimed the area as a regular hangout in the 50s, bringing with them handfuls of greenbacks and a new industry—tourism. More than 200 gringo RV parks now line the coast of the greater San Felipe area, and cashiers look positively perplexed if you try to pay in pesos. However, San Felipe offers a stellar selection of seafood and a beautiful stretch of beach teased by the warm, shallow waters of the Gulf. The town is laid-back and scenic, the perfect place to relax for a day or 10, and grab a drink or 20. As one local bar has written on the wall, "No worries—be happy."

**Orientation and Practical Information** San Felipe is 198km south of Mexicali at the end of sizzling-hot Rte. 5. The town is also accessible via a paved road from Ensenada—if coming from Tijuana, the latter makes for a more pleasant ride. A dirt and gravel road connects San Felipe to points farther south. **Los Arcos** (a tall arched structure) is immediately recognizable when entering the village; **Chetumal** is the street continuing straight from the arches toward the sea. Hotels and restaurants cluster on **Mar de Cortés,** one block from the beach. The **Malecón,** lined with seafood stands, is right on the beach. Almost all of the "action" (restaurants, hotels, services) are on these two last streets. All cross-streets named "Mar" run parallel to the beach; from south to north, **Manzanillo, Topolobampo, Ensenada, Chetumal,** and **Acapulco** run perpendicular. To get downtown from the **bus station,** walk north on Mar Caribe to Manzanillo and turn right toward the water. Hike until you see the Hotel Costa Azul, and you're on Mar del Caribe, one block from the beach.

The **tourist office,** Mar de Cortés 300 at Manzanillo (tel. 7-11-55), has English-speaking staffers and handy maps and brochures (open Mon.-Fri. 8am-7pm, Sat. 9am-3pm, Sun. 10am-1pm). **Bancomer,** Mar de Cortés Nte. at Acapulco (tel./fax 7-10-51), near Rockodile Bar, exchanges currency from 8am-2pm and has a 24-hour **ATM. Farmacia San Angelín,** Chetumal at Mar de Cortés, has **casetas** for **long-distance calls** (US$1 plus credit card charges). Some **LATADELs** line Mar Caribe. **Faxes** (tel. 7-11-12) can be sent from the yellow office on Mar Bermejo between Puerto Peñasco and Zihuatanejo (tel. 7-10-43; open Mon.-Fri. 8am-2pm).

Catch **buses** at the terminal on Mar Caribe (tel. 7-15-16), a 15-minute walk from the center of action. **Autotransportes de Baja California** runs buses to Ensenada (8am and 6pm, 3½hr., 87 pesos), Mexicali (6am, noon, and 4pm, 2½hr., 59 pesos), and "Plus" service to Mexicali (7:30am and 8pm, 2½hr., 64 pesos), and Tijuana (4 per day, 5hr., 121 pesos). Ticket sales daily 5:30am-10:30pm. **Luggage storage** at the bus station (5 pesos). The **Red Cross,** at Mar Bermejo and Peñasco (tel. 7-15-44), has English-speaking staffers (open 24hr.). **Farmacia San José,** Pto. Mazatlán 523 (tel. 7-13-87), is open 24 hours. The **Centro de Salud** is on Chetumal (tel. 7-15-21), near the fire and police station (English spoken; open 24hr.). In an **emergency,** dial 134. The **police** are on Mar Blanco Sur, just south of Chetumal (tel. 7-13-50 and 7-10-21). The **post office** is on Mar Blanco between Ensenada and Chetumal (tel. 7-13-30), five blocks inland from Cortés (open Mon.-Fri. 8am-3pm, Sat. 9am-1pm). **Postal Code:** 21850. **Phone Code:** 657.

**Accommodations** There are two kinds of accommodations in San Felipe: those with A/C, and those without. Travelers who prefer the former will end up paying *mucho dinero* for mediocre rooms. Sadly enough, San Felipe is one of the most expensive cities in one of the most expensive parts of the country; serious penny-pinchers will not find any cheap lodging. Those who plan on staying in this expensive little town should consider camping. A cheaper option is to rent a room in a private residence; check with the tourist office for a list. **Carmelita** (tel. 7-18-31), across from the Chapala Motel, is one of the private residences renting out rooms with A/C and private bath. Four rooms are available, housing single people or "married" couples only (US$25 per room). Crammed between curio shops and administered from the liquor store next door, **Motel El Pescador,** on Mar de Cortés at Chetumal (tel. 7-11-83 or 7-10-44), offers spacious and nicely furnished rooms overlooking the beach with A/C, color TV, and private baths. It's a real bargain (at least by San Felipe standards). Check-out time is noon (singles 175 pesos; doubles 200 pesos).

As any Californian with an RV can tell you, San Felipe is renowned for its trailer parks, which are remarkably safe and bountiful. The most famous is **Ruben's** (tel. 7-14-42), toward the end of Av. Golfo de California in Playa Norte. To reach Ruben's, turn left from Chetumal onto Mar de Cortés; it's a short drive up. Individual beach-front parking spaces are topped with two-story, open-air bungalows. Each spot easily accommodates carloads of folks with sleeping bags. RVs can hook up to electricity, hot water, and sewer connections (office open daily 7am-7pm; US$20 per vehicle, up to 3 people, US$2 per extra person). Smack dab in the middle of town on Mar de Cortés, **Campo San Felipe** (tel. 7-10-12) lures campers with a fabulous beachfront location. A thatched roof shelters each fully-loaded trailer spot (most spots US$17-27, a few US$9-10; depending on location and proximity to the beach; US$2 per extra person, children under 6 free; hookups US$1 extra; tent space US$10).

**Food** Mar de Cortés is crammed with restaurants advertising air-conditioned relief. Just one block over the Malecón, *ostionerías* and fish *taquerías* serve up fresh sea-food under shady thatched roofs for fewer clams. Shrimp tacos are US$1, full shrimp dinners US$5-6. **Los Gemelos**, on Mar de Cortés at Acapulco, near Bancomer (tel. 7-10-63), and its identical neighbor **Restaurant El Club** (tel. 7-11-75), feature beef, chicken, and shrimp enchiladas (22 pesos) and Veracruz-style fish (30 pesos) on pristine white tablecloths below hanging plastic turtles. The *cama-rones al mojo de ajo* (garlic shrimp 55 pesos) is one of the world's most perfect meals. Ice-cold *agua purificada* available free. Placemats feature octopi playing ten-nis—really (open daily 7am-11pm).

**Sights** People come to San Felipe to swim in the warm, tranquil, and invitingly blue Gulf waters. The beach in town follows along the Malecón and gets crowded on weekends. **Jet-skis** can be rented for around US$35 per hour. Try the beaches farther south for scuba and snorkeling—the water's clearer. A booth that rents jet-skis and beach buggies is located right next to Motel El Pescador (US$25 per hr., open 8am-6pm). **Banana boats** wait along the beach in front of Bar Miramar, ready to take you for a 20-minute spin (9am-6pm, 20 pesos per person, min. 5 people).

The whole Bahía is generally clean, safe, and appealing; beaches outside of town are more isolated, but might require a long walk or a drive. Every beach is accompa-nied by a commercialized RV trailer park, but, as always, beaches are free—you only need to pay if you're parking. **Playa del Sol, Playa Jalisco,** and **Playa de los Amigos** are all RV parks in the north of town, home to middle-age retirees. The only way to get there is by taxi (20 pesos).

Take time to visit the **Altar de la Virgen de Guadalupe,** a shrine to the virgin at the top of the *cerritos* (hills) near the lighthouse. After a scorching hike, you'll be rewarded with a spectacular view of San Felipe and the blue bay. Don't try to drive up unless you've got a 4-wheel-drive vehicle—the loose sand won't be forgiving. Sixty-four kilometers south of San Felipe is the **Valle de los Gigantes National Park.** With cacti up to 15m tall, the park was the original home of the giant cactus which represented Mexico at the 1992 World's Fair in Seville, Spain. Fossil hunters will be elated to find a vast array of petrified sea life.

**Entertainment** Because of all the tourists eager to spend dough, there's no dearth of dollars—or places to drink. Nowhere is this more evident than the high-priced, high-profile bar **Rockodile** on Malecón at Acapulco (tel. 7-12-19). Here, drunk customers write their names with magic marker on dollar bills and paste them up. Check out the volleyball court, pool table, and outdoor terrace. It's mellow during the day, but on weekend nights, it's a sweaty dance party; to begin inducing amnesia, try the electric-blue king-sized beverage, the "Adios motherfucker" (US$4). Cover $3-4 on Friday and Saturday nights (½-price happy hour Sun.-Fri. 11am-7pm; open daily 11am-2am).

Seasoned veterans nurse drinks at **Bar Miramar,** Mar de Cortés 315 (tel. 7-11-92). The oldest bar in San Felipe may look like a *cantina* from the 60s, but the patrons come for company, not glitz. Push a few cues over green felt on the pool tables out front (beer US$1.50, margaritas US$2; happy hour Mon.-Thurs. 3-7pm; open daily 10am-2am). **Beachcomber,** on Chetumal and Malecón (tel. 7-11-83), always has sports on TV and tourists tranquilly nursing a buzz. A well-stocked bar, long wooden counter, and jukebox featuring everyone's favorite sounds of the 1980s makes this a quiet, understated place to get trashed—and one of the cheapest (beer US$1.25, margaritas US$2; open daily 10am-2am).

# BAJA CALIFORNIA SUR

## ■ Guerrero Negro

Twenty degrees cooler than the bleak Desierto de Vizcaíno to the southeast, Guerrero Negro (pop. 10,000), though dusty and painfully industrial, might earn a soft spot in the hearts of heat-weary northbound travelers—there's always a cool breeze here, and even late summer nights can be positively chilly. Be prepared for lots of wind and gray. Guerrero Negro resembles a beach town without the beach; its sandy roads and salty breeze dupe travelers into thinking ocean waters are nearby.

In Guerrero Negro, salt is God, king, and country. So saline is Guerrero Negro that even breathing deeply of the town's air can send the hypochondriac's blood pressure soaring. The salt plant is now the world's largest, dominating the town's economy and attracting job-seekers from throughout the region. Although the locals are friendly and the cool breezes cathartic, Guerrero Negro's most attractive feature is its gas station, a beautiful PEMEX wonder. Fill up that tank, and burn, baby, burn.

**Orientation** Guerrero Negro sprawls along 3km of the Transpeninsular Highway. Its two main roads, the **highway** and **Avenida Baja California,** are home to basically all of the town's industrial and commercial centers; poor residential areas, filled with grim-looking shacks, lie one block off these roads to either side. The highway runs from the bus station at the south end to the riverbed and salt plant at the north end of town, where it turns. Av. Baja California continues into Guerrero Negro, veering to the left at the park and church.

**Practical Information** Change money at **Banamex** (tel. 7-05-55 to -57), on Av. Baja California, just in front of the plant (open Mon.-Fri. 8:30am-1pm). Travelers heading south should change currency here, as 24-hour **ATMs** (also in Sta. Rosalia and then La Paz) and bank services become sparse. **Telephones** are in Farmacia San Martín (tel. 7-09-11 or 7-11-11), on the Transpeninsular Highway, 100m north of the clinic (open Mon.-Sat. 8am-10pm, Sun. 9am-4pm). International collect calls or calling-card calls are free at the wall phone in the lobby of Motel Brisa Salina, on the highway across from the Union 76 ball (the one farther from the bus station).

The **ABC Autotransportes de Baja California** terminal (tel. 7-06-11) is one of the first buildings from the highway on the access road. ABC sends buses north (5 per day, 7pm-8am) to Ensenada (10hr., 173 pesos), Lázaro Cárdenas (7hr., 113 pesos), Punta Prieta (4hr., 49 pesos), El Rosario (6hr., 83 pesos), Rosarito (2hr., 29 pesos), San Quintín (8hr., 118 pesos), and Tijuana (11hr., 209 pesos); and south to La Paz (5 per day, 4:30am-9pm, 11hr., 228 pesos), Mulegé (4 per day, 4hr., 83 pesos), Santa Rosalía (4 per day, 3hr., 63 pesos), and points in between. Yellow **minivans** run up and down the Transpeninsular Highway (every 15min., 7am-10pm, 4 pesos).

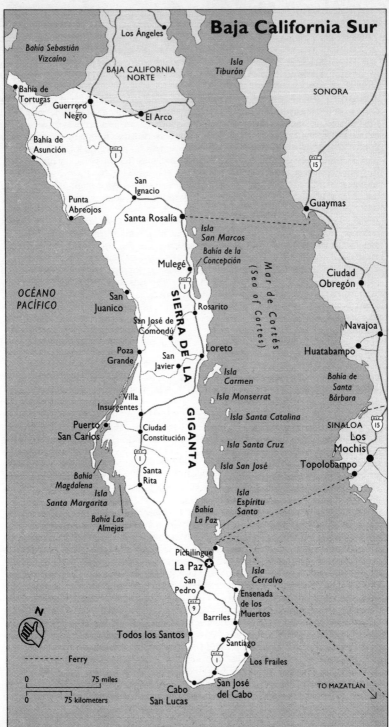

# Baja California Sur

Bahía Sebastián Vizcaíno

Los Ángeles

BAJA CALIFORNIA NORTE

Isla Tiburón

SONORA

Bahía de Tortugas

Guerrero Negro

El Arco

Bahía de Asunción

1

Punta Abreojos

San Ignacio

Santa Rosalía

Guaymas

15

Isla San Marcos

Bahía de la Concepción

Mulegé

1

San Juanico

SIERRA DE LA

Rosarito

Ciudad Obregón

OCÉANO PACÍFICO

San José de Comondú

Navajoa

Poza Grande

San Javier

Loreto

Huatabampo

Isla Carmen

Villa Insurgentes

GIGANTA

Isla Monserrat

Bahía de Santa Bárbara

Puerto San Carlos

Ciudad Constitución

Isla Santa Catalina

SINALOA

15

Mar de Cortés (Sea of Cortés)

Isla Santa Cruz

Los Mochis

1

Santa Rita

Isla San José

Topolobampo

Bahía Magdalena

Isla Santa Margarita

Bahía Las Almejas

Isla Espíritu Santo

Bahía La Paz

Pichilingue

La Paz

Isla Cerralvo

San Pedro

9

Ensenada de los Muertos

Barriles

N

Todos los Santos

Santiago

Ferry

Los Frailes

0        75 miles

0        75 kilometers

1

Cabo San Lucas

San José del Cabo

TO MAZATLÁN

For **groceries** and **stuff,** try the "Mercado" in front of Motel las Dunas (open daily 9am-11pm). An **IMSS Hospital and Clinic** is on the highway at Blvd. M. Zaragoza (tel. 7-04-33), half a kilometer north of the water tower, in Col. Rubic. The **police** (tel. 7-02-22) are in the Delegación Municipal, a few hundred meters before the salt plant. The **post office** (tel. 7-03-44) is off Av. Baja California, two blocks past the church (open Mon.-Fri. 8am-3pm). **Postal Code: 23940. Phone Code: 115.**

**Accommodations and Food** The best bargain in town is the **Motel Las Dunas** on the highway (tel. 7-00-55), below the water tank, a short walk north from the bus station. Immaculate rooms with large showers are as worthy as those at more expensive spots. Lukewarm *agua purificada* is available free, and the extremely courteous staff helps in every way possible (singles 66 pesos; doubles 77 pesos; triples 81 pesos; key deposit 10 pesos). **Hotel Ballenas** (tel. 7-01-10), off the highway toward the entrance to town (on your left as you drive in), has lovely, spacious red rooms with color TVs. Very friendly *mi-casa-es-su-casa* service might make you give the old salt' n' sand dump disguised as a town another chance (singles 90 pesos; doubles 120 pesos).

Many aspects of Guerrero Negro are a little hard to swallow, and the city's food is no exception. If you're looking for food after 9pm, particularly during the low season, bless you. The local specialty is lobster caught in the *laguna*. **La Palapa** (tel. 7-16-48) is on the highway across from the PEMEX station closer to the bus station. The dining room is decorated with model boats, shells, photographs of marine life, and plastic fish caught in nets. Try the local fish (20 pesos) or the absolutely delicious octopus (30 pesos). A large platter of french toast goes for 15 pesos (open daily 8am-9pm). Some of the best food in the town can be found at the brand-new **Restaurant Bar/Lupitas,** the highway between Motel las Dunas and Hotel las Brisas. Absolutely delicious home-cooked food in a large kitchen with only three tables. Watch the news with the friendly owners as you chow down on *camarones* (25 pesos) or *comida corrida.*

**Sights and Entertainment** Excitement comes to town between late December and early March with the thousands of gray whales who make the annual swim from the Bering Sea to reproduce in the waters offshore. During the rest of the year, more excitement might be found staring at a blank wall. If you time your visit correctly, you can commune with hundreds of whales in the **Parque Natural de las Ballenas Grises,** on the **Laguna Ojo de Liebre,** formerly a deep-water port facility of the salt company. In the early morning, whales swim right up to the docks; during the rest of the day, ascend a tall observation tower for a look. No public transportation is available to the park. To get there, head south on Rte. 1 toward Santa Rosalía for 8-15km. A sign points out the 30km dirt road to the *laguna*. Staffers at the park sometimes lead whale-watching tours in early January and February.

The **Bahía de los Ángeles** is populated by dolphins, blue and gray whales, sea lions, and many species of birds. From January to March, **Servicios Turísticos Mario** (tel. 7-07-88), on the highway near the PEMEX closer to the bus station, offers tours to the Bahía (min. 10 people) and of indigenous cave paintings in the Sierra de San Francisco. Most cave painting excursions, however, leave from San Ignacio (see p. 149). On a four-hour tour of the *laguna*, you'll visit the **Dunas de Soledad,** 10km of pearly white dunes whose configuration changes daily due to the movement of the tides. The dunes get their name from the first residents of the area, a solitary Sinaloa couple who settled here after a three-month overland trek. An archaeological site known for its unique and impressive rock paintings, **Mesa del Carmen** lies 68km southwest of Guerrero Negro. While it can only be reached by car, guides can be arranged in **El Arco,** a small town 10km southwest of Guerrero Negro. For more information, contact Jorge Serrano (tel. 8-25-31) in Ensenada.

# ■ San Ignacio

More than any other stop on the arid Baja Peninsula, San Ignacio (pop. 2000) seems like a tropical oasis. From a distance, the town appears to be a cruel illusion, a mirage of the mind—leafy date palms, flowering bushes, and broad swaths of green appear magically in the middle of the blistering desert. Chin up, kid—you're not dreaming. The area around San Ignacio is blessed with the most plentiful underground freshwater supply in all Baja California Sur; of late, they've been dammed up to form a murky lake used for swimming and irrigating local orchards.

Though hot during summer days, San Ignacio earns points for just about everything else. Locals are extremely amiable, and the whole town is one big, happy, close-knit family, relatively undisturbed by gringos (but also super-hospitable to them) for most of the year. San Ignacio's intimate atmosphere, beautiful nighttime starscapes, and historic mission overlooking the *zócalo* are but a few of the reasons why so many of the pleasure-seekers who set eyes on the town end up settling down here. San Ignacio is also a prime point of departure for cave painting and whale-watching tours.

**Orientation and Practical Information** A winding road canopied by swaying date palms leads from the Transpeninsular Highway to the *zócalo*. Within 10 minutes of pulling in, you'll know tiny San Ignacio better than your hometown. Life revolves around the wonderfully tranquil *zócalo,* which is delineated by **Juan Bautista Luyando** and the mission to the north, **Morelos** to the south, **Juárez** to the east, and **Hidalgo** to the west. Locals are more than happy to give directions.

There's no official tourist office in town, but to hear friendly, informative chatter about San Ignacio, visit the **elderly man** who owns the mini-mart next to Restaurant Chalita on Hidalgo (tel. 4-01-50, 4-01-60, and 4-01-90; open Mon.-Sat. 7am-7pm, Sun. 7am-1pm); he also leads tours to the cave paintings and whale expeditions. A lone **public phone** stands in the north side of the *zócalo;* you can place calls and send **faxes** at a pricier *caseta,* Hidalgo 24 (tel. 4-02-50; open Mon.-Fri. 8am-1pm and 3-6pm).

**Buses** pick up passengers at the sheltered bench 2km from San Ignacio on the Transpeninsular Highway. *De paso* buses leave at 7pm for Ensenada (13hr., 207 pesos), Guerrero Negro (3hr., 46 pesos), and Tijuana (14hr., 31 pesos), and at 10am and 6pm for La Paz (8hr., 122 pesos) and Rosarito (stopping at Santa Rosalía; 1hr., 20 pesos), Mulegé, and Loreto. **Nuevos Almacenes,** a good-sized **grocery store,** is on the corner of Juárez and Juan Bautista Luyando (tel. 4-01-22), facing the *zócalo.* They also carry a small collection of **unintentionally chic bargain basement clothes** in the back (open Mon.-Sat. 8am-noon and 2-7pm, Sun. 8am-noon). The pharmacy, **Boticas Ceseña,** is unmarked at Madero 24A (tel. 4-00-76, after hours 4-00-75), parallel to and east of Juárez and Hidalgo (open daily 8:30am-1pm and 3-7pm). To reach the **Centro de Salud,** walk five minutes away from the highway down Hidalgo, which turns into Ocampo. Turn right on Independencia, a tiny dirt road; it's the large white building on the right-hand side (open daily 8am-3pm). If you have a medical **emergency** after hours, call **Fischer Lucero** (tel. 4-01-90), the local doctor. Contact the health center or the police in an emergency only. The **police** (tel. 4-03-77) are in the Delegación Municipal on Ocampo and Zaragoza (open daily 8am-3pm). The **post office** is in the gray stone building on Juárez next to the *zócalo* (open Mon.-Fri. 8am-3pm). **Postal Code:** 23930. **Phone Code:** 115.

**Accommodations** San Ignacio has few accommodations, and they don't come cheap. Make reservations or call early if you're going to be in town during the Semana Santa or El Día de San Ignacio (July 31). The family living in **Restaurant Chalita,** Hidalgo 9 (tel. 4-00-82), rents bedrooms that ooze with local culture. The small, clean rooms have fans and black-and-white TVs (singles 75 pesos). **Hotel Posada,** on Ocampo and Indepencia (tel. 4-03-13), a three-minute walk down Ciprés from Hidalgo, has remarkably clean rooms with standing fans and private baths and a family-type atmosphere (singles and doubles 140 pesos). **El Padrino RV Park** (tel. 4-00-

89) is 500m from the *zócalo* on the road connecting San Ignacio to the highway. Full trailer hookup (US$10, without electricity US$7) comes with a complimentary margarita from the pleasant Flojo's Restaurant/Bar. Motorcycles cost US$3 to park. El Padrino also offers four brand spankin' new rooms with private baths (singles 70 pesos or US$10; doubles 140 pesos or US$20).

**Food** Most people chow down in the *zócalo*, partly because the food is great, and partly because they have no other choice—San Ignacio only has a handful of restaurants. Seafood dishes receive top billing on restaurant menus. Eat outdoors under the wonderfully starry sky at **Restaurant-Bar Rene's** (tel. 4-02-56), just outside the *zócalo* off Hidalgo. Wash down the house special, the delectable *calamar empanizado* (breaded squid, 35 pesos) with a beer (7 pesos). If you'd rather eat under a roof, head into their round thatched hut and stare out at the small adjoining pond. In any case, ask for Victor—he'll take care of you (open daily 7am-10pm). **Restaurant Chalita,** Hidalgo 9 (tel. 4-00-82), is housed in an old-fashioned Mexican kitchen. Sit on random furniture, listen to the caged birds sing, and find salvation in a warm plate of *pescado al mojo de ajo* (26 pesos), enchiladas (17 pesos), or *chiles rellenos* (20 pesos; open daily 7:30am-10pm). **Flojo's Restaurant/Bar** (tel. 4-00-89) is part of El Padrino RV Park (see p. 149) and a five-minute walk from town. Even you will become *flojo* (slack) when you overstuff yourself with three chicken burritos with rice and beans (29 pesos) or breaded Italian meat (34 pesos). Lean back, watch the stars shine between the reeds of the enormous *palapa*, and listen to the crickets chirp (open daily 7am-10:30pm).

**Sights** A colonial colossus towering over wild, leafy vegetation, the **Mission of San Ignacio,** on the northern side of the *zócalo*, was founded in 1728 by Jesuit missionary Juan Bautista. The construction of the mission proved a logistic nightmare; wood had to be hauled in from the Guadalupe mission in the Sierras, furniture was brought from Mulegé after a scorching four-day mule ride through the unpaved desert, and the paintings were carried by boat from the mainland. The mission is a beautiful achievement, well worth the difficulties—magnificent on the outside, cool inside, and heavenly at night, when illuminated by outdoor spotlights. The stately pinkish stone exterior has aged well; it is one of the most fantastic of the Baja missions. When you are inside, look up to see a flying gold angel seemingly suspended in the dome. A particularly striking outside view of the mission poking above palms and huts in the evening can be seen from halfway between the *zócalo* and Hotel Posada, on the small path. The newly opened **Mission Museum,** on Loyando (tel. 4-02-22), 30m west of the mission, tells the story of the nearby cave paintings and even has its own huge faux-cave painting (open Mon.-Sat. 8am-8pm; free).

The main tourist draw near San Ignacio are the **painted caves,** 75km away in the **Sierra de San Francisco.** Five hundred paintings, probably more than 10,000-years old, reside within a 12-square-kilometer area. **Oscar Fischer** of Hotel Posada and his son, **Dagoberto,** offer various tours to the caves (tel. 4-03-13 or 4-01-56). US$25 (during the tourist season) gets you a nine-hour trip to one cave and two petroglyphic zones. It leaves at around 8am and makes as many stops in between as requested. A two-day tour will take you to the impressive **La Pintada** and the minor **El Ratón** caves. For US$65, you'll get transportation, a guide, and a mule. If you're planning to sleep comfortably during the trip, you'll need a tent and an additional mule (US$10) to carry it. Some adventurous travelers make the trip from cave to cave on foot (about 8km each way), saving all mule costs but leaving their bodies worn, to say the least. US$80 plus tent and mule costs gets you the grandest tour of all: a three-day, eight-cave extravaganza that will show you more indigenous paintings than you probably ever wanted to see—all but the most resilient travelers will feel battle-worn. All trips must be cleared with the Mexican government, so it is recommended that you call well in advance. The managers also run trips to the Laguna San Ignacio to spy on **gray whales.** They leave before 7am and cost US$45 per person. Note that prices for all tours (caves and whales) assume groups of six or more; smaller parties can expect to pay more. Tours of the painted caves and whale-watching expeditions are also led by the owner of **Flojos Restaurant/Bar** and **El Padrino RV Park** (tel. 4-00-89).

# ■ Santa Rosalía

Not only is Santa Rosalía a convenient transportation hub for buses and ferries, it is also heir to a rich and colorful history. After an enormously rich copper ore was discovered here in 1868, Santa Rosalía was settled by a French-owned mining company. The town was settled on the sides of the mountain in an orderly fashion according to rank, so that the wealthier, higher-ranking officials literally lived higher up, and the town's cast-iron church, Iglesia Santa Bárbara, was designed by Gustave Eiffel. Today, mountains of abandoned machinery and railroad cars bristle with rust, returning their metals to the ground, and Santa Rosalia is nowhere as picturesque as its history might lead one to believe—even the public beaches are somewhat dirty and deserted, and the town shuts down by 9pm. If you're planning to visit Santa Rosalía, keep in mind that the town is unbearably hot and humid in the summer. The Gulf breezes don't cool it nearly enough. Still, Santa Rosalía's not a bad stopover—you'll get a chance to see jarring European architecture in the middle of Baja. The town is also often used as a departure or arrival point for the cross-Gulf ferry to and from Guaymas, Sonora.

**Orientation and Practical Information** To get from the **ferry** to **Obregón,** Santa Rosalía's main strip, turn right as you leave the ferry compound; Obregón is the second left. **Banamex,** on Obregón (tel. 2-00-10 or 2-09-84), changes traveler's checks, has a 24-hour **ATM,** and, most importantly, sports ice-cold A/C. Find some excuse to go in (open Mon.-Fri. 8:30am-1pm). **LADATELs** pepper the town; find some in front of the church and the Palacio Municipal. **Farmacia Central** (see listing below) has a long-distance *caseta.*

Most **buses** depart from the **ABC station** (tel. 2-01-50), across the street from the ferry office. Buses travel north to Ensenada (13½hr., 196 pesos), Guerrero Negro (3½hr., 52 pesos), Mexicali (18½hr., 257 pesos), Punta Prieta (7hr., 82 pesos), El Rosario (9hr., 128 pesos), San Ignacio (1hr., 20 pesos), San Quintín (9½hr., 143 pesos), and Tijuana (15hr., 222 pesos). Heading south, all buses go to Ciudad Constitución (4½hr., 80 pesos), Ej. Insurgentes (4hr., 71 pesos), La Paz (5 per day, 9:30am-11pm, 7hr., 117 pesos), Loreto (3hr., 49 pesos), and San Ignacio (1hr., 18 pesos). The **ABC Autotransportes bus office** is on Constitución, six blocks inland from the highway; from here, one bus heads south at 11am daily. From Santa Rosalía, you can catch the **ferry** connecting Baja to Guaymas on the mainland (Sun. and Wed. 8am, 7hr., *salón* 110 pesos, *turista* 222 pesos, *cabina* 330 pesos, *especial* 438 pesos). The boat leaves from the modern, blue and green **Sematur** office (tel. 2-00-13) on Rte. 1 (the Transpeninsular Highway), just south of town. To reach the docks, catch a bus from the **ABC Autotransportes** station, about 200m south of the ferry. Those with cars must purchase their spot in advance and show a tourist card, registration, and proof of their Mexican insurance (cars up to 5m long 993 pesos; motorcycles 174 pesos; office open Mon., Wed., Thurs., Sat. 8am-3pm, Tues., Fri. 8am-1pm and 3-6pm). Departure days and times, prices, and office hours are in constant flux, so be sure to call the office or talk to a travel agent to confirm the schedule.

**Farmacia Central,** Av. Obregón at Plaza (tel. 2-20-70; fax 2-22-70), is owned by English-speaking Dr. Chang Tam (open Mon.-Sat. 9am-10pm, Sun. 9am-1pm and 7-10pm). The **Centro de Salud** is at Juan Michel Costeau (tel. 2-13-37 or 2-13-36). Send letters home from the **post office** on Constitución between Calles 2 and Altamirano (open Mon.-Fri. 8am-3pm). **Postal Code:** 23920. **Phone Code:** 115.

**Accommodations and Food** If you're going to stay in sweltering Santa Rosalía, consider popping the few extra pesos for A/C. The budget standout is **Hotel Olvera,** Calle Plaza 14 (tel. 2-00-57 or -67), about three blocks from the shore on Constitución. From the bus station, take a left and walk along the water towards town until you come to the old train engine in front of the town's two main streets—follow

Constitución, the left one, and it's on your right at the bridge. Enjoy spacious bathrooms, large double beds with patriotic American bedspreads, and free lukewarm *agua purificada.* Rooms come with color TV and naturally hot water (in Baja during the summer, you might have trouble finding cold water; singles 100 pesos, with A/C 120 pesos; doubles 120 pesos, with A/C 190 pesos). Perhaps the cheapest room in town can be found at the cozy **Hotel Playa,** between Calles 1 and 2 on Constitución, behind the Hotel Olvera. There are only 12 rooms, and although they're run down, the mattresses are soft (singles 50 pesos; doubles 80 pesos; triples 110 pesos). **RV Park Las Palmas,** 3.5km south of town, has 32 spots with full hookups, a laundromat, and a restaurant (US$10 for 2 people, US$2 per additional person).

Santa Rosalía's best-known establishment, **El Boleo Bakery,** Obregón at Calle 4 (tel. 2-03-10), renowned for its French architecture, deserves a visit for its excellent baked goods as well. Otherwordly French bread (1.50 pesos), *pan dulce* (2 pesos), and doughnuts (2.50 pesos) thrill customers (open Mon.-Sat. 8am-10pm). **Asaderos,** a small corner taco stand, has more than just cheap food. The meat and salsas are super, and the roadside stools and black countertops are unrivaled for *ambiente.* Their delicious *quesatacos* (6 pesos) and *tostadas* (6 pesos) delight (open daily 1-10pm). To get there, head down Obregón for six blocks, make a left and walk straight one block, it should be on the right corner.

**Sights** The wooden houses, general stores, and saloons along Santa Rosalía's streets recall the town's mining-boom days. Startling specimens of 19th-century French architecture include the long and many-windowed **Palacio Municipal,** the **Hotel Francés,** and **El Boleo Bakery,** with their pure colors, simplicity of form, and modern use of glass and steel. The most serendipitous of artifacts is the pre-fabricated white cast-iron **Iglesia Santa Bárbara,** at Obregón and Calle 1. Designed by Gustave Eiffel (of Tower fame) for a mission in Africa, the church was never picked up by the company that had commissioned it. French mining *concessionaires* spotted the iron church at the 1889 Exhibition Universale de Paris and decided Santa Rosalía couldn't do without it. Observers either love it or hate it; its outside panels look like they fell off an industrial washing machine. The purple stained-glass windows are "interesting!" Those travelers looking for fun in the sun and abundant water sports would do better to make tracks south for the heavenly beaches in Bahía de la Concepción.

# ■ Mulegé

Good things often come in small packages. Mulegé (pop. 3500) is very small...and very good. Although many pass this tiny town while bookin' it north (or south), Mulegé offers much worth stopping for. Any one of Mulegé's 80-odd-and-growing expats will tell you that their half-desert, half-shady wonderland replete with date palms is the best little town in all Baja, and after a look around, you might just be compelled to believe them. Many people can't seem to stay away—the food is good, the people amiable, the town easily navigable in 15 minutes on foot. Best of all, Mulegé, located 136km north of Loreto and 300km south of Guerrero Negro, is the best place from which to explore the glistening beaches and storybook-blue sea of Bahía de la Concepción to the south (see p. 154). By day, most of the town's visitors—and many of its expats—abandon the little parcel of preciousness that is Mulegé proper and head for the heavenly sands of the Bahía.

**Orientation and Practical Information** Soon after bearing left off the Transpeninsular Highway, the road into Mulegé forks. To the left is **Moctezuma;** to the right is **Martínez.** Both are soon crossed by **Zaragoza;** take a right onto Zaragoza to get to the *zócalo,* which is one block away. **Madero** heads east from the *zócalo* (away from the highway) and, after following the Mulegé River for about 3km, hits the water at the town beach, **Playa de Mulegé.**

**El Candil** restaurant serves as the unofficial **tourist office.** English-speaking **Kerry "El Vikingo" Otterstrom** has written and published a 160-page book on Mulegé (50 pesos). He is a bartender at El Candil and can always be found here, unless he's out leading a tour. The **Hotel Las Casitas,** Madero 50 (tel. 3-00-19), also has tourist info. Ask for Javier—besides leading tours, he also has info on beaches, camping, and fishing. **Minisúper Padilla,** on Zaragoza at Martínez (tel./fax 3-01-90), one block north of plaza, has many **phones** for international calls; fax service may be available in 1998.

The **bus station** is simply a sheltered blue bench at the turnoff to Mulegé from Rte. 1. All buses are *de paso,* a phrase which might roughly be translated as "inevitably arrives late and full." Northbound buses stop by daily at 4, 5, and 7pm and head to Mexicali (19½hr., 307 pesos) via Santa Rosalía (1hr., 13 pesos), San Ignacio (2hr., 25 pesos), Rosarito (6hr., 99 pesos), Punta Prieta (8hr., 103 pesos), Santa Inés (9hr., 129 pesos), El Rosario (10hr., 141 pesos), San Quintín (10½hr., 158 pesos), Lázaro Cárdenas (11hr., 172 pesos), San Vicente (13hr., 209 pesos), Ensenada (14½hr., 228 pesos), Tijuana (16hr., 260 pesos), and Tecate (17hr., 273 pesos). Southbound buses stop by at 10 and 11:30am and go to La Paz (6hr., 110 pesos) via Loreto (2hr., 37 pesos), Insurgentes (3hr., 52 pesos), and Ciudad Constitución (3½hr., 71 pesos).

**Lavamática Claudia** (tel. 3-00-57) is next to the Hotel Terrazas (23 pesos per load; open Mon.-Sat. 8am-6pm). The **Red Cross** is on Madero (tel. 3-02-58 and 3-03-80, after hours 3-01-39; CB channel 14), 200m east of the plaza. **Farmacia Moderna** (tel. 3-00-42) is on Madero, on the plaza (open daily 8am-1pm and 4-10pm). **Centro de Salud B (ISSTE),** Madero 28 (tel. 3-02-98), treats medical emergencies (open 8am-2:30pm). The **post office** is on Martínez (tel. 3-02-05), across from the PEMEX station (open Mon.-Fri. 9am-3pm). **Postal Code:** 23900. **Phone Code:** 685.

**Accommodations**  Economical hotels crowd the center of town, but they're far from the beaches. Although Mulegé has plenty of cheap rooms (for such a tiny little town), those with sleeping bags often find the best deals on the shore. **Casa de Huéspedes Manuelita,** on Moctezuma (tel. 3-01-75), next to Los Equipales, around the corner from Zaragoza, has somewhat clean rooms with soft beds, table fans, and private showers. Campers who simply need to use the bathroom and shower pay 10 pesos (singles 50 pesos; doubles 70 pesos; all prices negotiable). **Casa de Huéspedes Nachita,** on Moctezuma (tel. 3-01-40), two doors down from Casa de Huéspedes Manuelita, has clean rooms, hot water, and even a miniscule courtyard for an unbeatable 40 pesos per room (some rooms have 2 beds). **Motel la Siesta** (tel. 3-05-55) is right near the bus station, on your left as you head into town. Live in luxury—all the big, tiled, and TVed rooms with spotless bathrooms adjoin a large outdoor patio with huge, shady trees. The frigid A/C is a blessing (singles 150 pesos; doubles 180 pesos). **Orchard RV Park** and **María Isabel RV Park,** both just south of town and accessible from the Transpeninsular Highway, are on Madero about 1km toward the beach, near a freshwater oasis lagoon (US$15 per night; space for tents US$6).

**Food**  For something informal and authentic, try **Taquería Doney,** known more commonly as **Doney's,** near the bus station across the street from Motel la Siesta. This is where locals go; in fact, they cram both the indoor tables and outdoor stools, wolfing down delicious tacos (15 pesos) or huge steak *tortas* (13 pesos). Plenty of opportunity to eavesdrop (open daily 10am-10pm). **Restaurant La Almeja,** at the end of Morelos near the lighthouse, about 3km from the center of town, is right on the beach. It offers outstanding seafood, including tasty and filling *sopa de siete mares* (seven seas soup, which includes just about every creature that ever swam in water, 35 pesos; open daily 8am-11pm). **El Candil Restaurant,** north of the plaza on Zaragoza near Martínez, serves an enormous Mexican combination platter with rice, beans, *chiles rellenos,* and tacos (37 pesos), and an excellent fish fillet (30 pesos; open daily 7am-10pm).

**Sights and Sand**  Mulegé's lovely **mission, Misión Santa Rosalía de Mulegé,** sits on a hill to the west. The awesome stone fortress/church is imposing. To get there, walk down Zaragoza away from the *zócalo,* go under the bridge, and turn right on the lovely shaded lane with all the palms. The mission is not a museum; mass is still held every Sunday. For a great view of the whole town, river, and palms, climb the steps to the top of the hill. Although the paths are not lit at night, the mission is a perfect place for a meditative stroll; walk where you will be immediately visible to cars.

Over seven hundred 14,000-year-old pre-Hispanic cave paintings are located at **La Trinidad** and the **Cuevas de San Borjita.** Kerry Otterstrom of El Candil Restaurant leads trips to La Trinidad that include hiking and swimming 200m in a narrow canyon (US$37.50 per person). The trip to San Borjita has a milder hike, no swimming, and more spectacular caves (US$50 per person). Longer trips can be arranged (up to 7 days, US$50 per person per day including hotel, food, and drink). The guide speaks English, Spanish, German, Thai, and Korean. Other tours available from **Salvador Castro Tours,** at Hotel Las Casitas (tel. 3-00-19).

Two beaches lie only 3km from the center of town. **El Faro** is at the end of Madero, which becomes a dirt road long before you reach the beach. Alternatively, reach the **public beach** by following the Mulegé River to the Sea of Cortés, where it drains. For a more isolated beach, walk to the PEMEX station about 4km south on the highway, continue about 20m south, and take the dirt road leading off to the left until you reach a lonely beach with sand dunes and desert hills overlooking somewhat rocky sand. Locals consider this area to be quite safe. Watch out for jellyfish, especially in June and July. Be warned, though—these beaches can't hold a candle to those 18km south in Bahía de la Concepción (see p. 154).

Mulegé's abundance of sea life makes for great **sport-fishing** and **clamming.** Isaiah Osuna Murillo can usually be found at his office in the **Hotel Serenidad** on the Mulegé River—he leads tours to do both. Fishing usually runs US$110 for three to four people, and he promises a delicious clambake and cookout (with all the clams you caught) for 500 pesos and as many people can fit in two cars.

**Mulegé Divers,** Madero 45 (tel. 3-00-59), down the street from Hotel Las Casitas, rents scuba equipment, leads boat excursions into Bahía de la Concepción, and sells Mulegé T-shirts (open Mon.-Sat. 9am-1pm and 3-6pm). If you already know how to scuba dive, try the five-hour trip (US$40, min. 2 people); otherwise, an instruction course helps you get your feet wet (US$70). They also organize five-hour-long snorkeling excursions (US$25 including equipment, minimum 2 people) and rent snorkeling gear (US$10). All excursions leave at 8am. Make reservations at least one day in advance. The best snorkeling is at nearby **Islas Pitahaya, San Ramón, Liebre, Blanca, Coyote,** and **Guapa.** Ask at the tourist office or at the dive shop for maps/orientation. October 2 promises loads of fun—this town celebration commemorates the battle in which the residents of Mulegé drove back the gringos from up north.

# ▩ Bahía de la Concepción

Heaven on earth may just be the 48km arc of rocky outcrops, shimmering beaches, and bright blue sea known as the Bahía de la Concepción. Forget the beaches of the northern peninsula; Bahía de la Concepción, beginning 16km south of Mulegé, is where it's at. Cactus-studded hills and stark cliffs drop straight down to white sand, translucent waters, and coves which look more perfect than those inhabited by Neverland's mermaids. Grown sport fishers and shell collectors weep at the variety and sheer size of the specimens caught here, and divers fall under the spell of underwater sights. As if this isn't enough, the Bahía remains relatively quiet and virginal, still untouched by running water and permanent electricity. While the Bahía is generally blissfully noiseless, Christmas holidays and Semana Santa bring rows of RVs stretching from the highway to the beach, strewn beer cans, and *mucho* noise. Come early to find some peace and a place to put your towel. All other times, Bahía de la Concepción might just be Mexico's most secret treasure. What are *you* waiting for?

**Playa Punta Arena,** 16km south of Mulegé, is far enough from the road that the roar of the waves drowns out the noise from muffler-less trucks. From the highway, travel 2km down a rocky dirt road. Bear right at all forks in the road. A dozen palm-frond *palapas* line the beach with sand-flush toilets in back (*cabañas* or parking US$3). The waters near the shore are great for clam fishing, but swimming may be hazardous due to manta rays. If you walk down the dirt road to Playa Punta Arena but take a left instead of a right at the second fork, you'll end up at **Playa San Pedro** and **Los Naranjos RV Park,** where payments for your space may be made with freshly caught fish.

**Playa Santispac,** the most popular beach on the Bahía, is connected to Playa Punta Arena by a dirt path that winds through mountains for a grueling 1km. The beach is most easily accessible by highway (about 20km south of Mulegé) where it is visible and clearly marked. During the winter, Santispac is the liveliest beach on the bay; in the summer, however, the sands are nearly deserted. On Playa Santispac, **Las Palapas Trailer Park** rents *palapas* and tent space (both US$5 per night; use of bathrooms and showers US$1). At **Ana's Restaurant,** guests enjoy fried fish (26 pesos) and shrimp omelettes (28 pesos) while marveling at the exotic shells on sale to the right of the counter (2 for US$1). The restaurant doubles as a bakery and sells cakes and huge loaves of bread (10 pesos; open in summer daily 7am-8pm, high season 7am-10pm). Ray and Diane Lima from Rosarito have just opened **Restaurant Santispac,** destined to become the biggest restaurant on the Bahía. With liquor license in hand, they plan for a fully stocked, TV-equipped bar to open in September 1997. The most important thing? Their fish tacos (6 pesos) are the best around (open daily; exact hours to be determined). **Kayak Concepción Bay** (tel. 3-04-09; fax 3-01-90), in front of Ana's, rents kayaks, mask-snorkel-fin sets, wetsuits, and VHF radios (open Oct.-April). They may also organize day-long tours which involve kayaking and snorkeling. Watch out in the water—there are mating sting rays in the spring and manta rays in the summer. In case of a sting, locals recommend treating the affected area with hot, salty water. The **hot springs** on the south end of Playa Santispac provide the perfect source. Check out these warm, bubbly (although somewhat dirty) waters even if you haven't been nipped by an underwater creature.

**Playa La Posada,** which looks essentially like a minuscule village, is covered by permanent homes, but large *palapas* house temporary visitors (US$10 with electricity, US$7 without; both include access to bathrooms). Two distant rocky islands and an overgrown islet are popular destinations for jet-skiers. **Playa Escondida** (Hidden Beach) is at the end of a 500m dirt path winding through the valley between two hills; look for a white sign with black letters at the southern end of Playa Concepción. True to its name, the short, facility-less Escondida is nicely hidden from all civilization. **Playa Los Cocos** is identified by its white garbage cans adorned with palm trees. Although people were once able to camp for free, the government has been granting concessions to many people (mainly, strangely enough, government employees). As a result, beaches are free, but any kind of facility usage is not. Still, the *cabañas* that line the shallow beach can be had for a pittance—5 pesos or so. A grove of trees and shrubs separates the strip from the highway. At **Playa El Burro,** you can rent a *palapa* next to hordes of RVs for 25 pesos per day.

Next is **Playa El Coyote,** perhaps the most populated beach after Santispac. Shelter and camping space can be had here for reasonable, completely negotiable prices. **Estrella del Mar** is a restaurant serving meat enchiladas (15 pesos) and fried chicken (28 pesos). The restaurant has a new volleyball court and baseball diamond (open Oct.-April daily 8am-8pm). The better sands and *palapas* are down on the southern end. Down the road another 15km is the exquisite (and even less populated) **Playa Resquesón,** which, unfortunately, is soon to be marred by current development. Even farther south, two more spots—**La Ramada** and **Santa Bárbara**—are currently undergoing development, and *palapas* have been built in these otherwise virgin beaches which are currently closed to the public. Another nearly deserted stretch of sand is the last before Rte. 1 climbs into the mountains separating Mulegé from Loreto. All of these beaches are marked from the highway. Enjoy the more secluded specimens before they start to look like Miami Beach.

Don't expect to find cold water or even remotely cold *anything* on the Bahía's beaches. Ice is rare, so unless you relish the idea of downing a boiling Coke in the pounding sun, bring a cooler with some drinks. The beaches are otherworldly after dark, illuminated by millions of stars, but only come at night if you plan to camp out or if you're equipped with wheels—it's impossible to hitch back, no buses run, and even stepping onto the curvy highway is dangerous due to oncoming cars.

**Getting There:** Check at the bus station for the next *de paso* bus south (10 and 11:30am). Wait to pay the fare until the bus arrives, and don't get on until the driver assures you that he plans to stop at one of the beaches. But don't count on a bus to take you back; bus service to the beaches is infrequent, and drivers may not stop along the busy highway. Beach-hoppers might also consider renting a car for the day, as access to and from the beaches farther south is limited. Many nomadic travelers hitch (known in Americanized Spanish as *"pedir"* ride") from Mulegé to the beaches, catching one of the RVs or produce trucks barreling down the Transpeninsular Highway towards the bay. Those who hitch are most successful getting rides right across the island from the bus stop, and tell the driver exactly where they are heading— "Playa Santispac" or "Playa Coyote" usually works well. Hitching back to Mulegé is reputedly even easier, since many people leaving the beach are heading back into town.

# ■ Loreto

Founded by Jesuit missionaries in 1697, Loreto (pop. 10,000) deserves homage for its history and beauty. It was the first capital of the Californias and its mission the first in a chain of Jesuit missions along the west coast of Baja—the legacy of Padre Kino. Although the town was wiped out by a freakish combination of hurricanes and earthquakes in the late 19th century, Loreto's loveliness didn't languor for long. The Jesuits were no aesthetic dummies—300 years after settlement, the town is quiet, restful, and a great place to adore nature. Sandwiched between the calm blue waters of the Sea of Cortés and golden mountains, Loreto remains an unassuming, simple town with a long, tranquil Malecón shaded by rows of palm trees and sprinkled with stone benches overlooking the rocky shore. Most of the few visitors are laid-back *norteamericanos* who come, by land or sea, to fish and enjoy happy hour at homey local bars.

**Orientation and Practical Information** The town is easy to navigate, as everything of interest is on the main road. The principal street in Loreto is **Salvatierra,** which connects the Carretera Transpeninsular to the Gulf. When Salvatierra becomes a pedestrian walkway, **Hidalgo** roughly becomes its continuation. **Independencia** intersects Salvatierra just as it turns into Hidalgo, and **Madero** intersects Hidalgo closer to the water. Away from the gulf, **Allende, León,** and **Ayuntamiento** cross Salvatierra before Independencia. **Malecón,** which leads north to the beach and outlines the entire width of the city at the coast, runs perpendicular to Hidalgo where Hidalgo ends. **Juárez** runs parallel to, and north of, Salvatierra and Hidalgo. The **zócalo** is at Hidalgo and Madero. To get to the *centro* from the **bus station,** walk down Salvatierra toward the distant cathedral (10min.) or indulge in a taxi (14 pesos).

The Palacio Municipal, on Madero between Salvatierra and Comercio facing the *zócalo,* houses the air-conditioned **tourist info center** (tel. 5-04-11). English is spoken (open Mon.-Fri. 8:30am-3pm and 6-8pm, but a sign asks you to call even if they're closed). An informal tourist info center is on Salvatierra between Independencia and Ayuntamiento (tel. 5-02-59), in a jewelry shop. **Bancomer,** on Madero (tel. 5-00-14 or 5-09-10), across from the *zócalo,* exchanges dollars (open Mon.-Fri. 8:30am-6pm). International **credit card calls** can be made on Salvatierra at Independencia (tel. 5-06-97) across from the supermarket (open daily 8am-9pm) and at the *nevería* across from Supermarket El Pescador (open Mon.-Sat. 8am-9pm, Sun. 9am-1pm and 4-8pm). The **telegram office** (tel. 5-03-87) is next to the post office (open Mon.-Fri. 8am-2pm).

**Águila buses** stop by the terminal on Salvatierra near Allende (tel. 5-07-67), just off the highway, about 2km from Madero. Northbound buses leave at 2, 3, 5, 9, 11pm, 1, and 3am, heading to Guerrero Negro (7½hr., 103 pesos) via Mulegé (2½hr., 37 pesos), Santa Rosalía (4hr., 57 pesos), and San Ignacio (5hr., 69 pesos); southbound buses go to La Paz (8am, 2, 3, 11pm, and midnight, 5hr., 74 pesos). **Thrifty** (tel. 5-08-15) rents cars for US$50 per day including insurance, tax, and mileage. Stock up for the day at **Supermarket El Pescador** on Salvatierra and Independencia (tel. 5-00-60; open daily 7:30am-10:30pm). **Lavandería El Remojón** is on Salvatierra and Independencia (tel. 5-02-59; up to 4kg 19 pesos; open Mon.-Sat. 8am-8pm, Sun. 8am-9pm). The **Red Cross** is on Salvatierra and Juárez (tel. 5-11-11; open daily 9am-1pm and 3-8:30pm). **Farmacia Misión,** Salvatierra 66 between Ayuntamiento and Independencia (tel. 5-03-41), is open daily 8am-10pm. The **Centro de Salud** is on Salvatierra (tel. 5-00-39), 1km from the bus terminal (open 24hr.). The **IMSS** can be reached at 5-62-70. **Medical emergency numbers** are 5-03-97, 5-09-06, and 5-00-62. The **post office** is on Salvatierra and Deportiva (tel. 5-06-47), near the bus station, behind the Red Cross (open Mon.-Fri. 8am-3pm). **Postal Code: 23880. Phone Code: 113.**

**Accommodations** The most economical hotel in town is the **Motel Davis** on Calle Davis about four blocks north of the *zócalo*. Both the unmarked motel and street are a little hard to find, so don't be afraid to ask. If you can put up with the muddy courtyard and sporadic service, it's a real deal. Rooms are small and clean, with beds, baths, and not much else for 50 pesos. **Motel Salvatierra,** on Salvatierra and Ocampo (tel. 5-00-21), close to the bus station, has clean, air-conditioned rooms that are a bit small but mercifully cold (singles 110 pesos, with cable TV 130 pesos; doubles 150 pesos, with TV 170 pesos). Another option is the nearby **Hotel San Martín,** on Juárez (tel. 5-04-42), two blocks north of the *zócalo,* near the water. Rooms have small baths, fans, and warm water, but the mattresses are rather wimpy (singles and doubles 90 pesos; triples 100 pesos). **El Moro RV Park,** Robles 8 (tel. 3-05-42), though not on the water, allows you to hook up a trailer (US$10) or just camp out (US$4). Showers are a two-dollar luxury. If no one is there, you can park on the honor system—leave your payment under the door (office open 7am-8pm).

**Food** Decent, cheap meals are served in establishments up and down Salvatierra, and a number of restaurants cluster conveniently near the bus terminal, offering roast chicken and the like for good prices. **Café Olé,** Madero 14 (tel. 5-04-96), south of the *zócalo,* offers huge portions, great food, excellent prices, and amazing gossip. Both tourists and locals chatter salaciously over their jumbo burritos (22 pesos) or fresh fish fillet with fries and *frijoles* (35 pesos). Huge omelettes with sides of beans and fries (20-25 pesos) will make breakfast buffs roar like the morning tigers they are. Vegetarians will delight in their cheese-stuffed *chile relleno* (22 pesos; open Mon.-Sat. 7am-10pm, Sun. 7am-2pm). The popular **Restaurant-Bar La Palapa,** on Hidalgo between Madero and López Mateos, fills the bellies of hungry diners with enormous Mexican combination platters (enchiladas or quesadillas, rice, and beans for 23 pesos). Lots of totally tranquil tourists eat and hang out here (open Mon.-Sat. 1-10pm). Although their famed pizza is expensive, you'll find your rainbow's end at **Tiffany's** (tel. 5-00-04) where you can sit outside while enjoying your huge "Breakfast at Tiffany's" (27 pesos), which will satisfy even super rats (open daily 8am-9pm).

**Sights** With shaded benches along the water and the sidewalk, the Malecón is a popular place for an evening stroll. Loreto's **public beach,** a few blocks north of Hidalgo, is nice enough. Though the beach is often crowded, the gray sand and the yellow and black fish that swim practically to shore can amuse you for hours as you soak up the sun. Equally enjoyable is the **Misión de Nuestra Señora de Loreto** and **Museo de las Misiones** (tel. 5-04-41), next to the reconstructed mission, one block west of the plaza. The museum recounts the complete history of the European conquest of Baja California. Here you can also receive information on Loreto's mission, built in 1697, and on other missions scattered throughout the peninsula (open Mon.-Sat. 10am-5pm, Sun. noon-5pm; admission 10 pesos).

If you're angling for a fresh seafood meal, rent a fishing boat and a guide (US$100 for 1 or 2 people, US$110 for 3 people; both 7hr.), or go it alone with some fishing equipment (US$7 per day) from **Alfredo's** (tel. 5-01-32). **Arturo's Sports Fishing Fleet** on Hidalgo (tel. 5-04-09 or 5-07-22), half a block from the beach, offers five-hour snorkeling trips (US$75, min. 3 people; equipment US$90 extra). **Tony,** owner of the

BAJA CALIFORNIA

**Happy Hour Bar,** off Salvatierra between the bus station and the *centro,* also offers sport-fishing excursions and the like for US$85-95; prices are negotiable. Try approaching these companies or others for a trip to **Isla Coronado,** where wide, sandy beaches and herds of sea lions await. **Isla Carmen,** another popular destination, contains an eerie ghost town and abandoned salt mines. North of Loreto, the road passes the beautiful **Bahía de la Concepción** (see p. 154)—with its incredible expanses of coves, blue-green water, and barren, cacti-dotted mountains jutting into the cloudless sky—on its way to Mulegé. South of Loreto, the road winds away from the coast into rugged mountains and the **Planicie Magdalena,** an intensively irrigated and cultivated plain. The striking white stripes on the first hillside beyond town are formed by millions of clams, conch, oyster, and scallop shells—refuse left by the region's Paleolithic inhabitants. Some caves on the hillside, inhabited as recently as 300 years ago, contain shells and polished stone.

Loreto celebrates the **festival** of its patron saint from September 5-8 with a great regional fair. From October 19-25, people from here and there come to celebrate the founding of the town with cultural and sporting events (boxing, wrestling, etc.).

## ▓ Puerto San Carlos

Puerto San Carlos (pop. 4000) is a pretty and strange little town. Completely seasonal, it hosts pods of tourists from around the world during whale-watching season and then settles down for an insanely quiet summer of boarded-up restaurants, vacant dirt roads, and the town's two policemen playing dominoes in the heat. Visit Puerto San Carlos from November to March, when an estimated 18,000 gray whales migrate yearly from the Bering Sea southward through the Pacific to **Bahías Magdalena and Almejas,** just south of town, easily accessible by boat. During mating season (mid-January to mid-March), the lovestruck creatures wow crowds with aquatic acrobatics. Few travelers have discovered Puerto San Carlos, and locals observe *extranjeros* with the same bemused fascination with which tourists view whales.

**Orientation and Practical Information** To get to San Carlos, take a transfer bus from **Ciudad Constitución** (1hr., 13 pesos), a nondescript tumbleweed town which has connections on **Autotransportes Águila** south to La Paz (every hr., 5am-11pm, 3hr.) and points in between, and north to Tijuana (every hr., 5am-11pm, 19hr.) and points in between. In Ciudad Constitución, basic hotels and restaurants abound; try the **Hotel Conchita** and the 24hr. **Ricos Tacos,** both on Olachea and Hidalgo, if you're stuck in town.

In Puerto San Carlos, most services are on the two main streets, **La Paz** and **Morelos,** which are perpendicular to each other. Both of these major roads are made of sand and marked by illegible street signs. Don't fret if the bus drops you off in what seems like the middle of nowhere—you're actually smack in the middle of town.

The **tourist office** is on La Paz (tel. 6-02-53), in a house next to the IMSS Hospital, marked by a cardboard sign. The extremely helpful English-speaking staff also leads whale-watching tours (open 24hr.; just don't ring late at night and wake them). The pink **information booth** at the edge of town near the PEMEX station provides maps of the bay and islands (closed in summer). **Phone** friends back home at the unmarked **Papelería Chokes,** at Morelos and La Paz (tel. 6-00-62; open Mon.-Sat. 8am-1pm and 3-7pm). **Autotransportes Águila** buses leave from the small white terminal on La Paz and Morelos—the waiting room is in some family's kitchen. Buses are few and far between, heading to Cabo San Lucas (1:45pm, 7hr., 90 pesos), Constitución (11am and 2pm, 45min., 13 pesos), and La Paz (7:30am and 1:45pm, 3½hr., 45 pesos). The **Red Cross** is on La Paz and Acapulco across from the church. **Farmacia Jazmín** is on La Paz and México (tel. 6-00-56), facing the church (open Mon.-Sat. 9:30am-12:30pm and 4-6pm). The **IMSS Hospital** is also on La Paz (tel. 6-02-11). The **Centro de Salud** is on La Paz in front of Hotel Alcatraz. The **police** are in the same building as the Red Cross. The **post office** is on La Paz near México (open Mon.-Fri. 8am-3pm). **Postal Code:** 23740. **Phone Code:** 113.

**Accommodations and Food** Finding rooms in San Carlos ain't easy. This town has few hotels, and they're pricey; come whale-watching season, the town turns into a big tourist trap. The best deal in town is the **Motel Las Brisas** (tel. 6-01-52 or 6-01-59). To get there from the bus station, turn right on La Paz, then left on Madero—the hotel will be on your left. Cheery, clean, yellow rooms with large fans surround a somewhat stark courtyard. If, for some very, very strange reason, you're here when the whales aren't, console yourself by studying the fading courtyard mural dedicated to these gentle giants (singles 80 pesos; doubles 100 pesos). **Hotel El Palmar,** Acapulco at Vallarta (tel. 6-00-35), near the bus station, lets you watch your modern color TV while lounging amid an endless variety of flowery bedspreads and curtains. While mattresses hardly cushion the hard bed-frames, bottled water more than appeases slightly sore-bottomed guests (singles 100 pesos; doubles 125 pesos). A **trailer park** at Playa la Curva outside of town offers full hookups for US$10.

Dining in San Carlos is homey—literally. A string of combination restaurant-living rooms along La Paz and Morelos allows you to meet locals, their kids, and pets while you enjoy delicacies from the sea. Chances are, the fish on your plate was alive the last time you brushed your teeth. **El Patio Restaurant-Bar** (tel. 6-00-17; fax 6-00-86), in front of Hotel Alcatraz on La Paz, welcomes you into white plastic Corona chairs under open skies. Enjoy an oyster cocktail (40 pesos) or chicken with *mole* (25 pesos) while you watch the palm trees sway (open daily 7am-10pm). An unnamed **torta shop** across the street from the IMSS on La Paz has killer tacos and *tortas* at some of the lowest prices in town—it's also one of the few eateries open year-round (open daily 9am-8pm).

**Sights** The islands and bays surrounding Puerto San Carlos teem with lifeforms. Both the **Bahía Magdalena** and **Bahía Almeja** lie just south of Puerto San Carlos. These bays are home to some of the best **whale-watching** in the world. From January to March, enormous numbers of whales **have sex** with each other. In a peculiar maneuver called "spy hopping," a huge hormonal whale will pop its head out of the water, fix an enormous eye on whatever strikes its fancy, and remain transfixed for minutes on end, staring hypnotically like a submarine periscope. The tiny **Islote de Patos** (Duck Islet) in the middle of Bahía Magdalena is home to numerous species of birds, including pelicans and white-necks. The gangly creatures crowd every inch of the beach, standing idly like expectant guests at a failed cocktail party. The sheer number of birds (and their malodorous excrement) make landing here difficult; it's best just to cruise by. Feisty Pacific waves at **Cabo San Lázaro** and **Point Hughes,** both on the western tip of **Isla Magdalena,** will keep even veteran surfers on their toes. Reed huts scattered along the beach offer protection from the oppressive midday sun. Fifteen species of clams and starfish inhabit the waters of these immaculate beaches. Farther south, the island narrows to less than 50m in width, tapering off into perfectly white sand tufted with occasional bits of foliage, unusual flowers, and cacti. An enormous colony of sea lions *(lobos marinos)* lives near the island's southern tip. **Crispin Mendoza Ramos** and his son, operating out of the tourist office (tel. 6-02-53), lead tours to the islands (US$35 per hr., min. 3hr., max. 6 people). A cheaper way to explore the islands is to make an ad-hoc deal with one of the fishermen departing from Playa la Curva in front of the PEMEX station. Unless you plan to camp out on the islands, make definite pick-up plans before you disembark.

# ▧ La Paz

The eclectic and beautiful capital of Baja California Sur, La Paz (pop. 140,000) is part pulsating port, part party town, and part peaceful paradise. Home to 10 tranquil beaches along the Sea of Cortés, this is where real, live Mexicans vacation, leaving the honky-tonk Cabos to Americans. In a past life, La Paz was a quiet fishing village, frequently molested by pirates for the iridescent white spheres concealed in the oysters off its coast; John Steinbeck's *The Pearl* depicted the town as a tiny, unworldly treasure chest. La Paz's hour of reckoning came in the 1940s, when the oysters sickened and died, wiping out the town's pearl industry; but within two decades, with the institution of Baja ferries and the completion of the Transpeninsular Highway in the 1960s, La Paz was rediscovered. That oyster town is now a city, and the row of night-clubs along the beach and snorkel stores may make La Paz (The Peace) feel sheepish about its name. No worries, though: the days are still hot and nonchalant, the fisher-men still friendly. At night, despite the reggae issuing from semi-gringoized dance clubs, pelicans still skip along the lamp-lit water, and a merciful breeze ruffles the hair of couples strolling along the rocky beach and the serene boardwalk pier at sunset.

## ORIENTATION

La Paz overlooks the **Bahía de la Paz** on Baja's east coast, 222km north of Cabo San Lucas and 1496km southeast of Tijuana, on the Transpeninsular Highway (Rte. 1). The city's main street, and loveliest lane for a stroll, is **Av. Obregón,** more commonly known as the **Malecón,** which runs along alternately sandy and rocky shore. Activity centers around the area delineated by **Constitución, Ocampo, Serdán,** and the shore. The **municipal bus system** in La Paz serves the city sporadically (approxi-mately every ½hr., 6am-10pm, 1.50-2 pesos). Flag buses down anywhere, or wait by the stop on Revolución and Degollado, next to the market. From the station, try to convince your driver to drop you off in the *centro.*

## CROSSING THE GULF

Ferries leave from the suburb of **Pichilingue;** they're the best way to get from La Paz to the mainland. Buy tickets at the **Sematur Company,** office 5 de Mayo and Prieto (tel. 5-46-66; open Mon.-Fri. 8am-1pm and 4-6pm, Sat.-Sun. 8am-1pm). Ferries go to Mazatlán (Sun.-Fri. at 3pm, 17hr., *salón* 166 pesos, *turista* 330 pesos, *cabina* 493 pesos, cars up to 5m long 1783 pesos, motorcycles 396 pesos) and Topolobampo, a suburb of Los Mochis (daily at 11am except for "cargo only" days—call for precise info, 8hr., *salón* 111 pesos, cars up to 5m long 1089 pesos, motorcycles 242 pesos). You cannot buy tickets from the office at the dock (open daily 8am-8pm).

In order to secure a ticket, be sure to get to the Sematur main office early, ideally right after it opens. Acquiring a *salón* ticket should be no problem on the day of departure, but for other classes, call one day ahead to make reservations. During hol-idays, competition for ferry tickets is fierce. A travel agency might be the most trou-ble-free way to make reservations—it costs the same and allows you to pick up the tickets at the agency instead of having to wait in the long lines at the ferry office. Agencies include **Operadora de Mar de Cortés,** on Bravo and Ortega (tel. 5-22-77; fax 5-85-99), in the CCC complex, a 15-minute walk from the center, and **Cabo San Lucas,** at Hidalgo and Madero (tel. 3-37-17; fax 3-37-07). Tickets can be picked up from 4 to 6pm the day before departure.

In order to get a vehicle on the ferry, you will need (at the very least) proof of Mex-ican insurance (or a major credit card with the car owner's name on it), car registra-tion, permission for the importation of a car into Mexico, and a tourist card. Oh, and three photocopies of each. You can get a permit at **Banjército** (tel. 2-11-16), at the ferry stop in Pichilingue, or through **AAA** in the U.S. (for more info on bringing your car into Mexico, see p. 41). Regardless of whether you have a car or not, you will need to obtain a tourist card (FMT) if you entered Mexico via Baja and are main-land-bound; get one from **Servicios Migratorios** (see p. 161). Clear all of the paper-work before purchasing the ticket; otherwise, Sematur will deny you a spot whether or not you hold reservations. For more information on ferries, see p. 126.

You need not hike 17km to the ferry dock in Pichilingue—**Autotransportes Águila** buses run between the dock and the downtown terminal on Obregón, between Independencia and 5 de Mayo (Mon.-Fri. 9am and 11-5pm, Sat.-Sun. and high season 9am and 11-6pm, approximately on the hr., 10 pesos). When you get off the ferry, hurry to catch the 9:30am bus to the *centro;* otherwise you'll have to wait for two hours. Buses also run from Pinchilingue to La Paz (9:30am and every hr., 11:30am-5:30pm, 10 pesos). A taxi from dock to downtown, or vice versa, will set you back a good 55 pesos.

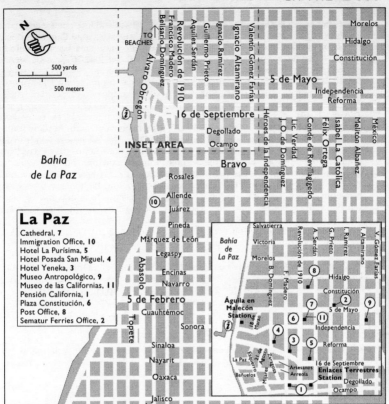

La Paz
- Cathedral, 7
- Immigration Office, 10
- Hotel La Purísima, 5
- Hotel Posada San Miguel, 4
- Hotel Yeneka, 3
- Museo Antropológico, 9
- Museo de las Californias, 11
- Pensión California, 1
- Plaza Constitución, 6
- Post Office, 8
- Sematur Ferries Office, 2

BAJA CALIFORNIA

## PRACTICAL INFORMATION

**Tourist Office:** Obregón at 16 de Septiembre (tel. 2-59-39), in a pavilion on the water. Excellent city maps and information about Baja Sur, especially Los Cabos. Cute English-speaking staff. Open Mon.-Fri. 8am-8pm.

**Tourist Police:** Fabulous folks recognizable by their starched white uniforms and big grins. Their job is "protection and orientation," but they'll do so much more.

**Immigration Office: Servicios Migratorios,** Obregón 2140 (tel. 5-34-93; fax 2-04-29). You must stop here to obtain a tourist card if you entered Mexico via Baja and are mainland-bound. Open Mon.-Fri. 8am-3pm. After hours, head to their outpost in the airport outside of town (tel. 2-18-29). Open daily 8am-10pm.

**Currency Exchange: Bancomer,** on 16 de Septiembre (tel. 5-42-48), ½ block from the waterfront. Open for exchange Mon.-Fri. 8:30am-4pm. 24hr. **ATM. BITAL,** 5 de Mayo at Revolución (tel. 2-22-89), has a 24hr. **ATM** and talking doors. Open for exchange Mon.-Fri. 8am-6:30pm, Sat. 9am-2pm.

**American Express:** Esquerro 1679 at La Paz (tel. 2-83-00; fax 5-52-72), off 16 de Sept., 1 block north of the sea. Open Mon.-Fri. 9am-2pm and 4-6pm, Sat. 9am-2pm.

**Telephones:** Sexy young **LADATELs,** as well as older, more mature payphones, pepper the downtown area and *zócalo.* **Librería Contempo,** Arreola 25A at Obregón (2-78-75), has a *caseta.* Open Mon.-Fri. 10am-9pm, Sun. 10am-5pm.

**Fax:** Tel. 2-67-07; fax 5-08-09. Upstairs from the post office. Open Mon.-Fri. 8am-6pm, Sat. 8-11am.

**Airport:** West of La Paz, accessible only by 70-peso taxis. If heading from the airport to the center, buy taxi tickets inside to avoid being swindled. Served by **Aeroméxico,** at Obregón and Hidalgo (tel. 4-62-88; central phone 12-00-91 through -93; open Mon.-Fri. 8am-6pm, Sat. 8:30am-5pm), and **Aerocalifornia** (tel. 4-62-88).

**Buses:** There are 3 stations. The **main station** is on Jalisco and Independencia, about 25 blocks southeast of downtown. Two municipal buses, "Central Camionera" and "Urbano," head to the terminal; catch them near the public market at Degollado and Revolución. Taxis cost 10 pesos. **Águila** and **ABC** (tel. 2-42-70) provide service to points north, including Ensenada (10am, 4, 8, and 10pm, 19½hr., 382 pesos), Loreto (8 per day, 9am-10pm, 5hr., 83 pesos), Mexicali (4pm, 24½hr., 444 pesos), Mulegé (8 per day, 9am-10pm, 7hr., 118 pesos), San Ignacio (5 per day, 10am-10pm, 9hr., 150 pesos), Santa Rosalía (8 per day, 9am-10pm, 8hr., 132 pesos), and Tijuana (10am, 4, 8, and 10pm, 21hr., 406 pesos). The new **Enlaces Terrestres station,** Degollado and Serdán (tel. 3-31-80), is more convenient for heading south. Buses run to Cabo San Lucas (7 per day, 6:30am-7pm, 3hr., 41 pesos), San José del Cabo (7 per day, 6:30am-7pm, 3½hr., 49 pesos), and Todos Santos (9 per day, 7am-8pm, 2hr., 23 pesos). Finally, the **Águila Malecón station,** Independencia at Obregón (tel. 2-78-98), is the best way of getting to nearby beaches. Buses run to Playas Palmira, El Coramuel, El Carmancito, Tesoro, and Pichilingue (every hr., 8am-6pm except 10am, up to ½hr., 3-8 pesos) and to Playas Balandras and Tecolote (Fri.-Sat. only, every hr., 8am-6pm, 45min., 10 pesos). The last bus back to La Paz leaves Tecolote Mon.-Fri. 5:45pm and Pichilingue at 5:30pm, Sat.-Sun. 6pm.

**Laundromat: Lavandería Yoli,** 5 de Mayo at Rubio (tel. 2-10-01), across the street from the stadium. Wash and dry a hefty load for 23 pesos. Open Mon.-Sat. 7am-9pm, Sun. 8am-3pm.

**Red Cross:** Reforma 1091 between Isabel la Católica and Félix Ortega (tel. 2-11-11). Open 24hr.

**Pharmacy: Farmacia Bravo** (tel. 2-69-33), next to the hospital, is open 24hr.

**Hospital: Salvatierra,** Bravo at Verdad (tel. 2-14-96 or 2-14-97), between Domínguez and the Oncological Institute.

**Emergency:** Dial 06.

**Police:** Colima at México (tel. 2-07-81). Open 24hr.

**Post Office:** Revolución at Constitución (tel. 2-03-88 or 5-23-58). Open Mon.-Fri. 8am-7pm, Sat. 9am-1pm. **Postal Code:** 23000.

**Phone Code:** 112.

## ACCOMMODATIONS

The city is full of inexpensive establishments bound to satisfy even the most finicky travelers. The cluttered artistic look, however, seems to be making a resurgence in the budget hotels of La Paz. A student of Mexican folk art could skip the Museo Antropológico and tour the lobbies of these hotels instead.

**Hotel Yeneka,** Madero 1520 between 16 de Septiembre and Independencia (tel. 5-46-88). Quite possibly the most unique hotel in all of Baja. The freshest and funkiest atmosphere around. Doubles as a museum of eccentric items, including a 1916 Model-T Ford, a pet hawk, and a live monkey who lives in the trees. Each Tarzan-hut room has been remodeled in matching twig furniture and painted with rainbow colors. You can see the painted handprints of the owner's little son on the walls, and the green hallways are a labor of love. All rooms come with fans, and a lucky few with small balconies. Singles 95 pesos; doubles 135 pesos. Adjoining **restaurant** was scheduled to re-open in September, 1997, after undergoing renovations.

**Pensión California Casa de Huéspedes,** Degollado at Madero (tel. 2-28-96). Bungalow rooms have concrete floors and beds on concrete slabs, but you have to admire the plastic turtle sculpture, sea shells, and dysfunctional washing machine. Prices include private baths and use of the communal kitchen and TV. If you're lucky, you might get a room that has a huge tree trunk running through the bathroom shower. Bring your own blanket. Padlocks on the doors provide security. Singles 55 pesos; doubles 80 pesos; triples 90 pesos. **Hostería del Convento** (tel. 2-35-08), across the street, belongs to the same owner and offers an identical setup.

**CREA Youth Hostel** (tel. 2-46-15), in Forjatero youth center, near the Technical University and at the 3km mark on the Transpeninsular Highway. From the unofficial bus station on the southeast corner of the market, on the corner of Degallado and Revolución, take a "CREA" bus (25 pesos) and ask the driver to point it out. The hostel offers small, clean rooms with bunk beds, bathrooms, and A/C, as well as a huge swimming pool, volleyball court, and a small eatery (open daily 7am-11pm). Unfortunately, it's terribly far from the center of town, approximately a 12-peso taxi ride, and local buses to the *centro* are sporadic (every 30-45min.) at best. All rooms 40 pesos per person. 10% discount with HI card.

**Hotel Posada San Miguel,** B. Domínguez 1510 just off 16 de Septiembre (tel. 5-88-88). Fountained courtyards, tiled arches, and wrought-iron scroll work on windows and railings. Cubical rooms with sinks and large, comfortable beds. Singles 60 pesos; doubles 80 pesos; triples 100 pesos.

**Hotel San Carlos,** 16 de Septiembre, between Revolución and Serdán. The place is worn, but rooms are pink, peach, and oh-so-clean. The staff is prompt and friendly. Singles 80 pesos; doubles 100 pesos.

## FOOD

On the waterfront you'll find decor, menus, and prices geared toward peso-spewing tourists. Move inland a few blocks and watch the prices plunge. Seafood meals are generally fresh. The **public market,** at Degollado and Revolución, offers a cheap selection of fruits, veggies, and fresh fish.

**Restaurante El Quinto Sol,** B. Domínguez at Independencia (tel. 2-16-92). One of the few vegetarian joints in Baja. Menu includes sausage a la soybean, as well as an assortment of juices. Yummy yogurt smoothie with fruit 18 pesos; vegetarian steak 28 pesos; tasty pastries 2 pesos. Open Mon.-Sat. 7:30am-9:30pm.

**Restaurant Palapa Adriana** (tel. 2-83-29), on the beach off Obregón at Constitución. Not just on the water, but practically in the water—cute kids swim up to the window and signal. *Huachinango* (red snapper) 40 pesos; *pollo con mole* 22 pesos; *pulpo al ajo* 30 pesos. Sea breeze *gratis.* Open daily 10am-10pm.

**La Luna Bruja,** on Playa Pichilingue, the 2nd *cabaña* on shore, farthest from the ferry dock. Defying the stereotype of the overpriced beachfront *palapa,* this quiet restaurant offers amazing seafood at good prices. *Tostados de ceviche* 25 pesos; fish about 35 pesos. Ice-cold beer 8 pesos, a real deal when it's hand-delivered to you on the beach. Open daily 9am-6pm.

## SAND AND SIGHTS

Instead of stretching curving expanses of wave-washed sand, the beaches of La Paz snuggle into small coves sandwiched between cactus-studded hills and calm, transparent water. To be sure, this is prime windsurfing territory. But be careful—La Paz lifeguards make appearances only on weekends and only on popular beaches.

The best beach near La Paz is **Playa Tecolote** (Owl Beach), 25km northeast of town. A quiet extension of the Sea of Cortés laps against this gorgeous stretch of gleaming white sand against tall, craggy mountains. Even though there are no bathrooms, Tecolote is terrific for **camping.** On Tecolote, jet-skis, banana boats, and boats to the nearby **Isla Espíritu Santo** are available. The snorkeling off **Playa Balandra,** just south of Tecolote, is excellent. Because facilities are sparse and sporadically open, it is best to rent equipment either in the city or at nearby Pichilingue or Tecolote. You may not be able to reach Tecolote or Balandra weekdays without a car; **Autotransportes Águila** buses get you there from the mini-station on Obregón and Independencia (spring break and July-Aug. daily, in the low season Sat.-Sun. only; 10 pesos).

Plenty of other beaches are easily accessible by taking the "Pichilingue" bus up the coast (10 pesos). Be forewarned that neither of these buses runs back to La Paz after 6:30 or 7pm. The "Pichilingue" bus goes as far as the ferry dock, at which point you need to walk 1km farther on the paved road to **Playa de Pichilingue.** This beach is a favorite among the teen set, who splash in the shallow waters and ride paddleboats in the winter (12 pesos per hr.). Along the same bus route lies **Playa El Coromuel,** near La Concha Hotel, where visitors and locals congregate on weekends. All the above beaches are out of walking distance from the city center, but just a short ride away. The farther you venture from La Paz, the better and more secluded the beaches get.

Some popular dive spots are also located around La Paz; the aquatic fun in this city doesn't stop at the shoreline. North of La Paz is **Salvatierra Wreck,** a dive spot where a 300 ft. boat sank in 1976. Also popular is the huge island east of La Paz, **Cerraluo Island.** This popular destination promises reefs, huge fish, and untouched wilderness. Both of these destinations (and many others) require guides because of strong currents, changeable weather conditions, and inaccessibility. For some of the lowest rates in town, try the newly opened **La Paz Dive Center,** on Esquerro off 16 de Septiembre (tel. 5-70-48), near the coast. They run tours to various points around the coast (dives around US$70, snorkeling tours US$30, snorkel sets US$5 per day). **Baja Diving and Service,** Obregón 1665 (tel. 2-18-26; fax 2-86-44), just north of B. Domínguez, organizes daily scuba and snorkeling trips to nearby reefs, wrecks, and islands, where you can mingle with hammer heads, manta rays, giant turtles, and other exotica (scuba trips US$77 per day without equipment, US$15 extra for equipment, snorkeling US$40 per day). Equipment is also rented (snorkeling US$8, scuba about US$45). Trips leave at 7:45am and return between 3 and 5pm. **Viajes Palmira,** on Obregón between Rosales and Allende (tel. 2-40-30), in front of Hotel Los Arcos, also offers whale-watching tours and one-day excursions to **Cabo San Lucas** and **Cabo Pulmo** (around US$150 including transport, torch, and equipment). Trips depart at 8am and return at 4pm, and include equipment, lunch, and drinks (snorkeling US$40, scuba US$73; snorkeling equipment US$10, scuba US$40).

45km south of La Paz along the transpeninsular highway is **El Triunfo,** an abandoned mining town. Marked by a huge tower/chimney, this lonely desert town offers lovely views, solitude, and a chance to see some works by locals in shell or stone.

## ENTERTAINMENT

**Structure,** Obregón and Ocampo (tel. 2-45-44), three blocks east of the center, is a brand-new, hoppin' disco with a dim interior and loud, terrific techno. The dance floor looks like a boxing ring. Many Thursdays feature live karate and sporting events while young couples drink beer (12 pesos) and watch Mexico's version of MTV on scattered TV screens (cover Tues. men 50 pesos, women 30 pesos (open bar); Fri. men 70 pesos, women 30 pesos (open bar); Sat. 2-for-1 specials; open in summer daily 10pm-late; in winter Tues.-Sat.). For something more mature, **La Cabaña,** Obregón 1570, on the 2nd floor in the Hotel Perla, is a gem. Every night, live music and bands crooning favorite Mexican ballads entertain a dressy, scotch-sipping, over-35 crowd. This joint is bizarre, kitschy, and really great. In the next six months, renovations will yield a "classical colonial" club designed to look like a decadent hacienda, and a stricter dress code will be enforced (cover Thurs.-Sun. 30 pesos; open Tues.-Sun. 10pm-5am). **Carlos 'n' Charlie's/La Paz-Lapa,** Obregón and 16 de Septiembre, is the most central and noticeable structure in town. You can savor huge 20-peso margaritas at C 'n' C, a staple of gringo nightlife, or go buck-wild at the very funny La Paz-Lapa, an outdoor booze and rockfest. U.S. and Mexican teens get down and sing along to Aerosmith. Funny signs like "Do not dive from balcony" turn into real warnings after about 3am. Cover and drink prices vary. Women usually pay much less; sometimes before 10pm they can enter and drink free (open Wed.-Sun. 10pm-late).

# ■ Todos Santos

Dick and Jane have moved to Todos Santos. She runs an outdoor fish market and has started surfing—at age 47. He got his ear pierced (3 times), and now makes sculptures out of chrome and cactus flowers. And yes, of course, they've never been happier. Todos Santos (pop. 3500) is paradise for the frugal surfer/painter/zoned-out vacationer/nature-lover/Deadhead/elderly expat set. Halfway between La Paz and Cabo San Lucas, this serene and sophisticated town is one of the few on the southern Baja coast which oozes culture, is easily accessible by bus, offers budget accommodations, and is largely unmutilated by resort development.

John Steinbeck used to hang his hat here; a large number of lesser-known (but more ecologically concerned) U.S. expats have recently fallen in love with Todos Santos's rolling cactus hills, huge surfing waves, dusty roads, and laid-back demeanor, and they've installed their own features: myriad gourmet shops, classy restaurants, and art galleries now inhabit the buildings whose large brick chimneys are all that remain of Todos Santos's sugar-cane-producing past. It's OK to ogle art, but don't think too hard. Follow Dick and Jane's example and rediscover yourself—slowly.

**Orientation** Todos Santos's two main streets, running parallel and east-west, are **Colegio Militar** and **Benito Juárez.** Juárez is just north of Militar; north of and parallel to Juárez run **Centenario** and **Legaspi.** South of Militar and parallel runs **Rangel.** From east to west, **Ocampo, Obregón, Topete, Hidalgo, Márquez de León, Morelos, Zaragoza,** and **Degollado** run north-south. Activity centers around the area between **Legaspi, Militar, Zaragoza, and Topete;** León crosses Militar and Juárez at the church and main plaza. You may be dropped off near Degollado and Juárez, as this is where the **Transpeninsular Highway** (from La Paz) turns to head toward Los Cabos.

**Practical Information** Todos Santos has no tourist office, but the American-owned **El Tecolote Libros,** on Juárez and Hidalgo, sells English-language newspapers, maps, and a comprehensive book on the town (96 pesos). Buy a book while you're there (16 pesos), or swap the one you're carrying (as long as it's not *Let's Go: Mexico 1998;* open Mon.-Sat. 9am-5pm). To exchange currency, head for the *casa de cambio,* half a block from El Tecolote (open daily 9am-6pm), or try the **Bancrecer** on the corner of Obregón and Juárez (open Mon.-Sat. 9am-1pm). Make long-distance calls from the **public phone** in front of the Delegación Municipal, or at the message center on the corner of Juárez and Hidalgo, adjacent to El Tecolote Libros (open Mon.-Sat. 8am-5pm). **Faxes** (tel./fax 5-03-60) can be sent at the Delegación Municipal on Centenario and Hidalgo (open Mon.-Fri. 8am-2pm).

The **bus** stop is at **Pilar's taco stand,** on the corner of Zaragoza and Colegio Militar (tel. 5-01-70). If you have any questions about bus times or anything else, Pilar is an excellent person to talk to. *De paso* **buses** run to Cabo San Lucas (8 per day, 8am-10pm, 1½hr., 22 pesos), La Paz (8 per day, 7am-11:30pm, 1hr., 21 pesos), and San José del Cabo (8 per day, 8am-10pm, 2hr., 28 pesos). Meet your recommended daily nutritional allowances at **Mercado Guluarte,** on Morelos between Colegio Militar and Juárez (tel. 5-00-06; open Mon.-Sat. 7:30am-9pm, Sun. 7:30am-2pm). Other markets are on Degollado and Juárez. The **laundromat,** on Pedrajo (tel. 5-03-41), three blocks west of Degollado, lets you take care of your dirty laundry for 23 pesos, including soap (open Mon.-Sat. 8am-3pm). **Farmacia Todos Santos,** on Juárez between Morelos and Zaragoza (tel. 5-00-30), is run out of a disheveled house but provides 24-hour service. For more standard pharmaceutical fare, try the **Farmacia de Guadalupe,** on Juárez and Zaragoza (tel. 5-00-76; open daily 8am-11pm). In case of an **emergency,** call the **hospital** on Juárez and Degollado (tel. 5-00-95; open 24hr.). The **police** are in the Delegación Municipal complex on Legaspi between León and Hidalgo. The **post office** is on Colegio Militar and León (tel. 5-03-30; open Mon.-Fri. 8am-3pm). **Postal Code:** 23300. **Phone Code:** 114.

**Accommodations** The town has four main hotels; two are in the center of town and the other two are a 15-minute jaunt away. Beware: red ants are everywhere. The **Hotel Miramar,** on Pedrajo at Mutualismo (tel. 5-03-41), offers an excellent value in an otherwise overpriced town. From the center, head to the west end of town and turn south onto Degollado. Walk five minutes down Degollado, past PEMEX and a supermarket, until you see a sign for "Hotel Miramar." Take the following right, and it's four blocks down on your left. Clean, centrally cooled rooms, large tiled bathrooms, color TVs, and *agua purificada* will reward you at the end of your hike (singles 90 pesos; doubles 130 pesos; triples 170 pesos). You don't need to shop around much to find the **Motel Guluarte,** at Juárez and Morelos (tel. 5-00-06). This tiny motel is run out of a grocery store in the Mercado Guluarte (see above). The pool is well-suited to those who enjoy bathing in full view of the street, but the adjacent outdoor *palapa* is shady and has an ice-cold *agua purificada* dispenser. Clean, cozy rooms have TVs and fans (singles 80 pesos; doubles 110 pesos; triples 170 pesos).

The best deals in town are the campgrounds. If you have the equipment, Todos Santos is an excellent place to camp, with plenty of gorgeous beach, scenic views of rolling hills, and pot-smoking, Kerouac-reading, surfing hardbodies. Two RV parks hide along the coast, south of town, both with great beaches and facilities. To reach the closer one, **San Pedrito Trailer Park** (tel. 2-45-20; fax 112-3-46-43), turn right off the Transpeninsular Highway, 6km south of town—you've missed the turnoff if you pass a beer store. Pass under an arch, drive 3km, bear left at the fork, and you're there. The friendly manager is almost always around (RV hookups US$15; simple, semi-sheltered *cabañas* where you can pitch your tent US$3; full-size, indoor *cabañas* with amenities US$25-35). To get to **Los Ceritos Trailer Park,** turn right 10km south of town at a blue and white sign that reads "RV Park." Past a fence and the old highway to Los Cabos, 2.6km down the dirt road, you'll hit the park. A pool, restaurant/bar, TV, and awesome surfing beaches await (RV hookups US$12).

**Food** Budget eats aren't hard to find in Todos Santos. Several *loncherías* line Colegio Militar near the bus station, offering triple tacos and the like for 10-12 pesos. Locals love **Carnitas y Chicharrones,** on Degollado near Colegio Militar, where they enjoy excellent meat tacos (6 pesos). **Pilar's Taco Stand,** on the corner of Zaragoza and Colegio Militar (tel. 5-01-46), is not only the town's de facto bus station but also an excellent place to indulge in glorious fish tacos (12 pesos) or fries (8 pesos; open daily 8am-8pm). **Restaurant Santa Monica,** on Degollado and Colegio Militar (tel. 5-02-04), has been open 22 years—try their *pescado a la veracruzana* (35 pesos) and you'll know why. Classy but casual decorations with colorful *piñatas* and cacti of Brobdingnagian proportions (open daily 7am-10pm).

---

### Stealing Home

If you're feeling energetic at night, you might want to take in a **baseball game** at the local stadium, off Degollado to the south. Follow the light towers—any local will show you the way. Admission is only 5 pesos, though a cold Tecate's another 5 pesos. Root, root, root for the home team—**Los Tiburones** (the Sharks)—while analyzing the odder aspects of Mexican League professional baseball: you'll see an all-sand playing field, umpires in bright blue pants, base-runners without batting helmets, players trading gloves between batters, lots of submarine-ball pitchers, some players on the same team in different uniforms, and huge crowds dancing between innings to popular dance music. Oh, and if, by chance, you catch a ball, don't even think about keeping it as a souvenir—you will first be swarmed by tiny kids paid by commission for every ball (and crushed beer can) they recover, and eventually you'll even be bothered by the police. Games are at 7pm some weeknights and 1 or 2pm on weekends.

---

**Sights** Modern art lovers are guaranteed to be wowed by the plethora and high quality of galleries. Todos Santos's new pride and joy (among art fans, at least) is the **Todos Santos Gallery,** on Legaspi and Topete (tel. 5-00-40), opened in 1995 by artist Michael Cope. The gallery is devoted strictly to the work of artists who reside in Baja California—exactly half of them Mexican, the other 50% from the U.S. and other countries (open Mon. and Wed.-Sat. 10am-5pm). Cutting-edge bronze and clay sculptures, off-the-wall wallclocks, and ornate mirrors are on parade at the **Santa Fe Art Gallery,** Centario 4 between Hidalgo and Márquez de León (open Wed.-Mon. 9:30am-5pm). **Casa Franco Gallery,** Juárez at Morelos (tel./fax 5-03-56), directly behind the Santa Fe gallery, has furniture, bowls, and pipes from Todos Santos, Guadalajara, and all over Mexico; the staff will be happy to tell you more (open Mon.-Sat. 9am-5pm).

If you overdose on art, don't forget that Todos Santos is surrounded by some of the region's most unspoiled (and unexplored) beaches. **La Posa,** only 2km from town, is perfect for that romantic stroll or uplifting solitary walk. Unfortunately, vicious undercurrents and powerful waves make this beach unequivocally unsuitable for swimming. To get there, go up Juárez and turn left on Topete. Follow the road as it winds across the valley and past a white building, and *voilà!* The beach. To reach **Punta Lobos,** the stomping ground of the local sea lion population and a beach popular with locals, turn left onto Degollado as you walk away from the town center. Roughly six blocks later, the city limits end. To catch a spectacular aerial view of the sea, turn right 1.5km south on the highway at the first possible fork in the road. Follow the main dirt path east for 2.5km; the path will bear left past an old fish plant and up a hill, which falls precipitously to the seashore. Most other beaches are accessible via the Transpeninsular Highway south of town. These sights are isolated, and therefore both attractive and hazardous. Bring a friend, and plan to return before nightfall.

A quiet and lovely beach by the highway is **San Pedrito,** 6km south of town. Lots of surfing and hangin' loose goes on here. It's easy to find a sunbathing spot, and on these Bohemian beaches, nobody cares if you bare all. Just watch out in the water— the current is not as friendly as the big, inviting waves. **Los Cerritos,** another 12km south of San Pedrito, is a popular picnic spot and family beach. The current is tamer here, but the waves are just as big, and there's always some sort of party going on.

A beautiful lake atop a mountain, **Sierra de la Laguna,** is accessible only by car (it's a 90-minute drive). One kilometer down the highway past the Punta Lobos turnoff, turn left at the fenced-off cattle ranch. A 45-minute drive brings you to **Rancho La Burera,** which serves as the trailhead for the *laguna.* Be social and make friends in town. Then invite them to show you the way. To reach the appropriately named **Playa de las Palmas,** travel another 4.6km from the Laguna down the highway, and turn right when you see the white buildings on the left. Travel another 2.6km and you'll be bowled over by palm trees; just past these is the beach. The serene and deserted shore here is excellent for swimming.

# ▓ Los Cabos

The towns of **Cabo San Lucas** and **San José del Cabo** comprise the southwestern part of the Los Cabos district (pop. 70,000), which includes much of the coastline of Baja California's southern end. Readily accessible via land, air, and water, Los Cabos (The Capes), the hottest honeymoon spot around, are much more developed than the majority of the peninsula. Visitors are drawn here by the stretch of beach leading from San José del Cabo to Cabo San Lucas, where luxury hotels form a glittering strip between the desert and the ocean, and travelers can choose between the calm green Sea of Cortés or the rougher, foamier Pacific Ocean. Don't expect wilderness or hidden pirate plunder, though: Bud-guzzling, sunbathing, sightseeing, gift-buying, jet-skiing *norteamericanos* congregate by the thousands. The *vía corta* bus from La Paz heads first to Cabo San Lucas, then to San José del Cabo, then back to La Paz.

## CABO SAN LUCAS

Perched on the southern tip of Baja, Cabo San Lucas is an eminent representative of the heavily Americanized resort industry of Mexico. Though small (pop. 8000), the town has surpassed such classic resorts as Acapulco in popularity among honeymooners and U.S. college spring-breakers due to its peaceful waters and ultra-modern pleasure domes. A favorite vacation spot among families looking for an easy, pampered escape from stress, Cabo is best suited to those who desire neither a peek into real Mexican culture nor the "inconvenience" of changing their dollars into pesos— or even of learning what a peso is. Cabo San Lucas now has the country's second highest cost of living, after Cancún, and it is quickly turning into the latter, with endless neon-lit, fog-machined discotheques, cigar shops, and American fast-food joints.

If all this sounds like it's not for you, then Cabo can be depressing; tensions between maltreated Mexicans, elderly resident U.S. expats, and carefree tourists run high. Local fishermen are finding it increasingly hard to survive, and the dolphins and whales that once flourished near the coast have all but disappeared. Recent legislation to diminish pollution may be just a little too late.

Despite its influx of dollar-rich, culture-poor tourists, Cabo San Lucas does have some appeal to the budget traveler, mostly due to its superb beaches and picturesque rock formations: **El Arco** is the famous arch rock that marks the very tip of the Californias. Cabo San Lucas has yet to develop extensive facilities for budget travelers. If you don't plan to spend lots of money, then stay in town only for the day and camp on the beach, or simply treat the town as a big supermarket—buy your sunscreen and make tracks for cheaper San José del Cabo.

**Orientation** Lázaro Cárdenas is the main street in Cabo San Lucas. It runs roughly southeast-northwest, diagonally through the town's grid of streets. **Paseo de la Marina** forks off Cárdenas where the resort zone begins, continues south, and winds around the marina. From west to east, north-south streets (all branching off Cárdenas) include **Ocampo, Zaragoza, Morelos, Vicario,** and **Mendoza.** Farther west, **Cabo San Lucas, Hidalgo, Matamoros,** and **Abasolo** cross Cárdenas and continue south into the resort zone, eventually meeting Marina. From north to south, the following streets are perpendicular to those above: **Obregón, Revolución, 20 de Noviembre, Libertad, 16 de Septiembre, Niños Héroes, Constitución,** and **5 de Mayo.** South of Cárdenas, **Madero, Zapata,** and **J. Domínguez** run east-west in the resort area. Continuing south on Marina, you'll pass the posh resorts, and eventually arrive at the beach, **Playa de Médano.** Restaurants and bars—and a high density of English-speaking Mexicans—are concentrated on Cárdenas between Morelos and the mountains on the western edge of town.

To get to the center of the action from the bus station, walk on Zaragoza for two blocks toward the water to Cárdenas. The grid-like pattern of the city makes it difficult to get lost. You might be dropped off at a remote bus station; from there, cross the street and walk across the sandy little park in front of the yellow complex; continue to the next street, and stand across the street from the bus stop to catch a local yellow bus to the center (every 15min., ½hr., 3 pesos).

**Practical Information** Tourist information and maps are dispensed by time-share hawkers all over the center of town. The "Marina Fiesta" salespeople have the best of the lot. To exchange money, try **Banca Serfin,** at Cárdenas and Zaragoza (tel. 3-09-90 or 3-09-91; open Mon.-Fri. 8:30am-1:30pm). It also has a friendly **ATM** that's fluent in English. Otherwise try **Bancomer** (tel. 3-19-50), across the street (open 8:30am-1pm), or the *casa de cambio* on Cárdenas at Zaragoza (tel. 3-19-50). Most hotels and restaurants will gladly exchange dollars at lower rates. There are **LADA-TELs** all over town, especially on Lázaro Cárdenas and Ocampo, and a long-distance *caseta* (tel. 3-00-25; fax 3-00-19) at Cárdenas and Hidalgo (open daily 8am-10pm).

**ABC Autotransportes** and **Águila buses** are located at Zaragoza and 16 de Septiembre (tel. 3-04-00). They head to San José del Cabo (every ½hr., 7am-10pm, ½hr., 13 pesos) and La Paz (6 per day, 3hr., 51 pesos) via Todos Santos (1½hr., 22 pesos). One bus per day leaving at 4:30pm heads north, stopping at La Paz (3hr., 51 pesos), Cd. Constitución (6hr., 74 pesos), Loreto (8½hr., 82 pesos), Mulegé (10½hr., 110 pesos), Santa Rosalía (11½hr., 127 pesos), San Ignacio (12½hr., 136 pesos), Guerrero Negro (14½hr., 203 pesos), San Quintín (19hr., 301 pesos), Ensenada (23hr., 389 pesos), and Tijuana (26½hr., 434 pesos). **Avis Rent-a-Car** (tel. 3-46-07) is at Plaza Los Mariachis, across from the Giggling Marlin. A VW Sedan, including insurance and unlimited mileage, costs US$44 per day (open daily 8:30am-6pm).

The **English-language bookstore,** at Marina and Cárdenas (tel. 3-31-71), in the Plaza Bonita Mall, has U.S. magazines, popular novels, and *USA Today* (open daily 9am-9pm). You have little choice but to get your groceries from **Supermercado Plaza,** at Zaragoza and Cárdenas (tel. 3-14-50). It's the only supermarket in town, uncontested and (surprise!) expensive (open daily 7am-11pm). **Farmacia Aramburo** (tel. 3-14-89) is next door to the supermarket, at Plaza Aramburo (open 7:30am-11pm). The **Red Cross** is on Delegación (tel. 3-33-02), on the outskirts of town towards San José del Cabo, 200m from the gas station. The **hospital** is on Zaragoza (tel. 3-01-02). You can access the Internet at **BajaTech,** on Blvd. Lázaro Cárdenas (tel. 3-42-40), across from

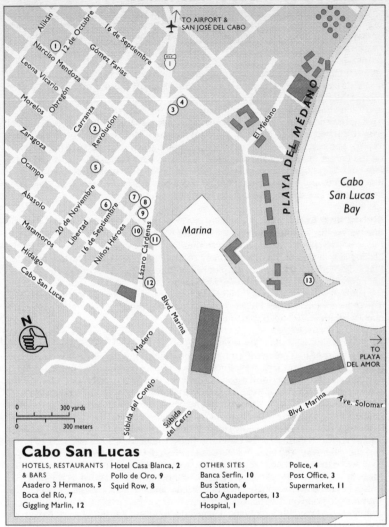

## Cabo San Lucas

| HOTELS, RESTAURANTS | Hotel Casa Blanca, 2 | OTHER SITES | Police, 4 |
|---|---|---|---|
| & BARS | Pollo de Oro, 9 | Banca Serfin, 10 | Post Office, 3 |
| Asadero 3 Hermanos, 5 | Squid Row, 8 | Bus Station, 6 | Supermarket, 11 |
| Boca del Río, 7 | | Cabo Aguadeportes, 13 | |
| Giggling Marlin, 12 | | Hospital, 1 | |

the PEMEX station. A hefty 40 pesos per hour, but you can charge what you want when you're the only place in town. In an **emergency,** dial the **police** (tel. 3-49-77). **Postal Code:** 23410. **Phone Code:** 114.

**Accommodations and Food** Multi-million-dollar resorts with every service imaginable dominate San Lucas's coast line; *ergo,* simple, cheap beds are seriously lacking. During the winter high season, make reservations early and be prepared to shell out more *dinero* than you would during the slower summer months. The only legitimate budget accommodation remaining may be the **Hotel Casa Blanca,** on Revolución and Vicario (tel. 3-02-60). Slightly less luxurious than its namesake, the hotel provides clean, simple, cement rooms with fans and functional private bathrooms (singles 100 pesos; doubles 120 pesos). To get to the **CREA Youth Hostel (HI;** tel. 3-01-48) from Cárdenas, walk 10 minutes down Morelos to Av. de la Juventud, and then turn right and hike five minutes to the Instituto Sur Californiano building. The street is not well-lit; lone travelers would be wise to check in before twilight or stay in town. Bring your own pillow (dorm bunk with communal bath 30 pesos; singles with private bath 40 pesos; bunk doubles with bath 50 pesos; camping 20 pesos).

Restaurant-bars along the water gang up on tourists; the cheap spots line Morelos, a safe distance from the million-dollar yachts. King of *taquerías*, **Asadero 3 Hermanos,** Morelos at 20 de Noviembre, serves up scrumptious, cheap, and safe tacos and *quesadillas* (5-6 pesos; open daily 9am-4am). Growling stomachs gravitate toward the enormous rotating chickens at **El Pollo de Oro,** Cárdenas at Morelos (tel. 3-03-10). Half a chicken goes for 28 pesos, a quarter bird 16 pesos (open daily 6am-11pm). The best and brightest new budget spot in town is **Uncle Tio's** (tel. 3-32-84), on the corner of Morelos and Cárdenas. It's owned by "Tio," a U.S. expat and excellent chef. This homey, serve-yourself cafeteria has 25-peso breakfast buffets, 35-peso lunch buffets, and 45-peso dinner buffets. Even better than the friendly folk and good home-cooked food is the fact that it's open daily 24 hours.

**Sights and Sand**  All major activity in Cabo San Lucas revolves around the pristine waters that surround the coast. **Playa del Médano,** one of the better beaches in the area, stretches east along the bay around the corner from the marina. Escape the blazing sun in one of the beach's many restaurants or *palapas.* The waters of the Playa de Médano are alive with parasailers and motorboats full of lobster-red, beer-guzzling vacationers. **Cabo Aguadeportes** (tel. 3-01-17), in front of the Hotel Hacienda, rents out water equipment (open 9am-5pm), as does **JT Watersports** (tel. 7-56-08), adjacent to Hotel Plaza Las Glorias (snorkeling gear US$9 per day; wave runners US$35 per ½hr.; open 9am-6pm).

The famous **Arch Rock** (El Arco) of Cabo San Lucas rises only a short boat ride from the marina. Although there are supposed to be tons of sea lions lolling about, there aren't—most of them are scarred by boat propellors and the noise from illustrious booze cruises. To get there, walk through the Plaza Las Glorias hotel or the big Mexican crafts market farther down Paseo Marina to the docks. Eager, English-speaking boat captains will be happy to take you on a 45-minute glass-bottom **boat ride** to El Arco and back (US$7). On the way, you may be treated to an inordinate number of tasteless or corny jokes. Other than the picturesque Arch and the creatures that visit it, the only thing you'll see are the summer dwellings of Sly Stallone, Michael Jackson, Madonna, Van Halen, and others—those budget travelers with weak stomachs can turn the other way. The boat also stops at **La Playa del Amor** (yes, that's the Beach of Loooove) right near El Arco and allows you to get out and head back later on a different boat for no additional charge. This beach, perennially mobbed, is the only one with access to both the rough, deep blue Pacific and the light, tranquil Sea of Cortés. Swimming is good on the gulf side, but beware of the Pacific's currents; two unlucky swimmers died recently after being dragged out to sea on this side. To get to the Love Beach and back, you can also take a water taxi (US$7). A beautiful and more secluded Pacific beach where you shouldn't swim is **Playa del Divorcio** (Divorce Beach). To get there, hop on a yellow bus (1.50 pesos) or walk out on Marina and turn right across from the Mexican crafts market. Slip out to the beach between massive condo complexes right after you pass the Terra Sol Hotel.

**Snorkeling** is popular on La Playa del Amor and around the rocks between the marina and the beach, where tropical fish abound. Bring your own gear or dish out those dollars for rented equipment from one of the vendors that populate the marina area (see above). The best snorkeling beach is said to be **Playa Santa María,** 13km from Cabo San Lucas on the highway between San Lucas and San José del Cabo.

The 8-peso bus ride to San José del Cabo provides access to more beaches along the way. Choose your spot carefully in order to avoid the crowds. **El Chileno,** halfway between the two towns (km 15), offers phenomenal opportunities for swimming as well as snorkeling in one of the only live coral reefs in the world. You can rent equipment from **Cabo Aguadeportes** right on Chileno Beach (open daily 9am-5pm). Just ask around to find names and descriptions of other good sites, and ask the driver to leave you at the beach of your choice. Beaches closer to (and in) San José, past El Chileno, are generally unswimmable due to the surf.

**Entertainment** If you want to go buck-wild, you can't pick a better place. At night, the couple of streets near the sea turn into a huge laser-lit party ground, and everyone stumbles down the street smoking Cuban cigars and shrieking. You too can join rich Americans and hip Mexican teens in the nightly ritual of alcohol-induced gastrointestinal reversal. Typical Cabo San Lucas bar decor is in the same booze-can-punish vein—off-the-wall signs like "Sorry, We're Open" and "Wrong Way—Do Not Exit" vie for space with assorted driver's licenses. Cabo is a great place to cut loose; just don't expect cheap booze—this ain't Tijuana. Here, those who play hard pay hard.

**La Concepción** (tel. 3-49-63), north of the Marina, next to Hotel Marina Fiesta. Probably Los Cabos's best-kept secret. The *ambiente* is amazing—sit outside in old hanging boats, listen to the latest in Mexican reggae, or sample one of 105 different tequilas. They'll give you a 20-page history of the drink (in Spanish) and explain tequila from A (agave) to W (worm). Laid-back atmosphere, clientele Mexican. Check out the ceiling, which is a rendition of an old pirate's map, while you nibble on delicious *botanas* (25 pesos) or tequila shots (20-230 pesos). The house drink, La Concepción, contains cranberry and pineapple juice, tequila, and *creme de cacao* (25 pesos). Open daily noon-2am.

**Squid Roe,** Cárdenas at Zaragoza (tel. 3-06-55), is the most popular spot in town, especially around 12:30am, when tourists from other clubs flock here to end their night (hopefully not alone). The pick-up scene is frantic. Conga lines, tequila everywhere, screaming whistles, and short-skirted, cigar-peddling salesgirls dancing on any and all surfaces. Mixed drinks 20 pesos. Open daily noon-3am.

**Carlos 'n' Charlie's,** Marina Blvd. 20, near Zaragoza (tel. 3-12-80 or 3-21-80). Although a bit expensive (beer 18 pesos, huge margaritas 36 pesos), this club (owned by the same franchise as Squid Roe) is hip, loud, and happening. Best of all, manager Francisco Castillo "Panaco" has promised a free drink to anyone carrying a copy of *Let's Go: Mexico 1998.* Young crowd drinks and dances to U.S. pop tunes from the 80s and 90s. Choreographed "waiter show" at 9 and 11pm. Open daily 11am-2am; kitchen closes at 11pm.

**Cool Hippo's/Sorry Charlie's,** on Marina in the Plaza de los Mariachis. Both outdoor and indoor bar and dining area, casual and fun with impromptu dancing whenever the urge (or beer rush) hits you. Not as taxing as some of the other nightspots. Specials include 4 tacos and a beer for US$5 or 3 chicken enchiladas, rice, beans, and a beer for US$5. Comparatively inexpensive drinks (beer 12 pesos, margaritas 15-18 pesos) and glorious 80s background music make this a great place to chill. Open daily 8am-3am; kitchen closes at 1am.

**Kokomo's,** on Blvd. Marina (tel. 3-06-00), near the Giggling Marlin, gets pumping at 10:30pm, when this brand-new club starts spouting fog from all corners and the lights really start acting up. The music is "contemporary"—late 80s top-40 (Aruba, Jamaica...) abounds. Beer 18 pesos, margaritas 25 pesos. Open daily 8am-11:30pm.

BAJA CALIFORNIA

## The Player

Timeshare vendors disguised as "tourist officials" roam the streets of Cabo San Lucas. If you want to take advantage of what they have to offer for free, you must be 25 years old (or tell them you're 25—they'll believe you) and possess a major credit card. If you have both, and a free afternoon, it's quite possible to go on the Arco boat ride for free and order anything you want at an expensive restaurant in exchange for an hour and a half of "listening," ears closed but eyes open, mouth pleasantly grinning, and head nodding to the English-speaking con man's pitch. He will try to convince you to dump US$15,000 into his hands in exchange for yearly time at an exclusive, American-oriented resort in Cabo. Don't admit until after dinner that you're not prepared to spend $15,000 (unless you want a struggle). Other lures include a free car rental for a day and a free day at a resort.

## SAN JOSÉ DEL CABO

If Los Cabos were two brothers, then José would be the more sedate of the two: unlike his ill-fated, party-animal, bad-boy younger brother Lucas, José would be charming, sincere, and polite, yet still lots of fun. San José del Cabo remains relatively untouristed and peacefully Mexican, a haven from the Resortville that dominates the rest of the cape. In fact, "Los Cabos," when said colloquially, often refers only to Cabo San Lucas and the surrounding beaches and resort, and does not include quieter, less commercial San José. Perhaps this will help preserve San José: while the town may be larger than its sister city, San José is strikingly tranquil and collected. Religious services with sing-alongs are held in the plaza every Wednesday, and snorkel shops snuggle peacefully with the *loncherías* next door.

**Orientation** The **Transpeninsular Highway** on the west and **Avenida Mijares** on the east, both running north-south, connect the town with San José's broad sweep of beautiful beach 2km away. From north to south, cross-streets, running east-west between the above two include **Obregón, Zaragoza, Doblado, Castro, Coronado, González,** and, much farther south along the resort-laden beach, **Paseo San José.** Between the two main north-south streets, **Green, Degollado, Guerrero, Morelos,** and **Hidalgo** run parallel from west to east. The conspicuous cathedral and *zócalo* are on Zaragoza near Hidalgo. To get to town from the **Águila/ABC bus station,** turn left out of the station and walk eight to 10 minutes down González until it hits Mijares. Turn left on Mijares, walk three blocks, make another left on Zaragoza, and presto! The town square and center of activity will appear like a happy dream.

**Practical Information** The **tourist center** on Zaragoza and Mijares (tel. 2-29-60, ext. 150), in the beige building next to the *zócalo*, offers a valuable map as well as plenty of brochures and info (open Mon.-Fri. 8am-3pm). Change money at **Bancomer,** on Zaragoza and Morelos (tel. 2-00-30 or 2-00-40; open for exchange 8:30am-4pm); traveler's checks can be cashed at most of the *casas de cambio* that line Mijares. **ATMs** can be found in many banks, including **Banco Unión** (tel. 3-34-34), near the *zócalo*. There are **LADATELs** all over the main plaza; **free local calls** can be made from the booth outside the tourist office. Make long-distance calls from the *caseta* beside the cathedral, Hidalgo 9 (tel. 2-04-53; fax 2-00-14), between Zaragoza and Obregón (open daily 8am-10pm).

Although they are working on another, San José de Cabo has but one bus station—on Gonzaléz, two blocks from the highway (tel. 2-11-00). **Águila** and **ABC Autotransportes** launch **buses** to Cabo San Lucas (every ½hr., ½hr., 12 pesos), La Paz (every hr., 6am-7pm, 3hr., 57 pesos), and Todos Santos (8 per day, 1½hr., 29 pesos). **Dollar Rent-A-Car** (tel. 2-01-00; at the airport 2-06-71), across from the supermarket (see below), will set you on the road for US$55 per day plus US$11 per day insurance and free mileage. You need a credit card and at least 25 candles on your last birthday cake. To corral a **taxi,** call 2-04-01. Buy groceries at the **Supermercado Aramburo** on Zaragoza and Guerrero (tel. 2-01-88 or 2-00-48; open daily 7am-9pm). **Farmacia La Moderna** is on Zaragoza and Degollado (tel. 2-00-50; open daily 8am-9pm). The ever-ready **Red Cross** is on Mijares (tel. 2-03-16), in the same complex as the post office, and offers 24-hour ambulance service. The **hospital** (tel. 2-37-13 or 2-38-13) is on Retorno Atunero, in Col. Clamizal; the **Centro de Salud** is at Manuel Doblado 39 (tel. 2-02-41). For **police,** call 2-03-61. For **internet access,** try **CaboNet** (tel. 2-29-05), just west of the Transpeninsular Hwy. just north of Valerio Gonzalez. The **post office** is on Mijares and González (tel. 2-09-11), several blocks toward the beach on the right-hand side (open Mon.-Fri. 8am-7pm, Sat. 9am-1pm). **Postal Code:** 23400. **Phone Code:** 114.

**Accommodations and Food** As prices rise with the approach of the megaresorts, rooms in the center of town look less and less appealing: imagine waking up US$16-40 poorer, then having to face a scorching 25-minute walk to the beach. Many

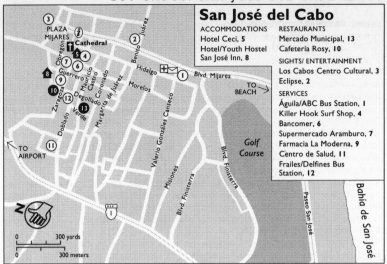

## San José del Cabo

**ACCOMMODATIONS**
Hotel Ceci, 5
Hotel/Youth Hostel
San José Inn, 8

**RESTAURANTS**
Mercado Municipal, 13
Cafetería Rosy, 10

**SIGHTS/ ENTERTAINMENT**
Los Cabos Centro Cultural, 3
Eclipse, 2

**SERVICES**
Águila/ABC Bus Station, 1
Killer Hook Surf Shop, 4
Bancomer, 6
Supermercado Aramburo, 7
Farmacia La Moderna, 9
Centro de Salud, 11
Frailes/Delfines Bus
Station, 12

**random rooms** are for rent for about 30-40 pesos per day; look for signs, especially on Obregón. Otherwise, you can enjoy multi-colored bedspreads and ancient paint jobs at **Hotel Ceci,** Zaragoza 22 (tel. 2-00-51), a block and a half up from Mijares. Spanking clean, cold rooms put guests in a positive mood, ready to appreciate the pastel curtains and matching lampshades. Bathrooms have colored glass windows—take a shower while admiring the lovely cathedral (singles 77 pesos, with A/C 95 pesos; doubles with A/C 95 pesos). **The Hotel Diana,** on Zaragoza (tel. 2-04-90), near the *centro*, has big, clean rooms with TVs and A/C. All rooms have one king-sized bed and one single bed. An ultra-friendly staff maintains this good location (all rooms 150 pesos). **Hotel San José,** on Obregón and Guerrero (tel./fax 2-24-64), has relatively clean and spacious pink rooms with fans, thick mattresses, and warm water. Although the hotel offers mail service, bike rentals, and long-distance phone calls, it can be a little desolate at times (singles 80 pesos; spacious doubles with TV 140 pesos). **Trailer Park Brisa del Mar,** just off the highway to San Lucas when it reaches the coast, provides beach campers, communal bathrooms, and a bar with TV (full hookup US$7 plus tax; US$5 for tent).

Budget restaurants in San José del Cabo are being pushed out by real estate offices and fancy tourist eateries, leaving few options between taco stands and filet mignon. A healthy suspicion of anglophone restaurants will save you money: if the menus are printed in flawless English, the food is probably more expensive than it ought to be. Good, moderately priced meals hide on Doblado and along Zaragoza, between the cathedral and the banks. The food at **Cafetería Rosy,** on Zaragoza and Green, will have you riveted. Seafood dishes like *sopa de camarones* (shrimp soup, 30 pesos), *pescado en mantequilla* or *al mojo de ajo* (fish in butter or garlic sauce, 38 pesos), and *pollo a la naranja* (chicken in orange sauce, 31 pesos) are tasty and hearty (open Oct.-May daily 8am-10pm; June-Sept. 8am-6pm). **Restaurante Vista al Mar,** on Castro and Doblado (tel. 2-06-32), offers homecooked meals and an authentic ambience absent elsewhere in town. Locals sit on the airy covered porch and heartily devour economical food prepared by the family, such as enchiladas (20 pesos) and *pollo frito* with chile, beans, and rice (26 pesos; open daily 8am-5pm). Follow locals to **El Nuevo Imperial,** Zaragoza and Green, a Chinese restaurant with great food and low prices. Entrees are usually below 20 pesos, and even the frighteningly named *paquete turístico* (tourist package) offers egg rolls, fried rice, and an entree for 30 pesos. People-watch on the outdoor patio, or if you must catch some sun, grab take-out (open daily 8am-9:30pm). The pricey and lovely **Restaurant Jazmin's,** at Zaragoza and Obregón (tel. 2-12-60), is a good place to enjoy breakfast. The Villafuerte

**BAJA CALIFORNIA**

family, also the owners of the Los Gorditos restaurant on Mijares, has decorated this place with exquisite taste (continental breakfast 20 pesos, *huevos rancheros* 25 pesos; open daily 8am-10pm).

**Sights** The most popular beach in town (for surfing, if not swimming) is **Costa Azul,** on Palmilla Pt., 1km south of the Brisa del Mar trailer park. To get there, take a bus headed for San Lucas (every ½hr.) and ask the driver to drop you off at Costa Azul; or take a bus from Valerio González (US$3). A 15-minute walk down Mijares will lead you to good beaches much closer to town. The newer luxury hotels mar the sand at some spots, but there's plenty of natural, clean coastline in the stretches between the artificial structures. If you want to swim, try either the **Playa Palmilla,** 3km toward Cabo San Lucas from Costa Azul, or **Playa Santa Mónica,** a prime spot for snorkeling. Some people hitch along that road.

Folks at the **Killer Hook Surf Shop,** on Hidalgo between Doblado and Zaragoza (tel. 2-24-30), are friendlier than the name suggests. They rent snorkel gear (US$8), fishing poles (US$10), and surfboards (US$15); they also repair surfboards and provide tips (open Mon.-Sat. 8am-9pm). **Trader Dick's** (tel. 2-28-28), next to La Jolla Resort, rents sand buggies (US$35 for 1½hr.).

If you can find time between trips to the beach, stop by **Los Cabos Centro Cultural** on Mijares. Feast your eyes on reproductions of wall paintings, regional antiques, and an original Pericúe home. Guided tours are available (open Mon.-Fri. 8am-3pm). At night, **Eclipse,** on Mijares (tel. 2-16-94), one block down from Doblado, pumps out rock tunes (beer 15 pesos, national drinks start at 10 pesos; open Tues.-Sun. 9pm-3am). Also of note is the **Huichol Gallery,** on Zaragoza and Mijares (tel. 2-37-99), that features beautiful handicrafts by local Huichol Indians, who've lived hundreds of years without much outside influence (open daily 9am-1pm and 5-10pm).

**Entertainment** San José del Cabo can't compete with its noisy neighbor, but it's still possible to have a good time here—just kick back, relax, and don't expect conga lines and table dancing. **Eclipse,** on Mijares and Guerro, is very upscale, pumping soft rock into tasteful decor. Dress "nicely" and make sure you have your wallet; beers will cost you 20 pesos each (Sat.-Sun. live bands, Wed.-Thurs. karaoke; cover Fri.-Sat. 20 pesos; open Mon.-Tues. 8pm-3am, Wed.-Sat. 10pm-4am). **Piso #2,** Zaragoza 21, two blocks from the church, is mellower. Red chairs, palm trees, and neon lights help you digest your Dos Equis (15 pesos). Huge mixed drinks are 30 pesos—don't try hitting the bar's pool tables after you've had one (Fri. 9-11pm free bar for women; open in summer daily 6pm-3am; in winter noon-3am).

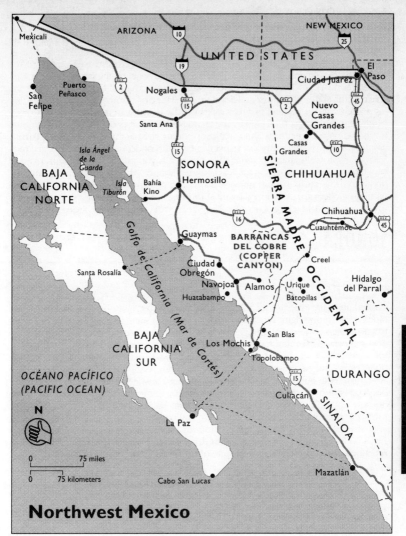

Northwest Mexico

# Northwest Mexico

The first taste of life south of the border for many gringos consists of nights of debauchery, rounds of tequila shots, gaudy felt sombreros, and blistering heat. In the midst of all this madness, many tourists overlook the rows of shantytowns, sadistic border-patrol battles, and miles of industrial wasteland just seconds away from all the gringo indulgence. But things calm down considerably as you venture farther south. The grime and frenetic madness of Ciudad Juárez and Nogales, Mexico's brawny border towns, give way to bustling markets, colonial mansions, iconoclastic museums, and a surreal cactus-studded landscape. In some parts, things slow to a virtual stand-still—you can hear the flies buzz and the wind whistle through the desert. Though swaggering *vaqueros* clad in tight jeans are almost obsolete, you may want to bring along a pair of cowboy boots and a wide-brimmed *sombrero*—the rugged terrain requires a lot of stamina, and the *noroeste* sun is merciless.

The Sierra Madre Occidental rips through the heart of Northwest Mexico. To the east of the mountains, the parched desert sprawl gives even the larger cities in **Chihuahua** a dusty frontier feel; frequent sandstorms enhance the mood. Along the coast, in the states of **Sonora** and **Sinaloa,** a melange of commercial ports, quiet fishing villages, and sprawling beaches overlook the warm waters of the Sea of Cortés. Landlocked **Durango,** traversed by the Sierra Madres, thrives on mining and is known for its Old-West ruggedness. But the most stunning sight in the *noroeste* is the Barrancas del Cobre (Copper Canyon), a spectacular series of deep gorges and unusual rock formations in Chihuahua, grander than Grand Canyon and brimming with tropical vegetation, all cut through by the Río Urique far, far below. The caves in the area are home to the reclusive Tarahumara Indians. The Northwest's diverse landscape and natural wonders are overlooked by most tourists, but those who look past the border towns and into the region's heartland and coast will be heavily rewarded.

# SONORA

## ■ Nogales

Pushed up against the border and straddled by two steep hills bearing tin houses and block-long Corona signs, Nogales (pop. 211,000) can seem like the archetypal border town—cheap curio shops and cheesy bars. The streets are crowded with street vendors expectantly waiting for pocketbook-happy Americans to dip below the border for a day and purchase tiny rag dolls to bring a little piece of Mexico back to their own homes and advertise. However, in spite of rampant off-track betting and English advertising, the cultural syncretism and fast-paced bustle which animate life in other border towns are notably absent here, especially in the precarious residential promontories and hills overlooking the city. On shack-lined, candle-lit dirt roads far above the border bustle, entire blocks watch TV and cook together each evening, exuding a sense of tight, cross-generational community little known in the U.S. Born out of the 1848 Mexican-American War as something of an unarmed fortress, Nogales has remained distinctively Mexican in spite of the under-21 gringo-party influx.

### ORIENTATION AND PRACTICAL INFORMATION

If you plan to venture beyond Nogales, obtain a **tourist card** at the border. It's much simpler to get the card here than farther south. When you cross the border through the new arched crossing complex, turn right into the first building you encounter; it's the immigration and **tourist office.**

The **bus terminal** and **train station** are directly across from each other on **Carretera Internacional,** 4.5km from town. A taxi from the bus station to the center of town will cost an exorbitant 35 pesos; instead cross the street and walk north to the end of the block, where you can board one of the white buses (2 pesos) marked "Parque Industrial" or "Villa Sonora." Downtown Nogales is the last stop. To get from downtown to the bus terminal and train station, wait at the bus stop across from the casino, one block south of the tourist office. Take the "Parque Industrial" bus and ask the driver to let you off before the bus terminal. A large supermarket should be to your right. Walk up the hill to the bus station.

Relatively small, Nogales makes for easy navigating. If you're crossing the border by foot, you'll be on **Pesqueira;** by car, you'll drive in on **Juárez.** From east to west, **Pesqueira, Juárez** (which becomes **López Mateos** several blocks south), **Morelos, Obregón** (the main tourist drag), **Hidalgo,** and **Ingenieros** run parallel to each other and perpendicular to the border. **Internacional** runs parallel to the tall picket fence that marks the border. Proceeding south, away from the border, **Campillo, Ochoa, Pierson, Aguirre, Vázquez, Díaz,** and **González** all run parallel.

**Tourist Office:** Tel. 2-06-66. To the left of the border from the Mexican side, in the Edificio Puerta de México, room #1. The friendly, English-speaking staff is best at directing visitors to curio shops or bars—the two main attractions for many Americans—but they will also hand out a crude map of the downtown area and (promotional) literature describing the rest of Sonora. Open Mon.-Sat. 8am-6pm.

**Currency Exchange:** Banks line Obregón near the border. **Banamex** has 2 central locations: one at Obregón and Ochoa (tel. 2-07-80 or 2-55-05) resembles the control tower of the Starship *Enterprise* (open Mon.-Fri. 9am-3pm); another on Pierson between Elias Calles and López Mateos (tel. 2-12-51 or 2-10-65) could pass for the *Enterprise*'s viewing deck (open Mon.-Fri. 9am-3pm). Both exchange dollars and traveler's checks and feature 24hr. **ATMs.**

**Telephones:** Downtown Nogales has a high concentration of **LADATELs.** Look for them at Obregón and Campillo, Obregón and Flores Guerra, and at the border in front of the tourist office. The *caseta* in the bus terminal (tel. 3-50-81, fax 3-50-82) offers overpriced international calls, but collect calls are free from the marked phone next to the *caseta* (open 24hr.).

**Fax: Puesta del Sol,** Campillo 115 at Obregón (tel. 2-00-16; fax 2-17-14), has an international-call-and-fax *caseta* (5 pesos per page for a local fax; local calls 3 pesos for 3min.; open daily 8am-9pm). Also, the **bus terminal** *caseta* (above) does faxes.

**Buses: Transportes Norte de Sonora** (tel. 3-16-03) runs to Guadalajara (26hr., 478 pesos), Hermosillo (every hr., 8:30am-6:30pm, 3½hr., 56 pesos), Los Mochis (7:30am-11:30pm, 11hr., 150 pesos), Mazatlán (16hr., 313 pesos), and Mexico City (3 per day, 32hr., 611 pesos). Check schedules. **Transportes del Pacífico** (tel. 3-16-06) goes to Guaymas (every 2hr., 8am-6:30pm, 6hr., 80 pesos), Hermosillo (3½hr., 55 pesos), Puerto Vallarta (26hr., 500 pesos), Querétaro (32hr., 580 pesos), and Tepic (22hr., 450 pesos); buses are *de paso* and leave every 2hr., 8am-8:30pm. Prices listed are for 1st-class fares. **Elite** (tel. 3-16-03) sends posh buses to Guadalajara (611 pesos), Hermosillo (62 pesos), Los Mochis (171 pesos), Mazatlán (348 pesos), and Mexico City (710 pesos). Call for schedules. **Greyhound** buses (tel. in Tuscon (520) 287-5628) leave for Tucson (every hr., 7am-7pm and 9pm, US$6.50) from their station ½ block from the U.S. side of the border.

**Trains:** Tel. 3-10-91. Two southbound trains depart daily; the slow *burro* (literally "donkey") leaves at 7am and the faster *estrella* leaves at 3:30pm, though times do change. Destinations include Guadalajara (175 and 313 pesos, respectively) and Mazatlán (*burro* 106 pesos, *estrella* 187 pesos). Tickets sold 6-7am and 8am-3:30pm. Reservations for the *estrella* can be made by phone.

**Luggage Storage:** Available 6am-10pm at the bus terminal (1 peso per hr.).

**Market: VH Supermarket,** Obregón 375 between Ramos and Rodríguez (tel. 2-41-24), 10min. from Av. Juárez. Open Mon.-Sat. 8am-10pm, Sun. 8am-8pm.

**Laundromat: Nuevas Lavanderas de Nogales,** Ingenieros 332 between Gonzáles and Díaz, under a large, white awning. Open Mon.-Sat. 8am-5pm, Sun. 7am-noon.

**Red Cross:** On Elías Calles and Providencia (tel. 3-58-00). Open 24hr.

**Pharmacy:** There's no shortage here, but most close early. If it's late at night and you've got that not-so-fresh *turista* feeling, try **Farmacia San Xavier,** Campillo 73 between Juárez and Morelos (tel. 2-55-03). Open 24hr. **Farmacia San Andrés** (tel. 2-02-36), behind the tourist office. Open daily 8am-8pm.

**Medical Assistance: Seguro Social,** Escobedo 756 at Obregón (tel. 3-59-85; take the "Parque Industrial" bus). English spoken. Open 24hr. Some English is spoken at the **Hospital Básico,** Dr. Francisco Arriola 1277 (tel. 3-07-94 or 3-08-59). Open 24hr.

**Police:** At González and Leal (tel. 2-01-16 or 2-01-14). English speakers on hand in the afternoon. Open 24hr. **Highway Patrol:** Tel. 4-18-30 or 4-18-33.

**Post Office:** Juárez 52 at Campillo (tel. 2-12-47). **Postal Code:** 84000.

**Phone Code:** 631.

## ACCOMMODATIONS AND FOOD

As in most of northern Mexico, rates in Nogales are steep. Fortunately, a string of (sort-of) budget hotels lines the block behind the tourist office on Av. Juárez and Obregón. The **Hotel San Carlos,** Juárez 22 between Internacional and Campillo (tel. 2-13-46 or 2-14-09), features a refreshing oasis—an ever-replenished, ice-cold purified water dispenser in the lobby. Large, clean rooms have A/C, color TVs with U.S. cable, massage-showers, and phones (singles 137 pesos; doubles 170 pesos). Right next door is the **Hotel Regis** (tel. 2-51-81 or 2-55-35). Clean rooms with A/C, phones, and TV will remind you of U.S. budget chains. If you're afraid you'll oversleep, don't worry: *norteño* tunes are piped in through the speakers in each room's ceiling. To adjust the volume, look for the black dial (singles 150 pesos; doubles 175 pesos).

Overpriced restaurants cluster around the *centro*. Ditch the tourist traps and head straight for **La Posada Restaurant,** Pierson 116 off Obregón (tel. 2-04-39), where you can mingle with the town's *petit-bourgeoisie*. Painted tiles and curious objects adorn the walls, while *burritos de machaca* (dried beef, 12 pesos) and *chimichangas* (15 pesos) grace the tables. The restaurant is kept comfortable not only by ceiling fans, but also by strings of dried chile peppers hanging in front of the windows, blocking the evil sunlight (open daily 7:45am-10pm). If you feel the Sonoran desert heat beating down on you, escape to **Super Tortas El Oasis,** Pierson 93 between Obregón and López Mateos (tel. 2-44-18). There, you can relax in a pine valley near a waterfall—an oasis indeed. Unfortunately, only your mind can escape: it's all just a big mural. The tasty *quesadilla especial* (15 pesos) and *burrito* (8 pesos), though, are real (open Mon.-Thurs. 8am-midnight, Fri.-Sun. 8am-1am).

## SIGHTS AND ENTERTAINMENT

Most of the curio and craft shops line Obregón. You may get good deals if you bargain and know something about quality. In fact, vendors *expect* shoppers to haggle. Often, low prices can be had by pretending to walk away uninterested. Before buying, ask turquoise vendors to put the rocks to "the lighter test." Plastic or synthetic material will quickly melt under a flame. Likewise, when buying silver, look for a ".925" stamp on the piece; if it's not there, the goods are (oxymoronically) bad.

At night, the usual bands of gringos patronize the bars on Obregón. **Coco Loco,** Obregón 69 between Campillo and Ochoa, is a good place for a little drinking and dancing (open Wed.-Sun. 1pm-2am). Other places to booze and boogie on the same street include **Sr. Amigo, La Cava Bar, Pancho Villa Bar,** and **Bora Bora.** Drinks start at around 12 pesos. Not in the mood to get intoxicated? Head for **Cinemas Gemelos** (tel. 2-50-02), on Obregón between F. Guerra and Torres, which shows first- and second-run American films (daily 3:30-9:30pm; 18 pesos; either dubbed or subtitled in Spanish). Top off your evening with some ice cream from **La Michoacana,** on the corner of Obregón and Aguirre (open daily 7am-7pm). A **paleta de fruta** (fruit popsicle) goes for only 3.50 pesos. Finally, there's always the option of gambling your fortune away: Off-track betting on dog or horse races can be done at the **Nogales Turf Club,** Campillo 77 between Obregón and Juárez, underneath the tall, pink building. Set to open in 1998, the **Casino de Nogales,** on Campillo between López Mateos and Elias Calles, is sure to be a popular gringo alternative to curios and bars.

# ■ Puerto Peñasco

The town with the English sobriquet—Rocky Point—caters more to American resortmongers than to budget travelers; always ask for prices in pesos instead of in dollars, even if the seller is reluctant. Just 105km off the border and about three hours from Tucson, Puerto Peñasco, like northern Baja, attracts a fair share of weekenders. Despite the throngs of *gringos*, somewhat tranquil beaches and clean streets make this dusty port still worth a trip. Once a launching pad for shrimp boats, Puerto Peñasco dried up when overfishing decimated the shrimp population of the Sea of Cortés. Economically widowed, the town now courts investors with a dowry of tax breaks and other incentives. Fifty kilometers north on the road to Sonoita lies the **El Pinacate** volcanic area.

**Orientation**   To reach the *centro* from the bus station, take a left past PEMEX and walk nine blocks down Puerto Peñasco's main road, **Blvd. Juárez;** continue south on

Juárez past the **Dársena**—the port area—and eventually to **Malecón,** Peñasco's old section, on the western edge of town. **Playa Hermosa** (Beautiful Beach) lies to the northwest, **Playa Miramar** to the south. Town activity centers around two intersections: **Fremont** and **Juárez** and **Constitución** and **Juárez.** Numbered *calles* run east-west and start with 1 at **Playa Miramar** (southernmost); boulevards run north-south.

**Practical Information**   Puerto Peñasco's **tourist office** (tel. 3-41-29) is on N. Bravo CP, Calle 18, off Blvd. Juárez and next to a travel agency. Little English is spoken (open daily 9am to mid-afternoon). **Bancomer,** on Juárez and Estrella (tel. 3-24-30), next to the plaza, exchanges currency and traveler's checks (open Mon.-Fri. 8:30am-3pm). **LADATELs** are not easy to find; there's one in front of the Hotel Paraíso, and another at Constitución and Simon Morva. *Casetas* are located at the Jim Bur Plaza, in Cheiky's Pizza Restaurant (tel. 3-36-27; local calls 2 pesos for 3min., calls to U.S. 7.50 pesos per min.; open daily 7am-11pm). The **fax and telegram office** (tel. 3-27-82) is in the same building (open Mon.-Fri. 8am-6pm, Sat. 9am-noon).

   **Buses** depart from Juárez and Calle 24. **Transportes Norte de Sonora** and **Autotransportes de Baja California** collectively go to Guaymas (4 per day, 9hr.), Hermosillo (3 per day, 7hr.), Mexicali (3 per day, 4hr.), and Tijuana (2 per day, 8hr.). **Trains** (tel. 3-26-10) leave from the station off Constitución, two blocks north of the intersection with Juárez, right behind the Hotel Paraíso del Desierto. *Estrella* trains leave at 1:40pm for Mazatlán (18hr.) with numerous stops along the way; *burro* trains start the crawl towards Mazatlán at 3am (21hr.).

   Get your supplies from **Supermarket Jim Bur,** on Juárez (tel. 3-25-61) at the Jim Bur Plaza (open Mon.-Sat. 8am-9pm, Sun. 9am-4pm). At **Lavamática Peñasco** on Constitución at Morúa across from Hotel Paraíso del Desierto, a wash costs six pesos; a dry costs five (open Mon.-Sat. 8am-7pm). The **Red Cross,** on Fremont at Chiapas (tel. 3-22-66), is open 24hr. Little English is spoken. **Farmacia Botica Lux,** Merchero Campo 146, off Blvd. Juárez, two blocks from the walking bridge, will meet your need for drugs (open daily 8am-midnight). **Hospital Municipal** is at Morúa and Juárez (tel. 3-21-10); little English is spoken (open 24hr.). **Police** wait at Fremont and Juárez (tel. 3-26-26) but speak little English (open 24hr.). The **post office** is at Chiapas (tel. 3-23-50), two blocks east of Juárez on Fremont (open Mon.-Fri. 8am-3pm). **Postal Code:** 83550. **Phone Code:** 638.

**Accommodations and Food**   Budget rooms in Puerto Peñasco are a rare commodity, since cheap accommodations are being torn down left and right to clear space for expensive resorts, condos, and time-shares. One of the last remaining quasi-budget hotels is the **Motel Playa Azul,** Calle 13 and Pino Suárez (tel. 3-62-96). It offers nicely furnished rooms with ancient TVs that receive a single channel, generous A/C, and yes, private bathrooms with hot water. Bargain with the manager. Singles 190-pesos. Doubles 270 pesos. Otherwise, **Playa Miramar RV Park** (tel. and fax 3-25-87), on (go figure) Playa Miramar, rents scenic spots year-round with cable TV, full hookup, and hot water. Washers, dryers, and showers available. Check-out time is noon. (90 pesos per day for 1 or 2 people, 15 pesos per day each additional person, 540 pesos per week, beachfront spaces slightly higher; key deposit 35 pesos).

   Most beachside restaurants cater to *gringos,* with their (high) prices quoted in U.S. dollars; insist on paying in good ol' *moneda nacional.*   As always, *taquerías* are the spot for budget grub; find some at Juárez between Constitución and Calle 24, near the bus station. Asaderos across from the bus station welcome the newly arrived with tasty tidbits such as handmade tortillas, chicken, and steak tacos.

**Sights and Entertainment**   Puerto Peñasco's clean and rarely crowded beaches are blessed with clear, warm waters. Shallow tide pools cradle clams, small fish, and colorful shells. **Sandy Beach** and **Playa Hermosa** are the best choices for swimming; both have curio shops, restaurants, and hotels galore. The beaches around **Rocky Point** and **Playa Miramar,** at the southern end of town, are less crowded, but also rockier, and rougher. Playa Miramar also brims with RV parks and

**NORTHWEST MEXICO**

condominiums. For the intellectual beach bum, the **Intercultural Center for the Study of Deserts and Oceans (CEDO)** at Playa Las Conchas, 9km from town (taxi 30 pesos), gives free tours of its wet lab and museum Tuesdays at 2pm and Saturdays at 4pm. Open Mon.-Sat. 9am-5pm, Sun. 10am-2pm.

To get to Playa Hermosa, turn left on Calle 13 when heading south on Juárez; the beach is straight ahead five or six blocks down. To reach Playa Miramar, head south on Juárez and turn left onto Campeche near the Benito Juárez monument. Continue uphill on the unpaved road for three blocks; Playa Miramar will be on your left. To reach Playa Las Conchas, head south on Juárez, turn left on Fremont near the Plaza del Camaronero, take a right onto Camino a las Conchas, and follow the rock-slab road for three or four kilometers. To reach Sandy Beach, head north on Encinas or Juárez until the intersection with Camino a Bahía Choya. Take a left and follow the road; turn left on the road labeled "To Sandy Beach."

## ■ Near Puerto Peñasco: El Pinacate

Forty-eight kilometers north of Puerto Peñasco on Rte. 8 to Sonora is the **El Pinacate** volcanic preserve, one of the largest and most spectacular biospheres in the world. Encompassing over four million acres, and including the upper reaches of the Sea of Cortés, the biosphere was created in June 1992 to limit volcanic rock excavation and protect endangered species. Pockmarked by over 600 craters and 400 cinder cones, the Pinacate lava fields form 30,000-year-old islands in a vast sea of sand. From inside the park, the only thing visible for kilometers around are fields of igneous rock and the monochromatic moonscape punctuated by purple, white, and red wildflowers. The people of the Tohono O'odham nation have lived in this region for tens of thousands of years, crossing the desert on foot from Arizona to bathe in the waters they consider to be sacred and healing, and extracting fresh water from *saguaro* cacti.

**Ecoturismo Peñasco** and **Ajo Stage Lines** (tel. 3-32-09 or 3-21-75) lead tours into the area; ask at the tourist office for details or talk to Peggy at **CEDO** (see (CROSS) above). Prices: $50 per person (1-2 people), $40 per person (3-4 people), $35 per person (5 or more people). The vast, isolated, climatically harsh region makes a guide necessary. If you do decide to tough it out alone, four-wheel-drive, high-clearance vehicles with partially deflated tires are a must. Bring tons of water, a shovel, a spare tire, and firewood. Camping is permitted, but don't leave anything behind and don't remove any souvenirs. The ideal time to visit is November to March, when temperatures range from approximately 60 to 90°F, as opposed to summer months, when temperatures can exceed 116°F.

# ■ Hermosillo

The capital of Sonora, Hermosillo (pop. 700,000) is an expansive metropolis and a center for commerce and education whose name comes from the Spanish word *hermoso*, "beautiful." With glorious cathedrals, majestic government palaces, stylish open-air malls, a remarkably endearing *zócalo*, and a lovely view of the mountains (if you ignore their huge radio towers), parts of Hermosillo certainly live up to its name. Daytrippers to the beaches of Kino will find hopping university nightlife in Hermosillo (if they seek it out), accompanied by few gringos, when they return home. Not all of this huge city, however, boasts such allure. The crowded, dusty thoroughfares of the *centro*, which scream during the day with the frenzied activity of urban life, are left by sundown without much more than garbage on the streets. Hermosillo's red-light district is prominent. If you get an early start and the buses run on time, you can breeze from Tucson to the beaches of Guaymas or Mazatlán in a single day (or vice versa), skipping the lonelier parts of Sonora entirely. But a layover in lively Hermosillo can become a pleasant surprise.

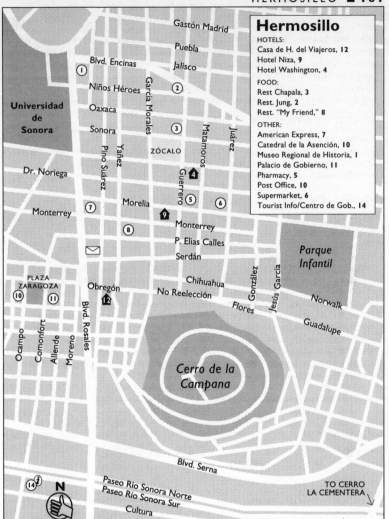

Hermosillo

HOTELS:
Casa de H. del Viajeros, 12
Hotel Niza, 9
Hotel Washington, 4

FOOD:
Rest Chapala, 3
Rest. Jung, 2
Rest. "My Friend," 8

OTHER:
American Express, 7
Catedral de la Asención, 10
Museo Regional de Historia, 1
Palacio de Gobierno, 11
Pharmacy, 5
Post Office, 10
Supermarket, 6
Tourist Info/Centro de Gob., 14

## ORIENTATION

Hermosillo lies 271km south of the border on Rte. 15, the main north-south highway connecting the western U.S. and central Mexico. **Buses** depart from the main terminal on Blvd. Encinas, 2km east of the city center. To get from the bus station to the center of town, cross the street and catch a bus marked "Circuito Norte-Mendoza" or "Centro" (every 10min., 5am-10:30pm, 2 pesos). Taxis will ask 35 pesos for a trip to *el centro;* haggle, and don't get in until settling a price. To get to the bus station from town, wait for a bus at Elías Calles and Matamoros, across from Óptica Morfín.

At the junction of **Blvds. Luis Encinas** (also known as Transversal) and **Rosales,** the **Hermosillo Flash** (an electronic bulletin board displaying daily news) helps the mapless orient themselves. Most of the activity lies inside the square area (the *centro*) bordered by **Rosales** on the west, **Juárez** on the east, **Serdán** on the south, and **Encinas** on the north. The *zócalo* is bounded by **Colosio, Sonora, Guerrero,** and **Garmendia.** The area surrounding Sonora west of the park should be avoided by lone female travelers at night. Listed from west to east, the principal north-south streets are **Rosales, Pino Suárez, Yañez, García Morales, Garmendia, Guerrero, Matamoros, Juárez,** and **González.** Listed from north to south, the east-west streets are **Encinas, Niños Héroes, Oaxaca, Sonora, Colosio, Dr. Noriega, Morelia, Monterrey, Plutarco Elías Calles,** and **Serdán.** Maps can be bought at one of the many local *papelerías* (20 pesos); better ones are free at the tourist office. If you get lost, remember that the antenna-capped mountain is always to the south if you're in the *centro*.

## PRACTICAL INFORMATION

**Tourist Office:** (tel. 17-29-64; fax 17-00-60), on the 3rd floor of the **Centro de Gobierno de Sonora,** Cultura and Comonfort. Walk south on Rosales over the canal, turn right, then walk one block west. Look for the big buildings crowned with indigenous drawings. If you need help, ask one of the officers wearing gray-and-brown camouflage. Open Mon.-Fri. 8am-3pm and 6-9pm.

**Currency Exchange:** Banks line Encinas and Serdán. **Bancomer,** Serdán and Yañez (tel. 17-36-81), cashes traveler's checks. Open Mon.-Fri. 8am-5pm. **Banamex,** Serdán and Matamoros (tel. 14-76-15), is closer to the center. Open Mon.-Fri. 8:30am-4:30pm. You'll see 24hr. **ATMs** at both.

**American Express: Hermex Travel,** Rosales at Monterrey (tel. 17-17-18). Open Mon.-Fri. 8:30am-1pm and 3-6:30pm, Sat. 9am-1pm.

**Telephones: LADATELs** in the *zócalo*, in front of the post office, at Serdán and Guerrero, and at Morelia 90 between Guerrero and Garmendia. *Casetas* can be found at nearly every pharmacy and...hair salon. Look for the blue *"teléfono público"* signs along the sidewalk. **Farmacia Margarita,** Morelia and Guerrero (tel. 13-17-73), has *casetas* for long-distance calls. Open daily 8am-9pm.

**Fax:** Tel. 12-03-56; fax 13-19-24. Same building as the post office. Also **telegram** and **telex** service. Open Mon.-Fri. 8am-7pm, Sat. 8:30am-4pm, Sun. 9am-12:30pm.

**Airport:** 10km west of town on Transversal toward Bahía Kino (tel. 61-00-08). Get there with the help of a small red bus called *taxi colectivo;* it departs from the bus or train station (2 pesos). **Aeroméxico** (tel. 16-82-59) to Guadalajara (9:05am, 4:35, and 4:50pm, 2hr., 1217 pesos), Mexico City (9:05am, 4:35, and 8:10pm, 2½hr., 1673 pesos), Tijuana (11:45am, 1hr., 947 pesos), and other destinations. **Mexicana** (tel. 61-01-12 or 17-11-03), to Mexico City (8:25am, 4hr., 1673 pesos) and more.

**Buses:** All service out of Hermosillo is *de paso;* during holidays and weekends you'll need to lace up your boxing gloves in order to win a seat. Buses to Tijuana and Mexico City fill up early, so buy tickets at least a day in advance. The cheapest carrier is **Transportes del Pacífico** (tel. 17-05-80). To Guadalajara (*primera clase* every hr., 22hr., 460 pesos; or *segunda clase* 24hr., 408 pesos), Guaymas (every hr., 1½hr., 26 pesos), Los Mochis (every hr., 7hr., 110 pesos), Mazatlán (every hr., 13hr., 250 pesos; or 14hr., 239 pesos), Mexicali (every hr., 9hr., 190 pesos; or 9hr., 173 pesos), Mexico City (every hr., 30hr., 670 pesos; or 32hr., 588 pesos), Nogales (3 per day, 4hr., 60 pesos; or 4hr., 56 pesos), and Tijuana (every hr., 12hr., 260 pesos; or 12hr., 230 pesos), among other destinations. **Transportes Norte de Sonora** (tel. 13-40-50) to most of the above, plus sunny, tourist-ridden Acapulco.

**Trains: Estación Pitíc** (tel. 14-32-00), north of the city on Rte. 15. Take the bus marked "Anapolas" to get to the train station. Northbound *estrella* (fast) to Nogales and Mexicali leaves at 7:50am, and the *burro* (slow) at 11am. The southbound train heads to Los Mochis and Guadalajara (*burro* 7:45pm, 313 pesos; *estrella* noon, 174 pesos). Reservations are needed for the *estrella* in advance.

**Supermarket: Ley Centro,** Juárez at Morelia (tel. 17-32-94). The size of two U.S. football fields, with public toilets and hundreds of young clerks decked out in red aprons. Takes U.S. dollars at a good exchange rate. Open daily 6:30am-10pm.

**Red Cross:** at Encina and 14 de Abril (tel. 14-07-69). Open 24hr. (Barely) English-speaking staff on hand daily 9am-5pm.

**Hospital:** Transversal at Reyes (tel. 13-25-56). Open 24hr. English spoken.

**Pharmacy: Farmacia Margarita,** Morelia 93 at Guerrero (tel. 13-15-90). Open 24hr.

**Emergency:** Dial 06. **Ambulance:** Tel. 76-75-27.

**Police:** Periférico Nte. and Solidaridad (tel. 18-55-64). Little English spoken. Open 24hr. **Transit Police:** Tel. 16-08-77.

**Post Office:** At Serdán and Rosales (tel. 12-00-11). Open Mon.-Fri. 8am-7pm, Sat.-Sun. 8am-noon. **Postal Code:** 83000.
**Phone Code:** 62.

## ACCOMMODATIONS

Hermosillo offers many budget hotels, allowing those who must watch every peso they spend to sleep comfortably and safely. Air conditioning is costly but indispensable, especially in the blistering summer heat.

**Hotel Washington, D.C.,** Dr. Noriega 68 Pte. between Matamoros and Guerrero (tel. 13-11-83). Friendly management. Just what you would want in a good budget hotel—good-sized rooms with A/C and clean bathrooms. You're set for a good night's sleep with the solid security and comfortable beds (though the hot water is erratic). You might just be serenaded by street music. LADATEL in the lobby. Singles 80 pesos; doubles 90 pesos; each additional person 20 pesos.

**Hotel Niza** (tel. 17-20-28 or 17-20-35), Elías Calles 66 between Guerrero and Garmendia. A grandiose Art Deco hotel of the bloated past. The pink atrium is graced with murals and a TV in the corner. Sit and chat with your fellow travelers as you watch the *partido de fútbol*. Rooms branching off this centerpiece have A/C, color TV, and comfy beds. Singles 120 pesos; doubles 160 pesos.

**Casa de Huéspedes del Viajero,** Sufragio Efectivo 90, between Pino Suárez and Yañez. Walk south on Rosales until you begin to pass the tall hill (Cerro de la Campana) to your left. Turn left onto S. Efectivo before reaching the canal. Unbelievably large rooms in an 84-year-old building. Adobe construction and fans keep the rooms cool. Aging outdoor bathroom. Lock your bags, since there's not always someone at the entrance, which might become a problem if you're trying to get in at odd times. Singles 40 pesos; doubles 70 pesos.

## FOOD

For a cheap and quick refuel, head for the **taco and torta** places around Serdán and Guerrero, where *taquitos* and *quesadillas* cost 7-8 pesos and *comida corrida* around 15 pesos. Alternatively, try the counters lining the inside of the **public market** at Matamoros, Guerrero, and Elías Calles. Although busy and smelly, some are sufficiently sanitary. Choose wisely: look out for flies and dirty pans and tabletops. Most offer tacos for a paltry sum, but *Let's Go* and your mother do not recommend eating foods containing uncooked vegetables in these establishments! Stick to enchiladas, burritos, and the like, also wonderfully cheap at about 5 pesos.

**Restaurant Jung,** Niños Héroes 75 at Encinas (tel. 13-28-81). A new-age vegetarian restaurant a mere 6 blocks from the center of town? Yes indeed. Relax to soothing music and the faint smell of incense as you savor the rejuvenating *comida corrida*, which comes with wheat rolls, soup, fruit juice, an entree, *frijoles*, whole-grain rice, and dessert (whew!...45 pesos). The adjoining herbal medicine, Eastern philosophy, and pseudo-psychology store is worth a peek, if only for the *agua purificada* it sells. Open Mon.-Sat. 8am-8pm. MC.

---

### Like Water for Chicharrones

In Mexico, there's no escaping the *chicharrónes* (pork rinds), and in some towns the popular snack has become...an ice cream flavor! On sweltering hot days, vendors push long carts loaded with rows of metal casks and scoop out ice cold salvation in a crazy variety of flavors—*elote* (cornmeal), *cerveza* (beer), *aguacate* (avocado), and tequila. Hand a vendor 5 pesos and he'll cram a mammoth portion into a cone or plastic cup. Mexican ice cream is known to harbor more than a few nasty amoebas, so verify the product's hygienic integrity by looking at the cleanliness of the stand before placing that spoon in your mouth. Then tuck a napkin into your shirt front, close your eyes, and lick away.

**Restaurant Chapala,** Guerrero between Sonora and Oaxaca (tel. 17-54-41). Mexican golden oldies blare from the jukebox while throngs of middle-aged men drown their sorrows in 40s of Tecate. Chicken, fish, or meat dishes come fried to crispy perfection and served with french fries, *frijoles,* tortillas, side salad, and a drink (29 pesos). The tipsy men aside, you might as well be in your Mexican aunt's house—if you're Mexican and you have an aunt, that is. Open daily 7am-10pm.

**Restaurant "My Friend,"** Plutarco Elías Calles and Yañez (tel. 13-10-44). This restaurant is definitely trying to make some American *amigos.* A framed photo of a cheeseburger (16 pesos), fries, and a soft drink beckons to starved and homesick gringos. Otherwise, enjoy yummy *huevos al gusto* (14 pesos) or a platter of 3 *tacos de cabeza y barbacoa* (12 pesos). Open Mon.-Sat. 7am-7pm, Sun. 8am-1pm.

**Cocina Económica Lupita,** on Obregón between Pino Suárez and Yañez. A few years ago, Lupita opened her home to boarding students. Now, she opens her dining room to budget travelers, serving up a homecooked meal for only 20 pesos and making great conversation all the while. Open sporadically Mon.-Fri. 7:30am-9pm.

**Tortas Hawaii,** Serdán 93 between Abasolo and Garmendia (tel. 17-55-46). In a rush? Try this fast-food-like restaurant. Juicy *tortas* are depicted in living color on the walls to help make that difficult decision (14-19 pesos). Open daily 10am-9pm.

## SIGHTS AND ENTERTAINMENT

The architecturally eclectic **Catedral de la Asunción** is on Tehuantepec and Comonfort (tel. 12-05-01; office and gift shop open Mon.-Fri. 9am-1pm and 4-7pm, Sat. 9am-1pm). Fugitives from the blistering sun can find refuge near the cathedral in the bee-yoo–tiful and refreshingly shady **Plaza Zaragoza,** where looming trees surround an open-air bandstand. Other shady parks dot the streets near the plaza, making this one of the more peaceful areas of Hermosillo, and a welcome change from the dusty, filth-ridden streets of the *centro.* This area is well-lit at night, making it safer than the lonely *centro.* For the kids, a **playground** (also very well-lit) complete with basketball courts dwells on the corner of Pino Suárez and Elías Calles.

On the other side of Rosales, at Encinas and Rosales by the University of Sonora, is **Museo Regional de Historia,** which contains exhibits on pre-Hispanic and colonial history (open Mon.-Fri. 9am-1pm and 4pm-6pm, Sat. 9am-1pm; free). **Cuartel Catorce,** on Guerrero and Colosio (tel. 13-13-79 for Sec. de Educación, ext. 23), is a rough structure with formidable walls of brown brick. The colonnaded inner courtyard is an oasis; the room in the back of the courtyard was once home to the army's cavalry (open Mon.-Fri. 8am-3pm). Don't kill yourself to get there, though.

Across the street from the Plaza Zaragoza is the majestic, grey-and-white **Palacio de Gobierno.** The Palacio, from which the state of Sonora is governed, should not be confused with the pink brick **Palacio Municipal** nearby, where city government functions are carried out. Both are worth investigating for their architecture. The Palacio de Gobierno contains four fascinating and detailed murals surrounding its beautiful, tree-laden inner courtyard, where statues immortalize Sonoran patriots and senators. Those in need of a bit more levity can head to **Multicinemas,** Blvd. Encinas 227 at Transversal and Reforma (tel. 14-09-70), to absorb U.S. movies with Spanish subtitles (a 5min. bus ride from the center of town; open daily 3pm-9pm; admission 17 pesos).

To find out what the Universidad de Sonora students do for fun, walk down Rosales south of Colosio, next to the university (itself worth seeing for its smooth, stream-lined modern architecture that resembles the front of an airplane if viewed from the Banamex across the street). Bars there include **La Fogata** at **Dr. Noriega, La Bella Epoca** at Morelia, and **Fook Lam Moon,** a Chinese restaurant and bar, also at Morelia. For a tougher bar-going experience, try **La Verbena** or **El Grito del Callejón** (literally, the scream of the dark alley), both at Obregón and Pino Suárez—La Verbena to the south and El Grito to the north. Adjacent to La Verbena is **Extasis Night Club,** located in what would be a beautiful colonial building if it weren't for the neon green glow.

## ■ Near Hermosillo

### CENTRO ECOLÓGICO DE SONORA

Hermosillo's **Centro Ecológico de Sonora** (tel. 50-12-25), 3km south of downtown off Vildosola, is more than just your token neighborhood zoo: it boasts an impressive array of animal life, a mini-aquarium (complete with outdoor sea lions), and hundreds of plant species from Sonora and elsewhere. Founded in 1985, the Centro is also home to groundbreaking biological research.

Among the animal exhibits, the Mexican grey wolf, bearded camels, and energetic monkeys stand out. The most spectacular feature of the Centro Ecológico, however, is its incredible collection of cacti; over 340 species are labeled and displayed throughout the animal exhibits or just outside the main pavilion. Keep your eyes peeled for the rare and beautiful *cina* and *biznaga*, from which fruit and candy are made, and the *maguey bacanova*, the fanned-out, spiked cactus which is the source of all those tequilas you've been downing.

The Centro is an excellent place for children; they delight in the clowns and Disney or Disney-esque flicks shown every Saturday and Sunday in the air-conditioned movie theater (noon-6pm; free). The enthusiastic and knowledgeable student staff is happy to answer any questions about the Centro and its flora and fauna. Cafeterias and *agua purificada* can be found throughout the park (open Wed.-Sun. 8am-7pm; admission 7 pesos, children 5 pesos).

**Getting There:** To get to the Centro, grab the orange-and-green striped bus marked "Luis Orci" from the corner of Guerrero and Dr. Noriega (20min., 2 pesos).

## ■ Bahía Kino

A pair of beach towns on the beautiful Sea of Cortés (or Golfo de California) comprise Bahía Kino, a 20km stretch of glistening sand, blue water, and radiant sun. **Kino Viejo**, a dusty, quiet fishing village, lies down the road from **Kino Nuevo**, a 4km-long Americanized strip of posh, secluded homes and condos where the satellite dishes are as abundant as the pelicans overhead. This is a place to kick back with your favorite book, watercolors, or a fishing pole. As the residents of Hermosillo who flock there on weekends will tell you, Kino (as the two towns are collectively known) is an ideal destination for a daytrip from dusty urbanity to the beach. The soothing breezes and vast expanses of sand make the hot, rickety ride from the city worthwhile.

**Orientation** Bahía Kino is located 120km west of Hermosillo. **Buses** in Hermosillo leave from the old **Transportes Norte de Sonora** station on Sonora between Jesús García and González, near the *zócalo* (10 per day, 5:40am-5:30pm, 2hr., 23 pesos one way). The bus stops in Kino Viejo before going on to Kino Nuevo. Look for water on your left and get off wherever you'd like. Early birds catch the daytrip-to-Kino worms—get an early bus from Hermosillo and sleep (if you can) during the ride. Missing the 5:30pm bus back to Hermosillo means spending the night in Kino.

To get from one Kino to the other or back to Hermosillo, flag down the bus (every hr., 2 pesos between Kinos) on Nuevo's main (and only) road, **Av. Mar de Cortés,** or on **Blvd. Kino** in Kino Viejo. If you choose to walk (4km), be sure to keep plenty of water or other hydrants on hand as well as adequate sun protection. It is also possible to hitchhike between the two towns.

**Practical Information** Long-distance phones are available at the clothing shop at Kino and Tampico in Kino Viejo. **Public bathrooms** are on the beach in Kino Nuevo, though not along the whole stretch. Try the end closer to Kino Viejo. In Kino Viejo itself, some downright pleasant potties are available at the **Centro de Salud,** at Tampico and Kino. Bring your own toilet paper. Near the post office and the police in Kino Viejo is the **Red Cross**, at Kino and Manzanillo, which has no phone but can be contacted via the Hermosillo **emergency** number (dial 06). **Dr. José Luís** (tel. 2-03-

95) speaks English. In any type of emergency, your best bet might be to look for the American-run **Centro Deportivo** (or for an American or Canadian license plate) and knock on their door; the friendly expatriate community takes good care of foreign visitors. The **police** are available at Santa Catalina and Av. Mar de Cortés (tel. 2-00-67) in Kino Nuevo, or at Kino and Cruz (tel. 2-00-32) in Kino Viejo. Next to the police in Nuevo is the **post office** (open Mon.-Fri. 8am-3pm). Small markets dot the road through Kino Nuevo under inviting "Tecate" signs. **Phone code:** 624.

**Accommodations and Food**  Options for the budget traveler are limited to renting a spot to pitch your tent or park your RV; nearby Hermosillo provides more choices. If you miss the bus, **Islanda Marina,** Guaymas and Puerto Peñasco (tel. 2-00-81), in Kino Viejo just off Blvd. Kino and right on the beach, charges 40 pesos per day for a spot (90 pesos with electricity). It also rents cabins (150 pesos for 4 people, 30 pesos for each additional person). It is run by two Arizona women who own a purified water plant—you'll never be short on that precious commodity. In Kino Nuevo, **Hotel Saro,** 5735 Mar de Cortés (tel. 2-00-07), is the cheapest you'll find at a stratospheric 280 pesos for a single with A/C, private bath, TV, fridge, and great view (doubles 300 pesos). The more adventurous traveler can easily camp for free under one of the many *palapas* (thatched umbrella structures) on the Kino Nuevo beach. Locals claim the area is fairly safe.

For a meal that's as economical as you want it to be, do as the Hermosillans do and pack a lunch to enjoy under a beach *palapa.* Otherwise, a decent budget meal can be found in Kino Viejo. Try the nice 'n' spicy **Dorita,** Av. Eusebio Kino and Sabina Cruz (tel. 2-03-49), decorated with Spice Girls paraphernalia, for relatively inexpensive breakfasts (35-22 pesos) or *carne asada* (35 pesos). Fill up on purified water there—it's free (open daily 7am-8pm). If you're looking for a taste of Acapulco, the **Acapulco Restaurant,** at Acapulco and Puerto Vallarta (tel. 2-03-22), won't provide it. However, it will provide you with a fine meal (breakfast 12 pesos; lunch 15 pesos; dinner 15-28 pesos; open daily 7:30am-9pm), and that's what matters, isn't it?

**Sand and Sights**  The **beaches** of Kino are peacefully deserted early in the week, but as the weekend approaches, so do the masses—although the masses of Kino are nothing compared with the masses at many other beach towns. Americans with homes in Kino tend to populate the beaches only during the winter, making for some long, lonely stretches of sand during the summer months. Beaches in Kino (as in all Mexico) are public by law, so you can plop down right in front of anyone's RV spot or satellite-laden faux-villa, and they can't do a damn thing about it. In general, the beaches are better in Kino Nuevo.

For water fun in Kino Nuevo, ask at **Hotel La Posada,** on Av. Mar de Cortés towards Kino Viejo, just before Kino Nuevo's main strip begins, for the names of people renting out scuba/snorkeling gear. For non-beach entertainment, the **Museo de los Seris,** on Mar de Cortés and Progreso, near the end of Kino Nuevo, offers air-conditioned refuge from shade-free Kino *and* teaches you more than you ever thought you'd learn about the Seris, a once-nomadic indigenous tribe whose specialty was fishing (open Wed.-Sun. 9am-4pm; admission 2 pesos).

# ■ Guaymas

Looking out over the Sea of Cortés, Guaymas (pop. 130,000) is the principal port in Sonora and the proud home of an active shrimping fleet and busy seafood-processing plants. Nearby, beachy San Carlos is a popular tourist destination for many *norteamericanos.*

Guaymas itself, however, is no resort town. Although its port area offers a pleasant view of the sea and nearby mountains and its charming cathedral and companion park serve as a haven for weary travelers, Guaymas suffers from an acute lack of convenient beaches. Nevertheless, it's a nice place to rest on the trip south to the more alluring resorts at Mazatlán, San Blas, and Puerto Vallarta: its cool ocean breezes, cleanliness, and civility give it a decided advantage over Hermosillo.

## ORIENTATION

Guaymas is 407km south of Nogales on Rte. 15. Municipal buses (2 pesos) run up and down its main strip, **Av. Serdán.** Running perpendicular to Av. Serdán are **Calle 1, Calle 2, Calle 3**...well, you get the idea. If you're walking along Av. Serdán and the numbers of the intersecting streets are increasing, you know you're headed east. The center of the city lies around the crossings of Calles in the low 20s and Serdán, and buses arrive right in the thick of things at Calle 14, right off (surprise) Serdán. To get to Serdán from the bus station, turn left if you're coming out of the Transportes del Norte station or turn right if you're coming out of the Transportes del Pacífico or the Transportes Baldomero Corral stations. Women should not walk alone more than two blocks south of Serdán after dark. The waterfront begins around Calle 23 and Serdán; coming up to the water, the cool ocean breeze will immediately provide relief from the heat.

Northbound vehicles, including buses, are often stopped by narcotics police. Have your identification ready and let them search whatever they want; it's better not to assert the right to privacy when dealing with humorless armed *federales*.

Along Serdán, you can also catch buses marked "Miramar" (2 pesos) and "San Carlos" (5 pesos) to reach the beaches north of the city; both buses run frequently 6am-8pm. Some daredevils also try thumbing as they wait for the bus at the junction of Serdán and the highway.

## PRACTICAL INFORMATION

**Currency Exchange:** Banks are located along Serdán. **Banamex,** Serdán at Calle 20 (tel. 4-01-23), exchanges traveler's checks and greenbacks, and has two 24hr. **ATMs** that accept Visa, MC, Cirrus, and Plus. Open Mon.-Fri. 8:30am-4:30pm.

**Telephones: LADATELs** are scattered all along Serdán. Two quieter locations are on Calle 19 Nte. at Av. 17 Pte. and in front of the Hotel Rubi. **Santa Martha Pañalera,** Serdán 80 at Calle 19 (tel./fax 4-03-54), has booths for long-distance collect calls (7 pesos per min. to the U.S., 4 pesos per min. within Mexico; Sun. and after 8pm 5 pesos to U.S., 2 pesos within Mexico). Open daily 8am-9pm. Another option is the long-distance **Computel** *caseta* at the Transportes Norte de Sonora station (tel./fax 2-95-18). Open daily 2-10pm.

**Fax:** Tel. 2-02-92. Next to post office. Open Mon.-Fri. 8am-5pm, Sat.-Sun. 9am-noon.

**Airport:** To reach it, catch a bus marked "San José" along Serdán (1.50 pesos). **Aeroméxico,** Serdán at Calle 15 (tel. 2-01-23), has daily flights to La Paz (4:25pm, 50min., 759 pesos one way), Mexico City (4:25pm, 4½hr., 1402 pesos one way), and Tucson (11am and 5:25pm, 55min., US$139 one way).

**Buses:** The town's 3 bus terminals are on opposite sides of the street at Calle 14 and Rodríguez. **Transportes Norte de Sonora** (tel. 2-12-71) goes to Ciudad Juárez (2:30pm, 13hr., 250 pesos), Culiacán (every hr., 9hr., 110 pesos), Guadalajara (every hr., 23hr., 380 pesos), Hermosillo (every hr., 1¾hr., 26 pesos), Los Mochis (every hr., 6hr., 70 pesos), Mazatlán (every hr., 12hr., 234 pesos), Mexicali (every hr., 12hr., 207 pesos), Mexico City (every 2hr., 31hr., 550 pesos), Nogales (every hr., 10hr., 180 pesos), Obregón (every hr., 1¾hr., 26 pesos), Puerto Peñasco (11am, 9hr., 162 pesos), San Luis (every hr., 6hr., 190 pesos), Tepic (every hr., 18hr., 310 pesos), and Tijuana (every hr., 15hr., 231 pesos). **Transportes del Pacífico** (tel. 4-05-76 or 2-30-19) offers fares to most of the above destinations for about 10% more, while their 2nd-class service runs 3-5% less. **Transportes Baldomero Corral,** across the street, offers service to Navojoa (every hr., 7:45am-midnight, 4hr., 40 pesos) and Nogales (4 per day, 5½hr., 62 pesos).

**Trains:** The old train station and current office (tel. 2-00-70 or 2-49-80) are located on Serdán at Calle 30. Open Mon.-Fri. 8am-noon and 2-5pm for info or reservations. Trains actually arrive and depart from the nearby city of **Empalme** (tel. 3-10-65 or 3-06-16), 10km south on the International Highway. To get there from anywhere along Serdán, take a municipal bus marked "Empalme" to the end of the route, then transfer to the bus marked "Estación." Tickets sold 1hr. before the train arrives. The faster *estrella* train leaves at 9:45pm; the slow *burro* leaves at 2:30pm. To Mazatlán (12hr., 160 pesos, or 17hr., 90 pesos), Tepic (15hr., 226 pesos, or 21¼hr., 121 pesos), and Guadalajara (21hr., 185 pesos, or 28hr., 160 pesos).

**Ferries:** Terminal on Serdán (tel. 2-23-24), about 1km past Electricidad. The boat steams to Santa Rosalía Tues. and Fri. at 11am (arriving at 6pm); tickets may be bought on the day of departure from 6-8am or on Mon., Wed., or Thurs. from 8am-2pm (*salón* 111 pesos, *turista* 220 pesos). To get to the terminal, hop on a bus heading away from the Carretera Internacional and get off at the "Transbordador" sign, on your right (see **By Sea,** p. 126).

**Luggage Storage:** Lockers are available at the **Transportes Nortes de Sonora** bus terminal. 10 pesos for first 8hr., 4 pesos every extra hr. Open 24hr.

**Market: VH Supermarket,** on Serdán between Calles 19 and 20 (tel. 4-19-49). You can't miss it. Open Mon.-Sat. 8am-10pm, Sun. 8am-9pm.

**Red Cross:** Carretera Internacional (tel. 2-55-55 or 4-08-76), at the 1980km mark, at the northern limit of Guaymas. No English spoken. Open 24hr.

**Pharmacy: Farmacia Sonora,** Serdán at Calle 15 (tel. 4-24-00). Open 24hr.

**Hospital: Hospital Municipal,** on Calle 12 between Av. 6 and 7 (tel. 4-21-38). Some English spoken. Open 24hr.

**Police:** On Calle 11 at Av. 9 (tel. 4-01-04 or 4-01-05), near the Villa School. Some English spoken. Open 24hr.

**Post Office:** Av. 10 between Calle 19 and 20 (tel. 2-07-57). Open Mon.-Fri. 8am-7pm, Sat. 8am-noon. **Postal Code:** 85400.

**Phone Code:** 622.

## ACCOMMODATIONS

Accommodations in Guaymas cluster around Av. Serdán, where tourists will find a handful of relatively inexpensive hotels. A few *casas de huéspedes* can be found on streets off Serdán.

**Casa de Huéspedes Lupita,** Calle 15 #125 (tel. 2-84-09), 2 blocks south of Serdán and across from the castle-like *cárcel* (jail). A mammoth "house" with 30 rooms and 12 communal baths, every last corner glowingly clean. Fans in every room provide much-needed ventilation; an ice-cold *agua purificada* dispenser awaits downstairs at the office. Towel deposit 10 pesos. Singles 35 pesos, with bath 45 pesos, with A/C 65 pesos; doubles 45 pesos, with bath 55 pesos, with A/C 85 pesos.

**Hotel Rubi,** Serdán at Calle 29 (tel. 4-01-69). Although the hike from the bus station may seem daunting, the friendly atmosphere and the spacious rooms equipped with black-and-white cable TV and A/C will reward your efforts. *Agua purificada*—yup. Singles with 2 beds 90 pesos; doubles 110 pesos; triples 130 peso; quads 140 pesos.

**Hotel Impala,** Calle 21 #40 (tel. 4-09-22, fax 2-65-00), 1 block south of Serdán. The hotel revels in its antiquity through the photos of Guaymas's past gracing the walls. Rooms, however, have been modernized with polyester bedspreads and curtains, A/C, and TV. Singles 120 pesos; doubles 150 pesos; triples 190 pesos.

## FOOD

Seafood is *the* Guaymas specialty. Local favorites include frog's legs (*ancas de rana*), turtle steaks (*cahuna*), and oysters (*ostiones*) in a garlic and chile sauce. Unfortunately, if you want to sample these local delicacies, you're going to have to pay a fair sum for them. Otherwise, the **Mercado Municipal,** on Calle 20, one block from Serdán, sells fresh produce; hot dog and taco vendors line Serdán.

**Los Barcos,** Malecón at Calle 22 (tel. 2-76-50). Gaze at the mural of the sea and nearby mountain peaks or look out the window at the real thing as you savor a seafood meal that won't bust your budget. Try a platter of *chimichangas de camarón, pescado, pulpo,* or *jaiba* (37 pesos), or the *machaca* (46 pesos). Open daily.

**Restaurant Todos Comen,** Serdán between Calles 15 and 16 (tel. 2-11-00). Take refuge from the crowd, heat, and noise of Serdán in this small, dark, and cave-like restaurant. Try the *filete de pescado* (35 pesos), *combinación mexicana* (30 pesos) or the *especialidad de la casa* (20 pesos). Open daily 7am-midnight.

**S. E. Pizza Buffet,** Serdán at Calle 20 (tel. 2-24-46). If you feel nostalgic for American entertainment, this is the place to be. Walls feature Power Rangers, Ziggy, and Shaq. Satisfy your appetite with their all-you-can-eat buffet of pizza, spaghetti, and salad (16 pesos). Open daily 11am-11pm.

**Las 1000 Tortas,** Serdán 188 between Calles 17 and 18 (tel. 4-30-61). The *torta* rules at this family-run joint (10-12 pesos each). Three types of delicious *comida corrida* (20 pesos) are prepared daily and served noon-4pm. Energetic customers sit upright in orthopedic wooden chairs while tired neighbors slouch in brown vinyl booths, but everyone munches on enchiladas and *gorditas* (18 pesos). Tasty *burritos de machaca con frijoles* (18 pesos). Open daily 7am-11pm.

## SIGHTS AND ENTERTAINMENT

Guaymas's **beaches,** popular with tourists and locals alike, are located to the north in **San Carlos** and **Miramar;** both are accessible by bus (15min.). In San Carlos, the beach gets better past the end of the bus route near Club Med and Howard Johnson's. The nicer (but smaller) beaches in Miramar are back along the bus route in front of the fancy villas. The beaches are safe, although campers should take special precautions. Overall, camping in this area is not advisable here; if you absolutely must, opt for San Carlos over Miramar.

Take a stroll in the **Plaza de los Tres Presidentes,** on Calle 23 at Serdán, in front of the **Palacio Municipal,** a classic Colonial-style structure built in 1899. The blue bay waters, the towering green-and-white **Catedral de San Fernando,** and three bronze statues of (rather obscure) Mexican presidents complete the scene. The best place to spend a quiet afternoon, however, is the small park directly in front of the cathedral; benches and many a shade-providing tree make for a prime nap area. **Cine Guaymas Plus,** Av. 11 (the Malecón) at Calle 20 (tel. 2-14-00) two blocks off Serdán, shows U.S. films with Spanish subtitles daily 3:40-11pm (admission 12 pesos). For the best view in town—of Guaymas, the mountains, the port, and the bay—seek out the shady benches of the **Plaza del Pescador,** just off Serdán towards the water, between Calles 24 and 25. Feel the soothing sea breeze and smile.

If you happen to be in the waterfront area at night, chances are you can find a bar or club in which to party. **Charles Baby Disco Video** and **Zodiakos,** both on Serdán between Calles 25 and 26, feature transvestite acts imitating popular Mexican singers. Cover varies according to the popularity of the acts, but it's usually about 20 pesos for men and free for women. Further down Serdán, between Calles 16 and 17, is **Cyrus**—the club with the wolf facade, where Sunday nights feature a "Sexy Levis" contest. For a mellower time, head to the **Sahuaro Paino Bar,** next door to Zodiakos, where beers will run you about 8 pesos.

# ■ Alamos

The sleepy town of Alamos (pop. 8000), in the scenic foothills of the Sierra Madre Occidental at the edge of the Sonoran desert, is a rambling collection of handsome colonial *haciendas*. Founded by Coronado in 1531, Alamos became the center of a rich mining district after the discovery of silver in the area in 1863. But when the silver veins ran dry around 1900, Alamos shrank to ghost-town proportions. In the last 50 years, Alamos has experienced a return to its architectural glory days with the arrival of wealthy gringos in search of winter homes. The town's current Old-Mexico feel may be less than authentic, but many buildings would not have been saved at all without American dollars.

**Orientation and Practical Information** All bus service to Alamos passes through **Navojoa,** 53km southwest of Alamos. From the **Transportes Norte de Sonora** and **Elite** bus stations in Navojoa, stand at the corner of Allende and Ferrocarril, looking down Ferrocarril as you face the bus stations. Then, walk one block to the

**Transportes del Pacífico** station and turn left (toward the center of town) on to Guerrero. Six blocks along Guerrero (passing the **Transportes de Baja California** bus station after 3 blocks) is the **Los Mayitos** bus station at Rincón, where you can catch a bus to Alamos (every hr., 6am-6:30pm, 1hr., 8 pesos). The return trip from Alamos starts from the bus station at Plaza Alameda (same times and price).

Once in Alamos, you can explore the small and compact town on foot. As you come into town on Calle Madero, you'll reach a fork in the road; the left branch leads to **Plaza Alameda,** the commercial center (where the bus stops), and the right branch leads to **Plaza de Armas,** in the historic district. A small alley known as the **Callejón del Beso** connects the Plaza de Armas with the market across from Plaza Alameda. The **cathedral** south of Plaza de Armas marks the northern edge of the **Barrio La Colorada,** where most of the *norteamericanos* have concentrated their hacienda-restoring efforts.

The **tourist office,** Calle Juárez 6 (tel. 8-04-50), is under the Hotel Los Portales on the west side of the Plaza de Armas (open Mon.-Fri. 9am-2pm and 4-7pm, Sat. 9am-2pm; erratic hours in summer). Currency can be exchanged at **Bancrecer** on Madero (tel. 8-04-44) before the fork in the road (open Mon.-Fri. 9am-5pm, Sat. 10am-2pm). A 24-hour **ATM** is right next door. Further out of the center of town on Madero is the **Hospital Básico** (tel. 8-00-25 or 8-00-26). The **post office** is also on Madero (tel. 8-00-09), between the Bancrecer and the hospital (open Mon.-Fri. 8am-3pm). **Postal code:** 85760. **Phone Code:** 642.

**Accommodations and Food** Unless you rediscover silver on your way into town, you'll probably have to turn away from the lush garden courtyards of the hacienda-hotels and head for hotels on the outskirts whose courtyards look a lot like parking lots. **Motel Somar,** Madero 110 (tel. 8-01-95), about 300m from Plaza Alameda, offers clean, spartan rooms with private showers and a chance to sit and chat with locals in the lobby. Loud fans cool the rooms (singles 100 pesos; doubles 120 pesos). Next door is the **Motel Dolisa,** Madero 72 (tel. 8-01-31). The rooms are similar to those at Somar, but with a few more amenities; A/C (15 extra pesos) and TVs are available (singles 160 pesos; doubles 180 pesos; triples 200 pesos; rooms with a kitchen 200 pesos; RV spaces for 100 pesos).

True peso-pinchers patronize the taco stands, such as **Taquería Blanquero,** in the Mercado Municipal by Plaza Alameda (open daily 7am-10:30pm). If you've yet to experience the joy of the mango, you can do so in the same market, where you can buy fruit grown within walking distance. **La Cita Cafe,** Madero 37, right before the fork, feels like a jungle lean-to with its brown wood walls, wire-wash windows, and the occasional birdcall in the distance. Citas and non-citas alike can enjoy a fish dish (32 pesos) or an *antojito* (around 20 pesos) as you admire how well the orange curtains, red and yellow tablecloths, brown chairs, and brown walls all match (open daily 7:30am-9:30pm). For a chance at a good view of the Plaza de Armas, the distant foothills, and an hacienda or two, eat outside under the arches at **Restaurant Las Palmeras,** Cárdenas 9 (tel. 8-00-65), northeast of the Plaza de Armas (breakfasts 12-17 pesos; *antojitos* 18-24; open daily 7am-10pm).

**Sights** The main reason to visit Alamos is to get a glimpse of Old Mexico. This can be achieved by strolling along the cobblestone streets and peeking into as many buildings as possible as you learn about the history of the town. One of the grandest homes in town was constructed in 1720 and refinished in the 19th century, when it became the home of Don José María, owner of one of the world's richest silver mines. The **Hotel Las Portales** now occupies most of the building, including Don Alameda's foyer and overgrown courtyard. Several other impressive restored homes, many of which are now hotels, can be found around the cathedral, including Hotel **Casa de los Tesoros** (a former convent), the **Hotel La Mansión,** and the **Casa Encantada.**

Today, the town **jail** and the **Mirador** offer excellent views from the same site Coronado chose for a fort in 1531. To get to the jail, walk along Madero west of the center of town and follow the signs. Signs to the Mirador will lead you in from Juárez. In 1630, the Jesuits established the first church in town; the current **cathedral** dates from 1805. A look inside at the height of the vault gives some dimension to Alamos's days of glory. In the mid-19th century, many Asians arrived in Alamos to work in the mines and in the growing silk industry. The only remainders of this period are a few mulberry trees and the **old silk factory** currently being restored as a private residence.

# CHIHUAHUA

## ■ El Paso, Texas

With its arid climate and disparate architectural landscape, modern El Paso (pop. 650,000) is part oversized strip mall, part Mexican mission town. At once a collegiate and military mecca, a symbol both of American westward expansion and its conversion to suburbia, and a city caught between two states, two countries, and two languages, El Paso suffers from a bona fide identity crisis.

The largest of the U.S. border towns, El Paso grew up in the 17th century as a stopover on an important east-west wagon route that trailed the Río Grande through "the pass" *(el paso)* between the Rockies and the Sierra Madres. As Spain extended its colonial reach into the New World, El Paso became a center for missionary activity; some old missions can still be seen today. More recently, the city has been dominated by Fort Bliss, the largest air defense base in the West, and the Biggs Army Airfield.

The city's San Jacinto Square, buzzing with pedestrians, is a pleasant place to while away the time. After dark, central El Paso turns into a ghost town: most activity leaves the relatively tame center of town and heads to the UTEP (University of Texas at El Paso) area or south of the border—to El Paso's raucous sister city, Ciudad Juárez.

### ORIENTATION

Before leaving the airport, pick up maps and information from the **visitor's center** at the bottom of the escalators descending from arrival gates. To get to the city from the airport, take Sun Metro bus #33. The stop is located on a traffic island outside the air terminal building, across from the Delta ticket window (Mon.-Fri. every ½hr., 6:27am-8:57pm; Sat. every ½hr., 7:57am-8:57pm; Sun. every hr., 8:12am-7:12pm; 40min. to downtown; US$1.10, students and children 6-13 50¢, seniors 30¢; exact change only). Get off when the bus arrives at San Jacinto Plaza and you'll find yourself right in the thick of it, near most hotels and restaurants.

When the bus stops running late at night, the only way to get to the city is to take a taxi (approximately US$20-25). Alternative approaches include I-10 (west/east) and US 54 (north/south). El Paso is divided into east and west by **Santa Fe Ave.** and into north and south by **San Antonio Ave.** Tourists should be wary of the streets between San Antonio and the border late at night.

### CROSSING THE BORDER

To reach the border from El Paso, take the north-south bus (every 10min., weekdays 6:30am-9pm, Sat. 8am-9pm, Sun. 9am-7pm, ½hr., US$1.10) to the **Santa Fe Bridge,** its last stop before turning around. Do not confuse the inexpensive bus with the costly trolley. Two pedestrian and motor roads cross the Río Grande: **El Paso Ave.,** an overcrowded one-way street, and **Santa Fe Ave.,** a parallel road lined with Western-wear stores, clothing shops, and decent restaurants. Entry to Mexico is 25¢ and the return trip costs a whopping 30¢. Capitalist pigs.

If entering Mexico by foot, walk to the right side of the Santa Fe Bridge and pay the quarter to cross. Daytrippers, including foreign travelers with a multi-entry visa, should be prepared to flash their documents of citizenship in order to pass in and out of Mexico. You might get your bag searched by a guard if you've got bad karma, but normally you won't even have to show ID. After stepping off the bridge, head to your right until you reach Av. Juárez. Then turn right until you get to the corner of Av. Juárez and Azucenas. On the northeast side you'll find the air-conditioned Juárez tourist office, where friendly, English-speaking employees await with maps and info.

To enter the United States, cross over the Santa Fe Bridge by the large *"Feliz Viaje"* sign. Be ready to deal with U.S. border guards and show a valid visa or proof of citizenship. You may be searched or asked to answer a few questions proving that you are who you say you are. Once in El Paso, wait at the stop on the right-hand sidewalk just across from the bridge for the north-south bus, which runs until 9pm to San Jacinto Plaza.

## PRACTICAL INFORMATION

**Tourist Office:** 1 Civic Center Plaza (tel. 544-0062), a small round building next to the Chamber of Commerce at the intersection of Santa Fe and San Francisco. Easily identifiable by the thin, water-filled moat that surrounds it. Well-stocked with brochures; sells **El Paso-Juárez Trolley Co.** tickets for day-long tours across the border leaving on the hour from the Convention Center. Tickets adults US$11, ages 4-12 US$8, under 4 free. Trolleys run 9am-4pm; there is also a 5pm trolley Wed.-Sat. during the summer; call 544-0062 for reservations, 544-0061 for recorded info.

**Mexican Consulate:** 910 E. San Antonio, on the corner of Virginia (tel. 533-5714). Dispenses **tourist cards.** Open Mon.-Fri. 9am-4:30pm.

**Currency Exchange: Valuta,** 301 E. Paisano at Mesa St. (tel. 544-1152). Conveniently near the border. Open 24hr. For **traveler's checks,** try **Bank of the West,** 500 N. Mesa St., on the corner of Missouri and Mesa (tel. 532-1000). Open Mon.-Thurs. 9am-4pm, Fri. 9am-5pm.

**American Express Office:** 3100 N. Mesa (tel. 532-8900). Open Mon.-Fri. 8am-5pm.

**Airport:** Northeast of the city center; to reach it, take bus #33 from San Jacinto Square or any other central location. Daily flights to locations in Mexico, the U.S., and elsewhere on a host of carriers, most with connections at Dallas/Ft. Worth.

**Buses: Greyhound,** 200 W. San Antonio (tel. 532-2365 or 1-800-231-2222), across from the Civic Center between Santa Fe and Chihuahua. Daily service to and from Los Angeles (10-15 per day, 16hr., US$35), Dallas, Phoenix, New York (7 per day, 48hr., US$99), and other U.S. cities. **Storage lockers** US$2 for up to 6hr., US$4 for 6-24hr. Open 24hr.

**Trains: Amtrak,** 700 San Francisco at Paisano (tel. 545-2247). Open Mon.-Sat. 10am-5:30pm.

**Public Transportation: Sun Metro** (tel. 533-3333), departing from San Jacinto Plaza, at the corner of Main and Oregon. Adults US$1.10, students and children US$.50, seniors $.30.

**Car Rental: Alamo** (tel. 774-9855), **Avis** (tel. 779-2700), **Budget** (tel. 778-5287), **Dollar** (tel. 778-5445), **Hertz** (tel. 772-4255), **Thrifty** (tel. 778-9236), and more, all at the airport.

**Hospital: Providence Memorial Hospital,** 2001 N. Oregon at Hague (tel. 577-6011), near UTEP. Open 24hr. Immunizations recommended but not required to enter Mexico. Call the **immunization department** (tel. 591-2050) of the **El Paso City County Health District,** 222 S. Campbell at First St. (tel. 543-3560). When approaching the Mexican border, turn left on Paisano St. and walk 3 blocks.

**Post Office:** 219 E. Mills between Mesa and Stanton (tel. 532-2652). Open Mon.-Fri. 9am-5pm, Sat. 8am-noon. **Postal code:** 79901.

**Area Code:** 915. To call Cd. Juárez from the U.S., first dial 011-52-16.

## ACCOMMODATIONS

El Paso offers safer, more appealing places to stay than Juárez. Budget hotels all cluster around the center of town, near Main St. and San Jacinto Square.

**Gardner Hotel/Hostel (HI-AYH),** 311 E. Franklin between Stanton and Kansas (tel. 532-3661). From the airport, take bus #33 to San Jacinto Park, walk 1 block north to Franklin, turn right, and head east 1½ blocks. The Gardner is 2 blocks up Mesa from San Jacinto Park. Clean rooms in the heart of downtown. Reception open 24hr. Locker rental 75¢, 50¢ for 4 or more days. **Hotel:** All rooms have color TV with cable (including HBO) and a phone. Singles $19-25, with bath $30-40; doubles and triples with bath $40-55. Deeply discounted weekend rates also available. **Hostel:** Small, 4-person dorm rooms and shared bathrooms. Beautiful, spacious kitchen, common room with pool table and cable TV, and couches for lounging and socializing in the basement. Check-out 10am. HI members $14, non-members $17. Linen $2 extra.

**Gateway Hotel,** 104 S. Stanton at San Antonio Ave (tel. 532-2611; fax 533-8100). A stone's throw from San Jacinto Square and a favorite stop for middle-class Mexicans. Clean and spacious rooms, large beds and closets, and thoroughly clean bathrooms, some with bathtubs. A/C upstairs; diner downstairs. Reservations accepted up to 5 days in advance, except during festivals and holidays. Parking US$1.50 for 24hr. Singles $23, with TV $30; doubles $35, with TV $37.

**Budget Lodge Motel,** 1301 N. Mesa at California (tel. 533-6821), a 10min. walk from San Jacinto Square (or take a Sun Metro bus going up Mesa St. until you get to River St.), 6 blocks from UTEP, 4 blocks from the hospital, and 2 blocks from the Catholic Church. Ample rooms are remarkably clean and have warm, strong running water, A/C, and cable TV. Small cafe, conveniently located on the first floor, serves breakfast and lunch at reasonable rates. And there is a swimming pool! Singles US$24; doubles $28.

## FOOD

El Paso is a hybrid species with North American and Mexican ancestors. Gringo chains coexist with small mom-and-pop restaurants; burritos are the undisputed local specialty. El Paso closes very early. If it's after 7pm, try **Hot Burger Restaurant,** at the Gateway Hotel, Stanton and San Antonio (open until 10pm).

**Sojourn's Coffeehouse,** 127 Pioneer Plaza, at El Paso and San Francisco (tel. 532-2817), above the San Francisco Grill. The only coffeehouse in downtown El Paso, Sojourn's boasts an outstanding selection of coffees, veggie fare, salads, and a small but delicious choice of sandwiches (US$5-6.50). Interesting decoration (Balinese) and crowd. Pick up a calendar of special events to catch an open-mike poetry reading, listen to some eclectic gypsy music, or have your palm read. Open Mon.-Thurs. 7:20am-10pm, Fri. 7:30am-late, Sat. 10am-late.

**Big Bun,** 500 N. Stanton at Franklin (tel. 533-3926). Mexican and American fast food butt heads at this mom-and-pop diner. Inexpensive tacos, burritos (US$1.09-1.29), hefty burgers (US$1.39), and sandwiches (US$2-4). Soda refills 25¢, free for iced tea. Open Mon.-Fri. 7:30am-7pm, Sat. 7:30am-6pm.

**Manolo's Café,** 122 S. Mesa between Overland and San Antonio (tel. 532-7661). Treat your stomach to the *menudo* (US$2) or burritos (US$1) and dig the bullfighter posters covering the walls. Open Mon.-Sat. 7am-5pm, Sun. 8am-3pm.

**Ben's Restaurant/Rinconcito Café,** 605 S. Mesa at Fourth Street (tel. 544-2236), between Ben's Grocery Store and Ben's Coin Laundry. Sit under the arches and pretend you're in an old hacienda while enjoying outrageously cheap—and tasty—burritos (US$1-1.75). Otherwise, try the generous *comida corrida* (US$3.25). Free delivery downtown. Open daily 8am-5pm.

## SIGHTS AND ENTERTAINMENT

The majority of visitors to El Paso are either stopping off on the long drive through the desert or heading south to Ciudad Juárez and beyond. For a whirlwind tour of the city and its southern neighbor, hop aboard the **Border Jumper Trolleys** that depart every hour from El Paso (see **Tourist Office,** p. 192).

Historic **San Jacinto Plaza** swarms with daily activity; street musicians play music that evokes El Paso's roots (*conquistadores* and cavalry). South of the square, on **El Paso St.,** hundreds of locals hurry along the thoroughfare and dash into stores in search of new bargains. To take in a complete picture of the Río Grande Valley, head northeast of downtown to Rim Rd. (which becomes Scenic Drive); **Murchinson Park** is at the base of the mountains. The park offers a commanding view of El Paso, Juárez, and the Sierra Madres. The **Cielo Vista Mall** boasts a variety of shops, as well as a movie theater, **Cinema 6** (take Sun Metro bus #63 from San Jacinto Plaza).

For nightlife, try **The Basement,** 127 Pioneer Plaza at San Francisco and San Antonio (tel. 532-7674), below the San Francisco Grill (open Fri.-Sat. 9pm-3am; cover US$10, under 21 $5; beer US$1.50 until 11pm). The gay hotspot is downtown at the dance club and bar **The Old Plantation,** 301 S. Ochoa at Paisano (tel. 533-6055), the brown brick building with the gray facade (open Thurs.-Sun. 9pm-2am). For rowdiness, no minimum drinking age, and ubiquitous nightlife, many people head to Juárez by night.

During the spring and summer, the **El Paso Diablos** (tel. 755-2000), pride of the fabled Texas League, play the best minor league baseball around (games April-May Mon.-Sun. 6:45pm; June-Aug. Mon.-Sat. 7:15pm, Sun. 6:45pm; call to confirm; general admission $3, box seats $4.75). To reach Cohen Stadium (9700 Gateway North), take Sun Metro bus #42 from San Jacinto Plaza as far north as it goes and walk the rest of the way. Ask the driver for directions.

# ■ Ciudad Juárez

Although Ciudad Juárez (pop. 1 million) is separated from El Paso only by the narrow Río Grande, one truly steps into another world upon entering Mexico. Visitors are immediately bombarded by commotion on all sides and treated to a feast of bright paint and neon. Near the border, the city is hectic, loud, and cheap; bands of carousing gringos infiltrate the area in search of cheap booze. The farther one proceeds towards the ritzy ProNaf area, the calmer, pricier, and more Americanized the establishments become. The incredibly high concentration of junkyards on the southern fringes of the city serve as a gauge of the excesses of Juárez. Fleeing in the face of the American advance, Mexican culture can be found in the city's cathedral square and Parque Chamizal, a pleasant respite from the sprawling industrial production centers and poor residential shantytowns that dot most of the cityscape. For more information on entering and leaving Mexico, see **El Paso: Crossing the Border** (p. 191) and **Entering and Leaving Mexico** (p. 16).

## ORIENTATION

Most of Old Juárez (the area immediately adjoining the Santa Fe and Stanton bridges) can be covered on foot. Street numbers start in the 600s near the two border bridges and descend to zero at **16 de Septiembre,** where **Av. Juárez** (the main street) ends. Both **Lerdo** and **Francisco Villa** run parallel to Juárez. To reach the **ProNaf center,** take public bus "Ruta 8A" (1.80 pesos). Most city buses leave from the intersection of **Insurgentes** and Villa or thereabouts; ask the driver whether your bus will take you to your destination. Taxis are always downtown, but fees are steep; negotiate before getting in. To get from the bus station to downtown, walk out the leftmost door (if you're facing the main station entrance) and up to the street. Don't be satisfied with just any bus that will take you to the *centro;* a bus driver's idea of *centro* may be bigger than a pedestrian's. Get on one that goes to Av. Juárez, or you'll be left a few blocks outside the real center. If you do happen to be dropped off among streets whose names are nowhere to be found in *Let's Go,* make your way to the cathedral (either by asking around or looking up). Walk down 16 de Septiembre away from Mariscal to get to Av. Juárez, Francisco Villa, and Lerdo. During the day, Juárez is relatively safe for the alert traveler. As darkness increases, however, so does the ratio of drunk to sober people wandering the streets. Women should not walk alone or in dark places; everyone should avoid the area more than two blocks west of Av. Juárez.

## PRACTICAL INFORMATION

**Tourist Office:** The main office is located in the Edificios de Gobierno del Estado, at Eje Vial Juan Gabriel and Aserraderos, a 10min. bus ride from the *centro.* A more conveniently located branch, the **Caseta de Información Turistica** (tel. 14-92-56), can be found on Av. Juárez Azucenas, 2 blocks from the border (tel. 29-33-00, ext. 5160 or 5649; fax ext. 5648). Few helpful brochures, but it has an amiable English-speaking staff. Open Mon.-Fri. 8:30am-2pm, Sat. 9am-1pm.

**U.S. Consulate:** López Mateos Nte. 924 at Hermanos Escobar (tel. 13-40-48 or 13-40-50). From Av. Juárez, turn left on Malecón and right on López Mateos, then walk for 15-20min. In an emergency, call the El Paso tourist office at 95-915-544-0062.

**Currency Exchange:** Banks congregate near the bus station, on Juárez, and on 16 de Septiembre. Most are open Mon.-Fri. 9am-3pm. Traveler's checks cashed by **Comisiones San Luis,** on the corner of 16 de Septiembre and Juárez (tel. 14-20-33). Open Mon.-Thurs. 9am-9pm, Fri.-Sat. 9am-9:15pm, Sun. 9am-6:15pm. Also try **Chequerama,** at Unión and Juárez (tel. 12-35-99). Open Mon.-Sat. 10am-6pm.

**Telephones: LADATEL** phones are scattered throughout the city. Look for them on Juárez near 16 de Septiembre. Secrefax (below) also has long-distance phones.

**Fax: Secrefax,** on Av. Juárez (tel. 15-15-10 or 15-20-49; fax 15-16-11), near the Santa Fe bridge, partially obscured under a white awning. Open daily 24hr.

**Airport:** Tel. 33-09-34. About 17km out on Rte. 45 (Carretera Panorámica). Catch the crowded "Ruta 4" bus and get off at the San Lorenzo Church; then board the "Ruta Aeropuerto" (1.80 pesos). **Aeroméxico** (tel. 13-80-89 or 13-87-19) flies to Chihuahua, Mexico City, and Monterrey.

**Buses: Central Camionera,** Blvd. Oscar Flores 4010, north of the ProNaf center and next to the Río Grande mall. To get there, take the **Chihuahuenses** bus from the El Paso terminal to Juárez (US$5) or cram into the "Ruta 1A" at Av. Insurgentes and Francisco Villa (1.50 pesos). Services include so-so eateries and an overpriced *caseta.* **Chihuahuenses** (tel. 29-22-29), **Ominbus de México** (tel. 10-64-45), **Estrella Blanca** (tel. 13-83-02), and others offer service to Chihuahua (every ½hr., 5hr., 122 pesos), Guadalajara (8:30am and 9pm, 24hr., 522 pesos), Hermosillo (10hr., 240 pesos), Mazatlán (24hr., 423 pesos), Mexico City (6 per day, 26hr., 614 pesos), Nogales (6pm, 8hr., 224 pesos), and more. **Greyhound** serves the U.S., including Dallas (US$70), El Paso (every hr., 50min., US$5), Los Angeles (US$35), San Antonio (US$79), and others.

**Trains:** Av. Eje Vial Juan Gabriel at Insurgentes (tel. 12-18-44). Walk down Lerdo until it ends and take Juan Gabriel. Service to Chihuahua and Mexico City.

**Supermarket: Smart,** López Mateos and Carretera Casas Grandes, a 15min. ride from Av. Juárez. The **Rio Grande Mall,** at Guerrero and López Mateos, sells groceries, clothes, furniture, and much, much more.

**Laundromat: Lavasolas,** Tlaxcala and 5 de Mayo (tel. 12-54-61). 12 other locations in town. Washers 9 pesos (large), 8 pesos (small); dryers 9 pesos. Open Mon.-Sat. 9am-9pm, Sun. 8am-5pm.

**Red Cross:** Tel. 16-58-06. In the ProNaf Center next to the OK Corral. English spoken. Open daily 24hr.

**Pharmacy: El Félix Super Farmacia,** 16 de Septiembre and Noche Triste (tel. 14-43-31), across from the cathedral. Turn right from Juárez. Open daily 8am-10pm.

**Hospital: Hospital Latinoamericano,** 250 N. López Mateos (tel. 16-14-67 or 16-14-15; fax 16-13-75), in the ProNaf area. English spoken. Open daily 24hr.

**Emergency:** Tel. 06.

**Police:** Oro and 16 de Septiembre (tel. 15-15-51). **Transit Police:** Tel. 12-31-97 or 41-10-28. English spoken at both.

**Post Office:** Lerdo at Ignacio Peña. Open Mon.-Fri. 8am-5pm, Sat.-Sun. 9am-1pm. **Postal Code:** 32000.

**Phone Code:** 16.

# ACCOMMODATIONS

In Juárez, a typical cheap hotel meets only minimal standards and charges some of the highest "budget" rates in Mexico. Inexpensive lodging can be found along the main strip, Avenida Juárez; pricier places are located in ProNaf, around López Mateos and Avenida de las Américas.

**Hotel del Río,** Juárez 488 near Mejía (tel. 12-37-76), is well worth the climb up the stairs. Clean rooms with comfortably thick beds, A/C, and color TVs await you. The environment is friendly and the place is safe. Big Brother has cameras set up in the reception area and hallways. Parking available. Singles, doubles, or tightly-squeezed triples 140 pesos.

**Hotel Juárez,** Lerdo 143 Nte. at 16 de Septiembre (tel. 15-02-98 or 15-03-58). Simple, small rooms in an old, yellow building, but one of the best deals you'll find in downtown Juárez. Room rates decrease as you move up the stairs (3rd floor: singles 73 pesos; doubles 84 pesos; additional person 11 pesos).

**Plaza Continental,** S. Lerdo 112 at 16 de Septiembre (tel. 15-00-84, 15-03-18, or 15-02-59). Centrally located, with all the makings of a luxury hotel: a spacious, elegant lobby with chandeliers, columns, and a wide staircase leading to large, comfortable, well-furnished rooms with A/C, color TV, and phones. *Agua purificada* dispenser and—joy—a Tecate vending machine are in the hall. Singles 168 pesos; doubles 201 pesos; triples 212 pesos.

## FOOD

Eateries vary from clean, air-conditioned restaurants catering to tourists to roadside shacks with picnic tables and TVs blasting *telenovelas* in Spanish. Weak-stomached travelers should avoid shacks. The quest for food that will not cause a bacteriological mutiny in gringo bellies is long; the prudent beat a path to Av. Juárez and Lerdo or to the ProNaf center. In general, *mariscos* (shellfish) are overpriced and less than fresh.

**Cafetería El Coyote Inválido,** Juárez 615 at Colón (tel. 14-27-27). We're still wondering about the name. A bustling, clean, American-style diner with heavenly A/C. Hamburgers (16 pesos), burritos (16 pesos), and an array of Mexican plates (16-32 pesos). Open daily 24hr.

**Hotel Santa Fé Restaurante,** Lerdo 675 Nte. and Tlaxcala (tel. 14-02-70), at the Hotel Santa Fe. Roll from here to there on the wheeled chairs. Then roll back. Sample chicken enchiladas or club sandwiches (17 pesos) and wash 'em down with a beer (9 pesos). Open daily 24hr.

**Restaurant/Bar Juárez de Noche,** Juárez 222 Nte. between Gonzáles and Carreño (tel. 15-20-02)—the place with the open-air facade. Let the tunes of the *grupo norteño* lead you to their taco platter, which comes with salad, french fries, beans, and more (24 pesos). Irrigate it all with a nice, cold beer (8 pesos).

## SIGHTS AND ENTERTAINMENT

The **Aduana Fronteriza** (tel. 12-47-07) stands in *el centro,* where Juárez and 16 de Septiembre cross. Built in 1889 as a trading outpost and later used for customs, it now houses the **Museo Histórico de la Ex-Aduana,** which chronicles the region's history during the Mexican Revolution. Peeking inside the antique wagons is not frowned upon (open Tues.-Sun. 10am-6pm; free). The **Museo de Arte e Historia** (tel. 16-74-14), at the ProNaf center, exhibits Mexican art of the past and present (open Tues.-Sun. 11am-6pm; admission 5 pesos, students free). Also at the ProNaf center, the **Centro Artesanal** sells handmade goods at sky-high prices; you'd be crazy not to haggle here. The "Ruta 8" bus will take you from *el centro* to ProNaf for 1.80 pesos; a taxi charges 20 times as much. Your call.

The deforested **Parque Chamizal,** near the Córdova Bridge, is a good place to escape the noise of the city, if not the heat, and enjoy a picnic with the Montoya family. Check out the newly inaugurated Mexican flag that's reputedly as big as a football field. The **Museo Arqueológico,** Av. Pellicer (tel. 11-10-48 or 13-69-83) in Parque Chamizal, houses plastic facsimiles of pre-Hispanic sculptures as well as trilobite fossils, rocks, and bones (open Tues.-Sun. 11am-8pm, Sat.-Sun. 10am-8pm). The **Misión de Nuestra Señora de Guadalupe,** on 16 de Septiembre and Mariscal (tel. 15-55-02), is the oldest building on both sides of the border for kilometers around. It features antique paintings and altars.

The *toro* and the *matador* battle in traditional bullfights on occasional evenings during the summer at the **Plaza Monumental de Toros,** Paseo Triunfo de la

República and López Mateos (tel. 13-16-56). General admission seating starts at 35 pesos, 60 pesos in the shade. Children 12 and under are free. The **Lienzo Charro,** on Av. Charro off República (tel. 27-05-55), also hosts bullfights and a *charreada* (rodeo) on Sunday afternoons during the summer. At the western edge of town, the **Juárez Racetrack** (Galgódromo; tel. 25-53-94) rises from Vicente Guerrero. Dogs run Wednesday to Sunday at 7:30pm; Sunday matinees during the summer at 2:30pm. Horse racing can be seen only on closed-circuit TV.

Juárez has so many bars that counting them could make you dizzy even before you start **drinking.** Many establishments are unsavory, and even some of the better ones can become dangerous; stick to the glutted strip along Av. Juárez or stay in the ProNaf area. On weekends, gringos swarm to Juárez in a 48-hour quest for fun, fights, fiestas, and inexpensive dental work. **Mr. Fog Bar,** Juárez Nte. 140 at González (tel. 14-29-48), is quite popular. A cartoon crocodile adorns the mirrored walls of this dark, reddish drinking establishment. The dance floor is in back (beer 8 pesos, liquor 9 pesos; open Sun.-Thurs. 11am-2am, Fri.-Sat. 11am-3am).

# ■ Nuevo Casas Grandes and Paquimé

Nuevo Casas Grandes belongs to a time when cowboys ruled the land. A quiet town (pop. 80,000) in the expansive Chihuahuan desert, this community arose at the beginning of this century after a group of pioneering families from (Viejo) Casas Grandes decided to move to the newly constructed railroad station. Today, cattle and agriculture continue to control the economy, and *vaquero* hats and boots remain ubiquitous. Eight kilometers southwest of Nuevo Casas Grandes, the ruins of Paquimé (pah-kee-MEH) in Casas Grandes are the remains of what was once the most important city in pre-Hispanic northern Mexico.

**Orientation and Practical Information**  From the **Estrella Blanca** bus station on Obregón and 16 de Septiembre, walk one block down 16 de Septiembre to reach **Constitución,** which runs along the railroad tracks. One block further is **Juárez.** These are the two main streets in town. Perpendicular to these is **5 de Mayo;** at the intersection of Juárez and 5 de Mayo is the **Plaza Juárez.** Taxis loiter on 16 de Septiembre at Constitución and on Minerva at Obregón. Everything listed below lies within the nine-block downtown area.

The **tourist office,** on the corner of Juárez and Domínguez (tel./fax 4-64-73), is on the second floor of the Cámara de Comercios office, across from La Mansión (open Mon.-Fri. 9am-5pm). Change money at **Casa de Cambio California,** Constitución 207 at 5 de Mayo (tel. 4-32-32; open Mon.-Fri. 9am-2pm and 3:30-7pm, Sat. 9am-2pm and 3:30-6pm). **Bancomer,** 16 de Septiembre at Constitución (tel. 17-52-22; open Mon.-Fri. 9am-3pm, Sat. 10am-2pm), has a 24-hour **ATM. LADATELs** cluster around the central square. **Estrella Blanca** and **Caballero Azteca** (tel. 4-07-80) **buses** run to Chihuahua (11 per day, 2am-midnight, 5hr., 95 pesos), Cuauhtémoc (3 per day, 6½hr., 88 pesos), and Cd. Juárez (12 per day, 5am-9pm, 3½hr., 75 pesos). **Chihuahuenses** (tel. 4-14-75) run all the way to Hermosillo (6:30pm and midnight, 8hr., 1st class 208 pesos, 2nd class 181 pesos), Monterrey (5, 11am, and 4pm, 16hr., 361 pesos), and Tijuana (3am, 2, 4, and 11pm, 16hr., 1st class 392 pesos, 2nd class 340 pesos). Next door, **Ómnibus de México** (tel. 4-05-02) sends buses to Chihuahua (7 per day, 5am-10:30pm, 5hr., 95 pesos). Stock up at **Hiperama,** Juárez at Minerva (tel. 4-55-55; open daily 9am-9pm). **Farmacia Benavides** is on Obregón at 5 de Mayo (tel. 4-55-55; open daily 8am-10pm). The **Red Cross** is on Carranza at Constitución (tel. 4-20-20; open 24hr.). The **police** can be found on Blanco and Obregón (tel. 4-09-75). The **post office** is at 16 de Septiembre and Madero (tel. 4-20-16; open Mon.-Fri. 8am-6pm, Sat. 8am-1pm). **Postal Code:** 31700. **Phone Code:** 169.

**Accommodations and Food**  Accommodations with modern conveniences cluster on Constitución and on Juárez between 5 de Mayo and Jesús Urueta. At Constitución 209 next to 5 de Mayo, you'll be welcomed to live it up at the **Hotel Califor-**

nia (tel. 4-22-14). It's a lovely place, with spacious, clean, air-conditioned rooms and bamboo-looking furniture. Ask for the economical rooms, which have black-and-white TV and cost 15 pesos less (singles 120 pesos; doubles 140 pesos; triples 160 pesos). At the **Hotel Juárez,** Obregón 110 (tel. 4-02-33), a block from the bus station, you can talk and talk and talk to the friendly, English-speaking owner, Mario. Show him your book and score a point for the good guys on his *Let's Go* vs. *Berkeley* scorecard. Clean rooms are small and not well-ventilated, but they have ample lighting, a bed, and a passable shower (singles 50 pesos; doubles 60 pesos; triples 70 pesos).

The low tourist count means that the food is cheap and the nightlife soporific. **Restaurante Constantino,** Juárez at Minerva (tel. 4-10-05), accompanies its *enchiladas de pollo* with fresh bread, chips, and salsa (25 pesos). The *comida corrida* is only 22 pesos (open daily 7:30am-midnight). The clean and icily air-conditioned **Dinno's Pizza,** Minerva and Constitución (tel. 4-02-40), has jalapeño, cherry, pineapple, and coconut pizzas (small 35 pesos, medium 40 pesos, large 50 pesos; open daily 8am-11:30pm). At **Restaurant Denni's,** on Juárez 600 at Urueta, you can sit beneath a wooden Aztec Calendar next to a framed *Dirty Dancing* poster. Syncretism, baby. Or something. After your *flautas de pollo* (22 pesos), top off your meal with *flan* (8 pesos) or a Denni's bumper sticker (free, if you're lucky; open daily 8am-midnight).

**Sights** The area around Nuevo Casas Grandes has a lot to offer the archaeology fan. Among the possible trips from Nuevo Casas Grandes are the **Cueva de Olla** (75km southwest), the **Arroyo de los Monos** (35km southeast), and **Mata Ortiz** (35km south). About 254km southeast of Nuevo Casas Grandes is **Madera,** from which the **Cuarenta Casas** archaeological site can be reached (54km north). Ask at the tourist office for more info. The most accessible and significant site, however, is the pre-Conquest city of **Paquimé** (a.k.a. **Casas Grandes**), 8km southwest of Nuevo Casas Grandes. Paquimé lay hidden underground for 600 years. Its architecture suggests that it grew out of two different cultures: its many-storied *pueblos* resemble those in the southwestern U.S., but other structures show the influence of central and southern Mexico. From AD 1000-1200, Paquimé was the most important agricultural and trading center in northern Mexico. The inhabitants kept parrots and turkeys in adobe pens and built indoor aqueducts and hidden cisterns to supply the *pueblos* in times of siege. They earned their livelihoods by farming and by trading sea shells brought from the Pacific coast. First exhumed in the early 1970s, Paquimé is now an archaeological zone administered by the Mexican government. Unfortunately, once it was exposed to archaeologists and tourists, its mud walls began to crumble. Visitors should avoid eroding the thin walls.

There are three principal maze-like mounds of ruins in Paquimé that form a striking scene with the dusty mountains and ice-blue sky as the backdrop. It's easy to tell the parts that have been restored (the darker, more solid walls) from the original (cracked-looking) walls, which are located primarily in the mound to the far right. Among the ruins lie a partially excavated **market** as well as a **ball court.** The short and narrow T-shaped doors allowed inhabitants to defend themselves by pummeling unwanted visitors as they lowered their heads to enter. Look for the **House of the Macaws,** the **House of Skulls,** and the **Cross Monument,** which points to the four cardinal directions. The **museum** (tel. 2-40-37) adjacent to the site is a terrific architectural achievement. Designed to blend in with the ruins and to have a low impact on the environment, the museum displays artifacts that have been found at Casas Grandes, with an emphasis on the many pieces of polychrome pottery. Southwestern U.S. history and natural history are foci of the "Sala de las Culturas," which features a large-scale model of Mesa Verde. A cafeteria, central patio with fountains, A/V room, gift shop, and a path directly out to the ruins round out the circular stone, wheelchair-accessible structure (museum and site open roughly 10am-5pm; admission 10 pesos, free Sun.).

On summer afternoons, the dry and shadeless ruins can become a blazing inferno, as temperatures approach or exceed 100°F. Be sure to bring sun protection, a broad-brimmed hat (cheap *sombreros* are available in town), and, most importantly, a gigantic bottle of water to quench your thirst. Some information on the site may be obtained at **Pueblo Viejo,** a store in the town square at Independencia and Juárez, or at the **Motel Piñón,** Juárez Nte. 605 at 5 de Mayo (tel. 4-06-55) back in Nuevo Casas Grandes. As always, be wary: wandering the area alone is not a wise idea.

**Getting There:** From Nuevo Casas Grandes, take the light yellow **municipal bus** at the corner of Constitución and 16 de Septiembre (1 per hr., 10min., 2 pesos). Get off by the main plaza, cross the street, and continue straight down a dirt road for 10 minutes. Follow the path as it turns right, then turn left at the next intersection. You have now arrived. Almost any **taxi** driver will take you to the site and walk around with you for about 60 pesos per hour.

# ■ Chihuahua

The capital of the Republic's largest state, Chihuahua (pop. 800,000) is the vibrant, historically rich mecca of Northern Mexico. Exposed to the sandstorms of Mexico's vast northern desert, the city may seem like little more than a far-flung outpost of the civilization to the south. While it may not fit your image of Mexico, Chihuahua's businesslike genuineness is quite endearing. Its relative seclusion convinced Pancho Villa to establish the headquarters of his revolutionary División del Norte here. During the conflict, his feisty gang of *bandidos* and vagabonds staged attacks against the Porfiriato, marching down from Chihuahua to assault social inequities. Quinta Luz, Villa's sprawling colonial home, shines as the city's major attraction, complemented by posh Euro-villas built by wealthy Americans and Europeans in the late 19th century.

The peoples who converge on Chihuahua and the surrounding area are as diverse as the land itself. Mennonites came here in flocks in the 1920s, attracted by the bountiful pastures. Today, they maintain their seclusion in the town of Cuauhtémoc and in other agricultural communities nearby. Equally secluded but quite different, the *indígena* Tarahumara people live isolated in the nearby Sierra Madres, venturing into the city only on market day to sell handmade crafts.

## ORIENTATION

*¡Ay!* Chihuahua sprawls in every direction. Skewered by Rte. 45 (the Pan-American Highway), the city serves as an important transportation hub for northern Mexico. Trains arrive at the **Estación Central de los FFNN,** just north of downtown. Trains headed for Los Mochis and Creel via the Barrancas del Cobre leave from the **Chihuahua al Pacífico** station, south of the city center off Ocampo, two blocks from 20 de Noviembre. To shorten the 20-minute walk to *el centro,* hop on one of the public buses (1.80 pesos) that run up and down Ocampo to Libertad; alternatively, snag a cab (about 20 pesos), but set the price before you step in. From the bus station, a municipal bus (1.80 pesos) will take you to the cathedral. The kiosk near the main entrance to the bus station has a map indicating the various municipal bus routes and standard prices for cab rides to different zones.

**Libertad** is a pedestrian-only shopping arcade between **Independencia** and **Guerrero.** Two other main streets, **Victoria** and **Juárez,** run parallel to Libertad. **Av. Ocampo** crosses Juárez one block past the cathedral. Starting with Av. Independencia, parallel streets *(calles)* have ascending even numbers to the south and odd numbers to the north. *Avenidas* running north-south are named. Don't let Chihuahua's sheer size intimidate you; while the city is large, most sights are within walking distance from the cathedral. Budget hotels and restaurants cluster on the streets behind the cathedral. With the exception of Av. Victoria, which perpetually celebrates victory with the flashing lights of bars and discos, the streets in Chihuahua are poorly illuminated. Women should avoid walking alone after dark.

**NORTHWEST MEXICO**

## PRACTICAL INFORMATION

**Tourist Office:** On Aldama between Carranza and Guerrero (tel. 10-10-77; fax 16-00-32), in the Palacio del Gobierno, across from the Plaza Hidalgo. Helpful, English-speaking staff dispenses maps and brochures. Open daily 9am-7pm.

**Currency Exchange: BanPaís,** on Victoria 104 (tel. 16-16-59), 1 block from the cathedral, past Independencia. No exchange fee for traveler's checks. Open Mon.-Fri. 9am-2:30pm. **Hotel San Francisco** (tel. 16-75-50), across the street, has 24hr. exchange. **ATMs** near the lobbies of all the tall banks downtown near the *zócalo.*

**American Express:** Vicente Guerrero 1207 past Allende (tel. 15-58-58), where Guerrero curves to become Bolívar. Open Mon.-Fri. 9am-6pm, Sat. 9am-noon.

**Telephones:** Silver **LADATELs** gleam in the sun all over the *zócalo.* Long distance service available in expensive hotels and the plaza, in front of the cathedral.

**Airport:** Tel. 20-51-04. 14km from town. **Aerolitoral,** Victoria 106 (tel. 20-06-16). **Aeroméxico,** Victoria 106 (tel. 15-63-03). **Aerovías de México,** Bolívar 405 (tel. 16-39-88). **Transportes Aéreos Ejecutivos,** Jiménez 1204 (tel. 16-03-71). All open Mon.-Fri. 9am-6:30pm. "Aeropuerto" buses get you there from Ocampo. Buses heading downtown wait outside of the baggage area.

**Buses:** The main station (tel. 20-22-86) is a 20min. ride on the "Central Camionera" bus from Ocampo and Victoria. **Ómnibus de México** (tel. 20-15-80) sends its luxurious fleet to Aguascalientes (4, 5:30, and 7pm, 14hr., 319 pesos), Casas Grandes (7 per day, 7:30am-6:30pm, 5hr., 95 pesos), Durango (11:30am, 6, 8:30, and 11pm, 9hr., 197 pesos), Guadalajara (7pm, 17hr., 400 pesos), Matamoros (2:40am and 9:30pm, 18hr., 377 pesos), Mexico City (4:30 and 9pm, 22hr., 490 pesos), Monterrey (6, 9:30, and 11pm, 12hr., 286 pesos), Querétaro (5 per day, 18hr., 415 pesos), Saltillo (6, 9:30, and 11pm, 10hr., 223 pesos), and San Luis Potosí (6 per day, 4:50am-9pm, 339 pesos). **Transportes Caballero Azteca** (tel. 29-02-42) sends buses to Hermosillo (2, 7:30, and 10pm, 14hr., 323 pesos), Tijuana (6:30 and 10pm, 22hr., 507 pesos), and Zacatecas (14 per day, 6am-11pm, 12hr., 209 pesos). **Transportes Chihuahuenses** (tel. 29-02-42) sends buses daily to Cd. Juárez (every hr. until 9pm, 5hr., 122 pesos), Mazatlán (10:15am and 5:30pm, 18hr., 298 pesos). **Turismos Rápidos Cuauhtémoc-Anáhuac** (tel. 10-44-33) has service to Cuauhtémoc (every ½hr., 5am-7:30pm, 1½hr., 27 pesos). **Estrella Blanca** has a slightly older fleet of buses that chugs to nearly all of the above cities for lower prices but requires more travel time.

**Trains: FFCC Chihuahua al Pacífico** (tel. 15-77-56; fax 10-90-59), the southern station near Quinta Luz. Walk south on Ocampo, turn right at 20 de Noviembre and left on Calle 24, at the end of the enormous prison. It's 2 blocks down. *Primera* trains leave at 7am for Creel (4½hr., 176 pesos) and Los Mochis (14hr., 380 pesos). *Segunda* trains leave at 8am for Creel (35 pesos) and Los Mochis (76 pesos). Tickets purchased on the train are 25% more expensive. Children travel at half-price. Tickets sold Mon.-Fri. 9am-2pm, Sat. 9am-10am. Only cash accepted. Two stopovers are permitted at an extra cost of 15%. The northern station, **FFCC Nacionales de México,** is on Av. Tecnológico.

**Car Rental: Hertz,** Av. Revolución 514 at José Nari Santos (tel. 16-64-73). VW Beetle with insurance and 300km per day cost 351 pesos per day.

**Red Cross:** Calle 24 and Revolución (tel. 11-22-11 or 11-14-84). Open 24hr.

**Pharmacy: Farmacia Mendoza,** Calle Aldama 1901 at Calle 19 (tel. 16-69-32 or 16-66-38), away from the cathedral past Plaza de Hidalgo. Open 24hr.

**Hospital: Hospital General,** Revolución and Colón (tel. 16-00-22), in Colonia Centro. **Clínica del Centro,** Ojinaga 816 (tel. 16-00-22).

**Police:** Av. Homero (tel. 13-30-98), across from the Ford plant, at the exit to Juárez.

**Post Office:** On Libertad between Guerrero and Carranza (tel. 37-12-00), in the Palacio Federal. Open Mon.-Fri. 8am-7pm, Sat. 9am-1pm. **Postal Code:** 31000.

**Phone Code:** 14.

## ACCOMMODATIONS

Hotels in Chihuahua are like the city itself—charm smiles through the grit. Economical hotels lie between Victoria and Juárez in the area behind the cathedral.

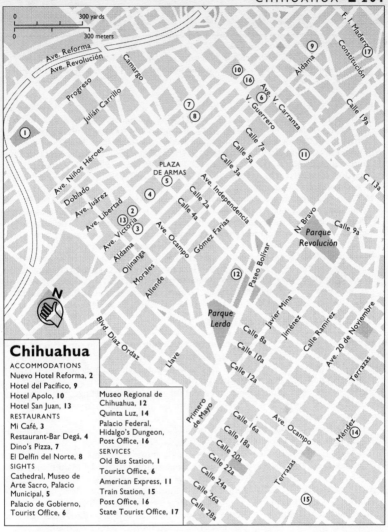

**Chihuahua**

ACCOMMODATIONS
Nuevo Hotel Reforma, 2
Hotel del Pacífico, 9
Hotel Apolo, 10
Hotel San Juan, 13
RESTAURANTS
Mi Café, 3
Restaurant-Bar Degá, 4
Dino's Pizza, 7
El Delfín del Norte, 8
SIGHTS
Cathedral, Museo de
Arte Sacro, Palacio
Municipal, 5
Palacio de Gobierno,
Tourist Office, 6

Museo Regional de
Chihuahua, 12
Quinta Luz, 14
Palacio Federal,
Hidalgo's Dungeon,
Post Office, 16
SERVICES
Old Bus Station, 1
Tourist Office, 6
American Express, 11
Train Station, 15
Post Office, 16
State Tourist Office, 17

**Hotel del Pacífico,** Aldama 1911 (tel. 10-59-13), at Calle 21, a few blocks from the
Palacio de Gobierno. A great bargain. Although the lobby is dark and musty, the
clean rooms have A/C, large bathrooms, and decent foam mattresses with cement
bases. Friendly management and a restaurant. Parking available. Singles 65 pesos;
doubles 75 pesos; triples 85 pesos; add 5 pesos for TV.

**Hotel Apolo,** Juárez at Carranza (tel. 16-11-00 or -01; fax 16-11-02), in the center. A
step up in price—and amenities. Dark but majestic lobby with sculptures, chandeliers, and paintings. All clean, bright rooms have A/C and nice, tiled bathrooms;
those on the 3rd and 4th floors come with color TVs. Cafeteria, bar, and parking.
Singles 133 pesos; doubles 143 pesos. Discounts for large groups.

**Nuevo Hotel Reforma,** Victoria 809 (tel. 10-68-48; fax 16-08-35). Unique and
delightful architecture. The old courtyard is covered by a warehouse-like roof and
is connected to the 2nd floor by an X-shaped staircase. The bug-free rooms have
fans, flabby beds, clean tile bathrooms, and incredibly tall ceilings. Singles 59
pesos; doubles 71 pesos; add 8 pesos for TV.

## FOOD

Eateries in Chihuahua are not geared toward tourists. Some of the best meals can be found in small *cantinas,* where bands serenade drunken (and often rowdy) men. For a quick, cheap bite to eat, try the shopping arcade along Libertad between Independencia and Guerrero.

**Rostícería Los Pollos,** Aldama 702 between Calle 7 and Guerrero (tel. 10-59-77). Cafeteria-style dining at its best and brightest. Plastic booths, mirrored walls, and A/C spice up your excellent *pollo en mole* with rice and tortillas (only 14 pesos). To finish it off, have some sweet *arroz con leche* (5 pesos). Open 9am-8pm.

**Dino's Pizza,** Manuel Doblado 301 (tel. 16-57-07), across from the Santa Regina. International crowd. Quaint decor and delectable pizza (4 different sizes: 25, 35, 45, and 49 pesos). The special (pizza, spaghetti, and salad) serves 5-6 people (79 pesos). Open 8:30am-midnight.

**Mi Café,** Victoria 1000 at Calle 10 (tel. 10-12-38), across from Hotel San Juan. Put on your sunglasses to enter this bright, laid-back, 50s-style diner with melon-colored vinyl booths and an orange and white checkered ceiling. A 27-peso order of chicken comes with bread, soup, rice, potatoes, and dessert—a huge meal. Burritos 12-13 pesos. Breakfast platter 20-24 pesos. Open daily 9am-midnight.

**Restaurant-Bar Degá,** on Victoria (tel. 16-77-70), at Hotel San Francisco near the *zócalo.* Oozing with class, this joint offers a rare (if pricey) chance at a vegetarian meal. The *plato vegetariano* (36 pesos) includes vegetarian soup, a soy steak, avocado, and white rice; the *ceviche vegetariano* (23 pesos) has mushrooms and olive oil. Fresh carrot, papaya, or grapefruit juice 12 pesos. Open 7am-10:30pm.

## SIGHTS AND ENTERTAINMENT

The stately and regal 19th-century **Palacio de Gobierno** stands in the center of Chihuahua on Aldama. Inside, Aarón Piña Moratell's famous and beautiful **murals** tell the story of Chihuahua. Look for a **nude Emiliano Zapata,** whose modesty is maintained by another soldier's conveniently placed rifle. Behind the Palacio de Gobierno is the **Palacio Federal,** housing the post office and the jail of Miguel Hidalgo, where he was detained before being shot. A few blocks from the palace, on Victoria and Calle 2, is the giant **cathedral.** While construction began in 1725, the church was actually finished more than a century later in 1826. The stone facade displays unique and creative talent from the Baroque period.

The area southwest of the *zócalo* offers an excellent, leafy retreat from downtown. At **Quinta Luz,** also called **Museo de la Revolución** (Pancho Villa's house; tel. 16-29-58), visitors can relive the turbulence of the revolution by looking through an extensive collection of documents and photographs, paintings of Señor Villa, the bullet-ridden Dodge in which he was assassinated, his household furnishings, and his vast collection of weapons (still enough to outfit a small army). Soldiers outside stand at attention. To reach Quinta Luz, hike 1.5km south on Ocampo, turn left on 20 de Noviembre, and go two blocks to Calle 10 and Méndez. Turn right, and Villa's house is two blocks down (open daily 9am-1pm and 3-7pm; admission 5 pesos).

On the way to the Villa household is another, equally worthy museum: the **Quinta Gameros Centro Cultural Universitario,** also called the **Museo Regional de Chihuahua.** This amazing architectural feat, on the corner of Calle 4 and Paseo Bolívar (tel. 16-66-84), is one of the more stunning mansions in Mexico. Mining engineer Don Manuel Gameros, the aristocrat who had it built, never lived in it—the Revolution drove him to El Paso, Texas. The house was seized by revolutionaries and at one point served as Pancho Villa's barracks. Some astounding art-nouveau furniture and rooms now wow observers; look for the 3m-high toilet and the beautiful mahogany dining room woodwork. Upstairs, local painters exhibit their works (open Tues.-Sun. 10am-2pm and 4-7pm; admission 10 pesos, children 5 pesos).

Back in *el centro,* the basement of the cathedral hides the **Museo de Arte Sacro,** Libertad and Calle 2 (tel. 10-38-77). Pastoral religious paintings from the 18th century mingle with photos and portraits from the Pope's most recent visit to Chihuahua (open Mon.-Fri. 10am-2pm and 4-6pm; admission 5 pesos, students and children 3 pesos). For those craving more secular pleasures, the recently opened **Museo de Arte Contemporáneo,** at Carranza and Aldama (tel. 29-33-00, ext. 3700), across from the Palacio del Gobierno, has a formidable collection of modern art. Sebastián's geometrical sculptures and Diego Rivera's sketch of a two-headed man/beast are among the highlights (open Tues.-Sun. 10am-8pm; admission 5 pesos, students and teachers 3 pesos; free Wed.).

At night, catch a flick at **Cinépolis,** Vallarta at Zaragoza (tel. 17-52-22; shows 3-9:30pm; 20 pesos, first show 15 pesos, Wed. 12 pesos). To get there, hop on a "Cerro de la Cruz" bus in front of the Héroes de la Revolución building, in the *centro* (every 8min. until 9:30pm, 15min., 1.80 pesos). If the buses have stopped running, you'll have to take a 20-peso cab back. Afterward, you can discuss the film at one of the many cafes in the center of town. **Café Calicanto,** Aldama 411 (tel. 10-44-52), serves snacks and a wide selection of coffees and beers. There is live music on weekends (open Sun.-Thurs. 4pm-midnight, Fri.-Sat. 5pm-3am). Nightclubs tend to be far away from the center, but taxis will get you there. **Quinto Sofía,** in front of Lerdo Park, brings out a twentysomething crowd to listen to live Spanish rock (beers 10 pesos; cover 15 pesos after 10:30pm). A somewhat older crowd flocks to **Old Town,** Juárez 3331 between Colón and Calle 39 (tel. 10-32-71). On weekends, there is a wild 20-minute **rodeo show** at midnight and country music after that (cover Fri.-Sat. 30 pesos; open Thurs. 9pm-1am, Fri.-Sat. 9pm-2:30am).

# ■ Cuauhtémoc Mennonite Colony

Among the masses of Mexican businesspeople, street vendors, and families around Cuauhtémoc's *zócalo,* a blond-haired, blue-eyed Caucasian in overalls or a long black dress will occasionally amble by—hardly a typical sight in Northwest Mexico. But not surprising in Cuauhtémoc, home to 40,000-60,000 Mennonites (out of a total population of 300,000). The Mennonites are a pacifist religious group founded in the 16th century in lower Germany. After being expelled from virtually every country in Europe due to their refusal to serve in the military and their steadfast determination to educate their children privately, a large number of Mennonites settled in the agricultural fields just outside Cuauhtémoc. The hard-working, almost compulsively clean group of Mennonites that now inhabits the area is renowned for the cheese that they produce. Most Mennonites speak Low German, an archaic 17th-century dialect that even those fluent in High (modern) German would have difficulty understanding. Although many Cuauhtémoc Mennonites have abandoned some of the stricter restrictions, such as the prohibition to use electricity, traditional dress is still standard: wide-brimmed, white hats and long, flowered dresses for women, tall hats and overalls for men. Cuauhtémoc, aside from its proximity to the *campos menonitas,* is not particularly thrilling; it's a bustling, working-class, usually friendly city.

**Orientation and Practical Information** Cuauhtémoc lies midway between Creel and Chihuahua, a two- to three-hour bus ride from each. The highway into Cuauhtémoc from Chihuahua continues past the city and into the **Mennonite area,** organized in small communities called **campos.** Each *campo* has a number and is laid out in an orderly manner, with a main street, several farms, a creamery, a church, and a school. *Campos* are organized by number: on the left, numbers start at one and go up; on the right they start in the mid-20s and count down, and after a certain point, the field numbers switch to the 100s. The center of Cuauhtémoc is at the beginning of the parallel numbered streets: Melgar (Calle 1) and Coello (Calle 2). Odd-numbered streets increase beyond Melgar to the east, and even-numbered streets increase beyond Coello to the west. The cross-streets Morelos and Allende delineate the *zócalo* with Melgar and Coello.

**Banca Serfín,** Melgar at Allende (tel. 2-63-33), has a 24-hour **ATM** (open Mon.-Fri. 9am-5pm). **LADATEL phones** surround the *zócalo* and dot the downtown area. Call friends back home at **Servicio Técnico García,** Allende at Calle 9 (tel. 2-04-48; open

Mon.-Sat. 9am-1pm and 3-7pm). The **Estrella Blanca bus station,** Allende at Calle 9 (tel. 2-10-18), runs buses to Basaseachi (8am, 12:30, and 4:30pm, 5hr., 61 pesos), Casas Grandes (6am, noon, and 9:30pm, 5hr., 80 pesos), Chihuahua (every ½hr., 8:30am-9:40pm, 1½hr., 27 pesos), Creel (every 2hr., 7:30am-7:30pm, 3½hr., 54 pesos), and Cd. Juárez (9hr., 125 pesos). The **Centro Comercial El Dorado,** Allende and Calle 3, across from the *zócalo,* is a big-time **supermarket** (open Mon.-Fri. 9am-8pm, Sat.-Sun. 9am-9pm). **Farmacia Cuauhtémoc** is on Morelos 321 between Calles 3 and 5 (tel. 1-48-77; open Mon.-Sat. 8am-midnight, Sun. 10am-6pm). The **police** can be reached at 2-28-56, and the **Red Cross** at 2-06-87. Dial 06 in case of an **emergency.** The **post office** is on Calle 4 and Guerrero (tel. 2-03-14; open Mon.-Fri. 8am-6pm). **Postal code:** 31500. **Phone code:** 158.

**Accommodations**  The best place to stay in Cuauhtémoc, hands down, is the **Motel Gasthaus** (tel. 1-43-33), the only Mennonite hotel, smack in the middle of the Mennonite area on the km 13 marker. To get there from the city, try the **Cumbres Friesen** travel agency (see **Sights and Entertainment** below). The place literally sparkles with an otherworldly cleanliness; you'll see your reflection in the spotless floors and immaculate walls. The rooms smell of roses, the beds are comfortable, and the bathrooms absolutely irreproachable (singles 100 pesos; doubles 110 pesos; huge suites with kitchen 150 pesos). If you must stay in the city, there are a only few options. Hotels in Cuauhtémoc tend to cluster around the *zócalo:* the more expensive hotels are on Allende and the budget hotels on Morelos, where simple singles run only 30-40 pesos. In between is the **Nuevo Hotel Gran Visión,** on Allende between Calles 7 and 9, across from the bus station, which offers tidy, smallish rooms with A/C, TV, and phones (singles 110 pesos; doubles 120 pesos; triples 140 pesos).

**Food**  If you're here to sample Mennonite culture, you might as well get out of the dirty city and into the ultra-clean kitchen of a Mennonite restaurant. Most have sinks with hand soap *outside* the bathroom because they're used so much. A few restaurants line the main highway through the *campos*—try the **Travelers Restaurant** (tel. 2-64-70), between *Campo* 3B and *Campo* 19 near the Motel Gasthaus. Traditional Mennonite foods are very rich and very tasty: the *empanadas de requesón* (dough filled with Mennonite cottage cheese, pirogi-like, and covered with cream sauce, 20 pesos) and *fideos con crema* (noodles with ham or sausage, also drowned in cream sauce, 19 pesos) are not exceptions. Eat here more than twice, however, and your cholesterol count may hit quadruple digits (open daily 9am-9pm). Also nearby is a tan brick structure housing **Pizzeria Los Arcos** (tel. 1-20-38), where you can enjoy non-Mennonite food such as hamburgers (7 pesos), burritos (6 pesos), or enchiladas (15 pesos) in traditional Mennonite style—that is, the floors are so clean you could eat off them. In the city, **El Den,** Allende at Coello (tel. 2-38-43), across from the *zócalo,* has cafeteria-style service including *comida corrida* (23 pesos) and an excellent vegetarian platter (26 pesos; open daily 7:30am-10:30pm).

**Sights and Entertainment**  There are a handful of ways to explore the Mennonite communities of Cuauhtémoc. **Public buses** head into the area (every hr., 20min., 8 pesos), letting passengers off anywhere along the way. Hitchhiking is reputedly extremely easy on and off the main highway. The Mennonite father-and-son team **Cumbres Friesen,** at Calle 3 between Rayón and Guerrero (tel. 2-54-57 or 2-30-64; fax 2-40-60), provide tours tailored to your interests for around US$10 per person, depending on the sights you want to cover and the duration of the tour (open Mon.-Fri 9am-7pm, Sat. 9am-1pm). The owner of **Motel Gasthaus** also offers tours. Tours typically include a look inside an authentic Mennonite home, a tour of a cheese factory and a machinery plant, and a meal (at your expense) at a Mennonite restaurant. If you want to check out the Mennonite colony on your own, you'll need a car to get from place to place. To see a Mennonite cheese factory in action, take a left at the 2-B/22 sign and follow the road heading down into the village. After passing a school and church (only open Sun.) on your left, take a right into the **Quesería**

**América,** one of the 20-25 cheese factories in the 80 or so Mennonite villages in the area. Make sure you visit in the morning, when the cheese is actually made. To see a genuine **Mennonite household,** take a left at the "Hotel La Estancia" sign at *Campo* 6A. Follow the road about 2km, then take a right down another road for a bit. You'll see a white house with a blue stripe around the bottom, surrounded by a white picket fence and tall trees; it's home to the **familia Guenther.** The friendly, Spanish-speaking family will show you their huge but stark kitchen with its jam-filled pantry, their living room, and their special guest room with a valuable wooden chair. Big families are standard among the Mennonites, and the Guenthers are no exception: Mrs. Guenther's 12 children all live nearby. After taking you on a tour of the house, Mrs. Guenther will offer her traditional Mennonite knitted crafts for sale. Outside, scope out the horizon for the **radio tower,** through which Mennonites communicated before they succumbed to that modern luxury, telephones. Before, they all had walkie-talkies. 10-4 *familia* Guenther.

# ■ Creel

High amid the startling peaks and gorges of the Sierra Madres and lodged among pine forests, log cabins, and rolling hills and valleys, the small village of Creel (pop. 5000, altitude 2340m) welcomes travelers with natural beauty, human warmth, and refreshing, mountain-pine air. The village resembles a frontier town of the late 1800s: smoke billows from the chimneys of the humble but picturesque huts to counter the chilly climate; the train rumbles through the middle of town at least twice a day; and horses, pigs, and cows are as common to Creel's streets as the rugged, cowboy-hat-wearing villagers to whom they sometimes belong.

Creel is most popular as a base from which to explore the stunning Copper Canyon. Although tourism to the town has increased of late, it hasn't damaged the unique ambience of the town nor substantially altered the lives of the Tarahumara Indians, at least those of whom are among the 50,000 living in the mountains surrounding the town. Of Mexico's many *indígena* groups, the Tarahumara have best warded off modern Mexican culture, living in isolated caves and wooden houses and resisting all efforts to settle them in villages. Well adapted to their rugged environment, the Tarahumara construct plows from the limbs of oak trees and are skilled in the preparation of 200 species of edible plants. They are famous for their non-stop long-distance sacred footraces, which last up to 72 hours. Tarahumara pine-needle baskets, blankets, figurines, and violins are sold throughout town.

While many Tarahumara come to Creel to sell their crafts or pick up supplies, they greatly value their seclusion and tend to shy away from contact with tourists. If you pass Tarahumara cave dwellings, look at the caves from the road, but don't take their obvious accessibility as an invitation to approach more closely or take photographs. The countryside around Creel is also home to a number of other *indígena* groups, including the Pima in the northwest, the Northern Tepehuan to the south, and the Guarojio to the west.

## ORIENTATION AND PRACTICAL INFORMATION

You can use the railroad tracks as a rough compass: towards Chihuahua is north and towards Los Mochis is south. The **train station** is located just northwest of the *zócalo,* and the **bus station** is right across the tracks and farther north. To reach the *zócalo,* walk one block along the tracks in the direction of Los Mochis and turn left. The main street, **Mateos,** runs parallel to the trains on the opposite side of the *zócalo.* Street numbers go up to the right and down to the left as you turn onto Mateos from the tracks. **Chapultepec,** farther north, runs parallel to Mateos and up to the tracks. **Avenidas Ferrocarril** and **Francisco Villa** run parallel to the train tracks on the opposite side of Mateos.

**Tourist Information: Artesanías Misión** (tel. 6-00-97), on the north side of the *zócalo.* Not an official tourist office, but the best source of information on Creel and the surrounding area. Sells books about the Tarahumara, crafts, and maps (12-40 pesos). The mission supports the Tarahumara's cultural development, and the local hospital receives store profits. English spoken. Open Mon.-Sat. 9:30am-1pm and 3-6pm, Sun. 9:30am-1pm.

**Currency Exchange: Banca Serfín** (tel. 6-02-50 or 6-00-60), next door to the Misión. Dollars exchanged 9am-1:30pm. Open Mon.-Fri. 9am-5pm.

**Telephones: No LADATELs** in town, but black coin-operated phones all around. Long-distance service is available at the **Papelería de Todo,** Mateos 30 (tel. 6-01-22 or 6-02-22). Open daily 9am-8pm.

**Fax:** In the same building as the post office. Open Mon.-Fri. 9am-3pm.

**Buses: Estrella Blanca** (tel. 6-00-73), in a small white and green building across the tracks from the *zócalo*. To Cuauhtémoc (3hr., 53 pesos) and Chihuahua (7 per day, 5hr., 80 pesos). From the Restaurant Herradero at Mateos 39, **Canyon buses** (tel. 6-02-79 or 6-02-30) leave for Batopilas (Tues., Thurs., and Sat. 7:15am, 6hr., 75 pesos; return trip leaves Batopilas Mon., Wed., and Fri. at 5:30am).

**Trains:** Av. Tarahumara 57 (tel. 6-00-15), right in town on the tracks—you can't miss it. Trains leave daily for Chihuahua (1st class 3:15pm, 6hr., 176 pesos; 2nd class 5pm, 7hr., 35 pesos) and Los Mochis (1st class 12:25pm, 9hr., 210 pesos; 2nd class 2pm, 10hr., 42 pesos). Ride out to the Divisadero station at Barrancas del Cobre on the Los Mochis-bound train (1st class 12:25pm, 1½hr., 71 pesos; 2nd class 2pm, 1½hr., 14 pesos). Tickets go on sale at 11:30am for the 1st-class train to Los Mochis and a half-hour before departure time for other trains. Some trains might be "full," in which case you should scramble on quickly and aggressively when the train arrives and purchase a ticket on board. Never count on a train leaving on schedule (station open Mon.-Fri. 10am-4pm, Sat. 10am-2pm).

**Bicycle Rental: Expediciones Umarike,** south along the tracks next to the 2-story cabin. Rents bikes (65-80 pesos per day, ½ day 40-50 pesos, 12 pesos per hr.) as well as helmet and gloves (15 pesos); they also offer a ½-day introductory rock climbing course (150 pesos per person, min. 2 people). Bikes can also be rented from **Complejo Turístico Arareko,** Mateos 33 (tel. 6-01-26), south of the *zócalo.*

**Market: Abarrotes Pérez,** on Mateos next to Cabañas Bertis. Fruit, vegetables, and purified water. Open daily 9am-9pm.

**Laundromat: Lavandería Veno,** Francisco Villa 112 (tel. 6-01-39). Across the tracks from the police. 15 pesos per load for wash and dry. Bring your load by 6pm if you want same-day service. Open daily 9am-8pm.

**Pharmacy: Farmacia Rodríguez,** Mateos 43 (tel. 6-00-52). Open Mon.-Sat. 9am-2pm and 3:30-9pm, Sun. 10am-1pm.

**Medical Services: Clínica Santa Teresita,** on Calle Parroquia (tel. 6-01-05) at the end of the street, two blocks from Mateos. Little English spoken. Open Mon.-Fri. 10am-1pm and 3-5pm, Sat. 10am-1pm. Open for emergencies 24hr.

**Police:** Tel. 6-04-50. In the Presidencia Seccional, on the south side of the *zócalo.*

**Post Office:** Tel. 6-02-58. In the Presidencia Seccional, on the south side of the *zócalo.* Open Mon.-Fri. 9am-3pm. **Postal Code:** 33200.

**Phone Code:** 145.

## ACCOMMODATIONS AND CAMPING

Due to Creel's flourishing popularity, the number of hotels here has multiplied and competition for tourists' pesos has become intense. Prices are often negotiable during low season, and budget rooms are never hard to find.

**Margarita's Casa de Huéspedes,** Mateos 11 (tel. 6-00-45), across from the *zócalo.* An international backpacker's mecca. You'll have no trouble finding it—a young emissary meets every train and bus to lead you to the house, where you mingle with Margarita's family, friends, and guests, who come from every corner of the globe. Make it clear that you want to go to the *casa,* not the hotel. Freshly renovated rooms are spacious and beautifully furnished with floor tiles and pine furniture. To top it all off, prices include two home-cooked meals. English-speaking staff. Tours offered. Bed in shared rooms 20-30 pesos; a spot on the floor costs just 10 pesos. If you must sleep alone, Margarita's has private rooms too: Singles 100 pesos; doubles 130 pesos. Prices are negotiable, and you may be able to work for room and board.

**Cabañas Bertis,** Mateos 31 (tel. 6-00-86). Log cabin feel with paneled walls, thick wool blankets, and a fireplace or wood stove in each abode. A/C and heater. Tours offered. Singles 50 pesos; doubles 120 pesos; triples 150 pesos.

**Pensión Creel,** Mateos 61 (tel. 6-00-71; fax 6-00-82). Walk down Mateos away from the *zócalo.* Budget rooms available farther from downtown near the trails and woods. Boasts a fully equipped kitchen, a large common room with a roaring fireplace and magazine shelf, and shared bathrooms. Complimentary bus service transports you to the *pensión,* though it is within walking distance. Prices range from 45 pesos (if you have your own sleeping bag) to 90 pesos (with continental breakfast). French and English spoken.

**Hotel Korachi,** Francisco Villa (tel. 6-02-07) across the tracks from the train station. A wanna-be hunting lodge. Clean bedrooms with dark, wood-paneled walls and comfy beds, and wood and gas heaters in the bathroom. Singles 80 pesos; doubles 120 pesos. Strange but clean *cabañas* with animal skins on the walls sit under shady trees and include private bath and wood supply. Singles 120 pesos; doubles 150 pesos.

For those who'd rather immerse themselves in nature, the campground and lodges around Lago Arareko are the way to go. The **campground** (10 pesos per person) is on the northwestern shore, on a hill overlooking the lake. The site sports 31 barbecue and fire pits, 12 latrines, hot showers, and picnic areas. The **Segórachi Cabin** fits 16 and contains a living room, kitchen, fireplace, and grill; guests are pampered with laundry service and a complimentary boat for use on the lake. The **Batosárachi Lodge,** on the southeast corner of this vast body of water, houses up to 50 in the three Tarahumara-style cabins (each has bunk beds, a common room, heaters, and hot water). At both places, guests can cook their own meals or let themselves be served. The lake is 8km from town, or a five-minute drive.

## FOOD

There are several inexpensive restaurants in town with friendly atmospheres and good, home-cooked fare. Picnicking spots lie on the quiet hillsides outside town.

**La Cabaña,** Mateos 36 (tel. 6-00-68), south of the *zócalo.* You can almost hear the birds chirping and the sap dripping as you recline in one of the pinewood stalls. Take in the stuffed game, the landscape drawings, and the big burritos (7 pesos). Open daily 8am-10pm.

**Jorge's,** Francisco Villa at Cristo Rey, south of the bus station. If thinking about the 80s leaves you hollow, don't fret; this is one place where you'll never have to ask "Where's the beef?" The super burgers (14 pesos) and enchiladas (18 pesos) practically burst at the seams with sizzling meat. Open daily 8am-11pm.

**Restaurante Todo Rico (All-Rich),** Mateos 37 at Chapultepec (tel. 6-02-05). Lip-smacking good food served up in a bright, clean, and friendly atmosphere. *Comida corrida* is a mere 15 pesos. Try the *caldo de oso* (fish, not bear, soup) for 25 pesos, or the tuna salad (19 pesos). Open daily 7:30am-11pm.

**Restaurante Veronica,** Mateos 34. This simple joint's a local favorite. Enjoy an order of eggs any style (15 pesos), or the *comida corrida* for 16 pesos. Open daily 7:30am-11pm.

## SIGHTS AND ENTERTAINMENT

The **Casa de las Artesanías del Estado de Chihuahua** is on Avenida Ferrocarril 178 (tel. 6-00-80), in the old railroad station. There, local and Tarahumara arts, crafts, and a random assortment of historical relics are on display. But what steals the show is the mummy in the back room, which some Tarahumara claim as a relative and upon which local schoolchildren periodically sprinkle flowers (open Tues.-Sat. 9am-1pm and 3-7pm, Sun. 9am-1pm; admission 5 pesos).

At night, a local *cantina* with a touch of class is **Laylo's Lounge and Bar,** inside **El Caballo Bayo** restaurant and hotel, López Mateos 25 (tel. 6-01-36). Its male-dominated crowd is classic *cantina,* but the shiny wood paneling and nice decor outdo most watering holes. A pitch-black entryway lies between you and the inside—you must knock on the door to get inside. This place is very popular with Margarita's guests (open daily 2pm-1am). Many local hotels, including the **Motel Parador** and the **Hotel Margarita's,** keep their guests entertained with night-time diversions at the bar, including *mariachis.* Parador rocks with live music and many all-too-willing dance partners—it is the job of the *animador* to get the women up and dancing with the male patrons. While most establishments in Creel close before 9pm, a few are open late, and the town usually has a few tourists roaming the streets or strumming guitars until near midnight. On Saturday nights, the **Casino de Creel** in front of the plaza offers outdoor and indoor dances, to which both locals and tourists are welcome (men 15 pesos, women 10 pesos; festivities run from 8pm-1am).

Creel's real draw, of course, is the canyon and surrounding countryside, and you'll need either a car, a tour guide, or a brave heart to get there. Read on.

# ■ Barrancas del Cobre (Copper Canyon)

Covering an area four times the size of Arizona's Grand Canyon, the **Barrancas del Cobre,** hidden deep within the Sierra Madres, are one of the more spectacular sights in all of Mexico. The Barrancas, comprised of five interlocking canyons in an area more generally known as the **Sierra Tarahumara,** hibernate under drifts of snow during the winter months and explode with color during the rainy season (July-Sept.) when the canyon's plants are in full bloom. The Copper Canyon is criss-crossed by the tracks of the **Chihuahua-Pacífico Railroad;** trains careen along canyon walls at death-defying angles, plunge into tunnels (there are 96 of them), and briefly skim the rim of the *barrancas.* The railroad stretches from Chihuahua to Los Mochis, crossing the Continental Divide three times and soaring to a height of 2240m. Passengers peering from train windows can glimpse a breathtaking series of landscapes—cactus-covered plateaus, mountains overgrown with cedars, unusual rock formations, snow-covered summits, blue skies, and canyon floors teeming with tropical vegetation.

Perhaps the most amazing thing about the expansive and magnificent Barrancas is what a well-kept secret they are. Few foreigners, even those familiar with Mexico, have ever heard of the Copper Canyon, and fewer still could place it. This bodes well for your visit: unlike the scene at the Grand Canyon, you certainly won't have to elbow your way through a crowd to look over the edge.

Two types of trains make the daily journey between Los Mochis and Chihuahua. The first-class train is for tourists: clean, air-conditioned, equipped with bathrooms, and blessed with large, comfortable seats. The second-class train screeches along the same tracks carrying both passengers and livestock; it's a much slower, sweatier ride. Trains go from Los Mochis to Chihuahua (1st class 6am, 386 pesos; 2nd class 7am, 76 pesos) and vice-versa (1st class 7am; 2nd class 8am). Creel is the most noteworthy stop on the trip, and makes a good base from which to explore the canyon (1st class Chihuahua to Creel 6hr., 176 pesos; Los Mochis to Creel 9hr., 210 pesos, 2nd class 13hr.). The serious mountain scenery lies between Creel and El Fuerte, so if you take the second-class Los Mochis-bound train, you'll zoom by some great views in the dark. For more expansive natural spectacles, grab a seat on the **left side** of the train heading towards Los Mochis, and the **right side** if you're on the way to Chihuahua. For more information, see Creel (p. 205).

At the **Divisadero station,** the jagged mountain edges overlap to create a maze of gorges and rocks at the rim of the Barrancas del Cobre. Eight hours out of Los Mochis, the first-class train stops here for 15 minutes of sightseeing. Everyone on board scrambles out, sprints to the brink, gapes, and sprints back. On the second-class train, it's less formal. Ask the conductor when the train is going to leave, and be back early. During this stop, you will have a chance to buy crafts directly from the Tarahumara

Barrancas del Cobre
(Copper Canyon)

Indians who live in the area. Also, you can take advantage of the opportunity to grab a good, cheap, quick bite to eat. Try a *gordita* for about 6 pesos.

## THE ROAD SOUTH TO BATOPILAS

Heading south from Creel, a road winds through the more scenic parts of the Copper Canyon. Buses rumble past nail-biting hairpin turns, balancing in one lane on the edges of steep cliffs that will make your heart pound both from excitement at the view and nervousness as you put your life in the hands of a stranger at the wheel. The road has been called North America's most spectacular by many, but, unpaved most of the way, it is also one of the continent's most treacherous. The first 75km section of the road just south of Creel is happily two-laned and paved.

On the right side heading south, still-inhabited **Tarahumara caves** are within view of the road. On tours, it's possible to go in and visit the homes for a small donation.

Beds and other furniture, woodstoves with chimneys, and kerosene lamps adorn the insides of many of the dismal, stone-walled caves.

Four kilometers down the road from Creel (and a left on a dirt road) lies the humble **San Ignacio Mission,** constructed in 1744 and still in use today—services are conducted in Rarámuri, the native language of the Tarahumara (Sun. 11am). The stone mission is dedicated to Saint Ignatius Loyola, the community's patron saint, and can easily be combined in a daytrip with the **Valle de los Hongos** (Valley of the Mushroom, a.k.a. Valley of the Frogs or Ducks). The valley contains immense, oddly shaped stones formed by the San Ignacio River. To reach the valley and mission by foot, walk down Mateos past the Motel Parador. When the road forks, take the smaller branch to the left, beside the cemetery. A kilometer or so out of town you will pass through the gates of the Tarahumara's *ejidos* (communal lands), containing the caves in which they live. After the cultivated fields, the valley is to the right and the mission at the bottom of the hill. On the way you will pass through small dells and plains surrounded by rocky cliffs, pines, and oak trees characteristic of the Tarahumara highlands.

Travelers can also hike to **Laguna Arareko,** an enormous lake 3km long and eight acres in area. Just bear right when the road forks past Mateos and follow the path 7km southeast. The water here is cold and contains dangerous weeds below the surface, so swimming is discouraged. From the small station next to the lake you can rent paddle boats. Nearby is **Recohuata Hot Springs,** where you can take a break from a long day of hiking in the soothing, warm waters (admission 10 pesos). A tour guide will take you for a one-and-a-half-hour ride and then send you on a 600m hike down into the canyon (around 60 pesos). The **Valle de las Monjas** (Valley of the Nuns), 9km away, makes for a great daytrip on horseback.

Twenty-two kilometers from Creel down the road to Batopilas is the town of **Cusárare,** which features its very own 18th-century Jesuit mission. Check out the mission's Tarahumara interior, with crude wood floors and indigenous designs. There are no pews—people sit on the floor when it's used on Sundays. A boarding house for children and a small Tarahumara craft museum are nearby, but the most popular attraction in the town's vicinity is the **Cusárare Falls,** a 3km hike uphill through a pine forest. While you can't swim in the falls, the view is spectacular.

Another 20km beyond Cusárare on the road to Batopilas, **Basíhuare** is an old overnight stop once frequented by silver carriers en route to Batopilas. Excellent views of the canyon can be had here. Twenty kilometers past Basíhuare is the crossing of the highest point of the **Río Urique.** Later, the road weaves around the narrowing canyon, offering spectacular vistas as it crawls up the **Cerro de 7 Pisos** (Seven-floor Hill), so named for the seven distinct layers that lead up along the rocky inner walls of the canyon on the most frightening stretch of this incredible one-lane path. The seven steps can best be seen from **La Bufa,** 60km from Basíhuare and past the fork, a scenic lookout that has the most magnificent view of all. If you have good vision, you can make out the tiny thread that is the Río Urique far, far below and the yellow wooden bridge that runs across it. If you're driving, pull off onto the shoulder, and try not to look down. Get out and gape. Then gape some more. If you go left at the fork, you'll come to **Norogachi,** a Tarahumara mission center at the river with beautiful (but touristy) Semana Santa services, and **Guachochi,** a rocky, frontier-like village with both colonial and Tarahumara influences.

The right fork will take you to the more impressive town of **Batopilas** (see below). On the way you'll pass the bridge that spans the Urique; you can get out and walk down into the bushes for a smashing view of the waterfall down below. Keep your eyes peeled for **Tescalama trees,** which have yellow flowers and grow out of the sides of sheer rock. The last quarter of the ride to Batopilas also has plenty of **piedra cobriza** (copper rock), which gives the canyon its copper tint.

**Getting There: Margarita's** and **Cabañas Bertis** in Creel (see p. 206) offer trips that cover Cusárare (mission and falls), Lake Arareko, a Tarahumara cave, and the **Elephant Rock.** It's a four-hour trip and runs about 60 pesos per person for at least five people. Bertis also runs trips to San Ignacio Mission, Lake Arareko, Valley of the Mushrooms, and the Elephant Rock (2hr., 50 pesos per person). Tours that go as far as La Bufa run 150 pesos per person from Margarita's, 120 pesos from Cabañas Bertis (min. 6 people; 10-hour round-trip). On any trip, remember to bring plenty of water and food, adequate footwear, and protection from the sun. If you're averse to walking, you can arrange to navigate on bikes, horses, or even donkeys for a few extra pesos. **Pensión Creel,** Mateos 61 (tel. 6-00-71; fax 6-02-00), **Hotel Nuevo,** and **Motel Parador,** Mateos 44 (tel. 6-00-75; fax 6-00-85), offer somewhat more expensive tours.

## BATOPILAS AND SATEVÓ

**Batopilas** (pop. 1200) is a tiny village nestled in the depths of the canyon, a mile below the rest of civilization, along the Río Urique, a rough 35km from La Bufa and a thrilling but scary 140km (6hr. by van, 8hr. by bus) from Creel. Batopilas was a silver-mining boom town founded in 1708. Its rich silver supply lasted until the late 1800s, which is why such a secluded place was the second city in all Mexico (after Mexico City) to receive electricity. Nowadays, phone service is limited to a single *caseta* in the center of town, a symbol of how little remains of the town's glory days. The wind whistles nostalgically through holes in once-proud hacienda walls, from which leafy vegetation has sprouted along Batopilas's steamy riverbank.

Everything in Batopilas centers around the **old stone plaza,** referred to as the *parque.* Streets do have names, but locals don't use them. The main street (which connects Batopilas to Creel and the rest of the world) splits off into two streets, one of which encounters a dead end while the other becomes Juárez. At the main plaza, Juárez splits off into two more streets. At the end of the northernmost of these (farther from the river) is a second, **smaller plaza** dedicated to Don Manuel Gómez Marín, founder of the PAN political party. Across from the north side of the plaza is the Presidencia Municipal, headquarters of the Batopilas **police.** For medical attention, try the **Red Cross** on the main street. The lonely *caseta* (tel. 6-06-32, 6-06-33, or 6-06-24) is on the east side of the plaza. Calls cost 2.50 pesos per minute (open Mon.-Sat. 9am-1pm and 3-7pm, Sun. 3-7pm). The **post office** is close to where the main street first forks (open Mon.-Fri 9am-4pm). **Postal code:** 33400. **Phone code:** 145.

A good choice for lodging in town is the **Hotel Mary,** Juárez 15, next to the church near the plaza. Large, rustic adobe rooms with ceiling fans are naturally cool (50 pesos per person). The nearby **Hotel Batopilas** offers dark, spacious rooms that could be cleaner (singles 25 pesos, with bath 30 pesos; doubles 40 pesos). Word has it that a new hotel, **Chula Vista,** is at the entrance of town, sporting A/C (singles 45 pesos, with bath 60 pesos; doubles 75 pesos, with bath 100 pesos). During low season, restaurants' opening and closing times are left to the whims of visitors. Try **Restaurant Carolina** on the main street near the entrance to town. The menu includes *carne machaca* and *tacos dorados de machaca* for 30 pesos. Another eatery in town that's reliably open is the Hotel Mary's **Quinto Patio.** Enchiladas with fresh cheese (20 pesos), an order of tacos (20 pesos), and *bistek* (27 pesos) are on the menu, but you're limited to whatever happens to be in the fridge at the time. Check out the old lightbulbs converted to flowerpots (open daily 7am-3pm).

The magnificent **haciendas** in ruins along the river are poignant reminders of the excesses of the owners in the silver-mining days of Batopilas. The brown, castle-like **Hacienda Shepard** belonged to an American, and its ruins now stand in contrast to the green of the surrounding trees and canyon. Look for the *tescalama* trees growing sideways out of the brown walls of the hacienda. Hikes from Batopilas leave daily for the **Porfirio Díaz mine** in town and the more interesting **Peñasquito,** an hour hike up a steep hill; for **Cerro Colorado,** a section of the old Camino Real to Chihuahua during the mining boom, a 12-hour hike; and for the lost mission of **Satevó** (see below). The best source of information about departing tours is the **Riverside Lodge,** in town diagonally across from the plaza on the bench side (not the basketball-court side). A restored hacienda, the lodge is now an incredibly posh package-tour inn—stop by and check out the luxuriant piano room and the view from the rooftop. The historical photos on the walls may be the most interesting exhibits. Check out an 1899 shot of Pancho Villa at age 22, a photo of gold bars stacked to the ceiling, and another of the day when the river ran as high as the hotel wall. **Artesanías Monse,** on the south side of the plaza, offers the opportunity to view and purchase handicrafts from Tarahumara *gentiles*—supposedly the least Christianized of the Tarahumara. You might get a chance to meet the artists who often hang out in the garden in the back. If you've yet to find a place to stay, the owner of Artesanías Monse might be able to offer some suggestions.

The most fascinating excursion from Batopilas is to **Satevó,** a minuscule town with a spooky and beautiful mission. It's a 40-minute drive (you'll need 4WD or, better yet, pixie dust) or a two-hour walk. In the middle of a fertile valley straddled by the towering canyon rises a lonesome, round mission shrouded in mystery. Why was it built here of all places? When was it built? (The 15th or 16th century are the best guesses, but no one knows.) And finally, how did the Tarahumara, barely able to find shelter for themselves, gather up the energy and desire to build such a thing? In any case, it's a sight to behold, especially at sunset, when the rays play off the red bricks of the roundhouse-like construction, combining with the clouds and valley to create a heavenly scene. In order to take a peek inside the mission, you'll have to tip the **family living next door;** they have the key. The inside of the mission is even eerier, with ancient tombs below and darkness above.

**Getting There:** Take the local bus from Creel to Batopilas (see p. 206). The bus makes a couple of stops during the six-hour trip, allowing you to grab a bite to eat or simply gape at spectacular scenery (the La Bufa stop is mind-blowing). If you want to step it up a notch, few places offer excursions to Batopilas. **Cabañas Bertis** (p. 207) offers a two-day trip for a minimum of six people that includes a one-night stay in the Hotel Mary (280 pesos per person). **Margarita's** (p. 206) does not organize formal trips to Batopilas, but if enough people are interested, a guide will travel with a group (min. 6 people) for 200 pesos per person.

## BASASEACHI FALLS NATIONAL PARK

With water cascading from a height of 246m, the **Basaseachi Falls** are one of the world's most spectacular waterfalls. Basaseachi (Tarahumaran for "place of the cascade" or "place of the coyotes") is the highest waterfall in Mexico and the fourth highest in North America. Few waterfalls are blessed with such gorgeous surroundings. This is the sight most associated with the region, and a not-to-be-missed excursion from Creel and the Chihuahua-Pacífico Railroad. From the village, a half-hour hike down leads to the "window"—the best view of the falls. The three-hour hike down to the base of the falls is picturesque and fascinating, but also steep and difficult.

**Getting There: Estrella Blanca** buses run to Basaseachi village from Cuauhtémoc (see p. 203). From Creel, trips through **Cabañas Bertis** (p. 207) to the village of Basaseachi run 140 pesos per person (min. 6). It's a 127km trip on unpaved roads or 210 less-scenic kilometers on paved roads. **Margarita's** (p. 206) runs the trip for 150 pesos per person.

## SOUTH OF CREEL TO URIQUE

It's a 154km jaunt from Creel to Urique. Along the way, partly on the Chihuahua-Pacífico railroad, are Divisadero, Bahuichivo, and Cerocahui. **Divisadero** is a train stop 51km south of Creel on the Chihuahua-Pacíficio railroad. It can also be reached by road from Creel. **Margarita's** (see p. 206) charges 70 pesos per person for an excursion. Aside from claiming an amazing vista of the canyon (perhaps the fullest view of the Barrancas anywhere), Divisadero is also home to **La Piedra Volada,** a large, precariously balanced stone. It is technically possible (though quite difficult) to attempt a full-day hike between Cusárare and Divisadero, but an experienced guide is a must. A far more manageable and popular hike from Divisadero (which might force you to stay at the pricey hotel, as camping is not recommended) is down into the canyon— you can go as far as you want. A four-hour, 4km round-trip hike leads to the Tarahumara village **Bacajipare,** while the 27km descent to the bottom of the canyon from

Divisadero takes eight hours each way. Guides for hire hang around the hotel, and they'll take you down to the Río Urique, to Bacajipare, or elsewhere.

**Bahuichivo,** in a clearing in the forest, is another stop on the railroad, 97km south of Creel. There's not much to see there, but it's often used as a departure point for spots deeper in the canyon or Cerocahui and Urique, farther south. The beautiful mountain village of **Cerocahui** (pop. 600, elevation 1525m) is 17km southeast of Bahuichivo. You can grab a white "Transportes Cañón Urique" bus or van (10 pesos), which also goes to Urique, right at the Bahuichivo train station. The main attraction is the **Jesuit Mission,** founded in 1681 by the priest Juan María de Salvatierra. **Sangre de Cristo** (gold and silver mines), the **Gallego Mountain** (38km away), the **Misión Churo,** and the **Yeparavo waterfall** (4km south) are among the possible excursions from Cerocahui.

The village of **Urique** sits in the **Barranca de Urique,** the deepest of the canyons. The three-hour, edge-of-your-seat ride from Bahuichivo to Urique takes you from a cool, frontier-like town in the forest to a warm, tropical village where the mango trees share the same humid air as the cacti beside them. About halfway down to Urique, the canyon will open up, mesmerizing you with magnificent cliffs, painted by lush, green vegetation and set against a pristine sky. Look down at the white spots along the Urique river—that's the village of Urique. The miniscule town (pop. 1000) is divided into two main streets, one of which heads straight into town. The limited services available in Urique are all in the plaza, including the **police** (at the pink building) and *caseta* (in the blue building; open Mon.-Sat. 8am-1pm and 2-7pm, Sun. 8am-noon). Accommodations in Urique are fairly cheap; options include the **campgrounds** on the main street, on the edge of town (15 pesos per person), and the **Hotel Cañon Urique,** on the main street, which offers clean, dark, spacious rooms (singles 40 pesos; doubles 80 pesos; triples 100 pesos). Travelers can also spend the night in Bahuichivo at **Hotel Cola de Caballo** or three or so other places in town. **Restaurant Jardín,** in the center, is a local pick.

**Getting There:** To get to Urique from Creel, take the Los Mochis-bound morning train and get off at Bahuichivo (1st class 12:25pm, 3½hr., 71 pesos). From there, take a bus to Urique (3hr., 40 pesos). If you arrive in Bahuichivo on the second-class train, there will be a van, instead of a bus, waiting to take you to Urique. To get back, the bus to Bahuichivo leaves Urique at 8:30am and supposedly arrives back in time for the Chihuahua-bound first-class train.

# SINALOA

## ▨ Los Mochis

The nucleus of an extremely fertile region of crops, Los Mochis (often just called "Mochis") is an important stop on a cross-country voyage, linked to the Baja peninsula (by a ferry departing from Topolobampo to La Paz) and the Barrancas del Cobre (by rail to Creel). Most travelers, repulsed by the city's congested, dirty streets, smoggy air, and cultural void, use Mochis as little more than a departure point.

**Orientation** The city is laid out in a simple grid. The main streets running parallel to one another are **Constitución, Degollado, Allende, Prieto, Zaragoza, Leyva,** and **Flores.** Perpendicular to these streets are **Ordoñez, Castro, Obregón, Hidalgo, Independencia, Juárez, Morelos, Madero, Bravo, Carranza,** and **Serdán.**

**Practical Information** Set office hours are the butt of town jokes. The **tourist office,** on Obregón and Allende (tel./fax 12-66-40), is in the Municipal Transit Building. As you walk into the main entrance on Ordoñez, follow the hallway on your left. After turning the first corner, the tourist office is the room at the end of the hall (open Mon.-Fri. 9am-3pm). For your banking needs, try the **Bancomer** on Leyva and Juárez (tel. 15-80-01; open Mon.-Fri. 8:30am-2pm and 3:30-7pm, Sat. 10am-2pm). Four 24-hour **ATMs** are at your disposal. The **Tourist Security** number is 91-800-90-392. **LADATELs** are scattered throughout downtown; when making local calls within the city, add "1" before any number with only five digits. Given the number of travel agencies in town, the residents of Los Mochis seem to be aware that their role in tourism is to help visitors get somewhere else. To purchase tickets in advance, try **Viajes Conelva,** Leyva 525 at Valdez (tel. 15-60-90 or 15-80-90), inside Hotel El Dorado (open Mon.-Sat. 8am-7pm, Sun. 9am-2pm).

The **ferry** to La Paz leaves from Topolobampo at 10am every day except Sunday and arrives at 8am the next morning (*salón*-class tickets 116 pesos per person; 1100 pesos per car). Buy tickets at the **Sematur** office in Topolobampo on Rendón 519 (tel. (686) 2-01-41; fax (686) 2-00-35; open Mon.-Fri. 8am-1pm and 3-7pm, Sun. 9am-1pm; hours erratic). Tickets must be purchased one day in advance (before 11am) at the Sematur office or on the day of departure on the ferry at Topolobampo. To get to the office, walk nine blocks from Juárez on Flores, then turn left on Rendón. In the mornings, a **bus** runs to Topolobampo (every 20min., starting at 6am, 5 pesos); the bus leaves from a side street between Hidalgo and Obregón near Hotel Santa Anita. It can also be flagged down on Cuauhtémoc between Prieta and Zaragoza.

The **Chihuahua al Pacífico train** (tel. 12-08-47) runs back and forth from Los Mochis to Chihuahua, passing through the Copper Canyon. At the Divisadero stop, just south of Creel, tourists are allowed to get off the train and gape for 15 minutes. Unfortunately, the train can be unreliable due to frequent problems, including **derailments** and **landslides.** The first-class train passes through at 6am (210 pesos to Creel; 380 pesos to Chihuahua); be in the station by 4:30am or earlier to get in the snail-paced ticket line. If the train looks like it's about to leave and you're still in line, you may want to ditch the line and push your way onto the train; what can the conductors do but sell you a ticket if you're already on? The train arrives in Creel around 4pm. A second-class train, which departs from Los Mochis on Tuesdays, Thursdays, and Saturdays, supposedly leaves at 7am and arrives in Creel after dark. A better alternative to waiting in the ticket line is buying your ticket beforehand from a travel agency. You'll have much more peace of mind come sunrise. After dark, or early in the morning, the train-bound become the captives of cagey taxi drivers (50 pesos to downtown). This desperate situation tempts otherwise scrupulous travelers to bluff their way onto the free bus to and from the Hotel Santa Anita. To catch a public bus from the station back to town during the daylight hours (every 15min., 3 pesos), just walk away from the station down the road about 100m. If you miss the train and must get to Chihuahua or Creel, the best alternative (the coolest spot in hell) is to get a bus to Hermosillo (8hr.) and then catch the overnight Hermosillo-Chihuahua bus (8pm, 14hr., 217 pesos). From Chihuahua, buses run regularly to Creel (5hr., 80 pesos).

**Transportes Norte de Sonora** (tel. 12-17-57), and **Elite** (tel. 18-49-67) **buses** operate out of the modern terminal at the corner of Juárez and Degollado. **Transportes Norte de Sonora,** usually the cheapest carrier, runs buses to Guyamas (every hr., 5hr., 70 pesos), Mazatlán (every hr., 5am-5pm, 5½hr., 128 pesos), Mexicali (7 and 8:15am, 18hr., 353 pesos), Mexico City (6pm, 24hr., 528 pesos) via Culiacán (3hr., 50 pesos), and Tijuana (4, 7, and 8:15pm, 22hr., 423 pesos) via Hermosillo (7hr., 99 pesos). **Transportes del Pacífico,** on Morelos between Leyva and Zaragoza (tel. 12-03-47 and 12-03-41), sends *de paso* buses south to Mazatlán and north through Guaymas, Hermosillo, and Mexicali to Tijuana. These buses are relatively cheap, but often packed by the time they reach Los Mochis. Seats are easier to obtain on the slower *local* buses to Guadalajara, Mazatlán, and Tijuana (approximately 3 per day). Buses to El Fuerte and other destinations leave from Zaragoza, between Ordoñez and Cuauhtémoc. **Norte de Sinaloa** (tel. 18-03-57) sends a large fleet of rickety green buses every 15 minutes to Culiacán (3½hr., 40 pesos), Guasave (1hr., 15 pesos), Guamuchil (2hr., 20 pesos). For **taxis,** call 2-02-83.

For fresh fish, fruit, and vegetables, check out the **market** in the area around Zaragoza between Castro and Ordoñez; on weekends it bustles with activity (most stores close around 7pm). Los Mochis's hippest threads get washed and dried at **Lavamatic,**

Allende 218 just before Juárez (20 pesos; open Mon.-Sat. 7am-7pm, Sun. 7am-1pm). The **Red Cross,** at Tenochtitlán and Prieto (tel. 15-08-08 or 12-02-92), one block off Castro, has 24-hour ambulance service. **Super Farmacia San Jorge,** Juárez and Degollado (tel. 18-18-19), is open 24 hours. Hit the **Hospital Fátima,** Blvd. Jiquilpán Pte. 639 (tel. 12-33-12), to check out the local medical scene. No English is spoken. The **Centro de Salud** can be reached at 12-07-74. In case of **emergency,** call 06. The **police** are at Degollado at Cuauhtémoc in the Presidencia Municipal (tel. 12-00-33). No English is spoken. The **post office** is at Ordóñez 226 (tel. 12-08-23), two blocks off Castro, between Prieta and Zaragoza (open Mon.-Fri. 8am-7pm). **Postal Code:** 81200. **Phone Code:** 68.

**Accommodations** Budget hotels of variable quality are sprinkled throughout the downtown area demarcated by Castro, Juárez, Leyva, and Constitución. Mention that you're a tourist when negotiating a price at a hotel—Los Mochis's crusade to enhance tourism includes offering tourists lower prices at hotels. **Hotel Montecarlo,** Flores 322 Sur (tel. 12-18-18), a gracefully aging blue building at the corner of Independencia, has large rooms surrounding a quiet, palatial indoor courtyard. A/C, fans, and cable TV make life much easier. Take a room downstairs if you can—they're much cooler (singles 110 pesos; for 2 people 120 pesos; doubles 140 pesos). At **Hotel Hidalgo,** Hidalgo 260 Pte. (tel. 12-34-56), between Prieta and Zaragoza, ceiling fans and chilly colors (deep blue furniture and baby blue walls) cool the small rooms. If there's a soccer game on the tube, the lobby becomes a local hang-out (singles 90 pesos, with A/C 100 pesos; doubles 110 pesos; each additional person 10 pesos). If you want to pamper yourself before or after your long trip, try the **Hotel Fenix,** on Flores Sur 365 between Independencía and Hidalgo (tel. 12-26-23 or 12-26-25; fax 15-89-48). Sit in the elegant wood lobby and hang with the businessmen also staying at the hotel before heading up to your carpeted, clean room with cable TV and A/C. Laundry service is available. The day's newspaper is delivered to you in the morning (singles 125 pesos; doubles 155 pesos; triples 175 pesos; additional person 15 pesos).

**Food** The crowning virtue of this farming region is the **public market** along Zaragoza between Castro and Ordóñez, where prices are low and quality is high. Be there before stores start to close around 7pm. The *taquerías* and *loncherías* in the market dish out cheap, home-brewed enigmas, many of which pack quite a wallop. Except for the *cantinas* (which women should avoid) and the corner *taquerías,* just about everything in town shuts down at 9pm; alcohol evaporates at 11pm. Good, cheap *tortas* can be found on Independencia and Hidalgo. Try **Tortas Moka,** Independencía 216 at Prieto (tel. 12-39-41), where you can enjoy a *torta* (8 pesos) while you people-watch. **El Farallón,** at Obregón and Flores (tel. 2-14-28 or 2-12-73), the first restaurant in the city to serve shellfish, and was also famous for its sea turtles before

NORTHWEST MEXICO

---

### Time Out: Topolobampo

Topolobampo is a decent place to spend the day, especially if you're stuck in life-less Los Mochis and willing to dish out the cash for an excursion—just about the only worthwhile activity there. When Albert Owen set out to forge his socialist utopia, he certainly didn't envision today's Topolobampo, a small fishing village helped along by the tourists who swim with the dolphins in the port's warm waters. From the bus station, hang a left and follow the street to the shore, where boats and taxis run trips to the outlying attractions. For 70 pesos, a boat will usher you to **Playa El Maviri,** a fairly well-developed beach. Perhaps more interesting is **El Farallón,** a distant island where sea lions and pelicans run (er, swim and fly) free, and a hill juts out to the waters. While there are no beaches on the island, snorkeling and swimming are still possible. A full-day boat trip costs a wallet-shrinking 500 pesos round-trip for 5-6 people. Other destinations include the **Cerro de los Patos,** an area rife with ducks; the **Copus,** a large beach with fine sand; and the **Isla Verde,** a shallow lagoon.

they were outlawed. Ornate fishing nets and stately wooden fish decorate the walls. Spectacularly good flounder and sea bass (48 pesos), California sushi (30 pesos), and frog's legs (49 pesos) flop onto your plate in huge portions. Air-conditioning mimics an ocean breeze (open 8am-10pm). At **El Taquito,** on Leyva between Hidalgo and Independencia (tel. 2-81-19), pink window shades provide shade from the offending sun, and cold A/C dries your sweaty skin and prevents the vinyl booths from sticking to the undersides of your thighs. Waiters in red jackets serve up *enchiladas suizas* (27 pesos), hamburgers and fries (20 pesos), and cheese-filled shrimp wrapped in bacon (42 pesos). Offers group discounts (open 24hr.).

**Sights and Entertainment** Los Mochis boasts a few modest amusements, but if you can, head to Topolobampo. Catch the bus at prieto and Cuauhtémoc (every 20min., 5 pesos). One of Los Mochis's founders, the sugar baron Benjamin Johnston, assembled the extraordinary collection of trees and plants standing in **Sinaloa Park,** on Prolongación and Castro. Hundreds of species inhabit this outdoor forest-museum, where *indígena* performers strut their stuff every Sunday beginning at 11am. Bark-watchers should check out the stump at the entrance to the park; a harem of wild animals and the insignia of the state of Sinaloa have been gouged into its roughened surface. The **Museo Regional del Valle del Fuerte,** Pte. Municipal at Castro (tel. 2-46-92), was once the home of another early settler and now houses his guns and personal diary. Photographs documenting the growth and development of Northern Mexico are also on display (open Tues.-Sun. 9am-1pm and 4-7:30pm; admission 5 pesos). Across the street is the **Plaza Solidaridad,** which hosts performances every Sunday at 6pm. For a schedule of upcoming festivals and musical events at the Pl. Solidaridad and the nearby **Plazuela 27 de Septiembre,** consult the **Secretaria de Cultura y Acción Social** (tel. 5-04-05, ext. 38 or 39). Adjoining the Plaza Solidaridad is the **Santuario del Sagrado Corazón de Jesús,** Los Mochis's oldest church, which was built after Johnston's wife donated the land to the people. Many locals find it ironic that she was not even Catholic. The **Cinema 70** is on Blvd. de la Plaza. If you spend the night in Mochis, head to the **Rodeo Bar,** on Obregón and Constitución, where you can down a few beers and take the mechanical horse for a ride (open 9pm-3am).

# ▓ Mazatlán

Mazatlán (pop. 315,000) means "place of the deer" in Náhuatl. A less appropriate name can hardly be imagined, since there is nothing even remotely pastoral or ruminant about this city. The only wildlife present—genus *Gringusmaximus,* species *norteamericanus*—roams the beaches in large herds.

However, Mazatlán is truly a city divided. The **old city** is traditionally Mexican, with a shady *zócalo,* busy streets, and bustling markets that lend it a genuine charm. Nearby on the shore is the **Olas Altas** (Tall Waves) neighborhood, with a peaceful, nearly empty beach, pleasant streets, and faded resorts of yesteryear that evoke Mazatlán's glory days. The wide, breezy Malecón is a favorite destination of Mexicans and a few foreign tourists out for a stroll along the beach.

Eight kilometers or so up the Avenida del Mar, however, lies another city entirely— the **Zona Dorada** (Golden Zone), home to high-rise hotels, Disney-castle clubs and pleasure palaces, dollar-dishing Americans, time-share condos, trinket shops, and patronizingly friendly tourism agents. But the numerous honeymooners, spring-breakers, and just plain sun-seeking families that come each year to dip into the fine waters and lie on the pristine beaches of Mazatlán's ritz zone will be greeted by lower prices and nicer beaches than its Floridian and Californian counterparts, and those virtues go a long way. Because of the city's layout, though, budget travelers looking to delve a little deeper can avoid entirely the swarms of tourists and fast-food franchises concentrated in this part of town.

Mazatlán offers little of historical or cultural interest to the traveler. The city's greatest assets are gifts of nature—glorious sunsets, a glittering ocean, and wide beaches. The *Zona Dorada* is the most popular, but not necessarily the best, way to appreci-

**Mazatlán**

Hotel Belmar, **2**
Hotel Cabinas, **7**
Hotel Club Playa Mar, **6**
Hotel del Centro, **9**
Hotel Fiesta, **8**
Hotel del Río, **3**
Hotel La Siesta, **1**
Hotel Lerma, **10**
Hotel San Fernando, **5**
Market, **4**

N

0        2 miles

0        2 kilometers

*Bahía de Puerto Viejo*

**Old Mazatlán**

N

Paseo Claussen

Zaragoza

*Cerro de la Nevería (Ice Box Hill)*

**High Divers of Mazatlán**

Olas Altas

Claussen

Venus
Ohina
Rojo

①

②

**Old Mazatlán**

Ave. del Mar

México

Miramar
Castelum
Flores

Najera

16 de Septiembre

Bolívar

Tampico

Quijano

Carrasco

Rosales/Cárdenas

Zúñiga

⑨

③

Zúñiga

5 de Mayo

Guillermo Nelson

Juárez

Serdán

Azueta

Zaragoza

Morelos

Hidalgo

Villahurbide

Germán Evers

Serrano

**Hospital**

Estrada

Ocampo

Ocampo

Estrada

④

Canizales

21 de Marzo

Leandro Valle

Canizales

21 de Marzo

⑩

Dominguez

⑤

Ángel Flores

Constitución

**Plaza Revolución**

Escobedo

Constitución

Guerrero

Juárez

Serdán

Carnaval

Cerval

Galeana

Roosevelt

Barragán

Niños Héroes

Arribo

Arribo

Dominguez

Avenida Miguel Alemán

*Estero del Sábalo*

**EL CID RESORT**

**ZONA DORADA**

ⓘ

Av. de la Marina

Av. Lomas de Mazatlán

Bugambilia

Calz. Rafael Buelna

*Laguna del Camarón*

Av. Loaiza

Laguna

Av. Insurgentes

⑥

Av. del Mar

⑦

Universidad

**Bus Station**

⑧

Tamazula

Pánuco

Beltrán

San Lorenzo

Carretera Internacional

Av. Benemérito de las Américas

Piaxtla

Gavitas

*Estero del Infiernillo*

*Isla de los Lobos*

*Isla de los Venados*

**OLD MAZATLÁN**
**(See Detail Map)**

Zaragoza

Olas Altas

*Bahía de Olas Altas*

5 de Mayo

Juárez

Serdán

16 de Sept.

Carnaval

Villahurbide

A. Flores

Constitución

Germán Evers

Azueta

G. Nájera

Carrasco

Paseo Claussen

Fuerte

Baluarte

Pánuco

Av. Benemérito de las Américas

Pesqueira

**Red Cross**

Potrero del Llano

Calz. Gabriel Leyva Solano

Av. Miguel Alemán

Serdán

Av. Emilio Barragán

*Canal de Navegación*

**Mazatlán**

ate those assets. It is the more senior Old Mazatlán, its shore, and its grand old hotels that the *mariachis* evoke when they sing the classic bittersweet song of lost youth in Sinaloa.

## ORIENTATION

Built on a rocky spur jutting southwest into the Pacific, Old Mazatlán's downtown area lies north of the *zócalo*. The main street running east-west is **Ángel Flores,** the southern boundary of the *zócalo*. Farther south, the **Malecón** follows the shore line. It starts as **Olas Altas** on the south end near Old Mazatlán, then runs to the Zona Dorada 8km north, serving as the Zona Dorada's one main street; there it is called **Avenida del Mar.** In between the two areas, to the south of the fisherman's statue and north of Olas Altas, it is called **Paseo Clausen;** and to the far north, past Valentino's in the *Zona Dorada*, it's known as **Sábalo.**

Mazatlán's **bus station** is three blocks behind the Sands Hotel and about 2km north of Old Mazatlán, in Olas Altas. To head downtown from the bus station, catch the "Insurgentes" bus stop across the street (1.80 pesos). A cab will make the trip for 15 pesos. The area around the bus station, with several reasonably priced hotels and restaurants, along with a good beach and the vital "Sábalo" bus line nearby, makes a convenient home base. You can catch the downtown-bound "Insurgentes" bus at the stand one block off the beach across from the chicken barbecue establishment. From the **train station,** on the far eastern edge of Mazatlán, the yellow "Insurgentes" or the green, beat-up "Cerritos-Juárez" buses will take you downtown. From the **airport,** 18km south of the city, the "Central Camionera" bus makes the trip; the only way to get back from downtown is a 70-peso cab ride. It's a grueling 20-minute walk from the *centro* to the **ferry** docks; the blue "Playa Sur" school bus (1.50 pesos) makes the trip, and, for 10 pesos, so will a taxi.

Mazatlán's efficient **bus system** makes getting around the city a breeze. At some point, all municipal buses pass the public market on Juárez, three blocks north of the *zócalo*. The most useful bus line is the **"Sábalo-Centro."** Serviced by smaller, white, buses, this line runs from the downtown market with stops a few blocks from the Malecón in Olas Altas and at Playa Sábalo in the *Zona Dorada*. The **"Cerritos-Juárez"** bus continues up to Playa Bruja at Puerta Carritos. The **"Insurgentes"** route services the bus and train stations, and **"Playa Sur"** goes to the ferry dock and lighthouse (every 15min., 5am-midnight, 1.80 pesos). Feel free to wave down a bus at any point on its route—no official stops exist. For late-night disco hopping, you'll have to take a cab or a *pulmonía* (pneumonia), an open vehicle which resembles a golf cart that putters along blasting raucous music. Always set the price before you commit yourself to a ride; standard fare between Old Mazatlán and the *Zona Dorada* is 10 pesos. If you want to save the fare, it'll take you over an hour to walk the long path between the two sections. Olas Altas and the *centro* both make a convenient home base. The infinitely more pleasant Olas Altas is a 10-minute walk from the noisy *centro* (take a right on Angel Flores from the Malecón) and is also well-connected by bus.

## PRACTICAL INFORMATION

**Tourist Office:** Av. Camarón Sábalo and Tiburón (tel. 16-51-62 or 16-51-65; fax 16-51-66 or 16-51-67), in the *Zona Dorada*, on the 4th floor of the pinkish Banrural building past El Cid resort on the "Sábalo Centro" bus line. Helpful staff doles out much-needed Mazatlán maps. English spoken. Open Mon.-Fri. 8:30am-2pm and 5-7:30pm. **Tourist Assistance:** Tel. 91-800-90-392.

**Tourist Police:** Gabriel Ruíz and Santa Mónica (tel. 14-84-44).

**Consulates: Canada,** Loaiza at Bugambilia (tel. 13-44-55) in Hotel Playa Mazatlán. Open daily 9am-1pm. **U.S.,** Loaiza at Bugambilia (tel. 16-58-89), in front of Hotel Playa Mazatlán. Open daily 9am-1pm.

**Currency Exchange:** Most banks open for exchange Mon.-Fri. 8:30-11am. *Casas de cambio* are open all day in the northern section of the downtown area but tend to sport less than thrilling rates.

**American Express:** Tel. 13-06-00; fax 16-59-08. In the Centro Comercial Plaza Balboa on Camarón Sábalo. Open daily 9am-5pm.

**Telephones:** Stainless-steel **LADATELs,** throughout the city, are best for international calls. *Caseta* at Serdán 1510 and 21 de Marzo (tel./fax 82-21-77) has **fax** and **email** (econet@red2000.com.mx; ½hr. for 25 pesos) as well. Open Mon.-Sat. 8am-8:30pm, Sun. 8am-2pm.

**Fax:** Tel. 81-22-20. In the same building as the post office. Open Mon.-Fri. 8am-7pm, Sat.-Sun. 8-11am. Also at the *caseta* above.

**Airport: Rafael Buelna International Airport** (tel. 82-21-77), 18km south of the city. **Aeroméxico,** Sábalo 310A (tel. 14-11-11 or 91-800-36-202). **Mexicana,** B. Domínguez and Av. del Mar (tel./fax 82-77-22). **Alaska Airlines** (tel. 95-800-426-0333; fax 85-27-30). **AeroCalifornia** (tel. 13-20-42), El Cid Resort. Call for schedules and fares. See **Orientation** above for info on getting to or from the airport.

**Buses: Transportes del Pacífico** (tel. 81-51-56) has service to Guadalajara (almost every hr., 7hr., 150 pesos) and Tepic (every hr., 5hr., 77 pesos). **Norte del Sonora** sends buses north to Monterrey (9pm, 17hr., 322 pesos) and Tijuana (11am, 2, and 6:30pm, 26hr., 462 pesos). **Transpacífico** (tel. 81-38-01) serves Culiacán (5, 6, and 8:30pm, 2½hr., 50 pesos), Durango (7:30pm, 7hr., 72 pesos), Los Mochis (every hr., 6am-4pm, 6½hr., 128 pesos), and Puerto Vallarta (7:30am, 7hr., 150 pesos). The following 3 lines offer posher buses: **Transportes Chihuahuauses** (tel. 81-53-81) runs to Ciudad Juárez (2pm and midnight, 24hr., 380 pesos) and Monterrey (7 per day, 18hr., 315 pesos). **Elite** (81-38-11) has service to Querétaro (2pm, 13hr., 303 pesos) and Tepic (every hr., 4½hr., 89 pesos). **Transportes del Norte** (tel. 81-23-35) has 1st-class service to Durango (5 per day, 7hr., 100 pesos), Monterrey (5 per day, 18hr., 277 pesos), and Saltillo (noon, 5, 7, and 10pm, 16hr., 279 pesos).

**Trains:** Tel. 84-67-10. In Colonia Esperanza on the eastern edge of town. One train leaves daily for Guadalajara (1st class 10am-2pm, 2nd class 5-7am, 13½hr., 1st class 128 pesos, 2nd class 70 pesos) and Nogales (1st class 7-11pm, 2nd class 11pm-2am, 18hr., 1st class 246 pesos, 2nd class 146 pesos). Call ahead on day of departure, as times are less than reliable.

**Ferry: Sematur,** at the end of Carnaval (tel. 81-70-20 or -21), south of Ángel Flores and *el centro.* Tickets are sold only on the day of departure. Arrive at the office at least 2hr. early to procure a spot, as capacity is very limited. Ticket office open Sun.-Fri. 8am-3pm, Sat. 9am-1pm. You can purchase tickets in advance at a local travel agency. During the high season (Dec., and Jul.-Aug.) make reservations at least 2 weeks ahead. Travels every day to La Paz, Baja California, arriving around 8am (3pm, 17hr., *salón* (a grungy seat—sleep on the deck instead) 163 pesos, *turista* (a decent bunk bed in a cabin) about double; children 2-11 ½-price).

**Car Rental: Hertz,** Sábalo 314 (tel. 13-60-60, airport office 85-05-48; fax 13-49-55). Starting around 300 pesos per day. Must be 21 years old.

**Laundromat: Lavamatic del Centro,** Serdán 2914 on the Malecón (tel. 81-35-56). Will wash and dry 3kg in a few hr. for 24 pesos. Open Mon.-Sat. 8am-7:30pm.

**Red Cross:** Zaragoza and Corona (tel. 85-14-51).

**Pharmacy: Farmacia Ibael,** Ángel Flores and Campana (tel. 822-62-49). English spoken. Open daily 8:30am-10:30pm.

**Hospital: Sharp Hospital,** Dr. Jesús Kumate and Rafael Buelna (tel. 86-56-76), near Zaragoza park. English spoken.

**Emergency:** 24hr. tel. 81-36-90

**Police:** on Rafael Buelna (tel. 83-45-10), in Colonia Juárez.

**Post Office:** Juárez and 21 de Marzo (tel. 81-21-21), across from the *zócalo.* Open Mon.-Fri. 8am-7pm, Sat. 9am-1pm. **Postal Code:** 82000.

**Phone Code:** 69.

## ACCOMMODATIONS AND CAMPING

High-quality cheap rooms do exist; simply avoid the *Zona Dorada,* where rates are exorbitant even at the shabbiest joints. Budget hotels cluster in three areas: in Old Mazatlán along the three avenues east of the main square (Juárez, Serdán, and Azueta), in the noisy area around the bus station, and on the pleasant waterfront along Olas Altas, southwest of the center of Old Mazatlán. Large groups can even find cheap beds on Sábalo, near the beaches. The busiest seasons in Mazatlán are Christmas and the month following Semana Santa—check in early. There's a trailer park, **La Posta,** on Av. Rafael Buelna (tel. 83-53-10; full hook-up and tent space 70 pesos).

## Olas Altas

Back in the 1950s, long before wily developers began constructing multi-million-dollar pleasure pits along the north shore, the focal point of Mazatlán's fledgling resort scene was Olas Altas, a winding, shore-hugging stretch southwest of town dotted with regal, colonial-style hotels. Although the majority of tourists now opt to stay in the flashy hotels to the north, Olas Altas is a calm oasis, only a 10-minute walk from the *centro* and connected to the rest of Mazatlán by several buses.

**Hotel Belmar,** Olas Altas 166 at Osuna (tel. 85-11-11). The second you get into Mazatlán, *run,* don't walk, to the Belmar, and plop down here; this absolute gem makes deciding where to stay in town a no-brainer. A resort of yesteryear, the Belmar glows with hazy marble floors, luxuriant dark wood paneling, and arches lined with colorful tiles. Cool, spotless rooms have gigantic bathrooms. Match other guests ping for pong at the table downstairs, take a dip in the pool, or crawl into an antique rocker with an English book in hand (they have a small collection). Singles with A/C and TV 85 pesos, with ocean view (no A/C) 100 pesos; doubles with A/C and TV 100 pesos, with ocean view (no A/C) 120 pesos.

**Hotel La Siesta,** Olas Altas Sur 11 and Escobedo (tel. 81-26-40 or 81-23-34, toll-free 91-800-69-770; fax 13-74-76). A jungly central courtyard spills over into huge, immaculate rooms. Slackers afflicted with *ennui* can toy with the A/C, TV, or phone, or just lounge on the balcony overlooking the sea. Singles 140 pesos; doubles 164 pesos. Ask for a room with a view.

## Old Mazatlán

This is the noisier part of town ("downtown"), and the hotels here are farther from the beach—therefore rooms are on the cheap side. This area, especially the cathedral square, is well-trafficked after sundown, mainly by old men watching passers-by, and for that reason is somewhat safer than other parts of town.

**Hotel Lerma,** Simón Bolívar 622 near Serdán (tel. 81-24-36). Riotously colored, centrally located, and clean. Fans make the heat bearable. Popular among backpackers who know a good deal when they see one. Singles 45 pesos; doubles 50 pesos.

**Hotel del Centro,** Canizales 705 between Serdán and Juárez (tel. 81-26-73). Somewhat small, cool, turquoise rooms have A/C, purified water, and tiny bathrooms. Singles and doubles 72 pesos.

**Hotel Central,** Domínguez 2 Sur and Escobedo (tel. 82-18-88). Spotless rooms decorated with funky wood carvings. Phone, TV, A/C, and sparkling bathrooms make this hotel a smart choice for larger groups. Singles, doubles, and triples 105 pesos.

## Near the Bus Station

Hotels in this area are closer to the ritzy *Zona Dorada* in proximity but not in quality. Be forewarned: buses do their noisy thing 24 hours a day.

**Hotel Fiesta,** Ferrosquila 306, in front of the bus station. Clean rooms have bathrooms, firm mattresses, and purified water. Aquamarine halls with fluorescent lights make you feel like you're in a fishbowl. Singles and doubles 60 pesos; 10 pesos extra each for A/C or TV.

**Hotel Económico,** Palos Prietos and Espinoza. As cheap (and basic) as it gets. All of the sunny, yellow rooms have fans, mirrors, and tiny bathrooms. Singles 30 pesos; doubles 40 pesos, with TV 50 pesos, with TV and A/C 60 pesos.

## FOOD

Mazatlán's restaurants serve up everything from *comida corrida* to charbroiled T-bone steak, a gringo favorite. Prices escalate as you get sucked toward the Golden Zone. Mazatlán's *centro* is the place to be for quality budget meals. The busy **public market,** between Juárez and Serdán, three blocks north of the *zócalo,* serves the cheapest food in the area. If you need a **headless pig,** look no further. Jumbo shrimp, *antojito* platters, and steak can be had for staggeringly low prices. Snacking opportunities exist outside in the *loncherías* and **taco stands.** For a more formal meal, try one of the *centro*'s many inexpensive restaurants or, for the view, a joint along the Malecón in Olas Altas. Enjoy your meal with **Pacífico** beer, the pride of Mazatlán.

**Restaurante Vegetariano,** Ángel Flores and Frías (tel. 82-61-43). Phenomenal veggie cuisine at unbeatable prices. Enjoy the enormous *comida corrida,* which includes salad, soup, a hearty main course, fresh wheat bread, juice, and dessert, all for only 23 pesos. A family joint. Open daily 8am-4:30pm.

**Restaurant de Esther,** Serdán 1605 and Canizales. Fans work furiously overhead to cool Mexican patrons feasting on Esther's home cooking. Beach photos help them imagine that the fans are working. *Comida corrida* around 18 pesos. *Enchiladas suizas* 15 pesos. Open daily 7am-10pm.

**Cafe Pacífico,** Constitución 501 (tel. 81-39-72), across from the Plazuela Machado. This famous pub is a relic, with all the charm of grand Old Mazatlán: good food and drink, a dark, artsy atmosphere and chummy service. Chat, chat, chat. A large-screen TV with ESPN and a pool table add to the fun. Let the cool tunes and A/C pump you up as you snack on chicken wings (35 pesos), tuna salad (18 pesos), or the platter of assorted cheeses (30 pesos). Open daily 10am-midnight.

**Las Cazuelas,** Canizales 723 and Juárez. Pottery-festooned walls and cheerful table-cloths spice up white plastic furniture. Good, cheap food. *Comida corrida* 15 pesos. Pancakes 8 pesos. *Tostadas* 4 pesos.

**Cafe Machado,** Constitución 515 (tel. 81-22-45), on the Plaza Machado. Funky art-work, cool tunes, and damn tasty food. *Comida corrida* 18 pesos. Impersonate Hemingway's Santiago with marlin tacos (22 pesos). Open Mon.-Sat. 8am-1am.

**El Mambo Lonchería,** Espinoza Ferrusquilla 204 (tel. 85-04-73), across from the bus station. Mexican pottery, hanging seashells, eclectic art, a macaw, and a parrot that speaks more Spanish than most of the patrons. Tasty, large, and cheap meals. Shrimp *al mojo de ajo* (in garlic) 28 pesos. Open Mon.-Sat. 7am-7pm.

## SAND AND SIGHTS

Mazatlán's greatest asset is its 16km of beach. Just north of Old Mazatlán and along Av. del Mar sprawls **Playa Norte,** a decent stretch of sand if you don't mind small waves and the stares of local *machos* who play soccer here. Solo women should con-sider doing their swimming farther north. As you hone in on the *Zona Dorada,* the beach gets cleaner, the waves larger, and Playa Norte eases into **Playa Las Gaviotas.** Just past Punta Sábalo, in the lee of the islands, basks **Playa Sábalo,** whose great waves and golden sand are enjoyed to the point of abuse by crowds of *norteameri-canos.* Most area beaches are patrolled by lifeguards, who use a color-coded flag sys-tem to inform bathers of local conditions: green, yellow, and red flags indicate the level of undertow; white flags mean *quemadores* (jellyfish) are around. "Sábalo-Cen-tro" buses pass by all of these beaches.

As Playa Sábalo recedes to the north, crowds thin rapidly and you can frolic on the glorious beaches all by yourself. Take the yellow "Sábalo" bus to the last stop and walk left; you'll soon reach nearly deserted **Playa Bruja,** with tons of beautiful sand and 1- to- 2m waves. Swim at your own risk: there are no lifeguards. Camping is per-mitted, but be cautious after dark and camp in groups whenever possible. Solo women should avoid Playa Bruja, as assaults have been reported. For a 360° view of Mazatlán, the sea, and the surrounding hills, climb to the top of **El Faro,** the second-tallest lighthouse in the world. The hike (about ½hr.) is almost unbearable in the sum-mer; avoid the heat by ascending in the early morning or late evening.

The **Acuario Mazatlán,** Av. de los Deportes 111 (tel. 81-78-15 or 81-78-16), keeps piranhas and other feisty fish (up to 250 breeds in all) in a slew of cloudy tanks. The aquarium, supposedly the largest in Latin America, also hosts performing sea lions and birds. In the aviary, check out the hooded orioles, bar-vented wren, and social fly-catchers in the trees. The Acuario is one block back from the beach and north of the Sands Hotel; the turn-off is marked by a shimmering blue sign (open daily 9:30am-6:30pm; admission 25 pesos, children 3-13 10 pesos).

Mazatlán's **tower divers** don't quite match the exploits of the cliff divers in Acapulco, but their acrobatic plunges are nevertheless dangerous and hence very entertaining. Performances take place during the day, but be forewarned that the divers will not perform unless they can pull in a sufficient number of "tips" beforehand. The best time to watch the divers is between 10-11am and 4:30-6:30pm when guided tour buses arrive and tourists fork over their pesos. The best viewing angles are just south of the towers; on days when the water is too rough for diving, climb the tower to watch the waves break below. Walk to the waterfront on Zaragoza and head south to get to the towers.

William Blake saw the universe in a grain of sand and eternity in an hour. You too may get bored at the beach. In this case, don't abandon Mazatlán—just hop on one of the boats to **Isla de la Piedra** (see below), where locals go to escape the crowds. Boats leave from the wharf on Av. del Puerto at Gutiérrez Najera. Buses to the wharf depart from near the public market (1.80 pesos). To walk there, take 21 de Marzo from the cathedral past Serdán to the water, then turn left on Av. del Puerto (7 pesos round-trip). **Islas Venados** (Deer Island) is a relatively deserted scrap of land with fine diving; catamaran boats leave for the island from the Agua Sports Center in the **El Cid Resort** (tel. 13-33-33, ext. 341) in the *Zona Dorada* (10am, noon, 2, and 4pm, 35 pesos). Waterpark mania has hit Mazatlán with the new **Mazagua** (tel. 88-00-41), located north of the *Zona Dorada* near Puerta Cerritos. Go bonkers in the wave pool or shoot down slippery slides (open March-Oct. daily 10am-6pm; admission 35 pesos, children under 4 free). To get there, take a "Cerritos Juárez" bus (1.80 pesos).

The newly restored and luxurious **Teatro Ángela Peralta** at Carnaval and Libertad near the Plaza Machado hosts an impressive variety of cultural programs and has a fascinating history to boot.

## ENTERTAINMENT

Hordes of *norteamericano* high schoolers ditch the prom and hit Mazatlán yearly to twist, shout, and drink. Supply rises to meet demand, and more than a dozen discos and bars clamor for gringo dollars. Inside, only the occasional Mexican rock tune will remind you you're in a foreign country. Most of the hot clubs are in the area known as **Fiesta Land,** in the *Zona Dorada*. If you address bartenders or bouncers in Spanish, they'll smile, pat you on the head, and answer in near-perfect English, never forgetting to address you as *amigo*. Cover charges can be hefty, especially during high season and holidays such as Semana Santa and Christmas.

**Bora-Bora,** on Paseo del Mar (tel. 86-49-49), at the southern end of the *Zona Dorada*, next to the beach. Always jam-packed with touring (and local) teenagers clad in neon (or nothing at all) and dancing on the bars. Those so inclined may dance in cages. Clubbers in search of more wholesome activities can head for the volleyball court and swimming pool (but many choose to have sex instead). Drinks start at 18 pesos. Cover Fri.-Sun. 20-40 pesos, including beer. Open daily 9pm-4am. Or try **Valentino's,** in the same building, which draws an older, more ritzy crowd. Dancing and drinks continue to pack 'em in. Open daily 9pm-4am.

**Cafe 808,** Calle Laguna 13 and Las Garzas (tel. 16-54-26). Acid jazz and techno are the house specialty. Long-haired locals clad in black sip drinks in the cool blue neon-lit interior. Open Tues.-Sun. 6pm-2am. Cover 20 pesos (includes one drink) on high-season weekends.

**Harley's,** Las Garzas 8 and Rodolfo Loaiza (tel. 16-54-14). Loud Doors tunes and baseball-cap-sporting waiters keep the beer flowing. Biker art and photos of rock legends enliven the walls. Live rock nightly. Open Tues.-Sun. 5pm-2am.

**Pepe Toro,** Las Garzas 18 and Loaiza. Caters to gay men and a few lesbians. The dance floor starts hoppin' after 11pm. Open daily 7pm-2am.

**El Toro Bravo,** Av. del Mar 550 (tel. 85-05-95). Watch twentysomething would-be cowpokes drink their bladders full of beer (15 pesos) and then attempt to ride the bucking saddle—guess where that beer goes next. Wed. is Ladies' Night. Cover Thurs.-Sun. 30 pesos. Open daily 9pm-4am.

## ■ Near Mazatlán: Isla de la Piedra

Just a five-minute boat ride from the mainland, Isla de la Piedra consists of 10km of glistening sand, crashing waves, and an assortment of marine life that would make the folks at Sea World gnash their teeth with envy. A popular spot among Mexican families, the island's beaches are gorgeous and don't have the intimidating undertow of the mainland.

**Orientation and Practical Information** To get to the island, take a green **"Independencia" bus** (2 pesos) from the *mercado* to the **Embarcadero de la Isla de la Piedra.** From there, take a **boat** (every 10min., 5min., 7 pesos round-trip) to the island; **trucks** (2 pesos) and **taxis** (6 pesos) will be waiting to take passengers to *la playa.* Alternatively, walk straight away from the boat landing and follow the gravel path across the island for about 15 minutes.

Obtain **tourist information** at any of the restaurants near the beaches; most owners have been on the island for ages and are more than willing to help. The island's one **telephone** (tel. 85-44-50) is located across from the dock (open daily 7am-1pm and 3-9pm). Adjacent to the phone is **Farmacia de la Piedra,** which also offers medical assistance (open daily 7am-1pm and 3-9pm).

**Accommodations and Food** The island is perfect for a daytrip or to camp out. **Carmelita's,** a few meters from the shore, offers space for tents, sturdy trees for hammock slinging, and use of bathroom and grill free of charge. If you can't camp out, she also offers clean rooms with the basics: electricity and private bathrooms with running water (60 pesos for 1-3 persons). **Lety's,** adjacent to Carmelita's, offers similar free lodging. It also has spacious rooms with modern bathrooms, desks, lighting, two beds, and a sofa-bed (60 pesos for 1-3 people). There's nothing nicer than camping out on a secluded beach and gazing at the stars, but be careful and don't stray too far from the center.

Seafood rules on the island. **Carmelita's** serves shrimp platters and fish fillets, both with *frijoles,* tortillas, salad, and rice (25 pesos; open 9am-6pm). If you're tired of seafood, head to **Lety's** for a quarter chicken (25 pesos) or quesadillas (20 pesos; open 9am-7pm). Listen to the cool tunes and watch folks play volleyball by the shore at **Restaurant Estebin,** a two-minute walk from Carmelita's. Same ol' grub: fish fillets (25 pesos), and chicken (22 pesos; open daily 9am-7pm).

**Sights** The main attraction is, of course, the beautiful **beaches.** Wriggle your toes in the cool sand, duck the waves, or bask in the radiant sun. If you're into water sports, then try a trip on a banana boat (25 pesos), rent snorkeling equipment (60 pesos per hr.), or borrow a boogie board (10 pesos per hr.). The restaurants will point you the right way. Aging horses may also be hired (50 pesos per hr.) further up the beach.

# DURANGO

## ▓ Durango

State capital and commercial center, Durango (pop. 490,000) is a busy, trafficky city caught up in Mexico's 20th-century push toward industrialization. The view of the impressive Baroque cathedral is partially obstructed by cars and buses busily cruising along the roads surrounding the central Plaza de Armas. Durango's residents revel in their city's Old-West flavor, and cowboy boots and hats are *de rigueur.* The city's collection of colonial architecture and handful of decent museums make it a deserving stopover on your way through the region, but it isn't likely to hold your interest for more than a day or two.

**Orientation and Practical Information** Durango's bus station is located on the eastern outskirts of town. To reach the *centro*, catch a "Centro" bus in front of the station (1.50 pesos); taxis are also available (9-10 pesos). Most sites of interest lie within a few blocks of the cathedral and its **Plaza de Armas. 20 de Noviembre** is a major east-west thoroughfare passing in front of the cathedral; Juárez runs north-south. Navigating downtown is fairly simple; the streets are in a grid and rarely change names.

Tourist information can be found at the **Dirección Estatal de Turismo y Cinematografía,** at Hidalgo 408. From the Plaza, walk one block in the opposite direction from the cathedral to 5 de Febrero, then turn right and walk about three blocks to Hidalgo and turn left. The very helpful staff provides maps and brochures. **Banco Serfin,** on the Plaza (tel. 12-80-33), is open 9am-5pm weekdays and has a 24-hour **ATM.** There is a *caseta* at 5 de Febrero 106 Pte. (open daily 8am-10pm). **Telecomm,** at Felipe Pescada and Zaragoya, about eight blocks from the Plaza, offers **fax** service (open Mon.-Fri. 8am-8pm, Sat. 9am-4pm).

**Estrella Blanca** and **Rojo de los Altos** (tel. 18-30-61) send buses to Aguascalientes (6 per day, 5:30am-7pm, 6hr., 102 pesos), Guadalajara (5 per day, 7:15am-7pm, 9½hr., 174 pesos), and Mazatlán (5 per day, 10am-10pm, 7hr., 82 pesos). **Transportes Chihuahuenses** has service to Mexico City (4, 6, 8am, and 10 pm, 11hr., 276 pesos), Monterrey (9 per day, 8½hr., 186 pesos), Torreón (18 per day, 3hr., 75 pesos), and Zacatecas (6 per day, 8am-11:15pm, 4½hr., 84 pesos). **Ómnibus** (tel. 18-33-61) sends buses to Ciudad Juárez (direct 6, 8, and 10pm, 8hr., 293 pesos; non-direct 5 per day, 8am-11:05pm, 12hr., 210 pesos), Matamoros (7:35, 9:15pm, 13hr., 278 pesos), Mexico City (direct 7:05, 8:05, 9, and 10:05pm, 12hr., 276 pesos; nondirect 7:30am, noon, 6:05 and 11:05pm, 13hr., 276 pesos), and San Luis Potosí (7 per day, 7:30am-11pm, 6hr., 136 pesos). **Turistar Ejecutivo** and **Futura** (tel. 18-37-84) serve Mazatlán (9am, 5, and 12pm, 7hr., 92 pesos), Monterrey (6 per day, 9am-10pm, 9hr., 186 pesos), and Nuevo Laredo (8 and 9:30pm, 12hr., 268 pesos). **Transportes del Valle Poanas** and **Transportes de Durango** send buses to points throughout the state of Durango, including Agua Vieja (every hr., 7am-8pm, 2½hr., 28 pesos), Los Angeles (about every hr., 7am-8pm, 1¼hr., 17.50 pesos), and Villa Unión (every ½hr., 7am-8pm, 2hr., 20 pesos).

**Hospital General,** 5 de Febrero and Norman Fuentes (tel. 11-91-15), is open 24 hours. The **police** are at Felipe Pescador and Independencia (tel. 17-54-06 or 17-55-50). In an **emergency,** dial 06. The **post office** is at 20 de Noviembre and Roncal (tel. 11-41-05), 12 long blocks from the Plaza de Armas (open Mon.-Fri. 8am-7pm, Sat. 9am-1pm). **Postal Code: 34000. Phone Code: 118.**

**Accommodations and Food** Inexpensive accommodations abound near the market, a few blocks west of the Plaza de Armas. The **Casa de Huéspedes El Hotelito,** Progresso 102 Sur (tel. 12-31-81), near the market, has clean, basic rooms with TV and bathroom. The elderly *dueña* also rents large furnished apartments with kitchen (singles 40 pesos; doubles 50 pesos; apartments 70 sweet pesos). Those who demand luxury will find it surprisingly affordable at the centrally-located **Posada Duran,** 20 de Noviembre 506 (tel. 11-24-12), just east of the cathedral, where wood-floored rooms surround a soothing fountain and enclosed courtyard that doubles as an upscale bar by night. Some rooms have balconies overlooking the cathedral (singles 76 pesos; doubles 93 pesos). Adequate and affordable rooms can also be found at **Hotel Buenos Aires,** Constitución 126 Nte. (tel. 11-31-28), and **Hotel El Gallo,** 5 de Febrero 117 (tel. 11-52-90), near the market.

Inexpensive meals aren't hard to find in Durango. Cheap *comedores* and taco stands cluster around the market, and most are open daily. The tiny, plant-filled cafe and whole grain bakery **Al Grano,** Negrete and Zaragoza, a few blocks west of the cathedral, serves super breakfast specials (12 pesos) and tasty Mexican fare (burritos 3.50 pesos), including vegetarian dishes (open Mon.-Sat. 8am-8pm). Watch your food being prepared in the open kitchen at the family-run **Cafe de la Mancha,** 20 de Noviembre 807 Pte. at Zaragoza (*comida corrida* 16 pesos; *gorditas* 3 pesos; *tortas* 5 pesos; open daily 9am-8pm). **La Terraza,** 5 de Febrero 603 Pte., overlooks the Plaza de Armas. Garish stained glass and neon set the stage for well-prepared food (small pizzas around 24 pesos; breakfast 11-13 pesos; beer 10 pesos; nightly *mariachi* madness around 11pm).

**Sights and Entertainment** The most imposing building in town is the enormous **cathedral** overlooking the Plaza de Armas. Its ornately-carved Baroque facade rests under two enormous bell towers and includes the figures of angels, an eagle, and a heavy iron cross. Its dim interior is filled with marble pillars, carved wood, and wrought iron. Just west of the cathedral on 20 de Noviembre waits the white brick **Teatro Ricardo Castro.** Construction of the building began in 1900; today it houses temporary exhibitions, theatrical productions, and film screenings. The huge **Palacio de Gobierno,** on 5 de Febrero between Martinez and Zaragoza, was built by a Spanish mining tycoon and expropriated by the government after Mexico won independence. Inside, a bronze likeness of Benito Juárez glares amid colorful murals depicting the city's history.

There are a few museums in town that may be worth a visit. The **Museo de las Culturas Populares,** at Juárez and Barreda, displays ceramics and textiles and hosts talks, dances, and other events (open Tues.-Sun. 10am-6pm; admission 1 peso). The **Museo Regional de Durango,** known (for some reason) as **El Aguacate,** at Madero Serdán and Negrete, houses some paintings of Miguel Cabrera as well as exhibitions regarding the state's history, indigenous groups, paleontology, and natural resources (open Tues.-Sun. 9am-4pm; admission 1 peso). The **Museo de Arte Contemporanea,** at Negrete and Pasteur, hosts temporary exhibits of local and national artists (open Tues.-Sun 10am-6pm; admission 3 pesos).

At night, live it up in the city's discos and bars. A popular disco is **La Covacha,** Pino Suárez 500 Pte. and Madero (tel. 12-39-69), where locals dance to international and Latin hits (cover 20 pesos; open Thurs.-Sun. 9pm-4am). **Excalibur,** at Mascareñas and Cárdenas, is a mellower hangout, with pool tables and live *mariachi* music on weekends (open daily 4pm-late).

On Sundays, city officials close off the streets in Durango's *centro* to celebrate **Domingo Familiar,** when vendors hawk kid-pleasing treats and street performers play to the crowds. For 10 days at the beginning of July, Durango celebrates the **Feria Nacional** in commemoration of the city's founding. Parades and fireworks liven things up, and reservations become a must. Over 200 films have been shot in the desert around Durango. Some of the **sets** have been left standing and have been turned into tourist attractions. The tourist office organizes trips to visit the sets. You try a do-it-yourself version by taking an Estrella Blanca bus to **Chupaderos** (every ½hr., 25min., 6 pesos). Ask the driver to let you off on the highway near the sets.

# Northeast Mexico

Dust-swept border towns, former colonial settlements, old mining hotspots, and congested urban centers make up Northeast Mexico. The incredible lack of tourists—one of the most constant features across the disparate towns and cities of the Northeast—can sometimes create an almost paradisiacal sense of calm amongst proud, parched-white missions, wide streets, and Americanized slang.

However, that sense won't hit you in the bad-ass, broken-down border towns of **Tamaulipas** and **Nuevo León.** Not for the faint of heart, these towns simulate an old country-western movie by combining the seediest elements of both U.S. and Mexican culture, with dust storms, cheap booze, arid landscapes, and a sun so scorching that it makes a high-noon showdown completely conceivable. Further south, the gringo influence and grubbiness fade. In Monterrey, a metropolis of millions, lovely cathedrals and gorgeous parks peek out of a sea of grey skyscrapers; recently, Monterrey has become a chic city without catering to tacky tourists. If it's beach you crave, *el Noreste* offers little more than a taste. Fresh, salty Tampico has never been able to draw flocks of tourists, but the newly beautified beaches and seafood brought in by local fishermen might change all that. Perhaps the most wonderful part of the Northeast lies within the state of **San Luis Potosí.** Even the town of Real de Catorce, ridden with peyote-hungry backpackers, is largely untouched by modernity, with one phone, hundreds of burros, and mountain views. Xilitla offers the eco-warrior caves, waterfalls, rivers, wild parrots, semi-tropical rainforests, and ruins an hour or two from congested city centers. The city of San Luis Potosí is a quiet jewel—the capital of the state, it is a playground of regional culture, awesome architecture, and colonial appeal. The **Zacatecas** state was blessed with a location smack in the middle of Mexico's legendary silver store; as a result, its capital, now a university town, is far more classically colonial, commercial, and cosmopolitan than is customary for the Northeast. While *El Noreste* might not feature prominently in the plans of most tourists, the quiet appeal and dry charm of its towns and cities might surprise you.

## ■ Brownsville, Texas

Make no mistake about it, once you've hit Brownsville (pop. 135,000), you've hit Mexico, if not physically then culturally. Lanky men sporting cowboy hats and the slew of late-model American cars only thinly veil the pervasive Mexican influence; a 90% Hispanic population and delightful wholesale markets blaring Mexican top-40 will make you doubt that you're actually above the border. Few tourists come to Brownsville, and for good reason: this gritty border town tries hard but offers little.

**Orientation and Practical Information** Most points of interest lie northwest of **International Blvd.,** which traverses the city before turning into the **International Bridge** that leads into Mexico. Numbered streets run parallel to International Blvd., starting at **Palm Blvd.** Those 3rd-grade American history classes will finally pay off, as perpendicular streets are named after American presidents in order, starting with Georgie **Washington** and tapering off before the Great Depression. **Elizabeth St.,** right near the border, is the city's main commercial thoroughfare and precedes the presidential streets. Street numbers correspond to location—770 Elizabeth is between 7th and 8th. What tourists exist are drawn to the old city near the border and the suburban hotel strip in the northwestern part of town. At night, the area around the border is desolate; women and solo travelers should probably avoid it, along with **Southmost Rd.,** perpendicular to and east of International Blvd., where there have been rumors of gang activity. **Local buses,** which travel long routes throughout Brownsville, run from 6am-7pm and cost $.75 (students and seniors $.50); all buses leave on the hour or the half hour from City Hall on E. Washington St. between E. 11th and E. 12th.

# Northeast Mexico

0 ——————— 50 miles
0 ——————— 50 kilometers

**N**

Corpus Christi

Nuevo Laredo — Laredo

TEXAS

UNITED STATES

S. Padre Island

Monclova

Sabinas Hidalgo

McAllen

COAHUILA

Reynosa — Brownsville

Monterrey

China

Matamoros

San Pedro de las Colonias

Saltillo

NUEVO LEÓN

SIERRA MADRE ORIENTAL

Linares

San Fernando

TAMAULIPAS

ZACATECAS

La Pesca

Real de Catorce

Matehuala

Ciudad Victoria

Golfo De México (Gulf Of Mexico)

Fresnillo

Ciudad Mante

Zacatecas

Guadalupe

SAN LUIS POTOSÍ

Ciudad Madero

AGUASCALIENTES
Aguascalientes

San Luis Potosí

Ciudad Valles

Tampico

Río Verde

Lagos Moreno

GUANAJUATO

Xilitla

VERACRUZ

JALISCO

The **tourist office** is at the **Chamber of Commerce,** 1600 E. Elizabeth (tel. 542-4341), across the street from the border crossing (open Mon.-Fri. 8am-5pm). Check out the **Brownsville City Web Page** (http://www.ci.brownsville.tx.us/City/). **Express Money Exchange,** 801 International Blvd. (tel. 548-0303), exchanges traveler's checks (open daily 10am-6pm). *Casas de cambio* line International Blvd.; rates are nearly identical to, if not better than, banks'. The best rates, though, are found across the border. **Brownsville and South Padre International Airport,** 700 S. Minnesota (tel. 542-4373), is served by **Continental** (tel. 541-2200 or (800) 231-0856), which currently offers eight flights per day to and from Houston. Taxis to downtown run US$9-11. The **Greyhound** station is at 1134 E. Charles St. (tel. 546-7171), two blocks from the International Bridge, and **buses** serve Dallas (6 per day, 13hr., US$49), Houston (5 per day, 9hr., US$24), Laredo (2 per day, 6hr., US$21), and San Antonio (6 per day, 7hr., US$31). **Valley Transit Company,** 1305 E. Adams at 13th (tel. 546-2264), also sends buses to Laredo (7:15am, 6hr., US$20), McAllen (every hr., 1:15-5:15pm, 7:15pm, and midnight, 2hr., US$8), and many other towns in Texas and Mexico. The **police** are at 600 E. Jackson (tel. 548-7000). For **internet access,** try the **Convention and Visitors Bureau** (contact jeffrey@brownsville.org for info). The **post office,** at Elizabeth and E. 10th, is in the beautiful Greek Revival/brick masonry courthouse building (open Mon.-Fri. 7am-7pm). **ZIP Code:** 78520. **Area Code:** 210.

**Accommodations and Food** Lodging in Brownsville—besides the pricey national chains—gently prepares the southbound traveler for the hotel life that is to come. Brownsville prices, however, are certainly American. Although more convenient, the downtown area is more dangerous at night than the distant area along the North Expressway. Downtown empties out by 9pm (Fri.-Sat. 10:30pm). After that, travel in groups or take cabs. At the **Cameron Motor Hotel,** 912 E. Washington (tel. 542-3551), you can take refuge from the interminable heat in the cool lobby/lounge. Rooms come with bath, cable TV (65 channels!), A/C, and telephones—enough equipment to drown out the car alarms and thumping Mexican rap music from the vehicles on the street below (singles US$36.60; doubles US$42). **Plaza Square Motel,** 2255 Central Blvd. (tel. 546-5104), is conveniently located across the street from the AmEx office and on the bus route 7.5km from downtown. The Plaza Square offers the usual amenities (pool, cable TV) amid quirky decor (singles US$28; doubles US$30; each additional person US$5).

Catering primarily to local residents, Brownsville restaurants serve up a colorless combination of simple Mexican dishes and bland American fare. Downtown, cafes open and close early following an American meal schedule; all offer similar menus of burgers and burritos. For the salsa-weary, **Artichoke Deli,** 108 E. Elizabeth (tel. 544-7636), a 10-minute walk from downtown, sports eclectic furnishings and walls adorned with chile peppers, cartoons, and colorful pop art. Perhaps the closest thing in Brownsville to a vegetarian-friendly eatery, the deli offers fresh salads and sandwiches for about US$5 (open daily for lunch 11am-4pm). **Rutledge's Restaurant,** 1126 E. Washington, is located in a narrow alleyway between two buildings next to Zepeda Hardware. The unique atmosphere and a wide selection of hearty food for under US$2 keep the crowds coming to this burger-lover's mecca.

**Sights and Entertainment** It may look like a humdrum run-down border town, but Brownsville is home to one of the top zoos in the nation for rare and endangered species, as well as several museums honoring the city's role in American history. The **Gladys Porter Zoo,** 500 Ringold St., off E. 6th (tel. 546-7187), offers a 31-acre tropical sanctuary where most animals live in open quarters surrounded only by waterways. The collection includes lowland gorillas, Sumatran orangutans, and white rhinos (open daily 9am-sunset, tickets sold only until 5pm; extended summer hours; admission US$6, children US$3).

After a long, hot day of wholesale shopping and exchanging money, kick back at the **Artemis Sports Bar and Grille,** 1200 Central Blvd. (tel. 542-2367), a block away from the medical center. Unlike others, the Artemis is hip, clean, and safe—even at night. TVs blare football games, and, on Fridays and Saturdays, live bands play everything from alterna-rock to Spanish pop (house beer US$2.50; happy hour 11am-7pm; open Mon.-Fri. 11am-2am, Sat.-Sun. noon-2am; kitchen closes at midnight).

# TAMAULIPAS

## ■ Matamoros

Texans joke that the narrow dusty roads of Matamoros were designed less for cars and trucks than for carts and horses. Indeed, Brownsville's sister city to the south is a bit dirty and provincial. You've got your basics here—a shady town plaza, vendors selling sandals and disposable razors, students from the *universidad* hand in hand. But lest this sound too peaceful, don't worry: the town has enough booze and border brawls (especially at night) that you'll need to dream up your own reasons to go.

**Orientation and Practical Information** If walking (sunscreen is a must) or traveling by car from Brownsville, you must cross the **International Bridge,** located at the northernmost part of Matamoros. The two best options for crossing the border are by foot or in a private car (bring along all documentation). Pedestrians pay a budget-busting 25¢ or 1 peso to leave either country. Autos pay US$1, but be sure you've checked your insurance before you cross—most U.S. insurance is null and void in Mexico (p. 43). Upon arrival in Mexico, you will pass the customs and tourist offices on your right. To reach the center of town from the border area, take one of the yellow minibuses labeled "Centro." To reach the **bus station,** take one labeled "Central" (1 peso). If you're returning to the border, catch a minibus marked "Puente" (1 peso). From the border crossing, the city extends out in a V-shape following the bend in the **Río Bravo;** the left (eastern) arm of the V is defined by **Calle 1,** which runs parallel to the river and leads directly to the **Central de Autobuses,** 2km down in the southeast corner of the city. As the city opens up to the right (west), the streets' numbers increase. **Álvaro Obregón,** which quickly changes name into the ubiquitous **Calle Hidalgo,** forms the other wing of the V. Heading south of the border, the main area of activity and importance is the *centro,* which emerges between **Calle 5** and **Calle 6.** Also of interest, the region located directly by the border, where numbered streets intersect flower streets (**Lilas** and **Gladiolas**), is filled with beautiful homes.

Get your Matamoros maps from the **Brownsville Chamber of Commerce,** only 2 blocks from the border. *Casas de cambio* dot the *centro,* particularly along Calles 5 and 6, but the best exchange rates await in the bus station (which is closed on Sun.) or from friendly **ATMs** like the one at **Bancomer** at Matamoros and Calle 6 (tel. 13-90-00). **Bus** traffic flows through the **Central de Autobuses,** on Canales at Aguiles, off Calle 1. **ADO** (tel. 12-01-81) goes to Tampico (2 per day, 8hr., 122 pesos), Tuxpan (1 per day, 12hr., 172 pesos), and Veracruz with numerous stops in between (2 per day, 303 pesos). **Noreste** (tel. 13-27-68) offers the cheapest and most frequent buses to Monterrey (16 per day, 6hr., 94 pesos), and also travels to Reynosa (14 per day, 2hr., 28 pesos). **Transportes del Norte** (tel. 12-27-77) runs to Mexico City (1 *ejecutivo* per day, 18hr., 426 pesos; 4 *primera* per day, 336 pesos), Saltillo (6 per day, 7hr., 120 pesos), and San Luis Potosí (3 per day, 8hr., 150 pesos). **Trains** move out from **Ferrocarriles Nacionales de México** on Hidalgo between Calles 9 and 10 (tel. 6-67-06). Slow, unreliable service is available to Reynosa and Monterrey beginning at 9:20am. Buy a train ticket ahead of time and arrive early for boarding. **Police** are always stationed around International Bridge and the border. They can also be reached 24hr. by telephone at 2-03-22 or 6-07-00. The **post office** is in the bus station (open Mon.-Fri. 7am-7pm, Sat. 9am-1pm; **postal code:** 87361). The **phone code** is 891.

**Accommodations and Food** Although prices in Matamoros are reasonable, expect the basics—and little more. The cheapest hotels cluster in the *centro.* The market area, where most of the budget accommodations are located, quickly loses its bustling crowds after nightfall—be careful, be very careful. **Hotel Colonial,** on the corner of Matamoros and Calle 6 (tel. 16-64-18), competes with its sister hotel across the border—choose your country. The rooms are bare and slightly dark but adequate. The staff is always eager to help, and you can't beat the prices (singles 37 pesos; doubles 55 pesos). **Hotel México,** Abasolo 87 (tel. 2-08-56), on the pedestrian mall between Calles 8 and 9, is the bargain basement of budget accommodations. Here, yellow walls and bare rooms put the spotlight on the running water and soft mattresses. Beware the noisy street-side rooms (singles 50 pesos, for 2 people 60 pesos; doubles for 3 people 120 pesos, for 4 people 140 pesos). **Hotel Sexta Avenida,** on Calle 6 between Zaragoza and Terán (tel. 16-66-66 or 16-66-96), is a bit more expensive, but definitely elegant (singles 150 pesos; doubles 175 pesos).

The food in Matamoros is typically overpriced and border-town bland. If you choose to follow the crowds heading to delectable **outdoor stands,** check for proper cleanliness and hygiene. There are some great small **cafés** between Calle 6 and Calle 9. **Café Planchado,** on Calle 6 (tel. 12-22-90), north of the plaza, has been a staple in town since 1953. The restaurant offers speedy service and yummy-to-the-tummy Mexican favorites at equally palatable prices. Ask for a table away from the main entrance (it'll be cooler and quieter) and sample tacos (12 pesos) or lunch specials at varying prices (open daily 6am-2pm). **Café y Restaurant Frontera,** on Calle 6 between N. Bravo and Matamoros (tel. 3-24-40), is filled with locals enjoying the optical-illusion floor while digging into Mexican specialties (15-20 pesos). Look for the heart-shaped sign (open daily 7am-10pm).

**Sights and Entertainment** Brash vendors pounce upon any sign of interest, so be wary and look weary. The old market, or **Pasaje Juárez,** has entrances on both Matamoros and Bravo between Calles 8 and 9. Bright *piñatas* and rows of glittering jewelry brighten the dim interior of **Mercado Juárez,** the new market on Abasolo between Calles 9 and 10. Remember, though—markets farther south offer higher quality and lower prices. For a cultured evening, stop by the **Teatro de la Reforma,** on Calle 6 between González and Abasolo (tel. 12-51-21). Renovated in 1992, this beautiful colonial brick building is home to everything from classical drama to contemporary Mexican theater. Ticket prices for most shows are 20-30 pesos. If you're in the mood to bar-hop, boogie, and booze, think twice. Most reasonably priced **bars** (and yes, real saloons too) near the border are very unsafe at night. More upscale drinking occurs in bars located in or near fancy hotels.

# ■ Reynosa

Despite its growth from a 1749 Spanish colony to its present size of over 600,000, the small-town atmosphere of Reynosa, across the border from McAllen, Texas, may recall old Zorro movies. However, the sight of local teens with body piercings speaking American slang is enough to quell false nostalgia. There isn't a lot to see or do in Reynosa. The wide, clean streets and shady plaza make it a marginally worthwhile daystop before venturing deeper into Mexico, but before nightfall, you'll likely get that further-south itch.

**Orientation and Practical Information** Reynosa is 150km from Monterrey and 645km from Mexico City; it can be reached from McAllen by taking 23rd St. 12km south into Hidalgo and then over the **International Bridge.** From Mexico, Rte. 2 from Matamoros and Rte. 40 from Monterrey both lead straight into town. The city forms a square with the International Bridge border crossing forming the northeast corner. The city rises to the **central plaza,** one square block bounded by Zaragoza on the north, Hidalgo on the west, Morelos on the south, and Juárez on the east. *Peseros* run in nearly all directions for about 1 peso; taxis will try to overcharge, so haggle.

The **tourist office,** Cámara de Comercio, at Chapa and Allende, has lots of free pamphlets with maps and brochures. Super-size your city map of the city for 30 pesos (open Mon.-Fri. 9am-5pm). *Casas de cambio* are scattered all along Hidalgo and the plaza area, but most will not accept traveler's checks; the **Centro de Cambios "Reynosa,"** Matamoros 505 (tel. 22-90-60), is one of the few that will. **Bancomer,** on the south end of the plaza, offers 24hr. **ATMs.** The **bus station** is on Colón in the southwest corner of town. **ADO** offers primarily evening service with routes to Tampico (2 per day, 11hr., 125 pesos), Veracruz (2 per day, 306 pesos), and Villahermosa (1 per day, 419 pesos). **Futurama** offers *ejecutivo* and *primera clase* service to Monterrey (4 per day, 4hr., 104 and 69 pesos), Mexico City (3 per day, 16hr., 429 and 289 pesos), and Guadalajara (2 per day, 15hr., 390 and 295 pesos). **Ómnibus de México** runs to Monterrey (15 per day, 4hr., 69 pesos), Saltillo (9 per day, 6hr., 69 pesos), and Chihuahua (2 per day, 15hr., 308 pesos). **Noreste** offers the most extensive service; it will take you to San Luis Potosí (9 per day, 10hr., 190 pesos), Matamoros (25 per day, 2hr., 28 pesos), Monterrey (30 per day, 4hr., 69 pesos), and many other destinations. The **train station,** located in a dirty, decrepit, unsafe part of town, 6 blocks south of the plaza on Hidalgo, boasts unreliable, slow service to Matamoros and Monterrey. The **police** (tel. 22-00-88 or 22-07-90) are housed south of the railroad, to the right off Blvd. Morelos. The **post office** is on the corner of Díaz and Colón by the train station (open Mon.-Fri. 8am-7pm, Sat. 9am-1pm; **postal code:** 88630). Should you desire to call, the **phone code** is 89.

**Accommodations and Food** The many hotels around the plaza are pricey. The cheapest are around south Díaz and Hidalgo streets near the train station. Although boisterous and congested during the day, this area becomes desolate, and even a little scary, at night. *Cuídate.* The amenities at **Hotel Rey,** 556 Díaz (tel. 22-26-32 or 22-29-80), overlooking the Hidalgo marketplace, are fit for a king. The phone in the lobby, with free local calls, just might have the fastest international operator access this side of the border (1 person 120 pesos; 2 people 150 pesos). **Hotel Avenida,** at Zaragoza 885 Ote. (tel. 22-05-92), is the best of both worlds—the central patio with flora and birds is traditionally Mexican, but carpeted floors and deodorized bathrooms make this bargain very reminiscent of a U.S. chain. With its proximity to the main plaza and an A/C-TV combo, you can't lose (singles 120 pesos; doubles 150 pesos). To find **Hotel San Miguel** (tel. 22-75-27), follow the arrows on signs for 2 blocks as you exit the bus station. Despite the dark rooms and bugs, crazy and colorful bathroom tiles and cable TV make you forget about your worries. Insist on a room with working A/C (singles 88 pesos, doubles 110 pesos).

A good man may be hard to find, but good sit-down restaurants are even harder to find in Reynosa. Locals eat at outdoor stands or at open-air family-run cafeterias (there are many near the border). Despite the classy paintings by Frida Kahlo and Diego Rivera at the immaculate and cool **Café Sánchez,** on Hidalgo (tel. 22-16-65) off the southwest corner of the plaza, it's the food that lures in the diverse crowd of businessmen, bus drivers, and families of ten. Entrees (18-25 pesos) are *riquísimos* (open daily 7am-8:30pm). Hidden behind brash vendors in the Hidalgo marketplace, **Café Veracruz,** Hidalgo 510 (tel. 22-12-68; open daily 10am-8pm), is illuminated by blue neon. A wide selection of seafood swims toward the yuppie in you. Entrees range from 15 pesos (certain types of *pescado*) to 54 pesos (*langostinos,* of course).

**Sights and Entertainment** At nightfall, the main plaza hosts congregating couples, young and old. The **Hidalgo marketplace** may not offer any substantial deals, but it is a great spot for people-watching. For an abridged history, check out the beautiful storefront mural on the corner of Zaragoza one block east of Canales, just a few blocks south of the border crossing. It was funded by Bacardí (their billboard forms the last scene of the mural). Doesn't it just make you want to sip a *Cuba Libre?*

Well...OK then, but be careful. Drinking in Reynosa is serious stuff. Most bars and boozing tend to be near the border. Most brawls and brain damage occur near the border. Coincidence? You decide.

Most nightspots have on- and off-seasons. For a month during spring breaks, Reynosa turns into a miniature Cancún; the off-season, on the other hand, is a mellow time. Some bars shut down completely, but not the **Alaska Grill,** a dark, cold discotheque with two levels, an enormous dance floor, and a fully-stocked bar. In summer, happy "hour" (noon-1am) means no cover, and all beers, all shots, and all mixed drinks for US$1. Whether empty or full, Javier the bartender will be happy to pump the music and get the fog machine going. Alaska never sounded this good before.

# ■ Laredo, Texas

Having served under seven flags in its history, Laredo (pop. 166,000), according to its tourist packets, is now the second-fastest-growing city in the U.S. This growth is painfully apparent to the onlooker: public buildings are being expanded and small family cafeterias being demolished to make way for ominous two-story fast-food chains. Still,

Laredo tries to keep its precarious grip on the friendly, small town at its heart; plenty of grassy knolls and highly wanderable historic districts set off the strip malls and new Marriott looming nearby.

## ORIENTATION

Laredo's downtown centers around **International Bridge #1,** which becomes **Convent St.** on the U.S. side and runs north. Seven blocks north of the border, and one block west of Convent **(Salinas St.)** is **Jarvis Plaza,** surrounded by all the main government buildings and delimited by **Matamoros** and **Farragut.** The other main thoroughfare is **San Bernardo,** which originates near the border and runs north past some of Laredo's finest historical buildings (the **Laredo Civic Center** and **Chamber of Commerce**), as well as most motels and restaurants. One block east lies **I-35,** what used to be the eastern border of town for most travelers. Many newer hotels and nightspots, however, now lie miles north and east of Jarvis Plaza and the border, accessible only by car and taxi. East-west streets are named after American and Mexican military and political figures.

Getting around town is easy thanks to **El Metro city buses** (tel. 795-2280), which run from Matamoros and Farragut streets on Jarvis Plaza (every ½hr., Mon.-Sun. 6am-9pm; 60¢, children 25¢). Get schedules from their office, in the **Laredo Intermodal Transit Center** on the south side of the Plaza (which is still in a state of heavy construction, although it was scheduled for completion in January 1997).

## PRACTICAL INFORMATION

**Tourist Office: Chamber of Commerce,** 2310 San Bernardo (tel. (800) 292-2122 or 722-9895), north of the border. Cordial staff offers colorful, informative, and easy-to-read maps and brochures directing you to a plethora of sights and eateries in the downtown area. The full-size map of Laredo and Nuevo Laredo (US$2) is a grand cartographic achievement. Open Mon.-Sat. 8:30am-5pm.

**Currency exchange:** *Casas de cambio* all along Convent, and a few sprinkled throughout downtown. **Laredo National Bank,** 600 San Bernardo, is the proud owner of a 24hr. **ATM.**

**Fax: Western Union,** 711 Salinas (tel./fax 722-08-50), by Jarvis Plaza. Postal boxes, fax, copies, FedEx, UPS, and pool cues available. Also located in the bus station and every HEB supermarket.

**Internet Access: Laredo Times,** 111 Esperanza Dr. (tel. 728-2505), provides email accounts (US$17 per month, negotiable).

**Airport:** On Maher (tel. 795-2000), northeast of town. **American Eagle** (tel. (800) 433-7300) serves Dallas (4 per day, 2hr.); **Continental Express** (tel. (800) 525-0208 and 723-3402) covers Houston (6 per day, 1½hr.); and **Taesa** ((800) 328-2372 and (956) 725-1022) goes to Mexico City (Mon., Tues., Thurs., and Fri., 2hr.).

**Buses:** The bus station is on San Bernardo and Matamoros (tel. 723-1321). **Greyhound**-affiliated service runs to cities throughout the U.S., as well as daily buses to San Luis Potosí (3 per day, US$48), León and Aguascalientes (1 per day, US$42), Querétaro (2 per day, US$40), and Monterrey (7 per day, US$25). However, traveling south from Nuevo Laredo is much cheaper and provides more destinations and departures. **Luggage lockers** (first 6hr. US$2, each additional 30min. US$1).

**Trains: Missouri Pacific Railroad,** just west of Jarvis Plaza. Service to Nuevo Laredo, but it's much quicker and cheaper to take a bus or just walk across.

**Market: HEB,** 1002 Farragut (tel. 791-3511), 2 blocks south of the courthouse downtown. Other locations throughout town. Open daily 8am-9pm.

**Laundromat: Sunshine Laundromat,** 2900 San Bernardo, north of the Chamber of Commerce. Do it yourself (75¢ per wash, US$1 per dry, detergent available), or get same-day full service (small load US$5, large load US$6.50). Open daily 8am-8pm.

**Pharmacy: J&A Pharmacy,** 201 West Del Mar Blvd. (tel. 717-3839), far northeast of town. Open Mon.-Fri. 9am-8pm, Sat. 9am-4pm.

**Hospital: Mercy Regional Medical Center,** 1515 Logan Ave. (tel. 718-6222).

**Police:** 1300 Matamoros (tel. 723-3643), in the Greek Revival building by Jarvis Pl.
**Post Office:** 1300 Matamoros (tel. 723-3643), on Jarvis Plaza, housed with police
headquarters. Open Mon.-Fri. 8:30am-5pm, Sat. 9am-noon. **Zip Code:** 78040.
**Area code:** 210.

## ACCOMMODATIONS

Nice hotels in Nuevo Laredo are cheaper than the most inexpensive Laredo lodgings. Nevertheless, those who value American motel amenities (drinkable tap water
or national-chain status) will find an ample selection along San Bernardo north of the
Chamber of Commerce, where budget hotels (U.S. style) are dime-a-dozen. Expect
good deals and nice, standard rooms from such big names as **Days Inn,** 4820 San
Bernardo (tel. 722-6321); **Best Western Fiesta Inn,** 5240 San Bernardo (tel. 723-
3603); or **Motel 6,** 5310 San Bernardo (tel. 725-8187). Most lodgings are accessible
by the #2 El Metro city bus. For something a bit different:

**Mayan Motor Inn,** 3219 San Bernardo (tel. 722-8181). The charming wooden furnishings, pig-leather trappings, bathtubs, A/C, TVs, parking, lobby with coffee
bar, and recreational pool are not Mayan. Singles US$25; doubles US$35.
**Cortez Hotel,** 3113 San Bernardo (tel. 727-1001). With jungle-print bedsheets,
dark wood panelling, and hanging Tiffany-style lamps, these are perhaps the
kitschiest rooms around. The best part? Prices are just a starting-off point for
negotiations and cutting deals. Come on now, don't be shy. Singles US$30; dou-
bles US$39.

## FOOD

Head downtown for a copious culinary selection with a strong emphasis on Tex-
Mex cuisine (who knew?). Salsa-phobes can find salvation in seafood restaurants or
Chinese buffets. Fast-food joints and yummy *taquerías* line San Bernardo.

**Tacolare,** 1206 San Bernardo (tel. 727-8100), just north of the railroad tracks. The
small storefront disguises a large and inviting restaurant, a favorite among locals,
with tiled decor and central kitchen area. Watch tacos being brought into the
world (great selection, under US$5). Open Mon.-Sat. 11am-10pm.
**Canton Plaza,** 900 Houston off San Bernardo (tel. 725-2690), near Laredo National
Bank. Don't be misled by the large aquarium, plush green curtains, faux-malachite
table-tops—the (albeit U.S.) prices for Chinese food are very reasonable. Entrees
US$5-8, but don't miss the extensive and excellent buffet, US$5 all day. Get there
early while the food is fresh and hot. Open Mon.-Thurs. 11am-9pm, Fri.-Sat.
11:30am-10pm, Sun. 11:30am-8pm.
**Danny's Restaurant,** 802 Juárez (tel. 724-3185), off Jarvis Plaza near the courthouse building. The striking similarities to Denny's make you wonder until you
taste the food (it's good). Lunch specials include heaping portions of enchiladas,
*caldo de res,* and your favorite *hamburguesa* for US$3-5. Danny encourages you
to eat three balanced meals a day—breakfast specials US$2.59. Open daily 6am-
11pm.

## SIGHTS AND ENTERTAINMENT

The **Civic Center,** on San Bernardo about 1km north of the border, is the place to
catch traveling performances or the **Laredo Philarmonic Orchestra** (tel. 727-8886;
concerts some nights Oct.-May at 8pm). Every February, Laredo turns into one big
**Washington's Birthday Celebration,** which includes a parade—led by the town
princess dressed as Pocahontas—and the Martha Washington Ball. For something a
bit more sinister, try **Yerbería de San Judas,** on 711 Salinas (tel. 725-83-36), a witchcraft store selling herbs and religious charms.

"Entertainment" in Laredo (e.g. drinking yourself into a stupor and losing $150 to
a pool shark) is complicated by the large distances between establishments and the
relative scarcity of taxis—most people drive into Laredo from the highway. On top

**NORTHEAST MEXICO**

of this, police are hyper-cautious and alert, especially at night, frequently arresting people for public drunkenness and drunk driving. The adventurous should try **Club Gastronómico,** 1802 San Bernardo (tel. 722-9235). Despite its indigestive name, this tiny shack-like building right off San Bernardo promises the coldest beer in town and a pool table. Prices are less than *astronómico.*

# ■ Nuevo Laredo

Nuevo Laredo pulses with commerce, from small souvenir shops to enormous tractor trailers passing through with NAFTA-spurred trade. Today, pesos and dollars pour through Nuevo Laredo (pop. 575,000) at a dizzying pace, leaving its residents to snatch the crumbs that fall through the cracks. Laredo's cheap liquor and abundant artisans attract over-the-border-for-an-afternoon tourists, but the city's gorgeous plazas and friendly inhabitants make it more desirable than most Mexican border towns.

## ORIENTATION

**International Bridge #1** is the main way for pedestrians to go into Mexico; simply plunk down the 35¢ (for information on crossing the border, see p. 16). Travelers stick to the *centro*. **Avenida Guerrero** emerges from **International Bridge #1** as the main thoroughfare running south from the border. Three plazas along Guerrero define the downtown, with small, inviting **Plaza Juárez** just two blocks from the border; large, central **Plaza Hidalgo** adjoining the **Palacio Federal** in the heart of the city; and **Plaza México** with its endearing fountain farthest south. The train station forms the extreme western boundary of downtown, and the bus station lies to the far south of town.

## PRACTICAL INFORMATION

**Tourist Office: Delegación Turismo** (tel. 12-01-04), at the Nuevo Laredo tip of the bridge before Mexican customs. Extensive supply of brochures in both Spanish and English.

**Currency exchange:** As usual, *casas de cambio* (especially the one at the border) offer the best exchange rates. Major banks line Guerrero near Plaza Hidalgo. **Banamex,** on Canales and Guerrero, has a 24hr. **ATM.**

**Telephones: LADATELs** are to be found throughout the downtown border area, particularly near Plaza Hidalgo and Plaza Juárez.

**Fax: Western Union,** on Valle on the east side of the Palacio Federal. Fax Mon.-Fri. 9am-7pm; telegrams Mon.-Fri. 9am-8pm; money wiring Mon.-Fri. 8am-6pm, Sat.-Sun. 9am-noon.

**Airport:** Tel. 14-07-05. At the extreme southwest of the city, off Rte. 2. Purchase **Aeroméxico** tickets at **Viajes Furesa,** Guerrero 830 (tel. 12-96-68), for the flight to Mexico City (11:50am direct, and 6pm via Guadalajara). **Mexicana** offers various direct and indirect flights to Mexico City as well.

**Buses:** Station is at Refugio Romo 3800, southwest of the city and quite a trek from the *centro*. To get to the border, take any blue-and-white or green-and-white bus marked *"Puente."* To get to the station from the border, take the bus marked *"Central."* 24hr. **luggage storage** 18 pesos. **Ómnibus de México** goes to Aguascalientes (5 per day, 11hr., 318 pesos), Guanajuato (4 per day, 13hr., 259 pesos), Xalapa (282 pesos), Saltillo (4½hr., 100 pesos), Zacatecas (5 per day, 9hr., 210 pesos), Monterrey (4 per day, 3hr., 59 pesos). **Noreste** travels to Matamoros (4 per day, 5½hr.) and Reynosa (8 per day, 3½hr.). **Turistar** can take you to Acapulco (22hr., 518 pesos), Morelia (17hr., 334 pesos), Mexico City (16hr., *ejecutivo* 461 pesos; *primera clase* 369 pesos), Querétaro (13hr., 400 pesos or 296 pesos). **Futura** travels to Guadalajara (16hr., *ejecutivo* 413 pesos; *primera clase* 318 pesos), León (12hr., 381 pesos or 289 pesos), and San Luis Potosí (11hr., 299 pesos or 220 pesos). **Transportes del Norte** boasts a bus to Monterrey (every ½hr., 3hr., 72 pesos).

**Trains:** Station on López de Lara near Mina St. The almost-defunct train station has switched from being government-owned to privately-owned, and service is dubious and arbitrary. The big event of the day is a train to Monterrey between 6-7pm.

**Market: Gigante,** Reforma 4243, on the southern extension of Guerrero.

**Pharmacy: Farmacia Calderón,** on Guerrero west of Plaza Hidalgo. Open 24hr.

**Hospital: ISSTE,** (tel. 14-80-16) on Victoria and Reynosa to the east of Plaza Juárez by the border. Limited English spoken.

**Red Cross:** On Independencia and Méndez (tel. 12-09-49), east of Plaza Hidalgo.

**Emergency:** Tel. 06.

**Police:** Tel. 12-21-46. In the Palacio Federal, facing Plaza Hidalgo.

**Post office:** In the Palacio Federal, on the northeast corner of Dr. Mier and Camargo. Open Mon.-Fri. 8am-7pm, Sat. 9am-12:30pm.

**Phone code:** 87.

## ACCOMMODATIONS

Most hotels of all prices are found within a few blocks of the city's main plazas. There are some great bargains if you're willing to look around. A bed, a toilet, and a lightbulb are standard equipment, but don't expect much more.

**Motel Don Antonio,** González 2435 (tel. 12-18-76), on the southeast corner of Plaza Hidalgo. Awake smack in the center of town to the pleasant chirping of songbirds. Every room is an imaginative mixture of eclectic furnishings like red carpets, velvet chairs, and Chinese-print bed covers. TV and central A/C. Arrive early to snag a room. Singles 90 pesos; doubles 120 pesos; triples 140 pesos; quads 160 pesos.

**Motel Las Vegas,** Arteaga 3017 (tel. 12-20-30), 1½ blocks west of Guerrero and 4 blocks south of Plaza Hidalgo. Recently renovated, spacious rooms now boast folkloric wooden furniture and immaculate bathrooms. A stellar value. Singles 50 pesos; doubles 70 pesos.

**Hotel Texas,** Guerrero 807 (tel. 12-18-07). Although the rooms aren't exactly Art Deco (read: they're bare-boned and sparse), the pink, yellow, and turquoise paint makes this more Miami Beach than Dallas. Central location (just off Plaza Hidalgo) and hard-to-beat prices compensate for puny standing fans and the "hot water only when needed" rule. Singles 50 pesos; doubles 70 pesos; triples 80 pesos.

**Hotel Mina Posada,** Mina 3521 (tel. 13-14-73), 3 blocks east of the train station. With just 6 rooms, this quiet inn boasts better-than-U.S. lodgings at slightly-less-than-U.S. prices. With carpet, TV, A/C, telephones, lush flora, you name it. Two-person staff offers great service and conversation. Singles US$20; doubles US$25.

## FOOD

Home to the oft-imitated, never duplicated fajita, Nuevo Laredo's culinary fortes are meat and seafood. *Cabrito,* the roasted goat kid found throughout the northeast, and fajitas, often sold by the kilo, are well worth the extra money. The good stuff is south of Herrera, around Guerrero 1700.

**Playa Azul** (tel. 14-55-35, ext. 735), around Guerrero 2001. Great place to kick back and relax as you enjoy your *ceviche* (marinated fish cocktail with lime juice) and *telenovelas* (soap operas). Homey dining room decorated with tasteful *campesino* furniture and a selection of seafood specialties (25-45 pesos) that will blow your mind. Open daily 8am-9pm.

**Al-Dahabi,** Guerrero 1791 (tel. 14-78-79). Despite its exotic name, Al-Dahabi serves up Mexican food, enchiladas and all (entrees about 21-27 pesos). From midnight-8am, the *menu nocturno* has only slightly less variety. Come get a sunrise snack of guacamole or *queso fundido.* Open daily 24hr.

## SIGHTS AND ENTERTAINMENT

What's a commercial center without a **market?** The largest (and most expensive) ones are concentrated around Guerrero near the border. Since an ample selection of sturdy wooden furniture, pottery, and practical goods exists, this may be just the place for travelers exiting Mexico to load up on souvenirs. Although better prices and higher-quality goods can be found further south, Nuevo Laredo has a tantalizing and terrific supply of liquor stores. Along Guerrero, for blocks south of the border, stores carrying lavish varieties of liquor all advertise the lowest prices in town. Pick up 750mL of Kahlua for US$7 or a liter of Cuervo Gold for US$4.50.

Those in search of cultural titillation can head to the **theater** on Victoria and Reynosa, near the border. Strolling up and down Guerrero can be relaxing in the evenings when the three plazas fill with people gaily chatting and whiling away the time; the fountain on Nacatez and Guerrero is a favorite resting spot. If all this ambling about is not your style, then head to **Señor Frog's,** the self-proclaimed "Home of the Mother Margarita," just blocks south of the border on Belden. Although beers and tequila shooters are steeply priced (US$2 or 15 pesos), the lack of cover charge, the expert bartending, and the wonderfully hilarious cartoons and comics that adorn every inch of the restaurant/bar never cease to amaze. El Señor packs 'em in on weekends. Ribbit. Ribbit.

The **Raux Winery,** 308 Matamoros, though decidedly less colorful and campy than Sonesh Chainani, provides cool green lights and lots of space. Once restaurant and bar, now just bar, extra tables and chairs make this a great place to hang out.

# ■ Tampico

If you've seen Humphrey Bogart in *The Treasure of the Sierra Madre,* you might think of contemporary Tampico (pop. 270,000) as the hot, dirty, unfriendly oil town that every gringo is itching to skip. Somewhat dirty and a lot hot, maybe, but Tampico is anything but unfriendly. The pleasant nearby beach is often uncrowded on weekdays, and Tampico's two main plazas are full of fabulous architecture and much-needed greenery. Founded in the 16th century on the ruins of an Aztec village, Tampico was destroyed by pirates in 1623. Two hundred years later, though, Santa Anna ordered the city re-settled, and it soon grew into one of the most important oil ports in the world. Despite the ominous oil tankers and loads of litter, Tampico is trying to carve out a new identity: *Tampiqueños* built the first beach resort in all of Tamaulipas, and their seafood is ridiculously fresh. Tampico may not be terrific yet, but it gets an "E" for "Effort." For a seaside getaway, **Playa Miramar** is accessible by either the "Playa" or "Escollera" bus (1.60 pesos from López de Lara and Madero).

**Orientation and Practical Information** The town centers around the **Plaza de Armas** and the **Plaza de la Libertad.** To the north of the Plaza de Armas is **Calle Carranza,** to the east is **Olmos,** and to the south is **Díaz Mirón.** To get to the city center from the bus stop, take a yellow taxi (27 pesos), minibus (1.80 pesos), or *colectivo* (1.80 pesos, 3 pesos with luggage).

The **tourist office,** 20 de Noviembre 218 Nte. (tel. toll-free from the U.S. (800) 633-3441, or 91-800-57-100 from Mexico), one block west and two blocks north of Pl. de Armas, has got the goods—maps 'n' guides to the city (open Mon.-Fri. 8am-7pm, 2hr. break in the late afternoon). Exchange currency at **Central de Divisa,** Hidalgo 215 Sur (tel. 12-90-00; open Mon.-Fri. 9am-6pm, Sat. 9am-1:30pm). **Banamex,** on Madero between Aduana and López de Lara, has a 24-hour **ATM. LADATELs** that work properly are clustered around the corners of the Pl. de Armas. Avoid the mushroom-cloud-layin' bus-station LADATELs; they're ill-tempered and could blow at any moment.

The **bus station,** on Zapotal, north of the city, has adjoining first- and second-class terminals. **Ómnibus de México** (tel. 13-45-47) serves Ciudad Valles (4 per day, 2hr., 39 pesos), Monterrey (1 per day, 8hr., 143 pesos), Saltillo (1 per day, 10hr., 168 pesos), and Tuxpan (4 per day, 3hr., 51 pesos). **ADO** (tel. 13-41-88) serves Xalapa (2 per day, 9hr., 120 pesos), Matamoros (3 per day, 8hr., 112 pesos), and Puebla (3 per day, 9½hr., 119 pesos). **Futura** (tel. 13-46-55) serves Mexico City (1 per day, 9½hr., 179 pesos). **Frontera** heads to Ciudad Mante (every ½hr., 2hr., 42 pesos), Guadalajara (1 per day, 295 pesos), and Reynosa (8 per day, 6½hr., 125 pesos). **Estrella Blanca** runs buses to Tuxpan (every 2hr., 3hr., 52 pesos).

The **Sixpack,** Díaz Mirón 405 Ote. (tel. 12-24-15), three blocks east of the southeast corner of the Plaza de Armas, is a **market** which sells more than just **beer** (open daily 9am-10pm). If you need a **pharmacy,** try **Benavides,** Carranza 102 Pte. on the corner of Olmos (tel. 19-25-25), at the northeast edge of the Plaza de Armas (open Mon.-Sat. 8am-11pm, Sun. 8am-10pm). The **Red Cross** (tel. 12-13-33 or 12-19-46) offers 24-hour ambulance service. English-speaking doctors can be found at the **Hospital General de Tampico,** Ejército Nacional 1403 (tel. 15-22-20 or 13-20-35), near the bus station. In an **emergency,** dial 06. The **police** are at Tamaulipas at Sor Juana de la Cruz (tel. 12-10-32 or 12-11-57). The **post office,** Madero 309 Ote. (tel. 12-19-27), is at the intersection with Juárez on Plaza de la Libertad (open Mon.-Fri. 8am-7pm, Sat. 9am-1pm). **Postal Code:** 89000. **Phone Code:** 12.

**Accommodations and Food**  Quality budget hotels are rare in Tampico, but for those willing to pay 140-200 pesos, many of the larger hotels near the plazas provide excellent rooms. In the downtown area, there is **Hotel Capri,** Juárez 202 Nte. between Calles Altamirano and Obregón (tel. 12-26-80). Clean, no-frills rooms with fans and free coffee are pleasant, except for the noise from the street below, but hey—at least you and a slew of fun-loving, beachfaring families are in the middle of things (singles 50 pesos; doubles 55 pesos). **Hotel Central** (tel. 17-09-18), across the street from the bus station, is an equally simple option. TV, hot water, soft beds, adjoining pharmacy—this is the pick of many businessmen and stopover travelers.

Seafood is the standard fare in Tampico. Be sure to try delicious *jaiba* (blue crab). If you're feeling adventurous, try eating at a seaside stand, or at the covered food court near the river (a few blocks from Plaza de la Libertad). As you walk upstairs, you will be accosted by small "restaurant" (read: moving countertop) owners pushing their fresh food and phat prices. Have fun—but investigate the kitchen before chowing down. More upscale, **Café Mundo,** López de Lara y Díaz Mirón (tel. 14-18-31), three blocks east of Pl. de Armas, glows with locals. It's *the* place to see and be seen. The menu is varied; most entrees come with beans, fresh bread, and coffee (20-32 pesos). *Torta de milanesa con queso amarillo* with fries goes for 18 pesos (open 24hr.). At **Cafetería Emir,** Olmos Sur 107 (tel. 12-51-39), catch up on the latest Perlson *telenovela* while downing a hearty meal from the *menús económicos* (7-16 pesos; open daily 6am-midnight).

# NUEVO LEÓN

## ■ Monterrey

Fast, frenetic, and fried (baking at an average summer temperature of 93°F), Monterrey has no tolerance for slackers. Three million people and growing, Mexico's third-largest city and industrial leader has expanded aggressively at the feet of Cerro de la Silla (Saddle Mountain). Although Monterrey is decked out with the unfortunate raiment of "progress" (traffic, pollution, and a sobering belt of factories and dingy, impoverished huts), the *centro* is a pleasantly cosmopolitan surprise. Gorgeous parks, chic, smoke-filled cafes, sun-drenched plazas, and modern art are all here—and all right next door to each other. Backed by some of the country's wealthiest corporations and families, modern development has given Monterrey a look that is bold, muscular, and at times incongruous: across the street from the old yellow cathedral, a 30-story red monolith which pays tribute to Monterrey's budding business sense shoots fluorescent blue laser beams into the semi-peaceful night.

## ORIENTATION

As the largest city in northern Mexico, Monterrey serves as an important transportation hub. The bus and train stations are in the northern part of town, 3km north of the *centro*. All buses in and out of the city pass through Monterrey's huge **Central de Autobuses** at Colón and Villagrán. To reach the city center from the **bus station,** take any bus going south on Pino Suárez, the thoroughfare to the left as you exit the station (#18 lets you off at the central Gran Plaza), or walk two blocks east to the gray subway station at Cuauhtémoc and Colón, and take the **metro** (Line 2, 2 pesos) to Padre Mier or Zaragoza. The **train station** is at Calzada Victoria, six blocks west of the bus station; to get to the bus station from there, walk straight ahead on Victoria for two blocks, turn right on Bernardo Reyes, and then turn left on Colón.

Downtown, **Avenida Constitución** runs east-west along the Río Catarina, a 10km-long dry river bed that has been converted into a series of athletic fields. From west to east, the most important streets running north-south across Constitución are **Gonzalitos, Pino Suárez, Cuauhtémoc, Benito Juárez, Zaragoza, Zuazúa,** and **Dr. Coss.** From north to south, running east-west and parallel to Constitución are **Colón, Madero,** and further south, **Washington, 5 de Mayo, 15 de Mayo, Matamoros, Padre Mier, Hidalgo,** and **Ocampo.** The *Zona Rosa* is bounded by Padre Mier to the north, Zaragoza to the east, Ocampo to the south, and Juárez to the west.

**Local buses** run usually head in only one direction on any given street except for Constitución and Juárez (6am-midnight; 1.90 pesos). Popular routes include the Gran Plaza (#18 or #42), points along Padre Mier and Hidalgo (#15), and points on the perimeter of the downtown area (#69). To get from the budget hotel area to the city center, take the #1 Central or #17 Pío X bus, both of which run the lengths of Pino Suárez and Cuauhtémoc. For more detailed route information, ask locals or the outstanding bilingual staff at the tourist office.

Monterrey's amazing **subway** system, however, has all but replaced the large and confusing bus system. Although buses are useful in providing transportation to points far away from *el centro* and especially near the city's periphery, the subway system is new, spanking clean, and efficient—only seven minutes from *el metro* near the bus stop to the Gran Plaza. Signs are clear and everywhere. Tickets are 1 for 2 pesos, 4 for 7 pesos, 14 for 21 pesos (open daily 6:30am-midnight).

## PRACTICAL INFORMATION

**Tourist Office: Oficina de Turismo,** Padre Mier and Dr. Coss (tel. 345-08-70 or 345-09-02; toll-free (800) 235-2438 from the U.S., 91-800-83-222 in Mexico). A small building on the corner. From the *Zona Rosa*, walk straight across the Gran Plaza on Padre Mier until Dr. Coss. Or take the subway (line 2) to **Zaragoza,** exit on Zuauzúa and cross the street. A must for all tourists. The staff is extraordinarily helpful, with abundant maps and brochures in both English and Spanish. Open Tues.-Sun. 10am-5pm.

**Consulates: Canada,** tel. 344-32-00. **U.K.,** Priv. Tamazunchale 104 (tel. 378-25-65, open Mon.-Fri. 8am-5pm). **U.S.,** Constitución Pte. 411 (tel. 345-21-20), downtown. Open Mon.-Fri. 8am-1pm for passports and citizen's concerns, 1-5pm for visas. For emergencies after hours, U.S. citizens should dial 344-52-61.

**Currency Exchange:** Banks dot Madero near the budget hotels and flood the *Zona Rosa,* lining Padre Mier in particular, but many refuse to cash traveler's checks. All have 24hr. **ATMs.** Most open Mon.-Fri. 9am-1:30pm. **Mexdollar Internacional,** 1136 Nte. Pino Suárez (tel. 374-43-11), right by the bus station and Cuauhtémoc subway stop, offers 24hr. currency exchange at a great rate and without a service charge. **Banco del Atlantico,** Hidalgo between Pino Suárez and Cuauhtémoc, exchanges traveler's checks. Open Mon.-Fri. 9am-5pm, Sat. 9am-1pm.

**American Express:** Calzada de Valle (tel. 343-09-10), across *el río.* Catch a bus headed for "San Pedro" on Ave. Piño Suárez about 1.5km west of the *centro.* Take the #4 bus on Padre Mier from the *Zona Rosa.* Your best bet for changing AmEx checks. Open Mon.-Fri. 9am-1pm and 3-6pm, Sat. 9am-1pm.

**Telephones:** Most **LADATELs** are clustered in the *Zona Rosa.*

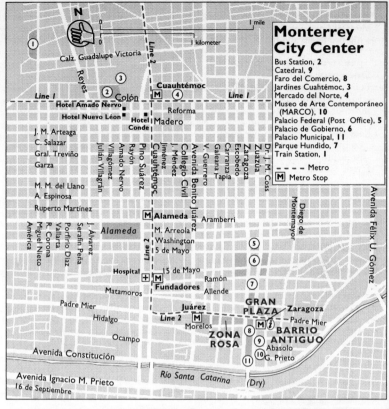

**Monterrey City Center**

Bus Station, 2
Catedral, 9
Faro del Comercio, 8
Jardines Cuauhtémoc, 3
Mercado del Norte, 4
Museo de Arte Contemporáneo (MARCO), 10
Palacio Federal (Post Office), 5
Palacio de Gobierno, 6
Palacio Municipal, 11
Parque Hundido, 7
Train Station, 1

- - - - Metro
Ⓜ Metro Stop

**Fax:** Service in the bus station between *Salas* 2 and 3, daily 7am-11pm.

**Airport:** Taxis charge 60 pesos for the 4km trip to the center, *colectivos* 40 pesos. Haggling for a lower price may work. **Aeroméxico,** Cuauhtémoc 812 Sur (tel. 343-55-60), at Padre Mier, and **Mexicana,** Hidalgo 922 Pte. (tel. 340-55-11), run flights to Mexico City, Guadalajara, and various other destinations. Offices open Mon.-Thurs. 9am-7pm, Fri. 9am-6pm, Sat. 9am-1pm and 3-6pm. Make reservations at least 2-3 days in advance, more for weekend travel.

**Buses:** Colón at Villagrán to Amado Nervo. 24hr. **pharmacy** and **emergency** medical unit. **Luggage storage:** Bag check 2 pesos per hr.; 24hr. lockers 18 pesos. **Ómnibus de México** to Aguascalientes (2 per day, 8hr., 166 pesos), Chihuahua (3 per day, 12hr., 241 pesos), Guadalajara (4 per day, 11hr., 238 pesos), Mexico City (2 per day, 12hr., 283 pesos), Querétaro (every hr., 10hr., 214 pesos), Zacatecas (3 per day, 6hr., 130 pesos), and more. **Noreste** goes to Laredo, Texas (4 per day, 3hr., *primera clase* 74 pesos, *regular* 54 pesos). **Frontera** (tel. 375-09-87) goes to Saltillo (every hr., 22 pesos), Leon (6 per day, 178 pesos), and other destinations. Similar service provided by **Estrella Blanca** (tel. 318-37-47), **Frontera** (tel. 375-09-87), **Líneas Americanas,** and luxurious **Futura** and **Turistar.**

**Trains: Región Noreste,** Calzada Victoria (tel. 375-46-04). Sometimes cheaper than buses, but always much, much slower. To Mexico City (154 pesos).

**Supermarket: Gigante,** on Colón, across from the bus station. Open Mon. and Wed.-Sat. 9am-10pm, Tues. 9am-9pm. Offers clothes, food items, *panadería,* and an adjoining **pharmacy. Mercado del Norte,** also known as La Pulga, is an endless maze of vendor stalls covering Reforma, the street just south of Colón; enter on Colón, 2 blocks east of the bus station. Haggle. Open from morning to dusk.

**Laundromat:** Padre Mier 1102 Ote. (tel. 42-11-08), in el Barrio Antiguo. Self-service. Open Mon.-Sat. 8am-7pm.

**Pharmacy:** In the bus station or **Benavides,** Pino Suárez at 15 de Mayo. Open 24hr.
**Medical Emergencies and Assistance: Red Cross** (tel. 342-12-12 or 375-12-12), at Alfonso Reyes and Henry. Open 24hr. **Cruz Verde,** at Ciudad Madero and Ciudad Victoria (tel. 371-50-50 or 371-52-59). English spoken. Open 24hr. Or try the hospital at subway stop "Hospital."
**Emergency:** Dial 06.
**Police:** on the corner of Gonzalitos and Lincoln (tel. 11-11-77, 342-00-53, or 342-00-55). For missing persons call **Locatel** (340-77-77). Little English spoken.
**Internet Access:** For internet information in Monterrey, email the tourist bureau of the government city at turismo@acme.net.
**Post Office:** Zaragoza at Washington (tel. 342-40-03), inside the Palacio Federal; or on the 2nd fl. of the bus station near *Sala* 3. Both open Mon.-Fri. 8am-7pm, Sat. 9am-1pm. **Postal Code:** 64000.
**Phone Code:** 8.

## ACCOMMODATIONS

Hotels conveniently located near the *Zona Rosa* inflate their rates to exploit tourists; budget accommodations, catering more to local businessmen, are sprinkled throughout the underdeveloped area near the bus stations. Many rooms are full by early afternoon. Bugs are an ever-present reality in congested Monterrey; if they become a problem, ask the management to spray your room. Take precautions when walking in this area at night; the streets become deserted by 10pm.

**Hotel Posada,** Amado Nervo 1138 (tel. 372-3908), across from the bus station. Cross the overhead walkway on Colón. More luxurious than the other hotels near the bus station: the walls are thicker, the rooms are quieter, the fans newer. Arrive early at this little inn—its prime location draws weary travelers quickly. 1-2 people 105 pesos, with A/C 117 pesos; 3-4 people 140 pesos, with A/C 163 pesos.
**Hotel Amado Nervo,** Amado Nervo 1110 Nte. (tel. 375-46-32). Well-furnished rooms with full-length mirrors and giant showers that spew out a steady stream of blissfully hot water. Management can be helpful in combatting insects. Singles 80 pesos; doubles 110 pesos.
**Hotel Nuevo León,** Amado Nervo 1007 (tel. 374-19-00). Sure, you'll wake up to the sound of blaring horns and other street noise, but who can complain with such soft beds, warm water, and a wonderful, doting staff? Hallway phone available for use by patrons. Singles 70 pesos; doubles 90 pesos.

## FOOD

Barbecued meats, especially *cabrito* (goat kid), are a specialty of northern Mexico; other popular dishes include *agujas* (collar bone), *frijoles a la charra* (beans cooked with pork skin, coriander, tomato, peppers, and onions), *machacado con huevos* (scrambled eggs mixed with dried, shredded beef), hot *tamales,* and for dessert, *piloncillo con nuez* (hardened brown sugar candy with pecans) or heavenly *glorias* (candy balls of goat's milk and nuts). Although the **Zona Rosa** is home to some of Monterrey's most expensive shopping (and some of northern Mexico's most expensive hotels), for food it can't be beat. Catering mainly to businesspeople on their lunch breaks or arduous shoppers, the service is good, the food *sabroso,* the prices more than reasonable. *Buen Provecho.*

**La Puntada,** Hidalgo 123 Ote. (tel. 340-69-85), east of Juárez in the *Zona Rosa.* Quickly served meals in the friendly, relaxing atmosphere. Join in lively conversation between mouthfuls of ultra-fresh tacos and tortillas. Although breakfast specials are only 10 pesos, their specialty is *comida americana* (10-16 pesos). The *hamburguesa especial* (16 pesos) comes complete with all of the toppings, including what else but *guacamole* and *jamón.* Open daily 7am-10pm.
**Las Monjitas** (The Little Nuns), Escobedo 903 (tel. 344-67-13), and 2 other locations in the *Zona Rosa.* This dark, abbey-like restaurant with servers dressed as

nuns is worth the delirious heat for more than its kitsch value. For a big dinner, tackle *Platillo Juan Pablo II* (38 pesos). Enchiladas and quesadillas run about 15 pesos, most varieties of *flautas* only 13 pesos? Good Lord! Open daily 8am-11pm.

**Los Kajones,** Padre Mier 619 Pte. (tel. 345-73-14). White and blue stucco walls, crêpe paper flowers, and little after-lunch candies make you feel like you're in a *piñata.* The menu changes every day but the good food and low prices (18-25 pesos) don't. Open daily 8am-6pm.

**El Dicho,** Naranjo 1003, at the far end of the Barrio Antiguo, near Av. Constitución. This brand-new cafe/restaurant is the perfect place to sip an ice-cold soda and watch TV. *Tortas* 15 pesos; tacos 2 pesos. Open Mon.-Fri. 8am-7pm, Sat. 8am-5pm.

## SIGHTS

Though their decisions may seem sketchy at times, at least Monterrey's architects were kind to tourists. They jam-packed virtually all of Monterrey's sights, art and historical relics (both new and old) into one grand plaza called, er, the Gran Plaza. The Gran Plaza is bounded by Washington on the north, Constitución on the south, Zaragoza on the west, and Dr. Coss on the east. The Gran Plaza is host to a slew of lovely government buildings including the **Palacio Federal,** the **Palacio del Gobierno** (at the north end of the plaza), and the **Palacio Municipal** (at the southern end). If the sun is too much for you, try dozing in the **Parque Hundido** (Sunken Park), just south of the Palacio del Gobierno, a cool and verdant garden paradise for lovebirds. One of Mexico's most notorious centers of public affection, the *parque* looks like Noah's Ark, with groups of two napping, nuzzling (and often just plain necking), all over the place. Farther along the Gran Plaza lies the **Fuente de La Vida** (Fountain of Life) which douses an immense statue of Neptune surrounded by cavorting nymphs and naiads. The most striking construction, however, is the bright orange **Faro del Comercio** (Commerce Lighthouse) topped with a laser beacon that circles the skies at night. The lighthouse serves a purely symbolic purpose, a testament to the economic ambitions of Monterrey's leaders. The laser doesn't begin to pulse until after 10pm, when hundreds pack the adjoining Barrio Antiguo in search of some late-night fun. Just across Zuazúa from the Faro de Comercio is the resplendent, pale yellow **Catedral de Monterrey.**

If you're weary of planting yourself in front of *palacios* or watching couples go at it in the park, perhaps a good dose of culture is what you need. Don't worry—Monterrey's got plenty of that, too. Just off the northeast corner of the Gran Plaza, the **Museo de Historia Mexicana,** Dr. Coss 445 Sur (tel. 345-98-98), mimics the ridges of the Saddle Mountain in the background. This geometric sandstone structure differs greatly from the gray edifices lining the plaza; its pyramidal form is an evocative reminder of Mexico's ancient past. Inside, two twisted staircases wind their way up to a permanent collection that includes state-of-the-art audio-visual resources, intriguing artifacts, and informative exhibitions (open Tues.-Thurs. 11am-6pm, Fri.-Sun. 11am-8pm; admission 8 pesos, students with ID 5 pesos). If you're feeling even more hip and progressive than usual, check out the **Museo de Arte Contemporáneo (MARCO)** (tel. 342-48-20), where changing exhibitions display the works of prominent avant-garde painters, photographers, and other artists. At worst, the art is pretentious and annoying. Most of it, however, is interesting and radically different work. An immense bronze dove that looks like a huge phallus guards the entrance (open Tues. and Thurs.-Sat. 11am-7pm, Wed. and Sun. 11am-9pm; admission 5 pesos, students with ID 8 pesos, free Wed.).

The **Obispado** (tel. 346-04-04), former palace of the bishop of Monterrey, is now a state museum displaying murals, paintings, and old weapons from the colonial era. The real draw is the spectacular view of the city (open Tues.-Sat. 10am-6pm, Sun. 10am-5pm; admission 10 pesos). Take bus #4 from Washington, and ask the driver to point out the stop. Also worth a visit are the **Grutas de García** (Caves of García), 45km northwest of the city and accessible by car or bus. Once there, take the cable-car railway in order to avoid the steep 700m uphill climb. Ticket for the cable car is included in the price of admission (open daily 9am-5pm; tickets 26 pesos, children 16 pesos). The Grutas are a network of natural chambers; the dozens of sedimentary layers in their walls reveal that 50 or 60 million years ago, the caves lay on the ocean floor. The easiest way to get to the Grutas is on a three-hour Grayline **tour** leaving from the Hotel Monterrey at 2:10pm (65 pesos) on Thursdays and Saturdays. Make reservations by calling 331-22-11 (open Fri.-Sun.11am-8pm; admission 8 pesos, students with ID 5 pesos). A cheaper alternative is to take an **Estrella Blanca** bus from the central bus station (every 20min.; 16 pesos).

## ENTERTAINMENT

If you want nightlife, then you want to hit the **Barrio Antiguo** (bounded by the Gran Plaza and Constitución). Silent by day and screaming by night, this neighborhood is positively anachronistic—these sleepy old buildings all turn into bars, concert spaces, and discotheques playing the newest and coolest music. After sundown, police cordon off the area to cars and although the action doesn't get started until 10:30pm or so (9:30pm on weekends), many places have no cover if you come early enough. For something a bit mellow and Bohemian, try **El Infinito,** Raymundo Jardón 904 Ote. (tel. 340-36-34). This cafe-cum-used bookstore-cum-art-house movie theater promises radical politics and killer conservation. Although no alcohol is served, if you donate a book, you get a free cup of coffee. On Thursdays and Saturdays, art-house international films are shown. **Café Paraiso** on Morelos and Mina, with its huge 8-peso frappucinos, will make you forget your summer spent sipping Sanka in Seattle (open daily 9pm-2am). Things get a little louder at **Real de Catorce,** Padre Mier 1062, a club featuring live music—everything from hard rock to sweet ballads. The space is small, neat, and classy; the bar is a work of supreme godliness (drinks 7-8 pesos; cover 20-25 pesos after 10pm; open daily 9:30pm-3am). Want something a little louder? No problem. **El Iskizzo,** on Padre Mier, has a dark, cave-like interior with an outdoor dance space and hard-core DJs. Playing the latest house, techno, trance, and rave, the primarily male-populated El Iskizzo seeks "open-minded people." Get your engines a-pumpin' and hearts a-thumpin' to go to **El Reloj,** one of the coolest clubs in town. With a young (read: pre-teen to 23-year-old) contingent, Reloj always has long lines and loud U.S. rock playing. People-watching outside may be even better than groovin' inside—your call (open daily 9pm-late; cover 26 pesos). The newly opened **Club Vongole** on Av. Constitución, east of Barrio Antiguo, is the most hip-hop, be-bop, and happening gay and lesbian night spot in town.

### Strange Brew

What do Mexican *beisból*, gardens, Monterrey's leading producer of beer, and modern art have to do with each other? If you said "nothing," you are 100% incorrect. Check out **The Cuauhtémoc,** 1½ blocks south of the General Anaya subway stop on Line 2. Featuring gardens, a **Hall of Fame** (tel. 528-57-96) that commemorates Mexican baseball legends, and the **Museo Deportivo** (a shrine to rodeos, boxing, soccer, etc.), the gardens also house a beer museum foaming over with beer-related artifacts (don't miss the mugs). Perhaps the most interesting part is the **Museo de Monterrey,** covered wall to wall with the best in modern Mexican art. The museum cafe serves (what else?) Carta Blanca beer and many others. (*Let's Go* does not recommend sampling 30 different kinds of beer and then proceeding to observe and analyze modern art—you will look and sound foolish.) Every spring, Banamex (a large national bank) funds a competition including painting and sculpture. Each year thousands of top-notch artists compete for this honor to have their work judged by a bank and displayed in an old beer factory. Go figure.

# COAHUILA

## ■ Saltillo

For a city of 700,000, Saltillo is small and dull. Despite the onslaught of car companies (including Chrysler and GM) that have drawn thousands of residents from nearby locales, the city is a fairly closed community. Early to bed and early to rise, *saltillenses* are proud of their dry climate and their pretty spot in the Sierra Madres. Only an hour from Monterrey, Saltillo's clean and relaxed downtown might best serve as a refuge of sorts for harried *regiomontanos* and a quiet break for those few who stop while flocking south to beaches and to Mexico City or north to Monterrey and the border.

**Orientation and Practical Information** Saltillo, the city in a valley between the jagged Sierra Madre mountains, lies 87km southwest of Monterrey, along desolate **Highway 40.** The **bus station** is located about 3km southwest of the city center on Blvd. Echeverría Sur. To get to the *centro,* exit the terminal, cross the pedestrian overpass, and catch minibus #10 from the small street perpendicular to Echeverría, across the street from the Restaurant Jaslo. All buses cost 1.80 pesos and run daily 6:30am-11pm. Catch a return bus (#9) at the corner of Aldama and Hidalgo, a block down the street from the cathedral, in front of the entrance to the furniture store. The *centro's* streets form a slightly distorted grid not quite aligned with the four cardinal directions. The quiet **Plaza de Armas** is home to the cathedral and is bordered by **Juárez** to the south (or right, facing the cathedral) and **Hidalgo** to the east (between the Plaza and cathedral). Walk one block to the west, past the **Palacio de Gobierno,** and one block north to arrive at **Plaza Acuña,** bordered on its west (far side) by the narrow **Padre Flores** and on the east by **Allende.**

The **Secretaría de Fomento Económico (tourist office)** is on Blvd. Luis Echeverría 1560 (tel. 15-17-14), on the 11th floor of the *über*-modern glass Edificio Torre Saltillo (not to be confused with the mushroom-shaped La Torre Hotel), on Saltillo's circular perimeter road; it's accessible by buses 2B (to catch it, walk several blocks north on Allende to Cárdenas) and 2A (continue walking north to Coss). It's worth the trek to obtain helpful maps and brochures (open Mon.-Fri. 9am-5pm). *Casas de cambio* offer the best exchange rates. **Banamex,** at Allende and Ocampo, behind the Palacio de Gobierno, has a 24-hour **ATM.** The **Central de Autobuses,** at Echeverría Sur and Garza, is accessible by minibus #9. **Transportes del Norte** (tel. 17-09-02) runs to Guadalajara (5 per day, 10hr., 213 pesos), Mexico City (1 per day, 10hr., 256 pesos), San Luis Potosí (4 per day, 5hr., 110 pesos), and Zacatecas (4 per day, 5hr., 95 pesos). **Ómnibus de México** (tel. 17-03-15) serves Aguascalientes (7 per day, 6hr., 145 pesos) and Reynosa (13 per day, 5hr., 87 pesos). **Frontera** runs buses to Matamoros (9 per day, 3hr., 66 pesos) and other places; their special draw is a shuttle to Monterrey every 20 minutes (25 pesos). The **police** are at Treviño and Echeverría Ote. (tel. 15-55-61 or 15-51-62). The **post office** is at Victoria 453 after Urdiñola (tel. 12-20-90; open Mon.-Fri. 9am-5pm, Sat. 9am-1pm). **Postal Code:** 25000. **Phone Code:** 84.

**Accommodations and Food** Blvd. Luis Echeverría, which runs along the bus station, teems with cheap places to rest your head. These two are a bit more pricey: At the modern **Hotel Saade,** Aldama Pte. 397 (tel. 12-91-20 or 12-91-21), a block west of Pl. Acuña, earth tones dominate the clean, well-furnished, and quiet rooms. Saade's location places you in the heart of it all. The rooftop restaurant offers a stunning panorama of the city and the Sierra. Rooms come in three styles, from *económico* (bed and bath) to *ejecutivo* (bed, bath, TV, phone, rug, etc.; 1 person 95-120 pesos; 2 people 125-140 pesos; 3 people 145-160 pesos.) **Hotel Urdiñola,** on Victoria 207 (tel. 14-09-40), behind the Palacio del Gobierno, is very swank, with an exquisite marble staircase, beautiful stained-glass window, and charming courtyard. This elegant retreat is also equipped with *agua purificada*, cable TVs, and phones; unfortunately, such grandeur is reflected in the prices (singles 130 pesos; doubles 154 pesos).

Be sure to sample delicious *pan de pulque* (bread made with tequila-like fermented cactus juice), a Saltillo specialty. Restaurants on Allende and Carranza cater more to tourists, while the cafes on smaller streets remain local picks. **Café and Restaurant Arcasa,** Victoria 215 (tel. 12-64-24), is a family-run cafe with a touch of class (breakfast 10 pesos, *antojitos* 14-17 pesos, *comida corrida* 18-21 pesos; open daily 7am-midnight). A tinkling fountain sets the mood in the cheerful **Restaurant Principal,** Allende Nte. 702 (tel. 15-00-15), seven blocks north of the Palacio de Gobierno, where the caged birds sing. Copious buffet options include vegetarian dishes (29-45 pesos). Their *cabecito* (19 pesos) will leave you with that invigorating after-the-hunt feel (open daily 8am-9pm).

**Sights**   Weary travelers rest assured: Saltillo does not lend itself to much sight-seeing. Saltillo's streets burst with artistry and cultural pride (they even host a series of rodeos and bull fights) during **Feria de Saltillo** from July 18 to August 3. Otherwise, the most alluring site in town is probably the newly-opened **Museo de las Aves** (tel. 14-01-68 or 14-01-69), home to an incredibly large number of species of birds.

**Plaza Acuña,** two blocks northwest of the Plaza de Armas, is a good place to people-watch. Vendors spill out of the **Mercado Juárez** in the northwest corner of the plaza, while marimbas resonate and guitar players and accordionists rove through the crowds (open daily 8:30am-8pm). Perched on a hill overlooking the city, **Plaza México** (or **El Mirador**) offers a smashing view of the whole area and the unconquerable mountains beyond. Take Miguel Hidalgo uphill for a kilometer, turn left on General Cepeda (unmarked, but the 900 block of Hidalgo just after the Centro Deportivo Ojo de Agua), and follow it for another 20-50m, turning onto the winding Gustavo Espinoza and up to the small plaza with benches and old street lamps.

# ZACATECAS

■ **Zacatecas**

At approximately 2400m above sea level, Zacatecas (pop. 1.3 million) is the second-highest city in Mexico (after Toluca)—don't be alarmed if the city's many hills leave you winded. The lifeblood of Zacatecas once flowed through rich veins of silver. A silver trinket, given to early Spanish colonists by an indigenous Cascane in the mid-1500s, triggered the mining frenzy that eventually stripped the surrounding hills of 6000 tons of silver. As far as mining towns go, Zacatecas was unusually fortunate: the arts flourished under the patronage of affluent silver barons, and the rows of grand colonial mansions downtown testify to an era of lavish consumption. When the mines ran dry, Zacatecas rose again as a busy, bustling university town and center of commerce and tourism. The town's colonial beauty continues to attract a largely Mexican crowd of tourists.

## ORIENTATION AND PRACTICAL INFORMATION

Zacatecas is 347km north of Guadalajara, 135km south of Aguascalientes, and 832km south of Chihuahua. All buses arrive and depart from the **central bus terminal** on the outskirts of town. City buses (1.25 pesos; Ruta 8 to the *centro*) and taxis (10 pesos to the *centro*) wait outside.

Zacatecas has no identifiable city center. Activity revolves around two streets, **Juárez** and **Hidalgo** (called **González Ortega** southwest of Juárez). Use the Juárez-Hidalgo intersection, which falls one block northwest of **Plaza Independencia,** as your point of orientation. Many of the city's colonial monuments are on or near Hidalgo. Zacatecas evenings can get chilly, so a sweater may come in handy.

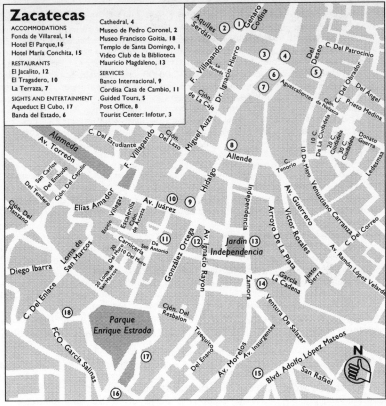

**Zacatecas**

ACCOMMODATIONS
Fonda de Villareal, 14
Hotel El Parque,16
Hotel María Conchita, 15

RESTAURANTS
El Jacalito, 12
El Tragadero, 10
La Terraza, 7

SIGHTS AND ENTERTAINMENT
Aqueduct El Cubo, 17
Banda del Estado, 6

Cathedral, 4
Museo de Pedro Coronel, 2
Museo Francisco Goitia, 18
Templo de Santa Domingo, 1
Video Club de la Biblioteca
Mauricio Magdaleno, 13

SERVICES
Banco Internacional, 9
Cordisa Casa de Cambio, 11
Guided Tours, 5
Post Office, 8
Tourist Center: Infotur, 3

**Tourist Office: Infotur,** Av. Hidalgo (tel. 4-03-93), across from the cathedral. Young, helpful staff distributes useful maps and lists of museum schedules. No English spoken. Open daily 9am-8pm. For more in-depth info about the city and state, visit the tremendously informative **Dirección de Turismo, Esplanada del Ferrocarril** (tel. 4-05-52; fax 2-93-29), near the train station. Open Mon.-Fri. 9am-3:30pm and 5-8pm. **TIPS,** a Spanish-language weekly listing cultural events and tourist services, is available during high season at hotels and at newsstands.

**Guided Tours: Asociación de Guías Turistas,** Calle del Ángel 202 (tel. 4-18-17 or 2-85-09), behind the cathedral. Guided tours of the city 90 pesos, including admission to museums and transportation. Open daily 10am-8pm.

**Currency Exchange: Cambios Zacatecas,** Gonzalez Ortega 136 (tel. 2-68-44), has excellent rates. Open Mon.-Fri. 9am-7pm, Sat. 10am-2pm. **Banca Promex,** Gonzales Ortega 122 (tel. 2-22-40) also has good rates and a 24hr. **ATM.** Open for exchange Mon.-Fri. 8am-7pm., Sat. 10am-2:30pm. **Cordisa Casa de Cambio,** González Ortega 142 (tel. 2-55-04), one block from Juárez, also changes traveler's checks and money orders. Open daily 9am-7pm.

**Telephones: LADATELs** throughout the city including the bus station. A somewhat noisy *caseta* is located inside the Centro Commercial Multicosas, on the Plaza de Independencia. Open daily 9am-2pm and 5-7pm.

**Fax:** Hidalgo at Juárez (tel. 2-00-60; fax 2-17-96). Telegrams too. Open Mon.-Fri. 8am-5pm, Sat. 9am-noon.

**Airport:** Tel. 498-03-38. Accessible by *combis* (tel. 2-59-46) from the Mexicana office (leave 1¼hr. before flight, 20min., 25 pesos). **Mexicana,** Hidalgo 406 (tel. 2-32-48). Open Mon.-Fri. 9am-7pm. **Taesa,** Hidalgo 306 (tel. 2-00-50 or 2-02-12). Open Mon.-Fri. 9am-7pm, Sat. 10am-6pm.

**Buses: Central de Autobuses** (tel. 2-11-12), Lomas de la Isabélica at Tránsito Pesado. From the *centro,* take the "Camionera Central" or Ruta 8 bus from González Ortega (1 block from Juárez). Ómnibus de México (tel. 2-54-95) has service to Durango (11 per day, 4½hr., 86 pesos), Guadalajara (16 per day, 5hr., 110 pesos), Matamoros (6 per day, 4:30am-1am, 11hr., 225 pesos), and Mexico City (11 per day, 1am-10:50pm, 8½hr., 195 pesos). **Futura** (tel. 2-00-42) sends buses to San Juan (1:50am and noon, 4hr., 60 pesos), and Reynosa (8:15 and 10:30pm, 9½hr., 196 pesos). **Estrella Blanca** (tel. 2-06-84) serves Mexico City (3:20, 8:30am, 6:40, and 10:05pm, 8hr., 165 pesos) and Torrean (about every hr., 6am-8:30pm, 6hr., 101 pesos). **Transportes del Norte** (tel. 2-00-42) sends buses to Monterrey (5 per day, 11:30am-5pm, 6hr., 130 pesos), Nuevo Laredo (7:30, 9:30, and 10pm, 11hr., 210 pesos), and Piedras Negras (4:30am, 7:45, and 9:15pm, 11hr., 247 pesos). **Transportes Chihuahuenses** (tel. 2-00-42) has service to Chihuahua (about every 45min., 12hr., 253 pesos), Irapuato (1:15, 1:40, 2:30, 10pm, and 12:30am, 4½hr., 70 pesos), and Puerto Vallarta (1am and 5pm, 12hr., 250 pesos). **Turistar Ejecutivo** sends buses to Fresnillo (6:30am, 45min., 22 pesos), and León (10:30am, 4½hr., 109 pesos). **Camiones de los Altos** (tel. 2-06-84) has service to Aguascalientas (every ½hr., 6am-8:30pm, 2hr., 32 pesos) and Nuevo Laredo (7:30pm, 9hr., 210 pesos).

**Trains: Estación de Ferrocarriles** (tel. 2-02-94). Within walking distance of downtown and accessible by the Ruta 8 bus. From Juárez, follow González Ortega until you see the train cars. To Mexico City (1st class 8:30pm, 13hr., 148 pesos; 2nd class 4:30am, 13hr., 74 pesos). Night tickets sold daily 7-9pm.

**Car Rental: Budget,** Mateos 104 (tel. 2-94-58). Minimum 300 pesos per day including insurance, taxes, and 200km daily. Must be age 25 with valid credit card and driver's license. Open Mon.-Fri. 9am-3pm and 5-8pm, Sat. 9am-2pm.

**Luggage Storage:** at the bus station, 12 pesos per day. Open daily 7am-10pm.

**Laundromat: Lavandería del Indio Triste,** Juan de Tolosa 826, an extension of Hidalgo, about 3 blocks past the cathedral. 7 pesos per kg; same-day service if dropped off before 5pm. Open Mon.-Sat. 9am-9pm.

**Red Cross:** Calzada de la Cruz Roja 100, off Héroes de Chapultepec (tel. 2-30-05 or 2-33-23), near the exit to Fresnillo. English spoken. Open 24hr.

**Pharmacy: Farmacia Central de Zacatecas,** Hidalgo 318 (tel. 2-03-21). Open Mon.-Sat. 9am-3pm, 5-9pm. **Farmacia Isstezac,** Callejón de las Campanas 103 (tel. 4-37-25, ext. 19), on the right side of the cathedral. Open 24hr.

**Hospital: Hospital General,** García Salinas 707 (tel. 3-30-04, 3-30-05, or 3-30-06). Open 24hr. **Dr. José Cruz de la Torre González** speaks English (tel. 4-07-03).

**Emergency:** Dial 06.

**Police:** Héroes de Chapultepec 1000 (tel. 2-05-07 or 2-43-79). No English spoken.

**Post Office:** Allende 111, off Hidalgo (tel. 2-01-96). Open Mon.-Fri. 8am-7pm, Sat. 9am-1pm. **Postal code:** 98000.

**Phone Code:** 492.

## ACCOMMODATIONS

The less expensive hotels in Zacatecas tend to be dingy, and middle-range accommodations are hard to come by. Unless you're willing to pay over 90 pesos for a single, hotels farther away from the *centro* are your best option.

**CREA Youth Hostel (HI),** Parque La Encantada (tel. 2-02-23, ext. 7), southwest of the city. Take the Ruta 8 bus on Gonzales Ortega (1.25 pesos) from Pl. Independencia or the bus station, and get off after about 10min. at the sign for La Encantada. Walk down Calle 5 Señores for about 15min., turn left on Calle Ancha, and walk up the hill until you see the grounds of the youth camp, and veer right around the red building. The sherbet green hostel is behind the pool to the left. Equipped with a soccer field and courts for basketball, volleyball, and racquetball. Small, sterile quads. Single-sex floors. Clean communal bathrooms. 15 pesos per person. Breakfast, lunch, and dinner 12 pesos each. Open daily 7am-11pm. **CREA Youth Hostel II (HI),** Av. de los Deportes (tel. 2-93-77), just behind the soccer stadium, is another option but is pretty far out of town (take the Ruta 11 bus for about ½hr.) and not as well-maintained. 15 pesos per person. Breakfast, lunch, and dinner 12 pesos each. Open daily 7am-11pm.

**Hotel del Parque,** González Ortega 302 (tel. 2-04-79), near the aqueduct. A tad out of the way, but in a nice area 3 blocks from Juárez just past the beautiful Parque Enrique Estrada. Vanilla decor. Clean rooms are sort of dark, though the TVs brighten things up. Singles 60 pesos; doubles 70 pesos.

**Conda de Villareal,** Plazuela de Zamora 303 (tel. 2-12-00). Within 1 block of the Plaza Independencia opposite Juárez. Central location, friendly management, and low prices are its only virtues. Lots of traffic and loitering outside at night. Singles 40 pesos; doubles 40 pesos.

**Hotel Gami,** López Mateos 309, (tel. 2-80-05), about 3 blocks from the Plaza de Independencia. Yellow walls brighten carpeted rooms complete with firm mattresses, desks, purified water, and a view of the traffic on the street below. Singles 65 pesos; doubles with 1 bed 75 pesos, with 2 beds 115 pesos.

**Hotel María Conchita,** Av. López Mateos 401 (tel. 2-14-94 or 2-14-96), 3 blocks south of the Jardín Independencia on a busy street. Looks like it was designed by Mike Brady but the less-than-sparkling rooms could use a cleaning by Alice. Rooms have tiny TVs and phones. Singles 60 pesos; doubles 70 pesos.

## FOOD

Budget meals in Zacatecas often fail to impress. Restaurant prices tend to be expensive; a better bet is to fill up on inexpensive tacos and *gorditas* (a fat tortilla stuffed with rice, beans, or tongue). Stands are scattered along Hidalgo and Juárez, and inexpensive *loncherias* serving basic Mexican fare may be found along Juan de Tolosa a couple of blocks past the cathedral. Get that sugar rush with a chunk of *dulce con leche, camote,* or *cocada,* sold by vendors throughout the *centro* (1 peso).

**Gorditas Doña Julia,** Av. Hidalgo 409 (tel. 3-79-55), across the street about 1 block from the cathedral. Locals gorge themselves on delicious *gorditas* (3.50 pesos). If you can't find a table at the restaurant, ask for your *gorditas* to go *(para llevar).* Open daily 8am-6:30pm.

**Mesón La Meña,** Av. Juárez 15 (tel. 2-27-73), just off the plaza de Independencia. As big inside as it is popular, this spacious local favorite serves up solid traditional Mexican fare. *Enchiladas verdes* 20 pesos. *Comida corrida* 25 pesos. Open daily 8am-11pm.

**Cafe Zas,** Av. Hidalgo 201 (tel. 2-70-89), about 3 blocks from the Cathedral. Students giggle over milkshakes (10 pesos) and professionals munch on burgers (12 pesos) and *chilaquiles* (19 pesos) as they read the newspaper. Open daily 8am-9pm.

**El Tragadero,** Av. Juárez 132 (tel. 2-43-32), just after the intersection with Hidalgo. The open kitchen and light decor keep this family-run joint nice and cozy. Yummy vegetarian platter 18 pesos. Enchiladas 14 pesos. Open daily 8am-10pm.

**La Terraza** (tel. 2-32-70), next to the cathedral. A lovely outdoor cafe. The menu is limited and servings are small, but it's still a great place to stop for coffee and a snack. Burgers 7 pesos. Ice cream 6 pesos. Open daily 10am-9:30pm.

**El Jacalito,** Av. Juárez 18 (tel. 2-07-71), near the Jardín Independencia. Belying its name (The Little Shack), there will always be a table waiting for you in this spacious white-walled restaurant. Popular with locals. Hot cakes breakfast combo 18 pesos. Enchiladas 16 pesos.

## SIGHTS

The 18th-century **cathedral,** on Hidalgo four blocks northeast of Juárez, has an intricately sculpted facade representing the Eucharist. Apostles, doctors, and angels jostle for space above the cathedral's main entrance. The Churrigueresque northern facade bears a representation of Christ on the cross, and the European Baroque southern facade pays homage to Nuestra Señora de las Zacatecas. The cathedral interior does not live up to the promise of its lavish exterior and is surprisingly plain (open daily 7am-1pm and 4-9pm). Next to the cathedral, the **Palacio de Gobierno** is notable for the mural which surrounds its interior stairwell. Painted in 1970 by Antonio Pintor

Rodríguez, the work traces the history of Zacatecas from the pre-Hispanic era until the present. Much of the mural devotes itself to the mugs of Zacatecas's historical players (open Mon.-Fri. 8am-8pm).

Across Hidalgo and up the steep Callejón de Veyna is the **Templo de Santo Domingo.** Built by the Jesuits in 1746, the church contains eight impressive Baroque altars of gilded wood and an elaborate 18th-century German pipe organ (open daily 7am-1pm and 3:30-9pm; quiet, respectful visitors are welcome during services). Next door, in a building whose past incarnations include a monastery and a jail, is the **Museo de Pedro Coronel** (tel. 2-80-21). Housing the tomb, sculptures, and paintings of the Zacatecan artist Pedro Coronel, the museum houses one of the best modern art collections in Latin America. Works by Picasso, Braque, Chagall, and Miró jostle for space. Mesoamerican and African masks, as well as Japanese, Chinese, and Tibetan pieces break the Eurocentric spell (open Fri.-Wed. 10am-2pm and 4-7pm, Sun. 10am-4:30pm; admission 10 pesos, students and seniors 5 pesos, children under 10 free).

The dramatic **Ex-Convento de San Francisco,** an attraction in itself, houses the **Museo Rafael Coronel** (tel. 2-81-16). To reach the museum from the cathedral, follow Hidalgo, bearing left at the first fork and right at the second. The museum is renowned for its fabulous collection of masks from around the world. (Open Mon.-Tues. and Thurs.-Sat. 10am-2pm and 4-7pm, Sun. 10am-5pm; admission 10 pesos, students, teachers, and seniors half-price, kids free. Ex-convent open same hours; free.) Southeast of the downtown area, 39 pink stone arches mark the end of Zacatecas's famous colonial aqueduct, **El Cubo.** Beside the aqueduct, the verdant **Parque Estrada** with winding stone pathways borders the former governor's mansion, now the **Museo de Francisco Goitia,** Enrique Estrada 101. (Tel. 2-02-11; open Tues.-Sat. 10am-1:30pm and 5-7:30pm, Sun. 10am-4:30pm; admission 10 pesos, seniors and children 12 and under free.)

The **Cerro de la Bufa,** named for its resemblance to a Spanish wineskin, peers down from the city's highest crag. La Bufa, as it is affectionately known, is lit by floodlights at night and is a favorite lookout point for the spectacular view it offers of Zacatecas and the surrounding area. Adjacent to the Cerro is the **Museo de la Toma de Zacatecas** (tel. 2-80-66). Erected to commemorate Pancho Villa's decisive victory over federal troops in the summer of 1914, the museum lays claim to an array of revolutionary memorabilia, including photographs, cannons, and small arms (open Tues.-Sun. 10am-4:30pm; admission 5 pesos, students, seniors, and teachers half-price, children under 11 free). On one side of the museum lies the 18th-century **Capilla del Patrocinio,** whose graceful facade and cloistered courtyards are carved from deep-red stone. Nearby shops sell arts, crafts, and loads of geodes. A short but steep walk up the hill leads to the ornate Moorish **Mausoleo de los Hombres Ilustres de Zacatecas,** worth the hike if only for the view of the city it affords (open daily 10am-6pm). There's an even better vista from the **Meteorological Observatory** behind the museum. Public buses run to La Bufa only on Sundays and holidays (take Ruta 9 from the Plaza de Armas), and a cab costs 20 pesos. The most appealing way to make the trip is by *teleférico* (suspended cable car; tel. 2-56-94), which runs between the peak of El Grillo and La Bufa every 10 minutes. Follow García Rojas northwest to its end to the cable car stop (open daily 10am-6pm; 5 pesos each way).

The **Mina de Edén** (tel. 2-30-02) was one of the region's most productive silver mines until about 30 years ago, when continual flooding made mineral extraction futile. You may enter the mine from either the top or the side. The top entrance is 100m to the right as you leave the *teleférico*. From there, walk into the mountain, take the elevator down, and begin the tour. Otherwise, follow Juárez northwest along the **Alameda,** a tree and fountain filled park lined by some of Zacatecas's grandest colonial mansions. Continue along Torreón until it ends, and then turn right and walk one block, veering to the left. From there, a mini-locomotive whisks tourists into the mountain. A one-hour guided tour (in Spanish) of the cool subterranean tunnels ensues. Tour groups cross rope bridges and learn about the haunting myths of the mine (open daily 11am-7:30pm; admission 12 pesos).

## ENTERTAINMENT

Zacatecas's nightlife kicks off on Thursday and Friday nights, when university students slam the books shut and head to the bars and discos. Not surprisingly, the tourist favorite is **El Malacate** (tel. 2-30-02), a rare opportunity to boogie in an old mine shaft. Solid rock walls are tastefully decorated with helmets, shovels, and plush green sectionals, and partiers quaff expensive drinks and dance to a mix of the latest U.S. top-40 hits and Latin rhythms (cover 40 pesos, beer 10 pesos, mixed drinks 20 pesos; open Thurs.-Sun. 9pm-3am). Revelers can also be found jamming to rock music just next to the *teleférico* station at **El Elefante Blanco,** Paseo Díaz Ordez 36 (tel. 2-71-04). The club offers a stunning view of the city at night, in addition to pool tables, foosball, and a happenin' dance floor (cover 30 pesos; open Thurs.-Sat. 9pm-3am; taxi to either club 8 pesos).

If you're feeling a bit more mellow, the **Video Club de la Biblioteca Mauricio Magdaleno,** Jardín Independencia 1 (tel. 2-59-29), is the place to be. It shows movies from just about every country and in just about every genre, including cartoons (free screenings Mon.-Fri. 11:30am and 5:30pm; look for the movie schedule in *TIPS* (see p. 245) or inquire at the library). Also check out **Nova Cinema,** Constituyentes 300 (tel. 2-54-04), for the latest in Mexican and American films. On Thursdays and Sundays at 7pm, take advantage of the free performance by the **Banda del Estado** in the Plazuela Goitia, next to the cathedral.

The yearly cultural highlight is **Zacatecas en la Cultura,** a festival during **Semana Santa** in which concerts and artistic activities are held in the elegant **Teatro Calderón,** on Hidalgo, near the cathedral, and throughout the city. For two weeks near the beginning of September, the city celebrates the **Feria Nacional de Zacatecas** with musical and theatrical events, bullfights, agricultural and crafts shows, and sporting events.

The **Museo de Arte Virreinal,** also known as the **Museo Regional de Guadalupe** (tel. 3-20-89), is in the village of Guadalupe, 7km east of Zacatecas on the highway to Mexico City. Highlights include the first series on the Virgin of Guadalupe, painted by the 18th-century artist Miguel Cabrera, and a 1621 Gutenberg volume on mining (open Tues.-Sun. 10am-4:30pm; admission 14 pesos, free Sun. and for students and teachers with ID, seniors, and children under 14). The collection of antique vehicles housed next door in the **Anexo al Convento de Guadalupe** (tel. 3-20-89) is also worth a peek (open Tues.-Sun. 10am-4:30pm; free). To get there, catch a Ruta 13 bus to Guadalupe (every 15min., 1.25 pesos) at the corner of Salazar and López Mateos, right outside the Centro Comercial car-park.

### I Wear My Sunglasses at Night

Donning shades south of the border is no easy business, especially if you want to do it right. In Mexico, sunglasses are a slightly dressier, more formal accessory than in some other countries, so men in business suits or women in dresses often wear them. Although large Ray-Ban type glasses may suit older men, they are generally to be avoided. Long, narrow ski-goggle type glasses, especially mirrorshades, the rage among Mexican adolescents a few years ago, are currently falling out of favor. Smaller, rounder, metal frames, especially when coupled with a casual button-down shirt and pants, convey a desirable cool-but-careless attitude. The right kind of glasses say, "Hey, you—are you talkin' to me?" and convey appropriate machismo. For women, strutting in sunglasses is more difficult. It is thought to be almost too stylish, too self-conscious—an admission of sexiness (and sexy intentions). Women who walk down the street peacefully one day might be cat-called or even solicited the next, all because of those *telenovela* stars who dangle tortoise-shell sunglasses from their painted lower lips during interviews. One thing everyone agrees on: no sunglasses are ever to be worn at night (unless you want to look like a chump). How 'bout actually wearing sunglasses to keep sun out of your eyes? Pshaw. Go buy a hat or something.

# AGUASCALIENTES

## ■ Aguascalientes

A charming city is the last thing a traveler expects to find in the prickly desert of Central Mexico—yet out of nowhere rises Aguascalientes (pop. 520,000). With its expansive Plaza de la Patria, beautiful churches and cosmopolitan feel, Aguascalientes makes for the perfect two- or three-day stopover en route to Zacatecas or Guanajuato. The pride and joy of the city is the eagerly anticipated **Feria de San Marcos,** two weeks of festivities between the second half of April and the first week of May. Aside from its yearly extravaganza, Aguascalientes offers a small range of attractions, including the impressive colonial architecture of its *centro histórico* and several worthwhile museums. Aguascalientes is a thoroughly modern city with the laid-back attitude one would expect of a smaller Mexican town.

**Orientation** Aguascalientes is 168km west of San Luis Potosí, 128km south of Zacatecas, and 252km northeast of Guadalajara. **Av. Circunvalación** encircles the city, while **Av. López Mateos** cuts through town east to west. The **bus station** is on Av. Convención, a few blocks west from Av. José María Chávez. All city buses are green and white; "Centro" buses (1.50 pesos) run from outside the bus station to the Mercado Morelos, two blocks north of the **Plaza de la Patria.** To return to the station, "Central Camionera" buses traverse the length of **Rivero y Gutiérrez** (parallel to and one block north of Madero). The drivers of Aguas are one of the city's miracles—due to a recent (and strictly enforced) city ordinance, everyone here wears a seatbelt. Those strapped-in *taxistas* charge about eight pesos from the bus terminal to the center of town. From the Plaza de la Patria, most sights are either on **Montoro** (the street that runs east from the southeast corner of the plaza) or on **Carranza,** which begins to the west of the plaza, behind the basilica. When you plan your day in Aguas, keep in mind that the city takes its siestas quite seriously; most sites and businesses are closed between 2 and 5pm.

**Practical Information** The **tourist office** (tel. 15-11-55 or 16-03-47) is on the first floor of the Palacio de Gobierno, on the Plaza de la Patria, the first door to the right of the main entrance. The helpful staff hands out a so-so map and answers questions (open Mon.-Fri. 8:30am-3pm and 5-7pm, Sat. 10am-1pm). **Moneytron** at Montoro 120 (tel.15-79-79), one block from the Plaza, has excellent rates and charges no commission (open Mon.-Fri. 9am-5pm, Sat. 9am-2pm). **Bancomer,** 5 de Mayo 112 (tel. 17-19-00), one block from the plaza, also offers good rates (open Mon.-Fri. 8:30am-5:30pm, Sat. 10am-2pm). **LADATELS** may be found along the Plaza and throughout town; there is a *caseta* at the **Tabaquería Plaza,** Colón 102 (tel. 15-56-51 or 15-68-95), on the corner of the Plaza (open daily 8:30am-9pm). **Telecomm,** Galeana at Nieto, (tel. 16-14-27), provides **telegram, fax,** and **money wiring service** (open Mon.-Fri. 8am-6pm, Sat. 9am-1pm).

The **bus station** is on Av. Circunvalación. **Flecha Amarilla** (tel. 78-26-61) has service to Guanajuato (8:50, 9:40am, and 8:30pm, 3½hr., 45 pesos), Irapuato (14 per day, 3½hr., 50 pesos), Mexico City (6 per day, 2am-8:20pm, 8hr., 133 pesos), and Uruapan (11:30am and 3pm, 8½hr., 120 pesos). **Primera Plus** (tel. 78-26-61) has first-class service to Mexico City (11 per day, 6hr., 178 pesos) and Querétaro (6 per day, 9am-11:30pm, 4½hr., 100 pesos). **Estrella Blanca** (tel. 78-27-58) serves Durango (1st class 3:30, 6:30, 10pm, and midnight, 7hr., 122 pesos; 2nd class 9, 11:15am, 3:15, and 5:20pm, 8hr., 103 pesos), Mexico City (direct every hr., 7am-4pm and 10pm-midnight, and 12:30am, 6hr., 165 pesos), and Zacatecas (every ½hr., 6am-8:30pm, 2½hr., 32 pesos). **Ómnibus** (tel. 78-27-70) has first-class service to Acapulco (11:30pm, 11hr., 278 pesos), Guadalajara (15 per day, 2¾hr., 78 pesos), and Zacatecas (6 per day, 6am-6pm, 2hr., 38 pesos). **Futura** sends first-class buses to

Mazatlán (11pm, 12hr., 233 pesos), and San Luis Potosí (12 per day, 6am-11pm, 3hr., 60 pesos). **Transportes de Norte** (tel. 78-27-58) has first-class service to Monterrey (12 per day, 9am-midnight, 8hr., 166 pesos) and Saltillo (11 per day, 9am-midnight, 6hr., 144 pesos). **Transportes Chihuahuenses** has first-class service to Durango (5 per day, 2:30pm-midnight, 6hr., 122 pesos) and Zacatecas (6 per day, 10am-9:45pm, 2hr., 38 pesos).

**Lavamatic,** Montoro 418 and Zaragoza (tel. 16-41-81), will deal with you and your laundry (open Mon.-Sat. 9am-8pm). **LOCATEL** (tel. 18-00-58) finds missing persons and some lost items. **Farmacia Sánchez,** Madero 213 (tel. 15-35-50), sells drugs one block from the plaza (open 24hr.; doors close at midnight, but don't hesitate to knock). **Hospital Hidalgo,** at Galeana 465 (tel. 17-19-30 or 17-29-83) is open for emergencies 24 hours. In an **emergency,** dial 06. The **police** are at the corner of Libertad and Gómez Orozco (tel. 14-20-50 or 14-30-43). The **post office** resides at Hospitalidad 108 (tel. 15-21-18), one block east of the plaza on Madero, then left on Morelos and right on Hospitalidad (open Mon.-Fri. 8am-7pm, Sat. 9am-5pm). **Postal Code:** 20000. **Phone Code:** 49.

**Accommodations** Budget accommodations in Aguascalientes lack the charm of colonial architecture and the sharpness of modern hotels. Stay in the *centro* rather than near the bus station; it's an infinitely nicer part of town. The hotels are better, the prices are about the same, and it isn't that far. During the Feria de San Marcos (mid-April to early May), reservations are a must. The **Hotel Señorial,** Colón 104 (tel. 15-16-30), is located right on the Plaza de la Patria. Rooms are somewhat small but provide all the amenities—cable TV, fan, carpet, purified water, and desk. Friendly staff will keep an eye on backpacks for free (singles 75 pesos; doubles 100 pesos). **Posada San Rafael,** Hidalgo 205 and Madero (tel. 15-77-61), is about 3 blocks from the Plaza. Ceiling fans and cable TV make up for the slightly stuffy rooms (singles 60 pesos; doubles 70 pesos). Peso-pinchers can try for the room with bath across the hall—it's half price. **Hotel San Jose,** at Hidalgo 207 (tel. 15-51-30 or 15-14-31) next to Posada San Rafael, has somewhat institutional rooms with TV and bright orange and green bedspreads. Laundry service is available (singles 70 pesos; doubles 85 pesos).

**Food** Fill up on meatless Mexican food at **Restaurant Vegetariano,** Madero 409 (tel. 15-79-89), four blocks from the Plaza. All-you-can-eat vegetarian buffet with dessert and *agua de frutas,* 18 pesos (2-5:30pm). Otherwise, cheerful staff serves up soy burgers (9 pesos), sandwiches (7 pesos), and huge platters of fruit, yogurt, and granola (12 pesos; open Mon.-Sat. 8:30am-7pm). A trip to **El Zodiaco,** Galeana Sur 113 (tel. 15-31-81), behind the Basílica, may be in the stars. Odd atmosphere includes an open kitchen, bright orange chairs, formica tables, live canaries, and a painted shrine to the Virgin. Friendly staff speaks some English. Try the nice *comida corrida* (22 pesos), a sandwich (7 pesos), or a hamburger (8 pesos; open daily 8:30am-11pm). Mingle with Mexican families in **La Maceta,** Madero 427, a sweet and cheerful mom and pop operation. Multi-colored walls give the place pizazz (tacos 2.50 pesos, *tortas* 5-7 pesos, *comida corrida* 14 pesos). The rose-colored walls and wood paneling at **Mitla,** Madero 220 (tel. 16-61-97), soothe its largely professional clientele (cheeseburger and fries 17 pesos, enchiladas 21 pesos; open Mon.-Fri. 8am-9pm).

**Sights and Entertainment** During the **Feria de San Marcos** (mid-April to early May) most events, which include everything from cockfights to milking contests, take place in the **Jardín de San Marcos,** a 5- to 10-minute walk on Carranza from the **Plaza de la Patria.** The area around the Jardín was originally an Indian *pueblo,* but around the year 1600, *indígena* labor erected the **Templo Evangelista San Marcos** at the site. The church is most notable for housing José de Alsivar's *La Adoración de los Reyes Católicos* (open daily 7am-2pm and 4-9pm). Walk two blocks to the left as you face the *templo* to reach the **Expo Plaza,** filled with shops and restaurants. If you can't stomach a real bullfight in the adjacent **Plaza de Toros,** just watch the little gold matador and shiny black bull exit the clock of Fiesta America (just behind the statue of the horseman and running bulls) and do their passes at noon, 3, 5, 7, and 9pm. Other seasonal events include the festival of the patron saint of Aguascalientes, **La Romería de la Asunción,** which takes place August 1-15. Festivities include dances, processions, and fireworks. The **Festival de las Calaveras,** one week during the second half of November, is another occasion for the city to cut loose and celebrate.

The **Museo de Guadalupe Posada,** on León (tel. 15-45-56), next to the Templo del Encino, four blocks south of López Mateos, displays morbidly witty turn-of-the-century political cartoons, replete with skulls and skeletons. The museum holds 220 original works by Mexico's most famous printmaker, including many figures caricaturing dictator Porfirio Díaz. The most famous image is that of *La Catrina,* a society lady-*calavera* (skull) wearing an outlandish hat. Diego Rivera used her figure in his *Sueño de Una Tarde Dominical en la Alameda,* now on display in Mexico City (see p. 100). The museum also shows 100 works by Posada's mentor, Manuel Manilla, and has rotating exhibits of contemporary art (open Tues.-Sun. 10am-6pm; admission 5 pesos, students 2.50 pesos, children under 12 free, free Sun.).

The soft grays and rose-colored Solomonic baroque facade of the **Basílica de la Asunción de las Aguascalientes** make it the most remarkable structure on the Plaza. Look out for the sculptures of church patrons San Gregorio, San Jerónimo, and San Agustín. The cathedral's interior is graced with high ceilings, gold trimmings, and ornate icons, as well as paintings by José de Alcíbar, Andrés López, and Miguel Cabrera (open daily 7am-2pm and 4-9pm). Another beautiful church is the **Templo de San Antonio,** on Pedro Parga and Zaragoza; from the plaza walk three blocks down Madero, then three blocks left on Zaragoza. Every inch of the interior is painstakingly decorated with a collage of soft blues, pinks, and gold leafing. The mix of patterns on the murals, frescoes, oil paintings, and delicate stained glass windows match the mix of architectural styles of the exterior, built by a local self-taught architect (open daily 7am-2pm and 4-9pm).

The **Instituto Cultural de Aguascalientes,** popularly known as the **Casa de la Cultura,** Carranza 101 and Galeana (tel. 15-34-43), hosts temporary sculpture, painting, and photography exhibits (open Mon.-Fri. 10am-2pm and 5-8pm, Sat.-Sun. 10am-9pm; free). Kiosks in the courtyard just drip with listings for cultural events; you can also check the Casa's monthly bulletin or call 16-62-70. The **Centro Cultural Los Arquitos,** on the Alameda at Héroes de Nacozari (tel. 17-00-23), served as public bathrooms from 1821 until 1973. After a magnificent restoration process, the building became a beautiful cultural center in 1994 with a bookshop, a video room that shows children's movies (Fri. 5pm), and a small museum (open Mon.-Fri. 9am-1pm and 3-8pm, Sat. 9am-1pm and 3-6pm, Sun. 9am-2pm; center open daily 9am-2pm and 4-8pm). For something less high-brow, test your skill against that of the local pool sharks and domino fiends at **Bol Kristal,** inside the Centro Comercial Plaza Kristal (open 9am-10pm daily; Sun. is the busiest day).

By city ordinance, *discotecas* in Aguascalientes are only allowed to operate Thursday to Saturday; bars operate every night of the week. Shake your caboose at **Disco El Cabús,** Blvd. Zacatecas at Colosia (tel. 73-04-32), in the Hotel Las Trojes (cover Thurs.-Fri. 20 pesos, Sat. 30 pesos; open Thurs.-Fri. 9pm-3am; no shorts). Another weekend hotspot is the *discoteca* **IOS,** Av. Miguel de la Madrid 1821 (tel. 12-65-76). Thursday and Friday women pay no cover but men pay 20 pesos; Saturdays no one gets through the door without forking over the pesos (open Sat.-Thurs. 9pm-3am). Also popular among Aguas residents is the bar **Jubilee,** Calle Laureles 602-101 (tel. 17-05-07 or 18-04-94), which features live music and dancing Thursday to Saturday (cover 20 pesos).

**San Luis Potosí**

| ACCOMMODATIONS | SIGHTS | SERVICES |
|---|---|---|
| Hotel de Gante, 10 | Palacio Municipal, 5 | Tourist Center, 12 |
| Hotel Plaza, 9 | Cathedral, 4 | Banamex, 6 |
| Hotel Progreso, 15 | Antigua Caja Real, 8 | Computel, 11 |
| RESTAURANTS | Casa Othón, 3 | 2001 Viajes, 14 |
| Restaurante-Cafetería | Iglesia de Carmen, 2 | Train Station, 1 |
| Posada del Virrey, 7 | Museo Regional | Police, 5 |
| Yu Ne Nisa, 13 | Potosino, 16 | |

# SAN LUIS POTOSÍ

## ■ San Luis Potosí

In San Luis Potosí, everyone smiles a lot. But there's a lot to smile about; *potosinos* are truly, madly, deeply in love with their city. With plazas galore, plenty of pedestrian walkways, and innumerable cathedrals gently and naturally dotting the landscapes as easily as overgrown trees, San Luis (pop. 820,000) is a crash course in urban planning. Founded in 1583 as a Franciscan mission, the city was later converted into a silver-mining boom town and became the power center of Northern Mexico before losing its political pull but growing more comfortable. Now, its "downtown," with bright, squat buildings and wide median strips harboring pineapple palms, is downright inviting; friendly and eager to embrace the surprisingly few tourists who arrive, it is the residents of San Luis who set the city apart. Bands, magicians, and soap-bubble blowers gather in the town plazas at dusk to entertain assembled crowds of young and old. Lanterns that dot the cathedrals and fountains are spectacularly lit. On a warm evening, it's hard not to feel that San Luis Potosí is the quiet capital of some magical world.

### ORIENTATION

San Luis Potosí is at the center of a triangle formed by Mexico's three largest cities—Monterrey, Guadalajara, and Mexico City. Five main highways (Rtes. 57, 85, 70, 49, and 80) snake their way into the city. To get downtown from the **bus station,** catch an "Alameda" or "Centro" bus (5:30am-10:30pm, 1.80 pesos) and hop off at **Parque Alameda,** the first big stretch of green. A **taxi** costs 15 pesos.

San Luis's main drag is **Avenida Carranza,** which runs east-west and passes the north side of the **Plaza de Armas** (also known as **Jardín Hidalgo**), the city's historic center. East of the plaza, Carranza is called **Los Bravos. Madero** runs parallel to Carranza one block south, touching the Plaza de Armas's south side. East of the plaza, Madero goes by **Othón.** Running parallel to Carranza one block north is **Av. Obregón,** the **Plaza del Carmen** is two blocks east of the plaza on Madero. A block farther east lies the **Alameda,** where the bus from the station drops off visitors. The **train station** is on Othón opposite the Alameda. **Zaragoza** forms the east side of

Plaza de Armas; north of the plaza, it goes by **Hidalgo.** On the west side of the plaza is **5 de Mayo,** known as **Allende** farther north. **Aldama** is one block west of 5 de Mayo.

## PRACTICAL INFORMATION

**Tourist Office:** Obregón 520 (tel. 12-30-68), one block west of Pl. de los Fundadores. Open Mon.-Fri. 8am-8pm, Sat. 9am-2pm. Even more helpful is a **tourist center** on the first floor of the Palacio Municipal, on the northeast corner of Pl. de Armas. Jeronimo, at the first desk as you walk in, is friendly and speaks English.

**Consulate: U.S.,** Mariel 103 (tel. 12-15-28); take the "Morales" bus. Open Mon.-Fri. 8:30am-1:30pm, but sometimes available in the afternoons. The police and the tourist office have consulate employees' home numbers in case of emergency.

**Currency Exchange: Casa de Cambio,** Morelos 400 (tel. 12-66-06). Better rates than the banks. Open Mon.-Fri. 9am-2pm and 4:30-8pm. Many banks are around Pl. de Armas (open Mon.-Fri. 9am-1:30pm); **Banamex,** at Allende and Obregón, one block east of Pl. de Armas, has a 24hr. **ATM.**

**American Express: Grandes Viajes,** Carranza 1077 (tel. 17-60-04); they do *not,* however, cash American Express traveler's cheques. **Sterling,** a *casa de cambio* around Carranza 1400, 3 blocks from the AmEx office, does.

**Telephones: LADATELs** scattered throughout the numerous plazas, particularly on Ave. Obregón and Carranza near the Plaza de las Armas and the Plaza de los Fundadores. **Computel,** Carranza 360, opposite the Hotel Panorama. International collect calls. Open Mon.-Sat. 7:30am-9pm.

**Fax: Computel** (see above); or try Escobedo 200 (tel. 12-33-18), at the south end of the Plaza del Carmen, up the stairs to your right. You can also send **telegrams** there. Open Mon.-Fri. 9am-5pm, Sat. 9am-1pm.

**Airport:** Tel. 2-22-29. 25min. north of the city. Tickets can be purchased at **2001 Viajes,** Obregón 604 (tel. 2-29-53). Flights to Mexico City begin at 462 pesos with **Aerocalifornia,** and flights to Monterrey start at 1373 pesos with **AeroLiteral.** Open Mon.-Fri. 9am-1:30pm and 4:30-7pm.

**Buses: Central de Autobuses** (tel. 12-74-11), 2 blocks south of the chaotic convergence of highways that wrap around the Glorieta Benito Juárez, 4km east of the city center along Av. Universidad. **Luggage** can be stored with the bus companies—negotiate a deal. **Estrella Blanca** (tel. 18-30-49) goes to Aguascalientes (6 per day, 2hr., 60 pesos), Chihuahua (2 per day, 14hr., 307 pesos), Cuernavaca (1 per day, 8hr., 148 pesos), Monterrey (every hr., 7hr., 124 pesos), Querétaro (6 per day, 2½hr., 51 pesos), and Zacatecas (8 per day, 3hr., 51 pesos). **Ómnibus de México** (tel. 12-75-16), to Guadalajara (1 per day, 5hr., 124 pesos), Reynosa (1 per day, 10hr., 182 pesos), Saltillo (2 per day, 5½hr., 89 pesos), and Tampico (3 per day, 6hr., 120 pesos). **Transportes Tamaulipas** and **Noreste** (tel. 18-29-15) jointly trek to Matehuala (6 per day, 2½hr., 52 pesos), Monterrey (5 per day, 7hr., 144 pesos), and Reynosa via Linares or Monterrey (3 per day, 7hr., 90 pesos). **Del Norte** (tel. 16-55-43) goes to Acapulco (2 per day, 10hr., 269 pesos), Querétaro (9 per day, 3hr., 62 pesos), and Uruapán (3 per day, 124 pesos).

**Trains:** Station on Othón near the north side of the Alameda. To Mexico City (10am, 6hr., 50 pesos), Monterrey (2 per day, 8hr., 50 pesos), and not much more.

**Car Rental: Hertz,** Obregón 670 (tel. 12-95-00). Most small cars 200-270 pesos per day plus insurance. Must be 25. Open Mon.-Fri. 9am-5pm, Sat. 9am-noon.

**Supermarket: Gigante,** with a sign that beams like a jolly blue giant. Cross the street from the bus station, turn left, and follow the curve until you see the sign. Open Mon.-Fri. 9am-9pm, Sat.-Sun. 9am-8pm.

**Laundromat: Lavandería La Burbuja Azul,** Carranza 1093. Open Mon.-Sat. 9am-8pm, Sun. 10am-2pm.

**Red Cross:** Tel. 15-33-22 or 15-36-35. On Juárez at Díaz Gutiérrez.

**Pharmacy: Botica Mexicana,** Othón 180 (tel. 12-38-80), by the cathedral. Open 24hr. Yessssir, this drugstore is always open.

**Hospital: Hospital de Nuestra Sra. Salud,** Madre Perla #435, on the corner with Industry Ave., a few km southeast of town. Open 24hr. Some English spoken.

**Emergency:** Dial 06.

**Police:** Tel. 12-55-83 or 12-72-28. In the Palacio Municipal.

**Internet Access: Ing. Carlos V. Águilar,** Enrico Martinez 115 (tel. 11-70-17) in Col. Virreyes (toward the airport), runs a private firm renting out Internet time. **El Instituto Tecnológico de San Luis,** east of the city center, on the right-hand side off Hwy. Francisco Sarabia, will also provide access for a fee.

**Post Office:** Morelos 235 between Salazar and Insurgentes (tel. 2-27-40), 1 block east and 4 blocks north of the Plaza de Armas. Open Mon.-Fri. 9am-5pm, Sat. 9am-1pm. **Postal Code:** 78000.

**Phone Code:** 48.

## ACCOMMODATIONS

Some good accommodations can be found near the bus station; for those who don't mind staying in this noisy part of town, the youth hostel is a viable option. Some past-their-prime hotels close to the *centro* still boast somewhat-commodious rooms and views of a plaza (which one? Take your pick!).

**Villa Juvenil San Luis Potosí CREA Youth Hostel (HI)** (tel. 55-73-60), near the Glorieta Benito Juárez (a circular convergence of highways a few km east of the *centro*). Turn left as you exit the bus station; walk straight ahead one block past the Glorieta—those are the sports fields for the hostel. Rooms are clean but small; 2 adjoining rooms with 2 tightly-packed sets of bunk beds could fit into many hotel doubles. Still, the sports complex with basketball courts, soccer fields, and track, plus the no-curfew rule (the lobby, however, closes at 11pm), makes for an interesting and eclectic group of kids. 20 pesos per person. Breakfast 9 pesos; lunch and dinner 13 pesos each. Make reservations.

**Hotel Plaza,** Jardín Hidalgo 22 (tel. 12-46-31), on the south side of the Pl. de Armas. This hotel, the first in San Luis Potosí, has seen better days, but how can you complain when the beds are so soft, the fans so soothing, and the view from the balcony so beautiful? Ask for a room facing the plaza and maybe you'll get it. Ask for some history of the hotel and you'll definitely get a tour replete with old photos and scrapbook clippings. Rooms 75 pesos, 80 pesos, or 95 pesos, graded by size.

**Motel Potosí,** next door to the bus station (the first building on your left as you exit), is shockingly affordable considering the prices of nearby hotels. With a private garage for each room, and little living rooms complete with lovable, mismatching desk and sofa, you might just be lured away from *el centro* and live it up near the bus station. Singles 105 pesos; doubles 130 pesos; triples 160 pesos.

**Hotel de Gante,** 5 de Mayo 140 (tel. 12-14-93), ½ block south of the Pl. de Armas. Enormous rooms have well-equipped bathrooms and a marvelous view of the plaza. The lounges on each floor provide space to hang out and chug the free bottled water. Singles 98 pesos; doubles 113 pesos.

## FOOD

Many touristy restaurants lie on Carranza or one block north on Arista. While prices are jacked up along this strip, so is originality and the chance for a nice atmosphere. Both *tacos potosinos* and *enchiladas potosinas* are stuffed with cheese and vegetables, then fried. *Nopalitos* are tender and absolutely delicious pieces of cactus (spines removed) cooked in a green, salty sauce of garlic, onion, and tomato. *Chongos coronados* (curdled milk in sweet maple water) is a popular dessert.

**Restaurante-Cafetería Posada del Virrey,** Jardín Hidalgo 3 (tel. 12-32-80), on the north side of the Plaza de Armas. A popular plaza restaurant with an unbeatable 21-peso *menú del día*. Famously fabulous Sun. breakfast buffet 28 pesos. Open daily 7am-midnight.

**Yu Ne Nisa,** Arista 360 (tel. 14-36-31). A Yucatec celebration of vegetarianism. Bright eating area is decorated with plants and matching green chairs. Veggie burgers are 15 pesos, and that quesadilla you've been craving is a rock-bottom 10 pesos. Watch them squeeze juice and make luscious *licuados* as you watch—you'll howl in ecstasy. Adjoins an herbal/homeopathic/vegetarian store. Large variety of fruit juices and yogurt concoctions. Open Mon.-Sat. 8:30am-8:30pm.

**Tortas Hawaii,** Carranza 765, before the big Burger King sign. A selection of big, fat, phenomenal sandwiches with everything from *salchicha* to *queso* to *aguacate* (9-13 pesos). *Tortas especiales* (combo sandwiches) 14-18 pesos. You'll need to hit the waves and exercise after this one. Open daily 9am-midnight.

## SIGHTS

San Luis Potosí has so many beautiful buildings and lovely sights that it's almost appalling. Dubbed the "City of Plazas," San Luis Potosí has three main town squares. The most central of these is the **Plaza de Armas,** replete with trees and peaceful *potosinos.* At the beginning of the 17th century, residents watched bullfights from the balconies of the surrounding buildings. Since 1848, a red sandstone gazebo bearing the names of famous Mexican musicians has graced the plaza; on Thursday and Sunday evenings, it hosts a local band that attracts a romantically-inclined older crowd.

The west side of the Plaza de Armas is marked by the Neoclassical facade of the **Palacio del Gobierno.** Constructed in 1798 and briefly serving as the capital of the country and the seat of the presidency in 1863, the structure was renovated in 1950 and continues to serve as San Luis Potosí's administrative seat. The building has interesting *salas* (living rooms on the 2nd floor) filled with murals, statues, plaques, history, and legend. Sound overwhelming? It is. Ask the guard to unlock the *salas* if rooms are closed (open Mon.-Fri. 9am-2:30pm; free).

Opposite the Palacio de Gobierno stands the **cathedral,** with two bell towers that toll a different melody every 15 minutes. Both magnificent and ominous, the cathedral was completed in 1710, but in 1855, when San Luis became a diocese, the building was "upgraded." Miners are said to have donated gold and silver to beautify the interior, and marble statues of the apostles (small copies of those at the Basilica of San Juan de Letrán in Rome) were placed in the niches between the Solomonic columns of the Baroque facade. Paintings are in the sacristy (cathedral open daily 8am-7pm; tourists should avoid visiting on Sun. or during mass).

Not as high-profile as its counterpart, Armas, but still worth seeing, is the **Jardín de San Francisco.** The plaza is distinguished by its bronze fountain, quaint cobblestone streets, and red sandstone buildings. Elderly *potosinos* often congregate here, carrying grandkids and tossing crumbs to the pigeons. Soon after the city's founding, construction began on the **Iglesia de San Francisco,** on the plaza's west side. Less ornate than its nearby counterparts, the orange stucco facade still boasts a highly Baroque interior, including a magnificent Churrigueresque fountain (open daily 8am-7pm). For a sight a little more secular (and sumptuous), check out **La Lonja,** across the street from the Jardín on Guerrero. Built in the 1860s, this building quickly became the center of high (*very* high) society. It is decorated in the style of a French salon with imported European furniture, and a huge ballroom on the second floor. Bizarrely, the building is still in use, owned by 150 men—San Luis's richest; despite the fact that it is open to tourists, it still hosts numerous private cotillions and balls.

Perhaps the most beautiful thing to see in the city is the **Templo de Carmen,** on the northeast corner of the plaza with the same name, two blocks east of the Plaza de Armas. Many *potosinos* claim that the church is the most beautiful religious building in the city; it features hanging chandeliers, golden altars, and a huge mural of the crucifixion. During the day, the light filters in through stained glass and the place really glows (open daily 7:30am-1:30pm and 4-9pm; avoid visiting during mass). Three blocks east along Manuel Othón from the Plaza de Armas is the expansive **Alameda Juan Sarabia.** As of summer, 1997, the park was closed to the public due to massive construction. Avoid the Alameda at night (when drunks and pickpockets roam). Finally, try **Parque Tangamanga,** with lakes for paddle-boating and fishing, a baseball field, electric cars, and bike paths. To get to the park, catch a "Perimetral" bus (0.80 pesos) on Constitución across from the Alameda. Get off at the Monumento a la Revolución and walk south for three blocks (open Tues.-Sun. 9am-6pm).

If you're wandering around a bit overwhelmed and clueless, perhaps a museum should be your guide. The pink sandstone **Museo Nacional de la Máscara,** Villerías 2 (tel. 12-30-25), in the Palacio Federal, half a block south of Pl. del Carmen along Villerías, displays hundreds of ancient and modern masks from every Mexican region, from *diablos* to dancing cows. This is a fascinating place; be sure to check all of the oversized *mojigangas* in the hall—these enormous, eccentric representations are used in seasonal festivals, taken out of the museum, and paraded around the streets (open Tues.-Fri. 10am-2pm and 4-6pm, Sat.-Sun. 10am-2pm; admission 1 peso).

The **Museo Regional Potosino,** Galeana 450 (tel. 12-51-85), along the street on San Francisco's southern side, occupies the grounds of the former Franciscan convent. The government seized the land in 1950 and converted part of it into a museum. On the museum's second floor is the marvelous **Capilla a la Virgen de Aranzazu.** A shepherd found the altar's image of the Virgin in a prickly thicket, hence the name (*aranzazu* means "from within the thorns"). The *ex-votos* along the walls are a tradition among Mexico's faithful; each depicts a miracle that a parishioner has experienced. The first floor exhibits artifacts from all of Mexico, including an exhibition of pre-Hispanic artifacts (open Tues.-Sun. 10am-5pm; free).

## ENTERTAINMENT AND SEASONAL EVENTS

Taxis are nearly impossible to catch on Saturday nights, so if you plan on hitting the clubs, leave early. Chic *potosinos* flock to **Arusha,** Muñoz 195 (tel. 17-42-30), the best club in town. To understand the kitschy grandeur of the club's decor—it consists of a gigantic elephant head (fake), some stuffed animals (real), and a light system (real) to create that jungle mood (fake)—you need to know that Arusha is a city in Tanzania. Now, party on. The music ranges from techno to top-40 to *tejano.* Don't come in shorts, sneakers, or sandals, or the fashion police at the door will turn you away (drinks 12-20 pesos; cover 35 pesos; open Thurs.-Sat. 9pm-3am). Two other totally classy discos are inside hotels. Both **Dulcinea,** Carretera Mexico km 5 (tel. 18-13-12), inside the five-star Holiday Inn del Quixote, and **Oasis,** Carretera Mexico km 1 (tel. 22-18-82), in the Hotel Maria Dolores, attract a young, stylin' crowd. Both are dark and pulsing (cover 35 pesos; both open Thurs.-Sat. 8pm-late). A little closer to *el centro* is **Staff,** Carranza 423 (tel. 14-30-74), where a young, gay-friendly crowd grooves to Latin and dance music (cover 20 pesos).

For those itching for a bit of visual arts, check out **El Teatro de La Paz,** behind the Templo de Carmen. This theater is one of the four most famous and fabulously constructed in Mexico—many performers don't even need microphones. The salon holds a collection of modern art, the foyer has lovely sculptures and murals, and the theater plays everything from traditional Mexican fare to 101 Dalmatians. The ticket booth opens Monday through Friday at 10am, and posters and flyers around the city advertise the latest production. If you'd rather spend money shopping and be totally hip, the area along Carranza west of the *centro* teems with trendy restaurants and clubs. Here, the swank **Jardín de Tequis** is a great place to relax and listen to the trickle of four beautiful fountains. This area is accessible via the "Morales" bus.

Finally, the last two weeks of August mark the **Fiesta Nacional Potosina.** Concerts, bullfights, fireworks, and a parade guarantee that a swell time will be had by all.

# ■ Matehuala

Although Matehuala derives its name from a Huachichil phrase meaning "don't come," the town is anything but unfriendly. The few tourists who do trickle in are usually hallucinogen-hungry backpackers en route to Real de Catorce. They may be surprised to find that this town of 100,000, once a base for Spanish silver and gold mining, is relaxing, open, and beautiful—well worth a stay. Unlike some other Mexican cities, Matehuala has slid into the modern age with grace and good nature.

## ORIENTATION

Matehuala is 261km from Saltillo and 191km from San Luis Potosí. The **Central de Autobuses** is located on Calle 5 de Mayo, just south of the city and near the large, red

NORTHEAST MEXICO

**Arco de Bienvenida. Calle 5 de Mayo** runs north-south through the center of town. From the station, a *pesera* labeled "Centro" will take you to the downtown area for 1.60 pesos—ask the driver to let you off near the cathedral, or easier still, get off at Hidalgo, next to the Chalita market. Taxis charge 12 pesos for the trip.

Constantly forking or changing names, the streets of Matehuala are even confusing for longtime residents. Try to procure a map at the tourist office on Highway 57. **Miguel Hidalgo** runs north-south through most of the city; **Benito Juárez** runs parallel to it, one block west; and **Morelos** runs one block east. Most points of interest lie somewhere on or between these streets.

## PRACTICAL INFORMATION

**Tourist Information: Cámara de Comercio,** Morelos 427 (tel. 2-01-10), 1 block east of Hidalgo. Low on maps, but high on knowledge. Open Mon.-Fri. 9am-1:30pm and 4-7:30pm. Small-scale **tourist office** (tel. 2-12-81), next to the Padregal Motel on Highway 57, north of the city. Open Mon.-Fri. 10am-4pm.

**Currency Exchange: Casa de Cambio San Luis Divisa,** at Colón and Hidalgo (tel. 2-31-46), north of Hotel Matehuala. They also cash traveler's checks. Open daily 9am-8pm. **Banca Serfin** (tel. 2-12-82), at Reyes and Hidalgo, has a 24hr. **ATM.**

**Telephones: LADATELs** are sparse: on Hidalgo across the street from Hotel Matehuala and on the corner of Juárez and Ocampo. Long-distance service at **Domi's,** Morelos 701, off Plaza de Armas. Open daily 7am-2pm.

**Fax: Telecomm,** Madero 119A (tel. 2-00-08). Also houses a **Western Union** office. Open Mon.-Fri. 9am-7pm.

**Buses: Central de Autobuses,** on 5 de Mayo south of the downtown area. Consolidated service of **Transportes del Norte, Frontera, Estrella Blanca** (tel. 2-01-50), and **El Águila** (tel. 2-28-60), to Mexico City (5 per day, 8hr., 1st class 185 pesos, 2nd class 159 pesos), Monterrey (10 per day, 5hr., 83 pesos), Nuevo Laredo (every hr., 3pm-6am, 10hr., 1st class 171 pesos, 2nd class 139 pesos), Querétaro (2 per day, 6hr., 1st class 114 pesos, 2nd class 101 pesos), Saltillo (5 per day, 3hr., 66 pesos), and San Luis Potosí (every hr., 2½hr., 52 pesos). **Noreste** (tel. 2-09-97) serves Monterrey (7 per day, 4hr., 92 pesos) and Reynosa (3 per day, 6hr., 140 pesos). **Tamaulipas** (tel. 2-27-71) to Monterrey via Saltillo (17 per day, 91 pesos), Real de Catorce (5 per day, 17 pesos), Reynosa (3 per day, 7hr., 106 pesos), and San Luis Potosí (7 per day, 35 pesos).

**Market: Chalita,** Hidalgo 413 between Constitución and Madero (tel. 2-03-26). Open Mon.-Fri. 9am-2pm and 3:45-8pm, Sat. 9am-2pm and 3:45-8:30pm, Sun. 10am-3pm. The **indoor market** next to the Templo de la Imaculada Concepción sells crafts and produce. Open daily 9am-6pm.

**Laundromat: Lavandería Acuario,** Betancourt and Madero (tel. 2-70-88). Self-service wash or dry 5kg for 25 pesos. Open daily 8:30am-2pm and 4-8pm.

**Red Cross:** Ignacio y Ramírez and Betancourt (tel. 2-07-26).

**Pharmacy: Farmacia Madero,** Morelos and Madero (tel. 2-15-81). Open daily 8am-10pm. Little English spoken.

**Hospital: Hospital General,** on Hidalgo (tel. 2-04-45), a few blocks north of *el centro.* To the right is a small, shady plaza and the hospital. Open 24hr. Little to no English spoken. **Emergency:** Dial 06.

**Police:** Tel. 2-06-47. Next to the bus station.

**Post Office:** Leandro Valle and Negrete (tel. 2-00-73). Open Mon.-Fri. 8am-3pm, Sat. 9am-1pm. **Postal Code:** 78700.

**Phone Code:** 488.

## ACCOMMODATIONS

Budget accommodations dot the *centro.* The *casas de huéspedes* on **Calle Bocanegra** are the cheapest options (singles 20 pesos; doubles 40 pesos), but spend more and get luxurious rooms and central location. This town's got some great hotels.

**Hotel y Casino Del Valle,** on Morelos (tel. 2-37-70), right off the Plaza de Armas. The lobby greets you with a counter of opaque glass and sandstone, black velour loveseats, and pink walls. TV and hyperactive ceiling fans in the rooms make this hotel swank as a Vegas casino. Well, maybe not that swank, but worth the extra pesos. 1 person 115 pesos, each extra person 10 pesos; maximum 4 to a room.

**Hotel Blanca Estela,** Morelos 426 (tel. 2-23-00), next to the video store. Fans cool small, super-clean, colorful rooms with TVs. Beautiful wooden furnishings lend a classy feel to the rooms in this narrow, small hotel. Check in early; this may well be the most crowded shindig in town. Singles 65 pesos; doubles 80 pesos.

**Hotel Matehuala,** Bustamante 134 (tel. 2-06-80), just north of the Plaza de Armas. Spacious and airy, with a huge, empty tiled courtyard, this hotel is monastic in the best way. Though the rooms are dark as confessional booths, the 25ft. ceilings with wooden rafters, white walls, and rust color bureaus and coat rack are not to be missed. Each room has a little balcony. Singles 60 pesos; doubles 70 pesos.

**Hotel María Esther,** Madero 111 (tel. 2-07-14). Whitewashed exterior encloses rooms with an outdoor balcony, a slightly beat-up couch, comfy beds, and big, bright bathrooms. With an indoor restaurant. Singles 65 pesos; doubles 78 pesos; add 13 pesos per additional person.

## FOOD

The few restaurants in Matehuela are family-owned, family-prone cafeteria types with good food and low prices. Get ready to practice your hard-core menu-ordering Spanish.

**Restaurant y Mariscos Santa Fe,** Morelos 709 (tel. 2-07-53), on the east side of the Plaza de Armas. Full of lively, hungry families, this restaurant offers great *comida corrida* (22 pesos) and savory seafood (under 30 pesos). Sit by the windows, a great place to watch people come and go in the Plaza. Open daily 7am-midnight.

**Restaurant Fontella,** Morelos 618 (tel. 2-02-93). Colorful hanging lamps illuminate a tranquil, flora-filled dining area, while the murals of the city evoke a sense of yesteryear. *Comida corrida* offers copious servings of fresh vegetable soup, rice, chicken or steak, and dessert for 20 pesos. Open daily 8am-4am.

**La Cava,** Callejón del Arte 1 (tel. 2-28-88), just east of Hotel Matehuala, in a little pedestrian walkway. The elegant dining room is a pleasant escape from the merciless sun. Traditional Mexican fare and an array of healthy sandwiches for around 15 pesos. Huge steaks 36 pesos. Smooth cocktails. Open daily 7:30am-10:30pm.

## SIGHTS

While there's not a lot of big-name sights in Matehuala, every wide street and little park will seem ripe for reclining. Standing solemnly at the center of Matehuala between Calles Juárez and Hidalgo is the almost completed **Templo de la Inmaculada Concepción,** a copy of Saint Joseph's cathedral in Lyon, France. Construction began in 1905, and although poor funding has slowed progress on the project, more than 90 years of Matehualans are proud of their all-but-finished cathedral. The large clock and seemingly impenetrable gray exterior of this Gothic-style edifice belie a beautiful interior flooded with light. Just in front of the main cathedral is the **Plaza Juárez,** now permanently occupied by vendor stalls and small, makeshift cafes. Sprawling out onto adjoining streets, the bazaar is collectively known as **Mercado Arista.** Leather and ceramic goods as well as the usual slew of cheap plastic toys and trinkets figure prominently here. The lovely **Alameda,** a few blocks south of the main plaza offers lots of shade and jungle-like lushness.

Two other large parks stand at the northeast and southeast corners of the downtown area. Approximately three blocks east of Hidalgo, between Bocanegra and Altamirano, is the soothing and peaceful **Parque Vicente Guerrero** (also called the **Parque del Pueblo**). Vicente Guerrero's counterpart is the more lively **Parque Álvaro Obregón,** just south of Insurgentes. With basketball courts and benches aplenty, Álvaro Obregón draws entire families in the early evening hours.

NORTHEAST MEXICO

# ■ Real de Catorce

Only a stretch of pavement separates the cobblestone streets of Real de Catorce from ultra-modern Matehuala, but the two towns seem light-years away. Once a thriving mining town with 30,000 inhabitants, Real de Catorce now looms mysteriously on the side of a mountain, a veritable ghost town with a population of barely 1500 people. Still, backpackers come from all over to see this town's *burro*-trodden paths and brick ruins rising up from the Sierra Madre like desert bloom. The clumsily-constructed cobblestone streets and carts full of holy candles may not seem like much, but Real de Catorce is a Mexican miracle—this little town was left behind by time. Tourists from all over Mexico travel to Real de Catorce to investigate this dusty anachronism of a town and to explore hallucinogens.

**Orientation and Practical Information** The town's main thoroughfare (read: rocky path) is Calle Lanzagorta, which runs from the **bus station** past the famed **cathedral** and a few hotels and restaurants to a little town square with a gazebo. Self-appointed guides, offering **tourist information** and **peyote,** can be found in the back streets of the city. Most services (i.e. the civil registry, **police** station, and municipal government) are run out of the **Presidencia Municipal,** just by the Plaza Principal. The **post office** is on Calle Constitución (open Mon.-Fri. 9am-1pm and 3-6pm). The town's single **telephone** (tel. 2-37-33) will put you in touch with the hotels.

**Accommodations and Food** Real de Catorce has a conspicuous lack of decent budget accommodations (hotels cater almost exclusively to gringo tourists, mainly dazed backpackers, and journalists) as well as a strange penchant for expensive Italian food. Many restaurants are open only during "tourist season," which is late June, July, and August. Your best option would be **El Mesón de la Abundancia,** Langazorta #11. The oldest edifice in town (it used to be the town treasury in the 1880s), this hotel is also an exercise in historical recreation. Most furniture is original, the blankets made of superior wool, and the rooms are large and lovely enough to hold money. Some rooms have private terraces and sitting rooms. Adjoining restaurant/bar offers original artesanry, hanging plants, and more. *Comida corrida* runs 25 pesos. **El Real,** Morelos 20, has colorful, spic-and-span rooms with candlelight and mosaics. Some rooms boast skylights and fireplaces, and the roof terrace offers a smashing view (singles 135 pesos; doubles 160 pesos). Italian dishes (20-30 pesos) are the *forte* of the hotel's restaurant. **Hotel Providencia,** Lanzagorta 29, is cheaper, and although the rooms are pretty bare-boned, extensive renovation and plumbing is taking place. Delight in the narrow staircases and gorgeous vistas as you ascend the hotel. Also, ask to see the newer rooms—at this writing, they cost the same as the old ones (singles 50 pesos; doubles 100 pesos). The **Eucalipto Restaurant** on Calle Lerdo offers reasonably priced *comida italiana.*

**Sights** Calle **Lanzagorta** runs past most major sights. The **Templo de la Purísima Concepción** is down the road on the right; ascend the white walkway to reach the entrance. Inside, the floor seems to be composed of rectangular blocks of wood; the blocks are actually doors to subterranean **tombs,** each of which contains several bodies. The **cathedral** resembles a brightly colored Fabergé egg, with pastel decor and plastic figurines. It houses a lifelike image of St. Francis, whose miracles have created a devoted following; on October 4, the saint's feast day, the town attracts a flock of pious visitors hoping to pray at the cathedral. The most amazing part of the cathedral is a side room filled with **letters** of thanks and devotion to St. Francis. Often hand-painted, stenciled, or filled with photographs, these thousands of letters spanning decades are full of hope and meticulously crafted. If this doesn't leave you feeling warm and fuzzy inside, something's wrong. Uphill on the right, after the cathedral (a steep climb) is the **Plaza Principal,** where today only a crumbling fountain remains. Next to the plaza is the **Casa de Moneda,** formerly a mint, whose third floor houses a photography exhibit of Real de Catorce. Enter the museum by the plaza (open daily 10am-4pm; free).

Turning right immediately after the Jardín, continue two blocks uphill, then head one painfully uphill block to the left. There the terraced steps of the **Palenque de Gallos** (cock-fight ring) replicate the layout of a classical Athenian theater (ask someone in the Casa de Moneda to unlock it for you). The cliff known as **El Voladero** offers breathtaking views of the surrounding mountains and valleys. To reach it, walk uphill on Calle Constitución and you'll be rewarded with visions of 1000 ft. drops, dry riverbeds crackling with heat, and herds of cows on distant hilltops. At the top of Calle Zaragoza stands the stark white **Capilla de Guadalupe** (also called the Panteón), which overlooks a cemetery tightly paved with the graves of local saints. For a **guided horseback tour** of the region, contact expert trail masters at Hotel El Real or a little unnamed restaurant-cum-shop on Larazagorta (on your right-hand side as you walk from the bus station into the heart of town toward the cathedral). They rent horses and guides who speak very limited English for only 30 pesos per hour.

**Getting There: Autobuses Tamaulipas** (tel. 2-08-40) runs buses from Matehuala to Real de Catorce (during peak season every 2hr., 6am-6pm, 1¼hr., 33 pesos; fewer buses during the rest of the year). Always check with the bus driver about the schedules, and always arrive 15-30 minutes early. Taking the last bus means spending the night at Real de Catorce. Buses from Matehuala leave from a station at Guerrero and Méndez near *el centro*. Finding the station is quite tricky; ask a local to point you in the right direction or catch a shuttle bus from the **Central de Autobuses,** the central bus station on Cinco de Mayo, for free. The ride to "Real de 14" is guaranteed to whiten the knuckles of the timid traveler: the bus rambles along a cobblestone road and a winding path chiseled into the mountainside.

# ■ Ciudad Valles

Ciudad Valles (pop. 350,000) is a major crossroads between the *noreste* and central Mexico. Valles (as it is commonly called) is a hot, dirty city, the second largest in the state after the capital; but it lacks the charm, culture, and beauty of San Luis Potosí. With wide, bus-worn streets and no central plaza, the city evokes the U.S. midwest but unfortunately doesn't hint at the rich Huastecan culture surrounding the area. Valles feels more like Industrytown, Anywhere.

**Orientation and Practical Information** Ciudad Valles's main thoroughfare is **Calle Hidalgo.** Most accommodations and points of interest lie between **Jardín Hidalgo** and **Glorieta Hidalgo.** Terrific maps of the town can be purchased for 6 pesos at the **Cámara de Comercio,** Carranza Sur 55 (tel. 2-01-44 or 2-45-11), a half block south of Hidalgo (open Mon.-Fri. 9am-1:30pm and 4-7pm, Sat. 9am-1pm), or at the first two hotels listed below. **Banamex,** on Hidalgo and Madero (tel. 2-11-17), has a 24-hour **ATM.** The **Central de Autobuses,** on the outskirts of town, is accessible by bus from Calle Hidalgo (1.80 pesos) or taxi (18 pesos). **Oriente** bypasses Asia to serve Guadalajara (3 per day, 10-12hr., 158-177 pesos), Matamoros (10 per day, 8hr., 145 pesos), Querétaro (2 per day, 8hr., 128 pesos), San Luis Potosí (every hr., 5hr., 85 pesos), Tampico (every hr., 2½-3hr., 44 pesos), and Xilitla (7 per day, 2½hr., 16.50 pesos). **Frontera** runs buses to Monterrey (2 per day, 8hr., 152 pesos) and Nuevo Laredo (2 per day, 11hr., 199 pesos). In case of an **emergency,** dial 91-800-90-392. The **police** can be reached at tel. 2-53-53. The **post office** is on Juárez 520 (open Mon.-Fri. 8am-7pm, Sat. 9am-noon). **Postal Code:** 79000. **Phone code:** 138.

**Accommodations and Food** Several hotels dot the *centro*. **Hotel Piña,** Juárez 210 (tel. 2-01-83), offers clean (if somewhat dated) rooms with private bath. Enormous, empty closets with shelves may give the budget traveler (that's you) a clothes-shopping craving. Three different ranges of rooms—some have TV and/or A/C (singles 73 to 113 pesos; doubles 117 to 132 pesos). Another great deal is **Hotel Rex,** Hidalgo 418 (tel. 1-04-11), smack dab in the middle of town. Feel positively kingly in the spacious, elegant rooms and kempt new bathrooms. Kick back in the shady lounge or balcony—the view will please those who like hot, dusty, deserted streets (singles 73 pesos, with TV 95 pesos; doubles 88 pesos, with TV 117 pesos; triples 102 pesos, with TV 132 pesos; quads 145 pesos). There are few restaurants in town, but *loncherías* are ubiquitous. **La Bella Napoli** (tel. 2-33-84), adjoining Hotel Piña, offers an eclectic assortment of delicious pizzas, from the good-sized *chico* (16 pesos) to the "you-want-a-piece-of-this" *jumbo* (52 pesos). Also sells pastas and *antojitos* (open daily 7:30am-midnight). An assortment of tiny hotel-side restaurants can be found near the bus station, offering tasty food and good prices: **El Restaurant Melania,** for one (entrees 14-26 pesos).

## ■ Near Ciudad Valles: Xilitla

A serpentine road winds through the rocky *huasteca* highlands to the tiny hamlet of Xilitla, 90 minutes from and 1000m above Ciudad Valles. Although the town itself (pop. 4000) is run-down and shabby, the gorgeous greenery and surrounding hills scream "paradise," and the cultural legacy and natural gifts are rich indeed. The area has over 150 caves, including El Sótano de las Golondrinas, a spelunker's dream, over 450m deep with a cave floor covering approximately six acres. Dozens of waterfalls, rivers ripe for rafting, horseback trails, unofficial sanctuaries of wild orchids, and rare animals are accessible from Edenish Xilitla. For more information, contact Avery and Lenore Danziger, owners of El Castillo, a resort down the hill from Xilitla's main plaza. This infinitely wise and fabulously friendly couple (tel. 5-00-38) is best contacted through email (junglegossip@compuserve.com), where they can direct you to their soon-to-be-finalized website. Besides running a lovely resort, these folks can provide information about nearby sites, Huastecan culture, hiking, rafting, and other outdoor opportunities.

Xilitla's main attraction is the **Enchanted Garden of Edward James,** better known to locals as **Las Pozas** (the pools). Son of a wealthy English nobleman, James was a good, old-fashioned eccentric, obsessed with cleanliness and tissue paper and sometimes requiring his secretaries to work in the buff. After early experiments with poetry and art, James created a universe of concrete, steel, and stone in often-wild colors and even wilder forms throughout the jungle. James' melange of bridges, arches, and artistic relics recall *Alice in Wonderland,* with winding staircases that lead to nowhere, a library without books, and other touches of madness. James channeled the waterfall running through Las Pozas' 36 structures into the pools themselves (there are 9). They're safe for swimming—bring your bathing suit. To get there, take a taxi from Xilitla (30 pesos), or, if you're adventuresome, walk down the two-lane road skirting the edge of the cliff, turning left onto the dirt road just past the bridge; then make another left onto the first quasi-respectable road and follow it about 4km. Las Pozas will be on your right (admission 5 pesos; open daily 9am-5pm).

Although the jungle is not conducive to sound sleeping, one can **spend the night** inside Las Pozas itself. It isn't cheap, but it's not as bad as you might think (120-160 pesos). Edward James' own house within the crazy compound goes for 200 pesos per night with kitchen, and can be creatively crammed with six or more people. A **restaurant** immediately outside Las Pozas, catering to tourists, serves good food at good prices (15-25 pesos) as well as quick snacks and drinks (open daily 9am-5pm).

Exchange currency at **Compra y Venta Dólares,** Escobedo 204, on the second floor, half a block east of the Plaza Principal. The **Red Cross** (tel. 5-02-47) is on the road descending Xilitla. **Farmacia San Augustín** is on Hidalgo (tel. 5-00-11), at the northwest corner of the Plaza Principal (open daily 8:30am-9pm). The Palacio Municipal, on the plaza, houses the **police.** Behind the Palacio on Calle Zaragoza (south side of the plaza) is the **post office,** located on the second floor (open Mon.-Fri. 9am-4pm). **Postal code:** 79902.

**Getting There: Oriente** runs frequent buses to Xilitla (1½hr., 16.50 pesos) from the Central de Autobuses in Ciudad Valles.

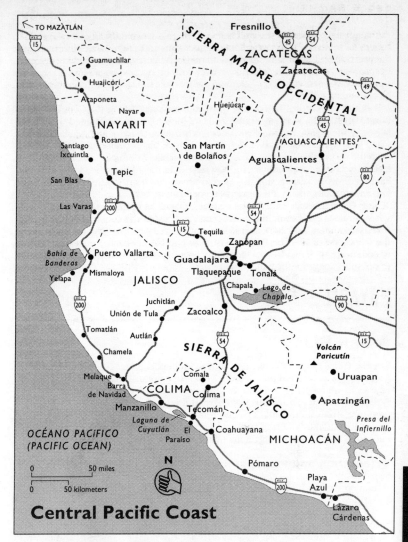

**Central Pacific Coast**

# Central Pacific Coast

Stretching from the quiet fishing villages near San Blas to the busy port of Manzanillo, the Central Pacific Coast boasts kilometer after kilometer of smooth sand massaged by the ebb and flow of the tide. Hot but not overly humid, the region's climate leaves little room for dissatisfaction, and the sun never fails to illuminate the azure skies.

A state with diverse terrain, **Nayarit** is marked by volcanic highlands, tropical jungles, and a network of lakes and rivers. This verdant and fertile region grows the lion's share of the nation's marijuana and served as the setting for *Journey to Ixtlán,* Carlos Castañeda's renowned book describing experiences with hallucinogens in a small town between Tepic and Guadalajara. Hallucinogen use has long been part of Cora and Huichol *indígena* traditions and is still common practice among shamans in their incantations.

It is not uncommon to see Huicholes in colorful native dress in even the state's larger cities. Men typically wear light-colored pants and a light, wide shirt belted at the waist, all brilliantly embroidered with religious figures and eye-catching designs. Peyote may be carried in colorfully woven knit or stitched bags worn across the shoulders. Women's traditional clothing consists of a similarly colorful embroidered blouse and long skirt.

South of Nayarit lies **Jalisco,** the most touristed state along the Central Pacific Coast. Much of the world's popular image of Mexico could be stamped "Hecho en Jalisco"—the *jarabe tapatío* (hat dance), *mariachis, charros,* and tequila all originated in this state. For much of its history, though, this province remained isolated from the rest of the Republic, possessing neither silver nor gold, jewels nor water, fertile land nor agricultural climate. It wasn't until the 1920s, when railroad tracks extended to Guadalajara, that this Sierran town (elevation 1552m) began to grow into a metropolis; today, it is Mexico's second largest city.

Tiny **Colima** boasts spectacular beaches as well as thoroughly pleasant towns where tourists can escape the resort scene and rest in the cool mountain air. The state is also home to Colima, a sparkling, untouristed gem of a city, and Manzanillo, the workhorse of Mexico's Pacific coast. This port has not paused once in 700 years of commerce with Asia to wipe its sweaty brow, and only recently has it attempted to polish its image for the benefit of visitors.

# NAYARIT

## ■ San Blas

San Blas (pop. 19,000) is a blend of shoe-worn buildings and crumbling relics from its glory days as a central port in Spain's colonial empire. Today, this tiny fishing village feeds off its ecological wealth: awesome beaches, over 300 species of birds (just listen as you exit the bus station), and the nearby jungle attract *norteamericano* expatriates, birdwatchers, and tourists en route to Puerto Vallarta. Also a mecca for surfers, San Blas's *zócalo* is a cool-dude sort of place; skate-rats, surfers, and video game junkies swagger about into the wee hours.

**Orientation and Practical Information**   San Blas is 69km northeast of Tepic by Rte. 15 and 54. **Calle Juárez,** San Blas's main drag, runs parallel to the bus station on the south side of the *zócalo.* **Batallón** runs perpendicular to Juárez from the *zócalo*'s center and leads to the closest beach, **Playa Borrego.**

The **Tourist Office,** Juárez 83, across from McDonald's, hands out maps and provides information about guides and trips to La Tovara (see p. 265) and hikes to some of Nayarit's more beautiful waterfalls (office open daily 9am-2pm, and 6-9pm). Change money at **Banamex,** on Juárez (tel. 5-00-30), east of the *zócalo* (open Mon.-Fri. 8:30-2pm; also has a 24hr. **ATM**). Make long-distance **phone** calls from the *caseta de larga distancia* at Juárez 3 (tel. 5-06-10 or 5-06-11; fax 5-06-65; open daily 8am-10pm). The **fax** office is at Sonora 56 and Juárez (tel. 5-01-15; open Mon.-Sat. 8am-2pm and 4-8pm).

**Transportes Norte de Sonora** (tel. 5-00-43) **buses** run to Guadalajara (9am, 6hr., 91 pesos), Mazatlán (5pm, 5hr., 83 pesos), Puerto Vallarta (7 and 10am, 3hr., 55 pesos), Santiago Ixcuintla (8:45, 11am, 1, and 4:30pm, 1¾hr., 21 pesos), and Tepic (every hr., 6am-7pm, 1¾hr., 21 pesos). **Farmacia Económica** is at Batallón 49 (tel./fax 5-01-11; open daily 8:30am-2pm and 4-9pm). The **Centro de Salud** is on Batallón and Campeche (tel. 5-02-32), five blocks south of the *zócalo.* No English is spoken (open 24hr.). Another medical center, the **Clínica IMSS,** at Batallón and Guerrero (tel. 5-02-27), is open for consultation daily 7am-6pm; at other times, enter on Canalizo. The **police** are on Sinaloa (tel. 5-00-28) opposite the bus station; it's the last door in the Palacio Municipal as you walk away from the *zócalo* (open 24hr.). The

**post office** is at Sonora and Echeverría (tel. 5-02-95), one block north and one block east of the northeast corner of the *zócalo* (open Mon.-Fri. 8am-1pm and 3-5pm, Sat. 8am-noon). **Postal Code:** 63740. **Phone Code:** 328.

**Accommodations and Food** Finding a place to sleep in San Blas isn't difficult during the off-season, but autumn storms bring mile-long waves and bed-seeking surfers. During September, October, Semana Santa, and Christmas, make reservations and expect higher prices. The blood-sucking mosquitoes near the water make camping a no-no; rooms inland are the best choice. **Bungalows Portolá,** Paredes 118 and Yucatán (tel. 5-03-86), has clean, furnished bungalows complete with fans, bath, and kitchen for up to four people (120-150 pesos; one single available for 50 pesos). The owner offers laundry and fax service and rents bicycles. **El Bucanero,** Juárez 75 (tel. 5-01-01), is reminiscent of a creaky pirate ship. It offers large, dim rooms with high ceilings, clean bathrooms, a swimming pool, and a huge, fading crocodile in the lobby. Hot water and fans make things comfy (singles 80 pesos, high season 100 pesos; doubles 130 pesos, high season 150 pesos; prices vary). **Posada Azul,** Batallón 126 (tel. 5-01-29) about four blocks from the *zócalo,* offers clean, white-brick rooms with hard-working fans and bathrooms. Sunglasses may come in handy when looking for this place—its bright blue exterior is practically blinding (singles 50 pesos; doubles 60 pesos). **Los Cocos,** on Batallón just before the Playa Borrego (tel. 5-00-55), is a trailer park with bathrooms, electricity, and a 24-hour guard (2 people 60 pesos).

**Restaurant McDonald,** Juárez 36, opposite the tourist office, is just as popular with locals and travelers as the real Mickey D's. Plaid flannel holiday tablecloths seem a bit out of place in the muggy climate, but the food is tried and true (*comida corrida* 20 pesos, *plato de frutas* 10 pesos; open daily 7am-10pm). **La Familia,** Batallón 18 (tel. 5-02-58), is a family joint, right down to the conversation-starting wall-mounted shark's teeth, sea bottles, and old drums. Don't worry, it's not Giorgio's (chicken 25 pesos; fresh fish 28 pesos; open daily 8am-10pm). **La Isla,** on Mercado and Paredes (tel. 5-04-07), lives up to its name—every space, crack, and crevice is covered with shells. The food will knock you out (fried fish 24 pesos; open Tues.-Sun. 2-10pm).

**Sand and Sights** San Blas, known for its perfectly symmetric waves and safe, sandy bottom, has churned out many a surfing champ. To rent surfing equipment or take lessons, drop by **La Tumba de Yako,** Batallón 219 (tel. 5-04-62), about six blocks from the *zócalo,* run by Juan García, president of San Blas's surfing club and technical director of Mexico's surf team. Also known as "Juan Bananas" (as in banana bread), he runs a vegetarian shop during high season (open daily 8am-8pm).

San Blas's main attraction is the smooth water, packed sand, and long waves of **Playa Las Islitas.** During the stormy months of September and October, surfers flock to San Blas in hopes of catching the famous yearly mile-long wave which carries them from Las Islitas all the way to Playa Matanchén. To reach Las Islitas, take a bus from the bus station (every hr., 7am-5pm, 3 pesos; returning every hr., 7:30am-4:30pm). There is another bus, leaving from the corner of Sinaloa at Paredes in front of the green trim building (8:20, 10:30am, 12:30, and 2:30pm, 15min., 3 pesos). The bus then continues to other beaches, passing by Las Islitas on its way back to town about one hour later. Don't settle for the first few stretches of sand that greet you—prettier coves and seclusion await farther along the shore.

At the southern end of Batallón, **Playa Borrego** is easily accessible from town and offers a relaxing, though somewhat bland, view of the coast. Borrego's sand is gray and its mosquitoes ravenous. Quiet and pretty **Playa del Rey,** off the coast of Borrego, has somewhat stronger currents. A *lancha* will take you there from the pier at the west end of Juárez (round-trip about 5 pesos; boats run daily about 7am-7pm).

Locals hype **La Tovara**—not the beaches—as San Blas's can't-miss attraction. While the winding jungle boat ride to La Tovara springs can be expensive, seeing a live crocodile just might make it worthwhile. Guides navigate the shallow, swampy waters, pointing out rare and interesting birds and the stilted huts left over from the set of the film *Cabeza de Vaca*. The path clears to reveal hordes of turtles and huge fish. Trips can be arranged through the tourist office or directly with a boat owner; find them at the small docking area on Juárez's eastern end. Trips last about four hours and can be made any day between 7am and 4pm, but it's best to journey to La Tovara early in the morning, when the water is still calm and the birds undisturbed by the *lanchas*. Expect to pay 130 pesos for a group of four, depending on the tour.

The short hike to the top of **La Contaduría,** the hill near town, affords a beautiful view of the city and coast. The splintering stone fortress that protected the city impresses from above, while an 18th-century church stands farther downhill. To get there, head east on Juárez as if leaving town. Just before the bridge and the sign that reads "Cape Victoria 7," turn right onto the dirt road behind the houses and restaurants, and veer right off that road onto the stone path that winds uphill.

The **Comunidad Cultural Huichol** of San Blas, a three-year-old non-profit organization, provides a non-exploitative forum of expression for Huichol artists. The **Huichol** Indians are believed to be the oldest native group in Mexico. For centuries, the Huichol have created unique crafts depicting scenes from their mythology. But the more than 15,000 Huichol who still live in rural mountain regions are easily taken advantage of by agencies that purchase their work for a paltry sum and sell it for 50 times the price the artisan was paid. Furthermore, Huichol artists are often coerced into reproducing identical designs and figures, a practice in conflict with traditional Huichol beliefs.

After hours in San Blas, there's not much to do except down a few at the local watering hole. **Mike's CantaBar** (tel. 5-04-32), above Restaurant McDonald, rarely gets wild or crazy, but it's an interesting place to pass the evening. Mike no longer performs vintage rock, but he sings live salsa in what looks like an antique airport lounge (no cover; open daily 6pm-1am, live music Thurs.-Sun. starting around 10pm).

## ■ Near San Blas: El Custodio de las Tortugas

**El Custodio de las Tortugas** (The Guardian of the Turtles, tel. (329) 2-29-54, toll-free from the US (800) 891-3670) is an eco-resort in the tiny village of **Platanitos,** an hour and a half south of San Blas and two hours north of Puerto Vallarta. Its villa, perched 9m on a precipice, overlooks 20km of virgin beach and the longest stretch of turtle camp in Nayarit. Between July and August, owners Min and Mona, in collaboration with the Mexican government and several ecological organizations, collect turtle eggs, protecting them from thieves and predators. The elegant two-bedroom, two-bath villa has TV, A/C, and huge, breezy terraces for whale watching and sunset worshipping. It's best enjoyed as a group (villa rental US$200 per person per week, min. 4 people; US$100 per person per weekend; or US$25 per night to help out and bunk in the turtle camp; some meals and kayak trips to the lagoon included). Don't miss going into town to try local specialty, *pescado sarandeado* (mesquite grilled fish, 40 pesos per kilo—enough to feed 3-4 people).

**Getting There: Transportes Norte de Sonora** gets you there from San Blas (tel. 5-00-43) or Puerto Vallarta (tel. 2-66-66; noon and 2:30pm, 2hr., 55 pesos). Ask the bus driver to let you off at Platanitos, then walk down the road and up the hill.

## ■ Tepic

The steam-belching, tree-guzzling woodchip plant situated directly across from Tepic's bus station provides an appropriate introduction to this blue-collar city. State capital and an important crossroads for the entire region, hard-working Tepic (pop. 450,000) fits its name well—it comes from the Náhuatl words *tetl* (rock) and *pic* (hard). Aside from a few historical sites and La Loma Park, there is little of tourist interest here. At best, the city can be used as a transportation hub and a base for exploring nearby towns. Tepic is 169km north of Puerto Vallarta, 228km northwest of Guadalajara, and 295km south of Mazatlán.

**Orientation and Practical Information** As you leave the bus station, *el centro* is down the highway (**Insurgentes**) to the left; cross the street and catch one of the yellow buses (6am-9pm, 1.50 pesos). Hustling *taxistas* charge 10 pesos for the short trip to the *centro*. **Avenida México,** running north-south six blocks west of the bus station, is downtown Tepic's main drag. Addresses on Av. México change from Norte to Sur about four blocks north of **Insurgentes,** the largest east-west street. The yellow minivan *combis* (6am-midnight, 1.50-2 pesos) run back and forth daily along Av. México and Insurgentes. At its northern terminus, the many-fountained **Plaza Principal** (officially the **Centro Histórico**) is incessantly active, dominated on one end by the cathedral and on the other by the **Palacio Municipal.** Six blocks to the south, **Plaza Constituyente** is shockingly desolate. Most tourist services lie on or near Av. México.

At **Dirección de Turismo Municipal,** Av. Puebla at the corner of Amado Nervo (tel. 16-56-61), one block from the cathedral, students of *turismo* hand out maps and brochures (open daily 8am–8pm). **Banks** (most open Mon.-Fri. 8am-1:30pm) and *casas de cambio* (commonly open Mon.-Sat. 9am-2pm and 4-7pm) clutter México Nte. Both **Banamex** and **Bancomer,** on Av. México Nte., a few blocks south of the plaza, have **ATMs.** There are card-operated **LADATELs** in the bus station and along Av. México, as well as two **computel** booths in the bus station (open daily 7am-9pm). For faxes, try **Telecomm,** on Av. México Nte. 50 (tel. 12-96-55), about one block from the cathedral (open Mon.-Fri. 8am-7pm, Sat.-Sun. 8am-2pm).

**Buses** leave Tepic from the newer long-distance station (the smaller one downtown, 3 blocks north of the plaza on Victoria, only serves local destinations). To get to the new station, take a 15-1 or "Mololoa Llanitos" bus from the corner of México Sur and Hidalgo (about a 20min. ride). **Norte de Sonora** (tel. 13-23-15) runs to Culiacán (about every hr., 8hr., 151 pesos), Guadalajara (every hr., 4hr., 79 pesos), Mazatlán (every hr., 5hr., 77 pesos), San Blas (every hr., 6am-7pm, 1½hr., 21 pesos), Santiago Ixcuintla (every ½hr., 5:30am-9pm, 1½hr., 21 pesos), and Tuxpan (about every hr., 6am-7:45pm, 2hr., 21 pesos). **Transportes del Pacífico** (tel. 13-23-20), provides first-class service to Mexico City (every hr., 11hr., 251 pesos) and Tijuana (every hr., 29hr., 507 pesos) and second-class service to Puerto Vallarta (every ½hr., 3am-8pm, 3½hr., 60 pesos). **Estrella Blanca** (tel. 13-13-28) serves Aguascalientes (5:30 and 7:45pm, 5hr., 160 pesos), Monterrey (4:30pm, 15hr., 317 pesos), and Zacatecas (5:30 and 7:45pm, 8hr., 179 pesos). **Ómnibus de México** (tel. 13-13-23) serves Ciudad Juárez (5:30pm, 28hr., 518 pesos) and Guadalajara (about every hr., 3½hr., 88 pesos). The station has **luggage storage** (1.50 pesos per hr. in the 1st-class terminal; 1 peso per hr. in the 2nd-class terminal), a **post office** (tel. 12-45-03; open Mon.-Fri. 8am-2pm, Sat. 7-11am), and a **telegram office** (tel. 13-23-27; open Mon.-Fri. 8am-noon). **Trains** leave from the station (tel. 13-48-61 or 13-48-93) on Allende at Jesús García; to arrive, hop on a "Ferrocarril" or "Estación Fresnosa" bus at the station or downtown at the corner of México Sur and Hidalgo.

**Farmacia ZMQ,** at Allende and Av. Mexico, and **Issstec Farmacia,** Puebla 192 Sur at Insurgentes (tel. 13-82-58), are both open 24 hours. The **Hospital General** is on Paseo de la Loma (tel. 13-79-37) next to La Loma Park. To walk there from the bus station (20min.), take a left as you leave the building and another left at the intersection with Avenida México. After three blocks, take the right-hand fork at the rotary; two blocks later the hospital is on your left (open 24hr.). Cabs to the hospital cost 10 pesos from the *centro.* The **police station** is at Avenidas Mina and Oaxaca (tel. 11-58-51), but cabs are the only way to get there (8 pesos). The **post office** is at Durango Nte. 33 and Allende (tel. 12-01-30; open Mon.-Fri. 8am-7pm, Sat. 8am-noon). **Postal Code:** 63000. **Phone Code:** 321.

**Accommodations and Food** Budget hotels in Tepic provide the basics at a reasonable price. Hotels in the *centro* are closer to Tepic's few sights, but those near the bus station may be more convenient for the traveler in Tepic for only a short stay. The best option in town may be the **Hotel Las Americas,** at Puebla 317 and Zaragoza (tel. 16-32-85). It's centrally located and has clean rooms with TV, fan, and tiled bathrooms. Wooden furniture and sunny patchwork quilts make it feel like Grandma's house (singles 50 pesos; doubles 70 pesos). To get to the **Hotel Nayar,** on Dr. Martínez 430 and República de Chile (tel. 13-23-22), make a left on your way out of the bus station and another left on the first street; continue for a block, turn right, and go up half a block. The rooms are large but sparsely furnished; bathrooms are roomy enough and clean, but lack shower curtains (singles 50 pesos; doubles 65 pesos). Warning: nearby buses start grinding at around 6am. The area just north of the Plaza Principal and west of Av. México hosts a slew of hotels. Try the **Hotel Sarita,** Bravo 112 Pte. (tel. 2-13-33), three and a half blocks west of Av. México. Sparse and clean concrete singles go for 60 pesos; doubles will run you 75 pesos.

Tepic has tons of agricultural goodies. Mangos and *guanábanas* (soursops) make their way to the stalls at the **mercado,** on Mérida and Zaragoza, four blocks south and three blocks east of the Museo Regional (see below). For a more formal meal, head to **Restaurant Vegetariano Quetzalcóatl,** León Nte. 224 at Lerdo, four blocks west of Plaza Principal. *Tranquilo* waiters serve yummy vegetarian food in a leafy courtyard decorated with local indigenous artwork. Sample the *comida corrida* (20 pesos) or stuff yourself with the buffet (Sat. only, 25 pesos; restaurant open Mon.-Sat. 8:30am-8:30pm). Grab a stool at the tile counter of **El Girasol II,** at Veracruz 169 Nte. and Lerdo, and feast your eyes upon delicious tacos (16 pesos) and *preparados de fruta* (4.50 pesos; open daily 7am-8:30pm).

**Sights** In front of the Plaza Principal is the **Catedral de la Purísima Concepción de María,** a church marked by twin 40m-tall towers. South of the Plaza Principal, at México Nte. 91 and Zapata, is the **Museo Regional de Antropologia e Historia** (tel. 12-19-00), which houses a small collection of Toltec and Aztec bones, pottery, and artifacts (open Mon.-Fri. 9am-7pm, Sat. 9am-3pm). The **Museo Casa de los Cuatro Pueblos,** Hidalgo Ote. 60 (tel. 12-17-05), displays the colorful artwork, embroidery, and beadwork, as well as replica houses, of Nayarit's four indigenous groups: the Coras, Huicholes, Náhuatls, and Tepehuanos (open Mon.-Fri. 9am-2pm and 4-7pm, Sat. 9am-2pm; free). Also south of the plaza, at Av. México and Abasolo, is the **state capitol,** a gracefully domed structure dating from the 1870s. At Av. México's southern end, turn west (uphill) on Insurgentes and you'll come to **La Loma,** a huge and enchanting park. If in service, a miniature train will take you through the park's many playgrounds (3 pesos).

About two hours out of Tepic, **Mexcaltitán** is a tiny, sleepy island with a population under 500, situated in the middle of a brown lagoon and accessible only by boat. The place comes alive during the yearly **Fiesta de San Pedro y San Pablo** (June 29), when the entire town makes a canoe pilgrimage to the lagoon to bless the waters from which it draws its livelihood. Unfortunately, on all other days, the aerial views of Mexicaltitán in the tourist office are better than the island itself; it's actually dusty and plain from down below. There are very basic hotels and restaurants on the island. To get there, travel first to **Santiago Ixcuintla** on Norte de Sonora (every ½hr., 5:30am-9pm, 1½hr., 21 pesos); coming out of the bus station, turn right, jog right half a block, then continue straight (uphill) for five blocks. Get a combi to **La Batanga,** the lagoon dock (8am, noon, 3, and 5pm, 40min.) from the end of the market on Ocampo (to your left). Finally, a boat will be waiting to take you to Mexcaltitán (4 pesos; return boats leave at 10am, 12:45, 3:45, and 5:15pm; miss the last one out and be stranded). Back in Santiago, buses to Tepic leave until 8pm.

# JALISCO

# ■ Guadalajara

More Mexican than Mexico itself, Guadalajara (pop. 5 million), capital of the state of Jalisco and the second-largest city of the Republic, is massive, mind-boggling, and magnetic. This crowning achievement of Spanish colonial urbanity has spawned many of Mexico's most marketable icons: bittersweet *mariachi* music, the *jarabe tapatío* (the Mexican hat dance), and tequila. These icons, now important symbols for the entire Republic, grew out of the distinctive *tapatío* culture forged by Spanish colonists who wanted to be both far from the capital and in a comfortably Spanish environment after pro-Independence convulsions disrupted life in 19th-century Mexico City. It certainly fit the bill: founded by Nuño de Guzmán, the most brutal of the *conquistadores*, Guadalajara was created out of a blood bath, as most of the region's *indígenas* were killed and few pre-Hispanic traditions survived. However, for better or for worse, it is this enduring and alluring *tapatío* legacy that colors most idealized images of colonial Mexico. Guadalajara is the image's finest incarnation, not built specifically for tourists but nevertheless fulfilling their hopes entirely.

Shockingly green, clean, and accessible, Guadalajara is an urban traveler's dream. The city's *centro*, with its wide, tree-lined avenues and pocket parks and plazas, is wonderfully crafted for walking; unlike much of Mexico, this metropolis boasts an excellent local bus system and speedy subways connecting its sprawling suburbs with its *centro*, so that most sights can be reached in 20 minutes or less. In a remarkable feat of city planning, the transit system was designed to preserve the splendor of Guadalajara's past; as Guadalajara evolved from colonial center into modern megametropolis, many streets were widened on only one side, wisely sparing the buildings which have since become architectural treasures. However, careful excavation does not preserve all, and the epic struggle against the blitz of development has seen some losing battles as well; though the treasures in the *centro* are still there, you sometimes need to squint to see them—industrial giants and endless rows of flat, unspectacular one-story houses reach far into the surrounding countryside.

As might be expected for a city of its scope, Guadalajara is a cultural mecca as well. Markets in and out of the city provide no shortage of *jalisciense* crafts, and local artists, thespians, dancers (including the renowned Ballet Folklórico), and street performers continue to celebrate Guadalajara's fine artistic tradition. Meanwhile, the university, the second-oldest in Mexico, keeps Guadalajara young and shades its urban bustle with a measure of high-brow intellectual sophistication.

## ORIENTATION

Guadalajara is divided into four sectors more or less along the major streets **Hidalgo/ Republica** and **Calzada Independencia Norte and Sur.** A map is very useful, as streets change names at the borders between these four sectors. The city's **shopping district** centers around the intersection of **Juárez** and **Alcalde/16 de Septiembre.** The oblong **Plaza Tapatía** contains the **cathedral,** the **Teatro Degollado,** many churches and museums, and countless stores. The area west of Tapatía and the University of Guadalajara, known as the **Zona Rosa,** has many of the most expensive hotels and restaurants, modern buildings, and the U.S. consulate.

The poorer *colonias* (suburbs) can be dangerous at any time of day. Check with the tourist office before blazing new trails. Throughout Guadalajara, it is wise to stick to lit streets after dark and to take taxis after 10pm. Solo women travelers may want to avoid **Calzada Independencia** after this hour as well, as the street has a magnetic field that attracts raucous, drunken men and supports a thriving prostitution trade at all hours of the day and night. As you move east from Calzada Independencia, conditions deteriorate—use common sense when deciding where to walk.

## PRACTICAL INFORMATION

**Tourist Offices: State Office,** Morelos 102 (tel. 658-22-22, 614-86-86, or toll-free within Mexico 91-800-363-22), in Pl. Tapatía. In addition to helpful information and maps, distributes *Guadalajara Weekly* (free tourist paper), *Tentaciones* (weekly listings of movies, exhibits, concerts, and theatrical events), and *Mexico Living and Travel Update* (detailed information for living in Mexico). English spoken. Ask about tours. Open Mon.-Fri. 9am-8pm, Sat.-Sun. and holidays 9am-1pm.

CENTRAL PACIFIC COAST

**Tours: Panoramex,** Federalismo 944 and España (tel. 810-51-09 or 810-50-05). Guadalajara and Tlaquepaque (Mon.-Sat. 9:30am, 5hr., 75 pesos); Chapala and Ajijic (Tues., Thurs., and Sat.-Sun. 9:30am, 6½hr., 100 pesos). Tours leave from the Jardín de San Francisco at 9:30am and from the Arcos de Ballanca at 9:45am. English tours available. Open Mon.-Fri. 9am-2:30pm and 4:30-7pm, Sat. 9am-1pm.

**Consulates:** Tons of 'em here. **Australia,** López Cotilla 2030 between López de Vega and Calserón de la Bara (tel. 615-74-18; fax 630-34-79). Open Mon.-Fri. 8am-1:30pm and 3-6pm. **Canada,** Local 30 (tel. 615-62-70, 616-56-42, or emergency 91-800-706-29; fax 615-86-65), at Hotel Fiesta Americana, on the Minerva traffic circle (catch a "Par Vial" bus). Open Mon.-Fri. 8:30am-5pm. **U.K.,** Quevedo 601 between Eulogio Parra and Manuel Acuña (tel. 616-06-29; fax 615-01-97). Open Mon.-Fri. 9am-3pm, and 5-8pm. **U.S.,** Progreso 175 (tel. 825-27-00 or 825-29-98; fax 826-65-49). Open Mon.-Fri. 8am-4:30pm. The **Oficina de la Asociación Consular,** at the U.K. consulate, can provide listings for other consulates.

**Currency Exchange:** The block of López Cotilla between Colón and Molina is a *mercado* with only one product: money. Rates don't vary much; most places open Mon.-Sat. 9am-7pm. **Banco Internacional,** Juárez 400 (tel. 614-88-00), at Galeana. Open Mon.-Sat. 8am-7pm. **Banamex,** Juárez at Corona (tel. 679-32-52). Open Mon.-Fri. 8:30am-5:30pm, Sat. 10am-2pm.

**American Express:** on Vallarta 2440 (tel. 615-89-10), at Plaza los Arcos. Take the "Par Vial" bus. Open Mon.-Fri. 9am-2:30pm, and 4-6pm, Sat. 9am-1pm.

**Telephones: LADATELs** are all over the *centro*. *Caseta* in Nueva Central bus station is open 24hr. Another is located at Gigante on Calzada Independencia 480 (open daily 8:30am-11pm).

**Fax: Palacio Federal,** Alcalde and Juan Álvarez (tel. 614-26-64; fax 613-99-15) and at the airport. Open Mon.-Fri. 8am-7pm, Sat. 9am-noon.

**Airport: Aeropuerto Internacional Miguel Hidalgo** (tel. 688-51-20, 688-51-27, or 688-97-66), 17km south of town on the road to Chapala. *Çombis* (tel. 688-59-25 or 812-43-08) run 24hr. and will pick you up from your hotel (40min., 60 pesos). A yellow and white "Aeropuerto" bus passes through the *centro* on Independencia to Los Angeles (every hr., 5:45am-8:45pm, 5 pesos). It makes the trip back from outside "Sala Nacional." Get off at 16 de Septiembre and Constituyentes. Don't pay more than 60 pesos for a cab. A major hub, served by **Aeroméxico** (tel. 669-02-02), **AeroCalifornia** (tel. 616-25-25), **American** (tel. 616-40-90 or 688-55-18), **Continental** (tel. 647-42-51 or 688-51-41), **Delta** (tel. 630-35-30 or 688-53-97), **Mexicana** (tel. 678-76-76), **Taesa** (tel. 679-09-00), and **United** (tel. 616-94-89).

**Buses: Nueva Central Camionera,** in nearby **Tlaquepaque.** Each of the station's 7 terminals has **LADATELs** and hotel info booths—don't trust quotes for hotels they don't promote. Fixed-fare buses and taxis (10-27 pesos) head downtown frequently, as do "Centro" buses. To reach the station from downtown, catch a #275, 275A, or "Nueva Central" bus on Av. Revolución or on Av. 16 de Septiembre, across from the cathedral. In a taxi, be sure to specify the *new* bus station. You can go just about anywhere directly from Guadalajara. Only partial listings are provided; call for more info. **Terminal 1: Primera Plus** and **Flecha Amarilla** (tel. 600-07-70) provide 1st-class service to Aguascalientes (4 and 8:15pm, 3hr., 85 pesos), Guanajuato (5 per day, 11am-8pm, 4hr., 100 pesos), Mexico City (every hr., 10hr., 208 pesos), Morelia (8 per day, 4:30am-9:30pm, 6hr., 102 pesos), Querétaro (every hr., 8hr., 118 pesos), and San Miguel de Allende (1 and 3pm, 5hr., 143 pesos). **Terminal 2: Autobuses de Occidente** (tel. 600-00-55), to Manzanillo (14 per day, 4am-11:45pm, 4½hr., 94 pesos) via Colima (3hr., 70 pesos), Uruapan (7 per day, 4:45am-5:15pm, 5hr., 77 pesos), and Toluca (8 per day, 3:30am-8pm, 11hr., 155 pesos). **Terminal 3: Transportes del Pacífico** (tel. 600-03-39), to Mexico City (7 per day, 5am-1pm, 8hr., 198 pesos) and Puerto Vallarta (11 per day, 4:30am-midnight, 6hr., 142 pesos). **Terminal 4: Transportes de Sonora** (tel. 679-04-63) goes to Hermosillo (14 per day, 24hr., 408 pesos) via Mazatlán (every hr., 8hr., 148 pesos) and points in between. **Terminal 5: Línea Azul** (tel. 600-62-31), to San Luis Potosí (1st class 15 per day, 5hr., 109 pesos; 2nd class every ½hr., 7am-11:30pm, 6hr., 95 pesos). **Terminal 6: Ómnibus de México** (tel. 600-02-91 or 600-04-69), to Ciudad Juárez (5 per day, 7am-10:30pm, 24hr., 475 pesos), Durango (7 per day, 7:30am-midnight, 10hr., 202 pesos), and Zacatecas (14 per

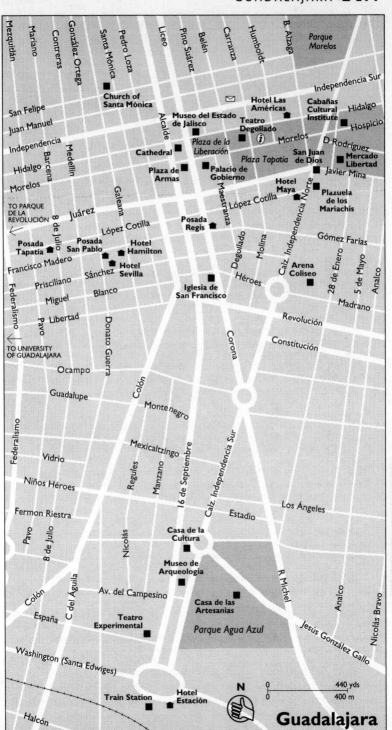

Guadalajara

day, 6:30am-midnight, 5hr., 110 pesos). **Terminal 7: Estrella Blanca** (tel. 679-04-04) is the parent company of numerous smaller lines, including **Rojo de los Altos** and **Transportes del Norte.** Serves Aguascalientes (13 per day, 5am-9pm, 3hr., 78 pesos).

**Local Buses:** Though usually crowded, always noisy, and sometimes uncomfortable, **minibuses** (2 pesos), **regular buses** (2 pesos), and the big blue **TUR** buses (4.50 pesos) are an excellent way to get just about anywhere in the city. Buses **#60** and **#62** run the length of Calzada Independencia, from the train station past the zoo and Plaza de Toros. The electrically wired **"Par Vial"** bus runs west on Independencia then Hidalgo, and turns onto Vallarta, turning just short of López Mateos. Coming back eastward, it cruises Hidalgo, 3 blocks north of Juárez. Bus **#258** from San Felipe, 3 blocks north of Hidalgo, runs from near the Plaza Tapatía down López Mateos to the Plaza del Sol—nightclub central. Bus **#24A** runs the length of López Mateos, from Zapopan to beyond the Plaza del Sol, in both directions. TUR bus **#707A** circles from the *centro* on Juárez west to López Mateos, down to Mariano Otero at the Plaza del Sol, up to Niños Héroes, and north on 16 de Septiembre and Corona to the start of the route. The big red **Cardenal** bus runs west on Madero to Av. Chapultepec along which is the **Zona Rosa,** the upper class shopping district west of the *centro*. The **aqua** TUR bus and Route **#45** return east on Lopez Cotilla. Bus route **#51** runs up and down Av. La Paz. Buses run from 6:30am-10:30 or 11pm.

**Trains:** Av. Washington and 16 de Septiembre (tel. 650-08-26 or 650-10-82), south of the *centro*. To get there, take bus #60 or #62 from the intersection of Independencia and Juárez. Taxis cost 10 pesos. Trains are unbearably slow. Advance ticket sales to points north Mon.-Fri. 9am-1pm, to Mexico City 9am-8pm daily. Same-day sales 7:30am-departure. Open daily 5am-10pm. Trains to Mexico City depart at 9pm; trains to points north depart at 9am (1st class) and noon (2nd class).

**Subway:** Tel. 853-75-70. Two lines run smoothly (every 5-10min., 6am-10:30pm, 2 pesos). It's a great alternative to the bus system if you're tired of breathing exhaust, but not so helpful if you don't know the stops. **Line 1** runs from the northern boundary of the city, Anillo Periférico Norte, more or less along Federalismo to Anillo Periférico Sur. There is a stop at Federalismo and Juárez. **Line 2** runs from Juárez and Av. Alcalde/16 de Septiembre to Av. Patria in the east.

**Car Rental: Dollar,** Av. Federalismo Sur 540-A and Mexicalcinco (tel. 826-79-59 or 825-50-80, at the airport 688-56-89; fax 826-42-21). Renters need a driver's license, major credit card, and 21 years under their belts. Prices start at 300 pesos per day plus 8% tax, including insurance and 300km. Delivers cars free of charge. Open daily 7am-9pm. **Hertz,** at the airport (open 24hr.) and at Av. 16 de Septiembre and Niños Héroes (tel. 688-54-83), has similar rates for drivers over 25.

**English Bookstores: Sandi Bookstore,** Tepeyac 718 (tel. 121-08-63), almost at the corner of Av. de las Rosas in Colonia Chapalita. Take bus #50 from Garibaldi or the green "Plus" bus from Juárez. Extensive selection of new books and newspapers. Open Mon.-Fri. 9:30am-2:30pm and 3:30-7pm, Sat. 9:30am-2pm. The **Hyatt** carries day-old copies of the *New York Times;* **Sanborn's** department store, at Juárez and Corona, carries a wide range of English-language magazines.

**Cultural Information: Dirección de Educación y Cultura,** 5 de Febrero and Analco (tel. 669-13-80 ext. 1487). **Instituto Cultural Cabañas,** Cabañas 8 in Pl. Tapatía (tel. 617-43-22). Open Mon.-Fri. 9am-3pm and 6-9pm.

**Supermarket: Gigante,** Juárez 573 between Medellín and 8 de Julio (tel. 613-86-38). It has just about everything. Open Mon.-Sat. 8am-9pm, Sun. 8am-3pm.

**Laundry: Lavandería Canadá,** Patria 1123 and Tepeyac (tel. 628-74-34). Open Mon.-Sat. 8am-8pm.

**Red Cross:** at Juan Manuel and San Felipe (tel. 613-15-50 or 614-27-07), on the 1st floor, behind Parque Morelos. Some English spoken. Open 24hr.

**Pharmacy: Farmacia Guadalajara,** Javier Mina 221 and Cabañas (tel. 617-85-55). Minimal English spoken. Open 24hr.

**Hospitals: México Americano,** Colones and América (tel. 641-31-41 or 641-44-58). English spoken. **Green Cross Hospital,** Barcenas and Veracruz (tel. 614-52-52 or 643-71-90). English spoken.

**Police:** Independencia Nte. 840 just before the *fuente olympica* (tel. 617-60-60 ext. 126 and 143).

**Internet Access: Cafe Arroba,** Lázaro Cárdenas 3286 and López Mateos (tel. 121-36-50 or 122-49-88), in Col. Chapalita on bus route #258. Email 14 pesos per ½hr. Open Mon.-Sat. 10am-9:30pm. Or try **Mailboxes Etc.,** Av. Chapultepec Sur 590 and Niños Héroes (tel. 616-26-81; fax 616-26-98). Open Mon.-Fri. 9am-8pm, Sat. 10am-2pm.

**Post Office:** (tel. 614-74-25 or 614-40-99), on Carranza, between Juan Manuel and Calle de Independencia (not Independencia Sur). Open Mon.-Fri. 8am-8pm, Sat. 9am-1pm. **Postal Code:** 44100.

**Phone Code:** 3.

## ACCOMMODATIONS

Guadalajara is full of cheap places to stay. *Posadas* are an intriguing option—they're small, family-run establishments (often beautiful, remodeled homes) that provide large, well-furnished rooms, good security, and, for a few extra pesos, frequently serve meals. The drawbacks are curfews and less privacy. Check at the tourist office for a list. Guadalajara also has an excellent hostel (see below). Outside of the hostel and the *posadas,* reservations are only necessary in February and October, the festival seasons.

### Near Plaza Tapatía

Rooms in hotels and *posadas* right in the *centro* are the best option: they're reasonably priced, relatively safe, and convenient to the sights, though often noisy. Be cautious in this area—even residents advise taking a taxi after dark.

**Hotel Las Américas,** Hidalgo 76 and Humboldt (tel. 613-96-22). Not the most exciting place on earth, but still comfortable—with plenty of hot water. Terrific location, but traffic noise can be problematic. Fake ficus trees rooted in cement clutter the hallways. Singles 72 pesos; doubles with 1 bed 78 pesos, with 2 beds 100 pesos. For an extra 11 pesos you can watch your fill of *telenovelas* while relaxing under a whirling ceiling fan.

**CODE Youth Hostel,** Av. Prolongación Alcalde 1360 (tel. 624-65-15). Take bus #52 or #54 from the Jardín de San Francisco or anywhere on Alcalde. The CODE is just past the traffic circle, across from the Foro de Arte y Cultura. Clean, single-sex rooms hold 20 metal bunks each. Bedding, pillows, and lockers provided, but bring your own lock. Water is hot and the management friendly. Reception open Mon.-Fri. 8am-2pm and 4-9pm, Sat.-Sun. 9am-3pm and 5-9pm. Curfew 11:30pm. 20 pesos per person. 25% discount with HI membership. Hostel closed during Semana Santa and Christmas.

**Hotel Hamilton,** Madero 381 between Ocampo and Galeana (tel. 614-67-26). Stalagtite ceiling makes the dim lobby feel like a cave. Somewhat small rooms with peeling paint, but hey, you can't beat the price: singles 40 pesos; doubles 50 pesos. Discounts for longer stays. Add 15 pesos for a TV.

**Posada Tapatía,** López Cotilla 619 (tel. 614-91-46). Peachy walls with bright colored trim, fuchsia sofas and spreads, and a leafy courtyard. Kempt rooms with private bath and fans. Singles 80 pesos; doubles 100 pesos.

**Posada San Pablo,** Madero 429 between Ocampo and Donato Guerra (tel. 613-33-12). Spacious rooms surround a cement courtyard in a remodeled mansion. Tons of hot water and a small paperback book collection, but not all rooms have fans. Singles 60 pesos; doubles 70 pesos. Add 10 pesos for private bath.

**Hotel Sevilla,** Sánchez 413 between Ocampo and Donato Guerra (tel. 614-91-72). Rooms have TVs, phones, sky-blue bathrooms with 24hr. hot water, and oh-so-tasteful landscape photos. Old but very clean. Singles 60 pesos; doubles with 1 bed 80 pesos, with 2 beds 90 pesos.

## East on Javier Mina

Javier Mina and the dark side streets off it can be dangerous at night. If the establishments above don't work out (or if you just want to be closer to Plaza de los Mariachis), these hotels are basic, modern, and clean.

**Hotel México 70,** Javier Mina 230 at Cabañas (tel. 617-99-78). White tile floors, red bedspreads, and aqua tile bathrooms make the head spin. Singles 55 pesos; doubles 65 pesos. Add 10 pesos for TV.

**Hotel Ana Ísabel,** Javier Mina 164 and Cabañas (tel. 617-79-20 or 617-48-59). Clean, small, somewhat dark rooms with ceiling fans and TV, all overlooking a green courtyard. Hot water in tiny bathrooms. Singles 65 pesos; doubles 80 pesos.

**Hotel San Jorge,** Javier Mina 284 (tel. 617-79-97). Plain but comfortable rooms with tile bathrooms and hot water. Dark hallways conserve energy. Singles 50 pesos; doubles 60 pesos. TV 10 pesos extra.

## West to The *Zona Rosa*

Hotels in the *Zona Rosa* are pricey. A pleasant option midway between the *centro* and the more expensive Av. Chapultepec is **Hotel La Paz,** La Paz 1091, between Donato Guerra and 8 de Julio (tel. 613-30-07), on bus route #51 or #321. Clean, basic rooms equipped with phones. Tranquil, but peace has its price—it's in the boonies. Singles 60 pesos; doubles 85 pesos; triples 100 pesos; add 10 pesos for TV.

## South to the Train Station

Before opting to bed down in this industrialized part of town, remember that there's nothing to do around here but sleep. Better hotels await in Guadalajara's lively *centro*. If you must, **Hotel Estación,** Independencia Sur 1297 (tel. 619-00-51), is just to the right as you leave the station, across six lanes of highways. The rooms and bathrooms are comfy enough. They have seen years of use, but the staff does its best to maintain them. Singles 55 pesos; doubles 65 pesos; add 15 pesos for TV.

# FOOD

Guadalajara has tons of budget eateries as well as many upscale restaurants with cuisine from around the world: French, Italian, Japanese, and more. *Birria* is a hearty local specialty made by stewing meat, typically pork, in tomato broth thickened with cornmeal and spiced with garlic, onions, and chiles.

## Near Plaza Tapatía

This is a great place to snack. Ice cream and fast-food are ubiquitous, sidewalk stands line the streets, and *panaderías* cluster around the area southwest of the plaza, primarily on the blocks enclosed by Pavo, Sánchez, Galeana, and Juárez.

**Hidalgo 112,** at...Hidalgo 112 (tel. 614-54-47), across from Teatro Degollado. No sign, so look for the brownish red awning. A glorified juice bar with pine tables and traditional blue glass. Squeeze in and chat with locals after the lunchtime rush. Fantastically cheap. Large fruit yogurt with granola in a glass 5 pesos. Whole wheat quesadillas (2 pesos) can't be beat. Open Mon.-Sat. 7am-10pm, Sun. 7am-5pm.

**Restaurant Acuarius,** Sánchez 416 (tel. 613-62-77), across from Hotel Sevilla. New Age, Mex-style. Don a peasant shirt and brandish your cosmic consciousness. *Jugo verde* 8.50 pesos. Soy burgers 13 pesos. Vegetarian *comida corrida* 29 pesos. Open Mon.-Sat. 9:30am-6pm, Sun. 10am-5:30pm.

**Cafe Madrid,** Juárez 264 and 16 de Septiembre (614-95-05). A bit pricey, but fun: a 1950s diner flourishing in the *centro*. Waiters sporting white jackets and bow ties serve breakfast (22-32 pesos), enchiladas (28 pesos), and divine cappuccino (6.50 pesos) to patrons seated on stools along the formica counter or at tables beneath an enormous Alfredo Santos mural. Open daily 7:30am-10:30pm.

**Restaurant Vegetariano Devachan,** López Cotilla 570 and 8 de Juio, inside the mysterious Instituto Devachan. Bountiful and tasty vegetarian *comida corrida* (18 pesos) served in a plant-filled yellow courtyard. On Saturdays, devotees and mystics gather to gorge themselves on the buffet (22 pesos). Open Mon.-Sat. 2-6pm.

**El Farol,** Moreno 466 and Galeana (tel. 613-03-49), 2nd fl. *Comida típica* at rock-bottom prices. Friendly owner makes a mean *chile relleno*. Complementary *buñuelos,* a fried dough dessert dripping with sugary syrup. Entrees 12-18 pesos, tacos 2 pesos, beer 5 pesos. Open daily 9:15am-11:30pm.

**Jugui Torti Pollo,** Corona 224 and Madero. What this tiny fast-food joint lacks in atmosphere it makes up for in taste. Burritos 5 pesos. *Tortas* 9 pesos. Juice 5 pesos. Open daily 6am-midnight.

### East on Javier Mina

Restaurants near Javier Mina will fill your stomach, but not with anything particularly thrilling. An exception is **Restaurant del Pacífico,** Plaza de los Mariachis 31 (tel. 617-82-28), where the *carne asada* (18 pesos) is orgasmic and the *mariachi* music a real mood-setter (open daily 9:30am-late).

### West to the *Zona Rosa*

Most places below cluster near the intersection of Vallarta and Chapultepec, on the "Par Vial" bus route. The #321 bus also does the trick. It's worth the trip—the extra pesos buy superior food and even a measure of elegance.

**Naló Cafe,** Justo Sierra 2046 (tel. 615-27-15), just off Chapultepec Nte. Tasty, amazingly cheap food served by fresh-faced teens in this airy, cool cafe. Excellent coffee and breakfast specials (10-18 pesos). Fettucini alfredo 14 pesos. Greek salad 8 pesos. Carrot cake 10 pesos.

**Restaurant Samurai,** Vidrio 1929 (tel. 826-35-54), the small street a block north of the Niños Héroes monument on Chapultepec. Japanese food served up in a room in a family's house. Very cozy, very quiet, very tasty. *Comida corrida* (Japanese style) with rice, soup, and main course 17 pesos. *Tonkatsu* 35 pesos. Open Mon.-Sat. noon-10pm, Sun. noon-7pm.

**Café Don Luis,** Chapultepec 215 and Av. de la Paz (tel. 625-65-99), at Libertad. Coffees and desserts. A great place to revive your sleepy bones after a *siesta;* Angel's Kiss (Kahlúa, coffee, and eggnog) is love at first sip (13 pesos). Open daily 9am-3pm and 5-11pm.

## SIGHTS

A great city for walking, Guadalajara fills in the evening with families out for a stroll in the cooling air. But don't limit your exploration to the *centro*—the city is huge, but its bus and subway systems make transportation into most areas a breeze. The sheer number of monuments testifies to the rich history and culture of Guadalajara. Statues commemorating everyone from the Niños Héroes to (who else?) Benito Juárez are ubiquitous. Guadalajara's plazas are clean and crowded, and often visited by party-hardy *mariachis.* The city's museums are the best introduction to Mexican culture and history outside of Mexico City.

### Downtown

Downtown Guadalajara's four plazas punctuate the city's concrete sidewalks with splashes of greenery. Horse-drawn carriages wait at the Independencia side of the Mercado Libertad, offering half-hour tours for about 50 pesos. The spacious **Plaza de la Liberación,** with its large, bubbling fountain, is surrounded by the cathedral, Museo Regional, Palacio de Gobierno, and Teatro Degollado. An enormous sculpture depicts Hidalgo breaking the chains of slavery in commemoration of his 1810 decree, signed in Guadalajara, to abolish the trade.

The **Palacio de Gobierno,** built in 1774 and on the plaza's south side, is a Churrigueresque building graced by a mural by José Clemente Orozco; check out Miguel Hidalgo's feverish eyes looking down from the wall. A second Orozco mural covers the ceiling in the echoing **Sala de Congreso.** The mural depicts enslaved *indígenas* and the heroism of Hidalgo and Juárez (both open Mon.-Fri. 9am-8:45pm, Sat.-Sun. 9am-3pm; guided tours available for a few pesos). Climb to the roof for a great view.

The imposing **cathedral** faces the Teatro Degollado across Plaza de la Liberación. Begun in 1558 and completed 60 years later, the cathedral is a melange of architectural styles. After an 1848 earthquake destroyed its original towers, ambitious architects replaced them with much taller ones. Fernando VII of Spain donated the cathedral's 11 richly ornamented altars in appreciation of Guadalajara's help during the Napoleonic Wars. One of the remaining original altars is dedicated to Our Lady of the Roses; it is this altar, and not the flamboyant flowers, that gave Guadalajara its nickname, "City of Roses." Inside the sacristy is the *Assumption of the Virgin,* a painting by the showy 17th-century painter **Bartolomé Murillo.** The towers, known as the *cornucopias,* can be climbed with the permission of the cathedral's administrators, who hole up in the side of the building facing the Teatro Degollado. There are entrances on this side, or just walk through the church to the back. The 60m jaunt to the top of the towers affords the best view in town. You may be able to take pictures of the church and sacristy, but be respectful (church open daily 7:30am-7:30pm; to avoid mass on Sun., visit after 2pm). On the cathedral's west side is the arboreal **Plaza de los Laureles;** to the north, the **Plaza de los Mártires** commemorates *tapatíos* who have died in various wars.

On the north side of the Plaza de la Liberación, the **Museo Regional de Guadalajara,** Calle Liceo 60 (tel. 614-99-57, 614-52-64, or 614-52-57), at Hidalgo, chronicles the history of western Mexico, beginning with the Big Bang. The first floor spans the country's pre-Hispanic history and includes meteorites, mammoth bones, metalwork, jewels, and some Aztec art lamenting the Spanish Conquest. Collections of colonial art, modern paintings, and an exhibit on the history of the Revolution occupy the second floor. Artsy and educational movie screenings, plays, and lectures take place in the museum's auditorium (open Tues.-Fri. 9am-7pm, Sat. 9am-6pm, Sun. 9am-3pm.; admission 14 pesos; free on Sun., Tues., and everyday for seniors, children under 12, and students with a Mexican ID—ISIC won't get you in).

Attend the Ballet Folklórico on Sunday mornings to get a good look at the breathtaking **Teatro Degollado,** a Neoclassical structure on the Plaza de la Liberación's east end. The theater's interior features gold and red balconies, a sculpted allegory of the seven muses, and Gerardo Suárez's depiction of Dante's *Divine Comedy* on the ceiling. You can visit anytime, provided there is no performance scheduled. Tickets (tel. 614-47-73) are available at the theater box office (see p. 277).

The crowded **Plazuela de los Mariachis** is on the south side of **San Juan de Dios,** the church with the blue neon cross at Independencia and Javier Mina. Immediately after you sit down, roving musicians will pounce. Using every trick in their musical bag, the *mariachis* will try to separate you from your pesos. Prices for songs are completely variable; a good *mariachi* who likes you or a bad one without much choice may perform a song for only 20-25 pesos, post-haggling.

From the **Plaza Tapatía,** constructed in 1982, you can spy the glinting dome of the 190-year-old **Hospicio Cabañas** at the corner of Hospicio and Cabañas, three blocks east of Independencia. It was here that Hidalgo signed his proclamation against slavery in 1810; the building has since served as an orphanage and an art school. For its main chapel, Orozco painted a nightmarish rendition of the Four Riders of the Apocalypse; some regard the work as Orozco's best. *Espejos* (mirrors) are available free for those who don't want to strain their necks; alternatively, lie down on one of the many benches set up for reclined viewing. The *hospicio* also houses a collection of Orozco drawings and lithographs (open Tues.-Sat. 10am-6pm, Sun. 10am-3pm; admission 8 pesos, with student ID 4 pesos, children under 12 free, free for all Sun.; 10 pesos for camera rights—no flash).

The cavernous **Mercado Libertad,** at Javier Mina and Independencia, is toted as the largest covered market in the Americas. It probably isn't, but there are still oodles of sandals, *sarapes,* jewelry, guitars, and dried iguanas and other witchcraft supplies filling tier after tier of booths. Savvy merchants expect customers to bargain; don't be shy (open daily roughly 9am-8pm, but some merchants don't open on Sun.). The weekly market **El Baratillo** on Javier Mina, approximately 15 blocks east of Mercado Libertad, offers bargain hunters even greater temptation. El Baratillo lasts all day Sunday and sometimes sprawls out over 30 or 40 blocks. Everything imaginable is peddled here, from hot *tamales* to houses. From Mercado Libertad, walk two blocks north to Hidalgo and catch bus #40 heading east or a "Par Vial" bus on Morelos.

### South

If you're tired of the hustle and bustle of the streets, take a stroll in the **Parque Agua Azul,** a lavish green park with tropical bird aviaries, an orchid greenhouse, a duck pond, and a butterfly house. The park is south of the *centro* on Calzada Independencia; take bus #60 or #62 heading south along this main street (open Tues.-Sun. 10am-6pm; admission 4 pesos, children 2 pesos). Almost everything is for sale inside the **Casa de las Artesanías de Jalisco** (tel. 619-46-64 or 619-51-79), on González Gallo, the street bisecting Parque Agua Azul. Pottery, jewelry, clocks, hammocks, china, blankets, *equipales,* chessboards, shirts, and purses are all high-quality and have all been carted over from Tlaquepaque and Tonalá (see p. 281). Prices are higher here than in the villages (open Mon.-Fri. 10am-7pm, Sat. 10am-4pm, Sun. 10am-2pm).

### Zona Rosa

Cultural activity in the city's wealthier areas focuses on the **Plaza del Arte,** one block south on Chapultepec from its intersection with Niños Héroes. National artists bare their souls on a rotating basis in the plaza's **Galería de Arte Moderno,** Mariano Otero and España (tel. 616-32-66; open Mon.-Fri. 10am-7pm, Sat.-Sun. 10am-4pm; free). The **Teatro Jaime Torres Bodet** (tel. 615-12-69), also in the Plaza del Arte, has book expositions, concerts, and more. Stand-up comedy and performance art enliven the premises with laughter and pretension (open Mon.-Fri. 9am-9pm).

### North

Lions and tigers and bears, oh my! If you're missing your furry friends, head out to the **Zoológico Guadalajara** (tel. 674-44-88 or 674-43-60), way north on Calzada Independencia, near the Plaza de Toros. The zoo also affords a spectacular view of the **Barranca de Huentitán,** a deep ravine (open Wed.-Sun. 10am-6pm; admission 15 pesos, children 12 and under 7 pesos). The **Centro de Ciencia y Tecnología** (tel. 674-41-06), a brief walk from the zoo, has exhibits on astronomy, aeronautics, and rock formations and houses a **planetarium** (open Tues.-Sat. 9am-7pm, Sun. 9am-6:30pm; admission 2 pesos, children under 12 free, 4 pesos for the planetarium). To get to any of the sights listed above, take Ruta #60 or #62 north on Calzada Independencia.

## ENTERTAINMENT AND SEASONAL EVENTS

Guadalajara is known for its cultural sophistication. There's almost always something going on, from avant-garde film festivals to bullfights. Listings of clubs and cultural events appear in *Tentaciones,* the Friday supplement to *Siglo 21;* in *The Guadalajara Weekly;* in *Vuelo Libre,* a monthly calendar of events; and on the kiosks and bulletin boards of places like Hospicio Cabañas. Be prepared to take a taxi at night, as many of Guadalajara's streets become deserted and dangerous after dark.

### Cultural Events

The **Ballet Folklórico** dazzles the world with amazingly precise rhythmic dance, authenticated with traditional regional garb and polished with amusing stage antics. There are two troupes in Guadalajara, one affiliated with the University of Guadalajara and the other with the state of Jalisco. The former, reputedly better, performs Sundays at 10am in the **Teatro Degollado** (tel. 614-47-73; open daily 10am-1pm and 4-7pm; tickets, 15-60 pesos, are sold a day in advance; spend the extra pesos for a seat up front and arrive half an hour early as seats are not reserved within sections). The **Ballet Folklórico de Cabañas,** the state troupe, performs Wednesdays at 8:30pm in the Hospicio Cabañas (tickets 25 pesos); arriving before 8pm will make you privy to a tour of some of the murals of the Hospicio.

University facilities, scattered throughout the city, have created a market for high culture on a low budget. The **Departamento de Bellas Artes** coordinates activities at a large number of stages, auditoriums, and movie screens throughout the city. The best source of information on cultural events is the blackboard in its lobby at García 720, which lists each day's attractions. The **Instituto Cultural Cabañas** presents live music on an open-air stage in the Hospicio Cabañas at least once a week. Drop by the Hospicio Cabañas ticket counter (see p. 276) or look for flyers with the Cabañas insignia (a building with pillars) for schedules.

For Luis Buñuel retrospectives and other vintage screenings, head to the cinema at Bellas Artes. The **Cinematógrafo**, at Vallarta 1102 (tel. 825-05-14), just west of the university, is a film house that changes its show weekly (tickets 20 pesos). Guadalajara has dozens of other cinemas with admission around 15 pesos; check the newspapers for listings. For more mature company and some live music, try the **Copenhagen**, Marcos Castellanos 120-2 between Juárez and López Cortilla (tel. 825-28-03; live music Mon.-Sat. 8pm-12:30am; open Mon.-Sat. 2:30pm-12:30am, Sun. 1-6pm). **La Terraza**, 442 Juárez at Ocampo (tel. 658-36-91), overlooks the *centro* and serves all-you-can-eat tacos (14.50 pesos, noon-5pm) and cheap beer (3.50 pesos; open daily noon-10pm). Otherwise try **La Hosta**, at México and Rubén Darío (open daily 1pm-1am).

## Bars and Clubs

Guadalajara has a thriving nightlife; determined partygoers can find something going on almost any night. For a more Mexican experience, skip the overpriced and generic *discotecas* and head instead to one of the city's many excellent bars. Live entertainment in these hot spots ranges from punk rock to *mariachi*.

**La Maestranza**, Maestranza 179 at López Cotilla (tel. 613-20-85). Bullfight regalia and posters crowd the walls of this local hangout. Tasty and surprisingly reasonably-priced food, good music, and, of course, plenty of alcohol. Enchiladas 24 pesos. Beer 8 pesos. Live trio daily 3-5pm. No cover. Open daily 10am-3am. In the same building, **Discoteca 1907** (tel. 613-39-15), featuring typical disco tunes and live rock on weekends. Cover 50 pesos for men on Wed. (including open bar; free for women), 25 equal-opportunity pesos for all Fri.-Sat. Open Wed.-Sat. 10pm-4am.

**La Cripta**, Tepeyac 4038 and Niño Obrero (tel. 647-62-07). Cool locals, mostly university types, down *cervezas* to live alternative tunes. Cover 20-40 pesos. Open daily 8pm-3am.

**Babel**, Av. Vallarta 1480 at Chapultepec (tel. 615-63-61), is the typical Mexican "video bar." Flashing screens and loud rockin' music in English and Spanish. No cover. Open daily 8pm-2am.

Although they close earlier than bars, many **cafes** are still happenin' nighttime spots. **Cafe La Paloma**, on López Cotilla 1855 at Miguel de Cervantes (tel. 630-00-91), is definitely a hipster hangout. The cool patio filled with wicker chairs makes for a welcome respite from the hustle of downtown. Local artwork spanks the imagination while the body enjoys tasty dishes and desserts (*cafe de olla* 10 pesos, chocolate cheesecake 12 pesos, quesadillas 6 pesos; open Mon.-Sat. 8:30am-11pm, Sun. 9am-10pm). **Bananas Cafe**, at Chapultepec 330 and Lerdo de Tejada (tel. 615-41-91), is slightly silly but fun and worth a visit for their unusual offering of drinks.

## Discotecas

Elegantly dressed partygoers line up to get into the classy joints along **Av. Vallarta** (taxi 15 pesos), while more classic discotheques with sophisticated track lighting and elevated dance floors cluster around **Plaza del Sol** (taxi 20-25 pesos).

**La Máquina**, Vallarta 1920 (tel. 615-23-25), near Plaza Los Arcos. Housed in an 18th-century mansion with gold leafing, high ceilings, chandeliers, and dapper waiters in red jackets and frilly blouses. Cover 80 pesos for men on Wed. (women free), 40 pesos for all Fri.-Sat. Open Wed.-Sat. 9pm-3am.

**La Marcha,** Vallarta 2648 at Los Arcos (tel. 615-89-99). Fancy artwork, fountains, and pretension, oh my. Cover Thurs.-Sat. men 80 pesos, women 40 pesos. Open Wed.-Sat. 10pm-3am.

**Lado B,** Vallarta 2451 and Queredo (tel. 616-83-23), at Plaza Los Arcos. A blazing inferno, complete with creepy murals, images of the sphinx and phoenix, and metal and wire furniture. Cover Fri. men 40 pesos, women 20 pesos, Sat. men 80 pesos, women 30 pesos. Open Wed., and Fri.-Sat. 9:30pm-3am.

**Pasaje,** Mariano Otero 1989 (tel. 121-13-63), by the Plaza de Sol. The ultimate in glam; thick smoke clouds a packed dance floor, while the crowd downs drinks amid flashing lights and big screen TVs. The attached video bar, **Forever,** is very popular. Cover Wed.-Thurs. men 50 pesos, women 20 pesos, Fri.-Sat. men 80 pesos, women 40 pesos, Sun. 30 pesos. Open Wed.-Sun. 10pm-2am.

There is more **gay nightlife** here than anywhere other than Mexico City, mostly along Chapultepec, on the upscale *Zona Rosa,* and at the Plaza de los Mariachis. The best-known gay disco is **Monica's,** Álvaro Obregón 1713 (nightly drag shows; cover 30 pesos; open Wed.-Sun. 11pm-4am). **S.O.S.,** La Paz 1413 (tel. 826-41-79), at Federalismo and Tolsa, has incredibly vibrant drag shows (Wed.-Sun. at midnight; cover 20 pesos; bar open Thurs.-Tues. 10pm-3am, disco open Wed.-Sun. 10pm-3am). **Mastara's,** Maestranza 238 and Madero (tel. 614-81-03), is a popular gay bar with 2-for-1 beers (10 pesos; open daily 9pm-1am). A mixed gay and straight crowd frequents **Chivas** at López Cotilla and Degollado (open daily 8pm-3am).

## Open-air Activities

Finding a bench in the Plaza de Armas, across from the Palacio de Gobierno, on Thursday and Sunday nights is an impossible task—the **Jalisco State Band** draws crowds of locals for free performances of gusto-packed music. The music doesn't get going until about 6:30pm, but seat-seekers should arrive before 6pm. The **Plaza de los Fundadores,** behind the Teatro Degollado, serves as a stage every afternoon for the clown-mimes who are popular among locals. Watch and give tips, but unless you like being the butt of jokes, keep out of the mime's eye.

Every October, Guadalajara explodes with the traditional **Fiestas de Octubre,** a surreal month-long bacchanal of parades, dancing, bullfights, fireworks, food, and fun. Each day of the month is dedicated to a different one of Mexico's 29 states, its 2 territories, or Mexico City. Revelers are treated to regional dance performances, concerts, and cultural celebrations for 31 consecutive days.

## Sports

**Bullfights** take place almost every Sunday from October to April in the **Plaza de Toros,** at Nuevo Progreso on the northern end of Independencia (take Ruta #60 or 62 north). Tickets (25-180 pesos) can be purchased at the Plaza de Toros (tel. 637-99-82 or 651-85-06; open Mon.-Sat. 10am-2pm and 4-6pm). More popular, colorful, and distinctly Mexican are the *charreadas* (rodeos), held every Sunday at noon at the **Lienzo Charro de Jalisco,** Dr. R. Michel 577 (tel. 619-32-32 or 619-03-15; take the #60 or 62 bus to the stadium; tickets are around 30 pesos).

Even by Mexican standards, *fútbol* is huge in Guadalajara. The *Chivas,* the local professional team, are perennial contenders for the national championship—conversations turn nasty, brutish, and short at the mention of the *Pumas,* the team's Mexico City rival. Matches are held September to May in **Jalisco Stadium** (tel. 637-05-63 or 637-02-99), at Calzada Independencia North in front of the Plaza de Toros (on the #60 or #62 bus route), and in **Estadio 3 de Marzo** (tel. 641-50-51), at the Universidad Autónoma (ticket office is at Colomos Pte. 2339).

# ■ Near Guadalajara

## TEQUILA

Surrounded by gentle mountains and prickly, blue-green agave plants stretching as far as the eye can see, Tequila is a typical Mexican *pueblo* with a difference: since the 17th century, Tequila has been dedicated solely to the production and sale of its namesake. The town is home to 11 tequila factories, and nearly every business in town is linked to the liquor in some way. Tourism sustains a slew of t-shirt and souvenir shops as well as numerous liquor stores in the *centro* and along the highway just outside of town. Though touristy by definition, this dusty town is lots of fun, and makes a great daytrip from Guadalajara.

Tequila's **tourist office** is located on the town's main plaza in front of the Presidencia Municipal (open daily 10am-5pm). They'll arrange tours of the tequila factories and the tequila museum. **Banamex**, at Sixto Gorjón and Juárez, has an **ATM** and changes dollars. The **police** wait on the Plaza Principal at José Cuervo 33, next to the tourist office. Don't plan to spend the night in Tequila—it's wiser to head back to Guadalajara at dusk than enjoy a Tequila sunrise. There's not a whole lot of choice in the dining department, either. One option is **Restaurant Bar El Sauzal,** Juárez 45 between Gorjón and Cuervo, which is home to a garish mural and beer-drinking locals (*bistec ranchero* 24 pesos; beer 6-7 pesos; quesadillas 5 pesos; *tostada* 7 pesos; open daily noon-11pm). True budget hunters will delight to find the *pollo* roaster **Aricola,** at Sixto Gorjón 20, where half a roasted chicken goes for about 20 pesos (open daily 7:30am-4pm). Tortillas available at the *tortillería* next door.

There's not much to do here besides drinking and the government-sponsored **factory tour,** but why else did you come to a town called Tequila? For the price of a couple shots, you'll learn more than you ever wanted to know about *agave* (the plant from which tequila is distilled), the distillation and aging processes, and the history of every *mariachi*'s favorite liquor. The **tour** includes a stop in a small **tequila museum** and **gift shop,** where you can sample the town's finest. Those who can spare the pesos will find good deals on hard-to-find varieties and tequila-related knick-knacks for the folks back home.

The best tequila, as the tour guides will tell you, bears a label boasting its content: 100% agave. Around 1600 varieties of this cactus exist in Mexico; only the blue *agave* is used to make tequila. Plants take eight to 12 years to mature, at which point their huge, dense centers (called *piñas*—pineapples—for their appearance) weigh 35-45kg. Though the *agave* plant's spiky leaves can tower above even tall *norteamericanos, agave* growers keep them trimmed short, as it is only the center that is used to produce tequila. Once harvested, each agave plant provides around 5L of tequila. Not bad for a cactus. From the field, the *piñas* are taken to the factory where they are cooked for 36 hours in enormous traditional ovens, or 12 hours in the modern and speedy autoclave. The *piñas* are then chopped and mixed with water. The mixture is then poured into huge tubs where it ferments, attracting bees, flies, ants, and other bugs which inevitably join this not-so-appetizing concoction. But don't try to blame these critters for your tequila trauma—in the several months or more before this brew finds its way to anyone's mouth, it will be carefully sterilized and diluted.

For 12 days at the beginning of December, Tequila celebrates its **Feria Nacional del Tequila.** Each of the town's factories has its own day on which to hold rodeos, concerts, cockfights, fireworks, and other festivities. And of course, there's always plenty of drink to go around as each company celebrates the past year's successes.

**Getting There:** Buses to Tequila leave from Guadalajara's Antigua Central about every 45 minutes (2hr., 15 pesos) and return on the same schedule.

## TLAQUEPAQUE

The "village" of Tlaquepaque is little more than the strip along Independencia, where upscale shops set in old colonial mansions sell silver, handicrafts, leather, ceramics, plastic toys, and junk. Though completely geared towards tourists, Tlaquepaque

---

### Gentlemen Prefer Blondes

*"¡Miren, miren, el güerito!"* shout the schoolgirls. *"Pss, pss, ¡güera!"* hiss the men. *"¡Qué güero!"* gasps the twentysomething woman. That's an average day, or half hour, in the life of a fair-skinned or -haired person in Mexico. *Güero (-a)* means blonde, and few Mexicans will hesitate to show their amazement and excitement upon seeing anyone with a full head of naturally yellow hair and a heartbeat. And it's no wonder: if you flip on the television while traveling in Mexico, you'll see mainly a cast that is fair-haired, fair-skinned, and light-eyed. Mexican media equates blonde with beautiful in a country that is mainly *mestizo* (of mixed indigenous and Spanish descent) and *moreno* (dark-haired, dark-eyed, and dark-skinned). Try to keep in mind that despite the frustration cat-calls may induce, the term is often used casually and with affection.

---

offers the best quality and prices for *artesanías* in the Guadalajara area. Just off its main square lies the *mercado,* where cheaper goods of lesser quality can be found.

The **Museo Regional de las Cerámicas y los Artes Populares de Jalisco,** Independencia 237 and Alfareros (tel. 635-54-04), sells an interesting collection of antique regional crafts as well as newer pieces (open Tues.-Sat. 10am-6pm, Sun. 10am-3pm; free). Another fun, if touristy, spot is **La Rosa de Cristal,** Independencia 232 and Alfareros (tel./fax 639-71-80), where artisans blow glass by hand then sell their work at inflated prices (glass-blowing Mon.-Fri. 10:30am-1:30pm, Sat. 10:30am-noon; shop open Mon.-Sat. 10am-6pm, Sun. 10am-2pm).

**Getting There:** Take the local #275 (or 275A) bus or the "Tlaquepaque" TUR bus (10min.). For the main markets, get off at Independencia, marked by a Pollo-Chicken joint to the left; if the driver turns left off Niños Héroes, you've gone too far. To get back to downtown Guadalajara, hop back on a #275 or TUR bus at the corner of Niños Héroes and Independencia.

## ZAPOPAN

Northwest of Guadalajara, the town of Zapopan is famous for the **Basílica de la Virgen de Zapopan,** a giant 16th-century edifice erected to commemorate a peasant's vision of the Virgin. The walls of the church are hung with many decades' worth of *ex-votos,* small paintings on sheet metal recognizing the Virgin's aid in curing diseases. The image of the Virgin was made by natives from corn stalks in the 16th century. Pope John Paul II visited the shrine in 1979, and a statue of the pontiff holding hands with a beaming *campesino* boy now stands in the courtyard in front of the church. During the early fall, the figure of Our Lady of Zapopan is frequently exchanged from church to church throughout the state—each move occasions serious partying. Then, on October 12 (*Día de la Raza,* the day Columbus landed in America), the figure makes her way from Guadalajara's cathedral to Zapopan, in the midst of a large procession. For tourists, the **Casa de Artesanías de los Huichol,** Eva Briseño 152, a museum and crafts market for Huichol handwork, remains Zapopan's focal point. Clothing, *ojos de dios* (eyes of God, crossed rods decorated with yarn designs), and *macramés* sold here tend to be pretty cheap (open Mon.-Fri. 9am-1pm and 4-7pm, Sat. 10am-1pm).

**Getting There:** To reach Zapopan, catch the local #275A bus northbound on Av. 16 de Septiembre (25min., 2 pesos); hop off at the big church.

## TONALÁ

A less accessible, mercifully less touristed version of Tlaquepaque, **Tonalá** is most fun on market days (Thurs. and Sun.), when the town springs awake from its near-perpetual *siesta.* Women weave multi-colored rugs and sew dolls, while patient ceramics merchants paint personalized messages onto their products. Here, the soft sell rules; merchants will take the time to talk with you, and you won't feel obligated to purchase anything. Tonalá specializes in inexpensive, conservatively-decorated ceramics; good-quality, low-priced silver also abounds.

**Getting There:** Local buses #103 and #104, which run through downtown Guadalajara along Moreno, or TUR bus #706, which runs along 16 de Septiembre (½hr., 4 pesos), are the best way to reach Tonalá.

## LAGO DE CHAPALA

Forty kilometers from the hustle and bustle of Guadalajara, the **Lago de Chapala,** Mexico's second largest lake, rests against the mountains which haunt its shore. Although industrial waste has made swimming in the lake unsafe, a visit to the small villages of **Chapala** and **Ajijic** is a pleasant daytrip. Home to a peaceful mix of Mexican tourists, *norteamericano* retirees, local artists, and residents, these villages lie tucked between the lake's serene northern shore and surrounding mist-cloaked mountains. English speakers will feel at home: half the signs, and conversations, are in English. But don't let the large number of gringos fool you—this is not a frenetic, hell-raising beach town, but rather a beautiful and tranquil setting for a romantic getaway or intense relaxation.

## AJIJIC

Hugging the shore of Lake Chapala and commanding a beautiful view of the surrounding mountains, this sleepy, peaceful village is a charming blend of the old and the new. Cobblestoned streets are dotted with old churches and buildings as well as high-tech telephone and fax services which are supported by the town's large expatriate community. The blending of cultures is also not new; it began years ago with the arrival in the 1920s of European intellectuals escaping political persecution. Market day in Ajijic is Wednesday.

The north-south strip is **Colón. Constitución,** another useful street, changes its name to **Ocampo.** The *plaza* is one block inland. While Ajijic lacks an official tourist office, longtime resident **Beverly Hunt,** owner of **Laguna Axixic Realty,** Carretera 24 (tel. (376) 6-11-74; fax 6-11-88), gets the job done, providing maps, brochures, English newsletters, tourist and realty tips, a friendly cup of coffee, and lots of tales. Hunt founded the well known **Guadalajara Reporter** with her husband years ago and has lived in Ajijic for nearly three decades. Exchange your greenbacks for more colorful bills at **Bancapromex,** Hidalgo and Morelos (tel. (376) 6-05-46), which has a 24-hour **ATM** (open Mon.-Fri. 8am-7pm, Sat. 10:30am-2:30pm). Call or fax home from the **computel** (tel. (376) 6-24-00; fax 6-20-28), conveniently located in the plaza (open daily 8am-9pm). If you're grungy, take your clothes to the **lavandería** at Colón 24-A, half a block up from the plaza (14 pesos per load; open Mon.-Sat. 8:30am-7pm, Sun. 8:30am-1pm). English is spoken at **Farmacia Jessica,** Parroquia 18 (tel. (376) 6-11-91), on the plaza (open daily 9am-10pm). The **post office** is at Colón 23 and Constitución (tel. (376) 6-18-88; open Mon.-Fri. 8am-3pm, Sat. 9am-1pm). The Wednesday market is centered around the intersection of Galeana and Constitución.

Accommodations in Ajijic are geared more towards retirees than students; prices may be out of reach of the budget-conscious. More reasonably-priced rooms and apartments are available for those planning a longer stay; check newspapers and bulletin boards for info. Two neighboring bungalows on the Carretera near its intersection with Juárez compete for tourist dollars. **Las Casitas,** Carretera Chapala Pte. 20 (tel. (376) 6-11-45), has the more charming interior with red tile floors, a dark wood dining set, a little kitchen, and a cozy living room with fold-out couch and chimney (bungalows for 2 people 150 pesos). Though the rooms next door at the **Posada Las Calandrias,** Carretera Chapala Pte. 8 (tel. (376) 6-10-52), are a bit plainer, there is a flower-filled garden, barbecue space, and a great view of the *laguna* from the terraces (small bungalow with 2 single beds 140 pesos; large bungalow with 4 single beds 234 pesos). Both establishments have pools. Ajijic is also host to a number of charming bed and breakfasts. Two of the best are the **Laguna Bed and Breakfast,** at Zaragoza 29, and the **Laguna Too,** at Guadalupe Victoria 30, both run by Laguna

Ajijic Realty (tel. 6-11-74). Beautifully-decorated rooms with Spanish tile floors and colorfully tiled bathrooms surround lush courtyards and communal living areas well-stocked with English books, cards, and board games (doubles US$25 including a hearty brunch; TV US$1 extra).

For a great lunch, try **Danny's,** Carretera Chapala Ote. 2A at Colón (tel. (376) 6-22-22), just off the highway half a block from the road to the *plaza.* Breakfasts, like the Grand Slam (eggs, pancakes, bacon, and sausage, 16 pesos) are for homesick gringos, while lunch goes native with Mexican combos from 15-24 pesos (open Mon.-Sat. 8am-5pm, Sun. 8am-1pm). For dinner, head upstairs to the newly opened **El Attic,** under the same management (open daily except Tues. 5-9pm). For something fancier, try the lunch buffet at **Hotel Nueva Posada,** Donato Guerra 9 (tel. (376) 6-14-44) on the lake. The sumptuous Italianate interior and sculpted gardens leading down to the lake are especially popular with retirees. Daily specials go for 32 pesos (open Sun.-Thurs. 8am-9pm, Fri.-Sat. 8am-11pm).

On weekends, both young and old swing to the live Latin rhythms at the old **Posada Ajijic** on the laguna at Colón (cover 15 pesos; live music Fri.-Sat. 9pm-1:30am). Or if you just want to float your troubles away, look for the **Barcaza del Cuervo,** the floating bar on the *laguna* roughly in front of the Posada Nuevo.

**Getting There:** From the *antigua* bus station in Guadalajara, take a **Guadalajara-Chapala** (tel. (376) 617-56-75) bus (every ½hr., 6am-9:40pm, 45min., 12 pesos); ask to be dropped off at Ajijic. Buses back to the big G can be caught along the highway (every hr., 6am-9:30pm, 45min., 14 pesos). From Chapala, take the bus to Ajijic at Madero and Manzanillo, one block north of the plaza (every 15min., 6:15am-8:30pm, 15min., 2 pesos). They first weave through the village of San Antonio, then go on to Ajijic. Catch a *camión* back to Chapala along Constitución.

## CHAPALA

Named after the Tecuexe Indian chief Capalac, who founded the village on the banks of the lagoon in 1510, Chapala's mix of history and geographic beauty has inspired artists for centuries. However, the charm of the town is somewhat obscured today by its size and modernity. Reeds thriving in the lake's now-polluted waters have caused the lake to shrink into its center, and traffic on the town's main north-south drag, Madero, makes strolling less than relaxing. The **bus station's** main entrance lies on Madero and Martinez. The lake is Chapala's southern and eastern boundary. **Hidalgo** (known as **Morelos** east of Madero) runs west to Ajijic from two blocks north of the lake. The *mercado de artesanías* is on the waterfront four blocks east of Madero's terminus, on Ramón Corona. D.H. Lawrence lived in Chapala at Zaragoza 4 during the 1940s, and it was here that he began *The Plumed Serpent.*

If you plan on spending the night in Chapala, the **Hotel Nido,** Madero 202 (tel. (376) 5-21-16), which once played host to dictator Díaz's weekend soirées, is the place to go. The airy hotel has clean, simple rooms with floral stencils, hot water, a pretty courtyard, and a pool (singles 115 pesos; doubles 145 pesos; add 15 pesos for TV). The hotel also has a somewhat pricey restaurant. A better choice for food is **Restaurant Superior,** at Madero 415 (tel. (376) 5-21-80) near the lake. Expatriates are practically cemented to the sidewalk tables outside. Decent grub goes for excellent prices: *pollo con mole* 24 pesos, hamburgers 10 pesos (open Wed.-Mon. 8am-10pm, Tues. 8am-5pm). More *típico* food is served at **Chabela's Fonda** (tel. (376) 5-43-80), at the far right corner of the plaza. Sunday swarms with locals brunching on the 12- to 14-peso *menú del día* (open daily 8am-7pm).

**Getting There:** From the *antigua* bus station in Guadalajara, take a **Guadalajara-Chapala** (tel. (376) 617-56-75) bus (every ½hr., 6am-9:30pm, 45min., 15 pesos). Buses back to Guadalajara leave from the station on roughly the same schedule; or head to Guadalajara's new bus station (every hr., 7:45am-5:45pm, 1¼hr., 12 pesos).

# ■ Puerto Vallarta

In 1956, tabloid headlines had the world fantasizing about Puerto Vallarta. The torrid affair between Richard Burton and Elizabeth Taylor while Burton was on location shooting John Huston's *Night of the Iguana* helped paint the city as the world headquarters of sensuality. Back then, neither highway nor telephone wire linked the town to the outside world. Forty years and billions of dollars later, Puerto Vallarta (pop. 100,000) is a world-class resort with carefully-groomed beaches, luxurious hotels, and showy mansions.

The three most important industries in Vallarta are tourism, tourism, and tourism, but resort-mania can take a variety of forms. The south end of town has virtually all the cheap hotels, best beaches, budget restaurants, and dance clubs. To the north, the hotels get more extravagant, and boutiques and restaurants alike cater almost exclusively to the thick-walleted. The artificiality of Vallarta's charm—the buildings are white-stuccoed, the roofs red-tiled, and the streets cobbled—doesn't bother the hordes of expats and retirees who call condos home in this ritzy resort. Still farther north, international resorts line the highway. On the outskirts, the mansions and property that are the fodder of glossy brochures sparkle in sensual luxuriance.

## ORIENTATION

Running roughly east-west, **Río Cuale** bisects Puerto Vallarta before hitting the ocean. The main streets in the southern half of town are **Insurgentes** and **Vallarta,** which run north-south two blocks apart, and **Francisco Madero** and **Lázaro Cárdenas,** which run east-west one block apart. Most buses and *combis* pass along Insurgentes between Madero and Lázaro Cárdenas at some point on their route. Rte. 200 from Manzanillo runs into town south of the river, becoming Insurgentes. Insurgentes and Vallarta run north from Lázaro Cárdenas to the two bridges that link the south and north sections. The main streets in the northern section are **Morelos,** the continuation of Vallarta, and **Juárez,** one block east. Four blocks north of the river is the **Plaza Mayor,** whose cathedral serves as a landmark. The ritzy waterfront between Plaza Mayor and 31 de Octubre, called the **Malecón,** contains overpriced restaurants, clubs, and cheesy shirt shops. **Paseo Díaz Ordaz** runs parallel to the Malecón, becoming **Av. México** to its north. Also, north of the Malecón, Morelos becomes **Perú** and runs through a working-class neighborhood before joining the coastal highway. North along the highway lie the **airport** and **marina.**

Taxis charge about 20 pesos to travel between the **Playa de los Muertos** and the entrance to the highway, 7 pesos within the *centro,* and about 25 pesos from the *centro* to the Marina Vallarta or to the airport in the north. Northbound **buses** and *combis* originate at the southern end of Insurgentes, run across the Insurgentes Bridge, head west on Libertad for a few blocks, north on Juárez, and onto the highway. In the opposite direction, buses enter the city on Av. México, which becomes Díaz Ordaz and then runs into Morelos, crossing the Vallarta Bridge before heading back. Any municipal bus operating south of the Sheraton or labeled "Centro" and all *combis* pass the Plaza. Buses and *combis* labeled "Hoteles" will pass the hotel strip. For the most part, buses stop only at the clearly marked *parada* signs and at the covered benches (buses and combis operate daily 6am-10:30pm, 1.50 pesos).

To get downtown from the airport, take a "Centro" or "Olas Altas" bus, or a taxi. To get to the airport from town, catch a "Novia Alta," "Marfil," or "Aeropuerto" bus on Lázaro Cárdenas, Insurgentes, or Juárez.

## PRACTICAL INFORMATION

**Tourist Office:** Tel. 2-02-42. In the Presidencia Municipal, on the north side of the Pl. Mayor (enter on Juárez) and at Av. Medina Ascencio 1712 (also known as Av. Las Palmas), 3rd fl. (tel. 3-07-44, 3-08-44; tel./fax 2-02-43). Free maps, brochures, and *Passport,* a publication that lists bars and restaurants and includes discount coupons. English spoken. Open Mon.-Fri. 9am-5pm.

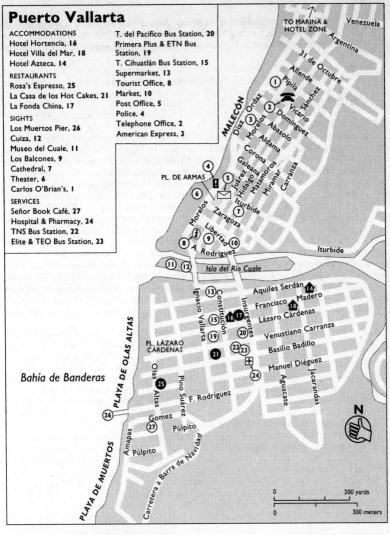

# Puerto Vallarta

**ACCOMMODATIONS**
Hotel Hortencia, 16
Hotel Villa del Mar, 18
Hotel Azteca, 14

**RESTAURANTS**
Rosa's Espresso, 25
La Casa de los Hot Cakes, 21
La Fonda China, 17

**SIGHTS**
Los Muertos Pier, 26
Cuiza, 12
Museo del Cuale, 11
Los Balcones, 9
Cathedral, 7
Theater, 6
Carlos O'Brian's, 1

**SERVICES**
Señor Book Café, 27
Hospital & Pharmacy, 24
TNS Bus Station, 22
Elite & TEO Bus Station, 23

T. del Pacifico Bus Station, 20
Primera Plus & ETN Bus Station, 19
T. Cihuatlán Bus Station, 15
Supermarket, 13
Tourist Office, 8
Market, 10
Post Office, 5
Police, 4
Telephone Office, 2
American Express, 3

**Consulates: Canada** (tel. 2-53-98 or 3-08-58; fax 2-35-17; open Mon.-Fri. 9am-5pm) and **U.S.** (tel. 2-00-69; open Mon.-Fri. 10am-2pm) are both at Zaragoza 160, on the Pl. Mayor above "Subway."

**Currency Exchange: Banamex,** at Juárez and Zaragoza (tel. 2-06-93 or 2-08-30), in front of the Presidencia Municipal. Open Mon.-Fri. 9am-5pm, Sat. 9am-2pm. **Ban Oro,** on Olas Altas at Badillo (tel. 3-04-84). Open Mon.-Fri. 9am-5pm, Sat. 9am-2pm. Both banks have **ATMs.** *Casas de cambio* are everywhere, especially near the Malecón. Their rates are lower than the banks; better deals are generally found away from the beach. Usually open daily 9am-9pm.

**American Express:** Morelos 660 at Abasolo (tel. 3-29-55; fax 3-29-26). English spoken. Open Mon.-Fri. 9am-6pm, Sat. 9am-1pm.

**Telephones:** Card-operated **LADATELs** can be found between Abasolo and Aldama, throughout the *centro* and along the beaches. There is a *caseta* at the **Transportes del Pacífico** bus station. Open daily 7am-10:30pm.

**Airport:** 8km north of town via the highway. **Alaska** (tel. 1-13-50 or toll-free 95-800-426-0333), **American** (tel. 1-17-99 or toll-free 91-800-36-270), **Continental** (1-10-25 or toll-free 91-800-90-050), **Mexicana** (4-81-00), and **Taesa** (1-15-21 or toll-free 91-800-90-463).

**Buses:** As of summer 1997, each bus line (all have competing routes) operates out of its own office-depot on the south side of the city. Construction has begun on a new central terminal located north of the *centro* near the airport—check for details. **Elite/Estrella Blanca,** Basilio Badillo 11 and Insurgentes (tel. 3-11-17), provides 1st-class service to Acapulco (6am, 18hr., 290 pesos), Aguascalientes (5:30pm, 9hr., 186 pesos), Ciudad Juárez and 21 points in between (5pm, 36hr., 555 pesos), Guadalajara (every hr., 6am-1:30am, 5½hr., 142 pesos), and Mexico City (1st class 8:30pm, 12hr., 424 pesos; 2nd class 4 per day, 5:15-9pm, 14hr., 327 pesos). **Primera Plus** and **ETN** both operate from Lázaro Cárdenas 258 and Ignacio Vallarta. **Primera Plus** (tel. 2-69-86) serves Aguascalientes (2:30pm, 9hr., 195 pesos), Colima (1pm, 6½hr., 146 pesos), León (10pm, 9hr., 245 pesos), Manzanillo (1st class 8am, 5hr., 100 pesos; 2nd class 5 per day, 7am-10:30pm, 6½hr., 80 pesos), Melaque (8am and 1pm, 4hr., 77 pesos), and Querétaro (9pm, 12hr., 262 pesos). **ETN** (tel. 3-29-99 or 3-06-46) serves Guadalajara (8 per day, 9am-1am, 5½hr., 185 pesos) and Mexico City's North Station (6:30pm, 14hr., 435 pesos). **Transportes del Pacífico,** Insurgentes 282 and Carranza (tel. 2-10-15), sends buses to Mexico City (6pm, 14hr., 326 pesos) and Tepic (every ½hr., 5am-8pm, and 10:30pm, 3½hr., 60 pesos). **Autocamiones Cihuatlán,** Madero and Constitución (tel. 2-34-36), has service south to Manzanillo (1st class 4:30 and 11:30pm, 5hr., 100 pesos; 2nd class 8 per day, 5am-4pm, 6½hr., 80 pesos). Second-class buses pass through Chamela (3½hr., 43 pesos), Melaque (5hr., 63 pesos), and Barra de Navidad (5hr., 65 pesos). First-class service to Manzanillo (4:30 and 11:30pm, 5hr., 79 pesos); also stops in Melaque and Barra de Navidad (3½hr., 62 pesos).

**Car Rental:** Almost all car rental companies have offices on Calle Francisco Medina Ascencio, the hotel strip. Prices are high. **National,** Medina Ascencio km 1.5 (tel. 2-27-42 or 1-12-26 at the airport), has the lowest rates—a VW with tax, insurance, and 200km goes for 295 pesos. **Thrifty,** Medina Ascencio km 5.5 (tel. 4-07-75), rents VWs for 380 pesos per day, including tax, insurance, and unlimited mileage.

**Bookstore: Señor Book Café,** Olas Altas 490 at Rodolfo Gómez (tel. 2-03-24). Used English books sold and exchanged—two of your old ones get you either one of theirs or a beer (how they make pesos is beyond us). Open daily 7:30am-10:30pm.

**Supermarket: Gutiérrez Rico,** at Constitución and Serdán (tel. 2-02-22). Open daily 6:30am-11pm. **La Ley,** México and Uruguay, is even bigger. Open daily 7am-11pm.

**Laundromat: Laundry Aguamatic,** 275 Constitución and Lázaro Cárdenas (tel. 2-59-78), charges 18 pesos to wash and dry 3kg. Open Mon.-Sat. 9am-2pm and 4-8pm, Sun. 10am-2pm.

**Red Cross:** At Río de la Plata and Río Balsas (tel. 2-15-33 or 2-49-73). Open 24hr.

**Pharmacy: Farmacia CMQ,** Basilio Badillo 365 (tel. 2-13-30 or 2-29-41), half a block inland from Insurgentes, plus 4 other locations. All open 24hr.

**Hospital: CMQ Hospital,** Basilio Badillo 365 at Insurgentes (tel. 3-19-19). English spoken. Open 24hr. Up the hill is **Hospital Medasist,** Manuel Diéguez 360 and Aguacate (tel. 3-04-44). Some English spoken. Open 24hr. **Dr. John H. Mabrey,** Basilio Badillo 365 (tel. 2-51-19, 3-00-88), speaks English.

**Police:** At Iturbide and Morelos (tel. 3-25-00 or 2-01-23). On call 24hr. Some English.

**Internet Access: The Net House,** Ignacio Vallarta 232 and Lázaro Cárdenas (tel. 2-57-64). Email 30 pesos per hr. Open 24hr. **Cyber Café,** Juárez 388 (tel. 2-02-04 or 2-02-35). Email 20 pesos per ½hr., 35 pesos per hr. Open Mon.-Sat. 9am-11pm.

**Post Office:** Juárez 628 (tel. 2-18-88 or 2-37-02). Open Mon.-Fri. 8am-7:30pm, Sat 9am-1pm. **Postal Code:** 48300.

**Phone Code:** 322.

## ACCOMMODATIONS AND CAMPING

The best budget hotels are south of Río Cuale, on or near Madero. Make sure the fan works before whipping out your wallet. June is the least expensive month of the year, December the most expensive. Reservations for November through January should be made two months in advance. Officially, Vallarta frowns on shiftless beach bums, but most travelers who choose to camp encounter few problems. Some beachfront clubs have night guards who may keep an eye on those who request their permission before bedding down. Many people dig into the sand behind the Hotel Los Arcos or the Castle Pelícanos, which is government property, or into the open space between the J. Newcombe tennis courts and the Sheraton. It's best to camp in a group whenever possible (this is much easier in high season, when Vallarta's hotels are filled to overflowing). Use caution.

**Hotel Azteca,** Madero 473 and Jacarandas (tel. 2-27-50). Clean and simple rooms—all you need, and at a great price. The brick exterior with wrought-iron details and the giant leafy jungle plants set it apart. Fans and *agua purificada*. Restaurant and long-distance phone for patrons. Singles 55 pesos; doubles 70 pesos; triples 80 pesos. Small suites with kitchen 90 pesos. 20-peso towel deposit.

**Hotel Villa del Mar,** Madero 440 (tel. 2-07-85 or 2-28-85), 2 blocks east of Insurgentes. Brick detailing and wooden doors give the well-scrubbed rooms a rustic feel. Modern tile bathrooms have plenty of hot water. Spiral staircases wind around Mexican and Cuban flags to a rooftop terrace with a fabulous view of the *centro*. Singles 64 pesos; doubles 80 pesos. Add 10 pesos for a balcony in high season.

**Hotel Ana Liz,** Madero 429 and Jacarandas (tel. 2-10-18), has basic, small, dark rooms with tiny bathrooms, but it's darn cheap, oh-so-tasteful landscape photos do their best to brighten things up. Singles 45 pesos; doubles 65 pesos.

**Hotel Hortencia,** Madero 336 and Insurgentes (tel. 2-24-84). Cheery bright blue walls are leafed up with a barrage of jungle plants. Ceiling fans and well-lit bathrooms. Singles 80 pesos, with TV or fridge 100 pesos; doubles 100 pesos, with TV or fridge 120 pesos.

**Hotel Escuela CECATUR,** Hidalgo and Guerrero (tel. 2-49-10; fax 3-02-94). Huge rooms with pink chiffon bedspreads are lovingly cared for by aspiring students of hotel management. Fans, TV, and *agua purificada*. Bathrooms are large enough to host a fiesta. Singles 90 pesos; doubles 125 pesos.

## FOOD

Puerto Vallarta's Malecón specializes in tourist traps with *norteamericano* cuisine, but some excellent, decently-priced restaurants can be found elsewhere on the north side. Near the beach on the south side, gringos can find many upscale restaurants built with them in mind, especially on the blocks enclosed by Basilio Badillo to the south, Olas Altas (the beachfront), Lázaro Cárdenas, and Constitución. Cheaper down-home eateries are plentiful along Madero, in the **market** on the north side, where Insurgentes crosses Río Cuale (open Mon.-Sat. 8am-8pm), and along Calle México to the north. Taco and quesadilla stands prosper south of the river.

**La Casa de los Hot Cakes** (The Pancake House), Badillo 289 and Constitución (tel. 2-62-72). A stupendously good breakfast. Indulge in the specialty pancake or waffle platters (22 pesos) or delectable cheese blintzes (25 pesos). Also serves lighter fare (scrambled egg whites 15 pesos, for those health freaks out there) and traditional Mexican *desayunos* (*chilaquiles* 16 pesos). Memo, the friendly owner, offers Mexican cooking classes in high season (winter). Open daily 8am-2pm.

**Café de Olla,** Basilio Badillo 168 (tel. 3-16-26), 1 block from the beach. A tourist joint with attentive waiters and reasonable prices (for Vallarta, that is). *Mariachis* weave between tables to serenade vacationers. Beautiful burgers 25 pesos; *chiles rellenos* 30 pesos. Open daily except Tues. noon-11pm.

**Mi Casa Buffet II,** Av. México 1121 and Rep. de Chile (tel. 2-09-65), near the Malecón. Gooood all-you-can-eat buffet. The spread, which changes daily, features 9 salads and 6 entrees. Lunch buffet (17 pesos), breakfast buffet (15 pesos), or the vacuum special: all you can eat and drink in one hour (25 pesos). Feels so much like Mexico, you'll forget you're in Vallarta. Open Mon.-Sat. 9am-noon and 1-8pm during high season, otherwise Mon.-Sat. 1-8pm.

**Rosa's Espresso,** Olas Altas 399 and Diéguez. This coffee house and multi-language book exchange will percolate your brain cells with one shot of their knock-your-socks-off coffee (5-9 pesos). Leaf through some mystery or self-help books, or chat with the throngs of new-agers between mouthfuls of banana split (15 pesos). Bulletin board announces tarot card readings, free kittens, rooms for rent, and language lessons. Open daily 8am-10:30pm.

**Restaurant Buffet Vegetariano,** Iturbide 270 and Hidalgo (tel. 2-30-73), a few blocks inland from Plaza Mayor and up the steep steps of Iturbide. 100% vegetarian cuisine, with a strong Indian influence. Small, white-walled, and simple. Buffet with beans, rice, soy patties, etc., 30 pesos (no menu). Open Mon.-Sat. noon-6pm.

**La Fonda Dianita,** Madero 243 and Vallarta. Find a table (if you can) in this teensy local favorite, and enjoy tasty and filling *comida corrida* (19 pesos). Clean and cheap. Open daily 11am-6pm.

**La Fonda China Poblana Restaurante y Bar,** Insurgentes 222 between Serdán and Madero (tel. 2-40-49). An open-air ground floor with wood and wicker tables to prop up the weary in the wee hours gives way to an airy second floor with a balcony. Breakfast 9 pesos, *comida corrida* 19 pesos, *enchiladas suizas* 22 pesos, beer 6-8 pesos. Open 7am-2am.

## SAND AND SIGHTS

Although the veneer of tourism detracts somewhat from Puerto Vallarta's natural beauty, the panorama of the city's 40km of coastline and surrounding mountains is still enchanting. Some of the least crowded and most gorgeous beaches stretch along the coast south of town on the road to **Mismaloya** (see p. 290) and north into Nayarit. The most popular beach within the Puerto Vallarta city limits is **Playa de los Muertos** (Beach of the Dead), a strip in front of the south side's costliest hotels. It begins at its southern end with a rocky cliff dotted with small white homes, and runs north to a small dock which separates it from the **Playa de Olas Altas** (Big Waves Beach). To get there, walk all the way west on Lázaro Cárdenas and then south along Playa de Olas Altas, or take the street of the same name and turn right on Rodríguez. Playa de Olas Altas continues to the Río Cuale, then becomes the rocky **Malecón** (boardwalk). Near the southern end of Playa de los Muertos is a small section of the beach known as **Las Sillas Azules** (the blue chairs), surely one of Mexico's only gay (male) beaches.

Water sports are very popular, particularly during the morning hours. This is your chance to go **parasailing** (US$30 a shot); parachutes are scattered on the Playa de Olas Altas and the beaches along the hotel strip, and their owners will descend upon you like vultures if you look even remotely interested. Wave runners (US$25 single, US$30 double for ½hr.) and banana boat rides (40 pesos per person) are also there for the taking. **Outcast Diving & Fishing,** Rodríguez 121 (tel. 3-17-33; 24hr. cellular (329) 41-544; email jacobel@pvallarta.icanet.net.mx), two blocks south of Hotel Los Arcos, rents scuba equipment (US$5 per piece, US$20 for a tank, plus deposit; license required) and offers diving lessons and trips (US$45 and up). Waverunners (US$35 pesos per ½hr.) and sea kayaks (US$10 per hr.) are also available. The best deal is to rent snorkeling equipment (US$5 each for mask and fins, plus deposit; open daily 9am-6pm). English is the first language here. **Chico's Dive Shop,** Díaz Ordaz 772 on the Malecón (tel. 2-18-95), also offers scuba and snorkeling trips, as well as a diving certification program (open daily 8am-10pm). **Equestrian** fanatics can boot the shore and take to the hills on horseback; rentals are available near Daiquiri Dick's on Olas Altas, at Carranza (horses 50 pesos per hr.; open daily around 9am-5pm).

Lots of new developments, condos, and resort facilities offer **freebies** to potential buyers. A common deal includes an invitation to eat a free meal at the resort, the opportunity to spend a few hours enjoying its facilities, half-price tickets to popular tours, and cruises, and gift certificates to local stores and restaurants. The catch is that you have to spend about two hours listening to their ultra-high-pressure sales pitch, which can verge on coercion. Don't relinquish your credit card number, no matter what; remember, you are under no obligation to buy anything.

**Isla Río Cuale** lies between and underneath two bridges spanning the ponderous **Río Cuale.** A cool pathway runs the length of the verdant island between small stores selling postcards, jewelry, and souvenirs. The **Museo del Cuale,** at the seaward end of the island, houses interesting displays on Mesoamerican culture and the region's history (open Tues.-Sat. 10am-3pm and 4-7pm, Sun. 10am-2pm; free). During the day, the walk along the river is pleasant, but anyone alone should avoid it after dark. The river can also be reached from the north via Zaragoza, which merits a walk. Stairs lead up the mini-mountain beginning behind the Church of Guadalupe, breaking out amid bougainvillea and hibiscus into the wealthy **Zaragoza** neighborhood, known locally as **Gringo Gulch.** The prominent bridge spanning the apex of the street connects Elizabeth Taylor's humble *pied-à-terre* with Richard Burton's.

## ENTERTAINMENT

After dark, Puerto Vallarta offers something for everyone, whether it's a cocktail in the moonlight or the chance to thrash across a crowded dance floor. On the **Malecón,** one can have a serious conversation about the latest melodramatic twist in *90210* or *Melrose Place* with any of the hundreds of American teeny-boppers who congregate there. Most of the upscale action is along **Díaz Ordaz** on the northern waterfront, where clubs and restaurants cater to suntanned professionals quaffing pricey rum drinks and bopping to U.S. top-40 tunes. Vallarta has sprouted a thriving **gay scene,** and boasts several clubs catering almost exclusively to gay men and the occasional lesbian. Discos are aimed at those who don't mind dropping 30 to 40 pesos for cover and 12-15 pesos for a cold one. For those clubs with covers, save a small fortune by obtaining free passes (which may not be honored during peak tourist season) from the condo-hawkers who lurk around the Malecón. Most discos aren't worth visiting until 11pm or midnight; the time before then is better spent tossing back drinks in cheap bars.

Nightlife transportation is greatly aided by the "Marina Vallarta" bus, which goes to the marina, and the "Pitillal" bus, which will take you just past the hotel strip. After 11pm, you're stuck with a cab (about 25 pesos to the *centro*). For cheap fun, nothing beats the **pool hall,** Madero 279 (tel. 2-24-57). Pool is 10 pesos per hour and dominoes 3 pesos per hour, but the middle-aged men don't look too highly upon (and sometimes look too long at) female visitors (open daily 9am-2am). For some entertaining air conditioning, take in a movie (15 pesos) at **Cine Bahía,** Insurgentes 63 (tel. 2-17-17), or **Cine Vallarta,** Perú and Uruguay (tel. 2-05-07). A **gay cruise,** departing daily at noon from the Los Muertos pier, ships partners, Noah's ark-style, to a private gay beach (includes drinks, snorkeling, and table dancing; around US$45). Tickets are available from travel agents or time-share hawkers, or ask at Paco Paco (below).

**Carlos O'Brian's Bar & Grill & Clothesline,** Díaz Ordaz at Pípila (tel. 2-14-44). The only things hanging out to dry here are totally trashed high-school students who've forgotten the names of their hotels. Teens bounce between here, **Kahlúa** (tel. 2-24-86), a few blocks south on the waterfront, and the **Zoo,** Díaz Ordaz 638 (tel. 2-49-45), next door (high-season weekend cover 40 pesos). It's the biggest party in town—block-long lines wrap around the building all night. Open daily 11am-4am.

**Paco Paco,** Ignacio Vallarta 578 and Lázaro Cárdenas, is Vallarta's hottest gay disco, with great music, lots of dance floor, and a somewhat plain decor. Friendly owner is a veritable fount of information on Vallarta's gay scene. Transvestite show Fri.-Sun. 1:30am. Weekend cover 20 pesos. Open daily 3pm-6am.

**Collage** (tel. 1-05-05), next to Marina Vallarta, is big enough to house all of Vallarta. Bowling, pool tables, video games, sushi bar (no, don't), and, of course, bars and a high-tech dance floor. Cover 50 pesos after 9pm. Open daily 11am-6am.

**J & B,** Medina Ascencio km 2.5 (tel. 4-46-16), toward the hotel zone. An older crowd dances the night away to salsa, merengue, and the occasional Michael Jackson tune. Raised dance floor makes it impossible to be shy here. Those determined not to dance can play pool instead. Cover 40 pesos. Open daily 9pm-late.

**Bar Dillinger,** Díaz Ordaz 668, next to Carlos O'Brian's. Just like John would have it: rockers and metalheads of all creeds down stiff beverages to loud AC/DC and Alice in Chains tunes. Oversized Cobain and Morrison portraits carefully watch over the crowd. No cover. Open daily 7pm-4am; live rock daily 10pm-4am.

CENTRAL PACIFIC COAST

**Cuiza** (tel. 2-56-46), on Isla Río Cuale, at the foot of the *puente nuevo*. Find a table on the shady patio, order a margarita, and listen to the jazz. Can't get any mellower than this. Mexican professionals and lots of new-waveish gringo couples. Live music Wed. and Fri.-Sun. 8-11pm. Open daily 6pm-1am, low season 8-11pm.

**Cactus,** Vallarta 399 at Diéguez (tel. 2-60-77). Popular with twentysomething tourists. Open bar Wed. (cover women 30 pesos, men 70 pesos). Open daily 10pm-late.

**El Faro** (tel. 1-05-41), in the Marina Vallarta. An elegant lighthouse bar 35m above ground provides a fantastic view of Puerto Vallarta, especially at sunset. Live flamenco music Wed.-Sat. 8-10:30pm, live Spanish guitar every night after 10:30pm. 1-drink minimum. Open daily 5pm-2am.

**Los Balcones,** Juárez 182 at Libertad (tel. 2-46-71). International gay crowd practices looking languid on the balconies. Scantily-dressed patrons sizzle on the neon-lit dance floor. Starts hopping at 11:30pm. Open daily 9pm-4am. No cover.

**Zótano,** Morelos 101 (tel. 3-06-77), on the Plaza Río next to the Vallarta Bridge. Art Deco coffee and video bar (with pool tables) sits above the vibrations of a rocking basement below. Wall-to-wall dancing—perhaps because there's no room at the bar. Almost exclusively gay men. Happy hour 9-11pm. Open daily 5pm-4am.

# ■ Near Puerto Vallarta

## SOUTH OF PUERTO VALLARTA

Vallarta's most popular beaches lie a few kilometers south of the city itself. The first few you'll come across are monopolized by resorts and condos, and though they're nicer and quieter than the ones back in town, access to them is usually only through the hotels. Farther down the coast lies **Los Arcos,** a group of pretty rock islands hollowed out in some spots by pounding waves. The coastline here lacks sand, but it still serves as a platform from which to start the 150m swim to the islands. Bring a mask or goggles, or risk missing the tropical fish that flit through the underwater reefscape. Flippers are useful against the heavy currents, and mind your step—the coral is sharp enough to draw blood. Use caution and swim with a friend. To get to Los Arcos, take the bus to Mismaloya and ask the driver to stop at Hotel de los Arcos. The beautiful crescent beach of **Mismaloya** lies just around the bend to the south. Best known as the setting of *Night of the Iguana* and Arnold Schwarzenegger's *cinéma vérité* classic, *Predator,* Mismaloya has recently been encircled by large hotels and is only slightly less crowded than the beaches in town. **Xanadu** is a gay club near this beach. Farther down, the road veers away from the coast just beyond the **Boca de Tomatlán;** this narrow cove contains only a small beach but offers a breather from the touristy hubbub of the northern coastline. The last place to check out on the southern road is **Chico's Paradise,** 5km inland from the Boca de Tomatlán. Wash down the view of the **Tomatlán Falls** with a drink at Chico's huge, airy *palapas.*

Farther south along the coast lie the beaches of **Las Ánimas, Quimixto,** and **Yelapa,** all of which are accessible only from the ocean. However, these lovely beaches are not deserted; they're inhabited by hordes of nacho-chomping tourists dropped off daily by cruise boats from Vallarta. Las Ánimas and Quimixto are twins—long stretches of unoccupied sand backed by small villages and a few *palapas.* Quimixto also offers a small waterfall to those who tire of the beach. The trip can be made in an hour by foot from the beach or in half an hour by rented mule. Scuba trips (organized by Outcast—see p. 288—and others) also make their way from downtown Vallarta and Mismaloya to these beaches. Yelapa, destination of the popular boat ride and highly touted by locals, is a bit of a fake. Supposedly a secluded peasant fishing village, its seemingly simple *palapa* huts were designed by a *norteamericano* architect whose definition of "rustic" apparently included interior plumbing and hot water. Many of these *palapas* are occupied for only part of the year, and short- and long-term rentals can be arranged easily for widely varying and sometimes surprisingly low prices. The beach fills with hawkers and parasailers during the day, but the town, a 15-minute walk from the beach, remains *tranquilo,* with waterfalls and nude bathing upstream and poetry readings downstream. Don't miss the secluded swim-

---

### Time Will Tell

You're wearing sandals from Ticul. A *huipil* from Valladolid. You sleep in a hammock from Mérida, sip *naranjadas* at lunch, and feign interest in the latest episode of "La Cente Bien" while downing an entire bowl of *chile habanero* (sans wincing). Slyly leaving your Tevas and *mochila* in storage, you could almost pass for one of the *indígenas*. So you blend in now, right? Not if you say "¡Buenos días!" when it's half past three, or "¡Buenas noches!" when it's only six. In Mexico, there are strictly adhered-to rules of greeting. *Buenos días* is for *good morning*. It's good until 11:59am. But come noon, sharp waiters and vendors alike won't bat an eyelash while correcting your greeting with a *Buenas tardes*. *Buenas noches* is only used when it's dark as *mole* outside. And for casual interactions, a muffled *Buenas* by itself is all it takes to get to business. So synchronize your watches, pay attention to the sun, and even if you roll out of bed at 1pm, remember to say *Buenas tardes*. Or they'll know. They'll see you're a *gabacho* under that poncho, no matter how many tequila shots you can take standing.

---

ming hole at the top of the stream that runs through town; follow the path uphill along the stream, and just before the restaurant, duck under the water pipes to the right of the trail and head up the track. About 15m before it rejoins the stream bed, an inconspicuous trail leads off to the left to a deep pool which overlooks the bay.

**Getting There:** Buses run to Mismaloya from the corner of Pino Suárez and Carranza in Puerto Vallarta (every 15min., 6:30am-10:30pm, 3 pesos; returning on the same schedule) and Chico's Paradise (8:25, 11:40am, 2:50, and 5:50pm, 1hr., 9 pesos; returning every 3hr., 10:40am-7:40pm). Taxis to Mismaloya cost 40 pesos. **Taxis Acuáticos** are the cheapest way to get to the boats-only beaches. They leave from the Muelle de los Muertos and stop at Las Ánimas, Quimixto, and Yelapa (10:30 and 11am, returning at 3:30 and 4pm, 45min., 50 pesos each way). If you prefer something more organized, **cruises** to points south of Vallarta leave the marina every day starting at 9am and return around 4pm. The cheapest cruises to Yelapa are 140 pesos including breakfast and music. Most are even more wallet-imploding, including a dinner and open bar. Information about these ritzy tours can be found in the tourist office, at any large hotel, from any condo-hawker, or in the marina.

## NORTH OF PUERTO VALLARTA

**Bahía de Banderas** (Bay of Flags), the name of the bay which Puerto Vallarta calls home, owes its name to a blunder: when Nuño Beltrán de Guzmán sailed here in 1532, he mistook the colorful headdresses of the thousands of natives waiting to meet him for flags. The northern edge of the bay has some of the prettiest and least-exploited beaches in the state of Nayarit and on all of Mexico's central Pacific coast. Nuevo Vallarta, the largest and southernmost of nine small towns on the north bay, is 150km south of Tepic and about 20km north of Puerto Vallarta.

Protected by a sandy cove, **Playa Piedra Blanca** has wonderfully calm waters. Farther north along the bay is **Playa las Destiladeras,** named for the freshwater pools formed by water trickling through the rocky cliff. Though the sandy bottom is colored with occasional rocks, the rougher waves make this strip of beach a haven for body-surfers and boogie-boarders. **Punta de Mita,** the northernmost point along the bay, is a lagoon sheltered by two rock islets. It is marked by the **Corral de Riscos,** a living reef. One-peso freshwater showers in Destiladeras make the bus ride home more comfy. Bring a bag lunch to avoid inflated prices in beachside *palapas*.

**Getting There:** From Puerto Vallarta, flag down a *Camiones del Pacífico* "Punta de Mita" second-class bus on Lázaro Cárdenas, Insurgentes, Juárez, or Medino Ascencio (every 20min., 6:20am-9pm, returning until 8pm; to Piedra Blanca 40min., 8 pesos; to Destiladeras 1hr., 10 pesos; to Punta de Mita 1¼hr. plus a 4km walk, 12 pesos).

## BAHÍA DE CHAMELA

The tranquil and secluded **Bahía de Chamela,** 60km northwest of Melaque, marks the northern point of Jalisco's "Ecological Tourism Corridor." A chain of small rocky islands breaks the horizon, while 11km of golden-brown sand dotted with gnarled driftwood and an occasional *palapa* beckon to the pensive beachcomber. Although Chamela receives its share of tourism, especially in December and April, the Midas touch has yet to spoil the natural beauty and seclusion of the bay. This, however, presents other problems; lone travelers (particularly women) and small groups should use common sense in deciding which beaches to visit, particularly during low season. Perula is the more populated of the two, but neither is comfortingly protected.

 **Punta de Perula,** the bay's northernmost point, shelters **Playa Perula,** making it perfect for swimming. A half-hour walk down the coast along completely virgin beach will bring you to the **Villa Polinesia Motel and Campsite,** marking **Playa Chamela.** Here and farther south, the rougher waves invite body-surfing and boogie-boarding—though they sometimes get a bit rough and have a strong undertow. **Perula** itself is a tiny fishing *pueblo* whose main attraction is, well, the beach. The town lacks most services, but has a couple hotels and seafood-serving restaurants and *palapas.* Continuing south will bring you to **Playa Rosada** and other even more secluded beaches. The occasional *palapa* refreshes the parched and weary bodysurfer. *Lanchas* from Playa Perula will transport wannabe Crusoes to the nearby islands (round-trip about 150 pesos).

 In Perula, **Tejamar Restaurante y Cuartos,** on Independencia (tel. 5-53-61) on the Jardín, one block south of Hotel Punta Perula and less than a block from the beach, is a small, family-run taco restaurant and *posada.* Its basic rooms have ceiling fans and open onto a small courtyard. The communal bathrooms are clean but lack hot water (singles 60 pesos; doubles 80 pesos). Friendly owners are eager to accommodate guests with bargain meals and trips to the nearby islands. The **Hotel Punta Perula** (tel. 5-50-20) is at the corner of Juárez and Tiburón, two blocks from the beach. Clean, simple rooms have ceiling fans, and bathrooms have hot water (singles 85 pesos; doubles 120 pesos). **Mariscos La Sirena** (tel. 5-51-14), one of the several *palapas* along the shore, serves shrimp (35 pesos) and fish (24 pesos). A cold one costs four well-spent pesos (open daily 7am-8pm, or until the last person leaves). **Tejaban,** on the highway near Chamela, serves breakfast (14-16 pesos) and *pollo frito* (18 pesos; open daily 7am-11pm).

 **Getting There:** Buses going from Melaque or Barra de Navidad to Puerto Vallarta (1½hr., 24 pesos) or Manzanillo (3hr., 34 pesos) pass through Perula, as do second-class buses from Puerto Vallarta to Manzanillo (3½hr., 40 pesos). Always tell the bus driver where you're going in advance so you don't miss the stop. To get to Playa Perula, get off by the big white "Playa Dorada" sign and walk a half hour down a winding dirt road—don't be surprised if friendly locals offer you a ride. To get to Playa Chamela, get off farther south at "El Súper," marked by the colorful figure directing passersby to the Villa Polinesia, and walk 15 minutes down the country road until you hit the beach. Perula is a half-hour walk along the shore. A dependable **taxi** service (tel. 5-50-31) will take you to either of the beaches for 20 pesos. Hotels in Perula will also come pick you up or send a taxi. There's a **LADATEL** outside the Primera Plus bus station next to Tejaban. To get back, catch a **Primera Plus** bus from that station. They head to Guadalajara (4pm, 6hr., 136 pesos), Manzanillo (1st class 10:15am and 2:30pm, 2½hr., 46 pesos; 2nd class every hr., 11am-7pm, and 8:30pm, 3½hr., 35 pesos) via Melaque (1st class 1hr., 30 pesos; 2nd class 1½hr., 24 pesos), and Puerto Vallarta (2nd class 9:30am, 12:30, and 4:30pm, 3½hr., 40 pesos).

# ■ Bahía de Navidad

Along with Guadalajara and Puerto Vallarta, Bahía de Navidad forms one vertex of Jalisco's "Tourist Triangle." Power is not shared equally within the triarchy, however: with the exception of December and Semana Santa, few tourists are spotted on the placid shores of Bahía de Navidad. The *bahía,* a sheltered cove of talcum sand and shimmering water, is home to the towns of **Melaque** and **Barra de Navidad.** Both towns boast sparkling white sand beaches framing spectacular crimson sunsets between the two spits of the cove. Given their dearth of tourism and smallness, both make for an excellent getaway. During high season, however, their growing pains are more evident, as the beach stretching between the towns is transformed into a seemingly endless river of bronzed bodies, and hotels in both towns are filled to overflowing with tourists. Change is in the air: Restaurants, hotels, and clubs are sprouting with great frequency; a Xanadu-esque hotel at the end of the bay opened in early 1997, and a 300-boat marina under construction threatens to overwhelm the bay with hordes of yachting foreigners.

Although Barra and Melaque lie only 5km apart if by land, two if by sea, Melaque is worlds better than its counterpart: better beach, better hotels, better everything. While Barra offers few places to eat and sleep and a steep beach with powerful undertow (better for surfing or boogie-boarding than swimming), Melaque treats visitors to gentle, choppy waves—a swimmer's dream—and its abundance of quality budget accommodations are the stuff such travel guides as this are made of. Visit Melaque—quick—before its small-town cream is skimmed off by tourist dollars.

Melaque and Barra de Navidad are 55km northwest of Manzanillo on Rte. 200 and 240km southwest of Guadalajara on Rte. 54. Melaque is the northernmost of the two They're well connected by road: **Municipal buses** and orange-and-white *combis* link the two towns (every 15min., 6:20am-9:30pm, 20min., 1.50 pesos). The larger buses heading to Manzanillo that leave on the hour from both towns' bus stations connect them at the same cost as municipal buses or *combis,* but are faster and more comfortable. Of course, the 40-minute walk along the beach is the hard-core budget option. Don't walk after sunset, as some incidents have been reported. Cabs cost 25 pesos.

## MELAQUE

**Orientation and Practical Information** Melaque's bus station (tel. 5-50-03) is on **Gómez Farías,** the parallel-to-the-beach main drag. From the bus station, turn left on Gómez Farías and walk two blocks to reach **López Mateos.** Another left turn takes you to the plaza, a few blocks inland. López Mateos and **Hidalgo** are the main cross-streets towards the ocean.

There is no bank in Melaque. **Cihuatlán,** a 25-minute bus ride away, has two: **Banamex,** Av. Alvaro Obregón 58 (tel. 5-23-38 or 5-20-48), and **Bancomer** (tel. 5-22-38 or 5-23-23), across the street (both open Mon.-Fri. 9am-5pm). Both have **ATMs.** In Melaque, a *casa de cambio* (tel. 5-53-43) across from the bus station past the pharmacy and inside the *centro comercial* changes dollars at a poor rate, but there's no commission and, well, it's the only option (open Mon.-Sat. 9am-2pm and 4-7pm, Sun. 9am-2pm). Melaque is home to several *casetas;* convenient to the bus station is **Jimmy's,** Gómez Farías 34 (tel. 5-63-10; fax 5-54-52), next to the station (open Mon.-Sat. 8:30am-9pm, Sun. 8:30am-3pm; open until 10pm daily during high season). The public telephones by the bus station will let you make long-distance collect calls, and LADATELs may be found around the town's main plaza.

**Autocamiones Cihuatlán** (tel. 5-50-03) sends **buses** to Guadalajara (1st class 7 per day, 9am-1:15am, 5hr., 111 pesos; 2nd class 14 per day, 4am-12:30am, 6½hr., 89 pesos), Manzanillo (every hr., 1½hr., 1st class 23 pesos, 2nd class 18 pesos), and Puerto Vallarta (1st class 9:15am and 1:30pm, 3½hr., 77 pesos; 2nd class 12 per day, 3am-11:30pm, 6hr., 63 pesos) via Chamela (1½hr., 18 pesos). A few doors down, **Primera Plus,** Gomez Farías 34 (tel. 5-61-10), has service to Guadalajara (1st class 8am, 3:15, 5, and 6:15pm, 5hr., 111 pesos; 2nd class 7 per day, 5am-8:30pm, 6½hr., 89 pesos), and Puerto Vallarta (1st class 1:15 and 4am, 4hr., 77 pesos; 2nd class 5 per day, 8am-7pm, 5hr., 73 pesos) via Chamela (1½hr., 18 pesos).

**Lavandería Industrial Hotelera,** a block from the bus station at Gómez Farías 26, picks up and delivers laundry (wash and dry 7 pesos per kg; open Mon.-Sat. 9am-6pm). The **Red Cross** (tel. 5-23-00) is 15km away in Cihuatlán, accessible by buses which leave from the plaza (every 15min., 4 pesos) or by taxi (40 pesos). **Súper Far-**

**macia Plaza,** López Mateos 48 (tel. 5-51-67), is on the south side of the plaza (open Mon.-Sat. 8am-3pm and 5-10pm, Sun. 8am-2:30pm and 6:30-10pm). The **hospital** (often called **Centro de Salud**) is on Cordiano Guzmán between Corona and Farías (on call 24hr.; consultations Mon.-Fri. 9am-2pm and 5-8pm). **Clínica de Urgencias,** Carranza 22 (tel. 5-61-44), two blocks from the bus station, also provides emergency service. **Dr. Marco Tiscarreño López** speaks English. The **police** are upstairs at López Mateos 52 (tel. 5-50-80), north of the plaza. The **post office,** José Clemente Orozco 13 (tel. 5-52-30), is two blocks left of the plaza as you face the beach and a block and a half towards the beach on Orozco, in the green building on your left (open Mon.-Fri. 8am-3pm, Sat. 8am-noon). **Postal Code:** 48980. **Phone Code:** 335.

## Accommodations and Camping
Melaque boasts a crop of snazzy budget hotels, and bargains aplenty await the persistent and inquisitive. Most budget accommodations in Melaque are inland, near the *centro*. A bargain occasionally lurks among the beachside bungalows. Expect rates to rise, of course, during high season. **Hotel Emanuel,** at Bugambilias 89 (tel. 5-61-07), is half a block from the beach and two blocks south of Restaurant Los Pelícanos. Look for the "Abarrotes Emanuel" sign. This new hotel has spacious rooms with clean, white-tile bathrooms and determined fans. No hot water, but a good deal (singles 40 pesos; doubles 60 pesos). **Casa Rafa,** Legazpi 5 (tel. 5-56-81), one block from the beach near Restaurant Los Pelícanos, sports brand-new, bright, oh-so-spiffy rooms. Cheerful periwinkle-blue bathrooms and colorfully striped comforters are clean, clean, clean (singles 50 pesos; doubles 80 pesos). **Hotel Hidalgo,** Hidalgo 7 (tel. 5-50-45), halfway between the plaza and the beach, is a friendly family affair. Cheery colors complement the fans, *agua purificada,* psychedelic curtains, and common kitchen (singles 40 pesos; doubles 60 pesos; additional people 10 pesos). A parrot- and mango-tree-laden courtyard greets visitors to the **Hotel Sierra Grande,** Ignacio Vallarta 18 (tel. 5-53-94). The attraction here is the posh, group-oriented bungalows with brick and wood details, TV, and fan (180 pesos for 1-6 people). **Playa Trailer Park,** at Gómez Farías and López Mateos (tel. 5-50-65), affords a great oceanfront view. Its 45 lots have electricity, water, and sewer hook-ups (2-person trailer spot or camping site 55 pesos); there are also public bathrooms (1 peso) and showers (8 pesos). Reservations are recommended. Many people park trailers or pitch tents at the far western end of Melaque, between the sandy beach and rock formations. However, this is not the safest option, even when the place is packed during high season.

## Food
During the summer, restaurants ship in shrimp from the north, but come high season, local fishing boats catch everything that is served on the waterfront. More authentic (and less expensive) Mexican places can be found near the central plaza. Cheaper still are the sidewalk food stands that materialize after the sun sets and the nameless, dirt-floored eateries in the *mercado* and near the bus station.

A trip to Melaque wouldn't be complete without a visit to **Los Pelícanos** (tel 5-54-15), at the end of the row of *palapas* on the beach, 200m beyond the huge pink Hotel Casa Grande. The proprietor, New Yorker "Phil" García, not only acts as the fairy godmother of the road-weary gringo, but also serves a mean *pulpo empanizado* (breaded octopus, 40 pesos) to boot. Watch live performances by the diving *pelícanos* in the bay while you eat (open daily 7am-11pm; off-season 10am-8pm). **La Flor Morena,** Juárez 21 on the plaza, welcomes locals and expats alike with great, filling Mexican food at unbelievably low prices. Owner Ambita, the sweetest woman in Jalisco, whips up cheap *tamales* (2 pesos) and enchiladas (8 pesos). Wash it down with a beer (4 pesos; open Tues.-Sun. 6-11pm). **César y Charly,** Gómez Farías 27A, midway down the beach, serves spaghetti (18 pesos), breaded steak (25 pesos), and an orgasmic flaming banana (10 pesos; open daily 7am-10pm). **Juguería María Luisa,** Corona 1 (tel. 5-61-15), has enough types of tasty and safe fruit and veggie juice to make your head spin (open daily 5am-11pm).

## Sights and Entertainment
The main attraction, of course, is the beach. Waves get smaller and the beach more crowded toward the western end of

Melaque's sandy strip. Rent **jet-skis** at the Restaurant Moyo (tel. 7-11-04), on the far west end of the beach (180 pesos per ½hr.; available daily 9am-7pm). Toonces-esque boat drivers tow banana boats and regularly dump unsuspecting riders in the ocean (15 pesos). Although not many come to Melaque for the nightlife, few refuse when it's thrust upon them (it's virtually dead in low season, though). **Disco Tanga,** where Gómez Farías runs into Vallarta (tel. 5-54-72 or 5-54-75), monopolizes the action and is the after-hours oasis of Melaque's under-30 (but over-18, mind you) tourist crowd (cover 15-20 pesos; open in high season, daily, Fri.-Sun. off-season, 10pm-late). For something a bit more mellow and smoky, you can always twirl cues with the middle-aged men at **Billiard San Patricio,** Melaque's pool hall, on Orozco and Juárez, up the street from the post office about three blocks from the plaza (pool and *carambola* 10 pesos per hr., dominoes 3 pesos per hr.; open daily 11am-11pm). Alternatively, head to Barra.

## BARRA DE NAVIDAD

**Orientation and Practical Information** Barra de Navidad is a narrow peninsula flanked on its eastern shore by a salty, sleeping *laguna;* the restless waves tug at her western shore. Virtually *everything* closes during low season. **Veracruz,** the main street, runs southeasterly, angling off at its end. There it meets **Legazpi,** another main street, which runs north-south, hugging the beach. Barra de Navidad's bus stop is at Veracruz 226, on the corner of Nayarit. Turn left on Veracruz from the bus station to get to the *centro.* The **tourist office** is at Jalisco 67 (tel. 5-51-00; tel./fax 5-64-00; open Mon.-Sat. 9am-4pm). The friendly Texans at **Crazy Cactus** (tel. 5-60-99), next to the church on Jalisco between Legazpi and Veracruz, can help you out with insider's advice. Barra has no bank, but a *casa de cambio,* Veracruz 212C (tel. 5-61-77), exchanges money at a poor rate (open Mon.-Sat. 9am-2pm and 4-7pm, Sun. 9am-2pm). **Telephones** are available at the *caseta* next to Hotel Pacífico on Legazpi. Public phones are on Veracruz next to the police.

Buses depart from **Autocamiones Cihuatlán,** Veracruz 228 and Michoacán (tel. 5-52-65), to Guadalajara (1st class 5 per day, 10am-midnight, 5hr., 112 pesos; 2nd class 12 per day, 3:15am-10:20pm, 6½hr., 90 pesos) and Puerto Vallarta (9am and 1pm, 3½hr., 79 pesos). **Primera Plus/Costa Alegre,** Veracruz 269 and Filipinas (tel. 5-61-11), has service to Guadalajara (1st class 7:45am, 3, 5:15, and 6pm, 5hr., 112 pesos; 2nd class 5 per day, 8:15am-8:15pm, 7hr., 90 pesos) and Manzanillo (1st class 11:45am, 2:30, and 7:30pm, 1¼hr., 17 pesos; 2nd class 9 per day, 8:45am-10:15pm, 1¾hr., 18 pesos), and Puerto Vallarta (1st class 1am, 3½hr., 79 pesos; 2nd class 5 per day, 7:45-midnight, 5hr., 64 pesos). The **travel agency** at Veracruz 204A sells tickets for ETN buses departing from Manzanillo. **Lavandería Jardín,** Jalisco 71, just left on Veracruz before Morelos, will wash and dry 3kg for 18 pesos (open Mon.-Fri. 9am-2pm and 4-7pm, Sat. 9am-noon). **Farmacia Marcela,** at Veracruz 69 (tel. 5-54-31), is open daily 9am-2pm and 4-10:30pm. The **Centro de Salud** (tel. 5-62-20), on Puerto de la Navidad, is down Veracruz and out of town. Make a right just after the signs for El Márquez, just before Veracruz becomes a highway; the Centro is the second building on the right, with the red and white gate. Emergency service is available 24-hour. **Police** wait 'round-the-clock at Veracruz 179 (tel. 5-53-99). The **post office,** Guanajuato 100, is one and a half blocks inland from the plaza, behind the market (open Mon.-Fri. 8am-3pm, Sat. 9am-1pm). **Postal Code:** 48987. **Phone Code:** 335.

**Accommodations and Camping** Budget accommodations in Barra are available only to the keen-eyed (or *Let's Go*-armed) traveler, and regardless, they lack the charm and cleanliness of Melaque's hotels. Reasonable accommodations are sometimes available in private residences—ask around and look for signs in restaurants. All prices are subject to hikes during the *temporada alta.* It's no longer possible to camp in Barra de Navidad; you're better off trying Melaque. **Casa de Huéspedes Caribe,** Sonora 15 (tel. 5-52-37), has decent rooms with fans and fluorescent-lit desks. Asymmetrical bathrooms lack hot water (singles 50 pesos; doubles 95 pesos). **Bungalows Karelia,** on Legazpi, on the beach between Hotel Bogavante and the Mexican armada, is a good deal for three or more people. Airy but worn suites house a refrigerator, table, stove, fan, and kitchen utensils (suites for 2-4 people around 200 pesos).

**Food** Try **Los Arcos,** Mazatlán 163 (tel. 5-58-76), across from the Posada Pacífico, for some of the best Mexican food in town. Enjoy *huevos al gusto,* juice, and coffee (15 pesos) in the outdoor patio; *chiles rellenos* go for 20 pesos (open daily 9am-9pm). For delicious, inexpensive Mexican food in a pleasant atmosphere, try **Restaurant Paty,** Jalisco 52 at Veracruz (grilled *pollo* 17 pesos, enchiladas 10 pesos; open daily 7am-11pm). Popular with travelers, **Pizzería Ivett,** Jalisco 56 (tel. 5-59-18), has cheesy pizzas (small for two, 25-33 pesos; open daily 6:30-11pm).

**Sights and Entertainment** **Crazy Cactus,** at the corner of Jalisco and Veracruz (tel. 5-60-99), rents out snorkeling equipment and boogie boards (12 pesos per hr., 60 pesos per day), surfboards (20 pesos per hr., 100 pesos per day), and bikes (80 pesos per day). It also organizes bilingual daytrips to secluded **Tenacatita Bay,** where you can snorkel along a coral reef (boat trip, seafood, drinks, and all the gear 350 pesos per person). Serious fishers will want to call **Z Pesca,** Legazpi 213 (tel. 5-64-64; fax 5-64-65), for rod, reel, and tackle (100 pesos per day) or a day-long deep-sea fishing expedition (800 pesos per day; open daily 9am-9pm).

The short trip across the lagoon to the village of **Colimilla** is pleasant; a *lancha* will deposit up to eight passengers at the far end of the lagoon or amid Colimilla's palms, pigs, cows, and open-air restaurants (50-60 pesos). Deserted **Playa de los Cocos,** 1km away, has larger breakers than those in Barra. If you don't want to swim back, remember to set a time to be picked up. Up to eight people can tour the lagoon behind Barra for 80 pesos. For 120-150 pesos per hour, up to four people can zoom off in a fully equipped *lancha* for tuna or marlin fishing. Operators have formed a cooperative, so prices are fixed. Their office and docks lie at the very end of Veracruz (open daily 7am-7pm).

Bibliophiles should not miss **Beer Bob's Book Exchange,** Mazatlán 61, a few blocks to the right as you face the Posada Pacífico. It's purely a book *exchange*—no cash involved. And what a collection! In the back room sit Bob and company, watching TV, playing cards, or engaging in "some serious beer-drinking" (open when the door's open, usually Mon.-Fri. 1-4pm). Everyone out past midnight parties at **El Galeón Disco,** Morelos 24 (tel. 5-50-18), in Hotel Sand's. Quaff a beer for 5 pesos or a mixed drink for 10 (cover 10 pesos; open Fri.-Sat. 9pm-3am, daily during high season). Things get pretty hot amid the potted plants next door at **Casablanca** (tel. 5-05-40; cover 10 pesos; open high season Fri.-Sat. 10pm-late). Those who prefer singing to dancing may want to mellow out at the **Terraza Bar Jardín,** Jalisco 71 (tel. 5-65-31), a local roof garden and karaoke bar. Somebody will sing "New York, New York" all night if you won't. Beer goes for 5-10 pesos (happy hour high season only 6-8pm; open 6pm-2am.) A number of two-for-one happy hours along Legazpi make the **giddy trip towards inebriation** that much cheaper.

# COLIMA

## ■ Manzanillo

Manzanillo (pop. 110,000) is home to the state's finest beaches, but you'd never know it from its dynamic, sweaty *centro* and the throngs of ships hugging the shore. Most tourists avoid central Manzanillo altogether and head to the glossy resorts on the city's two bays of golden-brown sand north and west of town. Thanks to a fortuitous combination of currents and latitude, Manzanillo is cooler in the summer than Puerto Vallarta and Acapulco. Reasonably priced hotels all lie in the midst of the loud and brazen port action—those seeking only sand and surf would do better to retreat to some secluded village, such as Cuyutlán or Barra de Navidad, where there is no metropolis between the hotels and the Pacific. But for those excited by the prospect of beautiful, immensely popular beaches *and* a real city, Manzanillo will deliver.

## ORIENTATION

Manzanillo lies 98km west of Colima and 355km south of Guadalajara. The **Jardín Obregón,** Manzanillo's *zócalo,* is the most useful orientation point in town. It faces north onto the harbor, but boxcars often obstruct the glorious view of oil tankers (sigh). **Morelos** runs east-west along the north (waterfront) edge of the plaza; **Dávalos,** becoming **Juárez,** runs along the south. **Avenida México,** Manzanillo's main street, runs south from the plaza; most hotels and services are nearby. The "Centro" bus runs from the station to the corner of 21 de Marzo and Hidalgo (1.50 pesos). From the corner, a right turn on Allende and another on México will take you to the *zócalo.* A taxi from the bus station to the center of town costs 6 pesos. White and blue "Miramar" buses provide the main transportation to Manzanillo's beaches and the main strip, **Blvd. Costera Miguel de la Madrid;** they run along México, around the Plaza, and turn on Morelos heading for the boulevard (about every 15min., 5am-11pm; price varies by destination).

## PRACTICAL INFORMATION

**Tourist Office:** Blvd. Costera Miguel de la Madrid 4960 (tel. 3-22-64 or 3-22-77), 2 blocks past Fiesta Mexicana. Catch a "Miramar" bus (3.50 pesos) and tell the driver where you're headed. Open Mon.-Fri. 8:30am-3pm and 6-8pm. Helpful **tourist police** (tel. 2-10-02) reside in the Palacio Municipal on the *zócalo* and distribute maps and brochures about Manzanillo and other locations throughout the state of Colima. **Information booths** are in front of the Palacio, around town, and along the beaches (open Mon.-Fri. 9am-7pm, daily in high season).

**Currency Exchange: Banco Internacional,** México 99 at 10 de Mayo (tel. 2-21-50), has slightly better rates and longer hours than most banks. Open Mon.-Fri. 8am-7pm, Sat. 9am-2:30pm. **ATM** across the street at **Banamex.**

**Telephones: Computel,** México 302 at Galindo (tel. 2-39-26); another on Morelos, ½ block east of the *zócalo,* next to Banca Serfín. Both open daily 7am-10pm.

**Fax: Telecomm** (tel. 2-30-30), in the Palacio Municipal, to the left of the stairs as you enter. You can send **telegrams** too, if you're an old-timer. Open Mon.-Fri. 8am-10pm, Sat.-Sun. 9am-12:30pm.

**Airport:** Tel. 3-11-19 or 3-25-25. In Playa de Oro, on the highway between Barra de Navidad and Manzanillo. **Mexicana** (tel. 3-23-23), **Aeromar** (tel. 3-01-51), and **Aerocalifornia** (tel. 4-14-14). **Viajes Vamos a...,** Carrillo Puerto 259 (tel. 2-17-11), 1 block west of México and 3 blocks south of the *zócalo,* can facilitate ticket purchase. Open Mon.-Fri. 9am-2pm and 4-7pm, Sat. 9am-2pm. Taxis cost 120 pesos. *Colectivos* (50 pesos) take passengers to the airport 2hr. before take-off (daily 9am-1:30pm and 5-7pm, 45min.); call the airport to make arrangements.

**Buses:** On Hidalgo, on the outskirts of town between Laguna Cuyutlán and the ocean. Not much more than bus offices lined up along a sidewalk. Taxis to the *centro* 6 pesos. **Autobuses de Occidente** (tel. 2-01-23) serves Mexico City (6 per day, 2:45am-7:30pm, 16hr., 224 pesos). **Autobuses de Jalisco** (tel. 2-01-23) provides 1st-class service to Colima (10 per day, 1½hr., 25 pesos), Guadalajara (10 per day, 7hr., 106 pesos), Morelia (10:45pm, 8hr., 152 pesos), and Uruapan (8:15pm, 8hr., 117 pesos). **Autocamiones Cihuatlán** (tel. 2-05-15) provides 2nd-class service to Guadalajara (12 per day, 7hr., 130 pesos) and Puerto Vallarta (10 per day, 4:30am-10pm, 6hr., 100 pesos), stopping at Melaque and Barra de Navidad (1½hr., 18 pesos). **Autotransportes del Sur de Jalisco** (tel. 2-10-03) serves Colima (5 per day, 1:15-7:40pm, 1½hr., 18 pesos). **Primera Plus** (tel. 2-02-10) sends deluxe buses to Puerto Vallarta (midnight, 5hr., 100 pesos) and Querétaro (7am, 8hr., 167 pesos). **Transportes Costalegre** (tel. 2-02-10) runs buses to Melaque and Barra de Navidad (11 per day, 6:30am-7pm, 1½hr., 18 pesos). **Elite** (tel. 2-04-32) provides cushy service to Acapulco (5am and 12:30pm, 12hr., 202 pesos), Mexico City (7:30 and 9pm, 14hr., 262 pesos), and Tijuana (4, 7:30, and 9pm, 36hr., 687 pesos) via

Tepic (7hr., 144 pesos), Mazatlán (11hr., 230 pesos), and Hermosillo (25hr., 541 pesos).

**Trains:** On Niños Héroes near Morelos (tel. 2-19-92). Office open daily 8am-2pm.

**Laundromat: Lavi-Matic,** Hidalgo 1 (tel. 2-08-44), all the way down México across the small plaza. Open Mon.-Sat. 8am-7pm.

**Red Cross:** Juárez 190 (tel. 6-57-70), 1 block from the plaza. Open 24hr.

**Pharmacy: Farmacia Manzanillo,** Juárez 10 (tel. 2-01-85 or 3-24-11), on the south side of the *zócalo*. English spoken. Open daily 8:30am-midnight. **Farmacia Continental** (tel. 3-02-86), at Playa Miramar, across from Restaurante Juanitos. **Dr. Joseph Cadet** speaks English. Open Mon.-Sat. 10am-2pm and 5-9pm.

**Hospital:** On Calle Hospital (tel. 3-03-41) in Colonia San Pedrito. Open 24hr.

**Police:** On Juárez (tel. 2-10-02 or 2-10-04) in the Palacio Municipal, facing the Jardín.

**Post Office:** Calle Miguel Galindo 3D (tel. 2-00-22). Open Mon.-Fri. 8am-7pm, Sat. 9am-1pm. **Postal Code:** 28200.

**Phone Code:** 333.

## ACCOMMODATIONS

Manzanillo's budget accommodations tend to be basic and plain, but you'll be on the beach the whole time anyway! Hotels near the *zócalo* are in a safer area than those near the bus station. **Camping** on Playa Miramar is feasible during Semana Santa and in December, when bathroom facilities are available and security is heightened.

**Hotel Emperador,** Dávalos 69 (tel. 2-23-74), 1 block west of the plaza. Spacious rooms with rustic wooden furniture, ceiling fans, and plenty of white tile. Singles 50 pesos; doubles 60-80 pesos.

**Hotel Flamingo,** Madero 72 (tel. 2-10-37), 1 block south of the *zócalo*. Old, Spanish-style rooms with stucco walls and heavy wooden furniture. Dimly-lit rooms are perfect for a siesta, although the place could use more ventilation. Clean bathrooms and joy in the form of purified water. Singles 50 pesos; doubles 70 pesos.

**Hotel Costa Manzanillo,** Madero 333 and Vicente Guerrero (tel. 2-27-40), has spotless rooms with fan, TV, and well-scrubbed, spacious bathrooms. Purified water adds to the fun. A definite step up. Singles 85 pesos; doubles 100 pesos.

## FOOD

Since tourists mostly put up closer to the beach, food at the market and in restaurants downtown is simple, local, and cheap. A few blocks from the plaza, at Cuauhtémoc and Madero, is a market of sorts with numerous family-run and inexpensive *fondas*.

**Restaurante Chantilly,** at Juárez and Moreno (tel. 2-01-94) on the plaza. Crowds of newspaper-reading professionals, flocks of families, and stragglers off the *zócalo* munch on fantastically good Mexican staples in a diner-like setting. Enchiladas 19 pesos. Mango *licuados* (5 pesos) are as good as it gets. Open Sun.-Fri. 7am-10pm.

**Restaurant Emperador,** Dávalos 69 (tel. 2-23-74), below the eponymous hotel. The blank walls, white tablecloths, and fluorescent lights aren't nearly as pleasing to the eye as the food is to the palate. Gargantuan *comida corrida* for a mere 15 pesos. *Chiles rellenos* only 10 pesos; hotcakes 6 pesos. Open daily 8am-10pm.

**Los Naranjos,** México 366. Look hard: the white and blue cafe is difficult to spot. When it rains, time stands still here; so do the flies and fans. Locals come here in droves to chow down on tasty entrees served with a mountain of tortillas, rice, beans, and a glass of juice (16 pesos). Open daily 7am-7pm.

## SIGHTS

Manzanillo's beaches stretch from west to east along two bays, **Bahía de Manzanillo** and **Bahía de Santiago,** formed by the Santiago and Juluapan Peninsulas. The Bahía de Manzanillo has more expensive hotels and cleaner golden sand. Unfortunately, its beach slopes steeply, creating a strong and sometimes dangerous undertow. The beaches at Bahía Santiago, though twice as far from the *centro* and bordered by a noisy highway, are better protected by the Juluapan peninsula, providing a panoramic vista of the rugged terrain and more tranquil surf. The bay is perfect for swimming and water sports and is very popular with sun worshippers.

The closest good beach on Bahía Manzanillo, **Playa Las Brisas,** has a few secluded spots but is for the most part crowded with luxurious hotels and bungalows. To get to Las Brisas from downtown Manzanillo, take a taxi (18 pesos) or the "Las Brisas" bus (2.50 pesos). Catch the bus on México or on the highway going toward the airport and Barra de Navidad. Alternatively, catch the "Miramar" bus and ask the driver to let you off at the *crucero* (crossroads), then turn left to populated shores or stake out a private piece of beach right at the junction.

The "Miramar" bus continues west of Peninsula Santiago, gear-grinding toward other excellent beaches on Bahía Santiago. Because this part of the bay is not used for shipping, the water is cleaner than at Las Brisas. Beyond **Olas Altas,** a beach popular with experienced (largely American) surfers but infamous for its powerful waves and dangerous undertow, is **Miramar Beach,** a stretch of golden beach with solid waves adequate for **boogie-boarding** or **body-surfing.** Get off where the footbridge crosses the highway. This is the most crowded section of the beach, but it boasts top-notch beachfront restaurants from which you can rent body boards and surfboards (5-10 pesos per hr.). Crowds thin out 20m to the east or west.

The calmer waters of the *palapa*-lined **Playa la Boquita,** the westernmost point on the Juluapan Peninsula, make this a popular spot for children and water sports. Two-seat **wave runners** (US$32 for ½hr.) or **banana boats** (15 pesos per person) can slip you around the bay. **Windsurfing** (60 pesos per hr.), **parasailing** (100 pesos per hr.), and **kayaks** (60 pesos per hr.) are also available. **Snorkeling** gear (70 pesos) is rented out at the last *palapa* on the shore (tel. 6-57-02; open daily 9am-5pm). If you're not much of a deep sea enthusiast, **Blas** at **Hotel Palma Real** (tel. 5-00-00) rents **horses** (70 pesos per hr.). To get to Playa La Boquita, take a "Miramar" bus to Club Santiago (3.50 pesos, 40min.). Walk through the white arches along the cobblestoned and palm-lined street, which becomes a dirt road; you'll hit the road after 25 minutes. Also reveling in its tranquility is **Playa Audiencia,** a small but magnificent cove with calm waters, light brown sand, a few small boats, and a gorgeous, rocky vista. To reach the *playa*, take a "Las Hadas" bus from Niños Héroes or anywhere on Miramar Highway to the Sierra Radison (3.50 pesos), then follow the path to the beach. The bus ride back to town offers a spectacular view of the peninsula.

## ENTERTAINMENT

Manzanillo doesn't sleep when the sun sets. After frolicking in the sun and splashing in the sea, locals and tourists alike show off their **tans** and **cool threads** at **Vog,** Av. Miguel de la Madrid (tel. 3-19-92) in the hotel strip. At 11:30pm, sophisticated track lighting rhythmically sprays beams across Flintstone-like walls (cover 30 pesos; open Thurs.-Sat. 10pm-4am, daily during high season). Next door at the **Bar de Félix** (tel. 3-18-75), funky topiaries welcome an older crowd. Weary revelers recline in plush red chairs while the packed dance floor pulsates to a melange of disco and Latin rhythms (2-drink or 35-peso minimum Fri.-Sat. during high season; open Tues.-Sun. 9pm-4am). "Miramar" buses run down the hotel strip. Taxis back to the *centro* cost 25 pesos.

# ■ Near Manzanillo

## CUYUTLÁN

With its lush vegetation, breathtaking black-sand beach, and mysterious lagoon, quiet **Cuyutlán** (pop. 1650) offers the traveler a few days of solitude. Medium waves roll up on the shore, making for fairly safe and exciting swimming. In the off-season, shut-up buildings and silent streets give the place a ghost-town feel, and the huge golden head of Benito Juárez is often the only face visible amid the palm trees of Cuyutlán's green and white *zócalo*. Summer weekends are slightly busier, but it is only during the high tourist season (Dec. and Semana Santa) that Cuyutlán truly comes to life. If you have to choose between Paraíso and Cuyutlán, the latter offers tourists a better beach, better hotels, and a greater variety of food.

**Orientation and Practical Information** Buses to Cuyutlán leave Armería from the Terminal Sub-Urbana (every ½hr., 7am-8pm, 20min., 4 pesos). (For information on how to get to Armería from Manzanillo, see **Paraíso: Getting There,** below.) Buses depart from Cuyutlán on the same schedule (sometimes a bit early) from the plaza. There is no direct public transportation between Paraíso and Cuyutlán.

The road from Armería, 15km from Cuyutlán, runs parallel to the coast and becomes **Yavaros** as it enters town. It intersects **Hidalgo,** which runs along the east side of the town square; a left at this intersection takes you to the beach. **Veracruz,** Cuyutlán's other mighty boulevard, runs parallel to and three blocks from Yavaros, one block off the beach.

Most of Cuyutlán's municipal services are within one block of the *zócalo*. The bilingual owners of the **Hotel Fenix** will **change money** if they have the cash. Bring an adequate supply of *pesos* just in case. The only *caseta* is at Hidalgo 47 (tel. 6-40-00), one block inland from the *zócalo*. **Farmacia del Carmen** is at Yavaros 6, facing the plaza (open daily 9am-2pm and 4-7pm). For those who fall sick, the blue and white **Centro de Salud** (tel. 6-42-10) is one block west of the *zócalo* on Yavaros at Madero. (Open 24hr. for emergencies, Mon.-Fri. 9am-2pm and 4-7pm for consultation; no English spoken.) The **police** reside at Hidalgo 144 (tel. 6-40-14, ext. 113), one block south of the *zócalo*. **Phone code:** 332.

**Accommodations and Food** Waves lap at the doorsteps of most nearby budget hotels. Most are well-maintained and very affordable. During high season (mainly Dec. and Semana Santa), expect rates to skyrocket to 130-150 pesos per person, with meals included to help justify the price. Make reservations a month in advance during this time. Almost all the food in Cuyutlán is served up in the **hotel restaurants,** and seafood is the obvious specialty. Most restaurants are on Yavaros. **Hotel Morelos,** Hidalgo 185 at Veracruz (6-40-13), offers plush rooms with clean bathrooms and carved wooden furniture. Tiled floors, festive colors, and what seems like all the flowers in Cuyutlán give the place pizazz (40 pesos per person). The rooms at **Hotel Fénix,** Hidalgo 201 at Veracruz (tel. 6-40-82), may be taller than they are wide, but there's a fan in each one, and the bathrooms are tidy. The friendly English-speaking owners run a popular bar that serves as the town watering hole (30-35 pesos per person; open during high season only). The **Hotel San Rafael,** Veracruz 46 (tel. 6-40-15), dishes out old Spanish style with white stucco walls, wooden-shuttered windows, leafy greens, and ocean views (75 pesos per person, high season 140 pesos per person). There's a **disco** next door.

**Cabañas Rafles,** at López Mateos, a 10-minute walk east along the beach (or along Veracruz past the Hotel San Rafael), offers basic rooms, access to showers and toilets, and campsites. The super-friendly caretaker Rafles will treat you right. Unofficial camping sites lie 200m from Cuyutlán's hotels, in a private patch of black sand. Some travelers string up a hammock in one of the *palapas* near the hotels. For 5 pesos, campers and daytrippers can use the toilets and showers at Hotel Fenix (or buy a drink at the bar).

**Sights** Aside from its gorgeous beach, Cuyutlán's biggest claim to fame is the **green wave,** a phenomenon that occurs regularly in April or May. Quirky currents and phosphorescent marine life combine to produce 10m swells that glow an unearthly green. The town itself reaches high tide during the **Festival de la Virgen de Guadalupe** (the first 12 days of December), when twice a day—at 6am and 6pm—men, women, and children clad in *traje de indios* walk 5km to the town's blue church. The celebrations peak on the twelfth day, when *mariachis* accompany the procession and the marchers sing tributes to the Virgin. Cuyutlán's **Tortugario,** 3.5km east of town along Veracruz, is a combination of a wildlife preserve and a zoo home to hordes of turtles, iguanas, and crocodiles. The camp also has saltwater pools for (human) swimming (admission 5 pesos; taxi to the camp 20 pesos).

## PARAÍSO

Paraíso may soon be destroyed by the gods for its hubris, but for now it outclasses its unsightly sister city, nearby **Armería.** A well-paved road connects the two towns, cutting through 7km of banana and coconut plantations before it dead-ends at the lava-black sands that surround Paraíso's few hotels and thatched, beachfront restaurants. A shoreline strewn with an endless row of lawn chairs and umbrellas backs the emerald green surf. Paraíso is a popular destination among Mexicans for daytrips and weekend vacations; during the high season and on Sundays, the beachfront has a true family atmosphere, and the town's single dirt road is often crammed with buses and cars blaring music. But on a lazy summer weekday, the beach is almost deserted, and a few lucky swimmers have the waters all to themselves.

Just before the main road becomes the beach, you'll see Paraíso's only other street, the dirt road **Av. de la Juventud** (called **Calle Adán y Eva** by locals) which runs along the back of the beachfront restaurants. The first building on the beach to your left is **Hotel Equipales** (call the town's *caseta* at tel. 2-14-80 or 2-00-25), where you'll find no-frills rooms with a view of the shore. The cramped bathrooms lack hot water (singles 40 pesos; doubles 60 pesos). Farther to the left lies **Hotel Paraíso** (tel. 7-18-25), a cut above Equipales. Spacious beachfront rooms have yellow-tiled floors, ceiling fans, and cold showers. A jungle-themed mural adds a splash of color to the popular pool (singles and doubles 138 pesos). At the opposite end of the strip lies **Posada Valencia,** where the beds are waist-high, the rooms clean, and the bathroom tiles scrubbed spotless. Alas, the plain cement floors put a damper on it all (singles 40 pesos; doubles 80 pesos).

Paraíso's extensive **beach** makes a soft pillow for campers, and the Hotel Paraíso provides showers (5 pesos) and free access to bathrooms. Hotel Equipales also offers bathroom (1 peso) and shower (5 pesos) use. Some *enramada* owners may let you hang your **hammock** under their thatched roofs. During the high season (Dec. and April), rooms may be available in **private houses;** ask in stores or in the *caseta.*

**Restaurants** run the slim gamut from rustic *enramadas* to cement-floored *comedores.* Not surprisingly, locally caught seafood dominates menus. **Restaurant Paraíso,** in the Hotel Paraíso, is as popular as the hotel pool. Uniformed waiters provide snazzy service, and string quartets and *mariachis* sometimes pop in the afternoon. Breakfast goes for 15 pesos and tasty shrimp dishes cost 42 pesos (open daily 8am-6pm). The restaurants at Hotel Equipales and Posada Valencia also offer pleasant atmospheres and reasonable prices. Long-distance **phone** calls can be made across the street from the bus stop in the *tienda rural* (open Mon.-Sat. 9am-9pm, Sun. 9am-6pm).

**Getting There: Autobuses Nuevos Horizonte y Rojos** (tel. 2-39-00) runs buses from Manzanillo to Armería (every 15min., 4:20am-10:30pm, 45min., 10.50 pesos). Get off at the blue "Paraíso" sign and cross the highway. Buses to Paraíso leave from **Terminal Sub-Urbano,** which provides service to Paraíso (every 45min., 6am-7:30pm, 15min., 3 pesos). Buses return from Paraíso to Armería on the same schedule and depart from where they leave passengers.

# ■ Colima

With 160,000 residents, the capital of the Colima state can hardly be called a *pueblo,* but it does manage to maintain a certain benevolence and informality: the streets and parks are magnificently groomed, the civic-minded inhabitants are remarkably friendly, and on Sundays, slews of stores close up shop as families head off to church. Blessed with cool mountain air, pleasant budget lodging, a string of museums, theaters, and a university, under-touristed Colima provides relief from the sweaty, well-trodden coastal route and proves a great place to shake the sand from your shoes.

## ORIENTATION

A string of plazas runs east to west across downtown Colima. The shady **Plaza Principal,** flanked by the cathedral and the Palacio de Gobierno on the east side, is the business center of town. Just past the cathedral and *palacio* is the smaller, quieter **Jardín Quintero,** marked by the large fountain in its center. Three blocks farther east on **Madero** (which runs along the north side of the plaza) is the large, lush **Jardín Núñez,** the other significant reference point in town. Many tourist services are on **Hidalgo,** which runs parallel to Madero one block to the south. The main **bus station** is 2km out of town, but mini-buses zip by incessantly (6am-8:30pm, 1.80 pesos). **Taxis** charge 5 pesos within the *centro,* 7 pesos to the outskirts.

## PRACTICAL INFORMATION

**Tourist Office:** Portal Hidalgo 20 (tel. 2-43-60 or tel./fax 2-83-60), on the west side of Pl. Principal, across the *zócalo* from the Palacio de Gobierno. Extremely helpful staff speaks English. Open Mon.-Fri. 8:30am-3pm and 5-9pm, Sat. 9am-1pm.

**Currency Exchange: Banamex,** Hidalgo 90 (tel. 2-01-03), 1 block east of Pl. Principal, has an **ATM.** Open Mon.-Fri. 9am-5pm. **Majapara Casa de Cambio,** Morelos 200 (tel. 4-89-98; fax 4-89-66), corner of Juárez at Jardín Núñez, has slightly better rates. Open Mon.-Sat. 9am-2pm and 4:30-7pm.

**Telephones: LADATELs** abound in the plazas. The *caseta* at **Comercializadora Sanvi** (tel. 3-50-80), Revolución 99 on the southeast corner of the Jardín Núñez, is open daily 8am-10pm.

**Fax:** Madero 243 (tel. 2-60-64), next to the post office. Telegrams (if that's your cup of tea) are another option. Open Mon.-Fri. 8am-6pm, Sat. 9am-noon.

**Buses: Autotransportes del Sur de Jalisco** (tel. 2-03-16) runs 2nd-class buses to Manzanillo (5 per day, 6am-11:40pm, 1¾hr., 20 pesos) via Armería (1hr., 10.50 pesos). **ETN** (tel. 2-58-99; fax 4-10-60) sends plush buses to the Guadalajara airport (9:30am, 3hr., 100 pesos) and Morelia by *autopista* (11:45pm, 6hr., 160 pesos). **Ómnibus de México** (tel. 4-71-90) goes to Aguascalientes (3:20pm, 6½hr., 146 pesos), Mexico City (7:45, 8:30, and 10pm, 10hr., 230 pesos), and Monterrey (6:50pm, 15hr., 300 pesos). **Primera Plus** (tel. 4-80-67) runs 1st-class buses to Aguascalientes (12:30pm, 6hr., 154 pesos), Guadalajara (10 per day, 5am-7:40pm, 3hr., 79 pesos), Manzanillo (9 per day, 1½hr., 22 pesos), and Mexico City (9 and 11:30pm, 10hr., 248 pesos), and 2nd-class buses to Querétaro (3:30 and 8:30pm, 8hr., 140 pesos). **Autobuses de Occidente** (tel. 4-81-79) has 2nd-class service to Lázaro Cárdenas (12:10 and 3:10am, 6hr., 85-98 pesos), Mexico City (6 per day, 5am-10pm, 11hr., 200 pesos) via Morelia (5, 8am, 2, and 10pm, 8hr., 105 pesos), and Uruapan (11am, 7hr., 85 pesos). **Flecha Amarilla** (tel. 4-80-67) provides 2nd-class service to Manzanillo (5 per day, 2:30am-8:50pm, 1¾hr., 20 pesos) and Morelia (6 and 11:15pm, 8hr., 105 pesos). **Elite** (tel. 2-84-99) sends 1st-class buses directly to Hermosillo (27hr., 539 pesos), Mazatlán (12hr., 240 pesos), Mexico City (9:30 and 11pm, 9hr., 230 pesos), and Tijuana (5pm, 36hr., 693 pesos) via Tepic (7hr., 165 pesos).

**Trains:** Av. Colón (tel. 2-92-50) by Parque Hidalgo, at the southern edge of town. The #6 and 7 buses go to the station. 2nd-class trains chug to Guadalajara (1:30am, 7hr., 35 pesos) and Manzanillo (3am, 2hr., 14.50 pesos). Offices open for information only daily 8am-3:30pm; tickets may be purchased daily after 1am.

**Luggage Storage:** At the bus station. 2 pesos per bag for 6hr., 0.50 pesos each additional hour. Open daily 6am-10pm. 24hr. restaurant can assist after hours.

**Laundromat: LavaTec,** Rey Colimán 4. Open Mon.-Sat. 8:30am-8:30pm.

**Red Cross:** Aldama at Obregón (tel. 2-14-51 or 2-22-42). Open 24hr.

**Pharmacy: Sangre de Cristo,** Obregón at Madero (tel. 4-74-74). Open 24hr.

**Hospitals: Hospital Civil,** San Fernando at Ignacio Zandoval (tel. 2-02-27 or 2-09-11). **Centro de Salud,** Juárez at 20 de Noviembre (tel. 2-00-64 or 2-32-38). **Dr. Armando López** speaks English. Open Mon.-Fri. 7am-2:30pm, Sat. 7am-1:30pm.

**Emergency:** Dial 06.

**Police:** Juárez at 20 de Noviembre (tel. 2-09-67).

**Post Office:** Madero 247 (tel. 2-00-33), on the northeast corner of the Jardín Núñez. Open Mon.-Fri. 8am-7pm, Sat. 8am-2pm. **Postal Code:** 28000. **Phone Code:** 331.

## ACCOMMODATIONS

Inexpensive, quality rooms can be difficult to find in Colima. If the options below don't work out, cheap lodging may be found near the Jardín Núñez. Higher-priced hotels tend to cluster around the university. Purified water is often not available.

**Hospedajes del Rey,** Rey Colimán 125 (tel. 3-36-83), ½ block from the southeast of the Jardín Núñez. "Fit for a king" couldn't describe it better: Enormous, plush rooms sport fans and wall-to-wall windows; hardwood floors and a beveled-glass dining table and chairs complete the royal ensemble. Bathroom floors are clean enough to eat from. Singles 75 pesos, with TV 80 pesos; doubles with TV 95 pesos.

**Hotel Colonial,** Medellín 142F, between Morelos and Nicolás Bravo (tel. 3-08-77), 1 block from the Pl. Principal. Spiffy rooms with fans, wicker chairs, wrought-iron beds, and enormous TVs (some with cable). Spotless, cheery, flower-tiled bathrooms make the hot water that much more enjoyable. A great budget spot. Singles 60-90 pesos; doubles 70-100 pesos.

**Casa de Huéspedes,** Morelos 265 (tel. 2-34-67), off the southeast corner of Jardín Núñez. A friendly family-run *posada* with breezy but decaying rooms and billions of blooming plants. Bathrooms could use a good scrub. Singles 30 pesos, with bath 35 pesos; doubles 55 pesos, with bath 60 pesos.

## FOOD

Restaurant fare in Colima reflects the town's dearth of tourism; inexpensive and authentic Mexican meals consist of traditional faves like *pozole blanco* and *sopitos*. A few pricey joints cluster around the Plaza Principal, but a jaunt down the smaller side-streets will lead to budget meals aplenty.

**Comedor Familiar El Trébol,** 16 de Septiembre 50 at Degollado (tel. 2-29-00), on the Pl. Principal. Colima at its best: popular and cheap. A family spot packed with kids laughing and stuffing their faces amid the festive decor. *Comida corrida* 12 pesos; breakfast 8 pesos; beer 5 pesos. Open Sun.-Fri. 8am-11pm.

**Samadhi,** Medina 125 (tel. 3-24-98), 2½ blocks north of Jardín Núñez. Walk down Juárez (the western border of the Jardín); Samadhi is next to the red and white church. Delicious, vegetarian-friendly cuisine served with new-age music in a leafy courtyard with soothing pastel walls. Breakfast buffet 25 pesos; soy burger with mushrooms and fries 13.50 pesos. Open Fri.-Wed. 8am-10pm, Thurs. 8am-5pm.

**Los Naranjos,** Barreda 34 (tel. 2-00-29), almost a block north of Madero, northeast of the Plaza Principal. Popular with those in the know. *Periódico*-perusing middle-aged men classily sip coffee, while glass vases and wicker chairs add Euro-flair. *Pollo a la Mexicana* 22 pesos. *Antojitos* 7-21 pesos. Open daily 8am-11:30pm.

**Cenaduría Morelos,** Morelos 299 at Domínguez (tel. 2-93-32), 1 block off the southeast corner of Jardín Núñez. Tasty, cheap *pozole, tostadas, taquitos,* and the regional favorite, *enchiladas dulces* (sweet enchiladas) served with a mountain of diced onion and hot-ass sauce (entrees 10 pesos). Cool it off with a beer (5-6 pesos). Open Tues.-Sat. 5-11pm, Sun. 5pm-1:30am.

## SIGHTS

In Colima's **Plaza Principal,** the gazebo and fountains of the **Jardín Libertad** lure bureaucrats on their lunch breaks to the garden's ornate white wrought-iron benches. The double arcade around the plaza encompasses the **Museo Regional de Historia de Colima.** On the east side of the plaza, much of the state government is housed in the **Palacio de Gobierno,** an unremarkable beige and white building with a breezy courtyard and a four-wall mural, completed in 1954 by Jorge Chávez Carrillo in honor of the bicentennial of Hidalgo's birth. The intricate mural moves counter-clockwise through Mexico's tumultuous history, beginning with a powerful depiction of the conquest and ending at the Mexican Revolution with Pancho Villa's infamous bravado. Adjoining Colima's municipal complex is the colonial **Santa Iglesia Cathedral,** a pawn in the battle between humanity and nature—or, depending on your perspective, between Catholicism and the ghost of indigenous religions. The Spanish first built a church on this spot in 1527, but an earthquake destroyed the original wood and palm structure; fire consumed its replacement. Undeterred, the Spanish built another church. The cathedral's Neoclassical interior sparkles with gilt paint, chandeliers, and polished marble. In the pulpit designed by Othón Bustos rests a statue of San Felipe de Jesús, the city's patron saint (open 6am-2pm and 4-8:30pm).

A block west of the tourist office stands **Teatro Hidalgo,** completed in 1883. Unmarred by the passage of time, the theater's four tiers of side-seating barely touch the high ceiling, and its swooping red curtains lend the stage a 19th-century ambience. Occasional performances enliven the majestic interior beyond those large wooden doors; inquire at the tourist office.

Colima's **Museo de Las Culturas de Occidente,** on Calle Calzada Galván at Ejército Nacional (tel. 2-84-31), is an excellent museum devoted to local pre-Hispanic art. Rarely seen outside the state, the Colima ceramic figurines on display here are among the most playful and captivating artifacts in Mexico. The figurines possess exaggerated, disproportionate bodies. The museum provides an excellent narrative of the artifacts' meaning and role in indigenous culture (open Tues.-Sun. 10am-2pm and 4-8pm). The **Casa de la Cultura** (same tel.), the university's cultural center, is the best source of information on cultural events in Colima (open daily 8am-9pm). To get to the museum, take the yellow "Ruta #3 Sur" bus on Av. Rey Colimán at Jardín Núñez.

Colima's newest museum, the **Museo de Historia,** Portal Morelos 1 at 16 de Septiembre and Reforma (tel. 2-92-28), on the south side of the Plaza Principal. The museum is home to a respectable collection of pre-Colombian ceramics and includes a creepy replica of a western Mesoamerican burial site, complete with two real skeletons. In the same courtyard is an eclectic gallery of art (both open Tues.-Sat. 9am-6pm, Sun. 5-8pm; free). Also sponsored by the institution is Colima's **Museo Universitario de Artes Populares** (tel. 2-68-69), at Barreda and Gallardo, which boasts a collection of traditional dresses and masks, figurines recovered from nearby tombs, and descriptions of the pre-Aztec western coast. A gift shop sells handmade reproductions of local ceramics (museum open Mon.-Sat. 9am-2pm and 5-7pm; free). Getting there is an easy 15-minute walk north on 27 de Septiembre from the Plaza Principal. Alternatively, catch the #7 bus on Gabino Barreda between Zaragoza and Guerrero, and take it to the corner of Barreda and Gallardo.

The **Parque Regional Metropolitano,** on Degollado (tel. 4-16-76), four blocks south of the Plaza Principal, offers nature-lovers an afternoon stroll along a human-made duck pond, home to two absurdly large pelicans who pester young children for fish. A miniature **zoo** houses monkeys, crocodiles, and lions. Children feed the deer ice cream cones through wire fences and frolic in the pool, zooming down the **waterslide.** (Zoo open daily 6am-7:30pm, 1 peso; pool and waterslide open Wed.-Sun. 10am-4:30pm; admission 4 pesos, waterslide and boat rides 5 pesos per hr., children 3 pesos.)

Erupting volcanoes aren't the only goings-on shaking things up in Colima. Night spots are populated largely by students. **Bariloche,** Av. Rey de Colimán 440 (tel. 4-55-00), near the Monumento Rey Colimán, may be the hottest spot in town. Huge-screen videos and two pool tables keep 'em coming (cover Wed. 50 pesos, including open bar, Fri.-Sat. 40 pesos without open bar; open Wed., and Fri.-Sat. 8pm-2am). Everybody knows your name at **Cheers,** on Zaragoza (tel. 4-47-00), a popular *discoteca* with copper ornaments on Alice-in-Wonderland-colored walls and rainbow seats (cover 20 pesos; open Fri.-Sat. 10pm-3am). **Atrium,** Sevilla de Río 174 at Castellanos (tel. 3-04-77), sports hockey and pool tables, peppy music, and a preppy crowd (open daily noon-2am). For some sappy tunes that'll make you cry in your beer, visit the Casa de la Cultura's cafe, **Dalí.** Prints by you-know-who drip from the walls under dim, smoky lights. The food isn't exactly cheap, but it's worth it just to drink *cervezas* or smoke cigars with the conflicted intellectuals. Weekend nights between 9 and 11pm, a **sensitive Mexican man** stands on the cafe's small platform wailing love songs, a guitar cradled in his arms. *Muy romántico* (open Mon.-Fri. 8am-midnight, Sat.-Sun. 4pm-midnight).

For an inexpensive couple of hours, check out some American flicks at **Cinemas del Rey,** Av. Rey Colimán and Juan José Ríos, or **Cine Jorge Sthal,** on Av. de los Maestros near the Centro Comercial San Fernando (10 pesos; Tues. 2-for-1 tickets).

# ■ Near Colima

## VOLCANOES

In Náhuatl, Colima means "place where the old god is dominant." The old god is **El Volcán de Fuego** (3820m), 25km from Colima city. Recorded eruptions date back to the pre-Conquest era, and lava was visible from the capital once again on June 24, 1994, when El Fuego reasserted its status as an active volcano (the tourist office assures visitors that the volcano is not a threat to the city). **El Nevado de Colima** (4240m) stands taller than its neighbor but is dormant and not much fun at parties. The **Joya Cabin,** near the summit, lacks all amenities except a roof. The park is only open sporadically; if you're planning a trip to the top, call the **police** ahead of time (tel. 2-18-01). As always, be cautious. The ascent should not be attempted by solo travelers or by those with little hiking experience.

**Getting There:** Guadalajara-bound *locales* (from the new bus station) pass through the town of **Atenquique,** 57km away. From here, a 27km unimproved dirt road runs to the summit of El Fuego. The trip is only recommended for 4-wheel-drive vehicles, though logging trucks based at the factory in Atenquique make trips up the road to spots near the summit. You can get to El Nevado by car or by bus. **Flecha Amarilla** (tel. 4-80-67) runs buses from Colima to **Guzmán,** 83km away (5 per day, 7am-5:30pm, 1¾hr., 28 pesos). Buses from Guzmán limp up to Joya, where you can make your epic assault on the summit.

## LAGUNAS CARRIZALILLO AND LA MARÍA

If you don't mind insects, frogs, and huge lizards, and just want to bask in peace, make a daytrip to **Laguna Carrizalillo,** 27km north of Colima. Larger, closer to the volcanoes, and more visited is **Laguna La María,** whose calm, green waters surrounded by a dense wall of plant life attract flocks of ornithologists in search of tiny yellow Singing Wilsons. If birds aren't your thing, try fishing at the shore or from a rented *lancha* (about 25 pesos per hr.). Two pesos buys access to either lagoon for a day. **Avitesa Agencia de Viajes,** Andador Constitución 43 (tel. 2-19-84), bordering Pl. Principal, can also make arrangements for *cabañas* at Laguna La María (180 pesos for up to 4 people; 200 pesos for up to 6; open Mon.-Fri. 9am-9pm, Sat. 9am-2pm).

**Getting There: Los Rojos** buses (tel. 3-60-85) destined for "San Antonio" or "Zapotitlán" leave the suburban bus station and chug up and down the mountain road to La María (7am, 1:20, 2:30, and 5pm, 1½hr., 18 pesos; buses return at 7:30am, 1:30, 3, and 4pm). Those who survive the painfully bumpy ride are rewarded with a magnificent view of the mountains just before the lagoon. To get to the entrance from the bus stop, follow the wooden sign that says "La María" (a 15min. hike). The bus back leaves from the same crossroads on the opposite side of the street.

## COMALA

South of the lagoons and just 9km north of Colima is the picturesque *pueblo* of **Comala,** known as "El Pueblo Blanco de América" (The White Town of America). Originally, all the facades in town were white, with red-tiled roofs, huge porches, and windows filled with flowers. Comala's cozy *zócalo* is surrounded by cobblestone streets and dotted with white benches, fountains, and orange trees. The south side of the *zócalo* is lined by lively restaurants in which *mariachis* perform and waiters supply patrons with a steady stream of free *botanas* (Mexican appetizers) to whet the appetite for *ponche* (warm rum and fruit punch), one of the region's vertigo-inducing traditional drinks.

Comala's main claim to fame is its colony of *indígena* artisans who craft wooden furniture, bamboo baskets, and more in accord with the dictates of pre-Hispanic traditions. The **Cooperativa Artesenal Pueblo Blanco** (tel. 4-47-90), a small *tianguis* (market), stands just outside Comala's *centro*, 200m past the restaurants on Progreso. It's a 20-minute walk from the *zócalo* (open Mon.-Fri. 8am-3pm, Sat. 9am-2pm).

To the east of the *zócalo* lies the **Iglesia San Miguel del Espíritu Santo,** whose unfinished bare-bricked rear gives it character. Watch your head as you enter, for perched above is a **sinister flock of pigeons.** Once inside, you are met not by ornate stained-glass windows but rather a sky-blue ceiling. The nave of the church is occupied by still more birds, chirping in deafening cacophony. On the other side of the *zócalo* are the city offices, where a four-wall mural commemorates Comala's 130 years as a city and celebrates the "richness of its soil." Unfortunately, the birds who have control of the church have also settled across the way, and have graciously added their own artistic expression to the mural. For more information, contact Ignacio Zamora, Director of Education, Culture, and Tourism, next door in the municipal building (tel. 5-50-22; available Mon.-Fri. 9am-1pm and 6:30-8:30pm).

**Getting There: Los Rojos** sends buses to Comala from Colima's suburban bus station (every 15min., 6am-10pm, ½hr., 3 pesos). Taxis charge about 20 pesos from Colima and, if you ask, the *taxista* may show you Colima's famous *magnético*—a segment of the road where cars may turn off their engines but still appear to run uphill. Optical illusion or miracle of science, it's loads o' fun.

# Southern Pacific Coast

Because many of the region's indigenous Purépecha lived by the rod and the net, the Aztecs dubbed the lands surrounding Lake Pátzcuaro **Michoacán** (Country of Fishermen). The distinctive Purépecha language (a variant of which is still widely spoken) and the terraced agricultural plots they built have convinced scholars that they were not originally indigenous to the area but in fact immigrants from what is today Peru. Purépecha hegemony lasted from around AD 800, when they first settled Michoacán, until the Spanish arrived in 1522. Michoacán's red, fertile soil, abundant rain, and mild weather make for bountiful crops, and agriculture swells the state's coffers. Today, many *indígenas* still dedicate their time to fishing; the forest-covered mountain ranges which surround Michoacán have attracted wildlife enthusiasts, and pretty beaches and inexpensive handicrafts have lured tourists.

The state of **Guerrero** has been blessed by fortune. During the colonial period, the rich mining town of Taxco kept not only the state but much of New Spain swimming in silver. More recently, the state's precious commodities have not come from high upon the rocky Sierra de Guerrero but rather from the rugged shores just past it, on the Pacific coast. In the 1950s, Acapulco became darling of the international resort scene; twenty-odd years later, wallflower Ixtapa and even quieter Zihuatanejo have almost managed to take their older sister's role. Today, most of the glitter has subsided, and Guerrero's beautiful colonial towns and Pacific beaches are almost as popular with budget travelers as those of the two states between which it is sandwiched.

**Oaxaca** is fractured into a crazy quilt by the rugged heights of the Sierra Madre del Sur. Despite its intimidating terrain, the land has inspired a violent possessiveness in the many people—Zapotecs, Mixtecs, Aztecs, and Spaniards—who have fought each other over the area. More than 200 indigenous tribes have occupied the valley over the past two millennia. Over one million *oaxaqueños* still speak an *indígena* language as a mother tongue, and more than one-fifth of the state's population speaks no Spanish whatsoever. This language barrier, and the cultural gap which it symbolizes and exacerbates, has long caused tensions between the Oaxacan government and its indigenous population. These tensions run through the veins of the enchanting highland colonial city of Oaxaca, a perennial tourist's favorite for its rich *indígena* culture, superb food, and sublime setting.

# MICHOACÁN DE OCAMPO

## ▓ Uruapan

Surrounded by red soil, rolling hills, and rows upon rows of avocado trees, Uruapan (pronounced ur-WA-pan, pop. 300,000) sits amid a checkerboard of farmland. Farmers and their families come to Uruapan to sell their produce and to buy bags of fried plantains, wristwatches, and other necessities of modern life. Cool mountain air and plenty of rain keep the city lush and green year-round. While Uruapan is developing into a important center of commerce, its residents still find time to relax with a cup of strong *michoacano* coffee in the city's excellent cafes. Tourists come to the Uruapan in droves to explore the nearby waterfall, national park, and Paricutín Volcano.

**Orientation** Uruapan lies 120km west of Morelia and 320km southeast of Guadalajara. Everything in town is within easy walking distance of the *zócalo,* known as **Jardín de los Mártires** on its west side and **Jardín Morelos** on its east end. The statue in the center faces south, looking down **Cupatitzio. Emiliano Carranza** runs into the southwest corner of the square from the west, and **Obregón** is its continuation on the eastern side of the plaza. **Venustiano Carranza** runs into the *zócalo*'s north side, and **Manuel Ocaranza** runs one block west of Cupatitzio into the plaza's south side. **Ocampo** runs along its western edge. To reach the center from the **bus station** on Benito Juárez in the northeast corner of town, hail a taxi (9 pesos) or hop aboard an "El Centro" bus (6am-9pm, 1.50 pesos).

**Practical Information** The friendly folks in the **tourist office,** Ocampo 64 (tel. 3-61-72), on the basement level of the Hotel Plaza Uruapan, provide a good map (open Mon.-Sat. 9am-2pm and 4-7pm, Sun. 9am-2pm). Good exchange rates and an **ATM** await at **Bancomer,** Carranza 7 (tel. 3-65-22; open Mon.-Fri. 8:30am-5:30pm, Sat. 10am-2pm). **LADATELs** line the plaza. Otherwise, make long-distance phone calls from **Computel,** Ocampo 3 (tel./fax 4-54-82), on the plaza (open 7am-10pm).

Buses leave from Benito Juárez, in the northeastern part of town, from the corner of Obregón and 5 de Febrero. To reach the station from the *zócalo,* take the "Central Camionera" or "Central" bus (1.50 pesos). A cab to the station costs 9 pesos. **Elite** (tel. 3-44-50 or 3-44-67) runs cushy first-class service to Mazatlán (5 and 7:30pm, 247 pesos), Mexico City (11:30pm, 6hr., 132 pesos), Monterrey (noon, 1, and 6:30pm, 15hr., 323 pesos), and San Luis Potosí (noon, 1, and 6:30pm, 8hr., 150 pesos). **Flecha Amarilla** (tel. 4-39-82) runs second-class buses to Aguascalientes (5:20, 7:40am, and 1pm, 8½hr., 120 pesos), Guadalajara (5 per day, 5hr., 87 pesos), Mexico City (7:30am, 7, and 10pm, 10hr., 152 pesos), Morelia (6 per day, 2hr., 37 pesos), Querétaro (5 per day, 6hr., 83 pesos), and San Luis Potosí (5, 9am, 6:10pm, and midnight, 9hr., 133 pesos). **ETN** (tel. 4-78-99) and **Primera Plus** (tel. 4-39-82) offer similar service. **La Línea** (tel. 3-18-71) is a good bet for Guadalajara (16 per day, 4½-6½hr., 68-87 pesos). **Transportes del Pacífico** (tel. 7-03-73) heads to points north. The station offers **luggage storage** (1.50 pesos per 3hr., 3 pesos per day; open daily 7am-midnight). The **train station** (tel. 4-09-81) is on Lázaro Cárdenas in the eastern part of town, and is accessible by the "Zapata" or "Zapata Revolución" buses.

**Autoservicio de Lavandería,** on Emiliano Carranza 47 at García (tel. 3-26-69), four blocks west of the *zócalo,* will wash and dry 3kg for 25 pesos (open Mon.-Sat. 9am-2pm and 4-8pm). Pharmacies rotate 24-hour shifts; call the Red Cross to find out which is on duty. **Farmacia Fénix** is on Carranza 1 at Ocampo (tel. 4-16-40; open daily 8am-9pm). The **Red Cross,** Del Lago 1 (tel. 4-03-00), is a block down from the **Hospital Civil** on Calzada Fray Juan de San Miguel 6 (tel. 3-46-60), seven blocks west of the northern edge of the *zócalo* (both open 24hr.). The **police** are at Eucaliptos and Naranjo (tel. 3-27-33). **Internet access** is available at **Logicentro,** Juárez 57 (tel. 4-94-94 or 4-77-40; email edelrio@compusep.com; email 18 pesos per 30min.; open Mon.-Sat. 9am-2pm and 5-9pm). The **post office,** on Reforma 13 (tel. 3-56-30), is three blocks south of the *zócalo* on Cupatitzio and left one block (open Mon.-Fri. 8am-7pm, Sat. 9am-1pm). **Postal Code:** 60000. **Phone Code:** 452.

**Accommodations** Uruapan's cheaper hotels oozing from the eastern edge of the *zócalo* tend to be sleazy, with tattered bedspreads, filthy bathrooms, prostitution, and a fraternity of jumbo *cucarachas* hosting 24-hour parties. Of the more reputable establishments, one of the best deals is **Hotel del Parque,** at Independencia 124 (tel. 4-38-45), 5½ blocks from the plaza and just half a block from the beautiful Parque Nacional. Clean rooms surrounding an airy patio and tree-filled *jardín* are popular with backpackers. Super-friendly *dueño* and 24-hour hot water add to the appeal (singles 50 pesos; doubles 70 pesos; 10 pesos for each additional person). Another bargain is **Hotel Los Tres Caballeros,** Constitución 50 (tel. 4-71-70). Go north up Portal Santo Degollado, the eastern border of the *zócalo,* into the market for about two blocks; the hotel is on the right. Red tile floors and stone stairways give the place old-world charm. Rooms are clean and loaded with furniture (singles 47 pesos; doubles 58 pesos). The posh **Hotel Regis,** Portal Carillo 12 (tel. 3-58-44 or 3-59-66), on the south side of the *zócalo,* offers spotless rooms, each with a TV, phone, and fan. Caged birds and sherbet-green walls covered with murals liven up the joint (singles 90 pesos; doubles 120 pesos; triples 135 pesos; quads 150 pesos; prices increase during high season).

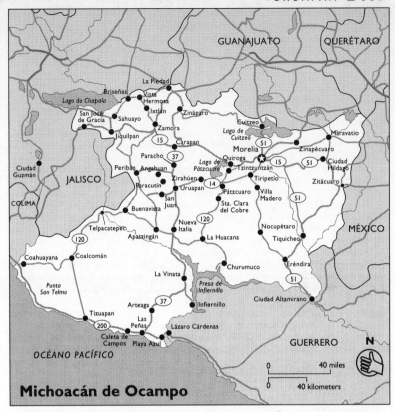

Michoacán de Ocampo

**Food** Uruapan's unique **Mercado de Antojitos,** between Constitución and Pátzcuaro y Quiroga, is an outdoor square where you can sample Michoacán specialties for a pittance. Don't miss the green chile *tamales* (2 pesos; open daily 7am-11pm). Hotel restaurants, like **Restaurant Fonda de la Villa,** in Hotel Villa de Flores, Carranza 15 (tel. 4-28-00; open 8am-10pm), are the most common option for a sit-down meal, and cafes specializing in coffees and desserts unleash their aromas up and down Carranza. Follow your nose to the **Café Tradicional de Uruapan,** Carranza 5B, where locals sit sipping their *café* so slowly that they might lose a race with a Mexican train. Dining here is like sitting inside a cigar box—the cafe's entire surface area is covered in richly stained wood, from the wood bannisters to the checkered ceilings and floors. Specialties are breakfast, snacks, and coffee. *Huevos rancheros* 11 pesos, *capuchino* 6.50 pesos (open daily 8:30am-10pm).

**Sights and Entertainment** The stunning **Parque Nacional Barranca del Cupatitzio,** at the western end of Independencia (tel. 4-01-97), should not be missed. A bit of jungle right on the edge of town, the park boasts frothy waterfalls, dense vegetation, and seemingly endless cool, shaded cobblestone walkways. The park makes for an excellent afternoon walk or picnic (open daily 8am-6pm; admission 2 pesos, children 1 peso). Uruapan's other attraction is the **Museo Regional de Arte Popular** (tel. 4-34-34), on the *zócalo,* which displays Michoacán crafts (open Tues.-Sun. 9:30am-1:30pm and 3:30-6pm; free).

Much of the after-hours scene is set in cafes, where locals spend hours chatting over strong and tasty coffee. The main *discoteca* in town is **La Scala Disco,** Madrid 12 (tel. 4-26-09), in Colonia Huerta del Cupatitzio, a bit outside of town on the road to

Tzaráracua and an 9-peso cab ride from the center of town. A young, local crowd dances to U.S. top-40 and Mexican dance tunes (cover Tues.-Thurs. 10 pesos, Fri.-Sat. 20 pesos; open Tues.-Fri. 9pm-2am). For a more low-key evening, saunter over to **Club 1910,** Cupatitzio 5 (tel. 3-20-25), less than a block from the *zócalo,* for some pool (12 pesos per hr.) or dominoes (6 pesos per hr.; open daily 10am-11pm).

# ■ Near Uruapan

## PARICUTÍN VOLCANO

A visit to the beautiful, black, still-active Paricutín Volcano makes a great daytrip from Uruapan. In 1943, the volcano began erupting. By the time it quit spewing lava eight years later, there was little dust left to settle—the land had been coated in a thick and hardening layer of porous lava. Along the way, entire towns had been consumed and a 700m dark-side-of-the-moon sort of mountain had sprung up. In one area, the lava covered the entire village of San Juan except for the church steeple, which now sticks out of a field of cold, black stone. The volcano's summit can be reached by foot and affords a spectacular view of the surrounding land and mountains. Numerous steaming hot-spots serve as a reminder of its might.

At the Angahuan **Centro Turístico** (tel. (452) 5-03-83), you can rent **horses** and a **guide** to ascend the volcano (100 pesos). Plan to get an early start to avoid afternoon thunderstorms, and bring along some warm clothing just in case. The trip is long, but worth the time and pesos. Decathlon contenders may consider the six- to eight-hour **walking tours** (30-40 pesos). Save yourself the centro's 8 peso entrance fee by arranging for your guide independently. Cabins also available for rent (1-6 people 250 pesos); 40 pesos buys a bunk in a communal cabin.

**Getting There: Paraíso Galeana** buses (tel. 4-33-50) headed for Los Reyes run to Angahuán (every 30min., 5am-8pm, 40min., 7 pesos).

## SAN JUAN NUEVO PARANGARICUTIRO

Ten kilometers west of Uruapan is the new **San Juan,** formed after the burial of the old village with the eruption of the Paricutín Volcano in 1934. Many devotees come to the village to see the **Lord of Miracles,** an image of Christ dating back to the late 16th century. The image is revered for answering countless prayers and miracles. When the volcano erupted, San Juan's 2000 inhabitants abandoned the village and began a three-day, 33km pilgrimage carrying their beloved Lord of Miracles. A beautiful rose brick **sanctuary** with blue and yellow tile *capillas* was eventually built to house the image. The interior's white walls and vaulted ceilings are adorned with gold leafing, delicate stained-glass windows, and sparkling chandeliers. Several colorful murals depict the figure's history and the eruption of the Paricutín volcano (open daily 6am-8pm; don't be a rude mass-interruptin' punk!). The **museum,** Av. 20 de Noviembre, around the corner from the sanctuary, exhibits photos depicting the volcano's eruption, as well as before-and-after shots of the village (open Mon.-Sat. 9:15am-7pm, Sun. 9:15-6:30pm; free).

At Uruapan's Parque Nacional Barranca del Cupatitzio, young children will give you a tour of **La Rodilla del Diablo** (The Devil's Knee) for a small fee. Legend has it that the river at one time dried up, leaving the people without food or water. One day, the friar Juan de San Miguel sprinkled some holy water on the Virgin's image and on the rocks at the river's mouth. Suddenly, Satan appeared, saw the Virgin, and with a tumultuous shaking of the earth, retreated into the rocks, resuming the flow of water. One rock still bears the imprint of the knee of the *Príncipe de la Tinieblas* (Prince of Darkness).

**Getting There:** Take a **Galeana** (tel. 4-33-50) bus to San Juan Nuevo (every 10min., 5am-9:30pm, 30min., 4 pesos).

## TZARÁRACUA AND TZARARECUITA

The waterfalls at **Tzaráracua** (sah-RA-ra-kwa), 10km from Uruapan, cascade 20m into a series of small pools, surrounded by dense lush vegetation. The first waterfall, Tzaráracua, is about 1km from the small parking lot—walk or ride a horse through steep, tree-lined paths (guides and horses await tourists at the lot). Expect to pay 25 pesos round-trip to the first waterfall. You can also hoof it to the waterfall on foot—the path descends a flight of cobbled stairs and culminates at the base of the falls after about 20 minutes. Look, but don't swim; there's a dangerous undercurrent. Use the recently-completed bridge (dig the view) or ask a worker to take you over the water in a suspended boxcar (2 pesos).

**Tzararecuita,** a privately-owned waterfall with two smaller pollution-free pools that are perfect for swimming, is another 1.5km beyond the large pool. Rumor has it that the owner doesn't mind visitors to the falls and that skinny-dipping is popular. Keep an eye on your clothes. The aid of a guide is necessary to find the falls; guides don't charge a set fee but expect a generous tip.

**Getting There:** "Tzaráracua" buses leave from the south side of the *zócalo* at the corner of Emiliano Carranza and Cupatitzio (every hr., 8am-5pm, 2.50 pesos). During the week, the schedule is so imprecise that you could be stuck there all day; Sundays are a bit more reliable. Taxis cost about 20 pesos.

## PARACHO

Thirty kilometers north of Uruapan, **Paracho** gives aspiring *guitarristas* a chance to strum their hearts out and unleash the *mariachi* within. Carefully crafted six-strings pack just about every store. Fantastic bargains are available for all varieties of guitar. In the first week of August the town holds an internationally renowned **guitar festival.** Musicians and craftspeople partake in a **musical orgy** that includes classical concerts, fireworks, dancing, and guitar-strumming competitions.

**Getting There:** Hop on a **Galeana** (tel. 4-33-50) bus bound for Zamora via Paracho (every 15min., 4am-8:30pm, 45min., 7 pesos) from the Central Camionera.

# ▓ Pátzcuaro

Michoacán's earthy jewel, Pátzcuaro (pop. 70,000), is slowly becoming a travelers' favorite. Set high in the mountaintops, the city is surrounded by land that bends and lilts, rolling up and over hills and extending to the shores of the expansive (and unfortunately polluted) Lake Pátzcuaro. The city center is nearly as striking as the surrounding landscape—the tolling of the bells resonates through cobblestone streets and white stucco colonial-style buildings. But Pátzcuaro is best known for its crafts. In order to further economic development, the Spanish bishop Vasco de Quiroga encouraged residents of each Purépecha village around the lake to specialize in a different craft. Today Pátzcuaro's plazas overflow with stacks of locally-produced woolen sweaters, meticulously carved wooden toys, and decorative masks.

## ORIENTATION

Pátzcuaro lies 56km southwest of Morelia and 62km northeast of Uruapan. To reach the *centro* from the **bus station,** catch a *combi* (7am-9:30pm, 2 pesos) or city bus (6:30am-10pm, 2 pesos) from the lot to the right as you leave the station. A taxi costs 10 pesos. The city consists of two distinct areas: the downtown, perched on a hill, and a residential part of town 2.5km to the north, fronting the lake. Downtown centers around Pátzcuaro's two main squares. The smaller **Plaza Bocanegra** is all bustle and thick crowds; it is bordered by **Padre Lloreda** to the north, **Dr. Bendito Mendoza** to the west, and **Iturbide** to the east. One block south on Dr. Benito Mendoza is the larger **Plaza Quiroga,** an elegant and quiet plaza with a fountain and well-shaded, rosebush-lined paths. Streets form a rough grid, changing names at each plaza. Addresses on the plazas are not given with the street name, but rather with the name of the *portal* (arcade). For example, at Plaza Quiroga, Benito Mendoza, which borders the plaza's western side, becomes **Portal Hidalgo.** Summers in Pátzcuaro can be wet and cool, so bring along some rain gear and a light sweater.

## PRACTICAL INFORMATION

**Tourist Office: Delegación Regional de Turismo,** Plaza Quiroga 50A (tel. 2-12-14). Staff speaks English and hands out a good map. Open Mon.-Sat. 9am-2pm and 4-7pm, Sun. 9am-2pm. A smaller **information booth** is on the west side of Pl. Quiroga, in Portal Hidalgo. Open daily 10am-2pm and 5-8pm.

**Currency Exchange: Banca Serfín,** Portal Morelos 54 (tel. 2-15-16), on the north side of Plaza Quiroga, has an **ATM** (open for exchange Mon.-Fri. 9am-2pm). **Sociedad Cambiaria Pátzcuaro,** Benito Mendoza 7 (tel. 2-02-40), also changes dollars. Open Mon.-Fri. 9am-4:30pm, Sat.-Sun. 10am-2pm.

**Telephones: LADATELs** can be found in the public library. There are public phones on the west side of Pl. Quiroga and in the bus station.

**Fax:** In the *caseta* in the bus station. Open daily 7am-9pm.

**Buses:** Off Circunvalación, 8 blocks south of the *centro.* **Herradura de Plata** (tel. 2-10-45) runs to Mexico City (1st class 10 per day, 8:15am-11pm, 5hr., 120 pesos; 2nd class 8 per day, 7:35am-9:50pm, 7hr., 109 pesos). **Galeana** (tel. 2-08-08) goes to Lázaro Cárdenas (every 2hr., 5:30am-9pm, 7hr., 70 pesos), Morelia (every 10min., 1hr., 17 pesos), and Uruapan (every 10min., 1½hr., 18 pesos). **Primera Plus** (tel. 2-01-70) has cushy service to Guadalajara (11:30pm, 5hr., 85 pesos), Mexico City (8 and 11:30am, 7hr., 120 pesos), Querétaro (11am and 1:40pm, 7hr., 75 pesos), and San Luis Potosí (10am, 8hr., 140 pesos). **Autobuses de Occidente** (tel. 2-00-92) sends buses to Guadalajara (12:15pm, 5hr., 85 pesos). **Elite** (tel. 2-14-60) goes to Nuevo Laredo (1 and 7:45pm, 16hr., 399 pesos) via Monterrey (14hr., 314 pesos). **Luggage Storage** available (3 pesos per 1½hr., 6 pesos per day). Open 7am-10pm.

**Trains:** At the bottom of Av. de las Américas (tel. 2-08-03), near the lakefront.

**Public Library:** On Pl. Bocanegra in the Ex-Templo de San Agustín. Small selection of English books. **LADATEL** inside. Open Mon.-Fri. 9am-7pm.

**Laundromat: Lavandería Automática,** Terán 14 (tel. 2-39-39), 2 blocks west of Plaza Quiroga. Open Mon.-Sat. 9am-8pm.

**Pharmacy: Principal,** Benito Mendoza 1, off Pl. Bocanegra. Open daily 9am-10pm. **Farmacia del Carmen** at the corner of Romero and Navarrete (tel. 2-26-52). Open 24hr. Doors open daily 8am-10pm; after hours, knock at the window on Navarrete.

**Hospital: Hospital Civil,** Romero 10 (tel. 2-02-85), next to San Juan de Dios church.

**Emergency: Cuerpo de Rescate,** (tel. 2-21-65). Open 24hr.

**Police:** On the corner of Ibarra and Tangara (tel. 2-00-04), 4 blocks from Pl. Quiroga.

**Post Office:** Obregón 13 (tel. 2-01-28), ½ block north of Pl. Bocanegra. Open Mon.-Fri. 8am-7pm, Sat. 9am-1pm. **Postal Code:** 61600.

**Phone Code:** 434.

## ACCOMMODATIONS

Pátzcuaro is home to a surprising number of hotels. Budget accommodations tend to be adequately kept and fairly priced. Expect to lodge with large numbers of Mexican, European, and some American travelers. The three rooms for rent at the **Mandala** restaurant (see below) are the best bargain in town. If you're lucky enough to find one open, you can enjoy super clean, beautiful rooms around a plant-filled courtyard and a complimentary breakfast, including homemade yogurt, for 50 pesos.

**Hotel Valmen,** Lloreda 34 (tel. 2-11-61), 1 block east of Pl. Bocanegra. Popular with international travelers. A great deal if you don't mind a mushy bed. Vibrant Aztec tile fills the lime-green courtyards. Well-lit rooms, some with balconies. Strict lockout 10pm. 40 pesos per person.

**Posada de la Rosa,** Portal Juárez 29, 2nd fl. (tel. 2-08-11), on the west side of Pl. Bocanegra. Red tiles and lots of sunlight. Simple rooms have a lone lightbulb hanging from the ceiling. Ask for a room overlooking the plaza. Singles and doubles 40 pesos, with bath 50 pesos.

**Pátzcuaro**

HOTELS &
RESTAURANTS
Hotel Valmen, 5
Mandala, 20
Posada de la Rosa, 3
Posada de la Salud, 8
Rest. El Monje, 17
Rest. Los Escudos, 12
Rest. Posada la Basilica, 6

SIGHTS & SERVICES
Basilica, 7
Casa de los Once
Patios, 19
Plazuela de San
Fransisco, 14
Hospital, 16
Laundry, 15
Mercado, 2
Museo, 9
Pharmacy, 18
Plaza Bocanegra, 4
Plaza Quiroga, 10
Police, 13
Post Office, 1
Tourist Office, 11

**Posada de la Salud,** Serrato 9 (tel. 2-00-58), 3 blocks east of either plaza, half a block past the basilica. Beautiful courtyard draped in tropical scarlet flowers, gorgeous carved furniture, cloud-soft mattresses, and clean bathrooms. Rooms can be cold and damp during the rainy season. Singles 80 pesos; doubles 120 pesos.

## FOOD

*Pescado blanco* is the most popular dish in Pátzcuaro. *Charales* (smelts), served in the restaurants along the lakefront and on Janitzio, are fried, sardine-like fish which are eaten whole and by the fistful. *Caldos de pescado* (fish broths) bubble in large clay vats outside open-air restaurants on Janitzio; loaded with fish, shrimp, crab, or squid, these spicy soups are a meal in themselves. Family-run *comedores* charging around 10 pesos for a full meal abound on Janitzio. More formal restaurants ring Plaza Quiroga, while the cheaper, more casual joints cluster around Plaza Bocanegra and the market.

**Mandala,** Lerín 14 (tel. 2-41-76), just behind the Casa de los Once Patios. Scrumptious and filling vegetarian *menú* includes soup, salad, a tasty entree, and dessert (25 pesos). Homemade whole wheat spaghetti (20 pesos) and organic veggies make for a new-age eating experience. Open Thurs.-Tues. 10am-8:30pm.

**Restaurant Los Escudos,** Portal Hidalgo 73 (tel. 2-12-90), on the west side of Pl. Quiroga, inside the Hotel Los Escudos. Linen tablecloths, attentive staff, and fresh flowers make for a relaxing atmosphere. Tasty food at reasonable prices. *Sopa tarasca* 10 pesos. *Comida corrida* 25 pesos. Take in a performance of the *danza de los viejitos* with your dinner Sat. at 8pm. Open daily 8am-10:30pm.

**Restaurant El Monje,** Portal Aldama 12 (tel. 2-13-13), on Pl. Quiroga. Outdoor tables are perfect for people-watching. Breakfasts 13-23 pesos; *enchiladas suizas* 18 pesos; steak *a la mexicana* 26 pesos. Open daily 8am-10pm.

**Restaurant Posada la Basílica,** Arciga 6 (tel. 2-11-08), in front of the basilica. A flowery courtyard leads to an elegant room with tiled floors, colorful tablecloths, and windows overlooking the town and nearby lakes. Steak *a la Mexicana* 25 pesos. Not the most inexpensive place in town, but the view is worth it. Open Wed.-Mon. 8am-5pm.

## SIGHTS

Pátzcuaro's unique handcrafts—hairy Tócuaro masks, elegant Sierran dinnerware, and thick wool textiles—are sold in Plaza Bocanegra's **market** and in the small shops along the passage next to Biblioteca Gertrudis Bocanegra. Bargaining is easier in the market or when you buy more than one item, but don't expect much of a discount on the stunningly handsome wool articles. The thick sweaters, brilliantly colored *saltillos* and *ruanas* (stylized ponchos), rainbow-colored *sarapes,* and dark shawls are Pátzcuaro's specialty. Most shops are open daily 8am to 8pm.

Some higher quality (though pricier) items may also be found in the **Casa de Artesanías,** (a.k.a. La Casa de los Once Patios, so named for the 18th-century building's 11 patios), down the street from the basilica, on Lerín near Navarette. Originally a convent for Dominican nuns, the complex now houses craft shops, a small gallery of modern Mexican art, and a mural depicting Vasco de Quiroga's accomplishments. The *casa* sells cotton textiles, wooden and copper crafts, and superb musical instruments (guitars, flutes, and *güiros*) at decent prices (guitars 150-700 pesos; open daily roughly 10am-2pm and 4-8pm). The **Museo Regional de Artes Populares** at the corner of Lerín and Alcanterillas (tel. 2-10-29), one block south of the basilica, is housed within old fort-like walls, stone floors, and a flower-filled arcaded courtyard. It displays pottery, copperware, and textiles, as well as an arresting collection of *maque* and *laca* ceramics (open Tues.-Sat. 9am-7pm, Sun. 9am-2:30pm; admission 14 pesos, free Sun. and for children under 13).

**Biblioteca Gertrudis Bocanegra,** on the plaza of the same name, occupies the former site of an Augustine convent. The library's multicolored mural illustrates the history of the Purépecha civilization from pre-Hispanic times to the 1910 Revolution (open Mon.-Fri. 9am-7pm). When the adjacent **Teatro Caltzontzín** (tel. 2-04-52), once part of the Augustinian convent, became a theater in 1936, an as-yet-unfulfilled prophecy was uttered: one Holy Thursday, the theater will crumble as punishment for the sin of projecting movies in a sacred place. Movies are still shown occasionally; catch a Mexican or U.S. film, if you dare (admission 5 pesos).

Statues of Pátzcuaro's two most honored citizens stand vigil over the town's principal plazas. The ceremonious, banner-bearing Vasco de Quiroga inhabits **Plaza Quiroga,** a vast and well-forested space which seems more like a humble city zoo than a *zócalo*. The massive, bare-breasted Gertrudis Bocanegra looks out from the center of **Plaza Gertrudis Bocanegra.** A martyr for Mexican independence, Bocanegra was executed by a Spanish squadron in the Plaza Quiroga in October of 1817. Locals claim that bullet holes still mark the ash tree to which she was tied.

When the Spanish bishop Vasco de Quiroga came to Pátzcuaro, he initiated not only social change but bold architectural projects as well. Quiroga conceived the **Basílica de Nuestra Señora de la Salud,** at Lerín and Serrato, as a colossal structure with five naves arranged like the fingers of an extended hand. Each finger was to represent one of Michoacán's cultures and races, with the hand's palm as the central altar representing the Catholic religion. Today, an enormous glass booth with gilded Corinthian columns and a dome protects the potentially edible statue of the *Virgen de la Salud*. When Vasco de Quiroga asked Tarascan artisans to design an image of the Virgin in 1546, they complied by shaping her out of *tatzingue* paste made from corn cobs and orchid honey, a typical 16th-century statue-making technique. The resulting statue is durable and incredibly light—only 5kg (open daily 8am-8pm).

Three kilometers east of the city, at the end of Av. Benigno Serrato, is **El Humillad-ero** (Place of Humiliation), where the cowardly king Tangaxhuán II surrendered his crown and his daughters to Cristóbal de Olid and his Spanish troops. Two peculiar features distinguish this chapel: on its altar stands a rare monolithic cross, undoubt-edly older than the date inscribed on its base (1553); and on the chapel's facade are images of gods which represent the sun and the moon. To reach it, take a *combi* marked "Panteón" or "El Cristo" (2 pesos).

## ENTERTAINMENT AND SEASONAL EVENTS

Aside from chilling in restaurants, there isn't much to do in Pátzcuaro at night. At **Charanda's N,** Plaza Vasco de Quiroga 61B, local students and aging intellectuals match wits in chess tournaments amid wood carvings and potted plants. Live music stirs things up on weekends (cover Sat.-Sun. 8-11pm 10 pesos; open Tues.-Sun. noon-1am). The off-beat **El Viejo Gaucho,** Iturbe 10 (tel. 2-03-68), a colorful Argentinian bar and restaurant with mask and painting exhibitions, features live Andean music, dra-matic readings, and an open mike (cover 10 pesos; open Tues.-Sun. 5pm-2am).

Pátzcuaro parties just about year-round. Its biggest celebration is without a doubt the spectacular **Noche de Muertos** (Nov. 1-2), which holds special importance for the Tarascans. Tourists from around the globe flock to Pátzcuaro and Janitzio to watch candle-lit fishing boats process to the tiny island. There families and neighbors keep a two-night vigil in the haunting graveyard, feasting at the graves of their loved ones. The first night commemorates lost children; the second remembers deceased adults. Soon after Christmas celebrations come to a close, the town is electrified by **Pastorelas,** celebrated on January 6 to commemorate the Adoration of the Magi, and on January 17 to honor St. Anthony of Abad, the patron saint of animals. On both occasions, citizens dress their domestic animals in bizarre costumes, ribbons, and flo-ral crowns. A few months later, Pátzcuaro's **Semana Santa** attracts devotees from all over the Republic. On Thursday, all the churches in town are visited to accompany the Nazareth, and on the night of Good Friday, the **Procesión de Imágenes de Cristo** is held, during which images of a crucified Christ are carried around town. The faith-ful flock from all over the state on Saturday for Pátzcuaro's **Procesión del Silencio,** celebrated everywhere else the day before. On this day, a crowd marches around town mourning Jesus's death in silence. Pátzcuaro and the surrounding regions party down with religious fervor on Sunday.

# ■ Near Pátzcuaro

## AROUND LAGO DE PÁTZCUARO

The tiny island of **Janitzio,** inhabited exclusively by Tarascan *indígenas* whose first language is Purépecha, subsists on its tourist trade. There are basically two directions in Janitzio—up and down. The town's steep main street is lined with stores selling woolen goods, hand-carved wooden chess sets, masks, and assorted knick-knacks. Between the shops, the bulk of which are quite pricey, numerous restaurants offer 10-peso meals of fresh *pescado blanco* and *charales*. A low hill towers over the island; atop it is a statue of Morelos so big it can be seen clearly from Pátzcuaro. Inside the statue, a mural traces the principal events in Morelos's life and the struggle for independence that he led. Morelos may not hold the world in the palm of his hand, but you can certainly see the world from his sleeve. Endless steps lead you to this fan-tastic lookout point. There are two paths to the monument—one steep, and the other steeper (and more direct); both are to your left as you leave the ferry docks (admission 2.50 pesos).

**Getting There:** First, hop on a "Lago" *combi* or bus at the corner of Portal Regules and Portal Juárez, at Plaza Bocanegra in Pátzcuaro (2 pesos). At the docks, buy a ferry ticket (ferries leave whenever they're full, 8am-6pm, 40min., 18 pesos round-trip). Find out when the last boat leaves the island for Pátzcuaro, as Janitzio does not accommodate the stranded.

## TZINTZUNTZÁN

The most exciting thing about **Tzintzuntzán** (Place of the Hummingbirds) may be saying the name—it is believed to be the phonetic sound of the many **hummingbirds** that flit through the sky. Tzintzuntzán was the last great city of the Tarascan empire. Before his death in the middle of the 15th century, the Purépecha lord Tariácori divided his empire among his three sons. When the empire was reunited some years later, Tzintzuntzán was chosen as its capital. Today, its claims to fame are the delicate, multicolored **ceramics** displayed on tables along Calle Principal.

**Yácatas**, a collection of peculiar pre-Hispanic temples, sits on a hill just outside the city on the road to Pátzcuaro. To reach the entrance, walk up the street in front of the market and convent. It's a bit of a hike—follow the road all the way around the hill until you reach the small museum/ticket booth. The bases of the structures, all that remain today, are standard rectangular pyramids. The missing parts, however, are what made them unique; each was originally crowned with an unusual elliptical pyramid constructed of shingles and volcanic rock. The pyramids are situated along the long edge of an artificial terrace. At the edge of the hill overlooking the lake is a sacrificial block from which victims were hurled; the bones of thousands of victims are said to lie at the base. The **Instituto Nacional de Anthropologia e Historia** at the entrance includes some Mesoamerican pottery, jewelry, and a narrative of Tarascan history (site open daily 9am-6pm; admission 10 pesos, free Sun.). Also of interest is the 16th-century Franciscan **convent** closer to town. The olive shrubs that now smother the extensive, tree-filled atrium were originally planted under Vasco de Quiroga's instructions over 450 years ago (open daily 10am-8pm).

**Getting There:** Tzintzuntzán is perched on the northeastern edge of the Lago de Pátzcuaro, about 15km from Pátzcuaro on the road to Quiroga and Morelia. Second-class **Galeana** (tel. 2-08-08) buses leave the Pátzcuaro bus station for Tzintzuntzán (every 15min., 6am-8:30pm, ½hr., 4 pesos) en route to Quiroga.

### SANTA CLARA DEL COBRE

**Santa Clara del Cobre,** 16km south of Pátzcuaro, truly shines when it comes to crafting copper. Long ago, rich copper mines filled the area, but they were hidden from the Spanish during the Conquest, never to be found again. The townspeople's passion for copperwork is unrivaled. When electricity was brought to the town, blackouts occurred when the artisans hammered the wires into pots and pans. Nearly every store in town sells unique decorative copper plates, pans, bowls, and bells. Prices here are only slightly better than elsewhere in Mexico, but Santa Clara is unbeatable for quality and variety. For a quick look at some highly imaginative pieces, step into the **Museo del Cobre,** near the plaza. Santa Clara celebrates the **Feria del Cobre** in early August. Like Quiroga, there is little to see in Santa Clara beyond *artesanías;* budget only a couple of hours for a trip here from Pátzcuaro.

**Getting There:** Take a **Galeana** bus from Lago de Zirahuén (every ½hr., 7am-8pm, 20min., 3 pesos).

### LAGO DE ZIRAHUÉN

If you have wet weather camping gear, the **Lago de Zirahuén** (Where Smoke Rose) makes for a fun trip from Pátzcuaro. Smaller than Lake Pátzcuaro, Zirahuén is bordered by green farmland and gently sloping hills unobstructed by marshes and islands. On weekends, the lakefront fills with locals in search of a *tranquilo* place to relax. To **camp,** hike up one of the ridges that border the lake and set up in any one of the spots overlooking the water; if the land is privately owned (usually fenced off), you may have to pay a few pesos. Ask before you pitch your tent. Another choice spot is the sizeable piece of lakefront on the west (left, as you face the lake) end of town. The strip, about 15m wide, is covered by grass cut short by grazing horses. The *cabañas,* a five-minute walk to the right along the dirt road bordering the lake, allow campers to use the bathrooms for 1 peso. Be forewarned: heavy afternoon rains during June and July can turn summer camping into a soggy experience.

After roughing it in the great outdoors, head to the *lancha* dock for a silky smooth one-hour ride around the lake (15 pesos in a collective boat; 120 pesos for a private ride, up to 10 people), then sit down at one of informal lakefront restaurants, where a stack of tortillas, rice, salad, and fresh fish will run you a mere 10 pesos.

**Getting There:** From Pátzcuaro, catch one of the Zirahuén-bound cabs from Obregón and Industrial, past the post office, a block north of Plaza Bocanegra (about every 20min., 8am-6pm, 9 pesos). Cabs returning to Pátzcuaro leave a block inland from the church at "La Posta," by the "Marilu" sign (about 15 pesos).

# ■ Morelia

At 500,000 inhabitants and growing fast, Morelia is a bustling city caught up in a dizzying whirl of growth and development. Sophisticated clothing stores and American fast-food joints squeeze in among colonial houses and imposing stone facades along the main streets. Vendors hawk traditional textiles and wooden crafts alongside bootleg cassettes, Levi's knock-offs, and spare blender parts in the crowded *centro;* nearby stand incongruous relics of Morelia's colonial magnificence—rose-colored stone arcades and grand, white-washed houses. A sizeable student population spices up the cultural scene with theater and dance productions and concerts. Blue exhaust clouds detract somewhat from the charm of Morelia's cobblestone side streets, but its bustling, eminently habitable spirit and sophisticated aura stimulate visitors without drawing crowds.

## ORIENTATION

The streets in Morelia form a large grid, so navigating the city is relatively uncomplicated. Most sights are within walking distance of the *zócalo* and the adjacent cathedral on **Av. Madero,** Morelia's main thoroughfare. North-south streets change name at Madero, while east-west streets change name every other block.

Getting downtown from the **bus station** is a quick 10-minute walk. Walk to the left (east) as you exit the building, take the first right onto Valentín Gómez Farías, walk three blocks, then make a left on Av. Madero—the *zócalo* is three blocks ahead. A taxi to the *centro* costs 8-10 pesos.

Buses and *combis* serve the city (daily 6am-10pm, 1.80 pesos). Most routes can be picked up on Nigromante and Galeana, one block west of the *zócalo,* and on Allende, south of the *zócalo.* Taxis cluster in front of the bus station. Morelia's streets empty out after 10pm, especially on streets parallel to Madero; consider the safety of a taxi.

## PRACTICAL INFORMATION

**Tourist Office: State Tourist Office,** Nigromante 79 at Madero Pte. (tel. 17-23-71), 2 blocks west of the *zócalo.* Staff distributes maps and a monthly list of cultural events. Free city tours Sun. 11am. Open Mon.-Fri. 8am-8pm, Sat.-Sun. 9am-8pm.

**Currency Exchange:** Banks cluster on Av. Madero near the cathedral. **Bancomer,** Madero Ote. 21 (tel. 12-29-90). Open Mon.-Fri. 8am-7pm, Sat. 9am-2pm. **BITAL,** Madero Ote. 24 (tel 13-98-00). Open Mon-Fri. 8am-7pm, Sat. 9am-2:30pm.

**Telephones:** Credit card-operated **LADATELs** are at Pino Suárez and Serdán, 1 block east of the *zócalo.* 24hr. long-distance *caseta* in the bus station, but no collect calls. **Fax: Computel,** Portal Galeana 157 (tel./fax 13-62-56), on the *zócalo* (open daily 7am-10pm). Also, Av. Madero Ote. 371 (tel. 13-86-72), in the Palacio Federal next to the post office. Open Mon.-Fri. 8am-8pm.

**Airport: Aeropuerto Francisco J. Múgica** on the Carretera Morelia-Cinapécuaro at km 27 (tel. 12-65-14). **Mexicana,** Pirindas 435 (tel. 24-38-08 or 24-38-18). Open Mon.-Fri. 9am-6:30pm. **Taesa,** Av. Acueducto 60 (tel. 13-40-50). Open Mon.-Fri. 9am-2pm and 4-7pm, Sat. 9am-1pm. **Aeromar** (tel. 12-85-45 and 13-05-55). All have offices at the airport. Taxi (tel. 12-22-21) to the airport 85 pesos.

**Buses:** Leave from the **Central** station on Ruiz at V. Gómez Farías (tel. 13-55-89). **Herradura de Plata** (tel. 12-29-88) goes to Mexico City (1st class 13 per day, 12:30am-11pm, 4½hr., 98 pesos; *plus* 22 per day, 4hr., 110 pesos). **Flecha Amarilla** (tel. 13-55-89) goes to Colima (7:40am and noon, 6½hr., 116 pesos), Guanajuato (every hr., 5:30am-4:30pm, 4hr., 55 pesos), Querétaro (12 per day, 4hr., 50 pesos), and San Luis Potosí (8 per day, 7:10am-8:30pm, 6hr., 107 pesos). **Ruta Paraíso/Galeana** (tel. 12-55-05) goes to Lázaro Cárdenas (every hr., 6:40am-7:50pm, 8hr., 105 pesos), Pátzcuaro (every 10min., 6am-9pm, 1hr., 17 pesos), and Uruapan (every 20min., 6am-9pm, 2¼hr., 37 pesos). **Elite** (tel. 12-24-62) sends buses to Acapulco (2nd class 5 per day, 7-2:30am, 12hr., 196 pesos), Nuevo Laredo (3, 6, and 9:30pm, 16hr., 428 pesos) via Monterrey (13hr., 331 pesos), Reynosa (5pm, 16hr., 364 pesos) via San Luis Potosí (6hr., 135 pesos), and Tijuana (1:15, 9, and 11:45pm, 40hr., 787 pesos) via Mazatlán (16hr., 288 pesos). **Transportes Fronteras** (tel. 12-24-62) serves Cd. Juárez (10:30am, 24hr., 563 pesos) via Zacatecas (9hr., 166 pesos). **Primera Plus** (tel. 13-55-89) runs 1st-class buses to Aguascalientes (2:30, 8:05am, 12:05, and 3:05pm, 6hr., 123 pesos), Guadalajara (9am, 1, 3:30pm, and midnight, 5hr., 108 pesos), Mexico City (8 per day, 4½hr., 110 pesos), and San Luis Potosí (8 per day, 6hr., 132 pesos). **Servicios Coordinados** (tel. 13-55-89) serves Aguascalientes (10:15am and 2pm, 6hr., 103 pesos), Guadalajara (8 per day, 5hr., 92 pesos), Querétaro (13 per day, 5:20am-7:20pm, 3½hr., 55 pesos), and San Luis Potosì (11 per day, 2am-3:20pm, 6hr., 120 pesos). **Autobuses de Occidente/La Linea** has 2nd-class service to Manzanillo (5 per day, 6:45-1:15am, 10hr., 129 pesos) and Mexico City (every 20min., 6hr., 80 pesos). **ETN** (tel. 13-74-40) has executive service to Manzanillo (10:30pm, 7¼hr., 195 pesos) and Mexico City (24 per day, 2am-midnight, 4hr., 155 pesos). **Parhikuni** (tel. 13-99-10) sends 1st-class and *plus* buses to Lázaro Cárdenas (10 per day, 6:20am-1:30am, 8hr., 115-123 pesos) and Uruapan (every 20min., 6am-8pm, otherwise every hr., 2hr., 40-43 pesos).

**Trains:** On Av. del Periodismo (tel. 16-39-65).

**Laundromat: Lavandería Cuautla,** Cuautla 152 (tel. 12-48-96), south of Madero. 16 pesos to wash/dry 3kg. Open Mon.-Fri. 9am-2pm and 4-8pm, Sat. 9am-1:30pm.

**Red Cross:** Ventura 27 (tel. 14-51-51 or 14-50-25), next to Parque Cuauhtémoc. Some English spoken. Open 24hr.

**Pharmacy: Farmacia Fénix,** Allende 69 (tel. 12-84-92), behind the *zócalo.* Open Mon.-Sat. 9am-9pm, Sun. 9am-8:30pm. Red Cross has a **24hr. pharmacy** (tel. 14-51-51, ext. 18).

**Hospital: Hospital General Dr. Miguel Silva,** Isidro Huarte and F. de Mogil (tel. 12-01-02). Open 24hr.

**Emergency:** Dial 06.

**Police:** On 20 de Noviembre (tel. 12-00-73 or 12-22-22), 1 block northwest of the Fuente de las Tarascas at the end of the aqueduct. Open 24hr.

**Post Office:** Av. Madero Ote. 369 (tel. 12-05-17), in the Palacio Federal, 5 blocks east of the cathedral. Open Mon.-Fri. 8am-7pm. **Postal Code:** 58000.

**Phone Code:** 43.

## ACCOMMODATIONS

Most budget hotels lie south of Madero and just west of the cathedral. The only time you may have trouble finding a room is during Semana Santa, although there is a slight influx of summer school students during July and August.

**IMJUDE Villa Juvenil Youth Hostel,** Chiapas 180 at Oaxaca (tel. 13-31-77). A 20min. walk from the *zócalo.* Walk west on Madero Pte., turn left on Cuautla, walk for 6 blocks, then turn right on Oaxaca and continue for 4 blocks to Chiapas. Very happening for a Mexican youth hostel. Exceptionally well-maintained dormitories, bathrooms, and red-tiled lobby. Sports facilities and pool. Curfew 11pm. 30 pesos per person. 50-peso linen deposit. Breakfast 12.50 pesos, lunch and dinner 15 pesos. 25% discount for HI members. Open daily 7am-11pm.

**Hotel Mintzicuri,** Vasco de Quiroga 227 (tel. 12-06-64), 2 blocks east and 1½ blocks south of the cathedral. Wrought iron railings overflowing with flowers enclose

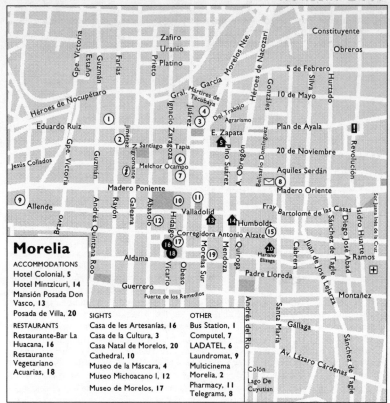

**Morelia**

ACCOMMODATIONS
Hotel Colonial, **5**
Hotel Mintzicuri, **14**
Mansión Posada Don Vasco, **13**
Posada de Villa, **20**

RESTAURANTS
Restaurante-Bar La Huacana, **16**
Restaurante Vegetariano Acuarias, **18**

SIGHTS
Casa de les Artesanías, **16**
Casa de la Cultura, **3**
Casa Natal de Morelos, **20**
Cathedral, **10**
Museo de la Máscara, **4**
Museo Michoacano I, **12**
Museo de Morelos, **17**

OTHER
Bus Station, **1**
Computel, **7**
LADATEL, **6**
Laundromat, **9**
Multicinema Morelia, **2**
Pharmacy, **11**
Telegrams, **8**

sparkling clean, cozy, wood-paneled rooms equipped with phones, cable TV, and hot water. Singles 78 pesos; doubles 92 pesos; triples 106 pesos; quads 121 pesos.

**Mansión Posada Don Vasco,** Vasco de Quiroga 232 (tel. 12-14-84), across from Hotel Mintzicuri. Rooms come with cable TV, phones, wood furniture, and purified water. 78 pesos for 1 person; 92 pesos for 2; 106 pesos for 3; 121 pesos for 4. Dark, no-frills rooms 50 pesos for 1 person, 60 pesos for 2.

**Hotel Colonial,** 20 de Noviembre 15 and Morelos Nte. (tel. 12-18-97). Cozy courtyard glows a deep yellow. Friendly staff. Rooms boast high ceilings, large windows, and private baths; some with balcony. Purified water. Singles 55 pesos; doubles 60-100 pesos. Add 15 pesos for TV.

**Posada de Villa,** Padre Lloreda 176 (tel. 12-72-90), 3 blocks south of the Museo de las Artesanías. Huge rooms with soft beds, light wood paneling, and funky green tile. Bathrooms are a bit trodden, but very clean. Singles 73 pesos; doubles 92 pesos. Pastel apartments for 1-2 people 1500 pesos per month.

## FOOD

Finding good, cheap food is a breeze in Morelia—almost every thoroughfare has at least one family-run restaurant that dishes out inexpensive *comida corrida* (usually around 10 pesos). Restaurants on the *zócalo* tend to be pricier but are good places for breakfast, since other eateries tend to open late and close early.

**Restaurante-Bar La Huacana,** Aldama 116 at Obeso (tel. 12-53-12). A gargantuan oil painting forms the backdrop for the large cafeteria-style dining area. Stone walls provide great acoustics for the *mariachis* who play Mon.-Fri. 3-5pm. *Comida corrida* 16 pesos. Enchiladas 15 pesos. Open Mon.-Sat. 9am-8pm.

**Restaurante Vegetariano Acuarias,** Hidalgo 75, at the end of the walkway south of the *zócalo*. Set in a blue-tiled courtyard littered with plants, bikes, and a random assortment of junk. Locals scarf down yummy vegetarian food as they listen to Mexican tunes. *Comida corrida* 16 pesos. Breakfast combos 14 pesos. Open daily 9am-4pm.

**Restaurant Vegetariano,** upstairs at Madero 549 (tel. 13-13-68), across from Salinas y Rocha store. Serves hearty, tasty vegetarian *comida corrida* (16-17 pesos), and veggie burgers (6 pesos). Open daily 8:30am-6pm.

**Súper Pozole,** Antonio Anzate 302B, just off Quiroga. Bright pink and purple trimmed walls enclose cafeteria-style rooms. Cheap grub and late hours. Enchiladas or *tamales* 12 pesos. Open Tues.-Sun. 6:30-10:30pm.

## SIGHTS

Still going strong at age 111, the **Museo Michoacano,** Allende 305 (tel. 12-04-07), one block west of the *zócalo* at Abasolo, has thorough exhibits divided into five categories: ecology, archaeology, the colonial period, the struggle for freedom, and independent Mexico. The most notable object on display is a huge, anonymous painting completed in 1738, *La Procesión del Traslado de las Monjas de una Universidad a su Convento Nuevo* (The Procession of the Nuns from the University to Their New Convent). The museum is also home to a large number of religious works by Miguel Cabrera and a trio of 19th-century *indígena* artists—Manuel Ocaraza, Félix Parra, and Jesús Torres. Near the stairway, a mural by Alfredo Zalce portrays Hidalgo, Morelos, and others who have shaped Mexico's history and skewers those who blindly admire U.S. mass culture (open Tues.-Sat. 9am-7pm, Sun. 9am-2pm; admission 14 pesos, free for children, seniors, and on Sun.).

Overlooking the *zócalo,* the massive **cathedral** has a stunning interior, graced by vaulted ceilings, chandeliers, tapestries, and beautiful stained glass windows. The church's oldest treasure is the *Señor de la Sacristía*, an image of Christ that was sculpted by *indígenas* out of dry corn cobs and orchid nectar; in the 16th century, Felipe II of Spain donated a gold crown to top off the masterpiece. In the 19th century, a bishop tipped the careful balance that had existed between Neoclassical and Baroque elements by removing the elaborate Baroque filigree from the altarpieces and frescoes and renovating the church's interior in the conservative Doric Neoclassical style (open daily 7am-9pm; free).

The former residence of José María Morelos, the parish priest who led the Independence movement after Hidalgo's death, is now the **Museo de Morelos,** Morelos Sur 323 (tel. 13-26-51), one block east and two blocks south of the cathedral. The museum displays Morelos's religious vestments, military ornaments, and uniform, as well as other mementos of the surge for independence (open Mon.-Sun. 9am-7pm; admission 10 pesos, free for children, seniors, and on Sun.). More of a civic building than a museum, the **Casa Natal de Morelos** (Birthplace of Morelos) is on Corregidora 113 at García Obeso (tel. 12-27-93), one block south of the cathedral. Glass cases preserve Morelos's wartime cartography, communiqués, and letters. Also notable are murals by Alfredo Zalce and a shady courtyard watched over by the martyr's bust (open Mon.-Sat. 9am-7pm; free).

The **Casa de Cultura,** Morelos Nte. 485 (tel. 12-41-51), is housed in the **Monasterio de los Carmelitas Descalzos,** four blocks north of Madero. A gathering place for artists, musicians, and backpackers, the *casa* houses a bookstore, art galleries, a theater, and a lovely cafe. Dance, voice, theater, guitar, piano, and sculpture classes are offered, and concerts, book presentations, art festivals, and literature workshops are held here (20-30 pesos). The on-premises **Museo de la Máscara** exhibits a small collection of masks from all over the Republic. (Center and museum open Mon.-Fri. 9am-3pm and 5-8pm, Sat.-Sun. and holidays 10am-6pm; free; cafe open Mon.-Fri. 10am-3pm and 5-9pm, Sat. 10am-3pm; for information on cultural events, call 13-12-15 or 13-13-20, ext. 233.)

The **Casa de las Artesanías,** Humboldt at Fray Juan de San Miguel (tel. 12-12-48), is a huge craft museum and retail store, selling colorful macramé *huipiles,* straw airplanes, pottery, carved wood furniture, and guitars (open Mon.-Sat. 10am-3pm and 5-8pm, Sun. 10am-6pm; free). Better prices await in Pátzcuaro.

## ENTERTAINMENT

Listings of events can be found at the Casa de Cultura and at the tourist office. Bright lights, musical celebrations, and thespian allure draw crowds to the **Teatro Morelos** on Av. Camelina at Calzada Ventura Puente (tel. 14-62-02), and the **Conservatorio de las Rosas** at the corner of Guillermo Prieto and Santiago Tapia (tel. 12-74-06). The **Casa Natal de Morelos** shows artsy films and holds cultural events on Fridays at 7pm (films screened the last Tues.-Thurs. of every month, noon and 7pm; admission 1 peso). **Multicinema Morelia** at Santiago Tapia and Bernal Jiménez (tel. 12-12-88), behind the Palacio Clavijero, features Hollywood's latest (open daily 3-10pm; 10 pesos). If you find heavenly bodies more fascinating than scantily clad ones, head for the **Planetario** Ventura Puenta and Ticateme (tel. 14-24-65), in the Centro de Convenciones at Calzada (shows Tues.-Sat. 7pm, Sun. 6:30pm; 10 pesos). To get there, take the "Ruta Rojo #3" *combi* from Av. Allende/Valladolid and watch for the *planetario* and convention center complex on the right. Both the *centro comercial* and Plaza Mexicana have spiffy multiplexes as well (take a red 3B *combi;* admission 15-20 pesos).

La **Casona del Teatro,** Aquiles Serdán 35 and Morelos (tel. 17-33-53), one block north of Madero, hosts comedies in Spanish (shows Tues.-Sat. 8:30pm, Sun. 7:30pm; 25 pesos, 50% discount for students). The coffee shop/theater is popular with students and bohemian types who play chess and drink coffee (6 pesos) until showtime (open Mon.-Sat. 9am-11pm). A similar hangout is the somewhat pricey bookstore and cafe **La Librería,** Calzada Fray Antonio de San Miguel 324 at Av. Acuedicto and Madero (tel. 12-02-87), about three blocks east of plaza de Villalongin, which sometimes has films and music.

Twentysomethings bounce to the latest Spanish and English pop tunes at **Dalí's,** Av. Campestre 100 (tel. 15-55-14; beer 15 pesos; cover 25 pesos; open Mon.-Sat. 8pm-2am, Sun. 5pm-2am). Another hotspot with a similar crowd is **Siglo 18** (tel. 24-07-47), Blvd. García León and Turismo, (cover 30-50 pesos; open Tues.-Sun. 9:30pm-3:30am). Down the street, tourists, local teens, and a handful of gringo students celebrate birthdays with ice-cold Coronas at **Carlos 'n' Charlie's,** Av. Camelinas 3340 (tel. 24-37-39), near the Hotel Calinda (open daily 1pm-2am). The dark interior at **Badierna,** Lázaro Cárdenas 2225 (tel. 15-53-54), lures an older, slicker crowd to salsa the night away. Domestic drinks run about 10 pesos (cover 10-20 pesos; open Thurs.-Sat. 9pm-3am). **Freedom,** Av. Campestre 374 (tel. 15-66-61), hosts local teeny-bopper rebels out past their curfew (open daily 1pm-3am).

# ▓ Lázaro Cárdenas

Named after *michoacano* President Lázaro Cárdenas, whose progressive socialist measures included nationalizing oil in 1938, the hot, noisy city of Lázaro Cárdenas (pop. 135,000) is Mexico's most important port on the Pacific. It also houses the largest steel factory in Latin America. The city's size, services, and location make it a likely departure point or pit stop on an exploration of Michoacán's 260km of deserted, rugged, beautiful coast, but Cárdenas itself is a filthy pit: get in and get out.

**Orientation and Practical Information** Lázaro Cárdenas lies near the border of Michoacán and Guerrero states, 382km southwest of Morelia and 122km northwest of Ixtapa. Most services lie on the town's principal thoroughfare, **Av. Lázaro Cárdenas,** usually near its intersection with **Corregidora.** The main *zócalo,* **Plaza de la Reforma,** is three blocks east of the *avenida's* intersection with Guillermo Prieto. *Combis* and buses run up and down Av. Lázaro Cárdenas and whisk passengers to nearby beaches. Get the maps and info needed to attack the coast from the **Delegación Regional de Turismo,** Nicolás Bravo 475 (tel./fax 2-15-47), one block east of Av. Lázaro Cárdenas and two blocks north of Corregidora, in the big white Hotel Casa Blanca (open Mon.-Sat. 9am-3pm and 5-7pm). **Banamex** (tel. 2-20-18) and **BITAL** (tel. 2-26-23), on Av. Lázaro Cárdenas, exchange currency and have **ATMs** (both open Mon.-Fri. 8:30am-4:30pm, Sat. 10am-2pm). Long-distance international **phone calls** can be made and **faxes** sent from **Caseta Goretti,** Corregidora 79 (tel. 7-31-55; open daily 7am-1am). The **airport** (tel. 7-17-18 or 2-19-20), named after you-know-whom, hosts carriers **Aerosudpacífico** (tel. 7-11-77 or 7-11-78), **Transporte Aeromar** (tel. 7-10-84 or 7-10-85), and **Aerolínea Cuahonte** (tel. 2-36-35).

**Buses** run out of independent stations on or close to the main drag. **Sur de Jalisco, Autobuses de Occidente,** and **Autobuses de Jalisco,** Av. Lázaro Cárdenas 1791 (tel. 7-18-50), run to Colima (1st class 10:30am, 7pm, 6hr., 98 pesos; 2nd class 2:30, 7am, and 1pm, 8½hr., 82 pesos), Guadalajara (*plus* 7 and 8:45pm, 9hr., 184 pesos; 1st class 10:45pm, 10hr., 161 pesos; 2nd class 2:30, 7am, and 1pm, 11hr., 143 pesos), **Estrella de Oro,** Corregidora 318 (tel. 2-02-75), travels to Mexico City (1st class 6, 10am, and 9pm, 10hr., 195 pesos). **Autotransportes Cuauhtémoc** and **Estrella Blanca,** Francisco Villa 65 (tel. 2-11-71), four blocks west of Corregidora, sends buses to Acapulco (1st class 6 per day, 6am-midnight, 6hr., 70 pesos; 2nd class 18 per day, 7hr., 58 pesos) and Tijuana (2:30pm, 48hr., 764 pesos), stopping at Mazatlán (20hr., 335 pesos) and points along the way. **Autotransportes Galeana,** Av. Lázaro Cárdenas 1810 (tel. 2-02-62), provides second-class service to Manzanillo (4:15, 5:30, and 11:30am, 6hr., 85 pesos), Morelia (15 per day, 2am-7pm, 8hr., 105 pesos) via Uruapan (6hr., 69 pesos) and Pátzcuaro (7hr., 84 pesos). The **Red Cross,** at Aldama 327 (tel. 2-05-75), is there for you day or night. **Farmacia Pans** resides at Av. Lázaro Cárdenas 2002 (tel. 2-14-35; open 24hr.). The **Hospital General** is on Av. Lázaro Cárdenas (tel. 2-08-21). The **police** (tel. 2-18-55) await at the Palacio Municipal, on Av. Lázaro Cárdenas at Av. Río Balsas. Send those postcards home from the **post office,** at Nicolás Bravo 1307 (tel. 2-05-47; open Mon.-Fri. 8am-7pm, Sat. 9am-1pm). **Phone Code:** 753.

**Accommodations and Food**   The condoms-for-sale atmosphere of most budget accommodations in town will make you happy to make your way to the reputable **Hotel Reyna Pío,** Corregidora 7A at Lázaro Cárdenas (tel. 2-06-20). Clean rooms boast A/C, telephone, mustard-yellow furniture, and 1970s TV sets (singles 80 pesos; doubles 100 pesos). Fill up that stomach at **El Chile Verde,** Francisco I. Madero 66 (tel. 2-10-85), across from Av. Lázaro Cárdenas. The casual, open-air cafe serves spicy *enchiladas verdes* (14 pesos) and *comida corrida* (14 pesos; open daily 7am-10pm). The slightly pricier but air-conditioned **El Paraíso,** on Lázaro Cárdenas near the Galeana bus station, offers traditional Mexican food in a dark funereal atmosphere. The *sopa de tortilla* (12 pesos) and fish (35 pesos) are both worth a try.

# ▓ Michoacán Coast

Michoacán's temperamental, wildly beautiful coastline offers solace and tranquility one moment, then suddenly erupts into ripping, turbulent surf. Rte. 200, the solitary coastal highway, twists up, down, and around Michoacán's angry terrain. Hills are pushed up against each other; rocks are defaced by crashing white waves spraying against blue skies. Lush tropical vegetation lends a loving touch of green to the state's 260km of virgin beaches.

Michoacán's coast is to be treated with cautious respect. Powerful waves make its beaches better suited for surfing than swimming, and the currents are strong even in the areas recommended for swimming. Since there are no lifeguards, exercise great caution. Rte. 200 tends to be deserted and dangerous at night; we recommend traveling during the day only.

## PLAYA AZUL

Playa Azul (pop. 5000), a small *pueblo* and nascent beach resort 26km west of Lázaro Cárdenas, is renowned for its long stretch of soft, golden sand and its majestic rose-golden sunsets. Here, the sea is temptress—the tide rises high onto the shore, tracing the base of a line of *palapa* restaurants, then quickly recedes under crashing waves, good for surfing and boogie-boarding. Swimmers shouldn't stray too deep, as this open stretch of sea has a strong undercurrent. The beach is crowded with Mexican tourists during December and Semana Santa, but quiet the rest of the year.

**Orientation and Practical Information** Far from being a polished tourist town, Playa Azul is typically *michoacano*. Unmarked dirt roads are the main thoroughfares, lined with thatched roof houses, open-air markets, and the occasional pig. The village is so small that street names are seldom used (or known) by locals. The **Malecón** borders the beach; it is called **Aquiles Serdán** to the west of the plaza and **Emiliano Zapata** to the east. The other streets bordering the plaza are **Montes de Oca** to the west, and **Filomena Mata** to the east. **Av. Lázaro Cárdenas** runs into Playa Azul from the highway, runs perpendicular to the beach, and intersects **Carranza, Madero,** and **Independencia,** the three main streets parallel to the beach.

Though Playa Azul doesn't have a bank or *casa de cambio,* it does offer most other services. For long-distance **phone calls,** visit the town's *caseta* (tel. 6-01-22 to -24), on Independencia (open Mon.-Sat. 8am-9pm, Sun. 8am-1pm). The **market** is on Flores Magón, two blocks east of the plaza. The **Centro de Salud** is next door to the post office (open 24hr.). The **police** (tel. 2-18-55 or 2-20-30) reside across from the PEMEX station. **Farmacia Eva Carmen,** Av. Lázaro Cárdenas at Madero, satisfies your drug needs (open daily 8am-9:30pm). The **post office** is on Madero at Montes de Oca, just behind Hotel María Teresa (open Mon.-Fri. 8am-3pm). **Phone Code:** 753.

**Accommodations and Food** Bucolic Playa Azul offers several adequate budget hotels from which to choose. Reservations are recommended in August, December, and during Semana Santa. **Hotel Costa de Oro,** on Madero three blocks away from Lázaro Cárdenas, is the best deal in town. White stucco walls and an elegantly scalloped bannister lead to clean, comfortable rooms with funky tile floors, fans, and mismatched bedspreads, but no hot water (singles 50 pesos; doubles or triples 70 pesos). **Bungalows de la Curva** (tel. 6-00-58 or 2-28-55), on Carranza at Lázaro Cárdenas, is a good deal for groups. Clean but worn bungalows have kitchenettes, basic furniture, and hot water (2 beds 115 pesos; 4 beds 172 pesos).

*Palapa* restaurants are so close to the shore that the waves will come up and tickle your toes. The bubbly owner of **Coco's Pizza** will make you feel right at home. The *camarones al diablo* (shrimp with *chile,* 35 pesos) are a spicy taste of heaven. Cool off with a beer (6 pesos; open daily 8am-7pm). Inland, **Restaurante Familiar Mitita,** on Flores Magón at Madero, is a cozy family-run restaurant with heavy, carved wooden chairs and fishnets on the walls. The *comida corrida* costs 20 pesos, while huge breakfast combos go for 18-20 pesos (open daily 7am-11pm).

**Getting There:** From Lázaro Cárdenas, take a "Playa Azul" *combi* on Av. Lázaro Cárdenas (every 2min., 5am-9pm, 35min., 6 pesos).

## CALETA DE CAMPOS

A tiny fishing village 47km west of Playa Azul, Caleta de Campos has a pleasant beach but little else to offer the fun-loving traveler. The entire town is laid out along its one main street; sneeze and you'll miss it. No one comes to Caleta for its urban thrills, though—its beach is the main act in town. The combination of green twisted terrain and brilliant blue surf massaging the shore is truly beautiful, and a dirt path climbs along the hills to the village above, offering a spectacular view of the coast. Because the water is somewhat sheltered, the surf is calmer than at Playa Azul, though the rolling waves still make for good boogie boarding and body surfing. For most of the year, Caleta's two hotels are empty, but they fill up during Semana Santa and Christmas.

**Orientation and Practical Information** From Lázaro Cárdenas, **Rutas de Transportación Colectiva** (tel. 2-02-62) buses run from the Galeana bus station to Caleta (every hr., 5:40am-8:10pm, 1½hr., 20 pesos). You can also board a "Caleta" *combi* anywhere along Av. Lázaro Cárdenas (every ½hr., 5:20-8pm, 1½hr., 18 pesos). To return to Lázaro Cárdenas from Caleta, pick up a bus or *combi* at the stop near the end of Av. Principal (5am-7:30pm). From Playa Azul, get on a "La Mira" *combi* across from the PEMEX gas station (every 10min., 5min., 2.50 pesos). Get off at La Mira and take a green and white *combi* to Caleta at the rotary in front of Autotransportes Galeana (every 30min., 5:45am-8:40pm, 1hr., 18 pesos). You'll also need to stop by La Mira on your way back to Lázaro Cárdenas.

Caleta de Campos has one paved main street, Melchor Ocampo, locally known as **Av. Principal.** There are few private telephones in town; almost everybody just uses the *caseta* located on the right-hand side of Av. Principal as you face away from the church at the far end of the street (tel. 6-01-92 or 6-01-93). Farther up the road is **Farmacia Morelia,** which will sometimes change dollars (open daily 7:30am-9pm). To get to the **Centro de Salud,** turn right on the side street before the paved road runs left and walk three blocks (open 24hr.). The **police, post office** (open Mon.-Fri. 8am-3pm), and **bus stop** are all on Av. Principal. **Phone Code:** 753.

**Accommodations and Food** Caleta is home to only two hotels, both of which are nice and affordable. The **Hotel Los Arcos** (tel. (755) 6-01-92 or 6-01-93), next to the church as Av. Principal turns left, has very clean rooms with golden doors, tiled floors and bathrooms, fans, and hot water. The rooms are perched on a bluff, providing a fantastic view of the coast (singles 60 pesos; doubles 80 pesos; triples and quads 120 pesos). It's always Christmas with the red and green bedspreads at **Hotel Yuritzi,** off Av. Principal after the church to the left, boasting spiffy rooms with hot water, fans, and TV. Restaurant downstairs open only in high season (singles 70 pesos; doubles 80 pesos; with A/C 130 and 150 pesos). To get to the beach from the hotels, walk to the end of Av. Principal. Pass the church and the Loncheria Bahía, on your right, and follow the dirt road as it bends to the right. The beach lies at the bottom of the hill. The entire walk takes about 10 minutes.

Across the street from Hotel Yuritzi is one of Caleta's only restaurants, **Lonchería Bahía.** The classy and laid-back cafe serves hamburgers (9 pesos), *tortas* (8-12 pesos), and fruit drinks (6 pesos; open daily 8am-10pm). Also popular is **Enramada Omar,** the third *palapa* restaurant on the sandy cove. It specializes in seafood and serves shrimp any style for 32 pesos (open daily 7am-9pm).

### Near Playa Azul and Caleta de Campos

Beautiful beaches cover the 43km of coast stretching from Playa Azul to Caleta de Campos. **Las Peñas,** 13km west of Playa Azul, is a beach that is better appreciated from the shore: its surf is terribly turbulent and its waters are infested with sharks. **El Bejuco,** only 2km farther west, has a sandy cove with tamer waves and fewer rocks. Another 12km west, you'll find **Chuquiapan,** a long stretch of sandy beach with reasonable waves and a shore studded with tall green palms. **La Soledad,** enclosed by rocky formations 4km farther west, is more secluded and cozy, lying at the base of a hill covered with dense vegetation. Its grey sands are strewn with rocks and driftwood. As usual in Michoacán's Pacific coast, rough waters don't make for safe swimming. **Mexcalhuacán,** 2km west, offers a fantastic view from a bluff overlooking a rocky coast. Caleta de Campos comes 7km later. **Nexpa,** a sandy beach with powerful waves, is a surfer's heaven 5km west of Caleta. *Palapa* restaurants, known as *enramadas,* line most of the beaches. To be safe, bring bottled water and a snack.

**Getting There:** Buses and *combis* running from Lázaro Cárdenas to Caleta de Campos pass by each of the beaches listed above, except Nexpa (every ½hr., 5am-7:30pm; Las Peñas ½hr., 10 pesos; Chuquiapan 40min., 12 pesos; La Soledad 45min., 13 pesos). The beaches are a five- to 10-minute walk from the highway. To return to Playa Azul or Caleta, you'll have to wave a towel and flag down a *combi*—be sure to confirm when the last one is expected. To get to Nexpa, take a white *combi* from the bus depot at the beginning of Av. Principal in Caleta de Campos (every 40min., 7am-7pm, 10min., 3 pesos).

**Guerrero**

# GUERRERO

## ■ Taxco

From the windows of a bus high up in the Sierra Madre del Sur, Taxco materializes like a strange and unreal apparition. White homes with rust roofs are built within feet of nearby waterfalls, and the whole beautiful town is built into the side of a preposterously steep hill. But this is no mirage—from the stunning Church of Santa Prisca to the glinting wares of silver shops, Taxco (pop. 110,000) is meant to be seen and savored from all angles. The two-way streets are so narrow that people flatten themselves along shop walls to let one VW bug pass. And, of course, beneath all the swarming confusion and old-fashioned beauty are the veins of silver which have shaped Taxco's history. When silver was discovered here in 1534, Taxco became the continent's first mining town, luring fortune seekers and artisans alike. Today, tourists buzz through the labyrinthine streets, drawn like bees to the sweet honey of countless jewelry shops.

### ORIENTATION

Taxco lies 185km southwest of Mexico City. The city consists of a maze of twisting streets leading up a hill to the *zócalo,* **Plaza Borda,** and the town's centerpiece, the **Catedral de Santa Prisca.** The main artery is **Av. de los Plateros.** From Mexico City, visitors enter Taxco on Plateros through white arches. The road winds past the **Flecha Roja** bus station and continues to the **Estrella de Oro** bus station before heading out of the city for Acapulco.

To reach the town center from the Flecha Roja bus station, walk uphill on J.F. Kennedy and turn left on **Juan Ruiz de Alarcón,** which runs past some nice hotels and eventually feeds into the *zócalo.* From the Estrella de Oro station, cross the street and walk up the steep hill known as **Pilita.** When you reach the **Plazuela San Juan,** with a small fountain and a **Bancomer,** veer left and you will come out facing Santa Prisca. Keep in mind that the streets are narrow and uncomfortably steep. A *zócalo combi* will take you to the center for 1 peso. Taxis charge 7 pesos.

## PRACTICAL INFORMATION

**Tourist Office: Info Booth,** J.F. Kennedy 1 (tel. 2-07-98). Take a "Garita" *combi* from the *zócalo*. Open daily 9am-7pm. Some English spoken. **Subsecretaría de Fomento Turístico** (tel. 2-22-74), at the entrance to town. "Los Arcos" *combis* end their route in front of the office. Open daily 9am-7pm. **Hotel Agua Escondida** on the Plaza Borda also offers maps. **Procuraduría del Turista** (tel. 2-22-64 or 2-66-16) offers assistance in emergencies. Open Mon.-Fri. 9am-7pm.

**Telephones: LADATELs** found around the main plazas (Pl. Borda and San Juan). **Farmacia Guadalupana,** Hidalgo 18 (tel. 2-03-95), near Pl. San Juan has a long-distance *caseta*. Open daily 8am-10pm.

**Fax:** Alarcón 2 (tel. 2-48-85), by the *zócalo*. Open Mon.-Fri. 9am-3pm.

**Currency Exchange: Confía** (tel. 2-45-10), on the *zócalo*. Has an **ATM.** Open Mon.-Fri. 9am-2:30pm.

**Buses: Estrella de Oro,** Kennedy 126 (tel. 2-06-48), at the southern end of town. From the *zócalo*, head downhill and hang a right on Kennedy. To Acapulco (5 per day, 6am-10pm, 2hr., 45 pesos), Cuernavaca (9am and 4pm, 1½hr., 20 pesos), and Mexico City (5 per day, 9am-6pm, 3hr., 46-54 pesos). **Flecha Roja,** Plateros 104 (tel. 2-01-31), downhill from the cathedral. To Cuernavaca (7 per day, 6am-6pm, 1½hr., 20 pesos) and Mexico City (12 per day, 5am-1am, 3hr., 41 pesos).

**Market: Mercado Tetitlán.** Take the street to the right of Santa Prisca, then descend the stairs to the right. At the bottom level are several *fondas* for meals.

**Red Cross:** J.F. Kennedy (tel. 2-32-32), next door to the tourist info *caseta*. Open daily 9am-8pm. 24hr. ambulance service. Little English spoken.

**Pharmacy: Farmacia Guadalupana,** Hidalgo 8 (tel. 2-03-45). Open daily 8am-10pm.

**Hospital: IMSS,** Kennedy 114 (tel. 2-03-36). 24hr. emergency service.

**Police:** (tel. 2-00-07). Always on duty.

**Post Office:** Kennedy 124 (tel. 2-05-01), near the Estrella de Oro station. Open Mon.-Fri. 8am-7pm, Sat. 9am-1pm. **Postal Code:** 40200.

**Phone Code:** 762.

## ACCOMMODATIONS

True budget accommodations and guest houses in Taxco are virtually nil. The up side? Even a moderately priced or cheap hotel will be classy and centrally located with silver shops, bars, and artisanry all over the place. Here's a place to live it up. Make advance reservations during local holidays.

**Posada de Los Castillo,** Alarcón 7 (tel. 2-13-96). Facing Santa Prisca, take the street to the left and turn right. As exquisite as the pricey silver shop downstairs. All the furniture, from the doors to the headboards, is carved in reassuring earth tones. Firm beds with fluffy pillows and first-rate bathrooms. Singles 115 pesos; doubles 150 pesos; triples 185 pesos.

**Hotel Los Arcos,** Alarcón 4 (tel. 2-18-36), across the street from Posada de Los Castillo. With black iron fixtures and cavernous rooms around a central courtyard, the hotel feels like a medieval manor. Well, except for the LATADEL. Tiled bathrooms and purified water. Singles 116 pesos; doubles 151 pesos.

**Hotel Casa Grande,** Pl. de San Juan 7 (tel. 2-11-08), on the small plaza down Cuauhtémoc from the *zócalo*. Worn rooms receive haphazard housecleaning, but the central courtyard and adjoining bar are definitely *padre* (cool). Hot water 24hr. Singles 80 pesos; doubles 100 pesos; triples 120 pesos; quads 150 pesos.

**Casa de Huéspedes Arellano,** Pajaritos 23 (tel. 2-02-15). From the *zócalo*, walk down the street to the right of the cathedral and descend the stairs; the hotel will be about 3 levels down. Box-like rooms pale next to the live birds and potted plants that enliven the terrace. A good space for laundry drying and sunbathing; a great place to smoke cigarettes and parlay with Euro-backpackers. Try to land a room with a private bath—or share it with up to 7 people. Singles 40 pesos; doubles 70 pesos; triples 100 pesos.

**Hotel Agua Escondida,** Guillermo Spratling 4 (tel. 2-07-26 or 2-07-36), on the Pl. Borda. Although upscale and expensive, this stunning hotel offers rooms with balconies practically *inside* the lovely Santa Prisca Church. Wake up to pink sand-

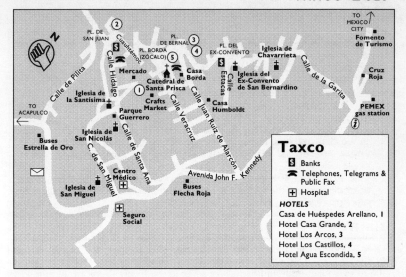

Taxco

$ Banks
☎ Telephones, Telegrams & Public Fax
✚ Hospital

**HOTELS**
Casa de Huéspedes Arellano, 1
Hotel Casa Grande, 2
Hotel Los Arcos, 3
Hotel Los Castillos, 4
Hotel Agua Escondida, 5

stone, flowers, and breakfast. Lounge, ping-pong, swimming pool, video arcade, and much more. Up for a splurge? Singles 200 pesos; doubles 250 pesos.

## FOOD

The narrow cobblestone streets of Taxco lack the push-cart vendors and sidewalk cafes that are so common in other Mexican cities. *Taquerías* and *torterías* are virtually extinct around Plaza Borda, but as you descend into the swarming market areas, their numbers increase.

**Restaurante Santa Fé,** Hidalgo 2 (tel. 2-11-70), ½ block down from Pl. San Juan. Locals flock here for filling Mexican food. Delicious *tortas* (7 pesos), tacos (12 pesos), and enchiladas (15 pesos). Open daily 7:30am-10:30pm.

**El Rincón del Abuelo,** Callejón del Nogal 1 (tel. 2-30-77), at Cuauhtémoc, before Pl. San Juan. The name (Grandpa's Corner) belies the sleek hipness of the cafe. Gringos come in droves for the dance music and healthy entrees. *Tortas* run 10-12 pesos, hamburgers 15-22 pesos, and *comida corrida* 24 pesos. Sit upstairs for more private chats above the din of rock music. Open daily 10am-midnight.

**La Concha Nostra,** Pl. de San Juan 7 (tel. 2-79-44), in the Hotel Casa Grande. A Bohemian hangout with a stage, old guitars hanging on the walls, and live music some Sat. nights. Slacker service to match the ambience. While you're waiting for your hotcakes (12 pesos), quesadillas (14 pesos), lasagna (24 pesos), or pizza (10-45 pesos), watch the city's language students blow smoke through their noses and scribble tormented prose in their notebooks. On a good weekday afternoon, you can have this den o' angst to yourself. Open daily 8am-midnight.

**Bora Bora Pizza,** Delicias 4 (tel. 2-17-21), on the unmarked street that slopes up to the right from Cuauhtémoc, just off the *zócalo*. Fishing nets and basket lamps dangle from the ceiling. Dimly lit with low tables and stools. Pizzas start at 18 pesos, spaghetti at 17 pesos. Open daily 1pm-midnight.

**Cactus Pizza** (tel. 2-59-51), on the hill, part of the Hotel Monte Taxco complex. This bright, chipper pizza joint and boutique is brand-new and very clean. Despite the presence of nearby country clubs, golf courses, and Corvettes, this place retains good old-fashioned pizza at good old-fashioned prices. A colorful place to spend an Art Deco afternoon. The piping-hot thin-crust pizzas start at 20 pesos. Open daily 9am-7pm.

> ### The Shining
>
> Although unscrupulous sellers and cheating craftspeople occasionally pass off *alpaca* (fool's silver) or *plateados* (silver-plated metals) as the real McCoy, buying silver in Taxco is usually a sure thing. Larger pieces, such as necklaces and bracelets, are consistently striking. Many proprietors speak English and accept U.S. currency, but if you stick with Spanish and talk in pesos while bargaining, you lower the risk of being charged tourist prices. In general, as one walks away from the Plaza Borda, the sterling products become cheaper and the employees more amenable to bargaining. Bargain at stores with silver workshops by faking out the clerk and heading straight for the artisan. Most shops have two prices: *menudeo* (retail) and *mayoreo* (wholesale), the latter for those profit-oriented people who load their bags with silver in Taxco to resell at lofty prices back home. Remember that only the official ".925" stamp on the object's side guarantees that your shiny new charm is indeed silver; inspect merchandise carefully before purchasing anything.

## SIGHTS

Over 300 shops cater to the busloads of tourists who are drawn to Taxco by the glint of silver. In general, the farther you go from *el centro,* the better the prices. Still, it's fun to ogle glamorous and expensive silver in the lovely shops around the Plaza Borda. Just don't josh around too much or you may get some looks from the tons of armed guards. If you're dipping so deep into your pockets that you can feel your knees, head for **El Mercado de Artesanías,** off Veracruz just behind Santa Prisca. Merchants sell silver and peddle pomegranates and painted ashtrays. The market is open daily from 10am to 6pm but is most crowded during *siesta,* when confused gringos hit Taxco's version of a mall instead of sleeping.

Even more impressive than the silver trinkets that shine from every shop window is the *zócalo*'s **Catedral de Santa Prisca,** with its beautiful Baroque facade of pink stone. Among the designs and figures on the facade, the standouts are the Churrigueresque *interestípite*—decorative inverted columns with a Corinthian flourish at the bottom. Despite its size, this gorgeous church looks light and other-worldly; at night, the sight of this pink monument is enough to bring even the least devout down to their knees.

To the left of the church is **Casa Borda,** a stately 18th-century building that was the home of José de la Borda; his family's coat of arms can still be seen beside the entrance. Enter through the bookstore on the *zócalo.* The interior gardens and several floors have been turned into the **Instituto Guerrerense de Cultura** (tel. 2-66-17). In addition to a library and dance studio, the center has ample gallery space for rotating exhibitions and photographs of daily life in Mexico (house open daily 9am-8pm, and galleries open daily 9am-3pm and 5-7pm).

The **Casa Humboldt,** Alarcón 12 (tel. 2-66-17), down the street past the Hotel Los Arcos, is one of the older colonial homes in town. With its unusual bas-reliefs in Moorish *mudéjar* style, the *casa* served as a temporary rest stop for explorer Alexander Von Humboldt for just one night, and it still bears his name (typical of dead white explorers). Nonetheless, this meticulously restored house now houses the collection of the **Museo de Arte Virreinal.** Exhibitions provide a detailed look at 18th-century Catholic rituals and dress (open Tues.-Sat. 10am-5pm, Sun. 9am-3pm; admission 10 pesos, students with ID 5 pesos).

The **Ex-Convento de San Bernandino,** in the Plaza del Convento, was built in 1592 as a Franciscan monastery. Destroyed by a fire two centuries later, the building was reconstructed in Neoclassical style in 1823. The struggle for independence officially ended when the Plan de Iguala was signed within the walls of this ex-convent in 1821. Now a school convenes under its roof. To get to the ex-convent, follow Juárez past the city offices (open daily 10am-5pm; free).

Perhaps the best sights in town are the vistas from surrounding hillsides. One of the more striking views of the city and the surrounding hills is from the **Church of Guadalupe.** The Neoclassical church becomes the center of festivities during the celebration of the Virgin in December. From the *zócalo*, take Ojeda, the street to the right of Cuauhtémoc, to Guadalupe, and veer right until you reach the plaza in front of the church. For a more sweeping vista, you can take a *teleférico,* or **cable car,** to Hotel Monte Taxco. Take a "Los Arcos" *combi* to the white arches at the entrance of the city (1.50 pesos). Before passing through the arches, turn left up a hill and bear left into the parking lot for the cable cars. The ride is exhilarating, with waterfalls on one side and the city on the other (open daily 8am-7pm; call 2-14-68 for more info; 22 pesos round-trip, free for hotel guests). **Góndolas** (tel. 2-14-68) run until 7pm.

## ENTERTAINMENT AND SEASONAL EVENTS

Taxco's crowded streets somehow accommodate a tsunami of tourists during its two major festivals. The **Feria Nacional de la Plata,** a national contest designed to encourage silver artisanship, takes place the last week in November. **Semana Santa** festivities are even more popular in Taxco. On Good Friday, hooded *penitentes* carry logs made out of cactus trunks on their shoulders or subject themselves to flagellation in order to expiate their sins and those of the town, including the ill-behavior of tourists. During the annual **Día del Jumil,** Taxco residents make a pilgrimage to the *Huizteco* hill, where they collect insects known as *jumil* to eat live or add, along with *chiles*, to salsa. The 1.5cm-long brown insects contain more protein per gram than beef.

After silver shops close, most of Taxco gathers at the **Plaza Borda** in front of the illuminated facade of Santa Prisca. Those still up for dancing after a day of hiking up and down Taxco's relentless hills will have to wait until the weekend. **Windows,** in the Hotel Monte Taxco (tel. 2-13-00), has the area's hottest dancing. Although accessible only by cable car or taxi, this bar/dance club is beautifully done up in crystal and glass and offers an unparalleled view of the city combined with a ritzy party atmosphere (cover 20 pesos; open Fri.-Sun. 10pm-late). **Cine Alarcón,** near Plaza de San Juan, shows American and "adult-interest" movies for about 10 pesos.

# ■ Near Taxco

## GRUTAS DE CACAHUAMILPA

While the scenery around Taxco has an awe-inspiring, rugged grandeur, it is the beauty of an extensive network of caves that compels tourists to forget about silver shopping and venture out of the city limits. According to lore, the **Grutas de Cacahuamilpa** were once a hideaway for runaway *indígenas.* Twenty huge *salones* (halls) are filled with stalactites, stalagmites, and rock formations in curious shapes, sizes, and colors. The columns and ceilings—some as high as 85m—are the work of the subterranean stream that developed into the **Río San Jerónimo.** Explorers hoping to traverse the caves have not always had great success—the makeshift grave of an English spelunker and his dog is the highlight of any tour of the *grutas.*

Tours leave on the hour from the visitor's center and afford little opportunity for traipsing about on your own. If your Spanish is good enough, the tour can be hilarious. You can only enter the caves with a tour guide, but once inside, you can discreetly wander about on your own. Shoes with good traction are helpful (caves open daily 10am-5pm; admission 15 pesos, children 10 pesos).

**Getting There:** "Grutas" *combis* leave from Taxco's **Flecha Roja** bus station, dropping passengers off at the parking lot for the caves (8 pesos). "Grutas" *combis* also leave the caves hourly to return to Taxco (8 pesos). Flecha Roja buses also make the trip (every hr., 10am-4pm, 45min., 8 pesos), but will drop you off at an intersection a short jaunt from the caves. To get to the parking lot at the caves, take a right, then another right after the curve.

## LAS GRANADAS AND IXCATEOPAN

Twenty-six kilometers away from Taxco, the ecological reserve of **Las Granadas** provides an Edenic respite from both Volkswagen-clogged streets and silver pushers. In addition to the flora and fauna, there are stunning natural waterfalls. There is no admission charge and no set hours.

Forty-two kilometers from Taxco, the town of **Ixcateopan** is known for both its beauty and its history. The marble and stone streets supply the former, while the **Museo de la Resistencia Indígena** provides information on the latter. The remains of Cuauhtémoc, the last Aztec emperor, are said to be kept here in the **Templo de Santa María de la Asunción.**

**Getting There:** *Combis* leave Taxco from in front of the Seguro Social, on J.F. Kennedy. To get to Las Granadas, head to the town of **Acuitlapan,** 20km from Taxco (every ½hr. until 7pm, 40min., 7 pesos). There you can get transportation to the reserve. To get to Ixcateopan, just take the eponymous vehicle (every ½hr., 6am-9pm, 1¼hr., 10 pesos).

# ■ Zihuatanejo and Ixtapa

Six kilometers and a gargantuan rift in lifestyle separate the twin beach towns of Zihuatanejo and Ixtapa. Both thrive on tourism, offering the requisite stretches of sand, the whole range of water sports, and the sunset-framing restaurants. Ixtapa has been meticulously constructed by Mexican pleasure engineers to cater to moneyed foreign visitors; this glitzy resort has no downtown, no budget accommodations, and a surfeit of fancy restaurants. Meanwhile, in Zihuatanejo, only a 15-minute bus ride away, even after prices were slapped on everything and menus reprinted in broken English, the serenity just wouldn't go away: Zihuatanejo hasn't shaken the grip of the net that marks it as a fishing town. In its downtown, there are actually budget hotels, and they're all a few steps from excellent beaches. The tourist brochures aren't kidding when they promise two vacations in one.

As a budget traveler, you're likely to spend one and a half of those vacations in Zihuatanejo. Ironically enough, the original plan designed the nascent resort paradise around Zihuatanejo Bay; complications with land rights forced development farther north to Ixtapa. A visit to only peaceful Zihuatanejo would be satisfying, yet the sanitized, glitzy Ixtapa, with its air-conditioned comfort and sophisticated nightlife, adds just the right amount of decadence. Together, the twin towns provide the complete escape that Mexico's other Pacific beaches hamper with pollution or lack of services.

## ORIENTATION

Buses arrive in Zihuatanejo. The **Estrella Blanca** station lies outside the *centro* and is connected to downtown by buses heading to the left as you leave the station (1.50 pesos) or taxis (8 pesos). **Estrella de Oro** is on the edge of town on **Paseo del Palmar.** To reach the *centro,* turn right from the station and walk until you reach a rotary with a Japanese-looking temple. Turn right on **Paseo de la Boquita,** which runs into the center of town. Resortgoers usually arrive at the **International Airport,** 15km outside of town. Taxis from the airport to Zihuatanejo charge 50 pesos.

As seen from the bay, downtown Zihuatanejo extends from the *muelle* (pier) on the left to the canal on the right. **Paseo del Pescador** runs along the waterfront. Seven blocks separate that walkway from **Av. Morelos,** which runs parallel to the water and marks the edge of the town. The two boundary streets perpendicular to the water are **5 de Mayo,** by the pier, and **Benito Juárez,** by the canal. Ixtapa's main road, **Blvd. Ixtapa,** parades past a phalanx of huge luxury hotels towards the water on the left, and overpriced stores to the right. Buses shuttling between the two cities leave Zihuatanejo from the intersection of Juárez and Morelos, across from the yellow Elektra store, and leave Ixtapa from various stops on the boulevard (every 15min., 6am-7pm, 15-25min., 2 pesos from any stop). Cab fare between the two towns runs

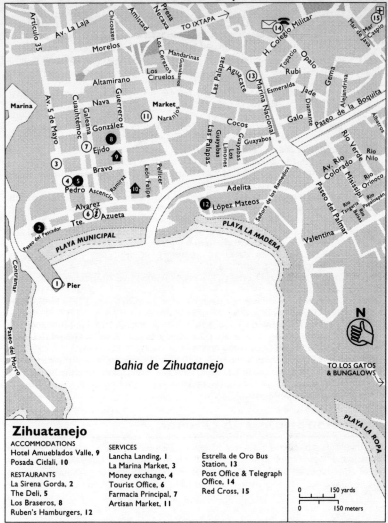

## Zihuatanejo

**ACCOMMODATIONS**
Hotel Amueblados Valle, 9
Posada Citlali, 10

**RESTAURANTS**
La Sirena Gorda, 2
The Deli, 5
Los Braseros, 8
Ruben's Hamburgers, 12

**SERVICES**
Lancha Landing, 1
La Marina Market, 3
Money exchange, 4
Tourist Office, 6
Farmacia Principal, 7
Artisan Market, 11

Estrella de Oro Bus
Station, 13
Post Office & Telegraph
Office, 14
Red Cross, 15

about 15 to 20 pesos by day, 25 pesos at night. Taxis in Zihuatanejo can always be found on Juárez, in front of the market.

If an address listed below is not on Blvd. Ixtapa, it is in Zihuatanejo.

## PRACTICAL INFORMATION

**Tourist Office: Info booth** (tel. 4-20-01), on Juan N. Álvarez, to the left of the small town square. Maps and basic information. Some English spoken. Open Mon.-Fri. 9am-3pm and 6pm-8pm, Sat. 9am-2pm. **SEFOTUR** (tel. 3-19-67), on Blvd. Ixtapa, across from Hotel Presidente. Comprehensive *Guía Turística Urbana* to beaches and services. Some English spoken. Open daily 9am-8pm.

**Currency Exchange: Banco Mexicano,** Los Mangos at Juárez (tel. 4-51-60). **Banca Serfín,** on Juárez (tel. 4-47-80), has an **ATM.** Both open Mon.-Fri. 9am-1:30pm. **Money Exchange,** on Galeana (tel. 4-35-22 or 4-36-22). From the beach, walk 1 block on Cuauhtémoc, take a right on Bravo, and make the first left onto Galeana. Worse rates than the banks, but no commission. Open daily 8am-9pm.

**Telephones: LADATELs** at the Estrella Blanca bus station and on streets downtown. Or try **Servicio Telefónico,** P. Ascencio at Galeana (tel. 4-28-10). Open Mon.-Sat. 8:30am-10pm, Sun. 8am-noon and 6-10pm.

**Airport:** Tel. 4-20-70. **Aeroméxico,** Álvarez 34 at 5 de Mayo (tel. 4-20-18), one block from the water. Open Mon.-Sat. 9am-6:30pm. **Mexicana,** Guerrero at Bravo (tel. 4-22-08). Open Mon.-Sat. 9am-5:45pm, Sun. 9am-2pm and 3-5:45pm.

**Buses: Estrella de Oro,** Paseo Palmar 54 (tel. 4-21-75), sends its crew to Acapulco (8 per day, 7am-5pm, 4½hr., 35 pesos), Cuernavaca (8am, noon, and 11pm, 10hr., 150 pesos), and Mexico City (*ordinario* 8am, noon, 8, and 11pm, 12hr., 195 pesos; *plus* 10pm, 9hr., 230 pesos; *deluxe* 9:15pm, 9hr., 325 pesos). **Estrella Blanca** (tel. 4-34-77) goes to Acapulco (every hr., 7am-5pm except 1pm, 4½hr., 45 pesos), Chilpancingo (4:20am and noon, 5½hr., 75 pesos), Huatulco (7:45pm, 13hr., 146 pesos), and Puerto Escondido (7:45pm, 11½hr., 123 pesos).

**Car Rental: Hertz,** Bravo 9 (tel. 4-22-55). Small VW US$45 per day with unlimited mileage. Insurance US$11. Open daily 8am-2pm and 4-8pm.

**Bookstore: Byblos,** Galeana 211 (tel. 4-38-11). English magazines, paperback novels, and the handy *Owen's English Language Guide to Ixtapa and Zihuatanejo* (written by a member of Cousteau's team). Open daily 9am-10pm.

**Market:** The *mercado* on Benito Juárez, 4 blocks from the water, sells fresh produce and has several small countertop eateries.

**Laundromat: Súper Clean,** Catalina González 11 at Galeana (tel. 4-23-47). 21 pesos per 3kg. Open Mon.-Sat. 8am-8pm.

**Red Cross:** On Av. de las Huertas (tel. 4-20-09) as you leave Zihuatanejo. 24hr. emergency and ambulance service.

**Pharmacy: Farmacia Principal,** Cuauhtémoc at Ejido (tel. 4-42-17), 3 blocks from the water. English spoken. Open Mon.-Sat. 9am-9pm.

**Medical Services: Centro de Salud,** Paseo de la Boquita at Paseo del Palmar (tel. 4-20-88). Open for consultations Mon.-Sat. 8am-3pm. **Dr. Rogelio Grayel** (tel. 4-79-00 or 7-04-52) speaks English and makes house calls for 100 pesos.

**Police:** In the Palacio Municipal (tel. 4-20-40 or 4-23-66) in front of Playa Principal.

**Post Office:** Off Paseo del Palmar (tel. 4-21-92). Walking away from the beach, turn right on Morelos, walk a block past the blue wall, then turn right. Open Mon.-Fri. 8am-6pm. **Postal code:** 40880.

**Phone code:** 753.

## ACCOMMODATIONS AND CAMPING

Zihuatanejo has plenty of budget accommodations within a few blocks of the Playa Municipal. Prices rise substantially during the high season (Dec.-April), as do the number of gringos per square foot. If you visit at an off-time, with a large group, or plan to stay several days, you will have excellent leverage for negotiating a discount. The tourist office discourages unofficial camping, possibly because they believe gringos can't do without the amenities of a five-star hotel, but also for safety reasons. If you insist on pitching a tent, **Playa Barra de Potosí** (p. 335) and **Playa Quieta,** near Club Med in Ixtapa, are the most sensible places to camp. For info on the countless *casas* and *departmentos* for long-term rent, call Mahara Heard-White at **RelMax Realty** (tel. 7-09-19). During the summers, you can also contact **Leigh Roth** (tel. 4-37-55).

**Hotel Casa Aurora,** Bravo 27 between Guerrero and Galeana (tel. 4-30-46). This budget mainstay features a friendly staff, clean, good-sized rooms, and funky 70s bedspreads. Rooms upstairs are nicer; all have overhead fan and hot water. A fine deal: 60 pesos per person, high season 75 pesos.

**Hotel Amueblados Valle,** Vicente Guerrero 14 between Ejido and Bravo (tel. 4-20-84). 8 fully-equipped apartments that would make any grad student jealous. Large kitchens, ceiling fans, balconies, hot water, and daily towel service. 1 bedroom (up to 3 people) 180 pesos; 2 bedrooms (up to 5 people) 280 pesos. Monthly rates available.

**Casa Elvira,** Juan N. Álvarez 8 (tel. 4-26-61), 1 block from the Playa Municipal. The first guest house in Zihuatanejo remains a bargain. Excellent location. Rooms are clean, if unspectacular, with portable fans, cold water, and small bathrooms. The treat is outside—an inviting courtyard filled with family members and close proximity to the beach. Singles 50 pesos; doubles 60 pesos; triples 80 pesos.

**Casa de Huéspedes La Playa,** Alvarez 6 at Guerrero (tel. 4-22-47). The best thing about this place is the location. The waves of the Pacific will lull you to sleep as you gaze out the window and see *la luna brillando en el mar*. Rooms basic and clean, with fans and no hot water. Rooms with 2 individual beds go for 80 pesos.

**Posada Citlali,** Vicente Guerrero 3 near Blvd. Álvarez (tel. 4-20-43). On the expensive side, but very cute. Vines dangle lazily in the central courtyard; wooden rockers on the terrace encourage you to do the same. All rooms have overhead fans and hot water. Singles 100 pesos; doubles 150 pesos; high season 20 pesos more.

## FOOD

Like the neighboring hotels, restaurants in Ixtapa are pricey. However, they are spotless and offer an array of authentic-tasting international cuisine—Italian food actually tastes Italian. The meal can be a reasonable splurge, especially if you eat at a cafe before they switch to the main menu (around 2pm). For consistent budget eats, restaurants in Zihuatanejo serve fish that were swimming in the bay the same morning. The farther you get from the beach, the cheaper and more authentic the restaurant.

**Los Braseros,** Ejido 21 (tel. 4-48-58). This exuberant open-air eatery specializes in heavenly stir-fried combinations of meat, veggies, and cheese (27-32 pesos). Large portions served with hot tortillas by an attentive waitstaff. Open daily 4pm-1am.

**La Sirena Gorda** (The Fat Mermaid), Paseo del Pescador 20A (tel. 4-26-87), next to the pier. Start your morning off with a stack of hotcakes (15-17 peso); dine on seafood tacos (20-38 pesos) when the sun goes down. The view of the water and fishing boats makes it all taste that much better. Open Thurs.-Tues. 7am-10pm.

**The Deli,** Cuauhtémoc 12 (tel. 4-38-50). With a mission to keep the gringos happy, the restaurant prides itself on purified everything, vintage music, and uncommonly clean bathrooms. The familiar food will also please foreigners (honey-mustard chicken sandwich 25 pesos). Sandwiches are good sized and come with fries; regular entrees are rather exorbitant. Open Mon.-Sat. 8am-11pm.

**Ruben's Hamburgers,** Adelita 1 on Playa Madera (tel. 4-46-17). Follow the Paseo del Pescador to the canal, turn left and cross the bridge. Walk straight down the street for 2 blocks—it's on the right, up the stairs. A loud, fun family joint, with booming jukebox and rolls of paper towels dangling overhead; get your drinks from the fridge and add up your own check. Delicious hamburgers (18 pesos) and sour-cream-stuffed baked potatoes (12 pesos). Open daily 6pm-midnight.

**Figaro's Restaurante** (tel. 3-14-52), Plaza Ixpamar off Blvd. Ixtapa, in the Ixtapa mall. Italian *comida del día* a multi-course bargain at 16 pesos. Individual pizzas start at 19 pesos. *Quesadillas* 18 pesos. Open daily 8:30am-11pm.

## SAND AND SIGHTS

Neither Zihuatanejo's self-conscious charm nor Ixtapa's resorts could ever eclipse the area's natural beauty. In Zihuatanejo, four stretches of sand line the water. They are, clockwise from the municipal pier, Playa Principal, Playa La Madera, Playa la Ropa, and Playa Las Gatas. Ixtapa overlooks the unbroken stretch of Playa del Palmar on the Bahía del Palmar, but the prettiest beaches lie beyond Laguna de Ixtapa: Playa Quieta, Playa Linda, and, at the bay's west edge, Isla Ixtapa.

### Zihuatanejo

Downtown Zihuatanejo's beach, **Playa Municipal,** in front of the Paseo del Pescador, is more suited to seashell stores and fishing boats than swimmers. The attractions here are the basketball court, the pier, and the hauls of fish the boats unload onto the dock. The beach ends at a canal that empties into the bay. Get your feet wet crossing over the rocks to **Playa Madera.** Its name refers to the local hardwoods that used to be exported from the shore, but the fine sand and gentle waves bear no trace of the lumberyard past. Good for bodysurfing, the shallow beach hosts a number of restaurants and bungalows.

Zihuatanejo's two best beaches cannot be reached by walking along the bay's shores. Protected from the rough Pacific by the shape of the bay, **Playa La Ropa's** crescent of sumptuous white sand attracts tourists from the hotels on the surrounding cliffs. Because La Ropa is nearly 1km long, it never feels too crowded. Taxis are the easiest way to reach La Ropa (10 pesos). The half-hour walk can be unshaded at points and close to traffic at others. Follow Paseo de la Boquita along the canal to the bridge, cross over and turn left, passing Playa Madera. The road curves to the right and passes Hotel Casa que Canta. Follow the stone road down to the left to the beach. At the opposite end of the beach, you can reward yourself with a meal at one of the waterfront seafood restaurants.

According to local lore, Tarascan King Calzontzin ordered the construction of the barrier reef in **Playa Las Gatas** as protection from the sharks that give the beach its name. Since then, coral and an abundance of marine life have taken over the stone barricade. The calm, transparent waters welcome snorkelers (equipment can be rented for 40 pesos per day). Escape the shops and restaurant tables by taking a path behind the last restaurant to the **Garrobo Lighthouse,** which offers a panoramic view. Since it's well-hidden, ask any of the waiters for specific directions to *"el faro."* To reach Las Gatas, take a *lancha* from the pier in downtown Zihuatanejo (boats leave every 15min., 9am-4pm, last boat leaves Las Gatas 6pm, 10min., round-trip 15 pesos). It is possible, but not easy, to walk to Las Gatas from La Ropa over the rocks. Or, continue walking on the road that led to La Ropa for another 45 minutes or so. Taxis from downtown Zihuantanejo are 20 pesos.

## Ixtapa

Guarded by a row of hotels, **Playa del Palmar** is a people-watching, wave-hopping, massage-receiving paradise. Not only is it one of the more attractive beaches around, it is perhaps the most active. Without the protection of a bay, the beach is pummeled by sizeable waves, attracting parasailers, scuba divers, and jet skiers. All along the sand next to the swimming pools, people play volleyball, soccer, and jog (swimmers should obey the lifeguards and red/yellow/green flags). The beach can be reached from public access paths at its two extremes, near the Sheraton hotel or near Carlos 'n' Charlie's. Otherwise, clutch your *Let's Go* confidently, wear your swimsuit proudly, and walk right through the hotel lobbies.

To the northwest of Ixtapa are less crowded and more stylish **Playa Cuatas, Playa Quieta,** and **Playa Linda.** To drive here from Ixtapa, follow the boulevard northwest beyond most of the hotels and turn right at the sign for Playa Linda. If you're driving from Zihuatanejo, the access road from Rte. 200 is more convenient; go past the exit for Ixtapa in the direction of Puerto Vallarta and take the next left, marked Playa Linda. The road skirts **Laguna de Ixtapa** and hits the beach farther northwest. A taxi to Playa Linda or Playa Quieta costs about 15 pesos from Ixtapa or 40 pesos from Zihuatanejo. There is a "Playa Linda" bus that begins in Zihuantanejo and passes through Iztapa on its way to Playas Quieta and Linda. Crystal clear water and body-surfing waves await at Playa Cuatas, across the street from the tennis courts at Club Med on Playa Linda. Both Playa Linda and Playa Quieta are known for their tranquil waters and calm swimming conditions. At Playa Linda it is possible to rent horses and ride all the way to the Ixtapa River.

Some claim that of all the area's beaches, the most picturesque are those on **Isla Ixtapa,** about 2km offshore from Playa Quieta. The island is a must for snorkeling enthusiasts. Activity picks up in a few shoreside restaurants by day, but the island's 10 acres remain uninhabited at night. The main beach is **Playa Cuachalalate,** frequented by fishermen and vacationers eager to waterski. **Playa Varadero** is a small beach with calm waters and *palapa*-covered restaurants. On the ocean side of the island, **Playa Coral** is the least-visited beach of the three. It has no services and is not great for swimming, but the coral makes for excellent scuba diving. To get there, take a boat from the pier at Zihuatanejo (boats leave at noon, return at 5pm, 1hr., 40 pesos). A cheaper alternative is to take a *microbús* from Ixtapa to the pier at Playa Linda (2 pesos) and catch a *lancha* from there (every 15min., 9am-5pm, round-trip 15 pesos).

## ENTERTAINMENT

The beaches of Ixtapa and Zihuatanejo may be similar, but by nightfall the contrast between the cities becomes clear. Ixtapa supports a varied collection of dance clubs and dress-up restaurants, all of them on Blvd. Ixtapa. The premier place for dancing is **Christine** (tel. 3-03-33), in the Hotel Krystal. With its tiered seats, hanging vines, and light show, it is as artificially beautiful as Ixtapa itself (cover 50 pesos; open daily 10pm-6am). A restaurant by day, **Los Mandriles,** in the commercial center, becomes a nightclub around 11pm (cover 30 pesos for men, 15 pesos for women). **Carlos 'n' Charlie's,** at the end of the Playa Palmar next to Hotel Posada Road, attracts a crowd to its bar and beachfront dancing (no cover, but on weekend nights there is a 50-peso drink minimum; open daily 4pm-3am). **Señor Frog's** (tel. 3-06-92) is a restaurant until midnight; at that point, American dancers climb on the tables and the party begins.

Choices for nightlife in Zihuatanejo are few. There is a disco, **Rocka Rock,** at 5 de Mayo, but it lacks pizzazz and attendance. Look for the green building facing the Mercado de Artesanías (cover 15 pesos; open Thurs.-Sun. 11pm-late). A recent addition to the scene is **D'Latino,** on the corner of Bravo and Guerrero. This spicy latin dance club features salsa and reggae, with occasional live music (cover 30 pesos; open Thurs.-Sun. 11pm-late). If you're in Zihuatanejo at night, dancing is probably not on your mind. Dinner at **Morro Viejo,** inside the **Hotel Puerto Mío,** Playa del Almacén 5 (tel. 4-27-48), may be expensive, but drinks are reasonable and the view of the sunset priceless. From the pier, cross the rickety wooden bridge over the estuary, then turn left. The road ends at the hotel; the restaurant is to the right.

# ▓ Costa Grande

The Guerrero coast north of Acapulco is often called the Costa Grande to distinguish it from its smaller counterpart (Costa Chica) to the south. Trade with Asia centuries ago explains the Polynesian features of some of the area's inhabitants—silk wasn't the only thing exchanged here. Of specific interest are **Barra de Potosí,** 20km southeast of Zihuatanejo, and **Papanoa,** another 60km farther along Rte. 200.

## BARRA DE POTOSÍ

For the gringo whose head is spinning from ruins, cathedrals, and souvenirs, there is no better tonic than a spell at the seemingly infinite stretch of sand known as **Playa Barra de Potosí.** Life here just couldn't get any more *tranquila*. Tourists bask in the sun, their words rolling lazily off their tongues and their thoughts drifting effortlessly out to sea. *Camionetas* putter along the single sandy road, bouncing the inhabitants back and forth to their secluded homes. Now and then, someone stirs for a bit of fishing. The owners of the 12 or so open-air *enramadas* (informal *palapa* restaurants), just past the strip that constitutes "town," are proud of Playa Potosí's laid-back friendliness—and its reasonable prices.

Visitors to Barra de Potosí are expected to sleep in the hammocks that adorn each *enramada*. The owners don't care if you sack out in their hammocks forever—as long as you buy a meal from them every now and then. *Baños*, too, are free of charge. The owners will let you leave your pack in the *enramadas* for as long as you like. The *enramadas* farthest from the lagoon avoid flooding and tend to be the most magical in Barra de Potosí. Flex your travel savvy and sleep on the diagonal, so as to support your back. The mosquitoes are also free, so bring plenty of repellent.

Those still unskilled in the art of hammock-snoozing can indulge themselves at **Hotel Barra de Potosí** (tel. 4-82-90, 4-82-91, or 4-34-45), an unfinished resort hotel that has nevertheless opened its doors for business. From the *enramadas,* walk away from the lagoon; you'll immediately see its name on the sidewalk. Rooms in the completed portion of the hotel include a view of the beach, TV, ceiling fan, washing machine, and kitchen. Not all rooms have the same amenities, but all have access to the beachside swimming pool and restaurant (4-person rooms with water view and kitchen 200 pesos, without kitchen 150 pesos; doubles without either 100 pesos).

In keeping with the casual spirit, restaurants do not have set menus; rather, they ask you what type of seafood you'd like to eat (expect to spend 20-30 pesos per person). **Enramada Bacanora,** the third restaurant from the right as you face the water, offers the friendliest atmosphere and cheapest prices (open daily 7am-6pm).

If you simply *must* exert yourself while in Barra de Potosí (something the locals may not understand), your only option is to hike up the dirt road to the lighthouse that sits atop **Cerro Guamiule** (2000m), the peak near the restaurants that guards the southern entrance to the bay. After a half-hour walk, you will be rewarded with a view of the bay and its 20km of beaches. After gaping, walk north along the shore of Playa Potosí, the southernmost beach on the bay, to the aptly named **Playa Blanca** (3km). You will pass **Playa Coacoyul** (8km), **Playa Riscaliyo** (19km), and pebbly **Playa Manzanillo** (24km) before reaching another lighthouse (26km), which overlooks the northern edge of the bay. All beaches are free of tourists in the summer months but fill up with a few hundred Mexican visitors during Christmas.

**Getting There:** From Zihuatanejo, "Petatlán" buses for Potosí leave from a station outside Restaurante La Jaiba on Las Palmas off Juárez (every 15min., 6am-9pm, ½hr., 3 pesos). Ask to be let off at Achotes, an unmarked intersection. A pick-up truck will be waiting (or will be arriving soon) on the side road to pick up passengers and make the bumpy trip to the *enramadas* (½hr., 4 pesos). Trucks return to the intersection from the same spot (every ½hr., until 5pm); the bus to Zihuatanejo leaves from the other side of the highway.

# ■ Acapulco

Once upon a time, Acapulco was the stunningly beautiful playground of the rich and famous. Hollywood legends once celebrated their silver-screen successes by dancing the Mexican nights away in its chic clubs, politicians spent their honeymoons hopping between its attractive shores, and scores of passengers on "The Love Boat" found televised love always exciting and new on the path from the Aloha Deck to the docks at Acapulco Bay. But time passes and fairytales fade: Acapulco's glamour went out at just about the time that Gopher hung up his cruise-ship whites and got himself elected to the U.S. Congress.

Today, Acapulco, a metropolis of 1.5 million, is two things—a slim, glitzy fingernail of a resort with beaches to one side and downtown to the other, and a slum that reaches up into the hills behind the resorts. This second, grimmer Acapulco was born when the heavily moneyed stopped vacationing on Acapulco's shore and hotel jobs could no longer keep pace with the waves of immigration drawn seaward from the interior by the prospect of plentiful pesos. Now more than ever, everyone in Acapulco is driven by money—either the need to spend it or the need to earn it. Vendors crowd the streets and cling to slow-moving or indecisive visitors; restaurant owners wave travelers inside with their menus. Peddlers of everything from Chiclets to "free information" run at tourists like eager bulls. But the high-rise hotels crowding the waterfront have lost the first flush of youth, and the Mexican families (as well as the older Europeans and *norteamericanos*) who come in droves to vacation here convey the sense that they are going through the obligatory holiday motions. Perhaps the best time to visit the city is at night, when darkness shrouds the grime and allows the glitter of the streetlamps to evoke Acapulco's fairytale past.

## ORIENTATION

Acapulco Bay lies 400km south of Mexico City and 239km southeast of Ixtapa/Zihuatanejo. Rte. 200 feeds into **La Costera (Avenida Costera Miguel Alemán),** the main drag. The traditional downtown area, with the *zócalo* and the cathedral, is in the western part of town (to the left as seen from the water). **Acapulco Dorado,** full of fast-food chains, malls, and luxury hotels, stretches from **Parque Papagayo** to the naval base. The ultra-chic resorts on **Acapulco Diamante,** farther east towards the airport, wipe out any dirty trace of Mexico that would disturb the paying guests. Most

**Acapulco**

Estrella Blanca buses, 13
Estrella de Oro Buses, 14
Casa de Huéspedes La
  Mamá Hélène, 10
Catedral de Nuestra Sra.
  de Solidad, 11
CICI Waterpark, 16
Fuerte de San Diego, 12
Hotel Angelita, 5
Hotel Asturias, 4
Hotel Coral, 9
Hotel Misión, 8
Hotel Torre Eiffel, 3
Jovito's, 15
Mágico Mundo Marino, 1
Muséo del Arqueologia, 17
Palacio Municipal, 6
Palladium, 18
Plaza de Toros Caletilla, 2
Post Office, 7

budget accommodations and restaurants lie between the *zócalo* and **La Quebrada**, the famous cliff-diving spot. In southwest Acapulco, a peninsula with **Playas Caleta** and **Caletilla** juts out into the bay.

"Hornos" or "Cici" buses run from Caleta along the Costera all the way to the naval base (2 pesos). "Cine Río-La Base" buses go from the *zócalo* to the base down Av. Cuauhtémoc. To get from the **Estrella de Oro** bus station to the *zócalo* (a 40min. walk), cross the street and flag down any bus heading southwest (1.80 pesos). A *"zócalo"* bus (2 pesos) will do the trick from the **Estrella Blanca** station. A **taxi** from the *zócalo* to the bus station costs 15 pesos, to the airport 75 pesos.

## PRACTICAL INFORMATION

**Tourist Offices: SEFOTUR,** Costera 187 (tel. 86-91-64), on Playa Hornos across from Banamex. Open Mon.-Fri. 9am-2pm and 4-7pm, Sat. 10am-2pm. In an **emer-**

**gency,** contact the **Procuraduría del Turista,** Costera 4455 (tel. 84-45-83), in the Centro Internacional in front of CICI waterpark. Open daily 9am-9pm.

**Tourist police:** Tel. 85-04-90. Officers clad in white wander around the *zócalo.*

**Travel Agency: M&M Tours,** Costera 26A (tel. 84-89-60), on Playa Condesa between McDonald's and the Fiesta Americana. Open daily 8am-10pm.

**Consulates: Canada,** Costera at Juan Pérez (tel. 86-50-45), in the Continental Hotel. Open daily 10am-2pm. **U.K., Australia,** and **New Zealand** (tel. 84-16-50 or 84-66-05), in the Hotel Las Brisas. Open Mon.-Fri. 9am-2pm and 4-7pm. **U.S.,** (tel. 69-05-56), in Hotel Club del Sol, next to the Canadian Consulate. Open Mon.-Fri. 10am-2pm. **Casa Consular** (tel. 84-70-50, ext. 116 or 117), in the Centro Internacional Acapulco, provides info on other consulates. Open Mon.-Fri. 9am-2pm and 4-7pm.

**Currency Exchange: Banks** on the Costera have decent rates. All open Mon.-Fri. 9am-3pm. *Casas de cambio* are ubiquitous, and often open until 8pm.

**American Express,** Costera 1628 (tel. 69-11-00 to -24; fax 69-11-88), on the bottom floor of the shopping center. Open Mon.-Sat. 10am-7pm.

**Telephones: LADATELs** line the Costera. **Caseta Carranza,** Carranza 9, is two blocks from the *zócalo* towards the strip. Open daily 8am-10pm.

**Fax:** (tel. 82-26-21; fax 83-84-82), on the Costera next to the post office. Open for **telegrams** and **money orders,** as well. Open Mon.-Fri. 8am-7pm, Sat. 9am-noon.

**Airport:** (tel. 66-90-35 or 66-95-34), on Rte. 200, 26km south of the city. **Aerocaribe** (tel. 84-23-42). **Aeroméxico** (tel. 85-22-80). **American** (tel. 66-92-33). **Continental** (tel. 66-90-63). **Delta** (tel. 84-14-28). **Mexicana** (tel. 84-68-90). **Taesa** (tel. 86-45-76).

**Buses: Estrella de Oro,** on Cuauhtémoc at Massiu (tel. 85-87-05), to Cuernavaca (10:30am, 3:40, 5:30, and 8pm, 4hr., 110 pesos), Mexico City (every hr., 6:45am-midnight, 5hr., 180 pesos), Taxco (7, 9, 11:30am, and 4:30pm, 4hr., 80 pesos), and Zihuatanejo (3pm, 3hr., 70 pesos). **Estrella Blanca,** Av. Ejido 47 (tel. 69-20-29), to Chilpancingo (every 30min., 3:40am-10pm, 2hr., 28 pesos), Cuernavaca (7 per day, 5hr., 100 pesos), Mexico City (1:30, 4:15, 5:30, and 11pm, 5hr., 135 pesos), Puebla (10:10am, 12:15, 10pm, and midnight, 7hr., 175 pesos), and Querétaro (5 per day, 8-10hr., 162-182 pesos).

**Car Rental: Hertz,** Costera 1945 (tel. 85-68-89), past La Gran Plaza on the left. Small VW with insurance 315 pesos per day. Open daily 8am-7pm.

**Bookstore: Sanborn's,** Costera 209, 2 blocks from the *zócalo* towards the hotel zone. Selection of English paperbacks. Open daily 7:30am-11pm.

**Markets: Mercado,** Av. Constituyentes at Hurtado. Open daily 6am-9pm. **Supermarket Comercial Mexicana,** near the tourist office. Open daily 8am-8pm.

**Laundromat: Lavadín,** on José Iglesias (tel. 82-28-90), 1 block left of the cathedral. Same day and delivery service. Open Mon.-Sat. 8am-8pm.

**Red Cross:** On Ruiz Cortínez (tel. 85-41-01), north of the *zócalo.* Take a "Hospital" bus. 24hr. emergency service. No English spoken. **Sociedad de Asistencia Médica Turística** (tel. 85-58-00 or 85-59-59) has a 24hr. doctor. English spoken.

**Pharmacy: Faber Farmacia,** Azueta 6, 2 blocks left of the cathedral. Open 24hr. **ISSTE Farmacias,** Quebrada 1 (tel. 82-34-77), directly behind the cathedral on the *zócalo.* The storefront faces Independencia. Open daily 8am-8pm.

**Hospital: IMSS,** Ruiz Cortínez 128 (tel. 86-36-08), north of the *zócalo* along Madero. Take a "Hospital" bus. 24hr. emergency service.

**Police: LOCATEL** (tel. 81-11-00 or 81-11-64), next door to the SEFOTUR office. Locates lost people and vehicles. Contacts police or ambulance. Open 24hr.

**Post Office:** Costera 215 (tel. 82-20-83), on the ground floor of the Palacio Federal. Open Mon.-Fri. 8am-7pm, Sat. 9am-1pm. **Postal Code:** 39300.

**Phone Code:** 74.

## ACCOMMODATIONS

Sleeping on the beaches of Acapulco Bay is unsafe. Fortunately, budget accommodations are easier to find here than anywhere else on Mexico's Pacific coast. Acapulco is a haggler's dream: be certain to inquire about discounts before paying for a room. However, during Semana Santa rooms are nearly double the off-season prices, and it's hard to find lodgings without a previous reservation. The first two hotels listed are near the *zócalo*. The last four are near La Quebrada; to get there, take Hidalgo and follow it to the right as it forks uphill.

**Hotel Misión,** Prof. J. Felipe Valle 12 at La Paz (tel. 82-36-43), 2 blocks left of the *zócalo*. The guests chatting over breakfast (9-15 pesos) in the courtyard and the lazy cats sprawled out on the stairway give it a homey feel. Colonial architecture and well-tended plants make staying here as soothing as possible. All rooms have ceiling fans and private baths; some have desks and sofas. 80 pesos per person.

**Casa de Huéspedes Mama Hélène,** Benito Juárez 12 at Felipe Valle (tel. 82-23-96; fax 83-86-97). French owner holds court over a posse of ping-pong-playing, coffee-drinking, chain-smoking Euro-backpackers. Haphazard collection of English novels. Flowery rooms with fans but no hot water. Singles 80 pesos; doubles 120 pesos.

**Hotel Angelita,** Quebrada 37 (tel. 83-57-34). A cool night's sleep is guaranteed here—2 fans keep all rooms well-ventilated. Everything is very clean and tidy. Welcoming proprietress and hot water make Angelita popular with foreigners and Mexicans. Singles 50 pesos; doubles 80 pesos; each additional person 40 pesos.

**La Torre Eiffel,** Inalámbrica 110 (tel. 82-16-83). At the top of La Quebrada, turn left and walk up a very steep hill. All rooms have hot water, fans, and TVs, making this a terrific value. Shady terrace offers a clear view of the ocean. Swimming pool. 40-50 pesos per person.

**Hotel Asturias,** Quebrada 45 (tel. 83-65-48), near Hotel Angelita. All rooms have fans, 24hr. hot water, and at least 2 beds. Guests enjoy attentive staff and a swimming pool. Singles 60 pesos; doubles 90 pesos. Each additional person 40 pesos.

## FOOD

Acapulco's restaurants are a godsend for Americans homesick for fast-food gringo cuisine. The many chic restaurants between Playa Condesa and the base cater mainly to tourists who apparently don't fret about money. If you insist on eating on the Costera, try **El Fogón,** across from the Continental Plaza (sandwiches 10 pesos; open 24hr.) or **Jovito's** (tel. 84-84-33), across from the Fiesta Americana at Playa Condesa (*tacos de mariscos* 23 pesos; open daily 1pm-midnight). As usual, *típico* spots serve cheaper meals; try the hundreds of **fondas** (food stands) throughout the city or the Mercado Central.

**Mariscos Nacho's,** Azueta and Juárez (tel. 82-28-91), 1 block from the Costera. An open-air *marisquería* serving seafood with rice (25 pesos) and delicious *camarones al mojo de ajo* (garlic shrimp, 45 pesos). Nacho's is always bustling, whether it's a sunburned family straggling in off the beach or a group of young hipsters dolled up for a night on the town. Open daily 8am-11pm.

**100% Natural,** Costera 248 at the corner of Sebastián Vizcaíno (tel. 85-13-12 ext. 100), across from the tourist office. Several other branches line the Costera. Health food restaurant serving hearty sandwiches with sprouts and lettuce (26-30 pesos), fruit salad (19-22 pesos), and chilly, smooth *licuados* (14-16 pesos). Lots of options for vegetarians. Open daily 8am-midnight. Other branches open 24hr.

**The Fat Farm/La Granja del Pingui,** Juárez 10 at La Paz, next door to Mama Hélène. Vegetable soup (9 pesos) is a specialty. Watch TV as you enjoy your poultry and meat (17-26 pesos) or fish (18-28 pesos) entree. Open daily 10am-10pm.

## SAND AND SIGHTS

### Península de las Playas

At **La Quebrada,** Speedo-clad daredevil *clavadistas* (divers) perform death-defying dives that make Olympians look like wusses (shows at 12:45, 7:30, 8:30, 9:30, and 10:30pm). Each performance includes at least two 25m dives and one 35m dive. The divers all pray rather theatrically (who can blame them?) at a shrine at the top of the cliff before the plunge. The show is a quintessential part of the Acapulco tourist experience. Though most spectators congregate at the bottom level, closest to the cliff, the view is better from the levels to the immediate right of the ticket booth. La Quebrada is a 15-minute walk from the *zócalo,* following the road that starts to the left of the cathedral's entrance. Continue until it ends at the parking lot of the hotel.

At the westernmost tip of Acapulco Bay, on the seaward side of the peninsula, lie **Playas Caleta** and **Caletilla.** Their gently rolling waves are ideal for swimming and attract hundreds of local families, making it hard for the Hart sisters to find an empty patch of sand anywhere. The narrow causeway that separates the two beaches leads to the island occupied by **Mágico Mundo Marino** (tel. 83-11-93), a water park with slides and pools (open daily 9am-7pm; admission 25 pesos, children under 12 15 pesos).

The **Plaza de Toros Caletilla,** Acapulco's main bull ring, sits beyond the abandoned yellow jai alai auditoriums 200m west of Caletilla beach. *Corridas* take place from Sundays at 5pm, December until Easter week, when the best-known *matadores* appear. Buy tickets at the Centro Kennedy box office, Costera at Álvaro Saavedra (tel. 85-85-40), or at the bull ring after 4:30pm on the day of the fight.

## From the Tourist Office to Parque Papagayo

The stretch of sand along the **Costera,** away from Old Acapulco, is blessed with few highrises and smaller crowds than the beaches at Caleta or farther down the bay. **Playas Tamarindo, Hornos,** and **Hornitos,** between Las Hamacas Hotel and the Radisson, are called the "afternoon beaches." This is where the fishermen bring in their catches. The waves are moderate, and the sand's great for beach sports. The only drawback is that these beaches are unmistakably urban—you can hear the traffic on Costera as you sunbathe.

Mexican families who seek an alternative to the beach come to **Parque Papagayo,** which sprawls from Costera to Av. Cuauhtémoc. Entering on Costera by the Gigante supermarket, you'll find a **roller skating rink** (admission 10 pesos, 8 pesos to rent regular skates, 10 pesos for rollerblades; open daily 4pm-midnight). The rest of the park has shaded paths for bikes and walkers. There's an aviary in the center, surrounded by an artificial lake where you can rent paddleboats (10 pesos). Kids will find a wading pool, exotic birds from Australia, and a zillion shady spots for hide and seek (tel. 85-71-77; open Mon.-Fri. 6am-7pm, Sat.-Sun. 6am-8pm).

## From La Diana to the Naval Base

A trip to **Playa Condesa,** at the center of the bay, is always exhilarating. Exercise caution: the waves are strong, and the sea floor drops without warning. The poor swimming conditions don't bother the throngs of sun worshippers who alternately lounge under their blue umbrellas and treat the beach as a runway for their minimal clothing fashion shows. Farther down the bay, between the golf course and naval base, is **Playa Icacos.** As you move toward the base, the waves become gentler.

**CICI,** Costera at Cristóbal Colón (tel. 84-80-33), is a state-owned **water park.** Let artificial waves toss and hurl you headfirst down the long, winding water slides, then rush to watch trained dolphins perform (shows at 12:30, 2:30, and 5pm; open daily 10am-6pm; admission 60 pesos, children under 11 50 pesos). To reach the park, follow Costera until you see the walls painted with bright blue waves and larger-than-life dolphins, or simply take a "CICI" or "Base" bus (2 pesos).

## Puerto Marqués

Lacking the pre-packaged polish of the strip only a few kilometers away, the beach town of **Puerto Marqués** encompasses an unremarkable ribbon of sand lined wall to wall with restaurants so close to the water that the bay's waves lap at diners' feet. The bus ride to this bay is the real attraction, thanks to a magnificent vista from the top of the hill before descending into town. Take a "Puerto Marqués" bus across the street from La Diana or by Comercial Mexicana supermarket at Playa Hornitos, on the beach side of the street (about every 30min., 5:30am-9pm, 45min., 1.80 pesos). As the bus rambles along, the Bahía de Puerto Marqués and the pounding surf of **Playa Revolcadero** come into full view. Beautiful **Playa Pichilingue,** a small, often-deserted patch of sand on the Bay, is inaccessible by land. From Puerto Marqués, it's possible to get to nicer beaches that have fewer crowds. catch a "Bonville" bus to get to **Playa Bonville**—a big improvement on the crowds and traffic of the downtown beaches.

## ENTERTAINMENT

In Acapulco, every night is Saturday night: the nightlife just *hums*. Most clubs pulsate with activity from 11pm to 5am and charge over 100 pesos for cover, which usually includes open bar. It's always easier and cheaper for women to get in; many clubs offer free admission (and open bar) to women on weeknights. The best clubs all cluster in the area around the CICI, the opposite side of the bay from the *zócalo*. Head and shoulders above the rest is **Palladium,** on the carretera Escenica Las Brisas (tel. 81-03-00). A space-age structure perched on a cliff with a truly fabulous view of the downtown lights, this hot spot features a wall of glass to enjoy the view, high-tech light and smoke effects, and watching the crowd is like attending a fashion show (cover 180 pesos for men, 130 pesos for women; open bar; open daily 10:30pm-5am). Sporting a medieval castle theme, **Andrómedas,** on Costera just past Planet Hollywood and the Hard Rock Café, is another happenin' place. Across Costera from Andrómedas is **Atrium,** Costera 30 (tel. 84-19-00). Mirrored exterior, smoke, laser lights, and a surreal underwater scuba projection behind the bar keep the young crowd entertained (cover 140 pesos for men, 100 pesos for women; open 10pm-late). Another 100km further down the Costera lies **Baby O's,** Costera 22 (tel. 84-74-74). This club is slightly less frenetic and more sophisticated (read: older) than its rambunctious neighbors (no cover weeknights; weekends 100 pesos for men, 50 pesos for women, no open bar; open 10:30pm-late). Alternatives to the hi-tech, exclusive discos include **Disco Beach** (tel. 84-82-30), on Condesa beach, which offers pool, video games, and free pizza on Saturday night, in addition to thumping dance tunes (cover 150 pesos men, 80 pesos women; open 11pm-whenever the dancing stops), and **Nina's,** Costera 2909 (tel. 84-24-00), on the beach side near CICI, with live tropical music (cover 110 pesos; open 10pm-5am).

Non-dancers flock to **Plaza Bahía,** a large shopping mall on Costera past La Gran Plaza on the water side, to satisfy the urge to acquire. Speed around a mini race course at **Go-Karts** (tel. 86-71-47), on the third floor (20 pesos for 5min., 25 pesos for 10min.; open daily 10am-1am), or bowl at the **Boliche** (tel. 85-09-70), on the fourth floor (130 pesos per hr., shoes 7 pesos; open daily 11am-2am). There is a snazzy movie theater on the second floor (15-20 pesos).

## ■ Near Acapulco: Pie de la Cuesta

**Pie de la Cuesta** is known for its truly magnificent sunsets—the lazy sun lingers beautifully over the Pacific horizon just before dropping out of view. A single-lane highway runs through Acapulco's hills to Pie de la Cuesta, ending at the narrow road that separates the Pacific from the placid waters of **Laguna de Coyuca,** and the hustle and bustle of Acapulco from the serenity of a small beach community.

At Playa Pie de la Cuesta, pleasure-seekers can choose between salt and fresh water. Since the Pacific's rough waves preclude swimming, many head to the lagoon instead, the site of the area's best **water skiing.** Several ski clubs line the lagoon (ski rental about 250 pesos per hr., 40 pesos for a lesson). Rest and relaxation is all too often interrupted, unfortunately, by aggressive *lancha* agents. Their tours of the lagoon include visits to the area where the exploding helicopter scene from *Rambo* was filmed (about 30 pesos per person in a *colectivo* boat). *Lancha* agents notwithstanding, the serenity of Pie de la Cuesta is worth at least a daytrip. The air is cleaner here, the water bluer, the surf stronger, the beach less crowded, and the scenery more stunning than in Acapulco. **Villa Nirvana** (tel. 60-16-31), a blue and white building a few blocks from the bus stop, carves out its own utopia complete with restaurant, swimming pool, and rooms with fans and private baths (60 pesos per person; high season 80 pesos). Beyond the pharmacy towards the base is **Acapulco Trailer Park** (tel. 60-00-10), with campgrounds, trailer hook-up sites, bathrooms, and ocean views (40 pesos per night).

SOUTHERN PACIFIC COAST

**Getting There:** Buses leave from Costera, across from the post office in Acapulco. Buses marked "Pie de la Cuesta Playa" go directly to the road along the beach; those labeled "Pie de la Cuesta Centro" stop on a parallel street in a small marketplace (40min., 2 pesos). From there, turn left down a dirt road; you should be able to see the shimmering ocean in the distance. At the end of the road, turn right and you're headed towards the base. A *combi* will take you as far as **La Barra,** the enchanted spot where the water from the lagoon flows into the ocean (2 pesos). To return to Acapulco, go back to the market and hail a bus going to the right.

# OAXACA

## ■ Tuxtepec

After years of neglect by Oaxaca's highland capital, Tuxtepec is now booming—signs of growth are everywhere, from the massive Corona brewery on the city's edge to dozens of new storefronts that lie in its shadow. In the past two decades, the city's population has skyrocketed from 20,000 to about 110,000. Boom and beauty rarely go hand in hand, and this is no exception: busy, hard-working Tuxtepec is a far cry from the sleepy colonial towns that lure tourists to the state. The city's only value to travelers is as a tolerable place to pass a night on the way to Oaxaca from the Gulf.

**Orientation and Practical Information** Tuxtepec is on the northern frontier of Oaxaca state, 222km from the state capital and 165km south of Veracruz. The Papaloapan River forms a U-shaped bend here, running along one edge of the city. The two main plazas—**Parque Juárez,** the *zócalo* proper, located at one end of the *centro,* and **Parque Hidalgo,** at the opposite side of downtown—are connected by **Av. Independencia,** where many of the restaurants, hotels, and banks cluster. From the **ADO** station at Ortiz and Primero de Mayo, exit the waiting area and turn right around the corner. Walk straight for one block and turn right on **Blvd. A. Camacho,** the wide thoroughfare; continue past the statue on **Matamoros.** The **AU** and **Cuenca** station is on the right as you head towards the river. Exiting from that station, turn right and follow Matamoros for 3½ blocks until it ends at Independencia. Taxis will take you for 8 pesos. Walking down Matamoros from the bus stations, the crossstreets will be, in order, **Carranza, Libertad, 5 de Mayo, 20 de Noviembre,** and then **Independencia.** To reach the *zócalo,* turn left on Libertad and follow it up to **Allende,** which constitutes one side of the *zócalo.* To get to **Parque Hidalgo,** turn right on 20 de Noviembre.

Tuxtepec has no tourist office, but the offices of **Ayuntamiento** on the second floor of the Palacio Municipal, located at the intersection of 5 de Mayo and Guerrero (tel. 5-15-66), can answer queries or give directions (open Mon.-Fri. 9am-2pm and 5-8pm). **Banamex,** Independencia 36 (tel. 5-23-28), just off the corner of the *zócalo,* accepts both cash and traveler's checks and has an **ATM** (open Mon.-Fri. 9am-3pm). There are **LADATELs** in the *zócalo* and Parque Hidalgo, among other spots. **ADO buses** (tel. 5-04-73) travel to Mexico City (5 per day, 8hr., 128 pesos), Oaxaca (12:30am, 10:30, and 11:15pm, 6hr., 51 pesos), Puebla (8:30am and 11:15pm, 6hr., 93 pesos), Veracruz (8 per day, 3hr., 42 pesos), Xalapa (5am, 5hr., 68 pesos), and other destinations. **AU,** on Matamoros (tel. 5-04-73), and **Cuenca** (tel. 5-02-37), in the same station, offer similar service.

**Farmacia Albatros,** 20 de Noviembre 996 (tel. 5-25-82), at Aldama is open 24 hours. The **Red Cross,** Madero 110 (tel. 5-00-57), one block west of Blvd. Benito Juárez, is open 24 hours (no English spoken). The **police** (tel. 5-31-66) are available 24 hours in the Palacio Municipal. In case of **emergency,** call the **Policía Preventiva** (tel. 5-15-45) anytime. The **post office** is at the corner of Independencia and Hidalgo (open Mon.-Fri. 8am-7pm). **Postal code:** 68300. **Phone Code:** 287.

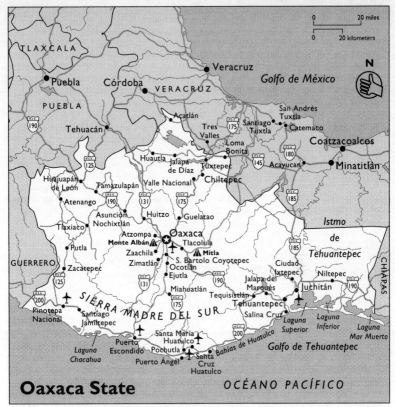

**Oaxaca State**

OCÉANO PACÍFICO

**Accommodations, Food, and Entertainment** Tuxtepec has several inexpensive hotels. Particularly well-located is **Hotel Posada Guadalupana,** Independencia 584 (tel. 5-11-95), between Matamoros and Aldama. From the second-class bus station, follow Matamoros until it hits Independencia, then turn left; the hotel will be on the left side of the block. The rocking chairs around the patio provide an escape from the bustle of Independencia. Newer rooms are more spacious and nicer than old ones, with cable TV and well-equipped bathrooms. All rooms have fans (singles 35-65 pesos; doubles 45-80 pesos; add 20 pesos for A/C). The bedrooms at **Hotel La Misión,** Hidalgo 409 (tel. 5-23-81), are spartan and rather somber. From Matamoros, turn left on Carranza and walk five blocks to Hidalgo towards the *zócalo;* the hotel is on the left side. It's got hot water all day and fans in the rooms (singles 45 pesos; doubles 50 pesos; triples 55 pesos).

Tuxtepec is a solidly working- and middle-class city, so there are lots of affordable restaurants along Independencia. For super-cheap eats, head to the **market** on Independencia and Calle Juárez and the stalls along Matamoros. Enjoy juice squeezed fresh from the cornucopia for 6 pesos at **Cocina Económica California,** Independencia 35, near Hidalgo. *Tortas* are 5 pesos; the *comida corrida* (12 pesos) is served quicker than you can chew it. The airy interior manages to combine juice-bar chic with friendly home cooking (open daily 7am-7pm).

In the evening, locals gather in the squares and on the few terraces along Independencia that offer views of the river. If so inspired, you might head to one of the two discos in town. **Fettiche** is at Av. 2 and Calle 3 (tel. 5-23-39), west of the ADO station (open Thurs.-Sat. 9pm-3am), while **Chichos** is on Blvd. Juárez (cover 15-20 pesos; open Thurs.-Sat. 9pm-3am and Sun. 6-11pm). **Bars** line Independencia and abound in the area bounded by Blvd. A. Camacho and Calle de la Felicidad. **Cinema Plus,** 20 de Noviembre 1364, shows English-language movies (10 pesos).

## ■ Near Tuxtepec

The area around Tuxtepec is renowned for its scenic beauty; unfortunately, most of it is not easily accessible by bus. The sites along the road to Oaxaca are perhaps the easiest to reach. They are served by an **AU** bus en route to **Valle Nacional,** a small tobacco-growing town 58km from Tuxtepec, where Porfirio Díaz once built a work camp for his political enemies. On the way there, the bus passes through **Chiltepec,** a town famous among gastronomes for its renditions of regional cuisine, and crosses a small suspension bridge on its way to **Jacatepec.** Another bus passes through **San Lucas Ojitlán** and **Xalapa de Díaz,** 42km and 70km from Tuxtepec, respectively. Ojitlán is notable for its *artesanías,* while Xalapa is known for its brightly colored *huipiles.* Other destinations are accessible by *colectivo* from the Mercado Flores Magón, on 20 de Noviembre between Riva Palacio and Blvd. Juárez, two blocks west of Parque Hidalgo. Consult the folks at the office for *cultura popular* to find out about musical events and crafts in nearby towns.

## ■ Oaxaca

Perched on a giant plateau that gracefully interrupts the Sierra Madre del Sur's descent into the Oaxaca valley, the city of Oaxaca de Juárez (pop. 250,000) is a rare beauty. The city's surname was added in honor of native son Benito Juárez, a Oaxacan Zapotec and Mexico's only *indígena* president. It earned its older nickname, "City of Jade," after Hernán Cortés began to build his beloved (but unfinished) estate here in 1535. Cortés's deep green stone buildings have since aged to a dignified yellow, and throughout the streets this style has been lovingly preserved and imitated, giving Oaxaca the feel of a city that lives and breathes its own remarkable history. Especially in the early morning, the city is strikingly beautiful; at first light, the city's high, green, gracefully aging silhouettes are spectacular.

A relatively affluent and cosmopolitan city, Oaxaca has recently become a major destination for tourists of all ages and nationalities who are lured by its prestigious museums, outstanding archaeological sites, and sheer attractiveness. For many visitors, one-month stays at a language school turn into whole summers of immersion, and those who do leave make plans to return to sip rich Oaxacan hot chocolate as soon as they can. In the face of the Teva-wearing crowds, the city manages to retain an air of authenticity rather than dilution. The *zócalo,* lined with sprawling jacaranda trees and outdoor cafes, is one of the most amiable in the Republic. Expect to see all of Mexico in evidence here: merchants, *indígenas,* and professionals jostling elbows; *norteamericanos* jabbering away at the city's fine language schools; and restless students, some tearing around on expensive motorcycles, others agitating for labor reform. But neither tourism nor politics can do anything to diminish Oaxaca's cultural richness—nor its colonial allure. Day and night, when streetlights play up and down the stone faces of its magnificent churches, Oaxaca is a wonder to behold.

### ORIENTATION

Oaxaca de Juárez rests in the Oaxaca Valley, between the towering Sierra Madre del Sur and the Puebla-Oaxaca range, 523km southeast of Mexico City, 435km south of Veracruz, and 526km west of Tuxtla Gutiérrez. Principal access to Oaxaca from the north and east is via Rte. 190. While most of Oaxaca's streets form a grid, many change names as they swing by the *zócalo.* The large, English-language maps posted around the *zócalo,* at the bus stations, and in the lobbies of fancy hotels clearly mark all sights. There are two main squares in the center of the historic district. The *zócalo,* or **Plaza de la Constitución,** is formed by the side of the cathedral and the arches of the Palacio de Gobierno opposite the cathedral. The main entrance to the cathedral faces the **Plaza Alameda de León,** bounded by the post office on the opposite side.

# Oaxaca

Casa Arnel, 1
Hotel Lupita, 7
Hotel Pasaje, 8
Hotel Pombo, 6
Hotel Reforma, 2
Iglesia de Santo Domingo, 5
Palacio Municipal
(Tourist Office), 3
Youth Hostel El Pasador, 4

NOTE: Streets generally change their names at ZÓCALO

SOUTHERN PACIFIC COAST

### Swingers

The main plaza in Oaxaca, with its live music and numerous cafes, draws out crowds of locals and foreigners every night. *"Zócalo* Boys," as everyone calls them, are an integral part of the culture that has developed around this international mix of people. These playful men tend to come from wealthy Oaxacan families and have artistic and intellectual leanings; they are well-dressed and often speak English. They spend their nights at the cafes, striking up conversations with foreign women sitting at nearby tables. Part of their attraction to their pastime is having the kind of flirtatious, carefree, frank conversation with a woman that would not always be possible within the norms of *machismo.* Undoubtedly, another explanation for their fascination with their game is the potential for physical intrigue with their conversational partners. Casual conversations easily turn into lunch or movie dates. *Zócalo* Boys are not confined to the *zócalo;* many frequent the salsa bar *Candela,* where they charm foreign women with their moves. One is so renowned for his rhythm that he offers dance lessons—*por supuesto,* only to women.

The street that runs between the two squares is **Av. Hidalgo,** one of the few streets that does not change names. The street running behind the cathedral and the *zócalo* begins as **Bustamante** below the *zócalo,* turns into **Valdivieso** behind the cathedral, and ends up as the **Andador Turístico (Av. Macedonio Alcalá),** a museum-lined pedestrian walkway, past the Plaza Alameda.

Oaxaca's downtown is circumscribed by a busy peripheral expressway, called the **Periférico** in the south, but known by other names as it loops above the Church of Santo Domingo. Avenida Hidalgo divides *el centro* into two principal areas: the budget district lies south of Hidalgo, while expensive hotels and restaurants cluster around the *zócalo* north of and on Hidalgo. Most of Oaxaca's sights are snuggled between lavish private residences in the neighborhood north of Hidalgo. The main street that runs to the left of the entrance to the cathedral is **Av. Independencia.** Banks, long-distance phones, and newsstands cluster around the two blocks between Independencia and **Trujano/Guerrero,** which runs along the *zócalo.*

The **first-class bus station** is on Calzada Niños Héroes de Chapultepec, 11 blocks from the *zócalo* past the Andador Turístico. To reach the *zócalo* from the bus station, cross the street and catch a bus marked "Centro" (1.20 pesos). The bus turns left on Juárez. If you get off at Hidalgo, the *zócalo* will be three blocks to your right. To make the 20-minute walk from the station, head left on Chapultepec for six blocks to Alcalá and turn left; then walk 12 blocks to the main plaza. From the **AU station,** take the *colectivo* marked "Centro," which will eventually head down Independencia. Ask to be let off at García Vigil, which will put you at the end of the Plaza Alameda away from the *zócalo;* the main square is one block towards the cathedral. If you care to make the 2km walk from the station (not recommended after dark), take a left coming out the door, walk to the stoplight, take a right onto Madero, and follow it to the **train station.** A 25-minute walk stretches ahead of you: turn right as if coming out of the station, walk five long blocks, then turn left onto Independencia, which will lead you to the *zócalo.* You can also catch the *colectivo* marked "Centro" at the train station. From the **second-class bus station,** exit the terminal, and cross the street to take a bus or taxi to the *centro.* Or, you could walk to the left, cross the busy Periférico at the stoplight, follow it for a block, turn on Trujano and follow it east for eight long blocks until you hit the *zócalo.* **Taxis** charge 10 pesos from any of these stations. It's a good idea to take a taxi when crossing town late at night, but be aware that cabbies charge extra from 11pm to 5am

## PRACTICAL INFORMATION

**Tourist Offices: SEDETUR,** 5 de Mayo 200 at Morelos (tel. 6-48-28), provides brochures, maps, assistance in finding hotel rooms, information on fairs, and details on the surrounding villages. English spoken. Smaller office at Independencia 607 (tel.

6-01-23), inside the Palacio Municipal. Both open daily 9am-8pm. **CEPROTUR,** Alcalá 407 (tel./fax 6-72-80), on the Andador Turístico at Allende, and in the Plaza Santo Domingo, provides assistance to tourists. Open daily 9am-9pm. **Info booth** at the airport (tel. 1-50-40).

**Consulates:** In an emergency, **CEPROTUR** (above) will get consular assistance. **Canada,** Dr. Liceaga 119 #8 (tel. 3-37-77; fax 5-21-47). Open Mon.-Fri. 9am-2pm. **Germany** and **U.K.,** Hidalgo 817 #5 (tel. 3-08-65 and 6-72-80). Open Mon.-Fri. 9am-8pm. **U.S.,** Alcalá 201 #204 at Morelos (tel. 4-30-54). Hidden under an arched doorway. Open Mon.-Fri. 9am-2pm.

**Currency Exchange: Banamex,** Hidalgo 821 at 3 de Mayo (tel. 6-59-00), 1 block from the *zócalo,* has an **ATM.** Open Mon.-Fri. 9am-11:30am. **Banco Serfín,** Independencia 705, to the left of the cathedral's entrance, also has an **ATM.** Open Mon.-Fri. 9am-2pm. **Cash Express,** Alcalá 201, exchanges money at more flexible hours. Open Mon.-Sat. 8am-8pm. **Western Union,** inside the Elektra Store at 210 Cristóbal Colón, 2 blocks from the *zócalo,* or in the telegram office, will wire money in minutes.

**Telephones: LADATELs** are in front of the post office, at La Iglesia de Santo Domingo, and at the ADO station. *Casetas* available at **Computel,** Hidalgo 204 (tel. 4-80-84). Discount rates after 7pm. Open daily 7am-10pm.

**Fax:** Independencia at 20 de Noviembre (tel. 6-49-02), around the corner from the post office. Open for fax and **telegrams** Mon.-Fri. 8am-6pm, Sat. 9am-noon. Open for money orders Mon.-Fri. 9am-6pm, Sat. 9am-noon.

**American Express:** Valdivieso 2 at Hidalgo (tel. 4-62-45 or 6-27-00). Open Mon.-Fri. 9am-2pm and 4-8pm, Sat. 9am-2pm. It also houses a travel agency that sells plane tickets and 1st-class bus tickets to Mexico City and Puebla. English spoken. Office open Mon.-Fri. 9am-2pm and 4-7pm, Sat. 9am-2pm for travel services.

**Airport: Aeropuerto Juárez,** on Rte. 175, 8km south of the city. **Airport Information:** Tel. 1-50-40. **Mexicana,** Independencia at Fiallo (tel. 1-52-29). **Aeroméxico,** Hidalgo 513 (tel. 1-50-55, airport 1-50-44). **AeroCaribe** (tel. 1-52-47). **Taxis** 40 pesos. **Transportes Aeropuerto** (tel. 4-43-50), next to the post office on the Plaza Alameda, will pick you up at your hotel (*colectivo* 12 pesos, *especial* 47 pesos; expect to pay more if you're not staying downtown). Arrange a day in advance. Office open Mon.-Sat. 9am-2pm and 5-8pm.

**Buses:** From Oaxaca, it is possible to go almost anywhere in the Republic at any time. The **1st-class station** is located at Niños Héroes de Chapultepec 1036. From this station, **ADO** (tel. 5-17-03) runs to Mexico City (17 per day, 9hr., 130 pesos), Puebla (6 per day, 7hr., 97 pesos), Tuxtepec (3 and 11:30pm, 6hr., 51 pesos), and Veracruz (8:30am and 8:30pm, 9hr., 131 pesos). **Cristóbal Colón** (tel. 5-12-14) goes to Puerto Escondido (9:30am and 10:30pm, 9hr., 118 pesos), San Cristóbal (7:30pm, 12hr., 135 pesos), Tehuantepec (9 per day, 5hr., 55 pesos), and Tuxtla Gutierrez (7:30 and 10:15pm, 11hr., 121 pesos). Tickets for ADO and Cristóbal Colón are also available at 20 de Noviembre 204. **Autobuses Cuenca del Paloapan** (tel. 5-09-03) offers similar service. The **UNO** bus to Mexico City is the next best thing to a corporate jet (6 per day, 9hr., 211 pesos), Puebla (6:30pm, 143 pesos). Open Mon.-Sat. 9am-2pm and 4-7pm, Sun. 9am-3pm. The **second-class station** is just past the Central de Abastos (big market), across the Periférico from the western end of Trujano. Small regional bus lines, many without signs or ticket windows, provide frequent service to every small town near Oaxaca, usually for under 3 pesos. **Estrella del Valle** (tel. 4-57-00 or 6-54-29) runs to Puerto Escondido (8 per day, 7am-11am, 8hr., 49 pesos). The **Hotel Mesón del Ángel,** Mina 518, between Mier y Terán and Díaz Ordaz, serves as a **bus stop** for **Autotransportes Turísticos** (tel. 6-53-27 or 4-31-61). Buses to Monte Albán (peak season every 30min., 8am-3:30pm, off-season 5 per day, 30min., round-trip 12 pesos).

**Trains: Ferrocarriles Nacionales de México,** Calzada Madero (tel. 6-26-76). In a stone building set back from the road on the western end of Madero. There is a 7:30am train to Puebla and a 7:20pm train to Mexico City. Tickets sold 6-11am and 3:30-7pm. Tickets must be bought at least a day in advance.

**Car Rental: Budget,** 5 de Mayo 305 (tel. 6-44-45). Must be over 21, with license and credit card. Small VWs cost 320-350 pesos per day, depending on the season. Free mileage. Open daily 8am-1pm and 4pm-7pm.

**Bike Rental: Bicicletas Bravo,** M. Bravo 214, 2 blocks from the Andador Turístico, rents mountain bikes (35 pesos per hr., 120 pesos per day, weekly and monthly rentals also available). Passport needed for a deposit. The cool English-speaking owner provides maps of trails to villages the tourist office doesn't even know exist and sponsors group tours—midnight full-moon run to Monte Albán, anyone? Open sometimes Mon.-Sat. 9am-noon and 4-7pm.

**Laundromat: Súper Lavandería Hidalgo,** J.P. García 200 (tel. 4-11-81), 2 blocks from the *zócalo.* Open Mon.-Sat. 8am-8pm.

**Bookstore: Librería Universitaria,** Guerrero 104 (tel. 6-42-43), off the corner of the *zócalo.* Small selection of English-language used paperbacks (10 pesos) and books on Mexico. Open Mon.-Sat. 9:30am-2pm and 4-8pm. **Códice,** Alcalá 403 (tel. 6-03-39), on the Andador Turístico. Books about Mexico and Oaxaca in Italian, French, Japanese, German, English, and Spanish. Open daily 9am-9pm.

**Libraries: Biblioteca Circulante,** Alcalá 305. A haven for displaced Americans. Everything from the New Yorker to Sports Illustrated. Open Mon.-Fri. 10am-1pm and 4-7pm, Sat. 10am-1pm. **Biblioteca Pública,** Alcalá 200 (tel. 6-47-14). Some English-language books on Oaxaca. Open Mon.-Fri. 9am-8:30pm. **Instituto Welte Para Estudios Oaxaqueños,** 5 de Mayo 412 (tel. 6-54-17). Large collection of English-language books and journals on Oaxacan history and anthropology. Open Mon.-Fri. 9:30am-1:30pm, plus Tues. and Thurs. 4-6pm.

**Cultural Center: Instituto Oaxaqueño de las Culturas,** Calz. Madero at Av. Técnica (tel. 6-24-83). Hosts plays, dance performances, and concerts. Check the monthly *Guía Cultura* for listings (5 pesos). **Casa de la Cultura,** González Ortega 403 at Colón (tel. 6-24-83). Poetry readings and art galleries. Open Mon.-Fri. 8am-8pm, Sat. 8am-2pm.

**Markets: Mercado Benito Juárez,** at the corner of 20 de Noviembre and Aldama 2 blocks from the *zócalo* away from the cathedral, sells crafts, produce, flowers, and clothing. Its annex, **Mercado 20 de Noviembre,** on the next block away from the *zócalo,* has gastronomic goodies. Both open daily 6am-9pm. Saturday is the big day at **Central de Abastos,** at the end of Trujano across from the 2nd-class bus station, but vendors offer up every type of product—including live animals—every day. Beware of pickpockets.

**Red Cross:** Armenta y López 700 between Pardo and Burgoa (tel. 6-44-55 or 6-48-09). Ambulance service. English spoken. Open 24hr.

**Pharmacies: Farmacia El Fénix,** Flores Magón 104 (tel. 6-60-11), next to the *zócalo* on the way to the market. Open Mon.-Sat. 7am-10pm, Sun. 8am-9pm. **Farmacia Héroes de Chapultepec** (tel. 3-35-24), half a block east of the 1st-class bus station. Open 24hr.

**Hospitals: Hospital Civil,** Porfirio Díaz 400 (tel. 5-31-81), 1.5km out of town. Free medical service. **IMSS,** Chapultepec 621 at Reforma (tel. 5-20-33). **Sanatorio Reforma,** Reforma 613 at Humboldt (tel. 4-62-77). Both open 24hr. English spoken.

**Police:** Aldama 108 (tel. 6-27-26), south of the *zócalo* between Miguel Cabrera and Bustamante. Some English spoken. Open 24hr. In an **emergency,** dial 06.

**Internet Access: Terra Nostra,** Morelos 600 at Virgil, 2nd fl. (tel. 6-82-92). 25 pesos per ½hr., 45 pesos per hr. Open Mon.-Fri. 9:15am-2pm and 4-8pm, Sat. 10am-2pm. **Antequera Red,** H. Colegio Militar 1009-4 (tel. 3-05-58; http://antequera.com). To get here, catch a "Gigante" bus on Díaz (1.40 pesos). Ask to be let off at the enormous red Gigante store and cross the street. Antequera Red is on the 3rd fl. Temporary accounts can be set up here; Internet access is 40 pesos per hr.

**Post Office:** Tel. 6-26-71. In the Pl. Alameda de León. Open Mon.-Fri. 8am-8pm, Sat. 9am-1pm. **Postal Code:** 68000.

**Phone Code:** 29.

## ACCOMMODATIONS AND CAMPING

As Oaxaca attracts more *norteamericanos,* some old budget standbys have upgraded their rooms in an attempt to lure more upscale tourists. But bargains still await the penny-pinching soul, especially in the busy blocks south of the *zócalo,* which are within easy walking distance of the second-class bus station and all major sights and services. Reservations are a must on *fiesta* weekends, especially during the *Guelaguetza* in July.

Outside the downtown area are a number of trailer parks. The **Trailer Park Oaxaca,** Violetas 900 (tel. 5-27-96), is near the *Zona Militar* in the northeast part of town. To get there, take the "Colonia Reforma" bus from the stop on García just north of Hidalgo. The **Trailer Park San Francisco,** Madero 705, in the northwest part of town, is accessible on the "Santa Rosa" bus from the same García stop.

For longer stays, many families rent rooms, advertising at the Biblioteca Circulante or the tourist offices. **Departmentos del Cuento,** Quintana Roo 107 (tel. 4-22-88), off Berriozabal past the Santo Domingo Church, rents six one- or two-person rooms with kitchen and bath (1300 pesos per month, utilities included).

### Near the First-Class Bus Station

This area is a residential neighborhood not far from the *zócalo* and the sights. **Parque Juárez** and the nearby movie theater lend a very laid-back feel to life here.

**Casa Arnel,** Aldama 404 at Hidalgo (tel. 5-28-56), in Col. Jalatlaco, a 20min. walk from the *zócalo*. Take a right coming out of the bus station, walk two blocks, and turn right on Aldama; it's 7 blocks down, across from a stone colonial church. From the *zócalo*, walk north on the *Andador Turístico,* make a right on Constitución, and follow it for 6 blocks. Turn left on Calz. de la República, and right several blocks later at the church. Spotless, homey rooms open onto a quiet, jungle-like courtyard, complete with parrots and laundry facilities. Large English-language library. Tourist information offered. An international backpacking crowd chats over breakfast. Curfew 11pm. Singles 40-50 pesos, 100 pesos with bath; doubles 80 pesos, 120 pesos with bath. Discounts for longer stays.

### North of the *Zócalo*

The northern part of town is more prosperous, residential, and tranquil. Hotels here offer desirable locations.

**Hotel Reforma,** Reforma 102 between Independencia and Morelos (tel. 6-09-39), 4 blocks past the left side of the cathedral. Kick back on the rustic, hand-carved wood furniture and pretend you're in an hacienda; the view from the rooftop table allows you to take in the city. Singles 75 pesos; doubles 85 pesos; triples 105 pesos; quads 125 pesos. Rooms are usually full; reservations help.

**Hotel Pombo,** Morelos 601 between Vigil and Díaz (tel. 6-26-73), 1 block from the Plaza Alameda. The superb location compensates for the small, musty rooms. Five rooms have no bathroom. Singles 35 pesos, with bath 55 pesos; doubles 45 pesos, with bath 65 pesos. Can accommodate quads.

### South of the *Zócalo*

South of the *zócalo,* you'll find a legion of budget hotels; often four or five share the same block, particularly along **Díaz Ordaz.** Because of their proximity to the market and second-class bus terminal, many of these hotels front noisy, dirty streets; ask for a room in the back. Be very cautious when walking in this area at night.

**Youth Hostel El Pasador,** Fiallo 305 (tel. 6-12-87). Walk 2 blocks on Guerrero then turn right. The hostel is on the left; ring the bell for an attendant. Three bunk beds are grouped together; the sexes are separated by bamboo. Bedding and laundry facilities provided. Though there are 3 bathrooms, the communal atmosphere fosters tooth brushing on the patio or in the group kitchen. No curfew, but quiet time after 11pm. 30 pesos per person per night, half-day 15 pesos. Somewhat private 2-person *cabaña* 60 pesos. Key deposit 10 pesos.

**Hotel Pasaje,** Mina 302 (tel. 6-42-13), 3 blocks south of the *zócalo*. Well-scrubbed rooms open onto a plant-filled courtyard. Rooms near the street are assaulted with traffic noise, but you can smell the chocolate from the nearby sweet shops. Singles 80 pesos; doubles 90 pesos.

**Hotel Posada de Carmen,** 20 de Noviembre 712 (tel. 6-17-79). Slightly darker-than-optimal rooms open onto a refreshingly peaceful courtyard. All rooms have overhead fans. Singles 65 pesos; doubles 75 pesos, with 2 beds 105 pesos.

**Hotel Lupita,** Díaz Ordaz 314 off Trujano (tel. 6-57-33), 3 blocks from the *zócalo*. Don't confuse this aqua-green hotel with its neighbor, the more expensive Hotel Fortín. Known for rock-bottom prices rather than their comfort. Often full. Singles without bath 40 pesos; doubles 50 pesos, with bath 60 pesos.

## FOOD

With food to please every palate, Oaxaca is a city to grow fat in. Even in heavily touristed areas, fresh, well-prepared meals at bargain prices await the jaded traveler. Oaxaca has seven versions of *mole,* a delicious sauce made of a myriad of ingredients including *chiles* and chocolate. Many restaurants also serve up **tlayudas,** large, crisp tortillas topped with just about everything. *Botanas oaxaqueñas* also make an appearance on menus throughout the city; they are plates full of regional goodies including *chile, quesillo* (boiled string cheese), *chorizo* (sausage), *guacamole,* and tiny, cooked and seasoned grasshoppers called *chapulines.* (They're good. Seriously.)

Sunny Oaxaca summers were made for *nieves,* sorbet-like treats. For the best frozen confections, head to the area in front of the Iglesia de la Soledad, three blocks past the post office on Independencia. You'll have several umbrella-covered stands to pick from and even more flavors. Two of the most common flavors are *leche quemada* (burnt milk) and *cajeta* (caramel). Also a must is Oaxaca's spicy cinnamon **hot chocolate.** The cafes in the *zócalo* are pricey, but if you find something on the cheaper side (breakfast, coffee, or drinks), you can watch Oaxaca for hours on end.

The **markets** offer *chapulines* and spiced *jícama* (a beet-shaped fruit), as well as the usual inexpensive fare. On **20 de Noviembre,** you'll find row after row of eateries. Avoid the ones with fancy lights and signs. Look for **Angelita's,** whose proprietor is used to serving foreigners and won't change her prices for them. At the adjacent Benito Juárez market, **Aqua Casilda** produces famous flavored waters (4 pesos) and fresh juices (4.50 pesos).

**Antojitos Regionales Los Olmos,** Morelos 403 at Crespo. Every night, the family that lives in this hedonist haven opens up their courtyard to share dinner with whomever is savvy enough to know about it. Almost always full of locals, with good reason. You won't find fresher, tastier food anywhere in Oaxaca. No menus, and you can watch the food being prepared. At 7 pesos, the *tamales de mole* is the most expensive item served. Open daily 8am-11pm.

**Restaurant Quickly,** Alcalá 100 on the Andador (tel. 4-7-76), just steps from the cathedral. The cheery atmosphere and central location attract scores of diners. Extensive menu includes breakfast (8-22 pesos), super-sandwiches (12 pesos), *comida corrida* (15 pesos), and a buffet (20 pesos). Open Mon.-Fri. 8am-10:30pm, Sat.-Sun. 2-10:30pm.

**Mariscos Los Jorges,** Pino Suárez 806 (tel. 3-43-08), across the street from Parque Juárez, toward the northern end of the park. This restaurant is more than worth the short walk from downtown. Tables are scattered throughout a secluded and leafy courtyard, and the waitstaff is friendly and eager to please. Excellent seafood at reasonable prices (shrimp tacos 24 pesos). Open Wed.-Mon. 8am-6:30pm.

**Café Morgan,** Morelos 601B, between Virgil and Díaz Ordaz. Morgan the Veronese chef serves up authentic pasta a variety of different ways, all for around 25 pesos. Though it may seem wrong to be eating Italian food while visiting Mexico, it tastes so right. Open Mon.-Sat. noon-2:30pm and 6:30-9:30pm.

**Restoran Café Alex,** Díaz Ordaz 218 (tel. 4-07-15). An extensive menu that runs the gamut of Mexican cuisine, with English explanations for the uninitiated. Garden seating available. Generous breakfasts (start at 15 pesos), *comida corrida* (20 pesos), and vegetarian specialties (22 pesos) are a cut above the grittier storefront fare in the neighborhood. Open Mon.-Sat. 7am-9pm, Sun. 7am-noon.

**La Tropical,** Mina 400 at J.P. Garcia (tel. 6-67-52). A juice bar serving exotic concoctions to complement the orange and green decor. A great place to watch Oaxaca pass by while sipping a banana or strawberry *licuado* (6.50 pesos). Medicinal concoctions 8 pesos. Open Mon.-Sat. 8am-8pm, Sun. 9:30am-4pm.

**Café del Portal,** located at the corner of Hidalgo and Valdivieso, on the northeast corner of the *zócalo*. Unlike many of the other cafes on the *zócalo*, this establishment doesn't charge a lot for the fascinating view of people passing by. Snag an outdoor table and enjoy *comida corrida* (18 pesos) or regional specialties starting at 16 pesos. Open daily 8am-11pm.

**La Olla Café,** Reforma 402 between Abasolo and Constitución (tel. 6-66-68), in front of Las Bugambilias B&B. A brightly decorated interior featuring rotating art exhibits and hand-painted ceramics makes the fresh, homemade food taste even better. Locals and tourists enjoy the tasty *comida corrida* (25 pesos) amidst the alluring ambience. Open Mon.-Sat. 8am-10pm.

**La Casa de Don Porfirio,** Porfirio Díaz 208 between Morelos and Matamoros (tel. 6-37-72). This bookstore/cafe features a beautiful garden courtyard that complements the funky wooden furniture and soothing classical music. A fairly bohemian clientele dines on bagels (12-14 pesos) and soy burgers (23 pesos). On weekend nights, the cafe becomes a forum for live music (cover 10 pesos). Open Mon.-Sat. 11am-11pm, Sun. 3-11pm.

## SIGHTS

Oaxaca's museums, churches, and historical venues offer something for everyone. From pre-Hispanic to colonial to contemporary, it's all here. Luckily for the weary traveler, the major sites are all located within walking distance on the pedestrian-only Andador Turístico. Don't leave without seeing the **Iglesia de Santo Domingo,** the **Museo de Arte Contemporáneo de Oaxaca (MACO),** and the **Museo de Arte Prehispánico de México Rufino Tamayo.**

### The Zócalo

The **Catedral de Oaxaca** and the **Palacio de Gobierno** (not to be confused with the Palacio Municipal, which contains the tourist office) sit on opposite sides of the *zócalo*. Originally constructed in 1535, the cathedral was damaged and finally destroyed by a series of earthquakes. It's worth sticking your head in to look around, but there's not much reason to linger. The ornate bishop's seat, in the central altar, provides a structural focus (open daily 7am-8pm).

Inside the **Palacio de Gobierno,** through the set of arches that don't shelter cafes, a mural by Arturo García Bustos presents an informative historical collage. This mural embodies a lot of what's great about Mexican art—it's colorful and fun to look at while addressing important historical and political themes with candor and frankness. On the left wall, scenes of pre-Hispanic life with maize cultivation, weaving, and temples give way to the political and religious figures that dominate the other panels. The center panel celebrates *oaxaqueño* Benito Juárez, his wife Margarita Masa, and one of his oft-repeated phrases, *"El respeto al derecho ajeno es la paz."* ("Respect for the rights of others is peace.") On the wall to the right as you ascend the staircase is a portrait of Sor Juana Inés de la Cruz, the 17th-century poet, nun, theologian, and astronomer. Considered Mexico's first feminist, she impersonated a man for several years in order to attend the university in Mexico City and penned a diatribe against misogynists called *Hombres Necios* (Foolish Men; palace open 24hr.).

### Along the Andador Turístico

To the left of the cathedral, a cobbled pedestrian street leads to museums, restaurants, and stores. A block down the Andador (also known as Alcalá), and on the right, is the **Museo de Arte Contemporáneo de Oaxaca (MACO),** Alcalá 202 (tel. 4-71-10), on the right. This beautifully constructed colonial building is known as the Casa de Cortés, although historians insist that it is not in fact Cortés's estate. The museum features both rotating and permanent exhibitions, and shows free movies on its large-screen TV. The permanent collection is especially impressive. It includes the works of *oaxaqueños* like Rufino Tamayó, Francisco Toledo, and Rodolfo Morales, whose pieces extend the city's historical legacy into the present. The bookstore carries a large number of art books and magazines plus English guidebooks to the region (10 pesos; open Wed.-Mon. 10:30am-8pm).

Following the walkway for three more blocks, the imposing **Iglesia de Santo Domingo** looms on the right. The church is the tallest building in Oaxaca, and it also wins the award for gaudiest interior. Upon entering, it takes a few seconds for the eyes to adjust to the dim interior. Further up, there is a retinal assault in the form of an explosion of gilt. The massive gold altar is echoed in waves of gilded stucco that cover the ceiling and walls. Construction on the church began in 1575, the structure was consecrated in 1611, and improvements and artistic work continued after that. Built 2m thick as protection against earthquakes, the walls served the convent well when it functioned as military barracks for both sides during the reform wars and the Revolution (open daily 7am-1pm and 4-8pm).

The Ex-convent next door was converted in 1972 into the city's prestigious **Museo Regional de Oaxaca** (tel. 6-29-91). Unfortunately, for the next year or so the large majority of the museum will be closed for renovations. The only exhibit on display is the Mixtec treasures from Tomb 7 of Monte Albán. There are two rooms full of exquisitely worked pieces of gold, silver, turquoise, bone, and obsidian. The treasure is definitely worth seeing, but at 14 pesos it's a little steep. If possible, plan to go on Sunday when admission is free (open Tues.-Fri., 10am-6pm, Sat.-Sun. 10am-5pm).

---

### Benito's Way

Five blocks north of the post office is the **Casa de Benito Juárez,** García Vigil 609 (tel. 6-18-60), once home to Mexico's famous ex-president. Although Juárez came from humble beginnings, the house hardly looks like the spot where a poor, 19th-century Zapotec *campesino* grew up. Benito's sister left the Juárez home in Guelatao to come to Oaxaca as the domestic servant of the wealthy Masa family who actually owned the house. The Masas were *paisanos* from Spain and good friends with the equally wealthy Salanueva family. The Salanuevas took interest in young Benito, adopted him, and brought him to Oaxaca. His subsequent education and upbringing qualified him to marry the Masas's daughter, Margarita, and to pursue a career in law and reform-minded politics. The house—living room, bedrooms, kitchen, well, and "bookbinding/weaving shop"—is a replica of a 19th-century upper-middle-class *oaxaqueño* home (open Tues.-Sat. 10am-6pm, Sun. 10am-5pm; admission 10 pesos, free Sun.).

---

### Near the Andador Turístico

The renowned **Museo de Arte Prehispánico de México Rufino Tamayo,** Morelos 503 between Díaz and Tinoco y Palacios (tel. 6-47-50), shows off the *oaxaqueño* artist's personal collection of pre-Hispanic objects. The figurines, ceramics, and masks that Tamayo collected are meant to be examined as cultural artifacts, as well as appreciated as works of art in their own right. Pieces are arranged in roughly chronological order rather than by culture, for a highly pleasurable viewing experience (open Mon., Wed.-Sat. 10am-2pm and 4-7pm, Sun. 10am-3pm; admission 12 pesos).

The **Teatro Macedonio Alcalá,** on 5 de Mayo at Independencia, two blocks behind the cathedral, is one of the most beautiful buildings in Oaxaca and an example of the art and architecture fostered by dictator Porfirio Díaz. Díaz's regime (1876-1911) had a taste for French art and intellectual formulas. Oaxaca, Díaz's birthplace, remained close to the dictator's heart. His support was instrumental in the theater's construction. On the ceiling, scantily clad Muses float above the giant candelabra (occasionally open for shows Mon.-Sat. 8pm, Sun. 6pm).

A minor but absorbing attraction is the funky museum of religious art at the **Basílica of Our Lady of Solitude,** Independencia 107 (tel. 6-75-66), three and a half blocks behind the post office. It houses an astonishing array of objects sent from around the world as gifts to the Virgin, who is said to have appeared here in 1620. Packed cabinets overflow with everything from model ships to shell-and-pasta figurines to wedding bouquets (open Mon.-Sat. 10am-2pm and 4-6pm, Sun. 11am-2pm; admission 1 peso).

For a breathtaking view of the city, head to the **Cerro de Fortín. The Escalera de Fortín** begins on Crespo; these stairs will take you up past the Guelaquetza amphitheater to the planetarium (tel. 6-69-84; open Tues.-Sun. 6-7pm; admission 8 pesos) and a great vista of Oaxaca and the surrounding hills. The stairs are a favorite destination for fitness fiends, be prepared to be passed by joggers loping effortlessly uphill.

Also worth a visit is the **Centro Fotográfico Alvarez Bravo,** Murguía 302, between Reforma and Juárez. The center displays rotating photography exhibits (open Wed.-Mon. 9:30am-6pm; admission free).

## ENTERTAINMENT AND SEASONAL EVENTS

Keeping track of Oaxaca's cultural and music events requires some effort. The *Guía Cultural,* distributed at the MACO and tourist offices (5 pesos), lists monthly activities, many of them free. The *Oaxaca Times,* published monthly in English, is a free guide to the city available at many hotels and tourist offices. During the summer, the streets fill with free music: Sundays at 12:20pm, the Oaxacan Orchestra plays in the Plaza Alameda; Mondays and Saturdays, marimba performers hammer away after 7pm in the *zócalo* kiosk; Tuesdays and Thursdays, the state band stages concerts— same place, same time.

Discos and bars are packed—and dripping with sweat—on weekend nights. Candela, Allende 211, two blocks over from the Santa Domingo church, is the place to go for salsa. Whether you are beginner or an expert, the live band will keep you moving all evening long. This establishment manages to be friendly and welcoming while showcasing moves that would put the cast of Dirty Dancing to shame. (Restaurant open Tues.-Sat. 12-5pm; music and dancing 9pm-2am. Cover 20 pesos.) The most popular club of the moment is Snob, at the intersection of Héroes de Chapultepec and Juárez, near the first-class bus station. The multi-colored exterior encloses an interior that is always packed and hopping. The crowd here seems to include a representative from nearly every nation in the western hemisphere (cover 20 pesos for men, 10 pesos for women; open Wed.-Sat. 10pm-3am). Tequila Rock, Porfirio Díaz 102 at Héroes de Chapultepec (tel. 5-15-00), is another popular destination. Around 11pm, the staff performs a short dance that eases the awkwardness of being the first one on the floor. Sweaty dance tunes soon take over (cover Fri.-Sat. 35 pesos; open Wed.-Sat. 9pm-3am). Back toward downtown is Universo Discoteca, Porfirio Díaz 219 at Matamoros (tel. 6-42-36). A young crowd boogies under plastic-and-pipe palm trees and groovy mood lighting (cover Fri. 10 pesos, Sat. 20 pesos; open Thurs.-Sat. 9pm-2:30am).

Watch a film at MACO or La Casa de la Mujer, or simply catch a recent flick in English with Spanish subtitles (15 pesos) at the **Plaza Alameda Cinema,** Independencia and Díaz (tel. 6-52-41). **Sala Versalles,** M. Ocampo 105 (tel. 6-23-35), three blocks behind the cathedral, hosts live shows as well as movies.

On the two Mondays following July 16, representatives from every part of Oaxaca state converge on a hill overlooking the city for the **Guelaguetza.** The event grew out of an indigenous tradition of making offerings on the **Cerro del Fortín** (The Hill with the Beautiful View); the days of dancing in the theater on the hill are called *los lunes del cerro* (Hill Mondays). "Guelaguetza" refers to the Zapotec custom of reciprocal gift-giving. During the two public gatherings, groups from the seven regions of Oaxaca give the audience a taste of their heritage through dance, music, and dazzling costumes. In between the gatherings, food and handicraft exhibitions, art shows, and concerts take place. Tickets cost up to 250 pesos, but a handful of free seats open up hours before the show begins. If you miss the Guelaguetza, sample dances are performed year-round at the Hotel Camino Real and Hotel Monte Albán for a hefty fee.

The night of December 23, Oaxacans celebrate the unique **Noche de los Rábanos** (Night of the Radishes). Masterpieces of historic or biblical themes expressed with radishes fill the *zócalo,* where judges determine the best. Hundreds of people admire the artistic creations and eat sweet *buñuelos.* Upon finishing the treat, you're supposed to make a wish and throw the ceramic plate down on the ground; if the plate smashes into pieces, your wish will come true. We promise.

# ■ Near Oaxaca

The villages surrounding Oaxaca are known both for their ancient Zapotec and Mixtec ruins and for their production of artisanry. As everyone from museums of folk art to the Nature Company took interest in the imaginative handicrafts made in these villages, many residents left farming work to devote themselves full-time to craft production. Villages often specialize in specific products: **Arrazola** and **San Martín Tilcajate** make wooden animals, **San Bartolo Coyotepec** black clay pottery, **Atzompa** green clay pottery, **Ocotlán** natural clay pottery, **Teotitlán del Valle** wool *sarapes,* and **Villa Díaz Ordaz** and **Santo Tomás Jalietza** textiles and weavings. All these villages can be reached by *colectivo* from the *Central de Autobuses;* or, for that adrenaline rush, rent a bike and transport yourself.

There is a lot to be said for getting out of the hustle and bustle of the city for at least part of the day. The surrounding countryside is lovely and it's always fun to ride in a bus that has to stop in order to let a herd of cows cross the road. The tourist office in Oaxaca (**SECTUR**, tel. 6-01-23 or 6-48-28) rents out guest houses in the communities of Abasolo, Papalutla, Teotitlán del Valle, Benito Juárez, Tlacolula, Quialana, Tlapazola, Santa Ana del Valle, and Hierve el Agua. Accommodations include four beds, kitchen, and clean bedding; proceedings benefit the community (cabin 120 pesos; 1 person 35 pesos; students 25 pesos; campers in the garden 10 pesos). Or try one of the *paseos culturales,* which introduce visitors to the traditional medicinal, agricultural, and artistic practices of 15 villages in the area. Contact **Museos Comunitarios de Oaxaca,** Tinoco y Palacios 311, *interior* (room) 16, for more information.

## ATZOMPA, ARRAZOLA, CUILAPAN, AND ZAACHILA

A culture and lifestyle different from the sophistication of Oaxaca de Juárez emerges in these small towns, all of which lie near Rte. 131. **Atzompa** (pop. 11,000) is where that magnificent blend of clay and sprouts, the **Chia Pet,** was invented. Pottery, the town's specialty, can be had here at better prices than in the city. Atzompa's *Casa de Artesanías* is a publicly funded forum that brings together the work of the town's specialized artisans. The selection is good at the *Casa,* but bartering is easier with the artisans themselves.

**Arrazola** is the hometown of **Manuel Jiménez,** one of Mexico's most famous artisans. Jiménez is the originator of *alebrijes,* the brightly colored figurines of demons that rank among Mexico's most sought-after handicrafts. While success has made his pieces simply unaffordable for most—think US$150 and upwards—his workshop is worth a visit. Cheaper versions of Jiménez's work, as well as wooden animals, are sold everywhere in town. Nearly all the households around the center of town make figurines to supplement income. Pick your way through yards full of goats and chickens to the workshop; the owners will happily show you their wares and haggle out a fair price. What the copies lack in grace and originality they make up for in intricacy and elaborate painting. Particularly interesting are Miguel Santiago Soriano's curvaceous iguanas and Maximiliano Morales Santiago's haughty lions. The central market opens at noon every day.

**Cuilapan de Guerrero** (pop. 11,000) has an isolated but hauntingly lovely 17th-century Dominican monastery, once home to one of the most powerful and wealthy religious orders in Mexico. Never finished, the ruined monastery's stone arcades frame the fields of the surrounding valley and the sinews of the hills that embrace it (gates open daily 10am-6pm; admission to grounds free, 7 pesos to interior).

**Zaachila** (pop. 15,000), the last political capital of the Zapotecs before they fell to the Spanish in 1521, hosts a fascinating market each Thursday. Drop your pesos on preserved bananas and squealing pigs. The fuchsia and yellow cathedral dominates the middle of town. Behind the church, a street heads uphill to a partially uncovered archaeological site. Until 1962, locals prohibited excavations to prevent outsiders from dissecting their Zapotec heritage. Little has since been explored, but two Mixtec tombs with well-preserved architecture and jewelry have been uncovered. The treasure of gold, turquoise, jade, and bone artifacts has been spirited away to museums in Oaxaca and Mexico City, but the tombs—the only decorated ones in Oaxaca—are easily accessible (open daily 8am-6pm; admission 7 pesos).

**Getting There:** Take a *colectivo* leaving from the parking lot on the side of the Central de Abastos in Oaxaca; destinations are labeled on the windshields (20min. to Cuilapán, 30min. to Aztompa, Arrazola, or Zaachila, 2.50 pesos). It's easy to hop from one town to the next; take a *colectivo* back to the main road and flag down another that's headed for your next destination. All four towns are ideally accessible in the course of a day, though your best bet is to start out in Arrazola or Atzompa and to head back to Oaxaca via Cuilapan or Zaachila.

## SAN BARTOLO COYOTEPEC AND POINTS SOUTH

The drive south from Oaxaca provides more spectacular scenery. Picturesque towns are nestled in the slopes of verdant hills, and for the eager consumer there are more distinctive crafts and artisanry for sale. **San Bartolo Coyotepec,** 12km south of Oaxaca on Rte. 175, is the source of the ink-black pottery that populates souvenir shops throughout the state. This is the only place in Mexico where the distinctive pottery is produced. Fine pieces are available here at fairly low prices. Valente Nieto, son of the creator of the craft, Doña Rosa, gives demonstrations for visitors. If you didn't pick up quite enough brightly colored animals in Arrazola, head to **San Martín Tilajete,** 21km south of Oaxaca and about 1km off the main road. Four kilometers farther south, **Santo Tomás Jalietza** specializes in weaving on back-strap looms. The town also boasts a 17th-century church dedicated to its patron saint. **Ocotlán de Morelos,** 33km out of the city, offers visitors a brightly colored church, a spacious *zócalo,* and a lively market, where there is a highly eclectic set of offerings. Leather goods, wrap-type traditional clothing, and herbal remedies can be had for a song. Swashbuckle your way through Mexico with one of the swords produced here. Market day is Friday; most of the action takes place between 10am and 5pm.

**Getting There:** Take one of the *colectivos* leaving from the end of the Central de Abastos opposite the second-class bus station (about 6 pesos). **Estrella del Valle** buses leave from their terminal on González Ortega for Ocotlán (every 8min., 5:45am-9:30pm, ½hr., 4 pesos) and will make stops at other villages.

## OAXACA TO MITLA

The road from Oaxaca east to Mitla, the Pan-American Highway (Rte. 190), cuts through a valley full of artisanal towns, *mezcal* distilleries, and archaeological sites. The first point of interest is the town of **Santa María El Tule** (pop. 7000). This friendly little town, just 14km outside the city, houses one of Mexico's great roadside attractions: the **Tule Tree.** The 2000-year-old and 40-meter-tall tree has an astounding perimeter at El Tule; then ask for *"el árbol."* There is a 2-peso fee to approach the fence closest to the tree, but the glory of this botanical behemoth can be appreciated from anywhere within a 100m radius. The **Dainzú** ruins, 22km from Oaxaca, just off the road branching to **Macuilxochitl,** date from Monte Albán's final pre-Hispanic epoch. A series of magnificently carved figures at the base of the tallest pyramidal monument represent ballplayers in poses similar to the "dancers" at Monte Albán (see p. 357). Two humans and two jaguars, gods of the sport, supervise the contest. Up the hill from the pyramid, another game scene is hewn in the living rock (open daily 10am-6pm; admission 7 pesos). Bring your walking shoes; the ruins are about 2km away from the main road.

The walls of the church in nearby **San Jerónimo Tlacochahuaya** (pop. 5300), 23km from Oaxaca, illustrate Zapotec decorative techniques as applied to Catholic motifs. It was built at the end of the 16th century by Dominicans seeking to escape worldly temptations (open daily 7am-noon). **Teotitlán del Valle,** 28km from Oaxaca, is the oldest community in the state. The source of extremely beautiful woolen *sarapes* and rugs, Teotitlán's 200 to 300 families earn their livelihood largely by spinning and weaving. Many allow tourists to visit their workshops and witness the process of natural-dye coloring and weaving. Unfortunately, Teotitlán is not quite as accessible as many of the other stops on the road; it's 4km away from where the bus drops you. There are *colectivo* taxis that run sporadically from the main road to the town. There are a few workshops scattered within walking distance of the main road; owners are happy to demonstrate and explain the process even if you don't end up buying anything.

**Tlacolula de Matamoros** (pop. 12,700), 33km from Oaxaca, is one of the larger towns in the area and adds a slightly gritty underside to the rural charm of the region. It hosts a lively market every Sunday morning—the specialty is the potent liquor *mezcal*. The market is officially open until 6pm, but activity starts to wind down at around 2pm.

**Yagul**, 36km from Oaxaca, was a Zapotec city inhabited from 700 BC-AD 1521 (guess what happened then). Less impressive archaeologically than Mitla, rarely visited Yagul is perhaps more striking aesthetically. A gorgeous 1km walk through cornfields and up a hill does an admirable job of prepping the visitor for the commanding view that awaits at the top. If you go on a weekday, chances are you'll be able to act out your fantasies of Zapotec kingship with lizards as your only audience. The city is built into the skirts of a hill overlooking a spectacular mountain-ringed valley. Most of the more famous buildings and tombs are in the **Acrópolis**, the area closest to the parking lot about 2km north of the highway. Bring some friends and you can start a pick-up ball game in the restored ballcourt, the largest of its kind in the Oaxaca valley. The **Court of the Triple Tomb** is on the left of the ballcourt. Carved with an image that is probably a jaguar, the tomb is in—you guessed it—three sections. Stone faces cover the largest portion. Beyond the ballcourt rises the **Council Hall;** behind lies the **Palace of the Six Patios,** believed to have been the home of the city's ruler. Heading back to the parking lot, take the trail that climbs uphill to the rocky outcropping to catch a spectacular view of the cactus-covered hills. Look for the small stone bridge; it's behind the tomb on your right as you climb the hill (open daily 8am-5:30pm; admission 7 pesos, free Sun.). There is also a *palapa*-style restaurant on the way to the ruins where you can slake your thirst or grab a quick bite (*comida corrida* 18 pesos).

Beyond Mitla, **Hierve el Agua** (The Water Boils), 57km from Oaxaca, takes its name from two springs of carbonated water that look like…boiling water. The waters are not actually hot and make for refreshing baths.

**Getting There:** All destinations listed above are accessible via a Mitla-bound bus, which leaves the second-class station in Oaxaca (every 15min., 8am-8pm, 5 pesos to Mitla). Ask the driver to let you off where you want to go. Most people visit these sites on daytrips, but the tourist office at Oaxaca can arrange for overnight stays in Teotitlán del Valle, Tlacolula, or Hierve el Agua (see p. 346).

# ▒ Mitla

Tucked away in a mostly Zapotec-speaking, dusty little village, the archaeological site at Mitla, 44km east of Oaxaca, is smaller and less popular with tourists than the immense Monte Albán. Mitla was built in AD 800 by the Zapotecs; it was later appropriated by the Mixtecs and eventually became the largest and most important of the late Mixtec cities. When the Spaniards arrived in the valley, Mitla was the only ceremonial center of the Mesoamerican Classical period still in use. Ironically, the Catholic archbishop of Oaxaca built his home to echo the horizontal lines of the Zapotec priest's residence in Mitla, thus paying architectural tribute to an ancient indigenous religion virtually exterminated by Catholicism. On the 2km walk through town to the ruins, you may have to weave your way through the herds of goats and cows that occasionally fill the streets; the ticket booth to the archaeological site is on the far side of the red-domed church. To the left of it, behind the church, are the three patios known as the **Group of the Church.** One of them has been almost completely buried by the church, and only a few of the original palace walls remain visible. The central patio is on the other side of the church; here and in the surrounding rooms you can still see pieces of Mixtec decorative paintings glowing red against the stone, supposedly telling Mitla's history.

More impressive ruins are across the road in the fenced-in area enclosing the **Group of the Columns.** Perhaps the most striking feature of these structures is the intricate geometric designs that decorate both exterior and interior. The interlocking stone squares and diamonds are slightly reminiscent of an abstract chain of Legos. These designs are used in many of the rugs produced in the valley. Beyond the entrance are two patios joined at one corner. On the first one lie the tombs of the pyramids, forming a cross. For years Spaniards thought this proved that the Mixtecs somehow knew the story of Jesus. On the second patio, two temples have tombs that are open to visitors. The tomb in the east temple has large stones covered with mosaic patterns. The roof of the tomb in the north temple rests on a single huge column known as the **Column of Life.** Pilgrims travel here each year to embrace the column; in exchange for the hug, the column tells them how much longer they will live. Explanatory signs throughout this area are in English (site open daily 8am-5pm; admission 10 pesos, free Sun.).

On the central plaza back in town, the unexciting **Frissell Museum** contains thousands of figurines from Mitla and other Mixtec sites, all arranged around a courtyard. Some descriptions are in English (open daily 9am-5pm; admission 10 pesos).

If you must stay in Mitla, try the **Hotel Zapoteca,** 5 de Febrero 12 (tel. 8-00-26), on the way from the bus stop to the ruins. The stucco-walled rooms are big and the bathrooms clean enough. Rooms upstairs are a bit nicer. The hotel's restaurant is not expensive (singles 50 pesos; doubles 70 pesos).

**Getting There:** Take a bus from Oaxaca's second-class terminal (every 15min., 8am-8pm, 45min., 5 pesos). The last Oaxaca-bound bus leaves Mitla at 8pm. The bus station is about 2km from the ruins. With your back to the station walk to your left and turn left at the sign for *"Las Ruinas."* Make another left onto the main road, and follow it for several blocks through town. Cut through the small *zócalo* on your right and walk uphill until you get to the church. The ruins will be on your right. **Autotransportes Turísticos Aragal** offers four-hour trips that leave from Oaxaca and visit Mitla, Yagul, and the Tule Tree (10am and 2pm, 25 pesos). Reservations (required) can be made at the **Hotel Trébol,** Las Casas at Flores Magón (tel. 6-38-66), across from the Benito Juárez market.

# ■ Monte Albán

The heart and soul of the Zapotec cosmos, the ancient mecca of the "Cloud People," regal Monte Albán now watches over its verdant mountaintop in utter calmness. Surrounded by rolling Oaxacan valleys and peaks, Monte Albán is one of the most important and spectacular pre-Hispanic ruins in Mexico. Monte Albán is to Oaxaca (only 10km away) what the *Mona Lisa* is to the Louvre—it's a travesty to leave without seeing it. The striking architecture of the monumental structures, the fascinating lay-out and organization of the city, and a stunning view of the surrounding area all make Monte Albán memorable. The fact that many of the structures are quite well-preserved means that visiting the ruins is truly a window into the past; standing in the central plaza, it isn't hard to imagine what the city must have looked like in its heyday.

The monolithic, geometrically precise stone structures that constituted the ceremonial center of the city are the culmination of Zapotec efforts to engineer a world that fused the religious, political, and social realms. As Monte Albán grew to become the major Zapotec capital, daily life was carefully constructed to harmonize with the supernatural elements. Architecture adhered to the orientation of the four cardinal points and the proportions of the 260-day ritual calendar. Residences were organized in families of five to 10 people in four-sided houses with open central courtyards. To emphasize the congruence between the household and the tripartite cosmos, families buried their ancestors underneath their house to correspond to the level of the underworld. Excavations of burials in Monte Albán have yielded not only dazzling artifacts, but also valuable information on social stratification.

Monte Albán flourished during the Classic Period (AD 300-750), when it shared the spotlight with Teotihuacán and Tikal as a major cultural and ceremonial center of Mesoamerica. This was the greatest of Zapotec capitals—maize was cultivated, water was supplied through complex drainage systems, and the city engaged in extensive exchange networks in Mesoamerica, especially with Teotihuacán (see p. 119). Teotihuacán's influence is visible in the murals painted and pottery made in Monte Albán. Artists used representations of divinities to legitimate the kings' power, and many stones share the theme of defeated enemies being sacrificed.

The history of Monte Albán is divided into five parts, spanning the years from 500 BC until the arrival of the Spaniards in the 16th century. Periods I and II saw the rise of Monte Albán as the Zapotec capital. There was also a great deal of contact with the Maya culture; the Zapotecs adopted the Maya *juego de pelota* (ball game) and steep pyramid structure, while the Maya appropriated the Zapotec calendar and writing system. The city reached its peak during the third period, AD 300-750.

Almost all of the extant buildings and tombs as well as several urns and murals of *colanijes* (richly adorned priests) come from this period. Burial arrangements of varying luxuriousness and size show the social division of the period: priests, clerks, and laborers lived apart, died apart, and were buried in very different tombs. For reasons that remain unknown, Monte Albán shriveled up and died around AD 750. Construction ceased, and control of the Zapotec empire shifted from Monte Albán to other cities such as Zaachila, Yagul, and later Mitla. Explanations for the abandonment of the city include drought, overexploitation of resources, or inability of the leaders to maintain stability. The subsequent periods IV and V saw the city taken over by the Mixtec people; this happened to many Zapotec cities. The Mixtecs used Monte Albán as a fortress and a sacred metropolis, taking over the tombs left by the Zapotecs. When the most noteworthy tomb, **Tomb 7,** was discovered in 1932 by Dr. Alfonso Caso, the treasure found within more than quadrupled the number of previously identified gold Mixtec objects. The treasures from Tomb 7 are now on display at the Museo Regional de Oaxaca (see p. 352).

As you enter the **Central Plaza,** the most prominent building to the right is the **Northern Platform.** Bear left as you enter the site, and walk along the edge of the Central Plaza; the first structure on the left is the ball court. Although the steps of the court seem to conjure up echoes of rowdy cheering, the "bleachers" were actually smothered in stucco and served as part of the playing area. After passing a series of related substructures, you'll reach two pyramids which dominate the center and southern end of this side of the plaza. The inclined walls were originally flat and covered with stucco.

**Building P,** the first of the two pyramids, fascinates archaeologists because of an inner stairway feeding into a tunnel to the central structures. The tunnel apparently allowed priests to pass into the central temples unseen by the public. The second pyramid, the **Palace,** was once a wealthy Zapotec residence; it is graced by a patio-courtyard and a garden in which a cruciform grave was discovered. The walls separating the palace rooms are still standing, giving a real sense of what the interior must have looked like.

Outside the palace are the four central monuments of the plaza. **Buildings G, H,** and **I** together constitute what was likely the **principal altar** of Monte Albán. Directly to the east, between the central Building H and Building P, is the small, sunken **Adoratorio,** where archaeologists dug up an intricate jade bat mask. This is Monte Albán's oldest structure, dating from Monte Albán II. A sacred icon and the most famous piece from this period, the mask contains 25 pieces of polished, forest-green jade with slivers of white conch shell forming the teeth and eyes of the bat. In 1994, in a famous heist, the mask was stolen from the Museo Nacional de Antropología in Mexico City.

The fourth of the central structures, **Building J** is formed in the bizarre shape of an arrowhead on a platform and contains a labyrinth of tunnels and passageways. Unlike any other ancient edifice in Mexico, it is asymmetrical and built at an angle to the other structures around the plaza. Its broad, carved slabs suggest that the building is one of the oldest on the site. Many of the glyphs depict an upside-down head below a stylized hill; the glyphs are thought to represent a place and a name. Archaeologists speculate that this image indicates a conquest, the head representing the defeated tribe and the name identifying the region conquered.

Behind Building J stands the highest structure at Monte Albán: the **Southern Pyramid.** On both sides of the staircase on the plaza level are a number of stelae carved with rain gods and tigers. The stela on the pyramid's right side contains a precise date, but archaeologists lack the point of reference needed to coordinate this date with the modern calendar. The neighboring stela is believed to depict the king of Monte Albán. If you climb only one pyramid in Mexico, make it this one: the top affords a commanding view of the ruins, the valley, and the mountains beyond.

Along the border of the Central Plaza, to the left as you descend the pyramid, are the foundations of **Building M,** followed by the **Platform of the Dancers** at the foot of Building L. The low platforms in front of Building M were apparently designed to make the plaza, which was built around inconveniently located rock formations, more symmetrical. In front of Building M and to the left as you face it are the haunting reliefs known as the **Dancers.** Among the most interesting examples of pre-Hispanic sculpture, the reliefs date from the 5th century BC, and are nearly identical to contemporary Olmec sculptures along the Gulf Coast. Many of the dancers show evidence of genital mutilation. There is much speculation whether these men were commoners or of high status. Beyond the Platform of the Dancers, the **Northern Platform,** which is almost as large as the Central Plaza itself, dominates the entire site. Steps rise to meet a sunken patio. **Building B,** to the left as you face north on top of the steps, is believed to be a Mixtec-influenced addition to the site.

The path exiting the site passes the gift shop and cafeteria on the way to **Tomb 104.** Duck underground, look above the entrance, and gaze at the urn. It is covered with a motif which interweaves images of the maize god and rain god. Near the parking lot is the entrance to **Tomb 7,** where the spectacular cache of Mixtec ornaments mentioned above was found.

The **museum** at the site's entrance was recently remodeled; it offers a chronological survey of Monte Albán's history and displays sculpted stones from the site's earlier periods. Unfortunately, the truly spectacular artifacts from the site have been hauled off to museums in Oaxaca and Mexico City (site open daily 8am-5pm; admission 14 pesos, 25 pesos if you want to use a camcorder, free Sun. and holidays).

**Getting There:** Buses to Monte Albán leave from the Hotel Mesón del Ángel, Mina 518 between Mier y Terán and Díaz Ordaz in Oaxaca. Monte Albán is only 10km from Oaxaca, but the ride through mountainous terrain takes 30 minutes. The normal procedure is to buy a round-trip ticket, with the return fixed two hours after arrival at the site (about the right amount of time for a full perusal); if you want to stay longer you can pay an extra 6 pesos to come back on one of the later buses. During high season, buses from the hotel leave daily every hour between 8:30am and 5:30pm; during low season, buses leave five times per day during the week and six times per day on Sunday (12 pesos round-trip). To avoid the tourist hordes, leave early. Travel agencies around the *zócalo* in Oaxaca arrange special excursions to the ruins, some with English-speaking guides (expect to pay around US$30 per person).

# ▓ Isthmus of Tehuantepec

East of Oaxaca de Juárez, the North American continent narrows to a slender strip of land just 215km wide known as the Isthmus of Tehuantepec, wedged between the Yucatán Peninsula and the highlands of south central Mexico. Scorching temperatures ensure that life in the isthmus towns progresses at a lethargic pace. The isthmus is known for its unique Zapotec matriarchal tradition, most visible in Tehuantepec.

## TEHUANTEPEC

Tehuantepec (pop. 60,000) is the oldest of the isthmus's principal cities. Tehuantepec is a matriarchal society; the birth of a daughter is cause for celebration, and men turn their wages over to their wives, who control family finances. This family structure is only apparent to tourists during the frequent *fiestas* that punctuate rural life. Women dance together, clothed in embroidered silk *huipiles* (blouses) and long, billowing *enaguas* (skirts). But liberation is limited even in Tehuantepec: while women enjoy a uniquely privileged social and economic status, they still can't ask men to dance, and women travelers are not free from the usual harassment.

For tourist information, visit the **Casa de la Cultura**, Callejón Rey Cosijopi (tel. 5-01-14; open Mon.-Fri. 9am-2pm and 5-8pm, Sat. 9am-2pm). Tehuantepec's real attractions are its *fiestas*. Each of the town's 14 *barrios* hosts an annual week-long celebration beginning on the eve of their patron saint's feast day. Since feast days are concentrated in the summer, *fiestas* tend to blend into an undifferentiated season of revelry. The festivities begin on May 1, with the *barrio* of Santa Cruz Tagolaba's *fiesta*, and continue through the second Sunday in October, when the *barrio* of Jaliso begins its celebration. There is a hiatus during most of July. Of all the festivals, the most colorful and spectacular are those of **Sandonga** (beginning May 28), **Santa María** (Aug. 14-20), and **Laborío** (Sept. 6-10). If you end up in Tehuantepec between *fiestas*, the entertainment pickings are decidedly slim, to say the least. Sixteenth-century structure's colonial frescoes vie for attention with modern paintings at the old Dominican **monastery,** now the **Casa de la Cultura,** down a short alley off Guerrero, next to the Centro de Salud (open Mon.-Fri. 9am-2pm and 5-8pm, Sat. 9am-2pm).

If you decide to spend the night, Tehuantepec has a few small but clean hotels and *casas de huéspedes*, all within a few blocks of the *zócalo*. **Hotel Oasis,** Melchor Ocampo 8 (tel. 5-00-08), on the right behind the Palacio, offers fans, faded tile floors, bathrooms with hot water, and a restaurant in the lobby (singles 60 pesos, with A/C 85 pesos; doubles and triples 85 pesos, with A/C 125 pesos). Food-wise, in the evenings, taco stands with outdoor seating fill the *zócalo;* pick the one with the biggest crowd. **Café Colonial,** Romero 66 (tel. 5-01-15), to the right of the Palacio, charms you despite the garish paintings on the wall; they serve breakfast (15-20 pesos), *antojitos* (22 pesos), and *comida corrida* (22 pesos; open daily 8am-7pm).

**Getting there and away:** Tehuantepec is four hours from Oaxaca. From the **bus station** on the highway, **Cristóbal Colón** and **ADO** (tel. 5-01-08 and 5-09-33) travel to Mexico City (5:30 and 9pm, 11hr., 183 pesos), Oaxaca (9 per day, 5:30am-midnight, 4hr., 55 pesos), and more; buses also go to nearby Juchitán (every ½hr., ½hr., 4 pesos) and Salina Cruz (every ½hr., 20min., 3 pesos). To get to town, make an immediate left as you leave the station. Follow this street, which becomes **Avenida Héroes**, as it veers to the right and eventually dead-ends. Turn right and walk a few more blocks; make a left on **Hidalgo** and follow it to the *zócalo*. Taxis will take you there for 3 pesos.

## JUCHITÁN

Characterized by the same Zapotec culture that distinguishes Tehuantepec, this bustling industrial center sees little to no tourist traffic. There is nothing packaged or refined about Juchitán, but the pace of life has a certain appealing raw energy. An exuberant market and excellent cultural center round out this friendly isthmus town.

The **Casa de la Cultura** is off 5 de Septiembre at the far end of the *zócalo*. It features a spacious, shady, blue and white courtyard and an interesting permanent collection of paintings; contemporary Mexican and *Zapatista* art is on display. Lodging options here are fairly limited. **Hotel La Mansión,** Prolongación 16 de Septiembre 34B (tel. 1-20-55), is near the bus station. Tastefully-appointed bedrooms and spacious bathrooms make this a great place to stay. Air conditioning compensates for slightly higher prices (singles 105 pesos; doubles 135 pesos). For some grub, **Mariscos Carmen,** 5 de Septiembre at Abasolo, features a colorful interior and a variety of creatures from the sea (fish fillets 30-40 pesos; open daily 8am-10pm).

**Getting there and away: Local buses** connect Juchitán with the isthmus towns of Tehuantepec (½hr.) and Salina Cruz (1hr.). **Cristóbal Colón** sends **buses** to Mexico City (8:30am, 9, and 9:30pm, 11½hr., 239 pesos), Oaxaca (6 per day, 4½hr., 68 pesos), and other destinations. The bus station is on Prolongación 16 de Septiembre. To get to town from the station, follow that street to the right upon leaving the station, and it soon splits into **5 de Septiembre** and **16 de Septiembre,** which run parallel and eventually form the sides of the *zócalo.* A taxi will bring you for 5 pesos.

## SALINA CRUZ

The huge mass of oil refineries that comes into view on the bus ride into Salina Cruz shows where this city's lifeblood lies. But like Juchitán, Salina Cruz moves with an infectious liveliness. The large, wind-swept *zócalo* provides a nice central focus, while a vigorous commercial area fills the streets to the north. A transportation hub for the rest of the isthmus, Salina Cruz is not a bad place to spend a night.

There are several hotels close to the *zócalo* and bus station. The best budget establishment is **Hotel Posada del Jardín,** Camacho 108 (tel. 4-01-62), two blocks north of the *zócalo,* with a beautifully leafy courtyard, clean, simple rooms, and overhead fans. Hot water flows only during cold weather (singles 45 pesos, with TV 60 pesos; doubles 70 pesos, with TV 85 pesos). **Restaurant El Lugar** is on the second floor at Av. 5 de Mayo and Acapulco (tel. 4-08-63). Windows offer a great view of the *zócalo,* while plaid tablecloths add a touch of New England. Breakfast runs 8-16 pesos, and *comida corrida* runs 18-20 pesos.

**Getting there and away: Local buses** connect Juchitán with the isthmus towns of Tehuantepec (½hr.) and Juchitán (1hr.). **Cristóbal Colón** runs **buses** to Huatulco (6 per day, 3hr., 36 pesos), Mexico City (7:30, 8:15, and 9:15pm, 11½hr., 250 pesos), Oaxaca (5 per day, 5hr., 66 pesos), and elsewhere. The main bus station is just a block away from the *zócalo* on 5 de Mayo; to get there, make a left upon exiting the waiting area.

# ▓ Bahías de Huatulco

With its wide, palm-lined streets, shiny, electric lights, and sprawling resorts, Huatulco is a paradise for those who like their vacations packaged, planned, and posh. If everything looks new here, that's because it is: Mexican government officials settled on the area as a prime candidate for resort development in the 1980s, and began building from the bottom up. As a result, the entire city feels something like a seaside country club; even the *zócalo* smacks of freshly poured concrete and professional landscaping. Visitors are primarily moneyed Mexicans, with a sprinkling of *norteamericanos* and Europeans. Though backpackers may feel out of place amidst the shining cars and bulging wallets, the place still merits a visit; Huatulco's nine bays remain naturally breathtaking, filled with sapphire-blue waters and lined with lush vegetation. But the days of Huatulco's virginal splendor are numbered—by 2018, every bay will be accessible by land, and the area will welcome two million visitors a year.

## ORIENTATION

Huatulco is 750km from Mexico City and 950km from Acapulco. The small downtown area, **La Crucecita,** is in the middle of the string of nine bays. It houses the bus stations and most budget accommodations. The *zócalo,* four blocks from the bus stations on **Gardenia,** is bordered by **Bugambilias** on the other side. **Carrizal,** one more block away from the *zócalo,* leads to the bays. **Santa Cruz,** the bay closest to downtown, is also the most developed of the lot. Hotels and an *artesanía* market clutter its main road, **Blvd. Santa Cruz.** From there, the bays of **Chahué, Tangolunda,** and **Conejos** lie to the south. Tangolunda is also known as the *zona hotelera* because it houses the Western hemisphere's largest Club Med and several other luxury lodgings. Its main road is **Blvd. Benito Juárez.** From Santa Cruz, the bays to the north are **El Órgano, Maguey, Cacaclutla, Chachacual,** and **San Augustín.**

SOUTHERN PACIFIC COAST

## PRACTICAL INFORMATION

**Tourist Office: Módulo de Información,** Bugambilias 210 (tel. 7-13-09), on the side of the *zócalo* opposite the church. Open daily 9am-8:30pm. **Asociación de Hoteles y Moteles,** Blvd. Santa Cruz at Monte Albán (tel. 7-08-48), in Santa Cruz. Open Mon.-Fri. 9am-2pm and 4-6pm, Sat. 10am-1pm.

**Currency Exchange:** Plan to get money ahead of time. There is a small **Bital** office on Gardenia across from the Colón bus station, but all ATMs and other banks are a 20min. walk away at Santa Cruz. **Bancomer,** Blvd. Santa Cruz at Pochutla (tel. 7-00-03), exchanges cash and traveler's checks. Open Mon.-Fri. 9am-1:30pm. **Banamex** (tel. 7-03-22), next door, houses a 24hr. **ATM.** Open Mon.-Fri. 9am-1:30pm. Large hotels also exchange money at slightly less favorable rates.

**Telephones: LADATELs** line Carrizal, Blvd. Santa Cruz, and Blvd. Benito Juárez. *Caseta* at the **Telefónica,** Bugambilias at Flamboyan (tel. 7-03-14). Open Mon.-Sat. 7:30am-9:30pm, Sun. 8am-1pm and 4-9pm.

**Fax: Telecomm,** (tel. 7-08-85) next to the post office. Telegrams, too. Open Mon.-Fri. 8am-6pm, Sat. 9am-12:30pm.

**Airport:** Tel. 1-03-10. 19km from Santa Cruz. Taxis charge 70 pesos for the 25min. trip; *microbuses* get you within a 200m walk from the terminal for 5 pesos. **Aerocaribe** (tel. 7-12-20) and **Mexicana** (tel. 7-02-43) serve the airport. **Bahías Plus Travel Agency** (tel. 7-08-11), Carrizal between Guamuchil and Guanacas, sells plane tickets (open Mon.-Sat. 9am–8pm; closed Wed. afternoons).

**Buses: Cristóbal Colón,** Gardenia at the corner of Ocotillo (tel. 7-02-61), has 1st-class service to Mexico City (5pm, 12½hr., 274 pesos), Oaxaca (*deluxe* 10pm, 7hr., 120 pesos; *ordinario* 5 and 11pm, 7hr., 101 pesos), Puebla (5pm, 11hr., 237 pesos), Puerto Escondido (6 per day, 5am-6pm, 2hr., 29 pesos), San Cristóbal (10:45am and 11:30pm, 10hr., 112 pesos), and Tuxtla Gutiérrez (10:45am, 7:05, and 11:30pm, 9hr., 94 pesos). **Estrella Blanca,** on Gardenia and Palma Real (tel. 7-01-03), sends buses to Acapulco (10 per day, 5:30am-7pm, 9hr., 1st class 100 pesos, *ordinario* 86 pesos), Mexico City (6pm, 13½hr., 180 pesos), Pochutla (10 per day, 5:30am-9pm, 1hr., 7 pesos), and Puerto Escondido (10 per day, 5:30am-9pm, 2hr., 20 pesos). **Estrella del Valle,** on Jasmín (tel. 7-01-93), at the corner of Sabali, provides service to Oaxaca (direct 10:15pm, 6½hr., 68 pesos; *ordinario* 8:30 and 12:30pm, 8hr., 51 pesos).

**Car Rental: Budget,** Ocotillo at Jazmín (tel. 7-00-10), 1 block from Cristóbal Colón station. Small cars 350-450 pesos per day, including mileage and insurance. Ask about special promotions. Open Mon.-Fri. 9am-1pm and 4-9pm.

**Market: 3 de Mayo,** on Guamuchil off the *zócalo*.

**Laundromat: La Estrella,** Carrizal at Flamboyan (tel. 7-05-85), across from Hotel Busanvi. 3kg for 21 pesos. Open Mon.-Sat. 8am-9pm.

**Red Cross:** On Carrizal (tel. 7-11-88) across from Gran Hotel Huatulco. Open 24hr.

**Pharmacy: Farmacia Aries,** Guamuchil at Carrizal (tel. 7-00-48), past the market. Open Mon.-Sat. 8am-9pm.

**Hospital: IMSS,** on Blvd. Chahué (tel. 7-02-64) past the government building. 24hr. service. No English spoken.

**Police:** At Blvd. Chahué 100 (tel. 7-02-10), in the pink government building 1½ blocks from the tourist office. Open 24hr. English-speaking interpreters and assistance available.

**Post Office:** Blvd. Chahué 100 (tel. 7-05-51), in the pink government building. Open Mon.-Fri. 9am-1pm and 3-6pm, Sat. 9am-1pm. **Postal Code:** 70989.

**Phone Code:** 958.

## ACCOMMODATIONS AND CAMPING

Camping is a way to escape Huatulco's high-priced hotel scene, but it's allowed only on Chahué, Cacaluta, and Conejos. The other bays are off-limits because they lack security and are hard to get to (they're accessible only by boat). Under no circumstances should you try to camp on Santa Cruz or Tangolunda; hotel security will not be kind. If camping isn't your thing, be prepared for slim pickings. All affordable rooms are located in La Crucecita, and tend to be overpriced even though they're somewhat removed from the ocean. Hot water is rare, but usually not too necessary.

Rates rise by about 50% during the high season (July-Nov.); the listings below indicate low-high season ranges.

**Hotel Posada San Agustín,** on Macuil at the corner of Carriza (tel. 7-03-68). From the bus station on Gardenia, walk 1 block to the left, turn left on Macuil, and walk for 2 blocks. In the midst of pastel monstrosities, this simple, blue and white building is a beacon for the budget traveler. Rooms are clean and bright; ask for one with a balcony. Fans but no hot water. Singles or 1-bed doubles 50-60 pesos; 2-bed doubles 80-90 pesos.

**Hotel Benimar,** Bugambilias 1404 at Pochote (tel. 7-04-47), 3 blocks from the bus station on Gardenia. Rooms come with ceiling fans and full bathrooms with hot water—if you tell management to turn it on. Homey common area with hammock and TV. Singles 80-120 pesos; doubles 100-140 pesos; triples 150-190 pesos.

**Hotel Busanvi II,** Macuil between Carrizal and Bugambilias. This hot-pink eyesore offers decent rooms for decent prices. All have fans and no hot water. Singles 80 pesos; doubles 100 pesos; triples 120 pesos.

## FOOD

Huatulco's cuisine runs the financial gamut from pricey French food to cheap *típico* kitchens. As a general rule, the closer the restaurant is to the *zócalo,* the more expensive it will be. Carrizal is lined with small places that offer cheap food.

**Comedor Gina,** Guarumbo 201 at Carrizal, 1 block from the *zócalo.* Standard *típico* fare served on standard plastic tables. Refreshingly free of pretension and resort-goers; you'll feel at home with the warm service. Fish soup or *comida corrida* 15 pesos. Open daily 7am-9pm.

**Restaurant-Bar La Tropicana** Guanacastle at Gardenia (tel. 7-06-61), across from Hotel Flamboyan. This restaurant may be the exception to the rule, "all restaurants on the *zócalo* must be overpriced." Sit outdoors and watch the folk saunter by while tapping your foot in rhythm to Mexican and American pop. Breakfast 10-22 pesos; *tortas* 12 pesos; fish 22 pesos. Open 24hr.!

**El Grillo Marinero,** Carrizal at Macuhitl. This outdoor *palapa* catches cool breezes as well as seafood-loving locals. There is no official menu, but the woman behind the stove will be happy to help you decide what to order. Fish fillets 30 pesos. Open Mon.-Sat. 9am-9pm.

## SAND, SUN, AND ENTERTAINMENT

Until the planners manage to finish paving the roads, Huatulco's nine bays and 36 beaches, spread across 35km, pose a transportation challenge; it's hard to get off the beaten track without shelling out for a taxi or boat to take you there. None of the bays can be seen from any of the others, and some are accessible only by boat. Santa Cruz, Tangolunda, and Chahué can all be reached by the blue and white *microbús* that leaves from Carrizal, near the Hotel Busanvi (2 pesos). A taxi will take you to a beach at Santa Cruz, Chahué, Tangolunda, Conejos, Maguey, or San Agustín and retrieve you at a pre-set time for 50 pesos.

To get from the *zócalo* to **Santa Cruz,** walk on Guamuchil two blocks past the market and turn right on the road behind the pink government building. As you descend, the sparkling water comes into view. Turn right on Blvd. Santa Cruz and then left on Mitla; the sands of **Playa Principal** are only a few meters away. This little strip of sand unfortunately gets crowded fast. A more spacious beach that is still conveniently accessible from downtown is **Tangolunda.** Hop on a *microbús* (2 pesos) or a *colectivo* taxi (3 pesos) and ask to be let off at the public beach entrance. Follow the dirt road to the gorgeous expanse of sand many posh resorts call home. The bus can also get you to within striking distance of the bay **Chahué;** its beaches, **Esperanza** and **Tejón,** are better for suntanning than swimming because of a strong undertow.

To get to any of the other bays, you'll have to hire a taxi. The tourist office arranges boat trips for a bit more. **Playa Entrega,** in Santa Cruz, and **Maguey** are best for snorkeling. Chahué and Tangolunda have slightly bigger waves and more surf. San

Agustín has no hotels, only outdoor *palapas*. **Cacaluta** is known for lush plant life and cooling breezes. In terms of crowds, Entrega, Maguey, and **San Agustín** are most popular; your best shots at solitude are Cacaluta, **Conejos,** and **El Órgano.**

The tourist office near the *zócalo* organizes a variety of excursions, all with bilingual guides. Make reservations a day in advance (tel. 7-13-09) to take a yacht to see **El Bufadero,** the **geyser** between Santa Cruz and El Órgano (200 pesos for up to 10 people), ride three and a half hours on horseback (250 pesos), or go on a 15-minute hot-air-balloon ride (Wed. nights, 75 pesos). They also rent snorkeling equipment (35 pesos per day) and arrange scuba diving trips (US$50). The tourist office also has info about renting bicycles, motor scooters, and go-cart-type vehicles.

Huatulco's night scene is just getting off the ground, leaving travelers with few options after the sunset. Most large hotels have their own bars, but the only full disco is **Magic Circus** (tel. 7-00-17), on Blvd. Santa Cruz next to the Hotel Marlin (cover Thurs.-Sun. 50 pesos; open bar Thurs.; open Wed.-Sun. 10pm-late). Buses stop running at 8pm, so a taxi from La Crucecita (7-10 pesos) will be necessary both ways.

# ■ Pochutla

Pochutla serves as the gateway to Puerto Ángel and Zipolite; if you're traveling by bus, you'll have to pass through. The lack of services in both beach towns makes Pochutla a good place to stock up on money, make any last phone calls, or buy stamps. Both Cristóbal Colón and Estrella Blanca have stations on Lázaro Cárdenas, a few blocks from downtown. Follow Cárdenas to the left and uphill to get to **Bital** and **Bancomer,** which both have **ATMs.** There are **LADATELs** near the bus stations and throughout the city. From the **bus** station on the left side of Lázaro Cárdenas just as you enter the city, **Cristóbal Colón** (tel. 4-02-74) sends first-class buses to Huatulco (9:45am, 7, and 9pm, 1hr., 12 pesos), Mexico City (4pm, 15hr., 284 pesos), Oaxaca (4 and 10pm, 8hr., 112 pesos), and Tehuantepec (9:45am, 7, and 9pm, 4½hr., 58 pesos). **Estrella Blanca,** on Lázaro Cárdenas (tel. 4-03-80) a block down from Cristóbal Colón, goes to Acapulco (semi-direct 6 per day, 6:15am-10pm, 8hr., 91 pesos; *ordinario* 6 per day, 9hr., 79 pesos), Huatulco (8 per day, 1hr., 7 pesos), and Mexico City (7am, 13hr., 201 pesos). There is a **supermarket, Super Compras,** on the left as you walk toward the banks on Cárdenas. To get to the **post office,** make a right on Juárez toward the church and the *zócalo;* it's to the left of the church, behind the Palacio Municipal (open Mon.-Fri. 8am-7pm, Sat. 9am-2pm). The **police** can be reached at 4-01-76. **Postal Code:** 70900.

If the wait for your bus will be a long one, you can spend a pleasant night in the **Hotel Posada San José** (tel. 4-01-53), down the alleyway next to the Estrella del Valle station. Rooms are well-kept and have generously sized bathrooms with hot water. A swimming pool and a pet monkey named Pancho provide the entertainment (singles 60-100 pesos; doubles 70-100 pesos).

# ■ Puerto Ángel

With no bank or newsstand and only a fledgling post office, Puerto Ángel's turquoise shores are a natural haven for urban escapists. The town is popular with Europeans, and most visitors are well-traveled, giving Puerto Ángel a touch of Bohemian flair. While many come expecting to use the town as a base for daytrips in the buff at Zipolite, lots find the comforts of Puerto Ángel even more seductive. The town has fairly advanced accommodations and tourist services, but is by no means a built-up resort town. Hotels and restaurants intermingle with homes and businesses, and nightlife is almost non-existent. Still, the food is good, the cove beautiful, and the living tranquil.

**Orientation and Practical Information** Puerto Ángel is 240km south of Oaxaca de Juárez and 68km east of Puerto Escondido. **Taxis** link between Puerto Ángel with nearby towns (to Pochutla, *colectivo* about 4 pesos, *especial* 20 pesos).

The road from Pochutla becomes Puerto Ángel's main drag at the edge of town; **Avenida Principal** descends a hill, then wraps around Playa Puerto Ángel, becoming **Blvd. Virgilio Uribe.** The main road crosses a small creek (really a glorified puddle) next to the naval base and forks at a sign for Hotel Ángel del Mar. The right-hand road rambles farther down the coast to Zipolite, while the left-hand road heads for Playa Panteón. The only significant side street climbs the hill near the entrance to town by Hotel Soraya. It starts out as **Vasconcelos,** then curves to the left, becomes **Teniente Azuela,** and arrives back at Uribe in front of the naval station.

Services in Puerto Ángel are minimal; most must be begged, borrowed, or imported from nearby Pochutla. There is a **long-distance *caseta*** at Vasconcelos 3 (tel. 4-03-98), around the corner from Hotel Soraya (open daily 7am-10pm). **Faxes** can be sent from the **Telecomm** office, next door to the post office (open Mon.-Fri. 9am-3pm). The *microbús* goes to Pochutla (every 20min., 6am-8pm, 2 pesos), returns to town, and leaves again for Zipolite (2 pesos) and Mazunte (3 pesos). Hop aboard anywhere along Uribe. **Farmacia Villa Florencia** is attached to the restaurant of the same name, on the main street (open daily 8:30am-9pm). There is a supermarket, **Super Puerto,** uphill on the right after the naval base. Limited **medical services** are available at the **Centro de Salud,** at the top of Vasconcelos to the left on a dirt path (open 24hr. for emergencies, Mon.-Sat. 8am-2pm and 4-8pm for consultation). The nearest **hospital** (tel. 4-02-16) is between Puerto Ángel and Pochutla. The **Agency of Public Ministry,** next to the base, will contact **police** in an **emergency.** The **post office** is on the main street, at the beginning of town (open Mon.-Fri. 9am-2pm). **Postal Code:** 70902. **Phone Code:** 958.

**Accommodations and Food** Puerto Ángel's cheap, attractive hotels and *casas de huéspedes* make the town a good base for daytrips to the sultry sands of Zipolite. Budget lodgings dot the hills on the inland side of the main road that runs behind the two beaches. Hammock spaces and ceiling fans are available in all of the following hotels, but hot water is not. The **Casa de Huéspedes Gundi y Tomás,** on Iturbide (tel. 4-31-02) just before the bridge and across from the naval base features stone-and-brick terraces overlooking the beach. Nets or screens render each room mosquito-proof. The communal bathrooms sparkle (singles 60 pesos; doubles 85-100 pesos, with bath 100-115 pesos; 10 pesos extra from July-Sept; hammocks 20 pesos). There is also a spectacular view at **Pensión Puesta del Sol** (tel. 4-30-96), past the naval base but before the road forks. Attractive common spaces and clean, freshly-painted rooms come with fans and screens. Breakfasts are available for 6-16 pesos (singles without bath 50 pesos; doubles without bath 65-75 pesos, with bath 85-100 pesos). Lie on the hammock in front of your room looking out over the cove at **Posada Rincón Sabroso** (tel. 4-30-95), on the high hill at the entrance to town (singles 80 pesos, high season 100 pesos; doubles 100 pesos, high season 120 pesos).

Seafood is the specialty of nearly every restaurant, though menus make some concessions for vegetarians—think grilled cheese sandwiches. Prices at the beachfront *palapas* aren't always in the budget range, but their tranquility is priceless. Cheaper restaurants tend to be inland, but they're often dim and hot. For some Italian fare, try the large, casual **Restaurant Villa Florencia** (tel. 4-30-44), in town on the landward side of Uribe, before the naval station (spaghetti 10-22 pesos; tortellini 30 pesos; pizzas 25-39 pesos). They also serve breakfast (5-10 pesos; restaurant and bar open daily 7am-11pm). **Beto's,** uphill past the naval base and supermarket on the right has the cheapest seafood dinner in town. Super-friendly service accompanies the 17-peso fish fillets, though the lack of a fan might dampen your brow (open daily 6-10pm). For a more expensive feast in a beautiful spot nestled in a sumptuous garden, head to **Buenavista,** on the right uphill immediately after the naval base. The restaurant is at the top of the hotel. The place commands a striking view of the bay and catches only passing breezes. The food is excellently prepared (fish and chicken dishes 35 pesos; veggie tamales 25 pesos; open for breakfast and dinner daily 8:30-11am and 7-11pm).

**Sand** Of Puerto Ángel's two beaches, the smaller **Playa Panteón,** on the far side of town, is the worthier. The water here is calm and warm, and the coves great for exploring. You can reach it via a cement walkway that begins on the left past the naval base or by car, driving uphill towards Zipolite and then turning left down a dirt road. Many of the restaurants on the beach rent equipment. **Luis y Vicente "Amigos del Mar"** (tel. 431-16) rents snorkel gear (20 pesos per hr., 55 pesos per day) and arranges boat trips (up to 5 people, 150 pesos per hr.; open daily 7am-11pm).

Away from the polluted waters of Playa Puerto Ángel and the restaurant-studded shores of Playa Panteón is the much less crowded **Playa Estacahuites** (pronounced "a Stack o Wheaties"). To get there, walk on the main road towards Pochutla and ascend the hill just past the post office until you find a yellow Corona sign. It takes 20 minutes to walk there from downtown. The three small bays have somewhat rocky sand and gentle water for swimming.

# ■ Zipolite

The road to paradise is newly paved. Zipolite, once a remote hippie beach, can now be easily reached by *colectivo* from Pochutla or Puerto Ángel. The word *zipolite* means "place of the dead"—it refers to those who have lost their lives in the unforgiving surf. Of course, cynics would note that for every person who has lost her life in the waves, 10 have lost their former lives to Zipolite's hypnotizing combination of wind, water, and marijuana. The lifestyle here is all about relaxation—eat when you're hungry, sleep as much as you want, and wear as little as you please. Come here to stroll naked down the long beach, check in with the international vagabond set, and generally partake of the fringe atmosphere. Do it soon, though—where paved roads go, clothes soon follow.

**Orientation and Practical Information** Zipolite lies just 4km west of Puerto Ángel; **microbuses** run back and forth between the two (every 20min., 2 pesos). Zipolite consists of one long stretch of beach. Get off the bus before it curves right in front of a thick grove of palm trees. Cross the street and walk towards the shining sea. If you need information, ask **someone who's naked**—those without tan lines have been here the longest. There is a **pharmacy** and a small **general store** and a place that exchanges money at pretty poor rates on the road near the entrance from Puerto Ángel. There are a number of **stands** scattered around the beach that sell purified water and sodas. You're better off buying supplies and munchies in Puerto Ángel or in Pochutla.

**Accommodations and Food** *Palapas* rent hammocks and the space to swing in (20 pesos a night). **Shambhala,** at the very far end of the beach across some rocks and up the stairs, is an international haven with a corresponding world-peace theme. Rooms have mosquito netting and lights (singles 40 pesos; doubles 50 pesos). All the food cooked in its cafe is health-conscious and purified. Unlike the other establishments it literally looks down on, Shambhala is drug- and alcohol-free. **San Cristóbal,** a cluster of *palapas* before the rocks that lead to Shambhala, has two floors of nicer-than-average wood and cement *cabañas* with lights and fans. Common bathrooms are conveniently located and clean (1 or 2 people 40 pesos, with bath 80 pesos). For just the essentials, try **Montebello,** a little further east from San Cristóbal. Slightly sandy *cabañas* with mosquito netting and common bath are 30 pesos for one person, 40 pesos for two.

For fish and seafood, the *palapas* are ready and waiting (most are open 8am-10pm and charge 20-30 pesos for their most expensive item). **Nuevo Sol** offers delicious pizzas prepared by the Italian owner. **3 de Diciembre,** 100m off the beach, offers vegetarian dishes and sweet desserts. **Lo Cósmico,** the last *palapa* before Shambhala, makes crêpes that are out of this world.

**Sand and Sights** The only sights in Zipolite are the other **sunbathers in the buff,** who are doing little more than allowing the rays to gleam off their naked curves. Waves break cataclysmically offshore, slamming the carefree souls who frolic in the surf. The waves come in from two directions, creating a series of channels that suck unsuspecting swimmers out to sea. Though ferocious, these channels are not very wide. If you find yourself being pulled away from shore, do not attempt to swim directly towards the beach; rather, swim parallel to the beach until you're clear of the seaward current.

Zipolite is unfortunately plagued by theft, so keep an eye on everything or leave it locked up. A final warning: scorpions frequent Zipolite, so either give your cut-offs a good shake before jumping into them or blend in by going about your business in the buff. If you *must* get out and do something, catch a bus to **Mazunte.** Its **Museo de la Tortuga** holds an impressive collection of turtles from all over the world. It is also an important venue for turtle research and conservation. Don't begrudge the admission price; your pesos go toward conservation (open Tues.-Sat. 10am-4:30pm, Sun. 10am-12:30pm; admission 10 pesos, children and students with ID 5 pesos; includes a guided tour in Spanish). Mazunte also offers some beaches better-suited to swimming than Zipolite, as well as—surprise!—more *palapa* restaurants. Playa Agustinillo is on the eastern edge of town, before the Turtle Museum. Playa Mazunte is accessible from the area where the bus stops. Both beaches offer fewer crowds and gentler surf, although there are still significant currents; keep your wits about you.

# ■ Puerto Escondido

Less than two decades ago, Puerto Escondido (pop. 20,000) was a quiet fishing village where only a handful of scantily clad *extranjeros* used to gleefully romp, wheedling overnight lodging from local families. Today, the proliferation of surfers, blondes, and bikinis makes Playa Zicatela reminiscent of Southern California. Hotels now outnumber hippies, nudity is uncommon, and excellent food, exotic drink, and kitsch trinkets compete for pedestrians' pesos. But Puerto Escondido is still a long way from *Baywatch*. Although no longer a remote outpost, this coastal town still entices mostly rugged-minded vacationers in search of a peaceful time.

## ORIENTATION

Like any self-respecting seaside village, Puerto Escondido has its very own airport. It's also connected to the rest of the world by land. Routes 175 (paved) and 131 (mostly unpaved) wind treacherously through the Sierra Madres toward the coast, while an expertly paved coastal road, Rte. 200, twists through ramshackle fishing towns and coastal forests on its way to Acapulco.

Puerto Escondido is built on a hill. The **Carretera Costera** (Rte. 200) cuts across the hill, bisecting it into an uptown of well-marked, perpendicular residential streets and a touristy downtown maze of paths leading to the beach. At *el crucero,* Rte. 131 from Oaxaca crosses Rte. 200 and becomes **Pérez Gasga,** which twists downhill and turns into the **Adoquín,** a pedestrian walkway leading to the beach. The bus station is near *el crucero.* To and from the airport, 3km away on Rte. 200, *colectivos* charge 15 pesos. Taxis can be found by the tourist information booth and along the Carretera Costera; they are the safer way of getting around after nightfall.

## PRACTICAL INFORMATION

**Tourist Office: Módulo de Información Turística** (tel. 2-01-75), a palm-shaded information booth with its back to the beach just before the beginning of the pedestrian walkway. Advice and counsel given with good humor and the wisdom of an insider (open Mon.-Fri. 9am-2pm and 5-8pm, Sat. 9am-2pm).

**Currency Exchange: Banamex,** Pérez Gasga on the corner of the Adoquín (tel. 2-03-52). Exchanges traveler's checks and has an **ATM.** Open Mon.-Fri. 9am-noon. **Bancomer,** 1 Nte. at 2 Pte. (tel. 2-04-11), near the bus station, also exchanges cash.

Open Mon.-Fri. 8:30am-3pm. **Money Exchange,** on the Adoquín (tel. 2-05-92), across from Farmacia Cortés, has bad rates but convenient hours. Open Mon.- Sat. 10am-3pm and 6-9pm.

**Telephones: LADATELs** line the beach side of the Adoquín. **Farmacia Cortés** sells 50-peso phone cards, along with other shops along the Adoquín.

**Telegrams:** Tel. 2-09-57. Next to the post office. Open Mon.-Fri. 8am-6pm.

**Airport:** Tel. 2-04-91. Airlines include **AeroMorelos** (tel. 2-06-53) and **Aerovega** (tel. 2-01-51). **Turismo Rodimar de Viajes,** Pérez Gasga 905B on the Adoquín (tel. 2-07-34), sells **Mexicana** plane tickets and daytrips. Open daily 7:30am-10pm.

**Bus Stations: Cristóbal Colón,** Calle 1 Nte. 207 (tel. 2-10-73), 2 blocks uphill from *el crucero* and to the right. To Huatulco (8 per day, 8:45am-9pm, 2hr., 29 pesos), San Cristóbal (8:45am and 9:30pm, 12hr., 160 pesos), and Tuxtla Gutiérrez (8:45am, 7, and 9:30pm, 10hr., 140 pesos). **Estrella Blanca** (tel. 2-04-27), just steps uphill from *el crucero,* goes to Acapulco (semi-direct 6 per day, 7:30am-11:30pm, 7hr., 78 pesos; *ordinario* 11 per day, 8½hr., 66 pesos), Huatulco and Pochutla (6, 7am, 2:50, and 7pm, ½hr., 18 pesos), Mexico City (9am and 7:30pm, 12hr., 163 pesos; deluxe 8pm, 12hr., 185 pesos), and Zihuatanejo (8:45pm, 11hr., 123 pesos). **Oax-aca-Istmo** (tel. 2-03-92), behind Estrella Blanca, travels to Pochutla and Salina Cruz (6, 8:30, 11:30am, and 1pm, ½hr., 10-39 pesos). **Estrella del Valle** (tel. 2-00-50), Hidalgo at 3 Ote., 3 blocks down, goes to Oaxaca (direct 8:15am and 10:15pm, 6½hr., 65 pesos; *ordinario* 6 per day, 7:30am-10pm, 8½hr., 54 pesos).

**Car Rental: Budget** (tel. 2-03-12) has an office in Hotel Posada Real in Bacocho, 3km west of *el crucero* on Rte. 200. Small cars 390 pesos per day, including insurance and unlimited mileage. Open daily 9am-2pm and 4-8pm.

**Market: Mercado Benito Juárez,** 8 Nte. at 3 Pte., 1 block past the post office all the way up Av. Oaxaca. Open daily 7am-6pm, but most lively Wed. and Sat. **Raya Sol,** on Pérez Gasga (tel. 2-02-87), is a small grocery store near the beginning of the pedestrian mall. Open daily 8am-11pm.

**Laundromat: Lavamática del Centro,** Pérez Gasga 405, uphill from the pedestrian walkway on the right. Cheap. Open Mon.-Sat. 8am-8pm, Sun. 8am-5pm.

**Red Cross:** Pérez Gasga (tel. 2-01-46), across from Hotel Nayar. Open 24hr.

**Pharmacy: Farmacia Cortés,** on the Adoquín (tel. 2-01-12). Open daily 7:30am-11pm.

**Hospital: IMSS,** 5 de Febrero at Calle 7 Nte. (tel. 2-01-42). Open 24hr. **Centro de Salud,** Pérez Gasga 409 (tel. 2-00-46), below and across from the Hotel Virginia. A small medical clinic open 24hr. for emergencies. No English spoken.

**Police:** On the Agencia Municipal on the Carretera Costera (tel. 2-01-11 or 2-01-55), shortly past *el crucero* on the way to the airport. No English spoken. The tourist booth will probably be more helpful—if it's open.

**Post Office:** Calle 7 Nte. at Av. Oaxaca (tel. 2-09-59), uphill from *el crucero* past the bus station. Open Mon.-Fri. 8am-7pm, Sat. 9am-1pm. **Postal Code:** 71980.

**Phone Code:** 958.

## ACCOMMODATIONS

The beach is not safe for camping, but a multitude of hotels cater to budget travelers, particularly during the off-season. During Semana Santa, Christmas, July, and August, reservations are an absolute must, and the least expensive places are the rented rooms, trailer parks, and *cabañas* along the beach—you'll feel like you're on Gilligan's Island, but without the coconut radio. In a pinch, **Farmacia Cortés** has listings of rooms and suites for rent. The first three listings are on the hill; the last two lie much closer to the beach. Price ranges reflect seasonal variation.

**Hotel Mayflower,** Andador Libertad (tel. 2-03-67). From the bus stations, cross *el crucero,* then take a left down a steep hill. The road will end, but stairs will descend on the right to the hotel entrance. The Mayflower will make you want to sing. Every guest receives a complimentary margarita in the upstairs bar where young international beachgoers dust off the sand and read back issues of *Newsweek* and *Glamour.* The hospitable, multilingual owner keeps rooms immaculate. Singles 79-99 pesos; doubles 99-120 pesos. Across the street, keeping with the pilgrim theme, **Plymouth Rock** has dorm rooms with communal bathrooms, mosquito nets, fans, and a kitchen. 30 pesos per person.

**Hotel Carrillo de Reyes,** Tel. 2-04-42. Follow Pérez Gasga from *el crucero;* the hotel is on the right. Rooms here are clean and spacious, with glossy wood furniture and fans. Courtyard bar is perfect for a round of drinks before dinner. Singles 65 pesos; doubles 82 pesos; triples 98 pesos.

**Casa de Huéspedes Naxhiely,** Pérez Gasga 301. At *el crucero,* cross and follow Pérez Gasga to the aqua-blue hotel on the left. A bit removed from the beach action. Provides cold water, sheets, and large plain rooms. Singles 40-115 pesos; doubles 50-150 pesos.

**Casas de Playa Acali** (tel. 2-02-78 or 2-07-54), at the beginning of Zicatela Beach just past the rocks. Wooden cabins have fans, mosquito netting, private bathrooms with 24hr. hot water, a jug of purified water on the porch, and a swimming pool. If that's not enough, cross the road to the ocean. (Most do.) Rooms start at 120 pesos for 2 people; add 30 pesos for each additional person.

**Restaurant y Cuartos Liza,** on Playa Marinero, past Carmen's Café and Hotel Flor de María. Among the safer of beach accommodations. Four rooms with fans, screens on the windows, and private bathrooms with hot water. Attached restaurant. Singles 80-100 pesos; doubles 120-140 pesos.

## FOOD

The restaurants on Pérez Gasga know their clientele: the ubiquitous "we accept dollars" signs should say it all. The pizza, pasta, and apple pie for sale on the pedestrian walkway are certainly prominent, but there are still some cheap seafood restaurants popular with the locals.

**Antojería Doña Claudia,** at the end of the Adoquín, past Coco's bar on the left. This casual, open-air spot specializes in typical Oaxacan *antojitos.* Not yet discovered by most tourists, Doña Claudia's offers great food without pricey frills. Delicious *empanadas amarillas* are 6 pesos, enchiladas 15 pesos, and *comida corrida* 16 pesos. Open daily 8am-10pm.

**Banana's** (tel. 2-00-05), the last restaurant on the beach side of Pérez Gasga, at the end of the pedestrian mall. Catering to the cable TV set, this popular hangout has a program for every meal. Enjoy your breakfast (10-18 pesos) with CNN Headline News, and your mid-day crepes (21 pesos) lit up by MTV. Every night they show recent movies, with closed-captioning for those who prefer to converse. Perfect with pizza (29-45 pesos). Happy hour 6-9pm. Open daily 7:30-12:30am.

**La Gota de Vida,** on Pérez Gasga (tel. 2-09-93), midway down Zicatela Beach. This vegetarian haven makes its own bread, pasta, yogurt, and tempeh, sterilizes all its vegetables, and prepares heavenly fruit *licuados* (12-14 pesos), tofu *tortas* (16-18 pesos), and salads (14-17 pesos). Watch surf acrobatics on Zicatela Beach as you eat. Open daily 8am-10pm.

**Carmen's Café** (tel. 2-08-60), on Playa Marinero, across from Hotel Flor de María. Follow the sign left up the alley, then turn right after crossing the bridge. One taste of the chocolate croissant (5 pesos) and you'll stop complaining about the gringo invasion of the beach. Fresh bread makes the peanut butter and banana sandwich (8 pesos) even more delicious. Extravagant fruit and yogurt salad with Carmen's own granola 13 pesos. Open Mon.-Sat. 7am-6pm, Sun. 7am-midnight. A second branch on Playa Zicatela is open daily 6am-9pm.

## SAND AND SIGHTS

Beach, beach, and more beach. Past Banana's, you'll encounter fishing boats; the stretch of sand from there to the rocks is **Playa Marinero,** great for swimming or sunbathing. Stepping over the rocks will take you to **Playa Zicatela,** one of the world's best surfing beaches. Those dudes bobbing up and down in the water waiting to ride the next killer wave all have several years of experience. Watching them is exhilarating, but *under no circumstances should you swim at Zicatela*—you risk a fate worse than wiping out. Past Carmen's on the road facing the beach, **Acuario** (tel. 2-

10-26) rents **snorkel** (20 pesos) and **scuba** gear (beginning at US$40 for a day's excursion). A few smaller beaches, suitable for snorkeling, lie on the other side of Playa Principal. The distance is short enough to walk, but you can also take a taxi (15 pesos) or a boat. From the tourist booth, walk to the right towards the lighthouse. A staircase will take you over the waves before climbing uphill to a road and a vista point. Follow the road and take the first left; stairs lead to **Playa Manzanillo.** On the other side of a rocky barrier is **Puerto Angelito.** Both tranquil beaches make for good swimming or languid lounging in the shaded hammocks or chairs (10 pesos per day). Even further removed from civilization is beautiful **Playa Carrizalillo,** offering fewer crowds and the best swimming around. It's accessible by boat or taxi from Puerto Angelito, but to walk there, head uphill from the beach on Pérez Gasga. When it forks at the Banamex, follow the left-hand side. You will pass a turn-off for Puerto Angelito; continue straight on the dirt road until you come to the Rotary Club basketball courts. Make a left and keep walking downhill. For those rugged adventurers dying to explore secluded beaches, be sure to exercise proper caution. Theft and violent crime are a serious problem in less-populated areas. It's probably best to stick to the established beaches. For a change of pace, head south to the more exotic locales of **Zipolite** (p. 366) and **Mazunte** (p. 367).

## ENTERTAINMENT

When the sun goes down, sun worshippers turn into bar crawlers, making their way to the many pubs along the strip. In the early evening, every restaurant and bar has a happy hour, which oddly enough lasts for three or four hours. Two-for-one drinks are one reason that everyone's happy. In addition to alcohol and TV, **Banana's** offers pool and foosball (20 pesos per hr.). Around 10pm, the music starts. **Discoteque Bacocho,** in the Bacocho residential district, is the only full-fledged dance club, meaning you'll have to shower and throw something nice over that thong bikini. Taxis will whisk you over there for 15 pesos (cover 25 pesos; open Sat.-Sun. 10pm-3am). More informal places line the pedestrian walkway. **El Tubo,** on the Playa Principal, plays reggae, salsa, and rock. The bacchanalian crowd spills out onto the beach by night's end (no cover; open daily 11pm-4am). **Montezuma's Revenge** and **The Wipeout Bar,** both on the Adoquín, feature live music every night. Keep your ears perked for Santana-esque tunes (no cover; music usually runs 10:30pm-1am).

# Central Mexico

The states of **Guanajuato** and **Querétaro** form a vast, bowl-shaped plateau of fertile soil, rolling farms, and verdant hillsides that are home to some of Mexico's most delightful colonial *pueblos* and cities. Since the 16th century, its silver-rich underground has brought the region prosperity and shaped its history. In the 18th century, the city of Guanajuato began to supply most of Mexico's minting silver and the area became one of the wealthier and more influential in the country. Guanajuato later became the commercial and banking center of this thriving region. Today, the region is home to a growing expat population in and around the culturally lively San Miguel de Allende. Nearby **Hidalgo,** one of the most mountainous states in Mexico, home to the pine-laden edge of the Sierra Madre Oriental, also lived on silver for much of its colonial history; though best-known for its archaeological sites, including Tula, Hidalgo is also home to slow-moving colonial towns like the pleasant Pachuca.

Although the first part of Mexico to bear the colonial mark of Hernán Cortés was Veracruz, the Conquest did not really pick up steam until his group ventured inland to **Puebla** and **Tlaxcala,** where many local tribes joined the entourage. Mexico's older churches, some built only months after the Spaniards' arrival, mark Cortés's trail through these states. But a glimpse into one of the region's 16th-century temples, where images from *indígena* mythology mingle with Catholic icons, shows that missionaries and *conquistadores* failed to fully subjugate indigenous peoples.

Contrary to popular conception, the **Estado de México** has more to offer than easy access to the thickly populated Mexico City. In the area outside of Mexico City's smog cloud, green plains creep up snowy volcanoes and swollen towns continue to grow, pushing against their natural barriers. The state is speckled with stellar archaeological sites, solemn convents, and vestiges of the colonial era. Forests seem to stretch forever, and small towns and villages within appear untouched by modernity.

After Emperor Maximilian built his summer home in Cuernavaca, thousands of Mexicans followed him and **Morelos** became a prime vacation spot. Once again, the state enjoyed the same interest that first brought the Olmecs from the Gulf Coast nearly 3000 years earlier. These days, Mexicans and foreigners alike march to Morelos to take advantage of Cuernavaca's "eternal spring," Xochicalco's underground observatory, and Tepoztlán's striking landscape. Unlike the overpopulated Federal District, parts of Morelos remain undeveloped, with plentiful tree-covered vistas and unspoiled streams. Morelos is just a short jaunt from the D.F.; you can easily spend a day in Cuernavaca or Tepoztlán and return to the capital in the evening.

# GUANAJUATO

## ▓ Guanajuato

Guanajuato is simply beautiful. The road into the city winds through lush mountains split at the base by winding streams, passing rows of *nopales* (prickly-pear cacti) that blend surreally into the landscape. The hills gradually give way to the city where the legacy of colonial days may be observed in the city's rich culture and fabulous architecture. Serpentine slate streets overflow with monuments to the silver barons who made Guanajuato one of the richest colonial mining towns in America, while *callejones* (stone alleyways) sneak through Spanish archways and courtyards, leading to the city's myriad museums, theaters, and cathedrals. The town's mining boom days are over, but Guanajuato is now livelier than ever. Its university students and musicians promote an animated and youthful lifestyle, and Guanajuato continues to enjoy its status as a favorite destination among Mexican and foreign tourists alike.

**CENTRAL MEXICO**

## ORIENTATION

Guanajuato lies 380km northwest of Mexico City. Navigating the city's tangled maze of streets and *callejones* (alleyways) can be a teeth-gnashing experience even with the best of maps. The **Plaza de la Paz**, the **Basílica**, and the **Jardín Unión** mark the center of town. **Av. Juárez** climbs eastward past the *mercado* and Plaza de la Paz. Just past the basilica, the street is called **Luis Obregón**; past Teatro Juárez, the street becomes **Av. Sopeña**. Roughly following the path of Juárez/Sopeña, the **Subterránea** is an underground avenue built beneath the former bed of the river, which now flows in an adjacent concrete channel. When you become lost (and you will), remember that the tunnel is always downhill from you.

Guanajuato's **bus station** is 3km west of town; from there, the "El Centro" bus takes you to the heart of the city, while the "Mercado" bus takes you to the market. Buses cross the city running westward above ground and eastward underground (daily 6am-10:30pm, 1.50 pesos). A taxi from the bus station to the *centro* will cost 10 pesos. Taxis within the city cost about 8 pesos.

## PRACTICAL INFORMATION

**Tourist Office: Subsecretaría de Turismo,** Plaza de la Paz 14 (tel. 2-15-74 or 2-19-82; fax 2-42-51; email turismo@quijote.ugto.mx.), on your left as you pass the front of the *basílica* going uphill. Multilingual staff distributes brochures *(folletos)* and so-so maps. Open Mon.-Fri. 8:30am-7:30pm, Sat.-Sun. 10am-2pm.

**Currency Exchange:** Banks line Juárez and Plaza de la Paz. **BITAL,** Plaza de la Paz 59 (tel. 2-00-18), is open for exchange Mon.-Sat. 9am-6pm. **Cronos InterDivisas,** Plaza de la Compañía 2 (tel. 12-79-94), one of the many *casas de cambio*, has good rates. Open Mon.-Sat. 9am-5pm. **ATM** inside same building as **Fax** (below).

**Telephones: LADATELs** are around Pl. de la Paz and throughout the city. **Lonchería y Caseta de Larga Distancia Pípila,** Constancia 9 (tel. 2-00-75), behind the Templo de San Diego. Open Mon.-Sat. 9:30am-9:30pm, Sun. 11am-3pm. **Computel,** Ayuntamiento 20 (tel. 2-06-48; fax 2-06-00), 1 block from the post office. A bit expensive but discounts on calls to the U.S. after 7pm. Also fax service. Open Mon.-Sat. 8am-9pm, Sun. 10am-5pm.

**Fax:** Sopeña 1 (tel. 2-04-29; 2-69-91), to your left facing Teatro Juárez. Open Mon.-Fri. 8am-6pm, Sat. 9am-noon. Also in **Computel** (see above).

**Buses: Central de Autobuses,** west of the *centro*. Take the "Central de Autobuses" bus from Plaza de la Paz to the station (1.50 pesos). **Flecha Amarilla** (tel. 3-13-26) sends buses to Aguascalientes (8 per day, 5:40am-5:50pm, 3hr., 45 pesos), Celaya (every 40min., 6am-8:40pm, 2hr., 29 pesos), San Luis Potosí (7:20am and 1pm, 4½hr., 62 pesos), and San Miguel de Allende (8 per day, 6:45am-6pm, 1½hr., 24 pesos). **Servicios Coordinados** (tel. 3-13-33) has 1st-class service to Manzanillo (7am, 8hr., 202 pesos), Puerto Vallarta (9:45pm, 10hr., 245 pesos), and Toluca (10, 12:15pm, and 1:45am, 6hr., 114 pesos). **Futura** sends 1st-class buses to Acapulco (9pm, 9hr., 204 pesos), Durango (4 and 9:30pm, 9hr., 158 pesos), and Monterrey (5 per day, 2-9:30pm, 9hr., 210 pesos). **Ómnibus de Mexico** (tel. 3-13-56) serves Ciudad Juárez (10:15am, 22hr., 449 pesos), Poza Rica (6:30pm, 7hr., 148 pesos), and Tuxpan (6:30pm, 8hr., 166 pesos). **ETN** (tel. 3-02-89 or 3-15-79) sends luxury buses to Guadalajara (8am, 12:30, and 5:30pm, 3¾hr., 135 pesos), Irapuato (5:30, 8:30am, and 6:30pm, 45min., 18 pesos), León (8am, 12:30, 5:30, and 7pm, 45min., 21 pesos), and Mexico City (5 per day, 5:30pm-1am, 4¼hr., 150 pesos).

**Laundromat: Lavandería Automática,** Manuel Doblado 28 (tel. 2-67-18). Self- and full-service. Open Mon.-Sat. 9am-2pm and 4-8pm.

**Red Cross:** On Juárez (tel. 2-04-87), 2 blocks beyond the *mercado*. Open for emergencies 24hr. Some English spoken.

**Pharmacy: San Francisco de Asis,** Ponceanu Aguilar 15 (tel. 2-89-16), just off the Plaza de la Paz. Open daily 7am-10pm.

**Hospital: Clínica Hospital de Especialidades,** Plaza de la Pazzo (tel. 2-23-05). English spoken by **Drs. Sanchez Leyva and López Márquez.** Open 24hr.

**Emergency:** Dial 06.

**Police:** At Alhóndiga 8 (tel. 2-02-66 or 2-27-17), 1 block from Juárez. Open 24hr.

Central Mexico

N

0 — 75 miles
0 — 75 kilometers

Golfo De México
(Gulf Of Mexico)

Océano Pacífico
(Pacific Ocean)

SIERRA MADRE ORIENTAL

SAN LUIS POTOSÍ

AGUASCALIENTES

JALISCO

GUANAJUATO

QUERÉTARO

HIDALGO

TLAXCALA

VERACRUZ

PUEBLA

OAXACA

MÉXICO

MORELOS

GUERRERO

MICHOACÁN

Aguascalientes
Lagos de Moreno
León
Guanajuato
Dolores Hidalgo
San Miguel de Allende
Salamanca
La Piedad
Zamora
Uruapan
Pátzcuaro
Morelia
Zitácuaro
Lázaro Cárdenas
Toluca
Querétaro
Tequisquiapan
Tula
Mexico City
Netzahualcóyotl
Popocatépetl
Cuernavaca
Cacahuamilpa
Taxco
Iguala
Cuautla
Cholula
Puebla
Tlaxcala
Pachuca
Tuxpan
El Tajín
Papantla
Xalapa
Veracruz
Córdoba
Tehuacán
Huajuapan de León
Huautla
Tuxtepec
Santiago Tuxtla
San Andrés Tuxtla
Catemaco

57
45
80
15
57
105
150
150
125
90
95
145

**Internet Access: Redes Internet Guanajuato,** Alonso 70 (tel. 2-06-11; email root@redes.int.com.mx). Email 25 pesos per hr. Open Mon.-Fri. 10am-2:30pm and 5-8pm, Sat. 10am-2pm.

**Post Office:** Ayuntamiento 25 (tel. 2-03-85), across from the Templo de la Compañía. Follow Truco, the street running behind the *basílica,* for 1 block and turn left. Open Mon.-Fri. 8am-7pm, Sat. 9am-1pm. **Postal Code:** 36000.

**Phone Code:** 473.

## ACCOMMODATIONS

The quiet, pretty neighborhood around the *basílica* is home to some inexpensive hotels, often occupied by young people from every corner of the globe; Guanajuato frequently serves as a two-day getaway spot for students at language institutes in San Miguel de Allende or Mexico City. More economic lodgings cluster near the *mercado* and the Alhóndiga. Those visiting Guanajuato on weekends, during the Festival Cervantino in October, or during Semana Santa in April should make hotel reservations far in advance and expect prices to double. The tourist office keeps a list of families who rent out rooms during the festival.

**Casa Kloster,** Alonso 32 (tel. 2-00-88). Leaving the *basílica,* pass the garden of Plaza de la Paz, turn left on Callejón de las Estrellas, and follow it to Alonso. A Garden of Eden right in the center of town. Clean, airy rooms overlook an open courtyard filled with flowers and birds. Communal bathrooms sparkle. Friendly guests and management. 50 pesos per person. Reservations recommended.

**Hotel La Condesa,** Plaza de la Pazzo (tel. 2-14-62), nestled in the corner of the Plaza. Neon signs and suits of armor brighten up the dark lobby. Each room's door is emblazoned with grim black-and-white scenes from around Guanajuato. Heavy wooden medieval chandeliers heighten the spooky but fun atmosphere. Never fear, rooms are clean and have bathrooms and 24hr. hot water. Singles 50 pesos; doubles 70 pesos (1 bed), or 100 pesos (2 beds).

**Posada Hidalgo,** Juárez 220 (tel. 2-31-45), 2 blocks past the market. Basic rooms with small bathrooms. Restaurant inside serves breakfast specials. Singles 30 pesos; doubles 70 pesos. Prices jump to 60 and 120 pesos in high season.

**Hotel Posada San Francisco,** Juárez 178 (tel. 2-24-67), at Plaza Gavira. The big pink hotel next to the market (be prepared for street noise). Clean, carpeted bedrooms with shiny, white bathrooms. All rooms come with TV, but if you feel lonely you can watch in the 2nd-floor lounge, with a suit of armor to keep you company (he won't talk, hog the remote, or steal your nachos). Singles 100 pesos; doubles 120 pesos. High season rates approximately 120 and 140 pesos.

## FOOD

Inexpensive restaurants cluster around Guanajuato's plazas and near the *basílica.* Prices rise near the Jardín Unión, as does the gringos-per-square-inch ratio. The **Mercado Hidalgo** has many fruit and taco stands.

**Truco No. 7,** Truco 7 (tel. 2-83-74), the first left beyond the *basílica.* Artsy, funky, and immensely popular with both local and foreign students. International pop music and the smell of cappuccino (7 pesos) fill the air. Granola and fruit 7 pesos. Burrito 4 pesos. Open daily 8:30am-11:30pm.

**La Loca Rana,** Pocitos 32, across the street from Diego Rivera's house. Catch a *fútbol* game on the tube with local students filling up on the tasty *menú del día* (13 pesos), *chilaquiles* (9 pesos), or *flautas* (5 pesos). Breakfast 11 pesos. Open Mon.-Fri. 8am-3pm.

**Cafetería y Restaurante Pinguis** (tel. 2-14-14), on the Jardín Unión. Look for the burnt orange awning across from Posada Santa Fe. Great location and rockbottom prices. Bulletin board advertises local cultural events while Diego Rivera and Charlie Chaplin look on. Clientele is a bizarre combination of students, *señores* sipping coffee over the newspaper, and whoever wanders in off the Jardín. *Menú del día*

CENTRAL MEXICO

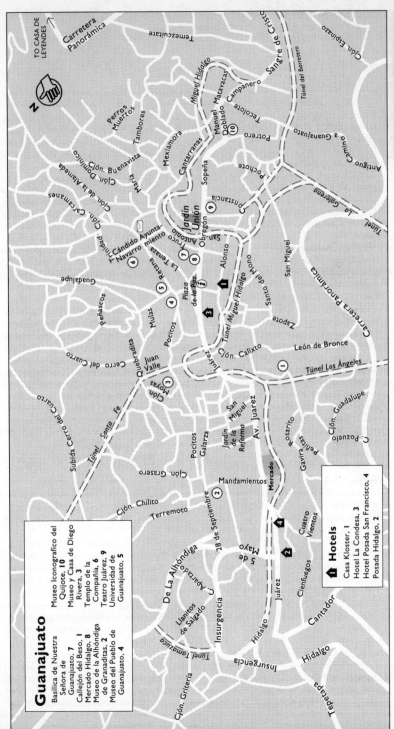

**Guanajuato**

Basílica de Nuestra
Señora de
Guanajuato, **7**
Callejón del Beso, **1**
Mercado Hidalgo, **8**
Museo de la Alhóndiga
de Granaditas, **9**
Museo del Pueblo de
Guanajuato, **4**

Museo Iconográfico del
Quijote, **10**
Museo y Casa de Diego
Rivera, **3**
Templo de la
Compañía, **6**
Teatro Juárez, **9**
Universidad de
Guanajuato. **5**

⬆ **Hotels**

Casa Kloster, **1**
Hotel La Condesa, **3**
Hotel Posada San Francisco, **4**
Posada Hidalgo, **2**

18 pesos. *Enchiladas meneras* 15 pesos (filled with carrots, cheese, and potatoes). Juice 3 pesos. Open daily 8:30am-9:30pm.

**La Abuela Lotty,** Juan Valle 2 (tel. 2-00-95 or 2-19-98), 2 blocks down Juárez from the Basílica, inside the antique shop Terracotta. Admire the colonial-era relics as you enjoy vegetarian *comida corrida* (18 pesos) or sandwiches (8 pesos).

## SIGHTS

The elegant Baroque exterior of the **Basílica de Nuestra Señora de Guanajuato** rises above the Plaza de la Paz. Inside, dozens of candelabra illuminate the Doric interior, including fine ornamental frescoes and paintings of the Madonna by Miguel Cabrera. The wooden image of the city's protectress, Nuestra Señora de Guanajuato, rests on a pure silver base and is believed to be the oldest piece of Christian art in Mexico (open daily 7am-8pm).

Next to the university and one block north of the *basílica* is the more interesting Jesuit **Templo de la Compañía** (tel. 2-18-27). Completed in 1765, the temple was shut down just two years later when the Jesuits were expelled from Spanish America. The ornate stone exterior is one of the more striking in the region and still has four of the original five Churrigueresque facades. Soft light streams in from the delicate cupola, catching on the gold brocade and brightening the gray and rose stone interior. The ex-sacristy in the back of the church holds an art exhibit containing some of the church's original collection. At the end of the exhibit is a spooky *relicario,* a wooden shelf enveloped in gold leaf, holding a collection of human bones. (Church open daily 7:30am-9:30pm; exhibit open daily 11am-2pm and 5-6pm; 5-peso donation requested to support the restoration process.)

The **Jardín Unión,** in the heart of the city and one block east of the *basílica,* is the town's social center. This triangular plaza boasts enough shops, cafes, and guitar-strumming locals to tame the wild beast of tourism. The **Teatro Juárez** (tel. 2-01-83) faces one corner of Jardín Unión. Built in 1903 for dictator Porfirio Díaz, the theater has an unabashedly gaudy facade—try 12 columns, 12 lampposts, eight statues, and two bronze lions. The auditorium betrays its Moorish design: half-circles, arabesques, and endlessly weaving frescoed flowers in green, red, yellow, and brown make the interior seem like a gigantic Persian rug. In addition to housing government offices, the Teatro Juárez still hosts plays and the main events of the Festival Cervantino. (Open Tues.-Sun. 9am-1:45pm and 5-7pm, except on days of performances. Admission 4 pesos.)

In addition to beautiful colonial architecture, Guanajuato is home to a number of unique museums. One of the best is the **Museo Iconográfico del Quijote,** Manuel Doblado 1 (tel. 2-62-21), east of the Jardín Unión. Housed in a gorgeous colonial mansion, its 10 large galleries contain over 600 works of art inspired by Cervantes's anti-hero Don Quijote, including paintings, sculptures, stained-glass windows, candlesticks, and clocks. Artists such as Dalí, Picasso, Daumier, Ocampo, and Coronel have all interpreted Quijote; so have scores of lesser-knowns, as you'll soon see (open Tues.-Sat. 10am-6:30pm, Sun. 10am-2:30pm; free).

Another excellent stop is the **Casa de Leyenclas,** Súbida del Molino and Panorámica, (tel. 2-13-57). To get there, catch a "La Presa" bus (1.50 pesos) in the subterranean and ask the driver to let you off at the Escuela Normal. From the Escuela, walk straight up the unmarked street to your left for two blocks, veering left at the fork. The museum will be directly in front of you. Dioramas complete with moving figures and loads of special effects recreate Guanajuato's many legends. Cringe as you watch the father of the famous lover from *Callejón del Beso* violently stab his daughter, then enter an elevator and "descend" into a mine filled with snakes, skeletons, and miners' unrealized dreams. Displays and guides only in Spanish. Open daily except Wed. 10am-2pm and 4-7pm, 20 pesos.

The **Museo y Casa de Diego Rivera,** Pocitos 47 (tel. 2-11-97), chronicles the life of Guanajuato's most famous native son. Works reveal the influence of Parisian friends Picasso and Modigliani, who encouraged Rivera's move from landscapes to Cubist sketches and elongated nudes, and Rivera's later fascination with Maya art. Visitors

## Peel it, Slice it, Suck it, Dice it

Mangos may be one of Mexico's more delicious offerings, but the fruit's sumptuous flavor is often passed over by foreigners who can't figure out how to eat the damn thing. There are many types of mangos, but the two most popular are the *paraíso,* which is the larger of the two and red and green, and the yellow *manila.* Mexicans often eat mango seasoned with chile powder and fresh lime juice, but for those with less adventurous taste buds, they're also available straight up. You can tell a lot about people from how they eat their mango. Some seem to find an acute enjoyment from sucking the fruit, turning it into almost an erotic art, while more prim folks can't stand the messiness involved. The easiest way to eat a mango is to pluck an end with your fingernail or fork, peel it like a banana, and suck away. But for hygiene's sake, consider a fancier option: cut along both sides of the seed, leaving yourself with two pieces and a seed with some fruit around the edges. Next, peel the skin around the seed and chomp away. Then take your two bowl-shaped pieces and cut down into the fruit, creating a grid in the pulp. Turn the skin inside-out and scrape your pieces onto a plate. Diced mango! Alternatively, cut the fruit into strips, shove them into your mouth, and use your teeth to scrape off the pulp. Mangos are sometimes sold on a stick, and one can eat the fruit like ice cream by turning and sucking—be sure to lean over as you eat. And the one vital rule of mango-eating: never, ever wear a white shirt.

can ogle furniture from this, his childhood home, then move upstairs to works arranged chronologically and representative of his different artistic periods. Don't miss the outstanding watercolor illustrations for the *Popol Vuh* (the sacred book of the Maya), which imitate Maya iconography. Note also Rivera's sketch for a section of the mural commissioned in 1933 by New York's Rockefeller Center—the mural was destroyed after a portrait of Lenin was discovered in it. This sketch, which portrays a woman enslaved by a machine with the head of Adolf Hitler, was not incorporated into the final composition. With money earned from the RCA mural, the revolutionary Rivera created a series of 21 paintings for the New Workers School of New York which so impressed Einstein that he sent a gushing letter of praise to Rivera's home in Mexico City. The museum also holds several photos of Rivera and his wife of 22 years, fellow artist Frida Kahlo. (Open Tues.-Sat. 10am-6:30pm, Sun. 10am-2:30pm. Admission 8 pesos, students and teachers 5 pesos, seniors and children free.)

The **Museo del Pueblo de Guanajuato,** Pocitos 7 (tel. 2-29-90), next to the university, was inaugurated in 1979 and houses a permanent collection of 18th and 19th century works by Mexican artists Herrera, Cabrera, and Bernal de Castillo among others. It also features rotating exhibits of work by contemporary Mexican artists. (Open Tues.-Sun. 10am-6:30pm; admission 8 pesos, students and teachers with ID 5 pesos, seniors and children under 13 free). The **Museo de la Alhóndiga de Granaditas,** on Calarza (tel. 2-11-12) at the west end of Pocitos, is fairly conventional. Constructed as a granary between 1797 and 1809, this building witnessed some of the more crucial and bloody battles of the fight for Mexican independence. Today, the Alhóndiga is an ethnographic, archaeological, and historical museum. A chamber on the first floor charts the course of Mexican nationhood. Other exhibits display the work of *indígena* artisans of the Bajío region—check out the masks, firecrackers, engraved machetes, tapestries, and candy horse skeletons designed for consumption on *El Día de los Muertos* (Day of the Dead). Another gallery shows Romualdo García's photographs of Mexicans on the eve of the 1910 Revolution. While the hall, which contains huge busts of the heroes of 1910, is nothing short of stunning, the museum's finest exhibition traces the social history of Guanajuato from the Conquest through the Revolution.

The museum's most impressive pieces are the three murals gracing the building's stairwells. The works are often mistaken for those of José Clemente Orozco, Diego Rivera, or David Alfaro Siqueiros; the actual painter, José Chávez Morado, was a contemporary of all three. *Abolición de Esclavitud* (1955), the earliest of the three murals, follows Mexico's history from the Conquest, when Indians were oppressed slaves, to the Revolution, by which time native groups had regained some measure of power (open Tues.-Sat. 10am-1:30pm and 4-5:30pm, Sun. 10am-2:30pm; admission 14 pesos, free for students, seniors, children under 12, and on Sun.; camera permit 1 peso).

Looking down on the Jardín from the nearby hill is the **Monumento al Pípila,** which commemorates the miner who torched the Alhóndiga's front door. The titanic Pípila looks most impressive at night, when he is illuminated by spotlights. While the view of Pípila from below is striking, the monument itself affords a magnificent panoramic vista of the city. To reach the statue, follow Sopeña to the east and take the steep Callejón del Calvario to your right (a 5min. climb), or hop a bus marked "Pípila" from Plaza de la Paz. If you're planning to walk up at night, take a friend.

The most famous alley in the city, the **Callejón del Beso** (Alley of the Kiss), is off Juárez, about two blocks down from the *basílica,* just as Juárez curves right towards the market. Local lore has it that a Spanish aristocrat living on one side of the Callejón surprised his daughter one night while she was kissing her lover, a poor miner, each from their respective balcony. Enraged by the lover's low breeding and occupation, the father cursed his daughter and forbade her to see her lover ever again. Ignoring her father, the young woman returned to her lover, at which point the Spaniard flew into a rage and stabbed his daughter to death rather than see her with a man of lesser social stature. Another block farther down Juárez is the **Mercado Hidalgo.** Constructed in 1910, the *mercado's* entrance is a monumental Neoclassical arch. While Guanajuato's famed ceramic mugs have declined in quality, woolen items are still cheap, and the wide variety of *sombreros* will satisfy even the most discerning of heads (most stalls open daily 9am-9pm).

Perhaps the most beautiful of Guanajuato's many natural attractions is the **Ex-Hacienda de San Gabriel de Barrera** (tel. 2-06-19). Seventeen glorious gardens, each laid out in a different style, cover about three acres. Cobbled paths, well-groomed flora, and whistling birds make the gardens a stroller's dream. The ex-hacienda itself, a 16th-century structure, abuts the gardens; its rooms contain furniture, silverware, and paintings from the era in which it was built. To get there, hop on a bus marked "Noria Alta/Marfil" across from the *mercado* (1.50 pesos), and tell the driver you're headed to San Gabriel de la Barrera (open daily 9am-6pm; free).

About 20km from Guanajuato, on top of a mountain 2850m above sea level, is the **Monumento a Cristo Rey,** completed in 1956. The mountain, called the **Cerro del Cubilete,** is considered the geographical center of Mexico. The dark bronze statue of Jesus which lords over it is 16m tall and weighs more than 80 tons. Although the statue is striking, you may spend more time observing the surrounding landscape; long stretches of blue hills are visible from the summit. Take the "Cristo Rey" bus from the bus station (8 per day 6am-4pm, 1hr., 7 pesos).

## ENTERTAINMENT AND SEASONAL EVENTS

Each year, Guanajuato explodes during the **Festival Internacional Cervantino** for two or three weeks in early October. The city invites repertory groups from all over the world to make merry with the *estudiantinas* (strolling student minstrels). Institutionalized in 1973, the festival got its start in 1954 as a production of the university's theater. The festivities take place mostly at local theaters, but Guanajuato's many museums and churches are also transformed into stages for the events. Dramatic productions are always sold out. Tickets are sold by TicketMaster one month in advance. The Office of the Festival Internacional Cervantino (tel. 2-64-87; fax 2-63-78) can provide more information.

At the end of June (the 24th is the big day), Guanajuato celebrates the **Feria de San Juan,** at the Presa de la Olla, with dancing, cultural events, fireworks, and sports. Shorter celebrations occur on **Día de la Cueva** (July 31), when residents walk to a cave's entrance to honor San Ignacio de Loyola, first patron saint of Guanajuato and founder of the Compañía de Jesús. After the worshippers hold mass, they party.

December religious celebrations include the famous *posadas,* which re-create Mary and Joseph's search for budget accommodations in Bethlehem (without use of the epic work, *Let's Go: Israel and Egypt*).

The rest of the year, theater, dance, and music are performed; check the tourist office for information, or consult posters around town. On Thursday and Sunday nights in the Jardín Unión, the state band performs three melodies of deceased *guanajuatense,* beginning at around 7pm. *Callejonadas,* sing-alongs with the student minstrels down Guanajuato's winding alleys, are organized on Friday and Saturday nights at 8:30pm, departing from the Teatro Juárez. These strolls are free for guests of sponsoring hotels, but sponsorship is rarely checked, and they're often open to the public. Student groups present films almost every day of the week. Call the **Teatro Principal,** Hidalgo 18 (tel. 2-15-26), the **Teatro Cervantes,** Plaza Cervantes (tel. 2-11-69), or the **Teatro Juárez** (tel. 2-01-83) for specifics (tickets about 10-15 pesos).

The core of Guanajuato's nightlife rests in the bar/cafe scene. Discos do exist, but they come to life only on weekends. The bars and cafes in the immediate vicinity of the Jardín Unión are friendly and comfortable, even for single women. If things slow down on the Jardín, it's because they're picking up at the **Guanajuato Grill,** Alonso 20 (tel. 2-02-87), one block behind the Jardín Unión. Neon palm trees, posters of sports heroes and scantily clad men and women, a nightly DJ with bass-booming speakers, and a *zócalo*-style gazebo in the center of the bar have the grill bursting at the seams with thirsty students when school's in session. The bouncers can be selective, and they generally discriminate against men. Beer costs 9 pesos (no cover; open Tues. and Thurs.-Sat. 9pm-3am).

A slightly more sophisticated crowd enjoys late night salsa and Latin rhythms at **Damas de las Camelias,** Sopeña 32. Decorated by Juan Ibañez, a student of the Spanish director Luis Buñuel, the bar's walls display cave-style paintings and pictures backed by tin foil (open Fri.-Sat. 6pm-6am, Sun.-Thurs. 6pm-late). Another place to chill, **Chez Santos,** at Juan Valle 19, takes mellowness to the extreme. Located off Juárez just before turning up into Plaza de la Paz, the bar is set in a former horse stable—its high stone walls and large wooden beams across the ceiling make you want to whinny. The dark, romantic atmosphere calls for candlelight. There is none, so it's a bit hard to see, which explains its reputation as a romantic rendezvous. The most offbeat club in town is **El Rincón del Beso,** Alonso 21A (tel. 2-59-12), east of Casa Kloster. Cozy candle-lit rooms divided by winding stairs and thick Spanish walls host nightly sing-alongs. The riotous poetry interpretations attract large crowds. Live music nightly. With tacos at 3 pesos each, you'd have to eat quite a few in order to make the *consumo minimo* of 25 pesos per person. Fortunately, drinks cost quite a bit more (mezcal 15 pesos, beer 15 pesos; open Mon.-Sat. 7:30-late).

Good coffee and even better conversation can be had at a number of artsy cafes in the *centro.* **Las Musas Arte y Cafe,** Baratillo 16, displays local artists' work and fills with university students daily. Breakfast is served 9am-noon (10-16 pesos, cappuccino 5.50 pesos; espresso 3.50 pesos; open Mon.-Sat. 8am-10pm). **Cafe Dada,** Truco 17, is another popular hangout serving excellent coffee, drinks, and a more extensive menu (cappuccino 5 pesos; espresso 4 pesos; pasta 20 pesos; Cajun chicken 22 pesos; open Mon.-Sat. 1:30-11:30pm).

# ■ San Miguel de Allende

Neal Cassady, the prototype of Kerouac's hero in *On the Road,* collapsed in San Miguel while walking near the railroad tracks, and died soon afterward. The plethora of expatriates and long-term tourists who call San Miguel (pop. 65,000, alt. 6400 ft.) home, though, have usually come for less morbid reasons. Yuppies bring their children in for a painless injection of Spanish skills and cultural consciousness, and tired suburbanites come to relax amongst mostly welcoming locals in the city's shady plazas, colonial churches, and quiet gardens bathed in green vegetation. Most comfortable in open air, San Miguel hosts numerous outdoor concerts and other performances along its cobblestoned streets, and its lofty spot in rolling highland hills brings a mild climate year-round (the average annual temperature is 18°C).

Though it is no feat here to find a Reuben sandwich or Häagen-Dazs ice cream, most gringos do not see San Miguel as a place to make like home, and they maintain a respectful attitude toward their surroundings, creating a peaceful *Mexicano-norteamericano* coexistence. Shopkeepers humor customers who want to practice their Spanish, and young blond children discuss Disney flicks fluently with their Mexican peers.

San Miguel boasts impressive colonial architecture and a number of truly beautiful churches. The town was founded by a Franciscan friar in 1542 and soon became an important stop on the route that connected the Zacatecas silver mines with Mexico City. San Miguel's moment in the spotlight came on September 16, 1810, when Hidalgo, the priest of nearby Dolores, led his rebel army into the city. Convinced by patriot Ignacio Allende of the righteousness of the pro-independence movement, the town rallied in opposition to Spanish rule. In 1826, the infant Republic recognized Allende's role in the drive for independence by adding his name to San Miguel's.

Now known more for artisanry and academics than rebelliousness, San Miguel grows more crowded during the winter months, when snowbirds follow the warmth south of the border. Also beware the doldrums of June and July, when cold afternoon drizzle or day-long downpours can turn the cobblestoned streets into gushing streams.

## ORIENTATION

San Miguel is 94km southeast of Guanajuato and 428km northwest of Mexico City. To get from the **bus station** to the center (known as the **Jardín Allende** or **Plaza de Allende**), take a "Centro" bus to the corner of **Colegio** and **Mesones,** near the statue of Allende on horseback (1.80 pesos). Walk two blocks down Mesones, then left one block on **Reloj** to the Plaza Allende. Alternatively, take a taxi (8 pesos). The **train station** lies 1km west of the bus station on the same road and bus route.

Most attractions are within walking distance of the Jardín, and the streets form a near-grid. **San Francisco, Reloj, Correo,** and **Hidalgo** border the Jardín. West of the Jardín, San Francisco becomes **Canal** and Correo becomes **Umarán.** Streets that run east-west south of the Jardín change their names every few blocks.

## PRACTICAL INFORMATION

**Tourist Office: Delegación Regional de Turismo** (tel./fax 2-65-65), on Pl. de Allende, to your left as you face the Parroquia. Knowledgeable and helpful staff speaks English and distributes maps. Also sells posters and the guidebook *The Insider's Guide to San Miguel de Allende* (100 pesos), useful for an extended stay. Open Mon.-Fri. 10am-3pm and 5-7pm, Sat. 10am-3pm, Sun. 10am-2pm.

**Consular Representatives: U.S.,** Macías 72 (tel. 2-23-57, after-hours emergencies only 2-00-68 or 2-06-53; fax 2-15-88), across the street from Bellas Artes. Open Mon. and Wed. 9am-1pm and 4-7pm, Tues. and Thurs. 4-7pm, or by appointment. **Canada,** Mesones 38 #15 (tel. 2-30-25, emergencies 91-800-7-06-29; fax 2-68-56). Open Mon.-Fri. 11am-2pm. For other countries, or to extend visas or visitors' permits, contact the **Delegación Regional de Servicios Migratorios,** Pl. Real del Conde shopping center, 2nd Fl. (tel. 2-25-42 or 2-28-35; open Mon.-Fri. 9am-3pm). Documents may be dropped off 9am-12:30pm and picked up 12:30-2pm. Allow at least 1hr. for processing.

**Currency Exchange:** Due to the huge foreign population in San Miguel, exchange spots abound. **Deal,** Correo 15, San Francisco 4, and Juárez 27 (tel. 2-29-32, 2-17-06, or 2-34-22), has good rates. **Helados Holanda,** Juárez 1 and San Francisco (tel. 2-05-67), serves tasty ice cream and doubles as a *casa de cambio* with excellent rates (money changed daily 10:30am-3:30pm). **Banamex,** on the west side of the Jardín, has a 24hr. **ATM,** but better yet, **Bancomer,** at Juárez 11, has 2.

**American Express:** Hidalgo 1 (tel. 2-18-56 or 2-16-95). Full financial and travel services. Open Mon.-Fri. 9am-2pm and 4-6:30pm, Sat. 10am-2pm.

**San Miguel de Allende**

✚ Hospital
✉ Post Office
ℹ Tourist Office

Bus Station, 1
Casa de Huéspedes, 11
Iglesia de la
Concepción, 3
Iglesia de San
Francisco, 9
Iglesia del Tercer
Orden, 8
Jardín Allende, 5

Mercado, 14
Museo Histórico de San
Miguel de Allende, 4
La Parroquia (Parish
Church), 6
Santa Casa de Loreto,
12
Templo del Oratorio
de San Felipe Neri, 13
**ACCOMMODATIONS**
Hotel Parador San
Sebastián, 10
Hotel Posada de
Allende, 7
San Miguel Hostel, 2

**Telephones: LADATELs** are scattered throughout town. **La Esquinita,** Correos at Recreo (tel. 2-36-21 or 2-39-39), charges 3 pesos for international collect calls. Open daily 10am-2:30pm and 5-10pm. **El Toro Caseta,** Macías 58A (tel. 2-11-00), allows credit card calls. Open Mon.-Sat. 8am-8pm, Sun. 8am-2pm.

**Fax: Telecomm,** Correo 16-B (tel. 2-32-15; fax 2-00-81), adjacent to the post office. Open Mon.-Fri. 9am-5pm; Sat., Sun., and holidays 9am-noon. Also offers telegrams and money wiring.

**Buses:** On Calzada de la Estación (tel. 2-22-06), 1km west of the center. Catch a "Central Estación" bus on Colegio at Mesones near the Plaza Cívica or on Insurgentes near the public library (1.80 pesos). **Ómnibus** (tel. 2-32-18) sends buses to Guanajuato (11:15am, 1¼hr., 29 pesos). **Primera Plus** (tel. 2-73-23) runs 1st-class service to Mexico City (9:40am and 4pm, 3½hr., 92 pesos), Guanajuato (7:45, 9:30am, and 5:30pm, 1½hr., 33 pesos), and León (7:45, 9:30am, and 5:30pm, 2½hr., 53 pesos). **Herradura de Plata** (tel. 2-07-25) runs to Querétaro (every ½hr., 5am-7:40pm, 1¼hr., 17 pesos), Dolores Hidalgo (every ½hr., 5am-7:40pm, 50min., 11 pesos), and Mexico City (every ½hr., 5am-7:40pm, 4hr., 75 pesos). Also has 1st-class service to Mexico City (6am and 1pm, 3½hr., 92 pesos). **Transportes del Norte** (tel. 2-22-37) serves Monterrey (7pm, 10hr., 210 pesos), and Nuevo Laredo (7pm, 12hr., 290 pesos), and also sells tickets to various destinations in Texas, with buses leaving Sat. and Sun. 10:30am. **Servicios Coordinados** (tel. 2-73-23) has service to Celaya (every 15min., 5am-9:30pm, 1½hr., 12 pesos), San Luis Potosí (6 per day, 7:40am-6:55pm, 4hr., 51 pesos), and Mexico City (12:30, 2:40am, and every 40min., 5:20am-8pm, 4hr., 75 pesos).

**Trains: Ferrocarriles Nacionales de México** (tel. 2-00-07), 2km west of town. Accessible by the "Central Estación" bus. To Mexico City (1:10pm, 6hr., 1st class 47 pesos, 2nd class 26.20 pesos) and Nuevo Laredo (2:35pm, 17hr., 1st class

134.60 pesos, 2nd class 75.10 pesos) via San Luis Potosí, Saltillo, and Monterrey. Reservations for 1st-class tickets may be made through a travel agent or in person but are not accepted over the phone.

**Car Rental: Gama Rent-a-Car,** Hidalgo 3 #1 (tel. 2-08-15). Prices start at 380 pesos per day, unlimited mileage, plus 50 pesos insurance. Special weekly rates. Drivers must be 24 with a license, a major credit card, and another form of ID. Open Mon.-Fri. 9am-2pm and 4-7pm, Sat. 9am-2pm.

**English Bookstore: El Colibrí,** Sollano 30, near Cuadrante (tel. 2-07-51). Paperback fiction and art supplies. Open Mon.-Sat. 10am-2pm and 4-7pm. **Lagundi,** Umarán 17 and Macías (tel. 2-08-30), has a large selection of English magazines, some books, and many art supplies. Open Mon.-Sat. 10am-2pm and 4-8pm, Sun. 11am-3pm.

**Public Library:** Insurgentes 25, between Reloj and Hidalgo (tel. 2-02-93). Art-filled courtyard serves as a gathering place for expatriates and students. Wide selection in both English and Spanish. Sells old paperbacks (4-5 pesos), postcards, and posters. Computers might be available (see **"Internet Access"** below). Open Mon.-Fri. 10am-2pm and 4-7pm, Sat. 10am-2pm. The building is also home to **Café Santa Ana,** which serves breakfast and lunch. Open Mon.-Fri. 9am-6pm, Sat. 9am-2pm.

**Market: Bonanza,** Mesones 43A, has a good selection of Mexican and American groceries. Open Mon.-Sat. 8am-2pm and 4-8pm, Sun. 8am-5pm.

**Laundromat: Lavandería El Reloj,** Reloj 34 and Mesones (tel. 2-38-43). Will wash and dry 4kg for 20 pesos. Open Mon.-Fri. 8am-8pm, Sat. 8am-6pm.

**Emergency:** Tel. 2-0-911. Direct contact with Red Cross, fire department, police. A few dispatchers speak English.

**Red Cross:** 1km on the Carretera Celaya (tel. 2-16-16). 24hr. emergency service.

**Pharmacy: Botica Agundis,** Canal 26 and Macías (tel. 2-11-98). Knowledgeable and helpful staff. Open daily 10:30am-11pm. Call police to find out which pharmacy is on call 24hr.

**Hospital: Hospital de la Fe San Miguel,** Libramiento Hwy. 43 to Dolores Hidalgo (tel. 2-22-33, 2-23-20, or 2-23-29; 24hr. emergency line 2-25-45; fax 2-29-00), near the bus station. English spoken.

**Internet Access: Estación Internet,** Recreo 11, 2nd Fl. between Correo and Hospicio (tel. 2-73-12). 8 pesos for 10min. email use; 30 pesos to surf the net for ½hr. Open Mon.-Fri. 9am-2pm and 4-8pm, Sat. 9am-2pm. **Unísono Net,** Macías 72 2nd Fl.(tel./fax 2-49-58 or 2-63-31; http://unisono.ciateq.mx; email info@unisono.ciateq.mx), across the street from Bellas Artes. 7 pesos for 10min. Email use, 40 pesos to surf the net for ½hr. Open Mon.-Fri. 9am-2pm and 4-6pm, occasionally on Sat. Unísono also runs a **San Miguel de Allende web page** (http://unisono.net.mx/sanmignew.html). **Mickler Computer Center** (email mickler@unisono.ciateq.mx) inside Biblioteca Pública, Insurgentes 25. 5 pesos per page to send or receive email, 15 pesos to surf the net for 15min. Less reliable than the two above. Open Mon.-Fri. 10am-2pm and 4-7pm, Sat. 10am-2pm.

**Post Office:** Appropriately at Correos 16 (tel. 2-00-89), 1 block east of the Jardín. Open Mon.-Fri. 8am-7pm, Sat. 9am-1pm. **Postal Code:** 37700.

**Phone Code:** 415.

## ACCOMMODATIONS

As with many hot spots on the gringo trail, budget accommodations can be hard to find in San Miguel, particularly during the winter, Semana Santa, and the entire month of September, when San Miguel throws a huge fiesta in honor of Independence Day (Sept. 15-16) and the city's founding. Reservations (if possible) are strongly recommended during these times and can also be a good idea during the rest of the year. If you are planning an extended stay, check newspapers and bulletin boards in popular *norteamericano* cafes and restaurants for information on rooms for rent.

**The San Miguel International Hostel,** Organos 34 (tel. 2-06-74). Walk 5 blocks down Calle Insurgentes from the Templo del Oratorio, turn right on Volanteros, then turn left onto Los Órganos. The hostel will be to your left. You'll come for a day and stay for a month. A communal effort: guests are expected to perform morning chores. Everybody joins in the courtyard conversations. Well stocked with English books, a sitting room, and a piano. Clean single-sex dorm rooms for 4-10 people. 40 pesos per person, 35 pesos with HI membership or ISIC. Also has 2 private rooms. Continental breakfast included. Free kitchen use. Washing machine (10 pesos per load, including soap). Reservations not accepted. Open daily 7am-11pm; if you'll be arriving later, call ahead.

**Hotel Parador San Sebastián,** Mesones 7 (tel. 2-70-84), about 6 blocks from the Jardín. Vibrant bougainvillea spill over arched stone walls enclosing the sunny courtyard. Pleasant rooms with tiled bathrooms and 24hr. hot water. Common sitting room off the courtyard is filled with books and a television set. Try for a recently renovated room (58.50 pesos per person). Reservations not accepted.

**Casa de Huéspedes,** Mesones 27 and Nuñez (tel. 2-13-78). More than just your generic "guest house." Serene, flower-filled patio and rooftop complete with ivy-covered arches, wooden lounge chairs, and back issues of the *New Yorker*. Wonderfully friendly staff. Rooms offer private bath with 24hr. hot water. Some rooms have kitchens. Singles 60 pesos, doubles 100 pesos. Month-long stays available (singles and doubles 1500 pesos). Reservations not accepted.

**Hotel La Huerta,** Cervada de Barrera (tel. 2-08-81). Walk up Mesones, 3 blocks past Colegio; when you see a stream to your left, turn right onto Atascadero. Follow the stone path about 1 block uphill—the hotel will be on your left. After your spooky journey through the woods, you'll be wearied—and you'll thank your lucky stars for the 2 friendly dogs, the amiable service, and the private bathrooms as you recline on your firm mattress at this *tranquilo,* castle-like establishment. Some rooms have great views of the town and surrounding trees. Singles 60-70 pesos, doubles 70-80 pesos, depending on location and quality.

## FOOD

The sweet aroma of international cuisine wafts through the cobbled streets of San Miguel, and restaurants and cafes grace almost every corner. Unfortunately, their prices can be as *norteamericano* as their clienteles. For cheap eats, try **Calle Insurgentes** and the streets around the **mercado** on Colegio.

**La Piñata,** on the corner of Jesús and Umarán (tel. 2-20-60), 1 block from the Jardín. A favorite among locals and travelers alike, this airy, vegetarian-friendly restaurant serves easily devourable food at prices that won't devour your wallet. A mellow mix of artists, students, backpackers, and Mexican families feasts upon *tostadas* (4 pesos), *tacos de guisado* (2 pesos), and sandwiches (8-12 pesos). Fresh juice 5 pesos. Breakfast 12-16 pesos. Open Wed.-Mon. 9am-8pm.

**La Villa de Pancho,** Insurgentes 144 and Macías (tel. 2-24-96), on the way to the San Miguel International Hostel. Welcome to the kitchen of Cristina, the bubbly owner; she and her friends will prepare tasty food while your hungry eyes follow each step of the process intimately. Enormously popular among backpackers. *Comida corrida* 20 pesos, 12 tacos 20 pesos. Open daily 9am-9pm.

**El Rincón del Quijote,** Macías 111 and Cuadrante (tel. 2-50-96 or 2-01-87), about 3 blocks form the Jardín. Nibble on freshly made whole wheat bread and listen to the wind rustle the bamboo in the mural-emblazoned patio as you live the impossible dream: to enjoy Mexican vegetarian selections which are actually creative. Not exactly off the gringo trail, El Rincón treats backpackers, retired expats, and men of La Mancha with the same respect and care. Don't be put off by the linen napkins and tablecloths—the prices don't reflect their presence. Try some carrot, lettuce, and alfafa juice (10 pesos), organic coffee from Chiapas (6 pesos), cheese and mushroom *tamales* (18 pesos), or, if you must, chicken enchiladas (22 pesos). Open Tues.-Sun. 10:30am-10pm.

**La Grotta,** Cuadrante 5 at Allende (tel. 2-41-19), 1 block behind the Parroquia. If you're a tortilla-weary traveler looking to splurge, you need only step a few feet below street level to enjoy a delectable small pizza (40 pesos) and join in the *extranjero* conversation at this tiny Italian restaurant. Pasta 33-42 pesos, beer 9 pesos. Open daily 1-11pm.

## SIGHTS

The best way to experience San Miguel is on your own two feet. Nearly all sites of interest (and there are many) lie within walking distance of the Jardín, and San Miguel's cobbled streets are easy to navigate.

**La Parroquia** (tel. 2-41-97 or 2-05-44), next to the Jardín, is one of the most distinctive churches in central Mexico. Its neo-Gothic facade and tower were designed by *indígena* mason Zeferino Gutiérrez, who is said to have learned the style from postcards of French cathedrals. The pointed arches and flute-like towers pull the eyes upward. Inside, the ceilings are graced by medieval-style banners, glittering chandeliers, and gold trim. At the front is a tremendous four-piece, gold-leaf altar. Former President Bustamante is buried in the basement (open daily 5:30am-9:30pm; mass Mon.-Fri. 6-8am, noon-1pm, and 7-9pm; Sat. 6-8am and 11am-1:30pm; all day Sun.).

The **Museo Histórico de San Miguel de Allende,** at Cuna de Allende 1 and Umarán (tel. 2-24-99), is just across the street from La Parroquia and is built on Allende's birthplace. Although some exhibits have not been completed, the museum is a respectable collection of ceramics, artifacts, tributes to the man known everywhere, and exhibits on the history of the region (open Tues.-Sun. 10am-4pm; free).

Founded in 1712, the **Templo del Oratorio de San Felipe Neri** (tel. 2-05-21) lies at the corner of Insurgentes and Loreto, two blocks east of the library. Rebuilt many times, the church is an amalgamation of styles—its interior is mainly Neoclassical, but its engraved Baroque facade shows syncretic *indígena* influences. The interior is incredibly ornate with pale pink walls, gold inlay, sparkling chandeliers, and a beautiful pink-and-mauve-toned dome. The altar holds a figure of Christ in red robes standing upon red carpets, and surrounded by gold-leaf and marble pillars; it looks like a giant wedding cake (open daily 6:30am-12:30pm and 6:30-8:30pm). On the west side of the church, the towers and the dome belong to the **Santa Casa de Loreto,** a reproduction of the building of the same name in Italy (enter on the right side of the altar in San Felipe Neri). The floors and the lower wall friezes are covered with glazed tiles from China, Spain, and faraway Puebla (Open daily Mon.-Sun. 8am-2pm).

At the corner of Canal and Macías, one block west of the Jardín, stands the enormous **Iglesia de la Concepción** (tel. 2-01-48) with its crumbling brick exterior and decaying grandeur. Graced by the representation of the Immaculate Conception which crowns its two-story dome, the church was finished in 1891. Inside is an ornate gold altar with a likeness of a virgin in blue metallic robes (open daily 7am-7pm; mass Mon.-Fri. 7:30am and 7pm, Sun. 9:30, 11:30am, and 7pm).

Next door to the Iglesia de la Concepción is **Bellas Artes,** at Macías 75 (tel. 2-02-89). Housed on an 18th century former convent, this cultural center and art school all rolled into one has galleries with rotating exhibits and a concert hall. Great murals enliven the wall surrounding the peaceful courtyard—look for *campesina* L. R. Santos lassoing a dreaded purple *chupacabras* (monster which sucks the blood of goats). Offers classes in ceramics, dance, art, guitar, and more, a few in English (open Mon.-Sat. 9am-8pm, Sun. 10am-2pm).

Another worthwhile stop is the **Instituto de Allende,** Ancha de San Antonio 20 (tel. 2-01-90), about a 15-minute walk up Zacateros from Iglesia de la Concepción. The Instituto also houses several galleries with exhibits by local artists and offers art, Spanish, and social studies classes (open Mon.-Fri. 10am-6pm, Sat. 10am-1pm).

Not to be missed is San Miguel's spectacular **Jardín Bótanico,** home to a dazzling array of cacti and succulents. About 1,900 species grow along the Jardín's 5 mi. of walking paths. To reach the garden, walk past the Mercado Ignacio Ramirez, then turn right at Homoband and continue on a steep uphill incline which flattens after about 10 minutes. Then walk straight for 20 minutes, following the signs; the Jardín will be to your left (open daily sunrise-sunset; admission 7 pesos, free Wed.). Proceeds benefit **Cante,** Mesones 71 (tel. 2-29-909; fax 2-40-15), a nonprofit conservation group.

A breathtaking view of San Miguel and the surrounding mountains may be had by visiting the **mirador** above the city. To get there from the Jardín, walk two blocks up

Correo to Recreo. Take a right and walk about 10 minutes. One block past the Plaza de Toros, take a left and walk uphill until you reach the main road called "Salida a Querétaro." The mirador is a few minutes to your left.

Every Tuesday, vendors from all around San Miguel converge upon the **Tianguis del Martes** (Tuesday market) near the municipal stadium to hawk their wares. Clothing, groceries, old doorknobs, and assorted odds and ends await the adventurous shopper. To get there, take a bus marked "Gigante" from Calle Juárez (1.80 pesos) or take a taxi (8 pesos). Most vendors set up around 7am and leave around 4pm.

Reverberating with the calls of tropical birds, **Parque Juárez,** three blocks south of the Jardín, is the greenest park in San Miguel. Relive those happy childhood moments with the Peggars in the pleasant grounds, or simply stroll through this shady oasis.

Hot springs fans will find their paradise at **La Gruta,** a 15-minute bus ride from San Miguel (3 pesos; catch the Dolores Hidalgo bus and let the driver know that you want to go to La Gruta).

During high season, groups gather in front of the church in the Jardín for 90-minute tours of the city (Tues. and Fri. 9am, 50 pesos—but the money goes to charity, so cough it up). The public library gives two-hour guided **home and garden walking tours** of the city in English (Sun. noon, 80 pesos; get there ½hr. early). San Miguel boasts some beautiful orchid-filled courtyards, but some say the tours are something of a real estate pitch. **Centro de Crecimiento,** Zamaro Ríos 6 (tel. 203-18), organizes trips to San Miguel's surroundings (Sat. 10:30am, 70 pesos).

## ENTERTAINMENT AND SEASONAL EVENTS

Did you think all these students came here just to learn? There are as many clubs as churches in San Miguel, and the arts pump through the city's veins daily. The magazine *Atención,* available every Monday, is the best source of information on upcoming concerts, theatrical productions, and lectures by both locals and *extranjeros* (5 pesos). **Bellas Artes** and the **Instituto Allende** also have bulletin boards crammed with posters advertising art exhibits, openings, and other events.

Nightlife for gringos centers around drinking and dancing. Expect cover charges at clubs to skyrocket during fiesta and especially Semana Santa. The listings below are for clubs; if you're not up for such a boisterous evening, there are cantinas all around town that you can stumble into—and out of, though women will feel more comfortable elsewhere (*cerveza* about 4 pesos).

**Mama Mía,** Umarán 8 (tel. 2-20-63), just off the Jardín, is a favorite destination of foreigners and friendly (especially *gringuita*-friendly) locals. Restaurant, bar, and *discoteca* in one, this enormous building is divided into several smaller establishments. **Mama Mía Bar,** to your right as you enter, attracts a twentysomething crowd and features jazz, soul, and rock music Mon.-Wed., salsa Thurs.-Sun. (cover 20 pesos Thurs.-Sun.). **Leonardo's,** across the entryway, scores points for its heavy bar stools and big-screen TV (open daily 7pm-3am). Directly in front of the entrance is a rather pricey **restaurant** appealing to mainly tourists and hosting nightly *música folklorica,* traditional music performances (open daily 7pm-late). The **terrace** upstairs pulses to the beat of live and loud rock performances Fri.-Sat. and has a great view of the city (open Fri.-Sat. 8pm-late).

**La Lola's,** Ancha de San Antonio 31 (tel. 2-40-50), across the street from the Instituto Allende, is a slightly less touristed bar attracting a mixed straight and gay clientele. More *tranquilo* than Mama Miá's, La Lola's also serves tasty (but pricey) food until 11pm. No cover. Open Tues.-Sat. 1pm-3am, Sun. 7pm-3am.

**Coco,** Macías 85 and Umarán (tel. 2-26-43), is another rather tranquil place. Live music 9pm-2am every night, including *boleros, trova,* and *música folklórica.* No dance floor, but wooden tables and candlelight make for an intimate atmosphere. Also serves pizza and burgers until 1am. Beers 13-15 pesos (2 for 16 pesos Wed.). Open Mon.-Fri. 5pm-late, Sat.-Sun. noon-late.

**Pancho and Lefty's,** Mesones 99 (tel. 2-19-58), has all the charm of your favorite American college bar. Loud rock and cover bands thrill the young and tightly packed crowd every night. On Saturdays, you'll pay 20 pesos for the right to pack yourself in. 2-for-1 beers Wed. Open Wed.-Sun. 8pm-3am.

**El Ring,** Hidalgo 25 (tel. 2-19-98 or 2-67-89), features standard *discoteca* fare and a late, lively, and very young Mexican crowd. Latin and U.S. dance hits will keep even the weariest club-hopper bouncing until the wee hours. Cover 20-40 pesos. Open Wed.-Sat. 8pm-late.

San Miguel is reputed to have more fiestas than any other town in Mexico. A celebration of some sort takes place nearly every weekend. In addition to national and religious holidays, San Miguel celebrates the **birthday of Ignacio Allende** on January 21 with parades and fireworks. The **Fiesta de la Candelaria,** which marks the start of spring, takes place each February 2. Nearly all of September is a party as San Miguel celebrates its **independence and founding.** On the third Saturday in September, San Miguel hosts a **Pamplonada** and bulls run around the Jardín. Watch yourself. The impressive **International Chamber Music Festival** is held in late July or early August at **Bellas Artes,** Macías 75 (tel./fax 2-02-89). Tickets start at 60 pesos and are sold beginning in July.

# ■ Near San Miguel

## DOLORES HIDALGO

*"Mexicanos, viva México!"*

-Miguel Hidalgo, "Grito de Dolores"

Nearly 200 years later, Hidalgo's rousing words still echo through Mexico's dusty "Cradle of Independence." Best seen as a daytrip from San Miguel, the small town of Dolores Hidalgo has little more to offer than hot, dirty streets, a thriving ceramics industry, and an amazing story. On Sunday, September 16, 1810, Don Miguel Hidalgo y Costilla, the town's priest, learned that the pro-independence conspiracy to which he belonged had been discovered by the government. He decided to take decisive action, and at 5am woke the entire town by tolling the parish church bell. The town's residents tumbled out of bed and gathered at the church; Hidalgo delivered a ringing speech proclaiming Mexico's independence from Spain—the *Grito de Dolores.* Then, calling his flock to arms, Hidalgo rallied an army to march on to Mexico City. Thus, the priest signed his own death warrant and paved the way for an independent Mexico years later. Today, Hidalgo is one of Mexico's most admired heroes, second only to Benito Juárez in the number of statues, streets, and plazas commemorating his heroism. However, coming to the actual locale of the *Grito* is worthwhile only for the most diehard history buffs.

**Orientation and Practical Information** Dolores Hidalgo (pop. 40,000, alt. 2000m) sits 50km northeast of Guanajuato and north of San Miguel de Allende. To get downtown from the bus station, walk straight out the door and take a left on **Hidalgo.** Three blocks down the street are the **Jardín,** the tourist office, **Plaza Principal,** and the **Parroquia. Río Batan** runs east-west through the city; streets are arranged in a grid parallel and perpendicular to the river. A map is useful since streets have different names on opposite sides of the plaza (there is a well-labeled map in the plaza). The town's points of interest all lie within a few blocks of the center.

Get that map from the **tourist office** (tel./fax 2-11-64) on the left side of the Plaza Principal, as you face the Parroquia (open Mon.-Fri. 10am-3pm and 4-7pm, Sat.-Sun. 10am-2pm and 3-6pm). **Bancomer,** on the left side of the plaza as you face the Parroquia, has a 24-hour **ATM. Intercambio del Bajío** is at Jalisco and Allende (tel. 2-13-35; open Mon.-Fri. 8am-7pm, Sat.-Sun. 9am-4pm). **LADATEL** phones may be found throughout town, including just outside of the bus station and in the Presidencia Municipal. There is a *caseta* in the **Restaurante Plaza** (tel. 2-01-52), on the south side of the plaza (open daily 9am-9pm). **Flecha Amarilla buses** (tel. 2-06-39) leave from the station on Hidalgo at Chiapas and go to Guanajuato (every 20min., 5:20am-

9:15pm, 1½hr., 16 pesos) and San Miguel de Allende (every 20min., 5am-8pm, 9, 10, and 11:30pm, 40min., 11 pesos).

Find **public toilets** in the narrow arcade around the corner from the tourist office (1 peso). **Botica San Vicente,** Zacatecas 2 (tel. 2-24-17), is on the corner of the plaza (open daily 9am-10pm; call the police to find out which pharmacy is on call 24hr.). English is spoken at the **Hospital Ignacio Allende,** Hidalgo 12 (tel. 2-00-13), one block from the plaza (open 24hr.). The **police** are in the Cárcel Municipal on San Luis Potosí (tel. 2-00-21), one block north of the Plaza Principal. The **post office** is on Puebla 22 at Jalisco (tel. 2-08-07), one block from the Plaza Principal (open Mon.-Fri. 9am-4pm, Sat. 9am-1pm). Inside the same building is a **Telecomm** office with **fax,** telegram, and money-wiring service. **Postal Code:** 37800. **Phone Code:** 418.

**Accommodations** Quality budget rooms are rather scarce in Dolores Hidalgo. Expect prices to rise around 50% and rooms to fill up September 8-17, when Dolores is overrun by Independence Day celebrants; reservations are advised. **Hotel Posada Cocomacán,** Plaza Principal 4 (tel. 2-00-18), on the Jardín, has rooms with wooden floors and tiled bathrooms. If it was good enough for Benito Juárez (on his way back south in 1867), it's good enough for you. Hot water is available from 7am to 1pm during the low season, 24-hours high season (singles 70 pesos, doubles 95 pesos). **Posada Hidalgo,** Hidalgo 15 (tel./fax 2-04-77 or 2-26-83), a block and a half south of the Jardín, has firm beds, warm, dark, and mostly clean rooms, and 24-hour hot water (singles 92 pesos, doubles 107 pesos). The restaurant in the lobby (open daily 8am-3pm) offers filling breakfasts (12 pesos) and tasty *tortas* (5-7 pesos). **Posada Dolores** is on Yucatán 8 (tel. 2-06-42), a block west of the Plaza Principal. Aging rooms and sparkling communal bathrooms fill a labyrinthine building (singles 30 pesos, with bath 50 pesos; doubles 50 pesos, with bath 60 pesos).

**Food** Around the Jardín, most restaurants are reasonably priced, and those that aren't betray themselves by their touristy clienteles. **Eduardo's Pizza,** Veracruz 5 (tel. 2-21-24), inside Plaza Veracruz, one block east and one block south of the Jardín, has good pizza and haphazard decor including "Green Musk Oil for Men" and iridescent purple swan napkin holders. Watch the hours go by on the digital watch collection suspended from the ceiling as you chomp on a small pizza (22-34 pesos) washed down with a cold one (5 pesos; open daily noon-11pm). Inexpensive and basic restaurants may be found along the west end of the Plaza, or near the **Mercado Hidalgo,** a block west of Plaza Principal (most open daily 7am-5pm).

**Sights and Entertainment** Most of Dolores's sights lie within four blocks of the bus station, and they revolve around the *Grito de Dolores.* The beautiful **Parroquia de Nuestra Señora de los Dolores,** where the *Grito* was sounded, still stands in the Plaza Principal, although the original bell now graces Mexico City's Palacio de Gobierno. Constructed between 1712 and 1778, the church, with an intricate facade and towers of pink stone, is the most awe-inspiring structure in town. On the west side of the plaza is the **Casa de Visitas,** built in 1786 and now host to each president of the Republic during his last year in office, when he reissues the *Grito.* In the center of the plaza is an enormous bronze statue of the Man with the Plan, Hidalgo.

The **Museo de la Independencia,** Zacatecas 6, lies less than one block northwest of the Parroquia. Gory technicolor paintings detailing life under Spanish rule and the fight for Independence add spice to Mexico's already exciting history. Relive Hidalgo's sounding of the *Grito* in an eerie life-sized diorama complete with wooden statues of an inspired Hidalgo and anxious *mexicanos.* The museum also includes an exhibit of Mexican *artesanía* and a shrine to Dolores Hidalgo's favorite musical son, Mariachi legend José Alfredo Jiménez. Open daily except Thursday from 10am to 5pm; admission 5 pesos (free for students and teachers with ID, seniors, and children under 13; free for everyone on Sun.). Hidalgo's home from 1804 until 1810, the **Museo Casa Hidalgo,** at Morelos and (what else) Hidalgo, one block from the Plaza Principal, is less than thrilling, but it does contain a somewhat interesting Metepec

**Tree of Life.** Other documents and works of art relating to the independence movement comprise the remainder of the collection (open Tues.-Sat. 10am-6pm, Sun. and holidays 10am-5pm; admission 14 pesos, free Sun. and holidays, free for teachers and students with ID, children under 13, and seniors).

## POZOS

**Pozos,** 25km northeast of San Miguel de Allende, is a lonely ghost town just waking up from a long slumber. Pozos was once a thriving mining town; the Jesuits worked the mines until their expulsion in 1767, at which point an American company took over. An eerie silence now cloaks the town's abandoned adobe homes and once-booming mines. Daytrippers from San Miguel come to Pozos to visit the mines, listen to the wind rattle in and out of the house-holes, stake out new hiking trails, and delight in the color contrast of the landscape beyond: prominent cacti and expansive sand set against an empty blue sky. The name "Pozos" refers to the deep craters on the town's outskirts.

**Getting There:** Though Pozos is a mere 25km from San Miguel de Allende, it takes a good two to three hours to reach the town, as you have to first travel to Dolores Hidalgo, then to San Luis de La Paz, and then to Pozos. **Flecha Amarilla** (tel. 2-00-84) runs buses from San Miguel to Dolores Hidalgo (every 20min., 6am-10pm, 45min., 11 pesos), and from Dolores Hidalgo (tel. (418) 2-06-39) to San Luis de La Paz (every 20min., 6am-10pm, 1hr., 15 pesos). From San Luis de La Paz, buses run to Pozos (every 20min., 20min., 6 pesos).

# QUERÉTARO

## ■ Querétaro

Situated between Mexico City and Guadalajara on the busiest stretch of highway in the Republic, Querétaro (pop. 500,000) lies at the crossroads of Mexico's geography and history. As the prosperous agricultural and industrial center of the Bajío, the outskirts of Querétaro assault the senses with whining grain elevators, monstrous warehouses, and truckloads of squealing pigs. Inside the commercial ring, however, the city center is a colonial masterpiece, with lantern-lit squares, an 18th-century aqueduct consisting of 74 graceful arches. In Querétaro's heart, university students and business people bustle past one another on centuries-old brick streets and *andares* (pedestrian walkways).

It was here that Emperor Maximilian, abandoned by Louis Napoleon and captured by Juárez's troops, ascended Cerro de las Campanas (Hill of the Bells) and uttered his famous last words: "Mexicans, I am going to die for a just cause: the liberty and the independence of Mexico." In the subsequent 50 years, Mexico was wracked by violence. Perhaps hoping to inaugurate the peaceful era Maximilian had prematurely proclaimed, the victorious Carranza drafted the new constitution in Querétaro. While Mexico gave up much here—the Treaty of Guadalupe Hidalgo, which compelled the Republic to cede its northern territories to the U.S., was signed in Querétaro—the many museums and monuments nevertheless indicate the city's pride in its history. Frequently overlooked by foreign travelers, Querétaro is a popular destination among Mexican tourists and is well worth a visit.

## ORIENTATION

Querétaro's streets form a grid, and nearly all important sites are within walking distance of the **Jardín Zenea.** The Jardín is bounded by **16 de Septiembre** (north), **Madero** (south), **Corregidora** (east), and **Juárez** (west). The **bus station,** whose modernity puts most international airports to shame, is on the very south side of town. To catch a bus to the *centro,* follow the signs marked "Transporte Urbano" to

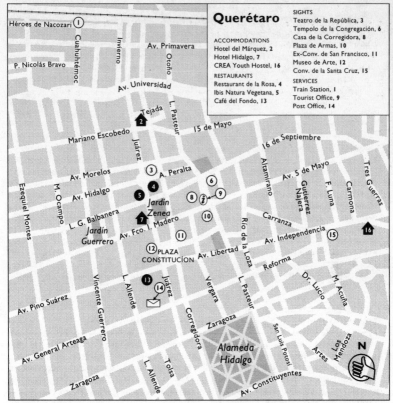

**Querétaro**

ACCOMMODATIONS
Hotel del Márquez, 2
Hotel Hidalgo, 7
CREA Youth Hostel, 16

RESTAURANTS
Restaurant de la Rosa, 4
Ibis Natura Vegetana, 5
Café del Fondo, 13

SIGHTS
Teatro de la República, 3
Tempolo de la Congregación, 6
Casa de la Corregidora, 8
Plaza de Armas, 10
Ex-Conv. de San Francisco, 11
Museo de Arte, 12
Conv. de la Santa Cruz, 15

SERVICES
Train Station, 1
Tourist Office, 9
Post Office, 14

Salida A, on the left-hand side of building "C" ("mercado") as you face the building. Buses for downtown leave every 5-10 minutes (2 pesos). A taxi will whisk you to your destination for 12 pesos—buy your ticket inside the station and give it to the driver.

## PRACTICAL INFORMATION

**Tourist Office: State Tourist Office,** Pasteur Nte. 4 (tel. 12-14-12, 12-09-07, or 12-12-87; email turismo@ciateq.mx). From the Jardín, take 5 de Mayo; the office is to your left at the end of the Plaza de Armas. Friendly English-speaking staff hands out maps and lists of local cultural events. City tours in English or Spanish depart at 10:30am and 6pm (10 pesos). Open Mon.-Fri. 9am-9pm, Sat.-Sun. 9am-8pm.

**Currency Exchange: Santander Mexicano,** Corregidora Nte. 55 (tel. 12-67-70), 1 block from the Jardín Zenea. Open Mon.-Fri. 9am-5pm, Sat. 9am-1pm. **ATM** next to the tourist office door on Pasteur Nte.; others by the Jardín and elsewhere.

**Telephones:** Blue international **LADATELs** abound, but most are coin operated. Also make long distance calls from the "Larga Distancia" caseta at 5 de Mayo 33 (tel. 12-11-67), ½ block from the Jardín. Open Mon.-Fri. 9am-3pm and 4:30-5pm.

**Fax: Telecomm,** Allende Nte. 4 (tel. 12-07-02), one block west of the Jardín. Telegrams and **Western Union,** too. Open Mon.-Fri. 8am-6pm, Sat.-Sun. 9am-4pm.

**Buses:** Station accessible via the "Ruta 25" on Allende and Zaragoza, "Ruta 8" on Ocampo and Constituyentes, and "Ruta 72" on Universidad—all are labeled "Central" (6am-10pm, 2 pesos). **1st-class service** in Acesos 1 and 2. **ETN** (tel. 29-00-17) sends plush buses to Guadalajara (6 per day, 4¾hr., 145 pesos), San Luis Potosí (1pm, 2¾hr., 82 pesos), and San Miguel de Allende (noon, 3:30, and 7:45pm, 1hr., 30 pesos). **Primera Plus** (tel. 11-40-01) serves Aguascalientes (6 per day, 4½hr., 100 pesos), Mexico City (every 20min., 4:30am-9pm, 10:30pm, and 2:45am, 2¾hr., 74 pesos), and Toluca (10 per day, 12:30am-6pm, 2½hr., 57 pesos). **Estrella Blanca** (tel. 29-00-22) offers service to points throughout the country, including Los Mochis (10:30am and 4:10pm, 20hr., 452 pesos), Saltillo (9:45am, 6, 7, and 10pm, 8hr., 191 pesos), and Torreón (8 per day, 4:15am-10:30pm, 11hr., 243 pesos). **Ómnibus** (tel. 29-00-29) serves León (2:40, 3:20am, and 1:15pm, 2hr., 54 pesos), Guanajuato (10am and 7:45pm, 3hr., 48 pesos), and Acapulco (Mon. and Fri., midnight, 8hr., 204 pesos). **Servicios Coordinados** (tel. 11-40-01) runs to León (11am and 6:30pm, 2¾hr., 54 pesos) and Ezequiel Montes (8:10am, 3:10, and 8:15pm, 45min., 14 pesos). **2nd-class service** in Acesos 3 and 4. **Estrella Blanca** (tel. 29-00-22) has service to Pachuca (every hr., 6:15am-8:15pm, 3hr., 55 pesos), Poza Rica (9:15pm, 6hr., 101 pesos), and Ixmiquilpan (every hr., 6am-8:15pm, 2hr., 36 pesos). **Oriente** (tel. 29-02-02) runs to Salamanca (10:10am and 6:45pm, 1½hr., 22 pesos), Matamoros (10:30pm, 12hr., 213 pesos). **Flecha Amarilla** (tel. 11-40-01) whisks passengers to Manzanillo (5 per day, 1:40am-8pm, 12hr., 190 pesos), San Luis Potosí (every hr., 6:15am-8:15pm, 3½hr., 53 pesos), and Aguascalientes (9:35, 11am, 1, and 3:30pm, 4½hr., 75 pesos). **Flecha Roja** (tel. 29-00-01) sends buses to San Mateo (every 20min., 2am-4:30pm, 4hr., 18 pesos). **Flecha Verde** (tel. 29-00-02) serves Coroneo (every hr., 6am-7pm, 1¾hr., 13 pesos) and Misión de Palmas (every ½hr., 8am-4pm, 2hr., 18 pesos). **Herradura de Plata** (tel. 29-02-45) runs to San Miguel de Allende (every 40min., 6am-10pm, 1¼hr., 17 pesos) and Toluca (every 40min., 2:30am-7pm, and 11:45pm, 2¼hr., 47 pesos). **Transportes Amealcences** (tel. 29-00-15) runs to Amealco (every hr., 6:30am-8:30pm, 1hr., 14 pesos) and San Juan del Río (every 15min., 6am-10:30pm, 1hr., 11 pesos). Finally, **Flecha Azul** (tel. 29-03-22) serves Tequisquiapan (every ½hr., 6:30am-8:15pm, 1hr., 12 pesos), Higuerillas (12:30 and 3:30pm, 2¾hr., 25 pesos), and San Joaquín (5 per day, 6:20am-4:20pm, 3hr., 30 pesos).

**Trains:** On Héroes de Nacozari, north of Av. Universidad (tel. 12-17-03). From the Jardín, walk 5 long blocks up Juárez to Av. Universidad, cross the bridge onto Invierno, and continue 2 blocks, turning left onto Héroes de Nacozari; the station is the blue building up 1 block to your right (about 20-25min.). "Ruta 8" and "Ruta 13" buses run up Ocampo and make the trip for 2 pesos. Service to Guadalajara, Cd. Juárez, Mexico City, Monterrey, and Nuevo Laredo.

**Laundromat: Lavandería Veronica,** Av. Hidalgo 153 and Ignacio Pérez (tel. 16-61-68). From Teatro de la República, turn left onto Hidalgo and walk for about 20min. Leave 3kg of laundry and 30 pesos and return in a few hours—the friendly staff will have your clothes washed, dried, and waiting. Open Mon.-Fri. 9am-2:30pm and 4:30-8pm, Sat. 9am-3pm.

**Red Cross:** At Balaustradas and Circuito Estadio (tel. 29-06-65 or 29-07-29), near the Estadio Corregidora.

**Pharmacy: Súper Farmacia Querétaro,** Av. Constituyentes Pte. 17 (tel. 12-44-23), 5 blocks south of the Jardín. Open 24hr. Omaha-esque **Woolworth Mexicana,** Madero 18 (tel. 12-24-13), a half block from the Jardín. Open Mon.-Fri. 10am-2pm and 4:30-8:30pm, Sat. 10:30am-2:30pm and 5-9pm, Sun. 10am-6pm.

**Hospitals:** English spoken at **Sanatorio San José,** Cezequiel Montes (tel. 12-61-36 or 12-30-13); **Grupo Médico Zaragoza,** Zaragoza Pte. 39-B, between N. Campa and E. Montes (tel. 16-76-38 or 16-57-86).

**Emergency:** Tel. 060. **LOCATEL** will find lost people and (supposedly) other missing items (tel. 14-33-11 or 14-11-49).

**Police:** Office at Pie de la Cuesta in Colonia Desarrollo San Pablo (tel. 20-83-83, 20-83-03, or 20-86-03). **Ángeles Verdes** (tel. 13-84-24) will rescue stranded motorists. Toll-free **medical, legal, and information service for tourists:** Tel. 91-800-90-392.

**Post Office:** Arteaga Pte. 5, between Juárez and Allende (tel. 12-01-15), 2 blocks south of the Jardín. Open Mon.-Fri. 8am-7pm, Sat. 9am-1pm. **Postal Code:** 76000.

**Phone Code:** 42.

## ACCOMMODATIONS

Despite a small-scale tourist industry, good and inexpensive accommodations are not difficult to find in Querétaro's *centro*.

**Hotel Hidalgo,** Madero Pte. 11 (tel. 12-00-81), a half block from the Jardín. Comfortable rooms with small bathrooms and cable TV. Hot water 24hr. The attached restaurant serves inexpensive and tasty food (Open Mon.-Sat. 8am-10pm, Sun. 8am-8pm). Singles 65 pesos; doubles with 1 bed 75 pesos, 2 beds 85 pesos.

**Hotel del Márquez,** Juárez Nte. 104 (tel. 12-04-14 or 12-05-54), 4 long blocks north of the Jardín. An enormous stained-glass depiction of Querétaro's aqueduct welcomes guests to this hotel. Purified water available in the lobby and from dispensers on each floor. Somewhat stuffy rooms have cable TV, telephones, tiled bathrooms, and 24hr. hot water. Singles 65 pesos, doubles 85 pesos.

**Posada Colonial,** Juárez Sur 19 (tel. 12-02-39), 2 blocks from the Jardín. Small, basic rooms with or without private bath. Communal bathrooms may be dark and damp, but, hey, your budget'll be happy. Singles 25 pesos, doubles 30 pesos. Singles or doubles with private bath and TV 50 pesos.

**Villa Juvenil Youth Hostel,** Av. Ejército Republicano (tel. 23-43-50). From the Jardín, walk 1 block south on Corregidora, then walk left on Independencia for 8 blocks. Veer right onto Ejército Republicano just past the Convento de Santa Cruz. The hostel is inside the sports and recreation complex surrounded by a stone wall and trees on the right side of the street. While a bit remote, it's a bargain; just beware flocks of athletes taking up all the rooms (call ahead). Single-sex dorms with 8 bunks per room. 20 pesos per person, 25% discount with HI. 20-peso bedding deposit.

## FOOD

Inexpensive restaurants face the Jardín Zenea, pricier *loncherías* and outdoor cafes rim the nearby Plaza Corregidora, and taco, *torta,* and other fast-food stands line 5 de Mayo. Many restaurants stop serving their *menú del día* at 5 or 6pm.

**Ibis Natura Vegetariana,** Juárez Nte. 47 (tel. 14-22-12), a half block north of the Jardín. Despite what you've heard, veggies in Mexico can be delicious *and* nutritious. Try a lip-smacking veggie cheeseburger (8.50 pesos), strawberry pancakes (9 pesos), or the hearty *menú del día* (18.50 pesos) while catching your reflection in the stainless-steel ceiling and chatting with gregarious patrons. Open daily 8am-9:30pm.

**La Mariposa,** Ángela Peralta 7 and Juárez (tel. 12-11-66 or 12-48-49). This cafeteria and *pastelería* is a local favorite. Enjoy enchiladas *verdes* (with green salsa, 18 pesos), fresh fruit juice (6 pesos), or a banana split (12 pesos) while you listen to patrons argue about *fútbol* or the day's business. Open daily 8am-9:30pm.

**Café del Fondo,** Av. Pino Suárez 9 (tel. 12-09-76), at Juárez, 1 block south of the Jardín. Good food and great prices make this local hangout an enticing stop for the budget traveler craving quesadillas (7.50 pesos) or sandwiches (6 pesos). Caffeine addicts, rejoice: this restaurant has a huge selection of exotic coffee drinks (from 6 to a whopping 19 pesos). Hearty breakfast specials 10.50-15 pesos. Open daily 7:30am-10pm.

**Restaurante de la Rosa,** Juárez Nte. 24 at Peralta (tel. 24-37-22), across from the Teatro Republicano. Tasty Mexican cuisine served by the swellest, sweetest women in town. Red wooden chairs, plaid tablecloths, and brick floors give the place a rustic feel. Food gets rave reviews from locals and tourists alike. Enchiladas *queretanas* 13 pesos. *Menú del día* 16-18 pesos. Open Mon.-Fri. 9am-9pm, Sun. 9am-1pm (breakfast only).

## SIGHTS

The most intriguing sight in Querétaro is the **Convento de la Santa Cruz** (tel. 12-02-35), south of the Jardín. Follow Corregidora to Independencia and turn left. After walking eight blocks, you'll reach the convent, which occupies a plaza dedicated to the founders of the city. Nearly everything inside Santa Cruz (founded in 1683) is original—the clay pipes and water-catching system date from the city's aqueduct days. Maximilian devotees can make a pilgrimage to the cell in which the emperor spent his last minutes; it has been left exactly as it was on the day of his execution. In one courtyard, trees grow thorns in the form of crucifixes. According to legend, the thorns began growing into crosses after a friar stuck his cane in the ground near the trees. It is said that these are the only trees of their kind in the world; attempts to plant seedlings elsewhere have supposedly failed. The tree is of the *mimosas* family, and is known simply as the *Árbol de la Cruz* (Tree of the Cross; open with 20min. guided tours in Spanish, English, French, or Italian Tues.-Fri. 9am-2pm and 4-6pm, Sat. 9am-5:30pm, Sun. and holidays 9am-4:30pm).

Along Calzada de los Arcos west of the *centro* stretches Querétaro's fascinating **Acueducto.** This distinctive structure, with its 74 arches of pink sandstone, was constructed between 1735 as a gift to a perpetually parched community from the Marqués de Villas del Águila. A *mirador* overlooking all 1280m of the aqueduct is located on Av. Ejército Republicano about three blocks past the Convento de la Santa Cruz. Up 5 de Mayo to the east of the Jardín is the **Plaza de la Independencia (Plaza de Armas),** a monument to the aforementioned Marqués. Stone dogs hang around his statue, drooling respectfully into a fountain. The plaza is bordered by old square-rimmed trees and beautiful colonial buildings, including the **Casa de la Corregidora,** home of Doña Josefa Ortíz de Domínguez, heroine of the Independence movement. The *casa* is now the seat of the state's government, so only the courtyard may be viewed (open Mon.-Fri. 8am-9pm, Sat. 9am-2pm); however, it's less than thrilling. One block north of the Casa de la Corregidora, at Pasteur and 16 de Septiembre, is the colorful **Templo de la Congregación** (tel. 12-07-32), with its two white towers and central dome. The church's frescoes and stained glass are splendid, and the pipe organ is one of the more elaborate in Mexico. The image of *La Guadalupana* is by Miguel Cabrera (open daily 7am-9pm; mass Mon.-Fri. at 8, 10am, and 8pm, and much more often Sat. and Sun.).

The entrance to the **Museo de La Ciudad,** Vicente Guerrero 27 and Hidalgo (tel. 24-36-50 or 14-34-54), is marked by a technicolor bird sculpture. To reach the museum, take a left on Hidalgo as you face the Teatro de la República and walk three blocks; turn left on Guerrero and look for the bird. The museum contains a well-organized display of religious art, a collection of railroad-related paraphernalia, an exhibit on traditional Querétaro fiestas, and an ever-changing exhibit of contemporary art (5 pesos; open Tues.-Sun. 11am-7pm). Another quality museum is the **Museo de Arte de Querétaro,** Allende 14 between Madero and Pino Suárez (tel. 12-35-23), about two blocks from the Jardín. The original edifice, an 18th-century Augustinian monastery, was rebuilt in 1889. An exhibition on local architecture supplements the bounty of Baroque paintings. European canvasses, 19th- and 20th-century Mexican art, and the work of the 20th-century *queretareano* Abelardo Ávila round out the formidable collection (open Tues.-Sun. 11am-7pm; admission 10 pesos, free for students with ID, seniors, children under 12, and for all on Tues.).

The **Museo Regional** is housed in the **Ex-Convento de San Francisco** (tel. 12-20-31; fax 12-20-36), at Corregidora and Madero, east of the Jardín Zenea. Exhibitions include various artifacts culled from the dustbin of history, such as the table upon which the 1848 Treaty of Guadalupe Hidalgo was signed with the U.S. While exhibitions of contemporary art and craftwork greet you at the entrance, the entire upstairs area is devoted to colonial-era religious paintings and artifacts relating to Querétaro's military and political history. (Tours Tues.-Fri. noon, Sat.-Sun. 11am and 2pm. Open Tues.-Sun. 10:30am-5pm. Admission 16 pesos, free for students and teachers with ID, seniors, children under 12, and for all on Sun.)

The **Cerro de las Campanas** (Hill of the Bells), named for the peculiar sound its rocks make when they collide, is where Emperor Maximilian first established his military headquarters and later surrendered his sword to General Escobedo in 1867. He was then taken to the cell in the Convento de la Santa Cruz. To reach the monument, walk a few blocks north of the Jardín Zenea on Corregidora and turn left onto General Escobedo. Proceed on Escobedo until the street ends at Tecnológico, then take a right and you will come to the monument (about a ½hr. walk). To the left of the Cerro de las Campanas and up a low hill, Maximilian's family built a small chapel over the ground where the emperor and two of his generals were shot. Three small white memorials inside designate the places where each took his last breath. Up the stairs

### La Virgen y La Malinche

The virgin/whore dichotomy was established early on in revolutionary Mexican lore. The **Virgin of Guadalupe,** Mexico's very own national virgin, purportedly appeared before *indígena* Juan Diego in 1531. Since then, this icon of chastity and virtue has become the object of a cult so passionate that it almost dwarfs Christ's. Every December 12, on the Virgin's name day, thousands of devout Christians make a pilgrimage on their bare knees to her basilica in Mexico City. On the flip side of the coin is **La Malinche,** the *indígena* woman who became Hernán Cortés's mistress, confidant, and interpreter. Changing her native name, Malintzin, to the Spanish Doña Marina, she aided her lover in a brutal conquest of her own people. She was later betrayed and abandoned by Cortés. While partly responsible for the conquest of Mexico, La Malinche is not seen entirely as a villain in legend; her story remains more of a cautionary tale on the dangers women risk by giving themselves to men.

to the left of the chapel stands a large stone sculpture of Benito Juárez, the man responsible for Maximilian's execution (open Tues.-Sun. 7am-6pm; 1 peso).

The newly remodeled **Teatro de la República** stands at Ángela Peralta and Juárez (tel. 24-00-40). Many historic events have transpired here: in 1867, the final decision on Emperor Maximilian's fate; in 1917, the drafting of the constitution; and in 1929, the founding of the Partido Nacional de la Revolución (PNR), the precursor of today's Partido Revolucionario Institucional (PRI). Inside, viewers can see the **Sala de Constituyentes,** where the constitution was drafted (both open Tues.-Sun. 10am-3pm and 5-8pm; free), but it's not much of a feast for the eyes.

For lazing around, nothing beats the shady trees of the **Alameda Hidalgo,** three blocks down Corregidora. The Alameda, which was built in 1790, includes a duck pond, green lawns, tree-lined paths, a skating rink, two soda fountains, and a monument honoring Hidalgo.

The **Andador Libertad,** two blocks from the Jardín and connecting the Plaza de la Independencia and Av. Corregidora, is host to a slew of mellow vendors and *artesanía* shops (open daily about 10am-9pm). **Andador 5 de Mayo,** off the Jardín, has several galleries with local artwork for sale.

## ENTERTAINMENT AND SEASONAL EVENTS

Local entertainment, like most everything else in Querétaro, revolves around the Jardín Zenea, where spectacular people-watching yields views of Querétaro's every human element each evening. Open-air brass-band concerts are given in the gazebo Sunday evenings from 6 to 8pm, and myriad jugglers, *mariachis,* and magicians perform there less regularly. Balloons in bunches big enough to fly you to Chicago are sold around the Jardín, enlivening the already-festive plaza. Jardín de los Platitos, where Juárez meets Av. Universidad north of the *zócalo,* dances to *mariachi* music. Things start to heat up at about 11pm on Fridays and Saturdays.

The *Cartelera de Eventos,* published monthly by the tourist office, is an excellent source of information about cultural events, concerts, performances, and festivals. Or call the **Academia de Bellas Artes** (tel. 12-05-70), Juárez Sur at Independencia, to find out what the students of the Universidad Autónoma de Querétaro have in store for the public. If you're lucky, you might catch a ballet recital, piano concert, theatrical event, or even a folk dance presentation. But call early; performances usually begin at 5pm.

More fun than monster trucks, **Querétaro 2000** (tel. 20-68-10 or -13), on Blvd. Bernardo Quintana, is a huge stretch of parks and facilities, including a pool, football field, basketball court, amusement park, library, open theater, and camping area (open daily 7am-7:30pm).

The local twentysomething crowd does its thing at **JBJ,** Blvd. Bernardo Quintana 109 (tel. 13-72-13 or 13-01-48). Booming rhythms and a merciless strobe light will pull you onto the dance floor (open Wed.-Sat. 7pm-3am; live music). Next to the disco is the **JBJ Bar,** which has karaoke and pool tables. Another happening spot is the disco **Van Gogh,** at Prolongación Pasteur Sur 285 (tel. 12-65-75; cover 20-25 pesos; open Fri.-Sun. 9pm-late). More convenient to the *centro* but less popular is **Tiffani's,** Zaragoza Pte. 67 (tel. 16-65-70). Women aren't charged a cover; sorry men— after 11pm you'll pay 15 pesos (open Thurs.-Sun. 9pm-late).

A more relaxed atmosphere can be found at **Quadros,** Andador 5 de Mayo 16 (tel. 12-04-45), one block from the Jardín. Local artwork covers the walls of this spacious but intimate cafe-bar, and each night from 8pm until closing, musicians playing anything from blues or jazz to *trova* (Silvio Rodriguez-esque music) treat the audience to hour-long sets. Friday and Saturday nights are open mike and twenty-ish would-be Selenas compete for drinks and prizes (cover 10-20 pesos after 8pm Fri.-Sat.; open Tues.-Sun. 6pm-3am).

The annual **Feria de Querétaro** usually takes place during the second week of December. The **Feria de Santa Ana,** complete with bulls running through congested streets, takes place July 26. The whole town dances during the **Celebración de la Santa Cruz de los Milagros** and the *Fiestas Patrias,* which take place during the second or third week of September.

## ■ Near Querétaro: Tequisquiapan

Situated on a high plateau 68km southeast of Querétaro, Tequisquiapan (pop. 40,000) sports narrow brick streets weaving in and out of flower-filled plazas and white stucco houses draped in bougainvillea. Still, it's not quite clear why it's become a tourist trap. Start with a pleasant setting and a relaxing spot to while away the time, and throw in a handful of sights, some overpriced *artesanía* stores, and a few expensive hotels and restaurants, and you've got Tequisquiapan. No more, no less.

To reach the *centro* from the bus station on the outskirts of town, walk along Calle Niños Héroes for about 10 minutes until you come to the Plaza Santa Rosa and behind it, the Plaza Principal. On your way into the town, you'll pass the **monument** marking the **geographical center of Mexico** at Niños Héroes and Av. Centenario Sur. In the Plaza Principal is **La Parroquia de Santa María de la Asunción,** a Neoclassic temple with a pink quarry facade, split-level columns, and a two-body tower trimmed in white brick. Also of interest is the **Museo de la Constitución de 1917,** housed in the Relox Hotel. This museum contains furniture and art from the early 20th century. In late May and early June, Tequisquiapan is host to the annual **Feria Internacional del Queso y del Vino,** marked by marginally amusing, touristy-as-hell musical and cultural events. The **tourist office,** Audador Morelos 7 (tel. (427) 3-02-95), will provide information (open Wed.-Sun. 10am-5pm). **Tequisquiapan Tours,** Callejón 20 de Noviembre 2A (tel. 3-13-62 or 3-13-02), can also be of help. **Shops** overflowing with baskets, rattan furniture, and other *artesanías* line Calle Ezequiel Montes. Pricey **restaurants** surround the Plaza; for less expensive eats, try Av. Moctezuma. **Cambios Express de Querétaro,** Juárez 5 (tel. 3-09-97 or 3-09-17), near Plaza Santa Rosa, offers good rates (open Mon.-Fri. 9am-6pm, Sat.-Sun. and holidays 9am-2pm).

**Getting There: Flecha Azul** (tel. 29-03-22) runs buses from Querétaro to Tequisquiapan (every ½hr., 6:30am-8:15pm, 1hr., 12 pesos).

# HIDALGO

## ■ Pachuca

On a hilltop overlooking the city, a monumental statue of *Cristo Rey* (Christ the King) extends its arms benevolently over Hidalgo's capital city. Whether or not the statue is responsible, Pachuca (pop. 220,000) is undeniably blessed in many ways. An important center for silver mining and processing since the 16th century, the city offers several lovely plazas, a few worthwhile museums, extremely friendly inhabitants, and invigoratingly crisp mountain air. Life moves at an orderly pace, but winding streets and hidden parks offer just the right degree of idiosyncratic charm. Pachuca exudes a sense of prosperity and contentment that is infectious, and the delightful streets are mostly free of tourists, making Pachuca a refreshing daytrip from the D.F.

## ORIENTATION AND PRACTICAL INFORMATION

Getting oriented is a bit difficult, as many streets curve and change names. The bus station is a fair distance from downtown. Frequent *combis* run from the bus station to the **Plaza de la Constitución** (1.50 pesos). To get from there to the *zócalo,* **Plaza de la Independencia,** make a left on Constitución and a right on Herrera. This will put you at the northeastern corner of the plaza. The street forming the eastern boundary of the square is **Matamoros;** it runs parallel to **Allende** (across the plaza) and **Guerrero** (one block west of the plaza). Matamoros and Guerrero converge a few blocks to the south at **Plaza Juárez. Juárez** and **Revolución** both begin at Plaza Juárez and run parallel to the south.

Pachuca's **tourist office** is in the bottom of the huge clock tower, on Plaza de la Independencia (open unreliably Mon.-Fri. 9am-6pm). **LADATELs** are scattered around the main plaza and throughout the city. **Banamex,** on the east side of the plaza on Matamoros, **changes money** 9am-1pm and has an **ATM. ADO** runs first-class **buses** to Mexico City's North Station (every 15min., 5am-10:15pm, 1hr., 23 pesos), Papantla (noon, 5hr., 56 pesos), and Tampico (10:45pm, 8hr., 129 pesos). **Autotransportas Valle del Mezouitan** has second-class service to Tula (every 15min., 4:20am-8:50pm, 2hr., 9 pesos). There is a **market** on the north side of Plaza de la Constitución. The **Red Cross** provides 24-hour ambulance service (tel. 4-17-20 or 4-32-53). For medical care, **Clínica IMSS,** off Maderos (tel. 3-78-33), is a bit far from downtown. The **police** (tel. 1-18-80) are in Plaza Juárez. The **post office,** Juárez at Iglesias, is two blocks south of Plaza Juárez (open Mon.-Fri. 8am-7pm, Sat. 9am-1pm).

## ACCOMMODATIONS AND FOOD

There is a dearth of true budget establishments in the immediate area. **Hotel Los Baños,** Matamoros 205 (tel. 307-00), just south of the main square, is a good value. A spacious, tiled courtyard gives rise to good-sized rooms with carpets, bottled water, telephones, and color TVs. Bathrooms are small but clean, and the central location is to die for (singles 75 pesos; doubles 85 pesos; triples 95 pesos). A couple blocks farther south on Matamoros is **Hotel Hidalgo,** Matamoros 503 (tel. 548-18). Rooms feature carpet, TV, and flowered bedspreads (singles 95 pesos; doubles 110 pesos).

In the 19th century there was an influx of Cornish miners to the Pachuca area. Their two lasting legacies are *fútbol* and *pastes*—pastry shells filled with meat, potatoes, and onions, with a dash of chile to keep it all tasting Mexican. *Pastes* make great, filling snacks; they are sold all over town for 1-3 pesos. On the east side of the *zócalo* is **Restaurante La Blanca,** Matamoros 201 (tel. 518-96). This friendly spot is popular with locals of all ages. The airy interior provides the perfect venue to enjoy *antojitos* (15 pesos), a sandwich (6-16 pesos), or the daily *comida corrida* (23 pesos). Tasty *pastes* (2.50 pesos) are available to go (open daily 8am-10pm). A bit of a walk south from downtown is **Girasol Restaurant and Bar,** Revolución 1107, about 10 blocks south of Plaza Juárez, across from the Revolución market. Brass fixtures, wood paneling, and forest-green walls are brightened by ubiquitous sunflower images. The lively ambience attracts a younger crowd, and the jazzy music keeps them happy while they munch on their *antojitos* (14-20 pesos; open daily 8am-midnight).

## SIGHTS AND ENTERTAINMENT

The Plaza de la Independencia is dominated by the impressive **Reloj Monumental.** This huge clock tower is a great example of the French architecture that was popular during the Porfirio Díaz regime. Four female statues represent Independence, Liberation, Constitution, and Reform. The clock and bell were made in England by the manufacturers of Big Ben. The **Centro Cultural Hidalgo** is in the **Ex-Convento de San Francisco.** To get there from the *zócalo,* follow Matamoros south for two blocks. Make a left on Allende, which soon ends in a traffic circle. Follow Arista to the left for two blocks, then make a right on Hidalgo (not to be confused with Nuevo Viaducto Hidalgo), the Ex-Convento is on the left. The cultural center contains the **Museo Nacional de la Fotografía,** an impressive survey of the technological history of photography. The museum also boasts a fascinating collection of Mexican photographs; gawk at Pancho Villa and Emiliano Zapata on their triumphal march into Mexico City in 1914. The center also contains the **Museo Regional de Hidalgo,** featuring exhibits on archaeology, history, crafts, and indigenous cultures. (Both museums open Tues.-Sun. 9am-6pm; free.) Adjoining the cultural center is the **Church of San Francisco.**

## ■ Near Pachuca: Mineral del Chico

Forty minutes of breathtaking scenery separates Pachuca from the tiny town of **Mineral del Chico** (pop. 500). Nestled in the **Parque Nacional el Chico,** the town has only a couple of restaurants, a small church, and a few houses. There are striking views of nearby rock formations, and it offers a great escape to nature for those sick of urban congestion and noise. There are several great hiking possibilities. Follow the road that runs uphill to the right from the *combi* stop to reach the spectacular vista point **Peña del Cuervo** (6km). Walking past the church and heading downhill to the left will take you through some old silver mines. That trail eventually leads up to the craggy rock formation dubbed **Tres Monjas** because of its resemblance to nuns bowed in prayer. Locals are very friendly and will happily suggest other trails to explore.

**Getting there:** *Combis* run from Pachuca to Mineral el Chico (every ½hr., 40min., 6 pesos). They leave from Galeana; to get there, follow Guerrero north of the *zócalo* and make a left on Galeana. Head uphill for about two blocks. If there isn't a *combi* waiting, there will be soon.

## ■ Tula

Tula (pop. 90,000) is not much to look at. Its *zócalo* empty, its streets moderately clean, this town is average in every way possible. It is Tula's excellent ruins that lure daytrippers here from Mexico City (80km) and Pachuca (75km). If you're eager for authentic Mexican life—chowing down at taco stands, bargaining for candles shaped like the Virgin of Guadalupe, and choking on exhaust in the small downtown—then Tula is the place for you. But don't expect much excitement.

**Orientation and Practical Information** Downtown Tula consists of a few commercial streets surrounding a central *zócalo.* To reach the *zócalo* from the **bus station,** turn right down Xicoténcatl and then left at Ocampo. Follow the signs to the *centro,* turn left down Zaragoza, and then right on Hidalgo. To get to Tula from Mexico City, take an **AVM** bus from the Central de Autobuses del Norte (every hr., 8am-8pm, 22 pesos), or **Metro** line 5, from the terminal Autobuses del Norte.

Currency can be exchanged at **Banamex,** Leandro Valle 102 (tel. 2-39-03), down Juárez from the *zócalo* (open Mon.-Fri. 9am-3pm). It also has a 24-hour **ATM.** Lovely **LATADELs** are found near the bus station and on Zaragoza and Hidalgo near *el centro.* **Buses** run out of the **AVM** terminal (tel. 2-02-25 or 2-02-64), on Xicoténcatl, to Mexico City (every 20min., 6am-8pm, 2hr., 19 pesos), Pachuca (every 20min., 4:30am-6:30pm, 2hr., 22 pesos), and Querétaro (9 per day, 7am-7pm, 2hr., 44 pesos). The **police** are at 5 de Mayo 408 (tel. 2-01-85). The **post office** is hidden on Av. Ferrocarril. From the top of Av. 5 de Mayo, head downhill on Av. Vicente Guerrero, along the train tracks, and continue straight ahead (open Mon.-Sat. 9am-3pm). **Postal Code:** 42800. **Phone Code:** 773.

**Accommodations and Food** Because Tula is a small town and the few travelers that show up only come to see the ruins, budget rooms don't come easy. The best deal in town is the **Auto Hotel Cuéllar,** 5 de Mayo 23 (tel. 91-800-2-04-42, toll-free in Mexico). Here, your car will have a place to sleep too. A smattering of wooden furniture and occasional patches of homey carpeting hug the rosy walls and tiled floors. The bathrooms are positively luxurious (singles 65 pesos; doubles 95 pesos). **Hotel Catedral,** Zaragoza 106 (tel. 2-08-13 or 2-08-33), near the *centro,* is also a good deal. A strange kitschy mixture of old and new, the worn rooms feature burlap lamp shades as well as gleaming automatic soap dispensers (far-out singles 75 pesos; doubles 90 pesos). **Restaurante Casa Blanca,** Hidalgo 114 (tel. 2-22-74), serves up a cheap five-course *comida corrida* (17 pesos) in a nice atmosphere. Some of the best and cheapest food in town lives at the **Restaurante El Ranchito** on Zaragoza (tel. 2-02-03), half a block before Hidalgo, a family-owned, family-style restaurant. A *comida corrida* with *postre* goes for only 13 pesos (open daily 7am-9pm).

**The Ruins** Once the Toltecs' greatest city, Tula was reputedly founded during the 9th century by the legendary Ce Acatl Topiltzin (a.k.a. that smarmy serpent Quetzalcóatl). Ce Acatl Topiltzin is the most venerated king in *indígena* history and mythology. After many years at Tula, the story goes, strife arose with neighbors who took issue with his peaceful ways, and he abandoned the city in AD 884 and led many of his followers to the Gulf coast, supposedly heading out to sea off the coast of Veracruz and vowing to return in the year "2 Reed." In the following years, several kings expanded Tula into the center of the mighty Toltec empire. Hundreds of years later, Cortés arrived in Veracruz, strangely enough, on the year "2 Reed." Because of his skin color and this coincidence, the Aztecs believed the *conquistador* was the same light-skinned Quetzalcóatl who had fled to the east so many years before, and Aztec Emperor Moctezuma brought about his own downfall by welcoming Cortés with open arms.

The Toltecs (see p. 51), whose name means "builders" in Náhuatl, relied on irrigation for their agricultural success and modeled their architecture after the style of Teotihuacán. During the 200-year-long Toltec heyday, the kingdom abandoned its once-pacific stance for violence and viciousness. When crop failures and droughts weakened the Toltec capital in AD 1165, the Chichimecs lashed out at the Toltecs and destroyed Tula. The ruins of the city (approx. 17 sq. km have been excavated) are architecturally mediocre, partly because of poor maintenance and partly because the Toltecs experienced internal instability—at one point Quetzalcóatl urged the Toltecs to evacuate the city, prompting some residents to bury their belongings and move to the region called Tlapallan. Tula was eventually absorbed by the Aztec empire, and Aztec ceramics and pottery can be found scattered among the ruins.

From the entrance area, a 600m dirt path zigzags through two sets of vendor stalls before arriving at the main plaza. Be sure to check out the super-prickly cacti that adorn the path—these ain't no houseplants. The first structure you see to your right (north) as you reach the main plaza is **Ballcourt #1,** just north of the large Edificio de los Atlantes. This court, nearly 60m long, once held a depiction of a ball player in ritual dress, which is now located in the archaeological sponge that is the Museo Nacional de Antropología in Mexico City. To the left (south) is the monumental **Edificio de los Atlantes,** also called the **Edificio de Tlahuizcalpantecuhtli,** likely the ceremonial worship building. Along its northern side and currently covered by a tin roof is the **Coatepantli,** which depicts jaguars and serpents in procession, as well as a deity in headdress and heart-devouring eagles. Reliefs of serpents feasting on live humans adorn the adjacent wall. Standing atop the pyramid are the Atlantes, figures of carved warriors. It is these structures that emblematize Tula on covers of National Geographic and on posters hanging in tourist offices throughout the country. Close inspection of the Atlantes (each a whopping 9.6m tall) reveals traces of red pigment, the only remnants of the many colors the statues once wore.

Immediately west of the Edifico de los Atlantes is the **Palacio Quemado** (Burnt Palace). It is thought to have been an administrative center in ancient Tula or perhaps the city market. A *chac-mool*, or messenger to the gods, was originally found in the central patio; now the black figure with a gaping mouth reclines near the steps to the Edifico de los Atlantes, under the awning. Like many other indigenous cultures, the Toltecs built their largest buildings on the eastern boundary of the plaza as witnesses to the sunrise. In this manner, Toltec leaders attempted to maintain sociopolitical control by inspiring awe and linking natural phenomena to the government. Tula's **Templo Principal** once towered over the others. On the east side of the expansive green plaza, this building may have served as living quarters for the high priests or rulers of the city. Not fully excavated and still overgrown with weeds, the Templo Principal can't be climbed from the front, but you can scramble up a steep rocky path in its southeast corner. Adjoining the ballcourt on the interior of the plaza is **El Tzompantli,** a small platform built by the Aztecs. Tzompantli means "place of skulls" and was used to display the victims of sacrifice.

During the week, few people come and it is possible to scale hills without seeing anyone in sight. **Taxis** will take you from Tula's plaza to the site (10 pesos). Taxis aren't available at the site for the return, but *peseros* pass frequently on the highway. The site is open daily 9:30am-4:30pm (admission 14 pesos, free for children under 13, students and teachers with ID, seniors, and on Sun. and holidays; museum free).

# ESTADO DE MÉXICO

## ■ Toluca

Capital of the Estado de México since 1846, Toluca (pop. 500,000) embodies many of the qualities that define the country as a whole. Industrial growth is rapidly expanding on the outskirts of town, traffic congestion is becoming a serious problem, and the not-so-invisible hand of American economic imperialism has clamped down in the form of a mammoth Wal-Mart. But while these signs of the changing times may not always please tourists, they are indicators of a city moving forward eagerly.

Despite these drawbacks, Toluca's downtown area remains truly striking for its beautifully preserved colonial architecture, complete with a traditionally elegant cathedral. Add a bunch of great museums and a breathtaking botanical garden enclosed in an enormous stained-glass mural, and you have the makings of a terrific escape from the sprawl of Mexico City, only an hour away.

### ORIENTATION AND PRACTICAL INFORMATION

Toluca is connected to Mexico City by the highway Paseo Tollocan. The *zócalo,* cathedral, and Portales shopping market constitute the *centro,* and are bounded by **Av. Hidalgo** on the south, **Lerdo de Tejada** on the north, **Juárez** on the east, and **Bravo** on the west. Independencia runs parallel to Hidalgo one block to the north and forms the south side of the *zócalo.* The **Alameda** lies three blocks west of the *centro* on Av. Hidalgo. The amazing stained-glass **Cosmovitral** is one block east of the *centro* on Lerdo de Tejada. *Peseros* link the bus station to the heart of Toluca.

**Tourist Office: State Tourist Office,** Urawa 100, Room #110, at Paseo Tollocan (tel. 14-78-30 or 14-79-17), about 6 blocks toward town from the bus station, in the orange municipal government building behind the Clínica IMSS and Wal-Mart.

**Telephones: LADATELs** are liberally scattered throughout the *centro* and bus station areas. A *caseta* in the bus station is open daily 7am-10pm.

**Fax: Telecomm,** in the bus station. **Telegrams** too. Open Mon.-Fri. 9am-3pm.

**Buses: Terminal Toluca** is tucked between Paseo Tollocan and Isidro Fabela, southeast of the *centro.* Tons of *peseros* run to the *centro* from the terminal, and return trips can be picked up on Juárez north of Independencia. **Estrella del Noreste** has constant service to Cholula (every 20min., 4 pesos) and Santiago (5.50 pesos). **Flecha Roja** (tel. 277-30-24) serves La Marquesa (every 10min., ½hr., 9 pesos),

Mexico City (every 10min., 1hr., 19 pesos), and Querétaro (every 2hr., 3hr., 52 pesos). **Naucalpan** goes straight to Mexico City's Metro stop Toreo (Line 2, every 5min., 1½hr., 15 pesos).

**Trains:** Av. de la Independencia at Electrificación. A 20min. walk east of the *zócalo*.

**Money Exchange:** There is a **BanCrecer** located in the bus station that will exchange money from 9am-1pm. A **Bancomer** with an **ATM** is on the corner of Juárez and Hidalgo.

**Market: Mercado 16 de Septiembre,** Manuel Gómez Pedraza between Ignacio Rayón and Sor Juana Inés de la Cruz, 2 blocks north of the Cosmovitral. Supplies and produce. Open daily 8am-6pm. **Super Wal-Mart,** so large it's impossible to miss it. A warehouse-like nirvana with 53 check-out aisles.

**Red Cross:** On Jesús Carranza (tel. 17-25-40), 1 block south of Paseo Tollocan and 1 block west of Paseo Colón, southwest of the *centro*. Open 24hr.

**Hospital: Clínica Hidalgo,** on Av. Hidalgo at Humboldt (tel. 17-07-33 or 14-91-11), 4 blocks east of Juárez, will patch you up or medicate you as necessary. Open 24hr. **Hospital Civil Adolfo López Mateos,** on M. Matamoros at Paseo Tollocan. Follow M. Galeana south of the *centro*. Open 24hr.

**Police:** In the Palacio Municipal, on Av. de la Independencia between Juárez and N. Bravo (tel. 14-93-51).

**Emergencies:** Dial 06 or call **LOCATEL** (tel. 12-11-21).

**Post Office:** On Av. Hidalgo, just east of Sor Juana Inés de la Cruz, 2 blocks east of Juárez. Open Mon.-Fri. 8am-7pm, Sat. 9am-1pm. There is also a small branch in the bus station. **Postal Code:** 50150.

**Phone code:** 72.

## ACCOMMODATIONS AND FOOD

Though far from stellar, accommodations are cheap and surround the *centro*. Avoid the noise and filth of rooms near the bus station. The centrally located **Hotel San Carlos,** Madero 210 (tel. 4-94-22), on the south side of Portales market in the *centro,* treats guests to peach rooms equipped with black-and-white TVs and comfortable bathrooms, some with phones. Ongoing renovation will result in a price increase when completed (singles 45 pesos; doubles 70 pesos). **Hotel Maya,** Hidalgo 413 (tel. 14-43-42), a couple of blocks west of the *centro,* is small and homey. Quirky home-spun quilts, clean communal bathrooms, and a flower-laden courtyard are welcome touches (singles 30 pesos; doubles 35 pesos, with 2 beds 50 pesos).

Restaurants and cheap stalls clutter the storefronts of the Portales. *Chorizo* (sausage), the local specialty, makes an appearance in everything from *queso fundido* (melted cheese) to *tortas*. Also popular are traditional candies like *palanquetas* (peanut brittle), candied fruits, and *dulces de leche* (burnt milk candy). At **Restaurant L'Ambiant,** Hidalgo 231, between Bravo and Galeana (tel. 5-33-93), red plaid tablecloths and red vinyl stools along the counter make this restaurant both cheery and cozy. The local lunch crowd is made up primarily of families and businesspeople (*comida corrida* 16 pesos; open daily 9am-9pm). **Taquería Las Brisas del Sur,** on Morelos, one block south of Hidalgo, between Juárez and Aldama, is not for vegetarians. This carnivorous paradise specializes in *carnes al carbon* (23 pesos). Typical plastic tables and chairs may not excite you, but the mouth-watering smell wafting onto the sidewalk is temptation enough (tacos 12-16 pesos; open daily 1-10pm).

## SIGHTS

The bulk of Toluca's offerings are found in the *centro*. The **Cosmovitral** and **Jardín Botánico** are housed in a building dating back to the turn of the century, located one block east of the northeast corner of the *zócalo*. The Cosmovitral, a stained glass mural, occupies 3000 square meters and is made of half a million pieces of glass. It depicts the universe converging into the vitality of humans. Its beauty enhances that of the many plants and pools of the Jardín. A small plaque and friendship lantern commemorate Toluca's sister city, Saitama, in Japan (open daily 9am-5pm; admission 5 pesos, children 2 pesos).

Toluca is bursting at the seams with museums. Happily, they are universally well-maintained and present their contents in easily digestible form. The museum mother lode lies 8km out of town; the **Centro Cultural Mexiquense** is accessible by buses that say "C. Cultural" and run along Independencia. The complex houses three museums. The **Museo de Culturas Populares** is a beautifully restored hacienda with a large collection of folk art and colorful, traditional Mexican crafts. The **Museo de Antropología e Historia** offers a large and informative collection of pre-Hispanic to modern Mexican artifacts and exhibits. The **Museo de Arte Moderno** provides an eclectic potpourri of modern art. (All museums open Tues.-Sun. 10am-6pm; admission 5 pesos, free Wed. and Sun; purchase tickets at the kiosk in the parking lot.)

The **Instituto Mexiquense de Cultura** sponsors five other museums in the *centro*. The **Museo José María Velasco** and the **Museo Felipe S. Gutiérrez** are housed in adjoining restored colonial structures off the northwest corner of the *zócalo*. Both artists were important 19th-century Mexican naturalists; the museums house visiting exhibitions as well as permanent collections of the two artists. The **Museo de la Acuarela,** two blocks west of the *portales,* displays all the watercolors you could possibly want to see. The **Museo de Numismática,** another half block west on Hidalgo, is ripe with coins galore. The **Museo de la Estampa,** on the south end of the Alameda, exhibits etchings, engravings, and graphic arts from all over the globe (all museums open Tues.-Sun. 10am-6pm; free).

# ■ Tepotzotlán

On the highway from Mexico City to Tula and Querétaro, the terrifically tiny town of Tepotzotlán (pop. 14,000) makes an easy and worthwhile daytrip from Mexico City. For those itching to escape the smog and bustle of the city, Tepotzotlán offers a glimpse of small-town life, and its church and monastery house exquisite examples of religious art. This idyllic old town is quiet and easily navigable by foot—what are *you* doing tomorrow afternoon?

In the 16th century, Jesuits established a convent in Tepotzotlán where *indígenas* could study language, art, theology, and mathematics. Martín Maldonado, an *indígena* convert, donated the land to the missionaries in 1582. Construction of the buildings continued until the end of the following century, and the huge bell in the tower was added in 1762. To the rear of the lavishly ornate Churrigueresque **Iglesia de San Francisco Javier** is the **Capilla de la Virgen de Loreto.** Behind it, the astounding **Camarín de la Virgen** (altar room) is fitted with a mirror so that visitors can see the decorations on the dome that crowns it. The interplay between sunlight and gold leaf is perhaps the most wonderful relic of Baroque godliness and glitziness.

After the expulsion of the Jesuits in 1767, the church and buildings became a reform school for priests. Early this century, they were returned to the Jesuits, and the whole complex of buildings became the **Museo del Virreinato** (tel. 207-91-37). This large, beautiful museum contains a mind-boggling amount of treasure from the colonial period. Exhibitions chronicle pre-Hispanic culture, colonial expansion, and missionary activities in the Republic. Jesuit imagery dominates the monastery's halls—St. Ignatius busts out all over the place, and St. Francis Xavier is only slightly less ubiquitous. Gregorian chants echo faintly throughout the halls, fitting the mood perfectly.

The **Iglesia de San Francisco Javier,** a church-cum-museum, is a masterpiece of the Churrigueresque style. All that glitters is indeed gold here, and the craftsmanship is among the most intricate and well-preserved in all of Mexico. Clerical vestments, murals lining the inner courtyard, and faded frescoes further enhance this divine religious collection. Look out for *El Crucifijo,* a 17th-century sculpture of Christ on the cross carved from a single piece of wood. Don't miss the concealed entrance to the upper floor near the exit; the hall contains more artifacts, and the balcony provides a great view of the surrounding area. Delight in the monastery's sweet-smelling orchard, crisscrossed by cobblestone paths (museum complex open Tues.-

Fri. 10am-5pm, Sat.-Sun. 10am-6pm; admission 14 pesos, free for seniors, students with ID, children, and on Sun.).

The plaza outside the church is packed with few eateries and even fewer hotels. Your best bet (and one of your only bets) is **Hotel Posada San José,** Plaza Virreynal 13 (tel. 876-08-35), nearly hidden right beside the Restaurant-Bar Pepe. The walls are bare brick, but the floors are carpeted and the bathrooms are tiled. If you're feelin' lazy, try some of the moderately priced room service. Rooms with a view of the church and beautiful *zócalo* cost extra, but it might be worth it (singles 60 pesos; doubles 90 pesos; add 20 pesos to each for a view). For eats, head to **Restaurante Los Pericos,** Plaza Virreynal 7A (tel. 876-23-72), on the far side of the plaza. Dining under the shaded balcony is perfect for people-watching, enjoying good food (most entrees 28-37 pesos), and ogling the bounteous bar (open daily 8am-10pm).

**Getting There:** To get to Tepotzotlán from Mexico City, take the Metro to Cuatro Caminos (Line 2), then the yellow or blue bus from *salida* H (buses leave about every ½hr., 6am-10pm, 5 pesos), or snag any bus going north on Highway 57 (to Tula or Querétaro) and ask to be left off at the *crucero* (6-10 pesos). From there you can walk or take a 10-peso cab ride to the *zócalo*. To get back to Mexico City, grab a bus across the street from the Hotel Posada San José to any of a number of Metro stations.

# ■ Ixtapan de la Sal

Why most people go to Ixtapan de la Sal: the $100-a-day resorts, upscale spas, and water park. Why you should go: *everything else.* Ixtapan de la Sal (pop. 40,000) is the real thing—clean, quiet streets, rustic life, home-cooked meals. The gorgeous and refreshingly simple rust and whitewashed cathedral and *zócalo* are among the most scenic in Mexico. Only a quarter mile of road links Ixtapan's *centro* to the ritzy slew of resorts and natural spas that have made this sleepy little town famous, but in Ixtapan proper, *burros* still amble down the streets and people arrange flower offerings for the Virgin Mary and sleep outdoors. Come quickly, before resorts swallow the town itself, but once you're here, rest easy—life is slow and damn good.

**Orientation and Practical Information** The **bus station** is on the main thoroughfare, **Juárez,** the same street that, ¼-½km ahead, ends in the huge *balenario* (spa and waterpark) and chain of resorts. Running parallel to Juárez is **Allende.** Some main streets running perpendicular to Juárez (listed in order, from the bus station toward the resorts): **20 de Noviembre, 5 de Febrero, 16 de Septiembre, Álvaro Obregón.** There is no tourist office, but an excellent **info booth** can be found at the end of Juárez, on the north side of the market in front of the water park. The **bus station** on Juárez sends buses to Mexico City (2nd class every 15min., 3:30am-7:40pm, 3hr., 22 pesos; *directo* every ½hr., 5am-7:30pm, 2hr., 27 pesos), Cuernavaca (every hr., 5am-7pm, 2nd class 3½hr., 17 pesos; 1st class 2½hr., 22 pesos), and Acapulco (10:45am, 1:15, and 5:15pm, 6hr., 73 pesos). The **Red Cross** (tel. 3-02-44), on the highway before the *unidad deportivo* (sports complex), is open 9am-9pm with 24-hour emergency service. **Farmacia El Fénix,** Plaza de Mártires 1, on the *zócalo*, is open daily 8am-10pm. The **post office** is located on 16 de Septiembre, two blocks from the cathedral (open Mon.-Sat. 9am-3pm). The **police** (tel. 3-02-44) can be reached 24-hour. **Postal Code:** 51900. **Phone code:** 714.

**Accommodations and Food** If you stay away from the obscenely high-priced resorts and spas, some real deals await you. **Casa de Huéspedes Sofia,** 20 de Noviembre 4 (tel. 3-18-51), is a short walk from the bus station. Go up Juárez three-quarters of a block, make your first right, and continue a block. This place offers small, clean rooms, some with carpets and all with hot water and super-friendly staff (50 pesos per person). The **Casa de Huéspedes Francis,** Obregón 6, near the cathedral, has a large, fern-filled lobby and bitchin' staircases. Rooms provide the basics, including 24-hour hot water. You can't beat the prices (40 pesos per person). The **Hotel Casa Sarita,** Obregón 1512, is refreshingly posh. This 11-room hotel features soft beds and rocking chairs. Prices include three phenomenal home-cooked meals upstairs and excellent service. Watch and learn as the cook picks out melons and chicken carcasses (150 pesos per person, including 3 meals). For one of the best meals in town, eat at **Restaurante Yolis,** Juárez 33 (tel. 3-02-05). The telephone number connects not to the restaurant but to Ms. Sara Medina Viuda de Castaneda's living room, where she'll be happy to talk to you in Spanish. The menu is posted every day. The huge *comida corrida* costs 25 pesos—breakfast (you tell 'em what you want and they'll make it) and *cena* each go for 20 pesos. Watch *telenovelas* with the family and enjoy your home-cooked food (open daily 8am-7pm). **Fonda Jardín,** Plaza 7 (tel. 3-02-74), offers both central location and cheap and yummy eats. The 12-peso enchiladas and ice-cold 4-peso beers (believe it) will make you want to wander around drunk and full for the rest of your days. For the do-it-yourself traveler, **Panificadora Ixtapan,** Obregón 101 near Allende, offers freshly-baked bread at 0.60 pesos per loaf. Or spring for the most expensive thing in the bakery—a 1-peso *biscocho* (pastry; open daily 5am-9:30pm).

**Sights** Most people come to Ixtapan to check out the massive water park/spa/thermal springs complex appropriately named **Ixtapan,** located at the end of Juárez (open daily 10am-6pm; admission 40 pesos, children 25 pesos). Back in town, however, lies a different kind of beauty. To get to the **Plaza de los Martires,** make a right from Juárez (facing the water park) onto Independencia and continue straight three or four blocks. This center of town life is surprisingly modern and lovely, with plenty of recycling bins and a new obelisk-like monument dedicated to all the martyrs of the revolution. Adjoining the plaza is the **Santuario de la Asunción de Maria,** an astonishing white church with burgundy and rust trim. This cathedral and its little plaza-like "yard" are one of the original reasons that cameras were invented. Completely open and airy, the church has a bulletin board filled with news of local weddings and a garden that sounds of buzzing bees and chirping birds. Adjoining this Mediterranean-like cathedral is the **Capilla del Santísima y del Perdon,** in which a glass case holds a silver Christ. Services take place here almost continually, sermons issued forth from the boom-box-like speakers on either side of the altar (open daily 7am-8pm).

# ■ Popocatépetl and Ixtaccíhuatl

Overlooking Morelos and Puebla are two snow-capped volcanoes veiled in Aztec mythology, **Popocatépetl** (5452m) and **Ixtaccíhuatl** (5282m), respectively the second- and third-largest peaks in the country. These magnificent mountains, which are open to both experienced climbers and less-seasoned backpackers, are shrouded in indigenous mythology. Legend has it that the warrior Popocatépetl ("Smoking Mountain" in Náhuatl) loved Ixtaccíhuatl ("Sleeping Woman"), the emperor's daughter. Once, when the warrior went off to battle, Ixtaccíhuatl came to believe that he had been killed; she subsequently died of lovesickness and grief. When Popo (as he was known to friends) learned of his lover's death, he built the two great mountains. On the northern one he placed her body (which you can see by looking at Ixtaccíhuatl from afar, with a little imagination), and on the southern one he stood vigil with a torch. Locals pay their respects to the supine, death-pale Ixtaccíhuatl on the mountain's snowy summit.

The passage between the two is called *Paso de Cortés,* because it is the route the Spanish conqueror took to the valley of Tenochtitlán. Popo is still active, and let loose a belch of ashes as recently as July 1997. In the towns surrounding the base of Popo, a cult following of films such as *Dante's Peak* and *Volcano* has developed. Both volcanoes can be climbed to a small degree on well-marked tourist trails; tourist organizations offer group trips to the peaks.

Before beginning your climb, register at the **Club Socorro Alpino** (Alpine Assistance Club) and inform them of your expected return date. Both mountains can be very dangerous and it is unwise to climb alone or without proper equipment. Travelers have lost their lives due to inclement weather, so (especially this year) inquire about the current conditions before making plans, and always bring both warm clothes and raingear. The small **Tlamacas Lodge** provides dorm-style housing and somewhat pricey meals in its cafeteria. The lodge organizes assaults on the mountains and rents equipment for about 120 pesos per person.

**Getting there:** The city of **Cuautla**, known mainly for having been Emiliano Zapata's stronghold during the Mexican Revolution and now notable only for the few *balnearios* (hot water springs) that dot the area, is the best jumping-off point for the volcanoes. Cuautla has two main **bus stations**, both of which are best reached from Cuernavaca (via Estrella Roja) or Mexico City's Tasqueña station. The large **Cristóbal Colón** station, on 2 de Mayo at Reforma, serves Amecameca (every 15min., 1½hr., 7.50 pesos), Mexico City (every 15min., 6:30am-9pm, 1½hr.), and Tlalmanalco (every 20min., 2hr., 7.50 pesos), while **Estrella Roja**, on Costeño at Vázquez, serves Cuernavaca (every 10min., 5am-8pm, 1½hr.).

To get to Popocatépetl, take a bus to **Amecameca** from Cuautla. In Amecameca, minibus drivers will charge you a hefty sum for the trip to **Tlamacas**, a small village at the base of the mountain. The minibuses from Amecameca generally do not operate on weekends. From there, another *pesero* runs to the beginning of the trail. To reach Ixtaccíhuatl, take a bus to **Tlalmanalco** from Cuautla. From there, a *pesero* runs to **San Rafael**, which rests at the base of Ixtaccíhuatl. Otherwise, several trips leave from the Tlamacas Lodge.

# MORELOS

## ■ Cuernavaca

No matter how you look at it, Cuernavaca is a blast. If you're heading into town, you'd better put on your party shoes and pool your pesos, because this once-mellow colonial town is now a chic weekend getaway and expatriate hotspot. The capital of Morelos, Cuernavaca (pop. 2 million) has long been seen as the quintessential colonial city, and has earned the nickname "City of Eternal Spring" for its temperature, which hovers around 68°F year-round. Situated in an enviable place in the hills and strewn with classic colonial architecture and serpentine streets, Cuernavaca has more going for it than just climate. A victim of its own popularity, the city has become more noisy and industry-oriented in the past 10 years, and chaos, commotion, and construction dominate its ambience. For such a center of movement, however, Cuernavaca still has plenty of shady places to relax, grab a beer, and meditate.

Before there were gringos here, or even Mexicans, there were Aztecs. The valley was first populated by the Tlahuica, an Aztec tribe; the city which grew up in the valley was called Cuauhnahuac, "Place on the Outskirts of the Grove." Mexico's *criollo* elite transformed the city into their private summer camp, and the name was corrupted into the Spanish quasi-homynym Cuernavaca. As word spread of the allure of Eternal Spring, Cuernavaca became a magnet for famous visitors like Cortés, García Marquez, Muhammad Ali, and the Shah of Iran; magnificent haciendas with vined fences too high for peeking began to radiate from the *zócalo*. Lately, the city's center of gravity has shifted away from the famous and toward the rich—wealthy Mexicans flock to Cuernavaca, and the city functions as a springtime playground for upper-class Mexico City residents fleeing bigger-city hassles. Unsurprisingly, this surge has been accompanied by equal, if not greater, swarms of foreigners (both tourists and residents), and innumerable foreign-language schools now draw them in by the bushel.

While penny-pinchers might snarl at Cuernavaca's cost of living, there's a reason people can't stay away—bars and clubs throb with nightly excitement, scores of fine restaurants pepper the streets, and an entire gringo scene has emerged. The city is hip, young, international, lovely, and full of art, culture, and Spanish instruction.

## ORIENTATION

**Route 95** from Mexico City intersects many of Cuernavaca's main avenues. To get to the city center, exit onto **Domingo Diez** if coming from Mexico City, or **Emiliano Zapata,** which splits into the northbound **José María Morelos** and the southbound **Avenida Obregón.** Morelos serves as the principal access road, running straight through the center of town. **Benito Juárez** is the main north-south thoroughfare east of the *zócalo.* Near the *centro,* Domingo Diez merges with **Cuauhtémoc** off the México-Acapulco expressway to become **Plan de Ayala,** which turns east to become the principal east-west axis in town. Ayala later rejoins the expressway.

Two plazas together make up Cuernavaca's *zócalo.* **Plaza de la Constitución,** the main square, is a few blocks east of Morelos via Hidalgo, at the intersection of Guerrero, Salazar, Juárez, and Hidalgo. Diagonally opposite the *zócalo*'s northwest corner is the smaller **Jardín Juárez.** Several blocks east of the *zócalo* is the market area, municipal bus center, and gathering place for locals. Cuernavaca is not an easy city to navigate—expect irregularities, unexpected turns, and name changes, especially near the plaza. Even and odd numbers usually stay on different sides of the street but, because of two different numbering systems, buildings opposite each other may have addresses several hundred numbers apart. As if this wasn't headache enough, by some strange governmental decree, the official address system changed. On Morelos and nearby streets, it's not uncommon to see two addresses on each building. "400/antes 17" means that the old address was 17 and the new "official" one is 400.

To reach the *centro* from the **Flecha Roja bus station,** take a right at the exit and head south on Morelos. Turn left onto Rayón, Hidalgo, or any nearby cross-street. If you arrive via **Pullman de Morelos** (make sure it's terminal #1, Terminal del Centro; if it's not, ask the bus driver to take you there) head straight uphill on Netzahualcóyotl to Hidalgo; most major sights can be accessed from there. Those arriving via **Estrella de Oro** should cross the street and flag down any northbound minibus on Morelos (1.70 pesos)—they all run past the center of town.

Frequent local buses (1.70-2.50 pesos), called *rutas,* run up and down Morelos; the *colonia* the bus is heading for is painted on the windshield. Taxis will go anywhere in the city for 7-15 pesos. After dark, because of Cuernavaca's active and spread-out nightlife, cabs charge 20-25% more (and get away with it). In any case, set prices before hopping in.

## PRACTICAL INFORMATION

**Tourist Offices: State Office,** Morelos Sur 187/antes 802 (tel. 14-38-72), a 15min. walk south from Hidalgo and Morelos. These great guys and girls will dole out lots of helpful information, including brochures and maps for Cuernavaca and the entire state of Morelos and info about language schools and study options. Open Mon.-Fri. 9am-9pm, Sat.-Sun. 10am-6pm. The informal white **info booth** on the north side of the cathedral also has brochures. Open daily 7am-7pm.

**Currency Exchange: Banca Serfín** (tel. 14-08-88), at the northwest corner of Jardín Juárez. **ATM.** Currency exchange daily 9am-5pm. **Casa de Cambio Gesta,** Morrow 9 at Comonfort (tel. 14-01-95 or 18-37-50). Open Mon.-Fri. 9am-2pm and 4-6pm, Sat. 9am-1pm. **Casa de Cambio Divisas de Cuernavaca,** Morrow 12A (tel. 12-85-68), also has offices at Guerrero 208 and in the Plaza Los Arcos, in the northern part of town. Open Mon.-Fri. 9am-5pm.

**American Express: Marín Agencia de Viajes** (tel. 14-22-66), in Las Plazas Shopping mall on the *zócalo.* Holds mail, provides travel services, and will usually exchange currency. Open Mon.-Fri. 9am-2pm and 4-6pm, Sat. 10am-2pm.

**Telephones: LADATELs** are easy to find around the *zócalo,* along Morelos Sur, and in the bus stations. For a good, old-fashioned *caseta,* there's **Telcom,** Salazar 8, on the eastern edge of the *zócalo.* Open Mon.-Fri. 8am-8pm, Sat. 9am-1pm.

**Fax: Telecomm** (tel. 18-05-67), to the right of the post office. Open for **telegrams** and fax Mon.-Fri. 8am-7pm, Sat. 9am-1pm.

**Buses: Flecha Roja,** Morelos 503 (tel. 12-81-90), 4 long blocks north of Jardín Borda. 1st-class service to Acapulco (8 per day, 8am-6pm, 5hr., 110 pesos), Grutas de

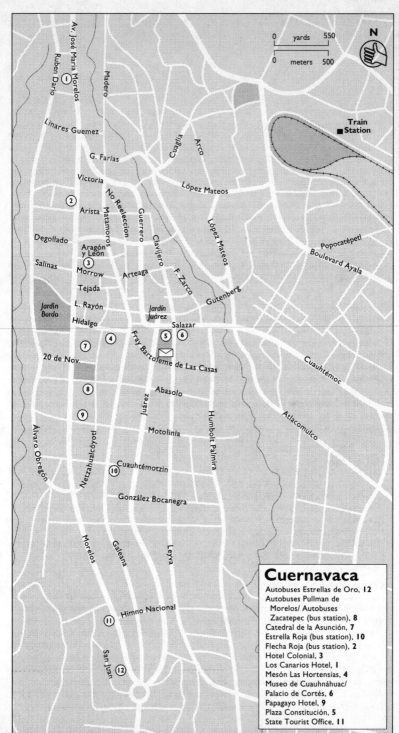

N

0 yards 550
0 meters 500

Train Station

Av. José María Morelos
Ruben Darío
Linares Guemez
Madero
Cuaglia
Arco
G. Farías
Victoria
No Reelección
Guerrero
López Mateos
Arista
Matamoros
Clavijero
López Mateos
Degollado
Aragón y León
Popocatépetl
Boulevard Ayala
Salinas
Morrow
Arteaga
F. Zarco
Tejada
Gutenberg
Jardín Borda
L. Rayón
Jardín Juárez
Hidalgo
Salazar
Cuauhtémoc
20 de Nov.
Fray Bartoleme de Las Casas
Abasolo
Atlacomulco
Juárez
Humbolt Palmira
Motolinía
Netzahualcóyotl
Cuauhtémotzin
Álvaro Obregón
González Bocanegra
Morelos
Galeana
Leyva
Himno Nacional
San Juan

# Cuernavaca

Autobuses Estrellas de Oro, 12
Autobuses Pullman de
  Morelos/ Autobuses
  Zacatepec (bus station), 8
Catedral de la Asunción, 7
Estrella Roja (bus station), 10
Flecha Roja (bus station), 2
Hotel Colonial, 3
Los Canarios Hotel, 1
Mesón Las Hortensias, 4
Museo de Cuauhnáhuac/
  Palacio de Cortés, 6
Papagayo Hotel, 9
Plaza Constitución, 5
State Tourist Office, 11

Cacahuamilpa (every 40min., 6am-6pm, 1hr., 11 pesos), Mexico City (every ½hr., 5:30am-9pm, 1¼hr., 26 pesos), Taxco (12 per day, 1½hr., 19 pesos), and northern cities including Guadalajara (6 and 10pm, 9hr., 272 pesos). The **Tres Estrellas del Centro** desk in the same building offers local service to Chalma (10am and 1pm, 1¼hr., 16 pesos), Santa Marta (10:30am and 1pm, 1hr., 9 pesos), Santiago (1 and 5pm, 1hr., 14 pesos), and Toluca (every ½hr., 6am-9pm, 17 pesos). The station has 24hr. **luggage storage** (5 pesos for the first 5hr., 1 peso per additional hr.) and long-distance phones. Open daily 6:30am-10pm. **México-Zacatepec (LASSER)/ Pullman de Morelos,** Netzahualcóyotl 106 at Abasolo (tel. 14-36-50), 2 blocks south of the *zócalo.* To Mexico City (every ½hr., 6:30am-10pm, 1hr., 26 pesos), Zacatepec (every hr., 9am-6pm, 7.50 pesos), and small cities throughout Morelos. **Estrella de Oro,** on Morelos Sur at Las Palmas Circle (tel. 12-30-55), 10 blocks south of the intersection of Reforma and Hidalgo. 1st-class service to Acapulco (4 per day, 10am-6pm, 3½hr., 110 pesos), Chilpancingo (4 per day, 1-8pm, 2hr., 65 pesos), Iguala (2pm, 1½hr., 20 pesos), Ixtapa/Zihuatanejo (11am and 3:30pm, 8hr., 119 pesos), Mexico City (5 per day, 1¼hr., 23 pesos), and Taxco (2 per day, 1½hr., 21 pesos). **Estrella Roja,** Galeana 401 at Cuauhtémotzin, 7 blocks south of the *zócalo.* 1st-class service to Cuautla (every 15min., 6:15am-10pm, 1hr., 9 pesos) and Puebla (every hr., 5am-7pm, 3hr., 28 pesos). 2nd class **Estrella Roja** and **Ome-tochtli,** on López Mateos at the south end of the Mercado. Buses load in the parking lot across the highway and run to Tepoztlán (45min., 5 pesos).

**Supermarket: Superama,** at Morelos (tel. 12-81-20), just behind Helados Holanda, north of the cathedral and south of the Flecha Roja bus station. Huge grocery and **pharmacy.** Open Mon.-Sat. 7am-10pm, Sun. 7am-9pm. The market on Blvd. Alfonso López Mateos sells excellent produce. Head east on Degollado, up the pedestrian bridge, and past the vendor stands.

**Laundromat: Lavandería Obregón,** Obregón and Salinas (tel. 12-94-98). Head down Morelos north past the *centro* and make a left on Salinas—the laundromat is at the bottom of the hill to your left. 6 pesos per kilo. Open Mon.-Fri. 9am-7pm, Sat. 9am-2pm.

**Red Cross:** Ixtaccíhuatl at Río Panuco (tel. 15-05-51 or 15-35-55).

**Pharmacy: Farmacia Morelos,** Morelos 233 (tel. 12-79-40), just north of the *zocálo.* Offers a 20-30% discount on most items. Open daily 8am-9pm.

**Medical Assistance: Centro Quirúrgico,** Juárez 507B (tel. 14-23-38). A pricey doctor for every ailment. Free help at **IMSS** (tel. 15-50-00).

**Hospital: Hospital Civil,** Morelos 197 (tel. 14-17-44 or 18-83-17), directly across the street from the cathedral. 24hr. emergency treatment free, except for the cost of supplies. English spoken and long lines at all hours.

**Emergency:** Dial 06.

**Police:** Emiliano Zapata 802 (tel. 17-11-15, 12-00-36, or 17-10-00). Take Morelos north until it becomes Zapata; it's a bit farther up on the left. For something more heavy-duty, call the **Policía Judicial** (tel. 17-17-19).

**Internet Access: Sports and Internet Café** on Morelos Sur. From the Jardin Borda, turn left down Morelos and walk a few blocks—the cafe is on your left, across from a huge supermarket. 20 pesos per ½hr. for email and the Web.

**Post Office:** Plaza de la Constitución 3 (tel. 12-43-79), on the southwest corner of the *zócalo.* Open Mon.-Fri. 8am-7pm, Sat. 9am-1pm. **Postal Code:** 62050.

**Phone Code:** 73.

## ACCOMMODATIONS

Although Cuernavaca's status as an upper-class getaway does not necessarily affect one's peaceful meanderings through town, it does reveal itself in the hotel department. Simply put, rooms are chronically overpriced. The cloud has a silver lining, though—even the barest of hotels are often outfitted with a swimming pool or lush courtyard. And if you don't mind some friendly old prostitutes standing in doorways and shady transactions, there are some extremely inexpensive *casas de huéspedes* on Aragón y León between Matamoros and Morelos. Just be sure they're clean.

For an extended stay (a couple of weeks or more), it's possible to lodge with a local family through one of the city's Spanish language schools. Students choose from a list of families willing to provide room, board, and language practice. **Cuauhnahuac,** Morelos Sur 1414 (tel. 12-36-73), is especially willing to lend their family list to backpacking visitors who wish to spend time with *cuernavaquenses*. Sharing a room with a student costs US$17 per day for room and board; for a private single, you pay US$32 (contact José Camacho at Cuauhnahuac). Also try the bilingual language school, **Experiencia,** Leyva 1130 (tel. 12-65-79), in Colonia Las Palmas.

**Villa Calmecac,** Zacatecas 114 (tel. 13-21-46; email meliton@mail.giga.com), in Col. Buenavista. Billing itself as an "ecotourist hostel," this unbelievable place offers lodging as well as numerous opportunities to bicycle, kayak, and participate in the great outdoors. With vegetable gardens, an art gallery, and ultra high-tech recycling and waste-management disposal, it's an earth-lover's dream. Facilities new and well-maintained. Dorm rooms 65 pesos; private double 190 pesos; private quad 360 pesos. Breakfast included.

**Hotel Colonial,** Aragón y León 104 (tel. 18-64-14), uphill and west of Matamoros. Despite the presence of nearby sketchy "hotels," this one is a gem. Pretty orange colonial home with a relaxing central courtyard and hospitable staff. Green and brown rooms enlivened by tiled floors and spotless bathrooms. Some of the singles even have cool bunk-bed-like fixtures. Singles 80 pesos; doubles 140 pesos; add 20 pesos for TV.

**Los Canarios,** Morelos 369 (antes 713) (tel. 13-00-00), 5 blocks north of *el centro*. Although some *cuernavaquenses* say this motor lodge is *de paso* (past its prime), it still groans merrily with groovy 50s decor and furnishings. Comfy, colorful rooms provide the basics, and 2 swimming pools and a restaurant complement your stay. All this, plus great prices, keeps packing vacationing Mexican families in. Some of them practically live here. Proprietor is often willing to offer discounts. Singles 60 pesos; doubles 110 pesos.

**Hotel Papagayo,** Motolinía 13 by Morelos (tel. 14-17-11), 5 blocks south of the cathedral. A budget resort. Geared towards bilingual clientele, although still mainly populated by wise national tourists. Features clean, well-furnished rooms, a pool with diving platforms, ping-pong, and restaurant service. Singles 125 pesos; doubles 205 pesos. Breakfast (8am-10am) included.

**Mesón Las Hortensias,** Hidalgo 13 Col. Centro (tel. 18-52-65), right near the Catedrál, across the street from the plaza. The key word is *location*. Step outside and you're in the middle of everything. The clean green rooms and gorgeous outdoor patio (also green) can't be complained about. TV, telephone, and continual cleanliness can be yours, but hurry—grab one of the 23 rooms before they're gone. Singles 150 pesos; doubles 132 pesos.

## FOOD

Overflowing with tourists, Cuernavaca has more than its share of budget eateries (as well as all major U.S. fast food chains, if you're truly desperate). For your main meal, take advantage of one of the excellent restaurants around the plaza. Head up the side streets (try Aragón y León) or larger thoroughfares Galeana and Juárez for lighter, less expensive fare. In the market, a *comida corrida* costs about 15-18 pesos *con refresco*. Along Guerrero, north of the plaza, street vendors sell mangos, *piñas* (pineapples), and *elotes* (corn on the cob). The health drinks sold at the Eiffel Kiosk in the Jardín Juárez include everything from the standard fruit and milk *licuados* to a spinach concoction not even Popeye could love (6-15 pesos).

**Marco Polo Pizzería,** Hidalgo 26 (tel. 12-34-84), on the 2nd floor. And after he helped facilitate the Italy-China spaghetti trade, this robust young explorer rested his weary butt and smiled. He liked the view of the mountains and the cathedral. More importantly, he liked the delicious puffy pizzas that come in 4 sizes (starting at 22 pesos). Cuernavacans have followed in Marco's footsteps; everyone who's anyone eats here. Try the tempting *tocino y cebollo* (bacon and onion) pizza for a special treat (24 pesos). Open Mon.-Thurs. 1-10:30pm, Fri.-Sun. 1-10pm.

**Restaurante Los Arcos,** Jardín de Los Héroes 4 (tel. 12-44-86), on the south side of the *zócalo*. Flanked by lush plants and a bubbling fountain, nice mosaic-inlaid outdoor tables are ideal spots from which to watch the day slip-slide away. Musicians of varying ages and abilities serenade the clientele. A great place to soak in the early morning sun. *Comida corrida* 23 pesos. Open daily 7:30am-midnight.

**Gin Gen,** Rayón 106 (tel. 18-60-46), 2½ blocks west of the Jardín Borda at Morelos. Pictures of Chinese pop stars adorn the walls. From 1-5pm, the super-filling *guisa-dos del día* provide soup, rice, 2 entrees, and dessert for only 33 pesos. Great tofu and vegetarian options, too (16-26 pesos). Open daily 8am-10pm.

## SIGHTS

Although Cuernavaca's popularity has little to do with scintillating sights, there is a lot to see besides the city's sunglass-clad elite sipping iced tea and speaking in newly-acquired Spanish or English (although that too can be frightfully exciting).

For starters, the city's main square, the **Plaza de la Constitución,** is notably lovely (though it's often notably noisy as well). Extending east from the Palacio de Gobi-erno, the plaza is not content to just hold the entire Morelos state bureaucracy. It is truly the heart and soul of its own city as well, shaded by trees colored by fiery red *flamboyanes* (royal poinciana), and speckled with cafes and wrought-iron benches. Food vendors and *mariachis* engage in a Darwinian struggle for pesos. A kiosk designed by Gustave Eiffel (bearing no resemblance to its more famous Parisian sibling) and commissioned by Cuernavaca's Viennese community stands in the **Jardín Juárez,** at the northwest corner of the Pl. de la Constitución, north of the Palacio de Gobierno. Thursdays and Sundays at 6pm, a merry but mediocre local band comman-deers the kiosk and belts out polkas, classical music, and Mexican country music. The kiosk houses a multitude of nutritionally-sound fruit drink stands.

At the southeastern corner of the Plaza de la Constitución, east of Benito Juárez, the **Palacio de Cortés** stands as a stately reminder of the city's grim history—Cortés set Cuernavaca on fire in 1521, then built this two-story fortress from the remains of local buildings, situating the fortress atop a sacred pyramid. It was completed in 1524 when Cortés craved another conquest (and left to raise hell in Honduras); the build-ing functioned as a prison in the 18th century and as the Palacio de Gobierno during the dictatorship of Porfirio Díaz.

A grant from the former British ambassador to Mexico (none other than Charles Lindbergh's father-in-law) transformed the Palacio de Cortés into the **Museo Cuauh-nahuac.** On the first floor of the museum, archaeological and anthropological exhib-its deal with pre-Hispanic cultures. One of the more interesting displays is the collection of indigenous drawings and depictions of the Spanish arrival, in which val-iant eagle and tiger warriors in full regalia battle the invaders. Second-floor exhibits on the Conquest and Mexican history include the first public clock ever to toll in Mesoamerica. The ubiquitous and astonishing Diego Rivera has yet another mural/masterpiece on the western balcony of the second floor. The mural, commissioned by then-U.S. ambassador to Mexico Dwight D. Morrow as a gift to the people of Cuer-navaca, depicts Mexico's history from the Conquest until the Revolution of 1910, proceeding chronologically from right to left. If you're not up on your Mexican his-tory, don't worry—a chart underneath the mural will explain it all (museum open Tues.-Sun. 10am-5pm; admission 14 pesos, free Sun. and for students with ID).

Black soot has darkened the tall walls and towers of the **Catedral de la Asunción,** three blocks down Hidalgo from the *zócalo,* at Morelos. Although it's one of the old-est churches in the Americas (construction began in 1525), it was only 20 years ago that the removal of the aisle altars revealed some fabulous Japanese frescoes depict-ing the persecution and martyrdom of Christian missionaries in Sokori, Japan. Histori-ans speculate that these startling frescoes were painted in the early 17th century by a converted Japanese artist who had settled in Cuernavaca. But ultimately, it's the sim-ple and sparse altar that makes this church special (and very unusual in a country of gold and gilded centerpieces). Here, seven plain baskets holding candles hang, seem-ingly suspended, within a faceless box (open daily 7am-7pm).

Quite different is the **Jardín Borda** (tel. 12-92-37), once the site of glamorous soi-rées during the French occupation of Mexico, now a Sunday gathering spot for young couples and families on picnics. The stone entrance is on Morelos, across from the cathedral. In 1783, the priest Manuel de la Borda built a garden of magnificent pools and fountains and, in 1864, Emperor Maximilian and his wife Carlota established a summer residence there. Today, it takes a vivid imagination to recognize the park's faded splendor amid the sometimes non-functional fountains and cracked sidewalks. Unlike the fountains and sidewalks, the flora—mango trees, tropical ferns, ornamental plants, and giant palm trees—have flourished through the years, thus accounting for the garden's heavy, overripe smell. Its modern amenities—an art collection near the entrance, a small theater, and a museum near Emperor Max's old summer home—make this more than just a garden well past its prime. Patchwork rowboats are available for rent (5 pesos per 15min., 10 pesos for ½hr., 15 pesos for 1hr.; park open Tues.-Sun. 10am-5:30pm; admission 5 pesos, students and teachers 2 pesos, free Wed.).

The **Pyramid of Teopanzolco** squats on a glistening green lawn at the center of a public park near the southern end of Teopanzolco, southeast of the market on Guerrero. Strangely deserted and unkempt, the pyramid actually consists of two pyramids, one within the other. The first stairway leads to a ledge, at the bottom of which a second stairway, belonging to the second pyramid, begins. An eerie partial staircase suggests that the new pyramid was unfinished when Cortés arrived. To get to the site from the marketplace or along Morelos, take a taxi (10 pesos) or hop on local bus #10 and ask the driver to let you off at the *pirámide*. If you're in the mood to break in those walking shoes, head north along Morelos (the cathedral will be on your left), turn right on Pericón, and go right on Río Balsas to Teopanzolco (open daily 10am-5pm; admission 10 pesos).

## ENTERTAINMENT AND SEASONAL EVENTS

Cuernavaca's popularity as a vacation spot fuels a fairly glitzy nightlife, and the city's *norteamericano* expatriates, now over 20,000 strong, as well as its plethora of soon-to-be bilingual students from the U.S., lend a north-of-the-border feel to many festivities. Bars in Cuernavaca are modern and highly commercialized, and most clubgoers are dressed to the hilt, heedless of high cover charges and the like. If you're up to it, a night on the town here promises a sleek, sophisticated time. Several of the clubs have live nightly entertainment. Around the *zócalo,* many of the clubs cater to tourists; some have no cover charge but expect patrons to buy drinks.

Discos are typically open from 9 or 10pm to 5am on Friday and Saturday. To deter the fistfights and *broncas* (brawls) that used to plague Cuernavaca's clubs, some now officially admit only male-female couples and require reservations; most, however, do not enforce these business-diminishing rules. The more popular discos in town are not on the *zócalo* but in different *colonias*. Most lie out of walking distance (especially at night) and are best reached by *rutas* or a taxi after 9pm. Most *rutas* end around 10:30pm, and Cuernavaca is nationally notorious for nightly rains. During the wet season, it rains at least an hour and a half without fail during the late afternoon or evening; cabs are your best bet. All the spots listed are familiar to cab drivers. Only Kaova is within walking distance of the *zócalo*. Sometimes lucky students from local language schools get free passes and avoid cover charges.

**Barba Azul,** Prado 10 (tel. 13-19-76). This club with long lines out the door would make Bluebeard shake his "booty." Good lighting and continually hip. A staple of Cuernavacan nightlife, popular with the early-20s, hard-hitting techno crowd. Drinks 15 pesos and up. Cover 50 pesos. Open Fri.-Sat. 10pm-5am.

**Kaova,** Av. Morelos Sur 241 (tel. 18-43-80), 3 blocks south of the cathedral. Rock-dance hybrid. Starts off mellow (i.e. Beatles and Elvis) and turns into a full-fledged dance party later. Senior citizens and college kids alike hit the small dance pit. Large Mexican contingent. No cover. Beer 15 pesos. National drinks 18 pesos and up. Live music Wed. and Sat. nights. Open Wed.-Sat. 9pm-late.

**Zumbale,** Chapultepec 13A (tel. 22-53-43 or 22-53-44), next to Ta'izz. This 2-story salsa club is unbelievable—an indoor waterfall, amazing live music, and some of the best Latin dancing around (tropical, salsa, rumba, merengue)—watch practiced pelvises grind. Don't worry, though—the friendly atmosphere (and copious bar service) encourages gringos to give it a go. Great fun. No cover Thurs. Free open bar 9-10pm. Cover 70 pesos Fri.-Sat. for men, women free. Beer 15 pesos, national drinks 24 pesos. Open Thurs. 9pm-4:30am, Fri.-Sat. 9pm-5am.

If you want to catch a flick for 10-12 pesos, try **Cinema Las Plazas** (tel. 14-07-93), downtown, across from the Jardín Juárez, screening imports and high-quality Mexican films. On Saturday and Sunday, the **market** in the Jardín Juárez specializes in silver jewelry; don't be afraid to bargain. The **Feria de la Primavera** (Festival of Spring) brings parades and costumes for 10 days a year at the vernal equinox (March 21-22).

# ■ Near Cuernavaca

## XOCHICALCO

Ceremonial center, fortress, and trading post rolled into one, **Xochicalco** (Place of the House of Flowers in Náhuatl) is the most impressive archaeological site in the state of Morelos, worth the trip if only for the awesome vistas. Although it was built around 200 BC and lasted to around AD 1100, Xochicalco had its peak between AD 60 and AD 900, just as the civilization at Teotihuacán was dwindling. Apparently, Xochicalco's ruins and central location explain the similarities in ruins as far apart as Teotihuacán and Tula. Besides being a center of Toltec culture, it's also thought that Xochicalco was a Maya outpost, thus explaining its influence on architecture as far south as Central America. Archaeologists speculate that the site may even be the mythical city of **Tamoanchan,** the place where wise men of different cultures, including Maya and Zapotec sages, came to begin the cult of the new god Quetzalcóatl, as well as to synchronize civil and religious calendars.

On the road right before the ruins, a stunning modern sight appears—the speckled green **Museo del Sitio de Xochicalco.** This museum was designed to mimic the ruins, greenery, and lush flora that pervades the area. It succeeds smashingly; inaugurated in April 1996, the museum's beautiful marble tiling and wall frescoes complement the site, and a gorgeous pyramidal motif is carried throughout the museum's skylights, tiling, and structure. Comprehensive exhibits on the site and invaluable brochures on the ruins (5 pesos) make the museum a useful stop before climbing on to the site itself (open Tues.-Sun. 10am-5pm; admission 14 pesos, free for children, students, and on Sun.).

From the museum, a rocky path leads to the ruins. The ruins are best explored in a generally circular manner, starting at the elevated plaza up to the left of the first patch of greenery. On the right side of the first plain, the **Pirámide de las Estelas** (Structure A) and the **Gran Pirámide** (Structure E) just south of it nearly dwarf the three smaller structures on the left. Although you'll want to bound up the pyramids full-speed, hold your horses. Guards (when they're present) are strict about hiking in non-designated areas. Anyway, later on you can scale up the back stairs and see the view. The Gran Pirámide forms the northern boundary of the **Plaza Central,** which can be reached by continuing straight (south) and taking the small slope down to the left. This area was most likely a trading center for the local and regional populations—many ancient roads converge here. Twin pyramids on the east and the west sides of the plaza, labeled **Structure C** and **Structure D,** were used in the worship of the sun, one oriented toward the sunrise, the other toward the sunset. At the center of the Plaza is a carved obelisk that bears two hieroglyphs related to the god Quetzalcóatl. Sadly, the coded inscriptions are faded and hard to see. Still, the lone obelisk is quite a sight—it looks like an alien outpost of the center of some old, obscene ritual. Apparently, by tracing the obelisk's shadow, priests plotted the sun's trajectory over the pyramids.

The southwest corner of this plaza offers a great overhead view of the **Juego de Pelota** (Ballcourt) below. To reach it, walk down the stone steps between Structures C and D. Straight ahead and off to the left lie unexcavated remnants of this sprawling city. Continue down the narrow rocky path directly to the right for the ballcourt.

Many experts believe that this ballcourt was the earliest one built; ballcourts as far south as Guatemala show signs of the heavy influence (a.k.a. virtual plagiarism) of Xochicalco's. In fact, a statue found here bears a remarkable likeness to another found in Copán, Honduras, a remote Maya outpost. All this is an indication of Xochicalco's once-great commercial and cultural scope.

After heading back up the hill to the central plaza, make your way to the base of the **Gran Pirámide** (Structure E). Atop this pyramid rest the remains of an even more ancient structure. Follow the path down to the left (west) and over to the stairway/portico section. This area was used to limit access to the main part of the city in case of invasion, but the design did not work well enough to prevent Xochicalco from falling prey to a revolution.

Past the portico and up two sets of impressive stairways rebuilt in 1994, the **Plaza Ceremonial,** served as the main ceremonial center of the city. As you enter, the top of the Pirámide de las Estelas is accessible and holds a small temple inside, enclosing a huge pit in the center that was the burial site for high priests and a place for ritual offerings. No bones or mangled skeletons are lying around, though. In the center of the plaza is the renowned **Pirámide de la Serpiente Emplumada** (Pyramid of the Plumed Serpent). Haphazardly reconstructed in 1910, it bears carved reliefs of Quetzalcóatl, the great feathered serpent who was a god-hero to a plethora of Indian groups including the Toltecs and the Aztecs. He wasn't just any old water moccassin, oh no—Quetzalcoatl's place in world myth and religion rivals that of Adam and Eve's salacious serpent. In fact, Xochicalco's aforementioned commercial partnership with southern cultures is reflected in the embrace that the plumed serpent Quetzalcóatl bestows upon a priest in an elaborate Maya headdress.

On the rear (west) end of the plaza is the tremendous **Montículo 2,** the highest area of the site, and supposedly the spot where the rulers of Xochicalco lived. The eastern side was intended for daily activities, while the west end was exclusively ceremonial. Exit the Plaza Ceremonial on the north side and head west down the slope to the **Hall of the Polichrome Altar,** where a colored altar rests beneath an authentic reconstruction of the roofing used by the Toltecs. Farther down is a cistern used for water storage, a sauna used for pre-game initiation rites, and **Teotlachtli,** the northern ballcourt. Here, two massive rings of rock are attached in the middle, unlike most ballcourts in Mesoamerica, which have only one ring. Teams competed for the privilege of being sacrificed atop the Pyramid of Quetzalcóatl, a true honor and a sign of good sportsmanship (they just don't make ballplayers like they used to). Nearby, the foundations remain of the **Calmecac,** the palace in which Toltec and Aztec priests underwent training and initiation.

Continue west along the weed-ridden path, around the back of the base of Montículo 2 until you reach a large stone amalgamation. A small opening in the corner (with steps leading up) allows access to the stuccoed interior of the underground **Observatorio,** where ancient astronomers followed the cosmos. On summer solstices, Aztec sages and stargazers peered through a shaft in the ceiling to trace the path of the sun; by so doing, they hoped to verify and adjust the Aztec calendar. A guide gives periodic presentations in Spanish as soon as a good-sized group has assembled. (Observatory open 11am-2pm.)

**Getting There:** From Cuernavaca, **Flecha Roja** runs buses directly to Xochicalco (every hr., 9am-5pm, 7.50 pesos). Alternatively, snag a bus to Miacatlán or Ixtapan de la Sal from the **Autos Pullman** station at Abasolo and Netzahualcóyotl, one block south of the cathedral (6.50 pesos). Ask the driver to drop you off at the *crucero de Xochicalco*. **Taxis** wait at the *crucero* and, for 7 pesos, will take you to the site. Otherwise, the uphill walk to the site (4km) will take about an hour. Because of the steep inclines and merciless sun, be prepared. Bring a hat, a tank top, or some water. Catch a bus back at the *crucero* or hail a nearby taxi and ask to go to the *caseta* (2 pesos), a nearby bus stop. Buses go back every half-hour or so. Taxis sometimes sit at the site entrance, but it may be smart to ask a driver to pick you up at a specified time.

## TEPOZTLÁN

In northern Morelos, the quiet *pueblo* of Tepoztlán occupies one of the state's more scenic and impenetrable sites—towering cliffs form a natural fortress that allows entrance only from the south. Proceeding along Rte. 95D toward Tepoztlán, keep your eyes peeled for **Popocatépetl** and **Ixtaccíhuatl,** the two massive volcanoes which surge from the ground (see p. 402). The cobbled *indígena* village preserves a colonial feel amid growing modernization such as pool maintenance and satellite television stores, and some indigenous people still speak Náhuatl. As of late, this lovely language has been revived. Many of Tepoztlán's youth are learning to speak it, even in Tepoztlán's schools. On Sundays, the *zócalo* comes alive with vibrant market activity. During the rest of the week, however, the town is quieter. Perched on a peak 360m above the village are the archaeological sites for which the town is famous. The thin air may leave you breathless and thirsty, so prepare accordingly.

The valley of Tepoztlán is charged with the myth, legend, and magic of ages gone by. It is thought that the god-hero of the Toltecs (and the Aztecs, and almost every other pre-Hispanic *indígena* group), Quetzalcóatl, was born here about 1200 years ago. Celebrations still take place every September 8, when the *pulque* flows and the dance floor fills in honor of Tepozécatl. *Los chinelos*—colorfully attired folk dancers—may invite you to join their traditional dance, *el salto.* Don't be shy; after pounding a couple of *pulques,* you'll be weeping cactus tears and dying to dance.

Tepoztlán's main draw is the **Pirámide del Tepozteco,** perched on the northern ridge of the cliffs that rise above one end of town, about 3km above the valley. Some say the pyramid was a Tlahuica observatory and defense post for the valley, while others swear it served as an Aztec sacrificial temple. The 10m-tall structure has a porch inscribed with barely-discernible Tlahuica glyphs. To reach the pyramid, follow Av. 5 de Mayo north out of town (passing the *zócalo* on your right) until you reach its end. The hour-long climb is steep and strenuous, but it's made bearable by the cooling shade of trees. If you intend to climb, equip yourself with appropriate footwear, water, and spirit. If you can't make it all the way up, don't worry—the view is spectacular from everywhere on the hill. Sunday excursions offer a fabulous people-watching experience; whole families, from newborn to great-grandfather, don their Sunday best and hike up this holy hill. Don't be surprised to see an eight-year-old carrying an ice chest overtake you (open Tues.-Sun. 10am-4:30pm; admission 10 pesos, free Sun. and for children under 13).

The **Museo de Arte Prehispánico** (more commonly known as the **Museo Carlos Pellicer**), at the rear of Capilla Asunción, holds a collection donated to the city by none other than the nationally renowned poet Carlos Pellicer. The impressive display includes pottery pieces and clay figures of Olmec, Zapotec, Maya, Totonac, and Aztec origin, as well as many objects from Teotihuacán (open Tues.-Sun. 10am-6pm; admission 3 pesos, students and teachers with ID 1.50 pesos).

Because of its natural beauty, vernal climate, and proximity to Mexico City, the area around Tepoztlán attracts an ever-growing population of wealthy *norteamericanos.* While the town and surrounding area are still lovely, prices are incredibly steep. Tepoztlán lacks moderately-priced anything—forget budget accommodations. Though expensive, perhaps your best bet is **Casa Iccemanyan,** Calle de Olvido 26 (tel. 5-08-99 or 5-00-96), on the first cross-street after the Pullman de Morelos station, all the way down the hill. This joint offers six bungalows for extended stays and gives travelers studying at neighboring language schools a chance to practice their skills with a Mexican family. Well-maintained and decorated rooms come with clean bathrooms and lots of privacy. Beautiful pool, lawn, and Tepozteco vistas are a plus (singles US$25; doubles US$46; rates include 3 meals and are negotiable).

**Getting There:** From Cuernavaca, **Ometochtli** buses leave from the market (6 pesos direct in the purple-and-green buses, 3.40 pesos by *pesero*). If you arrive at the Ometochtli depot, follow the main road; it will curve to become Av. 5 de Mayo. From Mexico City, take a **Pullman de Morelos** bus from the Tasqueña terminal (every ½hr.,

6am-10pm, 1¼hr., 21 pesos). In Tepoztlán, buses arrive and depart from the *zócalo,* close to the market, or from the bus depot just outside town.

## MALINALCO

**Malinalco's** Aztec ruins are one of four monolithic pyramids in the world—the other three are in India, Jordan, and Egypt. Malinalco was the sacred ground for the rituals that officially transformed an Aztec youth into a *guerrero tigre* or *guerrero águila* (tiger or eagle warrior). Because of the importance of these rituals and the ground they were performed on, the area was terraced and completely fortified from the outside. On the open circular stone platform—the first structure on the right as you enter—prisoners were bound to a pole with only arms left free and made to wrestle the recently initiated warriors. If the prisoner won consecutive bouts with two *águila* and two *tigre* warriors, he was matched against a left-hander. If the prisoner defeated the lefty, he was granted freedom. Defeat, on the other hand, had more unpleasant consequences; the small rectangular basin in front of the entryway to the pyramid was used to hold the prisoner's blood after his ritual sacrifice. Behind the pyramid, the bodies of the sacrificed were burned to ashes on the oval bed of rock.

The **Templo de la Iniciación** (Temple of the Initiation) for eagle and tiger warriors is a massive monolithic structure. All of its statues, rooms, and facades were carved from one giant slab of stone, and it was originally painted a brilliant crimson. To the right of the Templo de la Iniciación stand the remains of a *temascal,* an ancient predecessor to the sauna.

Though Malinalco has no tourist office, the **Casa de Cultura de Malinalco,** on one corner of the *zócalo,* can help you find the ruins and just about anything else you might need (open Mon.-Sat. 9am-2pm and 4-7pm, Sun. 10am-1pm).

**Getting There:** Malinalco is easily accessible from Cuernavaca, Mexico City, or Toluca. To get there, take a bus to **Chalma.** Once there, hail a taxi to Malinalco (20min., 20 pesos, 5 pesos if shared). To get to the ruins from the *zócalo,* follow the blue pyramid signs along Guerrero and go straight. Take a left on Milgar, a right at the next blue arrow, and another right at the blue sign that appears to lead visitors into someone's driveway (open Tues.-Sun. 10am-4:30pm; admission 16 pesos, free for students with ID and for all on Sun.).

# TLAXCALA

## ■ Tlaxcala

The approach to the capital of Mexico's smallest state is filled with vistas of cornfields, children riding on the backs of burros, and beautifully tiled churches. Although it might seem like things couldn't get any prettier, downtown Tlaxcala exceeds all expectations. Carefully maintained buildings and well-tended flowerbeds make for a picture-perfect *zócalo.* A symphony in shades of deep orange and red, the streets of the downtown area demonstrate a unique appreciation for aesthetic detail.

The people of Tlaxcala have a long history of welcoming foreigners. After being colonized by the Aztecs, the people of the Tlaxcalan Federation willingly allied themselves with Cortés and demonstrated such fierce loyalty in battle that they were recognized by Charles V. Today, *tlaxcalteños* limit their violent urges to the raising of bulls for fights throughout Mexico. Frequent regional fairs showcase artisans who weave *sarapes* or prepare dishes of maize. Although Tlaxcala is virtually untouristed by *norteamericanos,* weekenders flock here by the dozens, trading the noise and congestion of D.F. or Puebla for the alluring cafes along Tlaxcala's *zócalo* and safe, tree-lined streets. The city is also a useful base for visiting the archaeological sites of **Cacaxtla** and **Xochiténcatl.**

## ORIENTATION

Most services can be found in and around **Plaza de la Constitución,** the *zócalo,* and **Plaza Xicoténcatl,** diagonally adjacent to it. You'll know you're there when you see the blue-and-white tiled dome of the orange **Parroquia de San José.** To get there from the bus station, exit through the glass doors to a swarm of idling *colectivos.* Those facing to the right go to the downtown area, the market, and finally the hotel district on the northern edge of the city (2 pesos). To return to the bus station from the city center, take a "Central" *colectivo* from the market at 20 de Noviembre and Alonso Escalona, or flag it down behind San José at 20 de Noviembre and 1 de Mayo.

Facing the back of the church, the street behind you is **20 de Noviembre** and the street on the left is **Lardizábal.** Going around the church to the right will bring the entrance to the *zócalo* into view. The **Palacio de Gobierno** takes up the whole north side of the *zócalo* and will be on your left. At the end of the Palacio del Gobierno, at the corner of the *zócalo,* **Av. Benito Juárez** peels off to the left. After four blocks, Juárez veers right and becomes **Av. Guillermo Valle.** Several hotels are on the northern edge of town, where Guillermo Valle angles to the right and becomes **Blvd. Revolución.** To get there, catch a "Santa Ana" *colectivo* at 20 de Noviembre, three blocks from the *zócalo,* behind San José (2 pesos); it's a 40-minute walk from the *zócalo.*

## PRACTICAL INFORMATION

**Tourist Office:** Av. Benito Juárez 18 (tel. 2-00-27), at the intersection with Lardizábal. The *colectivo* from the bus station will drop you off on 20 de Nov. behind San José. A gold mine of information from a friendly, English-speaking staff. Sat. and Sun. they sponsor organized tours of the most popular sites (15 pesos). Open Mon.-Fri. 9am-7pm, Sat.-Sun. and holidays 10am-6pm.

**Currency Exchange: Banamex,** Plaza Xicoténcatl 8 (tel. 2-31-44) and **Banca Serfín,** Av. Independencia 4 (tel. 2-08-42), both in Plaza Xicoténcatl, have 24hr. **ATMs.** Open Mon.-Fri. 9am-2pm. Nearby, **Centro de Cambio Tlaxcala,** Av. Independencia at the corner of Calle Guerrero (tel. 2-90-85), buys or sells dollars in cash, money order, or traveler's checks. Open Mon.-Fri. 9am-4pm.

**Telephones: LADATELs** under the arches along the *zócalo.* Coin-operated phones in front of and behind **Parroquia de San José,** northwest of the *zócalo.*

**Fax: Telecomm,** Porfirio Díaz 6 (tel. 2-00-47), behind the post office. Telegraph service as well. Open Mon.-Fri. 8am-6pm, Sat.-Sun. 9am-12pm.

**Buses:** From the **Central Camionera, Autotransportes Tlaxcala** (tel. 2-02-17) runs to Mexico City (every 20min., 6am-8:30pm, 2hr., 34 pesos) and Veracruz, stopping in Xalapa (10:30am and 3:30pm, 6hr., 37 and 58 pesos). **Autotransportes México-Texcoco** has similar 1st-class service to Mexico City. **Flecha Azul** buses run to Puebla (every 5min., 5:45am-10pm, 45min., 6 pesos).

**Cultural Center: Palacio de la Cultura,** Av. Benito Juárez 62 (tel. 2-39-69), 4 blocks from the *zócalo* at the corner of Av. Justo Sierra. Announces and sometimes stages concerts, exhibits, and performances all over town. Open daily 10am-6pm.

**Markets:** The entire street of **Alonso Escalona** teems with *mercado* activity. From San José, cross to Lira y Ortega and walk 3 blocks, keeping the church behind you. The vendors spill outside onto Sánchez Piedras. Open daily 8am-8pm. **Gigante** is a behemoth of a supermarket on Blvd. Guillermo Valle, in the shopping center on the corner of Arévalo Vera. Open daily 8am-8pm.

**Laundromat: Lavandería de Autoservicio Acuario,** Lira y Ortega 3 (tel. 1-62-04). Go north from the *zócalo,* make an immediate left on Lardizábal, then take the first right on Lira y Ortega. Self-service 14 pesos, full service 15 pesos, 1hr. service with home delivery 30 pesos. Open Mon.-Sat. 9:30am-7:30pm.

**Red Cross:** Allende Nte. 48 (tel. 2-09-20). Go 2 blocks behind San José to Av. Ignacio Allende, then turn left and continue 1½ blocks past Muñoz Camargo. 24hr. walk-in emergency service. No English spoken.

**Pharmacy: Farmacia Ocotlán,** Av. Juárez on the corner of Guridi y Alcocer (tel. 2-04-50). Open 9am-7pm.

**Hospital: Hospital General,** Jardín de la Corregidora 1 (tel. 2-00-30, 2-03-57, or 2-35-55), 4½ blocks from the *zócalo* down Av. Muñoz Camargo, past the post office. No

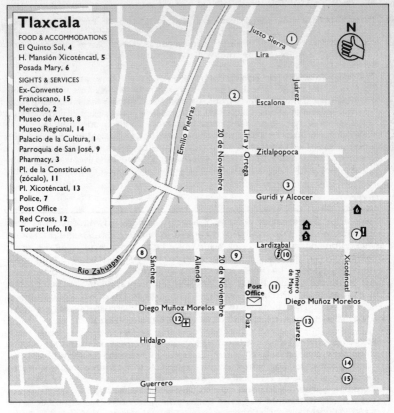

Tlaxcala

FOOD & ACCOMMODATIONS
El Quinto Sol, 4
H. Mansión Xicoténcatl, 5
Posada Mary, 6

SIGHTS & SERVICES
Ex-Convento
Franciscano, 15
Mercado, 2
Museo de Artes, 8
Museo Regional, 14
Palacio de la Cultura, 1
Parroquia de San José, 9
Pharmacy, 3
Pl. de la Constitución
(zócalo), 11
Pl. Xicoténcatl, 13
Police, 7
Post Office
Red Cross, 12
Tourist Info, 10

English spoken. Open 24hr. **IMSS,** Blvd. Guillermo Valle (tel. 2-34-00 or 2-34-22), across the street from the stadium. Take Av. Juárez from the *zócalo* until it turns into Blvd. G. Valle; the hospital is right after the Nestlé factory. Open 24hr.

**Police:** On Av. Lardizábal (tel. 2-10-79 or 2-07-35), 1 block past the tourist office, at the corner with Calle Xicoténcatl. Open daily 24hr.

**Post Office:** Plaza de la Constitución 20 (tel. 2-00-04), on the corner with Av. Muñoz Camargo. Open Mon.-Fri. 8am-8pm, Sat. 9am-1pm. **Postal Code:** 90000.

**Phone Code:** 246.

## ACCOMMODATIONS

There are few good budget accommodations in Tlaxcala. Establishments are either downtown near most sights and services, or in the hotel district on the northern edge of the city and accessible via the "Santa Ana" *colectivo.*

**Hotel Mansión Xicoténcatl,** Av. Juárez 15 (tel. 2-19-00), diagonally across from the tourist office. Calling this hotel a mansion is definitely a stretch. The location and price are right, however, and dark but clean rooms hold polyester-sheeted beds. Try to get a room with a window, as the naked bulb that provides light makes things a little grim. Singles 55 pesos, doubles 65 pesos.

**Posada Mary,** Xicoténcatl 19. From the tourist office, head away from the church on Lardizábal and take the first left; it's a ½ block away on the right. Their 8 small, moderately clean rooms are undergoing a slow but needed renovation. A restaurant is connected to the hotel. Ring bell persistently if locked. Private baths. Singles 50 pesos, doubles 60 pesos.

**Hotel Plaza Tlaxcala,** Blvd. Revolución 6 (tel. 2-78-52). Take the "Santa Ana" *colectivo* from the bus station or market (1.50 pesos). Recently renovated rooms in a pleasant 3-story hotel with a small garden and play area. Single rooms feature a huge king-sized bed. Private bath, wall-to-wall carpeting, and cable TV. Singles 80 pesos, doubles 90 pesos.

**El Centro Vacacional de Trinidad** (tel. 9-12-46). Located 15min. away from Tlaxcala city in Santa Cruz de Tlaxcala (4 pesos by *combi*), this resort offers an escape from typical sight-seeing. A former textile factory, the **Centro Vacacional** is a government-owned recreation facility. With a huge indoor pool, basketball and volleyball courts, and extensive grounds, there is no lack of activity. Also available for an extra fee: rowboats on 2 man-made lakes, horseback riding, and tennis courts. This budget Club Med caters mostly to Mexican families on vacation, though there are some business groups on retreats. Telephone, TV, and 24hr. hot water. Doubles 165 pesos, quads 250 pesos. Meal plan 90 pesos for 3 meals. Camping also available (adults 20 pesos, children 10 pesos).

## FOOD

Regional specialties include *pollo en xoma* (chicken stuffed with fruits and other meats), *barbacoa en mixiote* (meat cooked in *maguey* leaves), and *pulque,* an ancient, unrefined alcoholic drink made from the *maguey* cactus. You can either drink *pulque* straight, eat it with your chicken, or try *pulque verde,* a drink made with honeywater, *yerba buena* (spearmint), and lemon juice. The touristy restaurants on the *zócalo* are cheaper on weekday afternoons, when they cater to the lunch crowd rather than to tourists. Beware of *"comida típica"*—it is often a pricey journey into culinary mediocrity. There are good, inexpensive places along Av. Juárez, including the **market** on 20 de Noviembre at Alonso Escalona.

**El Quinto Sol** (tel. 2-49-28), on Av. Juárez diagonally across from the tourist office. A popular vegetarian joint full of tempting fruits to match the orange walls outside. Scrumptious breakfasts bring sunshine to the table in the form of freshly squeezed orange juice, yogurt, eggs, and coffee (14-18 pesos). Cheese or soybeef *tortas* 5-7 pesos; specialty cure-all juices 6 pesos. Open Mon.-Sat. 8am-8pm.

**Los Portales Restaurant-Bar,** Plaza Constitución 8 (tel. 2-54-19), on the side of the *zócalo* under the arches. Dapper waiters serve food *al fresco. Antojitos* 8-14 pesos, spaghetti 17-20 pesos, sandwiches 10-16 pesos, but the main attraction is the Parisian-cafe ambience. Open Mon.-Fri. 7am-11pm, Sat.-Sun. 24hr. After the sun goes down, *mariachis* prowl the arcade; if you're lucky, you'll get to hear a group of locals belting out their favorites.

## SIGHTS

On the north side of the *zócalo,* the 16th-century **Palacio de Gobierno** houses murals that illustrate the rich history of the city and the country with the vivid colors of Van Gogh and the controlled chaos of *Where's Waldo* (open daily 8am-8pm). On the northwest corner of the *zócalo* stands the **Palacio de la Justicia,** which was originally built in the 16th century as the Capilla Real de Indias to honor the Tlaxcaltecas who had served as Cortés's allies in the conquest of the Aztecs. Just beyond the northwest corner of the *zócalo* stands the 17th-century Baroque **Parroquia de San José.** While its interior is unremarkable, its peach-orange exterior and *mudéjar*-tiled dome gracefully punctuate the Tlaxcala sky. Cutting back along the *zócalo* under the arches and exiting its corner, you'll come to the **Plaza Xicoténcatl.** On weekends, the plaza is sometimes inhabited by musicians or a small fair.

At the opposite corner of the *zócalo,* a cobblestone way leads about 200m up a small hill to the cathedral, the **Ex-Convento Franciscano de la Asunción,** one of the most beautiful structures in 16th-century New Spain. *Mudéjar* woodwork and gilded eight-pointed stars accent the dark wooden rafters of the choir loft and ceiling. In the chapel at the end of the nave and on the right stands the stone baptismal font purportedly used to baptize the leaders of the Tlaxcalan Federation when they allied themselves with Cortés. Next door to the church is the **Museo Regional de Tlaxcala** (tel. 2-02-62), which covers pre-Hispanic and colonial cultures (open Tues.-Sun. 10am-5pm; admission 7 pesos, free Sun. and holidays).

The Ex-Convento shares the colonial limelight with the **Basílica de la Virgen de Ocotlán,** one of the masterpieces of the late Baroque Mexican style known as Churrigueresque. To get there, take an "Ocotlán" *colectivo* (1.50 pesos). It stops right in front of the church, where it waits to go back into town. To hike there, take a right on Av. Benito Juárez, head one block past the tourist office, and hang another right on Guridi y Alcocer. When the road forks, follow it up the hill to the left. The road climbs to the small **Capilla del Pocito de Agua Santa,** where it becomes a cobblestone street with a staircase alongside; the stairs lead directly to the square of the church. There, you'll be blinded by the brilliant white stucco facade, populated by figures of militant archangels and capped by a conch shell in stucco along its upper edge. The maritime theme is repeated in the interior, where golden conch shells top the pilasters and another giant shell frames the end of the nave. Its lines lead the eye up to the presbyter, which explodes in Churrigueresque splendor. The Virgin's *camarín* is a single piece that took 25 years to make. She allegedly appeared on this site in 1541, and is now the patroness of Tlaxcala.

On the other side of town is the **Museo de Artes y Tradiciones Populares** (tel. 2-23-37), where craftspersons from around the region demonstrate how their trades. The exhibits include a working indigenous steam bath (not for use by visitors), a loom, a demonstration of how *pulque* is made, and an exhibit of traditional carnival masks with eyes that blink. Many of these items can be bought at substantially inflated prices from the adjoining gift shop or from the artists themselves. To get there, go west on Lardizábal until it ends at Blvd. Mariano Sánchez, about four blocks from the tourist office. The museum is across the street on the left (open Tues.-Sun. 10am-6pm; admission 6 pesos, students 4 pesos).

For more indigenous beauty without the tourist packaging, the **Jardín Botánico de Tizatlán** (tel. 2-65-46) delivers Mexican plants in an otherworldly setting. From the hotel district on Blvd. Revolución, turn left at Camino Real before the brick bridge passes over the road. No bikes, balls, radios, or beer are allowed in this pastoral paradise. The rocky paths meander across a stagnant creek to reveal a tucked-away greenhouse (open daily 6am-11pm; free).

## ENTERTAINMENT

Tlaxcala has become something of a nightspot, at least on weekends. **Royal Adler's Disco,** Blvd. Revolución 4 (tel. 2-14-99), at the Hotel Jeroc, plays current hits (cover 15 pesos; open Fri.-Sat. 10pm-3am). Another local hotspot is **La Valentina,** 1 de Mayo 9 (tel. 2-64-57), a disco bar just two blocks west of the *zócalo* (cover 15 pesos; open Mon.-Wed. noon-7pm, Thurs.-Sat. 9pm-3am). Many of the restaurants and bars in the arcades feature live music on weekend nights as well. On weekdays, finding entertainment becomes a more difficult task, since much of the city shuts down by 10:30pm. Check the tourist office for concerts. **Cinevas,** at Guillermo Valle 113 and Calle de Bosque 1 (tel. 2-35-44), and **Cinema Tlaxcala** (tel. 2-19-62), on the south side of the *zócalo* across the street from the post office, show first-run American movies (10 pesos). It's fairly safe to walk the streets at night in Tlaxcala. If you do feel uncomfortable walking downtown after dark, hail one of the cabs at San José church.

# ■ Near Tlaxcala

## CACAXTLA AND XOCHITÉNCATL

The best preserved and best presented of the archaeological sites in the state are the hilltop ruins of **Cacaxtla,** 19km southwest of Tlaxcala. The Olmecas-Xicalancas, who once dominated the southwest corner of Tlaxcala State and most of the Puebla Valley, built and expanded the city between AD 600 and 750. Cacaxtla was abandoned by AD 1000, and its inhabitants were finally driven from the area by Toltec-Chichimec invaders in 1168. The approach to the site is marked by the walls and moats that protected the Olmec-Xicalancan inhabitants from their enemies. Excavation began at Cacaxtla in 1975, and the area is now reconstructed as the ceremonial center it once was.

Two discoveries distinguish this site from others. One is a **latticework window** on the west side, opposite the entrance. The window is the only one of its kind in any of Mexico's archaeological sites. It was produced by surrounding a latticework of twigs and branches with mud and stucco. Cacaxtla's other chief attraction is a series of murals scattered about the site, considered some of the best-preserved pre-Hispanic paintings in Mesoamerica. The largest of them, the **Battle Mural,** depicts a historical-mythological battle in which an army dressed in jaguar skins crushes the skulls of an army dressed as birds. It is believed to depict part of the culture's foundational mythology. The murals appear in all the glory of their original, mineral-based colors, which are still amazingly bright.

Beyond the entrance on the right is a museum that showcases some of the ceramics and fertility figures unearthed here. From the small museum, a dirt path leads towards the pyramid. Just past a small secondary pyramid is the staircase that goes up to the site by way of the **Gran Basamento,** the thick platform upon which the center was built. The pyramid is covered by the world's second-largest archaeological roof in order to prevent the erosion of the adobe structures. It makes for a refreshingly cool viewing experience. Once upstairs, visitors move clockwise around the excavations of ceremonial courtyards, temples, tombs, and what appears to have been a palace. Underneath the ruins, archaeologists have found the remains of 200 children, sacrificed during the final stages of construction.

From the Battle Mural, the official circuit takes you to an area whose bland name, **Building A,** belies its beauty. Five of the site's murals stand together, united by color and imagery into a symbolic unit. The leftmost mural depicts the god Quetzalcóatl and a human figure in jaguar skins, while the rightmost one shows a bird-man surrounded by symbols of rain god Tlaloc. Guides are available for 30 pesos per person, with reduced rates for large groups, but few speak English (open Tues.-Sun. 10am-4:30pm; admission 14 pesos; videocamera 25 pesos; free Sun.).

A ticket also offers admission to **Xochiténcatl,** the pyramid on the adjacent hill. This site features four pyramids, the largest of which is actually a pyramid on top of a pyramid. Civilization at Xochiténcatl predates Cacaxtla by several hundred years. In AD 300, the inhabitants of Xochiténcatl were conquered by the Olmecas-Xicalancas, who also took up residence at Cacaxtla. Interesting finds include a large snake sculpture and several large basalt founts. These founts are doubly impressive considering that they were made from a single large piece of stone without any steel tools. The site also offers a spectacular view of the surrounding volcanos: **Popocatépetel, Ixtac-cíhuatl,** and **La Malinche.** On clear days the Puebla valley is also visible.

There isn't really any public transportation that runs between Cacaxtla and Xochitécatl; however, it is only a 1.5km (½hr.) walk to climb up to Xochiténcatl. Follow the signs around the Cacaxtla pyramid to the path that leads up the hill.

**Getting There:** From Tlaxcala, *colectivos* labeled "Texoloc-Tlaxcala" and buses marked "Nativitas" leave from the bus plaza on 20 de Noviembre next to the market or along 20 de Noviembre behind San José. Ask whether the bus goes to Cacaxtla. Some go to the town San Miguel del Milagro (San Miguelito) at the base of the site; others travel past the main entrance (40min., 4.50 pesos). If dropped off in the town, walk up the windy road, following the signs to the entrance. To return to Tlaxcala, walk downhill from the ticket booth and turn right to go down to San Martín. *Colectivos* going right go to Xochiténcatl; across the street "Tlaxcala" *colectivos* return to the bus plaza next to the market (4.50 pesos). The tourist office offers guided trips to the two zones every Sunday for 15 pesos. The trip includes transportation and usually an English-speaking guide.

# PUEBLA

## ■ Puebla

A strategic wartime location throughout history and witness to such notable moments as the 5 de Mayo defeat of the French, Puebla has blossomed from a stopover between Veracruz and D.F. into an incredibly livable urban center for nearly two million inhabitants. Despite a steady flow of foreign visitors, *poblanos* have been careful not to lose their identity. The city has combined its splendid history with a dynamic present in a thoughtful and engaging manner. Gilt churches and trendy clothing stores share the same cobbled streets, and those tired of vying for bargains with the youngish shopping crowd can relax with the older generations in the shady *zócalo*. Although the tour buses line up alongside the cathedral, Puebla remains a vibrant city with a great deal of integrity in the face of a sizeable tourist industry.

According to legend, the angels in Puebla de los Ángeles (the city's full name) came from the dreaming mind of Don Julian Garcés, the Bishop of Tlaxcala. In a vision, he saw a beautiful field next to a sparkling river. Angels descended from the sky, planted stakes, and stretched cords for the streets of a new city. While hiking the next day, the Bishop recognized the land of his dreams and immediately erected the altar from which Fray Toribiode Benavente delivered Mexico's first Catholic mass in 1531. Puebla grew into a formidable fortress of Catholicism, commissioning more than 60 churches over the course of colonization.

Besides the trademark churches, the city has an exquisite culinary tradition that includes delicious *dulces* (candies) and *mole poblano,* a thick, dark sauce made with chocolate and chiles, among many other ingredients, and typically served over chicken, turkey, or enchiladas. While the angels may choke on the exhaust fumes and balk at the Kentucky Fried Chicken, they still smile down on amorous couples in the *zócalo,* foreign students exercising their new-found language skills at the discos, and citizens seeking redress from the state bureaucracy.

### ORIENTATION

Puebla, capital of the Puebla state, is connected through an extensive highway network to Mexico City (125km northwest along Rte. 150), Oaxaca (Rtes. 190, 125, or 131), Tlaxcala (Rte. 119), Veracruz (Rte. 150), and countless other cities. All **bus** companies operate out of the CAPU (Central de Autobuses Puebla) on Blvd. Norte and Tlaxcala, in the northwest corner of the city.

The *avenidas* and *calles* of Puebla form a near-perfect grid, with the northwest corner of the *zócalo* in the center. Everything changes names at that point: the main north-south street is called **5 de Mayo** north of it and **16 de Septiembre** south of it; the main east-west drag is **Avenida Reforma** to the west, and **Avenida Máximo Ávila Camacho** to the east. *Avenidas* run east-west and are designated either *Poniente* (*Pte.,* west) or *Oriente* (*Ote.,* east), depending on where they lie with respect to that intersection. Similarly, *calles* run north-south and are labeled *Norte* or *Sur* with respect to the critical point. Numerical addresses correspond to the order of the block away from the city center. For example, 4 Ote. 212 is located on the second block of the street, in the section bounded by Calle 2 Norte and Calle 4 Norte. On the following block away from the center, addresses will be in the 400s.

Official yellow **taxis** labeled *taxis controlados* will take you to the *zócalo* from the bus station for 12 pesos (14 pesos at night). If traveling with an independent *taxista,* set a price before getting in and don't be shy about haggling. Cabs from the train station to the *zócalo* run about 8 pesos. **Municipal buses** and *micros* or *combis,* white Volkswagen vans that operate like buses, cost 1.80 pesos. Anything labeled "Centro" should take you close to the *zócalo*. On Calle 9 Nte.-Sur you can catch buses to the bus station (marked "CAPU"), or to the train station (marked *"Estación Nueva Popular"*). CAPU buses also run along Av. Héroes de 5 de Mayo.

## PRACTICAL INFORMATION

**Tourist Office: State Office,** Av. 5 Ote. 3 (tel. 46-12-85 or 46-20-44), facing the cathedral's southern side, 1 block from the *zócalo*. Follow the blue signs with a white question mark to enjoy free maps, a monthly guide to cultural events in Puebla, and an interactive bilingual video guide to cities all over Mexico. Open Mon.-Sat. 9am-8:30pm, Sun. 9am-2pm. There is also a **booth** at the bus station.

**Currency Exchange:** Banks line Av. Reforma and Av. 16 de Septiembre around the *centro*. **Bital,** Reforma 126 (tel. 46-40-44), is blessed with a 24hr. **ATM** and will change money from 9am-6:30pm. *Casas de cambio* offer slightly better rates and cluster in the Zona Esmeralda along Av. Juárez further away from the *zócalo*. Try **Casa de Cambio Puebla,** Av. 29 Sur. 316-A at Juárez (tel. 48-01-99). Open Mon.-Fri. 9am-6pm.

**American Express:** Díaz Ordaz 6A Sur #2914, Suite 301 (tel. 40-30-18, 40-33-08, or 40-32-85), in the Plaza Dorada. Best bet for cashing and replacing AmEx checks; holds client mail for 10 days. Open Mon.-Fri. 9am-6pm.

**Telephones: LADATELs** are easy to find along 5 de Mayo and around the *zócalo*.

**Fax: Telecomm,** 16 de Septiembre 504 (tel. 32-17-79), just south of the post office. Telegrams too. Open Mon.-Fri. 9am-6pm, Sat. 9am-1pm; **money orders** Mon.-Fri. 9am-noon.

**Airport:** Tel. 32-00-32. In **Huejotzingo,** 22km away. Regional airlines fly to Guadalajara, Monterrey, and Tijuana.

**Buses: CAPU** (Central de Autobuses Puebla), at Blvd. Norte and Tlaxcala (tel. 49-72-11), in the northwest corner of the city. **ADO** (tel. 30-40-00), 1st class to Cancún (11:45am, 24hr., 419 pesos), Xalapa (every 2hr., 6:45am-9:15pm, 3hr., 47 pesos), Mérida (9:05pm, 22hr., 352 pesos), Mexico City (Tues.-Thurs. every 10min., Fri.-Mon. every 5min., 5am-midnight, 2hr., 38 pesos), Oaxaca (2 per day, 4hr., 113 pesos), Veracruz (5 per day, 4½hr., 98 pesos), and many other destinations. **Cristóbal Colón** (tel. 49-75-68), to Huatulco (9:45pm, 9hr., 181 pesos), Puerto Escondido (9:45pm, 10hr., 198 pesos), and Tehuantepec (9:45pm, 11hr., 177 pesos). **Estrella Roja** (tel. 49-70-99), 1st class to Mexico City (every 15min., 5am-9pm, 2hr., 44 pesos). **Estrella Blanca** (tel. 40-76-96), 1st class to Acapulco (5 per day, 7hr., 165 pesos); Chilpancingo (10:30am and 12:30pm, 6hr., 122 pesos), and Taxco (8am, 5hr., 60 pesos); Cuernavaca (2 per day, 32 pesos). **Estrella de Oro** (tel. 46-14-62), to Cuernavaca (every hr., 6am-8pm, 3¼hr., 28 pesos); Huejotzingo (5 per day, 45min., 6.50 pesos). **Flecha Azul** (tel. 49-73-55), to Tlaxcala (every 10min., 4:40am-10pm, 45min., 5 pesos).

**Trains: Estación La Unión,** more commonly known as **Estación Nueva,** Av. 70 Pte. and Calle 9 Nte. (tel. 20-16-64 for ticket info, 20-02-79 for general info). Just about the only tolerable route is to Oaxaca (2nd class 6am and midnight, 25 pesos; 1st class midnight, 44 pesos; both take 12-13hr.).

**Markets: Mercados** along 5 de Mayo, 1 block north of the *zócalo*, and along Av. 10 Pte. If you seek A/C and order, head for **Gigante,** at 4 Nte. and Blvd. Héroes del 5 de Mayo, to the north of the Templo de San Francisco. Open daily 9am-9pm. Also try **Comercial Mexicana,** Calle 5 Sur and Av. 19 Pte., by the large pelican sign. Open daily 8am-10pm.

**English Bookstore: Sanborn's,** Av. 2 Ote. 6 (tel. 42-39-61). News magazines and novels of the check-out stand variety. Open daily 7am-11pm.

**Laundromat: Lavandería Roly,** Calle 7 Nte. 404 (tel. 32-93-07). 14 pesos for 3kg self-service. Open Mon.-Sat. 8am-8pm, Sun. 8am-1pm.

**Red Cross:** At 20 Ote. and 10 Nte. (tel. 35-80-40). 24hr. ambulance service. Some English spoken.

**Pharmacies: Farmacias del Ahorro,** on the corner of Av. 2 Ote. and Calle 2 Nte. (tel. 31-33-83). Open daily 7am-11pm. **Sanborn's** also has a pharmacy where some English is spoken. Open Mon.-Fri. 7am-11pm, Sat.-Sun. 7am-1pm.

**Hospital: Hospital UPAEP,** Av. 5 Pte. 715 (tel. 46-60-99 and 32-91-51). **Hospital Universitario,** Calle 13 Sur at Av. 25 Pte. (tel. 43-13-77), 10 blocks south and 7 blocks west of the *zócalo*. 24hr. emergency service. Some English spoken.

**Emergency:** Tel. 06. Also try the **Policía Auxiliar** (tel. 88-18-63). Open 24hr.

**Police: Dirección de Policía,** 9 Ote. and 16 Sur. (tel. 32-22-23 or 32-22-22).

CENTRAL MEXICO

## Puebla

Hotel Avenida, 5
Hotel Imperial, 1
Hotel Teresita, 2
Hotel Victoria, 3
Las Chinas de Puebla, 7
Puente de Ovando, 6
Restaurant El Vegetariano, 4
Super Tortas Puebla, 8

# Puebla

TO CAPU (Bus Station)

TO TRAIN STATION

TO FORTS

TO AIRPORT

Av. 20 Oriente
Red Cross

Mercado el Alto Garibaldi

Av. 18 Oriente
Av. 16 Oriente
Av. 12 Oriente
Av. 8 Oriente
Av. 4 Oriente
Av. 2 Oriente

Templo de San Francisco

Blvd. Héroes del 5 de Mayo

Av. 5 Oriente

Calle 6 Norte

Teatro Principal

Av. 6 Oriente
Museo de Alfeñique

Mercado el Parián

Av. 2 Oriente

Av. Maximino Ávila Camacho

Av. 7 Oriente

Calle 4 Norte

Av. 16 Oriente
Av. 14 Oriente
Av. 12 Oriente
Av. 10 Oriente
Av. 8 Oriente

Casa de Aquiles Serdán

Av. 4 Oriente

Iglesia de la Compañía

Av. 3 Oriente

Av. 5 Oriente

Casa de Cultura and Biblioteca Palafoxiana

Museo Amparo

Av. 18 Ote.

Iglesia de Santo Domingo

La Casa de los Muñecos

Calle 2 Sur

Zócalo

Catedral

Av. 9 Oriente

Exconvento de Santa Mónica

5 de Mayo

16 de Septiembre

Calle 3 Norte

La Cocina de Santa Rosa

Av. 10 Poniente

Mercado Victoria

Museo Bello

Calle 3 Sur

Av. 8 Poniente

Calle 5 Norte

Av. 16 Poniente
Av. 14 Poniente
Av. 12 Poniente

Av. 6 Poniente

Calle 5 Sur

Calle 7 Norte

Av. Reforma

Av. 3 Poniente
Av. 5 Poniente
Av. 7 Poniente
Av. 9 Poniente

Hospital

Calle 9 Norte

Av. 4 Poniente
Av. 2 Poniente

Calle 11 Norte

Calle 11 Sur

Paseo Bravo

N

**Intiernet Access: RCP Electrónica,** Calle 4 sur 1922, south of Av. 19 Ote, upstairs in room 203. Ingeniero Juan Pablo Flores is the man to talk to. Projected cost 30 pesos per hr. Open Mon.-Fri. 9am-2pm and 4pm-8pm.

**Post Office:** 16 de Septiembre at Av. 5 Ote. (tel. 42-64-48), 1 block south of the cathedral, in the same building as the state tourist office. Open Mon.-Fri. 8am-8pm, Sat. 9am-1pm. **Northern office,** Av. 2 Ote. 411, on the 2nd floor. Open Mon.-Fri. 8am-7pm, Sat. 9am-noon. The 2 branches have separate *Listas de Correos,* so make sure you know where your mail awaits. **Postal Code:** 72000.

**Phone code:** 22.

## ACCOMMODATIONS

Puebla is well stocked with budget hotels, and most are within a five- or six-block radius of the *zócalo.* It's a good idea to ask to see your room first; same-priced rooms can vary widely in their size and decor. Hot water availability varies from hotel to hotel.

**Hotel Imperial,** Av. 4 Ote. 212 (tel. 42-49-80; fax 46-38-25). On the expensive side, but oh, the amenities! Telephone and TV in all rooms, 24hr. hot water supply, workout area, laundry service, pool table, and a Hershey's kiss on your pillow every night. Breakfast included. A 30% discount for proud *Let's Go* owners makes the Imperial's luxury more affordable. 15% discount for groups of over 10 people. Singles 120 pesos; doubles 180 pesos.

**Hotel Teresita,** Av. 3 Pte. 309 (tel. 32-70-72), 2 blocks west of the Cathedral. Ask for a remodeled room and you'll get carpeting, TV, a telephone, and a refreshingly unlumpy bed. There is 24hr. hot water in the sleek bathrooms, but not much space in the room to perform a dance celebrating the discovery of this budget-pleaser. Singles 100 pesos; doubles 140 pesos, with amenities 170 pesos.

**Hotel Victoria,** Av. 3 Pte. 306 (tel. 32-89-92), diagonally across from Hotel Teresita. Fluorescent lights illuminate the mismatched furniture in the large rooms. Tile floors lend an institutional feel. After 10pm, ring bell to enter. Singles 50 pesos; doubles 60-70 pesos.

**Hotel Avenida,** Av. 5 Pte 336 (tel. 32-21-04). Rooms are shabby but clean. Friendly staff, good location, and great prices make up for flaking paint and chipped plaster. Singles 40 pesos; doubles 55 pesos.

## FOOD

If you're going to splurge in one town, Puebla is the place to do it. Be sure to try the famous *mole poblano;* this heavenly dish is a mainstay on nearly every menu in town. Popular desserts are *yemas reales* (candied egg yolk), *camote poblano* (sweet potato), and a variety of almond-based sweets. Many restaurants line the streets near the *zócalo;* as always, for truly cheap eats the **mercados** are the way to go. A homey meal at the **Mercado San Francisco del Alto Garibaldi,** at Av. 14 Ote, between Calles 12 and 14 Nte., goes for only 5-15 pesos (open daily 7am-10pm).

**Las Chinas de Puebla,** Av. 5 Ote, in the same buildings as the tourist office. Although the location might suggest a rip-off in the making, this restaurant has ter-rifc food at good prices. Sit back in the colorfully painted chairs and enjoy the breeze from the large windows while eating the *comida corrida* (18 pesos). *Moles* go for 20 pesos, breakfast with eggs starts at 12 pesos. Open daily 9:30am-10pm.

**Restaurant El Vegetariano,** Av. 3 Pte. 525 (tel. 46-54-62). Popular in a city of carni-vores for one very good reason—terrific food. Don't worry about the *chorizo* and *jamón* listed on the menu; soy-based substitutes are used. Try the always tasty *comida corrida* (18 pesos), or opt for meatless *antojitos* (14 pesos). Their *energética,* a plateful of tropical fruits topped with yogurt and their very own gra-nola, is an unbridled breakfast joy (17 pesos). Open daily 7:30am-9pm. The same people operate **La Zanahoria,** Av. Juárez 2104, in the Zona Esmeralda.

**Puente de Ovando,** Av. 3 Ote. 1008 (tel. 46-10-44). Head east from the southeast corner of the *zócalo;* it's just across Blvd. Héroes 5 de Mayo, on the left. The *caf-*

*etería* on the first floor serves *poblano* classics in an enchanted garden setting. The sounds of the trickling fountain are almost as sweet as their excellent *mole poblano* (21 pesos). Soups (12-15 pesos) and meat entrees (28-42 pesos) in the pricier restaurant upstairs. Cafe and bar open daily 8am-11:30pm.

**Super Tortas Puebla,** Av. 3 Pte. 317. Hordes of Mexicans come here to indulge in the country's favorite lunchtime tradition, the *torta* (6-7 pesos). For a nostalgic dining experience, savor yours in the back room near a pastel-colored shrine to Marilyn Monroe. Open daily 9am-10:30pm.

## SIGHTS

Historic Puebla is a sightseer's paradise—which is, perhaps, the reason why busloads of Mexican students and *norteamericanos* from nearby language schools file into the *zócalo* every weekend, cameras in hand. Most sights are within walking distance of the city center. If you have only a short time in Puebla, the **Museo Amparo, Capilla del Rosario,** and **Casa de Aquiles Serdán** should top your list. For those interested in churches, the **cathedral** and **ex-convento de Santa Mónica** should not be missed. Churches close between 2 and 4pm; shorts are usually acceptable. Museums often give 50% discounts to students with ID.

### Near the *Zócalo*

In Puebla, modernity is tempered by many pre-18th-century architectural elements. The oldest buildings in town date from the 16th century and are notable for their Romanesque porches and smooth columns. While few original 16th-century edifices still stand, some later buildings on the west and north ends of the *zócalo* consciously attempt to imitate their style.

Puebla boasts over 100 churches. Gothic, classical, and even Baroque, many of them were built during the 17th century using oddly shaped red bricks and carefully painted *azulejos de talavera* (celebrated *mudéjar*-style Puebla tiles). For a prime example, head to the **Casa de los Muñecos** (House of the Dolls; Calle 2 Nte.; tel. 46-28-99) at the *zócalo's* northeast corner. Named for the *talavera* figures that populate the house, the building is a remarkable example of artistic spite: legend has it that the so-called "dolls" are actually caricatures of the architect's enemies.

The **Catedral Basílica de Puebla,** Av. 3 Ote. 302 at 5 de Mayo, stands adjacent to the *zócalo.* It was entirely constructed by *indígena* laborers working under Spanish direction between 1575 and 1649. Music sometimes echoes from the cathedral's two organs (one is 400 years old) and from the 19 bells of the bell tower. The interior of the cathedral gets its zing from chandeliers, gold plating, and Pedro Muñoz's fine woodwork choir-stalls on the pulpit's periphery. A guided tour goes for about 30 pesos. The tourist office can arrange authorized English-speaking guides. At 72m high, the cathedral is the tallest in Mexico (open daily 10am-12:30pm and 4-6pm). From 11am to noon, if the sexton is in the mood, visitors can climb the right tower of the cathedral for a panoramic view of Puebla (5 pesos). Two volcanoes, **Popocatépetl** and **Ixtaccíhuatl,** are visible to the northwest. To the northeast, you can see **La Malinche,** the volcano named in honor of Cortés's Aztec lover and interpreter. Be sure to start your climb by 11:30am; the lower door is locked at noon.

The art collection of the late textile magnate José Luis Bello is housed in the **Museo Bello,** Av. 3 Pte. at Calle 3 Sur (tel. 32-94-75), one block west of the southeast corner of the *zócalo.* The museum is crammed with ivory, iron, porcelain, earthenware, and *talavera* artifacts from different places and periods in world history; highlights include a collection of decorative keys and locks, a musical crystal door, and voluminous books of Gregorian chants from the 16th, 17th, and 18th centuries. A knowledgeable tour guide will spit out information about prominent pieces and answer questions in a spooky robot-like voice. Guided tours are offered in Spanish and English. (Open Tues.-Sun. 10am-5pm. Admission until 4:30pm. 10 pesos. Free Tues.)

## South of the *Zócalo*

The **Casa de la Cultura,** Av. 5 Ote. 5 (tel. 46-53-44), one block from the *zócalo* behind the Cathedral, in the same building as the tourist office, is an appropriate place to begin a visit to Puebla. Foreign students practice their Spanish in the court-yard while tourists view traveling art exhibits. Folk dances are performed every Satur-day and Sunday; movies are shown Thursday through Sunday. Check the board on the right as you walk in from the street for the latest schedules. The same building houses the impressive **Biblioteca Palafoxiana** (tel. 46-56-13), a beautiful library hold-ing 43,000 16th-century volumes. Belonging to no specific religious order himself, Don Juan de Palafox was a vocal critic of the Jesuits, condemning their aspirations to power, land, and money. His 6000-book library, which he donated to the city in 1646, includes a 1493 illuminated copy of the Nuremberg Chronicle (open Tues.-Sun. 10am-5pm; admission 10 pesos).

Around the corner from the *Casa de Cultura* and two blocks away from the *zócalo* is the **Museo Amparo,** Calle 2 Sur 708 (tel. 46-46-46). The exhibit begins with a time-line comparing the development of Mesoamerican art with that of Oceania, Asia, Africa, and Europe from 2400 BC to AD 1500. From there, the rooms guide you through the techniques, uses, and trends in the art of dozens of Mesoamerican indig-enous groups without losing the global perspective. Objects are presented in their contexts of use, in relation to other cultures, and finally as individual masterpieces. The last rooms of the museum jump to the colonial era, recreating the house as it once looked. As if Mexican pride hadn't been stroked enough, the exhibits open and close with two memorable paintings by Diego Rivera. Explanatory material is in both English and Spanish. Headphones provide visitors with more information on the pieces from the high-tech monitors in each room of the museum; explanations come in five languages (open Wed.-Mon. 10am-6pm; admission 16 pesos, students 8 pesos, free Mon. Guided tour Sun. at noon; headphones 8 pesos with 8-peso deposit).

## Northeast of the *Zócalo*

The extravagant, gilded **Iglesia de Santo Domingo** was constructed between 1571 and 1611 on the foundation of a convent. It lies two blocks from the *zócalo*'s north-west corner heading away from the Cathedral along 5 de Mayo, between Av. 4 and 6 Pte. Statues of saints and angels adorn the fantastic altar, but the church's real attrac-tion is the exuberant **Capilla del Rosario,** laden with enough 23½-karat gold to make Liberace wince. Masks depicting an *indígena,* a *conquistador* in armor, and a *mes-tizo* hang above each of the three doors along each side of the chapel. On the ceiling, three statues represent Faith, Hope, and Charity. The 12 pillars represent the 12 apos-tles; the six on the upper level are each made from a single onyx stone. Since there was no room for a real choir, designers painted a chorus of angels with guitars and woodwinds on the wall above the door (open daily 10am-12pm and 4-8pm).

**Casa de Aquiles Serdán,** originally the home of the eponymous printer, patriot, and martyr of the 1910 *Revolución,* serves today as the **Museo Regional de la Revolu-ción Mexicana** at Av. 6 Ote. 206 (tel. 32-10-76). Hundreds of bullet holes, both inside and out, bear witness to the assassination. The museum includes photos of Serdán, the bloody battles of the Revolution, the bedraggled battalions of Reyes and Obregón, and of the dead Zapata and Carranza. One room is dedicated to Carmen Serdán and other female revolutionaries (*las carabineras;* open Tues.-Sun. 10am-4:30pm; admis-sion 10 pesos, children 5 pesos).

When Benito Juárez's Reform Laws went into effect in 1857, they not only weak-ened the power of the Church but also forced the nuns at the **Convento de Santa Mónica,** on 5 de Mayo and 16 Pte., into hiding. The convent operated in stealth for 77 years before being accidentally discovered. Now an *ex-convento,* the building serves as a museum for religious art (open Tues.-Sun. 10am-5pm; admission 7 pesos, free Sun.). Regional clothing is sold at the tourist-happy **Mercado El Parián,** Av. 4 Ote. and Calle 6 Nte. (open daily 9am-7pm). The **Barrio del Artista,** on Av. 6 Ote. and Calle 6 Nte., is a pedestrian strip where local artists exhibit their work in small cubicles and

---

### How to Make a Mesoamerican Quilt

Inside the whitewashed **Iglesia del Espíritu Santo,** Camacho at Calle 4 Sur, is the tomb of the princess Mirrah, *la china poblana*. According to legend, this Indian noblewoman was abducted by pirates from China and brought to New Spain, where her captors sold her into servitude in 1620. The princess resigned herself to her fate, adopting Catholicism and a new name—Catarina de San Juan. She never forgot her blue blood, however, and distinguished herself from other *poblanas* by wearing elaborately embroidered dresses. By her death in 1668 at age 80, she had gained the town's appreciation by teaching many women to sew in the unique, multi-hued style that has been characteristic of the state ever since. Today, the *china* stands for *poblana* identity, strength, and beauty—an icon comparable to the Southern Belle.

---

paint the portraits of passers by. The best time to visit these markets is the weekend; they slow down considerably during the week.

The oldest church in Puebla, begun in 1535 and finished in 1575, is the **Templo de San Francisco,** Av. 14 Ote. and Calle 10 Nte. The church's dark bell tower was added in 1672. Near the church is the **Teatro Principal,** on Av. 8 Ote. at Calle 6 Nte. (tel. 32-60-85). The *teatro* is a prime example of Puebla's distinctive 16th-century architecture (open daily 10am-5pm, except when in use).

### In the Outskirts

A short trip from the *centro,* the **Centro Cívico 5 de Mayo** commemorates the Mexican army's victory over the French in the celebrated Puebla battle of 1862. To get there, walk three blocks from the *zócalo* away from Av. 5 de Mayo until you reach Blvd. Héroes del 5 de Mayo, where you can catch a #72 bus or #8 *colectivo* (both 1.50 pesos). They will drop you off by the cement octopus that memorializes Benito Juárez (don't ask). Facing the monument, cross the street to the left and walk uphill. On the road past an information center, a large, wavy representation of the Mexican flag marks a fork. To the right is the **Fuerte de Loreto,** which now houses the **Museo de La No Intervención.** The road to the left makes a loop; the first building is the **Museo de Historia Natural,** full of fossils, live snakes, and well-behaved school kids (open Tues.-Sun. 10am-5pm; admission 10 pesos, children 5 pesos, free for all Tues.). Next to it is the **Recinto Ferial,** an exposition center and fairgrounds; the tourist office distributes a pamphlet listing its monthly activities. The **Parque Rafaela Padilla de Zaragoza** comes next, providing a large, nature-filled oasis. Rambling trails descend to a theater, a playground, and benches that beckon to picknickers. The administration building near the entrance shows National Geographic-style videos (1 peso). The immersion in nature would be complete save for the oversized statues of animals and piped-in radio shows (open daily 9am-10pm). At the tip of the loop, the **Fuerte de Guadalupe** offers a panorama of the city and is "an altar to the patriotism of the heroes of the Fifth of May," as the signs so delicately put it. Finally, the **Museo Regional de Antropología** is on your right as you leave the fort and head back toward the flag (open Tues.-Sun. 10am-4:30pm; admission 14 pesos, free for all Sun.).

## ENTERTAINMENT

For evening entertainment, take a stroll along the **Zona Esmeralda,** on Av. Juárez, west of Calle 13 Sur. Enjoy the collection of movie theaters, shops, restaurants, and bars. A youngish Mexican crowd boogies to the beat of salsa and disco at **Pagaia,** Juárez 1906 after Calle 19 Sur (tel. 32-46-85; cover 20 pesos; open Fri.-Sat. 10:30pm-5am). **Charlie's China Poblana,** two blocks up at Juárez 2118 (tel. 46-31-59), is another hotspot. The neon-and-glass floor will make you feel like Michael Jackson singing "Billie Jean" (open daily 1pm-1am). If you're feeling mellower, the **Italian Coffee Company** (tel. 46-28-26) is just across Av. Juárez from Charlie's. A sophisticated set sits on the patio enjoying espresso and pastries (open daily 9am-midnight).

During the day, the **Plazuela de los Sapos,** on Calle 6 Sur between Av. 5 Ote and Av. 7 Ote., has no toads per se, but rather furniture and antique shops. After sundown, music from the bars lining the *plazuela* fills the air. At least three nightspots in the *plazuela* stand out. **El Cereso,** the last bar on the right side, features *botanas* and slick tunes (open 5pm-midnight on weeknights, 5pm-1:45am on weekends). If you're in a dancing mood, head to **Los Alambiques,** Calle 6 Sur 506, on weekend nights. For those who prefer to hear both sides of the conversation, bookstore/cafe **Teorema,** Reforma 540 at Calle 7 (tel. 42-10-14), is a hip hangout; lively banter and nightly live music pervade this literary lair (cover 8-13 pesos; open 9:30am-2:30pm and 4:30pm-2am; bookstore closes and music starts at 9:30pm).

To catch a flick, try the centrally located **Cine Continental,** Av. 4 Ote. 210 (tel. 32-19-55), next to the Hotel Imperial (10 pesos), or the brand new **Multicinemas** on Blvd. Héroes del 5 de Mayo 907, at the corner of Av. 9 Ote. (15 pesos).

The town of **Cholula** is 8km west of Puebla, making it an easy daytrip. To get there, take an Estrella Roja bus from the CAPU (every ½hr., ½hr., 3 pesos), or catch a colectivo on Av. 8 Pte (2.5 pesos). Eighty kilometers north of Puebla lies **Tlachichuca,** the town closest to Mexico's highest peak. The **Pico de Orizaba** is a 5747m volcano, the third-tallest mountain in North America. To get to Tlachichuca, head to the CAPU.

# ▓ Cholula

Legend holds that there are 365 churches in the city of Cholula. A photo mural in a bar near the *zócalo* depicts 128 of them, while the tourist office issues maps pointing out 38. Although the exact number may be in dispute, the prevalence of churches reminds the 69,000 residents of Cholula and the small number of foreign tourists of the city's sacred place in history. Founded in the 5th century BC, Cholula ("water that falls in the place of escape") was inhabited by several pre-Hispanic cultures—Olmecs, Zapotecs, Teotihuacanos, Toltecs, Chichimecs, and Cholutecs. Each successive culture group added a tier to the **Great Pyramid,** strengthening its reputation as a center for worship of the god Quetzalcóatl. When Cortés and his men entered the city in 1519, he decimated the townsfolk as well as the temples. On top of the religious ruins, the Spanish constructed Catholic churches, including the glittering **Santuario de los Remedios,** to outshine the pyramid. Together, the pyramid and its incongruous crown constitute Cholula's main attraction and a tangible symbol of the conquest. Many *poblanos* come to enjoy the college town nightlife (Cholula is home to the modern **Universidad de las Américas,** or **UDLA**), but despite the traffic the city remains unfazed; away from the archaeological zone and university, Cholula keeps resolutely to its own slow beat.

## ORIENTATION

Cholula is on **Route 150,** 122km east of Mexico City and 8km west of Puebla. The Estrella Roja **bus station** is located on **Av. 12 Pte.** near the intersection with **Av. 3 Nte.** Although the bus may not drop you off at the poorly marked station, you should head for the intersection of **12 Pte.** and **5 de Mayo.** To get to the center of town, walk 100m from the station and turn right on the first street, Av. 5 de Mayo. Next, walk four blocks downhill toward the large yellow church of San Pedro on the right side of the street. With the Church on the right, you are facing the edge of the *zócalo.* Colectivos to Puebla can be flagged down at a variety of locations in the city center, including the corner of **Av. 4 Pte.** and **Calle 3 Nte.,** as well as at **Morelos** and **Calle 4 Sur** (½hr. to Puebla's CAPU, 2 pesos). After the *colectivos* stop running at 8pm, you'll have to negotiate a price with a local taxi (20 pesos or more).

The numbered streets in Cholula form a grid with the *zócalo* roughly at the center. But beware: the municipality of Cholula encompasses two towns: **San Pedro Cholula** and **San Andrés Cholula.** The *zócalo,* tourist office, and majority of the restaurants are located in San Pedro; streets from the Archaeological Zone—where the **Pyramid** is—moving away from the *zócalo* are in San Andrés. As usual in Mexico, the same street may go by different names along different stretches.

Cholultecos insist that it is safe to walk around at night; crime seems to be directed against business establishments rather than individuals. The walk from San Andrés to Cholula past the pyramid can be uncomfortably lonely, but cabs travel the distance for about 7 pesos.

## PRACTICAL INFORMATION

**Tourist Office:** Av. 4 Pte. 103 (tel. 47-33-93). Facing the *zócalo* with the yellow Church of San Pedro on the right, turn right and walk toward the red-and-yellow arches; the office is inside a white building on the left side of the street just past the public library. Little English spoken, but you can always point your way to the free city map. Open Mon.-Fri. 10am-6pm, Sat.-Sun. at times.

**Currency Exchange: Casa de Cambio Azteca,** Av. Morelos 605 at 2 Sur (tel. 47-08-19). Open Mon.-Fri. 9am-7pm, Sat. 9am-2pm. Though they have more limited hours, the banks around the *zócalo* offer comparable rates. **Bancomer,** in the arcade on the side of the *zócalo* near the Church of San Pedro, is open for exchange Mon.-Fri. 9am-2pm. **Banamex,** Morelos 8, on the side of the *zócalo* opposite the Church of San Pedro, has an **ATM.** Open Mon.-Fri. 9am-5pm.

**Telephones: LADATELs** line the west side of the *zócalo,* but don't forget your phone card. Or try the phone inside the **Casa de la Cultura,** which takes coins.

**Fax: Telecomm,** Av. 5 Pte. 102A (tel. 47-01-30). Open Mon.-Fri. 9am-3pm. **Centro de Copiado Cholula,** Morelos 8B (tel./fax 47-14-72), on the south side of the *zócalo*. Open daily 8am-9pm.

**Buses: Estrella Roja,** at Av. 12 Ote. and 3 Nte. To Mexico City (every ½hr., 5am-8pm, 2hr., 29 pesos). Buses also run to Puebla (every ½hr., 5am-8pm, ½hr., 3 pesos). More destinations through the Puebla bus station.

**Market: Cosmo del Razo,** Av. Hidalgo and Av. 5 Norte, also in the *zócalo*. Cheap prices on meat, fruit, flowers, and clothing. Wed. and Sun. are *días de plaza* when the already crowded market swells with even more merchants.

**Laundromat: Lavandería Burbujas,** on Av. 14 Ote. (tel. 47-37-66), 1 block toward the *zócalo* from 5 de Mayo. 1kg for 5 pesos. Open Mon.-Sat. 9am-7pm.

**Red Cross:** Calle 7 Sur at Av. 3 Pte. (tel. 47-03-93), a bit of a hike from the *centro*. Walk-in service. Open 24hr. No English spoken.

**Pharmacy: Farmacia Moderna,** Morelos 12 (tel. 47-11-99), on the *zócalo*. Open daily 8am-8pm.

**Hospital: Clínica de IMSS** (tel. 47-53-14), Calle 4 Nte. and Av. 10 Ote. Open 24hr. **Hospital San Gabriel,** Av. 4 Pte. 503 (tel. 47-00-14), 2 blocks west of the *zócalo*. No English spoken.

**Police:** Tel. 47-05-62. At the Presidencia Municipal, Portal Guerrero 1, in the arcade under the arches on the side of the *zócalo*.

**Post Office:** At the intersection of Av. 7 and Av. 5 Pte. Open Mon.-Fri. 8am-7pm, Sat. and holidays 8am-noon. **Postal Code:** 72760.

**Phone Code:** 22.

## ACCOMMODATIONS

Though more expensive hotels have recently set up shop in increasingly touristed Cholula, two budget standouts hold firm:

**Hotel Reforma,** Calle 4 Sur 101 (tel. 47-01-49). From the zócalo, walk 2 blocks on Morelos towards the Great Pyramid, then turn right. Rooms feature full baths with hot water, and photographs of area churches. The real churches with their real bells lie just outside the hot-pink-accented courtyard, so alarm clocks are not necessary. Activity in the courtyard also makes for noisy nights. The front gate is locked from 10:30pm-8am; ring to enter. Singles 60-70 pesos; doubles 80 pesos.

**Hotel Las Américas,** Av. 14 Ote. 6 (tel. 47-09-91), in San Andrés, is well worth the hike. To reach the hotel from the *zócalo* or the *Estrella Roja* bus station, catch the San Andrés *colectivo* in front of the bus station (2 pesos) and ask to be dropped off at Av. 14 Pte.; the hotel is half a block west. If walking, pass the pyramid on Morelos; the hotel is on the right after Av. 5 de Mayo (San Andrés). Rooms on the 2nd and 3rd floor have more light and a possible view of a bougainvillea-laden courtyard. All rooms have TVs and phones. Singles 50 pesos; doubles 80 pesos.

## FOOD

Opportunities for the budget diner abound in the area around the *zócalo* and on Morelos/Hidalgo. For the cheapest eats in town, check out the food counters at the **mercados** on the north side of the *zócalo* and on Hidalgo and 5 Nte.

**Los Tulipanes,** Portal Guerrero 13, on the side of the *zócalo* near the Church of San Pedro. You can't beat this outdoor location. Shaded by the graceful arches of the arcade, you can watch the traffic of the *zócalo* go by. Breakfast starts at 13 pesos, *antojitos* 10-18 pesos, and *comida corrida* 22-24 pesos. Open daily 8am-9:30pm.

**Restaurant Colonial,** Morelos 605 (tel. 47-25-08), across the street from the entrance to the pyramid. Enjoy regional specialties from quesadillas (18 pesos) to fried chicken (32 pesos) while you are serenaded in a secluded courtyard by a variety of exotic birds, both in and out of cages. Open daily 9am-10pm.

**La Lunita,** (tel. 47-00-11), Av. Morelos at 6 Norte, occupies a graffiti-laden spot next to the railroad tracks and diagonally across from the steps up the pyramid. Serves complete breakfasts in the morning (20 pesos). At night, the orange-and-purple interior fills with mostly locals, drinking together genially. Open daily 8am-2am.

**La Chimenea,** 14 Pte. 605, 2 blocks past the pyramid in San Andrés. Not far from the Hotel las Américas and near most of the nightclubs, this sunny restaurant and bar happily serves up tasty fare. Breakfast 5-15 pesos, *antojitos* 8-15 pesos, *comida corrida* 20 pesos. Open daily 8:30am-9pm.

## SIGHTS

When Cortés destroyed the Toltec temple atop the misshapen hill that dominates Cholula, he was unaware that the hump of earth was actually the **Great Pyramid** of a culture that had dominated the area more than eight centuries before. This ancient civilization mysteriously collapsed in AD 700, and since then the pyramid's outer layers of adobe brick had disintegrated and sprouted trees. When the Toltec-Chichimec groups settled in Cholula in the 12th century, they named the pyramid Tlachiaualtepetl, or "man-made hill," and are believed to have practiced human sacrifice atop it. Twentieth-century archaeologists tunneled into the "hill," discovering three other pyramids built one on top of the other, the oldest of which dates from roughly AD 200. Sophisticated drainage systems preserved the structure, which is volumetrically the largest pyramid in the world. Today, the archaeological tunnels and some excavations on the south and west sides of the pyramid are open to visitors. Due to a lack of funding, only 5% of Cholula's ruins have been uncovered. The entrance to the tunnel is on Morelos, at the base of the pyramid. To reach the ruined structure, walk from the *zócalo* on Morelos, away from the red-and yellow-arches, and cross the railroad tracks; 50m farther on the right is the ticket booth. Avoid the pyramid's tunnels if you're claustrophobic. If you decide to brave it, guides will take you through the bewildering, unmarked excavation tunnels for 30-35 pesos. Look for the section of the main staircase that has been excavated from bottom to top to get an idea of the height of one of the smaller pyramids. Dioramas in illuminated sections of the tunnel demonstrate the evolution of the pyramid across the centuries (tunnel and ruins open Tues.-Sun. 10am-5pm; admission 14 pesos, 25 pesos to use a camcorder; free for children and seniors, and for all Sun.).

Just across the street from the tunnel, the **Museo del Sitio** displays a model of the pyramids in their original configuration; it makes the whole complex easier to understand. Fragments of the remarkable frescoes found on the second pyramid are exhibited in the back room. The fresco of the drinkers, as it was found on the pyramid, is 2.5m high and 65m long, making it one of the longest murals of pre-Hispanic Mexico. The museum's **bookstore** specializes in the art and culture of Cholula. (Museum open Tues.-Sun. 10am-5pm. Free admission with pyramid ticket.)

Upon exiting the tunnels, turn right on the path and follow it to the south of the pyramid to the **Patio de los Altares,** a large grassy area with extraordinary acoustics. Clap your hands while standing in the center of the courtyard. Wow. Follow the path as it takes you back to the railroad tracks; make an immediate right outside the fence where it ends, and begin climbing. No ticket is required to reach the **Santuario de Nuestra Señora de los Remedios,** the church built atop the pyramid in 1594 and the highlight of the Zone. Trekking up the pyramid demands as much effort as a Stairmaster workout, but the reward comes with the superb view of Cholula and its many churches. On a clear day, the snow-capped volcanoes **Popocatépetl** and **Ixtaccíhuatl** are visible in the distance. The inside of the church affords a stunning view as well—ornate gold decorations and fresh mums.

The only other churches worth visiting are the **Capilla Real** and the **Convento de San Gabriel,** on the side of the *zócalo* opposite the arches. The churches stand on the side of the **Templo de Quetzalcóatl,** yet another Spanish answer to pre-Hispanic temples. Unadorned but for its 49 domes, the Capilla Real possesses remarkable structural elegance. The steps in front of the entrance to San Gabriel are from the pyramid it replaced. (Open Mon.-Sat. 9am-1pm and 4-7pm, Sun. 9am-7pm.)

Aficionados of religious art and architecture should not miss the world-renowned church in the town of Tonantzintla, only 15 minutes away. Catch the bus marked "Chipilo" at Av. 6 Ote. and Av. 5 de Mayo (1.50 pesos). The bright saffron facade of **Santa María Tonantzintla** covers a startling interior, where over 450 stucco faces stare out from every spare inch of wall and ceiling. Saints, musicians, and chiefs congregate with animals and flowers in an explosion of spooky excess; it is the handiwork of the same indigenous artisan who executed the plans of European artists in Puebla's Capilla del Rosario (p. 424). Here the artisan reinterprets the colonial style in an indigenous rococo. Only a 15-minute walk (or an even shorter 1-peso minibus ride) away lies the town, and 15th-century church, of **San Francisco Acatapec.**

## ENTERTAINMENT

Thanks to its student population, Cholula sprouts distractions left and right. Bulletin boards at the **Casa de la Cultura,** Av. 4 Pte. 103A (tel. 47-19-86), in the same white building as the tourist office, advertise special events, films, local arts programs, new book clubs in the area, and the schedules of local aerobics classes (open Mon.-Sat. 9am-5pm; Spanish bookstore upstairs). Cholula has plenty of bars and nightclubs for those in search of more alcoholic adventures. Many popular bars and discos line the streets of San Andrés, within a block or two of the Hotel Las Américas. While there is a high rate of turnover among nightclubs, one constant has been **Club Keops,** on the corner of Av. 14 Ote. and 5 de Mayo. Catering to both gay and straight patrons, Keops nightly pulsates with the beat of house and techno music. Don't miss Travesty, the drag show put on at midnight on Friday and Saturday (open Wed.-Sat. 9pm-2am, cover 25 pesos). The video bar **La Tumba el Villa,** Av. Morelos 413, half a block away from the pyramid, features live music on weekend nights. Ignore the saccharine mural of cherubs on the back wall and enjoy the good music and super-exuberant local crowd (open daily 6pm-2am). Back under the arches on the corner of the *zócalo,* **Bar Enamorada** features music (sometimes live) and a young, hip clientele Thursday through Saturday nights (open daily 10:30am-midnight).

# Veracruz

The state of **Veracruz** is a thin strip of land that stretches 300km along the Gulf of Mexico. Unlike most of Mexico, its subsistence does not come from farming. Although many local residents make their living from farming, mainly tobacco or coffee, and small-scale cattle ranching, the state's main income comes from oil and fishing. But the state that works hard also parties hard: *veracruzanos,* also known as *jarochos,* are renowned for their delightful sense of humor, their wonderful seafood and coffee, and their Afro-Caribbean inspired music, which relies heavily on the marimba. The Afro-Caribbean influence dates back to the days when the city of Veracruz was the main slave trading port for the country and pervades not only the state's music, but also its cuisine and ethnic makeup. Local color is supplied by the over-hyped but still vital *curandero* culture. *Curanderos* (medicine men), called *brujos* (witches) by locals, practice a unique mixture of conjuring, devil-invocation, and natural healing.

Though Mexico's very first light-skinned visitors—Cortés and his ruthless band of *conquistadores*—first touched land in Veracruz in 1519 and began the first gringo trek to the capital from these shores, today the state of Veracruz, especially the verdant volcanic hills of La Sierra de los Tuxtlas, remains relatively untouristed; those who come are pleasantly surprised. Marimba rhythms and Caribbean colors flow through the steamy port city of Veracruz day and night, and the mountain city of Xalapa is endearingly artsy and colonial.

## ■ Xalapa (Jalapa)

Perched high upon a mountain slope, Xalapa (pop. 288,000) delights visitors with its decaying colonial beauty, its semitropical vegetation, and its subculture of talented artists. While other cities list countless churches as their most salient characteristic, Xalapa is home to a world-class museum, the University of Veracruz, and an emerald necklace of magnificent parks and gardens.

The capital of the state of Veracruz since 1885, Xalapa was first settled by Náhuatl speakers who dubbed the area "spring in the sand." After the Spanish conquest, Xalapa's annual fairs earned the city the economic importance it continues to enjoy today. Downtown Xalapa is the busy, giddy center from which the rest of the city ripples outward, merging gracefully with the raw beauty of the Veracruz landscape. Steep cobblestone streets provide a magnificent view of the verdant peaks surrounding Xalapa at every turn, while the bustling avenues give constant evidence of a city fairly bursting at the seams with artistic energy.

### ORIENTATION

Xalapa lies 104km northwest of Veracruz along Route 140 and 302km east of Mexico City. The **train station** is at the extreme northeast edge of the city, a 40-minute walk or 6 peso taxi ride from *el centro.* To get from the **bus station** to the *centro,* catch buses marked "Centro" or "Terminal" (1.80 pesos); a taxi will cost 8 pesos. There are two bus stations. **CAXA** is the major one for service to distant cities. The **Terminal Excelsior** is a stop where it's possible to catch buses to small neighboring towns. Make sure to clarify which bus station you want to go to.

Xalapa, like many other hilly towns, can be quite confusing. The *centro,* or downtown area, centers on the **cathedral** and **Palacio de Gobierno.** The street that separates them is **Enríquez,** which runs along **Parque Juárez.** Streets that branch from Enríquez towards the park and the Palacio de Gobierno run downhill; streets that split from Enríquez on the cathedral side run uphill. This uphill/downhill distinction works best for the streets near the center of town. Going away from the park towards the cathedral, Enríquez becomes two streets: **Xalapeños Ilustres** to the left and **Zamora** to the right. In the opposite direction, Enríquez becomes **Av. Camacho.**

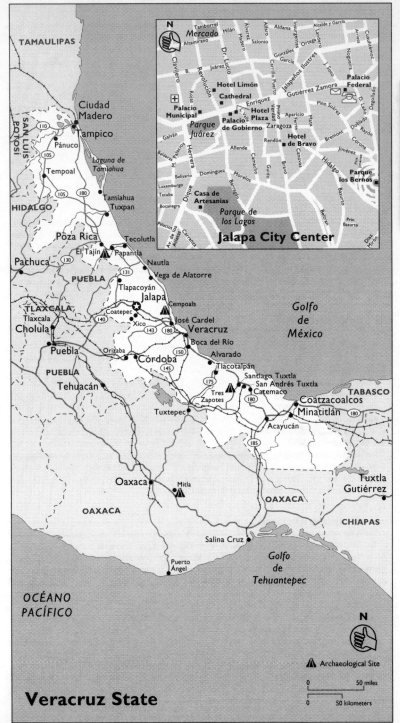

VERACRUZ

**Jalapa City Center**

N
Mercado
Tamborrel
Altamirano
Milán
Álvarez
Aldama
Alcalde y García
Insurgentes
Ortega
Salonio
Arteaga
Cuauhtémoc
Alfaro
Madero
Clavijero
B.
Juárez
Dr. Lucio
Revolución
González
García
Jalapeños Ilustres
Gutiérrez Zamora
Soto
J.
Landero
Palacio
Federal
Carrillo Puerto
Enríquez
Pino Suárez
D. León
Doblado
Topoyo
Palacio
Municipal
Hotel Limón
Cathedral
Rojas
Hotel
Plaza
Palacio
de Gobierno
Primo Verdad
Zaragoza
Aparicio
Maza
Rendón
Hotel
de Bravo
Rayón
Corona
Jiménez
Hidalgo
Parque
Juárez
Galván
Herrera
M. Palacios
Allende
Camacho
Guido
Bravo
Bremont
Canovas
Belisario
Domínguez
Morelos
Parque
los Bernos
Luxemburgo
Tacuba
Bocanegra
Dique
Barragán
Basurto
Beltrán
Casa de
Artesanías
Parque de
los Lagos
Priv.
Basurto
Palacios
Aldea
Carranza
Díaz
Mirón
An. de

Archaeological Site

TAMAULIPAS

SAN LUIS
POTOSÍ

Ciudad
Madero
110
Tampico
Pánuco
105
Tempoal
180
105
HIDALGO
Laguna de
Tamiahua
Tamiahua
Tuxpan
Poza Rica
130
El Tajín
Tecolutla
Papantla
Pachuca
Nautla
PUEBLA
131
Vega de Alatorre
Tlapacoyán
Jalapa
Cempoala
TLAXCALA
Coatepec
140
José Cardel
Tlaxcala
Xico
143
Veracruz
Cholula
180
Boca del Río
Puebla
Orizaba
150
Alvarado
PUEBLA
Córdoba
Tlacotalpán
145
Santiago Tuxtla
Tehuacán
175
San Andrés Tuxtla
Catemaco
TABASCO
Tres
Zapotes
180
Coatzacoalcos
Minatitlán
180
Tuxtepec
Acayucán
185
Golfo
de
México
Oaxaca
Mitla
Tuxtla
Gutiérrez
OAXACA
OAXACA
CHIAPAS
Salina Cruz
Puerto
Ángel
Golfo
de
Tehuantepec
OCÉANO
PACÍFICO
N
Archaeological Site
0          50 miles
0          50 kilometers

**Veracruz State**

## PRACTICAL INFORMATION

**Tourist Office:** Tel. 18-01-96. A kiosk in the bus station, to the far left as you enter the terminal, is the best source of information. Open daily 8am-10pm.

**Currency Exchange: Banamex,** at the corner of Xalapeños Ilustres and Zamora (tel. 18-17-13), is open Mon.-Fri. 9am-5pm and has a 24hr. **ATM.** Across the street, **Dollar Fast,** Xalapeños Ilustres 15 (tel. 17-28-91; fax 12-06-60), quickly buys and sells U.S. dollars and traveler's checks. Open Mon.-Fri. 9am-2pm and 4-6pm.

**American Express:** Carrillo 24 (tel. 17-41-14; fax 12-06-01), 3 blocks from Parque Juárez past the cathedral off Enríquez. Cashier open Mon.-Fri. 9am-2pm and 4-7pm. **Viajes Xalapa,** a full-service **travel agency,** shares the office.

**Telephones: LADATELs** outside the Palacio de Gobierno on Enríquez and outside the post office. *Caseta* at Calle Guerro 9, off the southwest corner of the Parque Juárez. Open daily 9am-10pm.

**Fax: Telecomm,** Zamora 70, around the corner from the post office. Open Mon.-Fri. 8am-7pm, Sat. 9am-noon. Also available at the bus station.

**Buses: CAXA,** in a state-of-the-art building at 20 de Noviembre 571, east of the city center. The station has long-distance phones, telegraph service, a pharmacy, shopping, food, and drink. **ADO** (tel. 18-99-88) travels 1st class to Catemaco (8am, 4½hr., 70 pesos), Mérida (8:15pm, 18hr., 275 pesos), Mexico City (23 per day, 12:30am-midnight, 5hr., 82 pesos), Papantla (7 per day, 4hr., 64 pesos), Puebla (8 per day, 3hr., 47 pesos), San Andrés Tuxtla (14 per day, 3½hr., 65 pesos), Santiago Tuxtla (10am, 2:30, and 7:30pm, 3½hr., 61 pesos), Tuxtepec (6am and 3:30pm, 5½hr., 68 pesos), and Veracruz (43 per day, 5:30am-11pm, 2hr., 28 pesos). Slightly slower, slightly cheaper 2nd-class service to almost identical destinations provided by **Autobuses Unidos (AU).**

**Market: Jaúregui,** Lucio at Altamirano, 2 blocks uphill from the right of the cathedral. Open daily 8am-6pm. **Chedraui** is a supermarket in the Plaza Crystal mall, on the corner of Independencia and Lázaro Cárdenas. Open daily 8am-9pm.

**Laundromat: Lavandería Los Lagos,** Dique 25 (tel. 17-93-38), around the corner from Casa de Artesanías. 3½kg for 15 pesos. Open Mon.-Sat. 9am-2pm and 4-7pm.

**Red Cross:** Clavijero 13 (tel. 17-81-58 for administration or 17-34-31 for emergencies), a block uphill from Parque Juárez. 24hr. ambulance service.

**Pharmacies: Farmacia Benavides,** Enríquez at Revolución (tel. 18-92-01), next to the cathedral. Open daily 7-midnight.

**Hospitals: Hospital Civil,** Pedro Rendón 1 at Bravo (tel. 18-44-00). 24hr. emergency care. **IMSS,** Lomas del Estadio (tel. 18-55-55). No English spoken.

**Emergency:** Dial 06.

**Police:** Helpfully sprinkled throughout the city, on the corner of Arteaga and Aldama (tel. 18-18-10), and at the Cuartel San José.

**Post Office:** At Zamora and Diego Leño (tel. 17-20-21), in the Palacio Federal. Open Mon.-Fri. 8am-7pm, Sat. 9-12am. **Postal Code:** 91001.

**Phone Code:** 28.

## ACCOMMODATIONS

And the Lord God, seeing the plight of the weary budget traveler, was moved to take pity upon her, and said, "Let there be Xalapa." The city is full of comfortable, economical, and convenient accommodations, many of them on **Revolución,** close to the *centro,* the market, and the parks. All rooms in the hotels listed have private baths with showers and 24-hour hot water.

**Hotel Limón,** Revolución 8 by Enríquez (tel. 17-22-04); go up past the left side of cathedral. Heaven. Immaculately clean, tastefully decorated rooms complete with color TV surround a beautifully tiled courtyard. Rooms close to the street can get a little noisy, the result of a great central location. Singles 45 pesos; doubles 55-65 pesos; triples 80 pesos; 10 pesos each additional person.

**Hotel Plaza,** Enríquez 4 (tel. 17-33-10), next to the Palacio de Gobierno. Faded but adequate rooms. Most 2nd-floor rooms wrap around an open-air patio and have elegant wooden doors and high ceilings. Singles 50 pesos; doubles 60-65 pesos.

**Hostal de Bravo,** Nicolas Bravo 11 (tel. 18-90-38). Walk away from the Palacio de Gobierno on Enríquez and turn right on Bravo. Walk 1½ blocks downhill; the hotel is on the left. Gorgeous rooms with huge windows look out onto a Mediterranean-style courtyard. Firm mattresses and color TVs round out this little piece of paradise. Singles 75 pesos; doubles 90 pesos.

## FOOD

Filled with high-quality cafes and cheap eateries, Xalapa is a true culinary paradise. As always in Mexico, particularly cheap cuisine can be found in the market. There are vegetarian restaurants on **Murillo Vidal,** downhill from the post office.

**La Sopa,** Callejón del Diamante 3A (tel. 17-80-69). 2 blocks from the park, past the Palacio de Gobierno, on a pedestrian street across from Banco Serfín. Another reason to love Xalapa. Inexpensive, delicious food in an irresistibly hip ambience. Advertisements for plays and exhibits cover the front doors. At night, musicians move in and tables move out to make way for dancing. *Comida corrida* 12 pesos. Open Mon.-Sat. 1-5:30pm and 7:30pm-midnight; music starts at 9pm.

**Café de la Parroquia,** Zaragoza 18 (tel. 17-44-36), 1 block downhill from the Palacio de Gobierno. Like its famous cousin in Veracruz, the cafe is always full and lively. Delicious *café con leche* 7 pesos. Breakfast is a little steep, starting at 17 pesos for toast, coffee, and juice, but *antojitos* are more reasonable (13-25 pesos). Open Mon.-Sat. 7:30am-10:30pm, Sun. 8am-11pm. Another location on Camacho on the way to the Teatro del Estado (tel 17-71-57).

**Enrico's Restaurant,** Enríquez 6 (tel. 17-64-47). Facing the Palacio de Gobierno, next to the Hotel Plaza. Hearty breakfast buffet (18 pesos) attracts a mature crowd. Don't miss what may be the world's best *enchiladas verdes* (18 pesos). Open Mon.-Sat. 8am-9pm.

**Café Chiquito,** Zamora 35 (tel. 18-93-30), directly across from the post office. Enjoy a morning coffee or an evening snack in this earth-toned nook. Clientele ranges from schoolgirls to retirees. Breakfast 10-15 pesos, *antojitos* 11-17 pesos. Open Mon.-Thurs. 8:30am-10pm, Fri.-Sat. 8:30am-11pm.

## SIGHTS

Xalapa's **Museo de Antropología** is probably the second-best museum in all of Mexico, after Mexico City's Museo Nacional de Antropología (see p. 102). The inscription above the entrance to the galleries admonishes the Mexican visitor to pause, for "this is the root of your history, your crib, and your altar." Below, a massive Olmec head stares grimly out across three millennia. Displayed in spectacular marble galleries and outdoor gardens, the museum's Olmec heads are perhaps the most impressive of its 3000 items. The heads commemorate leaders of the little-understood Olmecs, who ruled the Gulf Coast of Mexico around 1000 BC, but were unknown to archaeologists until the 1930s, when remains of them were found in the Veracruz rain forest (for more information, see **The Mysterious Olmecs,** p. 51). A group of Totonac figurines and masks subvert the austerity of the Olmec heads with their merry smiles, while nearby the Huastec deity Tlazoltéotl, associated with procreation, stands sculpted in soft, minimalist relief. The museum truly demonstrates the complexity and sophistication of Mesoamerican civilization, even for archaeology-phobes. The bookstore in the lobby sells an assortment of anthropology books; there is also a cafeteria. (Museum open daily 9am-5pm; admission 10 pesos, students 8 pesos; camera 6 pesos, video camera 30 pesos. Tours in English Mon., Wed., and Fri. 11am.) To get there, catch a yellow "Tesorería" bus on Enríquez (1.50 pesos); take a taxi (8 pesos); or walk on Enríquez/Camacho away from the cathedral, then left on Av. Xalapa, and on for several blocks until you see the museum on your left (45min.).

Some of Xalapa's most popular sights are its **public parks and gardens,** the hallmarks of a vibrant and livable city. The **Parque Ecológico Macuitépetl** is primarily a preserve for the flora and fauna indigenous to the Xalapa area, but also serves as one of the city's principal recreational areas. A brick path meanders past lip-locked lovers to the summit of an extinct volcano 186m above the city, where a spiral tower offers a commanding view of the city and mountains. To get there, take a "Mercado-Corona" *colectivo* (1.50 pesos) from Revolución and Altamirano (1.20 pesos), or hail a taxi (7 pesos; park open daily 6am-6pm). Downhill from Parque Juárez, on Dique, lies the **Paseo de los Lagos,** where a bicycle path traces the perimeter of several urban lakes. On sunny afternoons, the park is dotted with children, chirping birds, panting joggers, and still more amorous young couples. Like any urban park, it can be dangerous at night. At the west end of the park, near Dique, is the **Casa de Artesanías** (tel. 17-08-04), an activity center that hosts different fairs, festivals, and exhibits. Check at the tourist office or Agora de la Cuidad to see what's going on (open Mon.-Fri. 8am-8pm, Sat.-Sun. 10am-1pm).

Through the east entrance of the **Palacio de Gobierno,** off Enríquez opposite Parque Juárez, lies a marble courtyard with a staircase marching upward into the bureaucratic chambers above. The banister is guarded by bronze *conquistadores,* their swords beaten into lamp-posts instead of plowshares. The mural on the wall, by Mario Orozco Rivera, depicts a family overcoming ignorance and injustice. Note the gory figure on the left—no smooching here. Nearby, the terraces of **Parque Juárez,** built in 1892, share their view of the city and mountains with a small cafe. Carefully cut hedges line the walkways and enclose beds of flowers. One place where you'll be sure to avoid public displays of affection is the 18th-century **cathedral** on the corner of Enríquez and Revolución (open daily 9am-1pm and 4-7pm).

If you're in the mood to satisfy your sweet tooth while getting a dose of religion, head to the convent of **Los Madres Capuchinas,** on 20 de Noviembre Ote. 146. These nuns have been making exquisite marzipan candy/art for over 20 years. Good-sized boxes of delicately colored and delicious fruits, vegetables, and birds go for 25-35 pesos. The store also sells religious art and trinkets. The easiest way to get there is to take a cab (7 pesos; open Mon.-Fri. 9am-6pm). Don't let the deserted-looking grate deter you; ring the bell.

## ENTERTAINMENT

Xalapa is bursting with cultural opportunities. Ask at the bus station kiosk, or pick up a copy of a local newspaper for information about concerts, dance, and theater. The **Ágora de la Ciudad** cultural center, located at the bottom of the stairs in the Parque Juárez (tel. 18-57-30), has a screening room, gallery space, and loads of information and schedules about local events. The **Teatro del Estado** (tel. 17-31-10), a 10-minute walk from Parque Juárez on Enríquez/Camacho, at the corner of Ignacio de la Llave, holds enticing performances—the excellent **Orquesta Sinfónica de Xalapa** and the **Ballet Folklórico de la Universidad Veracruzana** appear regularly. A city with more than 6000 students, Xalapa is also one of the major destinations in Mexico for aspiring artists. **La Unidad de Artes,** Belisario Domínguez 25, posts announcements of exhibitions, plays, and recitals by students. For something much more low-brow, **Cine Xalapa,** Camacho 8, shows first-run movies from the U.S. The **Festival de las Flores** drowns the town in petals every April.

On weeknights, the cafes along Enríquez and Zaragoza brim with activity. The newly opened **Tierra Luna,** Diego Leño 28 (tel. 12-13-01), brews a great cappuccino (5 pesos) and has frequent live music (open Tues.-Thurs. 8am-10pm, Fri.-Sat. 8am-11pm, Sun. 10am-6pm). As the weekend approaches, however, people migrate from cafe tables to bars and dance floors. Near the *centro* is **B42,** on Camacho just west of Parque Juárez (tel. 12-08-93)—follow the throngs of teenagers to this fairly conventional club (cover 15 pesos; Thurs. is salsa night; open Thurs.-Sun. 9pm-2am). Just down the street from B42 is **Bistro Cafe del Herrero,** Camacho 8 (tel. 17-02-68), where a cool 20-something crowd drinks to the sounds of a peppy 80s dance mix. **7a Estación,** 20 de Noviembre 571 (tel. 17-31-55), just below the bus station, is the *grand dame* of Xalapa discos. With a crowd almost as diverse as your average college viewbook cover photo, 7a Estación caters to a wide variety of people. Get your groove-on steady on the spacious dance floor (cover 15 pesos; Thurs. is ladies night, no alcohol on Sun.; open Thurs.-Sat. 9pm-2am, Sun. 5pm-2am). For an avant-garde night out, head to the bar **Next** in the **Plaza Crystal** mall. A chic clientele lounges in this enclave of black lighting. To get to the Plaza Crystal, take a bus marked "Sumidero" or "Circunvalación" from the bus stop on Zaragoza, located down the stairs on the left side of the Parque Juárez. Be prepared to take a cab back (7 pesos).

# ■ Near Xalapa

## XICO AND CASCADA DE TEXOLO

It's hard to believe that **Xico** is located a mere 19km from Xalapa—here, there are almost as many mules on the road as there are automobiles. Xico is known for its cuisine (*mole xiqueño*, a slightly sweeter version of *mole poblano*, is a specialty) and its nine-day festival dedicated to Mary Magdalene, the town's patron saint. The festival begins on July 22 and includes bullfights and a running of the bulls.

Most tourists go to Xico for the awe-inspiring view of the **Cascada de Texolo** (Texolo Falls), 3km from the town. Immortalized in the film *Romancing the Stone*, the dramatic waterfall crashes into a gorge alive with vivid greenery, the songs of passing birds, and the constant drum of water as it spills into the river below. A restaurant and viewing area are across from the falls; from a bridge leading to the other side of the gorge, several paths yield stunning views of other waterfalls and dense vegetation.

The best viewing area is **Restaurante El Mirador.** The restaurant has a charming outdoor seating area and serves up regional specialties (10-15 pesos; open daily 9am-7pm). On the other side of the gorge, two gentle waterfalls are visible. The first appears as soon as you step off the bridge. Down a level by the white picket border, another waterfall, elegant and slender, plunges from the electricity plant to the river below. Only after returning across the bridge and turning right towards the white fence of the observation deck can you see the water whose rumble you had heard so loudly. Unlike the other two, this falls impresses with its brute force and sheer volume. To truly experience the falls in all their 80s cinematic glory, head to the left and go down the cement steps with the orange railings. The path gets a little rocky, but the reward is wading in the crystalline waters of the river below.

**Getting There:** To get to Xico from Xalapa, take the "Terminal" bus from the stop on Enríquez in front of the 3 Hermanos shoe store (to the right of the cathedral as you face it) to the Excelsior terminal (about 10min., 1.80 pesos). From there, cross the street towards the roundabout where buses are lined up and take a "Xico" bus (45min., 4.40 pesos).

To reach the falls, get off the bus as soon as the blue "Entrada de la Ciudad" sign appears on the right side of the road. Climb straight up the hill; soon the road will split at a restaurant called Las Artas. Take the left branch and turn left at the top of the hill, keeping a small vanilla and purple church on the right. Descending the hill, you will reach another fork guarded over by a makeshift shrine to the Virgin. Bear right after paying respects and keep her in mind as you lose hope on the interminable stone road ahead. The road curves to the right and then downhill to the viewing area, Restaurante El Mirador. To return to Xalapa and develop that film, re-trace your steps, but be aware that the walk will take 40 minutes and is not a smooth one. Even with a car, the trip will not be much shorter and certainly not any smoother. As you walk downhill past the Los Artas restaurant, stay on the right side of the street to hail a passing bus marked "Xalapa," which will deposit you back at the Excelsior Terminal.

# ■ Tuxpan (Tuxpam)

The first thing you notice when you step into the heart of Tuxpan is the funky smell, something like seafood, sweat, and sulphur. Although this may sound unappetizing, almost everything about Tuxpan (pop. 120,000) is actually quite palatable. Despite the bustle of the fresh *marisco* markets, couples amble up and down the Río Tuxpan, and the humidity and mellow plaza make for lovely, lethargic lounging. Much like their Olmec, Huastec, and Totonac predecessors, boys standing on the shore fling their nets into the water, draw them back, and fling them out again, and fruit vendors traverse the streets near the riverfront selling bananas and mangos by the bag. If everything seems too loud and crowded elsewhere, fear not—Tuxpan makes for terrifically easy living. For a sandy, salty break, **Playa Azul** is just 12km away. On weekends, the beach overflows with families splashing about.

**Orientation** Tuxpan, 347km northwest of Veracruz, spreads along the northern bank of Río Tuxpan. Activity centers around two park-like plazas. **Blvd. Reyes Heroles** is Tuxpan's main street, running along the river. One block north lies the omnipresent **Benito Juárez. Parque Rodríguez Cano** is on the waterfront, just south of the busiest part of town, and **Parque Reforma** is between Juárez and Madero. The bridge lies on the east edge of town. Streets perpendicular to the bridge and parallel to the water run roughly east-west. To get to the town center from the **ADO bus station,** head left 50m to the water, and then right (west) along Reyes Heroles for three blocks; you will be at Parque Rodríguez Cano. Walk one block north back to Juárez, then left (west) three blocks; Parque Reforma will be on your right. A taxi to Parque Reforma costs 7 pesos. To get to the beach, catch a "Playa" bus from the bench along the boardwalk by the ferry docks (every 10min., 6am-9pm, 2.80 pesos).

**Practical Information** The **tourist office,** Juárez 20 (tel. 4-01-77), is in the Palacio Municipal in Parque Rodríguez Cano. Enter on the Juárez side—it's a small office across from Hotel Florida. Try for maps (open Mon.-Sat. 8am-3pm and 4-7pm). **Bancomer** is on Juárez at Zapata (tel. 4-12-58; open Mon.-Fri. 9am-1:30pm). **Banamex** (tel. 4-08-40), just southwest of Parque Reforma, has a 24-hour **ATM. LADATELs** were last spotted in Parque Rodríguez Cano standing still.

Each **bus** line has its own station. **ADO,** Rodríguez 1 (tel. 4-01-02), three blocks east of Parque Cano down Reyes Heroles, has first-class service to Mexico City (5 per day, 6hr., 81 pesos), Papantla (8 per day, 2hr., 18 pesos), Tampico (every ½hr., 3hr., 52 pesos), Veracruz (8 per day, 6hr., 100 pesos), and Xalapa (5 per day, 6hr., 81 pesos). **Estrella Blanca,** Cuauhtémoc 18 (tel. 4-20-40), two blocks past the bridge, a left on Constitución, and then three blocks west, offers second-class service to Guadalajara (5 per day, 20hr., 180 pesos), Mexico City (10 per day, 9hr., 82 pesos), Monterrey (7 per day, 169 pesos), and nearly all points in between. **Ómnibus de México,** Vicente Guerrero 30 (tel. 4-11-45), at the bridge, has first-class service to Guadalajara (2 per day, 15hr., 216 pesos), Mexico City (5 per day, 6hr., 80 pesos), and Querétaro (1 per day, 8hr., 98 pesos).

**Farmacia Independencia,** Independencia 4 (tel. 4-03-12 or 4-92-64), is on the riverfront side of the market (open 24hr.). The **Red Cross,** Galeana 40 (tel. 4-01-58), is eight blocks west of *el centro* along the river, next to the police station. **Hospital Emilio Alcázar,** Obregón 13 (tel. 4-01-99), is one block west of the bridge, then a block and a half inland and up the inclined driveway on the right. No English is spo-

---

### Siempre Fidel

Mexico has a long tradition of close and friendly relations with Cuba. When Fidel Castro fled the island in the late 1950s, it was in Tuxpan that he organized the revolutionary forces that months later led the country in the fight against dictator Batista. The first hopeful years of the Cuban Revolution are celebrated in the **Casa de la Amistad México-Cuba.** Photographs of a young, beardless Fidel line the walls, and a colorful mural depicts the valiant leader and his fellow boatsmen disembarking under the watchful gazes of Latin American heroes Benito Juárez, José Martí, and Simón Bolívar. The final room on the tour displays pictures of doctors and farmers, symbolizing Cuba's social progress, as well as a proud look back through the guestbook and the diverse crop of visitors expressing support for the Cuban Revolution. To get to the museum, take a blue ferry (0.80 pesos) across the river. Walk right (west) along the sidewalk and continue straight up the dirt road, past the overgrowth to the paved sidewalk, turn left, and enter on the side of the two small, white buildings with the boat out front (open daily 9am-2pm and 3-7pm; free, but donations are always welcome).

ken (open 24hr.). In an **emergency,** dial 06. The **police** station (tel. 4-02-52) is located next door to the Red Cross, west of the *centro* (open 24hr.). To reach the **post office,** Mina 16 (tel. 4-00-88), from the Parque Reforma, make a right onto Morelos, and then the second left onto Mina (open Mon.-Fri. 8am-6pm, Sat. 8am-1pm). **Postal Code:** 92800. **Phone Code:** 783.

**Accommodations** Budget accommodations in Tuxpan cluster around the two central parks, ensuring a reasonable measure of safety into the evening hours. **Hotel Parroquia,** Escuela Militar 4 (tel. 4-16-30), to the left of the cathedral on Parque Rodríguez Cano, offers rooms with spacious bathrooms and balconies overlooking the park and river—all at rock-bottom prices. Full-length mirror, fan, and TV lounge provide all you need (singles 60-75 pesos; doubles 75-90 pesos; triples 92 pesos; quads 105 pesos). **Hotel El Huasteco,** Morelos 41 (tel. 4-18-59), is half a block east from the northeast corner of Parque Reforma. While extreme claustrophobes may do well to skip the small, windowless rooms, museum lovers should not—the mosaiced walls, skylights, immaculate upkeep, and freezing A/C make this feel like the Guggenheim (singles 58 pesos, with A/C 66 pesos). **Hotel Tuxpan,** Mina 2 between Juárez and Morelos (tel. 4-41-10), offers good, solid, somewhat boring rooms in a *great* location, halfway between parks. Watch TV in the lobby lounge with the hotel dog (singles 55 pesos; doubles 60 pesos; triples 70 pesos; quads 80 pesos).

**Food** Balancing traditional Mexican decor (simple, elegant wooden furniture and colorful tiles) with modernity (TVs to track *telenovelas* or *fútbol* matches), **El Mejicano,** Morelos 49 (tel. 4-89-04), at the corner of Parque Reforma, serves up tasty regional cuisine. Sample *pescado a la mexicana* (28 pesos) or *antojitos* like *tacos de bistec* (18 pesos). *Licuados* (6 pesos) are simply orgasmic, made only with fresh, seasonal fruit (open daily 7am-2am). The same owner operates **Cafetería El Mante,** Juárez 8 (tel. 4-57-36), one block west of Rodríguez. Enjoy your hotcakes (12 pesos) amidst a festive atmosphere—kiss-me-red tablecloths and hanging plants—and lots of locals. **Restaurant Don Carlos,** Escuela Amerigo Militar 12, near the Hotel Parroquia (above), is very small and very clean. The resident *familia* will whip up delicious dishes of seafood and meat right in front of your face (15-25 pesos). The *comida corrida* is an unbelievable 10 pesos (open daily 7am-10pm). Holy tamale, Batman!

**Sights and Entertainment** *Tuxpeños* are justly proud of their river's relaxed beauty and scenic shores. Palm trees line the boardwalk, and goods are sold up and down the river; under the bridge, piles of pineapples, bananas, shrimp, and fish can be had for a bare minimum at the huge open-air market which flows from the indoor market on Calle Rodríguez. Located on the waterfront, **Parque Rodríguez Cano** comes alive every Monday at 5:30pm for the **Ceremonia Cívica,** when government officials make speeches and schoolchildren march in an orderly procession.

Twelve kilometers from the city center, Tuxpan's **beach** can be crowded and slightly dirty, especially during the high season and hot weekends, but the wide expanse of fine sand stretches far enough for you to stake a private claim somewhere down the line. The beach is accessible by the "Playa" bus (every 15min., 6am-10pm, the last bus returns to Tuxpan at 8:30pm, 2.80 pesos).

There are a number of **bars** in Tuxpan's *centro,* and the town has had problems with brawls and rowdy nightgoers. Clubs and bars have short lifespans in Tuxpan, and places practically empty during the week are packed during the weekend. The best and safest nightlife in town can be found a few blocks down the river after the crowds in Parque Reforma thin out. At **Mantarraya,** Reyes Heroles at Guerrero (tel. 4-00-51), a young crowd grooves to American pop and techno hits. The enormous interior is the perfect place to chill, to dance, or to fall in love. Live music frequently includes elderly men crooning popular ballads while screaming teens drink and sing along (cover 20-40 pesos, including 2 drinks; open daily 9pm-3am). Your other option is the brand-new, quieter, and kitschier **La Veladora,** the town's only video bar. With electric candles barely lighting the place and life-size cartoon cut-outs of bullfights and small-town gaiety, the bar attracts a young (although older than Mantar-raya's pubescent) clientele. The bar plays everything from salsa to disco, and the dim interior is the perfect place to drink a beer (8 pesos) and watch soccer. Live Latin music on Friday (no cover; open Tues.-Sat. 7pm-late). Get that groove on.

# ■ Papantla

Papantla is almost picture-perfect. Crawling up the green foothills of the Sierra Madre Oriental, the city (pop. 156,000) looks out onto the magnificent plains of Veracruz. Despite its poverty, the city's white stucco houses have gorgeous Mediterranean tiled rooftops, and the plaza contains Indian stone carvings and beautiful art—even people climbing its insanely steep streets smile between huffs and puffs. Papantla is also one of the few remaining centers of Totonac culture. Conquered by the power-hungry Aztecs around 1450, the Totonac soon took their revenge, helping Cortés crush the Aztec Empire in the 16th century. In modern Papantla, Totonac rituals persist in the flight of the *voladores,* a thrilling acrobatic ceremony once laden with religious meaning, now performed for delighted tourists. Papantla is also a good base for exploring **El Tajín,** the highly impressive ruins of the Totonac capital, 12km south of the city (see p. 439). So take a deep breath and start up that mile-high street; every picture you take will look like a postcard.

**Orientation** Papantla lies 250km northwest of Veracruz and 21km southeast of Poza Rica along Rte. 180. Downtown activity centers around **Parque Téllez,** the white-tiled plaza. The cathedral on Nuñez and Dominguez rises on its southern side while **Enríquez** borders it on the north. Sloping downhill to the north are **Juárez** (on the east side) and **20 de Noviembre** (on the west side), both perpendicular to Enríquez. To get from the **ADO bus station** to *el centro,* turn left on Juárez out of the station and veer left at the fork. Taxis (5 pesos to the *centro*) pass frequently along Juárez. If you arrive at the **second class bus station,** turn left outside the station and ascend 20 de Noviembre three blocks to the northwest corner of the plaza.

**Practical Information** The **Chamber of Commerce,** Ramón Castaneda 100 (tel. 2-00-25), has excellent maps and brochures about Papantla and rudimentary info about El Tajín and the Veracruz state. To get there, follow Lázaro Muño (the narrow street running east from the plaza) four blocks downhill and turn right (open Mon.-Fri. 10am-2pm and 4-8pm, Sat. noon-8pm). The staff of the **tourist office** (tel. 2-01-23), on the second floor of the Palacio Municipal, on the west side of the plaza, is highly elusive (supposedly open Mon.-Fri. 10am-3pm and 6-8pm). A slew of banks on the northern side of the plaza, including **Banamex,** Enríquez 102 (tel. 2-00-01), have 24-hour **ATMs** (open Mon.-Fri. 9am-1:30pm). Sometimes-functioning **LADATELs** can be found on the north side of the plaza; collect calls can be made from **Hotel Tajín,** Núñez y Domínguez 104 (tel. 2-10-62; open 24hr.).

Papantla has two **bus stations.** The first-class **ADO** station, Juárez 207 (tel. 2-02-18), serves Mexico City (5 per day, 5hr., 66 pesos), Tuxpan (3 per day, 2hr., 17.50 pesos), Veracruz (5 per day, 4hr., 59 pesos), and Xalapa (7 per day, 4hr., 59 pesos). The second-class terminal, commonly called **Transportes Papantla,** 20 de Noviembre 200, heads off to Poza Rica (every 15min., 6am-11:30pm, ½hr., 5.50 pesos). Pay after boarding. **Poza Rica** (21km northwest of Papantla) is a nearby transportation hub. Their **ADO** station (tel. 2-04-29 or 2-00-85) runs buses to Mexico City (19 per day, 5½hr., 74 pesos), Papantla (23 per day, 30min., 6 pesos), Puebla (7 per day, 5hr., 73 pesos), Tampico (32 per day, 4½hr., 60 pesos), Tuxpan (35 per day, 2hr., 15 pesos), Veracruz (17 per day, 4½hr., 70 pesos), and Xalapa (17 per day, 4hr., 64 pesos).

Back in Papantla, the **Red Cross** is on Pino Suárez at Juárez (tel. 2-01-26; open 24hr.). **Farmacia Benavides,** Enríquez 103E (tel. 2-06-36), is at the northern end of the plaza (open daily 7:30am-1am). **Clínica IMSS,** on 20 de Noviembre at Lázaro Cárdenas, provides emergency medical care. From the ADO station, take a right and walk two blocks to Cárdenas, then turn left; IMSS is half a block up on your right (open 24hr.). The **police** (tel. 2-00-75 or 2-01-50) are in the Palacio Municipal (open 24hr.). The **post office** is on Azueta 198, second floor (tel. 2-00-73; open Mon.-Fri. 9am-1pm and 4-7pm, Sat. 9am-noon). **Postal Code: 93400. Phone Code: 784.**

**Accommodations and Food**  Few lodgings are available in tiny Papantla. A lovely, economical option is to stay at **Hotel Totanacapán,** 20 de Noviembre at Oliv (tel. 2-12-24 or 2-12-18), four blocks down from the plaza. Here, hallway murals, crazy colors, and large windows make things (unintentionally?) swank and totally cool. Rooms are a bit dark, but nice wooden furniture and a bedside TV will put you at ease. Enjoy the most affordable A/C around (singles 70 pesos, with A/C 95 pesos; doubles 90 pesos, with A/C 120 pesos). A step up in ritz, **Hotel Tajín,** Núñez y Domínguez 104 (tel. 2-01-21), half a block to the left as you face the cathedral, displays in its lobby a carved stone wall from El Tajín. Perched on a hill above the city, the balconies afford panoramic views. Amenities include bottled water, TV, and phones. Guided horseback tours of the area are available (for a fee). Unfortunately, a luxury hotel means luxury prices (singles 130 pesos, with A/C 170 pesos; doubles 180 pesos, with A/C 230 pesos; 30 pesos per extra person).

Papantla's few restaurants serve regional delicacies to tourists looking for authentic cuisine. Most eateries stick to beef and pork offerings with just a smattering of seafood. **Restaurant Plaza Pardo** (tel. 2-00-59), next door to Sorrento (below), serves up simply out-of-this-world food. Watch wise locals stuff their faces full of soft, delicious tamales (4 pesos) and *molotes* (10 pesos), or heavier meat dishes (16-30 pesos). This is the real thing. Large murals and a view of the plaza enliven **Sorrento,** Enríquez 105 (tel. 2-00-67), a popular breakfast hangout. No wonder, with early-morning *menús económicos* (6-14 pesos). Meal specials include *camarones fritos* (14 pesos) and steak enchiladas (18 pesos; open daily 7am-midnight).

**Sights and Entertainment**  Papantla's biggest attractions are the relics of its Totonac heritage. South of the plaza is the **Catedral Señora de la Asunción,** remarkable not so much for its interior, but for the stone mural carved into its northern wall, measuring 50m long and 5m high. Called **Homenaje a la Cultura Totonaca,** the mural was created by Teodoro Cano to honor local Totonac heroes and folklore figures. Its focus is the plumed serpent Quetzalcóatl, whose image runs along the full length of the carving. Brimming with history, the mural depicts such wonders as the discovery of corn and eager ballplayers vying for the right to ritualistic death and deification. The mural is truly massive, the most immediate and impressive structure in Papantla's *centro.*

The cathedral's spacious courtyard commands a view of the *zócalo.* Called the **Plaza de los Voladores,** the courtyard is the site of the ceremony in which *voladores* acrobatically entreat the rain god Tlaloc to water the year's crops. In early June, during the 10-day **Festival of Corpus Christi,** the *voladores* perform as often as three times a day. During the festival, Papantla comes alive with artistic expositions, fireworks, traditional dances, and cockfights. Papantla's latest effort to enshrine its *voladores* is the **Monumento al Volador,** a gigantic flute-wielding *indígena* statue erected in 1988 atop a hill and visible from all over town. To get to the monument, where you can read explanatory plaques and see all of Papantla, walk up Reforma along the right side of the cathedral and up the narrow alleyway, following the road as it curves left, then make a sharp left before the road starts to slope down and walk uphill.

The town's two markets are situated next to the central plaza. **Mercado Hidalgo,** on 20 de Noviembre off the *zócalo*'s northwest corner, beats **Mercado Juárez,** at Reforma and 16 de Septiembre off the southwest corner of the *zócalo,* hands down.

# ■ Near Papantla: El Tajín

The impressive ruins of El Tajín only hint at the thriving Totonac civilization that once spread across modern-day northern Veracruz. Named for the Totonac god of thunder, El Tajín served as the political and religious center of the Totonac people. Marked similarities between buildings at this site and those at Teotihuacán reflect the influence of the Aztec and Maya civilizations. Just by the entrance stands a large pole, the apparatus of the *voladores* (see p. 439). June through August, the *voladores* perform almost hourly; the rest of the year, they descend through the air only on weekends. These daring acrobats—who typically request a 10-peso donation when they are through—generally perform after a large group has finished touring the ruins. All explanatory information is in both Spanish and English. A tiny but useful brochure and map about El Tajín can be purchased at the **information desk** for 15 pesos. Besides selling overpriced plastic carvings, the **store** adjoining the information desk carries maps and excellent tour guides of Tuxpan, Papantla, and Veracruz state—better information than is frequently available at the cities themselves. To enter the ruins, one must pass through the **Museo del Sitio del Tajín** (in the same complex as the info booth; admission 16 pesos). The museum was recently refurbished, with original, still-painted fragments of murals and an eerie, fascinating display filled with sand and ancient skeletons, some with cracked skulls and visible bone injuries—a must for the secretly morbid maniac in you.

From the museum building, a straight path leads to the ruins themselves. Plaques are few, far between, and seldom in English. Besides a good guidebook, the best sources of information are the blue uniformed "rangers" stationed throughout El Tajín. Native Totonacs themselves, the rangers may offer to give you an *ad hoc* tour of a certain area and will eagerly answer any questions you pose, although their English proficiency may be limited.

The **Plaza del Arroyo,** the central rectangular plaza formed by four tiered pyramids, lies just to the left of the gravel road. Each pyramid points toward the northeast at a 20° angle, in a feat of architectural planning maintained in all the early buildings at this site. The heart of El Tajín is just past the pyramids. Two identical, low-lying, slanted constructions to the left of the observation area form a central ballcourt in which the famous one-on-one game called **pok-ta-pok** (see p. 520) was played. While the game vaguely resembled soccer, feet weren't allowed to make contact with the ball. Every 52 years, a contest was held between the most valiant ballplayers; some historians believe that the winner gained the honor of offering his heart for sacrifice. Puts the Vince Lombardi trophy to shame, no? Approximately 11 such courts grace the ruins of El Tajín.

Across from the plaza is an elevated central altar surrounded by two temples that can be climbed. Just left of the altar is a split-level temple that displays a statue of Tajín. This area was known as the **Central Zone,** and is unique because the styles and functions of the buildings here vary considerably. To the northwest stands **La Pirámide de los Nichos,** a fascinating structure with seven levels and a total of 365 niches corresponding to the days of the year. Each niche was once painted in red, crimson, and blue. The Totonacs marked time in 52-year epochs, during which a single flame was kept continuously burning. At the end of each epoch, the carefully-nurtured flame was used to ritually torch many of the settlement's buildings. Each new epoch of rebuilding and regeneration was inaugurated by the lighting of a new flame. Today, ritual ceremonies are held annually at the pyramid during the vernal equinox; farmers place seeds in the pyramid's niches and later retrieve them for planting.

Farther north and atop a hill is **Tajín Chico,** accessible either by a series of large stepping stones or an easy-to-ascend staircase off to the west. Whereas Tajín was a public religious and social center, archaeologists hypothesize that Tajín Chico was where the ruling class and political elite actually lived. Newly uncovered in the Tajín Chico area is **Building I,** where several colored paintings, representing different gods from the Tajín pantheon, are visible. While some buildings here are in good condition, most have yet to be excavated and are off-limits to the public. As a result, park officials don't mind if visitors scamper up the higher buildings to get a view of the site and surrounding hills. East of Tajín Chico, down the hill and around the curve in the gravel road, is the **Great Xicalcoliuhqui,** a tremendous recreational area (a separate jurisdiction from El Tajín, within the village of Xicalcoliuhqui) still being unearthed (open daily 9am-5pm; admission 16 pesos, free Sun. and holidays).

**Getting There:** El Tajín is accessible via *pesera* from the bus stop in Papantla behind the cathedral on Calle 16 de Septiembre. Buses are clearly marked "Tajín" (every 15min., early-6pm, 3 pesos). Your bus will first pass through El Chote and stop at the entrance to El Tajín, marked by a stone mural. To return to Papantla, walk down the access road to the main highway and cross the road to the bus stop to catch a *pesera* running back to El Chote (2.50 pesos). From El Chote, you can catch any one of the myriad buses leaving for nearby Papantla (2 pesos).

# ▓ Veracruz

The oldest port city in the Americas swelters in colonial decay and modern resurrection. Cortés landed here on Good Friday, 1519, christened the city "La Rica Villa de la Vera Cruz," was mistaken for the god Quetzalcóatl, and marched on to conquer the Aztec empire (see p. 53). Since then, Veracruz has been a place where Mexico has rubbed up against the rest of the world. Pirates long frequented the steamy port; after colonial contact, the city prospered as the only port in New Spain officially permitted to trade with the mother country. It was here that Juárez proclaimed the laws of the Reforma, and here that he staged the reconquest of Mexico from the Hapsburg Emperor Maximilian. Twice the city was occupied by American troops.

Today, Veracuz's streets continue to fill with sailors—as well as tourists—from around the world. Modern Veracruz (pop. 327,500) sprawls gracefully along Mexico's Gulf coast, merging gracefully with **Boca del Río** (pop. 143,800), the prosperous home of the area's best beach and most chic discos. Touristy beach glitz is undergirded by the numerous oil rigs and barges that fill the harbor. A hot, humid urban sprawl that drips with sweat into the night, the twin cities are buffeted by strong winds called *nortes,* a display of nature's force which some people find disagreeable and others spectacular. Despite the heat, tourists and citizens alike continue to enjoy the city's delicious *café con leche* by day and fall sway to a seductive, marimba beat by night. What impresses visitors most, however, is something distinctively *veracruzana*—the nearly untranslatable qualities of *sabor,* rich and alluring flavor, and *ambiente,* unique and enchanting atmosphere.

## ORIENTATION

Veracruz lies on the southwestern shore of the Gulf of Mexico, 104km south of Xalapa, 424km west of Mexico City, and 376km north of Oaxaca. To get to the *zócalo* from the **bus station,** take a "Díaz Mirón" bus (1.70 pesos) to Parque Zamora and walk away from the park on Independencia for seven blocks. To get back to the bus station from downtown, catch a Díaz Mirón bus heading toward Parque Zamora on 5 de Mayo. A taxi will cost you 8 pesos. From the **train station,** turn right at the exit and walk toward the opposite end of the Plaza in front of you. The Plaza ends at Lerdo; take a right and follow it into the *zócalo.*

Downtown Veracruz is laid out grid-style; streets run either parallel or perpendicular to the coast. **Díaz Mirón** runs north-south and converges with **Avenida 20 de Noviembre** at **Parque Zamora,** south of downtown. Here, the two streets become **Independencia,** the main drag. Independencia forms the boundary of the *zócalo* farthest from the water. **Miguel Lerdo,** to your left as you face the Palacio Municipal, has a string of hotels and restaurants. It runs towards the water and the **Plaza de la República,** home of the train station, the post office, and drop-off point for many municipal bus routes. To your right is **Zamora;** across **Zaragoza** toward the Gulf, it becomes **Malecón,** the boardwalk. At the edge of the water, Malecón makes a 90° turn to the right and becomes **Ávila Camacho,** which follows the Gulf to **Boca del Río,** a suburb housing some posh discos and restaurants.

The *centro* is generally safe, but visitors should be careful. Never give the name of your hotel to somebody you just met—thieves have been known to chum up to tourists in the *zócalo* and then rob them at their hotel. Do not walk far from the downtown area after dark. Women may find themselves the object of more male attention in Veracruz than in smaller towns, typically in the form of invitations from random men. A firm and polite refusal will be grudgingly accepted during the day, but at night it may well be taken as a challenge to overcome. Be firm.

## PRACTICAL INFORMATION

**Tourist Office:** Tel. 32-19-99. In the Palacio Municipal on the right side as you face it in the *zócalo*. Helpful staff speaks some English and hands out maps and brochures. Open Mon.-Sat. 9am-9pm, Sun. 10am-1pm. **Seguridad Para el Turista** (tel. 91-800-90-392) provides medical and legal services for tourists.

**Currency Exchange: Banamex,** on Independencia (tel. 32-82-70), 1 block from the *zócalo*, has 6 **ATMs.** Open for exchange Mon.-Fri. 9am-5pm. Virtually the only place open for exchange on the weekends is **Mini Súper Pete's,** Aquiles Serdán 797 (tel. 32-09-18), 2 blocks from the *zócalo* (open daily 8am-noon).

**American Express:** Camacho 222 (tel. 31-46-36), inside "Viajes Olymar," across from Villa del Mar beach. "Villa del Mar" bus stops at Serdán and Zaragoza. Won't cash traveler's checks. Open Mon.-Fri. 9am-1:30pm and 4-6pm, Sat. 9am-noon.

**Telephones: LADATELs** on the *zócalo* and by the Palacio Municipal and the cathedral.

**Fax:** Tel. 32-25-08. On Plaza de la República, next to the post office. Open Mon.-Fri. 9am-5pm, Sat. 9am-noon.

**Airport:** Tel. 34-00-08. 8km south of downtown Veracruz on Rte. 150. **Aeroméxico** (tel. 35-01-42). **Mexicana** (tel. 32-22-42, at airport 38-00-08). Both represented by **Viajes Carmi,** Independencia 837 (tel. 31-27-23), north of the *zócalo*. Open Mon.-Fri. 9am-1:30pm and 3:30-7:30pm, Sat. 9am-1pm.

**Buses: Central de Autobuses,** on Díaz Mirón 1698. **ADO** (tel. 37-57-88), with 1st-class service to Cancún (10:35pm, 21hr., 328 pesos), Catemaco (5 per day, 3hr., 40 pesos), Mexico City (19 per day, on the hr., 5½hr., 1st class 120 pesos, deluxe 140 pesos, ultra-deluxe 168 pesos), and Xalapa (48 per day, 1:25am-11pm, 1¾hr., 1st class 28 pesos). **Cristóbal Colón** (tel. 37-57-88), 1st-class service direct to Oaxaca (11pm, 6½hr., 145 pesos) and Tuxtla Gutierrez (6 and 7pm, 12hr., 151 pesos). **Cuenca** (tel. 34-54-05) sends 2nd-class buses to Oaxaca (7am and 8pm, 6½hr., 75 pesos) and Tuxtepec (every hr., 5am-7pm, 3hr., 32 pesos). **AU** (tel. 37-57-32; buses leave from La Fragua, 1 block behind ADO station), 2nd-class service to Córdoba (3:40, 5, and 6:20pm, 1½hr., 34 pesos), Mexico City (every hr., 6am-1am, 6½hr., 102 pesos), Orizaba (3:40, 5, and 6:20pm, 2½hr., 40 pesos), Puebla (every hr., 6am-7pm, 11pm, and midnight, 4½hr., 79 pesos), and Xalapa (1am and every hr., 6am-4pm, 1¾hr., 26 pesos). **Líneas Interunidas** (tel. 37-28-78) operates from the AU terminal to Catemaco (every ½hr., 2am-midnight, 3½hr., 35 pesos), San Andrés Tuxtla (every 10min., 2am-midnight, 3hr., 33 pesos), and Santiago Tuxtla (every 10min., 2am-midnight, 2½hr., 31 pesos).

**Trains: Ferrocarriles Nacionales de México** (tel. 32-33-38), at the far end of Plaza de la República, 1 block from the *zócalo*. 1st-class trains to Mexico City (10pm, 12hr., 62 pesos). Yup, twice as slow as buses. Tickets sold Mon.-Sat. 6-9am, 10-11am, and 4-9:30pm, Sun. 6-10am and 7-9:30pm.

**Taxis: Taxi Confort** (tel. 37-65-85 and 37-67-15) will pick you up and transport you in air-conditioned cars for about 3 pesos more than unaffiliated taxis. You may save money, though, since many unaffiliated taxis hike their prices for tourists.

**Car Rental: National InterRent,** in the lobby of the Hotel Emporio, on Serdán in between 16 de Septiembre and Xicoténcutl. The smallest car they offer goes for a budget-busting 350 pesos per day. Open daily 8am-1pm, 4-6pm.

**Bookstore: La Literaria,** Independencia 1415 (tel. 32-11-15), between the *zócalo* and Parque Zamora, on the right as you walk to the park. English magazines and a full-service stationery store. Open daily 9am-2pm and 4-8pm.

**Cultural Center: Instituto Veracruzano de la Cultura** (IVEC) (tel. 31-66-45), in a purple building on the corner of Canal and Zaragoza, 4 blocks from the Palacio Municipal. Sponsors dance classes, music recitals, and international exhibitions

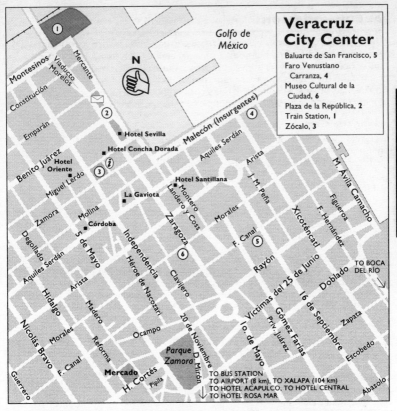

Veracruz City Center

Baluarte de San Francisco, 5
Faro Venustiano
  Carranza, 4
Museo Cultural de la
  Ciudad, 6
Plaza de la República, 2
Train Station, 1
Zócalo, 3

VERACRUZ

with topics like the Afro-Cuban influence in Veracruz. Bulletin boards announce events at other venues. Open Mon.-Sat. 9am-9pm, Sun. 9am-3pm. Free.

**Markets: Mercado Hidalgo,** on the corner of Cortés and Madero, 1 block from the Parque Zamora away from the Gulf. Fruit, vegetables, *piñatas,* seafood, flowers, meat, you name it. Open daily 8am-6pm. **Supermarket: El Alba,** M. Lerdo between Independencia and 5 de Mayo (tel. 32-24-34), just 1 block from the *zócalo.* Open Mon.-Sat. 9am-2:30pm and 5-9pm. **ATM** at Banco Serfín next door helps you fund those purchases.

**Laundromat: Lavandería Ultra-Clean,** Serdán 789 between Madero and 5 de Mayo (tel. 32-94-23). Same day service, 5 pesos per kg. Open Mon.-Sat. 9am-7pm.

**Red Cross:** On Díaz Mirón between Orizaba and Pérez Abascal (tel. 37-55-00), 1 block south of the Central de Autobuses. No English spoken. 24hr. emergency service and ambulance on call.

**Pharmacy: Farmacia del Ahorro,** Paseo del Malecón at Gómez Farías (tel. 37-35-25), 2 blocks from the *zócalo.* Open 24hr.

**Hospital: IMSS,** Díaz Mirón 61 (tel. 22-19-20). **Hospital Regional,** 20 de Noviembre 284 (tel. 32-36-90).

**Police:** Tel. 38-05-67 or 38-06-93. In the Palacio Municipal.

**Internet Access: Web Cafe,** Paseo Jardín 3C. To get there, catch a #6 bus (1.80 pesos) from behind the tourist office. Ask the driver to drop you on the corner of Costa Verde and Paseo Jardín; the cafe is on your left. 16 computers (16 pesos per hr.), limited refreshments. Open daily 10am-10pm.

**Post Office:** Plaza de la República 213 (tel. 32-20-38). Open Mon.-Fri. 8am-8pm, Sat. 9am-1pm. **Postal Code:** 91700.

**Phone Code:** 29.

VERACRUZ

## ACCOMMODATIONS

Veracruz has three peak seasons: *Carnaval* (the weeks before Ash Wednesday), Semana Santa (the week before Easter), and summer (July and August). The city is full of hotels, but many fill up well in advance during the first two peak periods, and some raise their rates. At other times, reservations are not necessary. Rooms with ceiling fans or large windows are not so pricey, but you'll have to pay more for the luxury of a room with air conditioning, often much needed in this steamy city.

### Near the *Centro*

Budget hotels cluster on Aquilés Serdán, two blocks over from the *zócalo*. The area, full of revelers all night every night, is fun, loud, and relatively safe. Hotels listed have private bathrooms with 24-hour hot water.

**Hotel Concha Dorada,** M. Lerdo 77 (tel. 31-29-96), on the *zócalo* to the left of the Palacio Municipal. Despite its premier location, the hotel's entrance is obscured by the labyrinth of cafe tables under the *zócalo*'s arches. Rooms are remarkably insulated from the hubbub outside. Singles 90 pesos, with A/C 110 pesos; doubles 100 pesos, with A/C 120 pesos; each additional person 21 pesos.

**Hotel Sevilla,** Morelos 359 (tel. 32-42-46), where the *zócalo* meets the Plaza de la República. Uninspiring, but adequate rooms with TV, fan, and street noise. Singles 80 pesos, peak season 115 pesos; doubles 100 pesos, peak season 135 pesos.

**Hotel Santillana,** Landery y Coss 208, at T.A. Dehesa (tel. 32-31-16). The lime green and purple courtyard has a certain garish charm. Big king-sized beds, huge bathrooms, TV, and fans in every room. Singles 70 pesos; doubles 90 pesos.

### On Díaz Mirón and Near the Bus Station

Not as central, but slightly cheaper and less likely to be full. Hotels close to the bus station tend to be very noisy, for obvious reasons. At night, take a cab back.

**Hotel Central,** Díaz Mirón 1612 (tel. 32-22-22), next to the ADO station. When the architects of Tomorrowland were done in Orlando and Anaheim, they designed this modern-looking hotel, complete with faux-marble lobby. Rooms have TV, phone, and large bathrooms; some even have balconies. Singles 100 pesos, with A/C 120 pesos; doubles 110 pesos, with A/C 140 pesos.

**Hotel Rosa Mar,** La Fragua 1100 (tel. 37-07-47), behind the ADO station. On a forgettable strip of aging storefronts, it valiantly tries to remain a clean, wholesome establishment. Convenient for catching early-morning buses. Singles 70 pesos; doubles 90 pesos, with 2 beds 120 pesos; add 15 pesos for A/C, 5 pesos for color TV.

## FOOD

Red snapper, shrimp, octopus, and a host of other sea beasts are hauled in daily from the Gulf. *Huachinango a la veracruzana* (red snapper decked out in olives, capers, onions, and olive oil) is the city's most brilliantly shining seafood star. The **fish market** on Landero y Coss, between Arista and Zaragoza, lets you enjoy them at incredibly cheap prices. The risk of cholera means that raw or partially cooked fish, including *ceviche* and sushi, should be avoided. Ice cream shops sell delicious flavored ices made with mango, coconut, strawberry, and purified water (4 pesos)—great for fighting the heat. And don't leave without trying what's arguably the best coffee in the country.

**Gran Café de la Parroquia,** Gómez Farías 34 at the corner of the Malecón (tel. 32-35-84). One of Veracruz's greatest traditions; the entire town always seems to be here. Sit back to people-watch, eavesdrop, and enjoy their famous *café con leche*. After your glass is half filled with syrupy coffee, clink your spoon against your glass to have it completed with steaming milk (7 pesos). Food 13-30 pesos. Open daily 6am-1am.

## Not Your Average Cup O' Joe

Every Mexican president since the 1810 Independence War has eaten at the **Gran Café de la Parroquia,** which has also served lesser politicians and luminaries such as Colombian author Gabriel García Márquez, and—judging from the nightly crowds—everyone in Veracruz. But a torrid story lies beneath the cafe's peaceful appearance. Years ago, La Parroquia decided to expand, and opened a smaller branch in addition to the original one a few blocks away on Paseo del Malecón. Eventually, however, the Gran Café lost its lease for the original location. Soon after, the **Gran Café del Portal** opened in that very space, veiling itself in la Parroquia's tradition. But **justice** prevailed, and folks in the know walk the extra few blocks to the corner of Malecón and Gómez Farías or to Parroquia's newest branch a few doors down Malecón. *Veracruzanos* remain loyal and still sip their *café* at la Parroquia, clinking their spoons against their glasses, and not the least confused by the number of Gran Cafés. Make sure you head to the original Café, not the imitator.

**El Cochinito de Oro,** Zaragoza 190, on the corner of Serdán (tel. 32-36-77). Serves not only seafood specials (22-30 pesos), but also *comida corrida* (20 pesos) and *antojitos* (8-14 pesos). Eating at this welcoming, roomy restaurant, you'll appreciate not only the locals' food but also their friendliness. Open daily 7am-5pm.

**Alaska** (tel. 31-78-73), in the Parque Zamora. Remember the diner in Happy Days? Alaska's got the jukebox and the soda fountain plus the lackadaisical ice cream licker. Frozen treats 8-14 pesos, *antojitos* 12 pesos; the view of the peachy-keen park is free. Open daily 8am-midnight.

**La Gaviota,** C. Triqueros 11, between Molina and Serdán (tel. 32-39-50). Sparkling linens and wood paneling give this restaurant and bar a touch of elegance. Fish specialties 25-35 pesos. Don't miss the *huachinango a la veracruzana* (35 pesos). Open daily 8am-3pm.

**Córdoba Cafe y Restaurant,** Miguel Lerdo 380, the side of Independencia away from the Gulf. Extensive selection of *refrescos;* the casual atmosphere attracts a younger crowd. *Antojitos* 5-13 pesos. Fish 25-35 pesos. Open Mon.-Sat. 7am-10:30pm.

## SIGHTS AND SAND

In the evening, the hymns of the cathedral spilling out into the *zócalo* yield to the sexy rhythms of marimba. Crowds gather on benches and outside bars to drink in music that doesn't relent until daybreak. On Tuesday, Thursday, and Saturday nights around 8pm, *veracruzanos* young and old gather for the slowly swaying *danzón,* an old Veracruz tradition. The band strikes up a tune, and couples—men in white wearing straw hats, women clutching their sandalwood fans—file out onto the makeshift dance floor where they sway to the nightly rhythms.

### Museums and Monuments

The **Castillo de San Juan de Ulúa** (tel. 38-51-51), Veracruz's most important historic site, rests on a fingertip of land that juts into the harbor. Spaniards first arrived at this point on the saint's day of San Juan; "Ulúa" was the greeting the native Totonacs offered the sailors as they disembarked. Construction, using coral as bricks, began in 1582 as part of the system of fortifications built around the Spanish Caribbean to protect the trade fleet and treasure from pirates. The fort has served many purposes since its inception, including a high-security prison much like Alcatraz. **Chucho el Roto,** Mexico's Robin Hood, was perhaps its most famous prisoner. Enter the site through the arched entrance and head for the last room on the right. As you enter, there are two openings in the wall to the left. The hole closer to the grass leads to some stairs and a dim, dank room that was known as **Purgatory.** The other room contains **Hell,** surrounded by walls 9m thick, where prisoners lost their sense of time and their sanity. To maintain yours, walk toward the row of 14 arches that hold a small museum. Through the arches, you can take in a panoramic view of the city and the hungry angelfish nibbling for crackers. To reach the fort, take a "San Juan de Ulúa" bus (1.40 pesos) in front of the Aduana building in the Plaza de la República (open Tues.-Sun. 9am-4pm; admission 15 pesos, video camera 25 pesos, guides in Spanish 20 pesos, free Sun. and holidays).

The bus from San Juan de Ulúa will drop you off at Plaza de la República. Walk straight one block and turn left on Malecón. Almost at the end of the street, you will see a yellow lighthouse on the right, between Hernández and Xicoténcatl. Outside is a larger than life statue of Carranza—Mexican revolutionary, constitution-drafter, president, and native *veracruzano*—coquettishly dressed with a *guayabera*. Upstairs and to the left is the **Museo Venustiano Carranza** (a.k.a. **Museo de la Revolución**), a four-room tribute displaying some of his belongings. The museum, owned by the Mexican Navy, proudly displays a gilded version of Article 32 of the 1917 Constitution. This provision, promulgated by Carranza, nationalized the Navy (open Tues.-Sun. 9am-5pm; free).

The **Baluarte de San Francisco,** on Canal between 16 de Septiembre and Gómez Farías, two blocks from the lighthouse on Xicoténcatl, is a 17th-century bulwark that protected inhabitants from swashbuckling pirates like Sir Francis Drake. It is all that remains of the old city wall that once enclosed the area between the train station and Parque Zamora. The museum inside displays a beautiful collection of pre-Hispanic gold ornaments; the roof affords a great view of the city (open Tues.-Sat. 10am-4:30pm; admission 14 pesos, Sun. and holidays free). Farther down Canal away from the water, turn right on Zaragoza to see the **Museo Cultural de la Ciudad,** Zaragoza 397 (tel. 31-84-10). Paintings, models, dioramas, and Spanish explanations tell the history of the city from pre-Hispanic times to the present. The museum's most interesting attraction is a relic from its days as an orphanage. In the back stairwell, a stained-glass window depicts Talinmasca, an orphan whose transgressions, legend has it, brought thunder, lighting, and the fierce autumn winds called *nortes* to the area (open Tues.-Sun. 9am-4pm; admission 8 pesos, students 5 pesos).

## Beaches and Beyond

The beaches in Veracruz are not world-class, but they are a refreshing break from the heat. The harbor is a case study on the toxic impact of big oil in big cities. Locals still swim in the water, but considering the health risk, a short trip south of the city is a better idea. **Playa Villa del Mar** is a fairly pleasant hour-long walk from the *zócalo* along the waterfront; it is also accessible via one of the frequent "Villa del Mar" or "Boca del Río" buses that stop on the corner of Serdán and Zaragoza (1.80 pesos). Villa del Mar attracts sunbathers, baseball players, soccer enthusiasts, and vendors of flavored ices called *glorias* and *raspados*. The **Acuario de Veracruz** (tel. 32-79-84), in Centro Comercial Plaza Acuario near the beach, has Sea World-like glass tunnels through communities of native Gulf Sea life and a display of exotic imports (aquarium open Sun.-Thurs. 10am-7pm, Fri.-Sat. 10am-7:30pm; admission 15 pesos, seniors 10 pesos, children 5 pesos; mall open daily 10am-10pm). Farther on Blvd. Camacho away from downtown Veracruz, luxury homes and pricey resorts hog the waterfront. A peaceful stretch of sand is **Costa de Oro** (Gold Coast), between the orange-pinkish hotels Fiesta Americana and Torremar.

The best beach in the Veracruz area is **Playa Mocambo,** next to the Hotel Torremar, in the neighboring city of Boca del Río. Take a "Boca del Río" bus from Zaragoza and Serdán (25min., 1.80 pesos) and ask to be dropped off at Mocambo. Walk past the air-conditioned Plaza Las Americas and follow the "Playa" sign across the street and down. At the bottom, veer left to head for the beach, or go straight into the **Balneario Mocambo** (tel. 21-02-88), which has a clean, Olympic-sized public pool surrounded by artificial palm trees, changing rooms, and a poolside bar-restaurant (open daily 9am-5pm; admission 16 pesos, children 8 pesos). Catch the bus back to Veracruz at the top of the drive.

## ENTERTAINMENT AND SEASONAL EVENTS

Neither rain nor darkness will prevent the nightly release of tension on the streets and in the clubs of Veracruz. Apart from the spontaneous singing in the *zócalo,* most action takes place along **Av. Camacho,** the stretch of road along the coast that connects Veracruz and Boca del Rio. **Café Andrade** is on Blvd. Camacho at the corner of Callejón 12 de Octubre (tel. 32-82-24), across the street from the Plaza Acuario and the Playa Villa del Mar. Rather than go the way of Starbucks, this chain retains local flavor and popularity. Beautiful people of all ages flock to the cool outdoor patio. They sell beans from nearby Coatepec for grinding at home, and the pungent smell permeates the place (open daily 8am-midnight). The other hopping night spots are about 3 mi. further down Blvd. Camacho away from Veracruz. A good landmark is the purple high-rise Hotel Lois. Just before the violet beacon, Ruiz Cortines branches off of Camacho. This is a good point to get off the bus. One block up Ruiz Cortines is **Ocean,** Ruiz Cortines 8 (tel. 22-03-55). A slick aluminum facade and its status as one of the older clubs in town make it a popular destination (cover 30 pesos; open Thurs.-Sat. 11pm-6am; no jeans, shorts, or tennis shoes). Head down Blvd. Camacho for about 200m and you'll hit **Master Club Billar,** Blvd. Camacho 4 (tel. 37-67-48), one of the friendlier, safer poolhouses you've ever seen, with TV, music, bar, A/C, and tables for dominoes or cards (open daily 1pm-2am; pool 25 pesos per hr.). Keep walking down Camacho and you'll hit **Blue Ocean,** Blvd. Camacho 9 (tel. 22-03-55), the offspring of Ocean. Outside, green lasers beckon to dancers; inside, a waterfall and a mix of English and Spanish tunes keep the crowd moving (cover women 20 pesos, men 80 pesos, same hours and dress code as Ocean). Señor Frog's, the touristy restaurant chain that just keeps on giving, has bestowed **Carlos 'n' Charlie's,** Blvd. Camacho 26 (tel. 22-29-09), on Veracruz. The restaurant regularly fills to the point of immobility—but that's okay, since everyone sits, drinks, and sings along merrily with the salsa music. Think TGIFriday's run by the Mad Hatter; if you tell the waiter it's your birthday, you'll get a whipped cream pie in the face…how, um, funny (no cover; open daily noon-2am). A recent addition to Veracruz nightlife is **Chalet,** Blvd. Camacho 18 (tel. 31-69-45), on the corner of Sporting, located back toward Veracruz about a 20-minute walk from downtown along the water, across from the pink La Bamba restaurant. This ultra-cool bar features live music every night (open daily 1pm-5 or 6am; cover Thurs.-Sat.15 pesos).

If two hours of air conditioning appeal to you, catch a movie—who cares what's showing? For English-language films, check out **Plaza Cinema,** Arista 708 (tel. 31-37-87), or **Cinema Gemelos Veracruz,** at Díaz Mirón 941 between Iturbide and Mina (tel. 32-59-70; 15 pesos).

Every midnight, December 31, *veracruzano* families dress in their Sunday best and fill Blvd. Camacho, looking east to the Gulf to witness the first sunrise of the year. With that auspicious start, a year of celebrations begins. The climax comes early, in

---

### If It's Good Enough for Ike…

Even if he's sitting at the right cafe, a guy can't claim to really know Veracruz until he's worn the traditional white shirt called a *guayabera.* The name comes from the word *guayaba,* Spanish for "guava." Cuban guava collectors got tired of shimmying up and down the tree countless times, so they designed a shirt with four pockets to expedite the task. From there, the *guayabera* shirt passed to Panama and then Mexico, where Carlos Cab Arrazate added the thin pleats that form vertical stripes connecting the pockets. His grandson continues the family business, **Guayaberas Finas,** Zaragoza 233 between Arista and Serdán (tel. 31-84-27; fax 31-33-43), in Veracruz city. Everyone who's anyone has bought one of their high-quality, hot-weather shirts—check out Dwight Eisenhower's note of appreciation on the store's wall. Fashion tip: shirts are not meant to be tucked in (*guayaberas* 150-1400 pesos, women's clothing also sold; open Mon.-Fri. 9:30am-8pm, Sat. 9:30am-7pm, Sun. 10am-4pm).

late February or early March, just before Ash Wednesday. **Carnaval** literally invades the *zócalo* and usurps the streets with parades, expositions, dance performances, and music. With the requisite ceremonies and parades, a king and queen are crowned. There's an entire office devoted to organizing the week-and-a-half-long event, the **Consejo Directivo del Carnaval** (tel. 32-31-31 ext. 149-172; fax 32-75-93). If you are able to, by all means come—but make hotel reservations early.

# ■ Near Veracruz

## ZEMPOALA RUINS

The ruins at **Zempoala** (sometimes spelled Cempoala), one of the most impressive archaeological sites in the state, lie 40km north of Veracruz, off Rte. 180. Zempoala was one of the larger southern Totonac cities, part of a federation that covered much of Veracruz in pre-Hispanic times. In 1469, the Aztecs subdued Zempoala and forced the Totonacs to join their federation. Cortés arrived in 1519, attracted to the glitter of the seashells in the stucco used to build the structures (thinking, of course, that they were gold). The Totonacs were happy to lend Cortés soldiers for his campaign against Moctezuma at Tenochtitlán in 1521.

Once a city of 30,000 people, the site's stone structures surround a grassy field next to present-day Zempoala. A museum, to your left as you enter, displays a small collection of pottery and figurines unearthed here. The structure closest to the entrance is the **Temple of Death.** Continuing to the left, you will see three **pyramids.** Climbing the narrow stairs is forbidden, just like in the old days, when only priests and sacrificial victims were allowed in the altars that topped the temples. The pyramid on the left is dedicated to Tlaloc (god of rain), the one on the right to the moon, and the one in the center, decorated with circular stone receptacles for the hearts of people sacrificed in religious offerings, to the sun. Turning to the right, you will encounter the largest structure on the site, the **Templo Mayor.** When Cortés arrived, the Spaniards erected an altar to the Virgin on top of the temple, literally imposing Catholicism on the Totonacs. In front of the Templo Mayor is the **throne** where the king sat to observe the sacrifices that took place on the platform next to him. The throne also faces the temple known as **Las Chimeneas.** Moving towards the entrance of the site, you will see a fenced-in structure. For the Totonacs, this piece played a central role in the "New Five Ceremony," a five-day fast that took place when a "century" of the ritual calendar ended every 52 years. Every spring equinox, people still come to the circle to expel negative energy and absorb positive energy (open daily 9am-6pm; admission 10 pesos, video camera 25 pesos, free Sun. and holidays).

**Getting There:** From the second-class bus station on La Fragua, in Veracruz, **Autobuses TRV** sends buses to **Cardel** (every 8min., 5am-9:15pm, 45min., 7 pesos), where you can take a bus to Zempoala (every 30min., 7am-7pm, 15min., 3 pesos). Ask the driver to let you out at **las ruinas,** at the intersection of Av. Prof. José Ruíz and Av. Fcodel Paso y Troncoso Norte. If driving from Veracruz, follow Rte. 180 past Cardel, take the Zempoala city turn-off, and proceed until an obscured "Zona Arqueológica" sign appears on the right (about 1km before town). To get back, stand across the street from where you were dropped off and hail a passing "Cardel" bus (3 pesos), where you can catch a bus to Veracruz (every 10min., midnight-8pm; every 15min., 8-10pm; 45min.; 7 pesos).

# ■ Catemaco

There can be no doubt that Catemaco is the most popular tourist destination in the Tuxtlas area. The 26 hotels, numerous lakeside restaurants, and annoying swarms of boat operators crying *"lancha?"* to every passerby all attest to a healthy tourist industry. But despite this fact, the town manages to retain some of the charm that attracted visitors in the first place.

The **Laguna Catemaco** and its islands are often compared to Switzerland, and the intense green of the surrounding foliage does suggest a degree of alpine seclusion. Another distinguishing characterisitic is Catemaco's status as a center for *brujería*, or witchcraft. *Curandero* culture is usually a hodge-podge of pre-Hispanic myth and New Age kitsch, but Catemaco's friendly residents provide a glimpse of a more authentic way of life.

**Orientation and Practical Information** Catemaco lies along Rte. 180 and is a frequent stop for both first- and second-class buses. Streets are poorly marked, but the basilica on the *zócalo* is usually visible. From the **Autotransportes Los Tuxtlas** stop, turn right and walk until you come to **Madero,** a large street with a strip of grass in the center. Turn left and walk toward the twin orange spires of the basilica, which awaits at the corner of **Boettinger** and Madero. To the left, **Carranza** runs past the Palacio Municipal. Straight ahead, the road becomes **Aldama.** One block downhill to the right is **Playa** and then **Malecón,** which follows the curves of the beach. The **ADO** station is on Aldama, one block behind the basilica.

Agustín Moreno, owner of Hotel Las Brisas, Carranza 3, next to the clock on the Palacio Municipal (tel. 3-00-57), provides **tourist information,** including maps of the region. Since there are no banks to exchange money, have pesos handy or obtain them from **Banamex** in San Andrés Tuxtla. If push comes to shove, **Hotel Los Arcos,** Madero 7 (tel. 3-00-03), on the lakes, will exchange dollars at extremely unfavorable rates. The **telephone *casetas*** in town do not allow international collect calls, so try the Hotel Catemaco, to the right of the Palacio Municipal, instead.

First-class **ADO** buses (tel. 3-08-42) leave for Mexico City (9am and 10pm, 9hr., 158 pesos), Puebla (9am and 10pm, 6hr., 123 pesos), Villahermosa (12:30pm, 5hr., 74 pesos), and Xalapa (6:15, 7am, 1, and 5pm, 3hr., 67 pesos). **AU** (tel. 3-07-77) goes to Mexico City (11:30am and 9pm, 9hr., 150 pesos), San Andrés (11:30am and 9pm, 20min., 3 pesos), and Veracruz (11:30am, 3½hr., 38 pesos). **Autotransportes Los Tuxtlas** goes to San Andrés (every 10min., 20min., 3 pesos) and Santiago (every 10min., 40min., 5 pesos).

The **market** is on Madero before the *zócalo* (open daily 6am-8pm). **Farmacia Nuestra Señora del Carmen** is at the corner of Carranza and Boettinger (tel. 3-00-91; open daily 7am-9pm). The **Centro de Salud,** on Carranza (tel. 3-02-47), is in a white building with a blue roof, three blocks south of the *zócalo,* on the left. Some English is spoken. Medical services are available 24 hours. The **police** (tel. 3-00-55) are in the Palacio Municipal, on the *zócalo.* The **post office** is on Mantilla, between the lake and Hotel Los Arcos (open Mon.-Fri. 9am-4pm, Sat. 9am-1pm). **Postal Code:** 95870. **Phone Code:** 294.

**Accommodations** Most hotels cluster around the *zócalo* and the waterfront. Although they fill up during Christmas and Semana Santa, you'll practically have the town to yourself on a weekday during the off-season. It is not safe to camp on the beaches, since crime has recently been a problem in the area. The **Hotel Julita,** Playa 10 (tel. 3-00-08), on the waterfront, one block downhill from the *zócalo,* is a very good deal, boasting an unbeatable location and large rooms with fans (singles 40 pesos, peak season 50 pesos; doubles 60 pesos). **Hotel Acuario** at Boettinger and Carranza (tel. 3-04-18), next to the Palacio Municipal, provides large, relatively clean rooms with 70s curtains, some with balconies (singles 50 pesos; doubles 80 pesos).

**Food** When choosing a waterfront restaurant, pay attention primarily to the view of the lake, as menus vary little. *Mojarra* and *topote* will hop right from the lake onto your plate, but make sure to have them well-cooked, since the waters can be polluted. *Mojarra* is prepared in a variety of ways, while the bite-sized *topote* is fried up whole and heaped with *tamales*. Shrimp, much of it from surrounding rivers, is also a local specialty. **Restaurant La Casona del Recuerdo,** Aldama 6 (tel. 3-05-76), just off the *zócalo,* is a haven from the busy waterfront. The terrace in back overlooks a peaceful wooded garden. Locals flock here for the excellent *comida corrida* (15 pesos; open daily 8am-8pm). On the waterfront, across from the Hotel Julita, **7 Brujas** (tel. 3-01-57) serves the standard seafood dishes (20-35 pesos). This is definitely not Kansas; what the idiosyncratic wooden structure lacks in the realm of flying monkeys it makes up for in funky ambience (open daily 8am-10pm). **Restaurant/Bar El Pescador,** just a few doors to the right of 7 Brujas as you face it, serves up good food with a nice view (seafood 25-35 pesos; open daily 9am-11pm).

**Sights, Entertainment, and Seasonal Events** The rocky beaches of **Laguna Catemaco** don't resemble Cancún, but a dip in the lake can be a refreshing break from the hot Veracruz sun. The water immediately in front of town is not safe for swimming. A hiking path runs along the edge of the lake—walk down from the *zócalo* to the waterfront and turn left. The trail, bordered by trees knotted with character, will guide you the 1.5km to **Playa Expagoya** and then another 0.5km down the road to the more secluded and sandy **Playa Hermosa,** the first swimmable beach on the trail. The path is not safe at night. It's also possible to swim off of a *lancha* in the deeper and sometimes clearer waters in the middle of the lake.

The lake is nearly circular, about 15km across. Several small islands dot its smooth surface. The waterfront is lined with long, flat-bottomed, brightly-colored *lanchas* equipped with chairs and canopies. These boats lie ready to take you on an hour-long trip to the best-known island of the lot, **Isla de Changos.** A group of semi-wild, red-cheeked *changos* (mandrills, a kind of baboon) was brought from Thailand for a scientific experiment by the University of Veracruz in 1979, who wanted to see if the animals could survive in their new environment. Lo and behold, 17 years later the *changos* are alive, well, and posing for snapshots. Knowing that the *lanchistas* bring coconuts and tortillas, the bravest *changos* climb right into the boat to pose for camera shots and collect their reward. En route to the island, you'll pass a cave-shrine that stands on the spot where a woman had a vision of the Virgin Mary over a century ago. Negotiate with the *lancheros* for longer trips, including an exploration of the rivers that feed the lake or a trip to the tropical forests of the nearby national park. The *lanchas* leave from the docking area below the *zócalo* (standard tour of the lake, including the Isla de Changos and the shrine of the Virgin, 150 pesos per boat, 30 pesos per person on a *colectivo;* go in the morning or on the weekend if you want to share the boat and save money).

Catemaco's **bars** and **discos** are the best in the Tuxtlas area, although that's not saying much. Nightlife only really heats up during the high tourist season—Semana Santa, July, and August. **Chanequa's,** in the Hotel Playa Azul (tel. 3-00-42 or 3-00-01), some distance from Catemaco, caters to the chic crowd that frequents this posh hotel. Walking there at night is difficult and dangerous; a boat will take you for 20 pesos. The road along the beach dominates nightlife in Catemaco. Four blocks from the Hotel Julita, one block away from the water on Madero, **Jahac 45** (tel. 3-08-50) is a video bar and disco that sometimes sponsors concerts by bands from the area (cover 12 pesos; open Fri.-Sat. after 9pm). Next on Playa, moving closer to the Hotel Julita, is **Luna 90,** a disco above Restaurant La Luna that features incredibly loud music (cover 15 pesos; open Fri.-Sat. after 9pm). Just past Hotel Julita is the bar portion of the restaurant **7 Brujas,** offering a more mellow atmosphere (open daily until 10:30pm). A few doors down is **Pescado Loco,** which plays a seafood salad of music from salsa and *rancheras* to English pop (cover 15 pesos; open Fri.-Sat. 9pm-3am).

In addition to Semana Santa and Christmas festivities, the town goes crazy on July 16, the day of its patron saint Carmen. May 30 is the Day of the Fisherman.

# ■ Near Catemaco: The Gulf Coast

Some say that the only reason to go to Catemaco is for its proximity to secluded beaches on the Gulf Coast. Waves, they will tell you, crash more crisply in the absence of Corona bars and souvenir shops. These beaches are off the beaten track— cattle roam the spaces between fishing villages with no telephone lines and only the most basic services. The state of Veracruz wants to pave the road to the coast and to develop the region for tourism. When this will happen is anyone's guess, but the sage traveler will visit the area before it does.

Getting to the Gulf Coast near Catemaco is an adventure. Public transportation to the area is limited to **Transportes Rurales**'s small **pick-up trucks,** affectionately dubbed *piratas* by locals. A four-door vehicle with wooden benches built into its caged-in bed, a *pirata* can carry the entire population of a small town. Men are expected to yield indoor seats to children and the elderly. From Catemaco, *piratas* depart from the intersection of two unmarked streets on the eastern edge of town. To get to them, follow the lakefront past 7 Brujas for several blocks until you pass the last restaurant before foliage takes over the street; then turn left and walk until the intersection of a paved road. Lines for the *piratas* begin to your left next to the trucks. A man with a clipboard can give you a general idea of when your ride will leave. Often you will have to wait until several passengers have congregated to go in your direction. There are two main routes: one ends at **Montepío** on the Gulf Coast and one goes to **Coyame** on the other side of Lake Catemaco. The *piratas* operate daily from 6am to 6pm.

## The Road to Montepío

The first point of interest on the way to Montepío (besides the jaw-dropping views) is **Sontecomapán,** 20km from Catemaco (6 pesos). This is also the end of the paved road. Hold on tight for the points beyond. Sontecomapán is a small town beside an eponymous saltwater lake that empties into the Gulf of Mexico. *Lanchas* are available for excursions on the lake. It is also possible to travel to other points further down the coast in a *lancha*. The going rate for a *lancha* from Sontecomapán to the small village of **La Barra** is 25 pesos; negotiate with the boat operators for longer trips. La Barra is a fishing community where Laguna Sontecomapán empties into the Gulf of Mexico. To get there, ride a *pirata* 8km beyond Sontecomapán until the road forks. Your *pirata* will normally follow the left fork; you can either negotiate with the driver to take the right fork instead, or you can hop off, take a right, and hike the 5-6km to La Barra yourself. Once there, locals will show you a modicum of hospitality if you introduce yourself politely; a friendly *viajero* will be allowed to camp near someone's home.

The *pirata* route comes closer to the coast near Playa Jicacal and Playa Escondida; ask the driver to let you off (50min., 12 pesos). A half-hour walk through a lush and remote rural area leads to **Playa Jicacal,** a true gem. The long, slightly stony beach is almost completely empty; the only footprints lead to a few modest fisherman's shacks and—inevitably—a *refresco* stand and snack bar (although there are plans to put in a hotel and restaurant). The beach is said to be safe for camping, and hammock-hanging sites may be available. Safety goes hand and hand with good manners, and campers who wish to crash on the beach would do well to ingratiate themselves with the *jicacaleños*.

Instead of turning right to Playa Jicacal, you can walk uphill to the left for **Playa Escondida** (Hidden Beach), a beach that lives up to its name. The simple white **Hotel Playa Escondida** (tel. 2-16-14 or 2-20-01 in San Andrés) appears like a mirage. The hotel is far enough off the beaten track that there are usually plenty of vacancies, but this is starting to change as the word gets out about this jewel on the coast, so reservations are not a bad idea. The hotel provides not only access to the small rocky beach below, but also the chance to explore the surrounding jungle. Rooms have fans (singles 90 pesos; doubles 100 pesos). This beach offers the safest camping in the area, as access is available only through the hotel. Be prepared to pay 15-20 pesos for this security. The remote hotel has a full-service restaurant perched high over the waves of the Gulf of Mexico. A complete lunch of soup, chicken, tortillas, and drink tastes all the more scrumptious because you had to trek so far to reach it (26 pesos). Swimming is possible at both beaches, but an undertow and big waves make for less than ideal swimming conditions. Access to the beach for nonguests is 5 pesos. For those who want a secluded beach without the half-hour walk through the jungle, have the *pirata* drop you off at **Balzapote** (1¾hr., 14 pesos). A handful of houses and a small restaurant-store are all that separates this empty beach from the dirt road.

At the end of the 40km *pirata* route is the tiny village of **Montepío** (2hr., 17 pesos). The town consists of a handful of buildings, including a little light-blue church whose facade is barely big enough to accommodate the door. There are some very modest restaurants, a **pharmacy** (open daily 10am-2pm), and a **health clinic** (open 24hr.) scattered around the church and along the road. Montepío is less spectacular than Playa Escondida, but it does offer a long, narrow beach framed by a tall bluff and volcanic rocks on one end and the green hills of the Sierra on the other. Locals rent **horses** for 15 pesos per hour. Pick-up trucks (every hr., 6am-6pm), take travelers to a nearby **biological research station,** where young scientists may tell you about the flora and fauna of the area and show you the snakes and monkeys they're studying. The new **Hotel Posada San José** (tel. 2-10-10 or 2-20-20 in San Andrés) stands on the bank of the small river leading to the beach. Colorfully painted rooms are clean and spacious (singles 100 pesos; doubles 120 pesos; add 20 pesos for each additional person). The *posada* also features a restaurant with a commanding view of the water; the *a la carte* menu offers most dishes for around 10 pesos. If your wanderlust urges you to go even farther afield, **Playa Hermosa** is another 8km down the beach from Montepío. It takes about an hour walking to get there, or a *lancha* will take you for 50 pesos. This beach features waterfalls and even more secluded sand.

### Coyame

Alternatively, you can take a *pirata* headed for Coyame, 12km from Catemaco, where you can watch the cool waters that are bottled to make the soft drink of the same name bubble up from underground springs. Seven kilometers *en route* to Coyamé, the **Proyecto Ecológico Educacional Nanciyaga,** or simply **Nanciyaga** (tel. 3-01-99; 3 pesos in *pirata*), has lured Hollywood producers, beauty queens, and uptight Americans to its cleansing font of pre-Hispanic therapy. From the highway, turn right and walk in front of the "Nanciyaga" sign on a dirt path that leads towards the shore of the lake. All of the vegetation in the area is part of a preserve, a fact that forced the makers of Sean Connery's *Medicine Man* to alter the landscape with styrofoam trees. Remains from the movie shoot as well as a facial mask of local mud and sips of natural spring water are part of the tour of the site (10 pesos; consultation with a real medicine man, who is a cross between a chiropractor and a faith healer, 40 pesos more). Guests can stay overnight in mosquito-netted bungalows and enjoy the Olmec *temazacal* sweat lodge, full-body mud baths, open-air concerts, and boat tours of the lake that sparkles through the trees (180 pesos; day pass 45 pesos; activities like massages and vegetarian meals require advance reservations). *Lanchas* or taxis will also take you to Nanciyaga (20 pesos). To return to Catemaco, walk back to the highway, cross the street, and flag down any *pirata* headed back to town.

## ■ San Andrés Tuxtla

Lodged between the lush lakeside resorts of Catemaco and the Olmec artifacts of Santiago, San Andrés Tuxtla (usually just San Andrés) is the relatively untouristed anchor of 125,000 inhabitants that keeps the Sierra de los Tuxtlas peacefully down to earth. A quiet little town, San Andrés serves mainly as a center for the tobacco and cattle industries of the surrounding countryside, and offers a cache of budget hotels, an entertaining *zócalo*, remarkably friendly people, and some nearby natural attractions. As the transportation hub of the region, San Andrés serves as a good base from which to stage daytrips to most locations in Los Dos Tuxtlas.

**Orientation and Practical Information** Located midway between Catemaco and Santiago Tuxtla on Rte. 180, San Andrés is built on and around a volcanic range that hugs the Gulf Coast. The downtown area lies in the slightly-raised center of a valley. To get there from the bus station, walk down **Juárez,** the city's main street. Branching off Rte. 180, Juárez descends a steep hill, crosses a small stream, and gradually ascends to meet the cathedral at the north corner of the *zócalo*. Right before reaching the cathedral, Juárez passes by the **Palacio Municipal** on the right and intersects **Constitución** to the left and **Madero** to the right, in front of the Palacio Municipal. Following Constitución to the left, you will come to the intersection of **Pino Suárez,** where some hotels are located. The walk takes 10 minutes from the bus station; a taxi costs 5 pesos.

The often-deserted **tourist office** is on the first floor of the Palacio Municipal, right in front of the cathedral (open Mon.-Fri. 9am-1pm and 4-6pm). You're more likely to find somebody at **Protux Viajes,** 16 de Septiembre 6 (tel. 2-21-75), around the corner. To get there, walk down Juárez toward the bus station and follow the road that veers almost immediately to the left. Protux Viajes is about three blocks down on the right. They provide pamphlets and information about San Andrés and environs (open Mon.-Sat. 8:30am-2pm and 4:30-8pm). Exchange your money at **Banamex** (tel. 2-03-50), on the south side of the *zócalo* (open for exchange Mon.-Fri. 9am-2:30pm). They have a 24-hour **ATM.** There are no **LADATELs** in San Andrés. Long-distance *casetas* can be found at **Pipisoles,** Madero 6B (open Mon.-Fri. 8am-10pm, Sun. 9am-1pm) and at **Protux Viajes.** Coin-operated phones are available outside the **Telmex** office on Carranza at the corner of Bernardo Peña; to get there, take Madero past the Palacio Municipal and turn right on Carranza (open Mon.-Fri. 8am-5pm). The telegram office, Constitución 93 (tel. 2-08-20), at the corner of Pino Suárez, has a **fax** machine (open Mon.-Fri. 8am-6pm, Sat. 9am-noon).

**Autotransportes Los Tuxtlas** (tel. 2-14-62), on Rte. 180 about 300m beyond the ADO station, sends **buses** to Catemaco (every 10min., 4am-10pm, 15min., 2.5 pesos), Coatzacoalcos (every 10min., 4am-10pm, 3½hr., 28 pesos), Santiago Tuxtla (every 10min., 4am-10pm, 20min., 2.50 pesos), and Veracruz (every 15min., 2am-10pm, 3½hr., 30.50 pesos). **ADO** (tel. 2-08-71), at the intersection of Juárez and Route 180 (also called **Blvd. 5 de Febrero**), serves Mexico City (1:30am, 9, 10:30, and 11:10pm, 7½hr., 156 pesos; comfy deluxe service 11pm, 7½hr., 180 pesos), Veracruz (37 per day, 5am-10:30pm, 2½hr., 34 pesos), and Villahermosa (13 per day, 12:45am-10:45pm, 5hr., 77 pesos). **AU** (tel. 2-09-84) goes to Puebla (9:50pm, 6hr., 112 pesos), Veracruz (noon and 9:50pm, 2½hr., 34 pesos), and Xalapa (noon and 9:50pm, 4hr., 60 pesos). **Cuenca** covers Tuxtepec (10 per day, 4am-6pm, 3hr., 37 pesos).

The **market, Mercado 5 de Febrero,** spills onto the streets several blocks from the *zócalo*. To get there, walk on Madero, turn right on Carranza and walk uphill (open daily 6am-10pm). **Lavandería Tintorería Roxy,** at Agosto 776 (tel. 2-12-94), will wash and dry 3kg of your dirtiest duds for 11 pesos (open Mon.-Sat. 8am-8pm). Be careful, as they charge 1-3 pesos per piece of clothing, depending on the size of each article. It gets pricey fast. The **Red Cross** is at Boca Negra 25 (tel. 2-05-00), north of the *zócalo* (open 24hr.). **Farmacia Garysa,** Madero 3, is in the "Canada" building to the left of the Palacio Municipal (open 24hr.). The **Hospital Regional** (tel. 2-31-99), at the edge of town, has an ambulance service. The **police** (tel. 2-14-99) are located on Pasaje Rascón, near the Palacio Municipal (open 24hr.). The **post office** (tel. 2-01-89) is at La Fragua and 20 de Noviembre, one block from the *zócalo* (open Mon.-Fri. 8am-8pm, Sat. 8am-12:30pm). **Postal Code:** 95700. **Phone Code:** 294.

**Accommodations and Food** Although San Andrés remains almost tourist-free, budget accommodations with private bath and hot water are abundant. Two of the best bargains are within spitting distance of each other, just to the left of the cathedral. Follow the street in front of the church to the left and turn right onto Pino Suárez at the orange Fénix supermarket. The **Hotel Colonial,** Pino Suárez 7 (tel. 2-05-52), has a spacious lobby and more modestly-sized rooms cooled vigorously by a ceiling fan. Mural-sized map behind the check-in desk gives a comprehensive overview of the area (singles 35-40 pesos; doubles 50-70 pesos). **Hotel Figueroa,** Pino Suárez 2 (tel. 2-02-57), is across the street. Rooms on the central courtyard look across to the home of the family that runs the place, while others line the arcaded balcony. All have portable fans (singles 35 pesos; doubles 50 pesos). The most affordable rooms with all-important air conditioning are in **Hotel Isabel,** Madero 13 (tel. 2-16-17), to the left of the Hotel Parque next to the *zócalo* (singles 80 pesos, with A/C 110 pesos; doubles 100 pesos, with A/C 130 pesos).

Several sidewalk cafes on the *zócalo* serve breakfast and coffee, and afford a pleasant view of simple small-town life. A number of good lunch spots line Madero, while the cheaper sidewalk stands proliferate in and around the market. **Restaurant La Caperucita,** Juárez 108 (tel. 2-05-11), downhill from the cathedral, specializes in large, filling fried *misantleca* (big disk-o'-dough stuffed with beans, ham, and cheese, 14 pesos). They also serve delicious tacos, fruit shakes, and *refrescos* at good prices (open daily 7am-midnight). The older and more affluent huddle at **Restaurant del Parque** (tel. 2-01-98), on the ground floor of the Hotel Parque on the *zócalo*. Food (breakfast 11-16 pesos, *antojitos* 10-20 pesos, *tortas* 10-17 pesos) is secondary to the socializing (open daily 7am-midnight). The friendly folks at **El Pequeño Archie,** on Pino Suárez just downhill from the hotels and across the street from the movies, serve up a delicious *comida corrida* (10 pesos) and *antojitos* (6-10 pesos; open Mon.-Sat. 8am-9pm, Sun. 8am-2pm).

**Sights, Entertainment, and Seasonal Events** Even nonsmokers will be impressed by the **Tabacos San Andrés Factory,** where Santa Clara cigars are made. From the *zócalo,* walk up Juárez to the ADO and turn right—it's about 200m down Rte. 180 (here called Blvd. 5 de Febrero) on the right. An open door and the smell of tobacco leaves invite you in. The amiable staff will gladly walk you through the entire process, from selecting the leaves to rolling the stogies to putting on the company seal. A skilled worker can produce 800 cigars a day. You can purchase some near the entrance: the bottom of the line starts at 100 pesos, while a box of 25 of their finest *puros* goes for 500 pesos (open Mon.-Sat. 7am-7pm; customs regulations may limit the number of cigars you can take back into your country—see p. 16).

The sheer number of video rental stores just about says it all: San Andrés is not exactly a town that parties until dawn. Unless you brought your VCR along, it might be hard to find nighttime entertainment. Most of the action centers on the *zócalo,* where folks in San Andrés gather to meet, gossip, see, and be seen. On Sunday nights, families bring their children, and the square becomes a little kiddie carnival with balloons and small electric cars for hire. **Cinemas San Andrés,** on Pino Suárez across from El Pequeño Archie, brings English-language movies to the big screen for 8 pesos. For anything more high-paced than people- and film-watching, catch the bus to **Catemaco** (p. 448), which offers a few bars and discos.

On Independence Day, September 16, giant balloons of colorful paper are flown over the *zócalo.* The town's patron saint is celebrated on November 30. December 12 is the day of Guadalupe, Mexico's patron virgin. As part of the celebrations, young people playfully hit each other with wooden figures called *majigangas.*

**La Laguna Encantada** is a volcanic lake 2km northeast of the city, surrounded by lush vegetation and known mainly for its weird tendency to rise during the dry season and fall during the rainy season. To get there, walk north on Serapio Rendón (perpendicular to, and a couple of blocks north of, Pino Suárez) until you hit Blvd. 5 de Febrero (Rte. 180); then walk east on 5 de Febrero until a sign for the lake appears on the left (40min.). The trail can be muddy and rocky, so come prepared. Taxis will take you there reluctantly, due to poor road conditions (20 pesos). The lake is very clean for swimming; it may be populated by washerwomen, fishermen, and birds, or even crowds of people, depending on the season, the weather, and the day of the week. As tempting as a solitary day in the woods may sound, for safety reasons it might be best to go with a friend.

On the opposite shore, which is accessible via the trail that circumnavigates the lake, a complicated series of unmarked trails leads to the spring whence the lake's waters flow, and then up a steep hill to **La Coberna del Diablo,** where witches from around Mexico gather on the first Friday in March. The remains of their ceremonial candles spot the rocks on the way up to the cave. Don't go in: if the devil doesn't get you, the sulfuric gases and tarantulas will.

## ■ Near San Andrés Tuxtla: Salto de Eyipantla

To reach the more accessible **Salto de Eyipantla** waterfall, take a minibus from the market that bears the name of these wide, bewilderingly powerful, spectacular falls (35min., 2.20 pesos). The bus will make a U-turn and stop at a small market. Walk straight behind the bus for a few minutes until you encounter a parking lot and children clamoring to give you flowers (beware, this will turn into pleas for money). Proceed through a restaurant at the end of the lot. Right after the entrance (admission a staggering 1 peso), you'll find the 244 steps descending to the base of the falls. A movie starring Lorenzo Lamas and a deodorant commercial were both filmed in this historic point. Don't expect a solitary communion with nature, though—you'll have to angle your camera so as not to include the kiosks in your pictures. The bus back to San Andrés stops every 10 minutes at the very stop where it left you (5am-8pm).

# ▓ Santiago Tuxtla

Of the three cities that constitute Los Tuxtlas, Santiago (pop. 50,000) has the least to offer visitors in terms of sights and recreational activities. Its attraction stems from its connection to two influential forces in Mexican history: the Olmecs and Hernán Cortés. The colossal stone heads and Catholic ceremonies that each left behind comingle in this community known for its superstition and elaborate festivals.

**Orientation and Practical Information** The **ADO bus station,** like everything else in Santiago, is just a few blocks from the *zócalo.* To reach the town center, walk downhill from Rte. 180 where the bus drops you. The first right is **Ayuntamiento,** which leads to the **Palacio Municipal** with its clock tower on the right and the *zócalo* in front of it. From the ADO bus station, walking downhill and then following **Morelos** will bring you to the **Autotransportes Los Tuxtlas** station on the left and **Calle Obregón** on the right.

The archaeology museum offers **tourist information. Currency exchange** is simply not possible in Santiago, so come armed with pesos. The closest bank is in San Andrés. Somebody at the **telephone office,** in the corner of the Palacio Municipal at the intersection with Ayuntamiento, should be able to help with long distance calls.

**ADO** (tel. 7-04-38) sends buses to Mexico City (9:20, 10:45, and 11:30pm, 7hr., 152 pesos), Veracruz (10, 11am, 1 and 6:45pm, 2¼hr., 33 pesos), and Xalapa (6:45, 7:50, and 9am, 4½hr., 61 pesos). **Cuenca** sends buses to San Andrés (every hr., 9am-10pm, except 4 and 7pm, 20min., 3 pesos) and Tuxtepec (every hr., 4:35am-6:35pm, 4hr., 34 pesos). **Autotransportes Los Tuxtlas** buses leave right next to the ADO station for Catemaco (every 10min., 8am-10pm, 40min., 6 pesos) and San Andrés (20min., 2.5 pesos).

The **market, Mercado Municipal Morelos,** begins to the left of the *zócalo* as you face it from the Palacio Municipal and continues one street over to the left (open daily 5am-8pm). The nearest **Red Cross** is in San Andrés; for **24-hour ambulance service,** dial 2-05-00. **Farmacia San Felipe,** just off the *zócalo* at Eduardo Murgía 13 (tel. 7-01-36), is open 24 hours. The **Clínica Doctores Castellanos,** across from the Hotel Castellanos (tel. 7-02-60), provides medical assistance day and night. Find the **police** (tel. 7-00-92) downstairs in the Palacio Municipal (open daily 24hr.).

**Accommodations** The **Hotel Castellanos,** on the corner of 5 de Mayo and Comonfort (tel. 7-03-00), at the far corner of the *zócalo,* is not only a place to stay, its also Santiago's most interesting attraction. The rooms fit together like wedges in a Trivial Pursuit game piece; each offers air conditioning, telephones, color TV, and a balcony with a panoramic view. If you can stop admiring the scenery or the painted ceramic bathroom sinks, there is also a pool and restaurant. Too bad it's so expensive (singles 115 pesos; doubles 138 pesos; triples 161 pesos). Both less stimulating and less expensive, **Casa de Huéspedes Morelos,** Obregón 15 (tel. 7-04-74), downhill from the bus stations, has basic small rooms with fans and bathrooms with hot water (singles 40 pesos; doubles 60 pesos; triples 70 pesos).

**Sights and Seasonal Events** The largest Olmec head ever discovered (45 tons) sits complacently at the far end of Santiago's *zócalo,* shaded from the sun by a large cupola. The sculpture is immediately recognizable as Olmec because of its distinctive facial features (heavy lips and slanted eyes), ears, and "helmet." The head is distinctive not only for its size but also because its eyes are closed. The **Museo Regional Tuxteco,** to the left of the head along the *zócalo,* displays terra-cotta masks of the Totonacs and another Olmec head, along with other artifacts from around the region (open Mon.-Sat. 9am-5pm; admission 10 pesos). Celebrations for the **fair** in honor of Santiago, the town's patron saint, take place July 20-29 and include a choreographed fight between Christians and Moors and a *torneo de cintas* in which men dress in medieval gear and ride horses.

# ■ Near Santiago Tuxtla

## TRES ZAPOTES RUINS

**Tres Zapotes,** one of the three main Olmec ceremonial centers, reached its peak between 300 BC and AD 300, but there is support for occupation as early as 900 BC. Today, calling the artifacts on display a "museum" would be either optimistic or an exaggeration. There are no written explanations to elucidate the small sheltered gathering of carved stones, nor are artifacts even located at their original sites. If you have at least a cursory knowledge of Spanish, solicit explanations from the attendant at the ticket booth.

The Olmecs did not construct great cities, but they did fill them with noteworthy art. The most imposing figure at Tres Zapotes is one of the trademark Olmec stone heads that always seems to carry the label "colossal." The monumentality of their sculpture contrasts with the delicate details and precise techniques they used to carve them. Archaeologists believe the heads are portraits of actual leaders. The helmet that adorns the head may have been worn during ritual ball games that appeared first in Olmec centers and then spread to Mesoamerica. The head at Tres Zapotes was discovered in 1862 by a *campesino* who first thought it was an overturned cooking pot. It was the first Olmec head ever found. To the left of the head is the **Stela C,** which, together with its more famous other half (now at the National Anthropology Museum in Mexico City (see p. 102), bears the oldest written date in the Americas— 31 BC, inscribed in late Olmec, or Spi-Olmec glyphs similar to those later used by the Maya. The date is visible on the back of the stela as a bar (representing "5") and two dots, giving a total of seven on their calendar. **Stela A** lies in the transept to the left. Decorations in the stela include the figure of a man, a serpent coiling upon itself (on the right side), and a man holding an axe (on the left side). **Stela D,** to the right of the head, again resembles a tablet. Within the mouth of a jaguar are renderings of three people whose relative heights symbolize their power and importance. The tallest figure, on the far right, is most likely a ruler; the central, skirted figure is perhaps an emissary; the kneeling figure on the left is probably someone making an offering or a prisoner of war. On the left side of the piece, the broad mouth of what is possibly a toad is visible; on the right side it's possible to discern a skeletal face (museum open daily 9am-5pm; admission 7 pesos, free Sun.).

**Getting There:** From the Museo Regional Tuxteco in Santiago, walk towards the clock tower and turn right on Zaragoza. Pass through the market and cross the bridge to Morelos, where you can take a *taxi-colectivo* to Tres Zapotes (½hr., 8 pesos). You will be let off in the town of Tres Zapotes. From the stop, turn left and walk to the first cross-street. Turn left and walk around the chain-link fence until you see the entrance on your right. The largest mound on the site is a few kilometers away from the museum. It's called Loma Camila and rises 12m above the surrounding countryside and sugar cane fields. Every May, a "Harmonic Convergence" is held on top of Loma Camila. Shirley MacLaine made the trip a few years ago, and every year crowds of new- age adherents descend upon Tres Zapotes. There's not much to see at the mound, but a taxi will take you to Loma Camila to experience the vibes for 7-8 pesos.

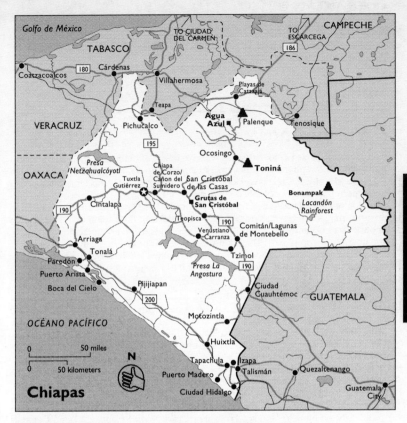

Chiapas

# Chiapas and Tabasco

**Chiapas** is special. Its climate is unique for southern Mexico—the chilly nights and crisp fresh air give the highlands a distinct flavor. Cortés had the Sierra de Chiapas in mind when, to demonstrate what Mexico looked like, he crumpled a piece of parchment and dropped it on the table. In these rugged green mountains, buses career around hairpin turns above deep valleys before hurtling down into jungles on rutted roads. One of Mexico's most beautiful cities, San Cristóbal de las Casas, known for cobblestone streets and surrounding *indígena* villages, rests high amid these peaks.

Throughout the state, you will hear diverse Mayan dialects and find markets and other public places filled with *indígenas*. Indeed, the state is part of the Maya heartland; the Lacandón Rainforest shields the remote ruins of Bonampak and Yaxchilán and is still home to the Lacandón Indians, whose isolation has kept them from both the Spanish Conquest and tourist invasion. Chiapas's *indígenas* remain fiercely traditional—in many communities, schools teach in the local dialect as well as in Spanish, and regional dress, while it varies across communities, is almost always maintained. The Zapatista rebellion of 1994 (see p. 60), while not of revolutionary proportions, succeeded in drawing the world's attention to the central Mexican government's lack of attention to the needs and rights of the highland region's poor *indígena* villages.

**Tabasco,** perched on the lush Isthmus of Tehuantepec, connects the Yucatán Peninsula to the Gulf coast and the rest of the country. *Tabasqueños* proudly boast that their state is one of the wettest places on earth, second only to the Amazon Basin. Tabasco, dotted by lakes and swamps, criss-crossed by rivers, and swathed in dense, humid jungle, certainly does see an awful lot of rainfall. The weather is like clock-work—be prepared for showers every afternoon during the rainy season (June-Sept.). Happy (and dry) is the well-prepared tourist.

# TABASCO

## ■ Villahermosa

By 1596, the Spanish colonists were weary enough of defending their coast against British and Dutch pirates that they migrated inland up the Río Grijalva to found Villa-hermosa. The city was relatively poor and substantially isolated, an agricultural center of minor importance, accessible only by river. In the past 50 years, however, the construction of railroad tracks and the discovery of oil have given the ailing city a shot in the arm, transforming Villahermosa (pop. 1.6 million), the capital of Tabasco, from boondock to boomtown, a dense urban forest of satellite antennae, luxury hotels, and apartment complexes. There's not much to do or see in this frenetic city; it is only Villahermosa's proximity to the ruins at Palenque and its position as a crossroads between Chiapas and the Yucatán that make it a common stopover for travelers.

### ORIENTATION

Tabasco's state capital lies 20km from the border with Chiapas and 298km west of Escárcega, the major crossroads for Yucatán-bound travelers. The spine of the downtown area is **27 de Febrero. Paseo Tabasco** runs north-south and connects the Tabasco 2000 complex to *el centro,* intersecting 27 de Febrero in front of the cathedral. *Saetas* (public buses) and *combis* (each 1.50 pesos) run from 6am to 10:30pm. First- and second-class **buses** depart from the eastern part of town. An **airport** lies northwest of the city, 14km from the downtown area; taxis shuttle between the airport and *el centro* (40 pesos *especial,* 15 pesos *colectivo*).

To reach downtown from the **first-class ADO station,** walk two and a half blocks to the right on Mina to Méndez. From there, take a *combi* labeled "Tierra Colorada Centro-Juárez" and get off a few minutes later at **Parque Juárez.** Most hotels are south of the park on either **Madero** or its parallel cousin **Constitución.** Walking from the station to Parque Juárez takes 15 to 20 minutes; upon exiting the terminal, head right down Mina for eight blocks, then turn left onto 27 de Febrero. Eight more blocks takes you to the intersection with Madero. To get downtown from the **second-class bus terminal,** cross Grijalva on the pedestrian bridge to the left of the station exit, then jump on a bus labeled "Indeco Centro" (1 peso) and disembark at Parque Juárez on Madero. To make the 25-minute walk from the station, cross the bridge and continue south on Mina for three blocks until you reach the ADO station (see above). A cab ride to the center of town costs about 10 pesos.

### PRACTICAL INFORMATION

**Tourist Offices: Instituto de Turismo,** Av. de los Ríos 113 (fax 16-51-43), 1 block behind the planetarium. Has more info than you'll ever need, but those colorful brochures will cost up to 25 pesos. Open Mon.-Fri. 9am-3pm and 6-9pm. **Tourist Information Booths** at the airport and Museo La Venta. Open daily 7am-4:30pm.

**Currency Exchange:** Villahermosa is the capital of ATMs. **Banamex,** Madero at Reforma (tel. 12-00-11). Open for exchange Mon.-Fri. 9am-5pm. 24hr. **ATM.**

**American Express:** Patriotismo 605 (tel. 91-800-5-00-44). Open Mon.-Sat. 9am-6pm.

**Telephones:** Calls are best made from the **LADATELs** all over town.

**Fax:** Lerdo 601 at Saenz (tel. 14-28-32 or 14-28-33), around the corner from the post office. Open for **telegrams** and fax Mon.-Fri. 8am-7pm, Sat. 9am-1pm.

**Airport:** On the Villahermosa-Macupana highway (tel. 56-01-57; fax 56-01-58). **Aeroméxico,** Camara 511, locale 2 (tel. 12-15-28). **Aviacsa,** Mina 1025 (tel. 14-57-70 or 14-57-80). **Mexicana,** Via 3 #120 (tel. 16-31-31 or 16-31-38).

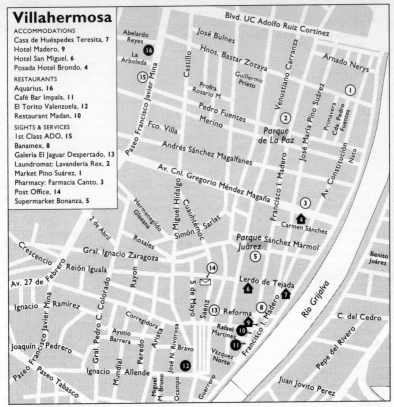

## Villahermosa

**ACCOMMODATIONS**
Casa de Huéspedes Teresita, 7
Hotel Madero, 9
Hotel San Miguel, 6
Posada Hotel Brondo, 4

**RESTAURANTS**
Aquarius, 16
Café Bar Impala, 11
El Torito Valenzuela, 12
Restaurant Madan, 10

**SIGHTS & SERVICES**
1st Class ADO, 15
Banamex, 8
Galería El Jaguar Despertado, 13
Laundromat: Lavandería Rex, 2
Market Pino Suárez, 1
Pharmacy: Farmacia Canto, 3
Post Office, 14
Supermarket Bonanza, 5

CHIAPAS & TABASCO

**Buses:** The 1st-class terminal is at Mina 297 at Merino, a couple blocks east of Juárez. **Cristóbal Colón** (tel. 2-86-00) runs to: Acaycan (7 per day, 4hr., 61 pesos), Agua Dulce (6:15pm, 2hr., 36 pesos), Balancan (5 per day, 3hr., 53 pesos), Campeche (5 per day, 5hr., 124 pesos), Cancún (8 and 10pm, 11hr., 254 pesos), Chetumal (9 and 11pm, 8hr., 152 pesos), Comalco (4 per day, 22 pesos), Escárcega (5 per day, 6hr., 85 pesos), Frontera (14 per day, 1hr., 19 pesos), Mérida (5 per day, 8hr., 171 pesos), Mexico City (5 per day, 11hr., 271 pesos), Oaxaca (6, 8, and 9:45pm, 11hr., 197 pesos), Palenque (8 per day, 2hr., 42 pesos), Paraíso (4 per day, 45min., 25 pesos), Playa del Carmen (8 and 10pm, 8hr., 228 pesos), Puebla (8:40pm, 8hr., 233 pesos), Tapachula (6:30am, 6, and 10pm, 12hr., 169 pesos), Teapa (5 per day, 45min., 13 pesos), Tuxtla Gutierrez (9 per day, 6hr., 75 pesos), and Veracruz (8 per day, 7hr., 134 pesos). **UNO** (tel. 14-58-18) has *servicio de lujo* (luxury); tickets must be purchased 5 days in advance. **Luggage storage** 7am-11pm (1 peso per piece per hr.).

**Car Rental:** There's no such thing as budget. **Renta de Autos Tabasco,** Paseo Tabasco 600 (tel. 15-48-30), next to the cathedral, is the lowest we could find at 391 pesos per day. Open Mon.-Fri. 8am-7pm, Sat.-Sun. 8am-2pm and 4-6pm.

**Radio Taxi:** Tel. 15-82-33, 15-23-39, or 15-83-33. On call 24hr.

**Market: Pino Suárez,** encompassed by Pino Suárez, Constitución, Hermanos Zozaya, and Grijalva, in the northeast corner of town. Open daily 6am-6pm.

**Supermarket: Bonanza,** Madero at Zaragoza (tel. 14-22-80). Open 7am-10pm.

**Laundromat: Lavandería Rex,** Madero 705, just past Méndez. High per-piece rates; try to swing a per-kg deal. Open Mon.-Fri. 9am-6:30pm, Sat. 9am-1pm.

**Red Cross:** On General Sandino (tel. 15-55-55 or 15-56-00), in Col. 1 de Mayo. Take the "1 de Mayo" bus from Madero. No English spoken.

**Pharmacy: Farmacia Canto,** Madero 602 (tel. 12-20-99). Open daily 7am-11pm.

**Medical Services: Clínica 39,** Zaragoza 1202, at Carmen Buen Día (tel. 12-20-49). English-speaking staff. Not free. Open daily 7am-8pm.
**Emergency:** Dial 06.
**Police:** 16 de Septiembre at Periférico (tel. 15-25-17). No English. Open 24hr.
**Post Office:** Saenz 131, at Lerdo (tel. 12-10-40), 3 blocks west of Madero. Open Mon.-Fri. 8am-7pm, Sat. 9am-1pm. **Postal Code:** 86000.
**Phone Code:** 93.

## ACCOMMODATIONS AND CAMPING

Most budget accommodations cluster around the 27 de Febrero and Madero intersection. **Camping** and **trailer parking** are allowed in **La Choca Park** in Tabasco 2000, but the site lacks facilities.

**Hotel Madero,** Madero 301 near 27 de Febrero (tel. 12-05-16). Great central location, but try to get a room off the street. Rooms of wildly varying quality; shop around. Most are clean, ample, and equipped with fans. Singles 70 pesos; doubles 80 pesos; triples 90 pesos.
**Hotel San Miguel,** Lerdo 315 (tel. 12-15-00). Right smack off a pedestrian-only street, in the heart of shop heaven. Small rooms have soft red beds and ceiling fans. The yellow bathrooms sparkle. Singles 50 pesos; doubles 60 pesos, with 2 beds 70 pesos; triples 80 pesos. TV 15 pesos extra. Additional person 15 pesos extra.
**Posada Hotel Brondo,** Pino Suárez 209 (tel. 12-59-61), 4 blocks north of the center on the left-hand side, just off Sanchez. Odd angles make every well-ventilated room unique. Rosy-clean private and communal baths. Singles and doubles without bath 50 pesos; singles with bath 73 pesos; doubles and triples with bath 85 pesos; 4-person suite with kitchenette 150 pesos.

## FOOD

It's hard to compete in the culinary world when you've got Chiapas to the south and all of Yucatán to the east. So, Villahermosa doesn't.

**Aquarius,** Av. Zaragoza 513 (tel. 12-05-79), downtown. Generous portions of healthy food at good prices, if the super-slow service doesn't faze you. Five-course *comida del día* is 26 pesos. Open Mon.-Sat. 8am-5:30pm. V, MC, AmEx.
**El Torito Valenzuela,** 27 de Febrero 202 at Madero (tel. 14-11-89), next to Hotel Madero. After-dinner mints from a *taquería?* Yup. And the steaming, veggie-filled tacos are even better. Huge *comida corrida* 26 pesos. Open daily 8am-midnight.
**Café Bar Impala,** Madero 421 (tel. 12-04-93). A cluttered hole-in-the-wall which serves up superb *tamalitos de chilipín, panuchos* (fried tortilla shells stuffed with meat and beans), and tacos (each a mere 1.50 pesos). Open daily 9am-8pm.

## SIGHTS

Villahermosa's hectic center has several areas of interest within walking distance—the Río Grijalva provides scenic walks along the city's eastern side, and the heart of downtown is a series of pedestrian streets lined with specialty *tiendas, licuado* stands, gurgling fountains, and shaded benches.

While exploring the ruins at La Venta, Tabasco in the early 1940s, U.S. archaeologist **M.W. Sterling** discovered six massive sculpted stone heads. Further studies indicated that La Venta was a principal ceremonial center of the **Olmecs** (see p. 51). Three of their remarkable massive heads, along with 30 other stone pieces, have been moved to the **Parque-Museo La Venta,** an archaeological park in northern Villahermosa. Doubling as archaeological park and zoo, the site is enchanting. La Venta's Olmec sculptures take center stage, displayed along a pathway which winds through a verdant jungle only minutes from the *Zona Remodelada*—only the traffic on Grijalva reminds you that you're actually in a city. At the park's northern edge, birds flit through the aviary, grand felines bask in the sun, and cheeky monkeys toy with those iguanas foolish enough to enter their pit. You can get a good look at the jaguars which roam around their enclosure in the south of the park, halfway around the archaeological walk, near the gift shop. To get to La Venta, take the "Tabasco 2000," "Carrisal," "Petrolera," or "Palacio" **bus** (1.50 pesos) from Madero in the center to the intersection of Tabasco and Ruiz Cortínez. Walk northeast on Cortínez for 10 minutes until you reach the entrance (site open daily 9am-4:30pm;15 pesos; 2hr. tours in Spanish or English about 25-45 pesos for 1-35 people).

Return to Paseo Tabasco through the **Parque Tomás Garrido Canabal,** which lies on the Laguna de las Ilusiones and surrounds the Parque-Museo La Venta. Landscaped alcoves hide benches and fountains. While the *mirador* claims to offer a panoramic view of Villahermosa, all you get in reward for your 40m climb is a good look at a few treetops. You can, however, also get a good look at the *lagunas* below. The main entrance is at the corner of Tabasco and Grijalva (free).

Northwest on Paseo Tabasco, away from the city center and Río Grijalva, is **Tabasco 2000,** a long strip of sparkling new buildings that includes the city's **Palacio Municipal,** a convention center, several fountains, a shopping mall, and a **planetarium** (tel. 16-36-41) with **OmniMax** shows dubbed in Spanish (shows Tues.-Fri. 6 and 7pm, Sat. 6 and 7:30pm, Sun. noon; 10 pesos). Take the "Tabasco 2000" bus from the city center and tell the driver where you want to get off.

The catalyst for the creation of the Parque-Museo La Venta was **Carlos Pellicer Cámara,** Tabasco's most famous poet. His name graces the **Museo Regional de Antropología Carlos Pellicer Cámara,** the main attraction at Villahermosa's new **Center for the Investigation of Olmec and Maya Cultures (CICOM).** The first floor focuses on the life, times, and arts of the Olmecs and the Maya, while the top floor includes representative pieces from all of Mexico's indigenous tribes. Guidebooks (in English or Spanish) are available at the ticket counter. The center also houses a public library, an arts school, and a theater. From the *Zona Remodelada,* the museum is best reached by a 15-minute walk south along the Río Grijalva. The #1 and "CICOM" buses pass often (open daily 9am-8pm; free).

Fourteen kilometers from the hustle and bustle of Villahermosa, elephants and zebras run free at the ecological reserve known as **Yumká** (Elf Who Tends the Jungle). A multitude of animals from around the world roam the three *tabasqueño* ecosystems: jungle, savannah, and wetlands (open daily 9am-5pm; admission 15 pesos, children 10 pesos; ticket counter closes at 4pm). A *colectivo especial* is the fastest way of getting there (60 pesos). Otherwise, go to the PEMEX station at Ruíz Cortinez in La Colonia; at the corner of Sierra and Cortinex, snag a 5 peso **bus** to the zoo.

## ENTERTAINMENT

Villahermosa presents two basic nightlife options: the discos in the luxury hotels or a myriad of cultural activities. The **Instituto de Cultura Tabasco,** on Magallanes (tel. 12-90-24), in the Edificio Portal del Agua, publishes a monthly calendar of musical, theatrical, and other cultural events; look for it in museums and major hotels.

The hottest mix of *salsa,* tropical music, and visual stimuli are found at **Video Bar Factory,** on Av. Méndez (open Tues.-Sat. 10pm-3am), **Tequila Rock** (tel. 16-53-63), on the part of Paseo Tabasco that extends into the Holiday Inn (open Wed.-Sat. 10pm-3am), and **Estudio 8,** on Paseo Tabasco (tel. 14-44-66), in the Hotel Maya, before Tabasco 2000 (open Thurs.-Sun. 9pm-2 or 3am). An older crowd frequents **Disco KU,** on Av. Sandino, and the ambitiously named **Snob,** Juárez 106 in the Hyatt (both open Tues.-Sat. 10pm-3am). Taxi drivers are well-acquainted with disco hot spots, and their vehicles are the only efficient means of reaching them.

For mellower diversion, head to **Galería El Jaguar Despertado,** Sáenz 117 (tel. 14-12-44), near Reforma in the *Zona Remodelada.* The cafe in the back sometimes features live classical music or jazz, but even without the tunes, fountain, original Mexican art, and gallery upstairs attract an interesting mix of intellectuals and romantics (open Tues.-Sat. 3-9pm). For entertainment that's closer to home, **Cinema Superior** on Madero, one block south of 27 de Febrero, has daily showings of American and English-language movies at 5pm and 7pm (17 pesos).

# ■ Near Villahermosa

## COMALCALCO

Whereas La Venta documents Tabasco's Olmec past, **Comalcalco** demonstrates the Maya's dominance over the area in the later Classic period (AD 200-700). One of the northernmost Maya settlements, Comalcalco has yielded evidence of contact with other Yucatecan Maya societies, as well as with the Toltecs, Mexica, and Totonacs. The site's most distinctive feature is its architecture: unlike those of other Maya cities, the pyramids and buildings of Comalcalco were constructed from packed earth and clay and later covered with stucco oven-fired bricks. Eroded but still imperial, the ruins contrast dramatically with the jungle behind them. Do not climb the temples—Uzi-toting guards are serious about the *"no subir"* signs.

With 10 levels, the hulking 25m-high **pyramid** to the left of the entrance to the site is Comalcalco's best-known landmark. The north face bears traces of the elaborate stucco carvings that once completely covered the structure's sides. Behind the pyramid lies the north plaza, surrounded by a series of ruined minor temples and mounds. If you look closely at the dilapidated walls, you'll be able to see the insides of Comalcalco's brickwork and oyster-shell mortar.

From the plaza, a well-worn path leads up the side of the acropolis area and passes a group of three temples on the way. As with the main pyramid, vestiges of elaborate decorative carvings can be seen on each of these temples. Farther up the acropolis, turn right to reach the **Tomb of the Nine Knights of the Night,** named after the nine bas-relief figures on the walls of the tomb. Visible from the acropolis, three sides of Comalcalco's **ballcourt** (to the left) remain unexcavated and covered with tropical vegetation. Several temples, including one known as **The Palace,** stand in pieces atop the acropolis against a backdrop of tall, square brick columns and several roofless rooms (site open daily 10am-5pm; admission 10 pesos).

**Getting There:** The site lies 34km northwest of Villahermosa, 2km from the town of Comalcalco, and is accessible by the bus that travels to Paraíso via Comalcalco. Get off at Comalcalco and walk back a block on Méndez to Rte. 187. From this corner catch a *combi* (about 2 pesos) and ask the driver to let you off at the access road to *las ruinas*. From here, the walk to the site is a pleasant 1km. You can also take a taxi *(especial)* directly to the site from the Comalcalco bus station (about 5 pesos).

# ■ Teapa

An hour's drive south of Villahermosa along roads flanked by banana groves, Teapa's sulfuric spa and splendiferous caverns lure daytrippers from the state capital. The town itself (pop. 35,000) is slow-moving; its dilapidated, leafy *zócalo* and quiet streets make for peaceful strolling.

**Orientation and Practical Information** The **Transportes Villermosa-Teapa** bus lets you off at the main bus terminal on Méndez, from which local buses whisk visitors to either the spa or the caves. If you arrive by **Cristóbal Colón,** walk 200m to the left to the main bus terminal, and an additional five minutes to reach the *zócalo.* Teapa's main drag is **Méndez.**

**Banamex,** Méndez 102 (tel. 2-02-84), next door to the church, offers a 24-hour **ATM** (open Mon.-Fri. 9am-1:30pm). **Cristóbal Colón** sends **buses** (tel. 2-03-52) to Tuxtla Gutiérrez (8 and 9:30am, 5hr., 48 pesos) and Villahermosa (5pm, 1hr., 9 pesos). Second-class buses run to Villahermosa (every hr., 5 pesos; station open daily 7am-10pm). You can check your **baggage** out back by the bathrooms. Villahermosa is much more easily reached by hopping into one of the red **taxis** in the center of town. They leave as soon as they have five people (approximately every 20min., 45min., 15 pesos). **Farmacia Espíritu Santo** is on Calle Dr. Ramón Medina 106, one and a half blocks north of the *zócalo* (open daily 8am-10pm, but provides 24hr. service if you ring the bell in the upper left-hand corner of the doorway). The **police** (tel.

2-01-10) are in the Palacio Municipal on Méndez (open 24hr.). The **post office** is at Calle Manuel Buelta 109, near the *zócalo* (open Mon.-Fri. 9am-3pm). **Postal Code:** 86800. **Phone Code:** 932.

**Accommodations and Food** Teapa's accommodations are a scant bunch without many bargains. Your best bet is **Casa de Huéspedes Miye,** Méndez 211 (tel. 2-00-11), in the center of town. Each bright room has its own color scheme, clean private bathroom, and fan. Birds and flowers make the outside as cheerful as the inside (singles 40 pesos; doubles 50 pesos; add 10 pesos for private bath). Across the park from the church on Av. Plaza de la Independencia, **Hotel Jardín** (tel. 2-00-27) is another possibility. Lime-green rooms have small windows and even smaller bathrooms (singles 50 pesos; doubles 60 pesos; triples 70 pesos). **Josegay,** Méndez 125, half a block west of the church, makes a divine *pollo en mole* (15 pesos; open daily 8am-midnight). **Fruit stands** and **panaderías** line Av. Méndez, but if you're in the mood for a long walk, **La Bella Sultana,** Av. Carlos Ramos 275, offers cheap food and heaping portions. From the *zócalo*, head out of town past the clock tower/arch, a dry bridge, and the PEMEX station; then cross the street and head for the airy, corrugated roof. The excellent service whisks out tacos starting at 2 pesos (open daily 6am-1pm and 4pm-12:30am).

## ■ Near Teapa: Las Grutas Coconá

Just a few kilometers from town, **Las Grutas Coconá** were discovered in the late 1800s. A path winds for 500m into the hillside, passing impressive caverns and underground lagoons along the way. Bringing along a flashlight or hiring an eight-year-old guide (a small tip is standard) will make your visit to the caves much more scintillating. Once you are 150m into the cave system, shine your light into the roof of the tunnel on the bend; sometimes you can catch the tiny bats during their *siesta*. Farther on, you'll enter a breathtaking, acoustically-funky domed cavern replete with mighty stalactites. Beyond, a wooden walkway leads over a pool into a dripping cave. The final cave is draped in gloom and can only be explored with the help of a flashlight. On the way back, look for a left-hand turnoff where a lone lightbulb has given life to a cluster of ferns. Here you can limbo beneath a 1m ledge to reach a secluded emerald pool (*grutas* open daily 9am-4pm; 10 pesos).

**Getting There:** *Combis* for the *grutas* leave from Calle Bastar on the right-hand side of the church (every 20min., 2 pesos). Taxis charge 8-10 pesos.

# CHIAPAS

## ■ Tuxtla Gutiérrez

An energetic young city, Tuxtla Gutiérrez (pop. 350,000) is the capital of Chiapas and the focal point of commerce and transportation for much of southern Mexico. The city was named for a progressive *chiapaneco* governor who, rather than succumb to imperialist right-wing forces, wrapped himself in the Mexican flag and dramatically leapt to his death from a church spire. While Tuxtla's rapid industrialization has left its grimy mark, the city has recently added some splashes of color to the urban landscape: young couples stroll arm-in-arm through verdant parks, and flaming red parrots squawk with pleasure in one of the best zoos in Latin America.

### ORIENTATION

Tuxtla Gutiérrez lies 85km west of San Cristóbal and 293km south of Villahermosa. *Avenidas* run east-west and *calles* north-south. The central axis of the city, upon which the *zócalo* rests, is formed by **Avenida Central** (sometimes called **Avenida 14 de Septiembre**) and **Calle Central.** Streets are numbered according to their distance from and geographical relation to the central axis. For example, Calle 2 Oriente Sur lies south of Av. Central and two blocks east of Calle Central. Fifteen blocks west of the town center, Calle Central becomes **Blvd. Dr. Belisario Domínguez;** 11 blocks east it is known as **Blvd. Ángel Albino Corzo.**

To get to the *centro* from the **ADO/Cristóbal Colón bus station,** walk left on 2 Nte. Pte. (away from the buses) for two blocks. The *zócalo* is two blocks to your left on Av. Central. The **Autotransportes Tuxtla Gutiérrez station** is in a cul-de-sac near Av. 3 Sur and Calle 7 Ote. From the station, turn right and then right again into the walled-in alley that doubles as a market. Make the first left onto Av. 2 Sur and continue west to Calle Central—the *zócalo* is two blocks to the right. Travelers from Chiapa de Corzo often disembark at a small station on 3 Ote. between 2 and 3 Sur. Facing the street from the bus stop, head left for Av. Central, then left again for the *zócalo.*

Major **bus** lines run west on 2 Sur, east on 1 Sur, north on 11 Ote., and south on 12 Ote. (daily 5am-11pm, 1.50 pesos). *Colectivos* run frequently through the city (6am-10pm, 1.50 pesos). As locals often crowd the *colectivos* in the *centro,* it may be more efficient to walk to your destination outside the *centro* and then catch a (less full) *colectivo* running back into town.

## PRACTICAL INFORMATION

**Tourist Office: Dirección Municipal de Turismo,** 2 Nte. Ote. at Calle Central (tel. 2-55-11, ext. 214), on the northwest corner of the *zócalo.* You'll need their city map. Open Mon.-Fri. 8am-4pm, Sat. 8am-1pm.

**Currency Exchange: Banamex,** 1 Sur Pte. 141 at Calle Central (tel. 2-87-44). Credit card cash advances. 24hr. **ATM.** Open for exchange Mon.-Fri. 9am-1pm.

**American Express:** Tel. 2-69-98. Plaza Bonampak, Local 14, on Blvd. Dr. Belisario Domínguez, across from the tourist office. Doubles as a travel agency. English spoken. Open Mon.-Fri. 9am-2pm and 4-6:30pm, Sat. 9am-1pm.

**Telephones: LADATELs** in town accept coins and credit or LADATEL cards.

**Fax:** 1 Nte. at 2 Ote. (tel. 3-65-47; fax 2-42-96), next to the post office. Open for **telegrams** and fax Mon.-Fri. 8am-6pm, Sat. 9am-1pm.

**Airport: Aeropuerto Francisco Sarabia** (tel. 5-01-11), 15km southwest of town. **Aerocaribe,** Av. Central Pte. 206 (tel. 2-00-20, at airport tel. 5-15-30). **Aviacsa,** Av. Central Pte. 1144 (tel. 2-80-81) or at the airport (tel. 5-10-11). **Taxtel** (tel. 5-31-95) run to the airport and charge 40 pesos; a cheaper option is to grab a cab off the street (12 pesos).

**Buses: Cristóbal Colón,** 2 Nte. Pte. 268 at 2 Pte. (tel. 2-16-39). 1st class to Campeche (7:30am and 3:30pm, 12hr., 150-192 pesos), Cancún (12:30 and 2:30pm, 18hr., 257 pesos), Chetumal (12:30 and 2:30pm, 13hr., 150-192 pesos), Comitán (every hr., 5am-11pm, 3½hr., 42 pesos), Escárcega (12:30 and 4:30pm, 9½hr., 143 pesos), Huatulco (9:35am, 8:15, and 11pm, 9½hr., 102-165 pesos), Mérida (7:30am and 3:30pm, 14hr., 181-240 pesos), Mexico City (6 per day, 15hr., 295-350 pesos), Oaxaca (11:30am, 7:15, and 9:30pm, 10hr., 122-152 pesos), Ocosingo (8 per day, 4hr., 50 pesos), Palenque (8 per day, 6hr., 70 pesos), Playa del Carmen (12:30pm, 17hr., 313 pesos), Puebla (6 per day, 13hr., 271 pesos), Puerto Escondido (9:35am, 8:15, and 11pm, 11hr., 140-173 pesos), San Cristóbal (every hr., 5am-11pm, 2hr., 19 pesos), Tapachula (every hr., 6am-11pm, 6hr., 102 pesos), Tonalá (every hr., 6am-11pm, 3½hr., 49 pesos), Tulum (12:30pm, 16½hr., 249 pesos), Veracruz (7:30 and 8:45pm, 12hr., 166-200 pesos), and Villahermosa (9 per day, 6hr., 70-95 pesos). **Autotransportes Tuxtla Gutiérrez,** 3 Sur 712 (tel. 2-03-22 and 2-02-88), between 5 and 6 Ote., has less frequent buses to the same destinations at cheaper fares. **Combis** leave from their stand on 2 Sur Ote., next to Hotel San Antonio, for San Cristóbal (every 20min., 1½hr., 16 pesos). To reach Chiapa de Corzo, hop on a **Transportes Chiapa-Tuxtla** *microbús* at the station at 2 Sur and 2 Ote. (every 10min., 25min., 5 pesos) You can also try hailing the bus as it leaves town on Blvd. Corzo.

**Car Rental: Budget,** Blvd. Dr. Belisario Domínguez 2510 (tel. 5-06-72). 406 pesos per day. Believe it or not, cheaper rates are hard to come by. Open daily 9am-7pm.

**Laundromat: Lavandería Automática Burbuja,** 1 Nte. 413A at 3 Pte. (tel. 1-05-95). 8 pesos per kilo. Open Mon.-Sat. 8am-8pm, Sun. 9am-1pm.

**Red Cross:** 5 Nte. Pte. 1480 (tel. 2-04-92), on the west side of town. Open 24hr.

**Pharmacy: Farmacia 24 Horas,** 1 Sur 716, between 6 and 7 Pte. Open 24hr.

**Hospital: Hospital Regional Dr. Domingo Chamona,** 9 Sur at 1 Ote. (tel. 2-14-40). 24hr. emergency service.

**Emergency:** Dial 08 or call **Policía de Seguridad Pública** (tel. 2-05-30 or 3-78-05).

**Police:** Tel. 2-11-06. In the Palacio Municipal, at the north end of the *zócalo*. Go left upon entering the building. No English spoken. Open 24hr.

**Post Office:** 1 Nte. at 2 Ote. (tel. 2-04-16), on the northeast corner of the *zócalo*. Open Mon.-Fri. 9am-2pm and 4-6pm, Sat. 9am-noon. **Postal Code:** 29000.

**Phone Code:** 961.

## ACCOMMODATIONS AND CAMPING

Budget hotels are a dime (we wish) a dozen around the *zócalo;* walking on any side and back streets off Av. Central will yield a plethora of cheap accommodations. Tuxtla also has a stellar youth hostel.

**Villas Deportivas Juvenil,** Ángel Albino Corzo 1800 (tel. 3-34-05), next to the yellow footbridge. Take a *colectivo* east on Av. Central (1 peso) and tell the driver it's next to the Ángel Corzo statue on Blvd. Corzo. Single-sex 4-person rooms have comfy beds at this hostel. Communal bathrooms and showers are well maintained. Free soccer fields and basketball courts, but admission to the pool is restricted. Beds 25 pesos per person. Breakfast 10 pesos; lunch and dinner 12.50 pesos.

**Hotel Oasis,** 11 Ote. Sur 122, off Av. Central (tel. 3-72-52). 11 blocks east of *zócalo*, but well worth the walk. Classy modern rooms have TV, phone, and super-nice private bath. Singles 82 pesos; doubles 94 pesos; triples 117 pesos; each additional person 20 pesos.

**Hotel San Antonio,** 2 Sur 540, between 4 and 5 Ote. (tel. 2-27-13). Cavernous rooms have fans and bathrooms that spout hot water. Singles 40 pesos; doubles with A/C 70 pesos; triples 80 pesos; 10 pesos per extra person.

**Hotel Avenida,** Av. Central 244 between 1 and 2 Pte. (tel. 2-08-07), 1½ blocks west of the *zócalo*. 70s decor gives this older hotel a unique twist. Right in the center of all Tuxtla's action, so ask for a room off the street. Singles 50 pesos; doubles 65 pesos; triples 90 pesos; quads 120 pesos.

## FOOD

Culinary miracles don't happen in Tuxtla, but the city is speckled with quality, inexpensive eateries. *Licuados* come in every flavor imaginable, from mango to spinach.

**Restaurante Imperial,** Calle Central Nte. 263 (tel. 2-06-48), 1 block from the *zócalo*. Surprisingly classy joint that serves delicious *comida corrida* for only 16 pesos. Popular with locals who don't mind street noise. Open daily 7am-7pm.

**La Antigua Fogata,** 4 Ote. Sur 115, just off Av. Central. They might only be a tin-roofed shack, but they've got 23 years of experience behind their scrumptious chicken *al carbón*. ¼ chicken 10 pesos. Open daily 7:30am-midnight.

**Restaurante Vegetariano Nah-Yaxal,** 6 Pte. 124 (tel. 3-96-48), just north of Av. Central. Peruse books on yoga theory and parenting as you enjoy your veggie *comida del día* (20 pesos). Smooth *licuados* 6-10 pesos. Open Mon.-Sat. 7am-9pm.

## SIGHTS

The shady forest foliage of the **Miguel Álvarez del Toro Zoo** offers a refreshing change of scenery from Tuxtla's gritty urban landscape. Renowned throughout Latin America, the zoo houses only animals native to Chiapas, including playful monkeys, stealthy jaguars, bright green parrots, and hairy tarantulas (open Tues.-Sun. 9am-5:30pm; free). To get to the zoo, take the "Cerro Hueco" or "Zoológico" bus, which leaves from 1 Ote. between 6 and 7 Sur (every ½hr., 1.50 pesos). The bus traces an indirect and sometimes unbearably slow route to the zoo's front gate. To return to the center, catch the same bus at the zoo's entrance as it goes up the mountain.

CHIAPAS & TABASCO

The **Conviviencia Infantil** (though many signs still read **"Parque Madero"**) unfurls in the northeast part of town at the intersection of 11 Ote. and 5 Nte. Its focal point is a large and modern theater, the **Teatro de la Ciudad Emilio Rabasa.** Films by Latin American directors and performances of *ballet folklórico* dominate the schedule (check the tourist information center for details). On the pleasant *paseo* east of the theater is a children's amusement park (open Tues.-Sun. 9am-10pm). Past the amusement park is the open-air **Teatro Bonampak,** where free folk dance performances are held (Sun. 5-8pm). The eastern extremity of Parque Madero is demarcated by a light aircraft next to the open-air theater, upon which several eight-year-old fighter-pilots-in-the-making usually clamber. A broad concourse, lined with fountains and bronze busts of famous Mexicans, leads west of the theater past the **Museo Regional de Chiapas,** which displays the region's archaeological finds (open Tues.-Sun. 9am-4pm; admission 14 pesos, free Sun.). Farther down the concourse, at the **Jardín Botánico Dr. Faustino Miranda,** you can amble under towering *ceibas* (silk-cotton trees) and admire the colorful grandeur of Chiapanecan flora (open Tues.-Sun. 9am-6pm). Across the concourse is the **Museo Botánico** (open Mon.-Fri. 9am-3pm, Sat. 9am-1pm). Back in the center, the air-conditioned **Cinema Vistarama Tuxtla,** at 1 Sur and 5 Ote. (tel. 2-18-31), shows mostly American films with Spanish subtitles (admission 15 pesos). Cheaper and more crowded, **Cine Chiapas,** at Avenida Central and 4 Pte., will give you two showings of American films for only 5 pesos.

# ■ Chiapa de Corzo

Most people look past the pleasant town of Chiapa de Corzo and head right to the **Cañón del Sumidero,** an impressive vegetation-clad canyon that stretches 32km to the north of the city. Carved out by the industrious Río Grijalva, the mist-enshrouded slopes of the gorge rise as much as 1200m above the water. According to local lore, nearly 15,000 Chiapan *indígenas* threw themselves into the canyon in 1528 after their chief, Sanguiem, was burned alive by the Spaniards.

The town of Chiapa de Corzo is adorable—friendly locals, quiet streets, and a gorgeous *zócalo* just might detain you a day or more.

**Orientation and Practical Information** Chiapa de Corzo overlooks the Río Grijalva, 15km east of Tuxtla and 68km west of San Cristóbal. Most sights lie near the *zócalo* **(Plaza Ángel Albino Corzo),** which is bounded on the north by 21 de Octubre (the Tuxtla-San Cristóbal highway), on the east by La Mexicanidad, on the south by Julián Grajales, and on the west by 5 de Febrero. **Boats** leave for **El Sumidero** from the riverbank, two blocks southwest of the *zócalo* on 5 de Febrero.

Contact the **tourist office** in **Tuxtla** for detailed tourist information. **Bancomer** (tel. 6-03-20) is on the eastern side of the *zócalo* (open Mon.-Fri. 8am-1pm; 24hr. **ATM**). **Transportes Chiapa-Tuxtla** *microbúses,* heading back to Tuxtla, stop on 21 de Octubre opposite the police station (every 10min., 25min., 3 pesos). **Farmacia Esperanza** (tel. 6-04-54) is on 21 de Octubre, one block east of the *zócalo* (open Mon.-Sat. 7am-11pm, Sun. 7am-2pm). The **police station** (tel. 6-02-26) is in the Palacio Municipal, on the northeast side of the *zócalo* (open 24hr.). The **post office** is on Calle Cenullo Aguilar 244, a block and a half north of the *zócalo* (open Mon.-Fri. 8am-6pm). **Postal Code:** 29160. **Phone Code:** 968.

**Accommodations and Food** Most people visit Chiapa de Corzo as a daytrip from Tuxtla. If you spend the night, **Hotel Los Ángeles,** Julián Grajales 2 at La Mexicanidad (tel. 6-00-48), on the southeast corner of the *zócalo,* is the only budget game in town. Tall-ceilinged rooms have wooden bed frames and firm mattresses. Private baths are adequate (singles 60 pesos; doubles 80 pesos; triples 110 pesos; quads 120 pesos). Since you've come to Chiapa to see the river, you may as well head to the waterfront for mid-range, filling food (cheaper food can be found at the **market,** open dawn to dusk at the left of the church). **Restaurant Comitán,** to the left as you hit the dock, offers a 20-peso breakfast special, occasional live marimba performances, and an airy, if fly-obscured, view of the lush, winding river banks (open daily 8am-7pm). **Restaurant Nancy,** around the corner to the right as you hit the dock, is shorter on atmosphere but long on selection—come here if you crave a wide variety of seafood goodies (25-35 pesos). When the marimba is played, it's not played shyly (open daily 6am-6pm).

**Sights** Carved out by the Río Grijalva, the **Cañón del Sumidero** stretches for 32 vegetation-clad kilometers north of Chiapa de Corzo. A two-hour round trip *lancha* journey begins with humble views of cornfields, but shortly after the Belisario Domínguez bridge, the hills jump to form near-vertical cliffs which rise as much as 1200m above water level. Protected as a natural park, these steep walls are home to troupes of monkeys, hummingbirds, and soaring falcons, while the murky waters harbor crocodiles and turtles. Along the meandering river lies a dripping cave and the park's most famous waterfall, the **Árbol de Navidad.** This spectacular *cascada* plummets from the sky, rambling over a series of scalloped rock formations before disintegrating into a fine mist that envelops passing boats. El Sumidero's northernmost extremity is marked by the 200m-high hydroelectric dam **Netzahualcóyotl,** which, with the Río Grijalva's three other dams, provides a quarter of Mexico's electricity.

**Boats** leave as soon as they're full from Chiapa's *embarcadero* (dock) at the end of 5 de Febrero, two blocks south of the *zócalo* (daily 7am-4:30pm; 50 pesos per person). Boats can also be taken up the canyon from **Cahuaré,** where the highway to Tuxtla Gutiérrez crosses the river near the Cahuaré Island Resort. The trip down the river is best made during August, at the height of the rainy season, when up to 42 waterfalls can be seen.

Back in Chiapa de Corzo, most architectural gems date from the city's colonial period. The *zócalo* contains two colonial structures: a small **clock tower** and a fountain shaped like the crown of Queen Isabel of Spain. Often called **La Pila,** this famous Moorish fountain taps underground waterways 5km long and provided the town with fresh drinking water during a 1562 epidemic. Inside the fountain, tile plaques tell the story of Chiapa's colonial-era history. The red-and-white **Catedral de Santo Domingo** is one block south of the *zócalo* near Río Grijalva. The most famous of the four bells dangling in its tower, "Teresa de Jesús," is named after a mystical Spanish saint (open daily 6am-2pm and 4-6:30pm). Alongside the cathedral, a 16th-century ex-convent houses the **Museo de la Laca,** which displays fine examples of Mexican lacquerwork, a handicraft practiced only in Chiapa de Corzo and four other cities (open Mon. 9am-1pm and 4-7pm, Tues.-Sun. 9am-7pm; free). You can also join one of the ongoing lacquering lessons during the summer months (check posted schedule).

During Chiapa's **Fiesta de San Sebastián** (Jan. 16-22), *los parachicos,* men in heavy costumes and stifling masks, dance from dawn to dusk. The fiesta's *gran finale* is the mock **Combate Naval** between *"españoles"* and *"indios."* More a beauty pageant than a battle, the *combate* features decorated boats, costumed sailors, and fireworks.

# ■ San Cristóbal de Las Casas

If San Cristóbal de Las Casas isn't on your list of destinations, make a new list. Nestled at an elevation of 2100m in the pine-filled Valley of Hueyzacatlán, San Cristóbal (pop. 75,000) derives its immense popularity from its picturesque, unsullied, red-tile-roofed, narrow-streeted colonial coziness, courtyards, and gardens, its invigorating highland climate, and its infusion by a remarkable diversity of Chiapas indigenous culture. Top off this combination with a 360° view of the lush green mountains, whose steeply rising slopes are clung to by San Cristóbal's outskirts, and you'll understand why herds of Mexican and foreign tourists alike have flocked here for years. A large resident contingent of North Americans and northern Europeans rounds out the populace and is mostly responsible for everything from clothing boutiques to English movies to yuppified but heartfelt campaigns to save the Lacandón jungle.

Though San Cristóbal is a well-touristed, aesthetic wonder, its life has long been animated by the age-old conflict between *mestizos* and *indígenas.* Founded in 1528 by the invading Spaniards and their Aztec allies, San Cristóbal de las Casas was once the colonial capital of the region, a *mestizo* enclave in the midst of Maya territory. Over the years, *mestizo* culture has became increasingly dominant in San Cristóbal, and some *indígenas* have adopted Western clothing and manners as their own. For most, however, tense syncretism has been the rule of the day. Catholicism mixes with shamanistic practices, and most women still wear braids with colorful ribbons and wear grand *rebozo* scarves. Fashionable ennui is pursued elegantly at the city's cafes, while Tzetzil women tread downtown streets barefoot. Local merchants walk 20 or more kilometers to Sunday markets, dressed in clothing whose patterns haven't changed in centuries, while even the most remote indigenous village is served by the Coca-Cola truck at least once a week. While Spanish is the city's official language, the Mayan tongues of Tzeltal or Tzotzil are spoken in the nearby villages.

On January 1, 1994, the day that NAFTA came into effect, a band of rebels, calling themselves Zapatistas (after the revolutionary leader Emiliano Zapata), rose up against the government in San Cristóbal. Led by a masked figure known as Subcommandante Marcos (now commercially commemorated by "Marcos dolls" sold by local vendors), the rebels insisted that land be redistributed to the poor, a demand that many San Cristóbal residents supported. While the city is still manned by military police, the overt political tension has seemingly died down and poses no threat to tourists; the 1997 Federal elections passed in peace, with little more than a few spray-painted houses and the *indígena* taking Zapatista advice to not vote.

## ORIENTATION

Nestled high in the Altos de Chiapas , San Cristóbal lies 83km east of Tuxtla Gutiérrez, 78km northwest of Comitán, and 191km southwest of Palenque. Rte. 190, the Pan-American Highway, cuts east from Tuxtla Gutiérrez, touches the southern edge of San Cristóbal, and then heads southeast to Comitán and Ciudad Cuauhtémoc at the Guatemalan border.

First- and second-class **bus stations** are scattered along the Pan-American Highway near Av. Insurgentes. From Cristóbal Colón, take a right (north) on Insurgentes and walk seven blocks to the *zócalo*. From the bus stations, walk east two or three blocks on any cross-street and turn left on Insurgentes. Since San Cristóbal is a popular destination for tourists, most of whom travel by bus, book seats as far in advance as possible during the Christmas season and Semana Santa. At other times, reservations made one day in advance will suffice.

Most of San Cristóbal's clearly labeled streets fall into a neat grid. The *zócalo*, also known as **Plaza 31 de Marzo,** is the city center. The four cardinal directions are indicated by prominent landmarks around town: the church and former convent of Santo Domingo are to the north, the blue-trimmed Templo de Guadalupe is on the hill to the east, the Cristóbal Colón first-class bus station lies to the south, and the Templo de San Cristóbal resides on the mountaintop to the west. Streets change names when crossing imaginary north-south and east-west axes centered at the *zócalo*. **Av. Insurgentes** connects the town center to the Pan-American Highway, becoming **Av. Utrilla** past the *zócalo*. Municipal buses and *colectivos* criss-cross town with destinations indicated on the window—just wave to catch one (1.50 pesos). Taxis (tel. 8-03-96) line up along the north side of the *zócalo*. Standard fare within town is 6 pesos, while prices to nearby villages are negotiable.

## PRACTICAL INFORMATION

**Tourist Office:** Hidalgo 2 (tel. 8-65-70), ½ block south of the *zócalo*. Open Mon.-Fri. 9am-9pm, Sat. 9am-8pm, Sun. 9am-2pm. The **Tourist Office** at the northwest end of the Palacio Municipal (tel. 8-06-60, ext. 126) has gobs of info in a find-it-yourself style. Open Mon.-Sat. 9am-8pm, Sun. 9am-2pm. **Information Booth** at the Cristóbal Colón terminal, with maps and brochures. Some English spoken. Open 24hr.
**Travel Agencies: Viajes Pakal,** Cuauhtémoc 6A between Insurgentes and Hidalgo (tel. 8-42-93; fax 8-28-19), 1 block south of the *zócalo*. Daytrips to Palenque, Agua Azul, Grutas de San Cristóbal, and nearby villages. Trips to Bonampak, Yaxchilán,

N

# San Cristóbal de las Casas

Del Clavel

Vicario

TO EL ARCOTETE

Iglesia de Guadalupe (Mirador)

Bernal Díaz del Castillo

Avenida Ísabel La Católica

Avenida J. M. Rojas

TO RANCHO SAN NICOLÁS

Diagonal Independencia

Almondanga

Real de Guadalupe

Posada Villa Betania

Guerrero

Tonalá

Museo Na-Bolom

Chiapa de Corzo

Comitán

Tapachula

Hotel Jovel

J.M. Santiago

Ejército Nacional

Paniagua

Ruiz

Casa de Huéspedes Margarita

Francisco Madero

Posada "Bed and Breakfast"

Dr. José Flores

Corzo

R. Corona

S. Esponda

Dr. Navarro

Flavio

Mercado

Diagonal Arriaca

Avenida General Utrilla

Catedral

Hotel "Posada del Barón"

Dr. Francisco León

Avenida Ortiz de Domínguez

Benito Juárez

Red Cross

Artisan's Market

20 de Noviembre

Palacio Municipal

Niños Héroes

Faculad de Derecho

Templo y Arco del Carmen

Convention Center

Insurgentes

Pino Suárez

Cristóbal Colón Station

Instituto Cultural de los Altos de Chiapas

Iglesia y Exconvento de Santo Domingo

Avenida 5 de Mayo

Miguel Hidalgo

Crescencio Rosas

La Casa de Gladit

1 de Marzo

5 de Febrero

Guadalupe Victoria

Diego de Mazariegos

Cuauhtémoc

Iglesia de San Cristóbal (Mirador)

Álvaro Obregón

Moreno

Transportes Lacandonia Station

Autotransportes Tuxtla Gutiérrez Station

Ignacio Allende

López Rayón

Gómez Farías

Carranza

Ramírez

TO GRUTAS DE SAN CRISTÓBAL, PALENQUE, COMITÁN & GUATEMALA

Cerro de San Cristóbal

Pan-American Highway

TO TUXTLA GUTIÉRREZ

and Guatemala by special arrangement. Open Mon.-Fri. 9am-2pm and 4-8pm, Sat. 9am-1pm. **Viajes Lacantún,** Madero 16 (tel. 8-25-88), ½ block east of the *zócalo,* for flights within Mexico and abroad. Open Mon.-Fri. 9am-2pm and 4-7pm, Sat. 9am-1pm.

**Currency Exchange: Bancomidad** (tel. 8-17-77; fax 8-01-99), on the southwest corner of the *zócalo.* 24hr. **ATM.** Open Mon.-Fri. 9am-2pm.

**Telephones:** Collect calls can be placed from public pay phones at the Palacio Municipal and throughout the *centro.*

**Fax:** Mazariegos 29 (tel. 8-42-71), 2½ blocks from the *zócalo.* Open for **telegrams** if you're old school (tel. 8-06-61). Mon.-Fri. 8am-6pm, Sat. 9am-noon.

**Buses:** The following listings include both **Cristóbal Colon** (tel. 8-02-91) and **Maya de Oro** buses, which both leave from the **station** at Pan-American Highway at Insurgentes, 7 blocks south of the *zócalo.* Open daily 6am-10pm. 1st-class service to Campeche (9:30am and 5:25pm, 10hr., 126-151 pesos), Cancún (2:30, 4:30, and 5pm, 17hr., 259-307 pesos), Chetumal (2:30, 4:30, and 5pm, 12hr., 166-196 pesos), Comitán (12 per day, 1½hr., 18 pesos), Escárcega (2:30 and 4:30pm, 8hr., 93-100 pesos), Guatemalan border (6 per day, 7am-12:30am, 3hr., 37 pesos), Mérida (9:30am and 5:25pm, 12hr., 162-218 pesos), Mexico City (1:50, 3:30, 4:30, and 5:30pm, 18hr., 218-356 pesos), Oaxaca (5 and 7:15pm, 12hr., 148-175 pesos), Palenque (12 per day, 5hr., 46-54 pesos), Puebla (1:50, 3:30, 4:30, and 5:30pm, 16hr., 278 pesos), Puerto Escondido (7:30am, 6:15, and 9pm, 12hr., 160 pesos), Tuxtla Gutiérrez (every hr., 2hr., 24 pesos), Tulum (2:30, 4:30, and 5pm, 13hr., 199 pesos).

**Car Rental: Budget,** Mazariegos 36 (tel. 8-18-71 or 8-31-00), 2 blocks west of the *zócalo.* With prices starting at 350 pesos per day, it's time they changed their name. Open Mon.-Sat. 8am-2pm and 4-8pm, Sun. 8-11am. MC, Visa.

**Bike Rental: Bicirent,** Belisario Domínguez 5B between Real de Guadalupe and Madero (tel. 8-63-68). 23 pesos per 3hr. or 50 pesos per day. Guided tours.

**Markets:** Between Utrilla and Domínguez, 7 blocks north of the *zócalo.* Best selection on Sat. Open daily 6am-2pm. Huge artisan's market forms around the Santo Domingo Church, 5 blocks north of the *zócalo* on Utrilla. Open daily 8am-5pm.

**Laundromat: Orve,** Domínguez 5 between Real de Guadalupe and Madero (tel. 8-18-02). 27 pesos for 1-3kg, 7 pesos per additional kg. Promises to wash loads separately and to separate colors, just like Mom. Open Mon.-Sat. 8am-8pm.

**English Bookstore: La Pared,** Hidalgo 2 (tel. 8-63-67), ½ block south of the *zócalo.* Buys, trades, sells, and, uh, rents used books. Open Mon.-Sat. 10am-2pm and 4-8pm, Sun. only during high season.

**Red Cross:** Ignacio Allende 57 (tel. 8-07-72), 3 blocks south of the Pan American Highway. No English spoken. 24hr. emergency service.

**Pharmacy: Farmacia Regina,** Mazariegos at Crescencio Rosas (tel. 8-02-41). No English spoken. Open 24hr.

**Hospital: Hospital Regional,** Insurgentes 24 (tel. 8-07-70), 4 blocks south of the *zócalo,* across from Santa Lucía, in Parque Fray Bartolomé. Open 24hr.

**Internet Access: Cybercafe,** in Pasaje Mezariegos (tel. 8-74-88), off Real de Guadalupe, 1 block east of the *zócalo.* Trendy and expensive, charging 10 pesos per 15min. Open Mon.-Sat. 9am-10pm, Sun. 11am-9pm. **La Llamada,** Real de Guadalupe 55, a few blocks west of the *zócalo,* has a handful of computers hooked up. 40 pesos per hr. Open Mon.-Sat. 8am-2pm and 4-9pm.

**Police:** Tel. 8-05-54. In the Palacio Municipal, on the west side of the *zócalo.*

**Post Office:** Cuauhtémoc at Crescencio Rosas (tel. 8-07-65), 1 block southwest of the *zócalo.* Open Mon.-Fri. 8am-7pm, Sat. and holidays 9am-1pm. **MexPost,** in the same office, open Mon.-Fri. 8am-7pm. **Postal Code:** 29200.

**Phone Code:** 967.

# ACCOMMODATIONS AND CAMPING

Budget travelers say *Amen.* San Cristóbal is stacked with inexpensive hotels. Most lie on **Real de Guadalupe, Madero, Insurgentes,** and **Juárez,** with prices decreasing relative to their distance from the *zócalo.* Camping is only available outside of town (see below). Due to the altitude, the temperature often drops below 10°C (50°F, 283 K), making hot water and blankets indispensable.

**Hotel Jovel,** Paniagua 28 (tel. 8-17-34), 2½ blocks east and 2 blocks north of the *zócalo*. Great natural lighting illuminates rooms with gorgeous wooden floors and colorful *sarape* bedspreads. Multi-leveled terraces and solarium offer a great view of the city and cozy reading areas. Hot water and medical service 24hr. Staff will watch luggage for a number of days. Singles 50 pesos; doubles 60 pesos; triples 70 pesos; add 30 pesos for private bath.

**Hotel Posada el Cerrillo,** Dominguez 27 (tel. 8-12-83), 2 blocks east and 2½ blocks north of the *zócalo*. Freshly painted rooms match the freshly painted courtyard adorned with fresh plants. This place screams fresh. Good communal bathrooms; 60 extra pesos for privacy. Singles 40 pesos; doubles 80 pesos; triples 110 pesos.

**Posada Villa Betania,** Madero 87 (tel. 8-44-67), 4 blocks east of the *zócalo*. Large, quiet rooms with big, firm beds, a table for two, private bath, and fireplace. Small gardens and intimate kitchen (5 pesos to use) complete the relaxed atmosphere. Singles 40 pesos; doubles 60 pesos; triples 80 pesos.

**Posada Bed and Breakfast,** Madero 83 (tel. 8-04-40), 4 blocks east of the *zócalo*. The second bed and breakfast on Madero, just before the Villa Betania. Small, dark rooms open to considerably cheerier dining area. Singles 25 pesos, with bath 30 pesos; doubles 40 pesos, with bath 45 pesos; triples 80 pesos; quads 90 pesos. Bed in a dormitory 20 pesos. The first B&B has similar prices, but only one bathroom for 25 beds.

**La Casa de Gladis,** Real de Mexicanos 16 (tel. 8-57-75), 6 blocks north and 2 blocks west of the *zócalo*. Worth the walk. Stars, moons, and hammocks decorate the colorful courtyard, while dorms come with hanging chairs, animal throws, and firm beds. Small, well-decorated private rooms. Communal bathrooms are exceptional. Hot water daily 8am-8pm. Doubles and triples 60 pesos; quads 80 pesos; 15 pesos to camp or sling a hammock; bed in a 7-person dormitory 20 pesos.

**Hotel Posada del Barón,** Belisario Domínguez 2 (tel. 8-08-81), 1 block east of the *zócalo*. A little pricey, but well worth it. Colonial architecture gives way to tasteful rooms and modern bathrooms (that actually have shower curtains). Singles 100 pesos; doubles 120 pesos; triples 150 pesos.

**Rancho San Nicolás,** on the extension of Francisco León (tel. 8-00-57), 1km east of town. If no one's around, ring the bell for the Hacienda across the road. Rooms, camping, and trailer park in a pastoral setting complete with whispering trees and hot water. During high season (Dec.-Feb.), rooms are often full, so call in advance. RVs 35 pesos; camping 15 pesos; rooms 25 pesos; each additional person 20 pesos. **Horse rental** 20 pesos per hr., 50 pesos per day.

## FOOD

Dining is delightful. Local specialties include *sopa de pan* (a doughy mass floating in vegetable broth), scrumptious *tacos al pastor,* full-bodied *chiles rellenos,* and grainy wheat breads from the Barrio San Ramón. Vegetarian restaurants are as plentiful as the *churro* stands. Top it all off with the exquisite *cerveza dulce* or some of Mexico's best coffee.

**Restaurante Madre Tierra,** Insurgentes 19 (tel. 8-42-97), opposite the Iglesia de San Francisco, 2½ blocks south of the *zócalo*. Immensely popular bakery whose breads are tastier than the restaurant's somewhat expensive dinners. A yuppie mecca. Breakfasts are healthy and tasty (13-20 pesos). Open daily 8am-9:30pm.

**Restaurante Paris México,** Madero 20 (tel. 8-06-95), 2½ blocks east of the *zócalo*. Offers French and Italian fares to the tortilla-tired tourist. Local dishes available. Extensive *menú del día* goes for 20 pesos. Open daily 8am-10pm.

**Cafetería del Centro,** Real de Guadalupe 15B (tel. 8-63-68), 2 blocks east of the *zócalo*. *Comida corrida* (soup, entree, rice, bread, *postre,* and coffee 15 pesos) is as good as it gets. Excellent breakfasts 9-13 pesos. Open daily 7am-9pm.

**La Salsa Verde,** 20 de Noviembre 7, 1 block north of the *zócalo*. Two *taquerias*. Same name. Same street. Different owners, who both swear they were first. The one at #7 is bigger, sporting pine needles on the floor (*indígena* tradition) and great service. The one at #11 is smaller and cozier, offering similar choices. Tacos 3 pesos each. Both open daily 8am-midnight.

**Centro Cultural El Puente,** Real de Guadalupe 55 (tel. 8-22-50), 3 blocks from the *zócalo*. Cafe-language school-cinema mixes in local art and silky jazz as well, all with a distinct leftist flavor. Vegetarians can feast on the cheese, tomato, and avocado omelette (13 pesos). Sandwiches 9-12 pesos. Hot breakfast croissants with cheese (6 pesos). Open Mon.-Sat. 8am-11pm.

**El Oasis,** 1 de Marzo 6C, 1 block north of the cathedral. Veggie cuisine. 4-course *comida corrida* 20 pesos. Excellent breakfasts. Open Mon.-Sat. 7am-9pm.

**Emiliano's Mustache,** Crecencio Rosas 7, 1 block west and 1 block south of the *zócalo*. Surprisingly elegant *taquería* serving up local dishes as well (25-35 pesos). Come for the tacos (2 pesos each)—all the locals do. Open daily 8am-1am. Taco stand open daily 6pm-1am.

**Café Altura,** 20 Noviembre 9 (tel./fax 8-40-38). The only organic vegetarian restaurant in town, also serving up some of the best coffee. At night, poets and musicians come to serenade well-caffeinated onlookers. Open daily 7am-11pm.

**Las Estrellas,** Ecuadrón 201, across from artisan market. Batik decor complements healthy vegetarian entrees. Hearty pesto pasta 10 pesos. Open daily 8am-10pm.

## SIGHTS

Since its construction by the Spanish in the 16th century, San Cristóbal's *zócalo* has been the physical and spiritual center of town. The colonial **Palacio Municipal** and the yellow-orange **cathedral,** with its white Corinthian columns and patterned wooden roof, dominate the heart of the city. Consecrated in 1528, the cathedral pews are filled with a bevy of devout followers, and its rafters with a flock of chirping birds (cathedral open daily 7am-7pm).

North on Utrilla and beyond the **Iglesia de la Caridad** is the **Iglesia y Ex-convento de Santo Domingo,** whose grounds make up the artisan market. While dirty and gigantic on the outside, Santo Domingo's inner walls are delicately covered in restless gold leaf which slithers in elaborate patterns up walls, around portraits, and over the left nave's exquisite pulpit (open daily 7am-8pm). Stashed in the Ex-convento is **Sna Jolobil** (tel./fax 8-26-46), which means "House of Weaving" in Tzeltal. It is a cooperative of 1500 weavers from 10 Tzotzil and Tzeltal villages in the *chiapaneco* highlands whose objective is to preserve and revitalize their ancestral weaving techniques. While many of the extremely high-quality, intricately embroidered *huipiles* will cost more than your plane ticket home, Sna Jolobil is a great place to window-shop and view the area's traditional garments (open Mon.-Sat. 9am-2pm and 4-6pm). Another cooperative, **J'pas Joloviletic,** is at General Utrilla 43 (tel. 8-28-48), on the opposite side of Santo Domingo (open Mon.-Sat. 9am-2pm and 4-7pm, Sun. 9am-1pm).

Next door to Sna Jolobil, the **Centro Cultural de Los Altos de Chiapas** houses an excellent multimedia exhibit on the history of San Cristóbal and Chiapas. On display are colonial artifacts, photographs, and a collection of Chiapanecan textiles, some of which are many hundreds of years old. During the summer, visitors bring along penknives to leave their mark on the avocado tree in the courtyard (open Tues.-Sun. 10am-5pm; admission 10 pesos, free Sun.; free group tours in Spanish).

San Cristóbal's most famous museum is **Na-Bolom,** Guerrero 33, at the end of Chiapa de Corzo. Located in the northeastern section of the city, Na-Bolom (House of the Jaguar) is a private house which turns into a museum twice daily. Guided tours will tell you more than you ever wanted to know about Trudy and Franz Blom, who worked and studied for many decades among the dwindling communities of the **Lacandón Rainforest** along the Guatemala border. After the death of her husband in 1963, Trudy Blom continued their work, winning acclaim as an ecologist, ethnologist, and photographer before her death in the winter of 1993. Many volunteers live at Na-Bolom, carrying out the jungle reforestation project begun by Mrs. Blom and conducting tours of the Fray Bartolomé de Las Casas library, the gardens, and the Bloms' personal museum. Travelers interested in **volunteering** at Na-Bolom should contact the main office at 8-14-18 at least two months prior to arrival. Positions last two to three months and include free housing and discounts on Na-Bolom meals. The library's manuscripts concentrate on Maya culture, with numerous periodicals, news clippings, and rare papers dealing with rainforest ecology and the plight of *indígena* refugees (library open Mon.-Fri. 10am-1:30pm). The small, ornate chapel (the building was originally intended as a seminary) now serves as a gallery of colonial *chiapaneco* religious art created by *ladinos* and *indígenas* alike. Other rooms are devoted to archaeological finds from the nearby site of **Moxviquil,** religious artifacts from the Lacandón Rainforest, and the work of artists in residence (museum open daily by self-congratulatory guided tour at 11:30am and 4:30pm in Spanish and 4:30pm in English, followed by a 15min. film; admission 15 pesos; museum shop open Tues.-Sun. 10am-2pm and 4-7pm; cafe open daily during meal times). You can also stay in one of Na-Bolom's 14 fabulously decorated rooms.

It's an arduous climb to the top of the **Iglesia de San Cristóbal de las Casas;** by the grace of God, the ascent has been broken into 285 steps. Behind the church stands a 6m-tall crucifix built of license plates. All that remains of the iron-frame Christ is his left arm, dangling grotesquely by the wrist. The monument dares you to feel any sense of reverence. To reach the stairs, walk three blocks south on Insurgentes and turn right on Domínguez; the stairs are three blocks ahead. Women traveling alone should avoid the area after dark (open daily dawn-dusk).

The **Facultad de Derecho** (Law School) of the Universidad de Chiapas, the fourth oldest law school in Mexico, is located on the corner of Miguel Hidalgo and Cuauhtémoc and boasts some fanciful murals painted in 1992 by Carlos Jurado. Enter the building, turn around, and you'll be greeted by Bosch-like lions, flying zeppelins, and blue devils (open daily 7am-8pm). A superb collection of **regional clothes** is displayed in **Sergio Castro's** home, Guadalupe Victoria 47 (tel. 8-42-89), west of the *zócalo*. In about an hour, Sergio can show you his collection of sartorial splendor. Call in advance for an informative and friendly tour. There is no admission charge, but a tip is appropriate (open daily 6pm-8pm).

San Cristóbal's daily morning **market** overflows with fruit, veggies, and an assortment of cheap goods. There aren't really any *artesanías* on sale though—look to the market around Iglesia de Santo Domingo for souvenirs. Try coming on Sunday, when *indígenas* from nearby villages turn out in droves (market open daily 7am-3pm or until the afternoon rain) or go to the villages themselves (see **Near San Cristóbal,** below). Utrilla and Real de Guadalupe, the two streets radiating from the northeastern corner of the *zócalo*, are dotted with colorful shops which sell *típico* attire for less than the market stands or neighboring villages. Locals do their shopping on Saturday mornings. Watch, listen, and learn—these experts wrote the book on bargaining.

## ENTERTAINMENT AND SEASONAL EVENTS

While the *zócalo* empties around 11pm, coffeeshops and restaurants host live music into the wee hours. A stroll down Madero or Guadalupe will offer any number of places to sip a cool *licuado*, kick back, and enjoy some Latin strumming. Try the **Restaurante Margarita,** next door to the Hotel Margarita for a trio offering Flamenco and classical selections (music daily 9:30pm-midnight). **La Galería,** Hidalgo 3 (tel. 8-15-47), is a chic courtyard restaurant with live music during the high season (nightly until 2am; cocktails around 10 pesos). **Café Altura** (see p. 472) serves up great coffee, hot poetry, and live music as well (daily, starting at 9pm).

Not to be outdone by the Yucatán, San Cristóbal has its own **Ruta Maya,** only here the temples are smoke-filled discos with throbbing bodies and flowing taps. Locals start around 11pm, gathering at Margarita's before heading to La Galería, then on to **Latinos** and **Las Vegas,** two discos off the *zócalo* on Madero. Hard-core throbbers twitching for more can try **Disco Palace,** Av. Crescencio Rosas 59 (tel. 8-26-00), on weekends, and **Disco Pop-Rock** (tel. 8-11-81), in the Hotel Maya Quetzal on the Pan American Highway, 300m west of the Cristóbal Colón bus station, on a Saturday night (open Sat. only after 10pm).

For those with aching feet, technophobia, or lack of disco get-up, **El Puente** features two films per day (6 and 8:30pm, 5 pesos), including a variety of American classics and foreign gems. **Cinemas Santa Clara,** on 16 de Septiembre between Escuadrón and 28 de Agosto (tel. 8-23-45), screens U.S. movies.

In San Cristóbal and the nearby villages, hardly a week goes by without some kind of religious festival. The city's Semana Santa celebration is rather *tranquila*. Many business establishments close their doors, and the processions and cultural events that take place are decidedly reverent and low-key. On Easter Sunday, however, Semana Santa gives way to the week-long **Feria de la Primavera y de la Paz.** Before the riotous revelry really gets going, a local beauty queen is selected to preside over the festivities, which include concerts, dances, bullfights, cock fights, and baseball games. Hotel rooms for either week must be reserved several months in advance. The *fiesta* of the city's patron, San Cristóbal, is celebrated July 18-25 with elaborate religious ceremonies and numerous concerts.

## ■ Near San Cristóbal de Las Casas

Sunday morning is the best and often the only time to visit the markets of nearby villages. However, because service is always routed through San Cristóbal, visiting more than one village in a single morning is almost impossible. Buses and *combis* leave from the lot one block past the market at Utrilla and Honduras. Destination signs next to the buses are only occasionally accurate; always ask drivers where they're going. Drivers don't leave until the *combi* is completely full, so be prepared to squeeze in.

Visiting the villages on your own can give you a greater sense of freedom and a lesser sense of herd animal, but it can also be like watching a chess game blindfolded without knowing the rules; there's a lot in each *pueblo* that happens behind closed doors. Sometimes joining the herd is a good idea, especially if the herd leader is the energetic and knowledgeable **Mercedes Hernández Gómez.** Something of an expert on local *indígena* culture and a splendid storyteller, Mercedes's five-hour tour includes political, domestic, and spiritual teachings while taking tourists into a private home, a saint's house, and the *pueblo* church (100 pesos for Chamula and Zinacantaíon; look for Mercedes and her huge golf umbrella at the *zócalo* every day at 9am). An equally viable option is the intelligent and gregarious **Raúl López** (tel. 8-34-41), a thirtysomething local who happily divulges a wealth of information on everything from regional customs to the Zapatista uprising to religion and back again, all with a refreshing frankness. Raúl, who only speaks Spanish (his *compañero* Manuel gives the same tour in English), meets interested travelers outside the cathedral daily at 9:30am (tour covers Chamula and Zinacantán; 60 pesos; van returns around 2pm).

## SAN JUAN CHAMULA

The community of San Juan Chamula (96 villages, 75,000 inhabitants) is the largest and most touristed of the villages around San Cristóbal. Located 10km northwest of San Cristóbal in a lush valley, Chamula's dirt roads, single-story houses, and wandering children are used to visitors. Chamula is known for its colors (black and blue), its *carnaval*, and its shamanic-Catholic church. Visitors come to Chamula to check out the spectacular traditional clothing and witness a civic and religious structure quite unlike any other in Mexico. Older Chamulan men wear traditional black wool *sarapes* tied with thick leather belts (black signifying *carga*, or duty), while the young men, still unburdened, sport either blue or white *sarapes*. Designs on the sleeves of the tunics indicate the wearer's *pueblito* or *colonia*. Village officials (elected by a hand-count) and elders drape ribbons over their large *sombreros*. If you should see officials in their official dress, stifle the urge to snap a shot—the men refuse to be turned into a tourist attraction while they are performing their *carga*.

Chamulans, who expelled their last Catholic priest in 1867, are famous for their fierce resistance to Mexico's religious and secular authority. Villagers have far more faith in the powers of the village shaman, and Catholic bishops are allowed into the church solely for baptisms. Similarly, the government medical clinic is used only as a last resort, after incantations with eggs, bubbly *refrescos,*and chickens have failed.

### True Colors

Chiapas is one of the few regions in the Republic where traditional dress codes are still strictly maintained. Each *indígena* group has distinctive clothing patterns and colors. Outsiders who wear *indígena* clothing may offend natives here, since the patterns and styles of garments are sometimes invested with social meaning. Women should avoid wearing broad, ribboned hats, which are reserved in most villages for men. Revealing clothing is often received coldly, so keep shorts hidden until you feel the ocean spray on your face. Under no circumstances should elders and church interiors be photographed and always make sure to ask before you go snap-happy on the locals. Sly, sneaky tourists have had whole rolls of film destroyed for not exercising shutter-control.

Before entering the brightly painted **church** (open 24hr.), you must obtain a permit (3 pesos) from the tourist office on the *zócalo* and show the permit to the guards inside the church. **Under no circumstances should you take pictures**—the church functions as a hospital, and it is disrespectful to the sick and disruptive to the shaman doctor to try to capture a very personal ceremony on film. The church's predominant color is green to recall the ancient Maya practice of praying in caves, hence the pine needles on the floor, the branches, and the flowers. Inside the church, families, candles, and chickens fill the pewless hall as shamans chant petitions to the Catholic saints on a conversational level. Different colored candles signify different levels of prayer-severity, and other Maya rituals are aided by the ubiquitous Pepsi bottle. The importance of carbonated beverages cannot be overstated; Chamulans believe that **burping** helps to purify the self by expelling evil spirits. Prior to the discovery of fizzy drinks, locals had to drink gallons of water to achieve the same cathartic effect.

To the left of the church stands a cluster of distinctive, green foliated Maya crosses. The crosses' origin is in the crucifix-shaped **Tree of Life,** featured on the sarcophagus of King Pakal at Palenque. When Fray Bartolomé de Las Casas showed up bearing the Christian cross, he waltzed right into Chamula, whose residents believed he was a messenger from the gods. Chamula's small but diverse artisan's **market** is behind the building that houses the tourist office; here the hungry tourist can find roasted corn (5 pesos) amidst the scattered taco stands and avoid the overpriced cafes at the *zócalo*.

Private homes usually have brick-mud walls, thatched roofs, and dirt floors, with beds on one end and an open fire on the other. No walls divide up the different sections, and most homes have little in terms of furniture. The village has a private house or chapel for each saint—just look for the leaf arches outside signaling the house's holy function. Inside the chapel are ceramic incense bowls, animal-shaped candle-holders, and a leaf curtain separating the holy altar from the seating area, which has little more than a few low benches lining the mud-caked walls and pine needles cushioning the floor. Homes and chapels are obviously not open to the public—join Mercedes and her tour for a peek into private Chamulan life (see p. 474).

The best time to visit Chamula is during **Carnaval,** which draws 40,000 *indígenas* and countless tourists, one week before Ash Wednesday. While they coincide with Lent, the festivities have their origins in the ancient Maya ritual concerning the five "lost" days at the end of the 360-day agricultural cycle. Expect to see religious leaders dashing through fire in order to purify themselves, as well as men decked out in monkey skins singing and dancing. In addition to Chamula's *carnaval* and the assumption of the *cargo* (Dec. 3-Jan. 1), the **fiestas** of **San Sebastián** (Jan. 20), **San Mateo** (Sept. 21-22), and **San Juan Bautista** (June 22-24) warrant a trip to the village.

**Getting There:** *Combis* to Chamula leave from San Cristóbal, on Utrilla near the market (about every ½hr., 6am-5pm, ½hr., 3 pesos). To reach Chamula by car from San Cristóbal, drive west from the *zócalo* on Guadalupe Victoria and bear right after crossing the small bridge on Diagonal Ramón Larraínzar. At the fork, bear right for Chamula, which is at the end of an 8km stretch of paved road.

CHIAPAS & TABASCO

## ZINACANTÁN

Just beyond Chamula lies the smaller community of Zinacantán (pop. 35,000), comprised of 36 villages. Your first vision will be a blur of deep red; here, the men (and even the young boys playing basketball in the *zócalo*) wear beautiful dazzlingly red *sarapes*, decorated with colorful stitched flowers and dangling tassels of deep red and purple. During **fiestas**, residents wear heel-guards on their *huaraches* (sandals) in accordance with ancient Maya custom. Many of the women walk about barefooted. This is not an indication of poverty but rather a reflection of the Maya emphasis on the importance of female fertility—they believe that women can draw fertility from the ground. Thus, as girls approach puberty, they begin to go without shoes. The unfortunate few women who are sterile are cast out of the village and must move, usually to San Cristóbal.

Somewhat exceptional for a *chiapaneco* village is the fact that Zinacantán has accepted the Catholic clergy. The village's handsome, whitewashed **church** dates back to the 16th century and features standard Roman columns and Corinthian arches. It is used exclusively for Catholic worship, while the small white convent has been set aside for ritual healing and pre-Conquest forms of worship. But you won't find confessionals in the church—confession here is a public act, directed at the effigies on the altar. The Catholic priest, independent of the village church, merely busies himself with confirmation, baptism, and wedding ceremonies. To enter the church you must pay a 3-peso visitor's fee at the tourist booth in front. Tourists who step inside the convent are expected to drop a small donation into the *limosna* box. As with all traditional communities, Zinacantán does not tolerate picture-taking, note-taking, or hat-wearing.

Of late, the village's flower industry has flourished and Zinacantán has gained a considerable economic edge over neighboring San Juan Chamula. Every Friday morning, town residents inaugurate what they hope will be a profitable weekend by marching down Av. Insurgentes in San Cristóbal. Today, many houses in Zinacantán contain stereos, TVs, and gas stoves, although these serve principally as status symbols and women prefer to cook directly on the ground. The children who bother tourists for pesos or pens will be severely scolded by their parents if caught. If you wander around town long enough, you'll stumble upon a backyard full of women **weaving**, and may well be invited in to browse the selection of clothes—you won't find souvenirs any more authentic than this.

Zinacantán's festivals include **Fiesta de San Sebastián** (Jan. 18-20), **Semana Santa, Fiesta del Patron San Juan** (July 24-29), and the **Fiesta de San Lorenzo** (Aug. 10-20).

**Getting There:** *Combis* to Zinacantán (3 pesos) leave San Cristóbal from the lot near the market as they fill up (daily 6am-8pm). If driving, follow Guadalupe Victoria west from the *zócalo* and turn right after crossing the small bridge on Diagonal Ramón Larraínzar. At the fork, turn left toward the "Bienvenido a Zinacantán" sign.

## SAN ANDRÉS LARRAÍNZAR

Site of the Zapatista negotiations during the summers of 1995 and 1996, San Andrés Larraínzar lies 26km northwest of San Cristóbal and 16km from Chamula. Because there are no convenient tours to the village, its 5000 citizens are better disposed toward the outsiders who do make the trip. The village colors are red, black, and white, appearing on most clothing and market items. Mexicans refer to the village as Larraínzar, but local Tzotziles prefer San Andrés. Since many of the villagers are reluctant to carry their produce all the way to San Cristóbal, the **market** (open Fri.-Sun. until 1pm) is better stocked here than at Chamula or Zinacantán. For a panoramic view of the beautiful green valleys and patches of cornfields which surround the city, walk up the hill from the main church to La Iglesia de Guadalupe.

**Getting There:** Starting at 6am, *combis* (50min., 5 pesos) make several trips to San Andrés from the small terminal behind the San Cristóbal market—continue on the dirt road for about a block and the stop will be on your right. It's best to return before 2pm, soon after the market begins to shut down and before the *combis* stop running.

To reach San Andrés by car, take the road northwest from San Cristóbal to Chamula and continue past the village. On a curve some 10km later, a prominent sign announcing "S.A. Larraínzar" points left to a road climbing the steep side of the valley; the village lies approximately 6km beyond the fork.

## CHENALHÓ

Chenalhó (pop. 6000) seems even more remote from San Cristóbal than 32km would suggest. Foreigners are rare birds here. In Chenalhó, typical dress for men varies from white or black ponchos worn over pants and bound with heavy belts, to short, light, white tunics. Women who have not adopted more current fashions dress uniformly in dark blue *nalgas* (skirts) and white *tocas* (shawls) embroidered with bright orange flowers. A small **store** behind the enclosed market supplies the town with nearly all its clothing. The **market** spreads out into the plaza in front of the church on Sunday and sells mostly foodstuffs, including *chiche,* a potent drink made from fermented cane. Villagers enthusiastically wave visitors into San Pedro, the church in the town's center, which serves as both a secular and a religious meeting place. Inside, the main aisle often shimmers with the light rising from candles. Chenalhó residents celebrate the **Fiesta de San Sebastián** (January 20) and the **Fiesta de San Pedro** (July 29) in grand style.

**Getting There: Autotransportes Fray Bartolomé de Las Casas** usually operates buses to Chenalhó and the even more remote town of **Pantelhó**. The bus leaves San Cristóbal from the station on Utrilla north of the market at about 2pm. The bus sometimes does not return until the next day, so make sure you have a ride back to San Cristóbal before you go. Bus trips take two hours. If you get stranded, Chenalhó does have some beds available—just ask nicely to be shown the way. Driving to Chenalhó can cut transit time in half, but the cost to your car's suspension system will be high—the dirt road northwest of Chamula is guaranteed to chatter some teeth.

## HIHKING TO EL ARCOTETE

Although a number of trails wind their way through San Cristóbal's countryside, the tourist office recommends that you not hike to or between the outlying villages—assaults (by bandits and poisonous snakes) are not uncommon. If you're desperate for a hike, consider undertaking the three- to four-hour round-trip trek to **El Arcotete,** a large natural arch formed where a small river cuts through a spur of rock. Unfortunately, the first half of the hike is alongside the highway, and then past a trash-filled park. Once on the ridge, however, the trail leads through beautiful pine forest with splendid views of the mountains.

**Getting There:** To reach the arch, head east on Calle Flavio Paniagua, in the northeast section of San Cristóbal. From a point level with the Iglesia de Guadalupe to your right, a 15-minute climb takes you steeply up to the *carretera.* Continue to climb along the roadside, as the city begins to spread out below you. A 30-40-minute walk brings you to a yellow "Prohibido Tirar Basura" sign, just as the highway begins to bear left. Leave the highway and continue to the right of the sign, through the forest. You'll eventually come upon a tiny *indígena* **village,** about 15 minutes from the highway. From here, the trail leads down through pristine pine forest to a gorgeous secluded clearing, 15 minutes from the village. At the bottom of the clearing to the right of an abandoned hut, a narrow trail leads 100m through the woods to a small river; El Arcotete is to your left. The water's not deep enough for swimming, but you can probably wade through the arch to the other side.

## GRUTAS DE SAN CRISTÓBAL

The Grutas de San Cristóbal lie just off the Pan-American Highway, 10km southeast of San Cristóbal. From the small entrance at the base of a steep wooded hillside, a tall, narrow fissure, incorporating a chain of countless **caves,** leads almost 3km into the heart of the rock. Because of the caves' unusual shape, the cave floor is not particularly friendly to the feet. Instead, a modern concrete walkway, at times 10m above the cave floor strewn with boulders, navigates 750m into the system. The dimly lit caves boast a spectacular array of stalactites and columns. If you're feeling youthful, stamping on the boardwalk at certain points generates a rumbling echo throughout the caves (caves open daily 9am-5pm; admission 3 pesos). Consider soliciting the help of one of the local youths who hang around outside to help uncover the natural light and shadow formations (a small tip is appropriate). Or bring your own flashlight and let your imagination run wild.

**Getting There:** Almost any east-bound *microbús* passing across the road from the Iglesia de San Diego passes the *grutas* (15min., 3 pesos). From the highway, a five-minute walk through the park brings you to the entrance. **Miguel Angel,** through the Café Tuluc at Av. Insurgentes 5 (1½ blocks south from zócalo) organizes horseback rides to the caves. For 60 pesos you get an energetic horse for four hours and a **sore bum** for days.

# ■ Comitán

Eighty-six kilometers southeast of San Cristóbal, Comitán is the last major town on the Pan-American Highway before the Guatemalan border (85km away). While rapid growth has transformed Comitán (pop. 85,000) into a dreary maze of tangled streets, the city can be active and genial; its verdant multi-terraced *zócalo*, filled with incessant marimba music, breeds a raucous, youthful fun—a striking contrast with the quiet lakes nearby. Even the military presence gets lost in the bustle; memories of large-scale Zapatista stunts are fading in the dusty trails of tourists who stream through Comitán going to and from Guatemala.

**Orientation and Practical Information** Streets increase numerically in both directions away from the *zócalo* and are named according to the geographical quadrant in which they fall. To reach the *zócalo* from the Cristóbal Colón bus station, cross over the **Pan-American Highway** and turn left. After 200m, take the first right onto **Calle 4 Pte. Sur.** Walk five blocks east, turn left, and walk three blocks north, past the post office, to the *zócalo* on **Av. Central.**

The **tourist office** (tel. 2-40-47), on the first floor of the Palacio Municipal, overflows with brochures and maps (open Mon.-Fri. 9am-3pm and 5-9pm). Guatemalan visas (see p. 490) can be obtained from the **Guatemalan Consulate,** Av. 1 Sur Pte. at Av. 2 Sur Pte. (tel. 2-04-91); look for the blue-and-white flag (open Mon.-Fri. 8am-4:30pm). **Banca Serfín,** at Av. 1 Sur Pte. 1 (tel. 2-12-96 or 2-15-70), just off the southwest corner of the *zócalo*, changes U.S. dollars only. They also have a 24-hour **ATM** (bank open Mon.-Fri. 9am-1:30pm).

**Cristóbal Colón,** on the Pan-American Highway between and Calles Sur Pte. 8 and 4 (tel. 2-09-80), runs to Mexico City (12:10 and 4:30pm, 16hr., 300 pesos), Palenque (10am, 6hr., 51 pesos), Puebla (12:10 and 4:30pm, 14hr., 270 pesos), Ocosingo (10am, 4hr., 24 pesos), San Cristóbal (12 per day, 1½hr., 19 pesos), Tapachula (7 per day, 6hr., 58 pesos), Tuxtla Gutiérrez (12 per day, 3½hr., 40 pesos), and Villahermosa (4pm, 9hr., 125 pesos). **Autotransportes Tuxtla Gutiérrez** on the Highway between Calles Sur Pte. 1 and 2 (tel. 2-10-44),, has first-class service to San Cristóbal (9 per day, 2hr., 20 pesos), continuing to Tuxtla (3hr., 30 pesos). Nine second-class buses also make the run to San Cristóbal and Tuxtla daily. You can shorten the walk to these stations by catching a *microbús* on the highway (1 peso). **Taxis** (tel. 2-01-27 or 2-01-05) can be found in the *zócalo* or along the highway.

Comitán's indoor **market** is on Central Benito Juárez, just before Av. 2 Ote. Sur, one block east of the *zócalo* (open daily dawn-dusk). Pick up groceries at **SúperMas,** Calle 2 Pte. 8 (tel. 2-17-27), one block south and one block east of the *zócalo* (open daily 8am-9pm). **Farmacia Regina,** Calle 1 Sur Ote. 1 (tel. 2-11-96 or 2-07-54), is on the south side of the *zócalo* (open daily 7am-10pm). The **Red Cross** is on Calle 5 Nte. Pte. (tel. 2-18-89), 2½ blocks west of the highway. In case of emergency contact the **Hospital Civil,** at Calle 2 Ote. Sur 13 and Av. 9 Sur Ote. (tel. 2-01-35 or 2-20-51). Get on the Internet at **Podernet,** Pasaje Morales 12 (tel. 2-22-50), to the right of the Palacio Municipal (30 pesos per hr.; open Mon.-Fri. 9am-2pm and 4-8pm, Sat. 9am-2pm) or at **Café Internet** (tel. 2-31-05), at Casa de la Cultura on the *zócalo*. The **police** (tel. 2-00-25) are on the ground floor of the Palacio Municipal. The **post office,** Central Dr. Belisario Domínguez 45 (tel. 2-04-27), is one-and-a-half blocks south of the *zócalo* (open Mon.-Fri. 9am-4pm, Sat. 9am-1pm).

**Accommodations and Food** Comitán is full of overpriced "budget" accommodations. A select few places stand out from the dregs, however. All establishments listed are within a few blocks of the *centro*. **Pensión Delfín,** Central Belisario Domínguez 21 (tel. 2-00-13), on the west side of the *zócalo,* offers an authentic, verdant, tile courtyard surrounded by wood-paneled rooms with firm beds and clean private baths (singles 70 pesos; 20 pesos per additional person, up to 7-person suites). **Hospedaje Montebello,** Calle 1 Nte. Pte. 10 (tel. 2-35-72), near Av. Central Nte., has brown, dark rooms with small windows that open to a concrete courtyard (30 pesos per person with communal facilities; private bath 10 whopping pesos). Several *taquerías,* clustered around the northwest corner of the *zócalo* and on Calle Central Nte., sell tacos for a pittance (2 pesos each).

# ■ Near Comitán

## PARQUE NACIONAL LAGUNAS DE MONTEBELLO

A hop, skip, and a 52km bus ride from Comitán lie the pine-covered hills of the **Parque Nacional Lagunas de Montebello.** Some 68 lakes peacefully await exploration in this scenic playground. Unfortunately, only 16 have trails leading from the main road, and some are notorious for bandit attacks. Be sure to inquire ahead at the Comitán tourist office or with guides at the lakes before undertaking any off-the-beaten-path hikes. Women traveling alone or in small groups should not try to hike the trails. But hey, you can get a great look at the lakes from the main paths. Buses unload passengers anywhere along the road to **Laguna Bosque Azul** or **Laguna Tziscao.** Camping is available at both of these sites, and Tziscao offers *cabañas* (30 pesos per person).

**Getting There:** From Comitán, the blue "Montebello" bus leaves the station on Av. 2 Pte. Sur, between Calles Sur Pte. 2 and 3 (every 15min., 5:30am-5pm, 1hr., 12 pesos). The bus swings by the Cristóbal Colón bus station for those who want to head straight to the lakes.

## OTHER SIGHTS

Just 22km south of the city lie the recently unearthed ruins of **Tenam Puente,** including a ballcourt and a handful of smaller pyramids. To reach the site, take the "Francisco Sarabia" bus from the Transportes Comitán-La Trinitaria station on Calle Sur Pte. 1, between Calles Pte. Sur 3 and 4 (Mon.-Fri. 8am and 2pm, ½hr., 3 pesos); it will drop you off at the access road, a couple of kilometers from the entrance. Check with drivers for return schedule (site open daily 8am-5pm; free).

Thirty-two kilometers from the Comitán-Cuauhtémoc (Pan-American) highway, on the way to Lagunas Montebello, lies another set of Maya ruins at **Chinkultic.** Perhaps more interesting than the 7th-century pyramid and ballcourt are the diminutive **cenote** (freshwater sinkhole) and the striking view of the lake region from the hilltop. The "Montebello" bus can drop you off at the access road, an easy 3km from the ruins (site open daily 9am-4pm; 10 pesos).

Popular with locals but more obscure than Montebello is the **Cascada de Chiflón,** a 250m waterfall 45km west of Comitán. The lake is relatively safe (albeit cold) for swimming, but don't venture too close to the waterfall, or you may take a once-in-a-lifetime plunge. There are some nice places to camp in this area, but no facilities. To get to Chiflón, take a *combi* to Tzimol from the Tuxtla Gutiérrez bus station on the highway (every ½hr. 5:45am-10am, 45min., 7 pesos). The waterfall is a 5km walk from the roadside.

CHIAPAS & TABASCO

# ■ Ocosingo

More rural than the bustling *zócalo* first lets on, tourist-free Ocosingo (pop. 24,000) straddles the hilltops of central Chiapas. As the nearest large settlement to the Lacandón rainforest, the fringes of which harbor the majority of Zapatista rebels, the military importance of Ocosingo's location is brutally obvious—and visibly so. Ocosingo's residents still bear painful memories of the January 1994 uprising, when a shootout in the market between the army and Zapatista-allied locals claimed dozens of lives. Despite the military backdrop, Ocosingo is a safe, albeit grimy, base from which to explore the nearby ruins of Toniná. Furthermore, it is the home of *quesillo*, huge balls of cheese that are sold from every window and doorway.

**Orientation and Practical Information** Ocosingo lies 72km northeast of San Cristóbal de las Casas and 119km south of Palenque. To get to the *zócalo* from the **Cristóbal Colón bus station,** walk uphill about 200m and take a left at the sign pointing to Ocosingo. Once on the road, take the first right and walk uphill six blocks to the *zócalo*. From the **Autotransportes Tuxtla station,** walk uphill two blocks and take a left at the "centro" sign. Three blocks downhill brings you to the *zócalo*. The town is laid out in the customary compass grid, but it's small enough that street names can be ignored almost entirely. From the *zócalo,* cardinal directions are marked by the Hotel Central to the north, the Iglesia de San Jacinto to the east, and the Palacio Municipal to the west.

**Banamex** (tel. 3-00-34), in the northwest corner of the *zócalo,* does not change U.S. dollars, but a lengthy procedure will get you cash advances on major credit cards (open Mon.-Fri. 9am-1:30pm). *Caseta* (tel. 3-00-54), is on 1 Ote. in an orange building on the left one and a half blocks north of the church (open Mon.-Sat. 9am-9pm).

**Autotransportes Tuxtla Gutiérrez** (tel. 3-04-31), on the highway, offers first-class service to Campeche (7:30am, 7hr., 115 pesos), Cancún (2:30 and 4:30pm, 14hr., 200 pesos), Mérida (8am, 10hr., 136 pesos), Mexico City (12:45pm, 18hr., 248 pesos), Palenque (8 per day, 2hr., 28 pesos), Puebla (3:30 and 6:30pm, 16hr., 248 pesos), and Villahermosa (4 per day, 5hr., 74 pesos). **Cristóbal Colón** (tel. 3-04-31) runs buses to Escárcega (4:30, 7:30pm, and 2:30am, 6hr., 73 pesos), Mexico City (3:30 and 6:30pm, 18hr., 300 pesos) via Puebla (16hr., 312 pesos), and Tuxtla Gutiérrez (10 per day, 3½hr., 40 pesos). **Luggage storage** will cost you 3 pesos per day.

The **market** is two blocks south and three blocks east of the *zócalo* (open daily 5am-7pm). Take dirty clothes to **Lavandería Automática "La Espuma,"** just off Calle Central Nte., two blocks north of the Hotel Central and to the left. Just knock at the closed gate and Mom will wash your clothes for 6 pesos per kg. A **pharmacy, Cruz Blanca,** 1 Ote. and 2 Sur (tel. 3-02-33), is one block south of the church (open daily 7am-10pm). In case of a **medical emergency,** contact **IMSS** (tel. 3-01-51), 1.2km south of the *zócalo* on 1 Ote. Sur (open 24hr.). In case of an **emergency,** contact the staff at the Palacio Municipal (tel. 3-00-15) or the police. The **police** roost on Calle Central between 1 Pte. and 2 Pte. (tel. 3-05-07; open 24hr.). The **post office** is at 2 Sur Ote. 12, one block south of the *zócalo* (open Mon.-Fri. 9am-1pm and 3-6pm, Sat. 9am-1pm). **Postal Code:** 29950. **Phone code:** 967.

**Accommodations and Food** **Hotel Central,** Av. Central 1 (tel. 3-00-24), on the north side of the *zócalo,* is smartly decorated in shades of aqua, well-lit, and spacious. Rooms come with mineral water, cable TV, and fans that go whoosh (singles 60 pesos; doubles 80 pesos; triples 100 pesos). **Hotel Margarita,** Calle Central Nte. 6 (tel. 3-02-80), half a block north of Hotel Central, is old, but features nice, firm beds (singles 75 pesos; doubles 85 pesos; triples 95 pesos; TV and A/C 20 pesos extra).

**Restaurant La Montura,** Av. Central 5 (tel. 3-05-50), in the Hotel Central on the north side of the *zócalo,* is somewhat overpriced, but the outdoor tables under the arcade are the most pleasant in town. Entrees are 25-30 pesos, delicious *tortas* stuffed with *frijoles* and avocado go for 10 pesos (open daily 7am-11pm). **Restaurante Las Cazuelas,** 1 Ote. 127, in the Hotel Agua Azul, serves up tasty food in a tiny log cabin

# Greetings from Let's Go Publications

The book in your hand is the work of hundreds of student researcher-writers, editors, cartographers, and designers. Each summer we brave monsoons, revolutions, and marriage proposals to bring you a fully updated, completely revised travel guide series, as we've done every year for the past 38 years.

This is a collection of our best finds, our cheapest deals, our most evocative description, and, as always, our wit, humor, and irreverence. Let's Go is filled with all the information on anything you could possibly need to know to have a successful trip, and we try to make it as much a companion as a guide.

We believe that budget travel is not the last recourse of the destitute, but rather the only way to travel; living simply and cheaply brings you closer to the people and places you've been saving up to visit. We also believe that the best adventures and discoveries are the ones you find yourself. So put us down every once in while and head out on your own. And when you find something to share, drop us a line. We're **Let's Go Publications,** 67 Mount Auburn St., Cambridge, MA 02138, USA (email: fanmail@letsgo.com; http://www.letsgo.com). And let us know if you want a free subscription to **The Yellowjacket,** the new Let's Go Newsletter.

# When in 172-1011,
# do as the 172-1011's do.

All you need for the
clearest connections home.

Every country has its own AT&T Access Number which makes calling from overseas really easy. Just dial the AT&T Access Number for the country you're calling from and we'll take it from there. And be sure to charge your calls on your AT&T Calling Card. It'll help you avoid outrageous phone charges on your hotel bill and save you up to 60%.* For a free wallet card listing AT&T Access Numbers, call 1 800 446-8399.

I t ' s     a l l     w i t h i n     y o u r     r e a c h .

**http://www.att.com/traveler**

with tree-trunk tables. The menu changes at the whim of the chef or the season. All meals cost 13 pesos (open daily 8am-9pm).

# ■ Near Ocosingo: Toniná Ruins

While the ruins of Toniná rarely surface on lists of Mexico's can't-miss sights, they're larger and more interesting than over-billed Bonampak and comparable in size, though not in splendor, to Yucatán's Ruta Puuc sites of Kabah, Sayil, and Labná. After a brief conflict-imposed absence, the archaeologists and their builders are back at the site, carefully reconstructing the main pyramid. As these ruins don't have the user-friendly plaques present elsewhere, a guide is more crucial than elsewhere.

The Toniná complex, encompassing 15 acres of ruins, was a religious and administrative capital for the Maya city-state that flourished from AD 300 to 1000. Structures at Toniná do not share the orthodox symmetry or precise floorplan of Monte Albán or Chichén Itzá. Many statues have lost heads and feet to decay and neglect, and because the governor of Ocosingo took stones from the site to build roads around the turn of the century, the pyramids will never be fully restored.

The entrance path, which leads across the river east of the ruins and up a small gully, emerges at the **Plaza of War,** the first artificially terraced level of the site. Trees and grass have overgrown a pyramidal mound on the left; nearer the river is the grassy depression of the unexcavated **main ballcourt,** beyond which lies a **sacrificial altar.** The ruins of a smaller ballcourt lie forgotten at the back of the plaza, next to chunks of statues scattered near the fence. Extensive glyphs on the back of these figures relate to the scenes on the front, often giving the *fechas fatales* (birth and death dates) of prominent characters. Three animals—the snake, the bat, and the jaguar—appear together repeatedly. The three stelae at the foot of the first level commemorate the inauguration of new governments.

Toniná's chief attraction is a massive **pyramid** which towers 60m over the plaza. The pyramid's seven tiers corresponded to the city's various social strata, from the general populace to the high priests, whose temples are perched on the seventh level. Well-preserved panels and sculptures survive from almost all the levels, but most have been moved to the on-site museum or hauled off to Mexico City. At the center of the pyramid's fifth level gapes a royal grave. Here, archaeologists discovered a stone sarcophagus made of a single piece of limestone, which held a king's body and two unidentified corpses. To the left of the grave on the same level is a shrine to Chac, the Maya rain god. The stone originally above the figure, carved in AD 300, is now in the museum. The **Altar de Monstruo de la Tierra** is on the right on the sixth level. The seventh level of the pyramid was Toniná's religious focal point, and it supports four large pyramids dedicated to a curious mix of cosmic and civic forces. The lowest and least impressive is the **Temple of Agriculture,** on the far right of the terrace. This crumbling pyramidal building contained private rooms for ranking priests and governors. Considerably higher, the **Pyramid of Life and Death** rises to the left of the Temple of Agriculture. Archaeologists believe this mound once housed the king and the royal family. Behind it loom Toniná's two most important temples. The higher **Pyramid of War,** on the right, served as an observatory; from the top of the structure, guards would scan the countryside for foreign heavies. Nearby, the **Pyramid of Finances** is aptly symmetrical. From the peak of either pyramid, you can enjoy a brilliant view and a cool breeze. Below the Pyramid of War is a newly excavated statue of **King Zotz-Choj** (the jaguar-bat king), whose giant headdress is adorned with an eagle, serpents, and symbols for wind, smoke, and fire.

**Getting There:** The ruins are located 15 bumpy kilometers from Ocosingo (a ½hr. drive). By car, follow Calle 1 Ote. south out of town, past the clinic on the right. Bear right past the radio station on the left. Follow the signs for "Toniná ruins" to the Rancho Toniná; the road to the left of the gate leads to ruins and museum. Inquire at the ranch about camping. Travelers without a car can catch a morning *colectivo,* dole out a steep **taxi** fare (80-100 pesos one way), or walk for days. You can catch a *colectivo* pickup truck from the market or go to the *crucero,* a juncture where several buses and trucks go by, some of which may take you near the ruins. To get to this *crucero,* walk 10 minutes to the right on the dirt road behind the market. If you're part of a group, consider chartering a *colectivo "especial"* to take you to the ruins (30 pesos one way). Nearly all *colectivos* stop on the highway just uphill from the "Tuxtla Gutiérrez" station.

# ■ Palenque

You've seen Uxmal. You made it to Chichén Itzá. Still, nothing can prepare you for Palenque, whose time-defying temples, grand palaces, and gigantic pyramids gleam like white diamonds against an emerald backdrop. The ruins of Palenque straddle a magnificent 300m high *palenque* (natural palisade) in the foothills of the Altos de Chiapas. One of the most important sights in all of Mesoamerica, Palenque's ruins are amazingly preserved. Dozens of waterfalls tumble into the dense *selva* (jungle), and the vast, misty rainforest echoes with birds, monkeys, and the whistle of branches pressing against one another. Visitors are mesmerized even without the aid of the hallucinogenic herbs and fungi that flourish in the moist shadows of the forest.

Eight kilometers away is the grimy town of Palenque (pop. 17,000), home to ruins of a different sort—unfinished construction projects and abandoned buildings. The town serves as little more than a base for exploring the ruins and famous cascades of Agua Azul and Misol-Ha.

## ORIENTATION

Palenque is in the northeastern corner of Chiapas, 274km from Tuxtla Gutiérrez. Streets running east-west are labeled *avenidas,* while those running north-south are *calles.* **Avenida Juárez** runs west, away from the *parque* (town square) towards the ruins and highway. Parallel to Juárez to the south are Av. **5 de Mayo** and **20 de Noviembre.** To the north lie **Miguel Hidalgo, Nicolás Bravo, Reforma,** and **Domínguez.** From west to east, the *calles* are **Allende, Aldama, Abasolo, Independencia, Jiménez,** and **Guerrero.** The *parque* is bounded by Hidalgo, 20 de Noviembre, Independencia, and Jiménez. To get to the *parque* from the bus station, walk five blocks uphill (east) on Juárez.

## PRACTICAL INFORMATION

**Tourist Office:** In the **Casa de las Artesanías,** at the corner of Juárez and Abasolo. Very friendly, helpful staff speaks some English and can provide excellent maps of the town and ruins. Open Mon.-Sat. 8am-8:30pm, Sun. 9am-1pm.

**Currency Exchange: Bancomer,** Juárez 40 (tel. 5-01-98), 2 blocks west of the *parque.* 24hr. **ATM.** Open for exchange Mon.-Fri. 9am-1:30pm. **Viajes Yax-Ha** (see travel agencies) has a *casa de cambio.*

**Telephones: Caseta California,** Juárez 4 (tel. 5-11-50 or 5-12-12; fax 5-09-97), half a block from the *parque.* Open daily 8am-3pm and 6-11pm.

**Fax:** On Hidalgo (tel. 5-03-68), 1½ blocks east of the *parque* in the Chaka-max building, next to the post office. Open Mon.-Fri. 9am-3pm, Sat. 9am-1pm.

**Travel Agencies: Yax-Ha,** Av. Juárez 123 (tel. 5-07-98; fax 5-07-67), next door to Bancomer. Trips to Misol-Ha, Agua Azul, Yaxchilán, and Bonampak. **VW rental,** starting at 260 pesos per day. Reasonable exchange rate for U.S. dollars. Open daily 8am-9pm.

**Buses:** All stations are located 5 blocks west of the *parque* on Juárez. **ADO** runs 1st-class buses to Campeche (8am, 6hr., 86 pesos), Cancún (8pm, 12hr., 196 pesos), Chetumal (8pm, 7½hr., 112 pesos), Escárcega (8am, 3hr., 54 pesos), Mérida (8am, 8hr., 130 pesos), Mexico City (6pm, 12hr., 280 pesos), Oaxaca (5:30pm, 13hr., 198 pesos), Playa del Carmen (8pm, 11hr., 181 pesos), Puebla (7pm, 10½hr., 240 pesos), and Villahermosa (11 per day, 2hr., 40 pesos). **Cristóbal Colón** sails for Campeche (noon, 6:30, and 10:30pm, 6hr., 76 pesos), Escárcega (noon, 6:30, and 10:30pm, 3hr., 48 pesos), Mérida (noon, 6:30, and 10:30pm, 8hr., 126 pesos), Ocosingo (4 per day, 2hr., 25 pesos), San Cristóbal (4 per day, 4½hr., 43 pesos),

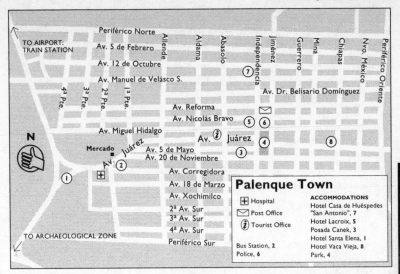

Palenque Town

| | |
|---|---|
| ✚ Hospital | **ACCOMMODATIONS** |
| ✉ Post Office | Hotel Casa de Huéspedes "San Antonio", 7 |
| ℹ Tourist Office | Hotel Lacroix, 5 |
| | Posada Canek, 3 |
| Bus Station, 2 | Hotel Santa Elena, 1 |
| Police, 6 | Hotel Vaca Vieja, 8 |
| | Park, 4 |

CHIAPAS & TABASCO

and Tuxtla Gutiérrez (4 per day, 6hr., 63 pesos). **Autobuses de Tuxtla Gutiérrez** (tel. 5-12-33) offers 1st- and 2nd-class service.

**Taxis:** Tel. 5-01-12 or 5-03-79. 20 pesos to the ruins; 7 pesos in town.

**Laundromat: Lavandería "Ela,"** 5 de Mayo at Allende, opposite the Hotel Kashlan. 30 pesos for 3kg. Same-day service. Open Mon.-Sat. 8am-1pm and 4-7pm.

**Pharmacy: Farmacia Central,** Av. Juárez near Independencia. Changes dollars at slightly unfavorable rates. Open daily 8:30am-10pm.

**Medical Services: Centro de Salud y Hospital General,** on Juárez (tel. 5-00-25), near the bus station, at the western end of town. Open 24hr. No English spoken.

**Police:** On Calle Independencia (tel. 5-08-28), in the Palacio Municipal. Open 24hr.

**Post Office:** Independencia at Bravo, north of the *parque*. Open Mon.-Fri. 9am-1pm and 3-6pm, Sat. 9am-1pm. **Postal Code:** 29960.

**Phone Code:** 934.

## ACCOMMODATIONS

Budget travelers can either stay in town or sack out at one of the hotels along the highway en route to the ruins. Of the two options, the latter tends to be much more expensive, with the exception of **Mayabell Trailer Park and Camping** (tel. 8-06-19; fax 5-07-67), which allows guests to pitch a tent, string up a hammock, or put down a sleeping bag under a *palapa* for about 15 pesos per person (10-peso deposit, 10 pesos for hammock rental). Electricity, water, and decent sewage facilities are available for trailers (10 pesos per car). The few rooms boast terra cotta honeycomb tiles, plaid bedspreads, standing fans, and private bathrooms (singles 85 pesos; doubles 105 pesos; triples 130 pesos; 10 pesos per additional person; 100-peso deposit). There's also a large swimming pool and attached restaurant. Three-hour guided horseback tours of the countryside available (120 pesos). Mayabell, 6km from town and 2km from the ruins, is accessible by *combi* (3 pesos).

All of the hotels listed below are in the town center, within easy walking distance of the *parque* and bus station. Camping outside of a campground can be unsafe.

**Posada Canek,** 20 de Noviembre 43 (tel. 5-01-50), between Independencia and Abasolo, half a block west from the *parque*. A glorified hostel with large, clean rooms, good bathrooms, and a view of the mountains to the south. Singles 25 pesos for a bed in a 5-person dormitory or 60 pesos for a room with private bath; doubles 60 pesos; triples 80 pesos; 20 pesos per additional person.

**Hotel Vaca Vieja,** 5 de Mayo 42 (tel. 5-03-77 or 5-03-88), 3 blocks east of the *parque* in a quiet part of town. Plain, spacious rooms with varnished wooden furniture, firm beds, and dauntless ceiling fans. Singles 60 pesos; doubles 75 pesos; triples 90 pesos. Prices rise by 10 pesos during the high season.

**Hotel Lacroix,** Hidalgo 10 (tel. 5-00-14), just off the *parque* and opposite the church. A large, gaudy Maya mural leads the way to blue rooms and bluer bathrooms. Cold water only. Singles 80 pesos; doubles 90 pesos; triples 100 pesos.

**Hotel Santa Elena** (tel. 5-10-29), on Jorge de la Vega Domínguez, around the corner from the ADO bus station. For once, the hotel next to the station is nice—well-ventilated rooms come with wood paneling, fans, and hot water. Singles 60 pesos; doubles 70 pesos; triples 100 pesos.

## FOOD

Thanks to the strong non-*indígena* presence in Palenque, local menus have taken on a sort of culinary condescension; prices are high for what is served. For cheap produce, try the **market** on Velasco Suárez, four blocks west and four blocks north of the *parque*. There is also a surprisingly decent restaurant at the ruins.

**Restaurante Las Tinajas,** 20 de Noviembre 41, at Abasolo. Family run food shack popular among tourists staying at Posada Canek across the street. Good local dishes (20-30 pesos) and *licuados* (7 pesos). Open daily 7am-11pm.

**Restaurant Rocamar,** 20 de Noviembre at Independencia, near the *parque*. Small seafood joint with plastic tables and chairs (entrees 25-35 pesos). Open daily 8am-8pm.

**Restaurant Yunuen,** 5 de Mayo 42 (tel. 5-03-88), at Chiapas annexed to the Hotel Vaca Vieja, 3 blocks east of the *parque*. Small, friendly, and very inexpensive. Feast on the *comida del día*—soup, meat dish, rice, tortillas, fruit, and coffee for a mere 20 pesos. Open daily 7am-11pm.

**Restaurant Maya,** Independencia at Hidalgo (tel. 5-00-42), right on the *parque*. Tourists crowd out locals for good service and tasty food. *Menús del día* go for about 25 pesos; sandwiches are 15-20 pesos. Open daily 7am-11pm.

## SIGHTS

During the Maya Classic Period (AD 300-900), one of Palenque's ancient names meant "Place of the Sun's Daily Death"—the city was obviously of great importance to the Maya. Though impressive, the ruins only hint at the former magnitude of the city, as less than 10% of the pyramids have been shorn of their dense jungle blanket. Excavation continues as you read.

Palenque owes much of its finery, including its unparalleled stucco bas-relief sculptures, to an early ruler, the club-footed god-man **King Pakal** (AD 615-683). According to inscriptions made at the time of his death, Pakal lived into his fifth *katan* (20-year period) and was then succeeded by his elderly son **Chan-Bahlum.** Chan-Bahlum celebrated his ascension by building a great pyramid-crypt (Temple of the Inscriptions) for his father. After Chan-Bahlum died, Palenque slipped into oblivion; some archaeologists speculate that the city had "fulfilled its purpose." When Cortés arrived in the 16th century, he marched right past the withered town without noting its existence.

Upon entering the site, you pass the tomb of Alberto Ruz, an archaeologist so devoted to restoring Palenque that he insisted on being buried there. To the right rises the steep **Temple of the Inscriptions.** Named for its magnificent tablets, the Temple was the burial place of King Pakal, and was the first substantial burial place discovered in the Americas. After his disappointing discovery of six unimpressive skeletons, Ruz bore into the interior of the crypt; he discovered the perfectly preserved, elaborately carved sarcophagus of the king. Visitors must scramble the long way down slippery stone steps in a steep and stuffy tunnel to view the royal crypt. The **hollow duct,** which allowed Pakal's spirit to exit the underworld and communicate with Palenque's priests, is visible on the right after the staircase.

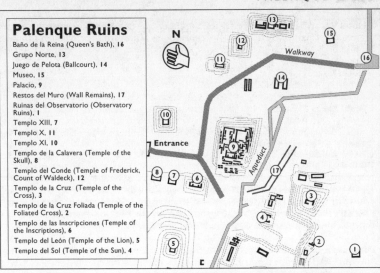

**Palenque Ruins**

Baño de la Reina (Queen's Bath), 16
Grupo Norte, 13
Juego de Pelota (Ballcourt), 14
Museo, 15
Palacio, 9
Restos del Muro (Wall Remains), 17
Ruinas del Observatorio (Observatory Ruins), 1
Templo XIII, 7
Templo X, 11
Templo XI, 10
Templo de la Calavera (Temple of the Skull), 8
Templo del Conde (Temple of Frederick, Count of Waldeck), 12
Templo de la Cruz  (Temple of the Cross), 3
Templo de la Cruz Foliada (Temple of the Foliated Cross), 2
Templo de las Inscripciones (Temple of the Inscriptions), 6
Templo del León (Temple of the Lion), 5
Templo del Sol (Temple of the Sun), 4

**CHIAPAS & TABASCO**

Next to the Temple is a trapezoidal **palace** complex, consisting of four patios and a four-story tower. This immense complex is replete with religious tributes, such as the relief on the north side depicting the nine gods of the underworld. Other carvings laud the godlike priests and royal families that inhabited its many chambers. The palace's T-shaped air tunnels cooled the air and doubled as representations of Ik, the god of the breezes. Clamber down the staircase from the top of the platform to explore the extensive, dimly lit network of underground passageways. Flat-nosed masks of the rain-god Chac, which glare accusingly off to the north end's stuccoed walls, reveal the influence of the Olmecs, and suggest a deep-seated societal fear of drought. An exclusively female steam bath and latrines have also been excavated.

A trail leads up the mountainside to the left of the Temple of Inscriptions. About 100m along this trail, on the right, is the **Temple of the Lion.** Descend the pitch-black stairwell inside the structure and you'll come upon the site of the ancient well where a few faint traces of paint are slowly surrendering to the green slime of the jungle. Bring a flashlight; the steps are wet and there's no light. The trail continues up the hill for 7km before reaching the tiny *indígena* village of Naranjo. Guides can be found for this difficult hike through beautiful terrain.

The path between the palace and the Temple of Inscriptions fords the recently reconstructed aqueduct before leading up to the **Sun Plaza,** another landscaped platform comprised of the **Temple of the Sun,** the **Temple of the Cross,** the **Temple of the Foliated Cross,** and the smaller **Temple 14.** The Temple of the Cross was named for a stucco relief of a cross which was found inside and which inspired a flurry of hopeful religious theories among the *conquistadores.* For the Maya, the cross represented the tree of life, with a snake as its horizontal branch, and a bird perched atop it. The outer layer of stucco has worn away, but the inner sanctum protects a large sculpted tablet and reliefs on either side of the doors.

About to be swallowed again by the jealous jungle, the **Temple of the Foliated Cross** lies across the plaza from the Temple of the Sun. Despite the overgrown path, the inner sanctum here contains a surprisingly clear carved tablet. The tablet was carved with an unusual tree (or cross) whose branches are remarkably similar to some of those found in a temple at Angkor-Wat, Cambodia, but nowhere else. Concoct your own elaborate alien fantasy explanation. To the south, through the wall of trees, several unreconstructed temples surround the uncleared **Plaza Maudslay.** Downhill from Temple 14 and past the palace lie the vestiges of a **ballcourt.** From the absence of stone rings, archaeologists speculate that wooden ones were used instead.

---

### Hoop Dreams

The great ballcourts found in Chichén Itzá and other Maya cities once witnessed an impressive game called **pok-ta-pok,** in which two contending teams endeavored to keep a heavy rubber ball in constant motion by using only their hips, knees, and elbows. Players scored by knocking the ball through the stone rings placed high on the court's side walls. The ball game was much more than just a cultural pastime for the Maya; it was a contest of **good** versus **evil** linked to a game of the gods. A Maya legend tells that every harvest, Hun Hunahpu, god of corn, was decapitated; his head was planted in the ground and became the seed of all corn plants. Every year, the evil gods of the nether-world stole the buried head in an attempt to destroy the Maya. The twins Xbalanque and Hunahpú (the sun and Venus respectively) would then descend to Xilbalba (the netherworld) and challenge the evil gods to an epic game of ball, using the god's head instead of a ball. Invariably, the twins were successful, and the seed was recovered. The new crop symbolized the god's resurrection and the Maya's salvation. It is believed that in response to the legend, the captain of the winning team would be decapitated and his head offered to the gods.

---

Plaenque is full of small paths leading to unrestored ruins and small cascades. Bring bug spray and a buddy if you intend to explore the not-so-frequented corners.

To the left of the ballcourt is the **Temple of Frederick, Count of Waldeck,** who lived here for three years while studying the ruins in the 1830s. The four other temples which share the platform with the Temple of the Count comprise the **North Group.** Waterfall enthusiasts may catch a glimpse of the **Queen's Bath** (so named for its exclusively female clientele), a small set of falls down the wide dirt path that leads right, away from the North Group. A second set of falls, **Cascada Montiepa,** is hidden in the jungle, 600m down the road from the ruins. At the right-hand bend follow the path into the woods. Sadly, overgrown banks and shallow water make swimming impractical. There is also an excellent **museum** 2km before the site near Mayabell (archaeological site and museum open daily 8am-4:45pm; crypt open daily 8am-4pm; admission 16 pesos, free Sun.; map 4 pesos).

**Getting There:** *Combis* to the site run daily from 6am-6pm (2 pesos); catch them off Juárez on Allende. Visiting the ruins at night is prohibited and extremely unsafe. Do not take shortcuts to the back entrance of the ruins from the campgrounds or the road—it is reported that rapes and robberies have occurred on these trails, and the dense jungle leaves you isolated even if there are many other tourists nearby.

## ■ Near Palenque

### CASCADAS DE AGUA AZUL AND MISOL-HA

Both of these large *cascadas* (waterfalls) have overflowed with tourists of late, and for good reason. **Agua Azul,** 62km south of Palenque, is a breathtaking spectacle: the Río Yax jumps down 500 individual falls, then slips into rapids, whirlpools, and calm swimming areas in between. Rainy season, however, brings rivers of mud down from the highlands into the once-azure falls. There is a tiny beach and swimming area 20 minutes upstream from the falls—if you swim, stay close to the bank and swim with a friend, as more than 100 people have met their watery end here.

The falls are best visited as a daytrip. If, however, the muddy, buggy, 4km walk from *el crucero* has you all tuckered out and you simply must spend the night, *cabañas* (doubles 110 pesos; quads 220 pesos) are available on site and space for tents or hammocks can be arranged.

The falls at **Misol-Ha,** smaller and less-visited than Agua Azul, are 24km from Palenque and only 2km from the highway crossing. There's a large cataract here, and the swimming area is clean and relatively safe. A small **restaurant** serves up a few good dishes at reasonable prices.

**Getting There:** The most painless way to visit Agua Azul and Misol-Ha is aboard a **Transportes Chambalu** *combi* (50 pesos round-trip). *Combis* leave daily from the Palenque station at Hidalgo and Allende at 10am and noon, and after a half-hour photo stop at Misol-Ha, proceed to Agua Azul. Passengers are then dropped off right by the falls for a three-hour swimming session. **Buses** between Palenque and Ocosingo or San Cristóbal will also stop at the crossroads for either Agua Azul or Misol-Ha (2 pesos). Since few buses pass after 4pm, you should leave the falls in the early afternoon. Hitchhikers report that steady pick-up truck traffic makes catching a ride fairly easy (admission to each of the falls 2 pesos, 5 pesos per carload).

# ■ Tonalá

If, while in Chiapas, you're hit by a sudden and irresistible urge to listen to the surf and wriggle your toes in the sand, then head for Tonalá. While the beaches near Tonalá don't compare with Oaxaca's golden stretches of sand, **Puerto Arista** and (especially) **Boca del Cielo** are pleasant enough spots to spend a few hours. During Semana Santa, Christmas, and weekends in July and August, these seaside stretches fill with Chiapanecan families. During all the rest of the year, however, their only guests are the *zancudos blancos,* vicious biting insects that exploit the holey nature of hammocks.

Tonalá is unfortunately a hot and inhospitable town. Crossing Avenida Hidalgo, the main street (which doubles as the coastal highway), often entails risking your life. Stop for lunch and head for the sand or further afield.

**Orientation and Practical Information** Tonalá lies 223km northwest of Tapachula and 172km southwest of Tuxtla Gutiérrez. All **bus stations** are on **Avenida Hidalgo,** Tonalá's main street. To get to the *zócalo* from the **Cristóbal Colón** bus station, take a left and head six blocks south. Both the **Autotransportes Tuxtla Gutiérrez** and **Fletes y Pasajes** bus stations are south of the *centro,* so you need to turn right and walk five blocks north. As the coastal highway, Av. Hidalgo runs roughly northsouth through town. To the east, **Av. Rayón** parallels Hidalgo, while to the west run **Avenidas Matamoros, Juárez,** and **Allende.** Listed from north to south, **Calles Madero, 16 de Septiembre, 5 de Febrero, Independencia,** and **5 de Mayo** run east-west, completing the grid that makes up the city center.

The **tourist office** is at Hidalgo and 5 de Mayo (tel. 3-27-87), two blocks south of the bus station, on the second floor of the Esmeralda building (no city maps; open Mon.-Fri. 9am-3pm and 6-9pm, Sat. 10am-1pm). Public **telephones** are located throughout the *centro.* Many long distance *casetas* line Hidalgo; don't be fooled into thinking those LADATEL booths work—their phones were ripped out long ago. **Banamex** is at Hidalgo 137 at 5 de Febrero (tel. 3-00-37 or 3-10-77), half a block south of the *zócalo* (open Mon.-Fri. 9am-1:30pm).

First-class **buses,** including Maya de Oro (tel. 3-05-40), leave from the **Cristóbal Colón** station, six blocks north of the *zócalo,* for Mexico City (8pm, 13hr., 280 pesos), Oaxaca (10pm, 6½hr., 115 pesos), Puebla (8 and 9pm, 10hr., 265 pesos), Tapachula (every hr., 3am-7pm, 3hr., 65 pesos), Tuxtla Gutiérrez (every hr., 3am-7:30pm, 3hr., 53 pesos), and Villahermosa (12:30am, 12hr., 130 pesos). **Autotransportes Tuxtla Gutiérrez,** Hidalgo 56, five blocks south of the *zócalo,* has first-class service to Mexico City (6:30pm, 13hr., 203 pesos) via Puebla (11hr., 178 pesos). **Fletes y Pasajes,** Hidalgo 52 (tel. 3-25-94), 50m south of the bridge and three and a half blocks south of the *zócalo,* sends second-class buses to Mexico City (4 per day, 13hr., 204 pesos), Puebla (4 per day, 11hr., 170 pesos), and Tapachula (6 per day, 3½hr., 56 pesos). From the same building, **TRF** (tel. 3-12-61) has first-class service to Tapachula (4 per day, 3hr., 43 pesos) and Tuxtla Gutiérrez (10 per day, 3hr., 40 pesos). **Taxis** (tel. 3-06-20) cruise up and down Hidalgo and hang out in the *zócalo* (40 pesos to Puerto Arista). If you're getting up early, the 24-hour **radio-taxis** (tel. 3-10-00) opposite the Colón bus station will come and rouse you at your hotel.

The **market** is on Matamoros, several blocks southeast of the *zócalo*. Walk south on Hidalgo and right on 5 de Febrero or Independencia to Matamoros (open until 2:30pm, though stalls outside stay open until 6 or 7pm). The **Red Cross** (tel. 3-02-76) is on Av. Joaquín Miguel Gutiérrez (open 24hr.). **Clínica de Especialidades,** Hidalgo 127 (tel. 3-12-90), at Independencia south of the *zócalo,* is a hospital and a pharmacy. One doctor speaks English (open daily 9am-1pm and 5-7pm; open 24hr. for emergency medical service). **Hospital General,** Av. 27 de Septiembre at Mina (tel. 3-06-87), is six blocks south of the *zócalo* and three blocks east before the gas station (open 24hr.). The **police** station is on Calle Libertad (tel. 3-01-03), two blocks north of Cristóbal Colón and to the right. The **post office** is on Zambrano 27 (tel. 3-06-83), two blocks north and half a block east of the *zócalo* (open Mon.-Fri. 8am-7pm, Sat. 9am-1pm). **Postal Code:** 30500. **Phone Code:** 966.

**Accommodations and Food**   Budget hotels in Tonalá are overpriced and undercleaned; there's not even one standout. Rooms at **Hotel Tonalá** (tel. 3-04-80), a few blocks south of the Cristóbal Colón station, are small, stuffy, and drab (singles 80 pesos; doubles 105 pesos; triples 150 pesos). Cheaper accommodations come at a price at **Hotel Thomás,** on Hidalgo (tel. 13-00-80) before the bridge, two blocks south of the *zócalo.* Blue, cell-like rooms are equipped with prehistoric ceiling fans, and the barely-flushing toilets are in need of repair (singles 50 pesos; doubles 65 pesos).

The pink **Restaurante Nora,** Independencia 10 just east of Hidalgo (tel. 3-02-43), a block from the *zócalo,* is a calm refuge from the heat and sun. The congenial owner will make you feel right at home (tasty 3-course *comida corrida* 24 pesos; open Mon.-Sat. 7am-6pm). At **Restaurant Sambors,** Madero and Hidalgo (tel. 3-06-80), right on the *zócalo,* you can watch people watch you sip your huge chocolate milk (10 pesos). The delicious *marisco* salad is worth every penny (open daily 8am-1am).

**Sand and Sights**   Eighteen kilometers southwest of Tonalá, **Puerto Arista** offers 32km of grey, sandy beach and the pounding waves of the Pacific. Be especially careful in the late afternoon, when the current flows out to sea. Most beachside restaurants can provide hammocks for the night (about 10 pesos), although they may not even charge if you enthusiastically patronize their establishment. Obviously, ask before setting up your own hammock or tent on someone else's property.

**Hotel Playa Escondida,** at the left end of the beach, offers rudimentary singles with fans and patchy paint (singles 60 pesos; doubles 80 pesos; 10 pesos less with communal bathroom; camping 20 pesos per person with trailer or 10 pesos per person with tent; hammocks 20 pesos). If *cabañas* by an estuary are a must, ask Hotel Playa Escondida to walk you to **Mayabel Cabañas.** You'll never find it on your own. Here, small, authentic *cabañas* come with fans, light, and mosquito nets. The friendly owner'll cook to order.

For calmer seas, head to the sheltered saltwater estuary of **Boca del Cielo,** 15km farther down the coast. As the estuary is less than 100m wide, you can wade and then swim across to the beachfront restaurants and open ocean. To get there with your wallet and clothes in a less-than-soaked condition, hop in a *lancha* (25 pesos). There are no hotels in Boca del Cielo, so you'll want to base yourself in Puerto Arista or Tonalá. Every 20 minutes, *colectivos* run to both Puerto Arista (5 pesos) and Boca del Cielo (8 pesos) from their stand on 5 de Mayo, one and a half blocks west of Hidalgo.

# ▓ Tapachula

Must be something about those border towns. Tapachula (pop. 300,000) is loud and dirty, crowded and crass, enormous and smelly...and let's not forget hot. But the all-out assault on the senses—completed by marimba music echoing through the hazy air from practically every street corner—might actually amuse you. If not, escape to the *zócalo,* where topiary trees, their leafy crowns trimmed square and joined to one another, form a green canopy over two square blocks, and relaxing outdoor cafes provide sanctuary. During the rainy season, hundreds of Guatemalan immigrants crowd under these trees, reading newspapers or socializing. For tourists, Tapachula is primarily a point of entry into Guatemala, and the businesses reflect this in their attitude—they know you're not staying, so they'll get you for what they can.

## ORIENTATION

Tapachula is 18km from Talismán at the Guatemalan border on Rte. 200 and 303km west of Guatemala City. Tonalá lies 220km to the northwest, along the Pacific coast. *Avenidas* run north-south, and *calles* run east-west. *Calles* north of **Calle Central** are odd-numbered, while those to the south are even-numbered. Similarly, *avenidas* east of **Av. Central** are odd-numbered, while those to the west have even numbers. Tapachula's main plaza is at **3 Calle Pte.** between **6** and **8 Av. Nte.,** northwest of the center. To get to the *zócalo* from the **bus station,** take an immediate right upon exiting onto 3 Av. Nte. Walk seven blocks south to 3 Calle Ote. and turn right; the *zócalo* lies five blocks ahead.

## PRACTICAL INFORMATION

**Tourist Office:** Tel. 5-54-09. In the Antiguo Palacio Municipal, south of the Iglesia de San Agustín on the west side of the *zócalo.* Brochures, maps, and enthusiasm. Open Mon.-Fri. 9am-3pm and 6-9pm, Sat.-Sun. 9am-2pm.

**Consulate: Guatemala,** 2 Calle Ote. 33, between 7 and 9 Av. Sur (tel. 6-12-52). Citizens of the U.S., Canada, and European Union countries don't need a visa. Your passport will get you across the border hassle-free. Citizens from other countries (Switzerland, South Africa, etc.) will need a visa (see p. 15). Go first to **Copias Motta,** on Calle Central and 9 Av. Nte., to photocopy the first page of your passport and obtain a visa application. Visas usually take less than ½hr.; arrive early, though, in case of crowds. Open Mon.-Fri. 9am-1:30pm and 3-5pm.

**Currency Exchange: Banamex,** Av. Central Nte. 9 (tel. 6-29-24). 24hr. **ATM.** Open Mon.-Fri. 9am-2pm.

**Telephones: LADATELs** at the Cristóbal Colón bus station, at the Cine Maya on 2 Av. Nte. at 1 Calle Pte., or anywhere around the *zócalo.*

**Airport:** On the road to Puerto Madero, about 17km south of town. Served by **Aeroméxico,** 2 Av. Nte. 6 (tel. 6-20-50), **Aviacsa,** Av. Central and Calle 1 Pte. (tel. 6-31-47 or 6-14-39), and **Taesa,** 1 Calle Pte. 11 (tel. 6-37-32; fax 6-37-02).

**Buses: Cristóbal Colón,** 17 Calle Ote. at 3 Av. Nte. (tel. 6-43-75 or 6-28-80). Open 24hr. To Brownsville, TX (10pm, 24hr., 569 pesos), Comitán (5 per day, 6hr., 65 pesos), Mexico City (5 per day, 16hr., 342 pesos), Oaxaca (6:30 and 8pm, 11hr., 195 pesos), Puebla (4:30, 5:30, and 8:15pm, 14hr., 305 pesos), Puerto Escondido (10:45pm, 7hr., 182 pesos), San Cristóbal (5 per day, 5hr., 80 pesos), Tampico (10pm, 16hr., 398 pesos), Tonalá (3 per day, 3hr., 65 pesos), Tuxtla Gutiérrez (every hr., 6hr., 108 pesos), Veracruz (10pm, 12hr., 180 pesos), and Villahermosa (9pm, 12hr., 168 pesos). **Autotransportes Tuxtla Gutiérrez** (tel. 6-95-13), 11 Calle Ote. 14, between 3 and 4 Av. Norte. Open 24hr. 2nd-class service to Mexico City (12:30 and 7pm, 16hr., 280 pesos) and Tuxtla Gutiérrez (7 per day, 7hr., 95 pesos). **Fletes y Pasajes,** 3 Av. Norte and 9 Calle Ote. (tel. 6-76-03), has 2nd-class service to Mexico City (1:45, 3:30, and 5pm, 17hr., 255 pesos) and Oaxaca (4am, 12:30, 1:30, and 6:30pm, 13hr., 140 pesos).

**Trains:** Av. Central Sur 150 (tel. 6-21-76), at the end of the *avenida* behind a miniature plaza. Slow, cheap, unreliable 2nd-class service.

**Red Cross:** 9 Av. Nte. at 1 Calle Ote. (tel. 6-19-49 or 5-35-06), across from the post office. 24hr. ambulance service. No English spoken.

**Pharmacy: Farmacia 24 Horas,** 8 Av. Nte. 25 at 7 Calle Pte. (tel. 6-24-80). No English spoken. Delivery to anywhere within the city available 7am-11pm.

**Hospital:** Tel. 6-80-80. On the highway to the airport. Open 24hr.

**Police:** 8 Av. Nte. and 3 Calle Pte. (tel. 5-28-51), in the Palacio Municipal. Open 24hr.

**Post Office:** 1 Calle Ote. 32 between 7 and 9 Av. Nte. (tel. 6-24-92). Open Mon.-Fri. 8am-6pm, Sat. 9am-1pm. **Postal Code:** 30700.

**Phone Code:** 962.

## ACCOMMODATIONS

Due to the huge influx of Guatemalan refugees, budget accommodations are a dime a dozen in Tapachula, especially near the market. Unfortunately, many hotel rooms are as noisy and dirty as the rest of the city. The two spots listed provide clean, pleasant accommodations at reasonable prices.

**Hotel San Agustín,** 12 Av. Nte. 14 between 1 and 3 Calle Pte. (tel. 6-14-53), 2 blocks west of the *zócalo.* Rooms are like nice, new garages: gigantic, empty, and made of white cement. 2-room suites have a bed in one room and nothing in the other. The floors and walls *radiate* heat; you won't need hot water from your clean private bath. For relief, try the pool and sundeck. TV in the lobby. One double bed 50 pesos; two 70 pesos; three 100 pesos; four 120 pesos. A/C 50 extra pesos.

**Hotel La Amistad,** 7 Calle Pte. 34 between Av. 10 and 10 Nte (tel. 6-22-93). A quiet, cool retreat from Tapachula's sweltering bustle. Peachy-keen rooms with private bathrooms, built around a lush courtyard. Singles 50 pesos; doubles 70 pesos; triples 80 pesos; quads 120 pesos; quints 150 pesos.

## FOOD

Food, like most things in Tapachula, is tasteless; to compound the problem, prices are high too. A *chinapueblito* is on 1 Calle Pte., one block southeast of the *zócalo,* but portions are often small. For cheap eats, head to the **San Juan food market** on 17 Calle Pte., north of the *centro* (open daily 5am-5pm). **Mercado Sebastián Escobar,** on 10 Av. Nte. between 5 and 3 Calles Pte., sells produce and baked goods.

**El Charco de las Ranas,** 4 Av. Nte. 21, between 1 and 3 Calle Pte., next to the Hotel Fénix. Friendly open-air joint with large quesadillas (5 pesos) and Godzilla lemonades to fight off Tapachula heat. Breakfasts 10-20 pesos. Open daily 7am-9pm.

**La Parrilla,** 8 Av. Nte. 20 (tel. 6-40-62), in the southwest corner of the *zócalo.* Might be the cheapest chow, but this cafeteria-style joint shamelessly charges 10 pesos for teeny lemonades. Better stick to beer (8 pesos). *Tortas* 10-15 pesos. Regular entrees 25-35 pesos. Open 7am-12:30am.

## CROSSING THE BORDER TO GUATEMALA

New policies have made border crossing that much easier. Almost no one needs a visa (see p. 15), and you'll get 30 days in Guatemala on your tourist card; if you stay longer, make sure to visit a consulate in Guatemala to ask (or beg) for more time. Otherwise, be prepared for a fee when you leave Guatemala. Plan to cross the border early in the day to avoid bureaucratic delay, early and unofficial closings, and wasted time in Talismán (right at the border). It's best to buy your **tourist card** (US$5) or get a visa from the Guatemalan consulate in Tapachula; the Talismán office has erratic hours.

From Tapachula, **Unión y Progreso buses** leave their station on 5 Calle Pte., a half-block west of 12 Av. Nte., for Talismán (every 5min., ½hr., 5 pesos). For those who don't want to spend any time in Tapachula, the bus swings by the Cristóbal Colón bus station, on 17 Calle Ote., on its way to the border. Buses from Tapachula drop off passengers at the entrance to the Mexican emigration office. Enter the building and present your **passport** and Mexican **tourist card** to officials behind the desk, then follow the crowd across the bridge, which charges a toll of approximately 3 pesos. Proceed to a small building on the left to have your passport stamped by Guatemalan authorities; there is a charge of five quetzales. A **taxi** from the *zócalo* to Talismán costs 50 pesos. Those crossing the border **on foot** will be besieged by money changers and self-appointed "guides."

The **money changers** on the Guatemalan side of the border generally give better rates for pesos than those on the Mexican side, but your best bet is to avoid small money changers and head for the **Banco de Quetzal,** on the Guatemalan side.

From Talismán, you can take a **bus** to Guatemala City (6 per day, 4am-midnight). Don't travel at night, since this route has been recently plagued by assaults. Should you have to spend the night, the **Hotel José Ricardo,** just past the official buildings on the right, offers nice, clean rooms with bathrooms and hot water. They lock the front door, which is reassuring. The various eateries in Talismán can turn seedy when the drunks come out of the woodwork. Women traveling alone should be very careful. The Tapachulan tourist office recommends that tourists not cross the border at Ciudad Hidalgo, as the bridge there is long and deserted, making travelers particularly vulnerable to assault.

# Yucatán Peninsula

Hernández de Córdoba mistakenly ran aground here in 1517. When the freshly disembarked sailors asked the locals where they were, the Maya, naturally not understanding Spanish, replied something to the effect of, "We haven't a clue what you're talking about." Unfamiliar with the Mayan language, Córdoba only caught the last few syllables of their reply, "Tectetán," and erroneously dubbed the region Yucatán. This encounter established a paradigm that would hold throughout Yucatán's history; misunderstood and continually molested by outsiders, it would never be fully conquered. Today, the peninsula's culture remains essentially Maya and thrives in the peninsula's small towns, where the only evidence of Western influence arrives in the form of the weekly Coca-Cola truck. Mayan is still the first language of most inhabitants, and *indígena* religions persist (often with a Catholic veneer). Yucatec women still carry bowls of corn flour on their heads and wear embroidered *huipil* dresses, and fishing, farming, and hammock-making out-produce big industry and commerce.

But foreign influence fights on: more workers are drawn by the dubious allure of the tourism industry, flooding the big cities and resorts to work in gringo-friendly restaurants, weave hammocks for tourists, or act as multi-lingual guides at archaeological sites. Burgeoning tourism is threatening the traditional *yucateco* way of life as international nomads discover the peninsula's fine beaches, beautiful colonial towns, and striking Maya ruins. After the Mexican government set an example by engineering the pristine pleasure-world of Cancún from the ground up, developers seized similar areas stretching further and further along the Yucatán coast; much of the virgin Caribbean beach land is currently under massive construction, as Maya ruin sites are plowed over to make room for new, palatial resorts. However, the surging popularity of eco-tourism in the past few years has shown dollar-seekers that some kinds of conservation can be lucrative as well.

The Peninsula's inter-state borders form a "Y" down its center. The Yucatán state sits in the crest of the "Y," Quintana Roo sees the Caribbean sun rise on the eastern coast, and Campeche faces the Gulf Coast to the west. The peninsula's geography consists mostly of flat limestone scrubland or rainforest dotted with *cenotes* (freshwater sinkholes). Because of the highly porous limestone subsoil, there are no above-ground rivers in Yucatán. Poor soil and the lack of water make farming difficult, so maize remains the staple crop. The prominence of the rain god Chac at most Maya ruins testifies to the eternal importance of the seasonal rains, which fall from May to late summer.

"The Yucatán" refers to the peninsula, not the state, whereas "Yucatán" without the article can refer to either entity. **Yucatán** state's rich history draws thousands of visitors each year, who come to scramble up and down the majestic Maya ruins such as the incomparable Chichén Itzá, marvel at old colonial towns, explore the area's many dark caves, and take a dip in the *cenotes*. **Quintana Roo**'s luscious rain jungle, fantastic coastline, and magnificent Maya ruins were idylls beneath the Caribbean sun until the government transformed the area from tropical paradise to tourist factory. Cancún rapidly became the beachhead for what some wryly call "the Second *Conquista*," and the nearby beaches and ruins were soon to follow. Although its countryside is dotted with Maya ruins and its coastline is over 200km long, **Campeche** pulls in fewer visitors than Yucatán to the north or Quintana Roo to the east, perhaps because it lacks a kind of swaggering grandeur—ruins are modest and relatively inaccessible, while the beaches are kept humble by wind and rocks.

# Yucatán Peninsula

MAR CARIBE

N

50 miles

50 kilometers

Isla Holbox

Isla Mujeres

Puerto Morelos

Playa del Carmen

Cozumel

Chiquilá

Cancún

180

Ideal

Xcaret

Akumal

Xel-Ha

Punta Allen

Kantunil Kin

X-Can

Cobá

Tulum

307

Felipe Carrillo Puerto

Sian Ka'an Biosphere Reserve

Punta Bravo

Majahual

San Felipe

Río Lagartos

295

Tizimín

176

Valladolid

Yaxuná

295

Santa Rosa

Chetumal

Dzibilchaltún

YUCATÁN

Grutas de Balankanche

Chichén Itzá

Polyuc

QUINTANA ROO

BELIZE

261

Mérida

Umán

Oxkutzcab

Grutas de Loltún

184

Kohunlich

Progreso

Oxkintok

Ticul

Labná

Hopelchén

Dzibilnocac

186

Becán

Xpujil

Sisal

Uxmal

Kabáh

Sayil

Grutas de Xtacumbilxunaan Xlapak

Hochob

Calokmul Biosphere Reserve

Chicaná

Xpujil

Calokmul Biosphere Reserve

GOLFO DE MÉXICO

Becal

Calkiní

261

Edzná

Escárcega

CAMPECHE

Celestún

Tenabó

180

24

Campeche

San Lorenzo

Seybaplaya

Champotón

186

GUATEMALA

180

Ciudad del Carmen

Villahermosa

TABASCO

# CAMPECHE

## ■ Escárcega

The bus stop—er, town—of Escárcega is a critical transit point at the intersection of Yucatán's Rtes. 261 and 186. The **first-class ADO station** serves gourmet food and Sauvignon Blanc. Just kidding. But it does serve the cities of Campeche (8 per day, 2hr., 37 pesos), Cancún (7 per day, 8hr., 147 pesos), Chetumal (7 per day, 5hr., 63 pesos), Mérida (7 per day, 5hr., 81 pesos), Mexico City (6 per day, 19hr., 307 pesos), Palenque (1pm, 3½hr., 49 pesos), Playa del Carmen (10:30pm, midnight, and 1:30am, 7hr., 132 pesos), Puebla (2am, 17hr., 272 pesos), Veracruz (10:30pm, 11½hr., 182 pesos), and Villahermosa (6 per day, 4hr., 69 pesos), all with a sprig of parsley. One kilometer down Av. Hector Martínez, the **second-class station** runs buses to similar locations and in between; it sells cheaper wine.

As buses leave around the clock for most destinations, it is unlikely you'll be stranded for very long in Escárcega. However, if you're too tired to continue (wuss), head into town on **Av. Héctor Martínez.** A good many blocks (about 1.5km), one railway crossing, and two stoplights later, take a right for Escárcega's small *zócalo.* The modern clock tower tells you you've made it. Escárcega and the long road leading to it are not the safest of places after dark, so take a taxi if it's late. For lodging, visit one of the sisters at **Hotel Las Tres Hermanas** (tel. (981) 4-01-10), right on the *zócalo,* which provides comfortable rooms with fans and cable TV (singles 50 pesos; doubles 60 pesos, with 2 beds 70 pesos; triples 100 pesos). If you think 5 pesos' worth of chiclets will make your hunger subside on the bus, think again. Better head on over to **Cocina Económica La Tabasqueña,** one block west of the post office on the *zócalo* and across the railroad tracks. Breakfast eggs cost 9 pesos and, if the owner likes you, so does everything else.

## ■ Campeche

Once called "Ah Kin Pech"—Mayan for "Place of the Serpents and Ticks"— Campeche is, thankfully, much more hospitable and pleasant that its original name suggests. When Francisco Hernández de Córdoba arrived, he transliterated the name to Campeche and, by 1540, had begun transforming the small city into an important trading port. As it grew, Campeche battled buccaneers and pirates, erecting stunning *baluartes* (bulwarks), fortified churches, and forts which still stand. Modern Campeche seems to have changed little since then; as if to underscore the immutability of the city's spirit, sections of the old stone fortifications still stand, now fragmented and crumbling. Recent efforts to attract tourism have had mild success; the city's cobblestone streets, crayon-colored facades, and rocky beaches may tempt those on their way to Mérida or Cancún to stop for a dose of rustic Old World beauty.

### ORIENTATION

Campeche lies 252km southwest of Mérida and 444km northeast of Villahermosa via Rte. 180. All major routes into the city intersect the peripheral highway that encircles it. A smaller road, **Circuito Baluartes,** circumscribes the old city. All main roads converge on the Circuito in the city center. **Avenida Gobernadores** comes in from the Mérida highway northeast of the city, crosses the peripheral highway, and passes the airport, train station, and bus terminals on its way to the Circuito.

To reach the *zócalo* from the **bus terminals,** catch the "Gobernadores" bus (1 peso) across the street from the station, and ask the driver to let you off at the **Baluarte de San Francisco.** Turn right into the old city and walk four blocks on **Calle 57** to the *zócalo.* Front-door hotel escorts by **taxi** cost only 10 pesos, but, if you'd rather walk (15min.), head left on Gobernadores and bear left when you reach the Circuito.

Three blocks later, turn right on Calle 57 through the stone arch and walk four blocks to the *zócalo*.

The *centro*'s east-west streets have odd numbers that increase to the south. **Calle 8** runs north-south between the *zócalo* and the western city wall. Parallel to Calle 8, to the east, lie Calles 10 to 16. The *zócalo* lies near the sea, bordered by Calles 8, 10, 55, and 57. To the west, outside the city wall, **Av. 16 de Septiembre** and **Av. Ruiz Cortínez** also run parallel to Calle 8. North of the *centro*, Calle 8 becomes **Malecón Miguel Alemán,** running past the Iglesia de San Francisco uphill to Fuerte de San José El Alto. **Av. Resurgimiento,** the main coastal drag south of the city, runs past the youth hostel and the Fuerte San Miguel on its way to San Lorenzo and Seybaplaya.

A confusing network of **buses** links Campeche's more distant sectors to the old city (1-2 pesos; daily 6am-11pm). The market, where Gobernadores becomes the Circuito, serves as the hub for local routes. Buses have no established stops, but it is possible to flag them down at the post office (see below) and at Jardín Botánico at Calle 51. You'll have to get around the city center on foot, since buses only come in as far as the Circuito.

## PRACTICAL INFORMATION

**Tourist Offices:** Calle 55 #3 (tel. 1-39-89), next door to the cathedral at the *zócalo*. Open Mon.-Fri. 8am-10pm.

**Travel Agencies: Prof. Augustín Zavala y Lozano,** Calle 16 #348 (tel. 6-44-26), gives 4hr. tours of Edzná (9am and 2pm, 90 pesos).

**Currency Exchange: Banamex,** at the corner of Calles 53 and 10 (tel. 6-52-51). Open Mon.-Fri. 9am-5pm. 24hr. **ATM.**

**Telephones: TelMex** phones throughout the city.

**Fax:** Tel. 6-43-90; opposite MexPost in the Edificio Federal. Money orders and telegrams too. Open Mon.-Fri. 8am-6pm, Sat. 9am-noon.

**Airport:** On Porfirio (tel. 6-31-09), 13km from the city center. **Aeroméxico** (tel. 6-56-78), at the airport. Taxis to the *centro* cost 25-30 pesos.

**Buses:** From the **second-class station,** Calle Chile just off Av. Gobernadores (tel. 6-28-02), **Camioneros de Campeche** goes to Dzibalchén (6 per day, 2hr., 15 pesos), Escárcega (5 per day, 2½hr., 20 pesos), Holpechén (11 per day, 1½hr., 12 pesos), Iturbide (5 per day, 2hr., 37 pesos), Muna (5 per day, 4½hr., 25 pesos), and Uxmal (5 per day, 4hr., 24 pesos). **Autobuses del Sur,** to Mérida (6 per day, 2½hr., 28 pesos), Palenque (10:30pm, 5½hr., 87 pesos), San Cristóbal (11pm, 12hr., 110 pesos), and Villahermosa (4 per day, 9hr., 76 pesos). The **1st-class station** lies on Av. Gobernadores #289, 4 blocks north of Circuito Baluartes at Baluarte San Pedro. **Autotransportes de Oriente (ADO),** to Cancún (10pm, 6hr., 106 pesos), Chetumal (noon, 7hr., 105 pesos), Escárcega (9:30am, noon, and 8pm, 2½hr., 40 pesos), Mérida (11 per day, 2½hr., 46 pesos), Mexico City (2:30 and 7pm, 16hr., 350 pesos), Palenque (10:45am and 10pm, 5hr., 90 pesos), Puebla (8:30 pm, 16hr., 315 pesos), Valladolid (4hr., 90 pesos), Veracruz (10pm, 12hr., 220 pesos), and Villahermosa (9:30am, 1:05, and 11pm, 7hr., 110 pesos). **Cristóbal Colón,** to Ocosingo (10pm, 8hr., 105 pesos), San Cristóbal (10pm, 10hr., 140 pesos), and Tuxtla Gutiérrez (10pm, 12hr., 150 pesos). **Maya de Oro** offers similar service to San Cristóbal (159 pesos).

**American Express:** Calle 59 between 16 Septiembre and shore (tel. 1-10-00). Open Mon.-Fri. 9am-2pm and 5-8pm, Sat. 9am-1:30pm.

**Taxis:** Tel. 6-23-63. 3 stands: Calle 8 at 55, to left of the cathedral; Calle 55 at Circuito, near the market; and Gobernadores at Chile, near the bus terminal. Intra-city travel 7-10 pesos.

**Car Rental: Hotel Baluartes** at Av. Cortinez, (tel. 1-18-84), a block from *zócalo*.

**Luggage Storage:** 3 pesos per day in the every hr. bus station.

**Market:** On Circuito Baluartes between Calles 53 and 55. Unexceptional handicrafts and cheap food. Open Mon.-Sat. sunrise-sunset, Sun. until 3pm.

**Supermarket: Súper Diez** (tel. 6-79-76), in the Pl. Comercial A-Kin-Pech on 16 de Septiembre, across the street from the post office. Open daily 7am-9:30pm.

**Laundromat: Lavandería y Tintorería Campeche,** Calle 55 #22 between Calles 12 and 14 (tel. 6-51-42). Same-day service 6 pesos per kg. Open Mon.-Sat. 8am-4pm.

**Red Cross:** On Av. Las Palmas (tel. 02 or 04), at the northwest corner of the city wall. Open 24hr.

**Pharmacy: Farmacia Gobernadores,** next to the ADO station. Open 24hr.

**Medical Services: Seguro Social,** on López Mateos (tel. 6-52-02), south of the city. **Hospital General,** Av. Central at Circuito Baluartes (tel. 6-09-20 or 6-42-33).

**Police:** On Calle 12 between Calles 57 and 59 (tel. 6-21-11). Open 24hr.

**Post Office:** 16 de Septiembre at Calle 53 (tel. 6-21-34), in the Edificio Federal. Open Mon.-Fri. 8am-8pm, Sat. 8am-1pm. **Express mail** next door at **MexPost** (tel. 1-17-30). Open Mon.-Fri. 9am-6pm, Sat. 9am-1pm. **Postal Code:** 24000.

**Phone Code:** 981.

## ACCOMMODATIONS

Few budget accommodations have cropped up in Campeche. Several middle-range establishments hover just out of the range of backpackers' pesos, and many of the cheaper places have sunk to unusually low levels of cleanliness and maintenance. The three hotels listed are in the old city, while the youth hostel is farther away, near the coastal highway.

**Hotel Regis,** Calle 12 #148 at Calle 57 (tel. 6-31-75), 1½ blocks from the *zócalo.* Colonial mansion, perfectly modernized and restored; rooms have high ceilings, large beds, and new bathrooms. Singles 90 pesos; doubles 135 pesos; triples 175 pesos; 30 pesos per additional person; 45 pesos for A/C.

**Colonial Hotel,** Calle 14 #122 between Calles 55 and 57 (tel. 6-22-22 or 6-26-30), 2½ blocks from the *zócalo.* Lime-green rooms with tiny windows. Showers barely have room for both you and the water. Singles 70 pesos; doubles 81 pesos; triples 101 pesos; 20 pesos per additional person; 30 pesos for A/C.

**Hospedaje Teresita,** Calle 53 #31 between Calles 12 and 14 (tel. 6-45-34). In a residential part of the old city, 3 blocks northeast of the *zócalo.* The cheapest place in the *centro,* and for good reason. Large, bare, concrete-walled rooms have wobbly fans. Lacks privacy. Communal bathrooms can be malodorous. Rooms 35 pesos. Two rooms have decent private baths (45 pesos).

**Youth Hostel Villa Deportiva Juvenil Campeche,** on Agustín Melgar (tel. 6-18-02), several blocks east of the water and the coastal highway. From the eastern section of the Circuito Baluartes, take the "Lerma" bus south along the coastal highway to the intersection with Melgar, then walk half a block toward the ocean. A black iron gate on the left marks the spot. Single-sex college dorm rooms with 2 bunks and spiffy bathrooms. Table tennis and swimming pool. No hot water. Full July-Aug. and Dec.; call to reserve. Bunk rental 20 pesos plus 20-peso deposit. Breakfast, lunch, and dinner, 12 pesos each.

## FOOD

*Campechanos* will tell you that there are two culinary experiences that visitors should not miss: dinner at San Pancho (see below) and a sampling of *pan de cazón* (stacked tortillas filled with baby shark and refried beans and covered with an onion, tomato, and chile sauce). Other local specialties include *pámpano en escabeche* (pompano broiled in olive oil and flavored with onion, garlic, chile, peppers, and a dash of orange juice). Except for San Pancho, all listings are near the *zócalo.*

**Restaurant Del Parque,** Calle 57 #8 at Calle 8 (tel. 6-02-40). Elegant yet inexpensive spot serving local fare, including *tortas* (8-12 pesos) and *pande cazón* (20 pesos). Open daily 7am-10:30pm.

**Cenaduría Portales** (tel. 1-14-91), better known as **San Pancho** for its proximity to Iglesia de San Francisco. Take any bus headed north on Malecón Miguel Alemán to the church. Cross the plaza east of the church and head left to another smaller square. The restaurant huddles beneath the arches straight ahead. An assembly line of highly trained sandwich makers jumps into action at your order and nearly instantly produces not just a sandwich, but a work of art. Sandwiches 7-10 pesos. Exceptional *horchata* (sweetened rice water, 4 pesos). Open daily 7pm-midnight. This area is not safe after dark—get back on the bus right away.

**Nutrivida,** on Calle 12 between 57 and 59 (tel. 6-12-21). Deli-cafe serves meatless burgers (7-13 pesos), delectable homemade yogurt, flaky bread, and fresh juice in a pleasant courtyard. Open Mon.-Fri. 8am-2:30pm and 5:30-9pm, Sat. 8am-2pm.

**Restaurant La Parroquia,** Calle 55 #9, between Calles 10 and 12 (tel. 6-80-86). Your standard Denny's-type all-night eatery. Cheap food, locals, and TV around the clock. Seafood starts at 20 pesos. Open daily 24hr.

## SIGHTS AND SAND

Campeche's pleasant corners and monuments are best seen at night, when spotlights warm up cold stone and the moonlight spills over the ocean. The most convenient way to see Campeche is by "Tranvia," the comfortable trolley that gives a historical tour of the major sights. Catch it at the *zócalo* in front of Los 3 Hermanos shoe store (Mon.-Fri. 9:30am, 6, and 8pm; Sat.-Sun. 9:30am, 6, 7, and 8pm; 1hr.; 7 pesos).

The **Fuerte de San Miguel** houses well-documented exhibits describing nearby ruins, and displays Maya jewelry, pottery, and several magnificent jade masks. On the top level, cannons still point out protectively over the sea and Campeche to the north. To reach the fort, take the "Lerma" bus from the eastern end of the Circuito Baluartes, and head south until the bus turns onto the coastal highway near the "Maxi" *tienda*. The road leading up to the fort is about a block ahead on the left (open Tues.-Sun. 8am-8pm; admission 4 pesos, free Sun.).

San Miguel's counterpart to the north, the **Fuerte de San José El Alto,** is a few kilometers from the *centro*. The "Bellavista" or "San José El Alto" bus from the market will drop you halfway up the hill; a five-minute walk will get you to the fort at the top. If you decide to walk, head north on Gobernadores, turn left on Cuauhtémoc, left on Calle 101, and right on Calle 7. Built in 1792, San José was amazingly defensible when in use. The path leading to the portcullis winds deliberately so that battering rams could not be used on the gate. The fort's moat, which encircles the building, was supposedly rife with vicious spikes; the water was obscured with chalk so as to hide them from anyone thinking about jumping in. The view from San José is spectacular; kilometers of green shoreline give way to the urban waterfront (open Tues.-Sun. 8am-8pm; admission 4 pesos, free Sun.).

In the **Baluarte de la Soledad,** across from the *zócalo,* off Calle 8 near Calle 57, the **Museo de Estelas Maya** houses a small collection of well-preserved Maya stelae and reliefs taken from sites in Campeche state, including a phallus the size of a torpedo. Informative texts in Spanish and pictographs elaborate on sculpted figures' occupations. Visitors may also climb the walls of the fort, which is surrounded by a park. A showroom across from the museum occasionally features free exhibitions (museum open Tues.-Sat. 8am-8pm, Sun. 8am-1pm; admission 3 pesos).

In the **Fuerte Santiago** at the northern corner of the city, the **Jardín Botánico Xmuch'haltún,** Calles 8 and 51 (tel. 6-68-29), makes an inviting stop. Over 250 species of plants thrive in a tiny open-air courtyard shaded by trees and marked by walkways, benches, and fountains—amble through the garden, soothe your mind, and refresh your soul (open Mon.-Fri. 8am-1pm and 4-8:30pm, Sat. 8am-1pm and 4-8pm, Sun. 9am-1pm; guided tours Mon.-Fri. 9am-3pm).

Campeche's **cathedral** looms above the *zócalo*. Don Francisco de Montejo first ordered the construction of the cathedral in 1540, but builders did not complete the massive structure until 1705. The cathedral's main attraction is its facade. Inside, you'll find the *Santo Entierro* (Holy Burial), a sculpture of Christ in a carved mahogany sarcophagus with silver trim. (Open daily 7am-noon and 5-8pm; free.)

A little farther from the center of town, the **Iglesia de San Francisco,** Av. Gustavo Díaz, built in 1518, claims to be the oldest church on the American mainland. Inside, yellow Corinthian arches project toward an ornate altar (open daily 8am-noon and 5-8pm). A few blocks south of the *centro,* the **Iglesia de San Román** houses El Cristo

Negro, greatly venerated by *campechanos* and supposedly one of only three black Christs in Mexico (open daily 6am-noon and 4-8pm; free).

Locals head south for **sand** and **sunbathing. San Lorenzo** is ideal for swimming, though the beach is pebbly. The closest half-decent stretch of sand is at **Playa Payucán.** The beach is great for snorkeling, but rentals are not available. Buses for **Seybaplaya,** 2km from the beach, leave from behind the market (4 pesos).

## ENTERTAINMENT AND SEASONAL EVENTS

Campeche sponsors various free outdoor musical events, including the **Ballet Folklórico** in the *zócalo*. Every Tuesday, Friday, and Saturday night at 8pm, an impressive **light and sound show** at Puerta de Tierra, Calles 59 and 18, recounts in Spanish the dramatic story of residents repelling pirates. The performers' awful acting is as entertaining as the historical account. Weather permitting, a Ballet Folklórico follows the conclusion of the show (light and sound show 10 pesos, 50% discount with student ID; translated text in 3 other languages is projected onto the wall). The wildly popular **Noche de Trova,** including music and performances by the Ballet Folklórico, is celebrated in the *zócalo* on Wednesdays and Thursdays at 8pm, but usually only during the high months of July, August, and December. For a complete schedule of events, ask for the *programa de actividades* at the tourist information center. San Román is Campeche's patron, and two weeks of both religious and secular festivities, starting September 15, celebrate his feast.

**Atlantis** (tel. 6-22-33), at the Ramada Inn on Av. Ruiz Cortínez, lords over Campeche's nightlife (cover 65 pesos for men, 35 pesos for women; Thurs. is singles night and free; open Thurs.-Sat. 10pm-3am). **La Cueva de Las Ranas,** near the university on López Mateos, attracts aspiring rock stars and a hip student crowd (open 9pm-3am). **Disco Dragon,** on Av. Resurgimiento 87 (tel. 6-42-89 or 1-18-10), is recommended by the tourist office as the local boogie. Ask them for more info.

## ■ Near Campeche

### EDZNÁ

If you're already in Campeche, visit the nearby ruins of **Edzná** (House of the Grimaces), where hieroglyphics date back to AD 652. Despite its lack of elaborately sculpted detail, the **Edificio de Cinco Pisos** (Building of the Five Floors), which towers over the surrounding valley atop the **Gran Acrópolis,** is supremely elegant. Sixty-five stairs, some adorned with hieroglyphics over 1300 years old, lead up to tiers of columns crowned by a magnificent five-room temple. During its Maya heyday, the perch atop the monument afforded a view of the network of irrigation canals criss-crossing the valley close to the Río Champotón, 20km to the west. The canals were built without the use of wheels, metal tools, or domesticated animals. Nearby, among the many thistle bushes, are the remains of a ballcourt and several other temples of a central plaza which are presently being excavated. Also on display are some of the 19 stelae found at Edzná, one crafted as early as AD 672, others made during the 10th-century evacuation of the ceremonial center.

Mosquitoes at Edzná can be so vicious that you may want to ask Luís at the tourist office what the current state of affairs is before you leave several pints of valuable blood in the jungle. A canteen of water and plenty of repellent are a must (site open daily 8am-5pm; admission 15 pesos, half-price with student ID, free Sun.).

**Getting There:** One bus makes three daily round-trips from the market in Campeche to Alfredo Bonfil (starting at 7am, 1½hr., 6 pesos), dropping you off at the Edzná access road. From there, a sign points the way and gives a distance 1500m too long. To avoid being stranded, be sure to ask the driver when he will return.

## DZIBILNOCAC AND HOCHOB

If you want to experience the ruins in solitude, head to Dzibilnocac or Hochob, way, *way* off the beaten path, about 400km from Ticul. Only Indiana Jones wannabes should visit the sites, as the effort it takes to reach them may exceed the effort it took to build them. **Dzibilnocac** consists of a set of three excavated temples in various states of decay: a mound of dirt, a mound of rocks, and a temple whose simple reliefs, masks, and rounded corners barely show themselves; the highlight is the third temple, a tall, narrow building with rounded corners and a stucco facade—climb to the top for a closer view of a gruesome mask of the rain god Chac. Simple reliefs at the middle levels resemble cave paintings. If you want to explore neighboring farms and cornfields, make sure you wear long pants and thick boots since the area is rife with poisonous snakes. **Hochob's** three short and squatty temples cluster around a central plaza that swells modestly from the flat rainforest. Deep-relief geometric patterns molded in stucco cover the well-preserved temple to the right of the entrance, the front of which once formed an enormous mask of Chac (the door representing his gaping mouth). Climb to the top for a view of the site and the rainforest (both sites open daily 8am-5pm; free).

**Getting There:** Dzibilnocac lies 61km off Rte. 261, near the small town of **Iturbide.** To reach it by car, exit Rte. 261 at Hopelchén and drive south; you'll see a sign at a fork pointing the way (straight on, *not* to the right) to Iturbide. When you reach the village, bear right at the end of the *zócalo,* and continue out of town (during the rainy season, the road can be treacherous; strongly consider walking). Fifty meters into the forest, the right branch of the fork in the road ends at the ruins. If you don't have a car, get to Iturbide through a **Camioneros de Campeche** bus from Campeche (5 per day, 3hr., 15 pesos) or from Hopelchén (12 per day, 1½hr., 9 pesos).

To reach Hochob, follow the signs from Dzibalchén (a tiny town between Iturbide and Hoplchén). The ruins are impossible to reach without a car, and even with wheels you may wonder if the trip was worth it.

## GRUTAS DE XTACUMBILXUNAAN

Twenty-seven kilometers from the Yucatán-Campeche border lie the **Grutas de Xtacumbilxunaan** (shta-kum-bill-shu-NAN, "Caves of the Sleeping Girl"). A custodian leads a tour past seven deep *cenotes* (natural wells) and points out barely discernible shapes on the cavern's walls and ceilings. These caves are poorly lit, a far cry from the high-roofed galleries of Loltún or the clean-cut passageways of Balankanché, but you can still have fun poking around (open daily 9am-6pm; tours in Spanish only; free, but guide expects a tip). Hard-core cave lovers who bring their own rock climbing equipment can take a two-day trip underground with the guides to visit the seven connected *cenotes* 150m below ground. Bring camping gear.

**Getting There:** The *grutas* lie 1km down the road that crosses Rte. 261 2km south of Bolonchén. Second-class buses drop passengers at the access road.

# YUCATÁN

## ■ La Ruta Puuc (The Maya Route)

**La Ruta Puuc** (a.k.a. La Ruta Maya) is a long stretch between Campeche and Mérida that traverses the Puuc Hills. This area was home to about 22,000 people during the Classic period of Maya civilization (4th to 10th centuries). Decimated by diseases introduced by the Spanish, the Maya slowly surrendered most of their cities and ceremonial centers to the jungle. Beginning in the 18th century, the Maya population began a slow recovery. While today's Puuc Maya live in towns with paved roads and plumbing, women continue to wear traditional embroidered *huipiles,* and Mayan remains the dominant language.

The Ruta Puuc refers specifically to the 254km on Rte. 261 between Campeche and Mérida and the Sayil-Oxkutzkub road which branches off just meters after the Campeche-Yucatán border. Taking this turnoff, **Sayil** is the first archaeological site to materialize (after 5km), followed by **Xlapak** (10km), **Labná** (13km), **Loltún** (25km), **Oxkutzkab** (45km), and **Ticul** (62km). Alternatively, if the turnoff is not taken, the road winds through **Kabah** (right after the border) and the stunning site of **Uxmal** (23km); 16km from Uxmal lies the junction at **Muna.**

The easiest way to see the ruins is by **renting a car** in Mérida (p. 509). The drive along the Ruta Puuc is also one of the most liberating and enjoyable on-the-road experiences, as small Maya villages and green jungle line the winding road.

Another option is an **organized tour.** These can be arranged through private companies in either Mérida or Campeche (ask in the tourist office). Public transportation is more difficult. Second-class **buses** traverse Rte. 261 frequently, and will stop when requested, but none travel the Sayil-Oxkutzkub road with the exception of the **Autotransportes del Sur "Ruta Puuc" bus** that leaves Mérida at 8am and visits Kabah, Sayil, Labná, and Uxmal, returning to Mérida at about 2:30pm. If you don't mind a whirlwind tour through the sites, this bus is an incredible bargain (40 pesos; admission to sites not included). But be on the bus promptly when it leaves each site; drivers have been known to leave stranded tourists at smaller sites. *Combis* are abundant in the morning and make frequent trips between Oxkutzkab, Ticul, **Santa Elena,** and Muna (it is easiest to get a *combi* to Uxmal from Muna), and they will make any trip if paid enough. Unfortunately, with both *combis* and buses, return trips are not always guaranteed. If you can only make it to one or two sights, don't miss Uxmal, and try to see Sayil—they have the best ruins of all.

The sites along the Ruta Puuc can best be explored using **Ticul** as a base; the town offers cheap accommodations and restaurants. Two to three days should be ample time for exhaustive exploration. Most sites sell *refrescos,* but the only one with accommodations (at ridiculously high prices) is Uxmal. Thank Chac for Ticul.

## TICUL

A bustling provincial town off the Campeche-Mérida highway, **Ticul** (pop. 40,000) is known for its cheap, durable shoes and its status as a convenient and inexpensive base from which to explore the Ruta Puuc sites of Uxmal, Kabah, Sayil, Xlapak, and Labná, as well as the Grutas de Loltún. Staying in Ticul is a relief from Mérida—the town's busy residents simply don't have time to heckle tourists. For those with wheels, a number of *cenotes* and colonial buildings await exploration in the nearby towns of **Teabo,** 30km southeast of Ticul, **Mayapán,** 45km to the northeast, and **Holcá,** 105km to the northeast. Maní, 15km east of Ticul, features a colonial monastery; **Tekax,** 35km to the southeast, a hermitage; and **Tipikal,** an impressive colonial church.

**Orientation and Practical Information** Ticul's streets form a grid with the main drag, Calle 23, passing east-west through the center. Even-numbered streets run north-south. Most commercial activity transpires between the *zócalo* (at Calle 24) and Calle 30, four blocks to the west.

**Banco del Atlántico,** Calle 23 #195, off the *zócalo,* changes U.S. dollars and traveler's checks (open Mon.-Fri. 9am-2pm). Nada LADA here—Ticul's version of a TelMex will charge you 30 pesos per minute (ouch!) for any international calls at the long-distance *caseta,* Calle 23 #210 between Calles 26 and 28 (tel. 2-00-00; open 8:30am-10pm). The **telegram office,** Calle 21 #192-C (tel. 2-01-46), is in the blue and white building behind the post office (open Mon.-Fri. 9am-3pm).

**Combis** leave from Parque de la Madre, Calle 23 between Calles 28 and 30, for Muna (7 per day, 5 pesos); from Calle 30 between Calles 25 and 25A, for Santa Elena, Uxmal, and Kabah (4 pesos); and from Calle 25 between Calles 26 and 28, for Oxkutzkub (every 15min., 5 pesos). From Muna, 5 **buses** run daily to Campeche (20 pesos) via Uxmal and Kabah, from the **Terminal** at the *zócalo.* Hourly buses head north to Mérida (7 pesos). The town's pedal-powered **taxis** transport passengers for a couple of pesos.

# Yucatán State

YUCATÁN PENINSULA

**N**

Airport
Archaeological Site

GOLFO DE MÉXICO

Mar Caribe

Isla Holbox

Isla Mujeres

Isla Cozumel

Laguna de Yalahau

Parque Nacional Río Lagartos

Parque Nacional San Felipe

Bahía de la Ascención

Puerto Carrillo Puerto Sian Ka'an Biospheric Preserve

Punta Allen

Cancún
Puerto Morelos
Cozumel
Akumal
Xel-Ha
Tulum
Playa del Carmen
Chiquilá
Kantunilkin
Colonia Yucatán
X-Can
Kucicán
Cobá
Valladolid
Tizimín
Panabá
Espita
Río Lagartos
San Felipe
Cenotillo
Tekom
Tepich
Felipe Carrillo Puerto
Ichmul
Santa Rosa
Peto
Polyuc
Grutas de Balankanchén
Yaxuná
Chichén Itzá
Parque del Estado de Quintana Roo

QUINTANA ROO
YUCATÁN
CAMPECHE

Dzilam de Bravo
Motul
Puerto Telchac
Dzibilchaltún
Mérida
Umán
Grutas de Loltún
Ticul
Grutas de Calcehtok
Muna
Oxkintok
Uxmal
Labná
Xlapak
Sayil
Kabah
Becal
Calkiní
Grutas de Xtacumbilxunaan
Hopelchén
Progreso
Chelem
Sisal
Hunúcma
Maxcanú
Tenabó
Edzná
Celestún
Campeche

50 miles
50 kilometers
0

180
307
295
184
293
281
80
261
176

**Farmacia San Jose,** Calle 23 #214J (tel. 2-03-93), is between Calles 28 and 30 (open 8am-1pm and 4-10pm; no English spoken). **Dr. Estela Sanabria** can be reached at the same number for 24-hour **medical assistance. Police** headquarters are on Calle 23 (tel. 2-00-10 or 2-02-10) at the northeast corner of the *zócalo* (open 24hr.). Ticul's **post office** (tel. 2-00-40) is in the Palacio Municipal on the *zócalo* (open Mon.-Fri. 8am-2:30pm). **Postal Code:** 97860. **Phone Code:** 997.

**Accommodations and Food** Ticul has several hotels and good restaurants. **Hotel San Miguel,** on Calle 28 (tel. 2-63-82), opposite Parque de la Madre, offers small, battleship-gray rooms with saggy beds and fans (singles 25 pesos; doubles 32 pesos, with 2 beds 38 pesos). **Hotel Sierra Sosa** on Calle 24 (tel. 2-00-08; fax 2-02-82), on the northwest corner of the *zócalo,* has modern rooms with firm beds, strong fans, and TVs. Rooms with windows come with street noise. Coffee and *agua purificada* come free. Rooms with A/C drown out the noise and heat (singles 60 pesos; doubles 70 pesos; triples 80 pesos; add 20 pesos for A/C).

Dining in Ticul can be tricky; only one restaurant stays open past 6pm. Luckily, **Los Almendros,** Calle 23 #207 between Calles 28 and 30 (tel. 2-00-21), is known worldwide for their *poc-chuc;* the chain of restaurants started here in little ol' Ticul. They also make a mean *pollo pibil* (chicken with herbs baked in banana leaves, 24 pesos; open daily 9am-9pm). **Restaurant Los Delfines** (tel. 2-04-01), Calle 27 between Calles 28 and 30, serves shrimp dishes, *chiles rellenos* (35 pesos), and jars of lemonade under a big airy *palapa* (open daily 11am-7pm). Ticul's **market** is just off Calle 23 between Calles 28 and 30 (open daily sunrise-sunset).

**Getting to the Ruins** The Ruta Puuc is a well-marked, *tope*-ridden road that can be driven without purchasing a road map. Simply follow signs to Uman from Merida, then head towards Muna. From there on, just follow "Ruta Puuc" in Ticul.

Without a car, you'll be faced with relay races. Public transportation in Ticul is not geared toward ruin-happy tourists. While Uxmal and Kabah are fairly accessible if you have luck with *combi* transfers, the lack of traffic on the Sayil-Oxkutzcab road will leave the carless traveler frustrated and stranded. In general, you should reconcile yourself to changing buses. To reach the ruins around Uxmal, take a Mérida-bound bus from the Ticul bus station on Calle 24 (tel. 2-01-62), behind the main church, and get off at Muna (every ½hr., 3 pesos). *Combis* for Muna leave from Parque de la Madre, Calle 23 between Calles 28 and 30. From Muna, board a southbound bus or *combi* for Uxmal, Kabah, or other sites from the *zócalo* (7 per day; 3 pesos). You can also reach the ruins by catching a *combi* on Calle 30 between Calles 25 and 25A, to Santa Elena (½hr., about 3 pesos). Change *combis* at Santa Elena for Uxmal, 16km from Mérida, or Kabah, south of Campeche. *Combis* are most plentiful in the morning. Considering the amount of time it will take to make connections as opposed to how long each sight really takes, you might want to reconsider the rush tour bus from Mérida (see p. 509).

To reach the Grutas de Loltún, snag a *combi* to Oxkutzcab at Parque de la Madre; you'll be let off at the intersection of Calles 23 and 26 (15min., about 3 pesos). *Combis* leave for Loltún from the lot across from Oxkutzcab's market, "20 de Noviembre." Tell the driver to let you off at the *grutas* (10min., about 3 pesos), as everyone else is probably headed for the agricultural cooperative 3km farther down the road. Because the road is more crowded with *combis,* it's easier to reach the Grutas than Uxmal or Kabah. Hitchhikers rarely find rides on any of these roads.

## UXMAL

Get here. Whatever it takes. Not many do, and that's part of the charm, not to mention the excellently restored pyramids, reliefs, and immense masks. Meaning "thrice built or occupied," it's not hard to see why **Uxmal,** once a capital with 25,000 inhabitants, kept drawing people.

**Orientation and Practical Information** Autotransportes del Sur (ATS) sends six buses per day from Mérida to Uxmal (1½hr., 11 pesos), as well as a "Ruta Puuc" bus which visits Uxmal, Kabah, Sayil, Xlapak, and Labná all in one day for just 40 pesos (see p. 509). From Campeche you'll have to take the **Camioneros de Campeche** bus to Mérida (5 per day, 3hr., 25 pesos). Ask the driver to stop at the access road to the *ruinas*. To return, grab a passing bus at the *crucero* just outside the entrance to the ruins. The last buses to Mérida and Campeche pass at 8pm and 7pm, respectively. A modern **tourist center** with a small museum, restaurant, gift shop, photographic supply shop, and bathrooms greets you at the entrance to the ruins. The **Kit Bolon Tun auditorium,** also in the tourist center, screens documentaries on the Ruta Puuc and gives 15-minute presentations of the Yucatán, Chichén Itzá, and Uxmal (6 shows per day in Spanish and 4 in English; free).

**Accommodations and Food** Even the bravest of ruins crumble under the huge prices of Uxmal's lodging and food. Consider staying 30 minutes away in Ticul, where hotel rooms cost half as much. In Uxmal, the cheapest option is **Rancho Uxmal** (tel. 2-02-77), 4km north of the ruins on Rte. 261. From the highway near Uxmal, you can reach Rancho Uxmal by hopping aboard a passing bus or *combi* (about 2 pesos). Thinly carpeted rooms have inviting bedspreads, hand-painted murals, and standard bathrooms. The pool is usually in service during peak season (singles 120 pesos; doubles 160 pesos; triples 180 pesos). The Ranch's restaurant serves up a complete menu for 35 pesos, and offers Maya folk dancers at 2pm Thursday and Friday (open daily 7am-10pm).

YUCATÁN PENINSULA

---

### Singing in the Rain

Uxmal's entire nightlife consists of a light-and-sound show celebrating Maya history and culture. The Spanish version (25 pesos) begins at 8pm and ends after the last of the Campeche-bound buses passes. Although it requires language fluency, it is usually more fun than the English version (one hour later, 35 pesos). While the lights and the sound remain identical (except for the fact that the text is translated), the crowd in the Spanish show is a spectacle in itself. Don't be shy to join in the clapping and chanting "¡Chaaaac!, ¡Chaaaac!" Guidebooks are available at the bookstore. Bring a raincoat—the chanting might actually work.

---

**Sights** According to the **Chilam Balam** (see p. 65), a Maya historical account written in phonetic Spanish, Ah Suytok Xiu and his warriors from the Valley of Mexico invaded Yucatán at the end of the 10th century. Xiu and his successors dominated Uxmal until the city's strength was sapped by civil warfare in the 12th century. Because their priests foretold the coming of white, bearded men, the Xiu did not resist when Spanish conquistadors attacked Uxmal. The last Xiu ruler of the city was Ah Suytok Tutul Xiu, whose descendants still live in the Puuc region. Tutul Xiu was baptized as an old man; his godfather was Francisco de Montejo, conqueror of the Yucatán.

The 40m-tall near-pyramid visible upon entering Uxmal is the **Temple of the Magician.** Built at a 60° angle, the narrow steep stairs make for a wicked climb. The pyramid, the legend goes, was built by a dwarf-magician who hatched from a witch's egg and grew to maturity in the space of a single year. The legend of the dwarf-magician's birth struck terror into the heart of the governing lord of Uxmal, who, it was prophesied, would be replaced by a man "not born of woman." He challenged the dwarf to a contest of building skills. The dwarf's pyramid, built overnight, easily outclassed the governor's Great Pyramid, still visible to the right of the Governor's Palace. Grasping at straws, the spiteful ruler complained that the base of the dwarf's pyramid was neither square nor rectangular but was actually elliptical. Having undermined the legitimacy of the dwarf-magician's triumph, the governor proposed that he and his adversary compete to see who could break a *cocoyol* (a small, hard-shelled fruit) on their heads. The dwarf-magician, in whose skull a turtle shell had been placed, easily cracked open the *cocoyol.* The governor crushed his unaltered skull trying to match the dwarf fruit for fruit.

The elegant south-facing arch leads to the **ballcourt.** Note the glyphs on the rings through which well-padded players tried to knock a hardened rubber ball. Emerging from the ballcourt, head right along a narrow path to the **Cemetery Group,** a small, leafy plaza bounded by a small pyramid to the north and a temple to the west. Stones that once formed platforms bear haunting reliefs of skulls and crossbones. Returning to the ballcourt, head south to the well-restored **Great Pyramid,** built by the governor in his contest with the dwarf-magician. The architecture and crude latticework reveal the influences of northern Campeche. To the west, the pyramid looks down on the jagged face of the Palomar, behind which lie the jungle-shrouded remains of the **Chenes Temple.**

The **House of Turtles** and the **Palace of the Governor** top a man-made escarpment east of the Great Pyramid. The two-story House is on the northwest corner of the escarpment and is adorned along its upper frieze with a series of sculpted turtles (turtles symbolized rain and were venerated by the Maya). The eastern frieze is covered by 20,000 decorations, which together form 103 masks of Chac.

From the Palace of the Governor, try to spot the overgrown, pyramidal **House of the Old Woman,** which lies to the east and can be reached by following the path directly to your left as you emerge from the entrance. About 400m south of the house is the **Temple of the Phalli.** Phallic sculptures hang from the cornices of this ruined building and spurt rain runoff from the roof. Experienced guides are available to give more detailed tours of the site (about 30 pesos per person as part of a group).

## KABAH

Once the second largest city in the northern Yucatán, **Kabah** was built with the blood and sweat of many slaves, whose effort has mostly succumbed to the ravages of time. The most elaborate of Kabah's structures is the **Codz Pop Temple** (rolled mat in Mayan), immediately to the right of the entrance, which was named for the odd shape of the rain god Chac's nose. The temple's broad facade displays nearly 300 masks of Chac, each comprised of 30 carved pieces. The elaborate Chenes style of the temple is unique to the Codz Pop—its neighbors to the east, **El Palacio** (a 25m pyramid) and **Las Columnas,** were executed in plainer fashion. The site is thought to have served as a court where justices settled disputes and the gods were the jury. Across the street by the parking lot, the short dirt road leads to rubble (right), more rubble (left), and the famous Kabah Arch (straight ahead). The arch marks the beginning of the ancient *sacbé* (paved, elevated road) which culminated in a twin arch at Uxmal. The perfect alignment of the archway with the north-south line is testimony to Maya astronomical understanding (site open daily 8am-5pm; admission 10 pesos, free Sun. and holidays).

**Getting There:** Bisected by Rte. 261, Kabah lies 23km southeast of its Ruta Puuc cousin, Uxmal. Because of its location on the Campeche-Mérida highway (*vía ruinas*), it can easily be reached by any second-class bus running between Mérida and Campeche (see p. 509 and p. 495). Buses will stop at Kabah only if a passenger notifies the driver beforehand or if the driver sees a person wildly gesticulating on the shoulder of the highway. Things are easier with the **ATS "Ruta Puuc" bus** (see p. 509). Since almost all the tourists who come to Kabah have cars, many try to hitch.

## SAYIL

The **Palace of Sayil** is an architectural standout among the region's ruins. While most of its buildings are now nothing more than glorified ant hills, Sayil's Palace is breathtaking. Between its three terraced levels, the building's 50 rooms exhibit unparalleled ornamental diversity. Walls are carved with rows of slender columns, the second-story frieze depicts the descending serpent-god's body, and elegant second-floor chambers open onto pleasant porticos, each graced by bulging columns. Climb to the top for a gorgeous panoramic view of the rolling, verdant Puuc hills. Behind the palace sits a *chultún* (plastered catch basin) that the Maya used to collect rainwater for use during the dry season.

The path continues past the palace to **El Mirador** (the lookout), a lofty temple with once-grandiose columns. Left of El Mirador, the path leads deeper into the jungle, where the extremely graphic **Estela del Falo** (Stela of the Phallus) will make even the most sexually liberated of visitors blush profusely. A few other temples are barely visible through the dense jungle undergrowth (site open daily 8am-5pm; admission 10 pesos, free Sun. and holidays).

**Getting There:** Sayil lies 9km past Kabah off Rte. 261 on the Sayil-Oxkutzcab road and 5km past Xlapak. The only public transportation to the site is the **Autotransportes del Sur "Ruta Puuc" bus** (see p. 509). Buses do run, however, from Mérida to Kabah, 10km away on the main highway. Some travelers hitch from Kabah to Sayil.

## LABNÁ

Labná's buildings were constructed towards the end of the late-Classic period (AD 600-900), when the Puuc cities were connected by a *sacbé* (white road). Today, a short reconstructed section of the *sacbé* runs between Labná's two most impressive sights: the palace and the stone arch. When the Yucatán flooded, the raised **sacbé** allowed the Maya to pass from one city to another. However, more common than floods were droughts. To deal with parched conditions, the Maya constructed huge *chultunes* (catch basins), many of which are found at Labná. The *chultunes* collected both water (up to 8000 gallons in each) and the bodies of peasants who couldn't afford to be buried. Many of Labná's buildings are too far gone to climb, giving rest to the tired and weak-kneed tourist.

Labná's **palace** is on the northern side of the site, to the left as you enter. While the construction of this building occupied the Maya for several centuries, the edifice was never actually completed. Labná's palace is reminiscent of the one at Sayil insofar as both boast exceptionally ornate second-floor facades. Nearby mosaics depict figures in palm huts, reminding present-day visitors that the stone palaces once housed only the privileged few. Now, they house scores of chipper birds.

Labná is famed for its picturesque **stone arch,** 3m wide and 6m high. Its western facade is intricately decorated in a trellis pattern, while the eastern side remains more bland. Previously thought to have been the entrance to another temple, archaeologists now believe that the arch served as a ceremonial point of entry for victorious warriors returning from the battlefield.

Beyond the arch, on the unrestored base of a pyramid, stands the **observatory,** also known as **El Mirador** (the lookout). Its notable facade rises over the box-like structure and bears sculptures attached by tenons and dowels. The terracing around the temple contained many *chultunes*. The top of the observatory affords a view of the entire site; keep your eyes peeled for falcons' nests (site open daily 8am-5pm; admission 10 pesos, free Sun.).

**Getting There:** The final destination on the "Ruta Puuc" bus, Labná lies 42km east of Uxmal, 4km beyond Xlapak, and 22km before Las Grutas (see below). Almost no *combis* come and go on this branch of the Ruta Puuc; hitching is reportedly tough.

## GRUTAS DE LOLTÚN

The Grutas de Loltún are 58km east of Uxmal on the Sayil-Oxkutzcab road. Below a dense jungle of mahogany and *ceiba*, kilometers of enormous caverns wind through the rock. Guides can be enticed to give longer tours (the caves go on forever) with the promise of a nice, fat tip. The ancient Maya first settled this area in order to take advantage of the Grutas' water and clay. Hundreds of years later, Maya *campesinos* returned to the caves seeking refuge from the Caste War (1847-1848). Important caverns include the **Room of the 37 Inscriptions,** which includes many still-visible markings (i.e., handprints), and the **Na Cab** (House of the Bees), where you can see the *ka'ob* (grindstones) left by the Maya. Ancient inhabitants broke off the stalactite tips in the **Gallery of Fallen Rocks** to use as spears and arrows. In the **Gallery of the Five**

**Chultunes,** a sculpted jaguar head drips water into cisterns while a huge warrior and eagle look on. The **Cathedral** is a palatial room that once hosted Maya feasts and assemblies. The shadowy silhouette above the entrance is popularly believed to represent the Virgin of Guadalupe. Several caves contain partially hollow stalactites and columns—thump one with the heel of your hand and listen to the soft booming sound *("Loltún...Loltún...")* reverberate throughout the cave system. Archaeologists speculate that the Maya used these formations as a musical means of underground communication.

Entrance to Loltún is only allowed when a guide leads a tour through the caves (9:30, 11am, 12:30, 2, 3, and 4pm). Guides will lead English tours, but Spanish ones tend to be more comprehensive. Bear in mind the exorbitant rates charged by aboveground guides when leaving a tip for the free guide service (admission 22 pesos, Sun. 7 pesos). As you exit the caves (0.5km from the entrance), you'll stumble upon the conveniently located **Restaurant El Huinoc de Loltún,** which serves up a good range of local dishes for about 25-40 pesos. Be prepared to wait—service is slow as molasses and the restaurant can be packed with tour buses.

**Getting There:** To get to Loltún, catch a bus as far as Muna or Ticul, hop in a *combi* headed for Oxkutzcab, then follow signs to *Centro.* Passing the market on your left, walk two blocks, turn right at the sign for Ruta Puuc, then pray for deliverance—Las Grutas are 7km down the road. A pick-up truck in Oxkutzcab's *zócalo* may be willing to make the trip, though it will cost you at least 20 pesos.

## GRUTAS DE CACHETOK

Located 30km west of Muna right off the Ruta Puuc, the Grutas de Cachetok are rarely visited by international tourists and remain an undiscovered gem. With sheer rock climbs aided by rope, holes barely big enough to squeeze through, and mud slicking every surface, these caves are for those living on the edge. The caves offer black paintings, rock silhouettes of Buddha, Christ, the Virgin Mary, and Maya Jaguar, and ancient Maya bones and grindstones litter dark corners. Entrance to the caves is always open, as there are no locks and no fences. But be warned; last year a couple ventured in alone and remained lost for 3 days in the pitch black caves when their lantern failed. Tricky footing, dangerous drops, and an unobvious path require "Roger" and his son, the only two men who know the caves well enough to lead tours. Roger can be found at the house off the main drag leading to the ruins with "Guya de grutas" scribbled on the facade, or you can call him at home (tel. 28-21-87; 2hr. tours, 10am-6pm; 20-30 pesos).

**Getting There:** Use a car; follow signs to Maxcanú from Muna. The caves are right before the town on the same turnoff to the ruins of Oxkintok.

# ■ Mérida

Built atop the ruins of the Maya capital of T'hó, modern Mérida is haunted by its pre-Hispanic history—the stones of the city's fortress-like cathedral even bear traces of the Maya temples from which they were stripped. The Maya called this site "place of the fifth point," to indicate that it was the center of the universe, the spot between the four points of north, south, east, and west. Today, elegant Mérida (pop. 1.5 million) is at least the center of Yucatán—it's the state's capital and key commercial center. Panama hats, made from the leaves of the *jipijapa* plant and the *guano* palm, come from Becal in the neighboring state of Campeche, hammocks arrive from nearby Tixcocób, and *henequén* is trucked to Mérida from all over Yucatán before being exported as hemp.

Of late, Mérida has become a magnet for immigrants from around the world. *Meri-deños* of recent Lebanese and Syrian descent have made their presence felt in the city, and a small French community is responsible for the Paseo Montejo, Mérida's version of the Champs-Elysées. Mérida is also a big destination for jet-setting tourists who arrive by the plane-load and spend days shopping and nights whispering sweet

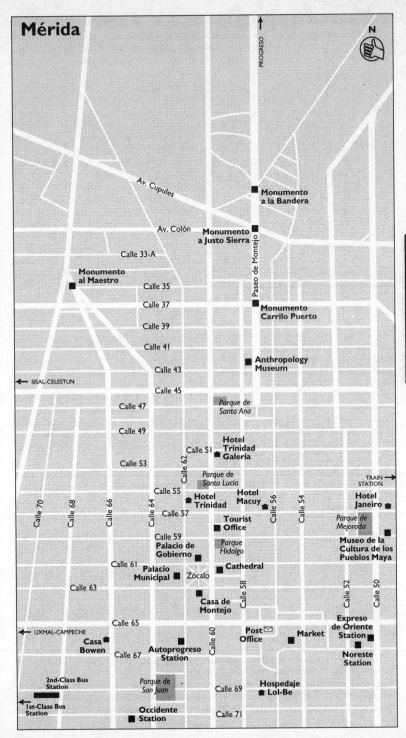

# Mérida

N

Av. Cupules

PROGRESO

Monumento
a la Bandera

Av. Colón

Monumento
a Justo Sierra

Paseo de Montejo

Calle 33-A

Monumento
al Maestro

Calle 35

Calle 37

Monumento
Carrilo Puerto

Calle 39

Calle 41

Calle 43

Anthropology
Museum

← SISAL-CELESTUN

Calle 45

Calle 47

Parque de
Santa Ana

Calle 49

Hotel
Trinidad
Galería

Calle 51

Calle 53

Calle 62

Parque de
Santa Lucía

TRAIN →
STATION

Calle 55

Calle 70

Calle 68

Calle 66

Calle 64

Hotel
Trinidad

Hotel
Macuy

Calle 56

Calle 54

Hotel
Janeiro

Calle 57

Tourist
Office

Parque de
Mejorada

Calle 59

Palacio de
Gobierno

Parque
Hidalgo

Museo de la
Cultura de los
Pueblos Maya

Calle 61

Palacio
Municipal

Zócalo

Cathedral

Calle 63

Calle 58

Casa de
Montejo

Calle 52

Calle 50

Expreso
de Oriente
Station

← UXMAL-CAMPECHE

Calle 65

Casa
Bowen

Calle 60

Post
Office

Market

Noreste
Station

Calle 67

Autoprogreso
Station

2nd-Class Bus
Station

Parque de
San Juan

Calle 69

Hospedaje
Lol-Be

← 1st-Class Bus
Station

Occidente
Station

Calle 71

nothings in music-filled parks. Although it is the largest city on the Yucatán Peninsula, Mérida has yet to succumb to big-city indifference. Street cleaners struggle to maintain its reputation as "The White City," intimate conversations swirl about the *zócalo*, and every Sunday promenading families come out to enjoy *Mérida en domingo*.

## ORIENTATION

Rte. 180 runs from Cancún (322km) and Valladolid (168km) to the east, becoming **Calle 65,** which passes through the busiest part of town, one block south of the *zócalo*. Those approaching on Rte. 180 from Campeche, 153km to the southwest, end up on **Avenida Itzáes** (also called **Avenida de la Paz**), which runs north-south, or on **Calle 81,** which feeds into the north-south **Calle 70.** Both intersect **Calle 59,** the best route to the center of town, which runs east to a point one block north of the *zócalo*. **Paseo Montejo** begins at **Calle 47,** running north as **Rte. 261.** The *zócalo* fills one city block, bordered by Calle 61 to the north, Calle 62 to the west, Calle 63 to the south, and Calle 60 to the east. To reach the *zócalo* from the **second-class bus terminal,** head east to Calle 62, walk three blocks, and turn left (north); the *zócalo* is three blocks ahead. Alternatively, take a taxi (10 pesos). From the **train station,** take a taxi (10 pesos), catch the "Seguro Social" bus, or walk six blocks west on Calle 55 and three blocks south on Calle 60.

Mérida's gridded one-way streets have numbers instead of names. Even-numbered streets run north-south, with numbers increasing to the west; odd-numbered streets run east-west, increasing to the south. Addresses in Mérida are given using an "x" to separate the main street from the cross streets and "y" ("and" in Spanish) to separate the two cross streets if the address falls in the middle of the block. Thus "54 #509 x 61 y 63" reads "Calle 54 #509, between Calles 61 and 63."

Mérida's **municipal buses** *(camiones)* meander along idiosyncratic routes. Precise information is available at the tourist information office, but the city is small enough so that a bus headed in the right direction will usually drop you off within a few blocks of your desired location. Locals and tourists tend to catch buses at their boarding points, usually in the center, a few blocks south from the *zócalo* at Calle 65 and 56. City buses run daily from 5am-11pm (1.50 pesos). **Taxis** do not roam the streets soliciting riders; it is necessary to phone or to go to one of the *sitios* (stands) along Paseo de Montejo, at the airport, and at the *zócalo*. Expect to pay at least 10-15 pesos for a trip within the *centro*. **Taxi-colectivos,** on the other hand, charge only 1.25 pesos for any destination in the city; **dropoffs** are on a first-come, first-serve basis.

## PRACTICAL INFORMATION

**Tourist Information: Central Office,** Calles 60 x 57 y 59 (tel. 24-92-90), in the Teatro Peón Contreras. Distributes *Yucatán Today,* a free monthly guide listing practical info and local events. Additional offices at the airport (tel. 46-13-00) and at the 2nd-class bus station, opposite the ADO info window. All open daily 8am-8pm.

**Telephones: LADATELs** are around the *zócalo*. Phone cards sold at a stand in the Palacio del Gobierno on the *zócalo*. Otherwise, you'll be left at the *casetas'* mercy.

**Fax:** Tel. 28-23-69; fax 24-26-19. In the same building as the main post office. Entrance around the corner on Calle 56A. Telegrams too. Open Mon.-Fri. 8am-7pm.

**Travel Agencies: Yucatán Trails,** Calle 62 #482 x 57 y 59 (tel. 28-25-82 or 28-59-13; toll-free in Mexico 91-800-2-02-85; fax 24-19-28). Canadian owner Denis Lafoy is a genial source of info on Mérida and the Yucatán. Arranges cheap Sat. daytrips to Ruta Puuc sites (280 pesos). Open Mon.-Fri. 8am-2pm and 4-7pm, Sat. 8am-1pm.

**Consulates: U.K.,** Calle 58 #498 x 53 (tel. 28-61-52; fax 28-39-62). Open Mon.-Fri. 9am-1pm. **U.S.,** Paseo de Montejo 453 at Av. Colón (tel. 25-50-11). Unless you have an emergency, try to go on Thurs. or Fri. Open Mon.-Fri. 7am-1pm.

**Currency Exchange: Banamex** (tel. 24-10-11 or 24-11-32), in Casa de Montejo on the *zócalo*. 24hr. **ATM.** Open Mon.-Fri. 9am-5pm.

**American Express,** Paseo de Montejo 494 #106 x 43 y 45 (tel. 42-82-00 or 42-82-10; fax 24-42-57). English spoken. Open Mon.-Fri. 9am-2pm and 4-6pm, Sat. 9am-1pm. Money exchange desk closes 1hr. early.

**Airport:** 7km southwest on Rte. 180. Bus #79, labeled "Airport," runs between the terminals and a midtown stop at the corner of Calles 67 and 60 (every 20min., 5am-9pm, ½hr., 80 pesos); a taxi charges 30 pesos for the trip. Post office, telegrams, long-distance telephone, and car rental are at the airport. **Aeroméxico,** Paseo Montejo 460 x 35 y 37 (tel. 27-90-00, at airport 46-13-05). **Mexicana,** Calle 58 #500 (tel. 24-66-33, at airport 46-13-32). **Aerocaribe,** Paseo Montejo 500B x 47 (tel. 23-00-02, at airport 46-13-61). **Aviateca** (tel. 24-43-54, at airport 46-12-96) Calles 58 x 45 y 43. Also at Calle 58 x 49 y 51.

**Buses:** Most bus lines operate out of the main **second-class** terminal, **Unión de Camioneros,** Calle 69 #544 x 68 y 70, 3 blocks west and 3 blocks south of the *zócalo.* **Autotransportes de Oriente (ADO)** (tel. 23-22-87) sends buses to Cancún (every hr., 4am-midnight, 6hr., 53 pesos), Chichén Itzá (every hr., 5am-midnight, 2hr., 20 pesos), Chiquilá (12:30am, 6hr., 52 pesos), Playa del Carmen (5 per day, 7hr., 64 pesos), Tizimín (5pm, 3½hr., 35 pesos), and Valladolid (every hr., 4am-midnight, 3hr., 24 pesos). **Autotransportes del Sur (ATS)** goes to Campeche (6 per day, 3hr., 28 pesos), Escárcega (10 per day, 5½hr., 42 pesos), Palenque (6 and 11:30pm, 14hr., 116 pesos), and Uxmal (6 per day, 1½hr., 11 pesos). **ATS** provides a special **Ruta Puuc** bus (8am, 40 pesos, admission to sites not included) which visits the archaeological sites of Uxmal, Kabah, Sayil, Xlapak, and Labná, returning around 2:30pm. **Línea Dorada** serves Chetumal (4 per day, 6hr., 93 pesos) and Ticul (every hr., 17 pesos). **Premier** goes to Tulum (6am, 6hr., 66 pesos), Cobá (6 per day, 3hr., 56 pesos), Playa del Carmen (8 per day, 5hr., 77 pesos), Chichén Itzá (8:45 and 9:30am, 2hr., 24 pesos), and Valladolid (5 per day, 2½hr., 35 pesos). Some buses leave from the **1st-class terminal,** called **CAME,** located around the corner on Calle 70 between Calles 69 and 71. **Autobuses de Occidente** runs to almost anywhere on the peninsula and Córdoba (4 per day, 17hr., 310 pesos), Mexico City (5 per day, 19hr., 350 pesos), Palenque (8am and 10pm, 8hr., 130 pesos), Puebla (5:45pm, 20hr., 352 pesos), Veracruz (9pm, 15hr., 262 pesos), and Villahermosa (9 per day, 9hr., 150 pesos). **Expreso** to Cancún (15 per day, 4hr., 63 pesos). The 9:15pm **Maya de Oro** or **Cristóbal** bus can take you to Campeche (2½hr., 42 pesos), Palenque (6½hr., 112 pesos), Ocosingo (8½hr., 140 pesos), San Cristóbal de las Casas (12½hr., 160 pesos), and Tuxtla Gutiérrez (16hr., 185 pesos).

**Trains:** Ferrocarriles Nacionales de México, on Calles 55 x 46 y 48 (tel. 23-59-44 or 23-59-66), northeast of the *zócalo.* Cheap and very, very slow. Buy tickets an hour before departure or on board. Or better yet, take the bus.

**Taxis:** Found at **Palacio Municipal,** on the northwest corner of the *zócalo* (tel. 23-13-17), **Mercado Municipal** at Calles 56 and 65 (tel. 23-11-35), in **Parque de la Maternidad** (tel. 28-53-22) at Teatro Peón Contreras, and dozens of other *sitios.* All are on call 24hr. It's much cheaper to use the *camiones* (municipal buses).

**Car Rentals: México Rent-a-Car,** Calle 57A Dept. 12 x 58 y 60 or Calle 62 #483A x 57 y 59 (tel. 27-49-16). VW Beetles, including insurance and unlimited *kilometraje,* for 200 pesos per day. Open Mon.-Sat. 8am-12:30pm and 6-8pm, Sun. 8am-12:30pm. V, MC, AmEx.

**Bookstore: Dante,** Calles 60 x 57 (tel. 24-95-22), in Teatro Peón Contreras. Guidebooks, maps, and magazines in English, French, and Spanish. Open Mon.-Fri. 8am-9:30pm, Sat. 8am-2pm and 5-9pm, Sun. 10am-2pm and 5-8pm.

**Laundromat: La Fe,** Calle 61 #518 x 62 y 64 (tel. 24-45-31), near the *zócalo.* 20 pesos per 3kg. Open Mon.-Fri. 8am-7pm, Sat. 8am-4pm.

**Market:** Four square blocks of covered stalls and street vendors extend south of Calle 65 and east of Calle 58. Open dawn to dusk. **Supermarket: San Francisco de Asís,** Calles 65 x 50 y 52, across from the market in a huge gray building. Open daily 7am-9pm.

**Red Cross:** Calle 68 #533 x 65 y 67 (tel. 24-98-13 or 28-53-91). 24hr. emergency and ambulance services (tel. 24-67-64). Some English spoken.

**Pharmacy: Farmacia Canto,** Calle 60 #513 x 63 y 65 (tel. 28-50-27). Open 24hr.

**Hospital: Centro Médico de las Américas,** Calle 54 #365, at Calle 33A (tel. 26-21-11 or 26-26-19). 24hr. service, including ambulances. **Clínica de Mérida,** Calle 32 #242 x 27 y 25 (tel. 25-41-00). English spoken in both.

**YUCATÁN PENINSULA**

**Police:** on Av. Reforma (Calle 72) x 39 y 41 (tel. 25-25-55 or 25-73-98), accessible with the "Reforma" bus. Some English spoken.

**Internet Access: PCS Suministros,** Calles 60 #483 x 55 y 57 (tel. 23-98-72), offers Netscape and Eudora for those trying to escape high phone bills. 30 pesos per hr. Open Mon.-Fri. 8:30am-8:30pm, Sat. 9am-2pm.

**Post Office:** on Calles 65 x 56 y 56A (tel. 24-35-90), 3 blocks from the *zócalo* in the Palacio Federal. Open Mon.-Fri. 7am-7pm, Sat. 9am-noon. Branches at Calles 58 x 49 y 51, at the airport, and at the main bus station. **MexPost** at Calles 58 x 53 y 55. **Postal Code:** 97000.

**Phone Code:** 99.

## ACCOMMODATIONS

Many of Mérida's budget accommodations are set in splendid colonial mansions. Though they may have lost the bustling servants and a coat or two of fresh paint, they nonetheless retain much of their original splendor. It is not every day that a few pesos will garner a room with tall ceilings, sun-bleached frescoes, and stained glass.

**Casa Bowen,** Calle 66 #521B x 65 y 67 (tel. 24-07-28 or 28-61-09), halfway between the main bus station and the *zócalo*. Pillared lobby with cable TV, LADATEL, dining room, and books of all languages leads up a grand staircase to questionably alluring rooms, each with fans, hot water, and private bath. Make 1-week reservations in Aug. and Dec. Singles 65 pesos; doubles 85 pesos. Rooms with kitchenette and fridge 100 pesos, with A/C 130 pesos; extra person 25 pesos.

**Hotel Montejo,** Calle 57 #507 x 62 y 64 (tel. 28-02-77 or 28-03-90), 2 blocks north and 1 block east of the *zócalo*. Beautiful, bold colonial mansion with rooms to match. Tall, wood-beamed ceilings. Bathrooms are in excellent condition. Singles 85 pesos; doubles 95 pesos; triples 150 pesos. Add 30 pesos for A/C and 25 pesos for an extra person.

**Hotel Macuy,** Calle 57 #481 x 56 y 58 (tel. 28-51-93; fax 23-78-01). 2 blocks north and 2 blocks east of the *zócalo*. Wake up to the chatting parrot or to tourists tinkering on piano. Sky-blue rooms are complemented by an excellent staff and a good selection of books. Laundromat next door. Singles 80 pesos; doubles 90 pesos; triples 100 pesos.

**Hotel Trinidad Galería,** Calle 60 #456 x 51 (tel. 23-24-63; fax 24-23-19). Huge colonial mansion with odd-angled rooms converted into both a modern-art gallery and hotel. Ask to see a room first, as each comes in a different size and shape (and price). The pool is a godsend. Singles 70-100 pesos; doubles 100-120; add 30 pesos for larger, multi-roomed quarters. Parking available. Similar rooms are available at the sister Hotel, Hotel Trinidad, calle 62 #464 x 55 y 57 (tel. 23-20-33).

**Hotel Latino,** Calle 66 #505 x 63 (tel. 28-58-27 or 23-50-87) is as cheap as it gets, and it shows. Singles 40 pesos; doubles 50 pesos; 10 pesos less per night for weekly stays, 20 pesos less per night for monthly stays.

**Hotel Janeiro,** Calle 57 #435 x 48 y 50 (tel. 23-36-02 or 23-83-73), a hike from the bus station. Though not "dah-ling", it is modern and practical. Peaceful, shallow pool and sun deck. Collection of English paperbacks. Parking available. Singles and doubles with fans 100 pesos; add 20 pesos for A/C; add 30 pesos per extra person.

## FOOD

Mérida's inventive specialties make good use of the fruits and grains that flourish in Yucatán's hot, humid climate. Try *sopa de lima* (frothy lime soup with chicken and tortilla bits), *pollo pibil* (chicken with herbs baked in banana leaves), *poc-chuc* (pork steak with onions doused in sour orange juice), *papadzules* (chopped hard-boiled eggs wrapped in corn tortillas served with pumpkin sauce), and the dish that raises eyebrows, *huevos motuleños* (refried beans, fried egg, chopped ham, and cheese on a tortilla garnished with tomato sauce, peas, and fried banana). Those who've been burned one too many times by over-seasoned chiles can rest assured—in Mérida, the local scorcher, *chile habanero,* does not lurk within dishes but instead waits patiently in a garnish bowl. The cheapest food in town awaits at the **market,** particularly on the second floor of the restaurant complex on Calle 56 at Calle 67. *Yucateco* dishes go for 5-10 pesos (open Mon.-Sat. 8am-8pm, Sun. 8am-5pm).

**Restaurante Amaro,** Calle 59 #507 x 60 y 62 (tel. 28-24-51). Finally, a respite from greasy dishes and stale tortillas. Excellent meals are healthy and delicious, offering lean meat and vegetarian options. Shady courtyard makes this a veritable oasis. Refreshing *horchata* (rice milk and almond shake) 9 pesos. Avocado and cheese sandwich 16 pesos. Huge, invigorating fruit salads 16-20 pesos. Meat entrees 25-30 pesos. Open Mon.-Sat. 9am-11pm.

**Los Almendros and Los Gran Almendros,** Calle 50 #493 x 57 y 59 on Parquet Mejorada (tel. 28-54-59), and at Calle 57 #468 x 50 y 52 (tel. 23-81-35). World-famous restaurant known for its *poc-chuc* (42 pesos). Music and picture menu add to this festive, if touristy place. *Pollo pibil* just 21 pesos. Los Almendros open daily 10am-11pm. Less touristy Gran Almendros open daily noon-6pm. V, MC, AmEx.

**El Rincón,** Calle 60 x 59 y 61 (tel. 24-90-22), situated right in Parque Hidalgo, is the restaurant for Hotel Caribe. Serves fantastic *sopa de lima* (13 pesos). Or try *arroz con plátanos* (9 pesos) or *pollo pibil* (30 pesos). Open daily 7am-11pm.

**Restaurante y Cafe Express,** Calle 60 x 59 y 61 (tel. 28-16-91), across the street from Parque Hidalgo. The best thing about this touristy, modern eatery is their huge, cheap breakfasts (14-18 pesos) and their beer (Bohemia at last!) for 8 pesos. Open daily 7am-11pm.

**El Louvre,** Calle 62 #499-D, on the northwest corner of the *zócalo*. A small diner popular with locals and tourists alike, due to an unbeatable location, great sandwiches (10-15 pesos), and the world's finest collection of art. Steer clear of bland main dishes. Open 24hr.

**El Tucho,** Calle 60 #482 x 55 y 57 (tel. 24-22-89). A loud and popular restaurant, El Tucho's mostly-male crowd is due to the mostly-female Las Vegas-style afternoon cabaret. While performers entertain you, troupes of waiters ferry trays of free *botanas* (hors d'œuvres) between customers. As long as you keep on drinkin', the food keeps on comin'. Real meals 25 pesos. Open daily 11:30am-9:30pm.

## SIGHTS

From cathedral towers outlined against a startlingly blue sky to couples getting up close and personal in the *confidenciales,* there is always something to see in Mérida's *zócalo.* The *zócalo* is busiest on Sundays, when street vendors cram in dozens of stalls, Yucatec folk dancers perform in front of the Palacio Municipal, and half the city comes out to people-watch.

The twin towers of the yellow **cathedral** loom over the eastern side of the *zócalo.* The fortress-like presence of the cathedral's Corinthian doors and stark, windowless facade recall the centuries of struggle between the Maya and missionaries. The sturdy stone blocks from which the cathedral was built were stolen from the Maya temples of T'hó. Built in the austere Herrericano style, the cathedral features rose-colored arched domes and a giant blistering Christ, the second-largest crucifix in the world (supposedly open daily 6am-6pm).

On the northern edge of the *zócalo* stands the **Palacio de Gobierno.** Built between 1883 and 1892, it fuses two architectural styles—Tuscan (main floor) and Dorian (upper floor). Inside, wonderful, gigantic murals narrate the strife-filled history of the Yucatán peninsula. The stairway painting illustrates the Maya belief that humanity comes from maize; an image of the *Popol Vuh,* the central document of Maya culture (see p. 51), dominates the next layout (open daily 8am-10pm).

Concerts and classes in *jarana,* the Yucatecan colonial dance, take place under the sheltering balcony of the **Palacio Municipal,** across the *zócalo* from the cathedral. A jail until the 1700s, the building was rebuilt in the colonial style in 1928 (open Mon.-Sat. 8am-8pm).

On the southern side of the *zócalo,* the **Casa de Montejo,** the oldest colonial structure in Mérida, was constructed in 1549 by order of city founder Francisco de Montejo. Built with stones from the Maya temple T'hó, the carved facade is a boastful depiction of Spanish conquest. The carving follows the Toltec tradition of representing warriors standing on their conquests' heads (open Mon.-Fri. 9am-5pm).

Mérida's most impressive museum, the **Museo de Antropología e Historia** (tel. 23-05-57), is housed in a magnificent Italian Renaissance-style building on the corner of Paseo Montejo and Calle 43. A long walk in the scorching Mérida sun yields a great facade but a surprisingly small collection inside. Most notable are the ancient Maya versions of plastic surgery (head-flattening devices for infants) and braces (enamel inserts of jade and silver). The shop downstairs sells comprehensive English-language guidebooks cheaper than they're sold at the ruins themselves (museum and shop open Tues.-Sat. 8am-8pm, Sun. 8am-2pm; admission 14 pesos, free Sun.).

Celebrating the indigenous crafts and artisans of Mexico, **Museo de la Cultura de los Pueblos Maya** is located six blocks east of the *zócalo* on Calle 59 x 48 y 50, behind the Convento de la Mejorada. Another long walk in the sun yields a sparse, somewhat hokey display of traditional costumes and masks (open Tues.-Sat. 8am-8pm, Sun. 9am-2pm; free).

On the corner of Calle 59 and Av. Itzáes (Calle 86) lies the **Centenary Park and Zoo.** Snag a bus at Calle 65 x 56 (2 pesos) and ask to be let off at the Centenario. The zoo is at the end of the park and is home to lions, tigers, preening peacocks, flamingos, antelope, Aztec dogs, and jaguars. A miniature train full of shrieking schoolchildren whizzes through periodically, but fails to rouse the catatonic creatures. (Park open Tues.-Sun. 6am-6pm; zoo open Tues.-Sun. 8am-5pm; both free.)

The **Museo de Historia Natural,** with its main entrance on Calle 59 x 84, one block east of Itzáes, also has a back entrance accessible from the park. Housed in a 19th-century hacienda, this small but ambitious collection is concerned with the history of life from the origin of the universe through the emergence of species (open Tues.-Sun. 9am-4pm; admission 10 pesos, free Sun.).

Decaying French-style mansions and local and international boutiques line the **Paseo Montejo;** promenades along the Paseo's broad pink sidewalks culminate in the **Monumento a la Patria.** In faux-Maya style, the stone monument, built in 1956, depicts major figures of Mexican history. For a tantalizing detour from the Paseo, veer left (southwest) onto **Avenida Colón,** a street flanked by closely grouped historic mansions in varying stages of decay.

Mérida takes special pride in the **Teatro Peón Contreras,** on the corner of Calles 60 and 57. The Italian Renaissance-style building is notable for its Rococo interior and its history—starting in 1624, it served as a university for nearly two centuries. The **Universidad Autónoma de Yucatán,** on Calle 57 x 60 y 62, is a Hispano-Moorish complex built in 1938. The ground floor contains a gallery exhibiting works by local artists and a screening room for films (*galería* and *videosala* open Mon.-Fri. 9am-1pm and 4-8pm, Sat. 4-9pm, Sun. 10am-2pm; free).

The many churches, statues, and pocket-sized parks scattered throughout Mérida's *centro* also invite exploration. Among the most noteworthy are the Franciscan **Convento de la Mejorada,** on Calle 59 x 48 y 50; the old **Arco** behind the park; the **Iglesia Santiago,** on Calles 59 x 72, one of the oldest churches in Mexico; and the **Iglesia de San Juan de Dios,** located on Calle 64 x 67 y 71, marking the *centro*'s southern limit.

## SHOPPING

All those pesos you saved by cramming two into a hammock at night, riding slow, dirty second-class buses, and eating *tortas* and *comidas corridas* will now come in handy. Nowhere else in the Yucatán is the shopping like it is in Mérida. The main **mercado** occupies the block southwest of the Palacio Federal, spreading outward from the corner of Calles 65 and 58. Behind the *palacio,* shops, awnings, and tin-roofed shacks ramble for a good many blocks both east and west. The only border is busy Calle 65 to the north, but even there, stands spill over onto the other side of the street and around the small square across from the Palacio Federal.

The second-floor **artisans' market,** part of a modern building behind and to the right of the Palacio Federal, sells mainly regional clothing: white *huipiles* with colorful embroidery skirting the neckline and hem go for 60-75 pesos, *rebozos* (woven shawls) cost around 150 pesos, and *guayaberas* (Yucatec men's short-sleeve shirts with distinctive vertical columns of double stitching) are between 60 and 80 pesos. Bargaining is expected, but those who get carried away are considered rude. Cheaper goods such as *huaraches* (hand-made leather sandals) are sold on the first floor of the market. Be sure to give them a try or two for good measure, as the sandals are sometimes hastily made. Although jewelry stores line the streets, the best prices are at the smaller *prestas* on the streets, in the market, or at the *zócalo* every Sunday.

## ENTERTAINMENT

Mérida's municipal government provides a never-ending series of free music and dance events organized by day. **Mondays** bring outdoor concerts with traditional Yucatec dancing and dress (9pm at Palacio Municipal). **Tuesdays** offer either a 1940s big-band concert (9pm at Santiago Park, Calles 59 x 72) or the University's wonderful **Ballet Folklórico** (9pm at Teatro Peón Contreras, Calles 60 x 57; 25 pesos). **Wednesdays** take you through a musical journey from the 18th century to the present (8pm at Ermita Park, Calles 66 x 77). **Thursdays** host **"The Serenade,"** the most traditional event in Mérida, with music, poetry, and folklore (9pm at Calles 60 x 55). **Sundays** bring **Mérida en Domingo,** when the *zócalo* and surrounding streets are crowded with vendors, strollers, food stalls, and live music (9am-8pm). Movie buffs can flock to **Cinema Fantasio,** at Parque Hidalgo, or **Plaza International,** on Calle 58 x 57 y 59, both offering American movies with Spanish subtitles for only 14 pesos (nighttime showings around 7 and 9:30pm only).

When in Mérida, do as *merideños* do—keep your eyes peeled for announcements of upcoming events glued to walls all over town. The **Teatro Peón Contreras** (tel. 23-73-54) hosts special events and frequent concerts. Just around the corner on the Parque de la Modernidad, an excellent acoustic guitar trio plays mellow tunes at the **Café Peón Contreras** (every night, 8pm-midnight). Avoid the cafe's pricey food— enjoy the music for free from one of the park benches. **Parque Hidalgo** has free **marimba concerts** each night; locals and tourists alike grab a margarita and some *botanas* (hors d'œuvres) at one of the many outdoor cafes and enjoy the (finally) cool breeze.

For a less high-brow evening, settle in for a **beer.** Mérida has many good local beers, such as the heavenly **Montejo León,** hard to find in other parts of the country. At local establishments, buy a few and you'll get free *botanas.* Enjoy comedians and live marimba music at **Pancho's,** Calle 59 x 60 y 62 (tel. 23-09-42), or **El Tucho** (p. 511). Another option is **Tulipanes,** Calle 42 #462A x 45 y 47; get ready for non-stop music, *yucateco* dance, and a chilling re-enactment of a Maya sacrifice (50 pesos). Air-conditioned, panchromatic discos are far from the center; a taxi ride will cost you 30-40 pesos. **Kalia,** Calle 22 #282 by Calle 37 (tel. 44-42-35), is where the young and sophisticated dance (open Wed.-Sat. 10pm-3am).

# ■ Near Mérida

## DZIBILCHALTÚN

Saying the name is half the fun. Situated 20km north of Mérida en route to the Gulf coast, Dzibilchaltún (dzib-ill-shahl-TOON, Place Where There Is Writing on Flat Stones) sprawls over 60 square kilometers of jungle brush. The site flourished as a ceremonial and administrative center from approximately 2000 BC until the Conquest. While its influence on Maya culture is of great interest to archaeologists and historians, the excavated site now open to tourists is neither as impressive nor as accessible as the other ruins near Mérida.

The site's **museum,** at the end of the covered walkway, to the left of the entrance just beyond the cactus garden, merits a quick visit, both for its blessed air-conditioning and for its attractive and informative displays. The first main room is for Maya history and artifacts (Chac! Chac!), and the second describes their Spanish conquest. Note the glass floor simulation of the ocean. Groovy.

From the museum, follow the path to **Sacbé No. 1** and turn left. Farther along this road, Dzibilchaltún's showpiece, the fully restored **Temple of the Seven Dolls**, possesses a rare harmony of proportion and style. The seven clay "dolls" discovered here are believed to represent illnesses or deformities and are now in the museum (they are the small, mangled figures that looked like some toddler really went at them). The temple also furnishes further proof of the genius of the Maya. Shortly after sunrise, a huge shadow mask of the rain god Chac is said to appear as the sun's rays pierce the temple (too bad the site opens at 8am). The temple is so carefully aligned that it can be used to verify the winter and summer solstices. At 5:30pm each summer solstice, the sun threads the tiny space between the doorjambs on the north side; at 7:30am each winter solstice, the phenomenon is repeated on the south side.

The other end of Sacbé No. 1 leads to a quadrangle, in the center of which stands a symbol of 400 years of history: a Maya temple converted into a chapel. Just beyond the eastern edge of the quadrangle is the **Cenote Xlacah,** reminiscent of Quintana Roo's oval, saltwater *lagunas.* Xlacah served as a sacrificial well similar to those at Chichén Itzá and as a source of water. Divers have recovered ceremonial artifacts and human bones from the depths of the 44m-deep *cenote.* While the *cenote* is not up to the Valladolid standard, the water invites a non-sacrificial dip among the water lilies and fish. A path to the south leads past a handful of smaller structures to the site's exit (site open daily 8am-5pm; museum open daily 8am-4pm; admission 22 pesos, free Sun. and for children under 13; wheelchair-accessible; parking 3 pesos).

**Getting There:** Getting to the ruins is cake—it's the return trip that might pose problems. Conkal-bound *combis* leave the Parque de San Juan in Mérida as soon as they fill up (about every 20min., 3 pesos). The *combi* will drop you off at the access road to the ruins, a five-minute walk from the entrance. To get back, you'll need to walk back to the Conkal road and pray (like any good Catholic in Mexico) for a *combi* to take you to Rte. 261. Some travelers hitch the 5km to the highway. **Autoprogreso buses** and Mérida-bound *combis* abound on Rte. 261, passing by in both directions every 15 minutes.

## CELESTÚN

The small, *tranquilo* beach town of Celestún is perfect for a daytrip (or two) from Mérida. The waves are soothing and the breeze refreshing, but the main draw is the **Río Celestún Biosphere Reserve,** home to 230 species of birds. Pelicans, cormorants, and the occasional stork all await the ooohs and aaahs of tourists, but the knock-kneed, splendidly pink **flamingos** hog center-stage. Mexican tourists and biologists flock here in July and August; call your hotel ahead to make sure there's room.

155 kilometers from Mérida, Rte. 281 runs into **Calle 11** in Celestún, on the western shore of the Yucatán. Calle 11 then passes the *zócalo,* **Calle 12** one block later, and hits the **shore** one block after that (as do all odd-numbered streets). Odd numbers increase to the south, while even numbers decrease moving away from the sand and run parallel to the waves. The *zócalo* is bounded by Calles 11, 13, 10, and 8.

Long-distance **phone** calls can be made from **Hotel Gutiérrez,** but be prepared for staggering rates. There is no LADATEL phone in all of Celestún. **Autobuses de Occidente** sends **buses** from a small booth at the corner of calles 8 and 11, at the *zócalo,* to Mérida (20 per day, 5am-8:30pm, ½-2hr., 1st class 20 pesos, second-class 11 pesos). **Farmacia Don San Luis,** Calle 10 #108 between Calles 13 and 15 (tel. 6-20-02), is open daily 8am-11pm. The **health center** is on Calle 5 between Calles 8 and 10 (tel. 6-20-46; open daily 8am-8pm). The **police** (tel. 6-20-15) stand guard at the Calle 13 side of the *zócalo.* The **post office** is on Calle 11 at the *zócalo,* and shares a building with the **telegram** service (both open Mon.-Fri. 9am-2pm). **Phone code:** 991.

Accommodations in Celestún are rare but serviceable, and the beach views can't be beaten. All are on Calle 12. **Hotel San Julio,** Calle 12 #93A (tel. 6-20-62), offers plain rooms with plainer bathrooms (singles 60 pesos; doubles 80 pesos; triples 90 pesos). **Hotel María del Carmen,** Calle 12 #11 (tel. 6-20-51), has rooms with sea views, balconies, billowing curtains, and immaculate bathrooms (singles 120 pesos; doubles 150 pesos; triples 180 pesos; 10% discount for students). **Hotel Gutiérrez,**

Calle 12 #127 between Calles 13 and 15 (tel. 6-20-41 or 6-20-42), has unimaginative blue rooms and matching bathrooms. Not all rooms have a view (130 pesos; cram in as many people as you like). Restaurants line Calle 12, both on and off the beach, and a few *loncherías* cluster in the *zócalo*. At **Restaurant La Playita,** Calle 12 #99 between Calles 9 and 11 (tel. 6-20-52), pack away a huge steaming plate of *jaiba frita* (fried blue crab) with rice and tortillas for just 20 pesos (open daily; schedule changes with the season). The lack of a beach view doesn't take away from the savory, cheap seafood at **Pelicano's,** Calle 12 #90 between Calles 9 and 11. Fifteen pesos will get you fried fish, and for 40 pesos, a heaping plate of crab claws will appear. At **Restaurant Celestún,** Calle 12 #101 (tel. 6-20-32), you can dine amid larger- (and pinker-) than-life painted flamingos. Fantastic fish *al mojo de ajo* (with garlic butter) 35 pesos (open daily 10am-8pm, sometimes until 11pm).

While the **flamingos** rest in large numbers at Río Lagartos (see p. 527), you can nevertheless spot some clusters along the breathtaking coastline by taking one of two tours offered. The first heads north to **Isla de Pájaros** (Island of Birds), playground for a plethora of winged pals. A stop along the way at a freshwater spring provides welcome relief. The second tour heads south through petrified forests and a tunnel with a watery floor and tree top roof before winding through the abandoned fishing village of **Real de Salinas.** Both tours can be arranged with *lancheros* at the bridge right before the entrance to the town (300 pesos for 1½-2hr.). Depending on the tide, this will accommodate five to eight people. If you want to combine both tours or explore other areas, fishermen can often be coaxed into acting as guides (400 pesos for 3½-4hr.). Hang out on the beach by the *lanchas* to find a ride, and a group to go with, as most guides won't leave without at least five people.

# ■ Progreso

Strategically located on the closest strip of coastline to Mérida, Progreso at first appears a small, typical, noisy fishing village with sand streets, unforgiving sun, weathered, wilting inhabitants, and one-story shacks. But as the Yucatán's premier commercial fishing port, Progreso has made a small fortune hauling in shrimp, red snapper, octopus, and tuna and exporting *henequén* (hemp). Old mansions outside the center attest to these profits. During the summer months, Progreso's proximity to the capital makes it a popular retreat with *merideños,* many of whom make the 33km jaunt northward to enjoy the clean, quiet beaches of the Gulf coast. At other times, the town is remarkably tranquil and tourist-free.

**Orientation and Practical Information** Calle 19, Progreso's **Malecón** (coastal avenue), runs east-west along the beach. Odd-numbered roads run parallel to Malecón, increasing to the south. North-south streets have even numbers and increase to the west. Progreso's *zócalo* is bounded by Calles 78, 80, 31, and 33. To reach the *zócalo* from the **bus station** (on Calle 29 between Calles 80 and 82; tel. 5-30-24), head east on Calle 29 to the end of the block, turn right, and walk two blocks on Calle 80. To reach the beach, follow Calle 80 in the opposite direction.

The often-bored but helpful staff of the **tourist office,** Calle 80 #176 between Calles 37 and 39 (tel. 5-01-04), can provide you with a tourist booklet, including a map (open Mon.-Fri. 9am-2pm and 4-7pm, Sat. 9am-noon; some English spoken). **Banamex,** Calle 80 #125 between Calles 27 and 29 (tel. 5-08-31), is open Mon.-Fri. 9am-2pm. **Long-distance phone calls** can be made from any one of the many TelMex *casetas* found throughout town.

**Autoprogreso buses,** Calle 62 between Calle 65 and 67, run to Mérida's Autoprogreso station (every 10min., 5am-9:45pm, 40min., 5 pesos one-way). *Combis* make the trip in slightly less time for the same price and leave from Calle 31 on the *zócalo*. **Lavamática Progreso,** Calle 74 #150A between Calles 29 and 31 (tel. 5-05-86), provides next-day service (4 pesos per kg; open Mon.-Sat. 8am-1:30pm and 4:30-7:30pm). The **supermarket San Francisco de Asís** is at Calle 80 #144 between Calles 29 and 31 (open daily 7am-9pm). **Farmacia YZA** is on Calle 78 at Calle 29

#143 (tel. 5-06-84; open 24hr.). Twenty-four-hour emergency service is provided by the **Centro Médico Americano**, at Calles 33 and 82 (tel. 5-09-51; some English spoken). The **police station** (tel. 5-00-26) is in the Palacio Municipal on the *zócalo* at Calle 80, between Calles 31 and 33 (supposedly open 24hr.). The **post office** is at Calle 31 #150, between Calles 78 and 76 (tel. 5-05-65), just off the *zócalo* (open Mon.-Fri. 7am-7pm). **Postal Code:** 97320. **Phone Code:** 993.

**Accommodations** When not flooded with vacationing urbanites from the south, budget accommodations are as plentiful as the shrimp. The **Hotel Progreso,** Calle 78 #142 near Calle 29 (tel. 5-00-39), has colorful rooms with spotless mosaic bathrooms and a breezy feel to boot (singles 60 pesos; doubles 70 pesos; add 60 pesos for A/C, 30 pesos for TV and telephone; 35 pesos per additional person). The **Hotel Miramar,** Calle 27 #124 between Calles 72 and 74 (tel. 5-05-52), offers two options with a simple rule: The more you pay, the cuter and cooler the rooms get. Choose from either well-kept rooms with bath and skylight or glorified port-a-potties with beds (*sans* the smell). The owner is very amiable (space-pod singles 60 pesos; doubles 75 pesos, with two beds 80 pesos; upscale singles 70 pesos, doubles 85 pesos; 20 pesos per extra person; long-term stays cheaper). Old but clean rooms in ghastly, bright colors are an economical option at the **Posada Juan Carlos,** Calle 74 #148 between Calles 29 and 31 (tel. 5-10-76; singles 40 pesos; doubles 60 pesos; 10 pesos per additional person, add 10 pesos for TV).

**Food** One fish. Two fish. Red fish. Blue fish. It's all about fish. And it's pretty darn cheap, too. Try the beach end of Calle 80. Fish with a view? Try Avenida Malecón, the main drag along the coast. Unfortunately, some restaurants only open during the summer. **Carabela,** just east of Calle 72 on Av. Malecón, serves up hearty fare and boasts a wide selection of seafood. *Filete empanizado* costs 25 pesos (open daily 7am-1am). If you like your fish *really* fresh, head to **Pescaría Los Cocos,** on Malecón between Calles 76 and 78, where you can enjoy a fish served whole, and practically still flopping around, for just 35 pesos (open daily 8am-8pm). At **El Cordobés,** Calle 80 #150 (tel. 5-26-28), right on the *zócalo,* you can treat yourself to *pescado en tikinxic,* a slow-cooked fish specialty with *chiles.* Most fish entrees go for 25-30 pesos (open daily 6:30am-midnight).

**Sights** Progreso's kilometers of clean beach and shallow water attract hordes in August, but remain calm in other months. For a more placid spot, head for the beach at **Chelém,** 8km west of town, or the wind-sheltered beach at Yaculpatén, just before Chelém. *Combis* leave for Chelém every 30 minutes from the parking lot outside Supermarket San Francisco on Calle 80 (2 pesos). If he's not too busy, the custodian of **El Faro** (the lighthouse), at Calle 80 near Calle 25, might let you climb the 120 bright red steps to the top. Step out on the balcony, from where you can see the ocean and the kilometers of marshy river that give the city its distinctive briny scent. The 2km *muelle* (pier) clings tenuously to the sandy beach; in the early morning it's a great spot from which to reel in fish.

## ■ Mérida to Chichén Itzá

The route from Mérida to Chichén Itzá harbors small villages that are quintessential Yucatán. Churches are oversized and blackened by time, *henequén* (hemp) is still harvested, and for many of the inhabitants, Spanish is a second language.

As Rte. 180 heads east from Mérida to Chichén Itzá, it passes the five private *henequén* haciendas of San Pedro, Teya, Ticopó, San Bernardino, and Holactún. Next come the villages of **Tahmek** and **Hoctún** (47km from Mérida). **Izamal** is only 24km northeast of Hoctún, but buses don't make the detour—catch a direct bus from Mérida (see p. 509). This tiny town contains the largest church plaza in Mexico, ringed with rows of yellow arches around the church and convent, and some of the oldest Spanish buildings in the region, dating from 1533 and built from the boulders of the

Maya pyramid that they replaced. Since almost all the buildings in Izamal are yellow, the city is sometimes referred to as **Ciudad Amarilla** (Yellow City). Near Izamal is the weather-worn pyramid of **Kinichkakmó,** Mayan for Macaw of Fire, which was plundered by the Spanish for stones to build the church and convent. The ancient *cenote* (freshwater sink-hole) of **Ixcolasc** is only 1km away.

Back on Rte. 180, you will find **Kantunil** (68km from Mérida). **Xocchel** (The Place Where the Chels Read) is an attractive town along Rte. 180 before Kantunil. Next is **Holcá,** and finally, **Libre Unión,** with a sizeable *cenote.* During squabbles between the territories of Yucatán and Quintana Roo, Libre Unión found itself smack on the border. The town voted to stick together and become part of the state of Yucatán—thus earning its name, Free Union.

Some travelers hitch or hop buses from one Maya village to another along the busy road between Mérida and Chichén Itzá. Those who choose to hitch should bring water—the waits can be long, and shade is sparse. Second-class bus drivers stop anywhere if requested, but a new fare is charged for each trip, and slow and irregular bus service limits the number of places you can visit in one day. If dusk arrives, be sure to take the next bus to Pisté or Mérida—you don't want to get stranded. If no buses are in sight, there are *palapas* for sleeping in Xocchel and most other towns; ask in the town store in the *zócalo.*

Tourists planning to drive a car through the Ruta Puuc will have an easier time and just as much of a chance to see small, rural villages, whose characteristic thatched huts, dirt roads, and Coca-Cola stands abound everywhere in the Yucatán.

# ■ Chichén Itzá

Chichén Itzá's reputation as the Yucatán's prize cultural attraction is well deserved. The combination of faultless ancient architecture and a backdrop of stunning natural beauty makes it a wondrous place. Yet this alone is not why Chichén Itzá, capital of the Maya empire at its zenith, continues to fascinate throngs of people some 1000 years after its creation. This dramatic window into the past illuminates the glaring paradoxes of Maya civilization: a people both intellectually advanced and brutally savage; a culture crushed by colonization, yet still thriving in the language, customs, and hearts of the present-day Maya. A visit to Chichén might just be the pinnacle of your Yucatán experience—don't miss it for the world.

## ORIENTATION

The ruins of Chichén Itzá lie 1.5km from **Route 180,** the highway running from Mérida (121km west) through Valladolid (43km east) to Cancún (213km east). As nearly every travel agency in Mexico pushes a Chichén Itzá package, the ruins tend to get overpopulated around noon. In order to avoid the stampede (and hot sun), use nearby **Pisté** (2.5km west of the ruins) as a base and get an early start, or visit late in the afternoon and head back to Pisté at nightfall.

Getting to the ruins is easy. From Pisté, catch a taxi (15 pesos) or flag down any eastbound bus (approximately every ½hr., 2-3 pesos). As with all Mexican buses, a vigorous, supplicatory wave to the driver gets you on the road. To get to Chichén Itzá from other towns, see bus listings for Mérida (p. 495), Cancún (p. 530), and Valladolid (p. 524). To head back to Pisté after a day at the ruins, hang out in the bus parking lot until a taxi or bus swings by (every hr.). From Pisté you can get to almost any city in the state (see listings below).

## PRACTICAL INFORMATION

Services are located in the dominant stone edifice at the site's western entrance. Across from the ticket counter is a small **information booth.** Refer specific questions about the ruins to official guides. The booth often provides free **luggage storage** (open daily 8am-5pm). There are also restrooms, a restaurant, an ice cream parlor, a gift shop (which changes U.S. dollars), a bookstore with guidebooks, an auditorium showing documentaries about the ruins, and a small museum. Parking is available right at the site (5 pesos; open daily 8am-10pm).

Pisté provides a few additional services. Across from the bus station, both **Centro Telefónico** (tel. 1-00-89; fax 1-00-88) and **Teléfonos de México** (tel. 1-00-58,1-00-59, or 1-00-60) let you phone home (open daily 7am-9pm). The town has no bank; **exchange** your money at the gift shop at the ruins, but be prepared for ruinous rates.

Pisté's **bus station** (tel. 1-00-52) is near the Stardust Inn on the eastern side of town. To Mérida (1st class 3pm, 1½hr., 27 pesos; 2nd class 11 per day, 2hr., 19 pesos), Cancún (1st class 5:30pm, 2½hr., 46 pesos; 2nd class 10 per day, 4hr., 34 pesos), Valladolid (10 per day, 1hr., 7 pesos), and Playa del Carmen (1:30 and 3:30pm, 5hr., 45 pesos). **Farmacia Isis,** Calle 15 #53, lies a short way past the *zócalo* toward the ruins (open daily 7am-10pm). For medical emergencies, the **Clínica Promesa,** Calle 14 #50 (tel. 6-31-98, ext. 198), in the blue-green building past the *zócalo* and 100m off Rte. 180 (open 24hr.). A single **police** officer sits at a desk in the *comisario* on the eastern side of the *zócalo*. The **post office** is in a small gray building near the *zócalo* across from Abarrotes "El Alba" (open Mon.-Fri. 9am-3pm). There is a **telephone** (tel. 1-01-24) right around the corner from the ticket counter. **Phone code:** 985.

## ACCOMMODATIONS AND CAMPING

Though a few luxury hotels snuggle right up to the ruins, the more economical options are located in **Pisté**—either on or just off Calle 15, the town's main road. You can pitch a tent in the **RV trailer park** right next to the bus station. Spaces have light and power outlets; there are communal bathrooms and a pool (25 pesos per person). The trailer park is administered by the Stardust Inn (tel. 1-01-22), on the other side of the bus station. The tentless can head over to the friendly **Posada Olalde** (tel. 1-00-86), just left of Calle 15 (Rte. 180), two blocks down the unmarked dirt road, directly across the street from the Carrousel Restaurant. An intimate courtyard leads to five pastel-colored rooms with large, firm beds and spotless white bathrooms (singles 100 pesos; doubles 140 pesos; triples 180 pesos). During high season, extra people can string up hammocks for 10 pesos per person. Haggle during the low season. **Posada Carrousel,** (tel. 1-00-78) on Calle 15, is in central Pisté at the large eponymous *palapa* restaurant. Colorful but stuffy rooms have fans, hot water, and *agua purificada* (singles 70 pesos; doubles 100 pesos; triples 130 pesos; quads 100 pesos). Hammocks lent at no extra cost. Nearby **Hotel El Paso,** Calle 15 #48, offers similar rooms with bouncy beds and small windows (singles 80 pesos; doubles 120 pesos; triples 130-150 pesos). Its restaurant offers a well-priced *menú del día* (25 pesos).

## FOOD

For daytrips to Chichén Itzá, the **restaurant** on site provides delicious, reasonable dishes (25-30 pesos) with sporadic entertainment. Picnickers can save a few pesos by packing a lunch from one of the **small grocers** that line Calle 15 in Pisté. Lugging fruit and *tortas* up El Castillo won't be too fun, however, and be prepared for your picnic to be as hot and wet as the inner Temple of the Jaguar. For those determined to save *dinero*, Pisté's Calle 15 is lined with small restaurants offering cheap and yummy *comida yucateca*. **El Carrousel** (tel. 1-00-78) serves three simple meals a day; try eggs any style (10-12 pesos) or enchiladas (15 pesos; open daily 7am-10:30pm). **Restaurant Sayil,** between El Carrousel and the Stardust Inn, is a peaceful place to savor local dishes like *pollo pibil* (chicken cooked in banana leaf, 12 pesos; open daily 7am-10pm). **Restaurant Poxil** (tel. 1-01-16), on the right just past the *zócalo,* serves a filling *comida típica* for just 30 pesos (open daily 8am-9pm).

## SIGHTS

As the Mayan name Chichén Itzá (Mouth of the Well) implies, the area's earliest inhabitants were drawn here by the two nearby freshwater *cenotes,* which are not so fresh today. Much of what is known about these sedentary people is based on the pottery shards recovered by diving archaeologists. Later periods in Chichén Itzá's history are illuminated by the **Chilam Balam,** one of the few pre-Hispanic Maya texts to survive the early missionaries' book-burnings. The *Chilam Balam* describes the construction of many buildings visible today, focusing on the period between AD 500 and 800, when construction was purely Maya.

Chichén was mysteriously abandoned at its height in the 7th century AD, and for the next 300 years it remained a crumbling ghost town. Sometime before AD 1000, the Toltec tribes of Tula (see p. 51) infiltrated the Yucatán and overcame peaceful Maya settlements, bringing with them the cult of the plumed serpent Quetzalcóatl (Kukulcán). The Toltecs fortified Chichén, which soon became the most important city on the peninsula. Toltec influence is visible in Chichén's buildings, which became more rounded, and in its iconography. Whereas the Maya depicted only warriors, eagles, and jaguars, the Toltecs brought in long-nosed representations of Chac (the rain god) and elaborate carvings of lesser gods. They also introduced *chac-mool,* reclining figures representing messengers to the gods that were used as altars for human sacrifice. In 1461, Chichén Itzá was again abandoned, this time due to war, but religious pilgrimages to the site continued well after Spanish conquest. Today, the relentless flow of tourists ensures that Chichén will never again stand in solitude.

For a deeper (not to mention air-conditioned) understanding of Chichén and its people, visit the **Centro Cultural Cecijema** (tel. 1-00-04), at Calle 15 #45 in Pisté. The modern gray building houses a small selection of Maya ceramic replicas as well as attractive rotating exhibits, and the well-stocked library offers books in both English and Spanish. A helpful staff will offer what amounts to a one-on-one tutoring session or just leave you alone to browse with a cup of coffee. Get your birthdate converted to Maya calendar format for a small fee (open daily 8am-5pm; admission free).

## The Ruins

The entire site of Chichén Itzá is open daily 8am-5pm (admission 30 pesos; free Sun. and for children under 14). From the main parking lot and visitor's center, the first group of ruins is up the gravel path and to the left. A small **museum** in the **visitor's complex** at the entrance to the site recaps the history of Chichén Itzá and displays some sculptures and objects removed from the **Sacred Cenote.** Its **auditorium** screens documentaries about the ruins in both Spanish and in English (showtimes vary; both open daily 10am-5pm; free).

If you are mainly interested in the architecture of the ruins, hiring a guide at the entrance is unnecessary. A guidebook (or even just a map) and the multilingual explanatory captions on plaques at each major structure are all you *need* to appreciate the ruins. Free maps are available at the telephone desk around the corner from the ticket counter. You'll need a guide to decipher some of the symbolism of the ruins or to follow the enigmatic recurrence of the number seven throughout the structures. Join one of the guided tours which begin at the entrance (Spanish or English, 6-8 people, 1½hr., 40 pesos per person) or get your own group together and hire a private guide (up to 20 people, 2hr., 150 pesos). Of course, eavesdropping on any of the tours is always free. If you do choose to hire a guide, ask to see identification, which guarantees certification and foreign language ability.

The first sight to meet your eyes is **El Castillo,** Chichén's hallmark. This pyramid, built in honor of Kukulcán, rises in perfect symmetry from the neatly cropped lawn, culminating in a temple supported by pillars in the form of serpents. El Castillo stands as tangible evidence of the astounding astral understanding of the ancient Maya: the 91 steps on each of the four faces, plus the upper platform, total 365 (the number of days in the non-leap year); the 52 panels on the nine terraced levels equal the number of years in a Maya calendar cycle; and each face of the nine terraces is divided by a staircase, yielding 18 sections representing the 18 Maya months. Even more impressive is the precision alignment of El Castillo's axes, which, in coordination with the sun and the moon, produce a bi-annual optical illusion. At sunrise during the spring and fall equinoxes, the rounded terraces cast a **serpentine shadow** on the side of the northern staircase. The sculpted serpent head at the bottom of the staircase completes the illusion. In March, the serpent appears to be sliding down the stairs precisely in the direction of the Sacred Cenote, while in September the motion is reversed. A light-and-shadow lunar serpent-god, identical to that of the equinoxes, creeps up and down the pyramid at the dawn of the full moon following each of the equinoxes. Twice a year people from all over the world converge on Chichén to see this incredible phenomenon, crowding accommodations with calendrical precision.

**Climbing El Castillo** is easier than coming down; many tourists do the entire descent on their behinds. That sight might elicit a chuckle, but the ambulance blatantly parked at El Castillo each day will sober you a bit. Nestled within El Castillo is an early Toltec **temple** which can be entered at the bottom of the north staircase on the western side. After climbing up steps whose walls sweat as much as you do, you'll be grimacing like the *chac-mool* located in the ceremonial chamber. Behind the chamber is a fanged, molding jaguar throne with jade eyes (open daily 11am-3pm and 4-5pm; free). West of El Castillo, or to the left of the entrance, lies the **ballcourt.** The enormous "I"-shaped playing field is bounded by two high, parallel walls with a temple at each end. The largest ballcourt in Mesoamerica, it also has an amazing side-to-side echo that repeats seven times and making it easy to catch free tidbits from tour guides going by. The game played here was called ***pok-ta-pok.*** Players of the two contending teams tried to keep a heavy rubber ball in constant motion by using only their hips, knees, and elbows. They scored by knocking the ball through the stone rings still visible today, high up on the walls in the middle of the "I". The elaborate game fascinated the Spanish so much that in 1528 Cortés took two entire teams back to Europe to perform before the crowned heads. After that, European ball games replaced their unyielding, dead wooden balls with lively, rubber ones.

The ball game was much more than just a cultural pastime for the Maya; it was a contest of **good** versus **evil** linked to a game of the gods. The Maya legend in the *Popol Vuh* tells that every harvest **Hun Hunahpú,** god of corn, was decapitated; his head was planted in the ground and became the seed of all corn plants. Every year, the evil gods of the netherworld stole the buried head in an attempt to destroy the Maya. The hero-twins **Xbalanque** and **Hunahpú** (the sun and Venus respectively) would then descend to **Xilbalba** (the netherworld) and challenge the evil gods to an epic game of ball, using the god's head instead of a ball. Invariably, the twins were successful and the seed was recovered. The new crop symbolized the god's resurrection and the Maya's salvation. In response to the legend, after a ball game (according to some historians) the captain of the victorious team would be decapitated and his head offered to honor the gods. The losers were left to live in shame.

A short distance from the ballcourt toward the grassy open area is the **Tzompantli,** Aztec for Platform of the Skulls. When the Spaniards conquered the Aztecs, they were shocked to find ritualized human sacrifice and horrified by the racks in Tenochtitlán designed to display the skulls of the sacrificed. Chichén's Toltec-designed structure served a similar macabre purpose. Today, eerie rows of skulls in bas-relief decorate the low platform's walls. Next to the Tzompantli stands the **Platform of Jaguars and Eagles,** named after the military men bearing the names of these ferocious animals and who were charged with obtaining prisoners from other tribes for human sacrifice. To either side of the feathered serpent heads on the balustrades, reliefs of jaguars and eagles clutch human hearts in their claws. East of the platform is the **Temple of Venus,** decorated with a feathered serpent holding a human head in its mouth. The temple's reliefs symbolize stars and give information on their motion.

The dirt path leading directly north from El Castillo, over the ancient Maya roadway, links the ceremonial plaza with Chichén Itzá's most important religious center, the **Sacred Cenote,** 300m away. The roughly circular sink-hole, about 60m across, induced vertigo in the sacrificial victims perched on the platform before their 25m plunge into the murky depths. The rain god Chac supposedly dwelt beneath the water's surface and needed frequent gifts to grant good rains. Human remains recovered by divers suggest that children and young men were the victims of choice. If they could keep afloat until noon, they were fished out and forced to tell what they had witnessed during the ordeal. Nowadays, the only thing sacrificed at the Sacred Cenote is the unbearable heat: with a snack shack nearby and lots of shade, the Cenote is a great place to take a bathroom break, cool off, and watch iguanas go by.

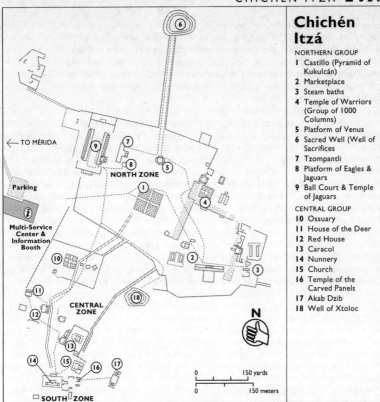

**Chichén Itzá**

**NORTHERN GROUP**

1 Castillo (Pyramid of Kukulcán)
2 Marketplace
3 Steam baths
4 Temple of Warriors (Group of 1000 Columns)
5 Platform of Venus
6 Sacred Well (Well of Sacrifices)
7 Tzompantli
8 Platform of Eagles & Jaguars
9 Ball Court & Temple of Jaguars

**CENTRAL GROUP**

10 Ossuary
11 House of the Deer
12 Red House
13 Caracol
14 Nunnery
15 Church
16 Temple of the Carved Panels
17 Akab Dzib
18 Well of Xtoloc

← TO MÉRIDA

NORTH ZONE

Parking

Multi-Service Center & Information Booth

CENTRAL ZONE

SOUTH ZONE

N

0        150 yards
0        150 meters

On the eastern edge of the central plaza, the **Temple of the Warriors** and **Group of the Thousand Columns** present an impressive array of elaborately carved columns which at one time supported a roof of some perishable material. On the temple itself (not open to the public), in front of two great feathered serpents and several sculpted animal gods, reclines one of Chichén's best-preserved *chac-mools*. The ornamentation of this building is largely Toltec; a nearly identical structure stands at Tula, the Toltec capital far to the west. The Temple of the Warriors marks the end of Chichén's restored monuments and the beginning of an overgrown area extending to the southeast of El Castillo. This corner houses the **Palace of the Sculptured Columns,** the back of which hides a couple beady-eyed masks of Chac. The rest of the quadrangle is comprised of the **Southeastern Colonnade,** the **market** and its courtyard, and the expansive **Western Colonnade.**

A red dirt path on the south side of El Castillo leads to the less photogenic **South Group** of ruins. Beyond the cafeteria and bathrooms, the first pyramid on the right is the **Ossuary,** or **High Priest's Grave,** its distinctive serpent heads mimicking El Castillo. A natural cave extends from within the pyramid 15m into the earth. The human bones and votive offerings found in this cavern are thought to have belonged to an ancient high priest. Past the Ossuary, the road forks, presenting two different routes to the second set of ruins in the South Group, often missed by tourists but well worth the visit. The most interesting structure in this group is the **Observatory,** the large circular building on the left-hand side. This ancient planetarium consists of two rectangular platforms with large, west-facing staircases and two circular towers. Because of the tower's interior spiral staircase (not open to the public), this structure is often called **El Caracol** (the Great Conch). The slits in the dome of the Observatory can be aligned with the important celestial bodies and cardinal directions. El Caracol was built in several stages by Maya and Toltec architects. Notice the small red hand-prints on the wall of the building just as you come up the stairs; these were suppos-edly the hands of the sun god Itzamná. Walking south from El Caracol, toward the Nunnery at the other end of the clearing, you will pass a tiny, ruined **sauna** and then the **Temple of the Sculptured Wall Panels** behind it. Though difficult to decipher, the panels on the exterior walls contain emblems of Toltec warriors—jaguars, eagles, and serpents—in three rows.

The largest structure in this part of Chichén is the misnamed **Nunnery,** on the south side of the quadrangle. Although it was probably a Maya royal palace, its stone rooms reminded Spaniards of a European convent—thus the misnomer. After several superimpositions and some decay, the building is now almost 20m high on a base 65m long and 35m wide. Above the entrance on the eastern side of the building, you can still see Maya hieroglyphs. Also on the eastern side, a smaller annex built at an angle is visible. Grab a flashlight and go exploring—many rooms in the nunnery have doorways that lead to dark corridors and small inner rooms. Play Indiana Jones by risking clean clothes and abrasions to uncover bats, frogs, and, unfortunately, water bottles left by other daring adventurers.

Diagonally across from the nunnery and annex is the **religious center,** its upper walls encrusted with intricate masks of the hook-nosed Chac. The religious center is remarkable for its fusion of cultural styles: over the doorway are Maya stone **lintels,** while the use of wood and inclined edges is evidence of Toltec influence. Above the door are representations of the four *bacabs,* that hold up the sky.

A poorly maintained path (which is sometimes closed during rainy months) runs about 130m east from the nunnery group, past the chapel, to the long **Akab-Dzib.** The oldest parts of this structure are believed to be Chichén's most ancient construc-tions. The two central rooms date to the 2nd or 3rd century AD, while the annexes on either side and to the east were added later. Inside the rooms, it is possible to make out the small, rose-red handprints of Itzamná on the ceiling. On the path is another cave, partly hidden by trees, whose narrow mouth yields more bats and water bottles nestled in its belly.

The overgrown **Cenote Xtoloc** hides in a dip behind the South Group ticket office. To reach it from the office, take the first left 20m into the site. The *cenote* is in the hollow, beyond the small, ruined temple of Xtoloc, the lizard god. There is no path down the steep slope through the undergrowth, and swimming is prohibited because of the dangerous underwater currents. A counterpart to the holy waters of the Sacred Cenote, this pool at one time provided all of Chichén with secular drink-ing water. Follow **sacbé No. 5,** which becomes a narrow, winding trail, to get to the back of the observatory.

As if Chichén Itzá couldn't muster enough daytime spectacle, those green panels (whose purpose you've been contemplating all day) pop open for the evening **light and sound show.** The buildings are splashed in red, blue, green, and yellow lights while booming voices detail the history of the site (Spanish version daily at 7pm, 12 pesos; English version daily at 9pm, 18 pesos). Avoid the poorly-lit and bug-infested nighttime walk from Pisté and cab it to and from the show (15 pesos each way).

## Chichén Viejo

Beginning about 1km south of the Nunnery, and spreading out southwest of the main site, Chichén Viejo is a collection of unrestored minor ruins scattered throughout the jungle. The **Group of the Initial Series** and the **Phallic Cluster,** the first set of ruins in Chichén Viejo, are easy enough to find on your own. Follow the dirt path (look for the "Chichén Viejo" sign) to the right of the Nunnery past the intersection of other dirt paths to a covered well. Shortly beyond the well, a right at the T-junction brings you to the cluster, set in a clearing. Chichén Viejo carries the only dated inscriptions at Chichén Itzá, one of which can be clearly seen on the one remaining lintel of the **temple** of the Initial Series. This **block,** upheld by two columns, features a hiero-glyphic inscription corresponding to July 30, AD 878. The rest of the temple stands in ruin. The main features of the appropriately named Phallic Cluster jut out proudly from the interior walls of the temple.

The remaining ruins, reached by taking the path to the right of the **House of the Phalli,** following the tracks, and then cutting through the bushes, are best located with the help of a guide. Though official guides will charge you almost as much as for the main site, you can ask some of the merchants at Chichén if they know of someone who would be willing to serve as guide for a cheaper flat fee. Unlicensed guides can be very knowledgeable, though few speak English. Shrouded by dense jungle, 10 minutes beyond the Phallic Cluster, lie the remains of the **House of the Four Lintels,** carrying another inscription dating to July 13, AD 881. In the **Principal Group of the Southwest,** hieroglyphs depict the Maya practice of compressing children's foreheads with stone plates (conically shaped heads were considered beautiful, as were crossed eyes and precious stones embedded in the flesh of the face). The Principal Group contains a magnificent **ruined pyramid,** the **Temple of the Three Lintels** (dating to AD 879), and the **Jaguar Temple,** where a handful of columns salute the ancient military order of the Jaguars.

Turning to the right through the jungle from the Southwest Group, do your best to stumble upon the **Bird Cornice Group,** featuring a strip of carved birds, the **Temple of the Turtle,** where a turtle-shaped stone was found, and the **Temple of the Sculpted Jambs,** whose doorjambs are molded into human figures.

## ■ Near Chichén Itzá

### GRUTAS DE BALANCANCHÉN

The inner caves of the **Grutas de Balancanchén** were only re-discovered in 1959 when a local amateur speleologist noticed a passageway blocked up with stones. Further exploration opened 300m of caves filled with stalactites carved to resemble leaves on the ceiling and a huge tree-like column surrounded by dozens of votive vessels with ghoulish masks. Archaeologists have come to believe that the cave was a center for Maya-Toltec worship of the gods Chac, Tlaloc (the Toltec rain god), and Kukulcán (Quetzalcóatl) during the 10th and 11th centuries. For unknown reasons, subterranean worship in Balancanchén stopped at the end of this period, and the offerings of ceramic vessels and stone sculptures rested undisturbed for eight centuries. The impressive **stalactites** and plethora of **ceramic offerings** definitely merit a visit, but be prepared for an almost incomprehensible Disney-esque tour which dramatizes the cave's history, keeping up with tour groups via a series of hidden speakers. A guide, available for questions, paces the group through the chambers along the 1km path. Self-guided tours are not permitted, and you'll need at least two people to start a tour (in Spanish, 9am, noon, 2, and 4pm; in English, 11am, 1, and 3pm; in French, 10am; 22 pesos, Sun. and holidays 7 pesos, children under 13 free).

**Getting There:** Located 6km east of Chichén Itzá and 2km past the Dolores Alba Hotel, the caves are easily reached by hopping on any bus traveling east on Rte. 180 (3 pesos). When you board, be sure to ask the driver to stop there. To get back, catch any westbound vehicle, but be prepared to wait a while for one.

### YAXUNÁ

**Yaxuná,** 30km southeast of Chichén Itzá, is home to the ruins of yet another ancient Maya city. The temple was built by the Maya of Cobá, who were planning to make war on the people of Chichén. A 100km *sacbé* (an wide, elevated, white stone road), the longest of the area, linked Yaxuná with Cobá. To keep a close eye on their enemy, the Maya of Cobá aligned their temple with El Castillo.

**Getting There:** There is no public transportation to Yaxuná, but it's possible to hire a truck in Pisté (about 150 pesos round-trip; arrange for your driver to wait for you and ask to stop at the *cenotes* and caves between Chichén and Yaxuná). Road conditions are incredibly poor: the trip is only possible during the dry season. The easiest route is take Rte. 180 to Libre Unión and then left to Yaxcabah, a small town 17km down the road and 8km from Yaxuná.

# ■ Valladolid

Valladolid (pop. 100,000) doesn't have the history of Mérida or the showiness of Cancún. It is a frenetic, crowded, noisy city. It sprawls. It screams. *Indígena* women and children besiege the *zócalo* to sell colorful *huipiles* and chewing gum, and whining mopeds buzz down narrow streets. But amidst all the bustle, Valladolid has a great hotel, good food, refreshing *cenotes* (freshwater sink-holes), and six churches. Not too shabby for a stopover on the way to Río Lagartos, Chichén Itzá, or Mérida.

**Orientation and Practical Information** Traversed by Rte. 180, Valladolid lies midway between Mérida and Cancún. Even-numbered streets run north-south, increasing westward. Odd-numbered streets run east-west, increasing to the south. *El centro* is bordered by Calles 27, 53, 28, and 60. Except for **Cenote X-kekén,** everything lies within comfortable walking distance from the *zócalo* (circumscribed by Calles 39, 40, 41, and 42). To get to the *zócalo* from the bus station, take a taxi (7 pesos) or walk one block south on Calle 54 to Calle 39. Turn left and follow Calle 39 for six blocks. Or better yet, get off before the bus station at the *zócalo* (look for a big cathedral; you can't miss it).

The *ayuntamiento* (city hall), on the Calle 40 side of the *zócalo,* provides **tourist information** and has a fantastic mural upstairs (open Mon.-Sat. 9am-1pm and 7-9pm). **Bancomer** (tel. 6-21-50), on the Calle 40 side of the *zócalo,* has a 24-hour **ATM** and good exchange rates (open for exchange Mon.-Fri. 9am-2pm). There are **LADATELs** on the east side of *zócalo.*

**Buses** leave from the station on Calle 54 and 37. **ADO,** Calle 37 at Calle 54 (tel. 6-34-49), sends buses to Cancún (7 per day, 2hr., 32 pesos), Chichén Itzá (8 per day, 1hr., 6 pesos), Mérida (9 per day, 2hr., 32 pesos), Playa del Carmen (noon, 2, and 3pm, 2½hr., 40 pesos), and Tizimín (every hr., 1hr., 8 pesos). To reach Tinum, buy a ticket on a Mérida-bound bus and ask the driver to drop you off (½hr., 6 pesos). **Luggage storage** costs 1 peso per piece per day (open 8am-7pm).

Buy the freshest, cheapest fruit at the **market,** bordered by Calles 35, 37, 30, and 32, 5 blocks northeast of the *zócalo* (open daily 5am-noon). **Lavandería Teresita,** Calle 33 and 42 (tel. 6-23-93), takes care of your dirty laundry (self-service 7 pesos for 3kg, full service 5 pesos per kg; open daily 7am-7pm). **El Descuento,** Calle 42 at 39 (tel. 6-26-44), on the northwest corner of the *zócalo,* is a **24-hour pharmacy.** In a medical emergency look for **Hospital S.S.A.** on Calle 41 (tel. 6-28-83), two blocks west of the *zócalo,* then five blocks southwest on Calle 41A (open 24hr.). The **police** (tel. 6-21-00) are on Calle 41 ten blocks east of the *zócalo.* The **post office** (tel. 6-23-26) is on the Calle 40 side of the *zócalo* (open Mon.-Fri. 8am-3pm). **Postal Code:** 97780. **Phone Code:** 985.

**Accommodations** The best hotels in town are on or near the *zócalo.* **Hotel Zací,** Calle 44 #191 between Calles 39 and 37 (tel. 6-21-67), is a standout. Fantastically furnished rooms with cable TV, fans, and sparkling bathrooms have a Spanish colonial air. A gorgeous pool and restaurant in the courtyard complete this paradise worth every peso (singles 80 pesos; doubles 90 pesos; triples 130 pesos; quads 160 pesos; add 20 pesos for A/C). **Hotel María Guadalupe,** Calle 44 #198 between Calles 39 and 41 (tel. 6-20-68), has sterile rooms with dark wood decor and brand new ceiling fans (singles and doubles 60 pesos; triples 70 pesos). **Hotel Mendoza,** Calle 39 #204 (tel. 6-20-02), is one and a half blocks west of the *zócalo.* The older rooms with springless mattressed beds and ceiling fans don't hide their history of use (singles 50 pesos; doubles 70 pesos; triples 90 pesos). Newer, larger suites have better baths and come with extra fans, cable TV, and a fridge (singles and doubles 120 pesos; triples 170 pesos).

**Food** Valladolid's greatest virtue may be its Yucatec food. Try the *poc-chuc* (thinly sliced grilled pork), *panuchos* (small tortillas filled with various combinations of chicken, pork, beans, lettuce, tomato, and chile), or *escabeche oriental de pavo* (a hearty turkey soup). **El Bazaar,** Calle 39 at 40, is a courtyard crowded with several

## Eat Drink Man Woman

If Chichén Itzá's ruins and Río Lagartos' National Park have failed to make you swoon, Valladolid's *Xtabentún* is sure to do so. As potent as whiskey, this popular Yucatec concoction of anise and honey has its origin here. According to legend, Zac-Nicté, a young woman whose beauty had attracted the wicked tribal chief's attention, fell in love with a warrior. Fearing what the chief might do to them, the young lovers sought refuge in the jungle. Coming across a beehive in a *balché* tree, the couple ate their fill of honey and left the rest in a hole in the trunk. The next day they discovered that the honey had magically become Xtabentún. When the chief finally caught up with them, he was so impressed with the drink's taste that he let them go…and they lived happily ever after. You too can sample this and other nectars at the **Sosa factory outlet,** on Calle 42 between Calles 47 and 49 (tel. 6-21-42), four blocks south of the *zócalo*. The Sosa family, which has been making the product for over 100 years, sell their entire line here at discounts (*Xtabentún* 25 pesos per bottle; open Mon.-Sat. 10am-1pm and 3-6pm).

cafes and juice bars right off the *zócalo* (open daily 6am-midnight). People-watch and be watched as you enjoy tacos (5 pesos) and *yucateco* entrees (12 pesos) from **La Rancherita.** Head to **Sergio's** for a pizza (15-25 pesos) or *chile relleno* (20 pesos). **Amigo Casiano** specializes in *comida yucateca* and does quite a job of it *(carne molida* 15 pesos). **Restaurante Cenote Zací,** on Calle 36 between Calles 37 and 39 (tel. 6-21-07), is a lovely thatched-roof restaurant overlooking the *cenote* with background music. The excellent liquor selection includes locally produced Xtabentún, a delectable concoction of rum, anise, and honey (4 pesos). Catch of the day costs 20 pesos (open daily 8am-6pm).

**Sights and Entertainment** The city's two main *cenotes* (freshwater sinkholes) are its most arresting attractions. **Cenote Zací** (sah-KEY) is only three blocks east of the *zócalo*, on Calle 36 between Calles 37 and 39. Well-worn stone stairs lead down into a cavernous hollow studded with plunging stalactites. Daredevil divers do their best to imitate those of Acapulco while unimpressed nesting finches and catfish look on (admission 4 pesos, children 2 pesos; free view from the *palapa* restaurant on the edge; free parking; open daily 8am-6pm). Though further from the center of town, **Cenote X-kekén** (chay-keh-KEN) is also more striking. Visit before noon, as plunging schoolkids disrupt the deliciously cool, turquoise, glassy surface of the *cenote's* water in the afternoon. At midday, light pours into the cove through the narrow hole in the roof, refracting into the water and reflecting off the jellyfish-like tree roots to create an eerie glow (open daily 7am-5pm; admission 5 pesos, children 2.50 pesos). To get there by car or bike (20min.), take Calle 39 to the highway and ride toward Mérida. Make a left at the sign for Dzitnup and continue to a damp stairway which leads down to the water's edge. Without your own wheels, take a taxi (15 pesos) or ask the driver of a second-class Mérida bus to drop you off.

The most famous church in town is **San Bernardino de Siena,** affiliated with the **Ex-Convento de Sisal,** Calle 41, four blocks southwest off Calle 46. Built in 1552, the church and convent are the oldest ecclesiastical buildings in the Yucatán. The walk along Calle 41A is fascinating. On the altar at the rear of the church is a large image of the Virgin of Guadalupe; original frescoes are visible behind two side altars (open Tues.-Sun. 8am-2:30pm and 5-8pm). The **Catedral de San Gervasio,** with its colonial-style twin towers, stands protectress over the *zócalo* on Calle 41. It would rival San Bernardino de Siena for the title of oldest church in the nation had residents not violated the sacred right to sanctuary. According to legend, two alleged criminals who took sanctuary in the church were discovered and brutally murdered by an angry mob. When the bishop learned of the mob's sinful actions, he closed the church and had it destroyed; it was later rebuilt facing in another direction. Needless to say, the outside is better than the inside (open daily 5am-noon and 3-9pm).

There are two forums of entertainment in Valladolid: people-watching at **El Bazaar** or viewing movies dubbed in Spanish at **Cinema Díaz,** just off the *zócalo,* on Calles 40 and 41 (screenings at 7 and 9pm).

# ■ Tizimín

If bustling cities can bustle slowly, Tizimín's lazy flow of traffic and pedestrians is a great example. Although it's the center of a large rural area, Tizimín (pop. 45,000) is less cosmopolitan than might be expected. The city has a handful of interesting sights, but the absence of tourists and souvenir shops indicates that Tizimín's best feature may be its languid lifestyle: It's one-thirty in the afternoon, no clouds, upper nineties. Not a soul within sight of the beautifully manicured *zócalo. It's too hot,* the locals say as they comfortably recline in their hammocks. Two-thirty, then three, then four. Clouds have gathered and things have cooled off considerably. It is pleasantly warm. Still no people. The locals lift their heads long enough to comment on the imminence of rain. It rains. Hard. Everything gets wet. An old man with leathery skin snores in sync with the swinging of the hammock. So goes life in Tizimín.

**Orientation and Practical Information** Tizimín lies 75km south of Río Lagartos by Rte. 295, and 120km west of Kantunil Kin by Rte. 175. Even-numbered streets run north and south, increasing to the west. Odd-numbered streets run west and east, increasing to the south. Most everything in Tizimín is centered around its *zócalo (el parque).* To get there, facing away from the bus station (east), walk west down the hill for two blocks on the street to your left, Calle 47. You'll pass a market on your left. Turn left on Calle 50 and walk south one block toward the large stone church (the **Ex-Convento**). **Bancomer,** on Calle 51 and 48 (tel. 3-23-81), exchanges currency on the little square behind the Ex-Convento (open Mon.-Fri. 9am-1:30pm). There is a **LADATEL** on Calle 50 one block north of the Ex-Convento on the right. Buses leave from the terminal at Calles 46 and 47. **ADO** (tel. 3-24-24) goes to Cancún (7 and 9am, 3½hr., 35 pesos), Chetumal (5 per day, 5hr., 58 pesos), and Valladolid (13 per day, 1hr., 9 pesos). **Autotransportes del Noreste** (tel. 3-20-34) has 1st-class service to Río Lagartos (9:15am, 6:45, and 7:45pm, 1hr., 12 pesos) Mérida (7 per day, 2hr., 40 pesos) and Kantunil Kin (10 per day, 1½hr., 13 pesos). **Farmacia Centro de Drogas** is on Calle 51 (tel. 3-37-26), behind the ex-convento, next to Bancomer (open Mon.-Sat. 7:30am-9:30pm). The **Centro Médico de Oriente San Carlos,** Calle 46 #461 (tel. 3-21-57), has a 24-hour pharmacy and ambulance service. The **post office** is at Calles 48 and 55 (open Mon.-Fri. 8am-3pm, Sat. 9am-1pm). **Postal code:** 97700. **Phone code:** 986.

**Accommodations and Food** Hotel **San Carlos,** Calle 54 #407 (tel. 3-20-94), is modern and inviting. From the southwest corner of the *zócalo* (by Tres Reyes restaurant) walk west one block and make your first right. The turtles in the gorgeous gardens will lure you into beautifully decorated, spotless rooms, each with two double beds and private bathrooms (singles 80 pesos; doubles 100 pesos; add 20 well-spent pesos for A/C). **Hotel San Jorge** (tel. 3-20-37), kitty-corner to Tres Reyes restaurant, has plain, big rooms with squishy beds and aging bathrooms. *Agua purificada* can be found in the lobby (singles 80 pesos; doubles 90 pesos; add 30 pesos for A/C). **Posada Marian** (tel. 3-28-57), in the *zócalo* on the southern side of the church, has a purple facade that leads to small purple rooms, each with two beds, hot water, a fan, and TV (singles and doubles 80 pesos; each additional person 10 pesos; add 15 pesos for A/C).

For the cheapest meal, buy some fruits, vegetables, and bread at the **market** on Calle 47 and picnic in the beautiful *zócalo.* The most popular eatery in Tizimín is the casual **Restaurante Tres Reyes,** on the *zócalo* (tel. 3-21-06). Hearty meals come with a high stack of tortillas (*pollo frito con papas* 28 pesos, *camarones al mojo de ajo* 45 pesos; open daily 7am-11pm). **Restaurante Portales** (tel. 3-35-05) provides cheap eats on a pleasant patio on the *zócalo* (huge breakfasts 20 pesos, sandwiches 8 pesos, tacos 12 pesos; open Mon.-Sat. 7:30am-12:30pm and 5:30-11:30pm, Sun. 5:30-11:30pm). **Restaurante Las Palmas,** Calle 51 #331A between Calles 38 and 40 (tel. 3-24-51), is a big, comfortable *palapa* that serves regional specialties (20-30 pesos) and occasionally hosts live music and dancing.

### Sights, Entertainment, and Seasonal Events

You want Maya ruins? Julio has them. You need maps? Julio's got 'em. Want info on folkloric dancing, Río Lagartos, El Cuyo? Yep, it's all about Julio. **Julio Caesar** (tel. 3-38-86), in the photography studio at Calle 50, Bazar Arce 8, between 47 and 49, (open Mon.-Sat. 8am-1pm and 5-8:30pm) is *the* tourist *jefe* in Tizimín. You can't get to the ruins at Kulubá without him, as the ruins lie on a private ranch whose owner works through Julio. The **archaeological site of Kulubá,** although largely in ruin, virtually untouristed, and somewhat hard to reach, is well worth a visit, as much for the beauty of the surrounding countryside as for the mind-boggling detail of the ruins themselves. The ruins date from the Late Classical period (AD 800-1000) and are the easternmost point of the Puuc architectural influence. The style here also shows some resemblance to the buildings at Chichén Itzá. Although neither building has survived the years intact, the details that remain are still impressive. **El Edificio de Las Úes,** a structure about 40m long, 8m high, and 7m wide, is carved with "U"s all along its facade. The original red stucco with which the whole building was once painted can still be seen on the carved portions of the stone. The second partially restored building, the more impressive of the two, features two surprisingly well-preserved pairs of masks of the rain god Chac, as well as other carved ornamentation. The building is 50m long, 10m high, and 8m wide, and at one time probably had three pairs of masks of the rain god, all with long curved noses. To get to the ruins, take the Tixcanal-bound bus a half-block from the *zócalo* and ask the driver to drop you off at Kulubá. **Taxis** from Tizimín charge 100 pesos for a round-trip jaunt to the ruins with a wait. Traveling to the site during the rainy season is especially difficult.

Tizimín's *zócalo* features a colonial church and ex-convent. The church, **La Venerada Iglesia de los Tres Santos Reyes,** is named after the patron saints of the town. The **festival** held each year in their honor (Dec. 30-Jan. 12) draws pilgrims from all over the region and provokes processions, dancing, bullfights, and lots of *típico* food. January 6 is the most important day of the festival, when the pilgrims file through the church to touch the patrons with palm branches. Every Sunday at the *zócalo* is a *ballet folklórica* around 7:30pm, free to public.

The tiny town of **Kikil,** 5km from Tizimín, has the enormous jungle-encroached remains of a colonial church and ex-convent and the fresh waters of a stunning *cenote*. The church, known to locals simply as **Iglesia Kikil,** is just to the right of the highway as you enter Kikil from Tizimín. The church was burned during the Caste War (1847-48) and has been utterly abandoned to vegetation, but with enormous trees growing atop it, the bulky ruin creates a sublime spectacle. Just inside the gate of the little courtyard to your left as you face the church stands an elaborately carved stone baptismal font which rings like a bell when you strike it with your hand. A beautiful fresh-water *cenote* hides just across the road from the church. Also to be seen in Kikil are traditional Maya ceremonies such as the **Ch-Chac,** a rain petition from May through June (taxi to Kikil 40-50 pesos round-trip with a wait).

# ■ Río Lagartos

Misnamed by Cortés when he chanced upon it, Río Lagartos (pop. 3000) is neither a *"río"* nor does it have *"lagartos"* (alligators). It is, however, an inlet of ocean water surrounded by beach and mangroves, now home to a small, arcadian, relatively gringo-free fishing village. Río's main attraction is the 47,000-hectare Río Lagartos National Park, home to some 30,000 pink flamingos, 211 other bird species, spider monkeys, white-tailed deer, jaguars, and crocodiles. A secluded, sugary beach, sumptuous seafood restaurants, and hospitable locals often extend travelers' planned stays.

**Orientation and Practical Information** Río Lagartos is easily accessed from Tizimín (48km), Valladolid (104km), and Mérida (156km). There is neither a post office nor a bank in the village; the town's services are limited to the long-distance **caseta** in the *zócalo* (tel. 3-26-68 or 3-26-65). **Autotransportes de Oriente (ADO)** has frequent buses to Tizimín (6 per day, 1hr., 9 pesos). If you're lucky, the cheerful owner of La Cueva de Macumba (see **Food** below) might arrange for someone to take you on his boat to **Isla Holbox** (p. 534), which is infinitely more convenient than traveling by land via Chiquilá, though the stunning journey along the coast may be a bit pricey. **Phone code:** 986.

**Accommodations** There is one. It's four huts, each with roofs and no locks. **Cabañas Los Dos Hermanos** (tel. 3-26-68, ext. 183) is on the same street as the bus station, three blocks to the east and almost on the beach. On the grounds of the owner's home, the buildings, like most in Río Lagartos, are lockless—a reflection of the town's relative safety. Each of the sizable *cabañas* has a double bed, cable TV, fans, and clean bathrooms with hot water (one room 80 pesos, fit as many people as you like; hammock hooks provided; reservations highly recommended).

**Food** Restaurante Isla Contoy (tel. 3-26-68, ext. 100) is right on the shore, three blocks south and two blocks west of the *zócalo;* from the bus station walk five blocks west and a few meters north. Enjoy the beach view and gregarious owner as you sup on delectable *fillete relleno* (breaded fish stuffed with shrimp and salsa, 30 pesos; open daily 6am-11pm). The restaurant also owns four **lanchas** that can be hired for a tour of the park (300-400 pesos, depending on the season). To sample the cooking and decorative tastes of an eclectic native, try **La Cueva de Macumba** (tel. 3-26-68, ext. 192), also on the waterfront, two blocks north of the *zócalo* near the lighthouse. The delightfully creative owner has decorated the place with a local-economy motif, complete with fishing gear, artfully arranged plumage, and a seashell chandelier. *Salbutes* (fried tortillas) cost 1.50 pesos apiece. Ask politely and he'll let you climb up to his loft/studio to see the creative process in action (open daily in the evening).

**Sights and Entertainment** Don't even think about exploring **Río Lagartos National Park** without talking to the people at the Restaurante Isla Contoy (see above). With maps, enthusiasm, and a great love of their Río, the guides will do their best to ensure flamingo sightings, and will take you to lesser-known treasures, such as the Maya Ruins, the colorful salt banks, and great hiking trails. To see flamingos, early mornings are best, and May through June is their courtship (from which the *flamenco* derives) and nesting time. When hiring a guide, always look for a badge verifying training in ecotourism; the qualified guides' enthusiasm is contagious.

Consistent with the tranquility and laid-back attitude of this fishing town, Río's nightlife is as calm as its days. Enjoy a few cold beers, people-watch at the *zócalo,* and be lulled into dreams by the lazy, broad sweeps of the lighthouse's beacon. On Saturday nights, **Titanic,** on Principal by the bus station, cranks up the disco. The town fiesta is July 20th, when parades and a circus liven up the narrow streets.

# QUINTANA ROO

## ■ Cancún

Mexico's biggest resort, Cancún (pop. 450,000) is also perhaps the world's most dramatic example of government-engineered tourism. Drunk on the success of Puerto Vallarta and Acapulco, Mexican entrepreneurs set about constructing Cancún from the ground up—literally—in the late 1960s after it was selected by a computer as the the most promising spit of sand in the country. The L-shaped island was a natural choice: blessed with miles of magnificent white beaches bordering storybook turquoise water accessible from 360° and ideal temperatures year-round, and is a short trip from many of the most celebrated Maya ruins. These features were fine-tuned by paradise engineers who dredged the ocean to enlarge the beaches, dug up earth to fill in the lagoon, and built bridges at either end of the island, connecting it to the mainland (where the older, cheaper Ciudad Cancún exists to complement the ritzy Isla and house its many employees).

First opened in 1974, the *Zona Hotelera* (Hotel Zone) was built up in its gilded high-rise splendor on Isla Cancún with the goal of avoiding the chaos of third-world urban growth that could scare tourists away. This complacent bubble encompasses every conceivable tourist need: there is a water purification system to provide to safe tap water, an enforced ban on panhandling, and strict zoning laws to prevent a scourge of skyscrapers. Here, in the middle of the *norteamericano* winter, you can parasail and scuba dive, shop in chic boutiques, snack at McDonald's and slam tequila at anything-goes Tex-Mex bars—all while speaking English, spending greenbacks, and being shuttled from hotel to beach to bar and back. Over two million tourists (many of them American) choose to sit back and enjoy "Mexico" here every year. But if you have fewer bills to throw around and are searching for the Yucatán of yore, abandon the mega-resort and seek enjoyment at nearby Tulúm or Isla Holbox.

## ORIENTATION

On the eastern tip of the Yucatán Peninsula, Cancún lies 285km east of Mérida via Rte. 180 and 382km north of Chetumal and the Belizean border via Rte. 307. The resort has two sections: **Ciudad Cancún,** where you'll find most services and shopping, and **Isla Cancún,** home of the *Zona Hotelera* and pure white beaches. The main drag in Ciudad Cancún, **Avenida Tulum,** runs parallel to **Yaxchilán** (Yash-chee-YAN), four blocks west. These two streets form a rough parallelogram with **Avenidas Cobá** and **Uxmal.** Facing the bus station (south), Av. Tulum is the busy throroughfare to the left (east) and Av. Uxmal is on the right (west). Downtown, *el centro,* lies south of the bus station. On the island, the *Zona Hotelera*'s main drag is **Paseo Kukulcán.**

To reach either section of town from the airport, buy a ticket for the shuttle bus TTC (50 pesos). Tickets are sold in baggage claim and buses leave from outside. A private taxi (white with green stripes) will charge around 75 pesos for that trip; it'll take at least 30 pesos to go from the beach to the stores, depending on how far into the *Zona Hotelera* you are. Always settle the price before getting into a cab. White buses marked *Hoteles* run the long stretch between the city's bus station and the island's tip around the clock. Buses can be caught at any blue sign along Av. Tulum and Paseo Kukulcán (3 pesos). To get off the bus in the *Zona Hotelera,* push one of the little square red buttons on the ceiling when in sight of your stop–if you don't know where you need to get off, mention the name to the bus driver as you board, with a *por favor.* While many places rent mopeds (useful for exploring the 18km of beaches which stretch from the Youth Hostel (p. 532) to Punta Nizuc), buses are much cheaper and just as convenient.

## PRACTICAL INFORMATION

**Tourist Offices:** On Av. Tulum 5 (tel. 87-3-11, ext. 114), inside the *Palacio de Gobierno* (open daily 8:30am-4pm). **Visitor office** located right next door in the little red building at Av. Tulum 26 (tel. 84-80-73), offers similar paraphernalia and help (open daily 9am-9pm). Ask for **Cancún Tips,** a free magazine full of useful information and maps (in English). Can also be found at Av. Tulum 29 (tel. 84-40-44), at Pl. Caracol in the *Zona Hotelera,* and at the airport.

**Consulates: Canada,** Av. Tulum 200 (tel. 83-33-60) in Pl. México. Open Mon.-Fri. 10am-2pm. For emergencies outside of office hours, call the embassy in Mexico City (tel. (91) 5-724-7900). **U.K.,** (tel. 85-11-66) in the Hotel Royal Caribbean. Open Mon.-Fri. 9am-5pm. **U.S.** (tel. 83-13-73 or 83-22-96), Plaza Caracol, 3rd fl. Open Mon.-Fri. 9am-1pm and 3-5:30pm.

**Currency Exchange: Bancomer,** Av. Tulum 20 (tel. 84-44-00), has the best rate of all banks on Av. Tulum. Open Mon.-Fri. 8:30am-5:30pm. Both **Banamex,** Tulum 19 (tel. 84-54-11), Mon.-Fri. 9am-4pm, and **Banca Serfín,** Av. Tulum at Cobá (tel. 84-14-24), give cash advances on Visa and MasterCard and have Cirrus **ATMs.** Equally competitive but more convenient is **CUNEX Exchange** (tel. 87-09-01), next to Banco Serfín on the corner of Tulum and Cobá. Open daily 8am-11pm.

**American Express:** Tulum 208 (tel. 84-17-01), 3 blocks past Cobá away from the city. Open Mon.-Fri. 9am-6pm, Sat. 9am-1pm.

**Telephones: LADATELs** and 20- or 50-peso phone cards make for easy and cheap long-distance calls. The **public phone** in Pl. Nautilus near the youth hostel is another option, provided you have a big pile of coins. *Casetas* throughout the city tend to charge hefty fees. For local calls, prefix the number you are dialing with "8" (we have already included the magic cipher in our listings).

**Fax:** Tel. 84-15-24. At the post office. Open Mon.-Fri. 9am-8:30pm, Sat. 9am-4:30pm. Telegram service available as well.

**Airport:** Tel. 86-00-28. South of the city on Rte. 307. *Colectivos* 50 pesos, taxis 80 pesos (fixed rates to downtown; buy a ticket at the desk). Airlines include **Aerocaribe** (tel. 87-44-97); **Mexicana** (tel. 86-01-48); **LACSA** (tel. 86-01-41); **American** (tel. 86-00-55 or 86-00-86); **Continental** (tel. 86-00-40); **Northwest** (tel. 86-00-44); **United** (tel. 86-01-58 or 86-00-25).

**Buses:** On Uxmal at Tulum (tel. 84-13-78). **ADO** travels to Valladolid (11:30am and 1:30pm, 2hr., 32 pesos); **Premier,** to Campeche (11:30am and 1:30pm, 6hr., 98 pesos), Chichén Itzá (8:45am, 2½hr., 47 pesos), Palenque (6pm, 12hr., 155 pesos), and Playa del Carmen (every hr., 45min., 13 pesos). You can save about 25% by hopping on the second-class buses that leave from the curbside and go to Mérida, Tulum, and Chetumal.

**Ferries:** To **Isla Mujeres:** take a bus or van marked "Pto. Juárez" to the 2 ferry depots north of town (Punta Sam for car ferries, Puerto Juárez for passenger ferries). Passenger ferries shuttle across (on the half-hour, 6am-8:30pm, 15 pesos). To **Cozumel:** from Playa del Carmen, south of Cancún and accessible by bus from the terminal in town (20 or 25 pesos).

**Taxis:** Tel. 88-69-90. The minimum fare within the *Zona* is 25 pesos; a ride into town can cost as much as 60 pesos. Within the *centro*, a taxi ride should run around 20 pesos. Prices are negotiable; be sure to settle the deal before getting in.

**Moped Rental:** Available from most major hotels; try **Hotel Las Perlas** (tel. 83-20-22), near the CREA youth-hostel (roughly US$65 per day).

**Luggage storage:** At the bus station (5 pesos for 24hr.).

**English Bookstore: Fama,** Tulum 105 (tel. 84-65-86). Newspapers, magazines, guidebooks, maps, and trashy beach books in English. Open daily 8am-10pm.

**Supermarket: Súper San Francisco** Av. Tulum (tel. 84-11-55) next to Banamex. Open Mon.-Sat. 7:30am-10pm, Sun. 7am-9pm. **Súper Deli,** a 24hr. grocery store, is conveniently located near the youth hostel.

**Laundry: Lavandería Automática "Alborada,"** Náder 5 (tel. 84-15-84), behind the Ayuntamiento Benito Juárez. Self-service 7 pesos. Mon.-Sat. 9am-8pm.

**Red Cross:** Av. Yaxchilán 2 (tel. 84-16-16). English spoken. Open 24hr.

**Pharmacies:** Several along Tulum and Yaxchilán. **Farmacia Paris,** Yaxchilán 32 (tel. 84-01-64), at the intersection with Calle Rosas, is open 24hr.

**Medical Assistance: Hospital Americano,** Calle Viento 15 (tel. 84-61-33, after hours 84-63-19), 5 blocks south on Tulum after its intersection with Cobá. **IMSS** (tel. 84-19-19), at Tulum and Cobá. For an ambulance call **Total Assist** (tel. 84-10-92 or 84-81-16), at Claveles 5 near Av. Tulum. English spoken.

**Emergency:** 06.

**Police:** Tel. 84-19-13. Av. Tulum next to City Hall.

**Post Office:** Av. Xel-Ha at Sunyaxchén (tel. 84-15-24). From Tulum, cut through any side street to Yaxchilán and head up Sun Yax Chén. The post office is 4 blocks farther. Open daily 8am-1pm and 4-8:30pm. **Postal Code:** 77500.

**Phone Code:** 98.

## ACCOMMODATIONS AND CAMPING

If you're not careful, Cancún will suck money out of you faster than you can sign your next traveler's check. Budget travelers often stay or camp at the **CREA Youth Hostel,** at the end of the *Zona Hotelera*. Even in Ciudad Cancún, some hotels will charge you

TO PUNTA SAM

TO ISLA
MUJERES

# Cancún

**CIUDAD CANCÚN**

Av. López Portillo

Av. Uxmal

Av. Cobá

Av. Banampak

Paseo Kukulcán

*Mar Caribe*

*Laguna
Morales*

*Playa las Perlas*

*Playa Juventul*

Blvd.

Av. Yaxchilán

Av. Kabah

**DETAIL MAP**

**CREA** Youth Hostel

*Playa Linda*

**Hotel
Suites
Albatros**

*Playa Langosta*

*Bahía de Mujeres*

*Playa
Tortugas*

*Playa Caracol*

Punta
Cancún

**Plaza Caracol**

*Laguna
Bojórquez*

*Playa Chac Mool*

*Laguna
Nichupté*

**ISLA
CANCÚN**
(ZONA HOTELERA)

**Sheraton Hotel**

*Playa Marlin*

*Laguna
del
Amor*

Paseo Kukulcán

*Playa Ballenas*

**Ruinas del Rey**

*Playa Delfines*

*Laguna
Río
Inglés*

*Mar Caribe*

Punta
Nizuc

TO
AIRPORT

Paseo Kukulcán

*Laguna
Caleta*

**Restaurante
Río Nizuc**

**Club Med**

TO
TULUM

**N**

------ Ferry

| 0 | 2 miles |

| 0 | |
| 2 kilometers | |

## DETAIL MAP

Av. Uxmal

**Bus Station**

Av. Uxmal

Rosas

Rosas

**Hotel
Canto**

Azucenas

Av. Carlos Nader

Av. Rubia

Mero

Cazón

Jazmines

Azucenas

Mero

Huachinango

Av. Sunyaxchén

Jazmines

Tulipanes

(i)

**Hotel
Coral**

Gladiolas

Margaritas

Tulipanes

Pargo

Av. Bonampak

**Hotel
Villa
Rossana**

Claveles

Cherna

Chiabal

Av. Yaxchilán

Claveles

Av. Tulum

Cherna

Crisantemos

Av. Cobá

Crisantemos

Av. Carlos Nader

Robalo

Av. Cobá

Av. Cobá

Av. X-Caret

Av. Cobá

Av. Kukulcán

upwards of US$20 for a room you wouldn't let your dog sleep in. Some daredevils sleep on the beach in the *Zona;* they must evade robbers and the police. With the exception of the CREA, all hotels listed are within a 10- to 15-minute walk from Av. Tulum in the city. During high season, phone reservations are a good idea.

**CREA Youth Hostel (HI),** Paseo Kukulcán km 3 (tel. 83-13-37). For those who plan to beach or club it, CREA is the closest and cheapest place to the *Zona Hotelera.* Just catch any *Hotelera* bus from the bus station or Av. Tulum and asked to be let off at "CREA." Old and dark, CREA's best asset is its location. 200 single-sex dorm rooms with 8 bunk beds apiece. Sheets and towels provided. Ceiling fans but no A/C. Use the personal lockers when you leave the room, even to shower. No hot water. Small pool, basketball court, and table-tennis. 15-night max. stay. Check-out 1pm. No curfew. 77 pesos, plus a 50-peso deposit. 10% discount with HI card. You can pitch a tent on the front lawn for 40 pesos per person, plus a 50-peso deposit. Locker not included, but place your stuff with hostel security.

**Hotel Coral,** Sunyaxchén 30 (tel. 84-20-97). Heading west from Av. Yaxchilán, the hotel is 2 blocks down on the left; look for the big, blue building. Peppy staff and life-giving fans add to the stark, simple rooms. *Agua purificada* in the hall. Hot water. All rooms have vigorous floor fans. Check-out 1:30pm. Singles 80 pesos, with A/C 100 pesos; doubles 100 pesos, with A/C 150 pesos; triples 120 pesos, with A/C 200 pesos; 20 pesos for each additional person. To make reservations, wire payment 10 days in advance.

**Hotel Villa Rossana,** Av. Yaxchilán 25 (tel. 84-19-43). On the right past Sun Yax Chén as you come down Yaxchilán. Large and well-lit rooms with ceiling fans, balconies, hot water, and big, comfortable beds. Check-out 1pm. Singles and doubles 110 pesos; triples 143 pesos; quads 176 pesos.

**Hotel Canto,** On Av. Yaxchilán (tel. 84-12-67). As you turn off Av. Uxmal onto Yaxchilán, look for the fading pink building on your right. Hot, wearied travelers will welcome the comforts of A/C, color TV, and phones in each spacious room. Spotless, groovy-blue bathrooms with good showers and hot water. *Agua purificada* in the lobby. Singles and doubles 165 pesos; triples 185 pesos; quads 200 pesos.

**Suites Albatros,** Yaxchilán 154 (tel. 84-22-42), 2 blocks south of Cobá and across the street from the Red Cross. Further from the action, but so nice, it's hard to believe you found it listed in a budget guide. Huge rooms have vividly tiled floors, kitchens, hot water, and A/C, and center around a large, shady courtyard with walkways, benches, bamboo, and a grill. Convenience store and laundromat next door. Upstairs rooms have balconies. Singles 140 pesos; doubles 160 pesos; 40 pesos for each additional person.

## FOOD

American tourists' reluctance to experiment with their taste buds has resulted in an overpriced and underspiced culinary experience. Don't even think of eating in the *Zona Hotelera;* but also avoid eating at the very bottom of the food chain—the roadside booths serving meats of dubious origin. For good, inexpensive food try the many joints along Avs. Cobá, Tulum, and Yaxchilán. **Mercado 28,** behind the post office and circumscribed by Av. Xel-Ha, is the best option for budget fare. Numerous cafes are located in its western courtyard; a hearty *comida corrida* at **Restaurants Margely, Acapulco,** or **La Chaya** costs well under 25 pesos. La Chaya offers vegetarian meals (all open daily 8am-6pm). Almost all restaurants listed below are in Ciudad Cancún.

**El Tacolote,** Av. Cobá 19 (tel. 87-30-45), 2 blocks east of Yaxchilán. Look for the sombrero-sporting, taco-gobbling, yellow chicken out front. Prices start at 16 pesos for a large plate of grilled meat and many small tortillas; the *alambre* goes for 25 pesos. Excellent, friendly service. Open daily 11am-2am.

**Restaurante Río Nizuc,** Paseo Kukulcán km 22. Take the *"Hoteles"* bus (3 pesos) to Río Nizuc, walk across the bridge, climb down left, then walk 3min. along left of the water (follow the wooden path). Those who make the effort will be well-rewarded with a breathtaking view of the Caribbean. The crowd of locals that gathers to enjoy the secluded sea-level dining attests to the popularity and quality of the food. Enormous servings of fresh, joyfully prepared barbecued fish (30 pesos) and *mariscos* (35 pesos). Open daily 11am-6pm.

**100% Natural,** Sun Yax Chén 6 at Yaxchilán (tel. 84-36-17); another location in Plaza Caracol. Shaded, leafy porch and modern Maya deco ease overheated spirits. Savory food (entrees 30-50 pesos) and tropical shakes made from fresh juicy fruit (10-15 pesos) soothe vegetarian stomachs. Open daily 7am-11pm.

## SIGHTS

Cancún is like America with fewer rules. Visitors do not come to Cancún to see Mexico. Most visitors do not even come to Cancún to see Cancún. And even the powdery white sand beaches and glistening blue surf provide only a backdrop for the sight most of the debauched gringos have come to see: each other's semi-nude, alcohol-soaked, sunburnt bodies. Cancún's name, meaning "snake nest" in Mayan, has proven to be oddly prophetic. Progress and culture have been summarily executed and buried in a neon tank top. Since fun here requires no more than a credit card and a brainstem, your mind won't be doing much wandering. If it does, however, you run the risk of becoming painfully aware of the reality of the poverty and inequality upon which the artifice of Cancún is built.

Even if you stay inland in Ciudad Cancún, you can still take advantage of the well-groomed beaches in front of the luxury hotels in the *Zona Hotelera*. Remember, all beaches in Mexico are public property, and travelers often discreetly use hotel restrooms, fresh-water showers, and lounge chairs. If you wisely choose to avoid the resort beach scene, head for the peaceful **Playa Langosta,** west of the CREA, or for the shores south of the **Sheraton Hotel,** some of the safest and the most pleasant in Cancún. Organized beach activities include volleyball, scuba classes, and Mexican-style painting lessons; become a visitor of the hotel for the day to join in. Boogie boards can be rented at the small marina on the beach (25 pesos for 2hr.), but Cancún's surf is a whimper to the roar of the rest of the *costa turquesa*. **Playa Chac-Mool,** where waves are about 1m high, is as exciting as it gets. **Playa Linda,** a 10-minute walk east, provides the closest decent (but shallow) swimming.

While walking along Paseo Kakulcán, keep your eyes open for the iguanas and exotic birds which take advantage of the *isla*'s cultured gardens. Grab a hammock and head towards the **International Vacation Club** (km 5), across from which is a waterfront park with huts to string it up. If your hammock leaves you stiff, head to the yellow and blue building next door; **Scuba Cancún** (tel. 83-10-11) offers diving lessons (US$70), snorkeling (US$24), and other services at comparatively reasonable prices. For those with more cash on hand, try the **Marina del Ray** (tel. 85-03-00), across from the Oasis Hotel, which provides wave runners, jet skis, and parasailing, scuba diving, snorkeling, water-skiing, and deep-sea fishing equipment—all at obscenely gringo-oriented prices. The dock to the right of the CREA hostel supports a dive shop which offers two hours of snorkeling, equipment included, for about US$20.

## ENTERTAINMENT

**Bullfights** occur every Wednesday at 3:30pm, in the bullring on Bonampak at Sayil (tel. 84-54-65). Tickets are available at travel agencies on Tulum (210 pesos per person including taxi fare, less if you're in a large group) or at the bullring on a bullfight day. Show includes a cockfight and a performance by the **Ballet Folklórico.** For less brutal entertainment, the right timing could mean enjoying Cancún's celebrated jazz festival (mid- to late-May) or the refreshingly native Caribbean festival (November). Check with the tourist office for info.

If it is burning greenbacks you have and frenetic, laser-lit partying you lack, you are the reason why Cancún was erected. **Discos and bars** are to be found both downtown (at the south end of Av. Tulum near Cobá) and in the *Zona Hotelera* at Plaza Caracol (km 9 on Paseo Kukulkán). Most establishments open at 9pm and close when the crowds leave, around 5-6am. Crowds differ according to time and season—

April is college spring-breakers, June is high school graduates, and late night year-round belongs to the Latinos. Dress code is simple; less is more, and tight is just right. Bikini tops often get women in for free.

**La Boom** and **Tequila Boom,** Tel. 83-11-52. Near the youth hostel (a 10min. walk toward the *Zona*). A nightclub, bar, and pizzeria under the same roof, Boom offers the least artificial atmosphere to young crowds. Serious dancers, get ready to boogie with lasers and (yes) phone booths on stage. Tequila Boom's huge video screens are always accessible free of cover; US$10 to get inside La Boom.

**Dady'O** (tel. 83-33-33), is the premier attraction on Plaza Caracol. Cave-like entrance makes you feel like you're heading for a disco inferno ("burn, baby, burn"). The cave-scape continues through to a stage and dance floor, surrounded by winding, layered walkways whose crevices sport tables, stools, and passed-out partiers. A cafeteria in the club serves snacks (12-25 pesos). Laser show nightly at 11pm. Cover US$10; free Tues. and for women on Fri. Open daily 9pm-late.

**Dady Rock,** Tel. 83-16-26. Next door to Dady'O. All-you-can-eat/drink deals (US$7-17) several nights per week (open daily 6pm-late). Behind Dady'O, **Tequila Rock** (tel. 83-13-02) bludgeons eardrums on several different green stages. Male eardrums US$15, female eardrums US$5; open bar on Mon.

**Cat's Reggae Club** is closer to Plaza Caracol and a little easier on the ears. Coziest dance floor in town. The reggae beat reverberates around colorful walls decorated with portraits of legendary reggae artists. Cover 45 pesos, free Mon. with *Cancún Tips* card, or between 9-11pm.

**Christine,** in the Hotel Krystal (tel. 83-11-33), offers a more classy environment for an over-21 crowd (ID checked). Abundant with lasers, plants, attentive waiters, and good bass, Christine is for the more experienced partier.

**Karamba,** on Tulipanes just off Tulum, in Ciudad Cancún. Gay disco with a spacious multi-level floor, funky pop-art murals, and a colorful variety of dance music. No cover.

# ■ Isla Holbox and Chiquilá

**Isla Holbox,** as in "This is Isla Olbosshhh. Don't tell anyone about it; I want it all to myself." The great thing is, you can just about have it. Aside from July and December, when Mexican tourists flood the place, this tiny island just off the northeastern tip of the Yucatán Peninsula is home to a handful of *holboxeños* and their fishing. The pace of life here is unbelievably *tranquila*, the beaches and surrounding tiny *islas* inspiring, and the people welcoming. If you think you've never seen such a beautiful sunset, stay another night. **Chiquilá** is the unfortunate embarkation point for passengers ferrying to the secluded beaches of Isla Holbox. The small settlement will not delay in-transit tourists, but after the last ferry chugs out, late arrivals usually prefer to head back to civilization for a meal and a bed for two simple reasons: there's no place to stay in Chiquilá, and the mosquitoes suck. Literally.

**Orientation and Practical Information** Getting there requires previous planning, but it's well worth it. The easiest way to go is to take the 8:30am bus from Cancún (26 pesos), which reaches Chiquilá at 11:30am, and hop on the *lancha* of "*Los 9 Hermanos*" (boats run every 2hr., 6am-5pm, 15 pesos; return to Chiquilá every 2hr., 5am-4pm). Returning from Holbox is much easier, since both Valladolid-bound and Cancún-bound buses and vans (35 pesos) meet the early boat. Be ready to leap off when the boat strikes the dock, because the buses wait for no one. If the Cancún bus doesn't show, take the Valladolid-Mérida bus to Kantunil Kin; the Cancún bus swings by there at 6:30am. You can always flag down a Valladolid-Cancún bus at Ideal, though waiting in the sun will be torturous.

Sloshing in an incompletely drained swamp, Chiquilá is neither a pleasant nor an inviting place, and it has neither accommodations nor eateries. If you miss the last ferry to Holbox, call a *lanchero* (5-20-21) and beg them to come get you; otherwise return to **Kantunil Kin,** a town 43km south of Chiquilá on the Chiquilá access road. In Kantunil Kin, beds are available at the red-and-white **Casa de Huéspedes "Del Parque"** (tel. 5-00-17), on the other side of the basketball court next to the church (singles 55 pesos; doubles 70 pesos; triples 90 pesos).

On the Isla, the main drag from the dock, **Avenida Juárez** leads to the *zócalo* and ends up at the beach. Holbox's **public telephone** *caseta* is a half-block east of the *zócalo* on Igualdad (open Mon.-Sat. 8am-1pm and 4-8pm; 2-3 pesos). The **Centro de Salud,** on the right side of Juárez in the blue-and-white building, houses a doctor who may be awakened in case of a serious emergency. The **police** force lounges in the station at the *zócalo* on the corner of Juárez and Díaz (open daily 9am-2pm and 4-8pm, but don't count on it). There is no bank on the island. Ask around nicely, however, and someone is bound to agree to change money (at a rate that would make the Mexican banks drool).

**Accommodations and Food** Two words: simple and fish. To talk shop with the local hotel mogul, look for Sra. Dinora in **Tienda Dinora** on the southwest side of the *zócalo*. She owns the store and the hotel of the same name, as well as **Posada Los Arcos,** on the southeast side of the *zócalo*. You'll find the same price at both, although at Posada Dinora, you'll get hot water and porches onto a cool, enclosed courtyard. All rooms have fans, closets, and tiled floors (singles 70 pesos; doubles 80 pesos; triples 90 pesos). Sra. Dinora also rents out similarly priced, crude beachfront *cabañas*—though her hotel rooms are a better value. **Posada D'Ingrid,** (tel. 5-20-70) one block to the left and two blocks toward the beach from the western corner of the *zócalo,* offers gleaming salmon-colored rooms with hot water, clean bathrooms, ceiling fans, and hooks for two hammocks in addition to the double bed (70 pesos). Super nice, new quads go for 100 pesos. **Hotel Flamingo** stands close to the dock and features a view of the mainland shaded by coconut palms (4 small rooms with a fresh coat of paint, fans, and hot water; 60 pesos per person, less for longer stays).

Restaurants in Holbox follow the pace of island life, meandering through time without a fixed schedule. Among them is **Zarabanda,** one block south of the *zócalo* and two blocks east of Juárez. The cooks will prepare excellent fish and meat dishes (20-35 pesos). **Lonchería El Parque,** off the *zócalo,* two doors down from Dinora's, also has fresh, cheap seafood, but no menu—the family serves you what they have. A chicken or beef dish and a frosty beer will cost about 30 pesos (open daily 9am-10pm).

**Sights** North Beach, on the island's north shore, is pleasant enough. For more, head about 8km west from North Beach to Punta Francisca, where begins a 25km stretch of raw, unspoiled beach. The main draws, aside from sunning and sleeping, are the boat trips provided by local fishermen (4hr. cruise 300-350 pesos; try to get a group together). East of the island is **Isla de Pájaros,** called **Isla Morena** by locals, home to nearly 40 species of birds, including flamingos and pelicans. Next stop is **Ojo de Agua,** an inlet on the mainland fed by a subterranean freshwater spring. Jump in and splash around in the shallow pools. Finally, you'll head across the lagoon which separates Isla Holbox from the mainland (look out for the many dolphins) to **Isla de la Pasión,** at the western end, so named for the couples of birds and *isleños* that relax there during the off-season. During the high season, this small island caters to day-trippers with its restaurant-bar, live music, and volleyball court. To see *holboxeños* at their liveliest, cruise the brightly lit *zócalo* at dusk, when old friends and families socialize daily. Be sure to head down to the north shore sometime during the night. There, you can witness *ardentía,* a rare and completely natural phosphorescent phenomenon. Microorganisms respond to movement in the water by turning bright green; just kick the water a bit to see the eery glow. Though closed for some stretches, **Cariocas Restaurant and Disco,** on Igualdad two blocks of the *zócalo,* is *the* place to be when it's open.

YUCATÁN PENINSULA

# ■ Isla Mujeres

When the Spaniard Francisco Hernández de Córdoba blew into this tiny island (7km by 1km, 11km northeast of the coast of Quintana Roo) in 1517 looking for slaves to work the Cuban mines, he found only women. With the men fishing out at sea, Córdoba saw an island seemingly ruled by the Maya goddess of fertility, Ixchel. Looking to the deity's numerous female attendants, he dubbed the site "Island of Women." After Córdoba left, the island remained in Spanish hands, existing variously as a private hacienda, a haven for pirates, and a home to Caribbean fishermen.

Some present-day inhabitants of the island (pop. 13,500) still fish, but many now sell souvenirs and cater to the daytrippers who arrive each morning from Cancún. Popular among British and Australian travelers, the island is free from the American culture and young crowds that characterize Cancún and offers its treasures at much cheaper prices. Those who choose to linger on Isla Mujeres will discover beaches of velvety sand, supremely good snorkeling, postcard-perfect azure water, and more breathing room than exists in all of Cancún.

## ORIENTATION

Walkers will enjoy getting around the island's small but lively *centro,* although crowds pack the streets from December through February. The town is laid out in a rough grid. Right in front of the dock is **Avenida Rueda Medina,** which runs the length of the island along the coastline, past **Playas Paraíso, Lancheros, Indios,** and the **Garrafón National Park.** Perpendicular to Medina are the six major streets of the *centro:* **Avenidas López Mateos, Matamoros, Abasolo, Madero, Morelos,** and **Nicolás Bravo,** from north to south. **Avenidas Juárez, Hidalgo, Guerrero,** and **Carlos Lazo,** in that order, run parallel to R. Medina. Turning left on any of these streets will quickly lead you to **Playa Norte.** Finally, on the southern tip of the island, beyond an abandoned lighthouse, are the remains of a Maya temple, **Ix-chel.** A good source of general information is *Islander,* a local publication available at travel agency shops, the ferry dock at Puerto Juárez, and the tourist office in the *zócalo.* Maps are available both on the ferry and in the many tourist offices. The best way to explore the island for yourself is by moped—the whole trip won't take more than three hours, even with a few stops for a swim. Public buses go only as far as Playa Lancheros (3 pesos). Taxis, on the other hand, roam the length of Mujeres; you should have no problem catching one unless you're returning from Garrafón in the wee hours.

## PRACTICAL INFORMATION

**Tourist Office:** Hidalgo 7, 2nd. fl. at Plaza Isla Mujeres, between Mateos and Matamoros. Most information, including a map of the town, is also available in Islander, Cancún Tips, and Isla Mujeres Tips.

**Telephones:** Call home from one of the ubiquitous polyphones, or try the long-distance *caseta* in the lobby of **Hotel María Jose,** on Madero by R. Medina (tel. 7-01-30). Open daily 9am-2pm and 4-7pm.

**Fax:** Guerrero 13 (tel. 7-02-45), next to the post office. Open Mon.-Fri. 9am-3pm. They also have a **telegram** service.

**Ferries:** To get to the island, catch a boat from **Puerto Juárez,** 2km north of Ciudad Cancún and accessible by a "Puerto Juárez" *colectivo* (15min., 3 pesos) or by taxi (25 pesos). Passenger ferries (every hr., 8am-8pm, 45min., 6.5 pesos) and speedier cruisers (every hr., 5:30am-8:30pm, 15min., 15 pesos). Arrive early—ferries are notorious for leaving ahead of schedule if they're full. A car ferry runs to Mujeres from Punta Sam, 5km north of Puerto Juárez (8 and 11am, 2:45, 5:30 and 8:15 pm; 6 pesos per person, 36 pesos per car).

**Taxis:** Tel. 7-00-66. Lines form near sights and beaches. Rides from town to Playas Paraíso and Lancheros, Garrafón, and the ruins cost 8, 20, and 25 pesos.

**Moped Rental:** Usually 40 pesos per hr., but shop around. At **El Zorro,** on Guerrero between Abasolo and Matamoros, they go for 150 pesos (gas included) per day— enough time for Sandrine Goffard to see the entire island. Open daily 8am-6pm.

**Markets: Súper Betino,** Morelos 3, on the *zócalo*. Non-resort prices. Open daily 7am-11pm. For a better selection of produce, try the **fruit stalls** just outside or the mini-market **Isla Mujeres,** on Hidalgo between Abasolo and Madero.

**Laundry Service: Lavandería Tim Phó,** Av. Juárez 94 at Abasolo. 4kg for 25 pesos, 2hr. turnaround. Open Mon.-Sat. 7am-9pm, Sun. 8am-2pm.

**Red Cross:** Tel. 7-02-80.

**Pharmacy: Farmacia Lily,** Madero 18 at Hidalgo (tel. 7-01-64). Open daily 8:30am-9:30pm.

**Medical Assistance: Centro de Salud,** Guerrero 5 at Morelos (tel. 7-01-17). White building at the northwest corner of the *zócalo*. Open 24hr. Some doctors speak English, such as **Dr. Antonio E. Salas** (tel. 7-04-77 or beeper (91) 98-88-78-68 code 1465), Hidalgo near Madero. Will make house calls. Open 24hr.

**Police:** Hidalgo at Morelos (tel. 7-00-98), in the Palacio Municipal. Open 24hr.

**Post Office:** Guerrero and López Mateos (tel. 7-00-85), at the northwest corner of town, around the corner from the Poc-Na Hostel. Open Mon.-Fri. 9am-6pm, Sat. 9am-1pm. **Postal Code:** 70085.

**Phone Code:** 987.

## ACCOMMODATIONS AND CAMPING

Lacking the flashiness and jaw-dropping prices of Cancún, Isla Mujeres offers a number of opportunities for economical lodging. Residents are too busy chasing the waves and enjoying the island breezes to concern themselves with swindling tourists. Prices tend to fluctuate, depending on the season and length of stay; inquire ahead. Camping on the beach is not strictly regulated; most people find **Playa Indios** (½km past Playa Paraíso on R. Medina) the most hospitable and unobtrusive spot to sack out. However, it's always wise to sample local opinion before settling in for the night. All hotels listed below are in town, north of the *zócalo*.

**Poc-Na Youth Hostel,** Matamoros 15 (tel. 7-00-90) on the beach. Revolves around its high-ceilinged *palapa* dining hall, which provides ample opportunities for socializing. So do the cramped, shady dorm-like rooms, each holding 8-14 people (both single-sex and mixed available). Popular among Aussies. Small additional fees for sheets, towels, and lock. Check-out 1pm, 13 pesos more to stay later. 25 pesos per person; 3 private rooms available (60-80 pesos). Cafeteria open 7am-10pm.

**Hotel Xul-Ha,** Hidalgo 23, between Matamoros and López Mateos (tel. 7-00-75). White and boxy—very Bauhaus. Great rooms with big beds, ceiling fans, and clean bathrooms. Two sets of screened windows provide good ventilation. Lobby with color TV, English paperbacks, and coffee. Quiet location. Check-out noon. Singles 100 pesos; doubles 130 pesos; triples 150 pesos. 20 pesos more during peak season. Discounts for longer stays.

**Hotel Marcianito,** centrally located at Abasolo 10 (tel. 7-01-11), between Juárez and Hidalgo. Great central location and cute pooch. Rooms have 2 double beds, ceiling fans, and hot water. Singles 100 pesos; doubles 120 pesos; triples 140 pesos; quads 160 pesos.

**Hotel Carmelina,** Guerrero 4 at Madero (tel. 7-00-06). Crisp, clean rooms with big beds and yellow bathrooms. Hot water and fans. Singles 75 pesos; doubles 120 pesos; triples 180 pesos. A/C 15 pesos extra. 15 pesos more during peak season.

## FOOD

Not surprisingly, seafood is ubiquitous. Try *pulpo* (octopus), delicious and actually not slimy, *caracol* (conch), and the refreshingly tangy *ceviche* (seafood marinated in lime juice, cilantro, and other herbs). For cheap grub, visit the *loncherías* on Guerrero between Matamoros and López Mateos, or look for roaming vendors selling seafood from gigantic pots. Many restaurants close between lunch and dinner.

**Café Cito,** Matamoros 42 (tel. 7-04-38), at Juárez. Newly redecorated and centrally located, Café Cito offers friendly service and an excellent variety of good, cheap food. Crepes (8 pesos), sandwiches (16 pesos), and *pez caribeño* (36 pesos). If the see-through sand tabletops don't mesmerize you, Sabina, offering spiritual consultations, will give props to any and all *citos*. Open Mon.-Wed. and Fri.-Sat. 8am-noon and 6-10pm, Thurs. and Sun. 8am-noon.

**La Lomita,** 2 blocks south of Bravo on Juárez. Popular with the locals; you'll wonder how such a small place makes such tasty food. Ask for daily specials. Feast on the *filete isleño*, the *comida corrida*, or the grilled octopus (35 pesos). Breakfast 10 pesos. Open Sun.-Fri. 9am-11pm.

**Chen Huaye** ("only here" in Mayan), just off the *zócalo*, on Av. Bravo. Behind its wagonwheels-and-bars facade lies a mecca of local dishes. Entrees 15-25 pesos. Try the zesty *pescado a la veracruzana* (24 pesos). Open Thurs.-Tues. 9am-11pm.

## SIGHTS AND SAND

If you want nature at her most beautiful, you've got it: soft white beaches, rocky promontories overlooking stormy seas, lighthouses, fishing boats, and mangroves. The most popular beach is **Playa Norte. Playas Lanchero** and **Paraíso** (km 3 on R. Martínez) look a lot like it. Snorkeling connoisseurs should head to **Garrafón National Park**, 1km past Lanchero and Paraíso, whose net-enclosed waters ensure the presence of shy marine life (park open daily 9am-5pm; 15 pesos). **Bahía Dive Shop** (tel./fax 7-03-40), on Rueda Medina across from the car ferry dock, rents quality snorkeling equipment; the staff can direct you to the best spots (open Mon.-Sat. 8:30am-7pm). Or join them year-round for organized reef snorkeling (US$15), diving (US$40), and fishing trips (US$10).

**La Isleña** travel agency (tel. 7-05-78), on Morelos a half block from the dock, offers snorkeling gear (30 pesos) and mopeds (50 pesos) and organizes trips to nearby **Isla Contoy**, a wildlife sanctuary rife with pelicans, cormorants, and about 5000 other bird species. The tours include reef snorkeling at **Isla-Che** (tour lasts 8:30am-4pm; equipment and 2 meals included; 230 pesos or US$30; deposit of at least 20 pesos required the previous day; agency open daily 7am-9pm).

Although not illustrative of how nature currently is, **PESCA,** km 5 on Carretera Sac Bajo, across the Laguna de Makax from the populated northern half of the island, is a heartening example of what it could be. This biological research station is engaged in a breeding program for two (soon to be three) species of sea turtles. Female turtles, captured by PESCA in May, lay their eggs in the safety of the station's beach throughout the summer and are returned to the wild in October. The young are reared for a year before they, too, are released. For 15 pesos, a guide will take you on a stroll through the center to see the turtles and their offspring at various stages of development depending on the time of year (open daily 9am-5pm).

Don't let the signs with the promise of Maya ruins fool you; what was once the temple of **Ix-chel** is now a small pile of rocks, courtesy of Hurricane Gilbert in 1988. The drive out to the South end of the island is spectacular, however, as well as the jutting promontory where the ruins lie.

**Entertainment** Isla Mujeres' nightlife is commensurate with its small size and laid-back demeanor. Nevertheless, a handful of *locales* do what they can to keep peace-loving visitors awake at night. **Restaurant La Peña,** Guerrero 5 at the *zócalo* (tel. 7-03-09), becomes a disco after 11pm. The thatched roof and stone archway house dancing in front, water-front dining in back. **Chimbo's,** on Playa Norte, just about accounts for the rest of Mujeres's nightlife. With a temporary dance floor laid out on the sand and plastic neon palm trees, this place makes up in energy what it lacks in decor. At **Pancho Tequila,** on Matamoros between Hidalgo and Guerrero, the small dance floor and lively mix of Mexican and international dance music are as refreshing as the air-conditioning. Swinging wooden doors recall Spaghetti Westerns. Things usually start up at the bars after 10pm, but as schedules are erratic, it's best to ask around. During rainy season, plan for nighttime showers to flood streets.

# ▨ Playa del Carmen

YUCATÁN PENINSULA

Smack in the middle of Quintana Roo's legendary *costa turquesa* (Turquoise Coast), Playa del Carmen (pop. 10,000) is a crossroads for archaeologically inclined travelers en route to inland ruins and beach hunters heading for Cozumel and Cancún. Though Playa (as locals call it) used to be a fishing village, its silky white sand and startlingly blue waters made it a tourist paradise. The last 10 years have seen a huge surge of shops, hotels, and restaurants; the vast majority of the town's residents now earn tourist pesos. As a consequence, it no longer is the budget paradise of yesteryear. The town seems to have lost touch with much of its culture and history, most of which is bundled into one token ruin the size of a beachfront *cabaña*. Focusing on the present rather than the past, the town's *palapas* and moderately priced seafood restaurants look out onto the breezy pedestrian walkway, where spray-paint artists and hammock vendors hawk their wares.

## ORIENTATION

Playa is centered around its main transportation centers, the ferry dock and the bus stations. The bus drops you off on the main drag, **Avenida Principal** (Juárez), which runs west from the beach to the Cancún-Chetumal Highway 1.5km away. Most services lie along this road. At the **bus station/plaza,** perpendicular to Avenida Principal, runs **Avenida Quinta,** which is parallel to the shore and encompasses most of the *tiendas* and restaurants. East-west *calles* increase by two in either direction; north-south *avenidas* increase by five. Playa's *playa* lies one block east of Quinta.

## PRACTICAL INFORMATION

**Tourist Office:** A wooden booth on the northwest corner of the plaza, diagonally across Av. Quinta from the bus station. Self-service pamphlets only. Open daily 7am-11pm.

**Currency Exchange: Banco del Atlántico,** Av. Principal (tel. 3-02-72), on the 1st block west of the plaza. Changes U.S. dollars only. Open Mon.-Fri. 8am-1:30pm. 24hr. **ATM. Bancomer** (tel. 3-04-00), 4 blocks up the street, offers similar rates and has another **ATM.** Open Mon.-Fri. 9am-2pm and 4-6pm.

**Telephones: LADATELs** dot Quinta. There is a *caseta* inside **Maya Laundry** (tel. 3-02-61; fax 3-02-04), on Quinta 1 block from the plaza. Open daily 8am-9pm.

**Buses:** From the corner of Quinta and Principal (tel. 3-01-09), **ADO** runs 1st-class buses to Chetumal (6 per day, 4½hr., 80 pesos), Coatzacoalcos (3 per day, 12hr., 280 pesos), Córdoba (7am, 22hr., 450 pesos), Escárcega (7am and noon, 6hr., 160 pesos), Mexico City (7am, noon, and 7pm, 25hr., 450 pesos), Orizaba (7pm, 14hr., 420 pesos), Puebla (6pm, 23hr., 460 pesos), San Andrés (3:30pm, 9½hr., 320 pesos), Veracruz (3:30pm, 12hr., 362 pesos), and Villahermosa (6 per day, 12hr., 230 pesos). **Cristóbal Colón** goes to Ocosingo (4:30pm, 13hr., 251 pesos), Palenque (4:45pm, 11hr., 210 pesos), San Cristóbal (4:45pm, 15hr., 260 pesos), and Tuxtla Gutiérrez (4:45pm, 16hr., 284 pesos). **ATS** has 2nd-class service to Tulum (11 per day, 1hr., 18 pesos). **Premier** goes to Mérida (8 per day, 5hr., 89 pesos) via Ticul (3½hr., 56 pesos).

**Laundromat: Maya Laundry,** on Quinta (tel. 3-02-61), 1 block north of the plaza, on the right. Wash and dry 8 pesos per kg. Dry cleaning too. Open daily 8am-8pm.

**Supermarket: El Súper del Ahorro,** on Principal (tel. 3-03-06), 3½ blocks west of Quinta. Open daily 6:30am-10:30pm.

**Pharmacy: Farmacia París,** on Av. Principal (tel. 3-07-44), opposite the bus station. Open daily 7am-midnight.

**Medical Care: Centro de Salud,** on Av. Principal (tel. 3-03-14), across from the post office. Some English spoken. Open 24hr.

**Police:** On Av. Principal (tel. 3-02-21), 2 blocks west of the plaza. Open 24hr.

**Post Office:** On Av. Principal (tel. 3-03-00), 3 blocks from the plaza. Open Mon.-Fri. 8am-7pm, Sat. 9am-1pm. **Postal Code:** 77710.

**Phone Code:** 987.

## ACCOMMODATIONS AND CAMPING

As Playa's accommodations begin to test the tempting waters of tourist-gouging prices, bargains become more and more scarce. Fortunately, as prices rise, so does quality. Most establishments lie along either Quinta or Principal, close to the beach.

**Hotel Lilly,** on Av. Principal (tel. 3-01-16), the flaming pink building 1 block west of the plaza. Convenient but noisy location near the bus stop. Enormous, cushy beds in ordinary but clean rooms. Fans and hot water. Singles 110 pesos; doubles 140 pesos; triples 160 pesos.

**Posada Las Flores** (tel. 3-00-85), on Quinta, 2 blocks north of the plaza. New and spotless white rooms have firm beds, ceiling fans, and alcove bathrooms. Hammock-filled courtyard perfect for taking that afternoon *siesta*. Hot water takes its time coming, but stays. Singles 150 pesos; doubles 190 pesos; triples 220 pesos.

**Campamento La Ruina** (tel. 3-04-05), on the beach 200m north of the ferry dock. Popular with Europeans. Hostel-style, with communal bathrooms and cooking facilities. Ceiling fans cool *cabañas rústicas* with tiny, stiff military-style beds. Bring a lock. Singles and doubles 72 pesos; triples 165 pesos. Hammock-space under the *palapa* 25 pesos, plus 5 pesos for a plastic hammock rental. Pitch a tent in the sand for 25 pesos, 50 pesos for 2 people, plus 15 pesos for every extra camper. Lockers 5 pesos.

**CREA Youth Hostel (HI)** (tel. 3-15-08), a 1km trek from the plaza. Walk 4 blocks on Principal and turn right before Farmacia La Salud (a.k.a. Lupita). Walk another 4 blocks, passing the big concrete IMSS building. The hostel is a block and a half farther on the left. Deserted during the low season. No curfew or max. stay. Bring a lock for your locker. Single-sex dorms with quaking bunk beds 30 pesos with a 30-peso deposit. *Cabañas* with private bathrooms 120 pesos plus an 80-peso deposit. 10% discount with HI card.

## FOOD

Many snazzy restaurants and aggressive restauranteurs (*psst, happy hour!*) line Quinta. Take the time to shop around, as high prices and quality don't necessarily go hand in hand. Cheaper fruit and *torta* experiences are found along breezy Principal.

**Sabor,** 1½ blocks north on Quinta. Easily missed if you're scurrying for shade on a hot day; look for the crowded, flowery, turquoise *parasoles* next to Pez Vela. Scrumptious sandwiches made with whole-wheat bread (10 pesos) and top-notch coffee. Bean and cheese burritos (15 pesos) are fit for Chac. Open daily 8am-10pm.

**Media Luna,** on Quinta (tel. 3-00-56), 3 blocks north of the plaza. Whether you're devouring one of their healthy breakfasts or simply sipping coffee, you'll want to linger in the padded wooden corners. Unusual and delicious mango crepes (35 pesos). Open daily 7am-11pm.

**Antojitos El Correo** (tel. 3-03-99). Walk up Principal 2 blocks to the clinic, then go left 1 block. Could it be? A genuine Mexican joint in Playa? A *palapa*-roofed setting for the *comida corrida* (25 pesos) and *desayunos* (15 pesos) served up to locals. Cheap but classy. Open daily 7am-midnight.

**Playa Caribe,** just north of the bus station on Quinta. Trés chic. Enjoy your soup, fish fillet, and beer (40 pesos) to the sound of happily sunburnt foot traffic. Food tends to be on the *picante* side. Open daily 6am-11pm.

## SAND, SIGHTS, AND ENTERTAINMENT

Decorated with an occasional palm tree and fringed by the turquoise waters of the Caribbean, Playa del Carmen's **beach** is simply beautiful. Though they are relatively free of seaweed and coral, the sands remain wrought with scantily clad sunbathing tourists; the wave that began in Cancún has officially splashed down in Playa. One kilometer north of town, the beach goes **nude.** If you want a water-escape, 60-100 pesos (depending on the place and your bargaining ability) will buy you an hour's worth of **windsurfing.** Windsurfing equipment and other gear can be rented from some of the fancier hotels just south of the pier, or from shacks a few hundred meters north. **Albatros** offers windsurfing lessons; just look for the pink sign. Although Playa has no snorkeling-friendly reefs nearby, there's a decent reef 200m past the Shangri-La Caribe Hotel. The high surf often hinders visibility. While the pace of life here is gentle and relaxed, there is one thing the locals do promptly: close shop. After dark, sun-lovers recuperate from the hot rays—relaxing in swaying hammocks with a cold beer or enjoying mellow guitar strumming can soothe even the meanest burn. Come nightfall, many move on to **Karen's Grill**, on La Quinta one and a half blocks north of the plaza, which is often embellished with popular local bands (happy hour 7-9pm). Quinta teems with late-night **bars** and local **bands**—just follow the music and the crowds to find the hottest places. If you're looking for a smaller place, hop onto a bar-side saddle at **La Bamba**, where you can drink and watch music videos until 11pm (or until you fall off the saddle, whichever happens first). Only the **Calypso Bar Caribeño**, its small dance floor lit an iridescent blue, stays open late, pumping out *salsa* until the first signs of dawn brighten the sea (open daily 10pm-4am). For those with a hankering for Hollywood, **Cinema Playa del Carmen,** four blocks west of the *zócalo* and one block north of Av. Principal, has evening showings of U.S. flicks (10 pesos).

# ■ Isla Cozumel

Cozumel (pop. 60,000) originally drew attention to itself as a key trading center for the Maya and later as a pirate refuge for Sir Francis Drake and Jean Lafitte. It took Jacques Cousteau in the 1950s to call worldwide attention to the natural wonders of the nearby Palancar Reef and the sea life it sustains. The reefs were too good to be left to idealistic research, however. Cozumel has been marketed lately as an "ecological getaway" for tourists wishing to "leave" Cancún's confines and "explore" Mexico (without saying goodbye to luxury, dollars, or sycophantic service). There is more to Cozumel, however, than over-priced dive shops and snorkeling tours; while the red and white diving banner has become the island's unofficial flag, much of the island is undeveloped. Miles upon miles of empty white beach greet the tourist who musters the energy to leave Cozumel the city and explore Cozumel the island. Isolated beach-front cafes and by-the-sea roads offer splendid views of gorgeous water and plenty of opportunities to explore the famous reefs that lie below.

## ORIENTATION

The island of Cozumel lies 18km east of the northern Quintana Roo coast and 85km south of Isla Mujeres. The island is most commonly accessed via ferry from Playa del Carmen (to the west) or **Puerto Morelos** (to the north). **Ferries** from Puerto Morelos (tel. 2-09-50) transport cars to and from Cozumel twice daily, docking in the island's only town, **Cozumel,** on the west shore (9am and 1pm, 2½hr., US$30 per car, US$4.50 per person). Tourist vehicles supposedly have priority, but the **car ferry** is inconvenient and unpredictable. The tourist office recommends that you secure a spot in line 12 hours in advance. **Water Jet Service** (tel. 2-15-08) sends three boats back and forth between Playa del Carmen and Cozumel. Tickets can be bought at the dock in Cozumel and from the booth on the Playa's plaza (12 trips daily from each shore, 4am-8pm, 40min., round-trip 50 pesos). If you are coming from Cancún, an alternative to the bus-ferry ordeal is the 20-minute **air shuttle** operated by Aerocaribe.

At 53km long and 14km wide, Cozumel is Mexico's largest Caribbean island. Although public transportation is literally nonexistent, downtown streets are clearly labeled and numbered with stubborn logic. If you don't mind occasionally spine-wrenching road conditions, the rest of the island is easily explored by bike or moped. Taxis are everywhere.

As you step off the ferry into Cozumel, **Avenida Rafael Melgar** runs along the shore, circling the entire island. **Avenida Juárez,** a pedestrian walkway for the first two blocks, is directly in front of you, running perpendicular east-west to the shore and crossing the town. Juárez continues on to cross the island as **Carretera Trans-**

**YUCATÁN PENINSULA**

versal, and joins Av. Melgar on the other side. *Calles* run parallel to Juárez and are labeled *Sur* and *Norte* (Nte.) with respect to Juárez. North of Juárez, *calles* increase in even numbers; south of Juárez, they increase in odd numbers. *Avenidas* run north-south, are numbered in multiples of five, and are designated *Norte* or *Sur* with respect to Juárez. **Avenida Adolfo Rosada Salas** is between Calles 1 and 3 Sur. Av. Melgar leads south to the main points of interest: the national park at **Laguna Chankanaab** and the popular beach at **San Francisco** are south of town on the western shore, and off the island's southern tip lies the **Palancar Reef.** The nearly deserted eastern coast is dotted by Maya ruins and supports only a few restaurants and camping spots.

## PRACTICAL INFORMATION

While there are no consulates on Cozumel, Mr. Bryan Wilson (tel. 2-06-54), who works closely with the Mérida U.S. consulate, provides unofficial, free assistance to English-speaking travelers. In an **emergency,** knock on the door of the white house at Av. 15 and Calle 13 Sur.

**Tourist Office:** Tel. 2-09-72. On the 2nd floor of "Plaza del Sol," the building to the left of Bancomer on the Plaza. *Cozumel Today* has a decent map. The *Blue Guide to Cozumel* is quite helpful. Supposedly open Mon.-Fri. 8am-2:30pm.

**Currency Exchange: BanPaís** (tel. 2-16-82), right off the dock, charges a 1% commission for exchanging traveler's checks. Open Mon.-Fri. 9am-12:30pm. **Bancomer** (tel. 2-05-50), on the plaza, has the same rates but charges a flat fee of US$.50 per check. Open Mon.-Fri. 8:30am-5:30pm, Sat. 10am-2pm. **Banco del Atlántico** (tel. 2-01-42), on the plaza, has a 24hr. **ATM.** Open Mon.-Fri. 9am-2pm, Sat. 10am-1pm. Cozumel is also a *casa de cambio* heaven.

**Telephones: LADATELs** throughout the city. The **Calling Station,** Av. Melgar between Calles 3 and 5 Sur (tel. 2-14-17), allows you to interface with loved ones.

**Fax:** Tel. 2-00-56. Next to the post office. From here, you can send faxes. You can send **telegrams,** too STOP Open Mon.-Fri. 8am-6pm STOP Sat. 9am-noon STOP

**Airport:** Tel. 2-04-85. 2km north of town. **Aerocaribe and Aerocozumel** (tel. 2-34-56), **Mexicana** (tel. 2-00-05), and **Continental** (tel. 2-08-47) serve Cozumel.

**Ferries:** Passenger ferries leave every hr. starting at 5am from the dock at the end of Av. Juárez (23 pesos). Arrive early, as ferry departures are frequently off-schedule. Buy tickets at the corner of Melgar and the dock. **Car ferries** leave from the dock south of main dock.

**Taxis:** Tel. 2-02-36. From the plaza, 20 pesos to the airport; 43 pesos to Chankanaab; 70 pesos to Punta Morena. Expect to pay more for more people.

**Car Rental: Smart Rent-a-Car,** Av. 5 between Calle 1 and Salas (tel. 2-43-81). VW Beetle US$35 per day, more in peak season. Open daily 7:30am-6:30pm. Will demand a driver's license and major credit card.

**Moped Rental:** Pretty expensive. Get one outside Hotel Posada Edem (see below) for about 160 pesos. Haggle for all you're worth.

**Bike Rental: Rentadora Cozumel,** Av. 10 at Calle 1 Sur (tel. 2-11-20 or 2-15-03). 40 pesos per day. Return by 6pm. US$20 deposit required. Open daily 8am-8pm.

**Bookstore: Agencia de Publicaciones Gracia** (tel. 2-00-31), on the plaza. Last week's *Newsweek* for the price of a meal (25-35 pesos). Open daily 8am-10pm.

**Laundromat: Margarita,** Av. 20 Sur 285 near Calle 3 Sur (tel. 2-28-65). Self service 10 pesos per machine, soap 3 pesos. Open Mon.-Sat. 7am-9pm, Sun. 9am-5pm.

**Red Cross:** Av. 20 Sur at Av. Adolfo Salas (tel. 2-10-57 or 2-10-58). Open 24hr.

**Pharmacy: Farmacia Kiosco** (tel. 2-24-85), on the *zócalo* near Hotel López. Everything for the sun-happy or sun-sick tourist. Open daily 8am-10pm.

**Medical Services:** There are several English-speaking private physicians in Cozumel. Try **Dr. M. F. Lewis,** Av. 50 at Calle 11 (tel. 2-09-12) for consultations or 24hr. tourist medical service. **Medical Center (CEM),** Av. 20 Nte. 425 between Calles 10 and 8 Nte. (tel. 2-29-19 or 2-14-19). For an **ambulance,** call 2-14-19.

**Police:** Calle 11 Sur near Rafael Melgar (tel. 2-00-92), in the Palacio Municipal. For English service, call 2-04-09 and ask for **James García** or another bilingual officer.

## San Miguel de Cozumel

**ACCOMMODATIONS**
Hotel Posada Edem, 3
Hotel Marruang, 11
Posada Letty, 8

**RESTAURANTS**
El Abuelo Gerardo, 4
Cocina Económica Mi Chabelita, 9

**SIGHTS & SERVICES**
Museo de la Isla de Cozumel, 2
Tourist Office, 5
Bancomer, 6
Banco del Atlántico, 7
Blue Bubble Divers, 13
Red Cross, 10
Medical Center (CEM), 1
The Calling Station, 12
Post Office, 14
Police, 15

Map not drawn to scale

YUCATÁN PENINSULA

**Post Office:** Off Rafael Melgar just south of Calle 7 Sur (tel. 2-01-06), along the sea. Open Mon.-Fri. 8am-8pm, Sat. 9am-noon. **Postal Code:** 77600. **Phone Code:** 987.

## ACCOMMODATIONS AND CAMPING

Although hotels in Cozumel are more expensive than in Playa, your extra pesos buy higher-quality rooms. Peak-season travelers should expect slightly higher prices and should hunt down a room before noon. Clean, reasonably cheap accommodations lie within blocks of the plaza—resist being roped into a pricey package deal when you step off the ferry. Secluded camping spots are at **Punta Morena** and **Punta Chiqueros,** on the island's Caribbean coast. Short-term campers should encounter no problems with the authorities, but for longer stays, you might want to consult the tourist office to find out what the best camping options are.

**Hotel Posada Edem,** Calle 2 Nte. 12 between Calles 10 and 15 (tel. 2-11-66). Upon docking, go left 1 block, turn right, and walk up 2 blocks. Astoundingly clean rooms with fresh linen, 2 beds, fans, fluffy towels, and hot water. English books in lobby. Up to 3 people 75 pesos; each additional person 20 pesos; add 82 pesos for A/C and TV.

**Hotel Marruang,** on Av. Adolfo Salas (tel. 2-16-78 or 2-02-08), just past Av. 20. Look for the dentist sign on the big blue building. Brand new, this hotel shines like freshly brushed teeth. Spotless floors lead to comfy beds, ceiling fans, and fantastic bathrooms with hot water. Singles and doubles 130 pesos; triples 160 pesos.

**Cabañas Punta Morena,** Carretera Transversal km 17. For those who have their own transportation. Next to a beachfront seafood restaurant, these *cabañas* have a fabulous view that beats any resort. Rooms lack hot water and furniture, but you'll be so mesmerized by the view, you won't even notice. At night during summer, turtles come to lay their eggs on the nearby shore. Volleyball court on the beach. Surfboards (100 pesos) and boogie boards (50 pesos) for rent. All rooms 85 pesos.

**Posada Letty,** Calle 1 Sur past Av. 10 (tel. 2-02-57). Their business card promises "Cleanliness-Order-Morality." We can only vouch for the former. Big green rooms have big windows, big beds, and little else. Feels more like a house than a hotel. Singles 110 pesos; doubles 120 pesos; triples 150 pesos; quads 180 pesos.

## FOOD

Food in Cozumel tends to be expensive, especially if you buy it near the beach or the plaza. Avoiding places that advertise in English will keep pesos in your pockets. There are several moderately priced restaurants a few blocks from the center, as well as some small *típico* cafes hiding on side streets. The **market,** on Av. Adolfo Salas between Av. 20 and 25 Sur, offers the standard items: meat, fish, and fruits. The five small restaurants outside the market offer generous portions of regional dishes. For a quick treat, stop by at the **Panificadora Cozumel,** on Calle 2 Nte. between Quinta and Melger (or another branch, Av. 10 Sur at Calle 3 Sur), where pastries and baked goods can be had for pocket change (open daily 6am-9:30pm).

**El Paso del Cedral,** opposite the road to the El Cedral ruins on the southwestern tip of the island. A bit far, but worth it. The seafood arrives on shore mere seconds before you do. Accompany Don Carlos, the chef, to choose the very fish you want. Get a few people together and go in for the house specialty, a monstrous red snapper (about 100 pesos—haggle). String up a hammock on the serene public beach for a post-feast *siesta* before you snorkel the nearby reef. Open daily 10am-6pm.

**Alfalfa's,** Calle 1Sur between Av. 10 and 15, across from Posada Letty. Chic vegetarian restaurant serves a huge *comida del día* (55 pesos) and lemonades to match. Some meat dishes. Good selection of English books. Open daily 11am-11pm.

**El Abuelo Gerardo,** on Av. 10 between Juárez and Calle 2 Nte. (tel. 2-10-12). A mellow place to grab an ice-cold afternoon beer. *Antojitos* 10-30 pesos. For something more substantial, try a fish fillet (28-35 pesos). Good breakfasts (7-20 pesos) with some of the best toast in Mexico. Open daily 7:30am-10:30pm.

**Restaurant Casa Denis** (tel. 2-00-67), across from the flea market on the *zócalo*. Ancient sketches and the 116-year-old (and aging!) *mamey* tree glorify this cheerful and sunny spot. Wide choice of breakfast (12-17 pesos). Sandwiches 7-20 pesos. Good view of rip-off restaurants across the plaza. *Comida regional*, including seafood plates, 28-48 pesos. Open daily 7am-10:30pm.

**Cocina Económica Mi Chabelita,** on Av. 10 Sur near Adolfo Salas (tel. 2-08-96). Great budget dining in a bright, coral-colored garage. Great *comida corrida* (18 pesos). Fried bananas (6 pesos) are simply orgasmic. Open Mon.-Sat. 8am-9pm.

## CORAL, SAND, AND SIGHTS

Most visitors to Cozumel have one sight in mind: the beautiful coral reefs around the island. Mopeds are the best way of getting to your favorite snorkeling spot or finding a new one. Be nice to yourself and get some wheels. Otherwise, expensive taxis will be your only option. Although hitchhiking is possible, it's uncertain, and dehydrating.

As you head south out of town on a counter-clockwise circuit of the island, **Hotel La Ceiba** makes a good stop-off point for snorkeling. You could walk through the hotel restaurant sporting a snorkel, fins, and a G-string, and the management still wouldn't care. Even if they did, all beaches in Mexico are public property, so you'd just be exercising your rights. The hotel has a beach perfect for swimming and a reef and plane wreck offshore waiting to be explored. The **Del Mar Aquatics** dive shop (tel. 2-08-44), 200m north of La Ceiba, rents out snorkeling gear (US$6 per day) and scuba equipment (US$35 per day), as well as offering deep-sea fishing, night/day dives, and snorkeling trips (open daily 7:30am-7:30pm).

**Chankanaab National Park,** a few more kilometers down the coastal highway, is comprised of the *laguna*, a botanical garden, museum, restaurant, snorkel area, and a

## Under the Sea

The **Palancar Reef** of Cozumel, the second-largest in the world, continually draws legions of scuba fanatics eager to explore its dramatic underwater formations. While the aesthetics are unmistakable, few visitors realize the biological importance of those majestic coral pillars. Coral is to a reef as topsoil is to a rainforest—without it, the basis of all life disappears. If the coral is destroyed, the entire reef's ecosystem disintegrates. International law prohibits the harvesting of coral, but it does not forbid the purchase or exportation of coral-derived jewelry and crafts. Several shops in Cozumel sell goods made from black coral, and, by patronizing these establishments, tourists heighten the demand for coral and adversely affect the splendorous reefs they have come to see.

few gift shops. A stroll through the endemic forest in the botanical garden, past the 1m-long beady-eyed, sunbathing iguanas, brings you to a few paltry ruins. The perfectly oval natural lagoon, once brimming with reef fish, is now home to the hardy survivors of years of gringo sunscreen attrition. Never mind; the real attraction is the abundant tropical fish and coral in the Caribbean a few meters away. Matching the crowds on land, the reef teems with eels, anemones, and gorgeous fish. The small museum focuses on the park's natural resources and houses some fantastic photographs of the underwater caves in the lagoon (open daily 7am-6pm; admission 35 pesos; for more info, contact the **Fundación de Parques** in town, tel. 2-09-14).

The best underwater sightseeing in Cozumel is likely to be on the offshore reefs, accessible by boat. You can rent snorkeling equipment anywhere on the island, including at Laguna Chankanaab and Playa de San Francisco. The standard rate is US$5-10 per day, plus deposit. Most of the numerous **dive shops** in town are on the waterfront or on Calle 3 Sur between Av. Melgar and Av. 10. Always consider safety before price; look for shops with a **CADO** (Cozumel Association of Dive Operators) insignia on their door. **Blue Bubble Divers** (tel. 2-18-65), Av. 5 and Calle 3 Sur, has a mellow, English-speaking staff and a choice of 20 reefs to visit (1½hr. single-tank dive US$41, snorkeling equipment US$6 per day; open daily 7am-9pm). Another option is **Aqua Safari,** Melgar at Calle 5 Sur (single-tank dive US$25, 2hr. snorkeling boat trip US$15; open daily 7am-1pm and 4-6:30pm).

The route along the eastern coast passes many secluded beaches that would make for good camping spots. Always ask before pitching a tent. While the beaches boast magnificent turquoise waters, the water is turbulent and somewhat dangerous; it should be treated with cautious respect. Midway along the coast, Carretera Transversal branches west and loops back through the jungle to town.

Between beach hops and reef drops, you may want to hunt down one of several small ruins in Cozumel's overgrown interior. You can visit **El Cedral** and the **Tumba de Caracol** ruins on a bumpy trek to the **Celarain Lighthouse,** on the island's southernmost point. The top of the lighthouse offers a thrilling view of the northern shores of the island. To get to the crumbled stone structures of **San Gervasio,** the only extensively excavated and partially reconstructed ruin on the island, take Juárez out of town. After 8km, a "San Gervasio" sign marks a gravel road branching to the left. The ruins are another 8km down this road (site open daily 8am-4pm; admission 17 pesos). The small, air-conditioned **Museo de la Isla de Cozumel** (tel. 2-14-75 or 2-14-74), on the waterfront between Calles 4 and 6, is filled with photographs and artifacts (open daily 9am-5pm; admission US$3). Check for other cultural events in the **Centro de Convenciones,** between the Plaza del Sol and Bancomer, or in the plaza itself, where locals gather on Sunday nights for family fun.

## ENTERTAINMENT

Though not as expensive as Cancún, Cozumel's nightlife is targeted towards the spendthrift gringos who jaunt into town from their cruise ships. Cozumel is emptier at night than might be expected for a town of its size, largely because the tour package herds tend to stay in their hotels after dinner. Obnoxiously boisterous all night long, **Carlos 'n' Charlie's,** on Rafael Melgar (tel. 2-01-91), just one block north of the dock, entertains *norteamericanos* with crazy drinks, slammer contests, and arm-wrestling matches. Occasional awards of free tequila to those willing to make fools of themselves (*cerveza* 14 pesos; open daily 10am-1:30am). A mellow, more native crowd enjoys reggae music and relives the swinging 70s at **Joe's Lobster Bar,** on Av. 10, between Calles 1 and 3 Sur (tel. 2-32-75). A live band starts up the action at 10:30pm and the place keeps kicking until 2 or 3am. For the best in live Mexican music (rock, reggae, salsa) under a hip groovy-colored *palapa,* head to **Raga,** on Salas between Calles 10 and 15. Live music begins and attractive *cozumeleños* converge nightly around 9pm (open daily 5pm-12:30am). The full-fledged disco **Neptuno** (tel. 2-15-37), five blocks south of the plaza, has multi-leveled dance floors bombarded with lasers and throbbing bass (open daily 9pm-early morning; cover 32 pesos).

For action and romance with happy endings and no alcohol, try **Cinema Cozumel,** on Av. Rafael Melgar between Calles 2 and 4, or **Cine Cecillo Borques,** on Juárez between Av. 30 and 35. Borques is cheaper (12 pesos) but more remote.

# ■ Tulum

On the eastern edge of the age-old Etaib (Black Bees) jungle, halfway down the Caribbean coast of the Yucatán, lies the walled Maya "City of the Dawn." Although the architecture of the ruins here may be less impressive than that at Uxmal and Chichén Itzá, the backdrop is stunning. Tulum's graying temples and nearly intact watchtowers rise above tall, wind-bent palm trees, clinging to a cliff above white sand pummeled by the steely-blue Caribbean Sea, forming one of Mexico's most photogenic scenes (see the cover of this book). Tulum brings together two of the best aspects of the Yucatán: archaeological wonders and Caribbean waters. First settled in the 4th century AD, Tulum was the oldest continuously inhabited city in the New World when the Spanish arrived. Today, sun worshippers of a different kind tramp through the ancient city, complementing their sightseeing with a healthy dose of swimming.

## ORIENTATION

Located 42km southeast of Cobá, 63km south of Playa del Carmen, and 127km south of Cancún, Tulum (pop. 12,000) is the southernmost link in the chain of tourist attractions on the Caribbean coast of Quintana Roo, and the eastern extreme of the major Maya archaeological sites. Although few people live here, Tulum sprawls out over three separate areas: *el crucero* (the crossroads), the beach *cabañas,* and **Pueblo Tulum.** Arriving in Tulum from Cancún on Rte. 307, buses first stop at *el crucero,* a few kilometers before town. Here, a couple of restaurants, hotels, and overpriced minimarts huddle together 800m west of the ruins. The well-paved access road turns south at the ruins, leading to food and lodging at *cabañas* 2km farther down the road. Pueblo Tulum, 4km south of *el crucero,* offers travelers a handful of roadside restaurants, minimarts, and some services.

Second-class **buses** provide cheap transportation from Tulum to nearby cities and to the sights and beaches which lie to the north on Rte. 307. Some travelers hitchhike from sight to sight along the highway. Taxis congregate at *el crucero* and at the bus stop at Pueblo Tulum.

## PRACTICAL INFORMATION

The few services available in Pueblo Tulum are along Rte. 307, which serves as the tiny town's main street. There is no tourist office, though a few stands at the ruins can provide sketchy maps. Those desperate to exchange money can do so at the *crucero* or next to the bus office in Pueblo Tulum.

**Telephones:** Shiny new public phones line Rte. 307 in Pueblo Tulum. **Caseta de Tulum** (tel./fax 1-20-09) is a block from the bus station. Open daily 7am-9pm.

**Buses:** A small waiting room sandwiched between 2 currency exchange booths opposite the Hotel Maya. **ADO** to Coatzacoalcos (8am, 11hr., 260 pesos), Córdoba (8am, 12hr., 390 pesos), Escárcega (8am, 4hr., 140 pesos), Mexico City (8am, 22hr., 480 pesos), San Andrés (4:30pm, 9hr., 300 pesos), Veracruz (4:30pm, 12hr., 340 pesos), and Villahermosa (4:30pm, 9hr., 221 pesos). Various **2nd-class buses** run to Cancún (14 per day, 2hr., 24 pesos), Chetumal (12 per day, 4hr., 44 pesos), Chichén Itzá (6 per day, 3½hr., 42 pesos), Cobá (9 per day, ½hr., 10 pesos), Escárcega (4:30pm, 8hr., 130 pesos), Mérida (4 per day, 5hr., 60 pesos), Ocosingo (4:30pm, 15hr., 180 pesos), Palenque (4:30pm, 14hr., 163 pesos), Playa del Carmen (14 per day, 1hr., 14 pesos), San Cristóbal (4:30pm, 16hr., 200 pesos), and Valladolid (5 per day, 25hr., 30 pesos).

**Taxis:** Available at *el crucero*, in Pueblo Tulum, along Rte. 307, and at various *cabañas*. From *el crucero* to Pueblo Tulum 10 pesos, to *cabañas* 25 pesos.

**Pharmacy: Súper Farmacia,** just past the post office. Open daily 8am-9pm. English-speaking **Dr. Arturo F. Ventre** available Mon.-Sun. 8am-noon and 6-9pm.

**Police:** Tel. 1-20-55. In the Delegación Municipal, 2 blocks past the post office.

**Post Office:** A few hundred meters into town on Rte. 307. Open Mon.-Fri. 9am-1pm and 3-6pm. **Postal Code:** 77780.

**Phone Code:** 987.

## ACCOMMODATIONS AND CAMPING

Tulum offers two lodging options: hotels at *el crucero* in town, or beachside *cabañas*. If you plan on staying only one night to visit the ruins, the road hotels can't be beat for sheer economy. However, your inner beach bum will be much happier in the *cabañas*. There you can chill with mellow international travelers and perfect your tan on the spectacular beach. Don't be afraid to ask for help with a hammock if it's (blush!) your first time. (Hint: protect your back by sleeping crosswise, not lengthwise.) *Let's Go* is not to blame if you end up staying for a month. Or two.

**Cabañas Santa Fe,** just off the paved road 1km south of the ruins. Follow the signs to Don Armando's and turn left. Diversity and a sandy ass are the twin hallmarks of the Cabañas Santa Fe experience. If you don't mind the perpetual sand, you can shack up here with backpackers from all over the world. Several sticks 'n' *palapa* combos to choose from: bare *cabaña* with sand floor and small hammock 40 pesos. 1-bed *cabaña* with cement floor 70 pesos; 2-bed *cabaña* 140 pesos; hammock rental 20 pesos per night. Mosquito-net rental 5-10 pesos per night.

**Don Armando Cabañas** (tel. 4-76-72 or 1-13-54), on the paved road 1km south of the ruins. A humble paradise with a volleyball court. Don Armando is absolutely delightful, the *cabañas* are generally solid and secure, and the communal facilities are spotless. *Cabaña* with 1 bed and 1 hammock 80 pesos, with 2 beds 100-120 pesos. Deposit 50 pesos. Camp or hang a hammock for 20 pesos per person.

**Hotel Maya,** on Rte. 307 across from the bus station in Pueblo Tulum. Small, stuffy singles—bigger rooms have more air, and more charm. Singles 70 pesos; doubles 100 pesos; triples 150 pesos.

## FOOD

Though the points of interest in Tulum tend to be rather spread out, a hearty and inexpensive bite of *típico* food is never too far away. Both the Pueblo and the *crucero* have satisfying and authentic restaurants as well as *mini-súpers;* the former are slightly cheaper and provide filling sustenance for daytrips.

**Restaurante El Crucero,** in Hotel El Crucero. Comfortable and shady interior provides respite from all that Maya sun. Get intimate with that old standby, *pescado al mojo de ajo* (35 pesos). Breakfast (fruit salad, orange juice, toast, and coffee) 19-30 pesos. Open daily 7am-9pm.

**Restaurante Santa Fe,** at the campground on the beach. Mellow reggae tunes, the rumble of surf, the newly reconstructed *palapa*, the *cabaña*-like sand floor, the fresh fish (30-40 pesos), and quesadillas (18 pesos) are the 6 hallmarks of the Restaurante Santa Fe experience. Restaurant and bar open daily 7am-11pm.

**Cocina Económica,** a block south of Hotel Maya in Pueblo Tulum. The name almost says it all, but leaves out the crucial "tasty" part. 15 pesos gets you the day's entree, served, of course, with beans and tortillas. Open daily 7:30am-10:30pm.

## SIGHTS

### The Ruins

The ruins would offer a great view of the sea, if only you could climb them (they're roped off). The murals would be beautiful, if only you could see them (they too are roped off). While all you can do is walk around the bases and stare at the ocean, the dramatically situated site certainly still merits a visit. The first thing you see in Tulum will be the still-impressive **dry-laid wall** that surrounded the city center's three landlocked sides. The wall, made of small rocks wedged together, was originally 3.6m thick and 3m high. It shielded the city from the aggression of neighboring Maya city-states and prevented all but the 150 or so priests and governors of Tulum from entering the city for most of the year. After Tulum's defeat at the hands of the Spanish in 1544, the wall fended off English, Dutch, and French pirates and, in 1847, gave rebel Maya refuge from government forces during the Caste War. Magnificent representations of a **figure diving into the water** cover the western walls. The images, depicting the Maya sunset god, are illuminated every evening by the rays of the setting sun. Other stone inscriptions (giant phallus, anyone?) show Tulum to have been the center of a religious fertility cult.

Just inside and to the left of the west gate stand the remains of platforms which once supported huts. Behind these platforms are the **House of the Halach Uinik** (the House of the Ruler), characterized by a traditional Maya four-column entrance; the **Palacio,** the largest residential building in Tulum; and the **Temple of the Paintings,** a stellar example of post-Classical Maya architecture. Well-preserved 600-year-old murals inside the temple depict deities intertwined with serpents, as well as fruit, flower, and corn offerings. Masks of Itzamná, the Maya Creator, occupy the northwest and southwest corners of the building.

**El Castillo,** the most prominent structure in Tulum, looms behind the smaller buildings and over the rocky seaside cliff. Serving as a pyramid and temple, it commands a view of the entire walled city. It also served as a lighthouse, allowing returning fishermen to find the only gap in the barrier reef just offshore. Its walls, like those of many buildings in Tulum, slope outward, but the doorposts slope inward. The castle's architectural and structural eccentricities are due to its numerous rebuildings.

In front of the temple is the sacrificial stone where the Maya held battle ceremonies. Once the stars had been consulted and a propitious day determined, a warrior-prisoner was selected for sacrifice. At the climax of the celebration, attendants painted the warrior's body blue—the sacred color of the Maya—and the chief priest cut his heart out and poured the blood over the idols in the temple. The body was given to the soldiers below, who were thought to acquire the strength to overcome their enemies through cannibalism.

To the right of El Castillo on the same plaza is the **Temple of the Initial Series.** Named after a stela found here, the temple bears a date that corresponded to the beginning of the Maya religious calendar in the year AD 761. The **Temple of the Descending God,** with a fading relief of a feathered, armed deity diving from the sky, stands on the other side of El Castillo's plaza. Perched on its own precipice on the other side of the beach, the **Temple of the Winds** was acoustically designed to act as a storm-warning system. Surely enough, before Hurricane Gilbert struck the site in 1988, the temple's airways dutifully whistled their alarm (site open daily 8am-5pm; admission 16 pesos, free Sun.; guided tours about 150 pesos for 1-5 people, 200 pesos for groups up to 25 people).

**Getting There:** Tulum's ruins lie a brisk eight-minute walk east of Rte. 307 from the *crucero.* For the supremely lazy, a dinky **train** (7 pesos) covers the distance in slightly less time. Admission tickets are sold at a booth to the left of the parking lot.

### The Beach

Hanging out on the beach in *cabañas* is a popular way to end a day at the ruins. Expect the Europeans to turn it into a topless affair; some even strip to their bare butts. Nude bathing is tolerated, and it usually takes one uninhibited soul to start the ball rolling, so to speak. The ever-vigilant Mexican Navy drops in occasionally to tell everyone to get back in uniform, but once the nudity-patrol is out of sight, the bathing suits are replaced by the birthday suits once again. *Cabaña* managers complain if you walk through the campgrounds in the buff.

Offshore, you can see the waves mysteriously breaking on Tulum's **barrier reef,** the largest in the Americas; it runs the full length of the Yucatán peninsula, including Belize. Although the water here is not as clear as at Xel-Ha or Akumal (see below), the fish are just as plentiful. To enjoy them, you can rent scuba and snorkeling equipment from the **dive shop** (tel. 1-20-96) at **Cabañas Santa Fe** (35 pesos per day for snorkeling; open daily 8am-3:30pm). The shop plans trips to the reef and a nearby *cenote* (US$15, including rental, *antojitos,* and *refrescos*). You can also get scuba certified here (US$30) or go diving in the Cenote Dos Ojos (you must be an experienced diver; US$50; see p. 550). Get fins if you snorkel; the 500m swim to the reef is often a struggle against a north-south current.

To escape the beaches, waves, and salty water, rent a bike from Cabañas Santa Fe (20 pesos per hr.) and visit one of the *cenotes* in the woods near Pueblo Tulum. Look for a small patch of gravel, large enough for two cars, on the right side of the road as you head toward Chetumal. Follow a rugged path to the serene **Cenote Escondido** or the smaller **Cenote Cristal** 100m farther down the road.

## ■ Near Tulum

A few kilometers south of Tulum on the coast road lies the 1.5-million-acre **Sian Ka'an Biosphere Reserve.** Sanctuary to over 345 species of birds as well as every endangered cat species of southern Mexico, the reserve also guards a wide range of wetland and marine habitats, as well as 27 Maya sites. Entrance is free but limited, and *lancha* tours are given exclusively by Sian Ka'an biologists. For more info, contact **Amigos de Sian Ka'an** in Cancún, Av. Cobá 5, (tel. (98) 84-95-83; fax 87-30-80; email sian@cancun.rce.com.mx), in Plaza América.

### XEL-HA AND AKUMAL

Though swimming is not permitted in the lagoon for which **Xel-Ha** (SHELL-ha) is famous, its natural aquarium, almost 2m deep, is a fun (and expensive) place for snorkeling. You can splash around all you want in the *caleta* (inlet) nearby. Don't bet on seeing any unusual fish life, but you can find parrot fishes and 1m-long barracudas toward the rope which marks the open sea. For relative peace during busy times, cross the inlet and explore the underwater caves, where an altar was once discovered. Be careful and don't go duck-diving under overhangs on your own. Note the bizarre incidence of cool seawater with a warm undercurrent of subterranean fresh water. It is the confluence of these water sources that sometimes impairs underwater visibility. The steep 120-peso entrance fee includes visits to two *cenotes,* a natural river, underground sea caves, and a hammock siesta. You still have to pay for rental of snorkel equipment, which is available near the inlet for 49 more precious pesos (no discounts this time). Visit before noon, when busloads of tourists from the resorts overrun the place. Lockers (7 pesos plus a 3-peso deposit) and towels (10 pesos plus a 30-peso deposit) are available at the shower area (open daily 8:30am-6pm).

Xel-Ha also maintains a small archaeological site on the highway, 100m south of the entrance to the inlet. **El Templo de Los Pájaros** and **El Palacio,** small Classical and post-Classical ruins, were only recently opened to the public. The former (the ruin farthest into the jungle) overlooks a peaceful, shady *cenote* where swimming is permitted. A strategically hung rope-swing makes the experience all the more Tarzan-esque. The jungle at Xel-Ha is rife with mosquitoes, so bring insect repellent (site open daily 8am-5pm; admission 10 pesos).

A few kilometers north of Xel-Ha towards Playa del Carmen lies the bay of **Akumal.** An older, wealthier crowd is drawn to its older, wealthier underwater attractions. The **Akumal Dive Shop** (tel. (987) 4-12-59) rents **snorkeling equipment** (US$6 per day), organizes **snorkeling** and **scuba trips** (US$20 per person; US$25 per one-tank dive), and offers **cavern-diving courses** (US$350; open daily 8am-1pm and 2-5pm).

**Getting There:** Xel-Ha lies 15km north of Tulum; Akumal is 10km farther north. Get on any northbound **bus** and ask to be let off at the site of your choice (5 pesos). Taxis charge exorbitant rates. Hitchhiking here is tough because the traffic is fast and the wait can be unnerving. Getting back to Tulum at the end of the day, when buses begin to come less and less frequently, can be more challenging than beating Dingle Hoggs in a match of wits. Vigorously wave down a bus on its way to Tulum or Cancún. Locals will usually be able to tell you when the next one is due to pass.

## CENOTE DOS OJOS

**Cenote Dos Ojos,** 1km south of Xel-Ha, is the second largest underwater cavern in the world, stretching for 33,855m. It was originally a dry cave system with beautiful rock formations in shades of amber as well as massive calcic stalactites, stalagmites, and natural wind-etchings. The whole system was flooded long, long ago, preserving the caves in their new underwater condition. It is now possible to **snorkel** and **dive** in the *cenote,* along with tetras, mollies, and swordfish. You must be an experienced diver with a minimum of 40 dives under your belt, including night dives.

The trip begins with a bumpy 20-minute ride in an open truck. Monstrous bugs, fit for any Indiana Jones movie, whiz by as you zip through the pristine jungle. A complete underwater circuit of the caves, at a depth of 10m, takes about 45 minutes. Meanwhile, snorkelers can explore the larger of the two (*dos ojos*—aha!) cave entrances. For divers and snorkelers alike, this is a unique opportunity to explore a spectacular unspoiled cave system which has only been open to the public since 1993. The dive costs US$50 (plus US$15 equipment rental). Snorkelers pay US$25. Three trips depart daily from **Dos Ojos Dive Center** (tel. (987) 4-12-71), several hundred meters south of the park entrance, at 10am, noon, and 2pm. Trips also leave from the **Cabañas Santa Fe** (see p. 547).

# ■ Cobá

Deep within the Yucatán jungle, Cobá receives less attention than her big sisters, Chichén Itzá and Tulum. The government has poured less money into the site, leaving an estimated 6500 buildings unexcavated. Here, for a change, mosquitoes outnumber tourists; Cobá is a site you can truly explore for yourself. In the jungle surrounding this ancient city (in its heyday, it is estimated, the city spread out over 10 square kilometers), lizards bask on private pyramids, spider monkeys rustle the tops of trees, and the ever-fierce *yucateco* mosquito is never far away. Early visitors can explore the site to a cacophony of birds, and just might find themselves alone atop a pyramid looking down on one of Cobá's four lakes. The site's isolation only heightens the impressiveness of its towering **Nohoch Múl,** which at 42m is the tallest Maya structure in the northern Yucatán. The town of Cobá itself, unfortunately, is little more than a glorified tourist trap.

**Practical Information** **Expreso de Oriente buses** head to Cancún (6:30am, 1:30, and 3:30pm, 2½hr., 28 pesos), Chichén Itzá (9:30am and 2pm, 1½hr., 27 pesos), Mérida (9am and 2pm, 2½hr., 46 pesos), Playa del Carmen (4 per day, 1½hr., 27 pesos), Tulum (5 per day, ½hr., 12 pesos), and Valladolid (9:30am, 1hr., 21 pesos).

**Accommodations and Food** Many houses near the ruins rent rooms. The **Hotel Bocadito,** right at the small ADO booth, has cement platform beds, un-hot water, and private baths that could use a wee bit more washing. Singles and doubles 70-80 pesos. Popular with tour buses—you'll likely have lots of company. For a comprehensive budget feast, try the hotel restaurant's *menú del día,* which includes soup, nachos, an entree with tacos, bread, dessert, and coffee (28 pesos). Good thing your bed is only a short stagger away (open daily 6:30am-9pm). **Nicté Ha,** on the shore a stone's throw west of the T-junction, is an idyllic spot for breakfast. Mexican crooners pluck out their heartstrings on the radio and early birds (before 8am or so) may catch a glimpse of an alligator paddling about just offshore. The super-friendly owner will let you browse through her Cobá guidebooks on request. Dinner entrees run 35-40 pesos (open daily 6am-9pm). Although the food at the **Hotel Villa Arqueológicas** is a bit expensive, a salad or drink will buy access to their garden-side pool. Take a break from the heat and revel in the courtyard of this resort, whose rooms start at 400 pupil-popping pesos.

**The Ruins** To get to the ruins, walk south on the main street in town as far as the T-junction at the lake. Here, take a left onto the Av. Voz Suave (Soft Voice); the ruins are a five-minute walk down the road. It's a good idea to find a guide at the entrance, as this will make the visit much more enlightening.

Once through the gate, the site's six attractions are laid out before you in a "Y"-formation, the entrance being at the base of the "Y." Take an immediate right to the **Grupo Cobá.** To the left looms the impressive **Temple of the Churches,** built over seven 52-year periods, each associated with a new chief priest. Only the front face of the temple has been excavated, revealing a corbel-vaulted passageway (to the left) which you can explore. Rising out of the jungle to the northeast are the grey steps of the ancient city's centerpiece, **El Castillo.** In front of the structure is a stone sacrificial table, upon which animal offerings were made to Chac, the rain god. The stela depicts Chac; another nearby features a kneeling Maya. Follow a second passageway farther south to the **Plaza del Templo,** where assemblies were once held. The red plant dye still visible on the walls of the passageway dates from the 5th century AD. A mortar here hints at the staple food of the ancient (and contemporary) Maya—maize. Return to the main path for a look at the **ballcourt.** The only arch which was standing when the site was discovered—it straddled the path—came tumbling down when Hurricane Gilbert struck Cobá in 1988.

A 1km walk up the "trunk" of the "Y" takes you to four other sites. Follow the right branch for another kilometer to reach a collection of eight stelae in the **Grupo Macanxoc.** On the way, you cross over one of the well-engineered Maya roads called a *sacbé* (white road). This particular road is 20m wide and raised 4m from the jungle floor. The ornate stone slabs of the Grupo Macanxoc were erected as memorials above the tombs of Maya royals. Especially impressive and well-preserved is the first, the **Retrato del Rey.** The king is shown standing on the heads of two slaves, bow and arrow in hand, wearing a *quetzal*-feather headdress.

Returning to the central part of the "Y" brings you to the **Conjunto de las Pinturas** (Assembly of the Paintings). Like the inscriptions on many of the stelae that hide off the side of the road, the murals lining the edges of the temple atop the pyramid have been badly eroded by heat and humidity, twin avatars of the jungle's destructive power. Nonetheless, the short climb to the top brings you face-to-face with an exquisitely carved detail of a few fish and Maya fishermen's faces. Plant dyes were used to create the red, orange, and blue colors. The stone slabs at the base of the pyramid are tombs. The small surface area is explained by the fact that the deceased were buried vertically rather than horizontally.

Continue north to the left-hand branch of the "Y." After 200m, follow an unmarked trail on the right to the three stelae of **Chumuc Múl.** The first stela depicts a kneeling Maya ballplayer. Sure enough, this is the tomb of a victorious captain. You can make out the *chicle* ball in the upper-left-hand corner. The second stela is of a princess, while the third is of a *sacerdote* (priest). His seal is stamped on top of the slab, along with a jaguar's head, a common Maya symbol of worship. Two hundred meters farther up this branch of the "Y," you'll run into **sacbé No. 1.** This thoroughfare ran from Chichén Itzá, 101km to the west, all the way to Tulum, 48km to the southeast. Runners were posted every 5km, so messages could be sent between settlements via a series of quick dashes. During the city's height (AD 900-1200), Cobá is believed to have been the major crossroads in a commercial region of 17 cities. Images of the honeybee god around the site are a reminder of this ancient economic hub—the Maya used honey (along with coconuts and jade) as a medium of exchange.

The tour climaxes with the breathtaking sight of the **Nohoch Múl.** If you believe the legend, which says that each of the nine platforms took 55 years to build, then Maya slaves labored for almost 500 years (without the wheel, metal tools, or domesticated animals) to complete this *castillo,* the highest in the Yucatán. While the view may not quicken your pulse, the 120-step climb surely will. The pyramid's nine levels, where Maya priests once led processions, display carvings of the "diving god." Just before the pyramid is **Stela No. 20.** The stela depicts a dignitary of high rank (note the plumed crest and rich clothing) standing on a board.

Regardless of when you arrive at the site, bring a water bottle and wear a hat. And unless you feel like being sacrificed to the mosquito god, bring plenty of repellent as well. During the high season, 11am-2pm are peak tourist hours (ruins open daily 8am-5pm;14 pesos).

# ■ Chetumal

Nestled in Quintana Roo's southeastern corner and straddling the border with Belize, Chetumal's one saving grace is that it sits on the Caribbean coast. No beaches, no ruins, but hey—*¡costa turquesa!* Established in 1899 to intercept shipments of arms to Maya rebels and to prevent illegal timber harvesting, this state capital (pop. 200,000) serves mainly as a stopover for travelers en route to Belize or Tikal.

## ORIENTATION

Tucked into the Yucatán's southeastern corner, Chetumal is just north of the Río Hondo, the natural border between Mexico and Belize. There are three principal approaches to the city: Rte. 186 from Escárcega (273km), along the Caribbean coast from Cancún (379km), and from Mérida via Valladolid (458km). The **bus terminal** at Av. de los Insurgentes and Av. Belice is Chetumal's ground transportation hub.

Take a taxi (5 pesos) into town or walk 4km through shadeless streets. Chetumal's thriving shopping district lines **Av. de los Héroes,** starting at **Av. Efraín Aguilar** at the city's market and extending 1km south to the bay. This compact commercial area encompasses most of Chetumal's hotels and restaurants. At the southern terminus of Héroes lies **Blvd. Bahía,** a wide avenue flanked by statues and small plazas that follows the bay for several kilometers. From here you can see part of Belize, the long spit of land stretching out to the right as you face the sea.

## PRACTICAL INFORMATION

**Tourist Office: Information booth,** on Héroes at Aguilar (tel. 2-36-63). Pick up a map of the city. Open Mon.-Sat. 8:30am-1:30pm and 6-9pm.

**Consulates: Belize,** on Obregón (tel. 2-01-00), west of Juárez next to Bancomer. To enter Belize for 30 days, all that is needed for U.S., Canadian, and EU citizens is a valid passport and a bus ticket. Open Mon.-Fri. 9am-2pm and 5-8pm, Sat. 9am-2pm. **Guatemala,** Chapultepec 356 at Cecilio Chi (tel. 2-30-45). Again, U.S., Canadian, and EU citizens don't need a visa. For those who do, the process is quick and almost painless (US$10). For stays longer than 30 days, you'll have to talk to the kind folk in Guatemala and show, dollar by dollar, how you plan to finance it. Open Mon.-Fri. 8am-2pm.

**Currency Exchange: Bancomer,** Juárez at Obregón (tel. 2-53-00), has good rates, short lines, and a 24hr. **ATM.** Open Mon.-Fri. 9am-1:30pm.

**Telegrams:** Tel. 2-06-51. In the same building as the post office, through the door to the left. Open Mon.-Fri. 8am-6pm, Sat. 9am-1pm.

**Airport:** Tel. 2-04-65. 5km south of the city on Aguilar. **Aviacsa** (tel. 2-76-76). **Bonanza** (tel. 2-83-06). **Aerocaribe,** Héroes 125 (tel. 2-66-75). Open Mon.-Sat. 8am-1pm and 5-8pm.

**Buses:** at Insurgentes and Belice (tel. 2-98-77). **ADO** (tel. 2-51-10) offers 1st-class service to Campeche (noon, 7hr., 117 pesos), Cancún (7 per day, 5hr., 98 pesos), Escárcega (6 per day, 4hr., 75 pesos), Mexico City (4 per day, 22hr., 380 pesos), Palenque (8pm, 8½hr., 150 pesos), Playa del Carmen (7 per day, 4hr., 86 pesos), Veracruz (6:30pm, 15hr., 270 pesos), Villahermosa (6 per day, 9hr., 142 pesos), and Xalapa (11:30am, 16hr., 300 pesos). **Línea Dorada** goes to Mérida (4 per day, 6hr., 100 pesos). **Cristóbal Colón** trucks to Ocosingo (9:15pm, 9hr., 125 pesos), San Cristóbal (9:15pm, 10hr., 170 pesos), and Tuxtla Gutiérrez (9:15pm, 12hr., 180 pesos). **Batty's Bus** goes south to Belize (4 per day, 3hr., 40 pesos). **TRP** goes to Tulum (6 per day, 4hr., 52 pesos). **Lockers** 1 peso per hr.

**Market:** Corner of Aguilar and Héroes. Vendors peddle everything from a diddle-eyed joe to a damned-if-I-know. Open daily 6am-3pm. **Súper San Francisco de Asis,** next to the bus station.

**Red Cross:** Chapultepec at Independencia (tel. 2-05-71), 2 blocks west of Héroes, in the back of Hospital Civil Morelos. Open 24hr.

**Pharmacy: Farmacia Canto,** Av. Héroes 99 (tel. 2-04-83), conveniently located at the northern end of the market. Open Mon.-Sat. 7am-11pm, Sun. 7am-5pm.

**Hospital: Hospital General,** at Quintana Roo and Juan José Sordio (tel. 2-19-99).

**Police:** Insurgentes at Belice (tel. 2-15-00), next to the bus station. Open 24hr. **Tourist Safety Line:** 91-800-90-392.

**Post Office:** Plutarco Elías Calles 2A (tel. 2-25-78), 1 block east of the Mercado. Open Mon.-Fri. 8am-7pm, Sat. 9am-1pm. **Postal Code:** 77000.

**Phone Code:** 983.

## ACCOMMODATIONS

Chetumal's budget accommodations aren't an extraordinary bunch, but they do score points for location. All are within easy walking distance of the *mercado*. A scenic **trailer park** in Calderitas, 9km northeast of Chetumal, offers electricity, water hookups, and clean bathrooms (vehicles 40 pesos; tent or hammock space 10 pesos per person; big bungalows with kitchen 70 pesos for 1-2 people).

**CREA Youth Hostel (HI),** Heroica Escuela Naval at Calzada Veracruz (tel. 2-34-65), at the eastern terminus of Obregón. For once, a youth hostel within manageable walking distance. Clean, modern, single-sex rooms with 2 bunk beds each. Bed with sheets, towel, and locker 30 pesos. Lawn for camping 15 pesos. 30-peso deposit. Breakfast 11 pesos; lunch and dinner 14 pesos. Front desk open daily 7am-11pm, but you can make arrangements to return later. Bathrooms open 24hr. Fills during July and August, so call to reserve.

**Hotel Brasilia,** Aguilar 186 at Héroes (tel. 2-09-64), across from the market. Sparkling white tiles enclose spacious rooms and bathrooms. Friendly management will store packs. Singles 46 pesos; doubles 63 pesos; triples 80 pesos; quads 96 pesos. Add 70 pesos for TV and A/C.

**Hotel María Dolores,** Obregón 206 (tel. 2-05-08), ½ block west of Héroes. Inspired by the chirpy image of Donald Duck at the entrance, you can quack all the way to your small, lime-colored room with dark wood decor and shiny bathroom. Singles 58 pesos; doubles 65-72 pesos; triples 84 pesos. U.S. dollars accepted.

## FOOD

Aside from a dish or two flavored with coconut (it's the *belizeño* influence), Chetumal offers standard Mexican fare. For cheap eats, try the cafe/restaurants at the end of Héroes, on 22 de Enero near the bay, or the eateries on Obregón, west of Héroes.

**Restaurante Pantoja,** M. Gandhi 181 (tel. 2-39-57), past Hotel Ucum, just north of the market. An extremely popular family restaurant, and with good reason: the food is *muy rica* and piping hot. Enchiladas (15 pesos) are *sabrosa*. Gigantic lemonades 4 pesos. Open Mon.-Sat. 7am-9pm.

**El Taquito,** Plutarco Elías Calles 220, near Juárez, 1 block west of Héroes. Groove with the locals as you savor *antojito* after *antojito*. Tacos 3 pesos. *Queso fundido* 18 pesos. Open Mon.-Sat. 9am-midnight.

**Arcadas Súper and Restaurante,** Av. Héroes at Zaragoza (tel. 2-08-84). A neatly packaged open-air cafe, bar, and supermarket. Aztec soup 10 pesos. *Fajitas* and chicken or meat specialties run 28-35 pesos. Open 24hr.

## SIGHTS AND SAND

People come from far and wide to visit **El Mercado.** If you think having your name written on a grain of rice is a pretty neat idea, you'll love this market. If you've been looking for plastics smeared with American iconography, Chetumal's got the goods. Everything from vibrators to packed cheese will make kitsch-fiends squeal with delight. Gaudy? Got it. Cheap? Check. Does a *mercado* get any more…mercado-ish?

The nearest beach is the *balneario* at **Calderitas,** a 10-minute bus ride from Chetumal. Buses leave from Av. Colón, between Héroes and Belice (every ½hr., 5am-10pm, 2 pesos). Although the water is turbid and the shores rocky, the beach looks like a *Where's Waldo* puzzle during summer and school holidays. Much nicer, both for atmosphere and for swimming, are the three watering holes near the town of **Bacalar,** 38km away. The local bus to Bacalar leaves from Chetumal's bus station (every hr., 5:30am-10:30pm, 5 pesos); *combis* leave from the corner of Hidalgo and Primo de Verdad in front of the public library (every 15min., ½hr., 6 pesos). The route passes **Laguna Milagros** and **Cenote Azul** before reaching Bacalar. Quieter than the Bacalar, both have bathing areas, dressing rooms, and lakeside restaurants. The huge dining room by Cenote Azul, though expensive, is right on the water.

Past the uninteresting Fuerte de San Felipe in Bacalar lie the docks of the **Laguna de Siete Colores,** named for the hues reflected in its depths. The fresh water is warm, perfectly clear, devoid of plant or animal life, and carpeted by powdery limestone, making it excellent for swimming. Nearby are bathrooms, dressing rooms, fruit vendors, expensive dockside restaurants, and a campground.

Much farther afield from Chetumal, the small seaside town of **Xcalac** (200km, 3hr.), the southernmost center of population on the spit of land extending south from the Sian Ka'an reserve, provides super-mellow bungalows, restaurants, snorkeling, and boat rentals. Nearby off the coast lies the enticing **Banco Chinchorro,** the second-largest shipwreck site in the world, making for a funky deep-sea treasure-hunting dive. Buses to Xcalac and the closer, less service-laden **Mahahval** (150km from Chetumal) depart daily at 7am from Av. 16 de Septiembre at M. Gandhi, 20m from the Restaurante Pantoja (20-30 pesos).

# Appendix

## HOLIDAYS AND FIESTAS

Granted, every day is a party in Mexico. But some days are better than others.

| Date | Festival | Notes |
|------|----------|-------|
| January 1 | New Year's Day | Have you made your resolutions? |
| January 6 | Three Kings' Day | Children awake to gifts from "the Magi." |
| January 6 | Festival of St. Anthony | Celebrated in Mexico City and other towns. |
| February 2 | Día de la Candelaria | Lanterned streets, processions, and bullfights. |
| February 5 | Día de la Constitución | Mexico's Constitution turns 81. |
| February 23-27 | Pre-Lenten Carnivals | Veracruz and Mazatlán lead the seaside storm. |
| March 21 | Benito Juárez Day | Happy Birthday, Benito! |
| March 21 | Spring Equinox Festival | Light and sound shows, dancers, and music. |
| April 5-12 | Semana Santa (Holy Week) | The big one. *Ferias,* processions, and crowds. |
| May 1 | Labor Day | Workers parade and speechify. |
| May 5 | Battle of Puebla (Cinco de Mayo) | Celebrates an 1862 victory over the French. |
| May 1-7 | San Marcos National Fair | Aguascalientes hosts rodeos and music. |
| May | Cancún Int'l Jazz Festival | A touch of class comes to party-central. |
| May | Acapulco Music Festival | Pop singers, starlets, and soap-opera actors. |
| June 10 | Feast of Corpus Christi | Mexico City |
| June 29 | Tlaquepaque | Guadalajara draws lovers of *artesanías.* |
| July | Guelaguetza Festival in Oaxaca | 3rd and last Thurs.; musicians and dancers. |
| August 15 | Feast of the Assumption | Huamantla, Tlaxcala. Flower-strewn streets. |
| August | International Festival | 1-2 weeks of performing arts in Mexico City. |
| September 15-16 | Independence Day | Particularly crazy in Mexico City's *zócalo.* |
| September 21 | Fall Equinox | Chichén Itzá hosts dancing and music. |
| October 12 | Día de la Raza (Race Day) | Celebrates Columbus's arrival in America. |
| late October | Festival Cervantino | Guanajuato celebrates Cervantes. |
| October | Fiestas de Octubre | Guadalajara parties the whole month away. |
| November 1-2 | Día de los Muertos (Day of the Dead) | Families keep vigil at the graves of relatives. |
| November 20 | Revolution | Patriotic parties remember 1910-21. |
| December 12 | Feast of the Virgin of Guadalupe | National displays of devotion. |
| late December | Christmas holidays | Songs, *piñatas,* and punch welcome Jesus. |

# CLIMATE

| Temp in °F Rain in inches | January Temp | Rain | May Temp | Rain | July Temp | Rain | November Temp | Rain |
|---|---|---|---|---|---|---|---|---|
| **Acapulco** | 88/72 | 0.5 | 90/77 | 0.0 | 91/77 | 8.0 | 90/75 | 0.6 |
| **Guadalajara** | 73/45 | 0.5 | 88/57 | 1.0 | 79/59 | 7.0 | 77/50 | 0.5 |
| **La Paz** | 73/55 | 0.3 | 91/63 | 0.0 | 97/73 | 1.0 | 84/63 | 0.5 |
| **Mérida** | 82/64 | 1.0 | 93/70 | 3.0 | 91/73 | 5.0 | 84/66 | 1.0 |
| **Mexico City** | 72/43 | 0.5 | 81/55 | 3.0 | 75/55 | 6.0 | 73/48 | 0.5 |
| **Monterrey** | 68/48 | 1.0 | 88/68 | 2.0 | 93/72 | 3.0 | 73/54 | 1.0 |
| **Oaxaca** | 82/46 | 2.0 | 90/59 | 5.0 | 82/59 | 8.0 | 82/50 | 2.0 |
| **San Cristóbal** | 68/41 | 2.0 | 72/48 | 7.0 | 72/50 | 7.0 | 68/45 | 3.0 |
| **Tijuana** | 68/43 | 2.0 | 73/54 | 0.2 | 81/61 | 0.0 | 73/50 | 1.0 |
| **Veracruz** | 77/64 | 1.0 | 86/77 | 4.0 | 88/75 | 9.0 | 82/70 | 2.0 |

To convert from °F to °C, subtract 32 and divide by 1.8. To convert from °C to °F, multiply by 1.8 and add 32.

| °C | 35 | 30 | 25 | 20 | 15 | 10 | 5 | 0 | -5 | -10 |
|---|---|---|---|---|---|---|---|---|---|---|
| °F | 95 | 86 | 75 | 68 | 59 | 50 | 41 | 32 | 23 | 14 |

# INTERNATIONAL TELEPHONE CODES

| Australia | 61 |
|---|---|
| Ireland | 353 |

| New Zealand | 64 |
|---|---|
| South Africa | 27 |

| U.K. | 44 |
|---|---|
| U.S./ Canada | 1 |

# TIME ZONES

Most of Mexico is six hours behind Greenwich Mean Time, as is U.S. Central Standard Time and Central America. It's always one hour earlier in Baja California Sur, Sinaloa, Sonora, and parts of Nayarit, which are on Mountain Standard Time. And you're yet another hour younger in Baja California Norte, which is always on Pacific Standard Time, like California.

# WEIGHTS AND MEASUREMENTS

Mexico, like most of the rational world, uses the metric system:

1 ounce = 28.35 grams (g)
1 pound = 0.454 kilograms (kg)
1 inch = 2.54 centimeters (cm)
1 foot = 0.305 meters (m)
1 yard = 0.91 meters (m)
1 mile = 1.61 kilometers (km)
1 quart = 0.94 liters (L)

1 gram = 0.04 ounces (oz.)
1 kilogram = 2.21 pounds (lb.)
1 centimeter = 0.4 inches (in.)
1 meter = 3.29 feet (ft.)
1 meter = 0.62 yard (yd.)
1 kilometer = 0.612 miles (mi.)
1 liter = 1.06 quart (qt.)

# LANGUAGE

**Pronunciation** is straightforward. Vowels are always pronounced the same way: a ("ah" in father); e ("eh" in escapade); i ("ee" in eat); o ("oh" in oat); u ("oo" in boot); y, by itself, is pronounced like i. Most consonants are the same as English. Important exceptions are: j, pronounced like the English "h" in "hello"; ll, pronounced like the English "y" in "yes"; ñ, which is pronounced like the "gn" in "cognac"; rr, the trilled "r"; h is always silent; x has a bewildering variety of pronunciations: sometimes it sounds like the "h" in "hello," sometimes like the "cz" in "czar." Stress in Spanish words falls on the second to last syllable, except for words ending in "r," "l" and "z," in which it falls on the last syllable. All exceptions to these rules require a written accent on the stressed syllable.

# PHRASEBOOK

| English | Spanish | English | Spanish |
|---------|---------|---------|---------|
| **The Bare Minimum** | | | |
| Child | Niño (m.)/Niña (f.) | I would like... | Quisiera.../Me gustaría |
| Church | Iglesia | In Spanish, how do you say...? | ¿Cómo se dice... en español? |
| Closed | Cerrado | Man | Hombre |
| Could you speak more slowly, please? | ¿Podría hablar más despacio, por favor? | Mr./Mrs./Miss | Señor/Señora/Señorita |
| Could you tell me...? | ¿Podría decirme...? | My name is... | Me llamo... |
| Do you speak English? | ¿Habla inglés? | No | No |
| Excuse me | Con permiso/Perdón | No smoking | No fumadores/ No fumar |
| Expensive | Caro | Open | Abierto |
| Good morning! | ¡Buenos días! | Please | Por favor |
| Good afternoon! | ¡Buenos tardes! | Thank you very much! | ¡Muchas gracias! |
| Good evening/night! | ¡Buenas noches! | What? | ¿Qué? |
| Goodbye! | ¡Adiós! or ¡Hasta luego! | What did you say? | ¿Qué dijo?/¿Mande? |
| Hello | Hola | What is your name? | ¿Como se llama? (form.) |
| | Bueno (phone) | | ¿Como te llamas? (inf.) |
| How are you? | ¿Cómo está? (formal) | What time is it? | ¿Qué hora es? |
| | ¿Cómo estás? (informal) | | |
| How do you say...? | ¿Cómo se dice...? | When? | ¿Cuándo? |
| I'm fine, thanks | Estoy bien, gracias | When is it open? | ¿A qué horas está abierto? |
| I'm sorry | Lo siento/Perdón | Where is the bathroom? | ¿Dónde está el baño? |
| I don't know | No sé | Woman | Mujer |
| I don't speak Spanish | No hablo español | Yes | Sí |
| I don't understand | No entiendo | You're welcome! | ¡De nada! |

| English | Spanish | English | Spanish |
|---------|---------|---------|---------|

## Crossing the Border

| English | Spanish | English | Spanish |
|---------|---------|---------|---------|
| **Age** | Edad | **Customs** | Aduana |
| **Backpack** | Mochila | **Immigration** | Migración |
| **Baggage** | Equipaje | **Passport** | Pasaporte |
| **Border** | Frontera | **Suitcase** | Maleta |

## Getting Around

| English | Spanish | English | Spanish |
|---------|---------|---------|---------|
| **Airplane** | Avión | **Road** | Camino |
| **Airport** | Aeropuerto | **Round-trip** | Ida y vuelta |
| **Arrivals & Departures** | Llegadas y salidas | **Second class** | Segunda clase |
| **Avenue** | Avenida | **South** | Sur |
| **Bus** | Autobús/Camión | **Stop!** | ¡Alto! |
| **Bus depot** | Estación de Autobuses/ Central Camionera | **Straight ahead** | (Siempre) Derecho |
| **Bus stop** | Parada | **Street** | Calle |
| **Caution!** | ¡Atención!/¡Cuidado! | **Subway** | Metro |
| **Daily** | Diario/diariamente | **Taxi depot** | Sitio |
| **Danger!** | ¡Peligro! | **Ticket** | Boleto |
| **Driver** | Chofer | **Ticket window** | Taquilla |
| **East** | Este or Oriente (Ote.) | **Toll** | Cuota |
| **Every half hour** | Cada media hora | **Train** | Ferrocarril/Tren |
| **Every hour** | Cada hora | **Train station** | Estación de ferrocarril/ Estación de trenes |
| **First class** | Primera clase | **West** | Oeste or Poniente (Pte.) |
| **(To) get aboard** | Subir | **All the way to the end** | Al fondo |
| **(To) get off** | Bajar | **How long does it take?** | ¿Cuánto tarda? |
| **Highway** | Autopista/Carretera | **How much is a ticket to...?** | ¿Cuánto cuesta un boleto a....? |
| **Hitchhike** | Pedir aventón/ Pedir ride | **I want a ticket to...** | Quiero un boleto a... |
| **Map** | Mapa | **What bus line goes to...?** | ¿Qué linea tiene servicio a...? |
| **North** | Norte | **What time does the bus leave to...?** | ¿A qué hora sale el camión a...? |
| **One-way** | Ida | **I lost my baggage.** | Se me perdió mi equipaje. |
| **On foot** | A pie | **Will you give me a ride to...?** | ¿Me da un aventón a...? |
| **Passenger** | Pasajero | **Where is ... Street?** | ¿Dónde está la calle...? |
| **Reserved seat** | Asiento reservado | **Where is the road to...?** | ¿Dónde está el camino a...? |
| **Reservation** | Reservación | **To the left/right** | A la izquierda/derecha |

| English | Spanish | English | Spanish |
|---------|---------|---------|---------|

## Accommodations

| English | Spanish | English | Spanish |
|---------|---------|---------|---------|
| Air conditioning | Aire acondicionado | Manager | Gerente |
| Bath or Bathroom | Baño/Servicio/W.C. | Motel | Motel |
| Bed/Double bed | Cama/Cama matrimonial | Pillow | Almohada |
| Blanket | Cobija | Private Bathroom | Baño privado |
| Boarding house/ Guest house | Casa de huéspedes | Room | Cuarto/Recámara/ Habitación |
| Cold/Hot water | Agua fría/caliente | Sheets | Sábanas |
| Dining room | Comedor | Shower | Regadera/Ducha |
| Fan | Ventilador/Abanica | Swimming pool | Alberga/Piscina |
| Hotel | Hotel | Do you have a room for two people? | ¿Tiene un cuarto para dos personas? |
| Inn | Posada | Do you have any rooms? | ¿Tiene cuartos libres? |
| Key | Llave | Do you know of a cheap hotel...? | ¿Sabe de algún hotel barato? |

## Eating and Drinking

| English | Spanish | English | Spanish |
|---------|---------|---------|---------|
| Apple | Manzana | Meal | Comida |
| Beer | Cerveza/Chela/Cheve | Meat | Carne |
| Bakery | Panadería | Menu | Menú/Carta |
| Bottle | Botella | Milk | Leche |
| Bread/Sweet Bread | Pan/Pan dulce | Napkin | Servilleta |
| Breakfast | Desayuno | Orange | Naranja |
| Coffee | Café | Purified water | Agua purificada |
| Dessert | Postre | Rice | Arroz |
| Dinner | Cena | Salt | Sal |
| Drink | Bebida | Seltzer Water | Agua mineral (con gas) |
| Eggs | Huevos | Snack | Antojito/Botana |
| Fixed Menu | Comida corrida | Soda | Refresco |
| Fish | Pescado | Spoon | Cuchara |
| French Fries | Papas Fritas | Spring Water | Agua mineral (sin gas) |
| Fork | Tenedor | Steak | Bistec |
| Glass | Vaso | Strawberry | Fresa |
| Ice Cream | Helado | Supermarket | Supermercado |
| Juice | Jugo | Tea | Té |
| Knife | Cuchillo | Vegetarian | Vegetariano |
| Lime | Limón | Wine | Vino |
| Liquor | Licor | I am hungry | Tengo hambre |
| Lunch | Almuerzo/Comida | Check, please | La cuenta, por favor |

APPENDIX

| English | Spanish | English | Spanish |
|---------|---------|---------|---------|
| **Bank, Post Office, and Telephone** | | | |

| English | Spanish | English | Spanish |
|---------|---------|---------|---------|
| **Address** | Dirección | **Money** | Dinero |
| **Air mail** | Correo aereo/Por avión | **Number** | Número |
| **Bank** | Banco | **Operator** | Operador |
| **A call** | Una llamada | **Package** | Paquete |
| **To call** | Llamar | **Postcard** | Postal/Tarjeta postal |
| **To cash** | Cambiar | **Post office** | Correo/Oficina de Correos |
| **Certified** | Certificado | **Signature** | Firma |
| **Change** | Cambio | **Stamp** | Estampilla |
| **Check** | Cheque | **Telephone** | Teléfono |
| **Collect** | Por cobrar/Cobro revertido | **Traveler's check** | Cheque de viajero |
| **Dollar** | Dólar | **Weight** | Peso |
| **Envelope** | Sobre | **Do you accept traveler's checks?** | ¿Acepta cheques de viajero? |
| **Letter** | Carta | **I would like to make a call to the U.S....** | Quiero llamar a los Estados Unidos... |
| **Long distance** | Larga distancia | **The number is...** | El número es... |

## Health and Medicine

| English | Spanish | English | Spanish |
|---------|---------|---------|---------|
| **Allergy** | Alergia | **It itches** | Me pica |
| **Antibiotic** | Antibiótico | **Medicine** | Medicina |
| **Aspirin** | Aspirina | **Pain** | Dolor |
| **Bandage** | Venda | **Pill** | Pastilla |
| **Birth control pills** | Anticonceptivos | **Prescription** | Receta |
| **Blood** | Sangre | **Shot** | Inyección |
| **Burn** | Quemadura/Quemada | **Sick** | Enfermo/Enferma |
| **Condom** | Condón/Preservativo | **Stomachache** | Dolor de estómago |
| **Cough** | Tos | **Sunburn** | Quemadura de sol |
| **Dentist** | Dentista | **Toothache** | Dolor de muelas |
| **Doctor** | Doctor/Médico | **i need aspirin, please.** | Necesito aspirina, por favor. |
| **Drugstore** | Farmacia | **Where is there a doctor?** | ¿Dónde hay un médico? |
| **Fever** | Fiebre | **I am sick.** | Estoy enfermo(a) |
| **Flu** | Gripe | **I have a stomachache/headache** | Me duele el estómago/la cabeza |
| **Hospital** | Hospital | **I have a cough/a cold** | Tengo tos/gripe |
| **Headache** | Dolor de cabeza | **Help!** | ¡Ayuda! or ¡Socorro! |

| English | Spanish | English | Spanish |
|---------|---------|---------|---------|

## Car Talk

| English | Spanish | English | Spanish |
|---------|---------|---------|---------|
| Brakes | Frenos | Parking lot | Estacionamiento |
| Car | Coche/Carro/Auto/Automóvil | Repair shop | Taller mecánico |
| To Drive | Manejar/Conducir | Tire | Llanta |
| Driver's license | Licencia de conducir/de manejar | Traffic light | Semáforo |
| Gasoline | Gasolina | Fill it up please. | Lleno, por favor. |
| Gas station | Gasolinera | Check the oil, please. | Revise el aceite, por favor. |
| Oil change | Cambio de aceite | The tire has a leak. | La llanta está ponchada |

## Days and Numbers

| English | Spanish | English | Spanish |
|---------|---------|---------|---------|
| Sunday | Domingo | Today | Hoy |
| Monday | Lunes | Tomorrow | Mañana |
| Tuesday | Martes | Day after tomorrow | Pasado mañana |
| Wednesday | Miércoles | Yesterday | Ayer |
| Thursday | Jueves | Day before yesterday | Antes de ayer/Anteayer |
| Friday | Viernes | Week | Semana |
| Saturday | Sábado | Weekend | Fin de semana |

| | | | |
|---|---|---|---|
| 0 | cero | | |
| 1 | uno | 6 | seis |
| 2 | dos | 7 | siete |
| 3 | tres | 8 | ocho |
| 4 | cuatro | 9 | nueve |
| 5 | cinco | 10 | diez |
| 11 | once | 16 | dieciseis |
| 12 | doce | 17 | diecisiete |
| 13 | trece | 18 | dieciocho |
| 14 | catorce | 19 | diecinueve |
| 15 | quince | 20 | veinte |
| 21 | veintiuno | 101 | ciento uno |
| 23 | veintitrés | 142 | ciento cuarenta y dos |
| 30 | treinta | 200 | doscientos |
| 38 | treinta y ocho | 300 | trescientos |
| 40 | cuarenta | 400 | cuatrocientos |
| 50 | cincuenta | 500 | quinientos |
| 60 | sesenta | 600 | seiscientos |
| 67 | sesenta y siete | 700 | setecientos |
| 70 | setenta | 800 | ochocientos |
| 80 | ochenta | 900 | novecientos |
| 90 | noventa | 1000 | mil |
| 100 | cien | 1 million | un millón |

APPENDIX

# Index

## A

AAA (American Automobile
  Association) 4
abortion 25
Academia de la Lengua
  Española 66
Acapulco 336
Acueducto de Querétaro 392
Aeroméxico 39
Agua Azul 486
aguas de horchata 70
aguas frescas 70
Aguascalientes
  city 250
  state 250
Aguilar, Jerónimo de 53
Agustín, José 67
Ah Suytok Xiu 503
AIDS 25
air travel 38, 46
airplanes, cocaine-filled 62
Ajijic 282
Akumal 550
Alameda (Mexico City) 79,
  98
Alamo, The 56
Alamos 189
Alfredo Bonfil 498
Allende, Ignacio 380, 384,
  386
Amecameca 403
antojitos 69
Arau, Alfonso 68
Árbol de la Cruz 392
architecture 63
Arco, El (Arch Rock) 148
Arcotete, El 477
Armería 301
Arrazola 354
Arroyo de los Monos 198
art 63
Atenquique 305
ATMs 20
Atzompa 354
Augustinian architecture 64
auto insurance 41
automobiles 41, 43
Avenida de la Revolución
  (Tijuana) 131
Axayácatl 105
Aztec Calendar 64, 103
Aztec Stadium (Mexico City)
  119
Aztecs 52, 64, 105, 413, 416,
  448
azulejos de talavera 423

## B

Babewatch 68

Bacajipare 212
Bacalar 554
Bahía Almeja 159
Bahía de Banderas 291
Bahía de Chamela 292
Bahía de la Concepción 154
Bahía de la Paz 160
Bahía de los Ángeles 148
Bahía de Manzanillo 298
Bahía de Navidad 292
Bahía de Santiago 298
Bahía Kino 185
Bahía Magdalena 159
Bahías de Huatulco 361
Bahuichivo 213
Baja Beach 141
Baja California 125
Baja California Norte 126
Baja California Sur 146
Balbuena, Bernardo de 66
Ballet Folklórico de México
  99
Balzapote 452
Banco Chinchorro 554
Barra de Navidad 295
Barra de Potosí 335
Barrancas del Cobre 208
Basaseachi Falls 212
baseball
  El Paso 194
  Monterrey 242
  Todos Santos 166
Basíhuare 210
Basílica de Guadalupe, La
  (Mexico City) 106
Batopilas 211
Battle of Puebla 56, 555
beaches
  Acapulco 336
  Acapulco area 341
  Akumal 550
  Bahía de Banderas 291
  Bahía de Chamela 292
  Bahía de la Concepción
    154
  Bahía de la Paz 160
  Bahía de Manzanillo 298
  Bahía de Navidad 292
  Bahía de Santiago 298
  Bahía Kino 185
  Baja Beach 141
  Barra de Navidad 295
  Barra de Potosí 335
  Boca de Tomatlán 290
  Boca del Cielo 488
  Cabo San Lázaro 159
  Cabo San Lucas 170
  Cacaluta 364
  Caleta de Campos 323

Campeche area 494
Cancún 528
Catemaco 450
Catemaco area 450
Celestún 514
Chahué 363
Chetumal 552
Chico's Paradise 290
Chuquiapan 324
Conejos 364
Costa Grande 335
Coyame 452
Cozumel 541
Cuyutlán 299
El Bejuco 324
El Chileno 170
El Custodio de las Tortugas
  266
El Órgano 364
Ensenada area 141
Guaymas 186
Guerrero Negro 146
Huatulco 361
Isla Cozumel 541
Isla de la Piedra 223
Isla Holbox 534
Isla Magdalena 159
Isla Mujeres 536
Ixtapa 334
La Barra 451
La Paz 163
La Soledad 324
Las Peñas 324
Loreto 156
Los Mochis 213
Maguey 363
Manzanillo 296
Mazatlán 216
Melaque 293
Michoacán Coast 322
Mismaloya 290
Montepío 452
Mulegé 152
Nexpa 324
Paraíso 301
Perula 292
Pie de la Cuesta 341
Playa Azul 322
Playa Barra de Potosí 335
Playa Blanca 336
Playa Carrizalillo 370
Playa Cuatas 334
Playa del Amor 170
Playa del Carmen 539
Playa del Divorcio 170
Playa Entrega 363
Playa Escondida 451
Playa Estacahuites 366
Playa Jicacal 451

Playa las Destiladeras 291
Playa Linda 334
Playa Manzanillo 370
Playa Panteón 366
Playa Payucán 498
Playa Piedra Blanca 291
Playa Principal 363
Playa Quieta 334
Playa Santa María 170
Playa Santispac 155
Playa Tecolote 163
Point Hughes 159
Progreso 515
Puerto Ángel 364
Puerto Angelito 370
Puerto Arista 488
Puerto Escondido 367
Puerto Peñasco 178
Puerto San Carlos 158
Punta de Mita 291
Río Lagartos 527
Rosarito 133
San Agustín 364
San Blas 264
San Felipe 144
San Francisco 542
San José del Cabo 174
Santa Cruz 363
Santa Rosalía 151
Sontecomapán 451
Tampico 236
Tangolunda 363
Todos Santos 166
Tonalá 487
Topolobampo 215
Tulum 546
Tuxpan (Tuxpam) 435
Veracruz 446
Xel-Ha 549
Zihuatanejo 330
Zipolite 366
beans 68
beer 70, 237
Bejuco, El 324
Bell of Dolores 97
Bergan, Nikia 132
Bernal de Castillo 377
bistek 69
Boca de Tomatlán 290
Boca del Cielo 488
Bogart, Humphrey 236
Bohemia (beer) 70
Boing! 70
Bolonchén 499
border crossing
   Brownsville, TX 226
   Ciudad Juárez 194
   customs 16
   documents and formalities
      9
   driver's license and vehicle
      permits 15
   driving across the border 41
   El Paso, TX 191
   Laredo, TX 231

Matamoros 229
Mexicali 134
Nogales 176
Nuevo Laredo 234
passports 11
Reynosa 230
Tapachula 490
Tijuana 128
tourist cards 9
visas 15
Bosque de Chapultepec
   (Mexico City) 102
bougainvillea 289
Bradley, Ryan 68
Bravo, Lola Álvarez 65
breakfast 69
Breakfast at Tiffany's 157
Brownsville, Texas 226
budget travel agencies 37
Budweiser 70
Buenavista (Mexico City) 79
Bufa, La (Barrancas del Cobre)
   210
Bufadero, El 364
Bufadora, La 142
Buñuel, Luis 68, 379
burping 475
burritos 69
Burton, Richard 284
buses 42

## C

Cabo San Lázaro 159
Cabos, Los 167
   Cabo San Lucas 167
   San José del Cabo 172
Cabrera 377
Cacaxtla 417
café con leche 69, 445
Caín en los Estados Unidos
   111
Cakchiquel 65
Calderitas 554
caldo 68
Caleta de Campos 323
Callejón del Beso 376, 378
Cámara, Carlos Pellicer 461
Campeche
   city 494
   state 494
camping 48
Canal de las Estrellas 68
Cancún 528
Cárdenas, Cuauhtémoc 62
Cárdenas, Lázaro 59, 108
Carlota 56
carne asada 69
Carranza, Venustiano 58,
   388, 424
Carrillo, Lilia 65
cars 41, 43
Carta Blanca (beer) 70
Casa de la Corregidora
   (Querétaro) 392
Casas Grandes 197

Cascada de Texolo 435
Cassady, Neal 379
Castillo, El (Chichén Itzá) 519
Catedral Metropolitana
   (Mexico City) 97
Catemaco 448
cavern-diving 550
caves
   Chichén Itzá 521
   Cozumel 545
   Creel 209
   Grutas Coconá 463
   Grutas de Balancanchén
      523
   Grutas de Cacahuamilpa
      329
   Grutas de Cachetok 506
   Grutas de García 241
   Grutas de Loltún 505
   Grutas de San Cristóbal 477
   Grutas de Xtacumbilxunaan
      499
   Guerrero Negro 148
   Loreto 158
   Mulegé 154
   San Ignacio 149, 150
   Sierra de San Francisco 148,
      150
   Xilitla 262
   Yaxuná 523
Celestún 514
Cenote Azul 554
Cenote Dos Ojos 550
Central Mexico 371
Central Pacific Coast 263
Centro Ecológico de Sonora
   185
Cerocahui 213
Cerraluo Island 164
Cerro Colorado 211
Cerro de las Campanas
   (Querétaro) 388, 392
Cerro del Cubilete 378
Cervantes 376, 378
cerveza 70
cerveza dulce 471
Chac 52, 189, 481, 485, 499,
   500, 504, 513, 519, 520,
   523, 527, 551
chac-mool 519, 520, 521
Chahué 363
Chainani, Sonesh 236
Chalma 413
Chamela, Bahía de 292
Chan-Bahlum 484
Chankanaab National Park
   544
Chapala 283
Ch-Chac 527
Chelém 516
Chenalhó 477
Chetumal 552
Chia Pet 354
Chiapa de Corzo 466
Chiapas 463

Zapatista rebellion in 60, 468, 476
Chichén Itzá 517
Chichimecs 397, 426
chicken 69
Chico's Paradise 290
Chihuahua
city 199
state 191
Chilam Balam 503, 519
chilangos 71
chile relleno 69
Chiltepec 344
chimichangas 69
china poblana, la 425
chinampas 52
Cholula 426
Christianization 54
Christmas 555
Chucho el Roto 445
chupacabras 384
Chuquiapan 324
Churrigueresque 64
científicos 57
cigars 454
Cihuatlán 293
Cinco de Mayo 56
Cirrus 20
cita 190
cito 193, 538
Ciudad Amarilla 517
Ciudad Constitución 158
Ciudad Juárez 194
Ciudad Valles 261
clamming 154
Classic Period 51, 484
climate 1, 556
clothing and footwear 36
Coahuila 243
Coar, Sean xii
Coatepec 52
Coatlicue 52, 64
Cobá 550
Cobain, Kurt 289
Coca-Cola 70
coco loco 70
cocoyol 503
coffee 444
Colima 296
city 301
Colimilla 296
Colosio, Luis Donaldo 61
Comala 305
Comalcalco 462
comida corrida 68
Comitán 478
condoms 25
Connery, Sean 452
Constitución, Ciudad 158
Constitution of 1917 59
contraceptives 25
Copper Canyon 208
Coras 268
Córdoba, Hernández de 492, 536

Corona (beer) 70
Coronel, Pedro 248
Corral de Riscos 291
Cortés, Hernán 53, 66, 96, 105, 413, 416, 426, 428, 448, 455
Costa Grande 335
Council Travel 4
Coyame 452
Coyoacán (Mexico City) 107
Coyolxauhqui 52
Cozumel 541
cream of coconut 70
credit cards 20
Creel 205
Cuarenta Casas 198
Cuauhtémoc Mennonite Colony 203
Cuauhtémoc, The (Monterrey) 242
Cuautla 403
Cuernavaca 403
Cuervo 1800 (tequila) 70
Cueva de Olla 198
Cuevas de San Borjita 154
Cuicuilco Archaeological Zone 112
Cuilapan de Guerrero 354
Cusárare 210
Cusárare Falls 210
Cuyutlán 299

D

Dainzú 355
dancing cows 257
Dante 276
de Kooning, Willem 103
de la Cruz, Sor Juana Inés 66
dengue 23
Desagüe General 71
Día de la Candelaria 555
Día de la Constitución 555
Día de la Raza (Race Day) 555
Día de los Muertos (Day of the Dead) 377, 555
diarrhea 23
Díaz, Porfirio 57, 58, 283, 344
dietary concerns 35
Dirty Dancing 353
disabled travelers 33
Distrito Federal (D.F.) 71
Divisadero 212
documents and formalities 9
Dolores Hidalgo 386
Dominican architecture 64
Don Juan de Palafox 424
Don Quijote 376
donkeys painted as zebras 131
Dos Equis (beer) 70
Drake, Sir Francis 541
drinking 22
drinks 70
driving 43

drugs 22
drunkenness, public 22
Dunas de Soledad 148
Durango
city 223
state 223
Dzibalchén 499
Dzibilchaltún 513
Dzibilnocac 499

E

Echave Orio, Baltazar de 64
eggs 69
Eiffel Tower 152
Eiffel, Gustave 151
Einstein, Big Al 377
Eje del Papaloto, El 143
ejidos 59
El Chileno 170
El Custodio de las Tortugas 266
El Humilladero 315
El Paso Diablos 194
El Paso, Texas 191
El Tajín 439
El Triunfo 164
elections, 1997 62
Elephant Rock 210
Elías Calles, Plutarco 59
Empalme 187
enchiladas 69
encomiendas 53
Ensenada 137
Ernst, Max 103
Escárcega 494
Esquivel, Laura 67, 68
Estadio Olímpico 1968 111
Estado de México 398
Estero Beach (Ensenada) 141

F

Feast of Corpus Christi 555
Feast of the Assumption 555
Feast of the Virgin of Guadalupe 555
feathered serpent 51
Ferdinand Maximilian of Hapsburg 56
Fernández, Emilio 68
Ferries
Isla Cozumel 541, 542
ferries 126
Boca del Cielo 488
Cancún 530
Chiquilá 534
Guaymas 188
Isla Holbox 534
Isla Mujeres 536
La Paz 160
Los Mochis/Topolobampo 214
Mazatlán 219

Puerto Morelos 541
Santa Rosalía 151
Festival Internacional
Cervantino 378
Festival of St. Anthony 555
fiestas 555
Fiestas de Octubre
(Guadalajara) 555
film 37, 68
First Empire, The 55
flaming banana 294
flautas 69
food and drink 68
fractals, nifty 81
Franciscan architecture 64
Franciscan friars 54
Fray Bartolomé de Las Casas
475
library 472
Frontón Mexico 119
Fuentes, Amado Carrillo 62
Fuentes, Carlos 67
fútbol 279

**G**

Gadsden Purchase 56
Gallego Mountain 213
García, Phil 294
Garibaldi Plaza (Mexico City)
117
GAW xii
gay and lesbian nightlife
Cholula 429
El Paso, Texas 194
gay cruise (Puerto Vallarta)
289
Guadalajara 279
Mazatlán 222
Mexico City 118
Mismaloya 290
Monterrey 242
Puerto Vallarta 289, 290
San Luis Potosí 257
San Miguel 385
gay and lesbian travelers 33
gay beach
Las Sillas Azules (Puerto
Vallarta) 288
geographical center of
Mexico 378, 394
Gertrudis Bocanegra 314
giant cactus 145
Giardia 23
Gladys Porter Zoo 228
glamour, the origins of 63
God, the existence of 100
Goffard, Sandrine 536
Goldstein, Rosie xii
Gómez, Mercedes Hernández
474
Gopher 336
government agencies 1
Gran Café de la Parroquia
(Veracruz) 445
Granadas, Las 330

Great Death, The 53
Great Pyramid (Cholula) 428
gringas 69
Gringusmaximus 216
Grito de Dolores 55, 386, 387
Gruta, La (near San Miguel de
Allende) 385
Grutas de Cachetok 506
Grutas de Loltún 505
Guachochi 210
Guadalajara 268
Guanajuato
city 371
state 371
Guatemala 490
guayabera 447
Guaymas 186
Guelaguetza Festival
(Oaxaca) 555
Guerrero 325
Guerrero Negro 146
guisado 68
Gulf Coast near Catemaco
450
Guzmán 305

**H**

half-man-half-jaguar beings 63
hallucinogens 260
Hart, Elissa, and sisters 340
headless pig 220
health 22
heat-related sickness 24
Hell 445
Hepatitis A 23
Hermosillo 180
Herradura (tequila) 70
Herrera 377
Herrera, Alonso López de 64
Hidalgo (state) 394
Hidalgo, Miguel 54, 275, 276,
304, 380, 386, 387
jail of 202
Hierve el Agua 356
hiking
Barrancas del Cobre
(Copper Canyon) 208, 213
Catemaco 450
Colima 305
Comitán 478
Ensenada 141
gear 36
health precautions 23
Huatulco 361
Lagunas de Montebello 479
Mineral del Chico 396
Mulegé 154
El Nevado de Colima 305
Palenque 482
Parque Nacional
Constitución de 1857 142
Punta Banda 141
Río Lagartos 528
San Andrés Tuxtla 454
San Blas 264

San Cristóbal de las Casas to
El Arcotete 477
San Miguel de Allende 379
Todos Santos 164
Veracruz gulf coast 450
Volcán de Fuego 305
Xilitla 262
hitchhiking 47
HIV 25
Hochob 499
Hoctún 516
Hoggs, Allyson 550
Holbox, Isla 534
Holcá 500, 517
holidays 555
hostels 48
Cabo San Lucas 169
Cancún 530
Chetumal 553
El Paso, Texas 192
La Paz 162
Mexico City 90
Morelia 318
Oaxaca 349
Playa del Carmen 540
Tuxtla Gutiérrez 465
hotels 47
huachinango 70
a la veracruzana 444
Huastec 433
Huatulco, Bahías de 361
Huerta, Victoriano 58, 110
huevos 69
al gusto 69
huge golf umbrella 474
Huichol 174, 266
Huicholes 268
Huitzilopochtli 52
Hun Hunahpú 520
Hunahpú 520
Hussong's Cantina 140
Huston, John 284

**I**

Iglesia de Santo Domingo 352
Ignacio Zamora 306
Ik 485
immunizations 23
Independence 55
insurance 25
internet access
Brownsville, TX 228
Cabo San Lucas 168
Comitán 478
Cuernavaca 406
Guadalajara 273
Guanajuato 374
Mérida 510
Mexico City 87
Monterrey 240
Oaxaca 348
Puebla 422
Puerto Vallarta 286
San Cristóbal de las Casas
470

San José del Cabo 172
San Miguel de Allende 382
Uruapan 308
Veracruz 443
sla Carmen 158
sla Coronado 158
sla Cozumel 541
sla de Changos 450
sla de la Piedra 223
sla de Pájaros 515
sla Espíritu Santo 163
sla Holbox 534
sla Ixtapa 334
sla Magdalena 159
sla Mujeres 536
slas Venados 222
slote de Patos 159
sthmus of Tehuantepec 359
turbide 499
turbide, Agustín de 55
xcateopan 330
xcolasc 517
xtaccíhuatl 402, 418, 423, 429
xtapa 330
xtapan de la Sal 401
zamal 516
zquierdo, María 65

**J**

acatepec 344
ackson, Michael 170
aiba 70, 237
alapa (Xalapa) 430
alapa de Díaz 344
alisco 268
amaica flower 70
ames, Edward 262
anitzio 315
arabe tapatío 269
arana 511
avier the bartender 231
esuits 66
iménez, Manuel 354
uárez, Benito 56, 97, 225, 275, 299, 344, 351, 386, 387, 393, 424, 425
   Benito Juárez Day 555
uárez, Ciudad 194
uchitán 360

**K**

Kabah 504
Kahlo, Frida 65, 97, 107, 377
   Museo de 107
Kahlúa 70
Kantunil 517
Kantunil Kin 535
King Pakal 484
Kinichkakmó 517
Kino Nuevo 185
Kino Viejo 185
Kino, Padre 156
kosher food 35
Kukulcán 519

Kulubá 527

**L**

La Barra 451
La Crucecita 361
La Merced (Mexico City) 97
La Paz 159
La Soledad 324
La Venta, Parque-Museo (Villahermosa) 460
Labná 505
Labor Day 555
Lacandón Rainforest 472
Lacandóns 54
Lago de Chapala 282
Lago de Zirahuén 316
Laguna Arareko 210
Laguna Bosque Azul 479
Laguna Carrizalillo 305
Laguna Catemaco 450
Laguna Chankanaab 542
Laguna de Coyuca 341
Laguna de Ixtapa 334
Laguna de Siete Colores 554
Laguna Encantada (near San Andrés Tuxtla) 454
Laguna Hanson 142
Laguna La María 305
Laguna Milagros 554
Laguna Ojo de Liebre 148
Laguna Tziscao 479
Lagunas de Montebello 479
Lake Texcoco 52
Lamas, Lorenzo 455
language 557
Laredo, Texas 231
Las Ánimas 290
Las Casas, Bartolomé de 54
Las Peñas 324
Lawrence, D.H. 283
Lázaro Cárdenas 321
Lázaro Cárdenas (Valle de San Quintín) 143
Legos 357
Lenin, Vlad 377
Libre Unión 517
licuados 70
Like Water for Chocolate 67, 68
liposuction 62
literature
   20th century 67
   colonial 66
livability 433
lobster 69, 70
López Mateos, Adolfo 59
López, Raúl 474
Loreto 156
Los Arcos 290
Los Mochis 213
Love Boat, The 336
luggage 36

**M**

MacLaine, Shirley 456

MACO (Oaxaca) 351
Macuilxochitl 355
Madera 198
Madero, Francisco I. 58, 110
Madonna 170
Mahahval 554
mail 48
malaria 23
Malinalco 413
Malinche, La 53, 108, 393
Malinche, La (volcano) 418, 423
Maneadero 142
mangos 377
Manzanillo 296
manzanita 70
MARCO (Monterrey) 241
margaritas 70
mariachis 67, 269
marijuana 366
marimba 430, 441, 445
Marín, Don Manuel Gómez 211
Mármol, Manuel Sánchez 66
Martí, José 100
marzipan 434
Masa, Margarita 351
Mata Ortiz 198
Matamoros 228
Matehuala 257
Maximilian, Emperor 388, 392, 393
Maya 51, 52, 63, 65, 358, 376, 462, 473, 475, 476, 481, 482, 484, 541, 548, 550
Mayapán 500
Mazatlán 216
Melaque 293
Melrose Place 68
Mennonites 203
Mérida 506
Mérida to Chichén Itzá 516
Mesa del Carmen 148
mestizo 468
metric system 556
Metro (Mexico City) 80
Mexcalhuacán 324
Mexcaltitán 268
Mexicali 134
Mexican hat dance, the 269
Mexican High Baroque 64
Mexicana (airline) 39
Mexico City 71
   accommodations 87
   airport 72
   Alameda 79, 98
   Basílica de Guadalupe, La 106
   Bosque de Chapultepec 102
   Buenavista 79
   buses 76
   buses, local 82
   Catedral Metropolitana 97

centro 79, 80, 96
Circuito Interior 79
Ciudad Universitaria 111
Coyoacán 107
driving 83
Ejes Viales 79
entertainment 114
Estadio Olímpico 111
food 92
Garibaldi Plaza 117
La Merced 97
Metro 80
Museo Nacional de Arte 100
newspapers 84
Palacio de Bellas Artes 99
peseros 82
safety 84
San Ángel 110
shopping 113
sights 96
sports 119
taxis 82
Templo Mayor 98
Tlatelolco 105
Torre Latinoamericana 101
trains 75
UNAM 111
Xochimilco 112
zócalo 96
Zona Rosa 79
México, Estado de 398
mezcal 70
Michoacán Coast 322
Michoacán de Ocampo (state) 307
Mineral del Chico 396
minority travelers 35
Miró, Joan 103
Mismaloya 290
Misol-Ha 486
Mitla 356
Moctezuma II 53
Modelo (beer) 70
mojo de ajo, al 70
mole 69
    mole poblano 70, 419, 422
    mole xiqueño 435
Mona Lisa 357
money 18
Monte Albán 357
Montepío 451, 452
Monterrey 237
Montoya, Ignacio, and family 196
Monumento a Cristo Rey 378
Moquíhuix 105
Morelia 317
Morelos (state) 403
Morelos, José María 55, 315, 320
Morrison, Jim 289
Moxviquil 473
Mulegé 152
Muna 500

Museo de Antropología, Xalapa 433
Museo Nacional de Antropología 111
Museo Nacional de Antropología 102
Museo Nacional de Arte (Mexico City) 100
music 67

## N

Na-Bolom 472
NAFTA 60
Náhuatl 65, 216, 268
Nahui Ollin 52
Nanciyaga, Proyecto Ecológico Educacional 452
Napoleon III 56
national parks
    Barranca del Cupatitzio 309
    Basaseachi Falls 212
    Chankanaab 544
    Constitución de 1857 142
    Garrafón 538
    Lagunas de Montebello 479
    Río Lagartos 528
    Valle de los Gigantes 145
Navojoa 189
Nayarit 264
Negra Modelo (beer) 70
Nevado de Colima, El 305
New Year's Day 555
newsgroups, Usenet 9
Nexpa 324
Night of the Iguana 284, 290
Niños Héroes 56, 275
Noche de Muertos 315
Nogales 176
Norogachi 210
Northeast Mexico 226
Northwest Mexico 175
nude bathing
    Playa del Carmen 540
    San Pedrito (Todos Santos) 167
    Tulum 549
    Yelapa 290
    Zipolite 367
Nuevo Casas Grandes 197
Nuevo Laredo 234
Nuevo León 237

## O

O.T.T. 71, 95, 96
Oaxaca
    city 344
    state 342
Obregón, Álvaro 58, 110, 424
Ocosingo 480
Ocotlán de Morelos 355
Ojos Negros 142
Olmecs 51, 63, 426, 433, 455, 456, 460, 485
omelettes 69
OmniMax 461
orgasm 68

Orozco, José Clemente 65, 275
Otterstrom, Kerry "El Vikingo" 152
Oxkutzkab 500

## P

Pachuca 394
Pacífico (beer) 70, 221
packing 36
Palacio de Bellas Artes (Mexico City) 99
Palancar Reef 542, 545
Palenque 482
Pamplonada 386
pan dulce 69
Pan-American Congress, Fifth 57
panda bears 105
Panino, II xii
Pantelhó 477
Papantla 438
Paquimé 197
Paraíso 301
parasites 23
Paricutín Volcano 310
Parque Nacional Constitución de 1857 142
Parque Nacional el Chico 396
Parque Natural de las Ballenas Grises 148
Parroquia de Nuestra Señora de los Dolores 387
Partido de Acción Nacional (PAN) 60
Partido de la Revolución Democrática (PRD) 62
Partido Nacional Revolucionario (PNR) 59, 393
Partido Revolucionario Institucional (PRI) 59, 60, 393
Paso de Cortés 402
passports 11
Pastry War 55
Pátzcuaro 311
Paz, Octavio 67
Peggar, Kathleen, and family 385
pelicans 159
Pellicer, Carlos 412
Peñasquito 211
Perula 292
phalli 497, 504, 505, 522, 548
phrasebook 557
    accommodations 559
    bank, post office, and telephone 560
    car talk 561
    crossing the border 558
    days and numbers 561
    getting around 558
    health and medicine 560

Picacho del Diablo 142
Picasso 248
Pico de Orizaba 426
Pie de la Cuesta 341
pigeons, sinister 306
piña colada 70
Pinacate, El (volcanic
  preserve) 180
Pintada, La (cave) 150
Pisté 517
Plan de Iguala 55, 328
Planicie Magdalena 158
Playa Azul 322
Playa del Carmen 539
Playa las Destiladeras 291
Playa Linda 334
Playa Payucán 498
Playa Piedra Blanca 291
Playa Quieta 334
Plus 20
Pochutla 364
Point Hughes 159
pok-ta-pok 520
ponche 306
Pope John Paul II 281
Popocatépetl 112, 402, 418,
  423, 429
Popol Vuh 51, 65, 377, 520
popular culture 67
Porfiriato 57, 66
Porfirio Díaz 252, 376
Post-Classic Period 51
Pozas, Las 262
Pozos 388
Predator 290
Pre-Lenten Carnivals 555
Progreso 515
pronunciation 557
publications 4
Puebla
  city 419
  state 419
Puerto Ángel 364
Puerto Arista 488
Puerto Escondido 367
Puerto Morelos 541
Puerto Peñasco 178
Puerto San Carlos 158
Puerto Vallarta 284
pulque 70, 117, 416, 417
Punta Banda 142
Punta de Mita 291
Purgatory 445
Puuc Hills 499
Puuc Maya 499
Pyramid of Cuicuilco 112
Pyramid of the Sun 120

**Q**

Querétaro
  city 388
  state 388
quesadillas 69
questionably alluring 510

Quetzalcóatl 51, 52, 53, 97,
  120, 268, 397, 410, 411,
  412, 418, 426, 429, 439,
  519, 523
Quiché Maya 51
Quimixto 290
Quinta Gameros (Chihuahua)
  202
Quintana Roo (state) 528

**R**

rain gear 37
rainfall, by city 556
ranchera 67
Ratón, El (cave) 150
Real de Catorce 260
Real de Salinas 515
Recohuata Hot Springs 210
Reuben sandwich 380
Revolution of 1810 54
Revolution of 1910 58
Reyes, Bernardo 424
Reynosa 230
rice 68
Río Celestún Biosphere
  Reserve 514
Río Lagartos 527
Río Urique 210
Rivera, Diego 65, 96, 99, 100,
  107, 108, 111, 203, 252,
  424
  Museo y Casa de 376
Robin Hood 445
Rockefeller, John D. 99
rodeo
  Chihuahua 203
  Guadalajara 279
  Monterrey 242
  Saltillo 244
Romancing the Stone 435
Rosarito 133
ruins
  Cacaxtla 417
  Cachetok, Grutas de 506
  Campeche 497
  Chichén Itzá 517
  Cobá 550
  Comalcalco 462
  Dzibilchaltún 513
  Dzibilnocac 499
  Edzná 498
  Hochob 499
  Holcá 500
  Isla Cozumel 545
  Kabah 504
  La Venta 460
  Labná 505
  Loltún, Grutas de 505
  Malinalco 413
  Mayapán 500
  Mexico City 98
  Monte Albán 357
  Muna 500
  Oxkutzkab 500
  Palenque 482

Paquimé 198
Ruta Puuc, La 499
Sayil 504
Sian Ka'an Biosphere
  Reserve 549
Tajín, El 439
Teabo 500
Tekax 500
Teotihuacán 119
Tepoztlán 412
Ticul 500
Tipikal 500
Tres Zapotes 456
Tulum 546, 548
Uxmal 502
Xlapak 500
Xochicalco 410
Zempoala 448
Ruta Puuc, La (The Mayan
  Route) 499
RV parks
  Acapulco 341
  Alamos 190
  Bahía de la Concepción 155
  Bahía Kino 186
  Calderitas 553
  Chetumal 553
  Chichén Itzá 518
  Ensenada 139, 141
  Loreto 157
  Mulegé 153
  Oaxaca 349
  Palenque 483
  Pie de la Cuesta 341
  Puerto Escondido 368
  Puerto Peñasco 179
  Punta Banda 142
  San Cristóbal de las Casas
    471
  San Felipe 145
  San Ignacio 149
  San José del Cabo 173
  Santa Rosalía 152
  Todos Santos 166

**S**

Sacred Cenote (Chichén Itzá)
  520
safety and security 21
Sainz, Gustavo 67
Saldivar, Yolanda 67
Salina Cruz 361
Salinas de Gortari, Carlos 59
Salinas, Raúl 61
salt 146
Saltillo 243
Salto de Eyipantla (near San
  Andrés Tuxtla) 455
San Andrés Cholula 426
San Andrés Larraínzar 476
San Andrés Tuxtla 452
San Ángel (Mexico City) 110
San Bartolo Coyotepec 355
San Blas 264
San Cristóbal de Las Casas 467

San Felipe 144
San Francisco 542
San Francisco Acatepec 429
San Ignacio 149
San Jerónimo Tlacochahuaya 355
San José del Cabo 172
San Juan Chamula 474
San Lorenzo 51
San Lucas Ojitlán 344
San Luis Potosí
  city 253
  state 253
San Marcos National Fair (Aguascalientes) 555
San Martín Tilajete 355
San Miguel de Allende 379
San Miguel del Milagro 418
San Pedrito 167
San Pedro Cholula 426
San Quintín 143
San Quintín, Valle de 142
San Rafael 403
San Telmo 142
Sangre de Cristo 213
Santa Anna 55, 96
Santa Anna, Antonio López de 55
Santa Clara del Cobre 316
Santa Cruz 363
Santa Elena 500
Santa María El Tule 355
Santa Rosalía 151
Santiago Ixcuintla 268
Santiago Tuxtla 455
Santo Tomás Jalietza 355
Santos, Laurie 379, 384
Satevó 212
Sayil 504
schnaz god 52
Schwarzenegger, Arnold 290
Sebastián 203
Selena 67
Semana Santa (Holy Week) 555
senior citizens 31
Serdán, Aquiles 424
Serdán, Carmen 424
Seris 186
shoes 36
shrimp 69, 70
Sian Ka'an Biosphere Reserve 549
Sierra de Juárez 142
Sierra de la Laguna 167
Sierra de San Francisco 150
Sierra San Pedro Martir 142
silver 328
Sinaloa 213
sincronizadas 69
Singing Wilsons 305
Siqueiros, David Álfaro 65, 104, 108
slavery, abolition of 55
smallpox 53

snorkeling
  Akumal 550
  Bahía de la Concepción 154
  Bahía Kino 185
  Cabo San Lucas 170
  Cancún 528
  Cenote Dos Ojos 550
  El Chileno 170
  Huatulco 361
  Isla Cozumel 544
  Isla Mujeres 536
  La Paz 163
  Loreto 156
  Los Arcos 290
  Mulegé 152
  Playa del Carmen 539
  Playa Payucán 498
  Puerto Ángel 364
  Puerto Escondido 367
  Puerto Vallarta 284
  San Felipe 144
  Tulum 549
  Xel-Ha 549
Sol (beer) 70
Sonora 176
Sontecomapán 451
sopa de lima 70
sopa de tortilla 70
Sor Juana Inés de la Cruz 351
Southern Pacific Coast 307
Spice Girls 186
Spring Equinox Festival 555
Stallone, Sly 170
Stein, Adam 379
Steinbeck, John 35
stelae 63
Sterling, M.W. 460
student demonstrations 59
study 27
Subcomandante Marcos 60, 468
sunglasses 249
super rats 157
Superior (beer) 70

**T**

Tabasco (state) 457
tacos 69
Tahmek 516
Tajín, El 439
talavera 423
Talismán 490
tamales 69
Tamaulipas 228
Tamayo, Rufino 65, 103
Tamoanchan 410
Tampico 236
Tapachula 488
Tarahumara 209
Taxco 325
taxis 46
Taylor, Elizabeth 284
Teabo 500
Teapa 462
Tecate (beer) 70

Tehuantepec 360
Tehuantepec, Isthmus of 359
Tekax 500
telenovelas 68
telephone codes, international 556
telephones 50
television 68
temperatures, by city 556
Temple of the Inscriptions (Palenque) 484
Templo Mayor 52
Templo Mayor (Mexico City) 98
Tenam Puente 479
Tenochtitlán 64, 96
Teotihuacán 119
Teotihuacanos 63, 119
Teotitlán del Valle 355
Tepehuanos 268
Tepic 266
Tepotzotlán 400
Tepoztlán 412
Tequila 280
tequila 70, 269
Tequisquiapan 394
Terrazas, Francisco de 66
Tescalama tree 210
Texas League 194
Tezcatlipoca 52
Three Kings' Day 555
Ticul 500
tierras baldías 53
Tijuana 126
Tilcajete 354
Tipikal 500
tipping 20
Tizimín 526
Tlachichuca 426
Tlacolula de Matamoros 356
Tlalmanalco 403
Tlaloc 120, 121, 418, 439, 448, 523
Tlamacas 403
Tlaquepaque 280
Tlatelolco 105
Tlatelolco Massacre 105
Tlaxcala
  city 413
  state 413
Tlaxcalan Federation 413, 416
Tlazoltéotl 433
Todos Santos 164
Toltecs 51, 397, 426, 428, 519, 520
Toluca 398
Tomatlán Falls 290
Tomorrowland 444
Tonalá 487
Toniná 481
Toonces the driving cat 295
Topolobampo 215
Torre Latinoamericana (Mexico City) 101

ortilla 68
ostadas 69
Totonacs 53, 433, 438, 439, 448
tourist cards 9
Tovara, La 265
trains 46
travel organizations 4
traveler's checks 18
traveler's diarrhea (turista) 23
Treasure of the Sierra Madre, The 236
Treaty of Córdoba 55
Treaty of Guadalupe Hidalgo 56, 388, 392
Tree of Moctezuma 103
Tres Zapotes 456
Trinidad, La 154
Trotsky, Leon 108
    Museo y Casa de 108
Tula 396
Tule Tree 355
Tulum 546
turista 23
Tuxpan (Tuxpam) 435
Tuxtepec 342
Tuxtla Gutiérrez 463
Tuxtlas, Los
    Catemaco 448
    San Andrés Tuxtla 452
    Santiago Tuxtla 455
Twain, Mark 35
typhoid fever 23
Tzaráracua 311
Tzararecuita 311
Tzintzuntzán 316

**U**

Universidad Nacional Autónoma de México (UNAM) 111
Urique 213
Uruapan 307
Uxmal 502

**V**

vale of shadows 61
Valladolid 524
Valle de las Monjas 210
Valle de los Gigantes National Park 145
Valle de los Hongos 210
Valle Nacional 344
Vámonos xii

Van Halen, Eddie 170
Vasconcelos, José 64
vegetarian food 35
vehicle permit 15
vehicle permits 15
Veracruz
    city 441
    state 430
Vicente Guerrero 55
Villa Díaz Ordaz 354
Villa, Pancho 58, 199, 211, 304
    house of 202
Villahermosa 458
Virgin of Guadalupe 97, 106, 249, 300, 393, 454, 506
Virgin on the Floor 107
visas 15
voladores 440
Volcán de Fuego, El 305
volunteering 29

**W**

War of the Reform 56
water 24
waterfalls
    Barranca del Cupatitzio National Park 309
    Basaseachi Falls 212
    Batopilas 210
    Cascada de Texolo 435
    Cascada Montiepa 486
    Cascadas de Agua Azul and Misol-Ha 486
    Chiapa de Corzo 467
    Las Granadas 330
    Nayarit 264
    Palenque 482
    Playa Hermosa (near Catemaco) 452
    Queen's Bath 486
    Quimixto 290
    Salto de Eyipantla 455
    Taxco 329
    Tomatlán Falls 290
    Tzaráracua and Tzararecuita 311
    Xico 435
    Xilitla 262
    Yeparavo 213
weights and measurements 556
Weiss, Jenny 379
Weiss, Taya 379

whale-watching
    Puerto San Carlos 159
whistling 137
witchcraft 449, 454
women travelers 31
women's health 24
work 29
World Wide Web 7
worthless peon 96

**X**

Xalapa 430
Xbalanque 520
Xcalac 554
Xel-Ha 549
Xico 435
Xilbalba 520
Xilitla 262
Xitle 112
Xlapak 500
Xocchel 517
Xochicalco 410
Xochimilco 112
Xochiténcatl 418

**Y**

Yácatas 316
Yaculpatén 516
Yagul 356
Yaxuná 523
Yelapa 290
Yeparavo waterfall 213
Yucatán (state) 499
Yucatán Peninsula 492

**Z**

Zaachila 354
Zacatecas
    city 244
    state 244
Zapata, Emiliano 58, 403, 424
    naked 202
Zapatistas 60, 468, 476
Zapopan 281
Zapotecs 355, 356, 357, 426
Zedillo, Ernesto 61
Zempoala 448
Zihuatanejo 330
Zinacantán 476
Zipolite 366
Zona Libre 41
Zona Rosa (Mexico City) 79
Zumárraga, Juan de 54

INDEX

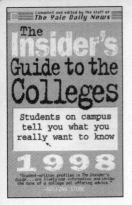

# ★Let's Go 1998 Reader Questionnaire★

> Please fill this out and return it to **Let's Go, St. Martin's Press,** 175 Fifth Ave., New York, NY 10010-7848. All respondents will receive a free subscription to **The Yellowjacket,** the Let's Go Newsletter.

**Name:** _____

**Address:** _____

**City:** _____ **State:** _____ **Zip/Postal Code:** _____

**Email:** _____ **Which book(s) did you use?** _____

**How old are you?** under 19   19-24   25-34   35-44   45-54   55 or over

**Are you (circle one)**   in high school   in college   in graduate school
employed   retired   between jobs

**Have you used Let's Go before?** yes  no  **Would you use it again?** yes  no

**How did you first hear about Let's Go?** friend   store clerk   television
bookstore display   advertisement/promotion   review   other

**Why did you choose Let's Go (circle up to two)?**   reputation  budget focus
price   writing style   annual updating   other: _____

**Which other guides have you used, if any?**   Frommer's $-a-day   Fodor's
Rough Guides   Lonely Planet   Berkeley   Rick Steves
other: _____

**Is Let's Go the best guidebook?**   yes  no

**If not, which do you prefer?** _____

**Please rank each of the following parts of Let's Go 1 to 5 (1=needs improvement, 5=perfect).**   packaging/cover   practical information
accommodations   food   cultural introduction   sights
practical introduction ("Essentials")   directions   entertainment
gay/lesbian information   maps   other: _____

**How would you like to see the books improved? (continue on separate page, if necessary)** _____
_____

**How long was your trip?**   one week   two weeks   three weeks
one month   two months or more

**Which countries did you visit?** _____

**What was your average daily budget, not including flights?** _____

**Have you traveled extensively before?**   yes  no

**Do you buy a separate map when you visit a foreign city?**   yes  no

**Have you seen the Let's Go Map Guides?**   yes  no

**Have you used a Let's Go Map Guide?**   yes  no

**If you have, would you recommend them to others?**   yes  no

**Did you use the Internet to plan your trip?**   yes  no

**Would you use a Let's Go:** recreational (e.g. skiing) guide   gay/lesbian guide
adventure/trekking guide   phrasebook   general travel information guide

**Which of the following destinations do you hope to visit in the next three to five years (circle one)?**   South Africa   China   South America   Russia
Caribbean   Scandinavia   other: _____

**Where did you buy your guidebook?**   Internet   chain bookstore
independent bookstore   college bookstore   travel store
other: _____

## Mexico City Metro

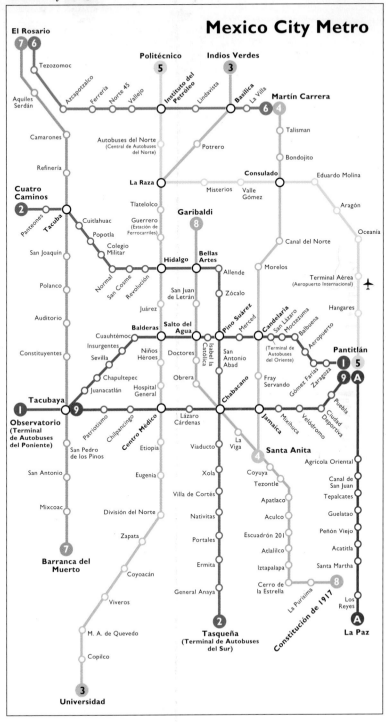

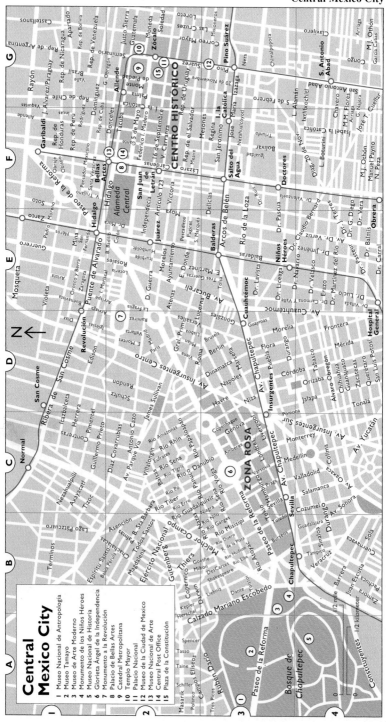

# Central Mexico City

**Central Mexico City**

1 Museo Nacional de Antropología
2 Museo Tamayo
3 Museo de Arte Moderno
4 Monumento de los Niños Héroes
5 Museo Nacional de Historia
6 Glorieta Ángel de la Independencia
7 Monumento a la Revolución
8 Palacio de Bellas Artes
9 Catedral Metropolitana
10 Templo Mayor
11 Palacio Nacional
12 Museo de la Ciudad de Mexico
13 Museo Nacional de Arte
14 Central Post Office
15 Plaza de la Constitución

CENTRO HISTÓRICO

ZONA ROSA

Bosque de Chapultepec

0   1/2 mile
0   1/2 kilometer